ANCIENT WORLD HISTORY

PATTERNS OF INTERACTION

Roger B. Beck

Linda Black

Larry S. Krieger

Phillip C. Naylor

Dahia Ibo Shabaka

HISTORY

HOLT McDOUGAL

 HOUGHTON MIFFLIN HARCOURT

Senior Consultants

Roger B. Beck, Ph.D.

Roger B. Beck is Distinguished Professor of African, World, and 20th Century World History at Eastern Illinois University. Having taught at international schools in Tokyo, Paris, and London, Dr. Beck also supervised student teachers and taught Social Studies Methods at Eastern for many years. In addition to a long teaching career at high school, college, and graduate school levels, Dr. Beck has published extensively, including authoring The History of South Africa and co-authoring the college world history text A History of World Societies. He has also published more than 100 book chapters, journal articles, and book reviews. He is a recipient of two Fulbright fellowships, and is an active member of the African Studies Association and the World History Association.

Linda Black, B.A., M.Ed.

Linda Black teaches World History at Cypress Falls High School in Houston, Texas, and has had a distinguished career in education as a teacher of world history, American history, and Texas history. In 1993–1994, Mrs. Black was named an Outstanding Secondary Social Studies Teacher in the United States by the National Council for the Social Studies. In 1996, she was elected to the Board of Directors of the National Council for the Social Studies. She is an active member of that council, the Texas Council for the Social Studies, and the World History Association. She served on the College Board Test Development for Advanced Placement World History from 1995 to 2003.

Larry S. Krieger, B.A., M.A., M.A.T.

Larry S. Krieger is the social studies supervisor for grades K-12 in Montgomery Township Public Schools in New Jersey. For 26 years he has taught world history in public schools. He has also introduced many innovative in-service programs, such as "Putting the Story Back in History," and has co-authored several successful history textbooks. Mr. Krieger earned his B.A. and M.A.T. from the University of North Carolina and his M.A. from Wake Forest University.

Phillip C. Naylor, Ph.D.

Phillip C. Naylor is an associate professor of history at Marquette University and teaches European, North African, and West Asian undergraduate and graduate courses. He was the director of the Western Civilization program for nine years where he inaugurated a "transcultural approach" to the teaching of the traditional survey. He has authored France and Algeria: A History of Decolonization and Transformation, coauthored The Historical Dictionary of Algeria, and coedited State and Society in Algeria. He has published numerous articles, papers, and reviews, and produced CD-ROM projects. In 1996, Dr. Naylor received the Reverend John P. Raynor, S.J., Faculty Award for Teaching Excellence at Marquette University. In 1992, he received the Edward G. Roddy Teaching Award at Merrimack College.

Dahia Ibo Shabaka, B.A., M.A., Ed.S.

Dahia Ibo Shabaka is the director of Social Studies and African-Centered Education in the Detroit Public Schools system. She has an extensive educational and scholarly background in the disciplines of history, political science, economics, law, and reading, and in secondary education, curriculum development, and school administration and supervision. Ms. Shabaka has been a teacher, a curriculum coordinator, and a supervisor of social studies in the Detroit Secondary Schools. In 1991 she was named Social Studies Educator of the Year by the Michigan Council for the Social Studies. Ms. Shabaka is the recipient of a Fulbright Fellowship at the Hebrew University in Israel and has served as an executive board member of the National Social Studies Supervisors Association.

Copyright © 2012 by Houghton Mifflin Harcourt Publishing Company

All rights reserved. No part of this work may be reproduced or transmitted in any form or by any means, electronic or mechanical, including photocopying or recording, or by any information storage and retrieval system, without the prior written permission of the copyright owner unless such copying is expressly permitted by federal copyright law. Requests for permission to make copies of any part of the work should be addressed to Houghton Mifflin Harcourt Publishing Company, Attn: Contracts, Copyrights, and Licensing, 9400 South Park Center Loop, Orlando, Florida 32819.

Maps on pages A1–A47 © Rand McNally & Company. All rights reserved.

Portions © 2010 A&E Television Networks, LLC. All rights reserved.

The History Channel, History, "H" logo and History Education are trademarks of A&E Television Networks, LLC. All rights reserved.

Printed in the U.S.A.

ISBN 978-0-547-49113-4

5 6 7 8 9 10   1421   19 18 17 16 15 14

4500466355   C D E F G

If you have received these materials as examination copies free of charge, Houghton Mifflin Harcourt Publishing Company retains title to the materials and they may not be resold. Resale of examination copies is strictly prohibited.

Possession of this publication in print format does not entitle users to convert this publication, or any portion of it, into electronic format.

Consultants and Reviewers

Content Consultants

The content consultants reviewed the content for historical depth and accuracy and for clarity of presentation.

Jerry Bentley
Department of History
University of Hawaii
Honolulu, Hawaii

Marc Brettler
Department of
Near Eastern and
Judaic Studies
Brandeis University
Waltham, Massachusetts

Steve Gosch
Department of History
University of Wisconsin
at Eau Claire
Eau Claire, Wisconsin

Don Holsinger
Department of History
Seattle Pacific University
Seattle, Washington

Patrick Manning
World History Center
Department of History
Northeastern University
Boston, Massachusetts

Richard Saller
Department of History
University of Chicago
Chicago, Illinois

Wolfgang Schlauch
Department of History
Eastern Illinois
University
Charleston, Illinois

Susan Schroeder
Department of History
Loyola University
of Chicago
Chicago, Illinois

Scott Waugh
Department of History
University of California,
Los Angeles
Los Angeles, California

Multicultural Advisory Board Consultants

The multicultural advisers reviewed the manuscript for appropriate historical content.

Pat A. Brown
Director of the Indianapolis
Public Schools
Office of African Centered
Multicultural Education
Indianapolis Public Schools
Indianapolis, Indiana

Ogle B. Duff
Associate Professor of English
University of Pittsburgh
Pittsburgh, Pennsylvania

Mary Ellen Maddox
Black Education
Commission Director
Los Angeles Unified
School District
Los Angeles, California

Jon Reyhner
Associate Professor and
Coordinator of the
Bilingual Multicultural
Education Program
Northern Arizona University
Flagstaff, Arizona

Ysidro Valenzuela
Fresno High School
Fresno, California

Teacher Review Panels

The following educators provided ongoing review during the development of prototypes, the table of contents, and key components of the program.

Patrick Adams
Pasadena High School
Pasadena, Texas

Bruce Bekemeyer
Marquette High School
Chesterfield, Missouri

Ellen Bell
Bellaire High School
Bellaire, Texas

Margaret Campbell
Central High School
St. Louis, Missouri

Nancy Coates
Belleville East High School
Belleville, Illinois

Kim Coil
Francis Howell North
High School
St. Charles, Missouri

Craig T. Grace
Lanier High School
West Austin, Texas

Katie Ivey
Dimmitt High School
Dimmitt, Texas

Gary Kasprovich
Granite City High School
Granite City, Illinois

Pat Knapp
Burgess High School
El Paso, Texas

Eric R. Larson
Clark High School
Plano, Texas

Linda Marrs
Naaman Forest High School
Garland, Texas

Harry McCown
Hazelwood West High School
Hazelwood, Missouri

Terry McRae
Robert E. Lee High School
Tyler, Texas

Joseph Naumann (retired)
McCluer North High School
Florissant, Missouri

Sherrie Prahl
The Woodlands High School
The Woodlands, Texas

Dorothy Schulze
Health Careers High School
San Antonio, Texas

Liz Silva
Townview Magnet Center
Dallas, Texas

Linda Stevens
Central High School
San Angelo, Texas

Leonard Sullivan
Pattonville High School
Maryland Hts., Missouri

Carole Weeden
Fort Zumwalt South
High School
St. Peters, Missouri

Rita Wylie
Parkway West Sr. High School
Ballwin, Missouri

Teacher Consultants

Glenn Bird
Springville High School
Springville, Utah

Michael Cady
North High School
Phoenix, Arizona

William Canter
Guilford High School
Rockford, Illinois

Nancy Coates
Belleville East High School
Belleville, Illinois

Paul Fitzgerald
Estancia High School
Costa Mesa, California

Craig T. Grace
Lanier High School
Austin, Texas

Tom McDonald
Phoenix Union HSD
Phoenix, Arizona

Joy McKee
Lamar High School
Arlington, Texas

Terry McRae
Robert E. Lee High School
Tyler, Texas

Myra Osman
Homewood Flossmoor
 High School
Flossmoor, Illinois

Dorothy Schulze
Health Careers High School
Dallas, Texas

Linda Stevens
Central High School
San Angelo, Texas

The following educators wrote activities for the program.

Charlotte Albaugh
Grand Prairie High School
Grand Prairie, Texas

Mark Aguirre
Scripps Ranch High School
San Diego, California

Sharon Ballard
L.D. Bell High School
Hurst, Texas

Bryon Borgelt
St. John's Jesuit High School
Toledo, Ohio

William Brown (retired)
Northeast High School
Philadelphia, Pennsylvania

Haley Brice Clark
DeBakey Health Prof. High School
Houston, Texas

John Devine
Elgin High School
Elgin, Illinois

Karen Dingeldein
Cudahy High School
Cudahy, Wisconsin

Joanne Dodd
Scarborough High School
Houston, Texas

Jan Ellersieck
Ft. Zummalt South High School
St. Peters, Missouri

Craig T. Grace
Lanier High School
Austin, Texas

Korri Kinney
Meridian High School
Meridian, Idaho

Jerome Love
Beaumont High School
St. Louis, Missouri

Melissa Mack
St. Margaret's High School
San Juan Capistrano, California

Harry McCown
Hazelwood West High School
Hazelwood, Missouri

Terry McRae
Robert E. Lee High School
Tyler, Texas

Joseph Naumann (retired)
McCluer North High School
Florissant, Missouri

Theresa C. Noonan
West Irondequoit High School
Rochester, New York

Robert Parker
St. Margaret's High School
San Juan Capistrano, California

Janet Rogolsky
Sylvania Southview High School
Sylvania, Ohio

Dorothy Schulze
Health Careers High School
San Antonio, Texas

Evelyn Sims
Skyline Center High School
Dallas, Texas

Brenda Smith
Colorado Springs School District 11
Colorado Springs, Colorado

Linda Stevens
Central High School
San Angelo, Texas

Leonard Sullivan
Pattonville High School
Maryland Heights, Missouri

Linda Tillis
South Oak Cliff High School
Dallas, Texas

Andrew White
Morrow High School
Clayton, Georgia

Reviewers (continued)

Student Board

The following students reviewed prototype materials for the textbook.

LaShaunda Allen
Weston High School
Greenville, MS

Brandy Andreas
Rayburn High School
Pasadena, TX

Adam Bishop
Jordan High School
Sandy, UT

Jennifer Bragg
Midlothian High School
Midlothian, VA

Nicole Fevry
Midwood High School
Brooklyn, NY

Phillip Gallegos
Hilltop High School
Chula Vista, CA

Matt Gave
Stevenson Senior High School
Sterling Heights, MI

Blair Hogan
Leesville Road High School
Raleigh, NC

Ngoc Hong
Watkins Mill Senior High School
Gaithersburg, MD

Iman Jalali
Glenbrook North High School
Northbrook, IL

Vivek Makhijani
Durfee High School
Fall River, MA

Todd McDavitt
Derby High School
Derby, KS

Teniqua Mitchell
Linden-McKinley High School
Columbus, OH

Cicely Nash
Edmond Memorial High School
Edmond, OK

Brian Nebrensky
Hillsboro High School
Hillsboro, OR

Jesse Neumyer
Cumberland Valley High School
Mechanicsburg, PA

Nora Patronas
Alba High School
Bayou La Batre, LA

Lindsey Petersen
Stoughton High School
Stoughton, WI

Nicholas Price
Central Lafourche Senior
  High School
Mathews, LA

Ben Richey
Fort Vancouver High School
Vancouver, WA

Karen Ryan
Silver Creek High School
San Jose, CA

Matt Shaver
Weatherford High School
Weatherford, TX

Richie Spitler
Atlantic High School
Port Orange, FL

Jessie Stoneberg
Burnsville High School
Burnsville, MN

Kelly Swick
Ocean Township High School
Oakhurst, NJ

Jason Utzig
Kenmore East High School
Tonawanda, NY

Justin Woodly
North Cobb High School
Kennesaw, GA

©2010 A&E Television Networks, LLC All Rights Reserved. 01762

HISTORY™ is the leading destination for revealing, award-winning, original non-fiction series and event-driven specials that connect history with viewers in an informative, immersive and entertaining manner across multiple platforms. HISTORY is part of A&E Television Networks (AETN), a joint venture of Hearst Corporation, Disney/ABC Television Group and NBC Universal, an award-winning, international media company that also includes, among others, A&E Network™, BIO™, and History International™.

HISTORY programming greatly appeals to educators and young people who are drawn into the visual stories our documentaries tell. Our Education Department has a long-standing record in providing teachers and students with curriculum resources that bring the past to life in the classroom. Our content covers a diverse variety of subjects, including American and world history, government, economics, the natural and applied sciences, arts, literature and the humanities, health and guidance, and even pop culture.

The HISTORY website, located at **www.history.com**, is the definitive historical online source that delivers entertaining and informative content featuring broadband video, interactive timelines, maps, games, podcasts and more.

"We strive to engage, inspire and encourage the love of learning..."

Since its founding in 1995, HISTORY has demonstrated a commitment to providing the highest quality resources for educators. We develop multimedia resources for K–12 schools, two- and four-year colleges, government agencies, and other organizations by drawing on the award-winning documentary programming of A&E Television Networks. We strive to engage, inspire and encourage the love of learning by connecting with students in an informative and compelling manner. To help achieve this goal, we have formed a partnership with Houghton Mifflin Harcourt.

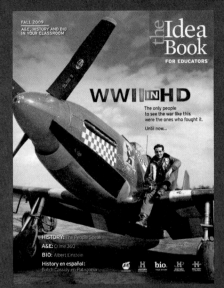
The Idea Book for Educators

Classroom resources that bring the past to life

Live webcasts

HISTORY Take a Veteran to School Day

In addition to premium video-based resources, **HISTORY** has extensive offerings for teachers, parents, and students to use in the classroom and in their in-home educational activities, including:

▷ *The Idea Book for Educators* is a biannual teacher's magazine, featuring guides and info on the latest happenings in history education to help keep teachers on the cutting edge.

▷ **HISTORY Classroom (www.history.com/classroom)** is an interactive website that serves as a portal for history educators nationwide. Streaming videos on topics ranging from the Roman aqueducts to the civil rights movement connect with classroom curricula.

▷ **HISTORY email newsletters** feature updates and supplements to our award-winning programming relevant to the classroom with links to teaching guides and video clips on a variety of topics, special offers, and more.

▷ **Live webcasts** are featured each year as schools tune in via streaming video.

▷ **HISTORY Take a Veteran to School Day** connects veterans with young people in our schools and communities nationwide.

In addition to **HOUGHTON MIFFLIN HARCOURT**, our partners include the *Library of Congress*, the *Smithsonian Institution, National History Day, The Gilder Lehrman Institute of American History*, the *Organization of American Historians*, and many more. HISTORY video is also featured in museums throughout America and in over 70 other historic sites worldwide.

4 million B.C.–200 B.C.
Beginnings of Civilization

🌐 RAND McNALLY Atlas   A1

Chapter 1 The Peopling of the World Prehistory–2500 B.C.   2

📺 VIDEO Stone Age Weapons   3
  1 Human Origins in Africa   5
     HISTORY THROUGH ART: *Cave Paintings*   12
  2 Humans Try to Control Nature   14
  3 Civilization
     CASE STUDY: *Ur in Sumer*   19
  Chapter 1 Assessment   24

Chapter 2 Early River Valley Civilizations 3500 B.C.–450 B.C. 26

📺 VIDEO Iconic Structures   27
  1 City-States in Mesopotamia   29
  2 Pyramids on the Nile   35
     SOCIAL HISTORY: *Work and Play in Ancient Egypt*   42
  3 Planned Cities on the Indus   44
  4 River Dynasties in China   50
  Chapter 2 Assessment   56

Tutankhamen death mask
(page 39)

Chapter 3 People and Ideas on the Move 3500 B.C.–450 B.C.   58

VIDEO King Solomon   59
  1 The Indo-Europeans   61
  2 Hinduism and Buddhism Develop   66
  3 Seafaring Traders   72
  4 The Origins of Judaism   77
  Chapter 3 Assessment   84

Chapter 4 First Age of Empires 1570 B.C.–200 B.C.   86

VIDEO Ramses' Egyptian Empire   87
  1 The Egyptian and Nubian Empires   89
  2 The Assyrian Empire   95
  3 The Persian Empire   99
  4 The Unification of China   104
  Chapter 4 Assessment   110

MULTIMEDIA CONNECTIONS China and the Great Wall   111 MC1

COMPARING AND CONTRASTING: *Ancient Civilizations*   112

Hebrew Flood Story art
(page 83)

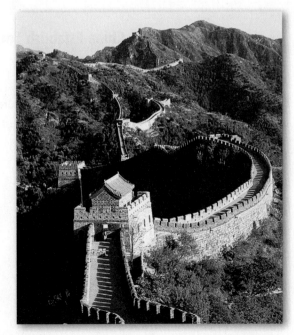

Great Wall of China
(page 108)

2000 B.C.–A.D. 700
New Directions in Government and Society

Roman fresco, Pompeii, Italy
(page 167)

Chapter 5 Classical Greece 2000 B.C.–300 B.C.   **120**

H **VIDEO** Delphi   121
1 Cultures of the Mountains and the Sea   123
2 Warring City-States   127
3 Democracy and Greece's Golden Age   134
   HISTORY THROUGH ART: *Greek Art and Architecture*   140
4 Alexander's Empire   142
5 The Spread of Hellenistic Culture   146
Chapter 5 Assessment   150

H **MULTIMEDIA CONNECTIONS** Ancient Greece   151 MC1

Chapter 6 Ancient Rome and Early Christianity 500 B.C.–A.D. 500   **152**

H **VIDEO** Ancient Rome: The Mobile Society   153
1 The Roman Republic   155
2 The Roman Empire   160
   SOCIAL HISTORY: *Life in a Roman Villa*   166
3 The Rise of Christianity   168
4 The Fall of the Roman Empire   173
5 Rome and the Roots of Western Civilization   178
Chapter 6 Assessment   184
H **MULTIMEDIA CONNECTIONS** Rome: Engineering an Empire   185 MC1

Chapter 7 India and China Establish Empires 400 B.C.–A.D. 550   **186**

H **VIDEO** China's Shortest Dynasty   187
1 India's First Empires   189
2 Trade Spreads Indian Religions and Culture   193
   HISTORY THROUGH ART: *Hindu and Buddhist Art*   198
3 Han Emperors in China   200
Chapter 7 Assessment   208

Asoka's lions (page 190)

Chapter 8 African Civilizations 1500 B.C.–A.D. 700   **210**

1 Diverse Societies in Africa   213
2 Migration
   CASE STUDY: *Bantu-Speaking Peoples*   220
3 The Kingdom of Aksum   225
Chapter 8 Assessment   230

Chapter 9 The Americas: A Separate World 40,000 B.C.–A.D. 700   **232**

VIDEO The Nazca Lines   233
1 The Earliest Americans   235
2 Early Mesoamerican Civilizations   240
   HISTORY THROUGH ART: *Olmec Sculpture*   244
3 Early Civilizations of the Andes   246
Chapter 9 Assessment   250

COMPARING AND CONTRASTING: *Classical Ages*   252

Kuba mask, Africa (page 224)

500–1500

An Age of Exchange and Encounter

Chapter 10 The Muslim World 600–1250   **260**

1 The Rise of Islam	263
2 Islam Expands	269
3 Muslim Culture	273
Chapter 10 Assessment	280

Dome of the Rock
(page 266)

WORLD RELIGIONS AND ETHICAL SYSTEMS   **282**

Buddhism	284
Christianity	286
Hinduism	288
Islam	290
Judaism	292
Confucianism	294

Chapter 11 Byzantines, Russians, and Turks Interact 500–1500   **298**

HISTORY VIDEO Byzantium's Call for Help	299
1 The Byzantine Empire	301
2 The Russian Empire	307
HISTORY THROUGH ART: *Russian Religious Art and Architecture*	312
3 Turkish Empires Rise in Anatolia	314
Chapter 11 Assessment	318

11th century Byzantine cross
(page 301)

Chapter 12 Empires in East Asia 600–1350   **320**

HISTORY VIDEO A Mongol Empire in China	321
1 Tang and Song China	323
SOCIAL HISTORY: *Tang and Song China: People and Technology*	328
2 The Mongol Conquests	330
3 The Mongol Empire	335
4 Feudal Powers in Japan	339
5 Kingdoms of Southeast Asia and Korea	344
Chapter 12 Assessment	348
HISTORY MULTIMEDIA CONNECTIONS Japan and the Samurai Warrior	349 MC1

Tang and Song China,
movable type (page 329)

Chapter 13 European Middle Ages 500–1200   **350**

1 Charlemagne Unites Germanic Kingdoms   353
2 Feudalism in Europe   358
3 The Age of Chivalry   364
4 The Power of the Church   370
Chapter 13 Assessment   374

Chapter 14 The Formation of Western Europe 800–1500   **376**

🅷 VIDEO **The Crusades: The Legacy**   377
2 Changes in Medieval Society   387
3 England and France Develop   393
4 The Hundred Years' War and the Plague   398
Chapter 14 Assessment   404

🅷 **MULTIMEDIA CONNECTIONS** The Crusades: Crescent & the Cross   405 MC1

Chapter 15 Societies and Empires of Africa 800–1500   **406**

1 North and Central African Societies   409
2 West African Civilizations   413
  HISTORY THROUGH ART: *Benin Bronzes*   420
3 Eastern City-States and Southern Empires   422
Chapter 15 Assessment   428

COMPARING AND CONTRASTING: *Trade Networks*   430

Illuminated manuscript
(page 354)

Emperor Charlemagne
(page 357)

Benin sculpture
(page 421)

UNIT
4

500–1800
Connecting Hemispheres

Elizabeth I of England
(page 493)

Chapter 16 People and Empires in the Americas 500–1500   **438**

VIDEO Ancient Maya: Power Centers	439
1 North American Societies	441
2 Maya Kings and Cities	446
HISTORY THROUGH ART: *Maya Architecture*	450
3 The Aztecs Control Central Mexico	452
4 The Inca Create a Mountain Empire	459
SOCIAL HISTORY: *Incan Mummies*	464
Chapter 16 Assessment	466
MULTIMEDIA CONNECTIONS The Maya	467 MC1

Chapter 17 European Renaissance and Reformation 1300–1600   **468**

VIDEO Humanism Triggers the Renaissance	469
1 Italy: Birthplace of the Renaissance	471
HISTORY THROUGH ART: *Renaissance Ideas Influence Renaissance Art*	478
2 The Northern Renaissance	480
SOCIAL HISTORY: *City Life in Renaissance Europe*	486
3 Luther Leads the Reformation	488
4 The Reformation Continues	495
Chapter 17 Assessment	502

Chapter 18 The Muslim World Expands 1300–1700   **504**

VIDEO Hagia Sophia	505
1 The Ottomans Build a Vast Empire	507
2 Cultural Blending	
CASE STUDY: *The Safavid Empire*	512
3 The Mughal Empire in India	516
HISTORY THROUGH ART: *Cultural Blending in Mughal India*	522
Chapter 18 Assessment	524

Safavid shah (page 506)

xiv

UNIT 4

Early globe (page 529)

Chapter 19 An Age of Explorations and Isolation 1400–1800   **526**

[H] HISTORY **VIDEO** Ming Dynasty Wall Building   527
  1 Europeans Explore the East   529
  2 China Limits European Contacts   536
  3 Japan Returns to Isolation   542
  Chapter 19 Assessment   548

Chapter 20 The Atlantic World 1492–1800   **550**

[H] HISTORY **VIDEO** Godspeed to Jamestown   551
  1 Spain Builds an American Empire   553
  2 European Nations Settle North America   561
  3 The Atlantic Slave Trade   566
  4 The Columbian Exchange and Global Trade   571
  Chapter 20 Assessment   576

[H] HISTORY **MULTIMEDIA CONNECTIONS** Ponce de Leon   577 MC1

COMPARING AND CONTRASTING: *Methods of Government*   578

1500–1900
Absolutism to Revolution

Louis XIV of France
(page 588)

Early telescope
(page 626)

Riots in Paris
(page 690)

Chapter 21 Absolute Monarchs in Europe 1500–1800   **586**

🅗 VIDEO Ivan the Terrible: Might and Madness   587
  1 Spain's Empire and European Absolutism   589
  2 The Reign of Louis XIV   596
  3 Central European Monarchs Clash   603
  4 Absolute Rulers of Russia   608
      SOCIAL HISTORY: *Surviving the Russian Winter*   612
  5 Parliament Limits the English Monarchy   614
  Chapter 21 Assessment   618

Chapter 22 Enlightenment and Revolution 1550–1789   **620**

🅗 VIDEO Sir Isaac Newton: The Gravity of Genius   621
  1 The Scientific Revolution   623
  2 The Enlightenment in Europe   629
  3 The Enlightenment Spreads   636
  4 The American Revolution   640
  Chapter 22 Assessment   646

🅗 MULTIMEDIA CONNECTIONS The American Revolution   647 MC1

Chapter 23 The French Revolution and Napoleon 1789–1815 **648**

🅗 VIDEO Napoleon Bonaparte: The Glory of France   649
  1 The French Revolution Begins   651
  2 Revolution Brings Reform and Terror   656
  3 Napoleon Forges an Empire   663
  4 Napoleon's Empire Collapses   668
  5 The Congress of Vienna   672
  Chapter 23 Assessment   676

Chapter 24 Nationalist Revolutions Sweep the West 1789–1900 **678**

🅗 VIDEO Miguel Hidalgo's Call to Arms   679
  1 Latin American Peoples Win Independence   681
  2 Europe Faces Revolutions   687
  3 Nationalism
      CASE STUDY: *Italy and Germany*   692
  4 Revolutions in the Arts   698
      HISTORY THROUGH ART: *Revolutions in Painting*   702
  Chapter 24 Assessment   704

COMPARING AND CONTRASTING: *Political Revolutions*   706

REFERENCES

Skillbuilder Handbook   R1

Section 1: Reading Critically
1.1 Determining Main Ideas   R2
1.2 Following Chronological Order   R3
1.3 Clarifying; Summarizing   R4
1.4 Identifying Problems and Solutions   R5
1.5 Analyzing Causes and Recognizing Effects   R6
1.6 Comparing and Contrasting   R7
1.7 Distinguishing Fact from Opinion   R8

Section 2: Higher-Order Critical Thinking
2.1 Categorizing   R9
2.2 Making Inferences   R10
2.3 Drawing Conclusions   R11
2.4 Developing Historical Perspective   R12
2.5 Formulating Historical Questions   R13
2.6 Making Predictions   R14
2.7 Hypothesizing   R15
2.8 Analyzing Motives   R16
2.9 Analyzing Issues   R17
2.10 Analyzing Bias   R18
2.11 Evaluating Decisions and Courses of Action   R19
2.12 Forming and Supporting Opinions   R20
2.13 Synthesizing   R21

Section 3: Exploring Evidence: Print, Visual, Technology Sources
3.1 Analyzing Primary and Secondary Sources   R22
3.2 Visual, Audio, and Multimedia Sources   R23
3.3 Evaluating Internet Sources   R24
3.4 Interpreting Maps   R25
3.5 Interpreting Charts   R27
3.6 Interpreting Graphs   R28
3.7 Analyzing Political Cartoons   R29

Section 4: Creating Presentations
4.1 Writing for Social Studies   R30
4.2 Creating a Map   R31
4.3 Creating Charts and Graphs   R32
4.4 Creating and Using a Database   R33
4.5 Creating a Model   R34
4.6 Creating/Interpreting a Research Outline   R35
4.7 Creating Oral Presentations   R36
4.8 Creating Written Presentations   R37

Glossary   R40
Glossary in Spanish   R51

Available @ hmhsocialstudies.com

- **Strategies for Studying History**
- **Strategies for Taking Standardized Tests**
- **Economics Handbook**
- **Primary Source Handbook**

    Rig Veda, *Creation Hymn*
    Bible, *Psalm 23*
    Confucius, *Analects*
    Thucydides, *History of the Peloponnesian War*
    Plato, *The Apology*
    Tacitus, *Annals*
    Qur'an
    Sei Shōnagon, *The Pillow Book*
    Magna Carta
    Popol Vuh
    Niccolò Machiavelli, *The Prince*
    Sir Thomas More, *Utopia*
    James Madison, *The Federalist, "Number 51"*
    Mary Wollstonecraft, *A Vindication of the Rights of Woman*
    Élisabeth Vigée-Lebrun, *Memoirs of Madame Vigée-Lebrun*
    Sadler Committee, *Report on Child Labor*
    Abraham Lincoln, *Second Inaugural Address*
    Elizabeth Cady Stanton, *The Natural Rights of Civilized Women*
    Woodrow Wilson, *The Fourteen Points*
    Elie Wiesel, *Night*
    Jeanne Wakatsuki Houston and James D. Houston, *Farewell to Manzanar*
    Nelson Mandela, *Inaugural Address*
    Martin Luther King, Jr., *I Have a Dream*
    Cesar Chavez, *An Open Letter*

World History Themes

While historical events are unique, they often are driven by similar, repeated forces. In telling the history of our world, this book pays special attention to eight significant and recurring themes. These themes are presented to show that from America, to Africa, to Asia, people are more alike than they realize. Throughout history humans have confronted similar obstacles, have struggled to achieve similar goals, and continually have strived to better themselves and the world around them.

Power and Authority

History is often made by the people and institutions in power. As you read about the world's powerful people and governments, try to answer several key questions.

• Who holds the power?
• How did that person or group get power?
• What system of government provides order in this society?
• How does the group or person in power keep or lose power?

Religious and Ethical Systems

Throughout history, humans around the world have been guided by, as much as anything else, their religious and ethical beliefs. As you examine the world's religious and ethical systems, pay attention to several important issues.

• What beliefs are held by a majority of people in a region?
• How do these major religious beliefs differ from one another?
• How do the various religious groups interact with one another?
• How do religious groups react toward nonmembers?

Revolution

Often in history, great change has been achieved only through force. As you read about the continuous overthrow of governments, institutions, and even ideas throughout history, examine several key questions.

• What long-term ideas or institutions are being overthrown?
• What caused people to make this radical change?
• What are the results of the change?

Interaction with Environment

Since the earliest of times, humans have had to deal with their surroundings in order to survive. As you read about our continuous interaction with the environment, keep in mind several important issues.

• How do humans adjust to the climate and terrain where they live?
• How have changes in the natural world forced people to change?
• What positive and negative changes have people made to their environment?

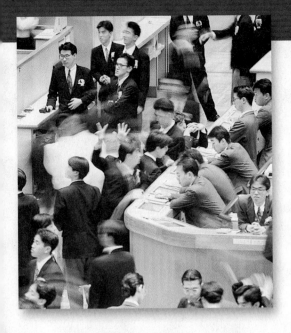

Economics

Economics has proven to be a powerful force in human history. From early times to the present, human cultures have been concerned with how to use their scarce resources to satisfy their needs. As you read about different groups, note several key issues regarding the role of economics in world history.

- What goods and services does a society produce?
- Who controls the wealth and resources of a society?
- How does a society obtain more goods and services?

Cultural Interaction

Today, people around the world share many things, from music, to food, to ideas. Human cultures actually have interacted with each other since ancient times. As you read about how different cultures have interacted, note several significant issues.

- How have cultures interacted (trade, migration, or conquest)?
- What items have cultures passed on to each other?
- What political, economic, and religious ideas have cultures shared?
- What positive and negative effects have resulted from cultural interaction?

Empire Building

Since the beginning of time, human cultures have shared a similar desire to grow more powerful—often by dominating other groups. As you read about empire building through the ages, keep in mind several key issues.

- What motivates groups to conquer other lands and people?
- How does one society gain control of others?
- How does a dominating society control and rule its subjects?

Science and Technology

All humans share an endless desire to know more about their world and to solve whatever problems they encounter. The development of science and technology has played a key role in these quests. As you read about the role of science and technology in world history, try to answer several key questions.

- What tools and methods do people use to solve the various problems they face?
- How do people gain knowledge about their world? How do they use that knowledge?
- How do new discoveries and inventions change the way people live?

RAND McNALLY
World Atlas

Contents

World: Political A2

World: Physical A4

North America: Political A6

North America: Physical A7

Mexico, Central America, and
the Caribbean: Political. A8

South America: Political A10

South America: Physical A11

Europe: Political A12

Europe: Physical A14

Africa: Political A16

Africa: Physical A17

Asia: Political. A18

Asia: Physical A20

Australia and Oceania. A22

Ancient World in the
7th Century B.C. A23

Roman Empire
About A.D. 120 . . . . A24

The Ottoman, Safavid, and
Mughal Empires in the 16th
and 17th Centuries A26

Revolutions in the Atlantic
World 1776–1826. . . . . A28

Latin America 1800–1850 . . . . . A30

Latin America 1850–1900 . . . . . A31

Industrialization of
Europe 1815. . . . . A32

Industrialization of
Europe 1910. . . . . A33

Europe 1922–1940. . . . . A34

Africa About A.D. 1400 . . . . A36

European Partition of
Africa: 19th Century A37

Resistance to
Colonialism 1870–1930 . . . . A38

Middle East/Israel
Political A40

Eastern Southern
Asia A.D. 750 . . . . A42

Asia 1900. . . . . A44

Russia and the Former
Soviet Union A46

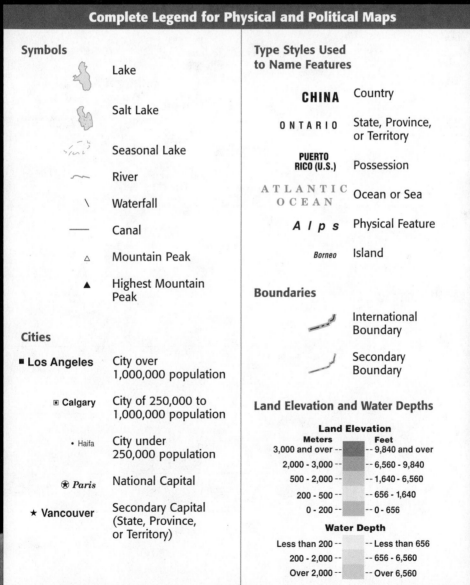

Complete Legend for Physical and Political Maps

Symbols

- Lake
- Salt Lake
- Seasonal Lake
- River
- Waterfall
- Canal
- △ Mountain Peak
- ▲ Highest Mountain Peak

Cities

- ■ Los Angeles — City over 1,000,000 population
- ▣ Calgary — City of 250,000 to 1,000,000 population
- • Haifa — City under 250,000 population
- ✸ Paris — National Capital
- ★ Vancouver — Secondary Capital (State, Province, or Territory)

Type Styles Used to Name Features

- **CHINA** — Country
- ONTARIO — State, Province, or Territory
- **PUERTO RICO (U.S.)** — Possession
- ATLANTIC OCEAN — Ocean or Sea
- *Alps* — Physical Feature
- *Borneo* — Island

Boundaries

- International Boundary
- Secondary Boundary

Land Elevation and Water Depths

Land Elevation

Meters	Feet
3,000 and over	9,840 and over
2,000 - 3,000	6,560 - 9,840
500 - 2,000	1,640 - 6,560
200 - 500	656 - 1,640
0 - 200	0 - 656

Water Depth

Less than 200	Less than 656
200 - 2,000	656 - 6,560
Over 2,000	Over 6,560

ARCTIC OCEAN

RUSSIA
ALASKA
Yukon (U.S.)
Anchorage·

Aleutian Islands

CANADA

Vancouver
Missouri

Chicago

UNITED STATES
Colorado

Los Angeles·

Houston

MEXICO
Gulf of Mexico

Mexico City ⊛

PACIFIC

MIDWAY IS.
(U.S.)

Tropic of Cancer

Hawaiian
Islands
(U.S.)

OCEAN

Equator

KIRIBATI

SAMOA
AMERICAN
SAMOA
COOK
ISLANDS (N.Z.)
TONGA

Tropic of Capricorn

FRENCH POLYNESIA

Easter Island
(Chile)

Baffin
Bay

GREENLAND
(Den.)

Arctic Circle

ICELAND

FAROE IS.
(Den.)

Hudson
Bay

Newfoundland

Montréal
Ottawa ⊛

New York
Washington, D.C.

Mississippi

ATLANTIC

BAHAMAS

CUBA
HAITI
DOM. REP.
PUERTO RICO (U.S.)

BELIZE
GUAT. HOND.
JAMAICA
EL. SAL. NIC.
Caribbean
Sea
COSTA
RICA
PANAMA

Caracas ⊛

TRINIDAD AND TOBAGO

VENEZUELA

GUYANA
SURINAME
FRENCH GUIANA

COLOMBIA

Galapagos Islands
(Ecuador)

ECUADOR

Amazon

BRAZIL

PERU
Lima ⊛

BOLIVIA

PARAGUAY

ARGENTINA

Santiago ⊛

URUGUAY

Buenos
Aires ⊛

C H I L E

0   1000   2000 Miles
0   1000   2000   3000 Kilometers
Copyright by Rand McNally & Co.
Robinson Projection
M-101519-2

Antarctic Circle

UNITED
KINGDOM
IRELAND
Lon

FRA

Azores
(Port.)
PORTUGAL

Ma

SP

Casablanca

Canary
Islands
(Sp.)

MAROC

W. SAHARA

CAPE
VERDE

MAURITANIA

SENEGAL

GAMBIA
GUINEA-BISSAU
GUINEA

SIERRA LEONE
COT
D'IVO
LIBERIA

Niger

OCEAN

ST. HELENA
(U.K.)

Rio de Janeiro

N

FALKLAND IS.
(U.K.)

South
Georgia
(U.K.)

South
Orkney Is.
(U.K.)

South
Shetland Is.
(U.K.)

Weddell
Sea

ARCTIC OCEAN

Franz Josef
Land

Novaya
Zemlya

sbergen
Nor.)

WAY

FINLAND

SWEDEN

DEN.

EST.
LAT.
LITH.

GERMANY

POLAND

BELARUS

Volga

Moscow

RUSSIA

Novosibirsk

Bering

Sea

Sea of Okhotsk

60°

45°

Yenisey

Ob'

Lena

SWITZ.
AUS.
Italy
CZO.
SLOV.
HUNG.
ROM.
BOS.
MONT.
ALB. MA.
BUL.
Rome
GREECE

UKRAINE

MOLD.

KAZAKHSTAN

MONGOLIA

NORTH
KOREA

Sea of Japan
(East Sea)

JAPAN

Black Sea

GEO.
ARM. AZER.

UZBEKISTAN

KYRG.

CHINA

Beijing

SOUTH
KOREA

Tokyo

45°

TURKEY

TURKMENISTAN

TAJIK.

Chang Jiang
(Yangtze)

Shanghai

30°

Mediterranean Sea

CYPRUS
LEB.
ISRAEL

SYRIA

IRAQ

IRAN

AFGHANISTAN

Crete

TUNISIA

JORDAN

KUWAIT

PAKISTAN

NEPAL

BHU.

Guangzhou

PACIFIC

Cairo

QATAR

BNGL.

ERIA

LIBYA

EGYPT

SAUDI
ARABIA

U.A.E.

Kolkata
(Calcutta)

TAIWAN

Tropic of Cancer

Nile

OMAN

Mumbai
(Bombay)

INDIA

MYANMAR

LAOS

NORTHERN
MARIANA ISLANDS
(U.S.)

WAKE ISLAND
(U.S.)

NIGER

Red Sea

YEMEN

Arabian
Sea

Bay of
Bengal

THAILAND

South China

Bangkok

VIETNAM

Sea

PHILIPPINES

GUAM (U.S.)

OCEAN

15°

CHAD

SUDAN

Addis
Ababa

DJIBOUTI

CAMBODIA

agos

CENTRAL
AFRICAN
REPUBLIC

SOUTH
SUDAN

ETHIOPIA

SRI LANKA

PALAU

FED. STATES OF
MICRONESIA

MARSHALL
ISLANDS

IGERIA

CAMEROON

SOMALIA

ATORIAL
GUINEA

UGANDA

KENYA

MALDIVES

BRUNEI

MALAYSIA

GABON

RWANDA

SINGAPORE

New Guinea

Equator

0°

EP. OF
ONGO

DEM. REP.
OF CONGO

BURUNDI

SEYCHELLES

Borneo

INDONESIA

PAPUA
NEW GUINEA

SOLOMON
ISLANDS

Congo

TANZANIA

Sumatra

Jakarta

Java

SAMBIQUE

COMOROS

INDIAN

TIMOR-LESTE

ANGOLA

ZAMBIA

Darwin

VANUATU

15°

NAMIBIA

ZIMBABWE

MADAGASCAR

MAURITIUS

Coral Sea

NEW CALEDONIA
(Fr.)

FIJI

BOTSWANA

MOZAMBIQUE

REUNION
(Fr.)

OCEAN

AUSTRALIA

Tropic of Capricorn

SWAZILAND

Darling

30°

SOUTH
AFRICA

LESOTHO

Perth

Sydney

Cape Town

Melbourne

Kerguelen
Islands
(Fr.)

Tasmania

NEW ZEALAND

Wellington

45°

SOUTHERN OCEAN

60°

Antarctic Circle

75°

ANTARCTICA

15°
30°
45°
60°
75°
90°
105°
120°
135°
150°
165°
180°

15°
30°
45°
60°
75°
90°
105°
120°
135°
150°
165°
180°

75°

ARCTIC OCEAN

Greenland

Baffin
Bay

Baffin
Island

Jan M

Iceland

Arctic C

Faroe Is

Br

Lon

Yukon

Mt. McKinley △
20,320 Ft.
6,194m

Mackenzie

Canadian Shield

Hudson
Bay

NORTH

AMERICA

Aleutian Islands

Vancouver

Rocky Mountains

Great Plains

St. Lawrence

Newfoundland

Azores

Los Angeles

Colorado

Mississippi

Appalachian Mts.

Washington, D.C.

Cape Hatteras

ATLANTIC

Iber
Pen

Atla
Mt

Midway Is.

Tropic of Cancer

Hawaiian
Islands

Baja
California

Gulf of Mexico

Yucatan
Peninsula

Cuba

Hispaniola

Puerto Rico

Jamaica

Caribbean
Sea

Canary
Islands

Cape
Verde
Islands

Cape Verde

Nig

PACIFIC

Orinoco

Trinidad

OCEAN

Palmyra

Galapagos Islands

Amazon

Amazon

SOUTH

Equator

Kiribati

OCEAN

Basin

AMERICA

Samoa
Islands

Marquesas Is.

Andes

Mato Grosso
Plateau

St. Helena

Tonga
Is.

Cook
Islands

Tahiti

Tropic of Capricorn

Easter Island

Andes

Paraná

Rio de Janeiro

N

Chatham Is.

Mt. Aconcagua
22,831 Ft.
6,959m

Buenos Aires

Archipiélago
Juan Fernández

Patagonia

Falkland Is.

South
Georgia

0   1000   2000 Miles

0   1000   2000   3000 Kilometers

Copyright by Rand McNally & Co.
Robinson Projection
M-101520-1

Cape Horn

Tierra del Fuego

South
Orkney Is.

South
Sandwich Is.

South
Shetland Is.

Antarctic Circle

Antarctic
Peninsula

Weddell
Sea

Ross
Sea

Marie
Byrd
Land

△ Vinson Massif
16,066 Ft.
4,897m

RAND McNALLY

15°   30°   45°   60°   75°   90°   105°   120°   135°   150°   165°   180°

ARCTIC OCEAN

75°

Spitsbergen

Franz Josef
Land

North Cape

Novaya
Zemlya

Scandinavian
Peninsula

Ob'

Yenisey

Siberia

Lena

60°

Bering
Sea

Ural Mts.

EUROPE

Volga

Moscow

Don

Altai Mts.

Amur

Sea of Okhotsk

Sakhalin

Kamchatka
Peninsula

45°

Alps

Balkan
Peninsula

Caucasus

Black Sea

Mt. Elbrus
18,510 Ft.
5,642m

Aral
Sea

Caspian Sea

ASIA

Pamir

Gobi Desert

Beijing

Huang

Hokkaidō

Honshū

Sardinia

Sicily

Crete

Cyprus

Mediterranean Sea

Zagros Mts.

Indus

Plateau
of
Tibet

Himalayas

Yangtze

East
China
Sea

Sea of Japan
(East Sea)

Kyūshū

30°

Cairo

Red Sea

Ganges

Mt. Everest
29,035 Ft.
8,850m

PACIFIC

hara Desert

Nile

Arabian
Peninsula

Taiwan

Tropic of Cancer

AFRICA

Sahel

Mumbai
(Bombay)

Deccan
Plateau

Arabian
Sea

Bay of
Bengal

Hainan
Island

South China
Sea

Luzon

Mariana
Islands

Wake
Island

Socotra

Lakshadweep

Guam

15°

OCEAN

Ethiopian
Plateau

Sri Lanka

Malay
Peninsula

Mindanao

Palau
Islands

Caroline
Islands

Marshall
Islands

Gulf
Guinea

Congo

Congo
Basin

Rift Valley

Maldive
Islands

Borneo

Celebes

0°

Equator

Kilimanjaro
19,340 Ft.
5,895m

Seychelles

Sumatra

Java

Timor

New Guinea

Solomon
Islands

INDIAN

Cocos
Island

Zambezi

Madagascar

Mauritius

Reunion

New
Hebrides

15°

Coral Sea

Fiji
Is.

New Caledonia

Kalahari
Desert

OCEAN

Great
Sandy
Desert

AUSTRALIA

Tropic of Capricorn

30°

ape of Good Hope

Cape Town

Cape Leeuwin

Darling

Great Dividing Range

Sydney

North Island

Kerguelen
Islands

Aoraki
(Mt. Cook)
12,316 Ft.
3,754m

Tasmania

South Island

45°

60°

SOUTHERN OCEAN

Antarctic Circle

een Maud
Land

Enderby
Land

Wilkes Land

Victoria Land

75°

ANTARCTICA

15°   30°   45°   60°   75°   90°   105°   120°   135°   150°   165°   180°

Land Elevation		
Meters		Feet
3,000		9,840
2,000		6,560
500		1,640
200		656
0		0

Water Depth		
0		0
200		656
2,000		6,560

ASIA

RUSSIA

Arctic Circle

North Pole

ARCTIC OCEAN

GREENLAND
(Denmark)

ICELAND
Reykjavik

Arctic Circle

Bering
Sea

Beaufort
Sea

Queen Elizabeth
Islands

Ellesmere Island

Devon
Island

Baffin Bay

Bering Strait

Aleutian Islands

U.S.

Anchorage

Fairbanks

Prudhoe
Bay

Banks
Island

Victoria Island

Baffin Island

Godthab

Valdez

Gulf of Alaska

Yukon

Mackenzie

Great
Bear
Lake

Devon
Island

Whitehorse

Great
Slave
Lake

Yellowknife

Hudson
Bay

Juneau

Peace

CANADA

Nelson

Newfoundland

PACIFIC

OCEAN

Edmonton

Calgary

Vancouver

Victoria

Seattle

Saskatoon

Saskatchewan

Lake
Winnipeg

Regina

Winnipeg

Thunder Bay

Lake Superior

Québec

Gulf of
St. Lawrence

St. John's

Spokane

Columbia

Portland

Missouri

Billings

Minneapolis

Milwaukee

Lake Michigan

Detroit

Lake Ontario

St. Lawrence

Montréal
Ottawa
Toronto

Saint John

Halifax

Boston

Sacramento

San Francisco

Great
Salt
Lake

UNITED STATES

Omaha

Chicago

Cleveland

New York

Philadelphia

Washington D.C.

Las Vegas

Denver

Colorado

Kansas City

Indianapolis

Cincinnati

St. Louis

Ohio

Nashville

Norfolk

Los Angeles

San Diego

Tijuana

Arkansas

Albuquerque

Oklahoma
City

Red

Memphis

Atlanta

Charlotte

BERMUDA (U.K.)

Phoenix

Ciudad
Juárez

Hermosillo

Dallas

Rio Grande

Houston

Mississippi

New Orleans

Jacksonville

ATLANTIC

OCEAN

Tropic of Cancer

Chihuahua

San Antonio

Tampa

BAHAMAS

Tropic of Cancer

MEXICO

Culiacán

Torreón

Monterrey

Gulf
of
California

San Luis Potosí

Miami

Nassau

CUBA

Havana

DOMINICAN
REPUBLIC

PUERTO
RICO
(U.S.)

Guadalajara

León

Mérida

Cancún

JAMAICA

HAITI

Port-au-
Prince

Santo
Domingo

Mexico City

Puebla

Veracruz

Kingston

Acapulco

GUATEMALA

BELIZE

Belmopan

HONDURAS

CARIBBEAN

SEA

Caracas

Guatemala City

Tegucigalpa

NICARAGUA

San Salvador

EL SALVADOR

Lago de
Nicaragua

Panama
City

VENEZUELA

Managua

COSTA RICA

San José

Golfo
de
Panamá

COLOMBIA

Bogotá

PANAMA

PACIFIC

OCEAN

SOUTH AMERICA

BRAZIL

Equator

⊛	National Capital
■	City over 1,000,000 population
▣	City of 250,000 to 1,000,000 population
•	City under 250,000 population

0   200   400   600   800   1000 Miles

0   300   600   900   1200   1500 Kilometers

Copyright by Rand McNally & Co.
Lambert Azimuthal Equal Area Projection

ASIA
RUSSIA
Arctic Circle
Bering Strait
Point Hope
Point Barrow
Prudhoe Bay
Bering Sea
Aleutian Islands
Alaska Peninsula
Gulf of Alaska
U.S.
Brooks Range
Yukon
Kuskokwim
Mt. McKinley 20,320 Ft. 6,194m △
Alaska Range
Anchorage
Mt. Logan 19,551 Ft. 5,959m △
Coast Mountains
Whitehorse
Queen Charlotte Islands
Vancouver Island
Mackenzie
Rocky Mountains
Columbia
Cascade Range
Coast Ranges
Sierra Nevada

ARCTIC OCEAN
North Pole
Queen Elizabeth Islands
Ellesmere Island
Devon Island
Beaufort Sea
Cape Bathurst
Banks Island
Victoria Island
Great Bear Lake
Great Slave Lake
Peace
Lake Athabasca
Saskatchewan
Edmonton
CANADA
Nelson
Lake Winnipeg
Churchill
Hudson Bay
James Bay
Albany
Canadian Shield
Foxe Basin
Baffin Island
Baffin Bay
Cape Adair
Cape Mercy
Péninsule d'Ungava
GREENLAND (Denmark)
Ice Cap
ICELAND
Cape Farvel
Norwegian Sea

PACIFIC OCEAN
Cape Blanco
Cape Mendocino
Vancouver
Great Basin
Great Salt Lake
Snake
Mt. Whitney 14,494 Ft. 4,418m △
Los Angeles
Colorado
Colorado Plateau
Missouri
UNITED STATES
Denver
Arkansas
Red
Rio Grande
Great Lakes
Lake Superior
Lake Michigan
Lake Huron
Chicago
Ozark Plateau
Ohio
Mississippi
Lake Ontario
Lake Erie
Niagara Falls
Montréal
Ottawa
St. Lawrence
Gulf of St. Lawrence
Newfoundland
New York
Washington D.C.
Appalachian Mts.
Cape Cod
Cape Hatteras
Coastal Plain
BERMUDA (U.K.)
ATLANTIC OCEAN

Houston
Baja California
Gulf of California
Sierra Madre Occidental
MEXICO
Sierra Madre Oriental
Cabo San Lucas
Mexico City
Gulf of Campeche
Yucatán Peninsula
GULF OF MEXICO
Cape Canaveral
The Everglades
Miami
Havana
CUBA
BAHAMAS
Tropic of Cancer
HAITI
DOMINICAN REPUBLIC
PUERTO RICO (U.S.)
JAMAICA
CARIBBEAN SEA
VENEZUELA
COLOMBIA

BELIZE
GUATEMALA
HONDURAS
EL SALVADOR
Lago de Nicaragua
NICARAGUA
COSTA RICA
PANAMA
Golfo de Panama

PACIFIC OCEAN

Tropic of Cancer
Equator

SOUTH AMERICA
BRAZIL

Land Elevation

Meters		Feet
3,000		9,840
2,000		6,560
500		1,640
200		656
0		0

Water Depth

0		0
200		656
2,000		6,560

N

0 200 400 600 800 1000 Miles
0 300 600 900 1200 1500 Kilometers

Copyright by Rand McNally & Co.
Lambert Azimuthal Equal Area Projection

RAND McNALLY

CALIFORNIA
Los Angeles
110°
ARIZONA
NEW MEXICO
OKLAHOMA
ARKANSAS
MISSOURI
90°
KENTUC
TENNES
UNITED STAT
Tijuana ★ Mexicali
Nogales
Ciudad Juárez
El Paso
TEXAS
LOUISIANA
MISSISSIPPI
ALABAM
30°
BAJA CALIFORNIA
SONORA
Hermosillo
CHIHUAHUA
Chihuahua
Houston
New Orleans
Isla Cedros
Ciudad Obregón
Rio Grande
Nuevo Laredo
COAHUILA
NUEVO LEÓN
GULF OF
MEXICO
Gulf of California
BAJA CALIFORNIA SUR
Los Mochis
DURANGO
Torreón
Saltillo ★
Reynosa
Monterrey
Matamoros
Canal de Yuca
Tropic of Cancer
La Paz ★
Culiacán
MEXICO
Durango
ZACATECAS
Ciudad Victoria
TAMAULIPAS
20°
SINALOA
Mazatlán
Zacatecas ★
San Luis Potosí
SAN LUIS POTOSÍ
Tampico
MÉRIDA
Cancún
Islas Marías
NAYARIT
Tepic
AGS
Aguascalientes
León
Irapuato
GTO.
Querétaro
QRO
HGO
Pachuca
YUCATÁN
Isla Cozumel
Islas Revillagigedo
Isla San Benedicto
Isla Roca Partida
Isla Socorro
Puerto Vallarta
Guadalajara ★
JALISCO
COLIMA
Morelia ★
MICHOACÁN
Toluca ★
Mexico City
MEX
DF
TLAX
Puebla ★
PUEBLA
Campeche ★
Gulf of Campeche
CAMPECHE
QUINTANA ROO
Chetumal ★
Xalapa ★
Veracruz
VERACRUZ
GUERRERO
Chilpancingo ★
Acapulco
Oaxaca ★
OAXACA
Coatzacoalcos
TABASCO
Villahermosa ★
Golfo de Tehuantepec
Tuxtla ★
Gutiérrez
CHIAPAS
Belmopan
BELIZE
Gulf of Honduras
San Pedro Su
HONDURAS
Tapachula
GUATEMALA
Guatemala City ★
San Salvador ★
EL SALVADOR
Tegucigalpa ★
León
Managua ★
Lago de Nicaragua
COST
PACIFIC OCEAN
10°

⊛ National Capital

★ Secondary Capital
(State, Province, or Territory)

■ City over 1,000,000 population

▣ City of 250,000 to 1,000,000 population

• City under 250,000 population

0   100   200   300   400 Miles
0   200   400   600 Kilometers
Copyright by Rand McNally
Lambert Conformal Conic Projection

N

Isla del Mapelo
(Col.)

110°
100°
90°

VIRGINIA

NORTH CAROLINA

SOUTH CAROLINA

GIA

FLORIDA
Lake
Okeechobee

ATLANTIC OCEAN

BERMUDA
(U.K.)

30°

Freeport
Abaco
Miami
Nassau   BAHAMAS
Eleuthera
Cat Island
Andros
Straits of Florida

Tropic of Cancer

Havana
Santa Clara
Isla de la
Juventud
CUBA
Camagüey
Holguín
Great
Inagua

TURKS AND CAICOS ISLANDS
(U.K.)

20°

W   e   s   t

CAYMAN ISLANDS
(U.K.)

Guantánamo

Santiago
de Cuba

Santiago

I   n   d   i   e   s

VIRGIN
ISLANDS
(U.S.)

BRITISH
VIRGIN
ISLANDS

Santo
Domingo

ANGUILLA
(U.K.)

ANTIGUA
AND
BARBUDA

Montego Bay

HAITI
Port-au-
Prince

San
Juan

Basseterre

Saint John's

JAMAICA

Kingston

DOMINICAN
REPUBLIC

PUERTO RICO
(U.S.)

SAINT KITTS
AND NEVIS

MONTSERRAT
(U.K.)

GUADELOUPE
(Fr.)

DOMINICA
Roseau
MARTINIQUE
(Fr.)

CARIBBEAN   SEA

Castries   SAINT LUCIA

SAINT VINCENT
AND THE
GRENADINES   Kingstown

Bridgetown
BARBADOS

ARAGUA

Isla de
San Andrés
(Col.)

ARUBA
(Neth.)
Curaçao   Bonaire
NETHERLANDS
ANTILLES

Saint
George's   GRENADA

Port of Spain
TRINIDAD AND TOBAGO

10°

Caracas

San José

Panama
Canal
Panama
City
PANAMA
Golfo de
Panamá

Maracaibo

Lago de
Maracaibo

Orinoco

VENEZUELA

Georgetown

GUYANA

Isla de Coiba

SURINAME

COLOMBIA

Bogotá

Orinoco

BRAZIL

80°   70°   60°

RAND McNALLY

A9

GULF OF MEXICO

Havana

NORTH AMERICA

CUBA

HAITI

DOMINICAN REPUBLIC

JAMAICA

MEXICO

BELIZE

GUATEMALA

HONDURAS

EL SALVADOR

NICARAGUA

COSTA RICA

PANAMA

PUERTO RICO (U.S.)

Lesser Antilles

CARIBBEAN SEA

ATLANTIC OCEAN

Barranquilla
Cartagena
Maracaibo
Caracas
TRINIDAD AND TOBAGO

Barquisimeto
Valencia
Cúcuta
Bucaramanga
VENEZUELA
Orinoco
Ciudad Guayana

Medellín
Bogotá
COLOMBIA
⊛Georgetown
GUYANA
⊛*Paramaribo*
SURINAME
Cayenne
FRENCH GUIANA

Cali

Macapá

Galapagos Islands (Ec.)

Quito
ECUADOR
Guayaquil

Putumayo
Japurá

Negro
Manaus
Amazon
Santarém
Tocantins
Belém
São Luis

Equator

Iquitos
Amazon
Juruá

Imperatriz
Fortaleza
Teresina

Chiclayo
Ucayali
P E R U
Madeira
Tapajós
B R A Z I L
Pôrto Velho

Natal

Trujillo

Recife
Maceió

Lima⊛

Feira de Santana
Aracaju

Cusco
Lake Titicaca
BOLIVIA
Cuiabá
Salvador

Arequipa
⊛*La Paz*
Cochabamba
Santa Cruz
Goiânia
⊛*Brasília*

Montes Claros

⊛*Sucre*
Uberlândia

Campo Grande
Paraná
Belo Horizonte
Vitória

Antofagasta
PARAGUAY
Campinas
Rio de Janeiro

Tropic of Capricorn

Isla San Ambrosio (Chile)

Salta
⊛*Asunción*
São Paulo

San Miguel de Tucumán
Curitiba

Isla San Félix (Chile)

Paraná
Caxias do Sul

Pôrto Alegre

Archipiélago Juan Fernández (Chile)

Córdoba
Santa Fe
URUGUAY

Valparaíso
Rosario

C
H
I
L
E
A
R
G
E
N
T
I
N
A

Mendoza
Santiago
Buenos Aires
⊛*Montevideo*
La Plata
Río de la Plata

Concepción

Bahía Blanca
Mar del Plata

PACIFIC OCEAN

N

ATLANTIC OCEAN

Chiloé

Archipiélago de los Chonos

Comodoro Rivadavia

⊛ National Capital

■ City over 1,000,000 population

▣ City of 250,000 to 1,000,000 population

• City under 250,000 population

FALKLAND ISLANDS (U.K.)
West Falkland
East Falkland

Strait of Magellan

Punta Arenas
Tierra del Fuego

South Georgia (U.K.)

0 200 400 600 800 1000 Miles

0 300 600 900 1200 1500 Kilometers

Copyright by Rand McNally & Co.
Lambert Azimuthal Equal Area Projection

Drake Passage

South Shetland Islands (U.K.)
South Orkney Islands (U.K.)

South Sandwich Islands (U.K.)

GULF OF MEXICO

90°   80°   70°   60°   50°   40°   30°

NORTH AMERICA

CUBA

Greater Antilles

HAITI   DOMINICAN REPUBLIC

JAMAICA

PUERTO RICO (U.S.)

BELIZE

MEXICO

GUATEMALA   HONDURAS

Gulf of Honduras

EL SALVADOR   NICARAGUA

CARIBBEAN SEA

Lesser Antilles

ATLANTIC OCEAN

20°

COSTA RICA

PANAMA

Gulf of Panama

Cristóbal Colón Peak 18,948 Ft. 5,775m

Caracas

TRINIDAD AND TOBAGO

10°

Galapagos Islands (Ec.)

Magdalena

Bogotá

COLOMBIA

Llanos

Orinoco

VENEZUELA

GUYANA

SURINAME   FRENCH GUIANA

Cape Orange

ECUADOR

Chimborazo 20,703 Ft. 6,310m

Putumayo   Japurá

Amazon

Negro

Amazon

Ilha de Marajó

Belém

Equator   0°

Amazon Basin

Manaus

PERU

Juruá

Selvas

Ucayali

Madeira

Tapajós

BRAZIL

Tocantins

Andes

Mt. Huascarán 22,133 Ft. 6,746m

Lima

Lake Titicaca

Mt. Illampu 21,066 Ft. 6,421m

BOLIVIA

Cordillera Oriental

Mato Grosso Plateau

Brasília

Recife

10°

São Francisco

Serra do Espinhaço

Atacama Desert

Mt. Sajama 21,463 Ft. 6,542m

Gran Chaco

PARAGUAY

Paraná

20°

Isla San Ambrosio (Chile)

Tropic of Capricorn

São Paulo

Rio de Janeiro

Tropic of Capricorn

Isla San Felix (Chile)

Mt. Ojos del Salado 22,615 Ft. 6,893m

Andes

Paraná

PACIFIC OCEAN

Archipiélago Juan Fernández (Chile)

Mt. Aconcagua 22,831 Ft. 6,959m

Santiago

CHILE

ARGENTINA

URUGUAY

Buenos Aires

Rio de la Plata

30°

Pampas

Land Elevation

Meters		Feet
3,000		9,840
2,000		6,560
500		1,640
200		656
0		0

Chiloé

San Matías Gulf

Península Valdés

Patagonia

San Jorge Gulf

40°

Water Depth

0		0
200		656
2,000		6,560

Point Medanoso

ATLANTIC OCEAN

Grand Bay

FALKLAND ISLANDS (U.K.)

West Falkland   East Falkland

Strait of Magellan

0   200   400   600   800   1000 Miles

0   300   600   900   1200   1500 Kilometers

Copyright by Rand McNally & Co.
Lambert Azimuthal Equal Area Projection

Tierra del Fuego

Cape Horn

South Georgia (U.K.)

South Sandwich Islands (U.K.)

50°

Drake Passage

South Shetland Islands (U.K.)

South Orkney Islands (U.K.)

60°

110°   100°   90°   80°   70°   60°   50°   40°   30°   20°   10°

National Capital
Secondary Capital
(State, Province, or Territory)
City over 1,000,000 population
City of 250,000 to 1,000,000 population
City under 250,000 population

0   100   200   300   400 Miles
0   200   400   600 Kilometers

Copyright by Rand McNally
Lambert Conformal Conic Projection
M-101521-2

Murmansk

WHITE SEA

Arkhangel'sk

Oulu

NLAND

Northern Dvina

Syktyvkar

RUSSIA

Petrozavodsk
Lake
Onega

Kirov

Perm'

Izhevsk

Ufa

Helsinki

St. Petersburg

Cherepovets
Rybinsk
Res.

Nizhniy
Novgorod

Kazan'

ASIA

of Finland

Tallinn

STONIA

Lake
Peipus

Yaroslavl'

Oka

Samara

Rīga

LATVIA

Tver'

Moscow

Ryazan'

Penza

ilnius

Vitsyebsk

Tula

Saratov

Syr Darya

Minsk

Bryansk

Don

Lipetsk

Voronezh

Ural

KAZAKHSTAN

BELARUS

Homyel'

Volgograd

Aral Sea

Amu Darya

Chernobyl

Kiev

Kharkiv

Luhans'k

UZBEKISTAN

L'viv

Vinnytsya

UKRAINE

Dnieper

Dnipro-
petrovs'k

Volga

Astrakhan'

Dniester

Kryvyy Rih

Donets'k

Rostov

CASPIAN

TURKMENISTAN

MOLDOVA

Iaşi

Chişinău

Zaporizhzhya

Mariupol'

Krasnodar

Stavropol'

Ashgabat

Cluj-Napoca

Odesa

Sea of Azov

SEA

ROMANIA

Galaţi

Simferopol'

Grozyy

Sevastopol'

Bucharest

Danube

BLACK SEA

GEORGIA

Tbilisi

Bākū

Craiova

BULGARIA

Varna

Yerevan

ARMENIA

AZERBAIJAN

AZER.

Sofia

Plovdiv

Tehran

Istanbul

IRAN

Thessaloniki

Ankara

TURKEY

REECE

AEGEAN

SEA

IRAQ

Baghdad

Euphrates

Tigris

Athens

SEA

SYRIA

Crete

CYPRUS

Nicosia

Beirut

LEBANON

ICELAND

Horn

Fontur

Surtsey

Arctic Circle

NORWEGIAN SEA

Lofoten Islands

Kebnekaise
6,926 Ft.
2,111m

Torne

A T L A N T I C

O C E A N

FAROE ISLANDS
(Den.)

Scandinavian

Peninsula

NORWAY

SWEDEN

Gulf of Bot

Umeälven

Galdhøpiggen △
8,100 Ft.
2,469m

Glåma

Klarälven

Dalälven

Hebrides

Orkney
Islands

Stockholm ✪

Vänern

Vättern

Öland

Land Elevation

Meters		Feet
3,000		9,840
2,000		6,560
500		1,640
200		656
0		0

Water Depth

0		0
200		656
2,000		6,560

N

Grampian
Mts.

UNITED

Cheviot
Hills

KINGDOM

N O R T H

S E A

DENMARK

Skagerrak

BALTIC SE

IRELAND

Irish
Sea

Great
Britain

Bornholm
(Den.)

St. George's Channel

Thames

London ✪

NETHERLANDS

Elbe

Berlin ✪

Oder

Northern Eu

RUS

English Channel

Strait of Dover

BELGIUM

Rhine

GERMANY

POLAND

0   100   200   300   400 Miles

0   200   400   600 Kilometers

Copyright by Rand McNally
Lambert Conformal Conic Projection
M-101522-2

LUX.

Paris ✪
Paris
Basin

Loire

Seine

CZECH
REPUBLIC

Bohemian
Forest

SLOVAKIA

Bay of Biscay

FRANCE

Saône

Black
Forest

Danube

AUSTRIA

Great Hungar
Plain

HUNGARY

Cantabrian Mts.

Dordogne

Pyrenees

Massif
Central

Jura

SWITZERLAND

LIECH.

A

l

p

s

SLOVENIA

Drava

Douro

Iberian Mts.

Ebro

Mt. Blanc
15,771 Ft.
4,808m

Rhône

Po

CROATIA

Duero

Rhône

ANDORRA

MONACO

SAN
MARINO

Apennines

Dinaric Alps

BOSNIA AND
HERZEGOVINA

SERBI

Lisbon ✪

PORTUGAL

Iberian

Peninsula

Tagus

SPAIN

Sierra Morena

Corsica
(Fr.)

Rome ✪

ITALY

Balearic Islands

Minorca

Sardinia
(It.)

MONTE
NEGRO

KOSO

ALBANIA

MA
DO

Balk

Strait of Gibraltar

Ibiza

Majorca

Vesuvius
4,190 Ft.
1,277m

TYRRHENIAN
SEA

GIBRALTAR
(U.K.)

M E D I T E R R A N

Pindus

Algiers

Mt. Etna
10,902 Ft.
3,323m △

Sicily

IONIAN
SEA

MOROCCO

A F R I C A

ALGERIA

TUNISIA

MALTA

Murmansk

Kola
Peninsula
Ponoy

WHITE SEA

Timan Ridge

Pechora

Ob'

ASIA

Mezen

Northern Dvina

Onega

Ural Mountains

Northern Uvals
(Uplands)

NLAND

Sukhona

Kama

Lake
Onega

Irtysh

Helsinki
of Finland

Lake
Ladoga

RUSSIA

Rybinsk
Res.

TONIA

Lake
Peipus

Valdai
Hills

★ Moscow

Oka

LATVIA

Plain

Central
Russian
Upland

Don

Khoper

Ural

Syr Darya

KAZAKHSTAN

Aral Sea

IA

Neman

BELARUS

Caspian Depression

UZBEKISTAN

Pripyat

Dnieper

Lowland

Donets Basin

Volga

Amu Darya

Kiev ★

Dnieper

UKRAINE

TURKMENISTAN

Dniester

MOLDOVA

Sea of Azov

CASPIAN

Crimean
Peninsula

athian Mts.

MANIA

sylvanian Alps

Caucasus

ninsula

Danube

BLACK SEA

Mt. Elbrus
18,510 Ft.
5,642m

GEORGIA

Baku

SEA

BULGARIA

ARMENIA

AZERBAIJAN

AZER.

Istanbul

★ Tehran

Olympus
70 Ft.
17m

TURKEY

IRAN

EGEAN SEA

REECE

Rhodes

IRAQ

SYRIA

Euphrates

Tigris

N

SEA

CYPRUS

LEBANON

Crete

ATLANTIC OCEAN

PORTUGAL

Azores (Port.)

Madeira Islands (Port.)

Strait of Gibraltar

SPAIN

Madrid

FRANCE
EUROPE
ITALY
Rome
BOS.
SERB.
ALB.
GREECE
Athens

AUS. HUNG.
ROMANIA
BUL.
Black Sea

UKRAINE
RUSSIA
GEORGIA
ARM. AZER.
TURKEY

KAZ.
Aral Sea
UZBEK.
Caspian Sea
TURKMENISTAN

Mediterranean Sea

MALTA

CYPRUS
LEBANON
ISRAEL
JORDAN
SYRIA
IRAQ
IRAN
KUWAIT

Algiers
Oran
Qacentina
Tunis
TUNISIA
Ghardaia

Rabat
Casablanca
MOROCCO
Marrakech

Canary Islands (Spain)

El Aaiún

WESTERN SAHARA (MOROCCO)

Tropic of Cancer

Tripoli
Gulf of Sidra
Banghāzī

Alexandria
Cairo
Suez
Asyut

Riyadh
SAUDI ARABIA
QATAR
U.A.E.
Persian Gulf
OM

ALGERIA
In Salah
Sabhā
LIBYA
EGYPT
Aswan
Lake Nasser

Tamanrasset

MAURITANIA
Nouakchott

Dakar
SENEGAL
Senegal
GAMBIA
GUINEA-BISSAU
GUINEA
Conakry
Freetown
SIERRA LEONE
Monrovia
LIBERIA

Timbuktu
MALI
Gao
Niger
Bamako
BURKINA FASO
Ouagadougou
COTE D'IVOIRE
GHANA
Lake Volta
TOGO
BENIN
Cotonou
Accra
Abidjan

NIGER
Agadez
Niamey
Kano
NIGERIA
Abuja
Benue
Lagos

CHAD
Lake Chad
Abéché
N'Djamena

SUDAN
Omdurman
Khartoum
Port Sudan
Red Sea
Nile
Blue Nile

ERITREA
Asmara
YEMEN
Gulf of Aden
DJIBOUTI
Djibouti
Lake Tana
ETHIOPIA
Addis Ababa
Dire Dawa
SOMALIA

CAPE VERDE

CENTRAL AFRICAN REPUBLIC
Bangui
CAMEROON
Douala
Yaoundé
Malabo
EQUATORIAL GUINEA
SAO TOME AND PRINCIPE
GABON
Libreville
REP. OF CONGO
Brazzaville
Kinshasa

Waw
Juba
SOUTH SUDAN
Nile
Mountains
Ubangi
Uele
Congo
Kisangani
DEM. REP. OF CONGO
UGANDA
Kampala
Lake Victoria
Kigali
RWANDA
Bujumbura
BURUNDI
Lake Turkana
KENYA
Nairobi
Mombasa
Mogadishu

INDIAN OCEAN
SEYCHEL

Equator

N

Ascension (St. Helena)

Luanda
Lobito
Huambo
ANGOLA

Mbuji-Mayi
Kolwezi
Lubumbashi
Ndola
ZAMBIA
Lusaka
Lake Kariba
Zambezi

Lake Tanganyika
Dodoma
TANZANIA
Dar es Salaam

MALAWI
Lake Nyasa
Lilongwe
Mayotte (Fr.)
COMOROS
Antsiranana
MOZAMBIQUE
Beira

Antananarivo
MADAGASCAR
MAURIT
Fianarantsoa
Reunion (Fr.)

ATLANTIC OCEAN

St. Helena (U.K.)

NAMIBIA
Windhoek
Okavango
BOTSWANA
Limpopo

Harare
ZIMBABWE

Mozambique Channel

Tropic of Capricorn

Gaborone
Pretoria
Johannesburg
Maputo
SWAZILAND
Maseru
LESOTHO
Durban

Orange
SOUTH AFRICA
Cape Town
Port Elizabeth

Tristan da Cunha Group (St. Helena)

0 200 400 600 800 1000 Miles
0 300 600 900 1200 1500 Kilometers
Copyright by Rand McNally
Lambert Azimuthal Equal Area Projection
M-101525-3

Prince Edward Islands (S. Af.)

Crozet Islands (Fr.)

⊛	National Capital
■	City over 1,000,000 population
▣	City of 250,000 to 1,000,000 population
•	City under 250,000 population

ATLANTIC OCEAN

Azores (Port.)

Madeira Islands (Port.)

PORTUGAL

SPAIN

Strait of Gibraltar

Canary Islands (Spain)

MOROCCO

Atlas Mountains

Algiers

Great Western Desert

Great Eastern Desert

TUNISIA

WESTERN SAHARA (MOROCCO)

Tropic of Cancer

ALGERIA

Ijafene

Tahat 9,541 Ft. 2,908m

S a h a r a   D e s e r t

Ahaggar Mts.

LIBYA

EGYPT

Libyan Desert

Qattara Depression

Cairo

FRANCE

EUROPE

ITALY

AUS. HUNG.

ROMANIA

BOS. SERB.

UKRAINE

ALB. GREECE

MALTA

Mediterranean Sea

BUL.

Black Sea

TURKEY

CYPRUS

LEBANON

ISRAEL

SYRIA

JORDAN

Gulf of Sidra

RUSSIA

GEORGIA

ARM. AZER.

KAZ.

Aral Sea

Caspian Sea

UZBEKISTAN

TURKMENISTAN

IRAQ

IRAN

KUWAIT

Persian Gulf

QATAR

U.A.E.

SAUDI ARABIA

OMAN

Lake Nasser

Red Sea

Nile

Nubian Desert

YEMEN

Gulf of Aden

Socotra (Yem.)

Cape Gwardafuy

PE VERDE

MAURITANIA

MALI

Sahel

NIGER

Aïr (Mts.)

Tibesti Massif

Mt. Koussi 11,204 Ft. 3,415m

Ennedi

CHAD

SUDAN

Khartoum

White Nile

Blue Nile

Lake Tana

ERITREA

DJIBOUTI

Cape Verde

SENEGAL

Dakar

GAMBIA

GUINEA-BISSAU

GUINEA

Sénégal

Niger

BURKINA FASO

BENIN

Niger

Lake Chad

NIGERIA

Jos Plateau

Benue

Ethiopian Plateau

Great Rift Valley

SIERRA LEONE

LIBERIA

COTE D'IVOIRE

GHANA

TOGO

Lake Volta

As Sudd

Mountain Nile

CENTRAL AFRICAN REPUBLIC

SOUTH SUDAN

SOMALIA

ETHIOPIA

Lagos

CAMEROON

Mt. Cameroon 13,451 Ft. 4,100m

Bioko

Gulf of Guinea

EQUATORIAL GUINEA

SAO TOME AND PRINCIPE

GABON

REP. OF CONGO

Ubangi

Congo

Uele

UGANDA

Lake Turkana

KENYA

Mt. Kenya 17,058 Ft. 5,199m

Equator

Congo Basin

Lake Victoria

Nairobi

RWANDA

BURUNDI

Serengeti Plain

Kilimanjaro 19,340 Ft. 5,895m

Masai Steppe

Zanzibar

INDIAN OCEAN

SEYCHELLES

DEM. REP. OF CONGO

Kinshasa

Kwango

Kasai

Cuanza

Great Rift Valley

Lake Tanganyika

TANZANIA

N

ATLANTIC

Ascension (St. Helena)

St. Helena (U.K.)

OCEAN

ANGOLA

Cunene

Okavango

ZAMBIA

Victoria Falls

Lake Kariba

MALAWI

Lake Nyasa

Zambezi

Mayotte (Fr.)

COMOROS

Cape Ambre

MOZAMBIQUE

MAURITIUS

Reunion (Fr.)

ZIMBABWE

Namib Desert

NAMIBIA

BOTSWANA

Kalahari Desert

Limpopo

Mozambique Channel

MADAGASCAR

Tropic of Capricorn

Barra Point

Vaal

Johannesburg

SWAZILAND

Cape Sainte-Marie

Orange

LESOTHO

Drakensberg

SOUTH AFRICA

Cape of Good Hope

Cape Agulhas

Land Elevation

Meters		Feet
3,000		9,840
2,000		6,560
500		1,640
200		656
0		0

Water Depth

0		0
200		656
2,000		6,560

Tristan da Cunha Group (St. Helena)

0 200 400 600 800 1000 Miles

0 300 600 900 1200 1500 Kilometers

Copyright by Rand McNally
Lambert Azimuthal Equal Area Projection
M-101526-3

Prince Edward Islands (S. Af.)

Crozet Islands (Fr.)

RAND MCNALLY

ATLANTIC

OCEAN

ARCTIC OCEA

ICELAND

FAROE
ISLANDS
(Den.)

Norwegian Sea

Arctic Circle

SVALBARD
(Nor.)

Spitsbergen

Franz Josef
Land

80°

Severnay
Zemlya

Barents
Sea

Novaya
Zemlya

Kara Sea

Noril'sk

PORTUGAL

SPAIN

MOROCCO

ANDORRA

GIBRALTAR
(U.K.)

IRELAND

UNITED
KINGDOM

London

North Sea

DENMARK

NORWAY

SWEDEN

FINLAND

ESTONIA

LATVIA
LITH.

RUSSIA

BELARUS

Ob'

Pechora

Yenisey

R U

Paris

FRANCE

NETH.

BEL.

GERMANY

CZECH
REP.

AUSTRIA

POLAND

SLOVAKIA

HUNGARY

Kiev

UKRAINE

Moscow

Volga

Yekaterinburg

Chelyabinsk

Novosibirsk

Omsk

Barnaul

Ishim

Irtysh

Ob'

Astana

KAZAKHSTAN

Karaganda

Semipalatins

Öskemen

ITALY

Adriatic Sea

SLO.

CRO.

BOS.

SERB.

MONT.

KOS.

MAC.

ALB.

ROMANIA

Danube

BULGARIA

GREECE

Black Sea

Istanbul

Izmir

Ankara

TURKEY

GEORGIA

Tbilisi

ARM.

Yerevan

AZER.

Caspian Sea

Aral
Sea

Syr Darya

Lake
Balkhash

ALGERIA

TUNISIA

Mediterranean Sea

LIBYA

CYPRUS

Beirut
LEBANON

Damascus

SYRIA

ISRAEL

Jerusalem

Euphrates

Tigris

Tabriz

Baku

TURKMENISTAN

UZBEKISTAN

Ashgabat

Tashkent

Bishkek

Almaty

Ürümq

KYRGYZSTAN

CHAD

EGYPT

Nile

JORDAN

Amman

IRAQ

Baghdad

Tehran

Esfahan

Mashhad

IRAN

Dushanbe

TAJIKISTAN

Kabul

Kuwait

KUWAIT

Persian Gulf

SUDAN

Nile

Red Sea

SAUDI

ARABIA

Riyadh

Jiddah

BAHRAIN

QATAR

Abu Dhabi

U.A.E.

Gulf of Oman

Muscat

OMAN

AFGHANISTAN

Islamabad

Lahore

Amritsar

PAKISTAN

Indus

Karachi

Hyderābād

Delhi

New
Delhi

Ganges

NEPAL

Kathmandu

Brahmaput

Kānpur

ERITREA

SOUTH SUDAN

DÉM. REP.
OF THE CONGO
(ZAIRE)

UGANDA

RWANDA

BURUNDI

KENYA

TANZANIA

ZAMBIA

MOZAMBIQUE

Blue Nile

ETHIOPIA

DJIBOUTI

SOMALIA

Gulf of Aden

YEMEN

Sanaa

Socotra
(Yem.)

Arabian

Sea

Ahmadābād

Mumbai
(Bombay)

Godavāri

Nāgpur

I N D I A

Hyderābād

Bangalore

Lakshadweep
(India)

Kolkata
(Calcutt

Ganges

Chennai
(Madras)

Bay of
Bengal

N

Colombo

SRI LANKA

MALDIVES

INDIAN OCEAN

0   200   400   600   800 Miles

0   200 400 600 800 1000 Kilometers
Copyright by Rand McNally
Lambert Azimuthal Equal Area Projection
MI-101523-3

National Capital
City over 1,000,000 population
City of 250,000 to 1,000,000 population
City under 250,000 population

New Siberian Islands
East Siberian Sea
Laptev Sea
Bering Sea
ALEUTIAN ISLANDS (U.S.)

Anadyr'
Palana
Kamchatka Peninsula
Petropavlovsk-Kamchatskiy

Lena
Yakutsk
Magadan
Sea of Okhotsk

ngara
aynoyarsk
Lake Baikal
Chita
Amur
Khabarovsk
Sakhalin
Kuril Islands

Irkutsk
sey
Ulaanbaatar
MONGOLIA

Qiqihar
Harbin
Vladivostok
Sapporo
Hokkaido

Changchun
Shenyang
NORTH KOREA
Seoul
SOUTH KOREA
Honshu
Tokyo
JAPAN
Nagoya

Beijing
Tianjin
Yellow Sea
Pusan
Osaka
Shikoku
Kyushu

Taiyuan
Jinan
Sea of Japan (East Sea)

Lanzhou
Huang
Huang
Nanjing
Shanghai
East China Sea

CHINA
Xi'an
Wuhan
Hangzhou

Chengdu
Chongqing
Chang (Yangtze)
Fuzhou
Taipei
TAIWAN

Guiyang
Guangzhou
Kaohsiung

Kunming
Nanning
Hong Kong
Luzon Strait

haka
Chittagong
Hanoi
Hainan Island
Luzon
PHILIPPINES

MYANMAR
LAOS
Gulf of Tonkin
South China Sea
Manila
Samar
Cebu

angon
Vientiane
THAILAND
Da Nang
Mindanao

Bangkok
CAMBODIA
VIETNAM
Davao

Phnom Penh
Ho Chi Minh City
Sulu Sea

Andaman Sea
Gulf of Thailand
Celebes Sea
Manado

cobar ands dia)
Bandar Seri Begawan
BRUNEI
MALAYSIA

MALAYSIA
Borneo
Ceram

Medan
Kuala Lumpur
Singapore
Banjarmasin
Celebes

Sumatra
INDONESIA
Banda Sea
Arafura Sea

Palembang
Jakarta
Bandung
Surabaya
Java
Java Sea
TIMOR-LESTE
Timor
Timor Sea

PACIFIC OCEAN
Tropic of Cancer

NORTHERN MARIANA ISLANDS (U.S.)

GUAM (U.S.)
Philippine Sea
FEDERATED STATES OF MICRONESIA

PALAU
Equator

New Guinea
PAPUA NEW GUINEA

Gulf of Carpentaria
Coral Sea
AUSTRALIA

RAND McNALLY

A19

ATLANTIC
OCEAN

ARCTIC OCEAN

Arctic Circle

ICELAND

FAROE
ISLANDS
(Den.)

IRELAND

UNITED
KINGDOM

London

North Sea

DENMARK

NORWAY

SWEDEN

FINLAND

Barents
Sea

Severn
Zem.

Novaya
Zemlya

Kara Sea

Yamal
Pen.

PORTUGAL

SPAIN

GIBRALTAR
(U.K.)

ANDORRA

MOROCCO

FRANCE

ITALY

MONACO

NETH.
BEL.
LUX.

GERMANY

CZECH REP.
AUS.
SWITZ.
SLOVAKIA

POLAND

LITH.

ESTONIA
LATVIA

RUSSIA

BELARUS

Moscow

Ural Mountains

Ob

West
Siberian
Lowland

Novosibir

Irtysh

Ob

ALGERIA

TUNISIA

SLOVENIA
CROATIA
BOS.
SERBIA
MONT.
KOS.
MAC.
ALB.

HUNGARY

ROMANIA

BULGARIA

UKRAINE

MOLD.

Volga

Astana

KAZAKHSTAN

Lake
Balkhash

Mediterranean Sea

GREECE

Black Sea

Ankara

GEORGIA

Caucasus

Caspian Depression

Ishim

Irtysh

LIBYA

CYPRUS

TURKEY

Mount Ararat
16,940 Ft.
5,165m

ARM.
AZER.

Caspian
Sea

Aral
Sea

Ust-Urt
Plateau

Syr Darya

Tian Shan

LEBANON
ISRAEL

SYRIA

Tigris

Kara Kum
(Desert)

UZBEKISTAN

KYRGYZSTAN

Cairo

EGYPT

JORDAN

IRAQ

Euphrates

Tehran

TURKMENISTAN

Amu Darya

TAJIKISTAN

Pamirs

K2 (Qogir Feng)
28,250 Ft.
8,611m

Tarim Basin

Nile

Sinai
Pen.

Red Sea

An-Nafud

SAUDI
ARABIA

Zagros Mts.

IRAN

Dasht-e Kavir

AFGHANISTAN

Hindu Kush

Kunlun M

KUWAIT

CHAD

SUDAN

Arabian
Peninsula

Persian Gulf

BAHRAIN
QATAR

U.A.E.

Gulf of
Oman

PAKISTAN

Indus

Great
Indian
Desert

New
Delhi

Ganges

HIMALAYA MT

NEPAL

Mt. Evere
29,035
8,

ERITREA

Rub Al-Khali

OMAN

INDIA

SOUTH SUDAN

DEM. REP.
OF THE CONGO

DJIBOUTI

ETHIOPIA

YEMEN

Gulf of
Aden

Socotra
(Yem.)

Mumbai
(Bombay)

Godavari

Deccan
Plateau

Western Ghats

Eastern Ghats

Bay
Ben

UGANDA

RWANDA

KENYA

SOMALIA

Arabian Sea

Lakshadweep
(India)

BURUNDI

N

SRI LANKA

TANZANIA

MALDIVES

INDIAN OCEAN

ZAMBIA

MALAWI

MOZAMBIQUE

0   200   400   600   800 Miles
0 200 400 600 800 1000 Kilometers

Copyright by Rand McNally
Lambert Azimuthal Equal Area Projection
M-101524-3

Land Elevation

Meters	Feet
3,000	9,840
2,000	6,560
500	1,640
200	656
0	0

Water Depth

0	0
200	656
2,000	6,560

New Siberian Islands

East Siberian Sea

Laptev Sea

...myr ...sula

...ntral ...berian ...plands

Indigirka

Kolyma

Arctic Circle

70°

60°

50°

40°

30°

Verkhoyansk Mts.

Lena

Kamchatka Peninsula

Bering Sea

Aleutian Islands (U.S.)

170°

RUSSIA

Siberia

Stanovoy Range

Amur

Lake Baikal

...ngara

Sea of Okhotsk

Sakhalin

Tatar Strait

Kuril Islands

PACIFIC

OCEAN

180°

Greater Khingan Range

Sikhote-Alin Mts.

Hokkaido

Tropic of Cancer

20°

...an Mountains

Sea of Japan (East Sea)

Honshu

Tokyo

MONGOLIA

...ai Mts.

Gobi Desert

NORTH KOREA

⊛ **Beijing**

Amur

SOUTH KOREA

Mt. Fuji 12,388 ft. 3,776m

JAPAN

Shikoku

Kyushu

Yellow Sea

CHINA

Qilian Shan

Huang

Chang (Yangtze)

Qinling Shandi

■ **Shanghai**

East China Sea

NORTHERN MARIANA ISLANDS (U.S.)

10°

GUAM (U.S.)

FEDERATED STATES OF MICRONESIA

...JTAN

...maputra

GL

Xi

TAIWAN

Philippine Sea

Luzon Strait

Luzon

Hainan Island

MYANMAR

LAOS

Irrawaddy

Salween

Red

Mekong

Gulf of Tonkin

South China Sea

PHILIPPINES

0°

Equator

180°

THAILAND

VIETNAM

⊛ **Manila**

Mindanao

PALAU

Bangkok ⊛

CAMBODIA

Sulu Sea

...man ...nds ...dia)

Andaman Sea

Gulf of Thailand

Celebes Sea

New Guinea

PAPUA NEW GUINEA

10°

MALAY PENINSULA

BRUNEI

MALAYSIA

Celebes

Moluccas

Ceram

...icobar ...slands (India)

MALAYSIA

Str. of Malacca

⊛ **Singapore**

Borneo

Banda Sea

Arafura Sea

Gulf of Carpentaria

Coral Sea

Sumatra

Greater Sunda Islands

INDONESIA

TIMOR-LESTE

Timor

Timor Sea

AUSTRALIA

20°

Jakarta ⊛

Java

Java Sea

100°

110°

120°

130°

140°

150°

⊛ **RAND MCNALLY**

A21

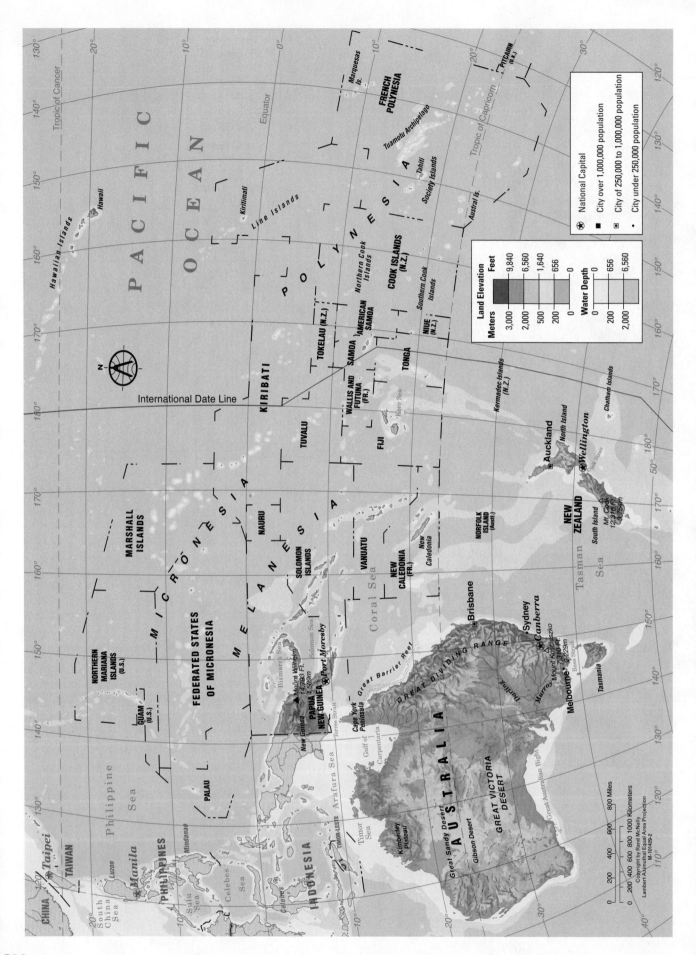

Australia and Oceania

Land Elevation

Meters	Feet
3,000	9,840
2,000	6,560
500	1,640
200	656
0	0

Water Depth

0	656
200	2,000	6,560

⊛ National Capital
■ City over 1,000,000 population
▣ City of 250,000 to 1,000,000 population
• City under 250,000 population

PACIFIC OCEAN

POLYNESIA

MICRONESIA

MELANESIA

Tropic of Cancer

Equator

Tropic of Capricorn

International Date Line

Marquesas Is.

FRENCH POLYNESIA

Tuamotu Archipelago

Tahiti
Society Islands

Austral Is.

Kiritimati

Line Islands

Northern Cook Islands

COOK ISLANDS (N.Z.)

Southern Cook Islands

NIUE (N.Z.)

TOKELAU (N.Z.)

AMERICAN SAMOA

SAMOA

KIRIBATI

WALLIS AND FUTUNA (FR.)

TONGA

Koro Sea

FIJI

TUVALU

MARSHALL ISLANDS

NAURU

NORTHERN MARIANA ISLANDS (U.S.)

GUAM (U.S.)

FEDERATED STATES OF MICRONESIA

SOLOMON ISLANDS

Solomon Sea

Bismarck Sea

VANUATU

NEW CALEDONIA (FR.)

New Caledonia

Kermadec Islands (N.Z.)

NORFOLK ISLAND (Aust.)

Chatham Islands

Auckland

North Island

Wellington

Cook Strait

NEW ZEALAND

Mt. Cook 12,316 ft. 3,754m

South Island

Tasman Sea

PITCAIRN (U.K.)

Hawaii

Hawaiian Islands

Taipei

TAIWAN

CHINA

Manila

PHILIPPINES

Luzon

Mindanao

South China Sea

Sulu Sea

Celebes Sea

Celebes

Philippine Sea

INDONESIA

TIMOR-LESTE

Timor Sea

Arafura Sea

PALAU

New Guinea

PAPUA NEW GUINEA

Mount Wilhelm 14,793 ft. 4,509m

Torres Strait

Cape York Peninsula

Gulf of Carpentaria

Great Barrier Reef

Coral Sea

Fort Moresby

Kimberley Plateau

Great Sandy Desert

Gibson Desert

GREAT VICTORIA DESERT

AUSTRALIA

Great Australian Bight

GREAT DIVIDING RANGE

Brisbane

Sydney

Canberra

Murray

Darling

Melbourne

Mount Kosciuszko 7,310 ft. 2,229m

Bass Strait

Tasmania

N

0 200 400 600 800 Miles
0 200 400 600 800 1000 Kilometers

Copyright by Rand McNally
Lambert Azimuthal Equal Area Projection
M-101439-2

⊛ RAND M?NALLY

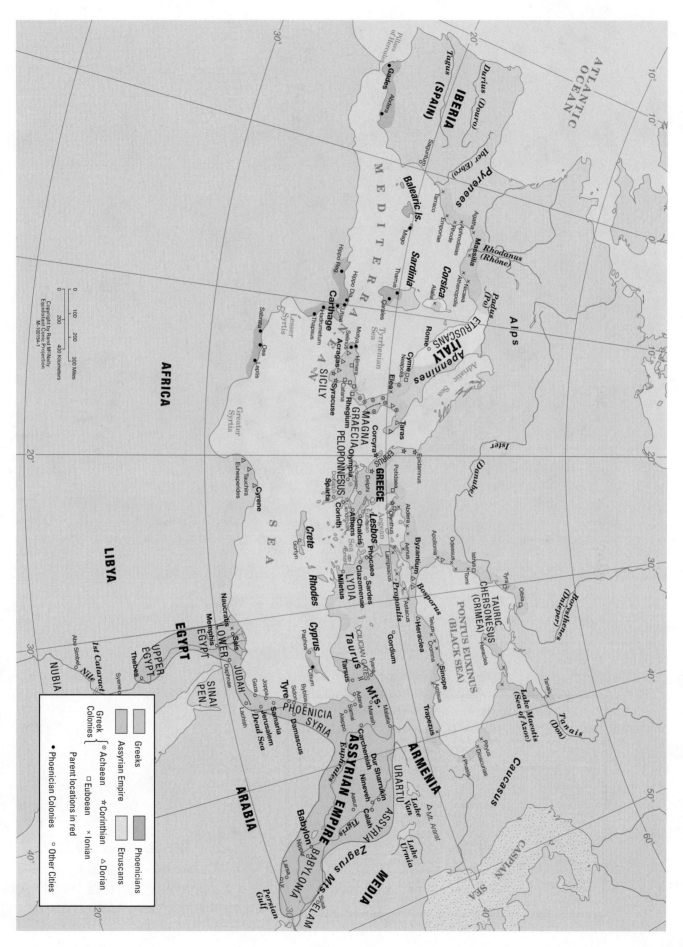

ATLANTIC OCEAN

IBERIA (SPAIN)

Tagus (Douro)
Durius (Douro)
Pillars of Hercules
Gades
Abdera
Iber (Ebro)
Saguntum
Pyrenees
Tarraco
Emporiae
Rhode
Agatha
Aphrodisias
Nicaea
Massilia
Rhodanus (Rhône)
Alps
Padus (Po)
ETRUSCANS
ITALY
Apennines
Alalia
Corsica
Athenopolis
Balearic Is.
Mago
Sardinia
Tharros
Caralles
Rome
Tyrrhenian Sea
Cyme
Neapolis
Adriatic Sea
Ister (Danube)

MEDITERRANEAN SEA

Hippo Reg.
Hippo Dia.
Utica
Carthage
Hadrumetum
Thapsus
Acragas
SICILY
Rhegium
Motya
Selinus
Himera
Catana
Syracuse
MAGNA GRAECIA
Taras
PELOPONNESUS
Sparta
Corinth
Olympia
Delphi
Athens
Chalcis
Eretria
Euboea
GREECE
Corcyra
EPIRUS
Potidaea
Epidamnus
Olynthus
Abdera
Aegean Sea
Lesbos
Phocaea
Clazomenae
Sardes
LYDIA
Miletus
Propontis
Byzantium
Bosporus
Aenus
Apollonia
Odessus
Istrus
Tomi
Tyras
Olbia
Borysthenes (Dnieper)
PONTUS EUXINUS (BLACK SEA)
TAURIC CHERSONESUS (CRIMEA)
Heraclea
Sinope
Amisus
Trapezus
Tanais
Lake Maeotis (Sea of Azov)
Tanais (Don)
Phasis
Dioscurias
Pityus
Caucasus
Mt. Ararat
CASPIAN SEA

AFRICA
LIBYA
Lesser Syrtis
Greater Syrtis
Sabrata
Oea
Lepcis
Cyrene
Euhesperides
Tauchira

Crete
Gortyn
Rhodes

Aegean Sea
Ionian Sea
Dodona

NUBIA
1st Cataract
Abu Simbel
Syene
Nile
Thebes
UPPER EGYPT
Memphis
LOWER EGYPT
EGYPT
Sais
Naucratis
Daphnae
SINAI PEN.
JUDAH
Jerusalem
Dead Sea
Samaria
Lachish
Gaza
Joppa
Tyre
Sidon
Byblos
PHOENICIA
SYRIA
Damascus
Aleppo
Simal
Carchemish
Til-Marash
Malatia
Mts
Tarsus
Taurus
Adana
CILICIAN GATES
Tyana
Gordium
Heraclea
Teum
Cius
Cyprus
Paphos
Citium
Lampsacus
Astacus

ASSYRIAN EMPIRE
ARMENIA
URARTU
Lake Van
Lake Urmia
ASSYRIA
Dur Sharrukin
Nineveh
Calah
Assur
MESOPOTAMIA
Tigris
Euphrates
Zagros
Babylon
BABYLONIA
Nippur
ELAM
Larsa
Ur
MEDIA
Persian Gulf

ARABIA

Copyright by Rand McNally
Equidistant Conic Projection
M-102154-1

0   100   200   300 Miles
0   200   400 Kilometers

Greeks
Assyrian Empire
Phoenicians
Etruscans

Greek Colonies {
⊙ Achaean
□ Euboean
✪ Corinthian
△ Dorian
× Ionian
}
Parent locations in red

● Phoenician Colonies
○ Other Cities

ATLANTIC

OCEAN

North Sea

Baltic Sea

IRELAND

BRITAIN

Wall of Antoninus

Wall of Hadrian

Deva

Eburacum

Lindum

BRITAIN

Camulodunum

Londinium

Lugdunum Batavorum

(Lost in 9 A.D.)

English Channel

Cantabrian Sea

LOWER GERMANY

Colonia Agrippina

GERMANY

Augusta Treverorum

Seine

BELGICA

Lutetia

Moguntiacum

LUGDUNENSIS

Elbe

Vistula

Liger (Loire)

Argentoratum

Rhine

GAUL

Augustodunum

UPPER GERMANY

CARPATHIANS

Carpathians

Bracara Augusta

Portus Cale

Douro

Asturica

Burdigala (Garonne)

AQUITANIA

Garumna

Rhone

Lugdunum

Vindonissa

Augusta Vindelicorum

RHAETIA

Vindobona

Carnuntum

NORICUM

Danube

Aquincum

TARRACONENSIS

Numantia

Iberus (Ebro)

Tolosa

Pyrenees

Alps

Comum

Mediolanum

Verona

Aquileia

Patavium

Po

ILLYRICUM

PANNONIA

Siscia

Sarmizeg.
(Colonia Ulpia)

DA

Salmantica

NARBONENSIS

Nemausus

Genua

Bononia

Ravenna

Florentia

Ancona

Sirmium

Olisipo

SPAIN

Caesar Augusta

Ilerda

Narbo

ALPINE PROVS.

Ligurian Sea

DALMATIA

Salonae

Narona

Viminiecium

Naissus

LUSITANIA

Emerita Augusta

Tagus

Toletum

Valentia

Massilia

Rome

ITALY

Adriatic Sea

Serdica

Tarraco

Ostia

Guadiana

Corduba

BAETICA

Hispalis

Munda

Castulo

Balearic Islands

CORSICA AND SARDINIA

Capua

Dyrrhachium

MACEDONIA

Philippop.

Gades

Tingis

Malaca

New Carthage

MEDITERRANEAN

Carales

Pompeii

Tarentum

Brundisium

Thessalonica

Corcyra

Ionian Sea

EPIRUS

Demetrias

Ac

Tyrrhenian Sea

MAURETANIA

Sitifis

Hippo Diarrhytus

Hippo Regius

Utica

Agrigentum

SICILY

Messina

Rhegium

Corinth

ACHAIA

Athen

Lambaesis

Cirta

Carthage

Syracuse

Sparta

Atlas Mountains

Thamugadi

Theveste

Hadrumetum

Thapsus

AFRICA

SEA

Crete

Gortyn

CRETE AN
CYREN

GAETULIA

NUMIDIA

Lesser Syrtis

Oea

Leptis

CRENA

Cyrene

CYRENA

Greater Syrtis

AFRICA

Roman City Names and Modern Equivalents

ROMAN NAME	MODERN NAME	ROMAN NAME	MODERN NAME
Ancyra	Ankara	Londinium	London
Aquincum	Budapest	Lugdunum	Lyon
Arelate	Arles	Lugdunum Batavorum	Leiden
Augusta Treverorum	Trier, Treves	Lutetia	Paris
Augusta Vindelicorum	Augsburg	Malaca	Malaga
Augustodunum	Autun	Massilia	Marseille
Bononia	Bologna	Mazaca Caesarea	Kayseri
Burdigala	Bordeaux	Mediolanum	Milan
Caesar Augusta	Saragossa	Moguntiacum	Mainz
Camulodunum	Colchester	Nemausus	Nimes
Carales	Cagliari	Olisipo	Lisbon
Colonia Agrippina	Cologne	Patavium	Padua
Deva	Chester	Salmantica	Salamanca
Eburacum	York	Thessalonica	Salonika
Emerita Augusta	Merida	Toletum	Toledo
Gades	Cadiz	Tolosa	Toulouse
Hispalis	Seville	Valentia	Valencia
Lindum	Lincoln	Vindobona	Vienna

	Roman Empire		Parthian Empire
	Armenia		Temporarily held by Rome

City of
ROME

Flaminian Gate
Pincian Gate
Salarian Gate
Nomentan Gate
Praetorian Camp
Mausoleum
of Augustus
Baths of Diocletian
C. NOMENTAN
Tiber
Virgo Aqueduct
FLAMINIAN ROAD
Mausoleum
of Hadrian
Sun Dial
Obelisk
Portico of Vipsania
Tiburtine Gate
Old Anio Aqueduct
CORNELIAN ROAD
Br. of Nero
Aurelian
Wall of Aurelian
Atellan Bridge
Baths
of Nero
Baths of Constantine
TRIUMPHAL ROAD
Stadium
Baths of Agrippa
Saepta Julia
Baths of
Constantine
Praenestine Gate
PRAENESTINE RD.
Circus Flaminius
Theater and Portico of Pompey
Forum
Temple of Venus and Rome
Portico of Livia
Baths of Trajan
LABICAN RD.
Bridge of Agrippa
Tem. of Juno
Temple of Venus
and Rome
Claudian Aqueduct
Theater of Balbus
Aurelian Bridge
Theater of Marcellus
Tom. of Jove
Colosseum
Aurelian Gate
RD.
Pal. of Augustus
Portico and Temple of the Emperor Claudius
Wall of Aurelian
Aemilian Bridge
Hippo-drome
Circus Maximus
Appian
Appian RD.
LATIN RD.
Tiber
Wall of Aurelian
Latin Gate
Emporium
Baths of Decius
Appian
Appian RD.
ARDEAN RD.
Baths of Caracalla
Granaries of Galba
Ostian Gate
ROAD TO OSTIA
Ardean Gate
Appian Gate

1 Column of Marcus Aurelius
2 Palace of Tiberius
3 Pantheon
4 Portico of the Argonauts
5 Portico of Philippus
6 Portico of the Gods
7 Temple of Aesculanius
8 Temple of Apollo
9 Temples of Juno and Jove

Dnieper
Dniester
SARMATIA
Tanais
Aral Sea
Olbia
Lake Maeotis
Panticapeum
Phanagoria
Danube
Tomi
Dioscurias
CAUCASUS
CASPIAN SEA
40°
Odessus
BLACK SEA
Sinope
Trapezus
Byzantium
Heraclea
Amisus
ARMENIA
Artaxata
Nicomedia
BITHYNIA
PONTUS
Halys
LESSER ARMENIA
ARMENIA
(114-117 A.D.)
Nicaea
Prusa
Ancyra
GALATIA
Melitene
L. Thospitis
L. Matianus
Pergamum
ASIA
Mazaca Caesarea
Amida
Ecbatana
Smyrna
Sardes
CAPPADOCIA
SOPHENE
Laodicea
LYCAONIA
Tyana
COMMA-GENE
Edessa
Rhesaena
Nisibis
ASSYRIA
(115-117 A.D.)
PARTHIAN
PISIDIA
Iconium
Adana
Carrhae
Halicarnassus
Rhodes
LYCIA
PAMPHYLIA
CILICIA
Tarsus
OSROENE
Singara
ZAGRUS MTS.
EMPIRE
Rhodes
Antioch
Nicephorium
Apamea
Dura
MESOPOTAMIA
SYRIA
Circesium
Euphrates
Tigris
Seleucia
Susa
CYPRUS
Emesa
Palmyra
Ctesiphon
Sidon
Damascus
Babylon
(115-117 A.D.)
Tyre
Caesarea
PERSIA
JUDEA
Jerusalem
Gaza
ARABIA PETRAEA
30°
Alexandria
Pelusium
Petra
ARABIA
Persian Gulf
Memphis
Arsinoe
Arsinoe
Oxyrhynchus
Nile
Antinoopolis
EGYPT
Red Sea
Coptos
Thebes
Syene
Berenice
30°
40°
50°

0   100   200   300 Miles
0   200   400 Kilometers
Copyright by Rand McNally
Equidistant Conic Projection
M-102156-1

RAND McNALLY

POLAND

HOLY ROMAN EMPIRE

FRANCE

ATLANTIC OCEAN

Dnepr

Danube

Vienna
1529,
1683

Budapest
1529

Ackerman
1484

Crimea

Milan

Venice

Mohács
1526

Genoa

Belgrade
1521

Nikopolis
1396

Varna
1444

Black S

Adriatic Sea

Kosovo
1389,
1448

Edirne
1360

Constantinople
(Istanbul)
1453

Naples

Otranto

Bursa
1326

Söğüd

Anka
140

PORTUGAL

Lepanto
1571

*Aegean
Sea*

Elbis

SPAIN

Rhodes
1522

Adana

Malaga

Granada

Crete
1669

Cyprus
1571
Be

Algiers

Tunis
1533,
1574

Mediterranean Sea

Fez

Tripoli
1551

Jerusale
151

Cairo
1517

Nile

	Ottoman Empire to 1360		Mughal Lands Conquered after 1635
	Ottoman Empire to 1481		Uzbek States in the 16th Century
	Ottoman Empire and its Dependencies in the 16th and 17th Centuries		Area disputed with Safavids
	Safavid Empire in the 16th Century		Area disputed with Uzbeks
	Kingdom of Babur in 1525		Area Disputed with Safavids and Uzbeks
	Mughal Empire in 1635		

- ○ Towns or Settlements
- ■ Main Portuguese Trade Settlements
- ☐ Towns with Large Portuguese Population

Mosul
1516 Date of Control

- ■ Ottoman Capitals
- ■ Safavid Capitals
- ■ Mughal Capitals

Chaldiran
1514 Site and Date of Important Battle

0   200   400   600   800 Miles
0 200 400 600 800 1000 1200 Kilometers
Copyright by Rand McNally & Co.
Miller Equal Area Projection

RAND McNALLY

MUSCOVY

Don

Volga

Ural

Don-Volga
Canal Project
1569

Azov

Caspian Sea

Aral
Sea

Syr Darya (Jaxartes)

Urganch

Amu Darya (Oxus)

rabzon
1461

Darband

Tiflis

Bukhara

Bashkent 1473

Erivan

Samarqand

Chaldiran
1514

Ardabil 1501

Ghujduvan
1512

Tabriz
1501

Marv

Balkh

arj Dabiq
516

Mosul
1516

Astarabad

Harat 1510

eppo
16

Qazvin

Mashhad

Kabul

Kirmanshah
1503

Hamadan
1503

Jam
1528

Indus

Tigris

Qum 1503

KASHMIR
1586

nascus
6

Kashan
1503

Lahore

Baghdad
1534

Isfahan
1503

Yazd
1504

Qandahar

Panipat
1526, 1556

Multan

Euphrates

Shiraz
1504

Kirman
1504

Delhi

Basra
1546

Kelat
1595

Kannauj
1540

Persian Gulf

Bandar
'Abbas

Hurmuz

Fatihpur Sikri

Agra

Chavsa
1539

Lucknow

Patna

Jaunpur

Medina

Gulf of
Oman

SIND
1591

Jodhpur

Chanderi
1572

GONDWANA

Masqat

Cambay
1572

Rissa

Mecca

Surat

d Sea

Daman

BERAR
1596

Diu
1538

Ahmadnagar
1598

Ramgir
1687

Arabian
Sea

Bidar

Golconda
1687

Bijapur
1686

Goa

Bay of
Bengal

Gulf of Aden

Mangalore

INDIAN
OCEAN

N

Cochin

Ceylon
(Sri Lanka)

Colombo

RAND McNALLY

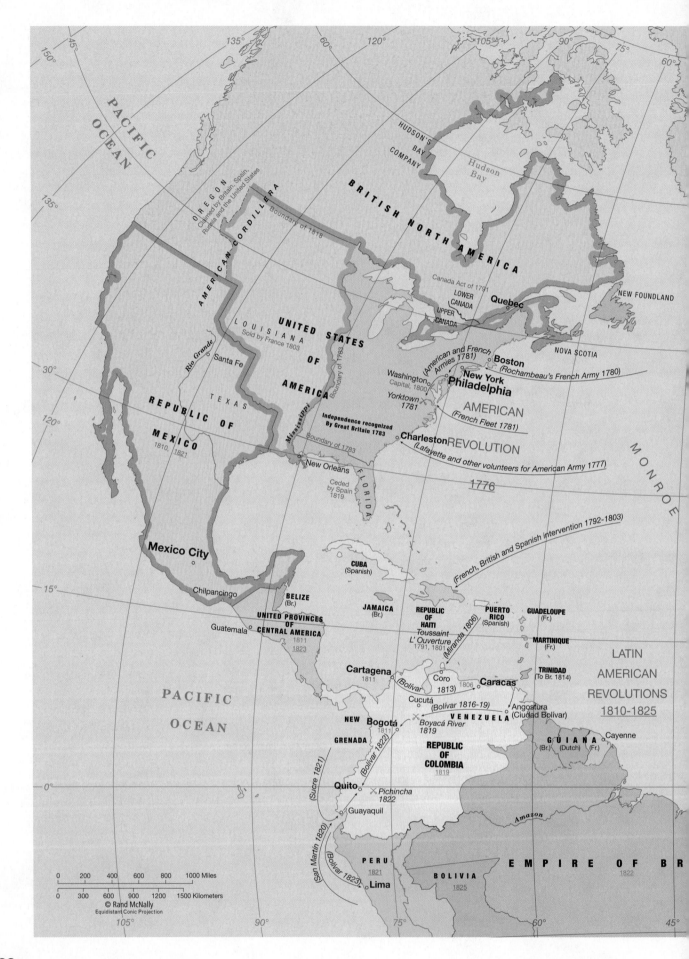

PACIFIC
OCEAN

HUDSON'S BAY COMPANY

Hudson Bay

BRITISH NORTH AMERICA

NEW FOUNDLAND

Canada Act of 1791

LOWER CANADA

UPPER CANADA

Quebec

NOVA SCOTIA

O R E G O N
Claimed by Britain, Spain,
Russia and the United States

Boundary of 1818

AMERICAN CORDILLERA

UNITED STATES OF AMERICA

LOUISIANA
Sold by France 1803

Boundary of 1783

Rio Grande

Santa Fe

TEXAS

REPUBLIC OF

MEXICO
1810, 1821

Mississippi

Independence recognized
By Great Britain 1783

Boundary of 1783

New Orleans

(American and French
Armies 1781)

Boston
(Rochambeau's French Army 1780)

Washington
Capital, 1800

New York
Philadelphia

Yorktown
1781

AMERICAN
(French Fleet 1781)

Charleston REVOLUTION

(Lafayette and other volunteers for American Army 1777)

1776

MONROE

FLORIDA

Ceded
by Spain
1819

Mexico City

Chilpancingo

BELIZE
(Br.)

CUBA
(Spanish)

JAMAICA
(Br.)

REPUBLIC OF HAITI
Toussaint L' Ouverture
1791, 1801

PUERTO RICO
(Spanish)

GUADELOUPE
(Fr.)

MARTINIQUE
(Fr.)

(French, British and Spanish intervention 1792-1803)

UNITED PROVINCES OF CENTRAL AMERICA
1811
1823

Guatemala

(Miranda 1806)

Cartagena
1811

(Bolívar)

Coro
1813

1806

Caracas

TRINIDAD
(To Br. 1814)

LATIN

AMERICAN

REVOLUTIONS

1810-1825

PACIFIC

OCEAN

Cucutá

(Bolívar 1816-19)

Angostura
(Ciudad Bolívar)

NEW

Bogotá
1811

GRENADA

(Bolívar 1822)

VENEZUELA

Boyacá River
1819

REPUBLIC OF COLOMBIA
1819

GUIANA
(Br.) (Dutch) (Fr.)

Cayenne

(Sucre 1821)

Quito

Pichincha
1822

Guayaquil

Amazon

(San Martín 1820)

(Bolívar 1823)

PERU
1821

Lima

BOLIVIA
1825

EMPIRE OF BR
1822

0   200   400   600   800   1000 Miles

0   300   600   900   1200   1500 Kilometers

© Rand McNally
Equidistant Conic Projection

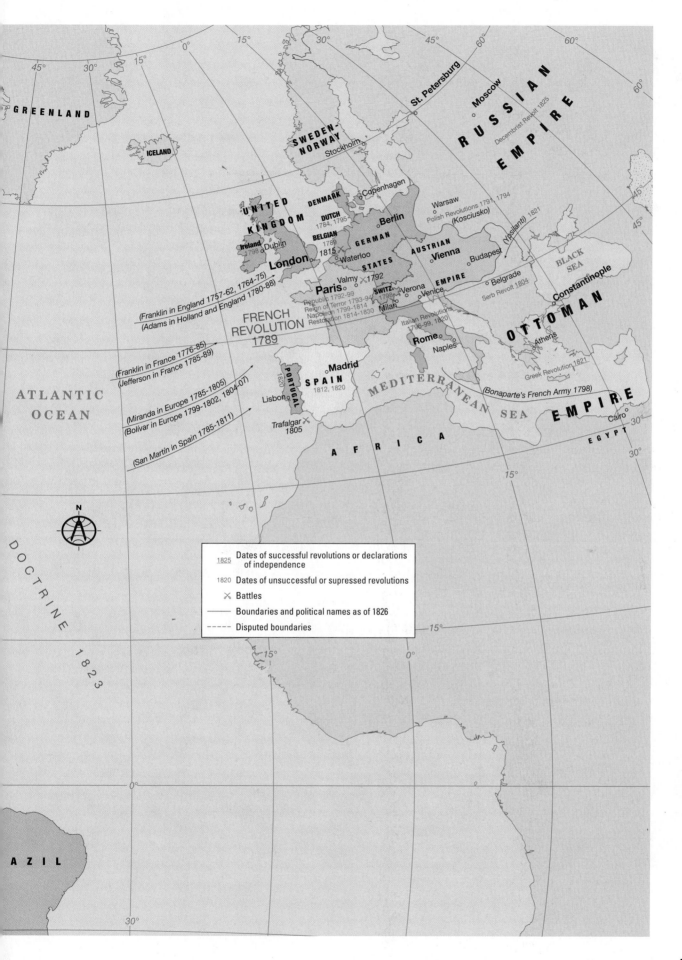

GREENLAND

ICELAND

SWEDEN-
NORWAY

Stockholm

St. Petersburg

Moscow

RUSSIAN

EMPIRE

Decembrist Revolt 1825

UNITED
KINGDOM

DENMARK

Copenhagen

Warsaw
Polish Revolutions 1791, 1794
(Kosciusko)

DUTCH
1784, 1795

Berlin

BELGIAN
1789

Ireland
1798 Dublin

1815

GERMAN

London

Waterloo

STATES

AUSTRIAN

Vienna

Budapest

(Ypsilanti) 1821

BLACK
SEA

Valmy ✕ 1792

EMPIRE

Belgrade
Serb Revolt 1804

Constantinople

(Franklin in England 1757-62, 1764-75)

Paris

Republic 1792-99
Reign of Terror 1793-94
Napoleon 1799-1814
Restoration 1814-1830

SWITZ.
1798

Verona

Venice

OTTOMAN

(Adams in Holland and England 1780-88)

FRENCH
REVOLUTION
1789

Milan

Italian Revolutions
1796-99, 1820

Athens

ATLANTIC
OCEAN

(Franklin in France 1776-85)
(Jefferson in France 1785-89)

Rome

Naples

Greek Revolution 1821

EMPIRE

(Miranda in Europe 1785-1805)
(Bolívar in Europe 1799-1802, 1804-07)

PORTUGAL

Madrid

SPAIN
1812, 1820

MEDITERRANEAN

SEA

(Bonaparte's French Army 1798)

EMPIRE

Cairo

Lisbon

Trafalgar
1805

AFRICA

EGYPT

N

DOCTRINE 1823

	Dates of successful revolutions or declarations of independence
1825	
1820	Dates of unsuccessful or supressed revolutions
✕	Battles
——	Boundaries and political names as of 1826
-----	Disputed boundaries

AZIL

Latin America 1800–1850

ATLANTIC OCEAN

Gila 110° 100° 90° 80° 70° 60° 50° 40°

U.S. 1846-48

TEXAS

U.S. annexation, 1845

Rio Grande ▲1836 from Mex.

Monterrey • Matamoros
MEXICO
▲ 1821 From Sp.
⚔ 1823
San Luis Potosí • Tampico
México •   Veracruz
U.S., 1848

Gulf of Mexico

U.S.,1822-25

Bahamas (Br.)

U.S. 1800

Havana   ⚔ 1844
CUBA
Santiago •   1844-61

U.S.,1824
Santo Domingo
PUERTO RICO
Virgin Is. (Den.)

YUCATÁN
⚔ 1847-53

Port-au-Prince   San Juan   ⚔ 1848
BELIZE   **JAMAICA**   **HAITI**   Guadeloupe
GUATEMALA   1804 from Fr.   1815, 1822
HONDURAS   Br.,   1806-20 ⚔   **DOMINICAN**   Martinique
Guatemala •   1846   **REPUBLIC**
San Salvador •   Tegucigalpa   *Caribbean   ▲1821 from Sp.*   St Lucia   Barbados
EL SALVADOR   León •   *Sea*   1844 from Haiti   St Vincent
Bluefields   Aruba   Bonaire   Grenada
NICARAGUA   **MOSQUITIA**   Curaçao   Tobago
(Miskito   Maracaibo   Caracas   Trinidad
San José •   *Indians)*   **VENEZUELA**
(CENTRAL AMERICAN STATES)   **COSTA RICA**   Cartagena   ▲1819 from Sp.   Angostura
▲ 1821 from Sp.   ⚔ 1842   1830 from
1823 from Mexico   Panamá   Gran Colombia   Georgetown
1838 From United Provinces   **BRITISH**   Paramaribo
of Central America   *Magdalena*   **GUIANA**   Cayenne
⚔1827-1829   Bogotá   **DUTCH**   **FRENCH**
NUEVA GRANADA   *Orinoco*   **GUIANA**   **GUIANA**
▲1819 from Sp.
1830 from Gran Colombia   *Negro*

0°   Quito •   *Galápagos Is.(Ec.)*   **ECUADOR**   Pará •   Maranhão •
Guayaquil •   ▲1822 from Sp.   *Amazon*   Ceará •
1830 from Gran
Colombia

PACIFIC OCEAN   *Marañón*   **BRAZIL**   Pernambuca •
Trujillo •   *Ucayali*   *ACRE*   ▲ 1822 from Port.
U.S., Br, Fr,   *Xingu*   ⚔ 1831-35
1835-36   **PERU**   *São Francisco*   Bahia •
Callao •   Lima •   ▲1821 from Sp.   *Araguaia*   *Tocantins*
Pisco •   Cuzco •   Minas Novas •
Lake   **BOLIVIA**   Mato Grosso
Titicaca   ▲ 1825 from Sp.   Diamantina •
Tacna •   ▲1839
Arica •   La Paz •   *Paraguay*   Rio de Janeiro •
Chuquisaca •   *GRAN*
Iquique •   Potosí •   *CHACO*   São Paulo •
1836-39   **PARAGUAY**
Antofagasta •   ▲ 1811 from Sp.
Jujuy •   Asunción •
Salta •
Copiapó •   Tucumán •   ⚔ 1835-45
CHILE   **LA PLATA**   Pôrto Alegre •
▲ 1818   ▲ 1816 from Sp.   1825-28
from Sp.   Córdoba •   ⚔ 1826,1838-39   **URUGUAY**
⚔1830   Santa   1825-28   ▲1814 from Sp., 1828 from Brazil
Valparaíso •   Fé •   1843-45   ⚔ 1836-52
Mendoza •   Rosario •   Montevideo •   Br.,1828, 1843
Santiago •   Buenos   *Rio de la Plata*
Aires •   U.S.,1833
Concepción •   Fr.,1806-07,1845
Br.,1838,1845

Valdivia •

PATAGONIA
(Mapuche   Indians)

Br.,1833
U.S.,1831-32

Falkland Islands   South Georgia

Legend:
- Independent state
- British colony
- Dutch colony
- French colony
- Spanish colony
- U.S. colony
- Disputed area
- → Latin American military forces
- → U.S. or European intervention
- ········· Projected canals
- ▲ Independence date and colonial power
- ⚔ Civil war

0   200   400   600   800   1000 Miles
0   400   800   1200   1600 Kilometers

Copyright by Rand McNally & Co.
Pseudo-Cylindrical Projection

120°   110°   100°   90°   80°   70°   60°   50°   40°   30°

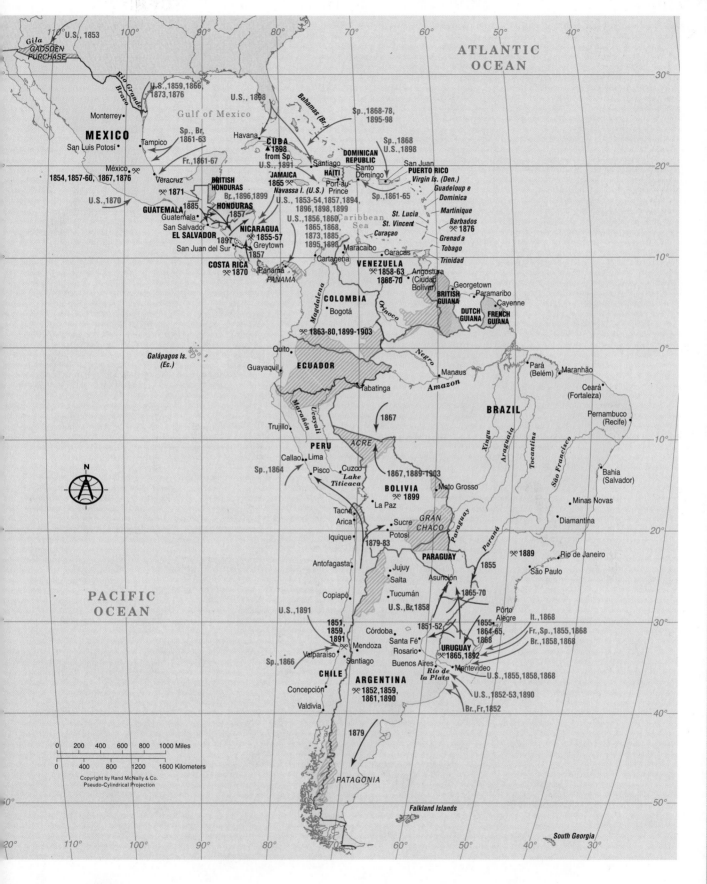

Gila
Gila
GADSDEN
PURCHASE
U.S., 1853

U.S., 1859, 1866,
1873, 1876

Rio Grande
Bravo

U.S., 1898

Bahamas (Br.)

Sp., 1868-78,
1895-98

ATLANTIC
OCEAN

Monterrey •

Gulf of Mexico

MEXICO

San Luis Potosí •

Sp., Br.,
1861-63

Havana •

CUBA
▲1898
from Sp.

Santiago •

Sp., 1868
U.S., 1898

San Juan

• Tampico

Fr., 1861-67

U.S., 1891

DOMINICAN
REPUBLIC

PUERTO RICO

México ✕
1854, 1857-60, 1867, 1876

JAMAICA
1865 ✕

HAITI

Santo
Domingo

Virgin Is. (Den.)

U.S., 1870

• Veracruz
✕ 1871

BRITISH
HONDURAS

Port-au-
Prince

Guadeloup e
Dominica

Br., 1896, 1899

Navassa I. (U.S.)

Sp., 1861-65

Martinique

GUATEMALA
1885

HONDURAS
1857

U.S., 1853-54, 1857, 1894,
1896, 1898, 1899

St. Lucia
St. Vincent

Barbados
✕ 1876

Guatemala •

U.S., 1856, 1860,
1865, 1868,
1873, 1885,
1895, 1898

*Caribbean
Sea*

San Salvador •
EL SALVADOR

NICARAGUA
✕ 1855-57
Greytown
1857

• Maracaibo

Curaçao

Grenad a
Tobago

San Juan del Sur
1897

• Cartagena

Caracas •

Trinidad

COSTA RICA
✕ 1870

Panamá •
PANAMA

VENEZUELA
1858-63
1866-70

Angostura
(Ciudad
Bolívar)

• Georgetown

• Paramaribo

BRITISH
GUIANA

Magdalena

COLOMBIA

Orinoco

DUTCH
GUIANA

• Cayenne

FRENCH
GUIANA

• Bogotá

✕ 1863-80, 1899-1903

Negro

Quito •

*Galápagos Is.
(Ec.)*

• Manaus

ECUADOR

Guayaquil •

Amazon

• Pará
(Belém)

Maranhão •

• Tabatinga

Marañón

Ucayali

• Trujillo

1867

BRAZIL

Ceará •
(Fortaleza)

• Pernambuco
(Recife)

Xingu

Araguaia

Tocantins

São Francisco

PERU

ACRE

Callao •
• Lima

Sp., 1864

• Pisco

• Cuzco
*Lake
Titicaca*

1867, 1889-1903

BOLIVIA
✕ 1899

Mato Grosso •

Bahia •
(Salvador)

• La Paz

Tacná •
Arica •

• Sucre

• Potosí

*GRAN
CHACO*

• Minas Novas

• Diamantina

Iquique •

1879-83

Paraguay

• Antofagasta

PARAGUAY

1855

✕ 1889

• Rio de Janeiro

• Jujuy

Asunción •

1865-70

Paraná

São Paulo •

U.S., 1891

PACIFIC
OCEAN

• Salta

• Tucumán

U.S., Br, 1858

Pôrto
Alegre •

It., 1868

Copiapó •

1851-52

1851,
1859,
1891

• Córdoba

Santa Fé •

Mendoza •

Rosario •

1855,
1864-65,
1868

Fr., Sp., 1855, 1868

Valparaíso •

Sp., 1866

• Santiago

Buenos Aires •

URUGUAY
✕ 1865, 1892

Br., 1858, 1868

CHILE

ARGENTINA
✕ 1852, 1859,
1861, 1890

Montevideo •
*Rio de
la Plata*

U.S., 1855, 1858, 1868

Concepción •

U.S., 1852-53, 1890

• Valdivia

Br., Fr., 1852

1879

PATAGONIA

N

0 200 400 600 800 1000 Miles

0 400 800 1200 1600 Kilometers

Copyright by Rand McNally & Co.
Pseudo-Cylindrical Projection

Falkland Islands

South Georgia

RAND McNALLY

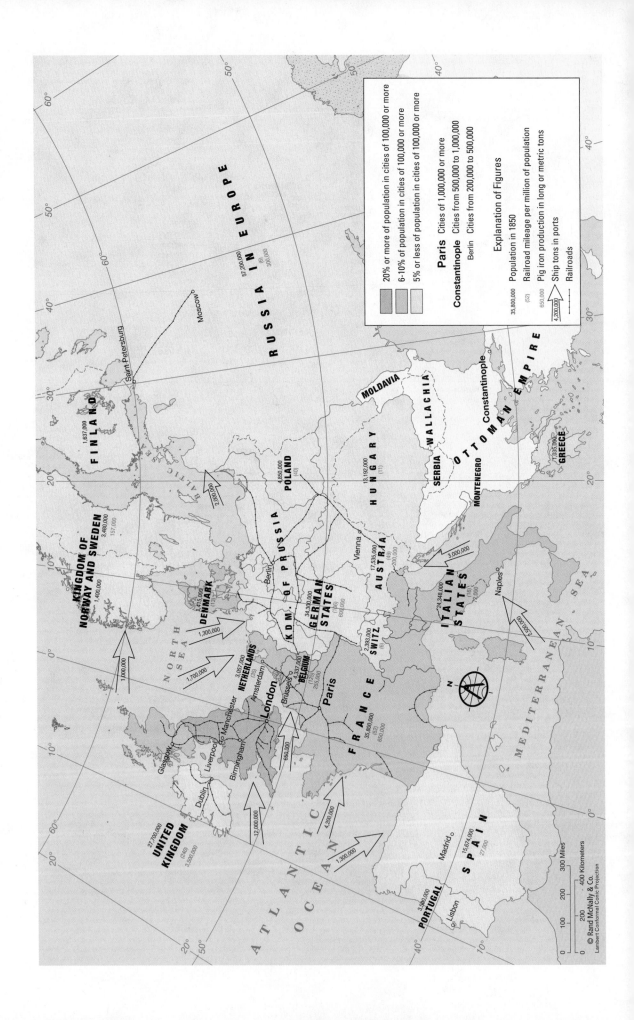

20% or more of population in cities of 100,000 or more
6-10% of population in cities of 100,000 or more
5% or less of population in cities of 100,000 or more

Paris Cities of 1,000,000 or more
Constantinople Cities from 500,000 to 1,000,000
Berlin Cities from 200,000 to 500,000

Explanation of Figures

35,800,000 Population in 1850
(52) Railroad mileage per million of population
650,000 Pig iron production in long or metric tons
4,200,000 Ship tons in ports
Railroads

RUSSIA IN EUROPE

57,200,000
(6)
300,000

FINLAND
1,637,000

Moscow

Saint Petersburg

MOLDAVIA

OTTOMAN EMPIRE Constantinople

SERBIA
WALLACHIA

MONTENEGRO

GREECE
1,035,000
(7,000)

BALTIC

KINGDOM OF
NORWAY AND SWEDEN
3,480,000
157,000

1,400,000

2,000,000

POLAND
4,850,000
(40)

HUNGARY
13,192,000
(11)

DENMARK
1,415,000
(13)

1,300,000

Berlin

KDM. OF PRUSSIA

GERMAN
STATES
34,300,000
(16)
604,000

Vienna

AUSTRIA
17,535,000
(49)
200,000

3,000,000

ITALIAN
STATES
24,348,000
(16)
72,000

NORTH
SEA

1,000,000

1,700,000

NETHERLANDS
3,057,000
(55)

Amsterdam

BELGIUM
4,337,000
(125)
255,000

Brussels

London

Paris

FRANCE
35,800,000
(52)
650,000

SWITZ.
2,393,000
(6)

Naples
2,500,000

MEDITERRANEAN SEA

N

Glasgow

Dublin

Liverpool Manchester

Birmingham

UNITED
KINGDOM
27,700,000
(240)
3,500,000

12,000,000

650,000

4,200,000

1,300,000

Madrid
SPAIN
15,674,000
27,000

PORTUGAL
3,390,000

Lisbon

ATLANTIC

OCEAN

60°

50°

40°

50°

60°

40°

30°

20°

50°

40°

30°

20°

10°

0°

10°

0°

10°

20°

0 100 200 300 Miles
0 200 400 Kilometers

© Rand McNally & Co.
Lambert Conformal Conic Projection

RAND MCNALLY

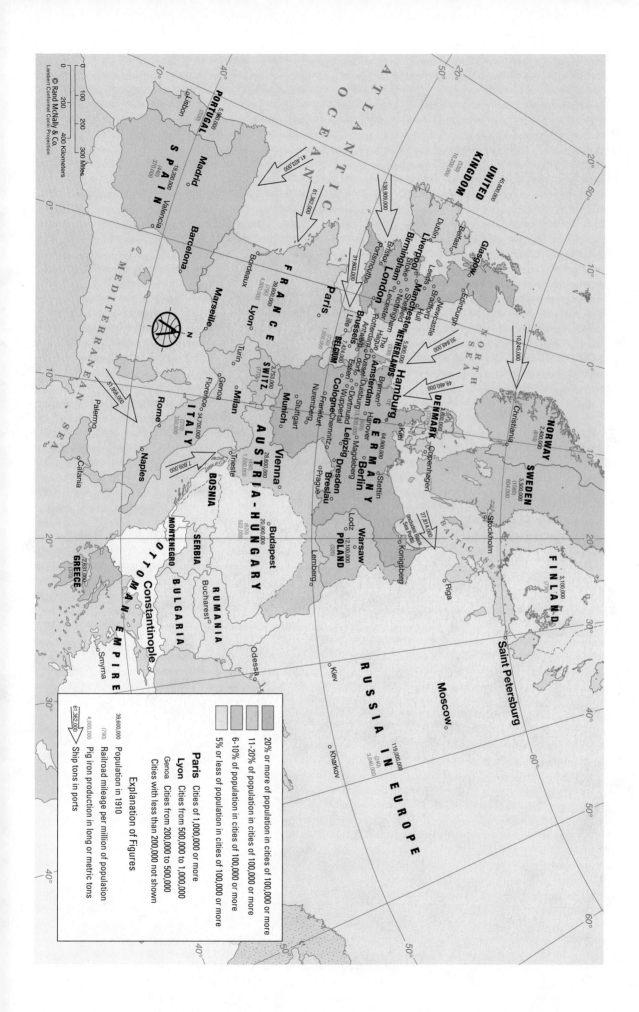

ICELAND

ATLANTIC

OCEAN

30° 20° 10° 0° 10° 70° 10° ARCTIC

Reykjavik

Faroe Islands
(Den.)

50°

Shetland
Islands

NORWAY

SWEDEN

Gulf of

Hebrides

Orkney
Is.

Bergen

Stavanger

Oslo

Åland Is.

North
Sea

SCOTLAND

Aberdeen

Uppsala

Stockholm

Glasgow Edinburgh

GREAT

Belfast

Gulf of

Göteborg

Baltic

Gotland

IRISH FREE
STATE

Dublin

Liverpool

Leeds

Hull

DENMARK

Aalborg

Helsingborg

Öland

Sea

LITHU

Cork

Manchester
Sheffield

BRITAIN

Birmingham

WALES ENGLAND

Cardiff

Oxford

Bristol

Copenhagen

Helgoland

Kiel

Lübeck
Hamburg

Bremen

Hanover

Bornholm

Stettin

Berlin

Danzig

MEMELAND
To Ger. 1939

Memel

EAST
PRUSSIA

Königsberg
(Kaun.)

Nazi-Soviet Pact Annexed
by Germany 1939

POLAN

Plymouth

Portsmouth

NETHERLANDS
Occ. by Ger. 1940

Amsterdam

Rotterdam

Weser

Magdeburg

Elbe

Leipzig

Dresden

Oder

SILESIA

Breslau

Bialystok

Brest-
Litovsk

English Channel

Channel
Is.

Brest

Le Havre

Amiens

Dover

London

Thames

Dunkirk

BELGIUM
Occ. 1940

Brussels

Essen

Cologne

GERMANY

Frankfurt

Potsdam

Cracow

Tannenberg

Tarnopol

Lublin

Przemysl

Rennes

Caen

Lille

Reims

Seine

Paris

LORRAINE

LUX.

Mainz

Nürnberg

Pilsen

Weimar

SAAR
To Germany
Plebiscite

Mannheim

Prague

Get at Munich 1938

CZECHOSLOVAKIA

Tesin

Košice

St. Nazaire

Nantes

Orleans

Fontainebleau

Verdun

Stuttgart

Strassburg

BAVARIA

Get at Munich 1938

RUTHEN

La Rochelle

Loire

Dijon

ALSACE

Basel

Zurich

Munich

Danube

Vienna
(Wien)

Bratislava
(Pressburg)

Annexed
by Hungary 1938

Bay

of

Biscay

FRANCE

Occupied by Germany 1940

Limoges

Saône

Lyon

SWITZERLAND

Geneva

Berne

LIECH.

Innsbruck

AUSTRIA

To Germany Anschluss 1938

Graz

Annexed by Hungary 1938

RUM

Corunna

Oporto

PORTUGAL

Coimbra

Duero

SPAIN

Bordeaux

Bayonne

Pyrenees

ANDORRA

VICHY FRANCE
1940

Toulouse

Grenoble

Garonne

Montpellier

Rhône

Avignon

Milan

TRENTINO

Innsbruck

Verona

Po

Trieste

Venice

Turin

Parma

Italy 1919

Ljubljana

Zagreb

Drava

CROATIA

Genoa

Bologna

Ravenna

Sava

BOSNIA

DALMATIA

YUGOSLAVIA

Budapest

Oradea

Mohacs

HUNGARY

TRANSYLVAN

Temisoara

WAL

Lisbon

Tagus

Salamanca

Valladolid

Burgos

Santander

San Sebastian

Ebro

Saragossa

Madrid

Toledo

Guadiana

Cordoba

Guadalquivir

Seville

Cadiz

Granada

Almería

Cartagena

Barcelona

Valencia

Balearic Islands
(To Spain)

Minorca

Majorca

Marseille

Toulon

Nice

San Remo

Ajaccio

Corsica
(To France)

Florence

Ancona

SAN
MARINO

ITALY

Rome

Naples

Adriatic

Sava

Zara

Split

Sarajevo

Novi
Pazar

MONTE-
NEGRO

Cattaro

Belgrade

SERBIA

Danube

Morava

Nish

Fiume

Dubrovnik
(Ragusa)

Lagosta
(To Italy)

Antivari

Durazzo

ALBANIA

Valona

Tirana

MACEDONIA

Vardar

Yannina

Corfu

Philippopolis

BU

Sofia

Sidra

Tangier

Gibraltar
(To Great Britain)

SPANISH AREA

Rabat

MOROCCO
To France

Atlas

Oran

Algiers

MEDITERRANEAN

Tyrrhenian Sea

Palermo

Messina

SICILY

Cagliari

Sardinia
(To Italy)

Bari

Taranto

Brindisi

Ionian

Sea

GREECE

Messolongi

Patras

Cephallenia

Sparta

Athens

Kavala

Salonika

Darda

Aeg

Les

Mountains

ALGERIA
To France

TUNIS
French Protectorate

Tunis

Malta
(Br.)

Crete

30°

0°

LIBYA

10°

20°

TRIPOLITANIA
To Italy

Tripoli

Bengazi

Gulf of
Sidra

CYRENAICA
To Italy

0   100   200   300 Miles

0   200   400 Kilometers

© Rand McNally & Co.
Equidistant Conic Projection

RAND McNALLY

	Principal status quo powers
	Principal Revisionist powers
	1914 Boundaries
	1922 Boundaries

CEAN

Pechenga
MURMAN COAST
Murmansk

KOLA
PENINSULA

Ceded to
USSR 1940

Archangel

White
Sea

Dvina

Vychegda

Pechora

Ob

FINLAND

Lake
Onega

Lake
Ladoga

nglors
sinki)

Viborg

Kronstadt

Leningrad
(Petrograd)

Novgorod

Vologda

Kirov

Sverdlovsk

Chelabinsk

NIA
(Tallin)

Vitebsk

Pskov

Kalinin
(Tver)

Yaroslavl

Volga

Gorkii (Nizhni Novgorod)

Kazañ

Kama

Uta

Tobol

Ishim

Akmolinsk

Kustanai

50°

IA
SSR

Smolensk

Moscow

Oka

Rizan

Tula

Penza

Belaia

Magnitogorsk

Borisov

W. Dvina

Mogilev

Tambov

Kuibyshev

Ural

Chkalov

Orsk

Minsk

Brianск

Orel

Voronezh

Saratov

Uralsk

UNION OF SOVIET SOCIALIST REPUBLICS

Pripet

Chernigov

Kursk

Aral
Sea

Zhitomir

Kiev

Dnieper

Don

Volga

40°

Bug

Poltava

Kharkov

Stalingrad

Kirovograd
(Elizavetgrad)

Czernowitz

Dniester

BESSARABIA

Dnepropetrovsk
(Ekaterinoslav)

UKRAINE

Prut

DAVIA

Annexed
by USSR
1940

Galatz

Taganrog

Rostov

Astrakhan

Kishinev

Odessa

Cherson

Sea
of
Azov

Kubañ

Voroshilovsk
(Stavropol)

Terek

CASPIAN SEA

TURKESTAN

ula
Bucharest

Constantsa

Sevastopol

Novorossiisk
(Anapa)

Krasnodar
(Ekaterinodar)

Grozni

Petrovsk

70°

astra

DOBRUJA

to Bulgaria 1940

Varna

BLACK SEA

Ordzhonikidze
(Vladikavkaz)

DAGHESTAN

Derbent

Krasnovodsk

Burgas

Sukhumi

REPUBLIC OF GEORGIA

Baku

ople

Bosporus

Sinope

Poti

Batum

Tiflis

Kura

REPUBLIC
OF
AZERBAIJAN

ïdia

Samsun

Kars

REPUBLIC

stanbul
Constantinople)

Skutari

Ereğli

Trebizond

OF

ARMENIA

Erivan

Lenkoran

TURKEY

Ankara (Angora)

Irma

Kizil

Tabriz

Teheran

30°

ASIA MINOR

L.
Urmia

PERSIA

Smyrna

Aidin

Konia

Adana

Mosul

Makri

Adalia

ALEXANDRETTA
Annexed by Turkey
1939

Aleppo

Rhodes

Nikosia

Latakia

Homs

SYRIA

Tigris

Baghdad

Cyprus
(Br.)

Limasol

Beirut

Fr. Mandate

Damascus

IRAQ

Independent since 1932

Euphrates

PALESTINE
Br. Mandate

Acre

Ammain

Jaffa

Alexandria

Jerusalem

TRANSJORDAN
Br. Mandate

Dead
Sea

ARABIA

KUWAIT

Kuwait

Persian Gulf

endent Kingdom with
ish Protective Rights

Port Said

EA

PT

30°

Nile

Cairo

Red Sea

60°

50°

40°

Strait of Gibraltar

Granada • Algiers
Tangier •
Fez • Tlemcen • Qayrawan • Tunis
Marrakech •
Sijilmasa • Ghadamès
Canary Islands
Taghaza •

Mediterranean Sea

Tripoli • Barqa •
Alexandria • Jerusalem
Cairo •
Siwa •
Awjila • Asyut •
Ghat •

ARABIA

Murzuq •
Aswan •
Mecca •
Bilma •
Akjoujt •
Dóngola •
Tademakka •
Takedda • Meroe •
Awlil •
Walata •
Senegal
Ghana • Timbuktu • Gao
Takrur • MALI SONGHAI
Darfur •
ALWA
Debarwa •
Sennar
Aksum
YEMEN
Aden •
Gambia
Djenné •
KANEM-
BORNU
Njimi •
Lake
Tana
Adefa
Sana
Zeila
Socotr
Mali •
Ouagadougou • Katsina •
HAUSA Kano
STATES Zaria
Lake Chad
SOLOMONID
ETHIOPIA
Harar •
ADAL
Berbera •
Kankan •
Kong •
Ife •
Benin City •
BENIN
Ke •
Bioko
Sanaga
Benue
Chari
Shebele
Juba

ATLANTIC
OCEAN

Ubangi
Congo
Lake
Albert Kibiro
Victoria Nile
Lake
Turkana
Mogadishu •

INDIAN
OCEAN

Bigo •
Ntusi •
Lake
Victoria
Tana
SWAHILI
Malindi
Loango •
Kasai
Lomami
Lualaba
Uvinza •
Mombasa
Pemba
Zanzibar
EAST AFRICAN
TRADING
STATES
Mpinda •
Congo
Mbanza Kongo •
KONGO
Kuango
Lake
Tanganyika
Sanga •
Ivuna •
Mafia
Kilwa
Luanda •
Karonga Rufiji
Lake
Malawi
Kapeni •
Mozambique •
Zambezi
Chedzurgwe •
Kuando
Great Zimbabwe •
GREAT ZIMBABWE
Zimbabwe •
Sofala •
Mozambique
Channel
Madagascar
Vohemar
Comoros
Manekweni •
Limpopo
Mapungubwe •
Orange
Vaal

Legend

Southern limits of Muslim influence, about 1400		Glass
State, empire, or dynasty with Muslim leader		Gold
KONGO State or Empire		Iron
Major trade route		Ivory
Cataract (rapids)		Jewelry, trinkets
Cattle		Kola nuts
Ceramics		Salt
Copper		Slaves
Foodstuffs		

0 200 400 600 800 Miles
0 200 400 600 800 1000 Kilometers
Copyright by Rand McNally & Co.
Robinson Projection

NORTH
ATLANTIC
OCEAN

EUROPE

Black Sea

Aral
Sea

ASIA

AZORES
Port.

MADEIRA IS.
Port.

CANARY IS.
Sp.

Algiers

Tunis

TUNIS
Fr.
Prot.
since
1881

Mediterranean Sea

Tripoli

Bengazi

Barca

Alexandria

Cairo

Suez
Canal
1869

Persian Gulf

SULTANATE OF MOROCCO

Fez

FRENCH
COLONY
OF
ALGERIA
1830

TRIPOLI
A Vilayet of Ottoman Empire until 1911-12

EGYPT
Tributary of
Ottoman Empire.
Occupied by
Great Britain
after 1882

Tuat

FEZZAN

RIO DE ORO
Spanish
Protectorate
Boundaries
Modified to 1900

René Caillié 1827

"Northern Limit of Arms and Spiritous Liquors Zone"
Import of arms and spiritous liquors zone. As a result of the Brussels Anti-Slavery Conference of 1889-90,
the import of arms was regulated and that of intoxicating drinks prohibited to the regions between 20 N. and 22 S. Latitude.

Red Sea

ARABIA

FRENCH COLONY
OF SENEGAL

Cape Verde

Tombouctu

FRENCH
SUDAN

Niger

L. Chad
Kuka

BORNU

Sokoto

Nile

Egyptian territory in revolt
under the Mahdi. Conquered by
Anglo-Egyptian forces, 1898

Omdurman

Khartoum

ITAL.
ERITREA

Aduwa

Gondar

L.
Tana

Assab
1882

Aden

SOCOTRA
(Br.)

Cape
Guardafui

PORT
GUINEA
Sp.

Freetown
SIERRA
LEONE

Monrovia
REP. of LIBERIA

FR. IVORY
COAST
COLONY

ROYAL   NIGER   CO.
1886

GOLD
COAST
COL.

TOGO
DAHOMEY

FRENCH

UBANGHI

KORDOFAN

DARFUR

Fashoda

FRENCH
SOM.

Obok
1883

Zeila

BR.
SOMALILAND
Protectorate 1884

Gulf of Aden

ADDIS
Abeba

ABYSSINIA
Italian Protectorate, 1889
Protectorate abandoned 1896

Frontier drawn by Anglo-Italian Treaty 1891

NIGER COAST
(OIL RIVERS)
PROT.
1884

LAGOS
COLONY

FERNANDO PO
Sp.

GERMAN
KAMERUN

CORISCO BAY
Rio Muni, Sp.

ANNOBAN
Sp.

Gulf
of Guinea

L. Albert
Nyanza

L. Victoria
Nyanza

L. Rudolf

ITALIAN SOMALILAND

COLONY OF
FRENCH CONGO

CONGO FREE
STATE
Under Sovereignty of
Leopold II of Belgium after 1885

Brazzaville

CABINDA
Port.

Leopoldville

Boma

Luanda

PORTUGUESE

ANGOLA

WEST

AFRICA

Benguela

Mossamedes

Cape Frio

Livingstone 1854

Ujiji

L.
Tanganyika

L.
Mweru

PEMBA

ZANZIBAR
British Prot.
1890

GERMAN
EAST
AFRICA
Leased from Zanzibar 1888
Purchased 1890

INDIAN

OCEAN

SOUTH
ATLANTIC
OCEAN

L.
Bangweolu

L. Nyasse

EAST
AFRICA

BRITISH CENTRAL AFRICA
PROTECTORATE
1891

Victoria
Falls

Zambezi

PORT.

Mozambique

Quelimane

MADAGASCAR

Tamatave

Antananarive

Mozambique Channel

BRITISH SOUTH AFRICA CO.
Chartered, 1889
Conquered Matabeleland, 1893

GERMAN

SOUTHWEST

AFRICA

WALFISH
BAY
Br. 1878

"Southern Limit of Arms and Spiritous Liquors Zone"

BECHUANALAND
PROTECTORATE
1885

SOUTH
AFRICAN
REP.
(TRANSVAAL)
Pretoria

Lourenco Marques

Luderitz Bay
(Angra Pequena)

Johannesburg

BECHUANALAND
British Colony
1885

Vaal

Limpopo

SWAZILAND

COLONY
OF
NATAL

Durban

Orange

ORANGE
FREE
STATE

Bloemfontein

BASUTOLAND

CAPE   COLONY

Capetown
Br. 1806

Cape of Good Hope

N

CONTROL OF TERRITORY

Great Britain 1885	Germany 1885
Great Britain 1898	Germany 1898
France 1885	Spain 1885
France 1898	Spain 1898
Turkey	Portugal 1885
Congo Free State 1885	Portugal 1898
Congo Free State (Belgium) 1898	Italy

0   200   400   600 Miles
0   200 400 600 800 Kilometers

© Rand McNally & Co.
Lambert Azimuthal, Equal Area Projection

ATLANTIC
OCEAN

RUSSIAN EMPIRE

Easter rising, 1916
Ireland *Britain*
UNITED KINGDOM

NETHERLANDS
BELGIUM
LUX.
GERMAN EMPIRE

AUSTRIA-HUNGARY

FRANCE
SWITZ.

ROMANIA

MONTENEGRO
SERBIA
ITALY
BULGARIA
ALBANIA
GREECE

Black Sea

Dagestani rebellion, 1877–78

Aral Sea

Muslim revolt in Turkestan, 1916

SPAIN
PORTUGAL
Azores

Corsica

Sardinia
Balearic Is.

Jailaz incident, 1911

Sicily
Malta
Crete
Dodecanese Is.
Cyprus

OTTOMAN EMPIRE

Russo-Afghan conflict, 1885

AFGHANISTAN

Anglo-Afghan War, 1878–1880

Madeira Islands

MOROCCO
Canary Islands
IFNI

Nationalist revolt, 1915-16

TUNISIA

Mediterranean Sea

Dinshaway incident, 1906

Urabi uprising, 1881-82

PERSIA

KUWAIT

QATAR

Persian Gulf

OMAN

ALGERIA

RIO DE ORO

TRIPOLITANIA (LIBYA)

Sanusi revolt, 1912-31

EGYPT

Red Sea

NEJD

TRUCIAL STATES

Arabian Sea

Cape Verde Islands

FRENCH WEST AFRICA

Mande revolt under Samori, 1884-98

Sokoto uprising, 1906

Rabih revolt, 1897-1900

Mahdist State, 1881-98

ERITREA

Abyssinia defeats Italians at Adowa, 1896

ADEN

BRITISH SOMALILAND

Socotra

GAMBIA

PORTUGUESE GUINEA

SIERRA LEONE

LIBERIA

Ashanti resistance, 1872-74, 1900

NIGERIA

Anyang revolt, 1904

ANGLO-EGYPTIAN SUDAN

ABYSSINIA (ETHIOPIA)

Somali resistance, 1891-1920

ITALIAN SOMALILAND

Mal

TOGO-LAND
Fernando Poó
GOLD COAST
KAMERUN
FRENCH EQUATORIAL AFRICA
RÍO MUNI

Sao Tomé-Príncipe

Equator

Bunyoro resistance, 1890-98

UGANDA

Tutsi/Hutu resistance, 1911-17

BRITISH EAST AFRICA

Nandi and Gusii revolt, 1895-1908

ATLANTIC
OCEAN

CABINDA

BELGIAN CONGO

Arab revolt, 1891-94

Arab revolt, 1887-89

GERMAN EAST AFRICA

Abushiri revolt, 1888-89

Hehe revolt, 1891-98

Maji-Maji revolt, 1905-09

Comoros

ANGOLA (PORTUGUESE WEST AFRICA)

Nationalist uprisings, 1913

NORTHERN RHODESIA

NYASALAND

Revolt under Chilembwe, 1915

MOZAMBIQUE (PORTUGUESE EAST AFRICA)

MADAGASCAR

Nationalist revolt, 1898-1904

Mauritius

Réunion

GERMAN SOUTHWEST AFRICA

WALVIS BAY

Herrero Hottentot uprisings, 1904-06

SOUTHERN RHODESIA

BECHUANA-LAND

Matabele and Mashona insurrections, 1896

SWAZILAND

Zulu resistance, 1879, 1906

BASUTOLAND

UNION OF SOUTH AFRICA

N

Legend

	Belgian
	British
	Dutch
	French
	German
	Italian
	Portuguese
	Russian
	Spanish
	United States
⫽	Area of anti-colonial resistance

Spheres of Influence

	British
	French
	German
	Russian
—	Japanese

0   200   400   600   800   1000 Miles

0   400   800   1200   1600 Kilometers

Copyright by Rand McNally & Co.
Times Projection

OUTER
MONGOLIA

Russians rejected
from Chinese
Turkestan
1877–78

Boxer
Rebellion,
1899-1900

KOREA

WEIHAI

CHINA

JAPANESE
EMPIRE

Sakhalin

Kuril Islands

Japanese sphere of influence

Aleutian Islands

PACIFIC
OCEAN

40°

SIKKIM

BHUTAN

NEPAL

INDIA

Nationalist
underground
in Bengal,
1905-09

Nationalist
under ground in
Maharashtra,
05-09

YANAM

DICHERRY

BURMA

Anglo-Burmese
War,
1885-91

Viet revolts in
Tonkin,
1885-1915

HONG KONG
MACAO
KWANGCHOWAN

Hainan

Bonin
Islands

20°

Bay of
Bengal

Andaman
Islands

Ceylon

Nicobar
Islands

SIAM

FRENCH
INDOCHINA

Cambodian revolt,
1885-87

Viet revolts in
Cochin China,
1885-86

Viet revolts in Annam,
1906-08

Philippine -
American War,
1898-1902

PHILIPPINE
ISLANDS
(U.S)

Moro (Muslim)
resistance,
1898-1913

Mariana
Islands

Guam

Marshall
Islands

Muslim revolt in
Atchin,
1881-1908

MALAYA

Singapore

Sumatra

BRUNEI

SARAWAK

NORTH
BORNEO

Borneo

Palau

Caroline Islands

KAISER-
WILHELMSLAND

Bismarck Archipelago

Equator

0°

Saminist peasant uprising,
1914-17

Java

DUTCH EAST INDIES

Celebes

Moluccas

New Guinea

Solomon
Islands

Bali

Nationalist
revolts, 1881-94

Lombok

Timor

TIMOR
(Port.)

PAPUA

INDIAN OCEAN

New
Hebrides
(Br.-Fr.)

20°

AUSTRALIA

New
Caledonia

NEW ZEALAND

40°

RAND McNALLY

Adriatic Sea
ITALY
Tirane
Skopje
MACEDONIA
Sofia
BULGARIA
ALBANIA
GREECE
Thessaloniki
Ionian Islands
Ionian Sea
Aegean Sea
Athens
Crete

20
30°
BLACK SEA
40°
Groznyy
GEORGIA
RUSSIA
Tbilisi
ARMENIA
AZERBAIJAN
Baku
Yerevan
AZER.
Erzurum
Istanbul
Bursa
Eskişehir
Ankara
Samsun
TURKEY
Kayseri
Konya
Diyarbakır
Lake Van
Lake Urmia
Orūmīyeh
Tabrīz
Rasht
Antalya
Adana
Gaziantep

MEDITERRANEAN
NORTH CYPRUS
CYPRUS
Nicosia
SEA
Aleppo
Mosul
Arbīl
SYRIA
Kirkuk
Hamadan
Bākhtarā
LEBANON
Hims
Euphrates
Tigris
Beirut
Damascus
Baghdād
Banghāzī
Tubruq
Gulf of Sidra
ISRAEL
Ar Rutbah
IRAQ
Tel Aviv-Yafo
Alexandria
Port Said
Gaza
Ammān
Jerusalem
Dead Sea
Karbalā'
An Najaf
Basra
30°
JORDAN
Suez Canal
KUWAIT
Giza
Suez
Kuw
El Fayoum
Cairo
Sinai Pen.
Al 'Aqabah
El Minya
Nile
Gulf of Aqaba
Gulf of Suez
LIBYA
EGYPT
Asyût
Ad M
Suhag
Buraydah
Luxor
Riyad
Tropic of Cancer
Aswân
Medina
Lake Nasser
RED SEA
SAUDI ARAB
Jiddah
Mecca
At Tā'if
20°
Port Sudan
20°
CHAD
Khamis Mushayt
SUDAN
ERITREA
Sanaa
Omdurman
Kassalā
Asmera
YEME
Khartoum
Al Hudaydah
Wad Madanī
Al Fāshir
Al Ubayyid
Ta'izz
Nyala
Aden
White Nile
Blue Nile
ETHIOPIA
Lake Tana
DJIBOUTI
Gulf of A
Djibouti
10°
CENTRAL AFRICAN REP.
Malakāl
Addis Ābaba
40
SOMA
30°

KAZAKHSTAN

UZBEKISTAN

TURKMENISTAN

Amu Darya

⊕ Ashgabat

Tehrān

AFGHAN.

I R A N

Mashhad ■

Eşfahān ■

Bīrjand

.Yazd

Daryacheh-ye Hamun

Kermān

Zāhedān

.Shīrāz

Bandar-e Būshehr

Bandar-e 'Abbās

Persian Gulf

Strait of Hormuz

OMAN

BAHRAIN

Manama

QATAR

⊕ Doha

Dubai ■

Abu Dhabi ⊕

UNITED ARAB EMIRATES

Gulf of Oman

Tropic of Cancer

Muscat ⊕

Sūr •

OMAN

ARABIAN SEA

Socotra (Yem.)

INDIAN OCEAN

0   100   200   300   400 Miles

0   200   400   600 Kilometers

Copyright by Rand McNally & Co.
Lambert Conformal Conic Projection

---

0 10 20 30 40   50 Miles

0   20   40   60   80 Kilometers

Copyright by Rand McNally
Lambert Conformal Conic Projection
M-101527-2

MEDITERRANEAN

SEA

Ⓐ Golan Heights. Captured by Israel in 1967; annexed in 1981.

Ⓑ West Bank. Controlled by Israel, parts administered by the Palestinian Authority. Permanent status to be determined.

Ⓒ Gaza Strip. Following withdrawal by Israel in 2005, administered first by the Palestinian Authority, 2005–6, then by Hamas, 2006–.

N

Beirut ⊛

Sidon •

LEBANON

Litani

Tyre •

Acre •

Haifa •

Golan Heights

Sea of Galilee

Ⓐ

Tiberias •

Nazareth •

Irbid •

Hadera •

Janīn •

Netanya •

Nābulus •

As-Salṭ •

Tel Aviv-Yafo •

West Bank

Ⓑ

Amman ⊛

Rehovot •

Jericho •

Ashdod •

✪ Jerusalem

Ashqelon •

Bethlehem •

Gaza •

Ⓒ

Hebron •

Gaza Strip

Khan Yunus •

Beersheba •

Al Karak •

ISRAEL

Dimona •

Aṭ-Ṭafīlah •

Port Said ■

JORDAN

Pelusium Bay

Suez Canal

El Qantara el-Sharqîya •

El Arish •

Ismailia •

Negev Desert

Ma'ān •

Great Bitter Lake

EGYPT

■ Suez

Gulf of Suez

Sinai Peninsula

Elat • Aqaba

Gulf of Aqaba

RAND M^cNALLY

A41

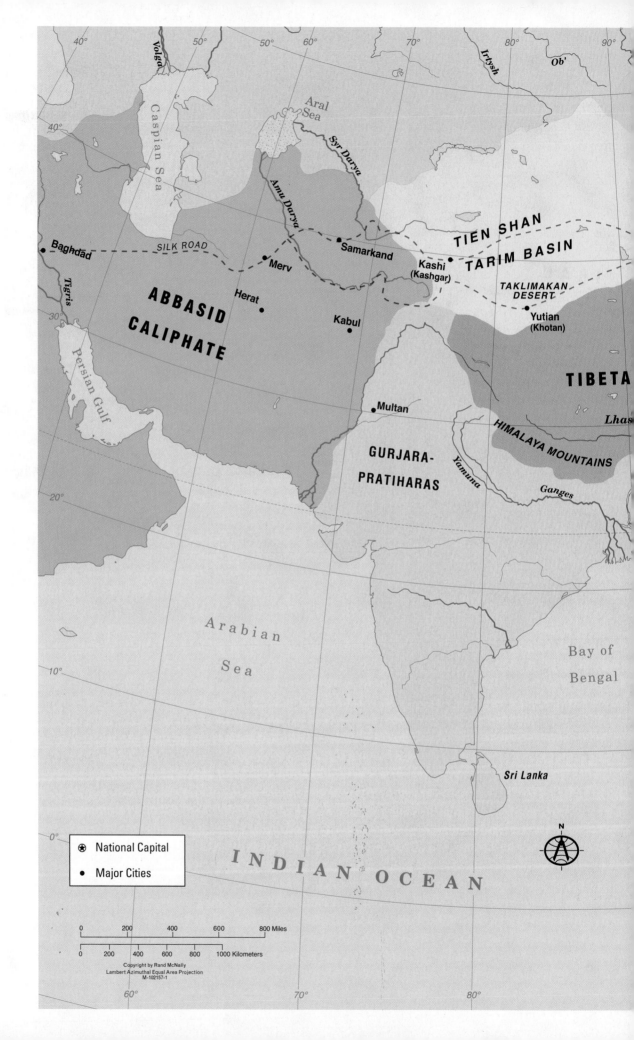

40°   50°   50°   60°   70°   80°   90°

Volga   *Irtysh*   Ob'

Aral Sea

40°

Caspian Sea

Syr Darya

Amu Darya

TIEN SHAN

TARIM BASIN

Baghdad   SILK ROAD   Samarkand   Kashi (Kashgar)

TAKLIMAKAN DESERT

Tigris   Merv

Herat   Kabul   Yutian (Khotan)

30°

ABBASID
CALIPHATE

Persian Gulf   TIBETA

Multan   Lhas

HIMALAYA MOUNTAINS

GURJARA-
PRATIHARAS

Yamuna

20°   *Ganges*

Arabian
Sea   Bay of
Bengal

10°

Sri Lanka

0°

⊛ National Capital

• Major Cities   N

INDIAN OCEAN

0   200   400   600   800 Miles

0   200   400   600   800   1000 Kilometers

Copyright by Rand McNally
Lambert Azimuthal Equal Area Projection
M-102157-1

60°   70°   80°

UIGHUR EMPIRE

GOBI DESERT

GREAT WALL

PARHAE

SILLA

Sea of
Japan
(East Sea)

Heian-kyo (Kyoto)
⊗ Nara

JAPAN

Dunhuang

SILK ROAD

Huang (Yellow)

Yellow
Sea

40°

30°

Grand Canal

Yangzhou

Luoyang

Chang-an
(Xi'an)

⊗

Hangzhou

East

China

Sea

Chang (Yangtze)

T'ANG EMPIRE
(CHINA)

PACIFIC

OCEAN

Taiwan

20°

hmaputra

EMPIRE

Xi (West)

Guangzhou
(Canton)

NAN-CHAO

South China

Sea

Philippine

Islands

Mekong

CHAMPA

CHEN-LA

10°

SRIVIJAYA

Borneo

Celebes

Sumatra

0°

⊗ Srivijaya
(Palembang)

10°

Java

100°

110°

120°

100°   110°   50°   120°   130°   140°

AUSTRIA-
HUNGARY

Moscow

20°
30°
40°
50°
60°
70°
80°

Ob'

R U S S I A N

50°

MONT.

SERB.

ROMANIA

BULGARIA

40°

Volga

Samara

Omsk

GREECE

Black Sea

Irtysh

Constantinople

O T T O M A N   E M P I R E

Cyprus
(Br.)

Mediterranean
Sea

Caspian Sea

Aral
Sea

Lake
Balkhash

Suez Canal

Euphrates

Tigris

Cairo

Jerusalem

Baghdad

Tehran

T U R K E S T A N

TIEN SHAN

Bukhara

Tashkent

TARIM BA

Samarkand

EGYPT

P E R S I A

TAKLIMAKAN
DESERT

Kabul

KASHMIR

KUWAIT

AFGHANISTAN

Red Sea

20°

ARABIA

BAHRAIN

Mecca

Persian Gulf

QATAR

TRUCIAL OMAN

BALUCHISTAN

PUNJAB

Indus

Delhi

HIMALAYA

NEPAL

SIND

RAJPUTANA

Yamuna

Ganga

OMAN

BEN

ERITREA

HADRAMAUT

B R I T I S H

ORISS

FR. SOM.

Aden
(Br.)

Bombay

HYDERABAD

10°

BRITISH
SOMALILAND

A r a b i a n

Hyderabad

ABYSSINIA

Goa
(Port.)

S e a

MYSORE

MADRAS

Madras

ITALIAN SOMALILAND

Ceylon

0°

Colombo

N

INDIAN OCEAN

0   200   400   600   800 Miles

0   200 400 600 800 1000 Kilometers

Copyright by Rand McNally
Lambert Azimuthal Equal Area Projection

10°

British
French
Dutch
Italian
Portuguese
United States

50°

60°

70°

80°

100° 110° 120° 60° 130° 140° 50° 150° 40° 160°

Lena

E M P I R E

Angara

Lake
Baikal

• Chita

• Irkutsk

Amur

M A N C H U R I A

Sakhalin

Hokkaido

• Vladivostok

Sea of
Japan
(East Sea)

Honshu

• Tokyo ⊛

M O N G O L I A

INNER MONGOLIA

KOREA

Lushun
(Rus.)

Seoul ⊛

JAPANESE
EMPIRE

30°

GOBI DESERT

Beijing ⊛

Tianjin •

Weihai
(Br.)

Shikoku

Kyushu

Huang (Yellow)

Qingdao
(Ger.)

Shanghai •

C H I N E S E   E M P I R E

Wuhan •

Hangzhou •

Ryukyu Islands
(Japan)

PACIFIC

BET

Chongqing •

(Yangtze)

Chang

Fuzhou •

Taiwan
(Japan)

OCEAN

20°

ahmaputra

Canton
(Guangzhou) •

Xi (West)

BHUTAN

ASSAM

Hong Kong •
(Br.)

Macao •
(Port.)

Luzon

PHILIPPINE
ISLANDS
(U.S.)

Calcutta

Kwangchowan •
(Fr.)

NDIA

BURMA

Mekong

ANNAM

South
China

Manila •

Rangoon ⊛

SIAM

FRENCH

Sea

Mindanao

ay of
engal

Bangkok ⊛

INDOCHINA

⊛ Saigon

Andaman
Islands
(Br.)

BRITISH
NORTH
BORNEO

BRUNEI

Nicobar
Islands
(Br.)

SARAWAK

Moluccas

MALAYA

Celebes

Singapore ⊛

Borneo

Sumatra

DUTCH EAST INDIES

TIMOR
(Port.)

10°

Batavia •

Java

90° 100° 110° 120°

10°

ARCTIC OCEAN

UNITED STATES

Bering Strait

Saint
Lawrence
Island

BERING
SEA

Wrangell
Island

EAST SIBERIAN
SEA

New Siberian Islands

Novaya
Sibir'
Island

LAPTEV
SEA

Kotelny
Island

Anadyr'

Zemlya

Srednekolymsk

Arctic Circle

Tiksi

Indigirka

Kolyma

Seymchan

Ust'-Kamchatsk

Komandorskiye
Islands

Verkhoyansk

Kamchatka
Peninsula

Petropavlovsk-
Kamchatskiy

Zhigansk

Lena

Magadan

SEA
OF
OKHOTSK

Tura · Lower Tunguska

Vilyuysk

Yakutsk

Aldan

Olëkminsk

Okha

A S I A

Angara

Bodaybo

Ust'-Kut

Nikolayevsk-na-Amure

Sakhalin

Amur

Komsomol'sk-
na-Amure

Kuril Islands

Bratsk

Zeya

Yuzhno-Sakhalinsk

Amur

Svobodnyy

Cheremkhovo

Lake
Baikal

Chita

Blagoveshchensk

Khabarovsk

Angarsk · Irkutsk

La Perouse Strait

Ulan-Ude

Birobidzhan

Hokkaido

JAPAN

PACIFIC
OCEAN

Ulan
Bator

Harbin

MONGOLIA

Vladivostok

Nakhodka

Shenyang

NORTH KOREA

P'yongyang

SEA OF
JAPAN
(EAST SEA)

★	National Capital
■	City over 1,000,000 population
▣	City of 250,000 to 1,000,000 population
•	City under 250,000 population

0   100   200   300   400   500 Miles

0   200   400   600   800 Kilometers

Copyright by Rand McNally
Lambert Azimuthal Equal Area Projection

Beginnings of Civilization

4 million B.C. – 200 B.C.

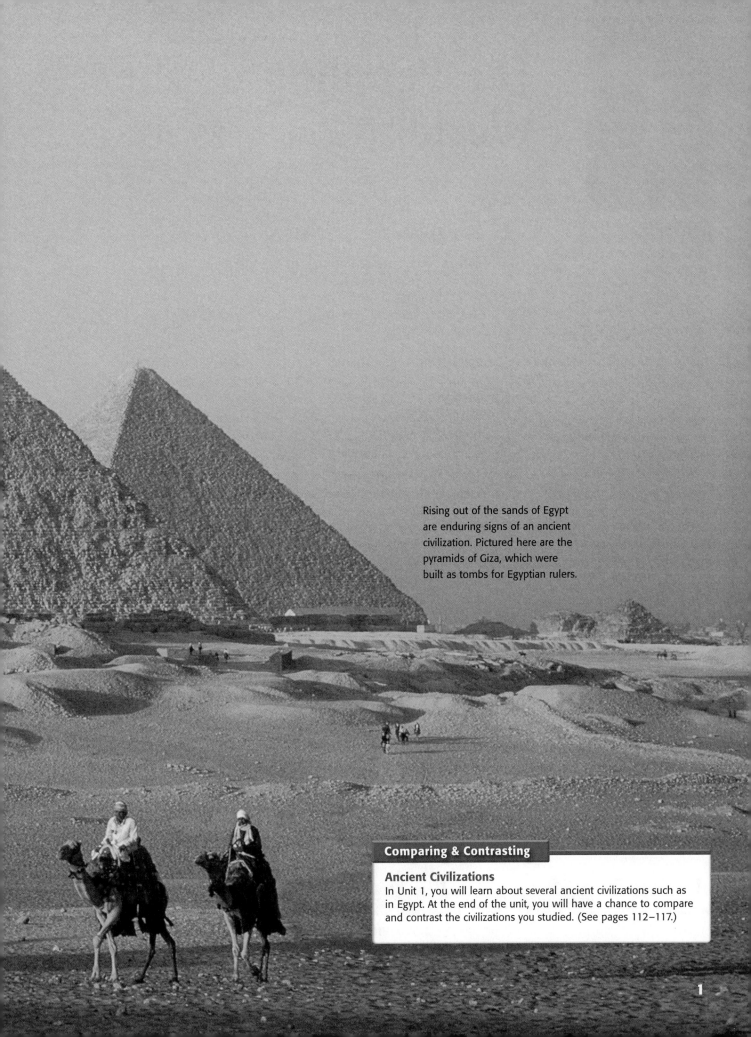

Rising out of the sands of Egypt
are enduring signs of an ancient
civilization. Pictured here are the
pyramids of Giza, which were
built as tombs for Egyptian rulers.

Comparing & Contrasting

Ancient Civilizations
In Unit 1, you will learn about several ancient civilizations such as
in Egypt. At the end of the unit, you will have a chance to compare
and contrast the civilizations you studied. (See pages 112–117.)

The Peopling of the World, Prehistory–2500 B.C.

Essential Question

Where did early human beings originate and what were some of their technological and artistic achievements?

 What You Will Learn

In this chapter you will learn about the origins, development, and achievements of early human life.

SECTION 1 Human Origins in Africa
Main Idea Fossil evidence shows that the earliest humans originated in Africa and spread across the globe.

SECTION 2 Humans Try to Control Nature
Main Idea The development of agriculture caused an increase in population and the growth of a settled way of life.

SECTION 3 Civilization Case Study: Ur in Sumer
Main Idea Prosperous farming villages, food surpluses, and new technology led to the rise of civilizations.

Previewing Themes

INTERACTION WITH ENVIRONMENT As early humans spread out over the world, they adapted to each environment they encountered. As time progressed, they learned to use natural resources.
Geography *Study the time line and the map. Where in Africa did human life begin?*

SCIENCE AND TECHNOLOGY The earliest peoples came up with new ideas and inventions in order to survive. As people began to live in settlements, they continued to develop new technology to control the environment.
Geography *Early humans began to migrate about 1.8 million years ago. What paths did these migrations take?*

ECONOMICS Early humans hunted animals and gathered wild plant foods for 3 to 4 million years. Then about 10,000 years ago, they learned to tame animals and to plant crops. Gradually, more complex economies developed.
Geography *Early settlement sites often were near rivers. Why might they have been located there?*

4,000,000 B.C.
First hominids appear in Africa.
(early hominid footprint) ▶

1,600,000 B.C.
Homo erectus
appears.

200,000 B.C.
Neanderthals
appear.

WORLD 4,000,000 B.C.

2,500,000 B.C.
Paleolithic Age begins.
(Paleolithic lunar calendar) ▶

Prehistoric World to 2500 B.C.

EUROPE

Cheddar
Neanderthal
Cro-Magnon
Lascaux
Çatal Huyuk
Jarmo
Shanidar
Uruk
Umma
Ur
Lagash

AFRICA

Hadar

Olduvai Gorge
Laetoli

N
W   E
S

HISTORY
Stone Age Weapons

↗ hmhsocialstudies.com   VIDEO

Homo erectus migration route

◆ Fossil or settlement site

Additional land, 18,000 B.C.

Extent of ice sheet, 18,000 B.C.

Glacial coastline, 18,000 B.C.

0   750   1500 Miles

0   750   1500 Kilometers

Winkel-Tripel Projection

20°W
40°N
20°N
0° Equator
20°S
0°
40°E
60°E
100°E

40,000 B.C.
Cro-Magnons
emerge. ▶

8000 B.C.
Neolithic Age begins;
first agriculture takes place.

3000 B.C.
◀ Bronze Age
well-established
in Mesopotamia.

2600 B.C.
◀ City of Ur
flourishes in Sumer.

2500 B.C.

How would these tools help early humans survive?

You have joined a team of scientists on an expedition to an ancient site where early humans once lived. The scientists' goal is to search for evidence that might unlock the mysteries of the past.

You're an eyewitness to their astounding discovery—human-made tools about 5,000 years old. They belonged to the so-called Ice Man, discovered in 1991. (See History in Depth, page 15.)

The remnants of a backpack

A birch-bark container

An axe

A dagger and its sheath

EXAMINING *the* ISSUES

- **What did early humans need to do to survive?**
- **What physical actions would these tools help humans do?**

As a class, discuss these questions. In your discussion, think about recent tools and inventions that have changed people's lives. As you read about the ancestors of present-day humans, notice how early toolmakers applied their creativity and problem-solving skills.

Human Origins in Africa

MAIN IDEA	WHY IT MATTERS NOW	TERMS & NAMES
INTERACTION WITH ENVIRONMENT Fossil evidence shows that the earliest humans originated in Africa and spread across the globe.	The study of early human remains and artifacts helps in understanding our place in human history.	• artifact • culture • hominid • Paleolithic Age • Neolithic Age • technology • *Homo sapiens*

SETTING THE STAGE What were the earliest humans like? Many people have asked this question. Because there are no written records of prehistoric peoples, scientists have to piece together information about the past. Teams of scientists use a variety of research methods to learn more about how, where, and when early humans developed. Interestingly, recent discoveries provide the most knowledge about human origins and the way prehistoric people lived. Yet, the picture of prehistory is still far from complete.

Scientists Search for Human Origins

Written documents provide a window to the distant past. For several thousand years, people have recorded information about their beliefs, activities, and important events. Prehistory, however, dates back to the time before the invention of writing—roughly 5,000 years ago. Without access to written records, scientists investigating the lives of prehistoric peoples face special challenges.

Scientific Clues Archaeologists are specially trained scientists who work like detectives to uncover the story of prehistoric peoples. They learn about early people by excavating and studying the traces of early settlements. An excavated site, called an archaeological dig, provides one of the richest sources of clues to the prehistoric way of life. Archaeologists sift through the dirt in a small plot of land. They analyze all existing evidence, such as bones and artifacts. Bones might reveal what the people looked like, how tall they were, the types of food they ate, diseases they may have had, and how long they lived. **Artifacts** are human-made objects, such as tools and jewelry. These items might hint at how people dressed, what work they did, or how they worshiped.

Scientists called anthropologists study **culture**, or a people's unique way of life. Anthropologists examine the artifacts at archaeological digs. From these, they re-create a picture of early people's cultural behavior. (See Analyzing Key Concepts on culture on the following page.)

Other scientists, called paleontologists, study fossils—evidence of early life preserved in rocks. Human fossils often consist of small fragments of teeth, skulls, or other bones. Paleontologists use complex techniques to date ancient fossil remains and rocks. Archaeologists, anthropologists, paleontologists, and other scientists work as a team to make new discoveries about how prehistoric people lived.

hmhsocialstudies.com
TAKING NOTES
Use the graphic organizer online to take notes on the advances of each hominid group discussed in the section.

Culture

In prehistoric times, bands of humans that lived near one another began to develop shared ways of doing things: common ways of dressing, similar hunting practices, favorite animals to eat. These shared traits were the first beginnings of what anthropologists and historians call *culture*.

Culture is the way of life of a group of people. Culture includes common practices of a society, its shared understandings, and its social organization. By overcoming individual differences, culture helps to unify the group.

Components of Culture

Common Practices	Shared Understandings	Social Organization
• what people eat • clothing and adornment • sports • tools and technology • social customs • work	• language • symbols • religious beliefs • values • the arts • political beliefs	• family • class and caste structure • relationships between individual and community • government • economic system • view of authority

How Culture Is Learned

People are not born knowing about culture. Instead, they must learn culture. Generally, individuals learn culture in two ways. First, they observe and imitate the behavior of people in their society. Second, people in their society directly teach the culture to them, usually through spoken or written language.

Media
Government
Religious Institutions
Family
School
Friends
Workplace

■ Observation and Imitation
■ Direct Teaching

↗ hmhsocialstudies.com

RESEARCH WEB LINKS Go online for more on culture.

> **DATA FILE**

CULTURAL DATA

Annual movie attendance, 2005 (per person)*

4.7 — U.S.
3.3 — India
0.6 — Chile

* UNESCO Institute for Statistics, last update 2006

Marriage rates, 2007 (per 1,000 population)*

7.3 — U.S.
5.7 — Japan
5.6 — Finland

* UN Demographic Yearbook 2007

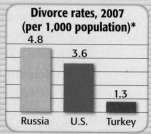

Divorce rates, 2007 (per 1,000 population)*

4.8 — Russia
3.6 — U.S.
1.3 — Turkey

* UN Demographic Yearbook 2007, Statistical Abstract of the United States 2010

Connect *to* Today

1. **Forming and Supporting Opinions** In U.S. culture, which shared understanding do you think is the most powerful? Why?

   See Skillbuilder Handbook, page R20.

2. **Making Inferences** Judging from the divorce rate in Turkey, what components of culture do you think are strong in that country? Why?

Early Footprints Found In the 1970s, archaeologist Mary Leakey led a scientific expedition to the region of Laetoli in Tanzania in East Africa. (See map on page 10.) There, she and her team looked for clues about human origins. In 1978, they found prehistoric footprints that resembled those of modern humans preserved in volcanic ash. These footprints were made by humanlike beings now called australopithecines (aw•STRAY•loh•PIHTH•ih•SYNZ). Humans and other creatures that walk upright, such as australopithecines, are called **hominids**. The Laetoli footprints provided striking evidence about human origins:

PRIMARY SOURCE
What do these footprints tell us? First, . . . that at least 3,600,000 years ago, what I believe to be man's direct ancestor walked fully upright. . . . Second, that the form of the foot was exactly the same as ours. . . . [The footprints produced] a kind of poignant time wrench. At one point, . . . she [the female hominid] stops, pauses, turns to the left to glance at some possible threat or irregularity, and then continues to the north. This motion, so intensely human, transcends time.

MARY LEAKEY, quoted in *National Geographic*

The Discovery of "Lucy" While Mary Leakey was working in East Africa, U.S. anthropologist Donald Johanson and his team were also searching for fossils. They were exploring sites in Ethiopia, about 1,000 miles to the north. In 1974, Johanson's team made a remarkable find—an unusually complete skeleton of an adult female hominid. They nicknamed her "Lucy" after the song "Lucy in the Sky with Diamonds." She had lived around 3.5 million years ago—the oldest hominid found to that date. **A**

Hominids Walk Upright Lucy and the hominids who left their footprints in East Africa were species of australopithecines. Walking upright helped them travel distances more easily. They were also able to spot threatening animals and carry food and children.

These early hominids had already developed the opposable thumb. This means that the tip of the thumb can cross the palm of the hand. The opposable thumb was crucial for tasks such as picking up small objects and making tools. (To see its importance, try picking up a coin with just the index and middle fingers. Imagine all of the other things that cannot be done without the opposable thumb.)

The Old Stone Age Begins

The invention of tools, mastery over fire, and the development of la[ng]... some of the most impressive achievements in human history. S[...] these occurred during the prehistoric period known as the Stone A[ge ...] vast length of time. The earlier and longer part of the Stone Age, [Old] Stone Age or **Paleolithic Age**, lasted from about 2.5 million to 800[0 ...] est stone chopping tools date back to this era. The New Stone Age [or Neolithic] **Age**, began about 8000 B.C. and ended as early as 3000 B.C. in some [places ...] who lived during this second phase of the Stone Age learned to polis[h ...] make pottery, grow crops, and raise animals.

MAIN IDEA

Drawing Conclusions

A Why were the discoveries of hominid footprints and "Lucy" important?

History Makers

The Leakey Family
The Leakey family has had a tremendous impact on the study of human origins. British anthropologists Louis S. B. Leakey (1903–1972) and Mary Leakey (1913–1996) began searching for early human remains in East Africa in the 1930s. Their efforts turned what was a sideline of science into a major field of scientific inquiry. Mary became one of the world's renowned hunters of human fossils.

Their son Richard; Richard's wife, Maeve; and Richard and Maeve's daughter Louise have continued the family's fossil-hunting in East Africa into the 21st century.

↗ **hmhsocialstudies.com**

RESEARCH WEB LINKS Go online for more on the Leakey family.

Australopithecines
- 4 million to 1 million B.C.
- found in southern and eastern Africa
- brain size 500 cm³ (cubic centimeters)
- first humanlike creature to walk upright

Homo habilis
- 2.5 million to 1.5 million B.C.
- found in East Africa
- brain size 700 cm³
- first to make stone tools

| 4 million years ago | 3 million years ago |

Much of the Paleolithic Age occurred during the period in the earth's history known as the Ice Age. During this time, glaciers alternately advanced and retreated as many as 18 times. The last of these ice ages ended about 10,000 years ago. By the beginning of the Neolithic Age, glaciers had retreated to roughly the same area they now occupy.

Homo habilis **May Have Used Tools** Before the australopithecines eventually vanished, new hominids appeared in East Africa around 2.5 million years ago. In 1960, archaeologists Louis and Mary Leakey discovered a hominid fossil at Olduvai (OHL•duh•vy) Gorge in northern Tanzania. The Leakeys named the fossil *Homo habilis,* which means "man of skill." The Leakeys and other researchers found tools made of lava rock. They believed *Homo habilis* used these tools to cut meat and crack open bones. Tools made the task of survival easier.

Homo erectus **Develops Technology** About 1.6 million years ago, before *Homo habilis* left the scene, another species of hominids appeared in East Africa. This species is now known as *Homo erectus,* or "upright man." Some anthropologists believe *Homo erectus* was a more intelligent and adaptable species than *Homo habilis. Homo erectus* people used intelligence to develop **technology**—ways of applying knowledge, tools, and inventions to meet their needs. These hominids gradually became skillful hunters and invented more sophisticated tools for digging, scraping, and cutting. They also eventually became the first hominids to migrate, or move, from Africa. Fossils and stone tools show that bands of *Homo erectus* hunters settled in India, China, Southeast Asia, and Europe.

According to anthropologists, *Homo erectus* was the first to use fire. Fire provided warmth in cold climates, cooked food, and frightened away attacking animals. The control of fire also probably helped *Homo erectus* settle new lands.

Homo erectus may have developed the beginnings of spoken language. Language, like technology, probably gave *Homo erectus* greater control over the environment and boosted chances for survival. The teamwork needed to plan hunts and cooperate in other tasks probably relied on language. *Homo erectus* might have named objects, places, animals, and plants and exchanged ideas. **B**

MAIN IDEA

Recognizing Effects

B How did *Homo erectus* use fire to adapt to the environment?

The Dawn of Modern Humans

Many scientists believe *Homo erectus* eventually developed into **Homo sapiens**—the species name for modern humans. *Homo sapiens* means "wise men." While they physically resembled *Homo erectus, Homo sapiens* had much larger brains.

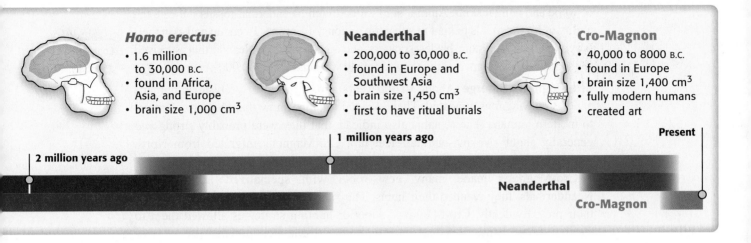

Homo erectus
• 1.6 million to 30,000 B.C.
• found in Africa, Asia, and Europe
• brain size 1,000 cm^3

Neanderthal
• 200,000 to 30,000 B.C.
• found in Europe and Southwest Asia
• brain size 1,450 cm^3
• first to have ritual burials

Cro-Magnon
• 40,000 to 8000 B.C.
• found in Europe
• brain size 1,400 cm^3
• fully modern humans
• created art

1 million years ago

Present

2 million years ago

Neanderthal

Cro-Magnon

Scientists have traditionally classified Neanderthals and Cro-Magnons as early groups of *Homo sapiens*. However, in 1997, DNA tests on a Neanderthal skeleton indicated that Neanderthals were not ancestors of modern humans. They were, however, affected by the arrival of Cro-Magnons, who may have competed with Neanderthals for land and food.

Neanderthals' Way of Life In 1856, as quarry workers were digging for limestone in the Neander Valley in Germany, they spotted fossilized bone fragments. These were the remains of Neanderthals, whose bones were discovered elsewhere in Europe and Southwest Asia. These people were powerfully built. They had heavy slanted brows, well-developed muscles, and thick bones. To many people, the name "Neanderthal" calls up the comic-strip image of a club-carrying caveman. However, archaeological discoveries reveal a more realistic picture of these early hominids, who lived between 200,000 and 30,000 years ago.

Evidence suggests that Neanderthals tried to explain and control their world. They developed religious beliefs and performed rituals. About 60,000 years ago, Neanderthals held a funeral for a man in Shanidar Cave, located in northeastern Iraq. Some archaeologists theorize that during the funeral, the Neanderthal's family covered his body with flowers. This funeral points to a belief in a world beyond the grave. Fossil hunter Richard Leakey, the son of Louis and Mary Leakey, wrote about the meaning of this Neanderthal burial:

PRIMARY SOURCE
The Shanidar events . . . speak clearly of a deep feeling for the spiritual quality of life. A concern for the fate of the human soul is universal in human societies today, and it was evidently a theme of Neanderthal society too.

RICHARD E. LEAKEY, *The Making of Mankind*

Neanderthals were also resourceful. They survived harsh Ice Age winters by living in caves or temporary shelters made

History *in* Depth

Time Line of Planet Earth
Imagine the 102 stories of the Empire State Building as a scale for a time line of the earth's history. Each story represents about 40 million years. Modern human beings have existed for just a tiny percentage of the life of this planet.

Present

1 billion years ago

2 billion years ago

3 billion years ago

40,000 years ago
Cro-Magnons appear.

200,000 years ago
Neanderthals appear.

4 million years ago
Australopithecines appear.

65 million years ago
Dinosaurs disappear; first mammals appear.

240 million years ago
First dinosaurs appear.

3.5 billion years ago
First single-cell life appears.

4 billion years ago

4.4 billion years ago
Earth is formed.

of wood and animal skins. Animal bones found with Neanderthal fossils indicate the ability of Neanderthals to hunt in subarctic regions of Europe. To cut up and skin their prey, they fashioned stone blades, scrapers, and other tools. The Neanderthals survived for some 170,000 years and then mysteriously vanished about 30,000 years ago. **C**

Cro-Magnons Emerge About 40,000 years ago, a group of prehistoric humans called Cro-Magnons appeared. Their skeletal remains show that they are identical to modern humans. The remains also indicate that they were probably strong and generally about five-and-one-half feet tall. Cro-Magnons migrated from North Africa to Europe and Asia.

Cro-Magnons made many new tools with specialized uses. Unlike Neanderthals, they planned their hunts. They studied animals' habits and stalked their prey. Evidently, Cro-Magnons' superior hunting strategies allowed them to survive more easily. This may have caused Cro-Magnon populations to grow at a slightly faster rate and eventually replace the Neanderthals. Cro-Magnons' advanced skill in spoken language may also have helped them to plan more difficult projects. This cooperation perhaps gave them an edge over the Neanderthals.

MAIN IDEA

Comparing

C How were Neanderthals similar to people today?

Early Human Migration, 1,600,000–10,000 B.C.

hmhsocialstudies.com | INTERACTIVE MAP

ARCTIC OCEAN

Heidelberg, Germany
600,000 years ago

Mladec, Czech Rep.
33,000 years ago

Malta, Russia
15,000 years ago

Diuktai Cave, Russia
14,000 years ago

EUROPE

Arctic Circle

NORTH AMERICA

ASIA

Ubeidiya, Israel
1 million years ago

Lantian, China
700,000 years ago

Blackwater Draw, U.S.
11,000 years ago

Meadowcroft Rockshelter, U.S.
12,000 years ago

40°N

Tighenif, Algeria
700,000 years ago

Qafzeh, Israel
92,000 years ago

Liujiang, China
67,000 years ago

PACIFIC OCEAN

Tropic of Cancer

ATLANTIC OCEAN

AFRICA

Area of Human Origins

Lake Turkana, Kenya
1.6 million years ago

Tabon Cave, Philippines
30,000 years ago

Trinil, Indonesia
700,000 years ago

INDIAN OCEAN

AUSTRALIA

Tropic of Capricorn

Pedra Furada, Brazil
12,000–30,000 years ago

SOUTH AMERICA

Klasies River Mouth, South Africa
100,000 years ago

Lake Mungo, Australia
38,000 years ago

Monte Verde, Chile
12,000–33,000 years ago

40°S

N

80°E   160°E   160°W   120°W

0   2,000 Miles
0   4,000 Kilometers

Legend:
- Homo erectus fossil site
- Homo sapiens fossil site
- Homo erectus migration route
- Homo sapiens migration route
- Extent of the last glacier, 18,000 B.C.
- Extent of land areas 18,000 B.C.

Famous Finds

CHAD

ETHIOPIA

TANZANIA

● **1960** At Olduvai Gorge, Tanzania, Louis Leakey finds 2-million-year-old **stone tools.**

● **1974** In Ethiopia, Donald Johanson finds "Lucy," a 3.5-million-year-old **hominid skeleton.**

● **1978** At Laetoli, Tanzania, Mary Leakey finds 3.6-million-year-old **hominid footprints.**

● **1994** In Ethiopia, an international team of scientists finds 2.33-million-year-old **hominid jaw.**

● **2002** In Chad, scientists announce discovery of a possible 6-million-year-old **hominid skull.**

GEOGRAPHY SKILLBUILDER: Interpreting Maps

1. **Movement** To what continents did Homo erectus groups migrate after leaving Africa?
2. **Human-Environment Interaction** What do the migration routes of Homo sapiens reveal about their survival skills and ability to adapt?

New Findings Add to Knowledge

Scientists are continuing to work at numerous sites in Africa. Their discoveries change our views of the still sketchy picture of human origins in Africa and of the migration of early humans out of Africa.

Fossils, Tools, and Cave Paintings Newly discovered fossils in Chad and Kenya, dating between 6 and 7 million years old, have some apelike features but also some that resemble hominids. Study of these fossils continues, but evidence suggests that they may be the earliest hominids. A 2.33-million-year-old jaw from Ethiopia is the oldest fossil belonging to the line leading to humans. Stone tools found at the same site suggest that toolmaking may have begun earlier than previously thought.

New discoveries also add to what we already know about prehistoric peoples. For example, in 1996, a team of researchers from Canada and the United States, including a high school student from New York, discovered a Neanderthal bone flute 43,000 to 82,000 years old. This discovery hints at a previously unknown talent of the Neanderthals—the gift of musical expression. The finding on cave walls of drawings of animals and people dating back as early as 35,000 years ago gives information on the daily activities and perhaps even religious practices of these peoples.

Early humans' skills and tools for surviving and adapting to the environment became more sophisticated as time passed. As you will read in Section 2, these technological advances would help launch a revolution in the way people lived.

Connect to Today

Chad Discovery
In 2002, an international team of scientists announced the discovery of a 6- to 7-million-year-old skull in northern Chad. The skull is similar in size to a modern chimpanzee, with a similar brain capacity. (See photograph.)

The team reported that the skull, nicknamed *Toumai,* or "hope of life," was the earliest human ancestor so far discovered. Its date is, in fact, millions of years older than the previous oldest-known hominid. The skull dates from the time that scientists believe the ancestors of humans split from the great apes.

Whether the skull is actually human or ape will require further study.

↗ **hmhsocialstudies.com**

INTERNET ACTIVITY Go online to create a TV news special on the Chad skull. Include conflicting theories on its origin.

SECTION 1 ASSESSMENT

TERMS & NAMES 1. For each term or name, write a sentence explaining its significance.
• artifact   • culture   • hominid   • Paleolithic Age   • Neolithic Age   • technology-   • *Homo sapiens*

USING YOUR NOTES
2. Which advance by a hominid group do you think was the most significant? Explain.

Hominid Group
Cro-Magnons

MAIN IDEAS
3. What clues do bones and artifacts give about early peoples?

4. What were the major achievements in human history during the Old Stone Age?

5. How did Neanderthals and Cro-Magnons differ from earlier peoples?

CRITICAL THINKING & WRITING
6. **RECOGNIZING EFFECTS** Why was the discovery of fire so important?

7. **MAKING INFERENCES** Why will specific details about the physical appearance and the customs of early peoples never be fully known?

8. **SYNTHESIZING** How do recent findings keep revising knowledge of the prehistoric past?

9. **WRITING ACTIVITY** ⟨INTERACTION WITH ENVIRONMENT⟩ Write a **persuasive essay** explaining which skill—toolmaking, the use of fire, or language—you think gave hominids the most control over their environment.

CONNECT TO TODAY CREATING AN ILLUSTRATED NEWS ARTICLE
Research a recent archaeological discovery. Write a two-paragraph **news article** about the find and include an illustration.

Cave Paintings

Cave paintings created by primitive people are found on every continent. The oldest ones were made about 35,000 years ago. Cave paintings in Europe and Africa often show images of hunting and daily activities. In the Americas and Australia, on the other hand, the paintings tend to be more symbolic and less realistic.

Scholars are not sure about the purpose of cave paintings. They may have been part of magical rites, hunting rituals, or an attempt to mark the events during various seasons. Another theory is that cave paintings (especially the more realistic ones) may simply be depictions of the surrounding world.

⌐ hmhsocialstudies.com

RESEARCH WEB LINKS Go online for more on cave paintings.

▼ Cave Paintings at Tassili n'Ajer, Algeria

These paintings depict women, children, and cattle. Located in Algeria, the Tassili n'Ajer (tah•SEEL•ee nah• ZHEER) site contains more than 15,000 images. They depict shifts in climate, animal migrations, and changes in human life. The oldest paintings date back to about 6000 B.C. Images continued to be painted until around the second century A.D.

▼ Cave Paintings at *Cuevas de las Manos* in Argentina

Cuevas de las Manos (Cave of the Hands) is located in the Rio Pinturas ravine, northeast of Santa Cruz, Argentina. Its rock walls display numerous hand paintings in vivid colors. The Tehuelches (tuh•WEHL•cheez) people created the paintings between 13,000 and 9,500 years ago. The cave is about 78 feet deep and, at the entrance, about 48 feet wide and 32 feet high.

3

▲ Replica of Lascaux Cave Painting, France

Discovered in 1940 , the Lascaux (lah•SKOH) cave contains more than 600 painted animals and symbols. These works were probably created between 15,000 and 13,000 B.C. In 1963, the cave was closed to the public. The high volume of visitors and the use of artificial lighting were damaging the paintings. A partial replica of the cave was created and is visited by about 300,000 people a year.

4

▲ Australian Aboriginal Cave Painting

This Aboriginal cave painting is in Kakadu (KAH•kuh•doo) National Park, Australia. Aboriginal people have lived in this area for at least 25,000 years. The painting depicts a Barramundi (bahr•uh•MUHN•dee) fish and a Dreamtime spirit. In the Aboriginal culture, Dreamtime is a supernatural past in which ancestral beings shaped and humanized the natural world.

Connect *to* Today

1. **Analyzing Motives** Why do you think primitive peoples used the walls of caves for their paintings?

   See Skillbuilder Handbook, page R15.

2. **Comparing and Contrasting** How are these paintings similar to or different from public murals created today?

13

Humans Try to Control Nature

MAIN IDEA	WHY IT MATTERS NOW	TERMS & NAMES
ECONOMICS The development of agriculture caused an increase in population and the growth of a settled way of life.	New methods for obtaining food and the development of technology laid the foundations for modern civilizations.	• nomad • hunter-gatherer • Neolithic Revolution • slash-and-burn farming • domestication

SETTING THE STAGE By about 40,000 years ago, human beings had become fully modern in their physical appearance. With a shave, a haircut, and a suit, a Cro-Magnon man would have looked like a modern business executive. However, over the following thousands of years, the way of life of early humans underwent incredible changes. People developed new technology, artistic skills, and most importantly, agriculture.

Early Advances in Technology and Art

hmhsocialstudies.com
TAKING NOTES

Use the graphic organizer online to take notes on the section's main ideas and details.

Early modern humans quickly distinguished themselves from their ancestors, who had spent most of their time just surviving. As inventors and artists, more advanced humans stepped up the pace of cultural changes.

Tools Needed to Survive For tens of thousands of years, men and women of the Old Stone Age were nomads. **Nomads** were highly mobile people who moved from place to place foraging, or searching, for new sources of food. Nomadic groups whose food supply depends on hunting animals and collecting plant foods are called **hunter-gatherers**. Prehistoric hunter-gatherers, such as roving bands of Cro-Magnons, increased their food supply by inventing tools. For example, hunters crafted special spears that enabled them to kill game at greater distances. Digging sticks helped food gatherers pry plants loose at the roots.

Early modern humans had launched a technological revolution. They used stone, bone, and wood to fashion more than 100 different tools. These expanded tool kits included knives to kill and butcher game, and fish hooks and harpoons to catch fish. A chisel-like cutter was designed to make other tools. Cro-Magnons used bone needles to sew clothing made of animal hides.

Artistic Expression in the Paleolithic Age The tools of early modern humans explain how they met their survival needs. Yet their world best springs to life through their artistic creations. Necklaces of seashells, lion teeth, and bear claws adorned both men and women. People ground mammoth tusks into polished beads. They also carved small realistic sculptures of animals that inhabited their world.

As you read in the Cave Paintings feature, Stone Age peoples on all continents created cave paintings. The best-known of these are the paintings on the walls and ceilings of European caves, mainly in France and Spain. Here early artists drew lifelike images of wild animals. Cave artists made colored paints from charcoal, mud, and animal blood. In Africa, early artists engraved pictures on rocks or painted scenes in caves or rock shelters. In Australia, they created paintings on large rocks.

The Beginnings of Agriculture

Vocabulary
Edible means "safe to be eaten."

For thousands upon thousands of years, humans survived by hunting game and gathering edible plants. They lived in bands of 25 to 70 people. The men almost certainly did the hunting. The women gathered fruits, berries, roots, and grasses. Then about 10,000 years ago, some of the women may have scattered seeds near a regular campsite. When they returned the next season, they may have found new crops growing. This discovery would usher in the **Neolithic Revolution**, or the agricultural revolution—the far-reaching changes in human life resulting from the beginnings of farming. The shift from food-gathering to food-producing culture represents one of the great breakthroughs in history.

Causes of the Agricultural Revolution Scientists do not know exactly why the agricultural revolution occurred during this period. Change in climate was probably a key reason. (See chart on page 17.) Rising temperatures worldwide provided longer growing seasons and drier land for cultivating wild grasses. A rich supply of grain helped support a small population boom. As populations slowly rose, hunter-gatherers felt pressure to find new food sources. Farming offered an attractive alternative. Unlike hunting, it provided a steady source of food.

Early Farming Methods Some groups practiced **slash-and-burn farming**, in which they cut trees or grasses and burned them to clear a field. The ashes that remained fertilized the soil. Farmers planted crops for a year or two, then moved to another area of land. After several years, trees and grass grew back, and other farmers repeated the process of slashing and burning.

VIDEO
Stone Age Weapons

hmhsocialstudies.com

History *in* Depth

The Neolithic Ice Man

In 1991, two German hikers made an accidental discovery that gave archaeologists a firsthand look at the technology of early toolmakers. Near the border of Austria and Italy, they spotted the mummified body of a prehistoric traveler, preserved in ice for some 5,000 years (upper right).

Nicknamed the "Ice Man," this early human was not empty-handed. The tool kit found near him included a six-foot longbow and a deerskin case with 14 arrows. It also contained a stick with an antler tip for sharpening flint blades, a small flint dagger in a woven sheath, a copper ax, and a medicine bag.

Scientific research on the body (lower right) concluded that the Ice Man was in his 40s when he died in the late spring or early summer from an arrow wound. Scientists also determined that in the hours before his death, he ate wild goat, red deer, and grains. The Ice Man is housed in a special museum in Bolzano, Italy.

Domestication of Animals Food gatherers' understanding of plants probably spurred the development of farming. Meanwhile, hunters' expert knowledge of wild animals likely played a key role in the **domestication**, or taming, of animals. They tamed horses, dogs, goats, and pigs. Like farming, domestication of animals came slowly. Stone Age hunters may have driven herds of animals into rocky ravines to be slaughtered. It was then a small step to drive herds into human-made enclosures. From there, farmers could keep the animals as a constant source of food and gradually tame them.

Not only farmers domesticated animals. Pastoral nomads, or wandering herders, tended sheep, goats, camels, or other animals. These herders moved their animals to new pastures and watering places.

Agriculture in Jarmo Today, the eroded and barren rolling foothills of the Zagros Mountains in northeastern Iraq seem an unlikely site for the birthplace of agriculture. According to archaeologist Robert Braidwood, thousands of years ago the environmental conditions of this region favored the development of agriculture. Wild wheat and barley, along with wild goats, pigs, sheep, and horses, had once thrived near the Zagros Mountains.

In the 1950s, Braidwood led an archaeological dig at a site called Jarmo. He concluded that an agricultural settlement was built there about 9,000 years ago:

PRIMARY SOURCE ⓐ
We found weights for digging sticks, hoe-like [tools], flint-sickle blades, and a wide variety of milling stones. . . . We also discovered several pits that were probably used for the storage of grain. Perhaps the most important evidence of all was animal bones and the impressions left in the mud by cereal grains. . . . The people of Jarmo were adjusting themselves to a completely new way of life, just as we are adjusting ourselves to the consequences of such things as the steam engine. What they learned about living in a revolution may be of more than academic interest to us in our troubled times.

ROBERT BRAIDWOOD, quoted in *Scientific American*

MAIN IDEA

Analyzing Primary Sources

ⓐ Why do you think Braidwood believes that we can learn from early peoples?

The Jarmo farmers, and others like them in places as far apart as Mexico and Thailand, pioneered a new way of life. Villages such as Jarmo marked the beginning of a new era and laid the foundation for modern life.

Villages Grow and Prosper

The changeover from hunting and gathering to farming and herding took place not once but many times. Neolithic people in many parts of the world independently developed agriculture, as the map at the right shows.

Farming Develops in Many Places Within a few thousand years, people in many other regions, especially in fertile river valleys, turned to farming.

- **Africa** The Nile River Valley developed into an important agricultural center for growing wheat, barley, and other crops.
- **China** About 8,000 years ago, farmers along the middle stretches of the Huang He (Yellow River) cultivated a grain called millet. About 1,000 years later, farmers first domesticated wild rice in the Chang Jiang River delta.
- **Mexico and Central America** Farmers cultivated corn, beans, and squash.
- **Peru** Farmers in the Central Andes were the first to grow tomatoes, sweet potatoes, and white potatoes.

From these early and varied centers of agriculture, farming then spread to surrounding regions. ⓑ

MAIN IDEA

Making Inferences

ⓑ What advantages might farming and herding have over hunting and gathering?

ASIA

EUROPE

40°N

Jarmo

TAKLIMAKAN DESERT

Huang He (Yellow R.)

Euphrates R.

Tigris R.

Jericho

Indus R.

Pan-po

CHINA

SAHARA

Nile R.

ARABIAN DESERT

INDIA

AFRICA

Tropic of Cancer

INDIAN OCEAN

NORTH AMERICA

SONORAN DESERT

ATLANTIC OCEAN

Tropic of Cancer

Tehuacán Valley

PACIFIC OCEAN

0° Equator

NAMIB DESERT

KALAHARI DESERT

SOUTH AMERICA

ATACAMA DESERT

Tropic of Capricorn

0   1,000 Miles
0   2,000 Kilometers

N

Major crops

Bananas	Grapes	Sorghum	Wheat
Barley	Olives	Soybeans	
Corn	Potato	Agriculture by 5,000 B.C.	
Cotton	Rice	Agriculture by 3,000 B.C.	

Agriculture by 2,000 B.C.

Agriculture by 500 B.C.

▲ A Neolithic grindstone and vessel used to grind grain

Agricultural Revolution

Temperature

60°
58°
56°
54°
52°
50°

Average Global Temperature (in Fahrenheit)

25 20 15 10 5 0
Years Ago (in thousands)

beginnings of agriculture

last ice age

Source: *Ice Ages, Solving the Mystery*

Population

150
125
100
75
50
25
0

World Population (in millions)

25 20 15 10 5 0
Years Ago (in thousands)

— Post-Agricultural Revolution
— Agricultural Revolution
— Hunting-gathering stage

Source: *A Geography of Population: World Patterns*

SKILLBUILDER: Interpreting Maps and Charts
1. **Map** What geographic feature favored the development of agricultural areas before 5000 B.C.?
2. **Chart** What effect did the agricultural revolution have on population growth? Why?

Catal Huyuk In 1958, archaeologists discovered the agricultural village now known as Catal Huyuk (chuh•TUL-hoo•YOOK), or the "forked mound." It was located on a fertile plain in south-central Turkey (about 30 miles from modern-day Konya), near a twin-coned volcano. Catal Huyuk covered an area of about 32 acres. At its peak 8,000 years ago, the village was home to 5,000 to 6,000 people who lived in about 1,000 dwellings. These rectangular-shaped houses were made of brick and were arranged side-by-side like a honeycomb.

▼ A 9,000-year-old baked-clay figurine found in Catal Huyuk

Catal Huyuk showed the benefits of settled life. Its rich, well-watered soil produced large crops of wheat, barley, and peas. Villagers also raised sheep and cattle. Catal Huyuk's agricultural surpluses supported a number of highly skilled workers, such as potters and weavers. But the village was best known at the time for its obsidian products. This dark volcanic rock, which looks like glass, was plentiful. It was used to make mirrors, jewelry, and knives for trade.

Catal Huyuk's prosperity also supported a varied cultural life. Archaeologists have uncovered colorful wall paintings depicting animals and hunting scenes. Many religious shrines were dedicated to a mother goddess. According to her worshipers, she controlled the supply of grain.

Vocabulary
Shrines are places where sacred relics are kept.

The new settled way of life also had its drawbacks—some of the same that affected hunter-gatherer settlements. Floods, fire, drought, and other natural disasters could destroy a village. Diseases, such as malaria, spread easily among people living closely together. Jealous neighbors and roving nomadic bands might attack and loot a wealthy village like Catal Huyuk.

Despite problems, these permanent settlements provided their residents with opportunities for fulfillment—in work, in art, and in leisure time. As you will learn in Section 3, some early villages expanded into cities. These urban centers would become the setting for more complex cultures in which new tools, art, and crafts were created.

SECTION 2 ASSESSMENT

TERMS & NAMES 1. For each term or name, write a sentence explaining its significance.
• nomad   • hunter-gatherer   • Neolithic Revolution   • slash-and-burn farming   • domestication

USING YOUR NOTES	MAIN IDEAS	CRITICAL THINKING & WRITING
2. Which effect of the development of agriculture was the most significant? *Humans Try to Control Nature* *I. Early Advances in Technology and Art* *A.* *B.* *II. The Beginnings of Agriculture*	3. How did Cro-Magnon's new tools make survival easier? 4. What factors played a role in the origins of agriculture? 5. What were the first crops grown in the Americas?	6. **MAKING INFERENCES** What kinds of problems did Stone Age peoples face? 7. **SUMMARIZING** In what ways did Neolithic peoples dramatically improve their lives? 8. **HYPOTHESIZING** Why do you think the development of agriculture occurred around the same time in several different places? 9. **WRITING ACTIVITY** SCIENCE AND TECHNOLOGY Write a two-paragraph **opinion paper** on the most significant consequences of the Agricultural Revolution.

CONNECT TO TODAY CREATING A CHART
Use text information on Jarmo and Catal Huyuk to make a **chart** listing the tools, weapons, and other artifacts that archaeologists today might find at an ancient site of a farming settlement.

Civilization

CASE STUDY: Ur in Sumer

MAIN IDEA	WHY IT MATTERS NOW	TERMS & NAMES
SCIENCE AND TECHNOLOGY Prosperous farming villages, food surpluses, and new technology led to the rise of civilizations.	Contemporary civilizations share the same characteristics typical of ancient civilizations.	• civilization • cuneiform • specialization • Bronze Age • artisan • barter • institution • ziggurat • scribe

SETTING THE STAGE Agriculture marked a dramatic change in how people lived together. They began dwelling in larger, more organized communities, such as farming villages and towns. From some of these settlements, cities gradually emerged, forming the backdrop of a more complex way of life—civilization.

Villages Grow into Cities

Over the centuries, people settled in stable communities that were based on agriculture. Domesticated animals became more common. The invention of new tools—hoes, sickles, and plow sticks—made the task of farming easier. As people gradually developed the technology to control their natural environment, they reaped larger harvests. Settlements with a plentiful supply of food could support larger populations.

As the population of some early farming villages increased, social relationships became more complicated. The change from a nomadic hunting-gathering way of life to settled village life took a long time. Likewise, the change from village life to city life was a gradual process that spanned several generations.

Economic Changes To cultivate more land and to produce extra crops, ancient people in larger villages built elaborate irrigation systems. The resulting food surpluses freed some villagers to pursue other jobs and to develop skills besides farming. Individuals who learned to become craftspeople created valuable new products, such as pottery, metal objects, and woven cloth. In turn, people who became traders profited from a broader range of goods to exchange—craftwork, grains, and many raw materials. Two important inventions—the wheel and the sail—also enabled traders to move more goods over longer distances.

Social Changes A more complex and prosperous economy affected the social structure of village life. For example, building and operating large irrigation systems required the labor of many people. As other special groups of workers formed, social classes with varying wealth, power, and influence began to emerge. A system of social classes would become more clearly defined as cities grew.

Religion also became more organized. During the Old Stone Age, prehistoric people's religious beliefs centered around nature, animal spirits, and some idea of an afterlife. During the New Stone Age, farming peoples worshiped the many gods and goddesses who they believed had power over the rain, wind, and other forces of

hmhsocialstudies.com
TAKING NOTES

Use the graphic organizer online to take notes on the characteristics of the civilization at Sumer.

nature. Early city dwellers developed rituals founded on these earlier religious beliefs. As populations grew, common spiritual values became lasting religious traditions.

How Civilization Develops

Most historians believe that one of the first civilizations arose in Sumer. Sumer was located in Mesopotamia, a region that is part of modern Iraq. A **civilization** is often defined as a complex culture with five characteristics: (1) advanced cities, (2) specialized workers, (3) complex institutions, (4) record keeping, and (5) advanced technology. Just what set the Sumerians apart from their neighbors?

Advanced Cities Cities were the birthplaces of the first civilizations. A city is more than a large group of people living together. The size of the population alone does not distinguish a village from a city. One of the key differences is that a city is a center of trade for a larger area. Like their modern-day counterparts, ancient city dwellers depended on trade. Farmers, merchants, and traders brought goods to market in the cities. The city dwellers themselves produced a variety of goods for exchange.

Specialized Workers As cities grew, so did the need for more specialized workers, such as traders, government officials, and priests. Food surpluses provided the opportunity for **specialization**—the development of skills in a specific kind of work. An abundant food supply allowed some people to become expert at jobs besides farming. Some city dwellers became **artisans**—skilled workers who make goods by hand. Specialization helped artisans develop their skill at designing jewelry, fashioning metal tools and weapons, or making clothing and pottery. The wide range of crafts artisans produced helped cities become centers of trade.

Complex Institutions The soaring populations of early cities made government, or a system of ruling, necessary. In civilizations, leaders emerged to maintain order among people and to establish laws. Government is an example of an **institution**—a long-lasting pattern of organization in a community. Complex institutions, such as government, religion, and the economy, are another characteristic of civilization.

With the growth of cities, religion became a formal institution. Most cities had great temples where dozens of priests took charge of religious duties. Sumerians believed that every city belonged to a god who governed the city's activities. The temple was the hub of both government and religious affairs. It also served as the city's economic center. There food and trade items were distributed. **A**

Record Keeping As government, religion, and the economy became more complex, people recognized the need to keep records. In early civilizations, government officials had to document tax collections, the passage of laws, and the storage of grain. Priests needed a way to keep track of the calendar and important rituals. Merchants had to record accounts of debts and payments.

Most civilizations developed a system of writing, though some devised other methods of record keeping. Around 3000 B.C., Sumerian **scribes**—or professional record keepers—invented a system of writing called **cuneiform** (KYOO•nee•uh•FAWRM), meaning "wedge-shaped." (Earlier Sumerian writing consisted of pictographs—symbols of the

Global Patterns

The Incan System of Record Keeping

Early civilizations other than Sumer also developed record keeping. The empire of the ancient Incan civilization stretched along the western coast of South America. Though the Inca had no writing system, they kept records using a *quipu*, a set of colored strings tied with different-size knots at various intervals (see photograph). Each knot represented a certain amount or its multiple. The colors of each cord represented the item being counted: people, animals, land, and so on.

The *quipucamayoc*, officials who knew how to use the *quipu*, kept records of births, deaths, marriages, crops, and historical events.

MAIN IDEA

Drawing Conclusions

A Why were cities essential to the growth of civilizations?

objects or what they represented.) The scribe's tool, called a stylus, was a sharpened reed with a wedge-shaped point. It was pressed into moist clay to create symbols. Scribes baked their clay tablets in the sun to preserve the writing.

People soon began to use writing for other purposes besides record keeping. They also wrote about their cities' dramatic events—wars, natural disasters, the reign of kings. Thus, the beginning of civilization in Sumer also signaled the beginning of written history.

Improved Technology New tools and techniques are always needed to solve problems that emerge when large groups of people live together. In early civilizations, some farmers harnessed the powers of animals and nature. For example, they used ox-drawn plows to turn the soil. They also created irrigation systems to expand planting areas.

Sumerian artisans relied on new technology to make their tasks easier. Around 3500 B.C., they first used the potter's wheel to shape jugs, plates, and bowls. Sumerian metalworkers discovered that melting together certain amounts of copper and tin made bronze. After 2500 B.C., metalworkers in Sumer's cities turned out bronze spearheads by the thousands. The period called the **Bronze Age** refers to the time when people began using bronze, rather than copper and stone, to fashion tools and weapons. The Bronze Age started in Sumer around 3000 B.C., but the date varied in other parts of Asia and in Europe.

▲ The wedge-shaped symbols of cuneiform are visible on this clay tablet.

> ## Analyzing Key Concepts

Civilization

As the history of Sumer demonstrates, civilization first developed in cities. In fact, the very word *civilization* comes from the Latin word for citizen. However, the development of cities is only one aspect of civilization. Many scholars define civilization as a complex culture with five characteristics. The graphic organizer to the right shows how Sumer displayed these five characteristics.

Specialized Workers
- merchants
- teachers
- soldiers
- metalworkers
- priests
- government officials
- potters
- farmers
- scribes
- weavers

Complex Institutions
- Formal governments with officials and laws
- Priests with both religious and political power
- A rigorous education system for training of scribes

CHARACTERISTICS OF CIVILIZATION in Sumer

Record Keeping
- Cuneiform tablets—records of business transactions, historical events, customs, and traditions

Advanced Cities
- Uruk—population of about 50,000, which doubled in two centuries
- Lagash—population of about 10,000 to 50,000
- Umma—population of about 10,000 to 50,000

Advanced Technology
By around 3000 B.C.:
- The wheel, the plow, and the sailboat probably in daily use
- Bronze weapons and body armor that gave Sumerians a military advantage over their enemies

SKILLBUILDER:
Interpreting Graphics
1. **Making Inferences** *Judging from the information on this graphic, what economic activities probably took place in Sumerian cities?*
2. **Drawing Conclusions** *What is the relationship between the development of specialized workers and the development of complex institutions?*

Civilization Emerges in Ur

Ur, one of the earliest cities in Sumer, stood on the banks of the Euphrates River in what is now southern Iraq. Some 30,000 people once lived in this ancient city. Ur was the site of a highly sophisticated civilization.

After excavating from 1922 to 1934, English archaeologist Leonard Woolley and his team unraveled the mystery of this long-lost civilization. From archaeological evidence, Woolley concluded that around 3000 B.C., Ur was a flourishing urban civilization. People in Ur lived in well-defined social classes. Rulers, as well as priests and priestesses, wielded great power. Wealthy merchants profited from foreign trade. Artists and artisans created lavish jewelry, musical instruments, and gold daggers. Woolley's finds have enabled historians to reconstruct Ur's advanced culture.

An Agricultural Economy Imagine a time nearly 5,000 years ago. Outside the mud-brick walls surrounding Ur, ox-driven plows cultivate the fields. People are working barefoot in the irrigation ditches that run between patches of green plants. With stone hoes, the workers widen ditches to carry water into their fields from the reservoir a mile away. This large-scale irrigation system was developed to provide Ur with food surpluses, which keep the economy thriving. The government officials who direct this public works project ensure its smooth operation. **B**

Life in the City A broad dirt road leads from the fields to the city's wall. Inside, city dwellers go about their daily lives. Most live in windowless, one-story, box-like houses packed tightly along the street. A few wealthy families live in two-story houses with an inner courtyard.

Down another street, artisans work in their shops. A metalworker makes bronze by mixing molten copper with just the right quantity of tin. Later, he will hammer the bronze to make spearheads—weapons to help Ur's well-organized armies

MAIN IDEA

Analyzing Causes

B How did Ur's agricultural way of life foster the development of civilization there?

The City of Ur

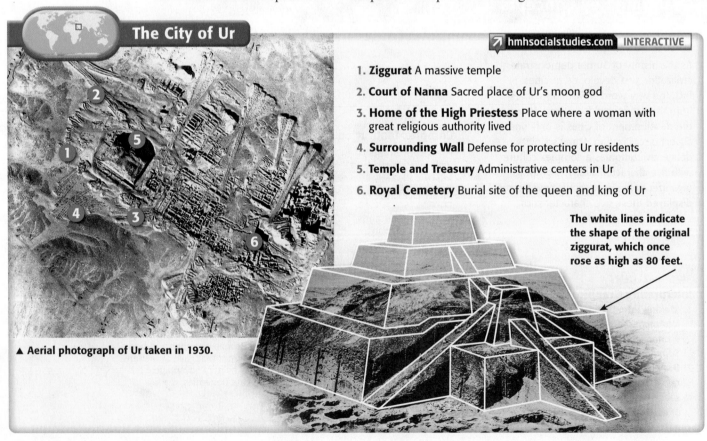

▲ Aerial photograph of Ur taken in 1930.

hmhsocialstudies.com **INTERACTIVE**

1. **Ziggurat** A massive temple
2. **Court of Nanna** Sacred place of Ur's moon god
3. **Home of the High Priestess** Place where a woman with great religious authority lived
4. **Surrounding Wall** Defense for protecting Ur residents
5. **Temple and Treasury** Administrative centers in Ur
6. **Royal Cemetery** Burial site of the queen and king of Ur

The white lines indicate the shape of the original ziggurat, which once rose as high as 80 feet.

defend the city. As a potter spins his potter's wheel, he expertly shapes the moist clay into a large bowl. These artisans and other craftworkers produce trade goods that help Ur prosper.

Ur's Thriving Trade The narrow streets open into a broad avenue where merchants squat under awnings and trade farmers' crops and artisans' crafts. This is the city's bazaar, or marketplace. Coins are not used to make purchases because money has not yet been invented. But merchants and their customers know roughly how many pots of grain a farmer must give to buy a jug of wine. This way of trading goods and services without money is called **barter**. More complicated trades require a scribe. He carefully forms cuneiform signs on a clay tablet. The signs may show how much barley a farmer owes a merchant for a donkey.

The Temple: Center of City Life Farther down the main avenue stands Ur's tallest and most important building—the temple. Like a city within a city, the temple is surrounded by a heavy wall. Within the temple gate, a massive, tiered structure towers over the city. This pyramid-shaped monument is called a **ziggurat** (ZIHG•uh•RAT), which means "mountain of god." On the exterior of the ziggurat, a flight of perhaps 100 mud-brick stairs leads to the top. At the peak, priests conduct rituals to worship the city god who looms over Ur. Every day, priests climb these stairs. They often drag a goat or sheep to sacrifice. The temple also houses storage areas for grains, woven fabrics, and gems—offerings to the city's god. Sumerians had elaborate burial rituals and believed in an afterlife.

An early city, such as Ur, represents a model of civilizations that continued to arise throughout history. While the Sumerians were advancing their culture, civilizations were developing in Egypt, China, and elsewhere in Asia.

Connect to Today

Iraq's Ancient Treasures at Risk

The ziggurat at Ur was damaged during the Persian Gulf War of 1991. In that conflict, Iraq parked military planes near the ziggurat, hoping coalition forces would not risk harming the ancient structure. While it was not attacked, bombs caused large craters nearby, and it was hit by stray machine gun fire.

During the 2003 war, the Iraqi National Museum in Baghdad was damaged and then attacked by looters. Some of the treasures of the area's ancient civilizations were either looted or destroyed.

SECTION 3 ASSESSMENT

TERMS & NAMES 1. For each term or name, write a sentence explaining its significance.
• civilization • specialization • artisan • institution • scribe • cuneiform • Bronze Age • barter • ziggurat

USING YOUR NOTES

2. Which characteristic is the most important for development of a civilization? Why?

Characteristics
1.
2.
3.
4.
5.

MAIN IDEAS

3. How did the social structure of village life change as the economy became more complex?

4. What role did irrigation systems play in the development of civilizations?

5. What are the key traits of a civilization?

CRITICAL THINKING & WRITING

6. **DRAWING CONCLUSIONS** How did life in Sumer differ from life in a small farming community of the region?

7. **RECOGNIZING EFFECTS** Why was writing a key invention for the Sumerians?

8. **MAKING INFERENCES** In what ways does the ziggurat of Ur reveal that Sumerians had developed an advanced civilization?

9. **WRITING ACTIVITY** ECONOMICS Choose a person from Ur who has a specialized skill, such as an artisan, a trader, or a scribe. Write an **expository essay** explaining that person's contribution to the economic welfare of the city.

MULTIMEDIA ACTIVITY CREATING A CHART

Use the Internet to create a **chart** showing the ten largest cities in the world, their populations, and the continent on which each is located.

INTERNET KEYWORD
city population

TERMS & NAMES

For each term or name below, briefly explain its connection to human prehistory.

1. artifact
2. culture
3. technology
4. hunter-gatherer
5. Neolithic Revolution
6. domestication
7. civilization
8. specialization
9. institution
10. Bronze Age

MAIN IDEAS

Human Origins in Africa Section 1 (pp. 5–13)

11. What kinds of evidence do archaeologists, anthropologists, and paleontologists study to find out how prehistoric people lived?

12. Why did the ability to walk upright and the development of the opposable thumb represent important breakthroughs for early hominids?

13. Why is the prehistoric period called the Stone Age?

14. What evidence supports archaeologists' beliefs that Neanderthals developed a form of religion?

Humans Try to Control Nature Section 2 (pp. 14–18)

15. Why do some archaeologists believe that women were the first farmers?

16. What role did the food supply play in shaping the nomadic life of hunter-gatherers and the settled life of farmers?

17. In what areas of the world did agriculture first develop?

Case Study: Civilization Section 3 (pp. 19–23)

18. What economic changes resulted from food surpluses in agricultural villages?

19. Why did the growth of civilization make government necessary?

20. Why did a system of record keeping develop in civilizations?

CRITICAL THINKING

1. **USING YOUR NOTES**

   In a chart, show the differences between Paleolithic and Neolithic cultures.

	Paleolithic	Neolithic
Source of food		
Means of living		
Technology		
Type of community		

2. **FORMING AND SUPPORTING OPINIONS**

   SCIENCE AND TECHNOLOGY Which technology of the New Stone Age had the most impact on daily life? Explain.

3. **ANALYZING CAUSES AND RECOGNIZING EFFECTS**

   ECONOMICS What effect did trade have on the development of civilization?

4. **SYNTHESIZING**

   What event or development in early human history do you think is of particular significance? Why?

5. **MAKING INFERENCES**

   How did the rise of cities affect government in early cultures?

VISUAL SUMMARY

The Peopling of the World

Hunting-Gathering Bands   **Growth of Villages**   **Rise of Cities**

SOCIAL ORGANIZATION

Beginning about **2 million** B.C.   Beginning about **8000** B.C.   Beginning about **3000** B.C.

KEY ACHIEVEMENTS

- Invention of tools
- Mastery over fire
- Development of language
- Creation of art

- Breakthroughs in farming technology
- Development of agriculture
- Domestication of animals
- Food surpluses

- Specialized workers
- Record keeping
- Complex institutions
- Advanced technology

Use the quotation and your knowledge of world history to answer questions 1 and 2.

PRIMARY SOURCE

Litter of the past is the basis of archaeology. The coins, the pottery, the textiles and the buildings of bygone eras offer us clues as to how our [early ancestors] behaved, how they ran their economy, what they believed in and what was important to them. What archaeologists retrieve from excavations are images of past lives. . . . [These images] are pieced together slowly and painstakingly from the information contained in objects found.

RICHARD LEAKEY in *The Making of Mankind*

1. According to Richard Leakey, what is the job of the archaeologist?

   A. to study coins to learn about an economy

   B. to clean out caves where early ancestors lived

   C. to create images of coins, pottery, and textiles

   D. to examine artifacts found at a location

2. What term applies to the behaviors, economic activities, and beliefs referred to by Richard Leakey?

   A. culture

   B. civilization

   C. case study

   D. artifacts

Use the illustration of the Stone Age cave painting from Argentina and your knowledge of world history to answer question 3.

3. What information might an archaeologist learn from this painting?

   A. the height of the humans living in the region

   B. the names of gods worshiped here

   C. types of animals found in the region

   D. the time of year this cave was visited

 hmhsocialstudies.com | **TEST PRACTICE**

For additional test practice, go online for:

• Diagnostic tests

• Strategies

• Tutorials

Interact *with* History

On page 4, you played the role of an amateur archaeologist as you tried to figure out the uses of some prehistoric tools. Now that you've read the chapter, what new clues have you discovered that would help you unravel the mystery of who made the tool with the wedge-shaped blade, and why? What evidence can you use to support your conclusions about its purpose? Discuss your ideas with a small group.

FOCUS ON WRITING

Consider the religious practices of the Neanderthals, the villagers of Catal Huyuk, and the city dwellers of Ur. Write a two-paragraph **essay** analyzing the development of religious beliefs over the course of the Stone Age. In your essay, consider the archaeological evidence that supports the scientific conclusions about beliefs, practices, and organization.

MULTIMEDIA ACTIVITY

NetExplorations: Cave Art

Go to *NetExplorations* at **hmhsocialstudies.com** to learn more about prehistoric cave art. Search the Internet for other examples of cave art—start with the list of sites at *NetExplorations* —and use some of the examples to create an online or classroom exhibit. Create a log and ask visitors to the exhibit to answer questions such as:

• What do you see in each cave art example?

• What do the materials used, the subject matter, and the style of each example suggest about the lives of prehistoric people?

• How does prehistoric art help historians learn about the people who created it?

CHAPTER 2

Early River Valley Civilizations, 3500 B.C.–450 B.C.

Essential Question

How did early peoples organize their societies and build advanced civilizations?

? What You Will Learn

In this chapter you will learn about the civilizations that developed on fertile river plains in Africa and Asia.

SECTION 1 City-States in Mesopotamia

Main Idea The earliest civilization in Asia arose in Mesopotamia and organized into city-states.

SECTION 2 Pyramids on the Nile

Main Idea Using mathematical knowledge and engineering skills, Egyptians built magnificent monuments to honor dead rulers.

SECTION 3 Planned Cities on the Indus

Main Idea The first Indian civilization built well-planned cities on the banks of the Indus River.

SECTION 4 River Dynasties in China

Main Idea The early rulers introduced ideas about government and society that shaped Chinese civilization.

Previewing Themes

INTERACTION WITH ENVIRONMENT The earliest civilizations formed on fertile river plains. These lands faced challenges, such as seasonal flooding and a limited growing area.

Geography *What rivers helped sustain the four river valley civilizations?*

POWER AND AUTHORITY Projects such as irrigation systems required leadership and laws—the beginnings of organized government. In some societies, priests controlled the first governments. In others, military leaders and kings ruled.

Geography *Look at the time line and the map. In which empire and river valley area was the first code of laws developed?*

SCIENCE AND TECHNOLOGY Early civilizations developed bronze tools, the wheel, the sail, the plow, writing, and mathematics. These innovations spread through trade, wars, and the movement of peoples.

Geography *Which river valley civilization was the most isolated? What factors contributed to that isolation?*

3000 B.C.
◄ City-states form in Sumer, Mesopotamia. (bronze head of an Akkadian ruler)

WORLD 3500 B.C.   2500 B.C.

2660 B.C.
◄ Egypt's Old Kingdom develops. (Egyptian scribe statue)

Four River Valley Civilizations

EUROPE

ASIA

AFRICA

HISTORY.
Ancient Egypt:
Iconic Structures

↗ hmhsocialstudies.com VIDEO

Black Sea

Caspian Sea

Mediterranean Sea

Tigris River

Euphrates R.

Babylon

Ur

Memphis

Persian Gulf

Nile River

Red Sea

ARABIAN PENINSULA

Indus River

Harappa

Kalibangan

Mohenjo Daro

HIMALAYAS

Huang He (Yellow River)

Anyang

Luoyang

Yellow Sea

Chang Jiang (Yangtze River)

Arabian Sea

Bay of Bengal

INDIAN OCEAN

N
W   E
S

Equator

0   500   1000 Miles

0   500   1000 Kilometers

Hyperelliptical Projection

45°N

30°N

15°N

45°E

60°E

75°E

90°E

105°E

	China, 3950–1000 B.C.
	Mesopotamia, 3500–1600 B.C.
	Ancient Egypt, 3000–2000 B.C.
	Indus Valley, 2500–1700 B.C.

1792 B.C.
Hammurabi develops
code of laws for
Babylonian Empire.

1027 B.C.
Zhou Dynasty forms in China.
(Zhou bronze vessel) ▶

1500 B.C.

500 B.C.

1750 B.C.
◀ Indus Valley civilization declines.
(fragment of a Harappan pot)

27

Why do communities need laws?

The harvest has failed and, like many others, you have little to eat. There are animals in the temple, but they are protected by law. Your cousin decides to steal one of the pigs to feed his family. You believe that laws should not be broken and try to persuade him not to steal the pig. But he steals the pig and is caught.

The law of the Babylonian Empire—Hammurabi's Code—holds people responsible for their actions. Someone who steals from the temple must repay 30 times the cost of the stolen item. Because your cousin is unable to pay this fine, he is sentenced to death. You begin to wonder whether there are times when laws should be broken.

1 The Babylonian ruler Hammurabi, accompanied by his judges, sentences Mummar to death.

2 A scribe records the proceedings against Mummar.

3 Mummar pleads for mercy.

EXAMINING *the* ISSUES

- **What should be the main purpose of laws: to promote good behavior or to punish bad behavior?**

- **Do all communities need a system of laws to guide them?**

Hold a class debate on these questions. As you prepare for the debate, think about what you have learned about the changes that take place as civilizations grow and become more complex. As you read about the growth of civilization in this chapter, consider why societies developed systems of laws.

City-States in Mesopotamia

MAIN IDEA	WHY IT MATTERS NOW	TERMS & NAMES
INTERACTION WITH ENVIRONMENT The earliest civilization in Asia arose in Mesopotamia and organized into city-states.	The development of this civilization reflects a settlement pattern that has occurred repeatedly throughout history.	• Fertile Crescent • Mesopotamia • city-state • dynasty • cultural diffusion • polytheism • empire • Hammurabi

SETTING THE STAGE Two rivers flow from the mountains of what is now Turkey, down through Syria and Iraq, and finally to the Persian Gulf. Over six thousand years ago, the waters of these rivers provided the lifeblood that allowed the formation of farming settlements. These grew into villages and then cities.

Geography of the Fertile Crescent

A desert climate dominates the landscape between the Persian Gulf and the Mediterranean Sea in Southwest Asia. Yet within this dry region lies an arc of land that provided some of the best farming in Southwest Asia. The region's curved shape and the richness of its land led scholars to call it the **Fertile Crescent**. It includes the lands facing the Mediterranean Sea and a plain that became known as **Mesopotamia** (MEHS•uh•puh•TAY•mee•uh). The word in Greek means "land between the rivers."

The rivers framing Mesopotamia are the Tigris (TY•grihs) and Euphrates (yoo•FRAY•teez). They flow southeastward to the Persian Gulf. (See the map on page 30.) The Tigris and Euphrates rivers flooded Mesopotamia at least once a year. As the floodwater receded, it left a thick bed of mud called silt. Farmers planted grain in this rich, new soil and irrigated the fields with river water. The results were large quantities of wheat and barley at harvest time. The surpluses from their harvests allowed villages to grow.

Environmental Challenges People first began to settle and farm the flat, swampy lands in southern Mesopotamia before 4500 B.C. Around 3300 B.C., the people called the Sumerians, whom you read about in Chapter 1, arrived on the scene. Good soil was the advantage that attracted these settlers. However, there were three disadvantages to their new environment.

- Unpredictable flooding combined with a period of little or no rain. The land sometimes became almost a desert.
- With no natural barriers for protection, a Sumerian village was nearly defenseless.
- The natural resources of Sumer were limited. Building materials and other necessary items were scarce.

hmhsocialstudies.com
TAKING NOTES

Use the graphic organizer online to take notes on Sumer's environmental problems and their solutions.

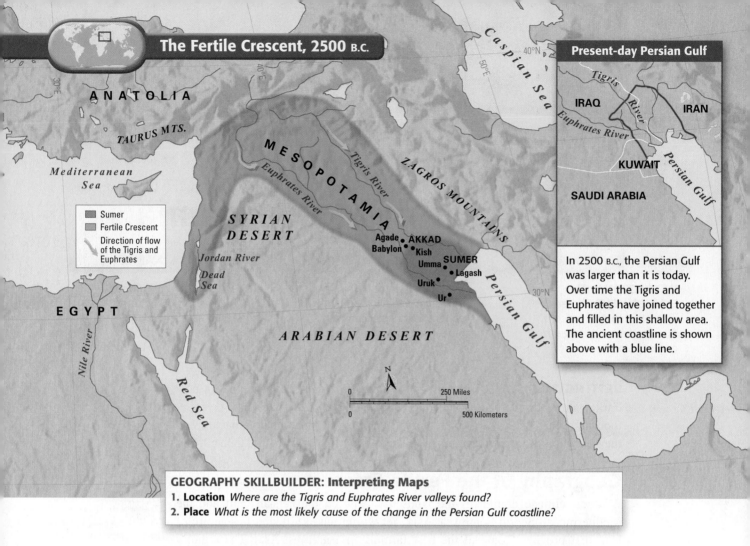

The Fertile Crescent, 2500 B.C.

ANATOLIA

TAURUS MTS.

Mediterranean Sea

MESOPOTAMIA

Tigris River

Euphrates River

ZAGROS MOUNTAINS

Caspian Sea

SYRIAN DESERT

Jordan River

Dead Sea

Agade • AKKAD
Babylon • • Kish
Umma • SUMER
• Lagash
Uruk •
Ur •

Persian Gulf

EGYPT

Nile River

ARABIAN DESERT

Red Sea

- Sumer
- Fertile Crescent
- Direction of flow of the Tigris and Euphrates

N

0 — 250 Miles
0 — 500 Kilometers

Present-day Persian Gulf

Tigris River

IRAQ   IRAN

Euphrates River

KUWAIT   Persian Gulf

SAUDI ARABIA

In 2500 B.C., the Persian Gulf was larger than it is today. Over time the Tigris and Euphrates have joined together and filled in this shallow area. The ancient coastline is shown above with a blue line.

GEOGRAPHY SKILLBUILDER: Interpreting Maps
1. **Location** *Where are the Tigris and Euphrates River valleys found?*
2. **Place** *What is the most likely cause of the change in the Persian Gulf coastline?*

Solving Problems Through Organization Over a long period of time, the people of Sumer created solutions to deal with these problems.

- To provide water, they dug irrigation ditches that carried river water to their fields and allowed them to produce a surplus of crops.
- For defense, they built city walls with mud bricks.
- Sumerians traded their grain, cloth, and crafted tools with the peoples of the mountains and the desert. In exchange, they received raw materials such as stone, wood, and metal.

These activities required organization, cooperation, and leadership. It took many people working together, for example, for the Sumerians to construct their large irrigation systems. Leaders were needed to plan the projects and supervise the digging. These projects also created a need for laws to settle disputes over how land and water would be distributed. These leaders and laws were the beginning of organized government—and eventually of civilization. **A**

Sumerians Create City-States

The Sumerians stand out in history as one of the first groups of people to form a civilization. As you learned in Chapter 1, five key characteristics set Sumer apart from earlier human societies: (1) advanced cities, (2) specialized workers, (3) complex institutions, (4) record keeping, and (5) improved technology. All the later peoples who lived in this region of the world built upon the innovations of Sumerian civilization.

MAIN IDEA

Summarizing
A What are three solutions to the environmental challenges of Mesopotamia?

By 3000 B.C., the Sumerians had built a number of cities, each surrounded by fields of barley and wheat. Although these cities shared the same culture, they developed their own governments, each with its own rulers. Each city and the surrounding land it controlled formed a **city-state**. A city-state functioned much as an independent country does today. Sumerian city-states included Uruk, Kish, Lagash, Umma, and Ur. As in Ur, the center of all Sumerian cities was the walled temple with a ziggurat in the middle. There the priests and rulers appealed to the gods for the well-being of the city-state.

Priests and Rulers Share Control Sumer's earliest governments were controlled by the temple priests. The farmers believed that the success of their crops depended upon the blessings of the gods, and the priests acted as go-betweens with the gods. In addition to being a place of worship, the ziggurat was like a city hall. (See page 22 for a ziggurat.) From the ziggurat the priests managed the irrigation system. Priests demanded a portion of every farmer's crop as taxes.

In time of war, however, the priests did not lead the city. Instead, the men of the city chose a tough fighter who could command the city's soldiers. At first, a commander's power ended as soon as the war was over. After 3000 B.C., wars between cities became more and more frequent. Gradually, Sumerian priests and people gave commanders permanent control of standing armies. **B**

In time, some military leaders became full-time rulers. These rulers usually passed their power on to their sons, who eventually passed it on to their own heirs. Such a series of rulers from a single family is called a **dynasty**. After 2500 B.C., many Sumerian city-states came under the rule of dynasties.

The Spread of Cities Sumer's city-states grew prosperous from the surplus food produced on their farms. These surpluses allowed Sumerians to increase long-distance trade, exchanging the extra food and other goods for items they needed.

By 2500 B.C., new cities were arising all over the Fertile Crescent, in what is now Syria, northern Iraq, and Turkey. Sumerians exchanged products and ideas, such as living in cities, with neighboring cultures. This process in which a new idea or a product spreads from one culture to another is called **cultural diffusion**.

Sumerian Culture

The belief systems, social structure, technology, and arts of the Sumerians reflected their civilization's triumph over its dry and harsh environment.

A Religion of Many Gods Like many peoples in the Fertile Crescent, the Sumerians believed that many different gods controlled the various forces in nature. The belief in more than one god is called **polytheism** (PAHL•ee•thee•IHZ•uhm). Enlil, the god of storms and air, was among the most powerful gods. Sumerians feared him as "the raging flood that has no rival." Demons known as Ugallu protected humans from the evil demons who caused disease, misfortune, and misery.

Sumerians described their gods as doing many of the same things humans do—falling in love, having children, quarreling, and so on. Yet the Sumerians also believed that their gods were both immortal and all-powerful. Humans were nothing but their servants. At any moment, the mighty anger of the gods might strike, sending a fire, a flood, or an enemy to destroy a city. To keep the gods happy, the

MAIN IDEA

Analyzing Causes

B How did military leaders gain power in the city-states?

▼ Iku-Shamagen, King of Mari, a city-state in Sumer, offers prayers to the gods.

▲ This gold and lapis ram with a shell fleece was found in a royal burial tomb.

Sumerians built impressive ziggurats for them and offered rich sacrifices of animals, food, and wine.

Sumerians worked hard to earn the gods' protection in this life. Yet they expected little help from the gods after death. The Sumerians believed that the souls of the dead went to the "land of no return," a dismal, gloomy place between the earth's crust and the ancient sea. No joy awaited souls there. A passage in a Sumerian poem describes the fate of dead souls: "Dust is their fare and clay their food."

Some of the richest accounts of Mesopotamian myths and legends appear in a long poem called the *Epic of Gilgamesh*. (See a selection from the Gilgamesh epic on page 83.)

(See a selection from the Gilgamesh epic on page 83.)

Vocabulary
epic: a long heroic poem that tells the story of a historical or legendary figure

Life in Sumerian Society With civilization came the beginning of what we call social classes. Kings, landholders, and some priests made up the highest level in Sumerian society. Wealthy merchants ranked next. The vast majority of ordinary Sumerian people worked with their hands in fields and workshops. At the lowest level of Sumerian society were the slaves. Some slaves were foreigners who had been captured in war. Others were Sumerians who had been sold into slavery as children to pay the debts of their poor parents. Debt slaves could hope to eventually buy their freedom.

Social class affected the lives of both men and women. Sumerian women could work as merchants, farmers, or artisans. They could hold property in their own names. Women could also join the priesthood. Some upper-class women did learn to read and write, though Sumer's written records mention few female scribes. However, Sumerian women had more rights than women in many later civilizations.

Sumerian Science and Technology Historians believe that Sumerians invented the wheel, the sail, and the plow and that they were among the first to use bronze. Many new ideas and inventions arose from the Sumerians' practical needs.

- **Arithmetic and geometry** In order to erect city walls and buildings, plan irrigation systems, and survey flooded fields, Sumerians needed arithmetic and geometry. They developed a number system in base 60, from which stem the modern units for measuring time (60 seconds = 1 minute) and the 360 degrees of a circle.

- **Architectural innovations** Arches, columns, ramps, and the pyramid shaped the design of the ziggurat and permanently influenced Mesopotamian civilization.

- **Cuneiform** Sumerians created a system of writing. One of the first known maps was made on a clay tablet in about 2300 B.C. Other tablets contain some of the oldest written records of scientific investigations in the areas of astronomy, chemistry, and medicine.

The First Empire Builders

From 3000 to 2000 B.C., the city-states of Sumer were almost constantly at war with one another. The weakened city-states could no longer ward off attacks from the peoples of the surrounding deserts and hills. Although the Sumerians never recovered from the attacks on their cities, their civilization did not die. Succeeding sets of rulers adapted the basic ideas of Sumerian culture to meet their own needs.

Sargon of Akkad About 2350 B.C., a conqueror named Sargon defeated the city-states of Sumer. Sargon led his army from Akkad (AK•ad), a city-state north of Sumer. The Akkadians had long before adopted most aspects of Sumerian culture. Sargon's conquests helped to spread that culture even farther, beyond the Tigris-Euphrates Valley.

By taking control of both northern and southern Mesopotamia, Sargon created the world's first **empire**. An empire brings together several peoples, nations, or previously independent states under the control of one ruler. At its height, the Akkadian Empire loosely controlled land from the Mediterranean Coast in the west to present-day Iran in the east. Sargon's dynasty lasted only about 200 years, after which it declined due to internal fighting, invasions, and a famine. **C**

MAIN IDEA

Contrasting

C How does an empire differ from a city-state?

Babylonian Empire In about 2000 B.C., nomadic warriors known as Amorites invaded Mesopotamia. Gradually, the Amorites overwhelmed the Sumerians and established their capital at Babylon, on the Euphrates River. The Babylonian Empire reached its peak during the reign of **Hammurabi**, from 1792 B.C. to 1750 B.C. Hammurabi's most enduring legacy is the code of laws he put together.

Hammurabi's Code Hammurabi recognized that a single, uniform code of laws would help to unify the diverse groups within his empire. He collected existing rules, judgments, and laws into the Code of Hammurabi. Hammurabi had the code engraved in stone, and copies were placed all over his empire.

> Analyzing Primary Sources

Hammurabi's Code of Laws

The image at the right shows the top of a pillar that had Hammurabi 's Code engraved on it. Hammurabi's law code prescribed punishments ranging from fines to death. Often the punishments were based on the social class of the victim. Here are some examples of the laws:

PRIMARY SOURCE

8. If a man has stolen an ox, a sheep, a pig, or a boat that belonged to a temple or palace, he shall repay thirty times its cost. If it belonged to a private citizen, he shall repay ten times. If the thief cannot pay, he shall be put to death.
142. If a woman hates her husband and says to him "You cannot be with me," the authorities in her district will investigate the case. If she has been chaste and without fault, even though her husband has neglected or belittled her, she will be held innocent and may return to her father's house.
143. If the woman is at fault, she shall be thrown into the river.
196. If a man put out the eye of another man, his eye shall be put out.
198. If he puts out the eye of a freed man or break the bone of a free man, he shall pay one gold mina.
199. If he put out the eye of a man's slave, or break the bone of a man's slave, he shall pay one-half of its value.

CODE OF HAMMURABI, *adapted from a translation by L. W. King*

DOCUMENT-BASED QUESTIONS
1. **Making Inferences** *Why might the punishments for the crimes be based on social class?*
2. **Forming Opinions** *What do you think the value was in making the punishments for the crimes known to all?*

History Makers

Hammurabi
? –1750 B.C.

The noted lawgiver Hammurabi was also an able military leader, diplomat, and administrator of a vast empire. Hammurabi himself described some of his accomplishments:

As for the land of Sumer and Akkad, I collected the scattered peoples thereof, and I procured food and drink for them. In abundance and plenty I pastured them, and I caused them to dwell in peaceful habitation.

⌐ hmhsocialstudies.com

RESEARCH WEB LINKS Go online for more on Hammurabi.

The code lists 282 specific laws dealing with everything that affected the community, including family relations, business conduct, and crime. Since many people were merchants, traders, or farmers, for example, many of the laws related to property issues. Additionally, the laws sought to protect women and children from unfair treatment. The laws tell us a great deal about the Mesopotamians' beliefs and what they valued.

Although the code applied to everyone, it set different punishments for rich and poor and for men and women. It frequently applied the principle of retaliation (an eye for an eye and a tooth for a tooth) to punish crimes.

The prologue of the code set out the goals for this body of law. It said, "To bring about the rule of righteousness in the land, to destroy the wicked and the evil-doers; so that the strong should not harm the weak." Thus, Hammurabi's Code reinforced the principle that government had a responsibility for what occurred in society. For example, if a man was robbed and the thief was not caught, the government was required to compensate the victim. **D**

Nearly two centuries after Hammurabi's reign, the Babylonian Empire, which had become much smaller, fell to the neighboring Kassites. Over the years, new groups dominated the Fertile Crescent. Yet the later peoples, including the Assyrians, Phoenicians, and Israelites, would adopt many ideas of the early Sumerians. Meanwhile, a similar pattern of development, rise, and fall was taking place to the west, along the Nile River in Egypt. Egyptian civilization is described in Section 2.

MAIN IDEA

Recognizing Effects

D How did Hammurabi's law code advance civilization?

SECTION 1 ASSESSMENT

TERMS & NAMES 1. For each term or name, write a sentence explaining its significance.
• Fertile Crescent   • Mesopotamia   • city-state   • dynasty   • cultural diffusion   • polytheism   • empire   • Hammurabi

USING YOUR NOTES

2. Which of the problems you listed required the most complex solution? Explain.

Problems	Solutions
1.	1.
2.	2.
3.	3.

MAIN IDEAS

3. What were the three environmental challenges to Sumerians?

4. How did the Sumerians view the gods?

5. What areas of life did Hammurabi's Code cover?

CRITICAL THINKING & WRITING

6. **DETERMINING MAIN IDEAS** How was Sumerian culture spread throughout Mesopotamia?

7. **RECOGNIZING EFFECTS** Why is the development of a written code of laws important to a society?

8. **ANALYZING CAUSES** How did the need to interact with the environment lead to advances in civilization?

9. **WRITING ACTIVITY** POWER AND AUTHORITY What advantages did living in cities offer the people of ancient Mesopotamia? Do modern cities offer any of the same advantages? Write a **compare-and-contrast essay** supporting your answer with references to the text.

CONNECT TO TODAY WRITING A STATUS REPORT

Research the South East Anatolian Water Project in Turkey. The project will place dams on the Tigris and Euphrates rivers. Create a **map** and write a **status report** that summarizes the current status of the project.

Pyramids on the Nile

MAIN IDEA	WHY IT MATTERS NOW	TERMS & NAMES
SCIENCE AND TECHNOLOGY Using mathematical knowledge and engineering skills, Egyptians built magnificent monuments to honor dead rulers.	Many of the monuments built by the Egyptians stand as a testament to their ancient civilization.	• delta • pyramid • Narmer • mummification • pharaoh • hieroglyphics • theocracy • papyrus

SETTING THE STAGE To the west of the Fertile Crescent in Africa, another river makes its way to the sea. While Sumerian civilization was on the rise, a similar process took place along the banks of this river, the Nile in Egypt. Yet the Egyptian civilization turned out to be very different from the collection of city-states in Mesopotamia. Early on, Egypt was united into a single kingdom, which allowed it to enjoy a high degree of unity, stability, and cultural continuity over a period of 3,000 years.

The Geography of Egypt

From the highlands of East Africa to the Mediterranean Sea, the Nile River flows northward across Africa for over 4,100 miles, making it the longest river in the world. (See the map on page 36.) A thin ribbon of water in a parched desert land, the great river brings its water to Egypt from distant mountains, plateaus, and lakes in present-day Burundi, Tanzania, Uganda, and Ethiopia.

TAKING NOTES
Use the graphic organizer online to take notes on Egyptian achievements.

Egypt's settlements arose along the Nile on a narrow strip of land made fertile by the river. The change from fertile soil to desert—from the Black Land to the Red Land—was so abrupt that a person could stand with one foot in each.

The Gift of the Nile As in Mesopotamia, yearly flooding brought the water and rich soil that allowed settlements to grow. Every year in July, rains and melting snow from the mountains of east Africa caused the Nile River to rise and spill over its banks. When the river receded in October, it left behind a rich deposit of fertile black mud called silt.

Before the scorching sun could dry out the soil, the peasants would prepare their wheat and barley fields. All fall and winter they watered their crops from a network of irrigation ditches.

In an otherwise parched land, the abundance brought by the Nile was so great that the Egyptians worshiped it as a god who gave life and seldom turned against them. As the ancient Greek historian Herodotus (hih•RAHD•uh•tuhs) remarked in the fifth century B.C., Egypt was the "gift of the Nile."

Environmental Challenges Egyptian farmers were much more fortunate than the villagers of Mesopotamia. Compared to the unpredictable Tigris and Euphrates rivers, the Nile was as regular as clockwork. Even so, life in Egypt had its risks.

Mediterranean Sea

Nile Delta
LOWER EGYPT

▲ Memphis

SINAI

UPPER EGYPT

W E S T E R N   D E S E R T

E A S T E R N   D E S E R T

Nile River

Thebes ●

Red Sea

NUBIA

First Cataract

Tropic of Cancer

N

Legend:
▲ Region of Great Pyramids
～ Prevailing winds
→ River current
▢ Nile Valley

The Mighty Nile
The Landsat image (left) shows the Nile flowing into its delta. An outline of the continental United States (below) shows the length of the Nile's course. The actual length of the Nile with all its twists and turns is more than 4,100 miles.

GEOGRAPHY SKILLBUILDER: Interpreting Maps
1. **Movement** *In which direction does the Nile flow?*
2. **Location** *Describe the location of Upper Egypt and Lower Egypt.*

VIDEO
How Does the Nile Measure Up?
HISTORY

⬈ hmhsocialstudies.com

- When the Nile's floodwaters were just a few feet lower than normal, the amount of fresh silt and water for crops was greatly reduced. Thousands of people starved.
- When floodwaters were a few feet higher than usual, the unwanted water destroyed houses, granaries, and the precious seeds that farmers needed for planting.
- The vast and forbidding deserts on either side of the Nile acted as natural barriers between Egypt and other lands. They forced Egyptians to live on a very small portion of the land and reduced interaction with other peoples.

However, the deserts shut out invaders. For much of its early history, Egypt was spared the constant warfare that plagued the Fertile Crescent. **A**

Upper Egypt and Lower Egypt Ancient Egyptians lived along the Nile from the mouth well into the interior of Africa. River travel was common, but it ended at the point in the Nile where boulders turn the river into churning rapids called a cataract (KAT•uh•rakt). This made it impossible for riverboats to pass this spot, known as the First Cataract, to continue upstream south to the interior of Africa.

Between the First Cataract and the Mediterranean lay two very different regions. Because its elevation is higher, the river area in the south is called Upper Egypt. It is a skinny strip of land from the First Cataract to the point where the river starts to fan out into many branches. To the north, near the sea, Lower Egypt includes the Nile **delta** region. The delta begins about 100 miles before the river enters the Mediterranean. The delta is a broad, marshy, triangular area of land formed by deposits of silt at the mouth of the river.

MAIN IDEA

Contrasting
A What was the main difference between the flooding of the Nile and that of the rivers in Mesopotamia?

The Nile provided a reliable system of transportation between Upper and Lower Egypt. The Nile flows north, so northbound boats simply drifted with the current. Southbound boats hoisted a wide sail. The prevailing winds of Egypt blow from north to south, carrying sailboats against the river current. The ease of contact made possible by this watery highway helped unify Egypt's villages and promote trade.

Egypt Unites into a Kingdom

Egyptians lived in farming villages as far back as 5000 B.C., perhaps even earlier. Each village had its own rituals, gods, and chieftain. By 3200 B.C., the villages of Egypt were under the rule of two separate kingdoms, Lower Egypt and Upper Egypt. Eventually the two kingdoms were united. There is conflicting historical evidence over who united Upper and Lower Egypt. Some evidence points to a king called Scorpion. More solid evidence points to a king named **Narmer**.

The king of Lower Egypt wore a red crown, and the king of Upper Egypt wore a tall white crown shaped like a bowling pin. A carved piece of slate known as the Narmer Palette shows Narmer wearing the crown of Lower Egypt on one side and the crown of Upper Egypt on the other side. Some scholars believe the palette celebrates the unification of Egypt around 3000 B.C.

Narmer created a double crown from the red and white crowns. It symbolized a united kingdom. He shrewdly settled his capital, Memphis, near the spot where Upper and Lower Egypt met, and established the first Egyptian dynasty. Eventually, the history of ancient Egypt would consist of 31 dynasties, spanning 2,600 years. Historians suggest that the pattern for Egypt's great civilization was set during the period from 3200 to 2700 B.C. The period from 2660 to 2180 B.C., known as the Old Kingdom, marks a time when these patterns became widespread.

Pharaohs Rule as Gods The role of the king was one striking difference between Egypt and Mesopotamia. In Mesopotamia, kings were considered to be representatives of the gods. To the Egyptians, kings were gods. The Egyptian god-kings, called **pharaohs** (FAIR•ohz), were thought to be almost as splendid and powerful as the gods of the heavens. This type of government in which rule is based on religious authority is called a **theocracy**.

MAIN IDEA

Making Inferences

B Why were Egypt's pharaohs unusually powerful rulers?

The pharaoh stood at the center of Egypt's religion as well as its government and army. Egyptians believed that the pharaoh bore full responsibility for the kingdom's well-being. It was the pharaoh who caused the sun to rise, the Nile to flood, and the crops to grow. It was the pharaoh's duty to promote truth and justice. **B**

Builders of the Pyramids Egyptians believed that their king ruled even after his death. He had an eternal life force, or *ka,* which continued to take part in the governing of Egypt. In the Egyptians' mind, the *ka* remained much like a living king in its needs and pleasures. Since kings expected to reign forever, their tombs were even more important than their palaces. For the kings of the Old Kingdom, the resting place after death was an immense structure called a **pyramid**. The Old Kingdom was the great age of pyramid building in ancient Egypt.

Connect to Today

Scorpion King

In 1999 Egyptologists discovered a series of carvings on a piece of rock about 18 by 20 inches. The tableau scene has symbols that may refer to a king named Scorpion.

The rock shows a figure carrying a staff. Near the head of the figure is a scorpion. Another artifact, a macehead, also shows a king with the scorpion symbol. Both artifacts suggest that Egyptian history may go back to around 3250 B.C. Some scholars believe the Scorpion is the earliest king to begin unification of Egypt, represented by the double crown shown below.

crown of Upper Egypt   crown of Lower Egypt   crown of Upper and Lower Egypt

These magnificent monuments were remarkable engineering achievements, built by people who had not even begun to use the wheel. Unlike the Sumerians, however, the Egyptians did have a good supply of stone, both granite and limestone. For the Great Pyramid of Giza, for example, the limestone facing was quarried just across the Nile. Each perfectly cut stone block weighed at least 2 1/2 tons. Some weighed 15 tons. More than 2 million of these blocks were stacked with precision to a height of 481 feet. The entire structure covered more than 13 acres.

The pyramids also reflect the strength of the Egyptian civilization. They show that Old Kingdom dynasties had developed the economic strength and technological means to support massive public works projects, as well as the leadership and government organization to carry them out.

Egyptian Culture

With nature so much in their favor, Egyptians tended to approach life more confidently and optimistically than their neighbors in the Fertile Crescent. Religion played an important role in the lives of Egyptians.

Religion and Life Like the Mesopotamians, the early Egyptians were polytheistic, believing in many gods. The most important gods were Re, the sun god, and Osiris (oh•SY•rihs), god of the dead. The most important goddess was Isis, who represented the ideal mother and wife. In all, Egyptians worshiped more than 2,000 gods and goddesses. They built huge temples to honor the major deities.

Vocabulary
deities: gods or goddesses

In contrast to the Mesopotamians, with their bleak view of death, Egyptians believed in an afterlife, a life that continued after death. Egyptians believed they would be judged for their deeds when they died. Anubis, god and guide of the underworld, would weigh each dead person's heart. To win eternal life, the heart could be no heavier than a feather. If the heart tipped the scale, showing that it was heavy with sin, a fierce beast known as the Devourer of Souls would pounce on the impure heart and gobble it up. But if the soul passed this test for purity and truth, it would live forever in the beautiful Other World.

People of all classes planned for their burials, so that they might safely reach the Other World. Kings and queens built great tombs, such as the pyramids, and other Egyptians built smaller tombs. Royal and elite Egyptians' bodies were preserved by **mummification**, which involves embalming and drying the corpse to prevent it from decaying. Scholars still accept Herodotus's description of the process of mummification as one of the methods used by Egyptians.

PRIMARY SOURCE C

First, they draw out the brains through the nostrils with an iron hook. . . . Then with a sharp stone they make an incision in the side, and take out all the bowels. . . . Then, having filled the belly with pure myrrh, cassia, and other perfumes, they sew it up again; and when they have done this they steep it in natron [a mineral salt], leaving it under for 70 days. . . . At the end of 70 days, they wash the corpse, and wrap the whole body in bandages of waxen cloth.

HERODOTUS, *The History of Herodotus*

MAIN IDEA

Analyzing Primary Sources
C What does this description suggest about the Egyptians' knowledge of the human body?

Attendants placed the mummy in a coffin inside a tomb. Then they filled the tomb with items the dead person could use in the afterlife, such as clothing, food, cosmetics, and jewelry. Many Egyptians purchased scrolls that contained hymns, prayers, and magic spells intended to guide the soul in the afterlife. This collection of texts is known as the *Book of the Dead*.

Pyramids and Mummies

Etched into some of the stones of the pyramids are the nicknames of the teams of workers who built them—"the Vigorous Gang," "the Enduring Gang," and "the Craftsman Gang," for example. Just as construction workers today leave their marks on the skyscrapers they build, the pyramid builders scratched messages for the ages inside the pyramids.

Who were the pyramid builders? Peasants provided most of the labor. They worked for the government when the Nile was in flood and they could not farm. In return for their service, though, the country provided the workers with food and housing during this period.

VIDEO
Pyramids at Giza **HISTORY**

↗ hmhsocialstudies.com

◀ The ancient Egyptians mummified the body so the soul could return to it later. Egyptian embalmers were so skillful that modern archaeologists have found mummies that still have hair, skin, and teeth.

▼ This solid gold death mask of the pharaoh Tutankhamen covered the head of his mummy. The mask, which weighs 22.04 pounds, is part of a popular exhibit in the Egyptian Museum in Cairo, Egypt.

▼ The largest of the pyramids is the Great Pyramid (right background) at Giza, completed about 2556 B.C. The diagram shows how the interior of a pyramid looks.

▲ These clay vessels are called Canopic jars. After preparing the mummy, embalmers placed the lungs, liver, and other internal organs of the mummy in these jars.

King's chamber

Air shaft

Grand gallery

Queen's chamber

Ascending passage

Escape passage

Unfinished chamber

SKILLBUILDER: Interpreting Visual Sources
1. **Making Inferences** *What does the elaborate nature of Egyptian burials suggest about their culture?*
2. **Comparing and Contrasting** *In what ways are modern burial practices similar to those of the ancient Egyptians? How are they different?*

Life in Egyptian Society

Like the grand monuments to the kings, Egyptian society formed a pyramid. The king, queen, and royal family stood at the top. Below them were the other members of the upper class, which included wealthy landowners, government officials, priests, and army commanders. The next tier of the pyramid was the middle class, which included merchants and artisans. At the base of the pyramid was the lower class, by far the largest class. It consisted of peasant farmers and laborers.

In the later periods of Egyptian history, slavery became a widespread source of labor. Slaves, usually captives from foreign wars, served in the homes of the rich or toiled endlessly in the gold mines of Upper Egypt.

The Egyptians were not locked into their social classes. Lower-and middle-class Egyptians could gain higher status through marriage or success in their jobs. Even some slaves could hope to earn their freedom as a reward for their loyal service. To win the highest positions, people had to be able to read and write. Once a person had these skills, many careers were open in the army, the royal treasury, the priesthood, and the king's court.

Women in Egypt held many of the same rights as men. For example, a wealthy or middle-class woman could own and trade property. She could propose marriage or seek divorce. If she were granted a divorce, she would be entitled to one-third of the couple's property. **D**

Egyptian Writing As in Mesopotamia, the development of writing was one of the keys to the growth of Egyptian civilization. Simple pictographs were the earliest form of writing in Egypt, but scribes quickly developed a more flexible writing system called **hieroglyphics** (HY•uhr•uh•GLIHF•ihks). This term comes from the Greek words *hieros* and *gluph,* meaning "sacred carving."

As with Sumerian cuneiform writing, in the earliest form of hieroglyphic writing, a picture stood for an idea. For instance, a picture of a man stood for the idea of a man. In time, the system changed so that pictures stood for sounds as well as ideas. The owl, for example, stood for an *m* sound or for the bird itself. Hieroglyphs could be used almost like letters of the alphabet.

Although hieroglyphs were first written on stone and clay, as in Mesopotamia, the Egyptians soon invented a better writing surface—**papyrus** (puh•PY•ruhs) reeds. These grew in the marshy delta. The Egyptians split the reeds into narrow strips, placed them crosswise in two layers, dampened them, and then pressed them. As the papyrus dried, the plant's sap glued the strips together into a paperlike sheet.

Egyptian Science and Technology Practical needs led to many Egyptian inventions. For example, the Egyptians developed a calendar to help them keep track of the time between floods and to plan their planting season. Priests observed that the same star—Sirius—appeared above the eastern horizon just before the floods came.

MAIN IDEA

Comparing

D How was the status of women similar in Egyptian and Sumerian societies?

History *in* Depth

The Rosetta Stone

In 1799, near the delta village of Rosetta, some French soldiers found a polished black stone inscribed with a message in three languages. One version was written in hieroglyphics (top inset). A second version was in a simpler form of hieroglyphics, and the third was in Greek (both are shown in the bottom inset).

Since ancient Greek was a well-known language, it provided clues to the meaning of the hieroglyphics. Still, deciphering the Rosetta Stone took many years. In 1822, a French scholar named Jean François Champollion (shahm•paw•LYAWN) finally broke the code of the hieroglyphics.

They calculated the number of days between one rising of the star and the next as 365 days—a solar year. They divided this year into 12 months of 30 days each and added five days for holidays and feasting. This calendar was so accurate that it fell short of the true solar year by only six hours.

Egyptians developed a system of written numbers for counting, adding, and subtracting. The system would have helped to assess and collect taxes. Scribes used an early form of geometry to survey and reset property boundaries after the annual floods. Mathematical knowledge helped Egypt's skillful engineers and architects make accurate measurements to construct their remarkable pyramids and palaces. Egyptian architects were the first to use stone columns in homes, palaces, and temples.

Egyptian medicine was also famous in the ancient world. Egyptian doctors knew how to check a person's heart rate by feeling for a pulse in different parts of the body. They set broken bones with splints and had effective treatments for wounds and fevers. They also used surgery to treat some conditions. **E**

MAIN IDEA

Summarizing

E What were the main achievements of the ancient Egyptians?

Invaders Control Egypt

The power of the pharaohs declined about 2180 B.C., marking the end of the Old Kingdom. Strong pharaohs regained control during the Middle Kingdom (2040–1640 B.C.) and restored law and order. They improved trade and transportation by digging a canal from the Nile to the Red Sea. They built huge dikes to trap and channel the Nile's floodwaters for irrigation. They also created thousands of new acres of farmland by draining the swamps of Lower Egypt.

The prosperity of the Middle Kingdom did not last. In about 1640 B.C., a group from the area of present-day Israel moved across the Isthmus of Suez into Egypt. These people were the Hyksos (HIHK•sahs), which meant "the rulers of foreign lands." The Hyksos ruled much of Egypt from 1630 to 1523 B.C.

Egypt would rise again for a new period of power and glory, the New Kingdom, which is discussed in Chapter 4. During approximately the same time period as the Old Kingdom and Middle Kingdom existed in Egypt, civilization was emerging in the Indus River Valley.

SECTION 2 ASSESSMENT

TERMS & NAMES 1. For each term or name, write a sentence explaining its significance.
• delta   • Narmer   • pharaoh   • theocracy   • pyramid   • mummification   • hieroglyphic   • papyrus

USING YOUR NOTES

2. Which of the Egyptian achievements do you consider the most important? Explain.

Egyptian Achievements

MAIN IDEAS

3. How did being surrounded by deserts benefit Egypt?

4. How did the Egyptians view the pharaoh?

5. Why did Egyptians mummify bodies?

CRITICAL THINKING & WRITING

6. **DRAWING CONCLUSIONS** Which of the three natural features that served as boundaries in ancient Egypt was most important to Egypt's history? Explain.

7. **RECOGNIZING EFFECTS** What impact did Egyptian religious beliefs have on the lives of Egyptians?

8. **COMPARING AND CONTRASTING** How were cuneiform and hieroglyphic writing similar? different?

9. **WRITING ACTIVITY** SCIENCE AND TECHNOLOGY Select an Egyptian invention or achievement. Write a **paragraph** about how your selected achievement changed the Egyptians' lives.

CONNECT TO TODAY CREATING A LANGUAGE

Devise a **set of symbols** to create a language. Write several sentences and have classmates try to decipher the message.

Work and Play in Ancient Egypt

For ancient Egyptians, life often involved hard work. When the weather was good, most worked in the fields, producing food for their families and for export. During flood season, thousands of these farmers were called upon to help build the pharaohs' temples.

But life was not all about work. Archaeological digs offer evidence that both upper-class Egyptians and the common people found ways to enjoy themselves.

↗ hmhsocialstudies.com

RESEARCH WEB LINKS Go online for more on life in ancient Egypt.

▼ **Games**

Games were popular with all classes of Egyptian society. The board shown below is for the game senet—also depicted in the painting. Players threw sticks or knuckle bones to move their pieces through squares of good or bad fortune. A player won by moving all his or her pieces off the board.

▲ **Farmers**

This detail from a tomb painting shows Egyptian farmers at work. Egyptians grew enough wheat and barley to have food reserves for themselves and for export to other civilizations. They also grew fruit and vegetables in irrigated fields.

▲ Cosmetics

Ancient Egyptians used cosmetics for both work and play. They protected field workers from sun and heat and were used to enhance beauty. Egyptian men and women applied makeup, called kohl, to their eyes. They made kohl from minerals mixed with water. They also soaked flowers and fragrant woods in oil and rubbed the oil into their skin. The dark eye makeup softened the glare of the sun. The oils protected their skin from the dry air. Egyptians kept their cosmetics in chests such as the one shown above.

▼ Temple Builders

The artist's colorful drawing of what the Karnak Temple Complex might have looked like explains why Egyptian pharaohs needed thousands of laborers to build their temples. Some historians believe the laborers may have been part of a rotating workforce drafted from the agricultural classes around Egypt. The photo at lower left shows the temple as it is today. Although faded and eroded, the temple still inspires awe.

> DATA FILE

MORE ON WORK

- **Surgeons** Ancient Egypt had skilled surgeons. Written evidence shows that Egyptian surgeons knew how to stitch cuts and set broken bones. Some Egyptian mummies even show evidence of being operated on. We know the names of about 150 physicians—2 of them were women.

- **Papyrus Growers** A large industry was built around the harvesting of papyrus. Papyrus was used to make the material Egyptians wrote on. Scrolls of various sizes could be made. One mathematics papyrus was 15 feet long and 3 inches wide.

MORE ON PLAY

- **Pets** Egyptians kept various animals as pets. Nobles would even have their pets mummified and buried with them. A single pet cemetery was discovered that contained 1,000,000 bird mummies.

- **Royal Dogs** The Pharaoh hound was very popular in ancient Egypt. Artifacts from 4000 B.C. show images of the breed. Today, a Pharaoh hound puppy bred for competition can cost up to $1,500.

Connect *to* Today

1. **Making Inferences** From what you have read here, what inferences can you make about Egyptian society?
   See Skillbuilder Handbook, page R10.

2. **Comparing and Contrasting** How are the work and leisure activities of ancient Egypt different from those in the United States today? How are they similar?

Planned Cities on the Indus

MAIN IDEA	WHY IT MATTERS NOW	TERMS & NAMES
INTERACTION WITH ENVIRONMENT The first Indian civilization built well-planned cities on the banks of the Indus River.	The culture of India today has its roots in the civilization of the early Indus cities.	• subcontinent • Harappan • monsoon civilization

SETTING THE STAGE The great civilizations of Mesopotamia and Egypt rose and fell. They left behind much physical evidence about their ways of life. This is the case in what today is the area known as Pakistan and part of India where another civilization arose about 2500 B.C. However, historians know less about its origins and the reasons for its eventual decline than they do about the origins and decline of Mesopotamia and Egypt, because the language of the culture has not been translated.

The Geography of the Indian Subcontinent

TAKING NOTES

Use the graphic organizer online to take notes on Indus Valley civilizations.

Geographers often refer to the landmass that includes India, Pakistan, and Bangladesh as the Indian **subcontinent**. A wall of the highest mountains in the world—the Hindu Kush, Karakorum, and Himalayan ranges—separates this region from the rest of the Asian continent.

Rivers, Mountains, and Plains The world's tallest mountains to the north and a large desert to the east helped protect the Indus Valley from invasion. The mountains guard an enormous flat and fertile plain formed by two rivers—the Indus and the Ganges (GAN•jeez). Each river is an important link from the interior of the subcontinent to the sea. The Indus River flows southwest from the Himalayas to the Arabian Sea. Much of the lower Indus Valley is occupied by the Thar Desert. Farming is possible only in the areas directly watered by the Indus. The Ganges drops down from the Himalayas and flows eastward across northern India. It joins the Brahmaputra River as it flows to the Bay of Bengal.

The Indus and Ganges and the lands they water make up a large area that stretches 1,700 miles across northern India and is called the Indo-Gangetic Plain. Like the Tigris, the Euphrates, and the Nile, these rivers carry not only water for irrigation, but also silt, which produces rich land for agriculture.

Below the Indo-Gangetic Plain, the southern part of the subcontinent is a peninsula that thrusts south into the Indian Ocean. The center of the peninsula is a high plateau cut by twisting rivers. This region is called the Deccan (DEK•uhn) Plateau. The plateau is framed by low mountain ranges called the Eastern and Western Ghats. These mountains keep moist air from reaching the plateau, making it a dry region. A narrow border of lush, tropical land lies along the coasts of southern India.

Monsoon Winter

Monsoon Summer

HINDU KUSH
KARAKORAM MTS.
KHYBER PASS
River
BOLAN PASS
• Harappa
Indus
• Kalibangan
• Mohenjo-Daro
INDO-GANGETIC PLAIN
H I M A L A Y A S
THAR DESERT
Ganges River
Brahmaputra R.
I N D I A
Arabian Sea
Godavari River
DECCAN PLATEAU
Krishna River
GHATS
EASTERN
WESTERN GHATS
Bay of Bengal
80°E

Dry monsoon winds
(October to May)
Wet monsoon winds
(June to September)
Indus Valley civilization

N

0   200 Miles
0   400 Kilometers

GEOGRAPHY SKILLBUILDER: Interpreting Maps
1. **Human-Environment Interaction** *What landforms presented natural barriers around the Indus Valley?*
2. **Movement** *Why do the winter monsoon winds carry so little moisture?*

Monsoons Seasonal winds called <u>monsoons</u> dominate India's climate. From October to February, winter monsoons from the northeast blow dry air westward across the country. Then, from the middle of June through October, the winds shift. These monsoons blow eastward from the southwest, carrying moisture from the ocean in great rain clouds. The powerful storms bring so much moisture that flooding often happens. When the summer monsoons fail to develop, drought often causes crop disasters.

Environmental Challenges The civilization that emerged along the Indus River faced many of the same challenges as the ancient Mesopotamian and Egyptian civilizations.

- Yearly floods spread deposits of rich soil over a wide area. However, the floods along the Indus were unpredictable.
- The rivers sometimes changed course.
- The cycle of wet and dry seasons brought by the monsoon winds was unpredictable. If there was too little rain, plants withered in the fields and people went hungry. If there was too much rain, floods swept away whole villages. **A**

MAIN IDEA

Identifying Problems

A What environmental challenge did the farmers of the Indus Valley face that the Sumerians and Egyptians did not?

Early River Valley Civilizations **45**

Civilization Emerges on the Indus

Historians know less about the civilization in the Indus Valley than about those to the west. They have not yet deciphered the Indus system of writing. Evidence comes largely from archaeological digs, although many sites remain unexplored, and floods probably washed away others long ago. At its height, however, the civilization of the Indus Valley influenced an area much larger than did either Mesopotamia or Egypt.

Earliest Arrivals No one is sure how human settlement began in the Indian subcontinent. Perhaps people who arrived by sea from Africa settled the south. Northern migrants may have made their way through the Khyber Pass in the Hindu Kush mountains. Archaeologists have found evidence in the highlands of agriculture and domesticated sheep and goats dating to about 7000 B.C. By about 3200 B.C., people were farming in villages along the Indus River.

Planned Cities Around 2500 B.C., while Egyptians were building pyramids, people in the Indus Valley were laying the bricks for India's first cities. They built strong levees, or earthen walls, to keep water out of their cities. When these were not enough, they constructed human-made islands to raise the cities above possible floodwaters. Archaeologists have found the ruins of more than 100 settlements along the Indus and its tributaries mostly in modern-day Pakistan. The largest cities were Kalibangan, Mohenjo-Daro, and Harappa. Indus Valley civilization is sometimes called **Harappan civilization**, because of the many archaeological discoveries made at that site.

One of the most remarkable achievements of the Indus Valley people was their sophisticated city planning. The cities of the early Mesopotamians were a jumble of buildings connected by a maze of winding streets. In contrast, the people of the Indus laid out their cities on a precise grid system. Cities featured a fortified area called a citadel, which contained the major buildings of the city. Buildings were constructed of oven-baked bricks cut in standard sizes, unlike the simpler, irregular, sun-dried mud bricks of the Mesopotamians.

Early engineers also created sophisticated plumbing and sewage systems. These systems could rival any urban drainage systems built before the 19th century. The uniformity in the cities' planning and construction suggests that the Indus peoples had developed a strong central government.

Harappan Planning Harappa itself is a good example of this city planning. The city was partially built on mud-brick platforms to protect it from flooding. A thick brick wall about three and a half miles long surrounded it. Inside was a citadel, which provided protection for the royal family and also served as a temple.

The streets in its grid system were as wide as 30 feet. Walls divided residential districts from each other. Houses varied in size. Some may have been three stories high. Narrow lanes separated rows of houses, which were laid out in block units. Houses featured bathrooms where wastewater flowed out to the street and then to sewage pits outside the city walls.

▼ A map of the citadel portion of Mohenjo-Daro shows an organized pattern of buildings and streets.

"College"

Granary

Stair

Tower

Assembly Hall

Fortifications

Plumbing in Mohenjo-Daro

From the time people began living in cities, they have faced the problem of plumbing: how to obtain clean water and remove human wastes? In most ancient cities, people retrieved water from a river or a central well. They dumped wastes into open drainage ditches or carted them out of town. Only the rich had separate bathrooms in their homes.

By contrast, the Indus peoples built extensive and modern-looking plumbing systems. In Mohenjo-Daro, almost every house had a private bathroom and toilet. No other civilization achieved this level of convenience until the 19th and 20th centuries. The toilets were neatly built of brick with a wooden seat. Pipes connected to each house carried wastewater into an underground sewer system.

↗ **hmhsocialstudies.com**

RESEARCH WEB LINKS Go online for more on water and waste management.

Plumbing Facts

- The ancient Romans also built sophisticated plumbing and sewage systems. Aqueducts supplied Roman cities with water.

- In the 17th century, engineers installed a series of water wheels to pump water for the fountains of Versailles, the palace of French king Louis XIV. The water was pumped from a river three miles away. This was the largest water-supply system powered by machine rather than gravity.

- The flush toilet was patented in 1775 by Alexander Cumming, a British mathematician and watchmaker.

1 In their private baths, people took showers by pouring pitchers of water over their head.

2 Wastes drained through clay pipes into brick sewers running below the streets. These sewers had manholes, through which sanitation workers could inspect the drains and clean out the muck.

Connect *to* Today

1. **Making Inferences** What does the attention the Indus people gave to the plumbing and sewer systems suggest about their culture?
   See Skillbuilder Handbook, Page R10.

2. **Comparing and Contrasting** Find out how water is supplied and wastewater disposed of in your home or community. How does the system in your home or community compare with what was used in Mohenjo-Daro?

47

Harappan Culture

Harappan culture spread throughout the Indus valley. Like the Egyptian and Mesopotamian civilizations you have studied, the culture was based on agriculture. Artifacts help to explain some aspects of the culture.

◀ Harappan seals show an elephant (top), an Indian rhinoceros (middle), and a zebu bull (bottom).

Language Like the other two river valley civilizations, the Harappan culture developed a written language. In contrast to cuneiform and hieroglyphics, the Harappan language has been impossible to decipher. This is because, unlike the other two languages, linguists have not found any inscriptions that are bilingual. The Harappan language is found on stamps and seals made of carved stone used for trading pottery and tools. About 400 symbols make up the language. Scientists believe the symbols, like hieroglyphs, are used both to depict an object and also as phonetic sounds. Some signs stand alone and others seem to be combined into words. **B**

Culture The Harappan cities show a remarkable uniformity in religion and culture. The housing suggests that social divisions in the society were not great. Artifacts such as clay and wooden children's toys suggest a relatively prosperous society that could afford to produce nonessential goods. Few weapons of warfare have been found, suggesting that conflict was limited.

The presence of animal images on many types of artifacts suggests that animals were an important part of the culture. Animals are seen on pottery, small statues, children's toys, and seals used to mark trade items. The images provide archaeologists with information about animals that existed in the region. However, some of the seals portray beasts with parts of several different animals—for example, the head of a man, an elephant trunk and tusks, horns of a bull, and the rump of a tiger. As in the case of the Harappan language, the meaning of these images has remained a mystery.

Role of Religion As with other cultures, the rulers of the Harappan civilization are believed to have close ties to religion. Archaeologists think that the culture was a theocracy. But no site of a temple has been found. Priests likely prayed for good harvests and safety from floods. Religious artifacts reveal links to modern Hindu culture. Figures show what may be early representations of Shiva, a major Hindu god. Other figures relate to a mother goddess, fertility images, and the worship of the bull. All of these became part of later Indian civilization.

Trade The Harappans conducted a thriving trade with peoples in the region. Gold and silver came from the north in Afghanistan. Semiprecious stones from Persia and the Deccan Plateau were crafted into jewelry. The Indus River provided an excellent means of transportation for trade goods. Brightly colored cotton cloth was a desirable trade item since few people at the time knew how to grow cotton. Overland routes moved goods from Persia to the Caspian Sea.

The Indus River provided a link to the sea. This access allowed Indus Valley inhabitants to develop trade with distant peoples, including the Mesopotamians. Seals probably used by Indus merchants to identify their goods have been found in Sumer. Ships used the Persian Gulf trade routes to bring copper, lumber, precious stones, and luxury goods to Sumer. Trading began as early as 2600 B.C. and continued until 1800 B.C.

MAIN IDEA

Clarifying

B What is the main reason Harappan language has not been deciphered?

Indus Valley Culture Ends

Around 1750 B.C., the quality of building in the Indus Valley cities declined. Gradually, the great cities fell into decay. The fate of the cities remained a mystery until the 1970s. Then, satellite images of the subcontinent of India revealed evidence of shifts in tectonic plates. The plate movement probably caused earthquakes and floods and altered the course of the Indus River.

Some cities along the rivers apparently suffered through these disasters and survived. Others were destroyed. The shifts may have caused another river, the Sarswati, to dry up. Trade on this river became impossible, and cities began to die. Harappan agriculture, too, would have been influenced by these events. It is likely that these environmental changes prevented production of large quantities of food. Furthermore, Harappan agriculture may have suffered as a result of soil that was exhausted by overuse. This too, may have forced people to leave the cities in order to survive.

Other factors had an impact on the Indus subcontinent. As Chapter 3 explains, the Aryans, a nomadic people from north of the Hindu Kush mountains, swept into the Indus Valley around 1500 B.C. Indian civilization would grow again under the influence of these nomads. At this same time, farther to the east, another civilization was arising. It was isolated from outside influences, as you will learn in Section 4. **C**

Vocabulary
tectonic plates: moving pieces of the earth's crust

MAIN IDEA

Analyzing Causes

C What factors may have contributed to the decline of the Indus Valley civilization?

▲ The bearded figure above might be a Harappan god or perhaps a priest king.

SECTION **3** ASSESSMENT

TERMS & NAMES 1. For each term or name, write a sentence explaining its significance.
- subcontinent
- monsoon
- Harappan civilization

USING YOUR NOTES	**MAIN IDEAS**	**CRITICAL THINKING & WRITING**
2. What is one conclusion you can draw about the Indus Valley civilization?	3. What problems can monsoons cause?	6. **DRAWING CONCLUSIONS** What evidence suggests Indus Valley cities were run by a strong central government?
	4. How were the planned cities of the Indus Valley different from other early cities?	7. **SYNTHESIZING** What skills would the construction of planned cities require? Explain.
	5. What reasons are suggested for the disappearance of the Indus Valley civilization?	8. **MAKING INFERENCES** How were the people of the Indus Valley connected to Mesopotamia?
		9. **WRITING ACTIVITY** INTERACTION WITH ENVIRONMENT Write a **comparison** of how Sumerians, Egyptians, and the people of the Harappan civilization made use of their environment. Then identify which group you think made better use of what they had.

Indus Valley	
Cities	fact
Language	fact
Trade	fact

MULTIMEDIA ACTIVITY CREATING A SKETCH

Use the Internet to research Harappan seals. Make some sketches of what you see. Then create a **sketch** of a seal that might have been found in a ruin in an Indus Valley civilization.

INTERNET KEYWORD
Harappan seals

River Dynasties in China

MAIN IDEA	WHY IT MATTERS NOW	TERMS & NAMES
POWER AND AUTHORITY The early rulers introduced ideas about government and society that shaped Chinese civilization.	The culture that took root during ancient times still affects Chinese ways of life today.	• loess • dynastic • oracle bone cycle • Mandate of • feudalism Heaven

SETTING THE STAGE The walls of China's first cities were built 4,000 years ago. This was at least 1,000 years after the walls of Ur, the great pyramids of Egypt, and the planned cities of the Indus Valley were built. Unlike the other three river valley civilizations, the civilization that began along one of China's river systems continues to thrive today.

The Geography of China

TAKING NOTES

Use the graphic organizer online to take notes on major events in early Chinese dynasties.

Natural barriers somewhat isolated ancient China from all other civilizations. To China's east lay the Yellow Sea, the East China Sea, and the Pacific Ocean. Mountain ranges and deserts dominate about two-thirds of China's landmass. In west China lay the Taklimakan (TAH•kluh•muh•KAHN) Desert and the icy 15,000-foot Plateau of Tibet. To the southwest are the Himalayas. And to the north are the desolate Gobi Desert and the Mongolian Plateau.

River Systems Two major river systems flow from the mountainous west to the Pacific Ocean. The Huang He (hwahng HUH), also known as the Yellow River, is found in the north. In central China, the Chang Jiang (chang jyhang), also called Yangtze (yang•SEE), flows east to the Yellow Sea. The Huang He, whose name means "yellow river," deposits huge amounts of yellowish silt when it overflows its banks. This silt is actually fertile soil called **loess** (LOH•uhs), which is blown by the winds from deserts to the west and north.

Environmental Challenges Like the other ancient civilizations in this chapter, China's first civilization developed in a river valley. China, too, faced the dangers of floods—but its geographic isolation posed its own challenges.

- The Huang He's floods could be disastrous. Sometimes floods devoured whole villages, earning the river the nickname "China's Sorrow."
- Because of China's relative geographic isolation, early settlers had to supply their own goods rather than trading with outside peoples.
- China's natural boundaries did not completely protect these settlers from outsiders. Invasions from the west and north occurred again and again in Chinese history.

China's Heartland Only about 10 percent of China's land is suitable for farming. Much of the land lies within the small plain between the Huang He and the

Extent of Shang Dynasty (Approximate)

Extent of Zhou Dynasty (Approximate)

Border of modern China

The Huang He, or Yellow River, is named for the color of its silt. This silt nurtured early development of Chinese civilization and is still a vital resource today.

GOBI DESERT

TAKLIMAKAN DESERT

CHINA

QIN LING

PLATEAU OF TIBET

HIMALAYAS

INDIA

Huang He (Yellow)

Anyang

Zhengzhou

Luoyang

Hao

Chang Jiang (Yangtze River)

Panlongcheng

Yangzhou

NORTH CHINA PLAIN

Yellow Sea

PACIFIC OCEAN

Xi Jiang

Ganges River

N

500 Miles

1,000 Kilometers

Yellow silt gives the Huang He a distinctive color.

GEOGRAPHY SKILLBUILDER: Interpreting Maps

1. **Location** *Describe the location of the Huang He and Chang Jiang in terms of where they begin and end.*
2. **Region** *What area did the Shang and Zhou dynasties control?*

Chang Jiang in eastern China. This plain, known as the North China Plain, is China's heartland. Throughout China's long history, its political boundaries have expanded and contracted depending on the strength or weakness of its ruling families. Yet the heartland of China remained the center of its civilization.

Civilization Emerges in Shang Times

Fossil remains show that ancestors of modern humans lived in southwest China about 1.7 million years ago. In northern China near Beijing, a *Homo erectus* skeleton was found. Known as Peking man, his remains show that people settled the river valley as much as 500,000 years ago.

The First Dynasties Even before the Sumerians settled in southern Mesopotamia, early Chinese cultures were building farming settlements along the Huang He. Around 2000 B.C., some of these settlements grew into China's first cities. According to legend, the first Chinese dynasty, the Xia (shyah) Dynasty, emerged about this time. Its leader was an engineer and mathematician named Yu. His flood-control and irrigation projects helped tame the Huang He and its tributaries so that settlements could grow. The legend of Yu reflects the level of technology of a society making the transition to civilization.

About the time the civilizations of Mesopotamia, Egypt, and the Indus Valley fell to outside invaders, a people called the Shang rose to power in northern China.

HISTORY

VIDEO
Omens in Ancient China

hmhsocialstudies.com

Lady Hao's Tomb

Lady Hao was a wife of king Wu Ding, a Shang ruler, during the 1200s B.C. Her relatively small grave contained some 460 bronze artifacts, 750 jade objects, and more than 6,880 cowry shells. Also found in the tomb beside Lady Hao's coffin were the remains of 16 people and 6 dogs.

Writings found in other places reveal a remarkable figure in Lady Hao. On behalf of her husband, she led more than one military campaign, once with a force of 13,000 troops. She also took charge of rituals dedicated to the spirits of Shang ancestors, a duty reserved for the most distinguished members of the royal family.

↗ **hmhsocialstudies.com**

INTERNET ACTIVITY Go online to create a multimedia presentation about Lady Hao's tomb and its contents.

The Shang Dynasty lasted from around 1700 B.C. to 1027 B.C. It was the first family of Chinese rulers to leave written records. The Shang kings built elaborate palaces and tombs that have been uncovered by archaeologists. The artifacts reveal much about Shang society.

Early Cities Among the oldest and most important Shang cities was Anyang (ahn•YAHNG), one of the capitals of the Shang Dynasty. Unlike the cities of the Indus Valley or Fertile Crescent, Anyang was built mainly of wood. The city stood in a forest clearing. The higher classes lived in timber-framed houses with walls of clay and straw. These houses lay inside the city walls. The peasants and craftspeople lived in huts outside the city.

The Shang surrounded their cities with massive earthen walls for protection. The archaeological remains of one city include a wall of packed earth 118 feet wide at its base that encircled an area of 1.2 square miles. It likely took 10,000 men more than 12 years to build such a structure. Like the pyramids of Egypt or the cities of the Indus Valley, these walls demonstrate the Shang rulers' ability to raise and control large forces of workers. **Ⓐ**

Shang peoples needed walled cities because they were constantly waging war. The chariot, one of the major tools of war, was probably first introduced by contact with cultures from western Asia. Professional warriors underwent lengthy training to learn the techniques of driving and shooting from horse-drawn chariots.

MAIN IDEA

Comparing

Ⓐ What did Shang cities have in common with those of Sumer?

The Development of Chinese Culture

In the Chinese view, people who lived outside of Chinese civilization were barbarians. Because the Chinese saw their country as the center of the civilized world, their own name for China was the Middle Kingdom.

The culture that grew up in China had strong unifying bonds. From earliest times, the group seems to have been more important than the individual. A person's chief loyalty throughout life was to the family. Beyond this, people owed obedience and respect to the ruler of the Middle Kingdom, just as they did to the elders in their family.

Family The family was central to Chinese society. The most important virtue was respect for one's parents. The elder men in the family controlled the family's property and made important decisions. Women, on the other hand, were treated as inferiors. They were expected to obey their fathers, their husbands, and later, their own sons. When a girl was between 13 and 16 years old, her marriage was arranged, and she moved into the house of her husband. Only by bearing sons for her husband's family could she hope to improve her status.

Social Classes Shang society was sharply divided between nobles and peasants. A ruling class of warrior-nobles headed by a king governed the Shang. These noble families owned the land. They governed the scattered villages within the Shang lands and sent tribute to the Shang ruler in exchange for local control.

Religious Beliefs In China, the family was closely linked to religion. The Chinese believed that the spirits of family ancestors had the power to bring good fortune

Vocabulary
tribute: payment made to keep peace

or disaster to living members of the family. The Chinese did not regard these spirits as mighty gods. Rather, the spirits were more like troublesome or helpful neighbors who demanded attention and respect. Every family paid respect to the father's ancestors and made sacrifices in their honor.

Through the spirits of the ancestors, the Shang consulted the gods. The Shang worshiped a supreme god, Shang Di, as well as many lesser gods. Shang kings consulted the gods through the use of **oracle bones**, animal bones and tortoise shells on which priests had scratched questions for the gods. After inscribing a question on the bone, a priest applied a hot poker to it, which caused it to crack. The priests then interpreted the cracks to see how the gods had answered.

Development of Writing In the Chinese method of writing, each character generally stands for one syllable or unit of language. Recall that many of the Egyptian hieroglyphs stood for sounds in the spoken language. In contrast, there were practically no links between China's spoken language and its written language. One could read Chinese without being able to speak a word of it. (This seems less strange when you think of our own number system. Both a French person and an American can understand the written equation $2 + 2 = 4$. But an American may not understand the spoken statement "Deux et deux font quatre.")

The Chinese system of writing had one major advantage. People in all parts of China could learn the same system of writing, even if their spoken languages were very different. Thus, the Chinese written language helped unify a large and diverse land, and made control much easier.

The disadvantage of the Chinese system was the enormous number of written characters to be memorized—a different one for each unit of language. A person needed to know over 1,500 characters to be barely literate. To be a true scholar, one needed to know at least 10,000 characters. For centuries, this severely limited the number of literate, educated Chinese. As a general rule, a nobleperson's children learned to write, but peasant children did not. **B**

▲ The earliest evidence of Chinese writing is seen on oracle bones like this one found in the city of Anyang.

MAIN IDEA

Recognizing Effects

B How did writing help unite China?

Chinese Writing

The earliest writing systems in the world—including Chinese, Sumerian, and Egyptian—developed from pictographs, or simplified drawings of objects. The writing system used in China today is directly related to the pictographic writing found on Shang oracle bones. As you can see in the chart below, the ancient pictographs can still be recognized in many modern Chinese characters.

	ox	goat, sheep	tree	moon	earth	water	field	heaven	to pray
Ancient symbol									
Modern character	牛	羊	木	月	土	水	田	天	祝

Early River Valley Civilizations **53**

Strong dynasty establishes peace and prosperity; it is considered to have Mandate of Heaven.

New dynasty gains power, restores peace and order, and claims to have Mandate of Heaven.

In time, dynasty declines and becomes corrupt; taxes are raised; power grows weaker.

Dynastic Cycle in China

Dynasty is overthrown through rebellion and bloodshed; new dynasty emerges.

Old dynasty is seen as having lost Mandate of Heaven; rebellion is justified.

Disasters such as floods, famines, peasant revolts, and invasions occur.

Zhou and the Dynastic Cycle

Around 1027 B.C., a people called the Zhou (joh) overthrew the Shang and established their own dynasty. The Zhou had adopted much of the Shang culture. Therefore, the change in dynasty did not bring sweeping cultural change. Nevertheless, Zhou rule brought new ideas to Chinese civilization.

Mandate of Heaven To justify their conquest, the Zhou leaders declared that the final Shang king had been such a poor ruler that the gods had taken away the Shang's rule and given it to the Zhou. This justification developed over time into a broader view that royal authority came from heaven. A just ruler had divine approval, known as the **Mandate of Heaven**. A wicked or foolish king could lose the Mandate of Heaven and so lose the right to rule. The Duke of Shao, an aide of the Zhou leader who conquered the Shang, described the mandate:

Vocabulary
mandate: a command or instruction from a higher authority

PRIMARY SOURCE
Heaven, unpitying, has sent down ruin on Yin [another name for Shang]. Yin has lost the Mandate, and we Zhou have received it. I dare not say that our fortune would continue to prosper, even though I believe that heaven favors those who are sincere in their intentions. I dare not say, either that it would end in certain disaster. . . .
The Mandate of Heaven is not easy to gain. It will be lost when men fail to live up to the reverent and illustrious virtues of their forefathers.

DUKE OF SHAO, quoted in *The Chinese Heritage*

The Mandate of Heaven became central to the Chinese view of government. Floods, riots, and other calamities might be signs that the ancestral spirits were displeased with a king's rule. In that case, the Mandate of Heaven might pass to another noble family. This was the Chinese explanation for rebellion, civil war, and the rise of a new dynasty. Historians describe the pattern of rise, decline, and replacement of dynasties as the **dynastic cycle**, shown above. **C**

Control Through Feudalism The Zhou Dynasty controlled lands that stretched far beyond the Huang He in the north to the Chang Jiang in the south. To govern this vast area, it gave control over different regions to members of the royal family and other trusted nobles. This established a system called **feudalism**. Feudalism is a political system in which nobles, or lords, are granted the use of lands that legally belong to the king. In return, the nobles owe loyalty and military service to the king and protection to the people who live on their estates. Similar systems would arise centuries later in both Japan and Europe.

At first, the local lords lived in small walled towns and had to submit to the superior strength and control of the Zhou rulers. Gradually, however, the lords grew stronger as the towns grew into cities and expanded into the surrounding territory.

MAIN IDEA

Synthesizing
C According to Chinese beliefs, what role did the Mandate of Heaven play in the dynastic cycle?

Peoples who had been hostile toward the lords gradually accepted their rule and adopted Zhou ways. As a result, the local lords became less dependent on the king. More and more, they fought among themselves and with neighboring peoples for wealth and territory.

Improvements in Technology and Trade The Zhou Dynasty produced many innovations.

- Roads and canals were built to stimulate trade and agriculture.
- Coined money was introduced, which further improved trade.
- Blast furnaces that produced cast iron were developed.

Zhou cast iron production would not be matched in Europe until the Middle Ages. The Zhou used iron to create weapons, especially dagger-axes and swords. They also used it for common agricultural tools such as sickles, knives, and spades. Iron tools made farm work easier and more productive. The ability to grow more food helped Zhou farmers support thriving cities.

A Period of Warring States The Zhou ruled from around 1027 to 256 B.C. The Zhou empire was generally peaceful and stable. Gradually, however, Zhou rule weakened. In 771 B.C., nomads from the north and west sacked the Zhou capital and murdered the Zhou monarch. A few members of the royal family escaped and set up a new capital at Luoyang.

However, the Zhou kings at Luoyang were almost powerless, and they could not control the noble families. The lords sought every opportunity to pick fights with neighboring lords. As their power grew, these warlords claimed to be kings in their own territory. As a result, the later years of the Zhou are often called "the time of the warring states."

Amidst the bloodshed, traditional values collapsed. The very heart of Chinese civilization—love of order, harmony, and respect for authority—had been replaced with chaos, arrogance, and defiance. As you will learn in Chapter 4, the dynastic cycle was about to bring a new start to Chinese civilization.

▲ These Chinese coins are made of bronze. Their shape resembles a digging tool such as a hoe or spade.

SECTION 4 ASSESSMENT

TERMS & NAMES 1. For each term or name, write a sentence explaining its significance.

- loess   • oracle bone   • Mandate of Heaven   • dynastic cycle   • feudalism

USING YOUR NOTES

2. Which event do you think was a turning point in Chinese history?

MAIN IDEAS

3. Between which two rivers is the heartland of China found?

4. What family obligations did a Chinese person have?

5. How is the dynastic cycle connected to the Mandate of Heaven?

CRITICAL THINKING & WRITING

6. **RECOGNIZING EFFECTS** In your judgment, what are the benefits and drawbacks of the belief that the group was more important than the individual?

7. **COMPARING** How did the social classes in Shang society differ from those in Egyptian society?

8. **ANALYZING MOTIVES** Do you think that the Zhou Dynasty's downfall resulted from its method of control? Why or why not?

9. **WRITING ACTIVITY** POWER AND AUTHORITY Study the dynastic cycle. Then write a **letter to the editor** suggesting that the current ruler should be replaced.

CONNECT TO TODAY CREATING A POSTER

Research the Three Gorges Dam Project in China. The project will place dams on the Chang Jiang. Create a **poster** showing the locations of the dams, some statistics about them, and an explanation of the project's purpose.

TERMS & NAMES

Briefly explain the importance of each of the following to early river valley civilizations from 3500–450 B.C.

1. Fertile Crescent
2. city-state
3. polytheism
4. empire
5. pharaoh
6. hieroglyphics
7. Harappan civilization
8. Mandate of Heaven

MAIN IDEAS

City-States in Mesopotamia Section 1 (pages 29–34)

9. What is the Fertile Crescent and why is it called that?
10. Name three disadvantages of Sumer's natural environment.
11. What circumstances led to the beginning of organized government?

Pyramids on the Nile Section 2 (pages 35–43)

12. Why did the Egyptians build pyramids?
13. Herodotus remarked that Egypt was the "gift of the Nile." What did he mean by this?

Planned Cities on the Indus Section 3 (pages 44–49)

14. What does the uniformity of Indus Valley cities tell us about their government?
15. What evidence exists to show that Indus Valley civilizations traded with Sumer?

River Dynasties in China Section 4 (pages 50–55)

16. What was the great advantage of the Chinese written language?
17. Explain the dynastic cycle in China.

CRITICAL THINKING

1. USING YOUR NOTES

Create a Venn diagram to indicate differences and similarities in religious beliefs among these ancient civilizations.

2. HYPOTHESIZING

POWER AND AUTHORITY Think about a massive public project that might be done today, such as building a large dam. In terms of government power and authority, how would this be similar to the building of the pyramids? How would it be different?

3. DRAWING CONCLUSIONS

SCIENCE AND TECHNOLOGY Why was it necessary to develop writing before civilization could advance?

4. MAKING INFERENCES

What reasons might be suggested for the location of civilizations along river valleys?

5. COMPARING

How was a theocracy different from a government run by warrior-kings?

VISUAL SUMMARY

Early River Valley Civilizations

	Sumer	Egypt	Indus Valley	China
Environment	• Tigris and Euphrates flooding unpredictable • No natural barriers • Limited natural resources	• Nile flooding predictable • Natural barriers: deserts • Nile an easy transportation link	• Indus flooding unpredictable • Natural barriers: mountains, deserts • Monsoon winds	• Huang He flooding unpredictable • Natural barriers: mountains, deserts • Geographically isolated
Power and Authority	• Independent city-states governed by monarchs • City-states united into first empires	• Pharaohs rule kingdom as gods • Pharaohs built pyramids	• Strong centralized government • Planned cities	• Community and family important • Sharp social divisions • Mandate of Heaven
Science and Technology	• Cuneiform • Irrigation • Bronze • Wheel, sail, plow	• Hieroglyphics • Pyramids • Mathematics, geometry • Medicine	• Writing (not yet deciphered) • Cities built on precise grid • Plumbing and sewage systems	• Writing • Silk • Coined money • Cast iron

Use the quotation and your knowledge of world history to answer questions 1 and 2.

PRIMARY SOURCE

The Lord of Fishes, He Who Makes the marsh birds to Go Upstream. There are no birds which come down because of the hot winds. He who makes barley and brings emmer [a kind of wheat] into being, that he may make the temples festive. If he is sluggish, then nostrils are stopped up, and everybody is poor. If there be thus a cutting down in the food offerings of the gods, then a million men perish among mortals, covetousness is practiced, the entire land is in a fury, and great and small are on the execution-block. . . . When he rises, then the land is in jubilation, then every belly is in joy, every backbone takes on laughter, and every tooth is exposed.

"Hymn to the Nile," from *Ancient Near Eastern Texts*

1. What natural phenomenon does the Lord of the Fishes represent?

   A. volcanic action

   B. monsoons

   C. the annual flooding of the Nile

   D. a major fish kill

2. Why are the people happy when the Lord of the Fishes comes to them?

   A. The wars they fight will be over.

   B. They will have food to eat.

   C. Corruption will stop.

   D. There will be a new pharaoh.

Use the map and your knowledge of world history to answer question 3.

World Climate Regions

Tropical-wet
Tropical-dry
Semidesert
Desert
Mediterranean
Humid subtropical
Continental
Subarctic
Mountain

3. How is the location of Anyang different from the other cities shown?

   A. It is located in the Western Hemisphere.

   B. It is not located in a river valley.

   C. Its climate is tropical.

   D. Its climate is not dry.

 hmhsocialstudies.com TEST PRACTICE

For additional test practice, go online for:

- Diagnostic tests
- Strategies
- Tutorials

Interact *with* History

On page 28, you looked at the justice of Hammurabi's Code. Now that you have read about the development of four civilizations, think about how laws differ from place to place. How have they developed and changed over time? What similarities do you see between Hammurabi's Code and the laws you live under today? How are they different? Discuss your opinions with a small group.

FOCUS ON WRITING

INTERACTION WITH ENVIRONMENT Write four **poems,** one for each civilization in the chapter. Include some reference to how each civilization interacted with the environment. Consider the following:

- the effect of the environment on life in the area
- responses to the environment by the people

MULTIMEDIA ACTIVITY

21ST CENTURY

Creating a Multimedia Presentation

Using the Internet, the library, or government resources, research the street structure of Washington, D.C., Boston, or the structure of your hometown streets. Identify their similarities and differences. Then research/work with a team to present your findings in a multimedia presentation.

- Which cities have a grid system? Which do not?
- What evidence is there of planning in the cities?
- What are the obvious similarities and differences of the two locations?

People and Ideas on the Move, 2000 B.C.–250 B.C.

Essential Question

How did migration and trade help spread goods and cultural ideas throughout the ancient world?

 What You Will Learn

In this chapter you will learn about how migrations and trade led to the foundations of Hinduism, Buddhism, and Judaism.

SECTION 1 The Indo-Europeans
Main Idea Indo-Europeans migrated into Europe, India, and Southwest Asia and interacted with peoples living there.

SECTION 2 Hinduism and Buddhism Develop
Main Idea The beliefs of the Vedic Age developed into Hinduism and Buddhism.

SECTION 3 Seafaring Traders
Main Idea Trading societies extended the development of civilizations beyond the Fertile Crescent.

SECTION 4 The Origins of Judaism
Main Idea The Israelites maintained monotheistic religious beliefs that were unique in the ancient world.

Previewing Themes

INTERACTION WITH ENVIRONMENT Early peoples often migrated from their lands to find new homes that promised a better life. Once they moved, they had to deal with a new environment.
Geography *Why did so many of the ancient trade routes cross the seas?*

RELIGIOUS AND ETHICAL SYSTEMS Three major world religions developed during this time. Hinduism and Buddhism originated in India, while Judaism developed in Southwest Asia.
Geography *What routes of communication existed between the Bay of Bengal near India and Phoenicia and Jerusalem in Southwest Asia?*

ECONOMICS Traders transported their goods to other parts of the world. Among the early trading peoples were the Phoenicians, who dominated the Mediterranean. Sea traders also traveled between India and Arabia.
Geography *How was the Arabian Peninsula well situated to take part in world trade?*

EASTERN HEMISPHERE

2000 B.C.
Hittites migrate to Anatolia.
(Hittite burial stone) ▶

1500 B.C.
Aryans invade India.

2000 B.C.   **1500 B.C.**

WESTERN HEMISPHERE

1200 B.C.
◀ Olmec civilization emerges in southeast Mexico.
(Olmec giant stone head)

The Ancient World, 1500 B.C.–250 B.C.

HISTORY™ King Solomon

↗ hmhsocialstudies.com VIDEO

EUROPE

ASIA

Massilia
Corsica
Rome
SPAIN
Sardinia
Balearic Is.
Gades
Sicily
Carthage
Knossos
Crete
Black Sea
Caspian Sea
GREECE
Athens
Cyprus
Byblos
PHOENICIA
Sidon
Tyre
Mediterranean Sea
Jerusalem
Memphis
ASSYRIA
Ashur
Babylon
BABYLONIA
Ur
PERSIA
Pataliputra
EGYPT
Thebes
Red Sea
ARABIAN PENINSULA
Persian Gulf
Arabian Sea
Bay of Bengal
15°N
AFRICA
INDIAN OCEAN
N
W   E
S
0° Equator
0° Equator

Early Indo-European Tribes, 1500 B.C.
Hittite Empire, 1500 B.C.
Phoenicians, 700 B.C.
Magadha, 600 B.C.
Trade route
▲ Phoenician colony

0   500   1000 Miles
0   500   1000 Kilometers
Winkel Tripel Projection

1100 B.C.
Phoenicians begin
to dominate
Mediterranean trade.
(Carthaginian glass bead) ▶

814 B.C.
Carthage founded
as a Phoenician
trade center.

586 B.C.
Jerusalem captured
by Babylonians.

1000 B.C.

250 B.C.

900 B.C.
Chavín culture
arises in Peru.

500 B.C.
Zapotecs found
Monte Albán.
(Zapotec jade mask) ▶

Why might you leave your homeland?

When your family, along with many others, decided to leave its homeland, you wondered whether you should go. It was hard to leave the land you love. Yet life there was becoming increasingly difficult. As your community grew larger, grazing for its many animals had become scarce. And lately, there had been rumors of coming invaders.

You have been walking and riding for days. Now you wonder whether you should have stayed. Will you find a new homeland, a better place in which to live? Will you survive the journey? Will you be welcome in a new land?

EXAMINING *the* ISSUES

- If you had stayed, would you have been able to adapt to changing conditions?

- Will you have to adopt the customs of the people living in a new land? How will you survive there?

As a class, discuss these questions. In your discussion, weigh the advantages and disadvantages of staying in your homeland and of leaving. As you read about migration in this chapter, see how old and new ways of doing things can blend together when groups of people move.

The Indo-Europeans

MAIN IDEA	WHY IT MATTERS NOW	TERMS & NAMES
INTERACTION WITH ENVIRONMENT Indo-Europeans migrated into Europe, India, and Southwest Asia and interacted with peoples living there.	Half the people living today speak languages that stem from the original Indo-European languages.	• Indo-Europeans • Aryans • steppes • Vedas • migration • Brahmin • Hittites • caste • Anatolia • *Mahabharata*

SETTING THE STAGE In India and in Mesopotamia, civilizations first developed along lush river valleys. Even as large cities such as Mohenjo-Daro and Harappa declined, agriculture and small urban communities flourished. These wealthy river valleys attracted nomadic tribes. These peoples may have left their own homelands because of warfare or changes in the environment.

Indo-Europeans Migrate

The **Indo-Europeans** were a group of nomadic peoples who may have come from the **steppes**—dry grasslands that stretched north of the Caucasus (KAW•kuh•suhs). The Caucasus are the mountains between the Black and Caspian seas. These primarily pastoral people herded cattle, sheep, and goats. The Indo-Europeans also tamed horses and rode into battle in light, two-wheeled chariots. They lived in tribes that spoke forms of a language that we call Indo-European.

The Indo-European Language Family The languages of the Indo-Europeans were the ancestors of many of the modern languages of Europe, Southwest Asia, and South Asia. English, Spanish, Persian, and Hindi all trace their origins back to different forms of the original Indo-European language.

Historians can tell where Indo-European tribes settled by their languages. Some Slavic speakers moved north and west. Others, who spoke early Celtic, Germanic, and Italic languages, moved west through Europe. Speakers of Greek and Persian went south. The Aryans (AIR•ee•uhnz), who spoke an early form of Sanskrit, located in India.

Notice the similarities of words within the Indo-European family of languages.

TAKING NOTES

Use the graphic organizer online to take notes on some of the languages that stem from Indo-European.

Language Family Resemblances				
English	**Sanskrit**	**Persian**	**Spanish**	**German**
mother	mātár	muhdáhr	madre	Mutter
father	pitár	puhdáhr	padre	Vater
daughter	duhitár	dukhtáhr	hija	Tochter
new	návas	now	nuevo	neu
six	sát	shahsh	seis	sechs

Indo-European Migrations, Starting about 1700 B.C.

Diverse Views

The origins and migrations of the Indo-European peoples are controversial topics among scholars. This map presents one view about where the Indo-Europeans came from and how they migrated. However, it is not the only view. In fact, there are many differing views.

Earliest Indo-European migrations
Later migrations

ASIA

Germans
Baltic Sea
Balts
Slavs
Celts
EUROPE
Italics
Illyrians
Early Indo-Europeans
STEPPES
Thracians
Indo-Europeans
CAUCASUS
Aral Sea
Aryans
ATLANTIC OCEAN
Black Sea
Caspian Sea
Aegean Sea
ANATOLIA
Greeks
Hittites
Luvians
Mediterranean Sea
AFRICA

GEOGRAPHY SKILLBUILDER: Interpreting Maps
1. **Location** *Which Indo-European people reached the farthest west?*
2. **Movement** *Describe the movement of the Indo-Europeans in their earliest migrations.*

An Unexplained Migration No one knows why these people left their homelands in the steppes. Whatever the reason, Indo-European nomads began to migrate outward in all directions between 1700 and 1200 B.C. These **migrations**, movements of a people from one region to another, happened in waves over a long period of time.

The Hittite Empire

By about 2000 B.C., one group of Indo-European speakers, the **Hittites**, occupied **Anatolia** (AN•uh•TOH•lee•uh), also called Asia Minor. Anatolia is a huge peninsula in modern-day Turkey that juts out into the Black and Mediterranean seas. Anatolia is a high, rocky plateau, rich in timber and agriculture. Nearby mountains hold important mineral deposits. Separate Hittite city-states came together to form an empire there in about 1650 B.C. The city of Hattusas (hah•TOO•sahs) was its capital.

The Hittite empire went on to dominate Southwest Asia for 450 years. Hittites occupied Babylon, the chief city in the Tigris-Euphrates Valley, and struggled with Egypt for control of northern Syria. Neither the Hittites nor the Egyptians were able to get the upper hand. So, the two peoples ended their conflicts by signing a peace treaty. They each pledged to help the other fight off future invaders.

Hittites Adopt and Adapt The Hittites used their own Indo-European language with one another. However, for international use, they adopted Akkadian, the language of the Babylonians they had conquered. The Hittites borrowed ideas about literature, art, politics, and law from the Mesopotamians. The Hittites thus blended their own traditions with those of other, more advanced peoples.

Chariots and Iron Technology The Hittites excelled in the technology of war. They conquered an empire against Egyptian opposition—largely through their superior chariots and their iron weapons. The Hittite war chariot was light and easy to maneuver. The chariot had two wheels and a wooden frame covered with leather and was pulled by two or sometimes four horses. The Hittite chariot proved itself a superb fighting machine.

The Hittites used iron in their chariots, and they owed many of their military victories to the skill of their ironworkers. Ancient peoples had long known that iron was stronger than bronze. They also knew that it could hold a sharper edge. However, the process of purifying iron ore and working it into weapons and tools is complex. Around 1500 B.C., the Hittites were the first in Southwest Asia to work with iron and harden it into weapons of war. The raw materials they needed—iron ore and wood to make charcoal—were easily available to them in the mountains of Anatolia. Knowledge of iron technology traveled widely with the Hittites—in both their trade and conquests. **A**

Despite its military might, the powerful Hittite empire fell quite suddenly around the year 1190 B.C. As part of a great wave of invasions, tribes attacked from the north and burned the Hittite capital city.

▲ This Hittite relief sculpture shows an archer in a chariot with his charioteer.

MAIN IDEA

Recognizing Effects

A How did environmental features in Anatolia help the Hittites advance technologically?

Aryans Transform India

Before 2000 B.C., the Hittites began establishing themselves in Anatolia. At the same time, some scholars believe, another Indo-European people, the **Aryans**, whose homeland was probably somewhere between the Caspian and Aral seas, crossed over the northwest mountain passes into the Indus River Valley of India. Other scholars believe the Aryans originated in India. There is no archaeological evidence to prove either hypothesis.

Though they left almost no archaeological record, their sacred literature, the **Vedas** (VAY•duhz), left a picture of Aryan life. The Vedas are four collections of prayers, magical spells, and instructions for performing rituals. The most important of the collections is the Rig Veda. The Rig Veda contains 1,028 hymns to Aryan gods. For many years, no written form of the Vedas existed. Instead, elders of one generation passed on this tradition orally to the next generation.

A Caste System Develops The Aryans fought their enemies, a people they called *dasas*. The Aryans differed from the *dasas* in many ways. Aryans were taller, lighter in skin color, and spoke a different language. Unlike the earlier inhabitants of the Indus Valley, the Aryans had not developed a writing system. They were also a pastoral people and counted their wealth in cows. The *dasas,* on the other hand, were town dwellers who lived in communities protected by walls.

Aryans were organized into four groups based on occupation: 1) **Brahmins** (priests), 2) warriors, 3) traders and landowners, and 4) peasants or traders. The group that an Aryan belonged to determined his or her role in society.

As the Aryans settled in India, they developed closer contacts with non-Aryans. To regulate those contacts, the Aryans made class restrictions more rigid. *Shudras*

The Aryan Caste System

The four major castes emerged from Purusha (the first human being) shown at the right. Purusha is identified with the creator god Brahma. The Brahmins (priests) were his mouth, the warriors were his arms, the landowners and traders were his legs, and the laborers and peasants were his feet.

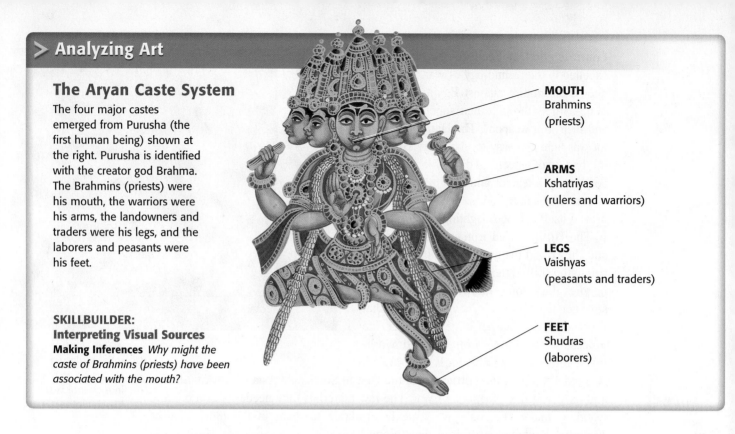

MOUTH
Brahmins
(priests)

ARMS
Kshatriyas
(rulers and warriors)

LEGS
Vaishyas
(peasants and traders)

FEET
Shudras
(laborers)

SKILLBUILDER:
Interpreting Visual Sources
Making Inferences *Why might the caste of Brahmins (priests) have been associated with the mouth?*

were laborers who did work that Aryans did not want to do. *Varna,* or skin color, was a distinguishing feature of this system. So the four major groups came to be known as the *varnas.* Later, in the 15th century A.D., explorers from Portugal encountered this social system and called these groups **castes** (kasts).

As time went on, the four basic castes gradually grew more complex—with hundreds of subdivisions. Classical texts state that caste should not be determined by birth. However, over time, some communities developed a system in which people were born into their caste. Their caste membership determined the work they did, whom they could marry, and the people with whom they could eat. Cleanliness and purity became all-important. Those considered the most impure because of their work (butchers, gravediggers, collectors of trash) lived outside the caste structure. They were known as "untouchables," since even their touch endangered the ritual purity of others. **B**

Aryan Kingdoms Arise Over the next few centuries, Aryans extended their settlements east, along the Ganges and Yamuna river valleys. (See map on page 62.) Progress was slow because of difficulties clearing the jungle for farming. This task grew easier when iron came into use in India about 1000 B.C.

When the Aryans first arrived in India, chiefs were elected by the entire tribe. Around 1000 B.C., however, minor kings who wanted to set up territorial kingdoms arose among the Aryans. They struggled with one another for land and power. Out of this strife emerged a major kingdom: Magadha. Under a series of ambitious kings, Magadha began expanding in the sixth century B.C. by taking over surrounding kingdoms. By the second century B.C., Magadha had expanded south to occupy almost all of the Indian subcontinent.

One of the great epics of India, the **Mahabharata** (MAH•huh•BAH•ruh•tuh), reflects the struggles that took place in India as the Aryan kings worked to control Indian lands. One part of the *Mahabharata* is the *Bhagavad Gita.* It tells the story of a warrior prince about to go to war. His chariot driver is Krishna, a god in human form.

MAIN IDEA

Making Inferences
B How were the more physical forms of work viewed by Aryans?

◄ This painting of Krishna battling with a demon in the form of a snake was created in 1785.

One of the most famous incidents in Indian literature occurs when Krishna instructs the young warrior on the proper way to live, fight, and die:

PRIMARY SOURCE
He who thinks this Self [eternal spirit] to be a slayer, and he who thinks this Self to be slain, are both without discernment; the Soul slays not, neither is it slain. . . . But if you will not wage this lawful battle, then will you fail your own [caste] law and your honor, and incur sin. . . . The people will name you with dishonor; and to a man of fame dishonor is worse than death.

KRISHNA, speaking in the *Bhagavad Gita*

The violence and confusion of the time led many to speculate about the place of the gods and human beings in the world. As a result, religion in India gradually changed. New religions were born, which you will read about in Section 2.

SECTION ❶ **ASSESSMENT**

TERMS & NAMES 1. For each term or name, write a sentence explaining its significance.
• Indo-Europeans • steppes • migration • Hittites • Anatolia • Aryans • Vedas • Brahmin • caste • Mahabharata

USING YOUR NOTES
2. Why did so many languages originate from Indo-European roots?

Indo-European

MAIN IDEAS
3. What were some of the technological achievements of the Hittites?

4. What were some of the borrowings of the Hittites?

5. Where do some historians think the Aryans lived before they arrived in India?

CRITICAL THINKING & WRITING
6. FORMING OPINIONS What important contributions did the Aryans make to the culture and way of life in India in terms of religion, literature, and roles in society?

7. DRAWING CONCLUSIONS Look at the Hittite chariot on page-63. What made it an excellent fighting machine?

8. COMPARING AND CONTRASTING What were some of the differences between the Aryans and the *dasas* in India?

9. WRITING ACTIVITY INTERACTION WITH ENVIRONMENT
Write an **expository essay** in which you discuss environmental reasons why the Indo-Europeans might have migrated.

MULTIMEDIA ACTIVITY **CREATING A CHART**

Use the Internet to create a **chart** that shows how a word in English is expressed in other Indo-European languages. Choose languages other than the ones listed on page 61 in this section.

INTERNET KEYWORD
words in Indo-European languages

People and Ideas on the Move **65**

Hinduism and Buddhism Develop

MAIN IDEA	WHY IT MATTERS NOW	TERMS & NAMES
RELIGIOUS AND ETHICAL SYSTEMS The beliefs of the Vedic Age developed into Hinduism and Buddhism.	Almost one-fifth of the world's people today practice one of these two religions.	• reincarnation • karma • Jainism • Siddhartha Gautama • enlightenment • nirvana

SETTING THE STAGE At first, the Aryans and non-Aryans followed their own forms of religion. Then as the two groups intermingled, the gods and forms of their religions also tended to blend together. This blending resulted in the worship of thousands of gods. Different ways of living and different beliefs made life more complex for both groups. This complexity led some people to question the world and their place in it. They even questioned the enormous wealth and power held by the Brahmin priests. Out of this turmoil, new religious ideas arose that have continued to influence millions of people today.

Hinduism Evolves Over Centuries

TAKING NOTES

Use the graphic organizer online to take notes on the beliefs and practices of Buddhism and Hinduism.

Hinduism is a collection of religious beliefs that developed slowly over a long period of time. Some aspects of the religion can be traced back to ancient times. In a Hindu marriage today, for example, the bride and groom marry in the presence of the sacred fire as they did centuries ago. The faithful recite daily verses from the Vedas.

From time to time, scholars have tried to organize the many popular cults, gods, and traditions into one grand system of belief. However, Hinduism—unlike religions such as Buddhism, Christianity, or Islam—cannot be traced back to one founder with a single set of ideas.

Origins and Beliefs Hindus share a common worldview. They see religion as a way of liberating the soul from the illusions, disappointments, and mistakes of everyday existence. Sometime between 750 and 550 B.C., Hindu teachers tried to interpret and explain the hidden meaning of the Vedic hymns. The teachers' comments were later written down and became known as the Upanishads (oo•PAHN•ih•shahdz).

The Upanishads are written as dialogues, or discussions, between a student and a teacher. In the course of the dialogues, the two explore how a person can achieve liberation from desires and suffering. This is described as *moksha* (MOHK•shah), a state of perfect understanding of all things. The teacher distinguishes between atman, the individual soul of a living being, and Brahman, the world soul that contains and unites all atmans. Here is how one teacher explains the unifying spirit of Brahman:

PRIMARY SOURCE
Thou art woman, Thou art man, Thou art the lad and the maiden too. Thou art the old man tottering on his staff: Once born thou comest to be, thy face turned every way! A dark-blue moth art Thou, green [parrot] with red eyes. Pregnant with lightning—seasons, seas: Thyself beginningless, all things dost Thou pervade. From Thee all worlds were born.

Svetasvatara Upanishad. IV. 3–4

When a person understands the relationship between atman and Brahman, that person achieves perfect understanding (*moksha*) and a release from life in this world. This understanding does not usually come in one lifetime. By the process of **reincarnation** (rebirth), an individual soul or spirit is born again and again until *moksha* is achieved. A soul's **karma**—good or bad deeds—follows from one reincarnation to another. Karma influences specific life circumstances, such as the caste one is born into, one's state of health, wealth or poverty, and so on.

Hinduism Changes and Develops Hinduism has gone through many changes over the last 2,500 years. The world soul, Brahman, was sometimes seen as having the personalities of three gods: Brahma, the creator; Vishnu, the protector; and Shiva, the destroyer. Vishnu also took on many forms or personalities, for example, as Krishna, the divine cowherder, and as Rama, the perfect king. Over the centuries, Brahma gradually faded into the background, while the many forms of Devi, a great Mother Goddess, grew in importance.

Hindus today are free to choose the deity they worship or to choose none at all. Most, however, follow a family tradition that may go back centuries. They are also free to choose among three different paths for achieving *moksha*. These are the path of right thinking, the path of right action, or the path of religious devotion. Ⓐ

Hinduism and Society Hindu ideas about karma and reincarnation strengthened the caste system. If a person was born as an upper-caste male—a Brahmin, warrior, or merchant—his good fortune was said to come from good karma earned in a former life. However, a person who was born as a female, a laborer, or an untouchable might be getting the results of bad deeds in a former life. With some exceptions, only men of the top three varnas could hope to achieve *moksha* in their present life. The laws of karma worked with the same certainty as the world's other natural laws. Good karma brought good fortune and bad karma resulted in bad fortune.

Together, the beliefs of Hinduism and its caste structure dominated every aspect of a person's life. These beliefs determined what one could eat and the way in which one ate it, personal cleanliness, the people one could associate with, how one dressed, and so on. Today, even in the most ordinary activities of daily life, Hindus turn to their religion for guidance.

New Religions Arise The same period of speculation reflected in the Upanishads also led to the rise of two other religions: Jainism (JY•nihz•uhm) and Buddhism. Mahavira, the founder of **Jainism**, was born about 599 B.C. and died in 527 B.C. Mahavira believed that everything in the universe has a soul and so should not be

MAIN IDEA

Making Inferences

Ⓐ How might the lack of a single founder result in Hinduism changing more over time than other religions?

▼ Vishnu grew to become a major Hindu god. He is seen here as the whole Universe in all its variety. He is blue, the color of infinity.

harmed. Jain monks carry the doctrine of nonviolence to its logical conclusion. They sweep ants off their path and wear gauze masks over their mouths to avoid breathing in an insect accidentally. In keeping with this nonviolence, followers of Jainism looked for occupations that would not harm any creature. So they have a tradition of working in trade and commerce. **B**

Because of their business activities, Jains today make up one of the wealthiest communities in India. Jains have traditionally preached tolerance of all religions. As a result, they have made few efforts to convert followers of other faiths. Because of this tolerance, Jains have not sent out missionaries. So, almost all of the nearly five million Jains in the world today live in India.

MAIN IDEA

Synthesizing

B How far might the Jain respect for life extend?

The Buddha Seeks Enlightenment

Buddhism developed out of the same period of religious questioning that shaped modern Hinduism and Jainism. The founder of Buddhism, **Siddhartha Gautama** (sihd•DAHR•tuh GOW•tuh•muh), was born into a noble family that lived in Kapilavastu, in the foothills of the Himalayas in Nepal. According to Buddhist legend, the baby exhibited the marks of a great man. A prophecy indicated that if the child stayed at home he was destined to become a world ruler. If the child left home, however, he would become a universal spiritual leader. To make sure the boy would be a great king and world ruler, his father isolated him in his palace. Separated from the world, Siddhartha married and had a son.

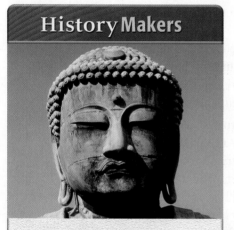

History Makers

Siddhartha Gautama
c. 563–483 B.C.

According to Buddhist tradition, Siddhartha Gautama's mother had dreamt of a beautiful elephant that was bright as silver. When asked to interpret the dream, Brahmin priests declared that the child to be born would either be a great monarch or a Buddha (an enlightened one).

Tradition also relates that at Gautama's birth, he exhibited the signs of a child destined for greatness. There were 32 such signs, including golden-tinged skin, webbed fingers and toes, a knob on the top of his skull, a long tongue, a tuft of hair between his eyebrows, and a thousand-spoked wheel on each foot. Some images of the Buddha display these traits.

Siddhartha's Quest Siddhartha never ceased thinking about the world that lay outside, which he had never seen. When he was 29, he ventured outside the palace four times. First he saw an old man, next a sick man, then a corpse, and finally a wandering holy man who seemed at peace with himself. Siddhartha understood these events to mean that every living thing experiences old age, sickness, and death and that only a religious life offers a refuge from this inevitable suffering. Siddhartha decided to spend his life searching for religious truth and an end to life's suffering. So, soon after learning of his son's birth, he left the palace.

Siddhartha wandered through the forests of India for six years seeking **enlightenment**, or wisdom. He tried many ways of reaching an enlightened state. He first debated with other religious seekers. Then he fasted, eating only six grains of rice a day. Yet none of these methods brought him to the truth, and he continued to suffer. Finally, he sat in meditation under a large fig tree. After 49 days of meditation, he achieved an understanding of the cause of suffering in this world. From then on, he was known as the Buddha, meaning "the enlightened one."

Vocabulary
fasted: ate very little.

Origins and Beliefs The Buddha preached his first sermon to five companions who had accompanied him on his wanderings. That first sermon became a landmark in the history of the world's religions. In it, he laid out the four main ideas that he had come to understand in his enlightenment. He called those ideas the Four Noble Truths:

The Four Noble Truths	
First Noble Truth	Life is filled with suffering and sorrow.
Second Noble Truth	The cause of all suffering is people's selfish desire for the temporary pleasures of this world.
Third Noble Truth	The way to end all suffering is to end all desires.
Fourth Noble Truth	The way to overcome such desires and attain enlightenment is to follow the Eightfold Path, which is called the Middle Way between desires and self-denial.

The Eightfold Path, a guide to behavior, was like a staircase. For the Buddha, those who were seeking enlightenment had to master one step at a time. Most often, this mastery would occur over many lifetimes. Here is how he described the Middle Way and its Eightfold Path:

PRIMARY SOURCE
What is the Middle Way? . . . It is the Noble Eightfold Path—Right Views, Right Resolve, Right Speech, Right Conduct, Right Livelihood, Right Effort, Right Mindfulness, and Right Concentration. This is the Middle Way.

BUDDHA, from *Samyutta Nikaya*

By following the Eightfold Path, anyone could reach **nirvana**, the Buddha's word for release from selfishness and pain.

As in Hinduism, the Buddha accepted the idea of reincarnation. He also accepted a cyclical, or repetitive, view of history, where the world is created and destroyed over and over again. However, the Buddha rejected the many gods of Hinduism. Instead, he taught a way of enlightenment. Like many of his time, the Buddha reacted against the privileges of the Brahmin priests, and thus he rejected the caste system. The final goals of both religions—*moksha* for Hindus and nirvana for Buddhists—are similar. Both involve a perfect state of understanding and a break from the chain of reincarnations. **C**

MAIN IDEA

Comparing
C In what ways are Buddhism and Hinduism similar?

▼ Buddhist tradition says that just before he died, the Buddha lay on his right side between two trees. This reclining Buddha is made of bronze.

The Religious Community The five disciples who heard the Buddha's first sermon were the first monks admitted to the *sangha,* or Buddhist religious order. At first, the *sangha* was a community of Buddhist monks and nuns. However, *sangha* eventually referred to the entire religious community. It included Buddhist laity (those who hadn't devoted their entire lives to religion). The religious community, together with the Buddha and the *dharma* (Buddhist doctrine or teachings), make up the "Three Jewels" of Buddhism.

Buddhism and Society Because of his rejection of the caste system, many of the Buddha's early followers included laborers and craftspeople. He also gained a large following in northeast India, where the Aryans had less influence. The Buddha reluctantly admitted women to religious orders. He feared, however, that women's presence would distract men from their religious duties.

Monks and nuns took vows (solemn promises) to live a life of poverty, to be nonviolent, and not to marry. They wandered throughout India spreading the Buddha's teachings. Missionaries carried only a begging bowl to receive daily charity offerings from people. During the rainy season, they retreated to caves high up in the hillsides. Gradually, these seasonal retreats became permanent monasteries—some for men, others for women. One monastery, Nalanda, developed into a great university that also attracted non-Buddhists.

The teachings of the Buddha were written down shortly after his death. Buddhist sacred literature also includes commentaries, rules about monastic life, manuals on how to meditate, and legends about the Buddha's previous reincarnations (the *Jatakas*). This sacred literature was first written down in the first century B.C.

Buddhism in India During the centuries following the Buddha's death, missionaries were able to spread his faith over large parts of Asia. Buddhist missionaries went to Sri Lanka and Southeast Asia in the third century B.C. Buddhist ideas also traveled along Central Asian trade routes to China. However, Buddhism never gained a significant foothold in India, the country of its origin. Several theories exist about Buddhism's gradual disappearance in India. One theory states that

Hinduism simply absorbed Buddhism. The two religions constantly influenced each other. Over time, the Buddha came to be identified by Hindus as one of the ten incarnations (reappearances on earth) of the god Vishnu. Hindus, therefore, felt no need to convert to Buddhism.

Vocabulary
pilgrimages: travels to holy places.

Nonetheless, despite the small number of Buddhists in India, the region has always been an important place of pilgrimages for Buddhists. Today, as they have for centuries, Buddhist pilgrims flock to visit spots associated with the Buddha's life. These sites include his birthplace at Kapilavastu, the fig tree near Gaya, and the site of his first sermon near Varanasi. Buddhists also visit the *stupas,* or sacred mounds, that are said to contain his relics. The pilgrims circle around the sacred object or sanctuary, moving in a clockwise direction. They also lie face down on the ground as a sign of humility and leave flowers. These three actions are important rituals in Buddhist worship.

⌐ hmhsocialstudies.com

INTERACTIVE MAP

Explore the spread of Buddhism in Asia.

Trade and the Spread of Buddhism As important as missionaries were to the spread of Buddhism, traders played an even more crucial role in this process. Along with their products, traders carried Buddhism beyond India to Sri Lanka. Buddhist religion was also brought southeast along trade routes to Burma, Thailand, and the island of Sumatra. Likewise, Buddhism followed the Central Asian trade routes, called the Silk Roads, all the way to China. From China, Buddhism spread to Korea—and from Korea to Japan. The movement of trade thus succeeded in making Buddhism the most widespread religion of East Asia. Throughout human history, trade has been a powerful force for the spread of ideas. Just as trade spread Buddhism in East Asia, it helped spread cultural influences in another major region of the world: the Mediterranean basin, as you will learn in Section 3.

Connect *to* Today

Buddhism in the West

Throughout the 20th century, large numbers of Asians have immigrated to the West, particularly to North America. Many of them brought Buddhism with them. Today, Buddhist temples are a common feature of many large cities in the West.

Since the 1950s, many non-Asians who were dissatisfied with the religions of the West have turned to Buddhism for insight into life's meaning. Today, Buddhism can claim about one million Asian and non-Asian believers in North America.

⌐ hmhsocialstudies.com

INTERNET ACTIVITY Go online to create a bar graph to show the number of Buddhists in some American cities.

SECTION 2 ASSESSMENT

TERMS & NAMES **1.** For each term or name, write a sentence explaining its significance.
• reincarnation   • karma   • Jainism   • Siddhartha Gautama   • enlightenment   • nirvana

USING YOUR NOTES

2. What are the terms for enlightenment in each religion?

> Buddhism only
> both
> Hinduism only

MAIN IDEAS

3. What are the Four Noble Truths of Buddhism?

4. How has Hinduism influenced social structure in India?

5. How did Buddhism spread?

CRITICAL THINKING & WRITING

6. MAKING INFERENCES How might the belief in reincarnation provide a form of social control?

7. COMPARING How are the Vedas and the Upanishads similar?

8. MAKING INFERENCES Look at the image of Vishnu on page 67. Why might blue represent infinity?

9. WRITING ACTIVITY `RELIGIOUS SYSTEMS` How did the experiences of Siddhartha Gautama influence his religious and ethical beliefs? Write a brief **biography** of his life. Include family background, accomplishments, and a list of his beliefs.

CONNECT TO TODAY **CREATING A MAP**

Where in the world is Hinduism the main religion? What about Buddhism? Copy an **outline map** of the world. Then color in those regions of the world where Buddhism and Hinduism are the dominant religions. Use a different color for each religion.

Seafaring Traders

MAIN IDEA	WHY IT MATTERS NOW	TERMS & NAMES
ECONOMICS Trading societies extended the development of civilizations beyond the Fertile Crescent region.	Traders spread knowledge of reading and writing, including an ancient form of the alphabet that we use today.	• Minoans • King Minos • Aegean Sea • Phoenicians • Knossos

SETTING THE STAGE Buddhism spread to Southeast Asia and to East Asia mainly through Buddhist traders. In the Mediterranean, the same process took place: traders in the region carried many new ideas from one society to another. They carried new ways of writing, of governing, and of worshiping their gods.

Minoans Trade in the Mediterranean

hmhsocialstudies.com
TAKING NOTES

Use the graphic organizer online to take notes on the accomplishments of the Minoans and Phoenicians.

A powerful seafaring people, the **Minoans** (mih•NOH•uhnz) dominated trade in the eastern Mediterranean from about 2000 to 1400 B.C. They lived on Crete, a large island on the southern edge of the **Aegean Sea** (ee•JEE•uhn). The Minoans produced some of the finest painted pottery of the time. They traded that pottery, along with swords, figurines, and vessels of precious metals, over a large area.

Along with their goods, Minoans also exported their art and culture. These included a unique architecture, burial customs, and religious rituals. Minoan culture had a major influence on Greece, for example. Trading turned Crete into a "stepping stone" for cultural exchange throughout the Mediterranean world.

Unearthing a Brilliant Civilization Archaeologists in the late 19th and early 20th centuries excavated **Knossos**, the Minoan capital city. There, they found the remains of an advanced and thriving culture. It must have been a peaceful one as well, since Minoan cities did not seem to need fortifications to protect them. The archaeologists named the civilization they found in Crete *Minoa* after **King Minos**

(MY•nuhs). According to legend, Minos was a king who owned a half-human, half-bull monster called the Minotaur (MIHN•uh•TAWR). He kept the monster locked inside a labyrinth, a complicated maze from which no one could escape.

The excavation of Knossos and its painted walls produced much information about Minoans. The wall paintings, as well as the official seals and vases, show the Minoans as graceful, athletic people who loved nature and beautiful objects. They also enjoyed sports such as boxing, wrestling, and bull leaping.

Many Minoan artworks depict women and their role in religious ceremonies. The art suggests that women held a higher rank than in most neighboring cultures. A great Mother Earth Goddess seems to have ruled over the other gods of Crete. Also, priestesses took charge of some shrines, aided by male assistants.

Bull Leapers of Knossos

The wall painting to the right captures the death-defying jump of a Minoan bull leaper in mid-flight. Many works of Minoan art show young men performing incredible acrobatic leaps over the horns of angry bulls. In one case, the gymnast jumps over the bull's horns, makes a somersault off its back, and lands behind its tail.

In another gymnastic feat, some team members hang on to the horns of a bull, using their bodies to cushion its horns and to force its head low, while another team member jumps over its back.

What was the reason for this bull leaping? Was it a sport? Just a "fun" activity? An initiation for young warriors? Or a religious ritual? Most likely it was all of these things.

The Minoans sacrificed bulls and other animals to their gods. In at least one case, a young man was sacrificed. Excavation of a mountain temple revealed the bones of a 17-year-old boy on an altar, along with the skeletons of three priests. The positions of the skeletons suggest that the priests carried out the human sacrifice just before the building collapsed.

Minoan Culture's Mysterious End The Minoan civilization finally ended about 1200 B.C. The reasons for its end are unclear. Could it have been the result of some natural disaster? Did the island become overpopulated? Or was it overrun by invaders?

The civilization had withstood previous disasters. In about 1700 B.C., a great disaster, perhaps an earthquake, destroyed most Minoan towns and cities. The Minoans rebuilt the cities with equal richness. Then in 1470 B.C. a series of earthquakes rocked Crete. The quakes were followed by a violent volcanic eruption on the neighboring island of Thera. Imagine the shaking of the earth, the fiery volcanic blast, then a huge tidal wave, and finally a rain of white volcanic ash.

The disaster of 1470 B.C. was a blow from which the Minoans never fully recovered. This time, the Minoans had trouble rebuilding their cities. Nonetheless, Minoan civilization did linger on for almost 300 years. After that, invaders from Greece may have taken advantage of their weakened condition to destroy them. Some Minoans fled to the mountains to escape the ruin of the kingdom. Crete's influence as a major sea power and cultural force was over. **A**

MAIN IDEA

Summarizing

A What adjectives might describe Minoan civilization?

Phoenicians Spread Trade and Civilization

About 1100 B.C., after Crete's decline, the most powerful traders along the Mediterranean were the **Phoenicians** (fih•NIHSH•uhnz). Phoenicia was mainly the area now known as Lebanon. Phoenicians never united into a country. Instead, they founded a number of wealthy city-states around the Mediterranean that sometimes competed with one another. The first cities in Phoenicia, such as Byblos, Tyre, and Sidon, were important trading centers.

The Phoenicians were remarkable shipbuilders and seafarers. They were the first Mediterranean people to venture beyond the Strait of Gibraltar. Some scholars believe that the Phoenicians traded for tin with inhabitants of the southern coast of Britain. Some evidence exists for an even more remarkable feat—sailing around the continent of Africa by way of the Red Sea and back through the Strait of Gibraltar. Such a trip was not repeated again for 2,000 years. The Greek historian Herodotus (hih•RAHD•uh•tuhs) relates the feat:

PRIMARY SOURCE
The Phoenicians set out from the Red Sea and sailed the southern sea [the Indian Ocean]; whenever autumn came they would put in and sow the land, to whatever part of Libya [Africa] they might come, and there await the harvest; then, having gathered in the crop, they sailed on, so that after two years had passed, it was in the third that they rounded the Pillars of Heracles [Strait of Gibraltar] and came to Egypt. There they said (what some may believe, though I do not) that in sailing round Libya they had the sun on their right hand [in reverse position].

HERODOTUS, in *History*, Book IV (5th century B.C.)

Alphabets—Ancient and Modern

Phoenician	Greek	English
⤫	A	A
⅁	B	B
∧	Γ	C
⊿	Δ	D
Ⅎ	E	E
Y		F
		G
	Z	
	H	H
⊗	Θ	
	I	I
		J
⅄	K	K
∠	Λ	L
ꟺ	M	M
Ч	N	N
	Ξ	
O	O	O
⌐	Π	P
⌐		Q
ዋ⊲	P	R
	Σ	S
‡	T	T
χ	Υ	U
	φ	V
		W
	X	X
∿	ψ	Y
Ɪ		Z
	Ω	

SKILLBUILDER: Interpreting Charts
1. **Comparing** *Which letters show the most similarity across the three alphabets?*
2. **Making Inferences** *Why might one language have fewer letters in its alphabet than another?*

Commercial Outposts Around the Mediterranean
The Phoenicians' most important city-states in the eastern Mediterranean were Sidon and Tyre, both known for their production of red-purple dye, and Byblos, a trading center for papyrus. (See map on page 59.) Phoenicians built colonies along the northern coast of Africa and the coasts of Sicily, Sardinia, and Spain. The colonies were about 30 miles apart—about the distance a Phoenician ship could sail in a day. The greatest Phoenician colony was at Carthage (KAHR•thihj), in North Africa. Settlers from Tyre founded Carthage in about 814 B.C.

The Phoenicians traded goods they got from other lands—wine, weapons, precious metals, ivory, and slaves. They also were known as superb craftspeople who worked in wood, metal, glass, and ivory. Their red-purple dye was produced from the murex, a kind of snail that lived in the waters off Sidon and Tyre. One snail, when left to rot, produced just a drop or two of a liquid of a deep red-purple color. Some 60,000 snails were needed to produce one pound of dye, which only royalty could afford.

Phoenicia's Great Legacy: The Alphabet As merchants, the Phoenicians needed a way of recording transactions clearly and quickly. So the Phoenicians developed a writing system that used symbols to represent sounds. The Phoenician system was phonetic—that is, one sign was used for one sound. In fact, the word *alphabet* comes directly from the first two letters of the Phoenician alphabet: *aleph* and *beth*. As they traveled around the Mediterranean, the Phoenicians introduced this writing system to their trading partners. The Greeks, for example, adopted the Phoenician alphabet and changed the form of some of the letters.

Phoenician Trade

Phoenicia was located in a great spot for trade because it-lay along well-traveled routes between Egypt and Asia. However, the Phoenicians did more than just trade with merchants who happened to pass through their region. The Phoenicians became expert sailors and went looking for opportunities to make money.

The Patterns of Ancient Trade, 2000–250 B.C.

— Ancient trade route
— Phoenician trade route

Merchant Ships

Phoenician sailors developed the round boat, a ship that was very wide and had a rounded bottom. This shape created a large space for cargo.

Foreigners wanted cedar, an aromatic wood that grew in Phoenicia.

Phoenician ships often were decorated with horse heads.

This wicker fence runs around the outer edge of the upper deck.

These pottery jars with pointed bottoms are called amphorae. They held oil or wine.

The most desired Phoenician trade item was dyed red-purple cloth.

SKILLBUILDER: Interpreting Visuals
1. **Drawing Conclusions** *Why would traders find it helpful to tow the cedar logs instead of storing them inside the ship?*
2. **Making Inferences** *What purpose does the wicker fence serve?*

75

▲ Phoenician inscription from a sarcophagus

Few examples of Phoenician writing exist. Most writings were on papyrus, which crumbled over time. However, the Phoenician contribution to the world was enormous. With a simplified alphabet, learning was now accessible to more people.

Phoenician trade was upset when their eastern cities were captured by Assyrians in 842 B.C. However, these defeats encouraged exiles to set up city-states like Carthage to the west. The Phoenician homeland later came under the control of the Babylonians and of the Persian empire of King Cyrus I. One of their most lasting contributions remains the spread of the alphabet.

Ancient Trade Routes

Trading in ancient times also connected the Mediterranean Sea with other centers of world commerce, such as South and East Asia. Several land routes crossed Central Asia and connected to India through Afghanistan. Two sea routes began by crossing the Arabian Sea to ports on the Persian Gulf and the Red Sea. From there, traders either went overland to Egypt, Syria, and Mediterranean countries, or they continued to sail up the Red Sea. To cross the Arabian Sea, sailors learned to make use of the monsoon winds. These winds blow from the southwest during the hot months and from the northeast during the cool season.

To widen the variety of their exports, Indian traders used other monsoon winds to travel to Southeast Asia and Indonesia. Once there, they obtained spices and other products not native to India.

Though traveling was difficult in ancient times, trading networks like those of the Phoenicians ensured the exchange of products and information. Along with their goods, traders carried ideas, religious beliefs, art, and ways of living. They helped with the process of cultural diffusion as well as with moving merchandise.

Phoenician traders made crucial contributions to world civilization. At the same time, another eastern Mediterranean people, the Jews, were creating a religious tradition that has lasted more than 3,000 years. This is discussed in Section 4.

Vocabulary
monsoon: a wind that affects climate by changing direction in certain seasons.

SECTION 3 ASSESSMENT

TERMS & NAMES 1. For each term or name, write a sentence explaining its significance.
• Minoans   • Aegean Sea   • Knossos   • King Minos   • Phoenicians

USING YOUR NOTES
2. Which of these achievements do you think was the most important? Why?

Minoan	Phoenician
1.	1.
2.	2.
3.	3.

MAIN IDEAS
3. What did the excavations at Knossos reveal about Minoan culture?

4. Where did the Phoenicians settle and trade?

5. Why did the Phoenicians develop a writing system?

CRITICAL THINKING & WRITING
6. **MAKING INFERENCES** What might have caused the collapse of Minoan culture?

7. **COMPARING** What were some similarities between the Minoans and Phoenicians in terms of trade?

8. **ANALYZING PRIMARY SOURCES** Go back to Herodotus' account of a voyage around Africa on page 74. What words show his doubt? Why was he doubtful?

9. **WRITING ACTIVITY** ECONOMICS The Phoenicians founded many city-states. These city-states often competed. Do you think it would have made more sense to cooperate? Write a brief **essay** explaining your opinion.

CONNECT TO TODAY MAKING A DATABASE

How might a commonly or widely accepted language make business and trade easier to transact? Make a **database** of bulleted points showing the ways a widely known language (such as English) would make it easier to conduct business around the world.

The Origins of Judaism

MAIN IDEA	WHY IT MATTERS NOW	TERMS & NAMES
RELIGIOUS AND ETHICAL SYSTEMS The Israelites maintained monotheistic religious beliefs that were unique in the ancient world.	From this tradition, Judaism, the religion of the Jews, evolved. Judaism is one of the world's major religions.	• Canaan • Moses • Torah • Israel • Abraham • Judah • monotheism • tribute • covenant

SETTING THE STAGE The Phoenicians lived in a region at the eastern end of the Mediterranean Sea that was called **Canaan** (KAY•nuhn). The Phoenicians were not the only ancient people to live in the area; for example, the Philistines were another people who lived in the region. Canaan was the ancient home of the Israelites, later called the Jews, in this area. Their history, legends, and moral laws are a major influence on Western culture, and they began a tradition also shared by Christianity and Islam.

The Search for a Promised Land

Ancient Canaan's location made it a cultural crossroads of the ancient world. By land, it connected Asia and Africa and two great empires, both eager to expand. To the east lay Assyria and Babylonia and to the west Egypt. Its seaports opened onto the two most important waterways of that time: the Mediterranean and the Red seas. The Israelites settled in Canaan, which lay between the Jordan River and the Mediterranean Sea. In fact, the Israelites often used the word *Canaan* to refer to all of ancient Canaan. According to the Hebrew Bible, Canaan was the land God had promised to the Israelites.

TAKING NOTES

Use the graphic organizer online to take notes on the major Jewish leaders.

From Ur to Egypt Most of what we know about the early history of the Israelites is contained in the first five books of the Hebrew Bible. Jews call these books the **Torah** (TAWR•uh) and consider them the most sacred writings in their tradition. Christians respect them as part of the Old Testament.

In the Torah, God chose **Abraham** (AY•bruh•HAM) to be the "father" of the Jewish people. God's words to Abraham expressed a promise of land and a pledge:

PRIMARY SOURCE
The LORD said to Abram, "Go forth from your native land and from your father's house to the land that I will show you. I will make you a great nation, and I will bless you; I will make your name great; and you shall be a blessing."
Genesis 12:1–2 (Hebrew Bible)

Abraham was a shepherd who lived in the city of Ur, in Mesopotamia. The Book of Genesis tells that God commanded him to move his people to Canaan. Around 1800 B.C., Abraham, his family, and their herds made their way to Canaan. Then, around 1650 B.C., the descendants of Abraham moved to Egypt.

The God of Abraham The Hebrew Bible tells how Abraham and his family migrated for many years from Mesopotamia to Canaan to Egypt and back to Canaan. All the while, God watched over them. Gods worshiped by other people were often local, and were associated with a specific place.

Unlike the other groups around them, who were polytheists, the Israelites were monotheists. They prayed to only one God. <u>Monotheism</u> (MAHN•uh•thee•IHZ•uhm), a belief in a single god, comes from the Greek words *mono*, meaning "one," and *theism*, meaning "god-worship." The Israelites proclaimed that there was only one God. In their eyes, God had power over all peoples, everywhere. To the Israelites, God was not a physical being, and no physical images were to be made of him.

The Israelites asked God for protection from their enemies, just as other people prayed to their gods to defend them. According to the Hebrew Bible, God looked after the Israelites not so much because of ritual ceremonies and sacrifices but because Abraham had promised to obey him. In return, God had promised to protect Abraham and his descendants. This mutual promise between God and the founder of the Jewish people is called a <u>covenant</u> (KUHV•uh•nuhnt).

▲ In this 14th-century painting, Moses holds a scroll inscribed with the story of God's appearance to Moses and commandment to lead the Israelites out of Egypt.

Moses and the Exodus

The Hebrew Bible says the Israelites migrated to Egypt because of a drought and threat of a famine. At first, the Israelites were given places of honor in the Egyptian kingdom. Later, however, they were forced into slavery.

"Let My People Go" The Israelites fled Egypt—perhaps between 1300 and 1200 B.C. Jews call this event "the Exodus," and they remember it every year during the

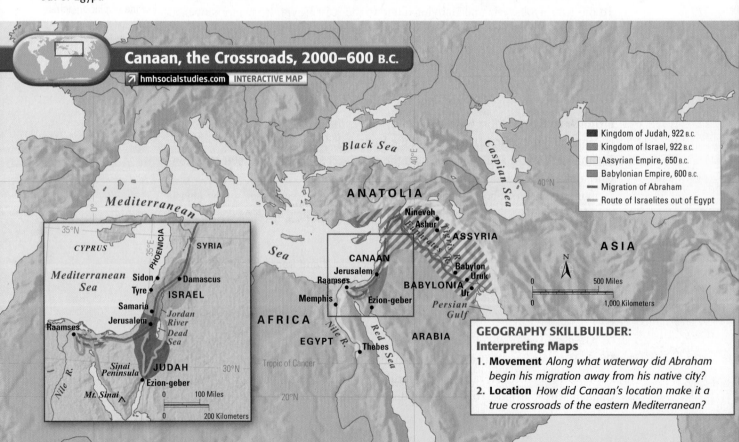

Canaan, the Crossroads, 2000–600 B.C.

hmhsocialstudies.com INTERACTIVE MAP

Kingdom of Judah, 922 B.C.
Kingdom of Israel, 922 B.C.
Assyrian Empire, 650 B.C.
Babylonian Empire, 600 B.C.
— Migration of Abraham
— Route of Israelites out of Egypt

Black Sea

Caspian Sea

ANATOLIA

Nineveh
Ashur

ASSYRIA

ASIA

Mediterranean

Sea

CANAAN
Jerusalem
Raamses

Babylon
Uruk

BABYLONIA
Memphis
Ezion-geber
Ur

AFRICA

Persian
Gulf

0   500 Miles

0   1,000 Kilometers

EGYPT

Nile R.

Red Sea

ARABIA

Thebes

Tropic of Cancer

20°N

GEOGRAPHY SKILLBUILDER:
Interpreting Maps
1. **Movement** *Along what waterway did Abraham begin his migration away from his native city?*
2. **Location** *How did Canaan's location make it a true crossroads of the eastern Mediterranean?*

35°N

CYPRUS
SYRIA

PHOENICIA

Mediterranean
Sea

Sidon
Tyre

Damascus

ISRAEL

Samaria
Jerusalem

Jordan
River
Dead
Sea

Raamses

Sinai
Peninsula

JUDAH

30°N

Ezion-geber

Mt. Sinai

Nile R.

0   100 Miles

0   200 Kilometers

The Ten Commandments

The Ten Commandments are a code of moral laws believed to have been given by God to Moses, which serve as the basis for Jewish law.

PRIMARY SOURCE

1. I the LORD am your God who brought you out of the land of Egypt, the house of bondage.
2. You shall have no other gods beside Me. You shall not make for yourself a sculptured image. . . .
3. You shall not swear falsely by the name of the LORD your God. . . .
4. Observe the sabbath day and keep it holy. . . .
5. Honor your father and your mother. . . .
6. You shall not murder.
7. You shall not commit adultery.
8. You shall not steal.
9. You shall not bear false witness against your neighbor.
10. You shall not covet . . . anything that is your neighbor's.

Deuteronomy 5:6–18

DOCUMENT-BASED QUESTIONS

1. **Comparing** Do the first four commandments concern themselves more with the Jews' relationship with God or with one another?
2. **Contrasting** What do the last six commandments have in common that distinguishes them from the first four?

▲ Tradition dictates that the Torah be written on a scroll and kept at the synagogue in an ornamental chest called an ark.

festival of Passover. The Torah says that the man who led the Israelites out of slavery was **Moses**. It is told that at the time of Moses' birth, the Egyptian pharaoh felt threatened by the number of Israelites in Egypt. He thus ordered all Israelite male babies to be killed. Moses' mother hid her baby in the reeds along the banks of the Nile. There, an Egyptian princess found and adopted him. Though raised in luxury, he did not forget his Israelite birth. When God commanded him to lead the Israelites out of Egypt, he obeyed.

A New Covenant While the Israelites were traveling across the Sinai (SY•ny) Peninsula, Moses climbed to the top of Mount Sinai to pray. The Hebrew Bible says he spoke with God. When Moses came down from Mount Sinai, he brought down two stone tablets on which God had written the Ten Commandments.

These commandments and the other teachings that Moses delivered to his people became the basis for the civil and religious laws of Judaism. The Israelites believed that these laws formed a new covenant between God and the Israelites. God promised to protect them. They promised to keep God's commandments. **A**

The Land and People of the Bible The Torah reports that the Israelites traveled for 40 years in the Sinai Desert. Later books of the Hebrew Bible tell about the history of the Israelites after their migration. After the death of Moses, they returned to Canaan, where Abraham had lived. The Israelites made a change from a nomadic, tribal society to settled herders, farmers, and city dwellers. They learned new technologies from neighboring peoples in ancient Canaan.

MAIN IDEA

Contrasting

A How did the religion of the Israelites differ from many of the religions of their neighbors?

When the Israelites arrived in Canaan, they were loosely organized into twelve tribes. These tribes lived in separate territories and were self-governing. In times of emergency, the Hebrew Bible tells that God would raise up judges. They would unite the tribes and provide judicial and military leadership during a crisis. In the course of time, God chose a series of judges, one of the most prominent of whom was a woman, Deborah.

Israelite Law Deborah's leadership was unusual for an Israelite woman. The roles of men and women were quite separate in most ancient societies. Women could not officiate at religious ceremonies. In general, an Israelite woman's most important duty was to raise her children and provide moral leadership for them.

The Ten Commandments were part of a code of laws delivered to Moses. The code included other rules regulating social and religious behavior. In some ways, this code resembled Hammurabi's Code with its statement "an eye for an eye and a tooth for a tooth." To Jews this meant to pay restitution and emphasize God's mercy. The code was later interpreted by religious teachers called prophets. These interpretations tended to emphasize greater equality before the law than did other codes of the time. The prophets constantly urged the Jews to stay true to their covenant with God.

The prophets taught that the Jews had a duty to worship God and live justly with one another. The goal was a moral life lived in accordance with God's laws. In the words of the prophet Micah, "He has told you, O mortal what is good; and what does the Lord require of you but to do justice, and to love kindness, and to walk humbly with your God?" This emphasis on right conduct and the worship of one God is called ethical monotheism—a Jewish idea that has influenced human behavior for thousands of years through Judaism, Christianity, and Islam. **B**

MAIN IDEA

Summarizing
B What does Jewish law require of believers?

> Analyzing Key Concepts

Judaism

Judaism is the religion of the Jewish people. In Judaism, one of the most important ways for a person to please God is to study the scriptures, or sacred writings, and to live according to what they teach. Many Jews keep a scroll of an important scripture passage in a mezuzah (a holder attached to a doorpost) like the one shown here.

SKILLBUILDER: Interpreting Charts
1. **Contrasting** *What is contained in the Hebrew Bible that is not in the Talmud? What is in the Talmud that is not in the Hebrew Bible?*
2. **Hypothesizing** *What kind of poetry would you expect to find in the Hebrew Bible? Explain what you think the subjects or themes of the poems might be.*

The Sacred Writings of Judaism

Sacred Writings	Contents
Hebrew Bible	**Torah** • first five books of the Bible • recounts origins of humanity and Judaism • contains basic laws of Judaism **Prophets** • stories about and writings by Jewish teachers • divided into Former Prophets and Latter Prophets • recounts Jewish history and calls for justice, kindness, right conduct, and faithfulness to God **Writings** • a collection of various other writings • includes psalms, poetry, history and stories, proverbs, and philosophical writings called wisdom literature
Talmud	**Mishnah** • written record of Jewish oral law **Gemara** • explanations and interpretations of the Mishnah

The Kingdom of Israel

Canaan—the land that the Israelites believed had been promised them by God—combined largely harsh features such as arid desert, rocky wilderness, grassy hills, and the dry, hot valley of the Jordan River. Water was never plentiful; even the numerous limestone formations soaked up any excess rainfall. After first settling in the south-central area of ancient Canaan, the Israelites expanded south and north.

Saul and David Establish a Kingdom The judges occasionally pulled together the widely scattered tribes for a united military effort. Nonetheless, the Philistines, another people in the area, threatened the Israelites' position in ancient Canaan. The Israelites got along somewhat better with their Canaanite neighbors.

From about 1020 to 922 B.C., the Israelites united under three able kings: Saul, David, and Solomon. The new kingdom was called **Israel** (IHZ•ree•uhl). For 100 years, Israel enjoyed its greatest period of power and independence.

Saul, the first of the three kings, was chosen largely because of his success in driving out the Philistines from the central hills. Saul is portrayed in the Hebrew Bible as a tragic man, who was given to bouts of jealousy. After his death, he was succeeded by his son-in-law, David. King David, an extremely popular leader, united the tribes, established Jerusalem as the capital, and founded a dynasty.

Solomon Builds the Kingdom About the year 962 B.C., David was succeeded by his son Solomon, whose mother was Bathsheba. Solomon was the most powerful of the Israelite kings. He built a trading empire with the help of his friend Hiram, the king of the Phoenician city of Tyre. Solomon also beautified the capital city of Jerusalem. The crowning achievement of his extensive building program in Jerusalem was a great temple, which he built to glorify God. The temple was also a permanent home for the Ark of the Covenant, which contained the tablets of Moses' law.

The temple that Solomon built was not large, but it gleamed like a precious gem. Bronze pillars stood at the temple's entrance. The temple was stone on the outside, while its inner walls were made of cedar covered in gold. The main hall was richly decorated with brass and gold. Solomon also built a royal palace even more costly and more magnificent than the temple.

The Kingdom Divides Solomon's building projects required high taxes and badly strained the kingdom's finances. In addition, men were drafted to spend one month out of every three working on the temple. The expense and labor requirement caused much discontent. As a result, after Solomon's death, the Jews in the northern part of the kingdom, which was located far from the south, revolted. By 922 B.C., the kingdom had divided in two. Israel was in the north and **Judah** (JOO•duh) was in the south. Eventually, the northern kingdom was destroyed and only the kingdom of Judah remained. As a result, the Israelites came to be called Jews, and their religion, *Judaism*. **C**

MAIN IDEA

Drawing Conclusions

C How might geographical distance make the split of Israel and Judah more likely?

VIDEO
King Solomon

↗ hmhsocialstudies.com

History Makers

King Solomon
962?–922? B.C.

In the Bible, Solomon prays to God for "an understanding mind," which God grants him.

Soon after, the story goes, two women and a baby boy were brought before him. Each woman claimed the baby was hers. After hearing their testimony, Solomon declared, "Divide the living boy in two; then give half to the one and half to the other."

One said: "Please, my lord, give her the living boy; certainly do not kill him!" However, the other woman accepted: "It shall be neither mine nor yours; divide it."

Solomon knew that the woman who would give up the child to save it was the real mother.

↗ hmhsocialstudies.com

RESEARCH WEB LINKS Go online for more on King Solomon.

The next 200 years were a time of upheaval for the two kingdoms of Israel and Judah. Sometimes they fought each other; sometimes they joined together to fight common enemies. Each of the kingdoms had periods of prosperity, followed by low periods of conflict and decline.

The Babylonian Captivity

Disaster finally struck as the two kingdoms lost their independence. In 738 B.C., both Israel and Judah began paying **tribute**—peace money paid by a weaker power to a stronger—to Assyria. By paying tribute, Israel and Judah hoped to ensure that the mighty Assyrian empire would not attack. But Israel revolted and withheld tribute and in 725 B.C. the Assyrians began a relentless siege of Samaria, the capital of Israel. By 722 B.C., the whole northern kingdom had fallen to the Assyrians' ferocious assault.

The southern kingdom of Judah resisted for another 150 years before it too was destroyed. The destruction of Judah was to come at the hands of the Babylonians. After conquering Israel, the Assyrians rapidly lost power to a rising Babylonian empire. The great Babylonian king Nebuchadnezzar (nehb•uh•kuhd•NEHZ•uhr) ran the Egyptians out of Syria and Judah, and he twice attacked Jerusalem. The city finally fell in 586 B.C. Solomon's temple was destroyed in the Babylonian victory. Many of the survivors were exiled to Babylon. During the exile in Babylon, the Hebrew Bible describes how the prophet Ezekiel urged his people to keep their religion alive in a foreign land.

Then about 50 years after the fall of Judah, another change in fortune occurred: in 539 B.C., the Persian king Cyrus the Great conquered Babylon. The next year, Cyrus allowed some 40,000 exiles to return to Jerusalem to rebuild the temple. Many, however, stayed in Babylonia.

Work on the second temple was completed in 515 B.C. The walls of Jerusalem were rebuilt in 445 B.C. Soon, however, other empires dominated the region—first the Persians, then the Greeks, and then the Romans. These new empires would take control both of Judah, now called Judea, and of the destiny of the Jewish people. **D**

> **MAIN IDEA**
>
> **Making Inferences**
>
> **D** The temple was rebuilt before the walls of Jerusalem. What does this fact indicate about the Jews after the Babylonian captivity?

SECTION 4 ASSESSMENT

TERMS & NAMES 1. For each term or name, write a sentence explaining its significance.
• Canaan • Torah • Abraham • monotheism • covenant • Moses • Israel • Judah • tribute

USING YOUR NOTES

2. Which of these leaders do you think was the most important? Why?

2000 B.C.

Abraham: father of Jewish people

MAIN IDEAS

3. Where did Abraham and his family originally come from?

4. What were some of the achievements of Solomon?

5. What was the Babylonian Captivity?

CRITICAL THINKING & WRITING

6. DEVELOPING HISTORICAL PERSPECTIVE What were the main problems faced by the Israelites between 1800 B.C. and 700 B.C.?

7. ANALYZING ISSUES What were some of the factors that made Canaan a good place for the Israelites to settle?

8. COMPARING In what ways are the laws delivered to Moses similar to Hammurabi's Code?

9. WRITING ACTIVITY | RELIGIOUS AND ETHICAL SYSTEMS | What might have been the advantages of monotheism? Write a **paragraph** in which you support your opinions.

CONNECT TO TODAY CREATING A PIE GRAPH

What are some of the important monotheistic religions in the world today? Create a **pie graph** in which you show the relative size of various monotheistic religions.

↗ hmhsocialstudies.com INTERACTIVE

The Flood Story

The tale of a devastating flood appears among the legends of ancient peoples throughout the world. In some versions, the story of the flood serves to explain how the world came to be. In others, the flood is heaven's punishment for evil deeds committed by humans.

A PRIMARY SOURCE

The Torah

Only one man, Noah, found favor in God's eyes.

———

God said to Noah, "I have decided to put an end to all flesh, for the earth is filled with lawlessness because of them. . . . Make yourself an ark of gopher wood. . . . And of all that lives, of all flesh, you shall take two of each into the ark . . .; they shall be male and female."

The rain fell on the earth forty days and forty nights. . . . At the end of forty days, Noah opened the window of the ark . . . and . . . sent out the dove. . . . The dove came back to him . . . and there in its bill was a plucked-off olive leaf! Then Noah knew that the waters had decreased on the earth. . . .

God spoke to Noah, saying "Come out of the ark. . . . Bring out with you every living thing of all flesh that is with you. . . . I now establish My covenant with you . . . never again shall there be a flood to destroy the earth. . . . I have set My [rain]bow in the clouds . . . as a sign of the covenant."

B PRIMARY SOURCE

The Epic of Gilgamesh

In this Mesopotamian legend, Utnapishtim, like Noah, escapes a worldwide flood by building an ark. Ea, the god of wisdom, warns Utnapishtim of the coming catastrophe in a dream.

———

O man of Shurrupak, son of Ubara-Tutu; tear down your house and build a boat, abandon possessions and look for life. . . .

I loaded into [the boat] all that I had of gold and of living things, my family, my kin, the beast of the field both wild and tame. . . .

For six days and six nights the winds blew, torrent and tempest and flood overwhelmed the world. . . . When the seventh day dawned the storm from the south subsided, the sea grew calm, the flood was stilled; I looked at the face of the world and there was silence, all mankind was turned to clay. . . . I opened a hatch and the light fell on my face. Then I bowed low, I sat down and I wept, the tears streamed down my face, for on every side was the waste of water.

C PRIMARY SOURCE

The Fish Incarnation of Vishnu

The Hindu god Vishnu, in his first earthly incarnation, took the form of Matsya, the fish, and saved humankind.

———

One day, as the sage Manu was praying at the river Ganges, a small fish asked for his protection. Manu put the fish in an earthen jar, but soon the fish was too big for the jar. So Manu put it into the river, but soon it outgrew the river. So Manu put the fish in the ocean. . . .

The fish told Manu there would be a great deluge [flood]. He advised Manu to build a large boat and take . . . the seeds of various kinds of plants, and one of each type of animal. When the deluge came, the fish said, he would take the ark . . . to safety.

Sure enough, when the deluge occurred, the fish was there. Manu tied the boat to the horns of the fish. . . . The fish then pulled the boat through the waters until it reached a mountain peak.

D PRIMARY SOURCE

Anonymous

This art dates from the fifth century A.D. It shows Noah and his ark in the Jewish flood story. In the picture, Noah is welcoming back the dove he had sent out from the ark at the end of 40 days. The dove is carrying in its beak an olive leaf.

Document-Based QUESTIONS

1. Based on Source A, what promise does God make to mankind?

2. What are some of the differences among the gods in Sources A, B, and C?

3. What are some of the similarities among the flood stories in Sources A, B, and C?

4. In Source D, what is the dove bringing to Noah and what might it represent?

TERMS & NAMES

For each term or name below, briefly explain its importance in the years 3500 B.C. to 259 B.C.

1. Indo-Europeans
2. caste
3. reincarnation
4. Siddhartha Gautama
5. Minoans
6. Phoenicians
7. monotheism
8. Moses

MAIN IDEAS

The Indo-Europeans Section 1 (pages 61–65)

9. What are three reasons that historians give to explain why Indo-Europeans migrated?
10. What are two technologies that helped the Hittites build their empire?
11. How were the Aryans different from the non-Aryans (*dasas*) that they encountered when migrating to India?

Hinduism and Buddhism Develop Section 2 (pages 66–71)

12. In Hinduism, how are the ideas of karma, reincarnation, and *moksha* connected?
13. Why were lower castes more likely to convert to Buddhism?

Seafaring Traders Section 3 (pages 72–76)

14. What did the Minoans export?
15. What is Phoenicia's greatest legacy to the world?

The Origins of Judaism Section 4 (pages 77–83)

16. What is ethical monotheism and why is it important?
17. What were some of the achievements of David?
18. What are two ways in which early Judaism differed from other religions of the time?

CRITICAL THINKING

1. USING YOUR NOTES

RELIGIOUS AND ETHICAL SYSTEMS In a chart, fill in information about three world religions.

Religion	Founder	Time Originated	Area Originated
Hinduism			
Buddhism			
Judaism			

2. DRAWING CONCLUSIONS

INTERACTION WITH ENVIRONMENT How important were the migrations of the Indo-European peoples? How lasting were the changes that they brought? Explain your conclusion.

3. RECOGNIZING EFFECTS

What were some of the effects of King Solomon's reign?

4. COMPARING

ECONOMICS How were the economic foundations of Minoan and Phoenician civilizations similar?

5. DEVELOPING HISTORICAL PERSPECTIVE

Why was monotheism unusual in its time and place?

VISUAL SUMMARY

Three Major Religions

	Hinduism	Buddhism	Judaism
Number of Gods	Many gods, all faces of Brahman	Originally, no gods	One God
Holy Books	Vedas; Upanishads, *Mahabharata*, and others	Books on the teachings and life of the Buddha	The Torah and other books of the Hebrew Bible
Moral Law	Karma	Eightfold Path	Ten Commandments
Leaders	Brahmins	Monks	Priests, judges, kings, prophets
Final Goal	*Moksha*	Enlightenment, Nirvana	A moral life through obedience to God's law

The following passage tells how the Israelites asked the prophet Samuel to appoint their king. Use the quotation and your knowledge of world history to answer questions 1 and 2.

PRIMARY SOURCE

Then all the elders of Israel gathered together and came to Samuel at Ramah, and said to him, ". . . appoint for us, then, a king to govern us, like other nations." . . . Samuel prayed to the Lord, and the Lord said to Samuel, "Listen to the voice of the people in all that they say to you; for they have not rejected you, but they have rejected me from being king over them. Just as they have done to me, . . . so also they are doing to you. Heed their demand, but warn them solemnly."

1 SAMUEL 8:4–8

1. What seems to be the Lord's reaction to the Israelites' demand for a king?

A. approval   **C.** indifference

B. disapproval   **D.** amusement

2. Who does this passage say was Israel's real king?

A. Samuel   **C.** Moses

B. The Lord   **D.** Solomon

Use the statue of a Hittite god and your knowledge of world history to answer question 3.

3. What does the fact that this statue is made of gold tell you about how the owner viewed it?

A. trivial   **C.** worthless

B. valuable   **D.** disposable

 hmhsocialstudies.com   TEST PRACTICE

For additional test practice, go online for:

• Diagnostic tests

• Strategies

• Tutorials

Interact *with* History

On page 60, you considered leaving your homeland before you knew what some of the consequences of your decision might be. Now that you've read the chapter, reconsider your decision. Would you still make the same choice, or have you changed your mind? Discuss the consequences of your decision on your life.

FOCUS ON WRITING

Write an **expository essay** describing how ironworking helped the Aryans to carry out their migrations to India, as well as their conquering and settling of territory.

Consider the effect of ironworking technology on the following:

• weapons and tools

• transportation

• conquest

• settlement

MULTIMEDIA ACTIVITY

Participating in a WebQuest

Introduction You are a member of a special committee commissioned by the Indian government to abolish the caste system.

Task Create an electronic presentation of the issues you had to consider and the problems you faced in abolishing the caste system.

Process and Procedures Assume the role of one of these committee members—religious leader, economist, historian, sociologist—to research Indian society and to present the issues. Use this chapter and the Internet as resources for your research.

Evaluation and Conclusion The caste system was officially abolished by the Indian government in 1955. How did this project contribute to your understanding of the caste system? What additional information would you like to know?

First Age of Empires,
1570 B.C.–200 B.C.

Essential Question

How did the first large empires in Africa and Asia develop between 1570 B.C. and 200 B.C.?

 What You Will Learn

In this chapter you will learn about the development of the early empires in Egypt, Nubia, Assyria, Persia, and China.

SECTION 1 The Egyptian and Nubian Empires
Main Idea Two empires along the Nile, Egypt and Nubia, forged commercial, cultural, and political connections.

SECTION 2 The Assyrian Empire
Main Idea Assyria developed a military machine and established a well-organized administration.

SECTION 3 The Persian Empire
Main Idea By governing with tolerance and wisdom, the Persians established a well-ordered empire that lasted for 200 years.

SECTION 4 The Unification of China
Main Idea The social disorder of the warring states contributed to the development of three Chinese ethical systems.

Previewing Themes

EMPIRE BUILDING Groups from Africa to China sought to conquer other groups and spread their influence across vast regions. These societies built the world's first great empires.

Geography *On the map, locate the Nile, Tigris, and Euphrates rivers, where many of the early empires arose. Why do you think the empire builders fought over these regions?*

CULTURAL INTERACTION For a long period, Egypt ruled Kush and the two cultures interacted. When the Kush Empire conquered Egypt, therefore, the Kushites adopted many Egyptian cultural values and ideas.

Geography *Study the map and time line. What other cultures might have adopted Egyptian values?*

RELIGIOUS AND ETHICAL SYSTEMS After the warring states period, Chinese philosophers developed different ethical systems to restore China's social order.

Geography *How might China's location have affected the spread of the ethical systems that began there?*

AFRICA, SOUTHWEST ASIA, CHINA

1570 B.C.
Egypt's New Kingdom is established. (temple at Karnak built during era) ▶

1570 B.C. • **1000 B.C.**

WORLD

1500 B.C.
◀ Mycenaean culture thrives on the Greek mainland. (gold death mask of a Mycenaean king)

1200 B.C.
Minoan civilization mysteriously ends.

Ancient Empires, 700 B.C.–221 B.C.

EUROPE

Black Sea

Caspian Sea

GOBI DESERT

ASIA

Huang He

Sardis

Nineveh

Tigris R.

Euphrates R.

Mediterranean Sea

LOWER EGYPT

JUDAH

Babylon

Sinai Peninsula

Ch'ang-an (Xi'an)

Yellow Sea

East China Sea

30°N

UPPER EGYPT

Persepolis

Indus River

Brahmaputra River

HIMALAYAS

Ganges River

Chang Jiang

Karnak

Thebes

Nile River

Persian Gulf

Abu Simbel

Napata

Red Sea

ARABIAN PENINSULA

Meroë

Arabian Sea

HISTORY

Ramses' Egyptian Empire

↗ hmhsocialstudies.com VIDEO

AFRICA

INDIAN OCEAN

N

W ✦ E

S

0   500   1000 Miles

0   500   1000 Kilometers

Hyperelliptical Projection

45°E   60°E   75°E   105°E

■	Kush Empire, 700 B.C.
▬	Assyrian Empire, 650 B.C.
■	Persian Empire, 500 B.C.
■	Qin Dynasty, 221 B.C.

850 B.C.
Assyrian Empire begins its rise to power.

751 B.C.
Nubian kingdom of Kush conquers Egypt. (Nubian pottery) ▶

550 B.C.
Persian Empire flourishes.

202 B.C.
The Qin Dynasty collapses. Civil war follows.

500 B.C.

200 B.C.

750 B.C.
Greek city-states begin colonization.

509 B.C.
Rome becomes a republic.

334 B.C.
Alexander starts to build his empire. ▶

How will the empire help you or harm you?

As a merchant traveling with your camel caravan, your life has become increasingly difficult. Bandits and thieves roam the roads, attacking traders like you. A new military empire is advancing through your region, putting down the outlaw bands. However, the military empire is also imposing harsh laws and heavy taxes on the regions it conquers.

Armed guards from the new empire battle bandits who were planning to attack the caravan, which carries a fortune in exotic goods.

Merchants traveling in caravans, such as this one, cross the Fertile Crescent and travel the Silk Roads from China.

An armed cavalry escort protects the caravan, bringing a new sense of order and safety to merchants and travelers.

EXAMINING *the* ISSUES

- Why might a merchant welcome the expansion of a strong empire?
- How might the empire oppress the region?

In small groups, answer the questions, then report back to the class. In your discussion, remember what you've learned about military conquest and the behavior of such groups as the Sumerians, Egyptians, and Hittites. As you read about the empires in this chapter, consider how the winners treat the people under their power and how the conquered people respond.

The Egyptian and Nubian Empires

MAIN IDEA	WHY IT MATTERS NOW	TERMS & NAMES
CULTURAL INTERACTION Two empires along the Nile, Egypt and Nubia, forged commercial, cultural, and political connections.	Neighboring civilizations today participate in cultural exchange as well as conflict.	• Hyksos • New Kingdom • Hatshepsut • Thutmose III • Nubia • Ramses II • Kush • Piankhi • Meroë

SETTING THE STAGE As you learned in Chapter 2, Egyptian civilization developed along the Nile River and united into a kingdom around 3100 B.C. During the Middle Kingdom (about 2080–1640 B.C.), trade with Mesopotamia and the Indus Valley enriched Egypt. Meanwhile, up the Nile River, less than 600 miles south of the Egyptian city of Thebes, a major kingdom had developed in the region of Nubia. For centuries, the Nubian kingdom of Kush traded with Egypt. The two kingdoms particularly influenced each other culturally.

Nomadic Invaders Rule Egypt

After the prosperity of the Middle Kingdom, Egypt descended into war and violence. This was caused by a succession of weak pharaohs and power struggles among rival nobles. The weakened country fell to invaders who swept across the Isthmus of Suez in chariots, a weapon of war unknown to the Egyptians. These Asiatic invaders, called **Hyksos** (HIHK•sohs), ruled Egypt from about 1640 to 1570 B.C. The Hyksos invasion shook the Egyptians' confidence in the desert barriers that had protected their kingdom.

hmhsocialstudies.com
TAKING NOTES
Use the graphic organizer online to take notes on important events in the history of Egypt and Nubia.

Israelites Migrate to Egypt Some historians believe that another Asiatic group, the Israelites, settled in Egypt during the rule of the Hyksos. According to the Hebrew Bible, Abraham and his family first crossed the Euphrates River and came to Canaan around 1800 B.C. Then, around 1650 B.C., the descendants of Abraham moved again—this time to Egypt. Some historians believe that the Hyksos encouraged the Israelites to settle there because the two groups were racially similar. The Egyptians resented the presence of the Hyksos in their land but were powerless to remove them.

Expulsion and Slavery Around 1600 B.C., a series of warlike rulers began to restore Egypt's power. Among those who helped drive out the Hyksos was Queen Ahhotep (ah•HOH•tehp). She took over when her husband was killed in battle. The next pharaoh, Kamose (KAH•mohs), won a great victory over the hated Hyksos. His successors drove the Hyksos completely out of Egypt and pursued them across the Sinai Peninsula into Canaan. According to some Biblical scholars, the Israelites remained in Egypt and were enslaved and forced into hard labor. They would not leave Egypt until sometime between 1500 and 1200 B.C., the time of the Exodus.

The New Kingdom of Egypt

After overthrowing the Hyksos, the pharaohs of the **New Kingdom** (about 1570–1075 B.C.) sought to strengthen Egypt by building an empire. As you may recall, an empire brings together several peoples or states under the control of one ruler. Egypt entered its third period of glory during the New Kingdom era. During this time, it was wealthier and more powerful than ever before.

Equipped with bronze weapons and two-wheeled chariots, the Egyptians became conquerors. The pharaohs of the 18th Dynasty (about 1570–1365 B.C.) set up an army including archers, charioteers, and infantry, or foot soldiers.

Vocabulary
A *dynasty* is a series of rulers from a single family.

Hatshepsut's Prosperous Rule Among the rulers of the New Kingdom, **Hatshepsut** (hat•SHEHP•soot), who declared herself pharaoh around 1472 B.C., was unique. She took over because her stepson, the male heir to the throne, was a young child at the time. Unlike other New Kingdom rulers, Hatshepsut spent her reign encouraging trade rather than just waging war.

The trading expedition Hatshepsut ordered to the Land of Punt (poont), near present-day Somalia, was particularly successful. Hatshepsut sent a fleet of five ships down the Red Sea to Punt in search of myrrh, frankincense, and fragrant ointments used for religious ceremonies and in cosmetics. In addition to these goods, Hatshepsut's fleet brought back gold, ivory, and unusual plants and animals.

Thutmose the Empire Builder Hatshepsut's stepson, **Thutmose III** (thoot•MOH•suh), proved to be a much more warlike ruler. In his eagerness to ascend to the throne, Thutmose III may even have murdered Hatshepsut. Between the time he took power and his death around 1425 B.C., Thutmose III led a number of victorious invasions eastward into Canaan and Syria. His armies also pushed farther south into **Nubia**, a region of Africa that straddled the upper Nile River. Egypt had traded with Nubia and influenced the region since the time of the Middle Kingdom.

Egypt was now a mighty empire. It controlled lands around the Nile and far beyond. In addition, it drew boundless wealth from them. Contact with other cultures brought Egypt new ideas as well as material goods. Egypt had never before—nor has it since—commanded such power and wealth as during the reigns of the New Kingdom pharaohs.

The Egyptians and the Hittites The Egyptians' conquest of parts of Syria and Canaan around 1400 B.C. brought them into conflict with the Hittites. The Hittites had moved into Asia Minor around 1900 B.C. and later expanded southward into Canaan.

After several smaller battles, the Egyptians and Hittites clashed at Kadesh around 1285 B.C. The pharaoh **Ramses II** (RAM•seez) and a Hittite king later made a treaty that promised "peace and brotherhood between us forever." Their alliance lasted for the rest of the century. **A**

An Age of Builders Like the rulers of the Old Kingdom, who built the towering pyramids, rulers of the New Kingdom

History Makers

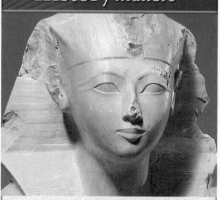

Hatshepsut
reigned 1472–1458 B.C.

Hatshepsut was an excellent ruler of outstanding achievement who made Egypt more prosperous. As male pharaohs had done, Hatshepsut planned a tomb for herself in the Valley of the Kings. Carved reliefs on the walls of the temple reveal the glories of her reign.

The inscription from Hatshepsut's obelisk at Karnak trumpets her glory and her feelings about herself:

I swear as Re loves me, as my father Amon favors me, as my nostrils are filled with satisfying life, as I wear the white crown, as I appear in the red crown, . . . as I rule this land like the son of Isis.

⬈ **hmhsocialstudies.com**

INTERNET ACTIVITY Go online to create a photo exhibit on the trading expeditions to Punt ordered by Hatshepsut. Include pictures of murals of goods collected.

MAIN IDEA

Recognizing Effects
A What were some of the political and economic effects of Egypt's conquests?

erected grand buildings. In search of security in the afterlife—and protection from grave robbers—they hid their splendid tombs beneath desert cliffs. The site they chose was the remote Valley of the Kings near Thebes. Besides royal tombs, the pharaohs of this period also built great palaces and magnificent temples. Indeed, the royal title *pharaoh* means "great house" and comes from this time period.

Ramses II, whose reign extended from approximately 1290 to 1224 B.C., stood out among the great builders of the New Kingdom. At Karnak, he added to a monumental temple to Amon-Re (AH•muhn•RAY), Egypt's chief god. Ramses also ordered a temple to be carved into the red sandstone cliffs above the Nile River at Abu Simbel (AH•boo SIHM•buhl). He had these temples decorated with enormous statues of himself. The ears of these statues alone measured more than three feet.

▲ Four statues of Ramses II guarded the entrance to the Great Temple at Abu Simbel.

The Empire Declines

The empire that Thutmose III had built and Ramses II had ruled slowly came apart after 1200 B.C. as other strong civilizations rose to challenge Egypt's power. Shortly after Ramses died, the entire eastern Mediterranean suffered a wave of invasions.

Invasions by Land and Sea Both the Egyptian empire and the Hittite kingdom were attacked by invaders called the "Sea Peoples" in Egyptian texts. These invaders may have included the Philistines, who are often mentioned in the Hebrew Bible. Whoever they were, the Sea Peoples caused great destruction.

The Egyptians faced other attacks. In the east, the tribes of Canaan often rebelled against their Egyptian overlords. In the west, the vast desert no longer served as a barrier against Libyan raids on Egyptian villages.

Egypt's Empire Fades After these invasions, Egypt never recovered its previous power. The Egyptian empire broke apart into regional units, and numerous small kingdoms arose. Each was eager to protect its independence.

Almost powerless, Egypt soon fell to its neighbors' invasions. Eventually, Libyans crossed the desert to the Nile Delta. There they established independent dynasties. From around 950 to 730 B.C., Libyan pharaohs ruled Egypt and erected cities.

But instead of imposing their own culture, the Libyans adopted Egypt's. When the Nubians came north to seize power, they too adopted Egyptian culture.

The Kushites Conquer the Nile Region

hmhsocialstudies.com

INTERACTIVE MAP

Explore the cataracts and fertile banks of the Nile Valley.

For centuries, Egypt dominated Nubia and the Nubian kingdom of **Kush**, which lasted for about a thousand years, between 2000 and 1000 B.C. During this time, Egyptian armies raided and even occupied Kush for a brief period. But as Egypt fell into decline during the Hyksos period, Kush began to emerge as a regional power. Nubia now established its own Kushite dynasty on the throne of Egypt.

The People of Nubia Nubia lay south of Egypt between the first cataract of the Nile, an area of churning rapids, and the division of the river into the Blue Nile and the White Nile. Despite several cataracts around which boats had to be carried, the Nile provided the best north-south trade route. Several Nubian kingdoms, including Kush, served as a trade corridor. They linked Egypt and the Mediterranean world to the interior of Africa and to the Red Sea. Goods and ideas flowed back and forth along the river for centuries. The first Nubian kingdom, Kerma, arose shortly after 2000 B.C.

The Interaction of Egypt and Nubia With Egypt's revival during the New Kingdom, pharaohs forced Egyptian rule on Kush. Egyptian governors, priests, soldiers, and artists strongly influenced the Nubians. Indeed, Kush's capital, Napata, became the center for the spread of Egyptian culture to Kush's other African trading partners.

History *in* Depth

Egyptian Influence on Nubian Culture

Nubia was heavily influenced by Egypt. This influence is particularly apparent in Nubian religious practices and burial traditions. But even though the Nubians adopted Egyptian ways, they didn't abandon their cultural identity. In many of these religious and funeral practices, the Nubians blended Egyptian customs with their own traditions.

Pyramids Unlike the Egyptian pyramids, the pyramids of Nubia had steeply sloping sides and were probably designed with a flat top.

Temples This stone ram, representing the Egyptian god Amen, lay at the entrance to a Nubian temple dedicated to that god. Although the Nubians worshiped many Egyptian gods, Amen's temple was located near another dedicated to Apedemak, a Nubian god.

Kushite princes went to Egypt. They learned the Egyptian language and worshiped Egyptian gods. They adopted the customs and clothing styles of the Egyptian upper class. When they returned home, the Kushite nobles brought back royal rituals and hieroglyphic writing.

With Egypt's decline, beginning about 1200 B.C., Kush regained its independence. The Kushites viewed themselves as more suitable guardians of Egyptian values than the Libyans. They sought to guard these values by conquering Egypt and ousting its Libyan rulers. **B**

Piankhi Captures the Egyptian Throne In 751 B.C., a Kushite king named <u>Piankhi</u> overthrew the Libyan dynasty that had ruled Egypt for over 200 years. He united the entire Nile Valley from the delta in the north to Napata in the south. Piankhi and his descendants became Egypt's 25th Dynasty. After his victory, Piankhi erected a monument in his homeland of Kush. On the monument, he had words inscribed that celebrated his victory. The inscription provided a catalog of the riches of the north:

MAIN IDEA

Making Inferences

B Why might the Kushites have viewed themselves as guardians of Egyptian values?

PRIMARY SOURCE

Then the ships were laden with silver, gold, copper, clothing, and everything of the Northland, every product of Syria and all sweet woods of God's-Land. His Majesty sailed upstream [south], with glad heart, the shores on his either side were jubilating. West and east were jubilating in the presence of His Majesty.

PIANKHI, monument in Cairo Museum

Statues These figurines represented Nubian slaves. They were buried with Nubian kings and meant to serve them in death. The figurines reflect traditional Egyptian style. The human faces, however, reveal Nubian features.

Kush Empire, 700 B.C.

Mediterranean Sea

LOWER EGYPT — Memphis
UPPER EGYPT
Thebes

ARABIAN DESERT

WESTERN DESERT

Nile River

Red Sea

Tropic of Cancer

NUBIA

Napata

Meroë

White Nile
Blue Nile

Kush Empire (at its greatest extent)
Egyptian Empire (at its greatest extent)
cataract

N

0   500 Miles
0   1,000 Kilometers

SKILLBUILDER: Interpreting Visual Sources
Forming Opinions Why did the Nubians combine Egyptian culture with elements of their own culture?

However, Piankhi's dynasty proved short-lived. In 671 B.C., the Assyrians, a war-like people from Southwest Asia, conquered Egypt. The Kushites fought bravely, but they were forced to retreat south along the Nile. There the Kushites would experience a golden age, despite their loss of Egypt.

The Golden Age of Meroë

After their defeat by the Assyrians, the Kushite royal family eventually moved south to **Meroë** (MEHR•oh•EE). Meroë lay closer to the Red Sea than Napata did, and so became active in the flourishing trade among Africa, Arabia, and India. (See the map on page 93.)

◄ This ring, bearing the head of a Kushite guardian god, was found inside a Meroë queen's pyramid. It dates from the late first century B.C.

The Wealth of Kush Kush used the natural resources around Meroë and thrived for several hundred years. Unlike Egyptian cities along the Nile, Meroë enjoyed significant rainfall. And, unlike Egypt, Meroë boasted abundant supplies of iron ore. As a result, Meroë became a major center for the manufacture of iron weapons and tools.

In Meroë, ambitious merchants loaded iron bars, tools, and spearheads onto their donkeys. They then transported the goods to the Red Sea, where they exchanged these goods for jewelry, fine cotton cloth, silver lamps, and glass bottles. As the mineral wealth of the central Nile Valley flowed out of Meroë, luxury goods from India and Arabia flowed in.

The Decline of Meroë After four centuries of prosperity, from about 250 B.C. to A.D. 150, Meroë began to decline. Aksum, another kingdom located 400 miles to the southeast, contributed to Meroë's fall. With a seaport on the Red Sea, Aksum came to dominate North African trade. Aksum defeated Meroë around A.D. 350.

Centuries earlier, around the time the Kushite pharaoh sat on the Egyptian throne, a new empire—Assyria—had risen in the north. Like Kush, Assyria came to dominate Egypt.

SECTION 1 ASSESSMENT

TERMS & NAMES 1. For each term or name, write a sentence explaining its significance.
• Hyksos • New Kingdom • Hatshepsut • Thutmose III • Nubia • Ramses II • Kush • Piankhi • Meroë

USING YOUR NOTES

2. Which empire was invaded more often? Why?

1570 B.C.   A.D. 350

Egyptian New Kingdom established   Aksum defeats Meroë

MAIN IDEAS

3. How did the New Kingdom of Egypt become so powerful and wealthy?

4. What cultural aspects of Egyptian civilization did the Kushites adopt?

5. Why was Kush able to thrive after losing Egypt to the Assyrians?

CRITICAL THINKING & WRITING

6. **DRAWING CONCLUSIONS** What role did geography play in Egypt's rise and fall?

7. **MAKING INFERENCES** How did trade help both Egypt and Nubia maintain their dominance in the Nile region?

8. **HYPOTHESIZING** What might have happened if the Kushites had imposed their own culture on Egypt?

9. **WRITING ACTIVITY** [CULTURAL INTERACTION] How did Egypt and Nubia strengthen each other at various times in their histories? Support your ideas in a one-paragraph **analysis**.

CONNECT TO TODAY CREATING A TIME LINE

Research to learn about the collapse of the Soviet Union—a modern-day empire—in 1991.
Create a **time line** of the events that led to the collapse.

The Assyrian Empire

MAIN IDEA	WHY IT MATTERS NOW	TERMS & NAMES
EMPIRE BUILDING Assyria developed a military machine and established a well-organized administration.	Some leaders still use military force to extend their rule, stamp out opposition, and gain wealth and power.	• Assyria • Medes • Sennacherib • Chaldeans • Nineveh • Nebuchadnezzar • Ashurbanipal

SETTING THE STAGE For more than two centuries, the Assyrian army advanced across Southwest Asia. It overwhelmed foes with its military strength. After the Assyrians seized control of Egypt, the Assyrian king Esarhaddon proclaimed, "I tore up the root of Kush, and not one therein escaped to submit to me." The last Kushite pharaoh retreated to Napata, Kush's capital city.

A Mighty Military Machine

Beginning around 850 B.C., **Assyria** (uh•SEER•ee•uh) acquired a large empire. It accomplished this by means of a highly advanced military organization and state-of-the-art weaponry. For a time, this campaign of conquest made Assyria the greatest power in Southwest Asia.

hmhsocialstudies.com
TAKING NOTES
Use the graphic organizer online to take notes on the causes of the rise and decline of Assyrian power.

The Rise of a Warrior People The Assyrians came from the northern part of Mesopotamia. (See the map on page 96.) Their flat, exposed land made them easy for other people to attack. Invaders frequently swept down into Assyria from the nearby mountains. The Assyrians may have developed their warlike behavior in response to these invasions. Through constant warfare, Assyrian kings eventually built an empire that stretched from east and north of the Tigris River all the way to central Egypt. One of these Assyrian kings, **Sennacherib** (sih•NAK•uhr•ihb), bragged that he had destroyed 89 cities and 820 villages, burned Babylon, and ordered most of its inhabitants killed.

Military Organization and Conquest Assyria was a society that glorified military strength. Its soldiers were well equipped for conquering an empire. Making use of the ironworking technology of the time, the soldiers covered themselves in stiff leather and metal armor. They wore copper or iron helmets, padded loincloths, and leather skirts layered with metal scales. Their weapons were iron swords and iron-pointed spears.

Advance planning and technical skill allowed the Assyrians to lay siege to enemy cities. When deep water blocked their passage, engineers would span the rivers with pontoons, or floating structures used to support a bridge. Before attacking, the Assyrians dug beneath the city's walls to weaken them. Then, with disciplined organization, foot soldiers marched shoulder to shoulder. The foot soldiers approached the city walls and shot wave upon wave of arrows. Meanwhile, another group of troops hammered the city's gates with massive, iron-tipped battering rams.

Assyrian Empire, 650 B.C.

Black Sea

ANATOLIA

TAURUS MTS.

CYPRUS

SYRIA

Nineveh

Ashur

Medes

MESOPOTAMIA

Caspian Sea

PHOENICIA • Sidon

Mediterranean Sea

JUDAH

Tyre

Jerusalem

Euphrates R.

Tigris R.

ZAGROS

Babylon

BABYLONIA

Chaldeans

ASIA

Persians

MTS.

Memphis

EGYPT

ARABIAN DESERT

Persian Gulf

SAHARA

Red Sea

Thebes

N

0   500 Miles

GEOGRAPHY SKILLBUILDER: Interpreting Maps

1. **Location** *What is the approximate distance between Nineveh and Thebes?*
2. **Location** *What is the southernmost part of the Assyrian Empire and to what other empire did it previously belong?*

When the city gates finally splintered, the Assyrians showed no mercy. They killed or enslaved their victims. To prevent their enemies from rebelling again, the Assyrians forced captives to settle far away in the empire's distant provinces and dependent states.

The Empire Expands

Between 850 and 650 B.C., the kings of Assyria defeated Syria, Israel, Judah, and Babylonia. Eventually, the Assyrians ruled lands that extended far beyond the Fertile Crescent into Anatolia and Egypt.

Assyrian Rule At its peak around 650 B.C., the Assyrian Empire included almost all of the old centers of civilization and power in Southwest Asia. Assyrian officials governed lands closest to Assyria as provinces and made them dependent territories. Assyrian kings controlled these dependent regions by choosing their rulers or by supporting kings who aligned themselves with Assyria. The Assyrian system of having local governors report to a central authority became the fundamental model of administration, or system of government management.

In addition, the military campaigns added new territory to the empire. These additional lands brought taxes and tribute to the Assyrian treasury. If a conquered people refused to pay, the Assyrians destroyed their cities and sent the people into exile. Such methods enabled the Assyrians to effectively govern an extended empire.

Assyrian Culture Some of Assyria's most fearsome warriors earned reputations as great builders. For example, the same King Sennacherib who had burned Babylon also established Assyria's capital at **Nineveh** (NIHN•uh•vuh) along the Tigris River. This great walled city, about three miles long and a mile wide, was the largest city of its day. In the ruins of Nineveh and other Assyrian cities, archaeologists found finely carved sculptures. Two artistic subjects particularly fascinated the Assyrians: brutal military campaigns and the lion hunt.

Nineveh also held one of the ancient world's largest libraries. In this unique library, King **Ashurbanipal** (AH•shur•BAH•nuh•PAHL) collected more than 20,000 clay tablets from throughout the Fertile Crescent. The collection included the ancient Sumerian poem the *Epic of Gilgamesh* and provided historians with much information about the earliest civilizations in Southwest Asia. The library was the first to have many of the features of a modern library. For instance, the collection was organized into many rooms according to subject matter. The collection was also cataloged. Europeans would not use a library cataloging system for centuries.

Assyrian Sculpture

This relief shows ferocious Assyrian warriors attacking a fortified city. A relief is a sculpture that has figures standing out from a flat background. The Assyrian war machine included a variety of weapons and methods of attack.

❶ Ladders

Assyrian archers launched waves of arrows against opponents defending the city walls. Meanwhile, Assyrian troops threw their ladders up against the walls and began their climb into the enemy's stronghold.

❷ Weapons

Troops were armed with the best weapons of the time, iron-tipped spears, as well as iron daggers and swords. They were also protected with armor and large shields.

❸ Tactics

The Assyrians were savage in their treatment of defeated opponents. Those who were not slaughtered in the initial attack were often impaled or beheaded, while women and children were sometimes murdered or sold into slavery.

❹ Tunnels

The Assyrian army used sappers—soldiers who dug tunnels to sap, or undermine, the foundations of the enemy's walls so that they would fall.

SKILLBUILDER: Interpreting Visual Sources

1. **Making Inferences** *What emotions might the relief have inspired in the Assyrian people?*
2. **Making Inferences** *How might the Assyrians' enemies have reacted to the sculpture?*

The Empire Crumbles

Ashurbanipal proved to be one of the last of the mighty Assyrian kings. Assyrian power had spread itself too thin. Also, the cruelty displayed by the Assyrians had earned them many enemies. Shortly after Ashurbanipal's death, Nineveh fell.

Decline and Fall In 612 B.C., a combined army of <u>Medes</u> (meedz), <u>Chaldeans</u> (kal•DEE•uhnz), and others burned and leveled Nineveh. However, because the clay writing tablets in Nineveh's library had been baked in a pottery oven, many survived the fire.

Most people in the region rejoiced at Nineveh's destruction. The Jewish prophet Nahum (NAY•huhm) gave voice to the feelings of many:

MAIN IDEA

Analyzing Primary Sources

Ⓐ What was Nahum's opinion on the collapse of the Assyrian Empire?

PRIMARY SOURCE Ⓐ

All who see you will recoil from you and will say, "Nineveh has been ravaged!" Who will console her? Where shall I look for anyone to comfort you? . . . Your shepherds are slumbering, O King of Assyria; your sheepmasters are lying inert; your people are scattered over the hills, and there is none to gather them.

NAHUM 3:7, 18 (Hebrew Bible)

Rebirth of Babylon Under the Chaldeans After defeating the Assyrians, the Chaldeans made Babylon their capital. Around 600 B.C., Babylon became the center

First Age of Empires **97**

of a new empire, more than 1,000 years after Hammurabi had ruled there. A Chaldean king named **Nebuchadnezzar** (NEHB•uh•kuhd•NEHZ•uhr) restored the city. Perhaps the most impressive part of the restoration was the famous hanging gardens. Greek scholars later listed them as one of the seven wonders of the ancient world. According to legend, one of Nebuchadnezzar's wives missed the flowering shrubs of her mountain homeland. To please her, he had fragrant trees and shrubs planted on terraces that rose 75 feet above Babylon's flat, dry plain.

▲ This is an artist's rendering of the legendary hanging gardens of Babylon. Slaves watered the plants by using hidden pumps that drew water from the Euphrates River.

Indeed, the entire city was a wonder. Its walls were so thick that, according to one report, a four-horse chariot could wheel around on top of them. To ensure that the world knew who ruled Babylon, the king had the bricks inscribed with the words, "I am Nebuchadnezzar, King of Babylon."

The highest building in Babylon was a great, seven-tiered ziggurat more than 300 feet high. It was visible for miles. At night, priests observed the stars from the top of this tower and others in the city. Chaldean astronomers kept detailed records of how the stars and planets seemed to change position in the night sky. They also concluded that the sun, moon, Earth, and five other planets belonged to the same solar system. The Chaldeans' observations formed the basis for both astronomy and astrology.

Nebuchadnezzar's empire fell shortly after his death. The Persians who next came to power adopted many Assyrian military, political, and artistic inventions. The Persians would use the organization the Assyrians had developed to stabilize the region.

SECTION 2 ASSESSMENT

TERMS & NAMES 1. For each term or name, write a sentence explaining its significance.
• Assyria   • Sennacherib   • Nineveh   • Ashurbanipal   • Medes   • Chaldeans   • Nebuchadnezzar

USING YOUR NOTES

2. Why did the Assyrians develop into a great military power? Why did their power decline?

Assyrian Power

Causes for Rise	Causes for Decline
Need to defend against attacks	Hated by conquered people

MAIN IDEAS

3. What methods did the Assyrians use when they attacked enemy cities?

4. What contributions to government administration and culture did the Assyrians make?

5. Why did the people in the region rejoice when the Assyrian Empire was defeated?

CRITICAL THINKING & WRITING

6. **FORMING OPINIONS** Do you think the Assyrians' almost exclusive reliance on military power was a good strategy for creating their empire? Why or why not?

7. **MAKING INFERENCES** Why might the Assyrian warrior kings have had such a great interest in writing and reading?

8. **COMPARING** In what ways were King Ashurbanipal and King Nebuchadnezzar similar?

9. **WRITING ACTIVITY** EMPIRE BUILDING Write a one-paragraph **essay** on how developments in technology influenced the rise and decline of the Assyrian Empire.

CONNECT TO TODAY CREATING A POSTER

Research an instance when a modern ruler used excessive force to govern or put down opposition. Create a **poster** that tells about and illustrates the ruler and the event.

The Persian Empire

MAIN IDEA	WHY IT MATTERS NOW	TERMS & NAMES
BUILDING By governing with tolerance and wisdom, the Persians established a well-ordered empire that lasted for 200 years.	Leaders today try to follow the Persian example of tolerance and wise government.	• Cyrus • satrap • Cambyses • Royal Road • Darius • Zoroaster

SETTING THE STAGE The Medes, along with the Chaldeans and others, helped to overthrow the Assyrian Empire in 612 B.C. The Medes marched to Nineveh from their homeland in the area of present-day northern Iran. Meanwhile, the Medes' close neighbor to the south, Persia, began to expand its horizons and territorial ambitions.

The Rise of Persia

The Assyrians employed military force to control a vast empire. In contrast, the Persians based their empire on tolerance and diplomacy. They relied on a strong military to back up their policies. Ancient Persia included what today is Iran.

hmhsocialstudies.com
TAKING NOTES

Use the graphic organizer online to take notes on the similarities and differences between Cyrus and Darius.

The Persian Homeland Indo-Europeans first migrated from Central Europe and southern Russia to the mountains and plateaus east of the Fertile Crescent around 1000 B.C. This area extended from the Caspian Sea in the north to the Persian Gulf in the south. (See the map on page 101.) In addition to fertile farmland, ancient Iran boasted a wealth of minerals. These included copper, lead, gold, silver, and gleaming blue lapis lazuli. A thriving trade in these minerals put the settlers in contact with their neighbors to the east and the west.

At first, dozens of tiny kingdoms occupied the region. Eventually two major powers emerged: the Medes and the Persians. In time, a remarkable ruler would lead Persia to dominate the Medes and found a huge empire.

Cyrus the Great Founds an Empire The rest of the world paid little attention to the Persians until 550 B.C. In that year, **Cyrus** (SY•ruhs), Persia's king, began to conquer several neighboring kingdoms. Cyrus was a military genius, leading his army from victory to victory between 550 and 539 B.C. In time, Cyrus controlled an empire that spanned 2,000 miles, from the Indus River in the east to Anatolia in the west.

Even more than his military genius, though, Cyrus's most enduring legacy was his method of governing. His kindness toward conquered peoples revealed a wise and tolerant view of empire. For example, when Cyrus's army marched into a city, his generals prevented Persian soldiers from looting and burning. Unlike other conquerors, Cyrus believed in honoring local customs and religions. Instead of destroying the local temple, Cyrus would kneel there to pray.

Cyrus also allowed the Jews, who had been driven from their homeland by the Babylonians, to return to Jerusalem in 538 B.C. Under Persian rule, the Jews rebuilt their city and temple. The Jews were forever grateful to Cyrus, whom they considered one of God's anointed ones. The Jewish prophet Ezra recounts Cyrus's proclamation:

PRIMARY SOURCE
Thus said King Cyrus of Persia: The LORD God of Heaven has given me all the kingdoms of the earth and has charged me with building Him a house in Jerusalem, which is in Judah. Anyone of you of all His people—may his God be with him, and let him go up to Jerusalem that is in Judah and build the House of the LORD God of Israel, the God that is in Jerusalem.

EZRA 1: 2–3 (Hebrew Bible)

Cyrus was killed as he fought nomadic invaders on the eastern border of his empire. According to the Greek historian Arrian, his simple, house-shaped tomb bore these words: "O man, I am Cyrus the son of Cambyses. I established the Persian Empire and was king of Asia. Do not begrudge me my memorial." Ⓐ

MAIN IDEA

Summarizing
Ⓐ What are some examples of Cyrus's tolerant method of governing?

Persian Rule

The task of unifying conquered territories fell to rulers who followed Cyrus. They succeeded by combining Persian control with local self-government.

Cambyses and Darius Cyrus died in 530 B.C. His son **Cambyses** (kam•BY•seez), named after Cyrus's father, expanded the Persian Empire by conquering Egypt. However, the son neglected to follow his father's wise example. Cambyses scorned the Egyptian religion. He ordered the images of Egyptian gods to be burned. After ruling for only eight years, Cambyses died. Immediately, widespread rebellions broke out across the empire. Persian control had seemed strong a decade earlier. It now seemed surprisingly fragile.

Cambyses's successor, **Darius** (duh•RY•uhs), a noble of the ruling dynasty, had begun his career as a member of the king's bodyguard. An elite group of Persian soldiers, the Ten Thousand Immortals, helped Darius seize the throne around 522 B.C. Darius spent the first three years of his reign putting down revolts. He spent the next few years establishing a well-organized and efficient administration.

Having brought peace and stability to the empire, Darius turned his attention to conquest. He led his armies eastward into the mountains of present-day Afghanistan and then down into the river valleys of India. The immense Persian Empire now extended over 2,500 miles, embracing Egypt and Anatolia in the west, part of India in the east, and the Fertile Crescent in the center. Darius's only failure was his inability to conquer Greece.

▼ Sculpted figures bring gifts to Darius. The relief sculpture, located in the ancient Persian capital of Persepolis, dates from around the sixth century B.C.

Persian Empire, 500 B.C.

hmhsocialstudies.com
INTERACTIVE MAP

Persian Empire under Cyrus, 530 B.C.
Persian Empire under Cambyses, 522 B.C.
Persian Empire under Darius, 500 B.C.
Former Assyrian Empire
— — The Royal Road

Black Sea
Caspian Sea
Aral Sea
MACEDONIA
CAUCASUS MTS.
ARMENIA
SOGDIANA
LYDIA
GREECE
• Sardis
ANATOLIA
TAURUS MTS.
SYRIA
• Nineveh
Ashur •
MEDIA
PARTHIA
BACTRIA
HINDU KUSH
CYPRUS
Euphrates R.
Tigris R.
ZAGROS MOUNTAINS
PERSIA
Mediterranean Sea
Sidon •
PHOENICIA
• Tyre
BABYLONIA
Babylon •
Susa •
• Persepolis
Indus R.
JUDAH
• Jerusalem
CHALDEA
Memphis •
ARABIAN
Persian Gulf
GEDROSIA
EGYPT
DESERT
SAHARA
Nile R.
Red Sea
N
• Thebes
0   500 Miles
0   1,000 Kilometers
Tropic of Cancer
Arabian Sea
INDIA

GEOGRAPHY SKILLBUILDER: Interpreting Maps
1. **Region** *What part of the ancient world did Cambyses add to the Persian Empire?*
2. **Region** *Compare the map of the Persian Empire with that of the Assyrian Empire on page 96. What areas did the Persians rule that the Assyrians did not?*

Provinces and Satraps Although Darius was a great warrior, his real genius lay in administration. To govern his sprawling empire, Darius divided it into 20 provinces. These provinces were roughly similar to the homelands of the different groups of people who lived within the Persian Empire. Under Persian rule, the people of each province still practiced their own religion. They also spoke their own language and followed many of their own laws. This administrative policy of many groups—sometimes called "nationalities"—living by their own laws within one empire was repeatedly practiced in Southwest Asia.

Although tolerant of the many groups within his empire, Darius still ruled with absolute power. In each province, Darius installed a governor called a **satrap** (SAY•TRAP), who ruled locally. Darius also appointed a military leader and a tax collector for each province. To ensure the loyalty of these officials, Darius sent out inspectors known as the "King's Eyes and Ears."

Two other tools helped Darius hold together his empire. An excellent system of roads allowed Darius to communicate quickly with the most distant parts of the empire. The famous **Royal Road**, for example, ran from Susa in Persia to Sardis in Anatolia, a distance of 1,677 miles. Darius borrowed the second tool, manufacturing metal coins, from the Lydians of Asia Minor. For the first time, coins of a standard value circulated throughout an extended empire. People no longer had to weigh and measure odd pieces of gold or silver to pay for what they bought. The network roads and the wide use of standardized coins promoted trade. Trade, in turn, helped to hold together the empire.

The Royal Road

One of the ways in which societies build and maintain empires is by establishing systems of communication and transportation. The Royal Road, built by the rulers of the Persian Empire, connected Susa in Persia to Sardis in Anatolia.

▶ This four-horse chariot dates from the 6th to 4th centuries B.C. It is the type of vehicle that would have traveled the Royal Road in the time of Darius. The studs on the wheels were designed to help prevent the chariot from slipping.

VIDEO
110 Guards for Persia's Royal Road

HISTORY

↗ hmhsocialstudies.com

A Ride Along the Royal Road

ASIA

EUROPE

Black Sea

Caspian Sea

Sardis • ANATOLIA
Nineveh

Mediterranean Sea

PERSIA

Susa •

AFRICA

SOUTHWEST ASIA

Arabian Sea

N

0   500 Miles
0   1,000 Kilometers

The Road

The road was 1,677 miles in length. There were 111 post or relay stations spaced about 15 miles apart along the road. Other roads branched off the main road to distant parts of the empire.

The Ride

Relay stations were equipped with fresh horses for the king's messengers. Royal messengers could cover the length of the Royal Road in seven days. Normal travel time along the road was longer. A caravan, for example, might take three months to travel the whole distance.

Strong road networks like the Royal Road enabled empires to expand and maintain control over people and places. Like the Persians, the Inca of South America created a-road system thousands of miles long. These roads allowed the Inca to extend their rule over as many as 16 million people. Empires throughout history have shared characteristics such as efficient communication systems, effective leaders, and powerful armies.

Connect *to* Today

1. **Recognizing Effects** How would the Royal Road enable a ruler to maintain power in the empire?

   See Skillbuilder Handbook, Page R6.

2. **Comparing** What systems of communication and transportation today might be compared to the Royal Road of the Persians?

The Persian Legacy

By the time of Darius's rule, about 2,500 years had passed since the first Sumerian city-states had been built. During those years, people of the Fertile Crescent had endured war, conquest, and famine. These events gave rise to a basic question: Why should so much suffering and chaos exist in the world? A Persian prophet named **Zoroaster** (ZAWR•oh•AS•tuhr), who lived around 600 B.C., offered an answer.

Zoroaster's Teachings Zoroaster taught that the earth is a battleground where a great struggle is fought between the spirit of good and the spirit of evil. Each person, Zoroaster preached, is expected to take part in this struggle. The Zoroastrian religion teaches a belief in one god, Ahura Mazda (ah•HUR•uh-MAZ•duh). At the end of time, Ahura Mazda will judge everyone according to how well he or she fought the battle for good. Similarities to Zoroastrianism—such as the concept of Satan and a belief in angels—can be found in Judaism, Christianity, and Islam.

After the Muslim conquest of Persia in the A.D. 600s, the Zoroastrian religion declined. Some groups carried the faith eastward to India. Zoroastrianism also was an important influence in the development of Manichaeism (MAN•ih•KEE•IHZ•uhm), a religious system that competed with early Christianity for believers. The followers of Mithra, a Zoroastrian god, spread westward to become a popular religion among the military legions in the Roman Empire. Today, modern Zoroastrians continue to observe the religion's traditions in several countries including Iran and India, where its followers are called Parsis. **B**

Political Order Through their tolerance and good government, the Persians brought political order to Southwest Asia. They preserved ideas from earlier civilizations and found new ways to live and rule. Their respect for other cultures helped to preserve those cultures for the future. The powerful dynasty Cyrus established in Persia lasted 200 years and grew into a huge empire. As you will learn in Section 4, great empires also arose in China and dominated that region.

MAIN IDEA

Comparing
B What ideas and world view did Zoroastrianism share with other religions?

SECTION 3 ASSESSMENT

TERMS & NAMES 1. For each term or name, write a sentence explaining its significance.
• Cyrus   • Cambyses   • Darius   • satrap   • Royal Road   • Zoroaster

USING YOUR NOTES
2. Which of the differences between Cyrus and Darius do you consider most important? Why?

Cyrus Only
Both
Darius Only

MAIN IDEAS
3. How did Cyrus treat the peoples he conquered?
4. What methods and tools did Darius use to hold together his empire?
5. What did Zoroaster teach?

CRITICAL THINKING & WRITING
6. **MAKING INFERENCES** What do the words that appeared on Cyrus's tomb suggest about his character?
7. **DRAWING CONCLUSIONS** How did the Royal Road help Darius maintain control over his people?
8. **DEVELOPING HISTORICAL PERSPECTIVE** What events led to the development of Zoroastrianism?
9. **WRITING ACTIVITY** EMPIRE BUILDING Write an **expository essay** explaining how Darius's methods of administration gave stability to the Persian Empire. In your essay, consider such topics as the structure of the empire, the policy of tolerance, and the role of the satrap.

MULTIMEDIA ACTIVITY CREATING A CHART

 Use the Internet to find information on modern Zoroastrianism. Create a **chart** to present your findings.

INTERNET KEYWORD
Zoroastrianism

The Unification of China

MAIN IDEA	WHY IT MATTERS NOW	TERMS & NAMES
RELIGIOUS AND ETHICAL SYSTEMS The social disorder of the warring states contributed to the development of three Chinese ethical systems.	The people, events, and ideas that shaped China's early history continue to influence China's role in today's world.	• Confucius • *I Ching* • filial piety • yin and yang • bureaucracy • Qin Dynasty • Daoism • Shi Huangdi • Legalism • autocracy

SETTING THE STAGE The Zhou Dynasty, as you read in Chapter 2, lasted for at least eight centuries, from approximately 1027 to 256 B.C. For the first 300 years of their long reign, the Zhou kings controlled a large empire, including both eastern and western lands. Local rulers reported to the king, who had the ultimate power. By the latter years of the Zhou Dynasty, the lords of dependent territories began to think of themselves as independent kings. Their almost constant conflict, which is known as "the warring states period," led to the decline of the Zhou Dynasty.

Confucius and the Social Order

TAKING NOTES

Use the graphic organizer online to take notes on how the chaos of the warring states affected the philosophy, politics, and cities of China.

Toward the end of the Zhou Dynasty, China moved away from its ancient values of social order, harmony, and respect for authority. Chinese scholars and philosophers developed different solutions to restore these values.

Confucius Urges Harmony China's most influential scholar was **Confucius** (kuhn•FYOO•shuhs). Born in 551 B.C., Confucius lived in a time when the Zhou Dynasty was in decline. He led a scholarly life, studying and teaching history, music, and moral character.

Confucius was born at a time of crisis and violence in China. He had a deep desire to restore the order and moral living of earlier times to his society. Confucius believed that social order, harmony, and good government could be restored in China if society were organized around five basic relationships. These were the relationships between: (1) ruler and subject, (2) father and son, (3) husband and wife, (4) older brother and younger brother, and (5) friend and friend. A code of proper conduct regulated each of these relationships. For example, rulers should practice kindness and virtuous living. In return, subjects should be loyal and law-abiding.

Three of Confucius's five relationships were based upon the family. Confucius stressed that children should practice **filial piety**, or respect for their parents and ancestors. Filial piety, according to Confucius, meant devoting oneself to one's parents during their lifetimes. It also required honoring their memories after death through the performance of certain rituals.

In the following passage, Confucius—the "Master"—expresses his thoughts on the concept:

PRIMARY SOURCE
Ziyou [a disciple of Confucius] asked about filial piety. The Master said: "Nowadays people think they are dutiful sons when they feed their parents. Yet they also feed their dogs and horses. Unless there is respect, where is the difference?"

CONFUCIUS, *Analects* 2.7

Confucius wanted to reform Chinese society by showing rulers how to govern wisely. Impressed by Confucius's wisdom, the duke of Lu appointed him minister of justice. According to legend, Confucius so overwhelmed people by his kindness and courtesy that almost overnight, crime vanished from Lu. When the duke's ways changed, however, Confucius became disillusioned and resigned.

Confucius spent the remainder of his life teaching. His students later collected his words in a book called the *Analects*. A disciple named Mencius (MEHN•shee•uhs) also spread Confucius's ideas.

Confucian Ideas About Government Confucius said that education could transform a humbly born person into a gentleman. In saying this, he laid the groundwork for the creation of a **bureaucracy**, a trained civil service, or those who run the government. According to Confucius, a gentleman had four virtues: "In his private conduct he was courteous, in serving his master he was punctilious [precise], in providing for the needs of the people he gave them even more than their due; in exacting service from the people, he was just." Education became critically important to career advancement in the bureaucracy.

Confucianism was never a religion, but it was an ethical system, a system based on accepted principles of right and wrong. It became the foundation for Chinese government and social order. In addition, the ideas of Confucius spread beyond China and influenced civilizations throughout East Asia.

Vocabulary
legend: a story handed down from earlier times, especially one believed to be historical

History Makers

Confucius
551–479 B.C.
Confucius was born to a poor family. As an adult, he earned his living as a teacher. But he longed to put his principles into action by advising political leaders. Finally, at around age 50, Confucius won a post as minister in his home state. According to legend, he set such a virtuous example that a purse lying in the middle of the street would be untouched for days.

After Confucius resigned his post as minister, he returned to teaching. He considered himself a failure because he had never held high office. Yet Confucius's ideas have molded Chinese thought for centuries.

Laozi
sixth century B.C.
Although a person named Laozi is credited with being the first philosopher of Daoism, no one knows for sure whether he really existed. Legend has it that Laozi's mother carried him in her womb for 62 years and that he was born with white hair and wrinkled skin. Laozi's followers claimed that he was a contemporary of Confucius.

Unlike Confucius, however, Laozi believed that government should do as little as possible and leave the people alone. Laozi thought that people could do little to influence the outcome of events. Daoism offered communion with nature as an alternative to political chaos.

hmhsocialstudies.com

RESEARCH WEB LINKS Go online for more on Confucius and Laozi.

Other Ethical Systems

In addition to Confucius, other Chinese scholars and philosophers developed ethical systems with very different philosophies. Some stressed the importance of nature, others, the power of government.

Daoists Seek Harmony For a Chinese thinker named Laozi (low•dzuh), who may have lived during the sixth century B.C., only the natural order was important. The natural order involves relations among all living things. His book *Dao De Jing* (*The Way of Virtue*) expressed Laozi's belief. He said that a universal force called the Dao (dow), meaning "the Way," guides all things. Of all the creatures of nature, according to Laozi, only humans fail to follow the Dao. They argue about questions of right and wrong, good manners or bad. According to Laozi, such arguments are pointless. In the following, he explains the wisdom of the Dao:

PRIMARY SOURCE

The Dao never does anything,
yet through it all things are done.

If powerful men and women
could center themselves in it,
the whole world would be transformed
by itself, in its natural rhythms.
People would be content
with their simple, everyday lives, in harmony, and free of desire.

When there is no desire,
all things are at peace.

LAOZI, *Dao De Jing,* Passage 37

MAIN IDEA

Analyzing Primary Sources

A What do you think is the Daoist attitude toward being a powerful person?

The philosophy of Laozi came to be known as **Daoism**. Its search for knowledge and understanding of nature led Daoism's followers to pursue scientific studies. Daoists made many important contributions to the sciences of alchemy, astronomy, and medicine.

Legalists Urge Harsh Rule In sharp contrast to the followers of Confucius and Laozi was a group of practical political thinkers called the Legalists. They believed that a highly efficient and powerful government was the key to restoring order in society. They got their name from their belief that government should use the law to end civil disorder and restore harmony. Hanfeizi and Li Si were among the founders of **Legalism**.

The Legalists taught that a ruler should provide rich rewards for people who carried out their duties well. Likewise, the disobedient should be harshly punished. In practice, the Legalists stressed punishment more than rewards. For example, anyone caught outside his own village without a travel permit should have his ears or nose chopped off.

The Legalists believed in controlling ideas as well as actions. They suggested that a ruler burn all writings that might encourage people to criticize government.

VIDEO
New Philosophies Emerge

hmhsocialstudies.com

Chinese Ethical Systems		
Confucianism	**Daoism**	**Legalism**
• Social order, harmony, and good government should be based on family relationships. • Respect for parents and elders is important to a well-ordered society. • Education is important both to the welfare of the individual and to society.	• The natural order is more important than the social order. • A universal force guides all things. • Human beings should live simply and in harmony with nature.	• A highly efficient and powerful government is the key to social order. • Punishments are useful to maintain social order. • Thinkers and their ideas should be strictly controlled by the government.

SKILLBUILDER: Interpreting Charts
1. **Comparing** *Which of these three systems stresses the importance of government and a well-ordered society?*
2. **Synthesizing** *Which of these systems seems to be most moderate and balanced? Explain.*

MAIN IDEA

Summarizing

B How did the Legalists think that a society could be made to run well?

After all, it was for the prince to govern and the people to obey. Eventually, Legalist ideas gained favor with a prince of a new dynasty that replaced the Zhou. That powerful ruler soon brought order to China. **B**

***I Ching* and Yin and Yang** People with little interest in the philosophical debates of the Confucians, Daoists, and Legalists found answers to life's questions elsewhere. Some consulted a book of oracles called *I Ching* (also spelled *Yi Jing*) to solve ethical or practical problems. Readers used the book by throwing a set of coins, interpreting the results, and then reading the appropriate oracle, or prediction. The *I Ching* (*The Book of Changes*) helped people to lead a happy life by offering good advice and simple common sense.

Other people turned to the ideas of ancient thinkers, such as the concept of **yin and yang**—two powers that together represented the natural rhythms of life. Yin represents all that is cold, dark, soft, and mysterious. Yang is the opposite—warm, bright, hard, and clear. The symbol of yin and yang is a circle divided into halves, as shown in the emblem to the upper right. The circle represents the harmony of yin and yang. Both forces represent the rhythm of the universe and complement each other. Both the *I Ching* and yin and yang helped Chinese people understand how they fit into the world.

▲ Traditional yin-and-yang symbol

The Qin Dynasty Unifies China

In the third century B.C., the **Qin Dynasty** (chihn) replaced the Zhou Dynasty. It emerged from the western state of Qin. The ruler who founded the Qin Dynasty employed Legalist ideas to subdue the warring states and unify his country.

A New Emperor Takes Control In 221 B.C., after ruling for over 20 years, the Qin ruler assumed the name **Shi Huangdi** (shihr-hwahng•dee), which means "First Emperor." The new emperor had begun his reign by halting the internal battles that had sapped China's strength. Next he turned his attention to defeating invaders and crushing resistance within China to his rule. Shi Huangdi's armies attacked the invaders north of the Huang He and south as far as what is now Vietnam. His victories doubled China's size. Shi Huangdi was determined to unify China.

Shi Huangdi acted decisively to crush political opposition at home. To destroy the power of rival warlords, he introduced a policy called "strengthening the trunk and weakening the branches." He commanded all the noble families to live in the capital city under his suspicious gaze. This policy, according to tradition, uprooted 120,000 noble families. Seizing their land, the emperor carved China into 36 administrative districts. He sent Qin officials to control them.

To prevent criticism, Shi Huangdi and his prime minister, the Legalist philosopher Li Si, murdered hundreds of Confucian scholars. They also ordered "useless" books burned. These books were the works of Confucian thinkers and poets who disagreed with the Legalists. Practical books about medicine and farming, however, were spared. Through measures

▼ Although a tyrant, Shi Huangdi is considered the founder of unified China. The word *Qin* is the origin of *China*.

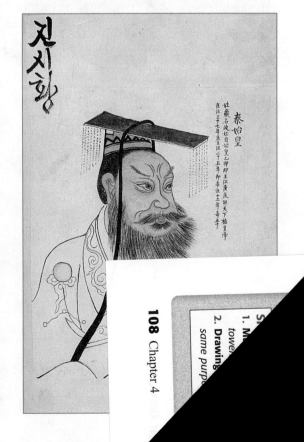

The Great Wall of China

From the Yellow Sea in the east to the Gobi Desert in the west, the Great Wall twisted like a dragon's tail for thousands of miles. Watch towers rose every 200 to 300 yards along the wall.

In the time of Shi Huangdi, hundreds of thousands of peasants collected, hauled, and dumped millions of tons of stone, dirt, and rubble to fill the core of the Great Wall.

Slabs of cut stone on the outside of the wall enclosed a heap of pebbles and rubble on the inside. Each section of the wall rose to a height of 20 to 25 feet.

VIDEO
HISTORY The First Emperor of China

↗ hmhsocialstudies.com

Although Shi Huangdi built the earliest unified wall, the wall as it exists today dates from the later Ming Dynasty (1368–1644).

The Qin Dynasty, 221–202 B.C.

- Qin Dynasty
- Extent of Zhou Dynasty (Approximate)
- ⌁ Great Wall

0 — 500 Miles
0 — 1000 Kilometers

MONGOLIA
KOREA
Anyang
Huang He
Yellow Sea
Luoyang
Wei He
Ch'ang-an (Xi'an)
Hao
East China Sea
TIBET
Chang Jiang
HIMALAYAS
Taiwan
Xi Jiang
INDIA
BURMA
South China Sea
Bay of Bengal
VIETNAM (ANNAM)

SKILLBUILDER: Interpreting Visual Sources

Making Inferences *What were the benefits of the watch towers along the wall?*

Draw Conclusions *What modern structures serve the same purpose as the watch towers?*

such as these, Shi Huangdi established an **autocracy**—a government that has unlimited power and uses it in an arbitrary manner.

A Program of Centralization Shi Huangdi's sweeping program of centralization included the building of a highway network of more than 4,000 miles. Also, he set the same standards throughout China for writing, law, currency, and weights and measures—even down to the length of cart axles. This last standard made sure that all vehicles could fit into the ruts of China's main roads.

Under Shi Huangdi's rule, irrigation projects increased farm production. Trade blossomed, thanks to the new road system. Trade pushed a new class of merchants into prominence. Despite these social advances, harsh taxes and repressive government made the Qin regime unpopular. Shi Huangdi had unified China at the expense of human freedom. **C**

Great Wall of China Scholars hated Shi Huangdi for his book burning. Poor people hated him because they were forced to work on the building of a huge defensive wall. Earlier, Zhou rulers had erected smaller walls to discourage attacks by northern nomads. Shi Huangdi determined to close the gaps and extend the wall almost the length of the empire's border. Enemies would have to gallop halfway to Tibet to get around it.

The Great Wall of China arose on the backs of hundreds of thousands of peasants. The wall builders worked neither for wages nor for love of empire. They faced a terrible choice: work on the wall or die. Many of the laborers worked on the wall and died anyway, victims of the crushing labor or the harsh winter weather.

The Fall of the Qin The Qin Dynasty lasted only a short time. Though fully as cruel as his father, Shi Huangdi's son proved less able. Peasants rebelled just three years after the second Qin emperor took office. One of their leaders, a peasant from the land of Han, marched his troops into the capital city. By 202 B.C., the harsh Qin Dynasty gave way to the Han Dynasty, one of the longest in Chinese history.

While the Chinese explored the best ways to govern, ancient Greece also was experimenting with different forms of government, as you will read in Chapter 5.

MAIN IDEA

Recognizing Effects

 C What were the positive and negative effects of Shi Huangdi's rule?

SECTION 4 ASSESSMENT

TERMS & NAMES 1. For each term or name, write a sentence explaining its significance.
• Confucius • filial piety • bureaucracy • Daoism • Legalism • *I Ching* • yin and yang • Qin Dynasty • Shi Huangdi • autocracy

USING YOUR NOTES

2. Which aspect of Chinese life was most affected by the chaos created by the warring states?

MAIN IDEAS

3. How did Confucius believe that social order, harmony, and good government could be restored in China?

4. What did the Legalists see as the key to restoring order?

5. What measures did Shi Huangdi take to crush political opposition at home?

CRITICAL THINKING & WRITING

6. **HYPOTHESIZING** How would followers of the three philosophical traditions in China react to the idea that "all-men are created equal"?

7. **ANALYZING CAUSES** Why did Shi Huangdi have his critics murdered?

8. **MAKING INFERENCES** Would a ruler who followed Confucian or Daoist ideas have built the Great Wall? Why-or why not?

9. **WRITING ACTIVITY** RELIGIOUS AND ETHICAL SYSTEMS
Write a **comparison-contrast paragraph** in which you discuss the-three Chinese ethical systems.

CONNECT TO TODAY **PREPARING AN ORAL REPORT**

Research to find out about the Great Wall today. Prepare an **oral report** in which you explain what the Great Wall looks like today and what it is used for.

Chapter 4 Assessment

TERMS & NAMES

For each term or name below, briefly explain its connection to the history of the first age of empires between 1570 and 200 B.C.

1. Ramses II
2. Kush
3. Assyria
4. Ashurbanipal
5. Cyrus
6. Royal Road
7. Zoroaster
8. Confucius
9. Daoism
10. Shi Huangdi

MAIN IDEAS

The Egyptian and Nubian Empires Section 1
(pages 89–94)

11. How did the Kushites treat Egyptian culture after they conquered Egypt?
12. When did Kush experience a golden age?

The Assyrian Empire Section 2 (pages 95–98)

13. How did Assyria acquire its empire?
14. What were the positive achievements of the Assyrian Empire?

The Persian Empire Section 3 (pages 99–103)

15. What is Cyrus's enduring legacy?
16. How far did Darius extend the Persian Empire?

The Unification of China Section 4 (pages 104–109)

17. Around what five basic relationships did Confucius believe society should be organized?
18. Why did Shi Huangdi have the Great Wall built?

CRITICAL THINKING

1. USING YOUR NOTES
EMPIRE BUILDING
Create a table and list the successes and failures of the leaders discussed in this chapter.

Leader	Successes	Failures
Thutmose III		
Sennacherib		
Cyrus		

2. DRAWING CONCLUSIONS
RELIGIOUS AND ETHICAL SYSTEMS Religious and ethical systems in Persia and China arose in response to what similar conditions?

3. DEVELOPING HISTORICAL PERSPECTIVE
How have Cyrus's and Sennacherib's contrasting ruling styles probably affected their legacies?

4. RECOGNIZING EFFECTS
CULTURAL INTERACTION What positive results occur when cultures interact? What negative results might there be?

5. SYNTHESIZING
What similar purpose was served by the Persians' Royal Road and by the Great Wall of China?

VISUAL SUMMARY

First Age of Empires

EMPIRE BUILDING

Egypt 1570–1075 B.C.

- Pharaohs set up a professional army.
- Pharaohs invaded territories in Africa and Southwest Asia.
- Egypt drew vast wealth from the lands it controlled.

Nubia 751 B.C.–A.D. 350

- Nubia and Egypt interacted and spread their culture through trade.
- The kings of Nubia conquered Egypt and maintained the Egyptian way of life.
- Nubia established trade among Africa, Arabia, and India.

Assyria 850–612 B.C.

- Assyria used a sophisticated military organization to conquer an empire.
- The empire engaged in brutal treatment of its conquered peoples.
- Kings used harsh taxes to control conquered peoples.

Persia 550–330 B.C.

- Persian kings were tolerant.
- Kings permitted a high degree of local self-government.
- The empire was divided into 20 provinces.

China 221–202 B.C.

- Ethical systems laid the groundwork for a strong central government.
- The Qin Dynasty defeated invaders, crushed internal resistance, and united China.
- China initiated a sweeping program of centralization.

Use the quotation and your knowledge of world history to answer questions 1 and 2.

PRIMARY SOURCE

> Guide the people with governmental measures and control or regulate them by the threat of punishment, and the people will try to keep out of jail, but will have no sense of honor or shame. Guide the people by virtue and control or regulate them by *li* [moral rules and customs], and the people will have a sense of honor and respect.
>
> **CONFUCIUS,** *Analects 2.3*

1. Which phrase best describes Confucius's belief about human nature and lawful behavior?

    A. People are naturally moral and can control their behavior on their own.

    B. People are best controlled by fear.

    C. People learn good behavior by example.

    D. People cannot be controlled by any means.

2. Which of the following rulers might have held a similar belief?

    A. Shi Huangdi

    B. Cyrus

    C. King Ashurbanipal

    D. Ramses II

Use the relief below depicting King Ashurbanipal and his queen at a garden party and your knowledge of world history to answer question 3.

3. What characteristic of the Assyrians does this relief seem to reflect?

    A. their love of luxury

    B. their military might

    C. their administrative organization

    D. their love of learning

 hmhsocialstudies.com TEST PRACTICE

For additional test practice, go online for:

- Diagnostic tests
- Strategies
- Tutorials

Interact *with* History

Recall your discussion of the question on page 88: "How will the empire help you or harm you?" You thought about the advantages and disadvantages of empire before studying the rise of the first great empires. Now that you've read the chapter, rethink the advantages and disadvantages of empire. Discuss the following questions with a small group:

- Do empires benefit conquered peoples?
- Do empires impose penalties on those they conquer?
- Which outweighs the other—the benefits or the penalties?

FOCUS ON WRITING

Study page 108, which deals with the Great Wall of China. Imagine that you are one of the workers who built the Great Wall. Write three **journal entries** describing the following:

- the work you carry out on the Great Wall
- your experiences
- your impressions

MULTIMEDIA ACTIVITY

21ST CENTURY

Creating a Web Site

Create a Web site on the first empires for a museum exhibit. Choose one of these empires to research: Assyria, Kush, Persia, or Qin. Consider including:

- art, artifacts, and maps
- a description of the empire with dates, location, and rulers
- information on major events and conflicts
- the rise and fall of the empire
- a discussion of the empire's legacy
- a list of Web sites used in your research

China and the Great Wall

Today, the Great Wall of China is an impressive symbol of the Asian giant's power, genius, and endurance. It wasn't always so. For much of its history, the Chinese people saw the Great Wall as a symbol of cruelty and oppression. This is just one way in which the wall differs from what we think we know. In contrast to popular notions, the wall that draws tourists to Beijing by the millions was not built 2,000 years ago. Nor is the Great Wall a single wall. Instead, it was patched together from walls built over many centuries. And for all its grandeur, the wall failed to keep China safe from invasion.

Explore facts and fictions about the Great Wall online. You can find more information, video clips, primary sources, activities, and more at hmhsocialstudies.com .

The Great Wall of China

Watch the video to learn the history and significance of the magnificent, mysterious walls that snake across northern China.

A Land of Walls Within Walls

Watch the video to learn how the Great Wall fits within the ancient Chinese tradition of wall-building.

The Human Costs of Building

Watch the video to learn about the miseries that awaited the men who built the wall.

Twentieth-Century China

Watch the video to examine the role that the wall has played in modern Chinese history.

The Rise of Civilizations

Thousands of years ago, several societies in different parts of the world changed from hunting and gathering to farming. Some began to produce surpluses of food. Those surpluses helped bring about the world's first civilizations.

In Unit 1, you learned that most historians define civilization as a complex culture with these five characteristics: (1) advanced cities, (2) specialized workers, (3) complex institutions, (4) record keeping and writing, and (5) advanced technology. You also learned about several early civilizations. In the next six pages, you will explore what those ancient civilizations had in common and how they differed.

EUROPE

ASIA

Indus Valley
The people of the Indus River valley lived in highly planned cities. Later, a new group moved into the area, creating a civilization that still influences South Asia.

Eastern Mediterranean
Various peoples settled in the hills and valleys of Palestine. One group— the Israelites—was unique because they worshiped only one God.

Ancient Egypt
Along the Nile River, powerful rulers led a dazzling civilization that produced monuments, art, and religion that still fascinate people today.

Mediterranean Sea

Caspian Sea

Tyre

Jerusalem

Babylon

Memphis

Ur

Euphrates R.

Tigris R.

Indus R.

Harappa

Mohenjo-Daro

Persian Gulf

H I M A

Thebes

A F R I C A

Nile

Red Sea

Mesopotamia
The Tigris and Euphrates rivers supported the different peoples of Mesopotamia. The first civilization there was based in city-states.

Arabian Sea

Bay of Beng

Ancient Civilizations over Time

Some of these ancient civilizations lasted only a few hundred years, but others lasted more than 3,000 years. Earlier civilizations often had influence on later ones that shared the same area. The civilizations shown here did not all develop in isolation of each other. Trade linked some. Some fought wars against each other.

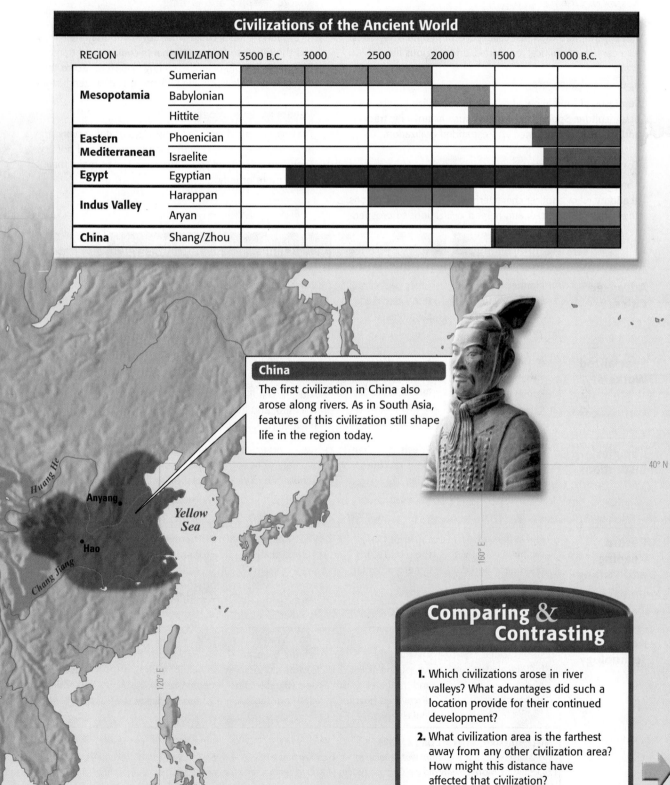

REGION	CIVILIZATION	3500 B.C.	3000	2500	2000	1500	1000 B.C.
Mesopotamia	Sumerian						
	Babylonian						
	Hittite						
Eastern Mediterranean	Phoenician						
	Israelite						
Egypt	Egyptian						
Indus Valley	Harappan						
	Aryan						
China	Shang/Zhou						

Civilizations of the Ancient World

China

The first civilization in China also arose along rivers. As in South Asia, features of this civilization still shape life in the region today.

Huang He

Anyang

Hao

Chang Jiang

Yellow Sea

40° N

160° E

120° E

Comparing & Contrasting

1. Which civilizations arose in river valleys? What advantages did such a location provide for their continued development?

2. What civilization area is the farthest away from any other civilization area? How might this distance have affected that civilization?

Characteristics of Civilizations

The civilizations you studied in Unit 1 each demonstrated the five characteristics that historians use to define a civilization.

Advanced Cities

Cities were key features of the ancient civilizations. These cities were more than just collections of people. They were also centers of political, economic, and religious life.

Specialized Workers

Surpluses of food allowed people to specialize in jobs outside of agriculture. Specialized workers such as artisans, traders, and soldiers strengthened and expanded civilization.

Complex Institutions

Complex institutions such as law codes, religion, and an economy were another characteristic of ancient civilizations. They organized, united, and helped civilizations to prosper.

Record Keeping and Writing

Each civilization developed a system of writing. Rulers could record laws. Priests could write down important religious dates and the rituals to follow. Merchants could record transactions. Eventually, people used the writing system to record their thoughts and ideas, creating literature and written history.

Advanced Technology

The civilizations developed new ways of doing work and new materials to work with, such as metals and pottery. They also developed tools like calendars to make their world more orderly.

	Indus Valley	Mesopotamia	China	Ancient Egypt	Eastern Mediterranean
Advanced Cities	• Planned cities had neatly laid-out streets and fortified areas.	• Cities had central temples called ziggurats.	• Cities had massive earthen walls for protection.	• Cities had power over the surrounding lands.	• Phoenician cities were busy ports. • Jerusalem had a large temple.
Specialized Workers	• Artisans made various goods, which traders exchanged with other peoples.	• Priests, warriors, scribes, artisans, and farmers all had special tasks.	• Warriors defended the land. • Artisans made beautiful and useful items.	• Rulers, officials, priests, and wealthy land-owners led society.	• Phoenician sailors carried goods. • Israelite religious leaders had great influence.
Complex Institutions	• Rulers organized the work of laying out the cities.	• Priests and then kings ran the cities. • Rulers created written law codes.	• Rulers organized workers to build canals and city walls.	• Pharaohs ordered people to build elaborate tombs. • Priests ran large temples.	• Israelites developed the belief in one God. They saw the law as a gift from God.
Record Keeping and Writing	• The system of writing has not yet been deciphered.	• Cuneiform was the world's first system of writing.	• The writing system helped unify peoples with different languages because characters stood for ideas.	• Hieroglyphic writing had symbols that stood for ideas and for sounds.	• The Phoenician alphabet became the basis of many alphabets.
Advanced Technology	• Engineers made sophisticated buildings and plumbing systems.	• Sumerians invented the wheel, the sail, and the plow, and discovered how to make bronze.	• The Chinese refined bronze casting technology and valuable silk cloth production.	• Advances were made in engineering, astronomy, and medicine.	• Phoenicians built ships with advances such as the steering oar and the sail.

SKILLBUILDER: Interpreting Charts
1. **Synthesizing** *How important was religion to these civilizations?*
2. **Analyzing Motives** *How did the Chinese system of writing contribute to the spread of Chinese civilization?*

Development of Law

Laws are a complex institution of civilizations. They are designed to do many things—settle conflicts between individuals, provide citizens with guidance on proper behavior, and outline an individual's relationship with the government. Thus, laws are important for building stable civilizations.

PRIMARY SOURCE

Hammurabi's Code

If a son has struck his father, they shall cut off his hand.

If a [noble] has destroyed the eye of a [noble], they shall destroy his eye.

If he has broken another [noble's] bone, they shall break his bone.

If he has destroyed the eye of a commoner or broken the bone of a commoner, he shall pay one mina of silver.

If he has destroyed the eye of a [noble's] slave or broken the bone of a [noble's] slave, he shall pay one-half [the slave's] value.

If a [noble] has knocked out the tooth of a [noble], they shall knock out his tooth.

If he has knocked out a commoner's tooth, he shall pay one-third mina of silver.

DOCUMENT-BASED QUESTION
Is the Code applied equally to all people? Explain your answer.

PRIMARY SOURCE

Hebrew Bible

When you reap the harvest of your land, you shall not reap all the way to the edges of the field, or gather the gleanings of your harvest. You shall not pick your vineyard bare, or gather the fallen fruit of your vineyard; you shall leave them for the poor and the stranger. . . .

You shall not defraud your fellow. You shall not commit robbery. The wages of a laborer shall not remain with you until morning. . . .

You shall not render an unfair decision: do not favor the poor or show deference to the rich; judge your kinsman fairly. Do not deal basely with your countrymen. . . .

You shall not hate your kinsfolk in your heart. Reprove your kinsman but incur no guilt because of him. You shall not take vengeance or bear a grudge against your countrymen. Love your fellow as yourself.

DOCUMENT-BASED QUESTION
What principle underlies these laws? How would you describe the concepts in these laws?

PRIMARY SOURCE

Confucius

The Master said, "A young man's duty is to behave well to his parents at home and to his elders abroad, to be cautious in giving promises and punctual in keeping them, to have kindly feelings towards everyone, but seek the intimacy of the Good."

The Master said, "Govern the people by regulations, keep order among them by chastisements, and they will flee from you, and lose all self-respect. Govern them by moral force, keep order among them by ritual, and they will keep their self-respect and come to you of their own accord."

DOCUMENT-BASED QUESTION
What behavior does Confucius expect of ordinary people and of rulers?

Comparing & Contrasting

1. How is the treatment of people in Hammurabi's Code different from the treatment of people in the Hebrew Bible and the writings of Confucius?

2. For which of the civilizations on the chart do you think laws were most important? Why?

Record Keeping and Writing

As institutions became more complex, people realized the need for record keeping. Officials tracked taxes and laws, priests recorded important rituals, and merchants totaled accounts. Record keeping provided stability for the complex institutions.

PRIMARY SOURCE

Indus Valley Seals

The system of writing used in the Indus Valley has not been deciphered. Scholars have identified about 400 symbols, but they do not know if these stand for ideas or sounds. Many of the examples are found on small seals. The seals might have been used to mark objects to show ownership. In that case, the symbols might give a person's name.

DOCUMENT-BASED QUESTION
Based on what you see on this seal, what are some possibilities for its translation?

PRIMARY SOURCE

Sumerian Cuneiform

Cuneiform originated in people's desire to keep track of goods they owned. By around 3000 B.C., Sumerians had more than 1,000 symbols. Each stood for an idea. Later, symbols stood for sounds. This system of writing was used in Mesopotamia for about 3,000 years. Different peoples adapted it for their own languages. At first, cuneiform was read from top to bottom. Later, it was read from left to right.

DOCUMENT-BASED QUESTION
What visual clue suggests that this cuneiform sample was read from left to right and not top to bottom?

PRIMARY SOURCE

Egyptian Hieroglyphics

Hieroglyphics were read in the direction that the human and animal heads faced. Usually this was from right to left. Sometimes, though, the direction could be changed to make a more pleasing appearance. Some symbols stood for ideas. Some stood for consonant sounds—vowels were not included. Some gave clues to how a word was used, such as whether a name referred to a person or a place.

DOCUMENT-BASED QUESTION
In the bottom row on the left, you can see an owl. What other symbols do you recognize?

PRIMARY SOURCE

Phoenician Alphabet

The alphabet used by the ancient Phoenicians had symbols for 22 consonants. This alphabet was adapted by the Greeks, and it became the basis for writing all European languages. The Phoenician alphabet also influenced how Hebrew and Arabic were written, and it was adapted to write the languages of India and Ethiopia.

DOCUMENT-BASED QUESTION
Do any of the letters in this Phoenician sample look similar to letters we use today? If so, which ones?

Advanced Technology

New technologies gave the ancient civilizations new ways of solving problems. Some solved age-old problems—for example, the plow made it easier to till the soil. Some solved new problems. Egyptians learned how to embalm the bodies of dead rulers as part of their complex beliefs about life after death.

PRIMARY SOURCE

Phoenician Sailing

The Phoenicians traded throughout the Mediterranean Sea and beyond. They were the most skilled sailors of their time. The first ships relied on rowers and did not have sails. They also lacked rudders for steering. By about 700 B.C., though, the Phoenicians had made advances. They added long steering oars in the back and a single sail, which could catch the wind and move the ship forward. Captains came to rely on the sails, though rowers had to work when the weather was calm or when the wind was not blowing from behind the ship.

DOCUMENT-BASED QUESTION
What is the advantage of having a sail on the ship?

PRIMARY SOURCE

Bronze from Shang China

During the Shang Dynasty, Chinese artisans grew highly skilled at making bronze. Bronze is a mixture of copper and tin. They made bronze weapons and vessels for religious ceremonies. Bronzes were made by creating pottery molds that were carved on the inside, in reverse, to leave the desired pattern on the final object. Hot liquid bronze was poured inside. When it had cooled, the pottery molds were broken.

DOCUMENT-BASED QUESTION
What does the intricate detail of this piece suggest about Shang society?

Comparing & Contrasting

1. How do the ancient systems of writing differ from the way words are written today?

2. What role did trade play in the development of writing?

3. Which technological advances do you think were more important—Chinese skill in making bronzes or Phoenician skill in sailing? Why?

EXTENSION ACTIVITY
Technological changes have continued throughout history. Choose one area of life, such as land transportation, communication, medicine, or raising food. Using this textbook or an encyclopedia, find out what technology one of these ancient civilizations had in that area. Then identify technological changes in that area over the centuries. Create an illustrated time line to show how that technology has changed.

New Directions in Government and Society

2000 B.C. – A.D. 700

This painting of Athens shows why the Greeks called the main district of government and religious buildings an acropolis, meaning city at the top. Such buildings were constructed in the highest, most easily defended part of the city.

Comparing & Contrasting

Classical Ages
In Unit 2, you will learn that Greece had a classical age, a time of great cultural achievement that left an enduring legacy. At the end of the unit, you will have a chance to compare and contrast Greece's classical age with several others. (See pages 252–257.)

CHAPTER 5

Classical Greece,
2000 B.C.–300 B.C.

Essential Question

What impact has ancient Greece had on the modern world?

 What You Will Learn

In this chapter you will learn about the history and culture of classical Greece and its impact on the modern world.

SECTION 1 Cultures of the Mountains and the Sea
Main Idea The roots of Greek culture are based on interaction of the Mycenaean, Minoan, and Dorian cultures.

SECTION 2 Warring City-States
Main Idea The growth of city-states in Greece led to the development of several political systems, including democracy.

SECTION 3 Democracy and Greece's Golden Age
Main Idea Democratic principles and classical culture flourished during Greece's golden age.

SECTION 4 Alexander's Empire
Main Idea Alexander the Great conquered Persia and Egypt and extended his empire to the Indus River in northwest India.

SECTION 5 The Spread of Hellenistic Culture
Main Idea Hellenistic culture, a blend of Greek and other influences, flourished throughout Greece, Egypt, and Asia.

Previewing Themes

POWER AND AUTHORITY In the Greek city-state of Athens, a new form of government developed—democracy—in which citizens exercised power.
Geography *What geographic factors might have confined democracy largely to Athens?*

CULTURAL INTERACTION Alexander the Great spread Greek culture throughout much of Asia. Greek, Egyptian, and Asian cultures then blended to create Hellenistic culture.
Geography *Why might the sea have been important to the spread of Greek culture?*

EMPIRE BUILDING Athens assumed control of a defense league and eventually built it into an empire. Later, Alexander conquered the Persian Empire and beyond to create a vast new empire of his own.
Geography *What geographic features might have strengthened the Macedonian desire to build an empire to the south and east?*

GREECE

2000 B.C.
Minoan civilization prospers on Crete.
(Minoan vase) ▶

1500 B.C.
Mycenaean culture thrives on Greek mainland.

2000 B.C.   **1500 B.C.**

WORLD

1780 B.C.
Hammurabi issues code of laws.

1472 B.C.
Hatshepsut, woman pharoah, begins her reign. (Head from statue of Hatshepsut) ▶

120

Greek City-States, 750 B.C.

MACEDONIA

Abdera   Maronea

Methone
Potidaea
Mt. Olympus

EPIRUS

Acanthus

Aegean Sea

LYDIA

Ionian Sea

Delphi
Thebes
Gulf of Corinth
West   Athens   East
Corinth
Mycenae
Olympia   Argos   Tiryns
Peloponnesus

Sparta

Delos
Cyclades

Ephesus

Miletus

Rhodes

HISTORY Delphi

hmhsocialstudies.com VIDEO

- Greek homeland in 750 B.C.
- City-State
▲ Greek Settlement

N
W   E
S

Topography

Elevation profile of Greece at 38°N

elevation (in feet)
5000
4000
3000
2000
1000
0

Athens

West   East

Mediterranean Sea

Crete
Knossos

0   50   100 Miles
0   50   100 Kilometers
Conic Projection

1200 B.C.
Trojan war
takes place.

750 B.C.
Greek city-states
flourish.

479 B.C.
Greece triumphs
in Persian Wars.

334 B.C.
Alexander starts
to build his empire.

1000 B.C.

300 B.C.

1027 B.C.
◄ Zhou Dynasty
begins in China.
(Zhou animal mask)

850 B.C.
Assyrians expand
their empire.

500 B.C.
◄ Zapotec of Mexico
build Monte Albán.
(Zapotec shield)

321 B.C.
Chandragupta
founds Mauryan
Empire in India.

What does this art tell you about Greek culture?

When you think of ancient Greece, what is the first thing that comes to mind? You can learn a lot about a culture from its works of art and literature, as well as from the statements of its leaders, philosophers, and historians. Look at these Greek works of art and read the quotations.

"As an oak tree falls on the hillside crushing all that lies beneath, so Theseus. He presses out the life, the brute's savage life, and now it lies dead."

EDITH HAMILTON, "Theseus," *Mythology*

▼ This plate shows Theseus, the greatest hero of Athens, killing the mythological beast the Minotaur.

▲ This stone relief panel of Democracy crowning Athens was placed in the marketplace, where citizens could see it daily.

"Our constitution is called a democracy because power is in the hands not of a minority but of the whole people."

PERICLES, an Athenian statesman

▲ The Greeks often adorned their public buildings with graceful sculptures of gods and goddesses.

"For we are lovers of the beautiful in our tastes."

THUCYDIDES, a historian

EXAMINING *the* ISSUES

- **What does the relief panel suggest about the role of democracy in Greek society?**
- **Why might the Greeks decorate pottery with a heroic scene?**
- **Why might the Greeks place graceful statues in and around their public buildings?**

Break into small groups and discuss what these artworks suggest about ancient Greek culture. Also discuss what the quotations tell you about the culture and its ideals. As you read about ancient Greece, think about how its culture influenced later civilizations.

Cultures of the Mountains and the Sea

MAIN IDEA	WHY IT MATTERS NOW	TERMS & NAMES
CULTURAL INTERACTION The roots of Greek culture are based on interaction of the Mycenaean, Minoan, and Dorian cultures.	The seeds of much of Western cultural heritage were planted during this time period.	• Mycenaean • Homer • Trojan War • epic • Dorian • myth

SETTING THE STAGE In ancient times, Greece was not a united country. It was a collection of separate lands where Greek-speaking people lived. By 3000-B.C., the Minoans lived on the large Greek island of Crete. The Minoans created an elegant civilization that had great power in the Mediterranean world. At the same time, people from the plains along the Black Sea and Anatolia migrated and settled in mainland Greece.

Geography Shapes Greek Life

Ancient Greece consisted mainly of a mountainous peninsula jutting out into the Mediterranean Sea. It also included about 2,000 islands in the Aegean (ih•JEE•uhn) and Ionian (eye•OH•nee•uhn) seas. Lands on the eastern edge of the Aegean were also part of ancient Greece. (See the map on page 121.) The region's physical geography directly shaped Greek traditions and customs.

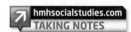

Use the graphic organizer online to take notes on the roots of Greek culture.

The Sea The sea shaped Greek civilization just as rivers shaped the ancient civilizations of Egypt, the Fertile Crescent, India, and China. In one sense, the Greeks did not live *on* a land but *around* a sea. Greeks rarely had to travel more than 85 miles to reach the coastline. The Aegean Sea, the Ionian Sea, and the neighboring Black Sea were important transportation routes for the Greek people. These seaways linked most parts of Greece. As the Greeks became skilled sailors, sea travel connected Greece with other societies. Sea travel and trade were also important because Greece lacked natural resources, such as timber, precious metals, and usable farmland.

The Land Rugged mountains covered about three-fourths of ancient Greece. The mountain chains ran mainly from northwest to southeast along the Balkan Peninsula. Mountains divided the land into a number of different regions. This significantly influenced Greek political life. Instead of a single government, the Greeks developed small, independent communities within each little valley and its surrounding mountains. Most Greeks gave their loyalty to these local communities.

In ancient times, the uneven terrain also made land transportation difficult. Of the few roads that existed, most were little more than dirt paths. It often took travelers several days to complete a journey that might take a few hours today.

Much of the land itself was stony, and only a small part of it was arable, or suitable for farming. Tiny but fertile valleys covered about one-fourth of Greece.

The small streams that watered these valleys were not suitable for large-scale irrigation projects. With so little fertile farmland or fresh water for irrigation, Greece was never able to support a large population. Historians estimate that no more than a few million people lived in ancient Greece at any given time. Even this small population could not expect the land to support a life of luxury. A desire for more living space, grassland for raising livestock, and adequate farmland may have been factors that motivated the Greeks to seek new sites for colonies. **A**

The Climate Climate was the third important environmental influence on Greek civilization. Greece has a varied climate, with temperatures averaging 48 degrees Fahrenheit in the winter and 80 degrees Fahrenheit in the summer. In ancient times, these moderate temperatures supported an outdoor life for many Greek citizens. Men spent much of their leisure time at outdoor public events. They met often to discuss public issues, exchange news, and take an active part in civic life.

MAIN IDEA

Analyzing Causes

A In what ways did Greece's location by the sea and its mountainous land affect its development?

Mycenaean Civilization Develops

As Chapter 3 explained, a large wave of Indo-Europeans migrated from the Eurasian steppes to Europe, India, and Southwest Asia. Some of the people who settled on the Greek mainland around 2000 B.C. were later known as **Mycenaeans**. The name came from their leading city, Mycenae (my•SEE•nee).

Mycenae was located in southern Greece on a steep, rocky ridge and surrounded by a protective wall more than 20 feet thick. The fortified city of Mycenae could withstand almost any attack. From Mycenae, a warrior-king ruled the surrounding villages and farms. Strong rulers controlled the areas around other Mycenaean cities, such as Tiryns and Athens. These kings dominated Greece from about 1600 to 1100 B.C.

Mycenaean Greece, c. 1250 B.C.

Legend:
- Mycenaean Greece
- Mycenaean city
- Other city
- Trade routes
- Battle

Black Sea

Troy
Lesbos · ANATOLIA
GREECE · Aegean Sea · Chios
Orchomenos · Gla · Euboea
Thebes · Athens · Samos
Mycenae · Tiryns · Miletus
Peloponnesus
Pylos
Rhodes
Ionian Sea
Sicily
HITTITE EMPIRE
Knossos
Crete
Mediterranean Sea
Cyprus
EGYPT

VIDEO
Greece: The Trojans
hmhsocialstudies.com

GEOGRAPHY SKILLBUILDER: Interpreting Maps
1. **Location** Where was the center of the Mycenaean Civilization located?
2. **Movement** Based on the map, how did Mycenaean traders conduct most of their trade?

Contact with Minoans Sometime after 1500 B.C., through either trade or war, the Mycenaeans came into contact with the Minoan civilization. From their contact with the Minoans, the Mycenaeans saw the value of seaborne trade. Mycenaean traders soon sailed throughout the eastern Mediterranean, making stops at Aegean islands, coastal towns in Anatolia, and ports in Syria, Egypt, Italy, and Crete.

The Minoans also influenced the Mycenaeans in other ways. The Mycenaeans adapted the Minoan writing system to the Greek language and decorated vases with Minoan designs. The Minoan-influenced culture of Mycenae formed the core of Greek religious practice, art, politics, and literature. Indeed, Western civilization has its roots in these two early Mediterranean civilizations. **B**

MAIN IDEA

Recognizing Effects

B How did contact with the Minoans affect Mycenaean culture?

▲ Greek stories tell of their army's capture of the legendary city of Troy by hiding soldiers in a hollow wooden horse.

The Trojan War During the 1200s B.C., the Mycenaeans fought a ten-year war against Troy, an independent trading city located in Anatolia. According to legend, a Greek army besieged and destroyed Troy because a Trojan prince had kidnapped Helen, the beautiful wife of a Greek king.

For many years, historians thought that the legendary stories told of the **Trojan War** were totally fictional. However, excavations conducted in northwestern Turkey during the 1870s by German archaeologist Heinrich Schliemann suggested that the stories of the Trojan War might have been based on real cities, people, and events. Further archaeological studies conducted in the 20th century support Schliemann's findings. Although the exact nature of the Trojan War remains unclear, this attack on Troy was almost certainly one of the last Mycenaean battle campaigns.

Greek Culture Declines Under the Dorians

Not long after the Trojan War, Mycenaean civilization collapsed. Around 1200 B.C., sea raiders attacked and burned many Mycenaean cities. According to tradition, a new group of people, the **Dorians** (DAWR•ee•uhnz), moved into the war-torn countryside. The Dorians spoke a dialect of Greek and may have been distant relatives of the Bronze Age Greeks.

The Dorians were far less advanced than the Mycenaeans. The economy collapsed and trade eventually came to a standstill soon after their arrival. Most important to historians, Greeks appear to have temporarily lost the art of writing during the Dorian Age. No written record exists from the 400-year period between 1150 and 750 B.C. As a result, little is known about this period of Greek history.

Epics of Homer Lacking writing, the Greeks of this time learned about their history through the spoken word. According to tradition, the greatest storyteller was a blind man named **Homer**. Little is known of his personal life. Some historians believe that Homer composed his **epics**, narrative poems celebrating heroic deeds, sometime between 750 and 700 B.C. The Trojan War forms the backdrop for one of Homer's great epic poems, the *Iliad*.

The heroes of the *Iliad* are warriors: the fierce Greek Achilles (uh•KIHL•eez) and the courageous and noble Hector of Troy. In the following dramatic excerpt, Hector's wife begs him not to fight Achilles:

PRIMARY SOURCE
"My dear husband, your warlike spirit will be your death. You've no compassion for your infant child, for me, your sad wife, who before long will be your widow. . . . As for me, it would be better, if I'm to lose you, to be buried in the ground. . . ."
Great Hector . . . replied, "Wife, all this concerns me, too. But I'd be disgraced, dreadfully shamed . . . , if I should slink away from war, like a coward. [F]or I have learned always to be brave, to fight alongside Trojans at the front, striving to win great fame for my father, for myself."

HOMER, the *Iliad* (translated by Ian Johnston)

Hector's response to his wife gives insight into the Greek heroic ideal of *aretē* (ar•uh•TAY), meaning virtue and excellence. A Greek could display this ideal on the battlefield in combat or in athletic contests on the playing field.

▲ This is a marble sculpture of Polyphemus—a cyclops, or one-eyed monster—who appears in another of Homer's epics, the *Odyssey*.

Greeks Create Myths The Greeks developed a rich set of **myths**, or traditional stories, about their gods. The works of Homer and another epic, *Theogony* by Hesiod, are the source of much of Greek mythology. Through the myths, the Greeks sought to understand the mysteries of nature and the power of human passions. Myths explained the changing of the seasons, for example.

Greeks attributed human qualities, such as love, hate, and jealousy, to their gods. The gods quarreled and competed with each other constantly. However, unlike humans, the gods lived forever. Zeus, the ruler of the gods, lived on Mount Olympus with his wife, Hera. Hera was often jealous of Zeus' relationships with other women. Athena, goddess of wisdom, was Zeus' daughter and his favorite child. The Greeks thought of Athena as the guardian of cities, especially of Athens, which was named in her honor. You will learn about Athens and other cities in Section 2.

SECTION 1 ASSESSMENT

TERMS & NAMES 1. For each term or name, write a sentence explaining its significance.
• Mycenaean   • Trojan War   • Dorian   • Homer   • epic   • myth

USING YOUR NOTES
2. Which of the cultures on your chart do you think contributed the most to Greek culture? Explain.

Culture	Contribution
Minoan	Writing System; pottery designs
Mycenaean	
Dorian	

MAIN IDEAS
3. What impact did nearness to the sea have on the development of Greece?
4. What aspects of culture did the Mycenaeans adopt from the Minoans?
5. Why were the epics of importance to the Greeks of the Dorian period?

CRITICAL THINKING & WRITING
6. **DRAWING CONCLUSIONS** How did the physical geography of Greece cause Greek-speaking peoples to develop separate, isolated communities?
7. **ANALYZING CAUSES** Other than the explanation offered in the legend, why do you think the Greeks went to war with Troy?
8. **MAKING INFERENCES** The Dorian period is often called Greece's Dark Age. Why do you think this is so?
9. **WRITING ACTIVITY** CULTURAL INTERACTION Write an expository **essay** explaining why the Greek epics and myths are so well known and studied in today's society.

CONNECT TO TODAY WRITING EXPLANATIONS
Many names and phrases from this period of Greek history have been absorbed into the English language. Use library resources to find examples, such as *Achilles heel, Homeric,* and *Trojan horse.* Write a brief **explanation** of each example.

Warring City-States

MAIN IDEA	WHY IT MATTERS NOW	TERMS & NAMES
POWER AND AUTHORITY The growth of city-states in Greece led to the development of several political systems, including democracy.	Many political systems in today's world mirror the varied forms of government that evolved in Greece.	• polis • tyrant • acropolis • democracy • monarchy • helot • aristocracy • phalanx • oligarchy • Persian Wars

SETTING THE STAGE During the Dorian period, Greek civilization experienced decline. However, two things changed life in Greece. First, Dorians and Mycenaeans alike began to identify less with the culture of their ancestors and more with the local area where they lived. Second, by the end of this period, the method of governing areas had changed from tribal or clan control to more formal governments—the city-states.

Rule and Order in Greek City-States

By 750 B.C., the city-state, or **polis**, was the fundamental political unit in ancient Greece. A polis was made up of a city and its surrounding countryside, which included numerous villages. Most city-states controlled between 50 and 500 square miles of territory. They were often home to fewer than 10,000 residents. At the agora, or marketplace, or on a fortified hilltop called an **acropolis** (uh•KRAHP•uh•lihs), citizens gathered to discuss city government.

hmhsocialstudies.com
TAKING NOTES

Use the graphic organizer online to take notes on important events in the development of Athens and Sparta.

Greek Political Structures Greek city-states had many different forms of government. (See the chart on page 128.) In some, a single person, called a king, ruled in a government called a **monarchy**. Others adopted an **aristocracy** (AR•ih•STAHK•ruh•see), a government ruled by a small group of noble, landowning families. These very rich families often gained political power after serving in a king's military cavalry. Later, as trade expanded, a new class of wealthy merchants and artisans emerged in some cities. When these groups became dissatisfied with aristocratic rule, they sometimes took power or shared it with the nobility. They formed an **oligarchy**, a government ruled by a few powerful people.

Tyrants Seize Power In many city-states, repeated clashes occurred between rulers and the common people. Powerful individuals, usually nobles or other wealthy citizens, sometimes seized control of the government by appealing to the common people for support. These rulers were called **tyrants**. Unlike today, tyrants generally were not considered harsh and cruel. Rather, they were looked upon as leaders who would work for the interests of the ordinary people. Once in power, for example, tyrants often set up building programs to provide jobs and housing for their supporters.

Athens Builds a Limited Democracy

The idea of representative government also began to take root in some city-states, particularly Athens. Like other city-states, Athens went through power struggles between rich and poor. However, Athenians avoided major political upheavals by making timely reforms. Athenian reformers moved toward **democracy**, rule by the people. In Athens, citizens participated directly in political decision making.

Building Democracy The first step toward democracy came when a nobleman named Draco took power. In 621 B.C., Draco developed a legal code based on the idea that all Athenians, rich and poor, were equal under the law. Draco's code dealt very harshly with criminals, making death the punishment for practically every crime. It also upheld such practices as debt slavery, in which debtors worked as slaves to repay their debts.

Vocabulary
The legal code prepared by Draco was so harsh that the word *draconian* has come to mean "extreme cruelty or severity."

More far-reaching democratic reforms were introduced by Solon (SO•luhn), who came to power in 594 B.C. Stating that no citizen should own another citizen, Solon outlawed debt slavery. He organized all Athenian citizens into four social classes according to wealth. Only members of the top three classes could hold political office. However, all citizens, regardless of class, could participate in the Athenian assembly. Solon also introduced the legal concept that any citizen could bring charges against wrongdoers.

Around 500 B.C., the Athenian leader Cleisthenes (KLYS•thuh•NEEZ) introduced further reforms. He broke up the power of the nobility by organizing citizens into ten groups based on where they lived rather than on their wealth. He also increased the power of the assembly by allowing all citizens to submit laws for debate and passage. Cleisthenes then created the Council of Five Hundred. This body proposed laws and counseled the assembly. Council members were chosen by lot, or at random.

The reforms of Cleisthenes allowed Athenian citizens to participate in a limited democracy. However, citizenship was restricted to a relatively small number of Athenians. Only free adult male were considered citizens. Women, slaves, and foreigners were excluded from citizenship and had few rights. **(A)**

MAIN IDEA

Contrasting
(A) How is Athenian democracy different from modern American democracy?

Athenian Education For the most part, only the sons of wealthy families received formal education. Schooling began around the age of seven and largely prepared boys to be good citizens. They studied reading, grammar, poetry, history, mathematics, and music. Because citizens were expected to debate issues in the assembly, boys also received training in logic and public speaking. And since the Greeks believed that it was important to train and develop the body, part of each day

Forms of Government

Monarchy	Aristocracy	Oligarchy	Direct Democracy
• State ruled by a king	• State ruled by nobility	• State ruled by a small group of citizens	• State ruled by its citizens
• Rule is hereditary	• Rule is hereditary and based on family ties, social rank, wealth	• Rule is based on wealth or ability	• Rule is based on citizenship
• Some rulers claim divine right	• Social status and wealth support rulers' authority	• Ruling group controls military	• Majority rule decides vote
• Practiced in Mycenae by 2000 B.C.	• Practiced in Athens prior to 594 B.C.	• Practiced in Sparta by 500 B.C.	• Practiced in Athens by about 500 B.C.

SKILLBUILDER: Interpreting Charts
1. **Summarizing** *Which forms of government feature rule based on wealth or property ownership?*
2. **Clarifying** *In which form of government do citizens have the most power?*

A Husband's Advice

In this excerpt from *The Economist*, the Greek historian Xenophon describes how a husband might respond to his wife's question about how she could remain attractive:

PRIMARY SOURCE

I counseled her to oversee the baking woman as she made the bread; to stand beside the housekeeper as she measured out her stores; to go on tours of inspection to see if all things were in order as they should be. For, as it seemed to me, this would at once be walking exercise and supervision. And, as an excellent gymnastic, I recommended her to knead the dough and roll the paste; to shake the coverlets and make the beds; adding, if she trained herself in exercise of this sort she would enjoy her food, grow vigorous in health, and her complexion would in very truth be lovelier. The very look and aspect of the wife.

XENOPHON, *The Economist,* Book 10 (Translated by H. G. Dakyns)

DOCUMENT-BASED QUESTIONS

1. **Making Inferences** *What is the husband suggesting in his advice to his wife?*
2. **Synthesizing** *How is the husband's advice representative of Athenian attitudes toward women?*

was spent in athletic activities. When they got older, boys went to military school to help them prepare for another important duty of citizenship—defending Athens.

Athenian girls did not attend school. Rather, they were educated at home by their mothers and other female members of the household. They learned about child-rearing, weaving cloth, preparing meals, managing the household, and other skills that helped them become good wives and mothers. Some women were able to take their education farther and learned to read and write. A few even became accomplished writers. Even so, most women had very little to do with Athenian life outside the boundaries of family and home.

Sparta Builds a Military State

Located in the southern part of Greece known as the Peloponnesus (PEHL•uh•puh•NEE•sus), Sparta was nearly cut off from the rest of Greece by the Gulf of Corinth. (See the map on page 121.) In outlook and values, Sparta contrasted sharply with the other city-states, Athens in particular. Instead of a democracy, Sparta built a military state.

Sparta Dominates Messenians Around 725 B.C., Sparta conquered the neighboring region of Messenia and took over the land. The Messenians became **helots** (HEHL•uhts), peasants forced to stay on the land they worked. Each year, the Spartans demanded half of the helots' crops. In about 650 B.C., the Messenians, resentful of the Spartans' harsh rule, revolted. The Spartans, who were outnumbered eight to one, just barely put down the revolt. Shocked at their vulnerability, they dedicated themselves to making Sparta a strong city-state.

↗ hmhsocialstudies.com **INTERACTIVE**

VIDEO
The Temple of Artemis at Ephesus
HISTORY
↗ hmhsocialstudies.com

Festivals and Sports

The ancient Greeks believed that strong healthy citizens helped strengthen the city-state. They often included sporting events in the festivals they held to honor their gods. The most famous sports festival was the Olympic games, held every four years. Records of Olympics winners started in 776 B.C. At first, the festival lasted only one day and had only one contest, a race called the stade. Later, many other events were added, including a long-distance race, wrestling, the long jump, the javelin, and the discus throw. The Olympics was expanded to five days in 472 B.C.

Women's Sports ►

Women had their own sports festival in ancient Greece. It was the festival devoted to Hera, the wife of Zeus. Like the Olympics, the Hera festival was held every four years. One of the main events was a foot race for unmarried women.

◄ Discus Thrower

Ancient athletes, such as this discus thrower, would be considered amateurs today because they received no pay for competing. However, they trained rigorously for months at a time. Victors were given lavish gifts and were hailed as heroes. Many athletes competed full-time.

▼ Mount Olympus

The ancient Olympics honored Zeus, the father of all Greek gods and goddesses. According to legend, Zeus hurled a thunderbolt from Mount Olympus at a spot in rural Greece. An altar for Zeus was built on that spot. Eventually, many buildings were erected around the altar. This area was called Olympia and became the site for the Olympic games.

SKILLBUILDER: Interpreting Visual Sources
1. **Evaluating Decisions** *Do you think it was a good decision for the Greeks to add more sporting events to the Olympics? Explain.*
2. **Comparing and Contrasting** *How are today's Olympics similar to and different from the Olympics in ancient Greece?*

Sparta's Government and Society Spartan government had several branches. An assembly, which was composed of all Spartan citizens, elected officials and voted on major issues. The Council of Elders, made up of 30 older citizens, proposed laws on which the assembly voted. Five elected officials carried out the laws passed by the assembly. These men also controlled education and prosecuted court cases. In addition, two kings ruled over Sparta's military forces.

The Spartan social order consisted of several groups. The first were citizens descended from the original inhabitants of the region. This group included the ruling families who owned the land. A second group, noncitizens who were free, worked in commerce and industry. The helots, at the bottom of Spartan society, were little better than slaves. They worked in the fields or as house servants.

Spartan Daily Life From around 600 until 371 B.C., Sparta had the most powerful army in Greece. However, the Spartan people paid a high price for their military supremacy. All forms of individual expression were discouraged. As a result, Spartans did not value the arts, literature, or other artistic and intellectual pursuits. Spartans valued duty, strength, and discipline over freedom, individuality, beauty, and learning. **B**

MAIN IDEA

Comparing

B How would you compare the ideals of Spartan and Athenian societies?

Since men were expected to serve in the army until the age of 60, their daily life centered on military training. Boys left home when they were 7 and moved into army barracks, where they stayed until they reached the age of 30. They spent their days marching, exercising, and fighting. They undertook these activities in all weathers, wearing only light tunics and no shoes. At night, they slept without blankets on hard benches. Their daily diet consisted of little more than a bowl of coarse black porridge. Those who were not satisfied were encouraged to steal food. Such training produced tough, resourceful soldiers.

Spartan girls also led hardy lives. They received some military training, and they also ran, wrestled, and played sports. Like boys, girls were taught to put service to Sparta above everything—even love of family. A legend says that Spartan women told husbands and sons going to war to "come back *with* your shield or *on* it." As adults, Spartan women had considerable freedom, especially in running the family estates when their husbands were on active military service. Such freedom surprised men from other Greek city-states. This was particularly true of Athens, where women were expected to remain out of sight and quietly raise children.

The Persian Wars

Danger of a helot revolt led Sparta to become a military state. Struggles between rich and poor led Athens to become a democracy. The greatest danger of all—invasion by Persian armies—moved Sparta and Athens alike to their greatest glory.

A New Kind of Army Emerges During the Dorian Age, only the rich could afford bronze spears, shields, breastplates, and chariots. Thus, only the rich served in armies. Iron later replaced bronze in the manufacture of weapons. Harder than bronze, iron was more common and therefore cheaper. Soon, ordinary citizens could afford to arm and defend themselves. The shift from bronze to iron weapons made possible a new kind of army composed not only of the rich but also of merchants, artisans, and small landowners. The foot soldiers of this army, called hoplites, stood side by side, each holding a spear in one hand and a shield in the other. This fearsome formation, or **phalanx** (FAY•LANGKS), became the most powerful fighting force in the ancient world.

Battle at Marathon The **Persian Wars**, between Greece and the Persian Empire, began in Ionia on the coast of Anatolia. (See the map on page 132.) The Greeks had long been settled there, but around 546 B.C., the Persians conquered the area.

↗ hmhsocialstudies.com

INTERACTIVE MAP

Follow the key battles of the Persian Wars.

When Ionian Greeks revolted, Athens sent ships and soldiers to their aid. The Persian king Darius the Great defeated the rebels and then vowed to destroy Athens in revenge.

In 490 B.C., a Persian fleet carried 25,000 men across the Aegean Sea and landed northeast of Athens on a plain called Marathon. There, 10,000 Athenians, neatly arranged in phalanxes, waited for them. Vastly outnumbered, the Greek soldiers charged. The Persians, who wore light armor and lacked training in this kind of land combat, were no match for the disciplined Greek phalanx. After several hours, the Persians fled the battlefield. The Persians lost more than 6,000 men. In contrast, Athenian casualties numbered fewer than 200.

Pheidippides Brings News Though the Athenians won the battle, their city now stood defenseless. According to tradition, army leaders chose a young runner named Pheidippides (fy•DIP•uh•DEEZ) to race back to Athens. He brought news of the Persian defeat so that Athenians would not give up the city without a fight. Dashing the 26 miles from Marathon to Athens, Pheidippides delivered his message, "Rejoice, we conquer." He then collapsed and died. Moving rapidly from Marathon, the Greek army arrived in Athens not long after. When the Persians sailed into the harbor, they found the city heavily defended. They quickly put to sea in retreat.

Thermopylae and Salamis Ten years later, in 480 B.C., Darius the Great's son and successor, Xerxes (ZURK•seez), assembled an enormous invasion force to crush Athens. The Greeks were badly divided. Some city-states agreed to fight the Persians. Others thought it wiser to let Xerxes destroy Athens and return home. Some Greeks even fought on the Persian side. Consequently, Xerxes' army met no resistance as it marched down the eastern coast of Greece.

When Xerxes came to a narrow mountain pass at Thermopylae (thur•MAHP•uh•lee), 7,000 Greeks, including 300 Spartans, blocked his way. Xerxes assumed that his troops would easily push the Greeks aside. However, he underestimated their fighting ability. The Greeks stopped the Persian advance for three days. Only a traitor's informing the Persians about a secret path around the pass ended their brave stand. Fearing defeat, the Spartans held the Persians back while the other Greek forces retreated. The Spartans' valiant sacrifice—all were killed—made a great impression on all Greeks.

Meanwhile, the Athenians debated how best to defend their city. Themistocles, an Athenian leader, convinced them to evacuate the city and fight at sea. They positioned their fleet in a narrow channel near the island of Salamis (SAL•uh•mihs), a few miles southwest of Athens. After setting fire to Athens, Xerxes sent his warships to

HISTORY

VIDEO
Greece: The Battle
of Thermopylae

hmhsocialstudies.com

The Persian Wars, 490–479 B.C.

hmhsocialstudies.com
INTERACTIVE MAP

Persian campaign, 490 B.C.
Persian campaign, 480 B.C.
Persian victory
Greek victory
Indecisive battle
Greek alliance
Persian empire and allies
Neutral Greek states

GEOGRAPHY SKILLBUILDER: Interpreting Maps
1. **Movement** By what routes did the Persians choose to attack Greece? Explain why.
2. **Location** Where did most of the battles of the Persian Wars occur? How might their citizens have been affected?

block both ends of the channel. However, the channel was very narrow, and the Persian ships had difficulty turning. Smaller Greek ships armed with battering rams attacked, puncturing the hulls of many Persian warships. Xerxes watched in horror as more than one-third of his fleet sank. He faced another defeat in 479 B.C., when the Greeks crushed the Persian army at the Battle of Plataea (pluh•TEE•uh). After this major setback, the Persians were always on the defensive.

The following year, several Greek city-states formed an alliance called the Delian (DEE•lee•uhn) League. (The alliance took its name from Delos, the island in the Aegean Sea where it had its headquarters.) League members continued to press the war against the Persians for several more years. In time, they drove the Persians from the territories surrounding Greece and ended the threat of future attacks.

Consequences of the Persian Wars With the Persian threat ended, all the Greek city-states felt a new sense of confidence and freedom. Athens, in particular, basked in the glory of the Persian defeat. During the 470s, Athens emerged as the leader of the Delian League, which had grown to some 200 city-states. Soon thereafter, Athens began to use its power to control the other league members. It moved the league headquarters to Athens, and used military force against members that challenged its authority. In time, these city-states became little more than provinces of a vast Athenian empire. The prestige of victory over the Persians and the wealth of the Athenian empire set the stage for a dazzling burst of creativity in Athens. The city was entering its brief golden age. **C**

MAIN IDEA

Recognizing Effects

C How did the Persian Wars affect the Greek people, especially the Athenians?

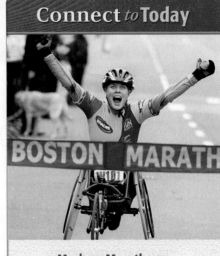

Connect to Today

Modern Marathons

Pheidippides' heroic act in the Persian Wars inspired officials at the first modern Olympic Games—held in Athens in 1896—to add a 26-mile race to their competition. The course of the race ran from Marathon to the Olympic Stadium in Athens.

Today, most of the world's major cities stage marathons every year. Many, like the one held in Boston, attract wheelchair competitors.

↗ **hmhsocialstudies.com**

INTERNET ACTIVITY Go online to create an illustrated history of the marathon.

SECTION 2 ASSESSMENT

TERMS & NAMES 1. For each term or name, write a sentence explaining its significance.
• polis • acropolis • monarchy • aristocracy • oligarchy • tyrant • democracy • helot • phalanx • Persian Wars

USING YOUR NOTES

2. Which of the events on your time line do you think was the most important for life today? Explain.

MAIN IDEAS

3. How does an aristocracy differ from an oligarchy?

4. What contributions did Solon and Cleisthenes make to the development of Athenian democracy?

5. How did Athens benefit from victory in the Persian Wars?

CRITICAL THINKING & WRITING

6. **CONTRASTING** How was living in Athens different from living in Sparta?

7. **MAKING INFERENCES** The introduction of cheap iron weapons meant that ordinary Greek citizens could arm themselves. How might the ability to own weapons change the outlook of ordinary citizens?

8. **ANALYZING MOTIVES** Why were the Spartan soldiers willing to sacrifice themselves at Thermopylae?

9. **WRITING ACTIVITY** [POWER AND AUTHORITY] Write a brief political **monologue** about democracy from an Athenian slave's point of view.

MULTIMEDIA ACTIVITY PREPARING AN ORAL REPORT

 New England town meetings are similar to the kind of democracy practiced in ancient Greece. Use the Internet to find information on the town meeting. Present your findings to the class in a brief **oral report**.

INTERNET KEYWORD
town meeting

Democracy and Greece's Golden Age

MAIN IDEA	WHY IT MATTERS NOW	TERMS & NAMES
CULTURAL INTERACTION Democratic principles and classical culture flourished during Greece's golden age.	At its height, Greece set lasting standards in art, politics, literature, and philosophy that are still influential today.	• direct democracy • classical art • tragedy • comedy • Peloponnesian War • philosopher • Socrates • Plato • Aristotle

SETTING THE STAGE For close to 50 years (from 477 to 431 B.C.), Athens experienced a growth in intellectual and artistic learning. This period is often called the Golden Age of Athens. During this golden age, drama, sculpture, poetry, philosophy, architecture, and science all reached new heights. The artistic and literary legacies of the time continue to inspire and instruct people around the world.

Pericles' Plan for Athens

hmhsocialstudies.com
TAKING NOTES

Use the graphic organizer online to take notes on Pericles' goals for Athens.

A wise and able statesman named Pericles led Athens during much of its golden age. Honest and fair, Pericles held onto popular support for 32 years. He was a skillful politician, an inspiring speaker, and a respected general. He so dominated the life of Athens from 461 to 429 B.C. that this period often is called the Age of Pericles. He had three goals: (1) to strengthen Athenian democracy, (2) to hold and strengthen the empire, and (3) to glorify Athens.

Stronger Democracy To strengthen democracy, Pericles increased the number of public officials who were paid salaries. Earlier in Athens, most positions in public office were unpaid. Thus, only wealthier Athenian citizens could afford to

Athenian and United States Democracy

Athenian Democracy	Both	U.S. Democracy
• Citizens: male; 18 years old; born of citizen parents	• Political power exercised by citizens	• Citizens: born in United States or completed citizenship process
• Laws voted on and proposed directly by assembly of all citizens	• Three branches of government	• Representatives elected to propose and vote on laws
• Leader chosen by lot	• Legislative branch passes laws	• Elected president
• Executive branch composed of a council of 500 men	• Executive branch carries out laws	• Executive branch made up of elected and appointed officials
• Juries varied in size	• Judicial branch conducts trials with paid jurors	• Juries composed of 12 jurors
• No attorneys; no appeals; one-day trials		• Defendants and plaintiffs have attorneys; long appeals process

hold public office. Now even the poorest citizen could serve if elected or chosen by lot. Consequently, Athens had more citizens engaged in self-government than any other city-state in Greece. This reform made Athens one of the most democratic governments in history.

The introduction of **direct democracy**, a form of government in which citizens rule directly and not through representatives, was an important legacy of Periclean Athens. Few other city-states practiced this style of government. In Athens, male citizens who served in the assembly established all the important government policies that affected the polis. In a speech honoring the Athenian war dead, Pericles expressed his great pride in Athenian democracy:

PRIMARY SOURCE Ⓐ
Our constitution is called a democracy because power is in the hands not of a minority but of the whole people. When it is a question of settling private disputes, everyone is equal before the law; when it is a question of putting one person before another in positions of public responsibility, what counts is not membership in a particular class, but the actual ability which the man possesses. No one, so long as he has it in him to be of service to the state, is kept in political obscurity because of poverty.
PERICLES, "The Funeral Oration," from Thucydides, *The Peloponnesian War*

MAIN IDEA

Analyzing Primary Sources

Ⓐ How accurate do you consider Pericles' statement that Athenian democracy was in the hands of "the whole people"?

Athenian Empire After the defeat of the Persians, Athens helped organize the Delian League. In time, Athens took over leadership of the league and dominated all the city-states in it. Pericles used the money from the league's treasury to make the Athenian navy the strongest in the Mediterranean. A strong navy was important because it helped Athens strengthen the safety of its empire. Prosperity depended on gaining access to the surrounding waterways. Athens needed overseas trade to obtain supplies of grain and other raw materials.

Athenian military might allowed Pericles to treat other members of the Delian League as part of the empire. Some cities in the Peloponnesus, however, resisted Athens and formed their own alliances. As you will read later in this section, Sparta in particular was at odds with Athens.

Glorifying Athens Pericles also used money from the Delian League to beautify Athens. Without the league's approval, he persuaded the Athenian assembly to vote huge sums of the league's money to buy gold, ivory, and marble. Still more money went to pay the artists, architects, and workers who used these materials.

Glorious Art and Architecture

Pericles' goal was to have the greatest Greek artists and architects create magnificent sculptures and buildings to glorify Athens. At the center of his plan was one of architecture's noblest works—the Parthenon.

Architecture and Sculpture The Parthenon, a masterpiece of architectural design and craftsmanship, was not unique in style. Rather, Greek architects constructed the 23,000-square-foot building in the traditional style that had been used to create Greek temples for 200 years. This temple,

History Makers

Pericles 495–429 B.C.

Pericles came from a rich and high-ranking noble family. His aristocratic father had led the Athenian assembly and fought at the Battle of Salamis in the Persian Wars. His mother was the niece of Cleisthenes, the Athenian noble who had introduced important democratic reforms.

Pericles was well known for his political achievements as leader of Athens. Pericles the man, however, was harder to know. One historian wrote: "[He] no doubt, was a lonely man. . . . He had no friend . . . [and] he only went out [of his home] for official business."

↗ **hmhsocialstudies.com**

RESEARCH WEB LINKS Go online for more on Pericles.

built to honor Athena, the goddess of wisdom and the protector of Athens, contained examples of Greek art that set standards for future generations of artists around the world. Pericles entrusted much of the work on the Parthenon to the sculptor Phidias (FIDH•ee•uhs). Within the temple, Phidias crafted a giant statue of Athena that not only contained such precious materials as gold and ivory, but also stood over 30 feet tall.

Phidias and other sculptors during this golden age aimed to create figures that were graceful, strong, and perfectly formed. Their faces showed neither joy nor anger, only serenity. Greek sculptors also tried to capture the grace of the idealized human body in motion. They wanted to portray ideal beauty, not realism. Their values of harmony, order, balance, and proportion became the standard of what is called **classical art**.

Drama and History

▼ This poster promotes an 1898 production of Euripides' *Medea*, starring the great French actress Sarah Bernhardt.

The Greeks invented drama as an art form and built the first theaters in the West. Theatrical productions in Athens were both an expression of civic pride and a tribute to the gods. As part of their civic duty, wealthy citizens bore the cost of producing the plays. Actors used colorful costumes, masks, and sets to dramatize stories. The plays were about leadership, justice, and the duties owed to the gods. They often included a chorus that danced, sang, and recited poetry.

Tragedy and Comedy The Greeks wrote two kinds of drama—tragedy and comedy. A **tragedy** was a serious drama about common themes such as love, hate, war, or betrayal. These dramas featured a main character, or tragic hero. The hero usually was an important person and often gifted with extraordinary abilities. A tragic flaw usually caused the hero's downfall. Often this flaw was hubris, or excessive pride.

In ancient times, Greece had three notable dramatists who wrote tragedies. Aeschylus (EHS•kuh•luhs) wrote more than 80 plays. His most famous work is the trilogy—a three-play series—*Oresteia* (ohr•res•TEE•uh). It is based on the family of Agamemnon, the Mycenaean king who commanded the Greeks at Troy. The plays examine the idea of justice. Sophocles (SAHF•uh•kleez) wrote more than 100 plays, including the tragedies *Oedipus the King* and *Antigone*. Euripides (yoo•RIP•uh•DEEZ), author of the play *Medea*, often featured strong women in his works.

In contrast to Greek tragedies, a **comedy** contained scenes filled with slapstick situations and crude humor. Playwrights often made fun of politics and respected people and ideas of the time. Aristophanes (AR•ih•STAHF•uh•neez) wrote the first great comedies for the stage, including *The Birds* and *Lysistrata*. *Lysistrata* portrayed the women of Athens forcing their husbands to end the Peloponnesian War. The fact that Athenians could listen to criticism of themselves showed the freedom and openness of public discussion that existed in democratic Athens. **B**

MAIN IDEA

Contrasting
B How did tragedy differ from comedy?

History As you learned earlier in this chapter, there are no written records from the Dorian period. The epic poems of Homer recount stories, but are not accurate recordings of what took place. Herodotus, a Greek who lived in Athens for a time, pioneered the accurate reporting of events. His book on the Persian Wars is considered the first work of history. However, the greatest historian of the classical age was the Athenian Thucydides (thoo•SID•ih•DEEZ). He believed that certain types of events and political situations recur over time. Studying those events and situations, he felt, would aid in understanding the present. The approaches Thucydides used in his work still guide historians today.

Athenians and Spartans Go to War

As Athens grew in wealth, prestige, and power, other city-states began to view it with hostility. Ill will was especially strong between Sparta and Athens. Many people thought that war between the two was inevitable. Instead of trying to avoid conflict, leaders in Athens and Sparta pressed for a war to begin, as both groups of leaders believed their own city had the advantage. Eventually, Sparta declared war on Athens in 431 B.C.

Peloponnesian War When the <u>Peloponnesian War</u> between the two city-states began, Athens had the stronger navy. Sparta had the stronger army, and its location inland meant that it could not easily be attacked by sea. Pericles' strategy was to avoid land battles with the Spartan army and wait for an opportunity to strike Sparta and its allies from the sea. **C**

Eventually, the Spartans marched into Athenian territory. They swept over the countryside, burning the Athenian food supply. Pericles responded by bringing residents from the surrounding region inside the city walls. The city was safe from hunger as long as ships could sail into port with supplies from Athenian colonies and foreign states.

In the second year of the war, however, disaster struck Athens. A frightful plague swept through the city, killing perhaps one-third of the population, including Pericles. Although weakened, Athens continued to fight for several years. Then, in 421 B.C., the two sides, worn down by the war, signed a truce.

Sparta Gains Victory The peace did not last long. In 415 B.C., the Athenians sent a huge fleet carrying more than 20,000 soldiers to the island of Sicily. Their plan was to destroy the city-state of Syracuse, one of Sparta's wealthiest allies. The expedition ended with a crushing defeat in 413 B.C. In his study of the Peloponnesian War, Thucydides recalled: "[The Athenians] were destroyed with a total

MAIN IDEA

Analyzing Motives
C What might have been Pericles' goals in the Peloponnesian War?

Peloponnesian War, 431–404 B.C.

16°E

42°N

24°E

Black Sea

THRACE

Byzantium

Adriatic Sea

MACEDONIA

Amphipolis (422 B.C.)

Aegospotami (405 B.C.)

Cyzicus (410 B.C.)

Spartalos (429 B.C.)

Cynossema (411 B.C.)

PERSIAN EMPIRE

Ionian Sea

Aegean Sea

Arginusae Islands (406 B.C.)

GREECE

IONIA

Thebes

Delium (424 B.C.)

Ephesus

Athens

Notium (407 B.C.)

✹ Athenian victory
✹ Spartan victory
■ Athens and allies
■ Sparta and allies
□ Neutral states

Corinth

Miletus

Mantinea (418 B.C.)

Sicily

Sparta

Syracuse (413 B.C.)

Sphacteria (425 B.C.)

N

0   100 Miles

0   200 Kilometers

Mediterranean Sea

Crete

GEOGRAPHY SKILLBUILDER: Interpreting Maps
1. **Location** Where were most of the allies of Athens located?
2. **Movement** Why was the sea important to Athens during the Peloponnesian War?

Classical Greece **137**

destruction—their fleet, their army—there was nothing that was not destroyed, and few out of many returned home." Somehow, a terribly weakened Athens fended off Spartan attacks for another nine years. Finally, in 404 B.C., the Athenians and their allies surrendered. Athens had lost its empire, power, and wealth.

Philosophers Search for Truth

After the war, many Athenians lost confidence in democratic government and began to question their values. In this time of uncertainty, several great thinkers appeared. They were determined to seek the truth, no matter where the search led them. The Greeks called such thinkers **philosophers**, meaning "lovers of wisdom." These Greek thinkers based their philosophy on the following two assumptions:

- The universe (land, sky, and sea) is put together in an orderly way, and subject to absolute and unchanging laws.
- People can understand these laws through logic and reason.

One group of philosophers, the Sophists, questioned people's unexamined beliefs and ideas about justice and other traditional values. One of the most famous Sophists was Protagoras, who questioned the existence of the traditional Greek gods. He also argued that there was no universal standard of truth, saying "Man [the individual] is the measure of all things." These were radical and dangerous ideas to many Athenians. **D**

MAIN IDEA

Making Inferences
D Why would philosophers start questioning traditional beliefs at this particular time in Athenian history?

Socrates One critic of the Sophists was **Socrates** (SAHK•ruh•TEEZ). Unlike the Sophists, he believed that absolute standards did exist for truth and justice. However, he encouraged Greeks to go farther and question themselves and their moral character. Historians believe that it was Socrates who once said, "The unexamined life is not worth living." Socrates was admired by many who understood his ideas. However, others were puzzled by this man's viewpoints.

In 399 B.C., when Socrates was about 70 years old, he was brought to trial for "corrupting the youth of Athens" and "neglecting the city's gods." In his own defense, Socrates said that his teachings were good for Athens because they forced people to think about their values and actions. The jury disagreed and condemned him to death. He died by drinking hemlock, a slow-acting poison.

▼ Surrounded by supporters, Socrates prepares to drink poison.

Plato A student of Socrates, **Plato** (PLAY•toh), was in his late 20s when his teacher died. Later, Plato wrote down the conversations of Socrates "as a means of philosophical investigation." Sometime in the 370s B.C., Plato wrote his most famous work, *The Republic*. In it, he set forth his vision of a perfectly governed society. It was not a democracy. In his ideal society, all citizens would fall naturally into three groups: farmers and artisans, warriors, and the ruling class. The person with the greatest insight and intellect from the ruling class would be chosen philosopher-king. Plato's writings dominated philosophic thought in Europe for nearly 1,500

History Makers

Socrates
470–399 B.C.

Socrates encouraged his students to examine their beliefs. He asked them a series of leading questions to show that people hold many contradictory opinions. This question-and-answer approach to teaching is known as the Socratic method. Socrates devoted his life to gaining self-knowledge and once said, "There is only one good, knowledge, and one evil, ignorance."

Plato
427–347 B.C.

Born into a wealthy Athenian family, Plato had careers as a wrestler and a poet before he became a philosopher. After Socrates, his teacher, died, Plato left Greece. He later returned to Athens and founded a school called the Academy in 387 B.C. The school lasted for approximately 900 years. It was Plato who once stated, "Philosophy begins in wonder."

Aristotle
384–322 B.C.

Aristotle, the son of a physician, was one of the brightest students at Plato's Academy. He came there as a young man and stayed for 20 years until Plato's death. In 335 B.C., Aristotle opened his own school in Athens called the Lyceum. The school eventually rivaled the Academy. Aristotle once argued, "He who studies how things originated . . . will achieve the clearest view of them."

years. His only rivals in importance were his teacher, Socrates, and his own pupil, Aristotle (AR•ih•STAHT•uhl).

Aristotle The philosopher <u>Aristotle</u> questioned the nature of the world and of human belief, thought, and knowledge. Aristotle came close to summarizing all the knowledge up to his time. He invented a method for arguing according to rules of logic. He later applied his method to problems in the fields of psychology, physics, and biology. His work provides the basis of the scientific method used today.

One of Aristotle's most famous pupils was Alexander, son of King Philip II of Macedonia. Around 343 B.C., Aristotle accepted the king's invitation to tutor the 13-year-old prince. Alexander's status as a student abruptly ended three years later, when his father called him back to Macedonia. You will learn more about Alexander in Section 4.

SECTION 3 ASSESSMENT

TERMS & NAMES 1. For each term or name, write a sentence explaining its significance.
• direct democracy • classical art • tragedy • comedy • Peloponnesian War • philosopher • Socrates • Plato • Aristotle

USING YOUR NOTES

2. Which of Pericles' goals do you think had the greatest impact on the modern world? Explain your choice.

Pericles' Goals

MAIN IDEAS

3. What steps did Pericles take to strengthen democracy in Athens?

4. What were the battle strategies of Athens and Sparta in the Peloponnesian War?

5. Why do you think some Athenians found the ideas of Socrates so disturbing?

CRITICAL THINKING & WRITING

6. **MAKING INFERENCES** How does the concept of hubris from Greek tragedy apply to the Peloponnesian War?

7. **DRAWING CONCLUSIONS** Was the rule of Pericles a "golden age" for Athens? Explain.

8. **FORMING AND SUPPORTING OPINIONS** Do you agree with Socrates that there are absolute standards for truth and justice? Why or why not?

9. **WRITING ACTIVITY** POWER AND AUTHORITY Write a two- or three-paragraph **essay** comparing the system of direct democracy adopted by Athens and the system of government Plato described in *The Republic*.

CONNECT TO TODAY CREATING AN ILLUSTRATED REPORT

One of Pericles' goals was to create magnificent sculptures and buildings to glorify Athens. Identify local buildings or works of art that were created to honor your community, state, or the United States. Write a brief **illustrated report** on these buildings.

Greek Art and Architecture

During ancient times, the Greeks established artistic standards that strongly influenced the later art of the Western world. The aim of Greek art was to express true ideals. To do this, the Greeks used balance, harmony, and symmetry in their art.

A major branch of Greek art was sculpture. Greek sculptors did not create realistic works, but instead made statues that reflected what they considered ideal beauty. Greek art also included pottery.

In Greek architecture, the most important type of building was the temple. The walled rooms in the center of the temple held sculptures of gods and goddesses and lavish gifts to these deities.

↗ **hmhsocialstudies.com**

RESEARCH WEB LINKS Go online for more on Greek art and architecture.

Nike of Samothrace ▶

Discovered in 1863, the Nike (or Winged Victory) of Samothrace was probably created around 203 B.C. to honor a sea battle. Through its exaggerated features and artful portrayal of flowing drapery, the Nike conveys a sense of action and triumph. Currently, it is displayed at the Louvre Museum in Paris.

◄ Red and Black Pottery

Greek art also included pottery, which is known for its beauty of form and decoration. The two major types of Greek pottery are black-figure pottery (shown on the vessel) and red-figure pottery (shown on the plate). The vessel shows a scene from Greek mythology. The god Zeus, disguised as a bull, carries off a young woman named Europa. The figures on the plate demonstrate the importance of the sea and seafood in Greek culture.

HISTORY VIDEO
Peter on the Parthenon

↗ hmhsocialstudies.com

The Parthenon ▲

Built between 447 and 432 B.C., the Parthenon was a Greek temple dedicated to Athena. It serves as an excellent example of the Greek expression of harmony, symmetry, and balance. Just as Greek philosophers tried to understand the basic laws of nature, so Greek architects looked to nature for guidance. They discovered a ratio in nature that they believed created pleasing proportions and used that ratio to design the rectangles in the Parthenon.

◄ Dramatic Masks and Theater

In the 6th century B.C., the Greeks became the first people to use theater for its own sake and not for religious rituals. They wrote two types of plays, comedy and tragedy. For both forms, actors wore theatrical masks that exaggerated human expressions. The plays were performed in outdoor theaters. The stage or dancing floor was partially surrounded by a semicircular seating area fitted into a hillside, such as the one shown here.

Connect *to* Today

1. **Drawing Conclusions** How does the Parthenon display the Greek preference for symmetry and balance?

   See Skillbuilder Handbook, Page R11.

2. **Hypothesizing** On what does our culture today base its standards of beauty? Give examples to support your hypothesis.

Alexander's Empire

MAIN IDEA	WHY IT MATTERS NOW	TERMS & NAMES
EMPIRE BUILDING Alexander the Great conquered Persia and Egypt and extended his empire to the Indus River in northwest India.	Alexander's empire extended across an area that today consists of many nations and diverse cultures.	• Philip II • Alexander the Great • Macedonia • Darius III

SETTING THE STAGE The Peloponnesian War severely weakened several Greek city-states. This caused a rapid decline in their military and economic power. In the nearby kingdom of Macedonia, King **Philip II** took note. Philip dreamed of taking control of Greece and then moving against Persia to seize its vast wealth. Philip also hoped to avenge the Persian invasion of Greece in 480 B.C.

Philip Builds Macedonian Power

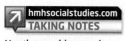

Use the graphic organizer online to take notes on the growth of Alexander's empire.

The kingdom of **Macedonia**, located just north of Greece, had rough terrain and a cold climate. The Macedonians were a hardy people who lived in mountain villages rather than city-states. Most Macedonian nobles thought of themselves as Greeks. The Greeks, however, looked down on the Macedonians as uncivilized foreigners who had no great philosophers, sculptors, or writers. The Macedonians did have one very important resource—their shrewd and fearless kings.

Philip's Army In 359 B.C., Philip II became king of Macedonia. Though only 23 years old, he quickly proved to be a brilliant general and a ruthless politician. Philip transformed the rugged peasants under his command into a well-trained professional army. He organized his troops into phalanxes of 16 men across and 16 deep, each one armed with an 18-foot pike. Philip used this heavy phalanx formation to break through enemy lines. Then he used fast-moving cavalry to crush his disorganized opponents. After he employed these tactics successfully against northern opponents, Philip began to prepare an invasion of Greece.

Conquest of Greece Demosthenes (dee•MAHS•thuh•NEEZ), the Athenian orator, tried to warn the Greeks of the threat Philip and his army posed. He urged them to unite against Philip. However, the Greek city-states could not agree on any single policy. Finally, in 338 B.C., Athens and Thebes—a city-state in central Greece—joined forces to fight Philip. By then, however, it was too late. The Macedonians soundly defeated the Greeks at the battle of Chaeronea (KAIR•uh•NEE•uh). This defeat ended Greek independence. The city-states retained self-government in local affairs. However, Greece itself remained firmly under the control of a succession of foreign powers—the first of which was Philip's Macedonia.

MAIN IDEA

Analyzing Causes

A How did the Peloponnesian War pave the way for Philip's conquest of Greece?

Although Philip planned to invade Persia next, he never got the chance. At his daughter's wedding in 336 B.C., he was stabbed to death by a former guardsman. Philip's son Alexander immediately proclaimed himself king of Macedonia. Because of his accomplishments over the next 13 years, he became known as **Alexander the Great**. **A**

Alexander Defeats Persia

Although Alexander was only 20 years old when he became king, he was well prepared to lead. Under Aristotle's teaching, Alexander had learned science, geography, and literature. Alexander especially enjoyed Homer's description of the heroic deeds performed by Achilles during the Trojan War. To inspire himself, he kept a copy of the *Iliad* under his pillow.

As a young boy, Alexander learned to ride a horse, use weapons, and command troops. Once he became king, Alexander promptly demonstrated that his military training had not been wasted. When the people of Thebes rebelled, he destroyed the city. About 6,000 Thebans were killed. The survivors were sold into slavery. Frightened by his cruelty, the other Greek city-states quickly gave up any idea of rebellion.

Invasion of Persia With Greece now secure, Alexander felt free to carry out his father's plan to invade and conquer Persia. In 334 B.C., he led 35,000 soldiers across the Hellespont into Anatolia. (See the map on page 144.) Persian messengers raced along the Royal Road to spread news of the invasion. An army of about 40,000 men rushed to defend Persia. The two forces met at the Granicus River. Instead of waiting for the Persians to make the first move, Alexander ordered his cavalry to attack. Leading his troops into battle, Alexander smashed the Persian defenses.

Alexander's victory at Granicus alarmed the Persian king, **Darius III**. Vowing to crush the invaders, he raised a huge army of between 50,000 and 75,000 men to face the Macedonians near Issus. Realizing that he was outnumbered, Alexander surprised his enemies. He ordered his finest troops to break through a weak point in the Persian lines. The army then charged straight at Darius. To avoid capture, the frightened king fled, followed by his panicked army. This victory gave Alexander control over Anatolia.

Conquering the Persian Empire Shaken by his defeat, Darius tried to negotiate a peace settlement. He offered Alexander all of his lands west of the Euphrates River. Alexander's advisers urged him to accept. However, the rapid collapse of Persian resistance fired Alexander's ambition. He rejected Darius's offer and confidently announced his plan to conquer the entire Persian Empire.

Alexander marched into Egypt, a Persian territory, in 332 B.C. The Egyptians welcomed Alexander as a liberator. They crowned him pharaoh—or god-king. During his time in Egypt, Alexander founded the city of Alexandria at the mouth of the Nile. After leaving Egypt, Alexander moved east into Mesopotamia to confront Darius. The desperate Persian king assembled a force of some 250,000 men. The two armies met at Gaugamela (GAW•guh•MEE•luh), a small village near the ruins of ancient Nineveh. Alexander launched a massive phalanx attack followed

Vocabulary

The Hellespont is the ancient name for the Dardanelles, the narrow straits that separate Europe from Asia Minor.

History Makers

Alexander 356–323 B.C.

When Alexander was only eight or nine years old, he tamed a wild horse that none of his father's grooms could manage. Alexander calmed the horse, whose name was Bucephalus, by speaking gently. Seeing the control that Alexander had over the horse, Philip II said: "You'll have to find another kingdom; Macedonia isn't going to be big enough for you."

Alexander took his father's advice. Riding Bucephalus at the head of a great army, he conquered the lands from Greece to the Indus Valley. When the horse died in what is now Pakistan, Alexander named the city of Bucephala after it. Maybe he was tired of the name Alexandria. By that time, he had already named at least a dozen cities after himself!

by a cavalry charge. As the Persian lines crumbled, Darius again panicked and fled. Alexander's victory at Gaugamela ended Persia's power.

Within a short time, Alexander's army occupied Babylon, Susa, and Persepolis. These cities yielded a huge treasure, which Alexander distributed among his army. A few months after it was occupied, Persepolis, Persia's royal capital, burned to the ground. Some people said Alexander left the city in ashes to signal the total destruction of the Persian Empire. The Greek historian Arrian, writing about 500 years after Alexander's time, suggested that the fire was set in revenge for the Persian burning of Athens. However, the cause of the fire remains a mystery.

Alexander's Other Conquests

Alexander now reigned as the unchallenged ruler of southwest Asia. But he was more interested in expanding his empire than in governing it. He left the ruined Persepolis to pursue Darius and conquer Persia's remote Asian provinces. Darius's trail led Alexander to a deserted spot south of the Caspian Sea. There he found Darius already dead, murdered by one of his provincial governors. Rather than return to Babylon, Alexander continued east. During the next three years, his army fought its way across the desert wastes and mountains of Central Asia. He pushed on, hoping to reach the farthest edge of the continent. **B**

Alexander in India In 326 B.C., Alexander and his army reached the Indus Valley. At the Hydaspes River, a powerful Indian army blocked their path. After winning a fierce battle, Alexander's soldiers marched some 200 miles farther, but their morale was low. They had been fighting for 11 years and had marched more than 11,000 miles. They had endured both scorching deserts and drenching monsoon rains. The exhausted soldiers yearned to go home. Bitterly disappointed, Alexander agreed to turn back.

MAIN IDEA

Analyzing Motives
B Why did Alexander continue his conquests after Darius was dead?

Alexander and His Successors, 336–300 B.C.

hmhsocialstudies.com INTERACTIVE MAP

- Alexander's empire at its height, 323 B.C.
- Path of conquest
- Major battle

GEOGRAPHY SKILLBUILDER: Interpreting Maps
1. **Region** Onto which continents did Alexander's empire spread?
2. **Place** Which kingdoms succeeded the empire of Alexander the Great after his death in 323 B.C.?

Alexander's Empire and Its Legacy, 336–306 B.C.

ALEXANDER'S EMPIRE

336 B.C.
Philip II was assassinated. Alexander became king of Macedonia at age 20.

334 B.C.
Alexander led 35,000 soldiers into Anatolia.

332 B.C.
Alexander entered Egypt and founded the city of Alexandria.

326 B.C.
Alexander's army reached the Indus Valley.

323 B.C.
Alexander died at age 32. His generals began a power struggle.

MACEDONIA

PERSIA

EGYPT

323 B.C.
Ptolemy became governor of Egypt.

312 B.C.
Seleucus took most of Persian Empire.

306 B.C.
Antigonus I became king of Macedonia.

By the spring of 323 B.C., Alexander and his army had reached Babylon. Restless as always, Alexander announced plans to organize and unify his empire. He would construct new cities, roads, and harbors and conquer Arabia. However, Alexander never carried out his plans. He became seriously ill with a fever and died a few days later. He was just 32 years old.

Alexander's Legacy After Alexander died, his Macedonian generals fought among themselves for control of his empire. Eventually, three ambitious leaders won out. Antigonus (an•TIG•uh•nuhs) became king of Macedonia and took control of the Greek city-states. Ptolemy (TAHL•uh•mee) seized Egypt, took the title of pharaoh, and established a dynasty. Seleucus (sih•LOO•kuhs) took most of the old Persian Empire, which became known as the Seleucid kingdom. Ignoring the democratic traditions of the Greek polis, these rulers and their descendants governed with complete power over their subjects. **C**

Alexander's conquests had an interesting cultural impact. Alexander himself adopted Persian dress and customs and married a Persian woman. He included Persians and people from other lands in his army. As time passed, Greek settlers throughout the empire also adopted new ways. A vibrant new culture emerged from the blend of Greek and Eastern customs.

MAIN IDEA

Hypothesizing
C Was the power struggle that followed Alexander's death inevitable?

SECTION 4 ASSESSMENT

TERMS & NAMES 1. For each term or name, write a sentence explaining its significance.
• Philip II   • Macedonia   • Alexander the Great   • Darius III

USING YOUR NOTES

2. Which of Alexander's conquests do you think was the most significant? Why?

I. Philip Builds Macedonian Power
 A.
 B.
II. Alexander Conquers Persia

MAIN IDEAS

3. How was Philip II able to conquer Greece?

4. Philip II's goal was to conquer Persia. Why did Alexander continue his campaign of conquest after this goal had been achieved?

5. What happened to Alexander's empire after his death?

CRITICAL THINKING & WRITING

6. **FORMING AND SUPPORTING OPINIONS** Do you think that Alexander was worthy of the title "Great"? Explain.

7. **HYPOTHESIZING** If Alexander had lived, do you think he would have been as successful in ruling his empire as he was in building it? Explain.

8. **MAKING INFERENCES** Why do you think Alexander adopted Persian customs and included Persians in his army?

9. **WRITING ACTIVITY** EMPIRE BUILDING In small groups, create **storyboards** for a video presentation on the growth of Alexander's empire.

CONNECT TO TODAY CREATING A MAP
Use atlases to find the modern countries that occupy the lands included in Alexander's empire. Create a **map** that shows the boundaries and names of these countries. Compare your map to the map of Alexander's empire on page 144.

The Spread of Hellenistic Culture

MAIN IDEA	WHY IT MATTERS NOW	TERMS & NAMES
CULTURAL INTERACTION Hellenistic culture, a blend of Greek and other influences, flourished throughout Greece, Egypt, and Asia.	Western civilization today continues to be influenced by diverse cultures.	• Hellenistic • Archimedes • Alexandria • Colossus of • Euclid Rhodes

SETTING THE STAGE Alexander's ambitions were cultural as well as military and political. During his wars of conquest, he actively sought to meld the conquered culture with that of the Greeks. He started new cities as administrative centers and outposts of Greek culture. These cities, from Egyptian Alexandria in the south to the Asian Alexandrias in the east, adopted many Greek patterns and customs. After Alexander's death, trade, a shared Greek culture, and a common language continued to link the cities together. But each region had its own traditional ways of life, religion, and government that no ruler could afford to overlook.

Hellenistic Culture in Alexandria

TAKING NOTES

Use the graphic organizer online to take notes on Hellenistic achievements in science and the arts.

As a result of Alexander's policies, a vibrant new culture emerged. Greek (also known as Hellenic) culture blended with Egyptian, Persian, and Indian influences. This blending became known as **Hellenistic** culture. Koine (koy•NAY), the popular spoken language used in Hellenistic cities, was the direct result of cultural blending. The word *koine* came from the Greek word for "common." The language was a dialect of Greek. This language enabled educated people and traders from diverse backgrounds to communicate in cities throughout the Hellenistic world.

Trade and Cultural Diversity Among the many cities of the Hellenistic world, the Egyptian city of **Alexandria** became the foremost center of commerce and Hellenistic civilization. Alexandria occupied a strategic site on the western edge of the Nile delta. Trade ships from all around the Mediterranean docked in its spacious harbor. Alexandria's thriving commerce enabled it to grow and prosper. By the third century B.C., Alexandria had become an international community, with a rich mixture of customs and traditions from Egypt and from the Aegean. Its diverse population exceeded half a million people.

Alexandria's Attractions Both residents and visitors admired Alexandria's great beauty. Broad avenues lined with statues of Greek gods divided the city into blocks. Rulers built magnificent royal palaces overlooking the harbor. A much visited tomb contained Alexander's elaborate glass coffin. Soaring more than 350 feet over the harbor stood an enormous stone lighthouse called the Pharos. This lighthouse contained a polished bronze mirror that, at night, reflected the

Vocabulary
Museum means "house of the muses."

light from a blazing fire. Alexandria's greatest attractions were its famous museum and library. The museum was a temple dedicated to the Muses, the Greek goddesses of arts and sciences. It contained art galleries, a zoo, botanical gardens, and even a dining hall. The museum was an institute of advanced study.

The Alexandrian Library stood nearby. Its collection of half a million papyrus scrolls included many of the masterpieces of ancient literature. As the first true research library in the world, it helped promote the work of a gifted group of scholars. These scholars greatly respected the earlier works of classical literature and learning. They produced commentaries that explained these works.

Science and Technology

Hellenistic scholars, particularly those in Alexandria, preserved Greek and Egyptian learning in the sciences. Until the scientific advances of the 16th and 17th centuries, Alexandrian scholars provided most of the scientific knowledge available to the West.

Astronomy-Alexandria's museum contained a small observatory in which astronomers could study the planets and stars. One astronomer, Aristarchus (AR•ih•STAHR•kuhs) of Samos, reached two significant scientific conclusions. In one, he estimated that the Sun was at least 300 times larger than Earth. Although he greatly underestimated the Sun's true size, Aristarchus disproved the widely held belief that the Sun was smaller than Greece. In another conclusion, he proposed that Earth and the other planets revolve around the Sun. Unfortunately for science, other astronomers refused to support Aristarchus' theory. In the second century A.D., Alexandria's last renowned astronomer, Ptolemy, incorrectly placed Earth at the center of the solar system. Astronomers accepted this view for the next 14 centuries.

Eratosthenes (EHR•uh•TAHS•thuh•NEEZ), the director of the Alexandrian Library, tried to calculate Earth's true size. Using geometry, he computed Earth's circumference at between 28,000 and 29,000 miles. Modern measurements put the circumference at 24,860 miles. As well as a highly regarded astronomer and mathematician, Eratosthenes also was a poet and historian.

Mathematics and Physics In their work, Eratosthenes and Aristarchus used a geometry text compiled by <u>Euclid</u> (YOO•klihd). Euclid was a highly regarded

▼ Hipparchus, who lived in Alexandria for a time, charted the position of 850 stars.

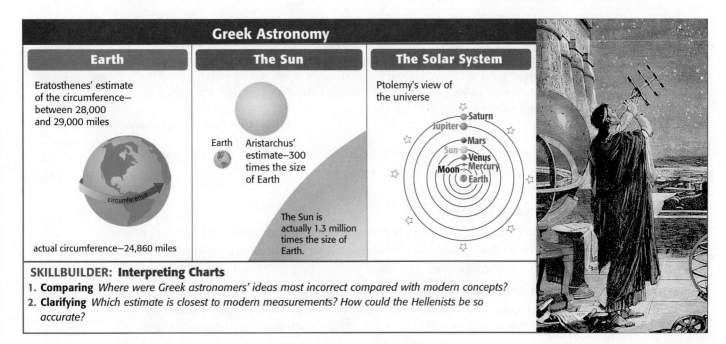

Greek Astronomy

Earth	The Sun	The Solar System
Eratosthenes' estimate of the circumference— between 28,000 and 29,000 miles	Earth Aristarchus' estimate–300 times the size of Earth	Ptolemy's view of the universe
actual circumference—24,860 miles	The Sun is actually 1.3 million times the size of Earth.	Saturn / Jupiter / Mars / Sun / Venus / Moon / Mercury / Earth

SKILLBUILDER: Interpreting Charts
1. **Comparing** *Where were Greek astronomers' ideas most incorrect compared with modern concepts?*
2. **Clarifying** *Which estimate is closest to modern measurements? How could the Hellenists be so accurate?*

Pythagorean Theorem

Geometry students remember Pythagoras for his theorem on the triangle, but its principles were known earlier. This formula states that the square of a right triangle's hypotenuse equals the sum of the squared lengths of the two remaining sides. Chinese mathematicians knew this theory perhaps as early as 1100 B.C. Egyptian surveyors put it to practical use even earlier.

However, the work of the school that Pythagoras founded caught the interest of later mathematicians. Shown are Euclid's proof in Greek along with a Chinese and an Arabic translation. The Arabs who conquered much of Alexander's empire spread Greek mathematical learning to the West. The formula became known as the Pythagorean theorem throughout the world.

Greek, A.D. 800

Arabic, A.D. 1250

Chinese, A.D. 1607

mathematician who taught in Alexandria. His best-known book, *Elements*, contained 465 carefully presented geometry propositions and proofs. Euclid's work is still the basis for courses in geometry.

Another important Hellenistic scientist, **Archimedes** (AHR•kuh•MEE•deez) of Syracuse, studied at Alexandria. He accurately estimated the value of pi (π)—the ratio of the circumference of a circle to its diameter. In addition, Archimedes explained the law of the lever.

Gifted in both geometry and physics, Archimedes also put his genius to practical use. He invented the Archimedes screw, a device that raised water from the ground, and the compound pulley to lift heavy objects. The writer Plutarch described how Archimedes demonstrated to an audience of curious onlookers how something heavy can be moved by a small force:

PRIMARY SOURCE

Archimedes took a . . . ship . . . which had just been dragged up on land with great labor and many men; in this he placed her usual complement of men and cargo, and then sitting at some distance, without any trouble, by gently pulling with his hand the end of a system of pulleys, he dragged it towards him with as smooth and even a motion as if it were passing over the sea.

PLUTARCH, *Parallel Lives: Marcellus*

Using Archimedes' ideas, Hellenistic scientists later built a force pump, pneumatic machines, and even a steam engine. **A**

Philosophy and Art

The teachings of Plato and Aristotle continued to be very influential in Hellenistic philosophy. In the third century B.C., however, philosophers became concerned with how people should live their lives. Two major philosophies developed out of this concern.

Stoicism and Epicureanism A Greek philosopher named Zeno (335–263 B.C.) founded the school of philosophy called Stoicism (STOH•ih•SIHZ•uhm). Stoics proposed that people should live virtuous lives in harmony with the will of god or the natural laws that God established to run the universe. They also preached that

MAIN IDEA

Summarizing

A What were some of the main achievements of the scientists of the Hellenistic period?

human desires, power, and wealth were dangerous distractions that should be checked. Stoicism promoted social unity and encouraged its followers to focus on what they could control.

Epicurus (EHP•uh•KYUR•uhs) founded the school of thought called Epicureanism. He taught that gods who had no interest in humans ruled the universe. Epicurus believed that the only real objects were those that the five senses perceived. He taught that the greatest good and the highest pleasure came from virtuous conduct and the absence of pain. Epicureans proposed that the main goal of humans was to achieve harmony of body and mind. Today, the word *epicurean* means a person devoted to pursuing human pleasures, especially the enjoyment of good food. However, during his lifetime, Epicurus advocated moderation in all things. **B**

MAIN IDEA

Drawing Conclusions

B What was the main concern of the Stoic and Epicurean schools of philosophy?

Realism in Sculpture Like science, sculpture flourished during the Hellenistic age. Rulers, wealthy merchants, and cities all purchased statues to honor gods, commemorate heroes, and portray ordinary people in everyday situations. The largest known Hellenistic statue was created on the island of Rhodes. Known as the **Colossus of Rhodes**, this bronze statue stood more than 100 feet high. One of the seven wonders of the ancient world, this huge sculpture was toppled by an earthquake in about 225 B.C. Later, the bronze was sold for scrap. Another magnificent Hellenistic sculpture found on Rhodes was the Nike (or Winged Victory) of Samothrace. It was created around 203 B.C. to commemorate a Greek naval victory.

Hellenistic sculpture moved away from the harmonic balance and idealized forms of the classical age. Instead of the serene face and perfect body of an idealized man or woman, Hellenistic sculptors created more natural works. They felt free to explore new subjects, carving ordinary people such as an old, wrinkled peasant woman.

By 150 B.C., the Hellenistic world was in decline. A new city, Rome, was growing and gaining strength. Through Rome, Greek-style drama, architecture, sculpture, and philosophy were preserved and eventually became the core of Western civilization.

SECTION 5 ASSESSMENT

TERMS & NAMES 1. For each term or name, write a sentence explaining its significance.
- Hellenistic
- Alexandria
- Euclid
- Archimedes
- Colossus of Rhodes

USING YOUR NOTES

2. Which Hellenistic achievement had the greatest impact? Why?

Category	Achievements
astronomy	
geometry	
philosophy	
art	

MAIN IDEAS

3. How did trade contribute to cultural diversity in the Hellenistic city of Alexandria?

4. How did Euclid influence some of the developments in astronomy during the Hellenistic period?

5. What did Stoicism and Epicureanism have in common?

CRITICAL THINKING & WRITING

6. **SYNTHESIZING** Describe how the growth of Alexander's empire spread Greek culture.

7. **MAKING INFERENCES** What do you think was the greatest scientific advance of the Hellenistic period? Why?

8. **COMPARING** How was the purpose served by architecture and sculpture in the Hellenistic period similar to the purpose served by these arts in the Golden Age of Athens?

9. **WRITING ACTIVITY** CULTURAL INTERACTION The Hellenistic culture brought together Egyptian, Greek, Persian, and Indian influences. Write a brief **essay** showing how American culture is a combination of different influences.

CONNECT TO TODAY CREATING A COLLAGE

Archimedes developed, or provided the ideas for, many practical devices—the lever, for example. Consider some of the everyday implements that are related to these devices. Create a **collage** of pictures of these implements. Accompany each visual with a brief annotation.

TERMS & NAMES

For each term or name below, briefly explain its connection to Classical Greece.

1. Trojan War
2. Homer
3. polis
4. democracy
5. classical art
6. Aristotle
7. Alexander the Great
8. Hellenistic

MAIN IDEAS

Cultures of the Mountains and the Sea
Section 1 (pages 123–126)

9. Why was sea travel important to early Greece?
10. Why did the Greeks develop myths?

Warring City-States Section 2 (pages 127–133)

11. What were the two most powerful city-states in early Greece?
12. What were the consequences of the Persian Wars?

Democracy and Greece's Golden Age
Section 3 (pages 134–141)

13. What were Pericles' three goals for Athens?
14. Who were the three renowned philosophers of the golden age?

Alexander's Empire Section 4 (pages 142–145)

15. Why was Greece so easily conquered by Macedonia?
16. What was the full extent of Alexander's empire before his death?

The Spread of Hellenistic Culture
Section 5 (pages 146–149)

17. What four influences blended to form Hellenistic culture?
18. What are some of the scientific achievements of the Hellenistic period?

CRITICAL THINKING

1. USING YOUR NOTES

In a diagram like the one below, show the development of direct democracy in Athens.

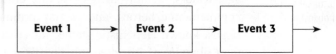

| Event 1 | → | Event 2 | → | Event 3 | → |

2. DRAWING CONCLUSIONS

POWER AND AUTHORITY "Years of uncertainty and insecurity have changed the country. It once was Athens, but now it has become Sparta." What do you think this statement means? Use information from the chapter to illustrate your answer.

3. ANALYZING ISSUES

CULTURAL INTERACTION Based on the Visual Summary below and your review of the chapter, how do you think Classical Greece has influenced the United States? Support your answer with examples.

4. MAKING INFERENCES

EMPIRE BUILDING Consider Pericles and Alexander the Great. What qualifications or characteristics do you think are needed for a leader to build an empire? Why?

VISUAL SUMMARY

The Legacy of Greece

Culture

- Greek language
- Mythology about gods and goddesses
- Olympic games
- Philosophers search for truth

Science and Technology

- Disagreement whether Sun or Earth at center of universe
- Euclid's geometry textbook
- Accurate estimate of Earth's circumference
- Development of lever, pulley, and pump

Arts

- Drama and poetry
- Sculpture portraying ideals of beauty
- Painted pottery showing scenes of Greek life
- Classical architecture

Government

- Direct democracy; citizens rule by majority vote
- Citizens bring charges of wrongdoing
- Code of laws
- Expansion of citizenship to all free adult males, except foreigners

Use the quotation and your knowledge of world history to answer questions 1 and 2.

PRIMARY SOURCE

Where ought the sovereign power of the state to reside?-.-.-. The state aims to consist as far as possible of those who are alike and equal, a condition found chiefly among the middle section. . . . The middle class is also the steadiest element, the least eager for change. They neither covet, like the poor the possessions of others, nor do others covet theirs, as the poor covet those of the rich. . . . Tyranny often emerges from an over-enthusiastic democracy or from an oligarchy, but much more rarely from middle class constitutions.

ARISTOTLE, *Politics*

1. Why does Aristotle support the middle class as the location of power?

   A. He finds poor people too backward to rule.

   B. He thinks the rich are too greedy.

   C. The middle class is very enthusiastic about democracy.

   D. The middle class is steady and is less eager for change.

2. According to Aristotle, what often emerges from an "over-enthusiastic democracy"?

   A. tyranny

   B. oligarchy

   C. monarchy

   D. aristocracy

Use this scene pictured on a piece of Greek pottery and your knowledge of world history to answer question 3.

3. This scene shows a battle formation used by the Greeks. What is the formation called?

   A. shield and spear

   B. massed formation

   C. phalanx

   D. acropolisv

 hmhsocialstudies.com TEST PRACTICE

For additional test practice, go online for:

• Diagnostic tests

• Strategies

• Tutorials

Interact *with* History

On page 122, you drew certain conclusions about Greek culture and values without knowing details of Greek history. Now that you have read the chapter, reexamine the artworks and reread the Greeks' words. Conduct a class debate about how the art and ideals of Greece have influenced modern society.

FOCUS ON WRITING

Write an **epic poem** (between two and three pages long) about an event or an individual that you read about in Chapter 5. Possible subjects you might select include the Trojan War, the Persian Wars, the Peloponnesian War, Hector, Pericles, and Alexander. In writing your poem, try to imitate the style of the *Iliad* or the *Odyssey.*

MULTIMEDIA ACTIVITY

21ST CENTURY

NetExplorations: The Parthenon

Go to *NetExplorations* at **hmhsocialstudies.com** to learn more about the Parthenon. Search the Internet for additional information on the Parthenon and the sculptor Phidias, who oversaw its construction. Use the information you gather to record a mock radio or television interview with Phidias, and play it in class. Have Phidias answer questions about

• his designs for the statues and carvings that adorned the Parthenon.

• the significance of the Parthenon for his fellow Athenians.

• other works of art he created.

ANCIENT GREECE

The Acropolis of Athens symbolizes the city and represents the architectural and artistic legacy of ancient Greece. *Acropolis* means "highest city" in Greek, and there are many such sites in Greece. Historically, an acropolis provided shelter and defense against a city's enemies. The Acropolis of Athens—the best known of them all—contained temples, monuments, and artwork dedicated to the Greek gods. Archaeological evidence indicates that the Acropolis was an important place to inhabitants from much earlier eras. However, the structures that we see today on the site were largely conceived by the statesman Pericles during the Golden Age of Athens in the 5th century B.C.

Explore the Acropolis of ancient Greece and learn about the legacy of Greek civilization. You can find a wealth of information, video clips, primary sources, activities, and more at 🔗 hmhsocialstudies.com.

▶ The Parthenon

Watch the video to see what the Parthenon, one of the most important temples on the Acropolis, might have looked like after it was completed.

▶ The Persian Wars

Watch the video to find out how Athens emerged as the principal Greek city-state at the conclusion of the Persian Wars.

▶ The Goddess Athena

Watch the video to learn how, according to Greek mythology, Athena became the protector of Athens.

▶ Legacy of Greece

Watch the video to analyze *The School of Athens*, a painting by the Italian Renaissance artist Raphael, which pays tribute to the legacy of ancient Greece in philosophy and science.

CHAPTER 6

Ancient Rome and Early Christianity, 500 B.C.–A.D. 500

Essential Question

What impact did the rise and fall of the Roman Empire have on culture, government, and religion?

 What You Will Learn

In this chapter you will trace the rise, fall, and impact of the Roman Empire and the spread of Christianity.

SECTION 1 The Roman Republic
Main Idea The early Romans established a republic, which grew powerful and spread its influence.

SECTION 2 The Roman Empire
Main Idea The creation of the Roman Empire transformed Roman government, society, economy, and culture.

SECTION 3 The Rise of Christianity
Main Idea Christianity arose in Roman-occupied Judea and spread throughout the Empire.

SECTION 4 The Fall of the Roman Empire
Main Idea Internal problems and invasions spurred the division and decline of the Roman Empire.

SECTION 5 Rome and the Roots of Western Civilization
Main Idea The Romans developed many ideas and institutions that became fundamental to Western civilization.

Previewing Themes

POWER AND AUTHORITY Rome began as a republic, a government in which elected officials represent the people. Eventually, absolute rulers called emperors seized power and expanded the empire.
Geography *About how many miles did the Roman Empire stretch from east to west?*

EMPIRE BUILDING At its height, the Roman Empire touched three continents—Europe, Asia, and Africa. For several centuries, Rome brought peace and prosperity to its empire before its eventual collapse.
Geography *Why was the Mediterranean Sea important to the Roman Empire?*

RELIGIOUS AND ETHICAL SYSTEMS Out of Judea rose a monotheistic, or single-god, religion known as Christianity. Based on the teachings of Jesus of Nazareth, it soon spread throughout Rome and beyond.
Geography *What geographic features might have helped or hindered the spread of Christianity throughout the Roman Empire?*

ROME

500 B.C.

509 B.C.
Rome becomes a republic.

300 B.C.

264 B.C.
First Punic War begins.

218 B.C.
In the Second Punic War, Hannibal invades Italy.

100 B.C.

WORLD

321 B.C.
Chandragupta Maurya founds Mauryan Empire in India.

202 B.C.
◄ Han Dynasty takes power in China. (sculpted figure from Han period)

The Roman World, 265 B.C.–A.D. 117

HISTORY

Ancient Rome:
The Mobile Society

↗ hmhsocialstudies.com VIDEO

BRITAIN

EUROPE

GAUL

Rhine River

Danube River

DACIA

Po River

Massilia

Corsica

Tiber R.

Rome

ITALY

MACEDONIA

THRACE

Black Sea

Byzantium

ANATOLIA

Tigris R.

SPAIN

Balearic Is.

Sardinia

Athens

Ephesus

Antioch

Euphrates R.

Gades

Sicily

Crete

Cyprus

SYRIA

Damascus

Tyre

Caesarea

JUDEA

Mediterranean Sea

Cyrene

Alexandria

Memphis

ARABIA

AFRICA

EGYPT

Nile River

Red Sea

Thebes

Roman Republic, 265 B.C.

Areas added to Empire, A.D. 117

0   250   500 Miles

0   250   500 Kilometers

Conic Projection

31 B.C.
Octavian defeats the forces
of Antony and Cleopatra.
(bust of Cleopatra) ▶

A.D. 284
Diocletian becomes
emperor of Rome.

A.D. 476
▲ Western Roman Empire
falls. (Roman horseman)

A.D. 100   A.D. 300   A.D. 500

A.D. 100
Moche culture arises in
South America. (gold
toucan from Moche era) ▶

A.D. 300
Aksum kingdom emerges
in east Africa.

What makes a successful leader?

You are a member of the senate in ancient Rome. Soon you must decide whether to support or oppose a powerful leader who wants to become ruler. Many consider him a military genius for having gained vast territory and wealth for Rome. Others point out that he disobeyed orders and is both ruthless and devious. You wonder whether his ambition would lead to greater prosperity and order in the empire or to injustice and unrest.

▲ This 19th-century painting by Italian artist Cesare Maccari shows Cicero, one of ancient Rome's greatest public speakers, addressing fellow members of the Roman Senate.

EXAMINING *the* ISSUES

- **Which is more important in measuring leadership—results or integrity?**

- **Does a leader have to be likable in order to succeed?**

As a class, discuss these questions. Based on your discussion, think about what you have learned about other leaders in history, such as Alexander the Great and Darius of Persia. What qualities helped them to be successful or caused them to fail? As you read about Rome, see how the qualities of its leaders helped or hindered its development.

The Roman Republic

MAIN IDEA	WHY IT MATTERS NOW	TERMS & NAMES
POWER AND AUTHORITY The early Romans established a republic, which grew powerful and spread its influence.	Some of the most fundamental values and institutions of Western civilization began in the Roman Republic.	• republic • senate • patrician • dictator • plebeian • legion • tribune • Punic Wars • consul • Hannibal

SETTING THE STAGE While the great civilization of Greece was in decline, a new city to the west was developing and increasing its power. Rome grew from a small settlement to a mighty civilization that eventually conquered the Mediterranean world. In time, the Romans would build one of the most famous and influential empires in history.

The Origins of Rome

According to legend, the city of Rome was founded in 753 B.C. by Romulus and Remus, twin sons of the god Mars and a Latin princess. The twins were abandoned on the Tiber River as infants and raised by a she-wolf. The twins decided to build a city near the spot. In reality, it was men not immortals who built the city, and they chose the spot largely for its strategic location and fertile soil.

hmhsocialstudies.com
TAKING NOTES
Use the graphic organizer online to take notes on the section's main ideas and details.

Rome's Geography Rome was built on seven rolling hills at a curve on the Tiber River, near the center of the Italian peninsula. It was midway between the Alps and Italy's southern tip. Rome also was near the midpoint of the Mediterranean Sea. The historian Livy wrote about the city's site:

PRIMARY SOURCE
Not without reason did gods and men choose this spot for the site of our city—the [salubrious] hills, the river to bring us produce from the inland regions and sea-borne commerce from abroad, the sea itself, near enough for convenience yet not so near as to bring danger from foreign fleets, our situation in the very heart of Italy—all these advantages make it of all places in the world the best for a city destined to grow great.

LIVY, *The Early History of Rome*

The First Romans The earliest settlers on the Italian peninsula arrived in prehistoric times. From about 1000 to 500 B.C., three groups inhabited the region and eventually battled for control. They were the Latins, the Greeks, and the Etruscans. The Latins built the original settlement at Rome, a cluster of wooden huts atop one of its seven hills, Palatine Hill. These settlers were considered to be the first Romans.

Between 750 and 600 B.C., the Greeks established colonies along southern Italy and Sicily. The cities became prosperous and commercially active. They brought all of Italy, including Rome, into closer contact with Greek civilization.

Ancient Rome and Early Christianity **155**

hmhsocialstudies.com

INTERACTIVE MAP

Explore the geography and learn about the early settlers of ancient Rome.

The Etruscans were native to northern Italy. They were skilled metalworkers and engineers. The Etruscans strongly influenced the development of Roman civilization. They boasted a system of writing, for example, and the Romans adopted their alphabet. They also influenced Rome's architecture, especially the use of the arch.

The Early Republic

Around 600 B.C., an Etruscan became king of Rome. In the decades that followed, Rome grew from a collection of hilltop villages to a city that covered nearly 500 square miles. Various kings ordered the construction of Rome's first temples and public centers—the most famous of which was the Forum, the heart of Roman political life.

The last king of Rome was Tarquin the Proud. A harsh tyrant, he was driven from power in 509 B.C. The Romans declared they would never again be ruled by a king. Instead, they established a republic, from the Latin phrase *res publica,* which means "public affairs." A **republic** is a form of government in which power rests with citizens who have the right to vote for their leaders. In Rome, citizenship with voting rights was granted only to free-born male citizens.

Patricians and Plebeians In the early republic, different groups of Romans struggled for power. One group was the **patricians**, the wealthy landowners who held most of the power. The other important group was the **plebeians**, the common farmers, artisans, and merchants who made up the majority of the population.

The patricians inherited their power and social status. They claimed that their ancestry gave them the authority to make laws for Rome. The plebeians were citizens of Rome with the right to vote. However, they were barred by law from holding most important government positions. In time, Rome's leaders allowed the plebeians to form their own assembly and elect representatives called **tribunes**. Tribunes protected the rights of the plebeians from unfair acts of patrician officials. **A**

Twelve Tables An important victory for the plebeians was to force the creation of a written law code. With laws unwritten, patrician officials often interpreted the law to suit themselves. In 451 B.C., a group of ten officials began writing down Rome's laws. The laws were carved on twelve tablets, or tables, and hung in the Forum. They became the basis for later Roman law. The Twelve Tables established the idea that all free citizens had a right to the protection of the law.

MAIN IDEA

Making Inferences

A Why did patricians want to prevent plebeians from holding important positions?

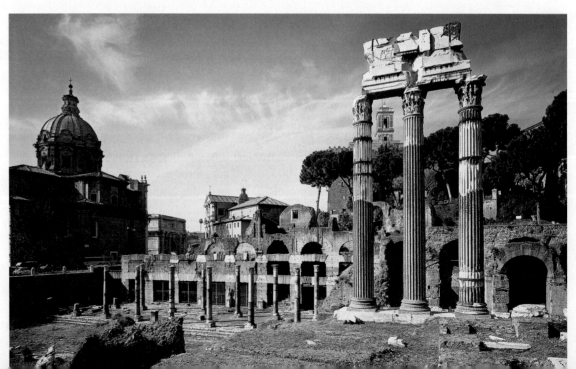

▶ Ruins of the Forum, the political center of the Roman Empire, still stand in present-day Rome.

Comparing Republican Governments		
	Rome	**United States of America**
Executive	• Two consuls, elected by the assembly for one year—chief executives of the government and commanders-in-chief of the army.	• A president, elected by the people for four years—chief executive of the government and commander-in-chief of the army.
Legislative	• Senate of 300 members, chosen from aristocracy for life—controls foreign and financial policies, advises consuls. • Centuriate Assembly, all citizen-soldiers are members for life—selects consuls, makes laws. • Tribal Assembly, citizens grouped according to where they live are members for life—elects tribunes and makes laws.	• Senate of 100 members, elected by the people for six-year terms—makes laws, advises president on foreign policy. • House of Representatives of 435 members, elected by the people for two years—makes laws, originates revenue bills.
Judicial	• Praetors, eight judges chosen for one year by Centuriate Assembly—two oversee civil and criminal courts (the others govern provinces).	• Supreme Court, nine justices appointed for life by president—highest court, hears civil and criminal appeals cases.
Legal code	• Twelve Tables—a list of rules that was the basis of Roman legal system	• U.S. Constitution—basic law of the United States
Citizenship	• All adult male landowners	• All native-born or naturalized adults

SKILLBUILDER: Interpreting Charts
1. **Comparing** *What similarities do you see in the governments of the Roman Republic and the United States?*
2. **Drawing Conclusions** *Which government seems more democratic? Why?*

Government Under the Republic In the first century B.C., Roman writers boasted that Rome had achieved a balanced government. What they meant was that their government had taken the best features of a monarchy (government by a king), an aristocracy (government by nobles), and a democracy (government by the people—see the comparison above of Rome to the United States). Rome had two officials called **consuls**. Like kings, they commanded the army and directed the government. However, their power was limited. A consul's term was only one year long. The same person could not be elected consul again for ten years. Also, one consul could always overrule, or veto, the other's decisions.

The **senate** was the aristocratic branch of Rome's government. It had both legislative and administrative functions in the republic. Its 300 members were chosen from the upper class of Roman society. Later, plebeians were allowed in the senate. The senate exercised great influence over both foreign and domestic policy.

The assemblies represented the more democratic side of the government. For example, an assembly organized by the plebeians, the Tribal Assembly, elected the tribunes and made laws for the common people—and later for the republic itself.

In times of crisis, the republic could appoint a **dictator**—a leader who had absolute power to make laws and command the army. A dictator's power lasted for only six months. Dictators were chosen by the consuls and then elected by the senate.

The Roman Army In addition to their government, the Romans placed great value on their military. All citizens who owned land were required to serve in the army. Seekers of certain public offices had to perform ten years of military service. Roman soldiers were organized into large military units called **legions**. The Roman legion was made up of some 5,000 heavily armed foot soldiers (infantry). A group of soldiers on horseback (cavalry) supported each legion. Legions were divided into smaller groups of 80 men, each of which was called a century. The military organization and fighting skill of the Roman army were key factors in Rome's rise to greatness.

Vocabulary
The word *veto* comes from the Latin for "I forbid."

Vocabulary
The term *legion* also means a multitude.

Ancient Rome and Early Christianity **157**

Rome Spreads Its Power

For hundreds of years after the founding of the republic, Rome sought to expand its territories through trade and conquest.

Rome Conquers Italy Roman power grew slowly but steadily as the legions battled for control of the Italian peninsula. By the fourth century B.C., the Romans dominated central Italy. Eventually, they defeated the Etruscans to the north and the Greek city-states to the south. By 265 B.C., the Romans were masters of nearly all Italy.

Rome had different laws and treatment for different parts of its conquered territory. The neighboring Latins on the Tiber became full citizens of Rome. In territories farther from Rome, conquered peoples enjoyed all the rights of Roman citizenship except the vote. All other conquered groups fell into a third category, allies of Rome. Rome did not interfere with its allies, as long as they supplied troops for the Roman army and did not make treaties of friendship with any other state. The new citizens and allies became partners in Rome's growth. This lenient policy toward defeated enemies helped Rome to succeed in building a long-lasting empire. For more than two centuries after 265 B.C., Roman power spread far beyond Italy. **B**

Rome's Commercial Network Rome's location gave it easy access to the riches of the lands ringing the Mediterranean Sea. Roman merchants moved by land and sea. They traded Roman wine and olive oil for a variety of foods, raw materials, and manufactured goods from other lands. However, other large and powerful cities interfered with Roman access to the Mediterranean. One such city was Carthage. Once a colony of Phoenicia, Carthage was located on a peninsula on the North African coast. Its rise to power soon put it in direct opposition with Rome.

War with Carthage In 264 B.C., Rome and Carthage went to war. This was the beginning of the long struggle known as the **Punic Wars**. Between 264 and 146 B.C., Rome and Carthage fought three wars. The first, for control of Sicily and the western Mediterranean, lasted 23 years (264–241 B.C.). It ended in the defeat of Carthage. The Second Punic War began in 218 B.C. The mastermind behind the war was a 29-year-old Carthaginian general named **Hannibal**. Hannibal was a brilliant military strategist who wanted to avenge Carthage's earlier defeat.

Hannibal assembled an army of 50,000 infantry, 9,000 cavalry, and 60 elephants with the intent of capturing Rome. Instead of a head-on attack, however, Hannibal sought to surprise the Romans with a most daring and risky move. He led his army on a long trek from Spain across France and through the Alps. Despite losing more than half his men and most of his elephants, the general's move initially worked. For more than a decade, he marched his forces up and down the Italian peninsula at will. Hannibal won his greatest victory at Cannae, in 216 B.C. There his army inflicted enormous losses on the Romans. However, the Romans regrouped and with the aid of many allies stood firm. They prevented Hannibal from capturing Rome.

HISTORY

VIDEO
Carthage: Hannibal

hmhsocialstudies.com

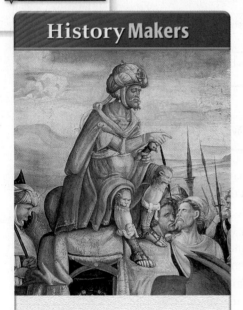

History Makers

Hannibal 247–183 B.C.

When Hannibal was only a boy of nine, his father, Hamilcar Barca, a general in Carthage's army, made him swear that he would always hate Rome and seek to destroy it.

After his defeat at the battle of Zama and Carthage's loss in the Second Punic War, Hannibal took refuge among Rome's enemies. He fought against Roman forces as an ally of the kings of Syria and Bithynia. When Roman agents came for him in Bithynia on the Black Sea in Anatolia in 183 B.C., he committed suicide rather than submit to Rome.

hmhsocialstudies.com

INTERNET ACTIVITY Go online to create an annotated map of Hannibal's journey through the Alps.

MAIN IDEA

Analyzing Issues

B How did its treatment of conquered people affect Rome's expansion?

Vocabulary
The term *Punic* comes from the Latin word for Phoenician.

Punic Wars, 264–146 B.C.

GAUL

ALPS

ITALY

DALMATIA

Adriatic Sea

Danube R.

Black Sea

N

0   400 Miles
0   800 Kilometers

ATLANTIC
OCEAN

40°N

PYRENEES

SPAIN

Tagus R.

Corsica

Rome

Sardinia

Balearic
Islands

Sicily

Cannae
(216 B.C.)

MACEDONIA

GREECE

Corinth Athens

Pergamum

ANATOLIA

Carthage

NUMIDIA

Zama (202 B.C.)

Mediterranean Sea

AFRICA

Alexandria

EGYPT

40°E

☐ Extent of Carthage's rule, 264 B.C.
☐ Extent of Roman rule, 264 B.C.
☐ Additional Roman territory, 146 B.C.
← Hannibal's invasion route
← Scipio's invasion route
✳ Major battle

GEOGRAPHY SKILLBUILDER: Interpreting Maps
1. **Movement** *How many miles did Hannibal's forces march to reach Cannae?*
2. **Region** *What territory did Rome add between 264 B.C. and 146 B.C.?*

Rome Triumphs Finally, the Romans found a daring military leader to match Hannibal's boldness. A general named Scipio (SIHP•ee•oh) devised a plan to attack Carthage. This strategy forced Hannibal to return to defend his native city. In 202 B.C., at Zama near Carthage, the Romans finally defeated Hannibal.

During the Third Punic War (149–146 B.C.), Rome laid siege to Carthage. In 146 B.C., the city was set afire and its 50,000 inhabitants sold into slavery. Its territory was made a Roman province.

Rome's victories in the Punic Wars gave it dominance over the western Mediterranean. The Romans then went on to conquer the eastern half. By about 70 B.C., Rome's Mediterranean empire stretched from Anatolia in the east to Spain in the west. As you will read in Section 2, however, such growth and power brought with it a new set of difficulties. **C**

HISTORY

VIDEO
Carthage:
Victory at
Cannae

🔗 hmhsocialstudies.com

MAIN IDEA

Drawing Conclusions
C Why were the Punic Wars important?

SECTION **1** **ASSESSMENT**

TERMS & NAMES 1. For each term or name, write a sentence explaining its significance.
• republic   • patrician   • plebeian   • tribune   • consul   • senate   • dictator   • legion   • Punic Wars   • Hannibal

USING YOUR NOTES
2. What do you consider to be the key characteristic of the early Roman Republic? Why?

I. The Origins of Rome
   A.
   B.
II. The Early Republic
   A.
   B.
III. Rome Spreads
   Its Power
   A.
   B.

MAIN IDEAS
3. What limits were there on the power of the Roman consuls?
4. What was the significance of the Twelve Tables?
5. How was Hannibal's attack on Rome daring and different?

CRITICAL THINKING & WRITING
6. **FORMING OPINIONS** Do you think the Roman Republic owed its success more to its form of government or its army? Why?
7. **ANALYZING ISSUES** Do you agree with claims that early Rome had achieved a "balanced" government? Explain.
8. **CLARIFYING** How did Rome expand its territory and maintain control over it?
9. **WRITING ACTIVITY** POWER AND AUTHORITY Write a brief **essay** explaining what problems might arise from appointing a dictator during times of crisis.

CONNECT TO TODAY PREPARING AN ORAL REPORT
Use the library and other resources to locate any monuments built to either Hannibal or the Punic Wars. Then present what you found and the circumstances surrounding the monument's creation in an **oral report.**

The Roman Empire

MAIN IDEA	WHY IT MATTERS NOW	TERMS & NAMES
EMPIRE BUILDING The creation of the Roman Empire transformed Roman government, society, economy, and culture.	The Roman Empire has served throughout history as a model of political organization and control.	• civil war • triumvirate • Julius • Augustus Caesar • *Pax Romana*

SETTING THE STAGE As Rome enlarged its territory, its republican form of government grew increasingly unstable. Eventually, the Roman Republic gave way to the formation of a mighty dictator-ruled empire that continued to spread Rome's influence far and wide.

The Republic Collapses

hmhsocialstudies.com
TAKING NOTES
Use the graphic organizer online to take notes on the ways in which Rome changed as it became an empire.

Rome's increasing wealth and expanding boundaries brought many problems. The most serious were growing discontent among the lower classes of society and a breakdown in military order. These problems led to a shakeup of the republic—and the emergence of a new political system.

Economic Turmoil As Rome grew, the gap between rich and poor grew wider. Many of Rome's rich landowners lived on huge estates. Thousands of enslaved persons—many of whom had been captured peoples in various wars—were forced to work on these estates. By 100 B.C., enslaved persons formed perhaps one-third of Rome's population.

Small farmers found it difficult to compete with the large estates run by the labor of enslaved people. Many of these farmers were former soldiers. A large number of them sold their lands to wealthy landowners and became homeless and jobless. Most stayed in the countryside and worked as seasonal migrant laborers. Some headed to Rome and other cities looking for work. They joined the ranks of the urban poor, a group that totaled about one-fourth of Roman society.

Two brothers, Tiberius and Gaius (GUY•us) Gracchus (GRAK•us), attempted to help Rome's poor. As tribunes, they proposed such reforms as limiting the size of estates and giving land to the poor. Tiberius spoke eloquently about the plight of the landless former soldiers:

PRIMARY SOURCE
The savage beasts have their . . . dens, . . . but the men who bear arms and expose their lives for the safety of their country, enjoy . . . nothing more in it but the air and light . . . and wander from place to place with their wives and children.

TIBERIUS GRACCHUS quoted in Plutarch, *The Lives of Noble Greeks and Romans*

The brothers made enemies of numerous senators, who felt threatened by their ideas. Both met violent deaths—Tiberius in 133 B.C. and Gaius in 121 B.C.

A period of **civil war**, or conflict between groups within the same country, followed their deaths.

Military Upheaval Adding to the growing turmoil within the republic was a breakdown of the once-loyal military. As the republic grew more unstable, generals began seizing greater power for themselves. They recruited soldiers from the landless poor by promising them land. These soldiers fought for pay and owed allegiance only to their commander. They replaced the citizen-soldiers whose loyalty had been to the republic. It now was possible for a military leader supported by his own troops to take over by force. Eventually, one would do just that.

Julius Caesar Takes Control In 60 B.C., a military leader named **Julius Caesar** joined forces with Crassus, a wealthy Roman, and Pompey, a popular general. With their help, Caesar was elected consul in 59 B.C. For the next ten years, these men dominated Rome as a **triumvirate**, a group of three rulers.

Caesar was a strong leader and a genius at military strategy. Following tradition, he served only one year as consul. He then appointed himself governor of Gaul (now France). During 58–50 B.C., Caesar led his legions in a grueling but successful campaign to conquer all of Gaul. Because he shared fully in the hardships of war, he won his men's loyalty and devotion.

The reports of Caesar's successes in Gaul made him very popular with the people of Rome. Pompey, who had become his political rival, feared Caesar's ambitions. In 50 B.C., the senate, at Pompey's urgings, ordered Caesar to disband his legions and return home.

Caesar defied the senate's order. On the night of January 10, 49 B.C., he took his army across the Rubicon River in Italy, the southern limit of the area he commanded. He marched his army swiftly toward Rome, and Pompey fled. Caesar's troops defeated Pompey's armies in Greece, Asia, Spain, and Egypt. In 46 B.C., Caesar returned to Rome, where he had the support of the army and the masses. That same year, the senate appointed him dictator. In 44 B.C., he was named dictator for life.

Caesar's Reforms Julius Caesar governed Rome as an absolute ruler, one who has total power. However, he started a number of reforms. He granted Roman citizenship to many people in the provinces. In addition, he expanded the senate, adding his friends and supporters from Italy and

History Makers

Julius Caesar
100–44 B.C.

In 44 B.C., on March 15, Caesar prepared to go to speak to the Senate, unaware that important senators plotted his death. According to legend, his wife, Calpurnia, begged him not to go. She said she had seen him in a dream dying in her arms of stab wounds.

When Caesar arrived at the Senate chamber, he sat in his chair. Soon the plotters encircled him, took knives hidden in their togas, and stabbed him 23 times, as depicted in the painting below. They were led by Gaius Cassius and Caesar's friend Marcus Brutus. Caesar's last words were "Et tu, Brute?" ("You, too, Brutus?")

↗ **hmhsocialstudies.com**

RESEARCH WEB LINKS Go online for more on Julius Caesar.

other regions. Caesar also helped the poor by creating jobs, especially through the construction of new public buildings. He started colonies where people without land could own property, and he increased pay for soldiers.

Many nobles and senators expressed concern over Caesar's growing power, success, and popularity. Some feared losing their influence. Others considered him a tyrant. A number of important senators, led by Marcus Brutus and Gaius Cassius, plotted his assassination. On March 15, 44 B.C., they stabbed him to death in the senate chamber. **(A)**

Beginning of the Empire After Caesar's death, civil war broke out again and destroyed what was left of the Roman Republic. Three of Caesar's supporters banded together to crush the assassins. Caesar's 18-year-old grandnephew and adopted son Octavian (ahk•TAY•vee•uhn) joined with an experienced general named Mark Antony and a powerful politician named Lepidus. In 43 B.C., they took control of Rome and ruled for ten years as the Second Triumvirate.

Their alliance, however, ended in jealousy and violence. Octavian forced Lepidus to retire. He and Mark Antony then became rivals. While leading troops against Rome's enemies in Anatolia, Mark Antony met Queen Cleopatra of Egypt. He fell in love with her and followed her to Egypt. Octavian accused Antony of plotting to rule Rome from Egypt, and another civil war erupted. Octavian defeated the combined forces of Antony and Cleopatra at the naval battle of Actium in 31 B.C. Later, Antony and Cleopatra committed suicide.

While he restored some aspects of the republic, Octavian became the unchallenged ruler of Rome. Eventually he accepted the title of **Augustus** (aw•GUHS•tuhs), or "exalted one." He also kept the title *imperator,* or "supreme military commander," a term from which *emperor* is derived. Rome was now an empire ruled by one man.

A Vast and Powerful Empire

Rome was at the peak of its power from the beginning of Augustus's rule in 27 B.C. to A.D. 180. For 207 years, peace reigned throughout the empire, except for some fighting with tribes along the borders. This period of peace and prosperity is known as the **Pax Romana**— "Roman peace." **(B)**

During this time, the Roman Empire included more than 3 million square miles. Its population numbered between 60 and 80 million people. About 1 million people lived in the city of Rome itself.

A Sound Government The Romans held their vast empire together in part through efficient government and able rulers. Augustus was Rome's ablest emperor. He stabilized the frontier, glorified Rome with splendid public buildings, and created a system of government that survived for centuries. He set up a civil service. That is, he paid workers to manage the affairs of government, such as the grain supply, tax collection, and the postal system. Although the senate still functioned, civil servants drawn from plebeians and even former slaves actually administered the empire.

After Augustus died in A.D. 14, the system of government that he established maintained the empire's stability.

History Makers

Augustus
63 B.C.–A.D. 14

Augustus was the most powerful ruler of the mightiest empire of the ancient world. Yet, amid the pomp of Rome, he lived a simple and frugal life. His home was modest by Roman standards. His favorite meal consisted of coarse bread, a few sardines, and a piece of cheese—the usual food of a common laborer.

Augustus was also a very religious and family-oriented man. He held to a strict moral code. He had his only child, Julia, exiled from Rome for not being faithful in her marriage

↗ hmhsocialstudies.com

RESEARCH WEB LINKS Go online for more on Augustus.

MAIN IDEA

Analyzing Motives-
(A) Why did Caesar's rivals feel they had to kill him?

MAIN IDEA

Summarizing
(B) To what does the term *Pax Romana* refer?

Vocabulary
The term *civil service* refers to persons employed in the civil administration of government.

Trade in the Roman Empire, A.D. 200

Trade Goods

- Grain
- Olive oil
- Slaves
- Wine
- Metals
- Textiles
- Wild animals

Roman Empire, A.D. 200

ATLANTIC OCEAN

BRITAIN
Londinium

EUROPE

GAUL
Loire R.

ALPS

Aquileia

DACIA

Danube R.

CAUCASUS MOUNTAINS

Caspian Sea

Massalia
Narbo
ITALY
Rome
Salonae
Adriatic Sea
Black Sea

PYRENEES
40°N
SPAIN
Tarraco

Byzantium

GREECE
ANATOLIA
Ephesus
Corinth

Gades

Carthage

Antioch
Damascus
Caesarea
Jerusalem
Ctesiphon
ZAGROS MOUNTAINS

ATLAS MOUNTAINS

AFRICA

Mediterranean Sea

N

0   500 Miles
0   1,000 Kilometers

EGYPT
Nile R.
Alexandria

ARABIA

Tropic of Cancer

GEOGRAPHY SKILLBUILDER: Interpreting Maps
1. **Movement** *From what three continents did trade goods come to Rome?*
2. **Location** *Which goods were supplied by all three areas?*

This was due mainly to the effectiveness of the civil service in carrying out day-to-day operations. The Romans managed to control an empire that by the second century A.D. reached from Spain to Mesopotamia, from North Africa to Britain. Included in its provinces were people of many languages, cultures, and customs.

Agriculture and Trade Agriculture was the most important industry in the empire. All else depended on it. About 90 percent of the people were engaged in farming. Most Romans survived on the produce from their local area. Additional food (when needed) and luxury items for the rich were obtained through trade. In Augustus's time, a silver coin called a denarius was in use throughout the empire. Having common coinage made trade between different parts of the empire much easier.

Rome had a vast trading network. Ships from the east traveled the Mediterranean protected by the Roman navy. Cities such as Corinth in Greece, Ephesus in Anatolia, and Antioch on the eastern coast of the Mediterranean grew wealthy. Rome also traded with China and India.

A complex network of roads linked the empire to such far-flung places as Persia and southern Russia. These roads were originally built by the Roman army for military purposes. Trade also brought Roman ways to the provinces and beyond.

The Roman World

Throughout its history, Rome emphasized the values of discipline, strength, and loyalty. A person with these qualities was said to have the important virtue of *gravitas.* The Romans were a practical people. They honored strength more than beauty, power more than grace, and usefulness more than elegance.

Ancient Rome and Early Christianity **163**

Roman Emperors, A.D. 37–A.D. 180

Bad Emperors			Good Emperors		
Caligula • 37–41 • Mentally disturbed	**Nero** • 54–68 • Good administrator but vicious • Murdered many • Persecuted Christians	**Domitian** • 81–96 • Ruled dictatorially • Feared treason everywhere and executed many	**Nerva** • 96–98 • Began custom of adopting heir **Trajan** • 98–117 • Empire reached its greatest extent • Undertook vast building program • Enlarged social welfare	**Hadrian** • 117–138 • Consolidated earlier conquests • Reorganized the bureaucracy **Antoninus Pius** • 138–161 • Reign largely a period of peace and prosperity	**Marcus Aurelias** • 161–180 • Brought empire to height of economic prosperity • Defeated invaders • Wrote philosophy

Caligula

Trajan

Most people in the Roman Empire lived in the countryside and worked on farms. In Rome and smaller cities, merchants, soldiers, slaves, foreigners, and philosophers all shared the crowded, noisy streets. Here, people from all walks of life came together to create a diverse society.

Slaves and Captivity Slavery was a significant part of Roman life. It was widespread and important to the economy. The Romans made more use of slaves than any previous civilization. Numbers of slaves may have reached as high as one-third of the total population. Most slaves were conquered peoples brought back by victorious Roman armies and included men, women, and children. Children born to slaves also became slaves. Slaves could be bought and sold. According to Roman law, slaves were the property of their owners. They could be punished, rewarded, set free, or put to death as their masters saw fit.

Slaves worked both in the city and on the farm. Many were treated cruelly and worked at hard labor all day long. Some—strong, healthy males—were forced to become gladiators, or professional fighters, who fought to the death in public contests. Other slaves, particularly those who worked in wealthy households, were better treated. Occasionally, slaves would rebel. None of the slave revolts succeeded. More than a million slaves lost their lives attempting to gain their freedom.

Gods and Goddesses The earliest Romans worshiped powerful spirits or divine forces, called *numina,* that they thought resided in everything around them. Closely related to these spirits were the Lares (LAIR-eez), who were the guardian spirits of each family. They gave names to these powerful gods and goddesses and honored them through various rituals, hoping to gain favor and avoid misfortune.

In Rome, government and religion were linked. The deities were symbols of the state. Romans were expected to honor them not only in private rituals at shrines in their homes but also in public worship ceremonies conducted by priests in temples. Among the most important Roman gods and goddesses were Jupiter, father of the gods; Juno, his wife, who watched over women; and Minerva, goddess of wisdom and of the arts and crafts. During the empire, worship of the emperor also became part of the official religion of Rome.

Society and Culture By the time of the empire, wealth and social status made huge differences in how people lived. Classes had little in common. The rich lived extravagantly. They spent large sums of money on homes, gardens, slaves, and luxuries. They gave banquets that lasted for many hours and included foods that were rare and costly, such as boiled ostrich and parrot-tongue pie.

However, most people in Rome barely had the necessities of life. During the time of the empire, much of the city's population was unemployed. The government supported these people with daily rations of grain. In the shadow of Rome's

History *in* Depth

Gladiator Games

Thumbs up or thumbs down—that is how a match often ended for a gladiator (shown in this mosaic battling a tiger). When one of the combatants fell, the organizer of the games usually determined his fate. A thumbs up sign from him meant that the fighter would live. Thumbs down meant his death.

The crowd usually played a key role in these life-and-death decisions. If the masses liked the fallen gladiator, he most likely would live to fight another day. If not, he was doomed.

great temples and public buildings, poor people crowded into rickety, sprawling tenements. Fire was a constant danger.

To distract and control the masses of Romans, the government provided free games, races, mock battles, and gladiator contests. By A.D. 250, there were 150 holidays a year. On these days of celebration, the Colosseum, a huge arena that could hold 50,000, would fill with the rich and the poor alike. The spectacles they watched combined bravery and cruelty, honor and violence. In the animal shows, wild creatures brought from distant lands, such as tigers, lions, and bears, fought to the death. In other contests, gladiators engaged in combat with animals or with each other, often until one of them was killed.

During this time of *Pax Romana,* another activity slowly emerged in the Roman Empire—the practice of a new religion known as Christianity. The early followers of this new faith would meet with much brutality and hardship for their beliefs. But their religion would endure and spread throughout the empire, and eventually become one of the dominant faiths of the world.

SECTION 2 ASSESSMENT

TERMS & NAMES 1. For each term or name, write a sentence explaining its significance.
- civil war
- Julius Caesar
- triumvirate
- Augustus
- *Pax Romana*

USING YOUR NOTES

2. What changes do you consider negative? Why?

Changes in Rome
• Dictator claims sole power
•
•

MAIN IDEAS

3. What factors contributed to the fall of the Roman Republic?

4. What were the main reasons for the Romans' success in controlling such a large empire?

5. What measures did the government take to distract and control the masses of Rome?

CRITICAL THINKING & WRITING

6. **ANALYZING CAUSES** What role did Julius Caesar play in the decline of the republic and the rise of the empire?

7. **ANALYZING ISSUES** What aspects of Roman society remained similar from republic to empire?

8. **RECOGNIZING EFFECTS** What was Augustus's greatest contribution to Roman society? Why?

9. **WRITING ACTIVITY** EMPIRE BUILDING Write a brief **dialogue** in which various members of society comment on conditions in the Roman Empire during the *Pax Romana*. Participants might include a senator, a civil servant, a slave, a merchant, and a former soldier.

CONNECT TO TODAY CREATING A POSTER

Create a **poster** depicting the sporting events and other forms of entertainment that you enjoy watching. Include an introductory paragraph that explains what about them appeals to you.

Life in a Roman Villa

Much of what we know about Roman homes comes from archaeological excavations of the ancient cities of Pompeii and Herculaneum. In A.D. 79, Pompeii and Herculaneum were buried in volcanic ash by a tremendous eruption of Mount Vesuvius. The illustration you see here is modeled after a home in Pompeii. Notice the rich artwork and refined architecture of this home.

VIDEO
Ancient Rome: The Rise of Apartments

↗ hmhsocialstudies.com

↗ **hmhsocialstudies.com**

RESEARCH WEB LINKS Go online for more on life in a Roman villa.

▼ **The Villa**
Very few Romans could afford to live in such luxury, but those who could left a legacy that still inspires wonder.

1 Center of Activity
Owners of such villas were usually noted citizens, and their homes had frequent visitors.

2 Entrance Hall Beautiful floor mosaics sometimes decorated the villa's entrance. Skilled artisans created the intricate designs like the one shown in the entry of this home.

3 Kitchen Well-stocked kitchens kept family members and guests well fed. A dinner from this kitchen might consist of eggs, vegetables, shellfish, meat, cakes, and fruit.

▲ Frescoes

A fresco is a painting made on damp plaster. Roman artists used this technique to brighten the walls of Roman homes. This fresco from the ruins of Pompeii reflects a couple's pride at being able to read and write—she holds tools for writing and he a scroll.

4 Gardens Wealthy Romans maintained gardens decorated with fountains, sculptures, and frescoes.

► Archaeological Excavation

When Mount Vesuvius erupted, ash rained down, covered everything, and hardened. Bread (shown above) carbonized in the bakeries. Bodies decayed under the ash leaving hollow spaces. An archaeologist developed the technique of pouring plaster into the spaces and then removing the ash. The result was a cast of the body where it fell.

> DATA FILE

Pompeii

- Of the 10,000 to 20,000 people who lived in Pompeii, only 2,000 bodies have been uncovered.
- About three-fourths of the city has been excavated.

Mount Vesuvius

- Scientists believe there may be a reservoir of magma 400 kilometers (about 249 miles) wide sitting below Mount Vesuvius.
- Today, in the first 15 minutes of a medium-to-large-scale eruption, an area within a 4-mile radius of the volcano could be destroyed—about 1 million people live and work in this area.

Number of Major Recorded Volcanic Eruptions

Years	Number of Eruptions
A.D. 1–500	3
501–1000	5
1001–1500	2
1501–2000*	20+

Number of Eruptions: 0 5 10 15 20

* The last eruption occurred in 1944.
Source: *Encyclopaedia Britannica*

Connect *to* Today

1. Making Inferences What other types of rooms or activities can you identify in the illustration?

See Skillbuilder Handbook, page R10.

2. Comparing and Contrasting How are homes today similar to a Roman villa? How are they different?

167

The Rise of Christianity

MAIN IDEA	WHY IT MATTERS NOW	TERMS & NAMES
RELIGIOUS AND ETHICAL SYSTEMS Christianity arose in Roman-occupied Judea and spread throughout the Roman Empire.	Christianity has spread throughout the world and today has more than a billion followers.	• Jesus • Constantine • apostle • bishop • Paul • Peter • Diaspora • pope

SETTING THE STAGE While religion played an important role in Roman society, the worship of Roman gods was impersonal and often practiced without a great deal of emotion. As the empire grew, so, too, did a new religion called Christianity. Born as a movement within Judaism, it emphasized a personal relationship between God and people—and attracted many Romans.

The Life and Teachings of Jesus

hmhsocialstudies.com
TAKING NOTES

Use the graphic organizer online to take notes on the events that led to the spread of Christianity.

Roman power spread to Judea, the home of the Jews, around 63 B.C. At first the Jewish kingdom remained independent, at least in name. Rome then took control of the Jewish kingdom in A.D. 6 and made it a province of the empire. A number of Jews, however, believed that they would once again be free. According to biblical tradition, God had promised that a savior known as the Messiah would arrive and restore the kingdom of the Jews. Roughly two decades after the beginning of Roman rule, many believed that such a savior had arrived.

Jesus of Nazareth Although the exact date is uncertain, historians estimate that sometime around 6 to 4 B.C., a Jew named **Jesus** was born in Bethlehem in Judea. Historical records of the time mention very little about Jesus. The main source of information about his life and teachings is the Gospels, the first four books of the New Testament of the Christian Bible. According to the Gospels, Jesus was raised in the village of Nazareth in northern Judea. He was baptized by a prophet known as John the Baptist. As a young man, he took up the trade of carpentry.

At the age of 30, Jesus began his public ministry. For the next three years, he preached, taught, did good works, and reportedly performed miracles. His teachings contained many ideas from Jewish tradition, such as monotheism, or belief in only one God, loving others, and the principles of the Ten Commandments. Jesus emphasized God's personal relationship to each human being. He stressed the importance of people's love for God, their neighbors, their enemies, and even themselves. He also taught that God would end wickedness in the world and would establish an eternal kingdom after death for people who sincerely repented their sins. (Refer to pages 286–287 for more about Christianity.)

A Growing Movement Some of the Gospels are thought to have been written by one or more of Jesus' disciples, or pupils. These 12 men later came to be called **apostles**.

As Jesus preached from town to town, his fame grew. He attracted large crowds, and many people were touched by his message. Because Jesus ignored wealth and status, his message had special appeal to the poor. "Blessed are the meek, for they shall inherit the earth," he said. His words, as related in the Gospels, were simple and direct:

PRIMARY SOURCE
Love your enemies, do good to those who hate you, bless those who curse you, and pray for those who mistreat you. If anyone hits you on the cheek, let him hit the other one too; if someone takes your coat, let him have your shirt as well. Give to everyone who asks you for something, and when someone takes what is yours, do not ask for it back. Do for others just what you want them to do for you.

Luke 6:27–31

Jesus' Death Jesus' growing popularity concerned Roman leaders. According to the New Testament, when Jesus visited Jerusalem about A.D. 29, enthusiastic crowds greeted him as the Messiah, or king—the one whom the Bible had said would come to rescue the Jews. The Roman governor Pontius Pilate accused Jesus of defying the authority of Rome. Pilate arrested Jesus and sentenced him to be crucified, or nailed to a large wooden cross to die like thousands of other opponents of Rome.

After Jesus' death, his body was placed in a tomb. According to the Gospels, three days later his body was gone, and a living Jesus began appearing to his followers. The Gospels go on to say that then he ascended into heaven. The apostles were more convinced than ever that Jesus was the Messiah. It was from this belief that Jesus came to be referred to as Jesus Christ. *Christos* is a Greek word meaning "messiah" or "savior." The name *Christianity* was derived from "Christ." **A**

MAIN IDEA

Hypothesizing

A Why did the followers of Jesus think he was the Messiah?

Christianity Spreads Through the Empire

Strengthened by their conviction that he had triumphed over death, the followers of Jesus continued to spread his ideas. Jesus' teachings did not contradict Jewish law, and his first followers were Jews. Soon, however, these followers began to create a new religion based on his messages. Despite political and religious opposition, the new religion of Christianity spread slowly but steadily throughout the Roman Empire.

▼ *Christ's Charge to Saint Peter* by Renaissance artist Raphael depicts Jesus calling the apostle Peter to duty as the other apostles look on.

Paul's Mission One man, the apostle <u>Paul</u>, had enormous influence on Christianity's development. Paul was a Jew who had never met Jesus and at first was an enemy of Christianity. While traveling to Damascus in Syria, he reportedly had a vision of Christ. He spent the rest of his life spreading and interpreting Christ's teachings.

The *Pax Romana*, which made travel and the exchange of ideas fairly safe, provided the ideal conditions for Christianity to spread. Common languages—Latin and Greek—allowed the message to be easily understood. Paul wrote influential letters, called Epistles, to groups of believers. In his teaching, Paul stressed that Jesus was the son of God who died for people's sins. He also declared that Christian converts were not obligated to follow Jewish law. It was this universality that enabled Christianity to become more than just a local religion.

Jewish Rebellion During the early years of Christianity, much Roman attention was focused on the land of Jesus' birth and on the Jews. In A.D. 66, a band of Jews rebelled against Rome. In A.D. 70, the Romans stormed Jerusalem and destroyed the Temple complex. All that remained was a western portion of the wall, which today is the holiest Jewish shrine. The Jewish fortress near Masada (see map at right) held out until A.D. 73. About a half million Jews were killed in the course of this rebellion.

The Jews made another attempt to break free of the Romans in A.D. 132. Another half-million Jews died in three years of fighting. Although the Jewish religion survived, the Jewish political state ceased to exist for more than 1,800 years. Most Jews were driven from their homeland into exile. This dispersal of the Jews is called the <u>Diaspora</u>.

Persecution of the Christians Christians also posed a problem for Roman rulers. The main reason was that they refused to worship Roman gods. This refusal was seen as opposition to Roman rule. Some Roman rulers also used Christians as scapegoats for political and economic troubles.

By the second century, as the *Pax Romana* began to crumble, persecution of the Christians intensified. Romans exiled, imprisoned, or executed Christians for refusing to worship Roman deities. Thousands were crucified, burned, or killed by wild animals in the circus arenas. Other Christians and even some non-Christians regarded persecuted Christians as martyrs. Martyrs were people willing to sacrifice their lives for the sake of a belief or a cause.

A World Religion

Despite persecution of its followers, Christianity became a powerful force. By the late third century A.D., there were millions of Christians in the Roman Empire and beyond. The widespread appeal of Christianity was due to a variety of reasons. Christianity grew because it

- embraced all people—men and women, enslaved persons, the poor, and nobles;
- gave hope to the powerless;
- appealed to those who were repelled by the extravagances of imperial Rome;
- offered a personal relationship with a loving God;
- promised eternal life after death. **B**

HISTORY

VIDEO
Jesus' Jerusalem
↗ hmhsocialstudies.com

Global Impact

The Jewish Diaspora
Centuries of Jewish exile followed the destruction of their temple and the fall of Jerusalem in A.D. 70. This period is called the Diaspora, from the Greek word for "dispersal." Jews fled to many parts of the world, including Europe.

In the 1100s, many European Jews were expelled from their homes. Some moved to Turkey, Palestine, and Syria. Others went to Poland and neighboring areas.

The statelessness of the Jews did not end until the creation of Israel in 1948.

Vocabulary
Scapegoats are groups or individuals that innocently bear the blame for others.

MAIN IDEA

Making Inferences
B Why were the citizens of the Roman Empire so drawn to Christianity?

North
Sea

BRITAIN

Rhine R.

Danube R.

ATLANTIC
OCEAN

GAUL

Christian areas, 325
Additional Christian areas, 500
Boundary of Roman Empire, 395

ITALY

Rome

SPAIN

Black Sea

Constantinople

Nicaea

Caspian Sea

40°N

GREECE

Corinth

ANATOLIA

ARMENIA

Mediterranean

Sea

Hippo

Antioch

SYRIA

N

JUDEA

Jerusalem

0   500 Miles

0   1,000 Kilometers

Alexandria

EGYPT

Nile R.

Red Sea

Persian Gulf

GEOGRAPHY SKILLBUILDER: Interpreting Maps
1. **Location** *Where was Christianity most widespread in A.D. 325?*
2. **Region** *What was the extent (north to south, east to west) of Christianity's spread by A.D. 500?*

Constantine Accepts Christianity A critical moment in Christianity occurred in A.D. 312, when the Roman emperor **Constantine** was fighting three rivals for leadership of Rome. He had marched to the Tiber River at Rome to battle his chief rival. On the day before the battle at Milvian Bridge, Constantine prayed for divine help. He reported that he then saw an image of a cross—a symbol of Christianity. He ordered artisans to put the Christian symbol on his soldiers' shields. Constantine and his troops were victorious in battle. He credited his success to the help of the Christian God.

In the next year, A.D. 313, Constantine announced an end to the persecution of Christians. In the Edict of Milan, he declared Christianity to be one of the religions approved by the emperor. Christianity continued to gain strength. In 380, the emperor Theodosius made it the empire's official religion.

Vocabulary
A *hierarchy* is a group of persons organized in order of ranks, with each level subject to the authority of the one above.

Early Christian Church By this time, Christians had given their religion a structure, much as the Roman Empire had a hierarchy. At the local level, a priest led each small group of Christians. A **bishop**, who was also a priest, supervised several local churches. The apostle **Peter** had traveled to Rome from Jerusalem and became the first bishop there. According to tradition, Jesus referred to Peter as the "rock" on which the Christian Church would be built. As a result, all priests and bishops traced their authority to him.

Eventually, every major city had its own bishop. However, later bishops of Rome claimed to be the heirs of Peter. These bishops said that Peter was the first **pope**, the father or head of the Christian Church. They said that whoever was bishop of Rome was also the leader of the whole Church. Also, as Rome was the capital of the empire, it seemed the logical choice to be the center of the Church.

A Single Voice As Christianity grew, disagreements about beliefs developed among its followers. Church leaders called any belief that appeared to contradict the basic teachings a heresy. Dispute over beliefs became intense. In an attempt to end conflicts, Church leaders tried to set a single, official standard of belief. These beliefs were compiled in the New Testament, which contained the four Gospels, the Epistles of Paul, and other documents. The New Testament was added to the Hebrew Bible, which Christians called the Old Testament. In A.D. 325, Constantine moved to solidify further the teachings of Christianity. He called Church leaders to Nicaea in Anatolia. There they wrote the Nicene Creed, which defined the basic beliefs of the Church.

The Fathers of the Church Also influential in defining Church teachings were several early writers and scholars who have been called the Fathers of the Church. One of the most important was Augustine, who became bishop of the city of Hippo in North Africa in 396. Augustine taught that humans needed the grace of God to be saved. He further taught that people could not receive God's grace unless they belonged to the Church and received the sacraments.

One of Augustine's most famous books is *The City of God*. It was written after Rome was plundered in the fifth century. Augustine wrote that the fate of cities such as Rome was not important because the heavenly city, the city of God, could never be destroyed:

PRIMARY SOURCE **C**

The one consists of those who live by human standards, the other of those who live according to God's will. . . . By two cities I mean two societies of human beings, one of which is predestined to reign with God for all eternity, the other is doomed to undergo eternal punishment with the Devil.

AUGUSTINE, *The City of God*

MAIN IDEA

Analyzing Primary Sources

C Why would Augustine write his book after Rome had been attacked?

While Christianity continued its slow but steady rise, the Roman Empire itself was gradually weakening. Under the weight of an increasing number of both foreign and domestic problems, the mighty Roman Empire eventually began to crumble.

SECTION 3 ASSESSMENT

TERMS & NAMES **1.** For each term or name, write a sentence explaining its significance.

• Jesus • apostle • Paul • Diaspora • Constantine • bishop • Peter • pope

USING YOUR NOTES	MAIN IDEAS	CRITICAL THINKING & WRITING
2. What event do you think had the biggest impact? Explain.	**3.** What did Jesus emphasize in his early teachings?	**6. HYPOTHESIZING** Do you think Christianity would have developed in the same way if it had arisen in an area outside the Roman Empire? Explain.
	4. Why did the early Christians face persecution from the Romans?	**7. FORMING AND SUPPORTING OPINIONS** Who did more to spread Christianity—Paul or Constantine? Why?
	5. What was the importance of the Nicene Creed?	**8. ANALYZING ISSUES** Why do you think Roman leaders so opposed the rise of a new religion among their subjects?
		9. WRITING ACTIVITY RELIGIOUS AND ETHICAL SYSTEMS Imagine you are a resident of Judea during the time of Jesus. Write a **letter** to a friend in Rome describing Jesus and his teachings.

Rome takes over Jewish kingdom.

CONNECT TO TODAY OUTLINING A SPEECH

Locate a recent speech by the pope or the leader of another Christian church and **outline** its main ideas. Then read some of the speech to the class and discuss its main points.

The Fall of the Roman Empire

MAIN IDEA	WHY IT MATTERS NOW	TERMS & NAMES
EMPIRE BUILDING Internal problems and invasions spurred the division and decline of the Roman Empire.	The decline and fall of great civilizations is a repeating pattern in world history.	• inflation • mercenary • Diocletian • Constantinople • Attila

SETTING THE STAGE In the third century A.D., Rome faced many problems. They came both from within the empire and from outside. Only drastic economic, military, and political reforms, it seemed, could hold off collapse.

A Century of Crisis

Historians generally agree that the end of the reign of the emperor Marcus Aurelius (A.D. 161–180) marked the end of two centuries of peace and prosperity known as the *Pax Romana*. The rulers that followed in the next century had little or no idea of how to deal with the giant empire and its growing problems. As a result, Rome began to decline.

Rome's Economy Weakens During the third century A.D., several factors prompted the weakening of Rome's economy. Hostile tribes outside the boundaries of the empire and pirates on the Mediterranean Sea disrupted trade. Having reached their limit of expansion, the Romans lacked new sources of gold and silver. Desperate for revenue, the government raised taxes. It also started minting coins that contained less and less silver. It hoped to create more money with the same amount of precious metal. However, the economy soon suffered from **inflation**, a drastic drop in the value of money coupled with a rise in prices.

Agriculture faced equally serious problems. Harvests in Italy and western Europe became increasingly meager because overworked soil had lost its fertility. What's more, years of war had destroyed much farmland. Eventually, serious food shortages and disease spread, and the population declined.

Military and Political Turmoil By the third century A.D., the Roman military was also in disarray. Over time, Roman soldiers in general had become less disciplined and loyal. They gave their allegiance not to Rome but to their commanders, who fought among themselves for the throne. To defend against the increasing threats to the empire, the government began to recruit **mercenaries**, foreign soldiers who fought for money. While mercenaries would accept lower pay than Romans, they felt little sense of loyalty to the empire.

Feelings of loyalty eventually weakened among average citizens as well. In the past, Romans cared so deeply about their republic that they willingly sacrificed their lives for it. Conditions in the later centuries of the empire caused citizens to lose their sense of patriotism. They became indifferent to the empire's fate.

hmhsocialstudies.com
TAKING NOTES

Use the graphic organizer online to take notes on what caused the problems facing the Roman Empire.

Emperors Attempt Reform

Remarkably, Rome survived intact for another 200 years. This was due largely to reform-minded emperors and the empire's division into two parts.

Diocletian Reforms the Empire In A.D. 284, <u>Diocletian</u>, a strong-willed army leader, became the new emperor. He ruled with an iron fist and severely limited personal freedoms. Nonetheless, he restored order to the empire and increased its strength. Diocletian doubled the size of the Roman army and sought to control inflation by setting fixed prices for goods. To restore the prestige of the office of emperor, he claimed descent from the ancient Roman gods and created elaborate ceremonies to present himself in a godlike aura.

Diocletian believed that the empire had grown too large and too complex for one ruler. In perhaps his most significant reform, he divided the empire into the Greek-speaking East (Greece, Anatolia, Syria, and Egypt) and the Latin-speaking West (Italy, Gaul, Britain, and Spain). He took the eastern half for himself and appointed a co-ruler for the West. While Diocletian shared authority, he kept overall control. His half of the empire, the East, included most of the empire's great cities and trade centers and was far wealthier than the West.

Because of ill health, Diocletian retired in A.D. 305. However, his plans for orderly succession failed. Civil war broke out immediately. By 311, four rivals were competing for power. Among them was an ambitious young commander named Constantine, the same Constantine who would later end the persecution of Christians.

Constantine Moves the Capital Constantine gained control of the western part of the empire in A.D. 312 and continued many of the social and economic policies

Multiple Causes: Fall of the Western Roman Empire

Contributing Factors

Political	Social	Economic	Military
• Political office seen as burden, not reward • Military interference in politics • Civil war and unrest • Division of empire • Moving of capital to Byzantium	• Decline in interest in public affairs • Low confidence in empire • Disloyalty, lack of patriotism, corruption • Contrast between rich and poor • Decline in population due to disease and food shortage	• Poor harvests • Disruption of trade • No more war plunder • Gold and silver drain • Inflation • Crushing tax burden • Widening gap between rich and poor and increasingly impoverished Western Empire	• Threat from northern European tribes • Low funds for defense • Problems recruiting Roman citizens; recruiting of non-Romans • Decline of patriotism and loyalty among soldiers

Immediate Cause

Invasion by Germanic tribes and by Huns

FALL OF ROMAN EMPIRE

SKILLBUILDER: Interpreting Charts

1. **Analyzing Issues** *Could changes in any contributing factors have reversed the decline of the empire? Why or why not?*
2. **Analyzing Causes** *Which contributing factors—political, social, economic, or military—were the most significant in the fall of the Western Roman Empire?*

Eastern Roman Empire
Western Roman Empire
Burgundians
Franks
Huns
Ostrogoths
Saxons, Angles, Jutes
Vandals
Visigoths
409 Date of invasion

450

North Sea

BRITAIN

EUROPE

406

428

Rhine R.

Dnieper R.

450

451

Huns under Attila 452

433

Don R.

410

380–454

412

GAUL

Danube R.

376

415

Alaric 410

399–400

Black Sea

395

ITALY

Adriatic Sea

Rome

410

Bosporus Strait

ATLANTIC OCEAN

40°N

Constantinople

SPAIN

407

Gaiseric 455

ANATOLIA

460

N

395

Carthage

SYRIA

ASIA

0   500 Miles

427–432

AFRICA

Mediterranean Sea

0   1,000 Kilometers

Jerusalem

Alexandria

EGYPT

GEOGRAPHY SKILLBUILDER: Interpreting Maps
1. **Movement** *What group of invaders came the greatest distance?*
2. **Location** *What areas of the empire were not threatened by invasion?*

of Diocletian. In 324 Constantine also secured control of the East, thus restoring the concept of a single ruler.

In A.D. 330, Constantine took a step that would have great consequence for the empire. He moved the capital from Rome to the Greek city of Byzantium (bih•ZAN•tshee•uhm), in what is now Turkey. The new capital stood on the Bosporus Strait, strategically located for trade and defense purposes on a crossroads between West and East. **A**

With Byzantium as its capital, the center of power in the empire shifted from Rome to the east. Soon the new capital stood protected by massive walls and filled with imperial buildings modeled after those in Rome. The city eventually took a new name—<u>**Constantinople**</u> (KAHN•stan•tuhn•OH•puhl), or the city of Constantine. After Constantine's death, the empire would again be divided. The East would survive; the West would fall.

MAIN IDEA

Analyzing Motives-

A Why did Constantine choose the location of Byzantium for his new capital?

The Western Empire Crumbles

The decline of the Western Roman Empire took place over many years. Its final collapse was the result of worsening internal problems, the separation of the Western Empire from the wealthier Eastern part, and outside invasions.

Germanic Invasions Since the days of Julius Caesar, Germanic peoples had gathered on the northern borders of the empire and coexisted in relative peace with Rome. Around A.D. 370, all that changed when a fierce group of Mongol nomads from central Asia, the Huns, moved into the region and began destroying all in their path.

In an effort to flee from the Huns, the various Germanic people pushed into Roman lands. (Romans called all invaders "barbarians," a term that they used to refer to non-Romans.) They kept moving through the Roman provinces of Gaul,

▲ This skull, still retaining its hair, shows a kind of topknot in the hair that some Germanic peoples wore to identify themselves.

Spain, and North Africa. The Western Empire was unable to field an army to stop them. In 410, hordes of Germans overran Rome itself and plundered it for three days.

Attila the Hun Meanwhile, the Huns, who were indirectly responsible for the Germanic assault on the empire, became a direct threat. In 444, they united for the first time under a powerful chieftain named <u>Attila</u> (AT•uhl•uh). With his 100,000 soldiers, Attila terrorized both halves of the empire. In the East, his armies attacked and plundered 70 cities. (They failed, however, to scale the high walls of Constantinople.)

The Huns then swept into the West. In A.D. 452, Attila's forces advanced against Rome, but bouts of famine and disease kept them from conquering the city. Although the Huns were no longer a threat to the empire after Attila's death in 453, the Germanic invasions continued.

An Empire No More The last Roman emperor, a 14-year-old boy named Romulus Augustulus, was ousted by German forces in 476. After that, no emperor even pretended to rule Rome and its western provinces. Roman power in the western half of the empire had disappeared. **B**

The eastern half of the empire, which came to be called the Byzantine Empire, not only survived but flourished. It preserved the great heritage of Greek and Roman culture for another 1,000 years. (See Chapter 11.) The Byzantine emperors ruled from Constantinople and saw themselves as heirs to the power of Augustus Caesar. The empire endured until 1453, when it fell to the Ottoman Turks.

Even though Rome's political power in the West ended, its cultural influence did not. Its ideas, customs, and institutions influenced the development of Western civilization—and still do so today.

MAIN IDEA

Hypothesizing
B Do you think Rome would have fallen to invaders if the Huns had not moved into the west? Explain.

SECTION 4 ASSESSMENT

TERMS & NAMES 1. For each term or name, write a sentence explaining its significance.
• inflation • mercenary • Diocletian • Constantinople • Attila

USING YOUR NOTES	**MAIN IDEAS**	**CRITICAL THINKING & WRITING**
2. How did these problems open the empire to invading peoples?	3. What were the main internal causes of the empire's decline?	6. **DRAWING CONCLUSIONS** How do you think the splitting of the empire into two parts helped it survive for another 200 years?
	4. How did Diocletian succeed in preserving the empire?	7. **IDENTIFYING PROBLEMS** Which of Rome's internal problems do you think were the most serious? Why?
	5. Why did so many Germanic tribes begin invading the Roman Empire?	8. **ANALYZING ISSUES** Why do you think the eastern half of the empire survived?

Causes	Effects
	Inflation
	Untrust-worthy army
	Political Instability

9. **WRITING ACTIVITY** [EMPIRE BUILDING] Imagine you are a journalist in the Roman Empire. Write an **editorial** in which you comment—favorably or unfavorably—on Constantine's decision to move the capital of the empire.

MULTIMEDIA ACTIVITY CREATING A TRAVEL BROCHURE

Use the Internet to gather information and create a **travel brochure** about modern-day Constantinople, now known as Istanbul. Include an introductory paragraph about the city and any facts you think a traveler might want to know.

INTERNET KEYWORD
Istanbul tourism

↗ hmhsocialstudies.com INTERACTIVE

The Fall of the Roman Empire

Since the fifth century, historians and others have argued over the empire's fall. They have attributed it to a variety of causes, coming both from within and outside the empire. The following excerpts are examples of the differing opinions.

A SECONDARY SOURCE

Edward Gibbon

In the 1780s Gibbon published *The History of the Decline and Fall of the Roman Empire*. In this passage, Gibbon explains that a major cause of the collapse was that the empire was simply just too large.

———

The decline of Rome was the natural and inevitable effect of immoderate greatness. Prosperity ripened the principle of decay; the causes of destruction multiplied with the extent of conquest; and, as soon as time or accident had removed the artificial supports, the stupendous fabric yielded to the pressure of its own weight. The story of its ruin is simple and obvious; and instead of inquiring why the Roman Empire was destroyed, we should rather be surprised that it had subsisted so long.

B SECONDARY SOURCE

Arther Ferrill

In his book *The Fall of the Roman Empire* (1986), Arther Ferrill argues that the fall of Rome was a military collapse.

———

In fact the Roman Empire of the West did fall. Not every aspect of the life of Roman subjects was changed by that, but the fall of Rome as a political entity was one of the major events of the history of Western man. It will simply not do to call that fall a myth or to ignore its historical significance merely by focusing on those aspects of Roman life that survived the fall in one form or another. At the opening of the fifth century a massive army, perhaps more than 200,000 strong, stood at the service of the Western emperor and his generals. The destruction of Roman military power in the fifth century was the obvious cause of the collapse of Roman government in the West.

C SECONDARY SOURCE

Finley Hooper

In this passage from his *Roman Realities* (1967), Hooper argues against the idea of a "fall."

———

The year was 476. For those who demand to know the date Rome fell, that is it. Others will realize that the fall of Rome was not an event but a process. Or, to put it another way, there was no fall at all—ancient Roman civilization simply became something else, which is called medieval. [It evolved into another civilization, the civilization of the Middle Ages.]

D PRIMARY SOURCE

Jerome

This early Church leader did not live to see the empire's end, but he vividly describes his feelings after a major event in Rome's decline—the attack and plunder of the city by Visigoths in 410.

———

It is the end of the world . . . Words fail me. My sobs break in . . . The city which took captive the whole world has itself been captured.

Document-Based QUESTIONS

1. Compare the reasons for the fall of Rome given in Sources A and B. How might they be considered similar?

2. What became of Rome according to Source C? Do you agree or disagree with that conclusion?

3. Source D is different from the other sources. How?

Rome and the Roots of Western Civilization

MAIN IDEA	WHY IT MATTERS NOW	TERMS & NAMES
POWER AND AUTHORITY The Romans developed many ideas and institutions that became fundamental to Western civilization.	Evidence of Roman culture is found throughout Europe and North America and in Asia and Africa.	• Greco-Roman culture • Pompeii • Virgil • Tacitus • aqueduct

SETTING THE STAGE Romans borrowed and adapted cultural elements freely, especially from the Greek and Hellenistic cultures. However, the Romans created a great civilization in their own right, whose art and architecture, language and literature, engineering, and law became its legacy to the world.

The Legacy of Greco-Roman Civilization

hmhsocialstudies.com
TAKING NOTES

Use the graphic organizer online to take notes on the accomplishments of Roman civilization.

Under the Roman Empire, hundreds of territories were knitted into a single state. Each Roman province and city was governed in the same way. The Romans were proud of their unique ability to rule, but they acknowledged Greek leadership in the fields of art, architecture, literature, and philosophy.

By the second century B.C., Romans had conquered Greece and had come to greatly admire Greek culture. Educated Romans learned the Greek language. As Horace, a Roman poet, said, "Greece, once overcome, overcame her wild conqueror." The mixing of elements of Greek, Hellenistic, and Roman culture produced a new culture, called **Greco-Roman culture**. This is also often called classical civilization.

Roman artists, philosophers, and writers did not merely copy their Greek and Hellenistic models. They adapted them for their own purposes and created a style of their own. Roman art and literature came to convey the Roman ideals of strength, permanence, and solidity.

Roman Fine Arts Romans learned the art of sculpture from the Greeks. However, while the Greeks were known for the beauty and idealization of their sculpture, Roman sculptors created realistic portraits in stone. Much Roman art was practical in purpose, intended for public education.

The reign of Augustus was a period of great artistic achievement. At that time the Romans further developed a type of sculpture called bas-relief. In bas-relief, or low-relief, images project from a flat background. Roman sculptors used bas-relief to tell stories and to represent crowds of people, soldiers in battle, and landscapes.

Roman artists also were particularly skilled in creating mosaics. Mosaics were pictures or designs made by setting small pieces of stone, glass, or tile onto a surface. Most Roman villas, the country houses of the wealthy, had at least one colorful mosaic. (See the Social History feature on pages 166–167.)

In addition, Romans excelled at the art of painting. Most wealthy Romans had bright, large murals, called frescoes, painted directly on their walls. Few have survived. The best examples of Roman painting are found in the Roman town of **Pompeii** and date from as early as the second century B.C. In A.D. 79, nearby Mount Vesuvius erupted, covering Pompeii in a thick layer of ash and killing about 2,000 residents. The ash acted to preserve many buildings and works of art.

Learning and Literature Romans borrowed much of their philosophy from the Greeks. Stoicism, the philosophy of the Greek teacher Zeno, was especially influential. Stoicism encouraged virtue, duty, moderation, and endurance.

In literature, as in philosophy, the Romans found inspiration in the works of their Greek neighbors. While often following Greek forms and models, Roman writers promoted their own themes and ideas. The poet **Virgil** spent ten years writing the most famous work of Latin literature, the *Aeneid* (ih•NEE•ihd), the epic of the legendary Aeneas. Virgil modeled the *Aeneid*, written in praise of Rome and Roman virtues, after the Greek epics of Homer. Here he speaks of government as being Rome's most important contribution to civilization:

PRIMARY SOURCE
Romans, never forget that government is your medium! Be this your art:—to practice men in habit of peace, Generosity to the conquered, and firmness against aggressors.

VIRGIL, *Aeneid*

While Virgil's writing carries all the weight and seriousness of the Roman character, the poet Ovid wrote light, witty poetry for enjoyment. In *Amores,* Ovid relates that he can only compose when he is in love: "When I was from Cupid's passions free, my Muse was mute and wrote no elegy."

Global Patterns

The Epic

While many know the epics of Virgil and the Greek poet Homer, other cultures throughout history have created their own narrative poems about heroic figures. India's *Mahabharata* tells the story of a battle for control of a mighty kingdom, while the Spanish epic *El Cid* celebrates a hero of the wars against the Moors. And while it is not a poem, *The Lord of the Rings,* the fantasy trilogy by English writer J.R.R. Tolkien, is considered to contain many aspects of the epic.

Most epics follow a pattern derived from the works of Homer. However, the emergence of epics around the world was not so much the result of one writer but the common desire among civilizations to promote their values and ideals through stories.

▶ Depictions of scenes from *The Lord of the Rings* (left), *El Cid* (top right), and *Mahabharata* (bottom right)

Western Civilization

Western civilization is generally seen as the heritage of ideas that spread to Europe and America from ancient Greece and Rome. Some historians observe, however, that Western civilization does not belong to any particular place—that it is the result of cultures coming together, interacting, and changing. Still, the legacy of Greece and Rome can be seen today.

The diagram below shows how ancient Greek and Roman ideas of government, philosophy, and literature can be traced across time. As with many cultural interactions, the links between the examples are not necessarily direct. Instead, the chart traces the evolution of an idea or theme over time.

Influence of Greek and Roman Ideas

Government	Philosophy	Literature
509 B.C. Rome developed a form of representative government.	**300s B.C.** Aristotle developed his philosophical theories.	**ABOUT 800 B.C.** Homer wrote the *Odyssey*.
400s B.C. Greece implemented a direct democracy.	**A.D. 1200s** Thomas Aquinas attempted to prove the existence of a single god using Aristotelian ideas.	**19 B.C.** Virgil used the *Odyssey* to guide his *Aeneid*.
1600s England became a constitutional monarchy.	**1781** Philosopher Immanuel Kant wrote that Aristotle's theories on logic were still valid.	**1922** James Joyce patterned his epic, *Ulysses*, after Homer's work.
1776 The United States declared independence from England and began building a republican democracy.	**Present** Scholars still hold conferences focusing on questions Aristotle raised.	**2000** The Coen brothers' film *O Brother, Where Art Thou?* brought a very different adaptation of the *Odyssey* to the big screen.

> ⁊ **hmhsocialstudies.com**

RESEARCH WEB LINKS Go online for more on Western civilization.

---

180 Chapter 6

> **DATA FILE**

DEMOCRACY

- Theoretically, 40,000 people could attend the Greek Assembly—in practice, about 6,000 people attended.
- In 1215, King John of England granted the Magna Carta, which largely influenced subsequent democratic thought.
- In the 1970s, there were 40 democratic governments worldwide.
- In 2002, over 120 established and emerging democracies met to discuss their common issues.

Current Forms of World Governments

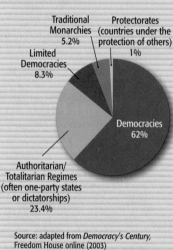

Traditional Monarchies 5.2%
Protectorates (countries under the protection of others) 1%
Limited Democracies 8.3%
Democracies 62%
Authoritarian/ Totalitarian Regimes (often one-party states or dictatorships) 23.4%

Source: adapted from *Democracy's Century*, Freedom House online (2003)

Connect *to* Today

1. **Hypothesizing** Why do you think ancient Greek and Roman cultures have had such a lasting influence on Western civilization?

   See Skillbuilder Handbook, page R15.

2. **Comparing and Contrasting** From what you know of ancient Greece and Rome, what is another element of either culture that can still be seen today? Provide an example.

water

▲ This Roman aqueduct in modern France has survived the centuries. The cross section indicates how the water moved within the aqueduct.

The Romans also wrote excellent prose, especially history. Livy compiled a multivolume history of Rome from its origins to 9 B.C. He used legends freely, creating more of a national myth of Rome than a true history. **Tacitus** (TAS•ih•tuhs), another Roman historian, is notable among ancient historians because he presented the facts accurately. He also was concerned about the Romans' lack of morality. In his *Annals* and *Histories*, he wrote about the good and bad of imperial Rome.

Here, Tacitus shows his disgust with the actions of the Emperor Nero, who many consider to be one of Rome's cruelest rulers.

PRIMARY SOURCE

While Nero was frequently visiting the show, even amid his pleasures there was no cessation to his crimes. For during the very same period Torquatus Silanus was forced to die, because over and above his illustrious rank as one of the Junian family he claimed to be the great grandson of Augustus. Accusers were ordered to charge him with prodigality [wastefulness] in lavishing gifts, and with having no hope but in revolution. . . . Then the most intimate of his freedmen were put in chains and torn from him, till, knowing the doom which impended, Torquatus divided the arteries in his arms. A speech from Nero followed, as usual, which stated that though he was guilty and with good reason distrusted his defense, he would have lived, had he awaited the clemency of the judge.

TACITUS, *Annals*

The Legacy of Rome

The presence of Rome is still felt daily in the languages, the institutions, and the thought of the Western world.

The Latin Language Latin, the language of the Romans, remained the language of learning in the West long after the fall of Rome. It was the official language of the Roman Catholic Church into the 20th century.

Latin was adopted by different peoples and developed into French, Spanish, Portuguese, Italian, and Romanian. These languages are called Romance languages because of their common Roman heritage. Latin also influenced other languages. For example, more than half the words in English have a basis in Latin. **(A)**

Master Builders Visitors from all over the empire marveled at the architecture of Rome. The arch, the dome, and concrete were combined to build spectacular structures, such as the Colosseum.

Arches also supported bridges and **aqueducts**. Aqueducts were designed by Roman engineers to bring water into cities and towns. When the water channel spanned a river or ravine, the aqueduct was lifted high up on arches.

MAIN IDEA

Clarifying

(A) What impact did the Romans have on our English language?

hmhsocialstudies.com

INTERACTIVE HISTORY

Explore the marvels of Roman engineering.

Science & *Technology*

The Colosseum

The Colosseum was one of the greatest feats of Roman engineering and a model for the ages. The name comes from the Latin word *colossus*, meaning "gigantic." Its construction was started by the Emperor Vespasian and was completed by his sons, emperors Titus and Domitian. For centuries after its opening in A.D. 80, spectators, both rich and poor, cheered a variety of free, bloody spectacles—from gladiator fights to animal hunts.

▲ The Colosseum in Rome as it appears today

↗ **hmhsocialstudies.com**

RESEARCH WEB LINKS Go online for more on the Colosseum.

exits—giant staircases that allowed the building to be emptied in minutes

Elevators and ramps led from the cells and animal cages in the Colosseum basement to trapdoors concealed in the arena floor.

arena—central area where spectacles took place

passageways—walkways that led to seats

velarium—a retractable canvas awning that shielded spectators from sun and rain

Facts About the Colosseum

- Built—A.D. 72–81
- Capacity—45,000–50,000
- Materials—stone and concrete
- Size—157 feet high, 620 feet long
- Arena—287 feet long, 180 feet wide

entrances—80 in all

Connect *to* Today

1. **Comparing** The Colosseum has been the model for sports stadiums worldwide. How is the design of modern stadiums patterned after that of the Colosseum? What are the similarities?

   See Skillbuilder Handbook, page R7.

2. **Drawing Conclusions** What do the kind of spectacles the Romans watched tell us about them as a people and about their leaders?

Because Roman architectural forms were so practical, they have remained popular. Thomas Jefferson began a Roman revival in the United States in the 18th century. Many large public buildings, such as the U.S. Capitol and numerous state capitols, include Roman features.

Roman roads were also technological marvels. The army built a vast network of roads constructed of stone, concrete, and sand that connected Rome to all parts of the empire. Many lasted into the Middle Ages; some are still used.

Roman System of Law Rome's most lasting and widespread contribution was its law. Early Roman law dealt mostly with strengthening the rights of Roman citizens. As the empire grew, however, the Romans came to believe that laws should be fair and apply equally to all people, rich and poor. Slowly, judges began to recognize certain standards of justice. These standards were influenced largely by the teachings of Stoic philosophers and were based on common sense and practical ideas. Some of the most important principles of Roman law were:

- All persons had the right to equal treatment under the law.
- A person was considered innocent until proven guilty.
- The burden of proof rested with the accuser rather than the accused.
- A person should be punished only for actions, not thoughts.
- Any law that seemed unreasonable or grossly unfair could be set aside.

MAIN IDEA

Analyzing Issues

B) How did Roman law protect those accused of crimes?

The principles of Roman law endured to form the basis of legal systems in many European countries and of places influenced by Europe, including the United States of America. **B)**

Rome's Enduring Influence By preserving and adding to Greek civilization, Rome strengthened the Western cultural tradition. The world would be a very different place had Rome not existed. Historian R. H. Barrow has stated that Rome never fell because it turned into something even greater—an idea—and achieved immortality.

As mighty as the Roman Empire had been, however, it was not the only great civilization of its time. Around the same period that Rome was developing its enduring culture, different but equally complex empires were emerging farther east. In India, the Mauryan and Gupta empires dominated the land, while the Han Empire ruled over China.

SECTION 5 ASSESSMENT

TERMS & NAMES 1. For each term or name, write a sentence explaining its significance.

- Greco-Roman culture   • Pompeii   • Virgil   • Tacitus   • aqueduct

USING YOUR NOTES

2. Which accomplishment do you consider most important? Why?

Fine Arts	Literature
Law	Engineering

MAIN IDEAS

3. What is Greco-Roman culture?

4. In what way did Roman art differ from Greek art?

5. What influence did Latin have on the development of Western languages?

CRITICAL THINKING & WRITING

6. **DRAWING CONCLUSIONS** Which principle of law do you think has been Rome's greatest contribution to modern legal systems?

7. **FORMING AND SUPPORTING OPINIONS** Do you agree with Horace's claim on page 178 that when it came to culture, Greece in essence conquered Rome? Explain.

8. **HYPOTHESIZING** Describe how the world might be different if Rome had not existed.

9. **WRITING ACTIVITY** POWER AND AUTHORITY Imagine you are a historian. Write an **expository essay** describing the importance of Rome's legacy.

CONNECT TO TODAY PRESENTING A REPORT

Locate several Latin phrases still in use today. Use the necessary materials to help translate those phrases, and then explain in a brief **report** the meaning and intent of those phrases.

VISUAL SUMMARY

Ancient Rome and Early Christianity

Early Rome

1000 B.C.	Latins enter region
753 B.C.	Rome founded

Roman Republic

509 B.C.	Republic created
451 B.C.	Twelve Tables written
405–265 B.C.	Italy conquered
264–146 B.C.	Punic Wars fought
44 B.C.	Julius Caesar assassinated

Roman Empire

27 B.C.	Empire and *Pax Romana* begin with reign of Augustus
A.D. 29	Jesus crucified
A.D. 64	Christian persecution begins
A.D. 79	Pompeii destroyed
A.D. 180	*Pax Romana* ends
A.D. 253	Germanic tribes enter frontier regions
A.D. 285	Diocletian divides empire into East and West
A.D. 313	Christianity given recognition
A.D. 324	Constantine reunites empire
A.D. 370	Huns invade frontier
A.D. 380	Christianity made official religion
A.D. 395	Empire permanently split
A.D. 476	Last emperor deposed

Timeline markers: 900 B.C., 600 B.C., 300 B.C., A.D. 1, A.D. 300, A.D. 600

TERMS & NAMES

For each term below, briefly explain its connection to ancient Rome or the rise of Christianity.

1. republic
2. senate
3. Julius Caesar
4. Augustus
5. Jesus
6. Constantine
7. inflation
8. Greco-Roman culture

MAIN IDEAS

The Roman Republic Section 1 (pages 155–159)

9. Name the three main parts of government under the Roman republic.
10. How did Rome treat different sections of its conquered territory?

The Roman Empire Section 2 (pages 160–167)

11. How did Augustus change Roman government?
12. How did Rome's population fare during the golden age of the *Pax Romana*?

The Rise of Christianity Section 3 (pages 168–172)

13. How did the apostle Paul encourage the spread of Christianity?
14. Why did the Roman emperors persecute Christians?

The Fall of the Roman Empire Section 4 (pages 173–177)

15. What was the most significant reform that the Emperor Diocletian made?
16. How did the Western Roman Empire fall?

Rome and the Roots of Western Civilization
Section 5 (pages 178–183)

17. Why did so much of Roman culture have a Greek flavor?
18. What aspects of Roman culture influenced future civilizations?

CRITICAL THINKING

1. USING YOUR NOTES

In a diagram, compare the Roman Republic with the Roman Empire when both were at the peak of their power.

republic only
both
empire only

2. ANALYZING ISSUES

RELIGIOUS AND ETHICAL SYSTEMS   What type of person do you think became a martyr? Consider the personal characteristics of individuals who refused to renounce their faith even in the face of death.

3. EVALUATING DECISIONS AND COURSES OF ACTION

POWER AND AUTHORITY   What do you think of Diocletian's decision to divide the Roman Empire into two parts? Was it wise? Consider Diocletian's possible motives and the results of his actions.

4. CLARIFYING

EMPIRE BUILDING   Explain more fully what the historian R. H. Barrow meant when he said on page 183 that Rome never really fell but instead achieved immortality.

Use the quotation and your knowledge of world history to answer questions 1 and 2.

Whereas the divine providence that guides our life has displayed its zeal and benevolence by ordaining for our life the most perfect good, bringing to us Augustus, whom it has filled with virtue for the benefit of mankind, employing him as a saviour for us and our descendants, him who has put an end to wars and adorned peace; . . . and the birthday of the god [Augustus] is the beginning of all the good tidings brought by him to the world.

Decree from the Roman Province of Asia

1. Based on the passage, the author of the decree
   A. greatly approved of the rule of Augustus.
   B. feared the amount of power Augustus had.
   C. considered Augustus's birthday a national holiday.
   D. thought Augustus should grant Asia its independence.

2. During which period in Roman history was this passage most likely written?
   A. the Punic Wars
   B. the *Pax Romana*
   C. the founding of the republic
   D. the fall of the Western Empire

Use this scene depicted on a Roman monument to answer question 3.

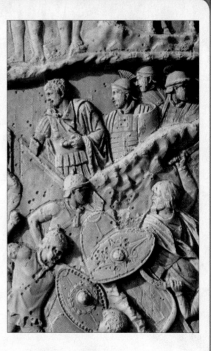

3. What aspect of society does the image show the Romans celebrating?
   A. education
   B. commerce
   C. government
   D. military strength

 hmhsocialstudies.com **TEST PRACTICE**

For additional test practice, go online for:
• Diagnostic tests
• Strategies
• Tutorials

Interact *with* History

On page 154, you considered the qualities that made a successful leader before knowing what the Romans thought about leadership. Now that you have read the chapter, reevaluate your decision. What qualities were needed for Roman leaders to be effective? What qualities hindered their success? How would you rate the overall leadership of the Roman Empire? Discuss your opinions in small groups.

FOCUS ON WRITING

Study the information about Rome's impact on the development of Western civilization in the Key Concepts feature on Western Civilization on page 180. Write an **essay** of several paragraphs summarizing the empire's impact on the Western world that developed after it. Provide the following:
• how the empire influenced later governments
• what influence the empire had on philosophy
• what impact the empire had on literature
• why you think Roman culture has been so enduring

MULTIMEDIA ACTIVITY

Creating a Virtual Field Trip

Plan a two-week virtual trip through the Roman Empire. After selecting and researching the sites you'd like to visit, use the historical maps from this chapter and contemporary maps of the region to determine your itinerary. Consider visiting the following places: Rome, Carthage, Pompeii, Hadrian's Wall, the Appian Way, Bath, Lepcis Magna, Horace's Villa, the Pont du Gard, and the Roman theater at Orange. You may want to include the following:
• maps of the Roman Empire
• pictures of the major sites on the field trip
• audio clips describing the sites or events that took place there
• reasons each site is an important destination

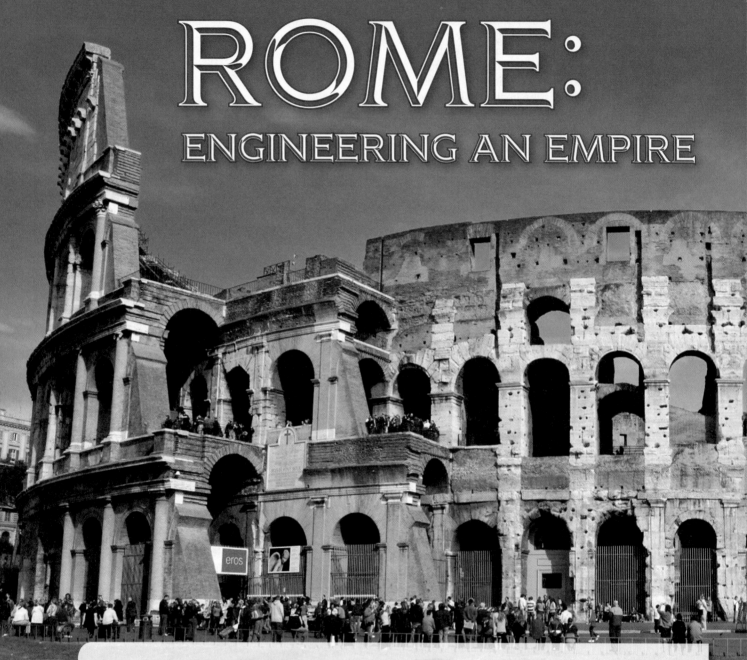

ROME:
ENGINEERING AN EMPIRE

The Roman Empire was one of the largest and most powerful empires in ancient history. With its strong military, the Roman Empire expanded to dominate the entire Mediterranean region, including much of western Europe and northern Africa. Keys to this expansion were the engineering and construction innovations made by Roman engineers. As the empire grew and prospered, Roman engineers made advances in city planning, road and bridge design, water and sewage systems, and many other areas.

Explore some of the incredible monuments and engineering achievements of the Roman Empire online. You can find a wealth of information, video clips, primary sources, activities, and more at

↗ **hmhsocialstudies.com**

The Glory of the Colosseum

Watch the video to go inside the Colosseum, Rome's premier entertainment venue and one of the most famous buildings of the Roman Empire.

Caesar Builds an Empire

Watch the video to learn why Julius Caesar built a bridge across the Rhine River as a demonstration of Roman power.

Growth of the Roman Empire

Explore the map to analyze the growth of one of the largest empires of the ancient world.

Arches, Angles, Innovations

Watch the video to learn about Roman engineering advances and the construction of aqueducts.

India and China Establish Empires,
400 B.C.–A.D. 550

How did India and China establish powerful empires and develop vibrant cultures?

 What You Will Learn

In this chapter you will learn about the establishment and development of empires in India and China.

SECTION 1 India's First Empires
Main Idea The Mauryas and the Guptas established empires, but neither unified India permanently.

SECTION 2 Trade Spreads Indian Religions and Culture
Main Idea Indian religions, culture, and science evolved and spread to other regions through trade.

SECTION 3 Han Emperors in China
Main Idea The Han Dynasty expanded China's borders and developed a system of government that lasted for centuries.

Previewing Themes

POWER AND AUTHORITY In both India and China in the 200s B.C., military leaders seized power and used their authority to strengthen the government.
Geography *Study the map. What geographic factors might have made further expansion difficult for both empires?*

CULTURAL INTERACTION From the time of the Aryan nomads, Indian civilization was a product of interacting cultures. In China, the government pressured conquered people to adopt Chinese culture.
Geography *What geographic feature was the main connection between the empires of India and China?*

RELIGIOUS AND ETHICAL SYSTEMS Hinduism and Buddhism were India's main religions by 250 B.C. The ethical teachings of Confucius played an important role in Chinese life. Buddhism also took root in China.
Geography *What dates on the time line are associated with religious changes in China and India?*

INDIA AND CHINA

321 B.C.
Chandragupta Maurya founds Mauryan Empire.

202 B.C.
Liu Bang establishes China's Han Dynasty. (Han Dynasty bronze horse) ▶

400 B.C.

200 B.C.

WORLD

264 B.C.
Punic wars between Rome and Carthage begin.

200 B.C.
Nazca culture emerges in Peru.

India and China, 321 B.C. – A.D. 9

- Han Empire, A.D. 2
- Mauryan Empire, 250 B.C.
- Silk Road
- ★ Capitals

0   500   1000 Miles
0   500   1000 Kilometers
Robinson Projection

GOBI DESERT

TAKLIMAKAN DESERT

Merv

Dunhuang

Huang He (Yellow River)

Luoyang

Ch'ang-an (Xi'an)

Yellow Sea

Taxila

PLATEAU OF TIBET

HIMALAYAS

Indus River

Ganges River

Brahmaputra River

Chang Jiang (Yangtze River)

30°N

East China Sea

Patala

Pataliputra ★

Bay of Bengal

Arabian Sea

Tamil States

N
W   E
S

INDIAN OCEAN

75°E   90°E   105°E   120°E

HISTORY. China's Shortest Dynasty

↗ hmhsocialstudies.com   VIDEO

A.D. 65
Buddhism takes root in China. ▶

A.D. 105
Chinese invent paper.

A.D. 220
Han Dynasty falls.

A.D. 320
Gupta Empire forms in India and encourages a renewal of Hindu faith. (Hindu god Shiva) ▶

A.D. 200

A.D. 400

A.D. 500

A.D. 29
Jesus is crucified in Jerusalem.

A.D. 100
Bantu speakers begin massive migrations throughout Africa. (Bantu mask) ▶

A.D. 476
Western Roman Empire falls.

Would you spy for your government?

You are a merchant selling cloth out of your shop when a stranger enters. You fear it is one of the emperor's inspectors, coming to check the quality of your cloth. The man eyes you sternly and then, in a whisper, asks if you will spy on other weavers. You would be paid four years' earnings. But you might have to turn in a friend if you suspect he is not paying enough taxes to the government.

1 This person comments to his friend on something he sees in the street.

2 This soldier's job is to check that everyone pays taxes. He seems suspicious of the man carrying bananas.

3 This man, who stands behind a wall watching, may be a spy.

EXAMINING *the* ISSUES

- Is it right for a government to spy on its own people?
- What kinds of tensions might exist in a society where neighbor spies upon neighbor?
- Is there a time when spying is ethical?

As a class, discuss these questions. In your discussion, review what you know about how other emperors exercised power in places such as Persia and Rome. As you read about the emperors of India and China, notice how they try to control their subjects' lives.

India's First Empires

MAIN IDEA	WHY IT MATTERS NOW	TERMS & NAMES
POWER AND AUTHORITY The Mauryas and the Guptas established empires, but neither unified India permanently.	The diversity of peoples, cultures, beliefs, and languages in India continues to pose challenges to Indian unity today.	• Tamil • Gupta Empire • patriarchal • matriarchal	• Mauryan Empire • Asoka • religious toleration

SETTING THE STAGE By 600 B.C., almost 1,000 years after the Aryan migrations, many small kingdoms were scattered throughout India. In 326 B.C., Alexander the Great brought the Indus Valley in the northwest under Macedonian control—but left almost immediately. Soon after, a great Indian military leader, Chandragupta Maurya (chuhn•druh•GUP•tuh-MAH•oor•yuh), seized power.

The Mauryan Empire Is Established

Chandragupta Maurya may have been born in the powerful kingdom of Magadha. Centered on the lower Ganges River, the kingdom was ruled by the Nanda family. Chandragupta gathered an army, killed the unpopular Nanda king, and in about 321 B.C. claimed the throne. This began the **Mauryan Empire**.

Chandragupta Maurya Unifies North India Chandragupta moved northwest, seizing all the land from Magadha to the Indus. Around 305 B.C., Chandragupta began to battle Seleucus I, one of Alexander the Great's generals. Seleucus had inherited part of Alexander's empire. He wanted to reestablish Macedonian control over the Indus Valley. After several years of fighting, however, Chandragupta defeated Seleucus. By 303 B.C., the Mauryan Empire stretched more than 2,000 miles, uniting north India politically for the first time. (See map on page 191.)

To win his wars of conquest, Chandragupta raised a vast army: 600,000 soldiers on foot, 30,000 soldiers on horseback, and 9,000 elephants. To clothe, feed, and pay these troops, the government levied high taxes. For example, farmers had to pay up to one-half the value of their crops to the king.

Running the Empire Chandragupta relied on an adviser named Kautilya (kow•TIHL•yuh), a member of the priestly caste. Kautilya wrote a ruler's handbook called the *Arthasastra* (AHR•thuh• SHAHS•truh). This book proposed tough-minded policies to hold an empire together, including spying on the people and employing political assassination. Following Kautilya's advice, Chandragupta created a highly bureaucratic government. He divided the empire into four provinces, each headed by a royal prince. Each province was then divided into local districts, whose officials assessed taxes and enforced the law.

Life in the City and the Country To stay at peace, Seleucus sent an ambassador, Megasthenes (muh•GAS•thuh•neez), to Chandragupta's capital.

hmhsocialstudies.com
TAKING NOTES
Use the graphic organizer online to take notes on the Mauryan and Gupta empires.

Megasthenes wrote glowing descriptions of Chandragupta's palace, with its gold-covered pillars, many fountains, and imposing thrones. The capital city featured beautiful parks and bustling markets. Megasthenes also described the countryside and how farmers lived:

PRIMARY SOURCE Ⓐ

[Farmers] are exempted from military service and cultivate their lands undisturbed by fear. They do not go to cities, either on business or to take part in their tumults. It therefore frequently happens that at the same time, and in the same part of the country, men may be seen marshaled for battle and risking their lives against the enemy, while other men are ploughing or digging in perfect security under the protection of these soldiers.

MEGASTHENES, in *Geography* by Strabo

MAIN IDEA

Analyzing Primary Sources

Ⓐ What information in this quotation indicates that Mauryan India valued agriculture?

In 301 B.C., Chandragupta's son assumed the throne. He ruled for 32 years. Then Chandragupta's grandson, **Asoka** (uh•SOH•kuh), brought the Mauryan Empire to its greatest heights.

Asoka Promotes Buddhism Asoka became king of the Mauryan Empire in 269 B.C. At first, he followed in Chandragupta's footsteps, waging war to expand his empire. During a bloody war against the neighboring state of Kalinga, 100,000 soldiers were slain, and even more civilians perished.

Although victorious, Asoka felt sorrow over the slaughter at Kalinga. As a result, he studied Buddhism and decided to rule by the Buddha's teaching of "peace to all beings." Throughout the empire, Asoka erected huge stone pillars inscribed with his new policies. Some edicts guaranteed that Asoka would treat his subjects fairly and humanely. Others preached nonviolence. Still others urged **religious toleration**—acceptance of people who held different religious beliefs.

Asoka had extensive roads built so that he could visit the far corners of India. He also improved conditions along these roads to make travel easier for his

Vocabulary
Edicts are official, public announcements of policy.

▲ This pillar, on which Asoka's edicts are written, is located at Vaishali.

History Makers

▲ This grouping of Asoka's lions is used as a symbol of India.

Chandragupta Maurya
?–298 B.C.

Chandragupta feared being assassinated—maybe because he had killed a king to get his throne. To avoid being poisoned, he made servants taste all his food. To avoid being murdered in bed, he slept in a different room every night.

Although Chandragupta was a fierce warrior, in 301 B.C., he gave up his throne and converted to Jainism. Jains taught nonviolence and respect for all life. With a group of monks, Chandragupta traveled to southern India. There he followed the Jainist custom of fasting until he starved to death.

🔲 hmhsocialstudies.com

RESEARCH WEB LINKS Go online for more on Chandragupta Maurya and Asoka.

Asoka
?–232 B.C.

One of Asoka's edicts states,

If one hundredth part or one thousandth of those who died in Kalinga . . . should now suffer similar fate, [that] would be a matter of pain to His Majesty.

Even though Asoka wanted to be a loving, peaceful ruler, he had to control a huge empire. He had to balance Kautilya's methods of keeping power and Buddha's urgings to be unselfish.

Asoka softened Chandragupta's harsher policies. Instead of spies, he employed officials to look out for his subjects' welfare. He kept his army but sought to rule humanely. In addition, Asoka sent missionaries to Southeast Asia to spread Buddhism.

officials and to improve communication in the vast empire. For example, every nine miles he had wells dug and rest houses built. This allowed travelers to stop and refresh themselves. Such actions demonstrated Asoka's concern for his subjects' well-being. Noble as his policies of toleration and nonviolence were, they failed to hold the empire together after Asoka died in 232 B.C. **B**

MAIN IDEA

Clarifying

B Which of Asoka's actions show the influence of Buddha's teaching of "peace to all beings"?

A Period of Turmoil

Asoka's death left a power vacuum. In northern and central India, regional kings challenged the imperial government. The kingdoms of central India, which had only been loosely held in the Mauryan Empire, soon regained their independence. The Andhra (AHN•druh) Dynasty arose and dominated the region for hundreds of years. Because of their central position, the Andhras profited from the extensive trade between north and south India and also with Rome, Sri Lanka, and Southeast Asia.

At the same time, northern India had to absorb a flood of new people fleeing political instability in other parts of Asia. For 500 years, beginning about 185 B.C., wave after wave of Greeks, Persians, and Central Asians poured into northern India. These invaders disrupted Indian society. But they also introduced new languages and customs that added to the already-rich blend of Indian culture.

Southern India also experienced turmoil. It was home to three kingdoms that had never been conquered by the Mauryans. The people who lived in this region spoke the **Tamil** (TAM•uhl) language and are called the Tamil people. These three kingdoms often were at war with one another and with other states.

GEOGRAPHY SKILLBUILDER: Interpreting Maps

1. **Region** Compare the region occupied by the Gupta Empire to that occupied by the Mauryan Empire. Discuss size, location, and physical characteristics.
2. **Place** Why did neither the Mauryan nor the Gupta Empire expand to the northeast?

The Gupta Empire Is Established

After 500 years of invasion and turmoil, a strong leader again arose in the northern state of Magadha. His name was Chandra Gupta (GUP•tuh), but he was no relation to India's first emperor, Chandragupta Maurya. India's second empire, the **Gupta Empire**, oversaw a great flowering of Indian civilization, especially Hindu culture.

Chandra Gupta Builds an Empire The first Gupta emperor came to power not through battle but by marrying a daughter of an influential royal family. After his marriage, Chandra Gupta I took the title "Great King of Kings" in A.D. 320. His empire included Magadha and the area north of it, with his power base along the Ganges River. His son, Samudra (suh•MU•druh) Gupta, became king in A.D. 335. Although a lover of the arts, Samudra had a warlike side. He expanded the empire through 40 years of conquest.

▲ This terra-cotta tile, showing a musician playing a stringed instrument, is from a Hindu temple of the Gupta period.

Daily Life in India The Gupta era is the first period for which historians have much information about daily life in India. Most Indians lived in small villages. The majority were farmers, who walked daily from their homes to outlying fields. Craftspeople and merchants clustered in specific districts in the towns. They had shops on the street level and lived in the rooms above.

Most Indian families were **patriarchal**, headed by the eldest male. Parents, grandparents, uncles, aunts, and children all worked together to raise their crops. Because drought was common, farmers often had to irrigate their crops. There was a tax on water, and every month, people had to give a day's worth of labor to maintain wells, irrigation ditches, reservoirs, and dams. As in Mauryan times, farmers owed a large part of their earnings to the king.

Southern India followed a different cultural pattern. Some Tamil groups were **matriarchal**, headed by the mother rather than the father. Property, and sometimes the throne, was passed through the female line. **C**

MAIN IDEA

Contrasting
C How were the family systems of north and south India different?

Height of the Gupta Empire While village life followed unchanging traditional patterns, the royal court of the third Gupta emperor was a place of excitement and growth. Indians revered Chandra Gupta II for his heroic qualities. He defeated the Shakas—enemies to the west—and added their coastal territory to his empire. This allowed the Guptas to engage in profitable trade with the Mediterranean world. Chandra Gupta II also strengthened his empire through peaceful means by negotiating diplomatic and marriage alliances. He ruled from A.D. 375 to 415.

During the reign of the first three Guptas, India experienced a period of great achievement in the arts, religious thought, and science. These will be discussed in Section 2. After Chandra Gupta II died, new invaders threatened northern India. These fierce fighters, called the Hunas, were related to the Huns who invaded the Roman Empire. Over the next 100 years, the Gupta Empire broke into small kingdoms. Many were overrun by the Hunas or other Central Asian nomads. The Empire ended about 535.

SECTION 1 ASSESSMENT

TERMS & NAMES 1. For each term or name, write a sentence explaining its significance.
• Mauryan Empire   • Asoka   • religious toleration   • Tamil   • Gupta Empire   • patriarchal   • matriarchal

USING YOUR NOTES

2. Which similarity of the empires do you consider the most significant? Explain.

Mauryan	Gupta
1.	1.
2	2
3	3

MAIN IDEAS

3. Why was Asoka's first military campaign also his last campaign?

4. Who were the Tamil people?

5. What caused the fall of the Gupta Empire?

CRITICAL THINKING & WRITING

6. **SUPPORTING OPINIONS** Which Indian ruler described in this section would you rather live under? Explain.

7. **DRAWING CONCLUSIONS** What impact did the Greeks, Persians, and Central Asians have on Indian life between the Mauryan and Gupta empires?

8. **ANALYZING ISSUES** Which empire, Mauryan or Gupta, had a more significant impact on Indian history? Explain.

9. **WRITING ACTIVITY** POWER AND AUTHORITY For three of the rulers in this section, choose an object or image that symbolizes how that ruler exercised power. Write **captions** explaining why the symbols are appropriate.

CONNECT TO TODAY CREATING A PIE GRAPH

Use the Internet or library sources to create a **pie graph** showing the percentage of the population in India today that is Hindu, Buddhist, or a follower of other religions.

Trade Spreads Indian Religions and Culture

MAIN IDEA	WHY IT MATTERS NOW	TERMS & NAMES
CULTURAL INTERACTION Indian religions, culture, and science evolved and spread to other regions through trade.	The influence of Indian culture and religions is very evident throughout South Asia today.	• Mahayana • Vishnu • Theravada • Shiva • stupa • Kalidasa • Brahma • Silk Roads

SETTING THE STAGE The 500 years between the Mauryan and Gupta empires was a time of upheaval. Invaders poured into India, bringing new ideas and customs. In response, Indians began to change their own culture.

Buddhism and Hinduism Change

By 250 B.C., Hinduism and Buddhism were India's two main faiths. (See Chapter 3.) Hinduism is a complex polytheistic religion that blended Aryan beliefs with the many gods and cults of the diverse peoples who preceded them. Buddhism teaches that desire causes suffering and that humans should overcome desire by following the Eightfold Path. Over the centuries, both religions had become increasingly removed from the people. Hinduism became dominated by priests, while the Buddhist ideal of self-denial proved difficult for many to follow.

hmhsocialstudies.com
TAKING NOTES

Use the graphic organizer online to take notes on the specific developments of Indian culture.

A More Popular Form of Buddhism The Buddha had stressed that each person could reach a state of peace called nirvana. Nirvana was achieved by rejecting the sensory world and embracing spiritual discipline. After the Buddha died, his followers developed many different interpretations of his teachings.

Although the Buddha had forbidden people to worship him, some began to teach that he was a god. Some Buddhists also began to believe that many people could become Buddhas. These potential Buddhas, called bodhisattvas (BOH•dih•SUHT•vuhz), could choose to give up nirvana and work to save humanity through good works and self-sacrifice. The new ideas changed Buddhism from a religion that emphasized individual discipline to a mass religion that offered salvation to all and allowed popular worship.

By the first century A.D., Buddhists had divided over the new doctrines. Those who accepted them belonged to the **Mahayana** (MAH•huh•YAH•nuh) sect. Those who held to the Buddha's stricter, original teachings belonged to the **Theravada** (THEHR•uh•VAH•duh) sect. This is also called the Hinayana (HEE•nuh•YAH•nuh) sect, but Theravada is preferred.

These new trends in Buddhism inspired Indian art. For example, artists carved huge statues of the Buddha for people to worship. Wealthy Buddhist merchants who were eager to do good deeds paid for the construction of **stupas**—mounded stone structures built over holy relics. Buddhists walked the paths circling the stupas as a part of their meditation. Merchants also commissioned the carving of

▲ This Buddha is carved in the Gandharan artistic style, a blend of Greco-Roman and Indian styles.

cave temples out of solid rock. Artists then adorned these temples with beautiful sculptures and paintings.

A Hindu Rebirth Like Buddhism, Hinduism had become remote from the people. By the time of the Mauryan Empire, Hinduism had developed a complex set of sacrifices that could be performed only by the priests. People who weren't priests had less and less direct connection with the religion.

Gradually, through exposure to other cultures and in response to the popularity of Buddhism, Hinduism changed. Although the religion continued to embrace hundreds of gods, a trend toward monotheism was growing. Many people began to believe that there was only one divine force in the universe. The various gods represented parts of that force. The three most important Hindu gods were **Brahma** (BRAH•muh), creator of the world; **Vishnu** (VIHSH•noo), preserver of the world; and **Shiva** (SHEE•vuh), destroyer of the world. Of the three, Vishnu and Shiva were by far the favorites. Many Indians began to devote themselves to these two gods. As Hinduism evolved into a more personal religion, its popular appeal grew. Ⓐ

MAIN IDEA

Drawing Conclusions

Ⓐ Why did the changes in Buddhism and Hinduism make these religions more popular?

Achievements of Indian Culture

Just as Hinduism and Buddhism underwent changes, so did Indian culture and learning. India entered a highly productive period in literature, art, science, and mathematics that continued until roughly A.D. 500.

Literature and the Performing Arts One of India's greatest writers was **Kalidasa** (KAH•lee•DAH•suh). He may have been the court poet for Chandra Gupta II. Kalidasa's most famous play is *Shakuntala*. It tells the story of a beautiful girl who falls in love with and marries a middle-aged king. After Shakuntala and her husband are separated, they suffer tragically because of a curse that prevents the king from recognizing his wife when they meet again. Generations of Indians have continued to admire Kalidasa's plays because they are skillfully written and emotionally stirring.

Southern India also has a rich literary tradition. In the second century A.D., the city of Madurai in southern India became a site of writing academies. More than 2,000 Tamil poems from this period still exist. In the following excerpt from a third-century poem, a young man describes his sweetheart cooking him a meal:

PRIMARY SOURCE

There dwells my sweetheart, curving and lovely,
languid of gaze, with big round earrings,
and little rings on her tiny fingers.
She has cut the leaves of the garden plantain
and split them in pieces down the stalk
to serve as platters for the meal.
Her eyes are filled with the smoke of cooking.
Her brow, as fair as the crescent moon,
is covered now with drops of sweat.
She wipes it away with the hem of her garment
and stands in the kitchen, and thinks of me.

ANONYMOUS TAMIL POET, quoted in *The Wonder That Was India*

In addition to literature, drama was very popular. In southern India, traveling troupes of actors put on performances in cities across the region. Women as well as men took part in these shows, which combined drama and dance. Many of the classical dance forms in India today are based on techniques explained in a book written between the first century B.C. and the first century A.D.

Entertainment in India: Bollywood

Today, drama remains hugely popular in India. India has the largest movie industry in the world. About twice as many full-length feature films are released yearly in India as in the United States. India produces both popular and serious films. Indian popular films, such as *Monsoon Wedding,* are often love stories that blend music, dance, and drama. India's serious films have received worldwide critical praise. In 1992, the Indian director Satyajit Ray received a lifetime-achievement Academy Award for making artistic films. His films brought Indian culture to a global audience.

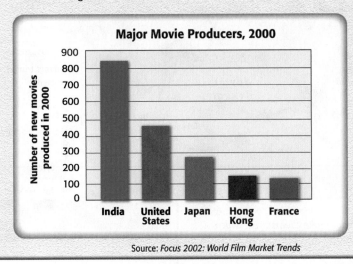

Major Movie Producers, 2000

Number of new movies produced in 2000 (vertical axis: 0–900)

India, United States, Japan, Hong Kong, France

Source: *Focus 2002: World Film Market Trends*

Astronomy, Mathematics, and Medicine The expansion of trade spurred the advance of science. Because sailors on trading ships used the stars to help them figure their position at sea, knowledge of astronomy increased. From Greek invaders, Indians adapted Western methods of keeping time. They began to use a calendar based on the cycles of the sun rather than the moon. They also adopted a seven-day week and divided each day into hours.

During the Gupta Empire (A.D. 320 to about 500), knowledge of astronomy increased further. Almost 1,000 years before Columbus, Indian astronomers proved that the earth was round by observing a lunar eclipse. During the eclipse, the earth's shadow fell across the face of the moon. The astronomers noted that the earth's shadow was curved, indicating that the earth itself was round.

Indian mathematics was among the most advanced in the world. Modern numerals, the zero, and the decimal system were invented in India. Around A.D. 500, an Indian named Aryabhata (AHR•yuh•BUHT•uh) calculated the value of pi (π) to four decimal places. He also calculated the length of the solar year as 365.3586805 days. This is very close to modern calculations made with an atomic clock. In medicine, two important medical guides were compiled. They described more than 1,000 diseases and more than 500 medicinal plants. Hindu physicians performed surgery—including plastic surgery—and possibly gave injections. **B**

MAIN IDEA

Drawing Conclusions

B What achievements by Indian mathematicians are used today?

The Spread of Indian Trade

In addition to knowledge, India has always been rich in precious resources. Spices, diamonds, sapphires, gold, pearls, and beautiful woods—including ebony, teak, and fragrant sandalwood—have been valuable items of exchange. Trade between

To Rome
Caspian Sea
Merv
Antioch
Ecbatana
Tyre
Ctesiphon
Herat
PERSIA
Gaza
Charax
Taxila
Alexandria
Persepolis
Aelana
Persian Gulf
Harmozia
EGYPT
ARABIA
Pattala
Pataliputra
Omana
Barbaricum
GUPTA EMPIRE
Barygaza
Nanhai (Guangzhou)
CHINA
Ch'ang-an (Xi'an)
Luoyang
Huang He (Yellow R.)
Chang Jiang (Yangtze R.)
Indus R.
Ganges R.
Tigris R.
Euphrates R.
Red Sea
Adulis
KINGDOM OF AKSUM
Cane
Arabian Sea
Muziris
Sopatma
Bay of Bengal
Takkola
Oc Eo
Tropic of Cancer
40°N
120°E
0° Equator

N
0   500 Miles
0   1,000 Kilometers

Trade route
Products traded
Cloth
Grains
Ivory
Metal
Precious stones
Silk
Slaves
Spices
Timber
Tortoise shell

GEOGRAPHY SKILLBUILDER: Interpreting Maps

1. **Movement** *Since people usually trade for goods they do not make themselves, which products were most likely to travel from Gupta India to Arabia?*

2. **Movement** *How far did trade goods travel to get from Luoyang in China to Alexandria in Egypt?*

India and regions as distant as Africa and Sumeria began more than 4,000 years ago. Trade expanded even after the Mauryan Empire ended around 185 B.C.

Overland Trade, East and West Groups who invaded India after Mauryan rule ended helped to expand India's trade to new regions. For example, Central Asian nomads told Indians about a vast network of caravan routes known as Silk Roads. These routes were called the **Silk Roads** because traders used them to bring silk from China to western Asia and then on to Rome.

Once Indians learned of the Silk Roads, they realized that they could make great profits by acting as middlemen. Middlemen are go-betweens in business transactions. For example, Indian traders would buy Chinese goods and sell them to traders traveling to Rome. To aid their role as middlemen, Indians built trading stations along the Silk Roads. They were located at oases, which are fertile spots in desert areas. **C**

Sea Trade, East and West Sea trade also increased. Traders used coastal routes around the rim of the Arabian Sea and up the Persian Gulf to bring goods from India to Rome. In addition, traders from southern India would sail to Southeast Asia to collect spices. They brought the spices back to India and sold them to merchants from Rome. Archaeologists have found hoards of Roman gold coins in southern India. Records show that some Romans were upset about the amount of gold their countrymen spent on Indian luxuries. They believed that to foster a healthy economy, a state must collect gold rather than spend it.

MAIN IDEA

Hypothesizing

C How might the Asian trade routes have spread Indian sciences and math to other civilizations?

Rome was not India's only sea-trading partner. India imported African ivory and gold, and exported cotton cloth. Rice and wheat went to Arabia in exchange for dates and horses. After trade with Rome declined around the third century A.D., India's sea trade with China and the islands of southeast Asia increased. The Chinese, for example, imported Indian cotton cloth, monkeys, parrots, and elephants and sent India silk.

Effects of Indian Trade Increased trade led to the rise of banking in India. Commerce was quite profitable. Bankers were willing to lend money to merchants and charge them interest on the loans. Interest rates varied, depending on how risky business was. During Mauryan times, the annual interest rate on loans used for overseas trade was 240 percent! During the Gupta Empire, bankers no longer considered sea trade so dangerous, so they charged only 15 to 20 percent interest a year. **D**

A number of Indian merchants went to live abroad and brought Indian culture with them. As a result, people throughout Asia picked up and adapted a variety of Indian traditions. For example, Indian culture affected styles in art, architecture, and dance throughout South and Southeast Asia. Indian influence was especially strong in Thailand, Cambodia, and on the Indonesian island of Java.

Traders also brought Indian religions to new regions. Hinduism spread northeast to Nepal and southeast to Sri Lanka and Borneo. Buddhism spread because of traveling Buddhist merchants and monks. In time, Buddhism even influenced China, as discussed in Section 3.

MAIN IDEA

Analyzing Causes

D Why would dangerous conditions make bankers charge higher interest on loans for trade?

Global Impact

↗ hmhsocialstudies.com INTERACTIVE MAP

The Spread of Buddhism

Buddhism became a missionary religion during Asoka's reign. From his capital city (1), Asoka sent out Buddhist missionaries. After Indians began trading along the Silk Roads, Buddhist monks traveled the roads and converted people along the way.

Buddhist monks from India established their first monastery in China (2) in A.D. 65, and many Chinese became Buddhists. From China, Buddhism reached Korea in the fourth century and Japan in the sixth century.

Today, Buddhism is a major religion in East and Southeast Asia. The Theravada school is strong in Myanmar, Cambodia (3), Sri Lanka (4), and Thailand. The Mahayana school is strong in Japan and Korea.

SECTION 2 ASSESSMENT

TERMS & NAMES 1. For each term or name, write a sentence explaining its significance.
• Mahayana • Theravada • stupa • Brahma • Vishnu • Shiva • Kalidasa • Silk Roads

USING YOUR NOTES

2. Which of the developments listed had the most lasting impact?

Religion	
Arts	
Science/Math	
Trade	

MAIN IDEA

3. How did Buddhism change after the Buddha's death?

4. What were India's main trade goods in the fifth century?

5. What were some of India's contributions to science during the Gupta period?

CRITICAL THINKING & WRITING

6. **RECOGNIZING EFFECTS** What do you think was the most significant effect of the changes in Buddhism and Hinduism during this period? Explain.

7. **MAKING INFERENCES** Why did Indian culture flourish during the Gupta Empire?

8. **FORMING AND SUPPORTING OPINIONS** Which do you think was more important to India's economy, overland trade or sea trade? Provide details to support your answer.

9. **WRITING ACTIVITY** CULTURAL INTERACTION Cite three of the cultures that interacted with India. Explain in a brief **expository essay** the result of each cultural interaction.

MULTIMEDIA ACTIVITY PREPARING A CHART

Use the Internet to research Indian trade today. Then prepare a **chart** listing the type of goods bought and sold and the trading partner for each type.

INTERNET KEYWORD
India trade

Hindu and Buddhist Art

The main difference between Buddhist art and Hindu art in India was its subject matter. Buddhist art often portrayed the Buddha or bodhisattvas, who were potential Buddhas. Hindu gods, such as Vishnu and Ganesha, were common subjects in Hindu art.

Beyond the differences in subject, Hindu and Buddhist beliefs had little influence on Indian artistic styles. For example, a Hindu sculpture and a Buddhist sculpture created at the same place and time were stylistically the same. In fact, the same artisans often created both Hindu and Buddhist art.

⬀ hmhsocialstudies.com

RESEARCH WEB LINKS Go online for more on Hindu and Buddhist art.

▼ The Great Stupa

Built during the third to first centuries B.C., the Great Stupa is a famous Buddhist monument in Sanchi, India. This stone structure is 120 feet across and 54 feet high; it has a staircase leading to a walkway that encircles the stupa. Stupas serve as memorials and often contain sacred relics. During Buddhist New Year festivals, worshipers hold images of the Buddha and move in processions around the circular walkway.

▼ Buddha

This bronze Buddha was made in India during the sixth century. Each detail of a Buddhist sculpture has meaning. For example, the headpiece and long earlobes shown here are lakshana, traditional bodily signs of the Buddha. The upraised hand is a gesture that means "Have no fear."

▲ Devi Jagadambi Temple in Khajuraho

Hardly any Hindu temples from the Gupta period remain. This temple, built in the 11th century, shows architectural trends begun in Gupta times. These include building with stone rather than wood; erecting a high, pyramidal roof instead of a flat roof; and sculpting elaborate decorations on the walls.

▲ Ganesha

Carved in the fifth century B.C., this stone sculpture represents the elephant-headed god Ganesha. According to Hindu beliefs, Ganesha is the god of success, education, wisdom, and wealth. He also is worshiped as the lifter of obstacles. The smaller picture is a recent image of Ganesha, who has gained great popularity during modern times.

Connect *to* Today

1. **Contrasting** How do the Buddhist stupa and the Hindu temple differ? According to the information on page 198, what might be the reason for those differences?

   See Skillbuilder Handbook, Page R7.

2. **Making Inferences** Why do you think Ganesha is a popular god among Hindus today? Explain.

Han Emperors in China

MAIN IDEA	WHY IT MATTERS NOW	TERMS & NAMES
ETHICAL SYSTEMS The Han Dynasty expanded China's borders and developed a system of government that lasted for centuries.	The pattern of a strong central government has remained a permanent part of Chinese life.	• Han Dynasty • centralized government • civil service • monopoly • assimilation

SETTING THE STAGE Under Shi Huangdi, the Qin Dynasty had unified China. Shi Huangdi established a strong government by conquering the rival kings who ruled small states throughout China. After Shi Huangdi died in 210 B.C., his son proved to be a weak, ineffective leader. China's government fell apart.

The Han Restore Unity to China

Use the graphic organizer online to take notes on the section's main ideas and details.

Rumblings of discontent during the Qin Dynasty grew to roars in the years after Shi Huangdi's death. Peasants were bitter over years of high taxes, harsh labor quotas, and a severe penal system. They rebelled. Rival kings were eager to regain control of the regions they had held before Shi Huangdi. They raised armies and fought over territory.

Liu Bang Founds the Han Dynasty During the civil war that followed, two powerful leaders emerged. Xiang Yu (shee•ANG-yoo) was an aristocratic general who was willing to allow the warlords to keep their territories if they would acknowledge him as their feudal lord. Liu Bang (LEE•oo-bahng) was one of Xiang Yu's generals.

Eventually, Liu Bang turned against Xiang Yu. The two fought their final battle in 202 B.C. Liu Bang won and declared himself the first emperor of the Han Dynasty. The **Han Dynasty**, which ruled China for more than 400 years, is divided into two periods. The Former Han ruled for about two centuries, until A.D. 9. After a brief period when the Han were out of power, the Later Han ruled for almost another two centuries. The Han Dynasty so influenced China that even today many Chinese call themselves "people of the Han."

▼ Emperor Liu Bang

Liu Bang's first goal was to destroy the rival kings' power. He followed Shi Huangdi's policy of establishing **centralized government**, in which a central authority controls the running of a state. Reporting to Liu Bang's central government were hundreds of local provincials called commanderies.

To win popular support, Liu Bang departed from Shi Huangdi's strict legalism. He lowered taxes and softened harsh punishments. People throughout the empire appreciated the peace and stability that Liu Bang brought to China.

The Empress Lü When Liu Bang died in 195 B.C., his son became emperor, but in name only. The real ruler was his mother, Empress Lü. Although Lü had not been Liu Bang's only wife, she had powerful friends at court who helped her seize power. The empress outlived her son and retained control of the throne by naming first one infant and then another as emperor. Because the infants were too young to rule, she remained in control. When Empress Lü died in 180 B.C., people who remained loyal to Liu Bang's family, rather than to Lü's family, came back into power. They rid the palace of the old empress's relatives by executing them.

Such palace plots occurred often throughout the Han Dynasty. Traditionally, the emperor chose the favorite among his wives as the empress and appointed one of her sons as successor. Because of this, the palace women and their families competed fiercely for the emperor's notice. The families would make alliances with influential people in the court. The resulting power plays distracted the emperor and his officials so much that they sometimes could not govern efficiently.

Vocabulary
Martial means warlike.

The Martial Emperor When Liu Bang's great-grandson took the throne, he continued Liu Bang's centralizing policies. Wudi (woo•dee), who reigned from 141 to 87 B.C., held the throne longer than any other Han emperor. He is called the "Martial Emperor" because he adopted the policy of expanding the Chinese empire through war.

Wudi's first set of enemies were the Xiongnu (shee•UNG•noo), fierce nomads known for their deadly archery skills from horseback. The Xiongnu roamed the steppes to the north and west of China. They made raids into China's settled farmland. There they took hostages and stole grain, livestock, and other valuable items. The early Han emperors tried to buy off the Xiongnu by sending them thousands of pounds of silk, rice, alcohol, and money. Usually, the Xiongnu just accepted these gifts and continued their raids.

Han Dynasty, 200 B.C.–A.D. 220

hmhsocialstudies.com INTERACTIVE MAP

Former Han, 200 B.C.

Han Empire at its greatest extent, A.D. 220
Han protectorate (influence)
Xiongnu regions
Great Wall
Silk Road

GEOGRAPHY SKILLBUILDER: Interpreting Maps
1. **Place** What was the approximate size, in square miles, of the Han Empire at its greatest extent?
2. **Location** Along which border did the Chinese build the Great Wall? Why did they build it there and not in other places?

When Wudi realized that the bribes were simply making the Xiongnu stronger, he sent more than 100,000 soldiers to fight them. To help defeat the Xiongnu, Wudi also made allies of their enemies:

PRIMARY SOURCE
The Xiongnu had defeated the king of the Yuezhi people and had made his skull into a drinking vessel. As a result the Yuezhi . . . bore a constant grudge against the Xiongnu, though as yet they had been unable to find anyone to join them in an attack on their enemy. . . . When the emperor [Wudi] heard this, he decided to try to send an envoy to establish relations with the Yuezhi.

SIMA QIAN, *Records of the Grand Historian*

After his army forced the nomads to retreat into Central Asia, Wudi attempted to make his northwest border safe by settling his troops on the Xiongnu's former pastures. Although this tactic succeeded for a time, nomadic raiders continued to cause problems during much of China's later history.

Wudi also colonized areas to the northeast, now known as Manchuria and Korea. He sent his armies south, where they conquered mountain tribes and set up Chinese colonies all the way into what is now Vietnam. By the end of Wudi's reign, the empire had expanded nearly to the bounds of present-day China.

A Highly Structured Society

Chinese society under the Han Dynasty was highly structured. (See Social History below.) Just as Han emperors tried to control the people they conquered, they exerted vast control over the Chinese themselves. Because the Chinese believed their emperor to have divine authority, they accepted his exercise of power. He was the link between heaven and earth. If the emperor did his job well, China had peace

Social History

Chinese Society

Under the Han Dynasty, the structure of Chinese society was clearly defined. At the top was the emperor, who was considered semidivine. Next came kings and governors, both appointed by the emperor. They governed with the help of state officials, nobles, and scholars.

Peasant farmers came next. Their production of food was considered vital to the existence of the empire. Artisans and merchants were below them.

Near the bottom were the soldiers, who guarded the empire's frontiers. At the bottom were enslaved persons, who were usually conquered peoples.

hmhsocialstudies.com

INTERNET ACTIVITY Go online to create a photo exhibit on Chinese society today. Include pictures of people from various walks of life.

Emperor

King

Governor

State Officials

Nobles & Scholars

Peasants

Artisans

Merchants

Soldiers

Slaves

and prosperity. If he failed, the heavens showed their displeasure with earthquakes, floods, and famines. However, the emperor did not rule alone.

Structures of Han Government The Chinese emperor relied on a complex bureaucracy to help him rule. Running the bureaucracy and maintaining the imperial army were expensive. To raise money, the government levied taxes. Like the farmers in India, Chinese peasants owed part of their yearly crops to the government. Merchants also paid taxes.

Besides taxes, the peasants owed the government a month's worth of labor or military service every year. With this source of labor, the Han emperors built roads and dug canals and irrigation ditches. The emperors also filled the ranks of China's vast armies and expanded the Great Wall, which stretched across the northern frontier.

Confucianism, the Road to Success Wudi's government employed more than 130,000 people. The bureaucracy included 18 different ranks of <u>civil service</u> jobs, which were government jobs that civilians obtained by taking examinations. At times, Chinese emperors rewarded loyal followers with government posts. However, another way to fill government posts evolved under the Han. This method involved testing applicants' knowledge of Confucianism—the teachings of Confucius, who had lived 400 years before.

The early Han emperors had employed some Confucian scholars as court advisers, but it was Wudi who began actively to favor them. Confucius had taught that gentlemen should practice "reverence [respect], generosity, truthfulness, diligence [industriousness], and kindness." Because these were exactly the qualities he wanted his government officials to have, Wudi set up a school where hopeful job applicants from all over China could come to study Confucius's works. **Ⓐ**

After their studies, job applicants took formal examinations in history, law, literature, and Confucianism. In theory, anyone could take the exams. In practice, few peasants could afford to educate their sons. So only sons of wealthy landowners had a chance at a government career. In spite of this flaw, the civil service system begun by Wudi worked so efficiently that it continued in China until 1912.

Han Technology, Commerce, and Culture

The 400 years of Han rule saw not only improvements in education but also great advances in Chinese technology and culture. In addition, the centralized government began to exert more control over commerce and manufacturing.

Technology Revolutionizes Chinese Life Advances in technology influenced all aspects of Chinese life. Paper was invented in A.D. 105. Before that, books were usually written on silk. But paper was cheaper, so books became more readily available. This helped spread education in China. The invention of paper also affected Chinese government. Formerly, all government documents had been recorded on strips of wood. Paper was much more convenient to use for record keeping, so Chinese bureaucracy expanded.

Another technological advance was the collar harness for horses. This invention allowed horses to pull much heavier loads than did the harness being used in Europe at the time.

MAIN IDEA

Making Inferences

Ⓐ Why would Wudi want his officials to have qualities such as diligence?

Vocabulary
Commerce is the buying and selling of goods.

Global Impact

Papermaking

People in ancient China wrote on pottery, bones, stone, silk, wood, and bamboo. Then, about 2,000 or more years ago, the Chinese invented paper. They began to use plants, such as hemp, to make thin paper. In A.D. 105, Ts'ai Lun, a Han official, produced a stronger paper by mixing mulberry bark and old rags with hemp fiber.

The art of papermaking slowly spread to the rest of the world. First, it moved east to Korea and Japan. Then, it spread westward to the Arab world in the 700s, and from there to Europe.

The Chinese perfected a plow that was more efficient because it had two blades. They also improved iron tools, invented the wheelbarrow, and began to use water mills to grind grain. **B**

Agriculture Versus Commerce During the Han Dynasty, the population of China swelled to 60 million. Because there were so many people to feed, Confucian scholars and ordinary Chinese people considered agriculture the most important and honored occupation. An imperial edict written in 167 B.C. stated this philosophy quite plainly:

MAIN IDEA

Making Inferences
B Which of these inventions helped to feed China's huge population?

PRIMARY SOURCE

Agriculture is the foundation of the world. No duty is greater. Now if [anyone] personally follows this pursuit diligently, he has yet [to pay] the impositions of the land tax and tax on produce. . . . Let there be abolished the land tax and the tax on produce levied upon the cultivated fields.

BAN GU and **BAN ZHAO** in *History of the Former Han Dynasty*

Although the same decree dismissed commerce as the least important occupation, manufacturing and commerce were actually very important to the Han Empire. The government established monopolies on the mining of salt, the forging of iron, the minting of coins, and the brewing of alcohol. A **monopoly** occurs when a group has exclusive control over the production and distribution of certain goods.

For a time, the government also ran huge silk mills—competing with private silk weavers in making this luxurious cloth. As contact with people from other lands increased, the Chinese realized how valuable their silk was as an item of trade.

Global Impact: Trade Networks

hmhsocialstudies.com **INTERACTIVE MAP**

Silk Roads

Why would anyone struggle over mountains and across deserts to buy fabric? Ancient peoples valued silk because it was strong, lightweight, and beautiful. Traders made fortunes carrying Chinese silk to the West. Because of this, the caravan trails that crossed Asia were called Silk Roads, even though many other valuable trade goods were also carried along these routes. The Silk Roads also encouraged cultural diffusion.

Camel Caravans ▶

No trader traveled the whole length of the Silk Roads. Mediterranean merchants went partway, then traded with Central Asian nomads—who went east until they met Chinese traders near India. Many traders traveled in camel caravans.

From this point, ships carried silk and spices to Rome. The Romans paid a pound of gold for a pound of Chinese silk!

Because of this, the techniques of silk production became a closely guarded state secret. Spurred by the worldwide demand for silk, Chinese commerce expanded along the Silk Roads to most of Asia and, through India, all the way to Rome.

The Han Unifies Chinese Culture

As the Han empire expanded its trade networks, the Chinese began to learn about the foods and fashions common in foreign lands. Similarly, expanding the empire through conquest brought people of different cultures under Chinese rule.

Unification Under Chinese Rule To unify the empire, the Chinese government encouraged <u>assimilation</u>, the process of making conquered peoples part of Chinese culture. To promote assimilation, the government sent Chinese farmers to settle newly colonized areas. It also encouraged them to intermarry with local peoples. Government officials set up schools to train local people in the Confucian philosophy and then appointed local scholars to government posts.

Several writers also helped to unify Chinese culture by recording China's history. Sima Qian (SU•MAH chee•YEHN), who lived from 145 to 85 B.C., is called the Grand Historian for his work in compiling a history of China from the ancient dynasties to Wudi. To write accurately, Sima Qian visited historical sites, interviewed eyewitnesses, researched official records, and examined artifacts. His book is called *Records of the Grand Historian*. Another famous book was the *History of the Former Han Dynasty*. Ban Biao (BAHN bee•OW), who lived from A.D. 3 to 54, started the project. After his death, his son Ban Gu (bahn goo) and later his daughter Ban Zhao

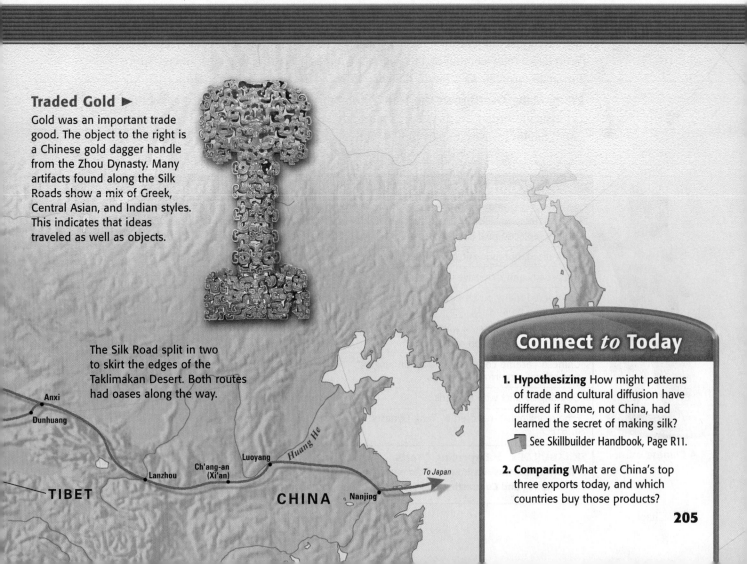

Traded Gold ▶
Gold was an important trade good. The object to the right is a Chinese gold dagger handle from the Zhou Dynasty. Many artifacts found along the Silk Roads show a mix of Greek, Central Asian, and Indian styles. This indicates that ideas traveled as well as objects.

The Silk Road split in two to skirt the edges of the Taklimakan Desert. Both routes had oases along the way.

Anxi
Dunhuang
Lanzhou
Ch'ang-an (Xi'an)
Luoyang
Huang He
Nanjing
To Japan
TIBET
CHINA

Connect *to* Today

1. **Hypothesizing** How might patterns of trade and cultural diffusion have differed if Rome, not China, had learned the secret of making silk?

   See Skillbuilder Handbook, Page R11.

2. **Comparing** What are China's top three exports today, and which countries buy those products?

(bahn jow) worked on it. Ban Zhao also wrote a guide called *Lessons for Women*, which called upon women to be humble and obedient but also industrious.

Women's Roles—Wives, Nuns, and Scholars Although Ban Zhao gained fame as a historian, most women during the Han Dynasty led quiet lives at home. Confucian teachings had dictated that women were to devote themselves to their families. However, women made important contributions to their family's economic life through duties in the home and work in the fields of the family farm.

Some upper-class women lived much different lives. As explained earlier, a few empresses wielded great power. Daoist—and later, Buddhist—nuns were able to gain an education and lead lives apart from their families. Women in aristocratic and landowning families also sometimes pursued education and culture. Some women ran small shops; still others practiced medicine.

The Fall of the Han and Their Return

In spite of economic and cultural advances, the Han emperors faced grave problems. One of the main problems was an economic imbalance caused by customs that allowed the rich to gain more wealth at the expense of the poor.

The Rich Take Advantage of the Poor According to custom, a family's land was divided equally among all of the father's male heirs. Unless a farmer could afford to buy more land during his lifetime, each generation inherited smaller plots. With such small plots of land, farmers had a hard time raising enough food to sell or even to feed the family. Because of this, small farmers often went into debt and had to borrow money from large landowners, who charged very high interest rates. If the farmer couldn't pay back the debt, the landowner took possession of the farmer's land.

Large landowners were not required to pay taxes, so when their land holdings increased, the amount of land that was left for the government to tax decreased. With less money coming in, the government pressed harder to collect money from the small farmers. As a result, the gap between rich and poor increased.

Wang Mang Overthrows the Han During this time of economic change, political instability grew. At the palace, court advisers, palace servants, and rival influential families wove complex plots to influence the emperor's choice of who would

▲ Chinese warrior

Comparing Two Great Empires: Han China and Rome	
Han Dynasty—202 B.C. to A.D. 220	**Roman Empire—27 B.C. to A.D. 476**
Empire replaced rival kingdoms	Empire replaced republic
Centralized, bureaucratic government	Centralized, bureaucratic government
Built roads and defensive walls	Built roads and defensive walls
Conquered many diverse peoples in regions bordering China	Conquered many diverse peoples in regions of three continents
At its height—area of 1.5 million square miles and a population of 60 million	At its height—area of 3.4 million square miles and a population of 55 million
Chinese became common written language throughout empire	Latin did not replace other written languages in empire
Ongoing conflict with nomads	Ongoing conflict with nomads
Empire fell apart; restored by Tang Dynasty in 618	Empire fell apart; never restored

SKILLBUILDER: Interpreting Charts
1. **Drawing Conclusions** *How long did each empire last? When did they both exist?*
2. **Comparing and Contrasting** *How were Han China and the Roman Empire similar? Different?*

▲ Roman soldier

succeed him as ruler. From about 32 B.C. until A.D. 9, one inexperienced emperor replaced another. Chaos reigned in the palace, and with peasant revolts, unrest spread across the land as well.

Finally, Wang Mang (wahng mahng), a Confucian scholar and member of the court, decided that a strong ruler was needed to restore order. For six years, he had been acting as regent for the infant who had been crowned emperor. In A.D. 9, Wang Mang took the imperial title for himself and overthrew the Han, thus ending the Former Han, the first half of the Han Dynasty.

Vocabulary
A *regent* is a person who rules temporarily while a monarch is too young.

Wang Mang tried to bring the country under control. He minted new money to relieve the treasury's shortage and set up public granaries to help feed China's poor. Wang Mang also took away large landholdings from the rich and planned to redistribute the land to farmers who had lost their land. But this plan angered powerful landholders. Wang Mang's larger supply of money disrupted the economy, because it allowed people to increase their spending, which encouraged merchants to raise prices.

Then, in A.D. 11, a great flood left thousands dead and millions homeless. The public granaries did not hold enough to feed the displaced, starving people. Huge peasant revolts rocked the land. The wealthy, opposed to Wang Mang's land policies, joined in the rebellion. The rebels assassinated Wang Mang in A.D. 23. Within two years, a member of the old imperial family took the throne and began the second period of Han rule—called the Later Han. **C**

MAIN IDEA

Recognizing Effects

C How did Wang Mang's policies help cause his own downfall?

The Later Han Years With peace restored to China, the first decades of the Later Han Dynasty were quite prosperous. The government sent soldiers and merchants westward to regain control of posts along the Silk Roads. But this expansion could not make up for social, political, and economic weaknesses within the empire itself. Within a century, China suffered from the same economic imbalances, political intrigues, and social unrest that had toppled the Former Han. By 220, the Later Han Dynasty had disintegrated into three rival kingdoms.

In the next chapter, you will learn about the early civilizations and kingdoms that developed in Africa.

▲ Silk was the trade good that linked the Han and Roman empires. This fragment of silk was found along the Silk Roads.

SECTION **3** **ASSESSMENT**

TERMS & NAMES 1. For each term or name, write a sentence explaining its significance.
• Han Dynasty • centralized government • civil service • monopoly • assimilation

USING YOUR NOTES
2. What was the most lasting development of the Han Empire? Explain.

> Han China
> I. The Han Restore Unity to China
>   A.
>   B.
>   C.
> II. A Highly Structured Society
> III. Han Technology, Commerce, and Culture

MAIN IDEAS
3. How did Wudi encourage learning?
4. What role did women play in Han society?
5. How did the Han Chinese attempt to assimilate conquered peoples?

CRITICAL THINKING & WRITING
6. **IDENTIFYING PROBLEMS** What problem do you think was most responsible for weakening the Han Dynasty? Explain.
7. **ANALYZING CAUSES** How important were Confucian teachings in the lives of people of the Han Empire? Provide details to support your answer.
8. **DRAWING CONCLUSIONS** Why was agriculture considered the most important and honored occupation in Han China?
9. **WRITING ACTIVITY** RELIGIOUS AND ETHICAL SYSTEMS Review the five qualities Confucius said gentlemen should have. Write one **sentence** for each describing the action a government official could take to demonstrate the quality.

CONNECT TO TODAY CREATING AN ORGANIZATIONAL CHART
Research information about the current government of the People's Republic of China. Then create an **organizational chart** showing its structure.

India and China Establish Empires **207**

VISUAL SUMMARY

India and China Establish Empires

300 B.C. — 100 B.C. — A.D. 100 — A.D. 300 — A.D. 500

Mauryan Empire

321 B.C. **Chandragupta Maurya** seized throne and began Mauryan Empire.

269 B.C. **Asoka** began rule; conquered Kalinga; regretted slaughter and converted to Buddhism; sent out missionaries.

232 B.C. **Asoka** died; empire started to break apart.

185 B.C. Greeks invaded India, beginning five centuries of turmoil.

Han Dynasty

202 B.C. **Liu Bang** started Han Dynasty; strengthened central government.

141 B.C. **Wudi** began reign; conquered neighboring regions; started civil service.

A.D. 9 **Wang Mang** temporarily overthrew the Han.

- 1st century A.D. Later Han rulers encouraged Silk Road trade with West.
- Chinese invented paper, collar harness, water mill.

Gupta Empire

A.D. 320 **Chandra Gupta I** began empire.

A.D. 375 **Chandra Gupta II** started reign. Indian art, literature, and dance flowered.

A.D. 500 Indian astronomers realized Earth was round; mathematician calculated value of pi and length of solar year.

- Buddhism and Hinduism developed more popular forms.
- Trade spread Indian culture, Hinduism, and Buddhism.

TERMS & NAMES

For each term or name below, briefly explain its connection to the empires in India and China between 321 B.C. and A.D. 550.

1. Mauryan Empire
2. Asoka
3. religious toleration
4. Gupta Empire
5. Kalidasa
6. Silk Roads
7. Han Dynasty
8. centralized government
9. civil service
10. assimilation

MAIN IDEAS

India's First Empires Section 1 (pages 189–192)

11. What were three significant accomplishments of the Mauryan rulers?
12. How did India change during the 500 years between the decline of the Mauryan Empire and the rise of the Gupta Empire?
13. How did the southern tip of India differ from the rest of India?

Trade Spreads Indian Religions and Culture
Section 2 (pages 193–199)

14. How did changes in Buddhism influence art in India?
15. What advances in science and mathematics had been made in India by about 500?
16. What were the economic and cultural links between India and Southeast Asia?

Han Emperors in China Section 3 (pages 200–207)

17. Why was Wudi one of China's most significant rulers? Explain.
18. Under the Chinese civil-service system, who could become government officials?
19. How did silk influence China's government, economy, and culture during the Han period?
20. How did economic problems lead to the decline of the Han?

CRITICAL THINKING

1. USING YOUR NOTES

In a diagram like the one to the right, fill in the information comparing the Mauryan, Gupta, and Han empires.

Empire	Period of Influence	Key Leaders	Significant Achievements
Mauryan			
Gupta			
Han			

2. CONTRASTING

RELIGIOUS AND ETHICAL SYSTEMS   Contrast Buddhism's influence on India's government with Confucianism's influence on China's government.

3. EVALUATING

POWER AND AUTHORITY   Which of the three empires—the Mauryan, Gupta, or Han—was most successful? Explain and support your opinion.

4. DRAWING CONCLUSIONS

CULTURAL INTERACTION   How significant were the Silk Roads to the economy of India? Defend your viewpoint with text references.

5. DEVELOPING HISTORICAL PERSPECTIVE

What was the importance of the Chinese invention of paper?

Use the quotation and your knowledge of world history to answer questions 1 and 2.

PRIMARY SOURCE

Kalinga was conquered by his Sacred and Gracious Majesty when he had been consecrated eight years. 150,000 persons were thence carried away captive, 100,000 were slain, and many times that number died. . . . Thus arose his Sacred Majesty's remorse for having conquered the Kalingas, because the conquest of a country previously unconquered involves the slaughter, death, and carrying away captive of the people.

ASOKA in *A History of Modern India* by Percival Spear

1. Why was Asoka remorseful about the campaign against Kalinga?

   A. His army was not victorious.

   B. The battle took too long to fight.

   C. Many people were killed or made captives.

   D. He was not able to play a more active role in the battle.

2. What did the conquest of Kalinga cause Asoka to realize about the nature of war?

   A. War leads to the deaths of innocent people.

   B. War is the best means possible to expand an empire.

   C. War cannot be avoided.

   D. War is very expensive to fight.

Use the photograph of this 16-inch, bronze sculpture from Han China and your knowledge of world history to answer question 3.

3. What does this sculpture reveal about life in Han China?

   A. that the Chinese invented the wheel

   B. that the Chinese used chariots in warfare

   C. that only privileged classes used this form of transportation

   D. that the Chinese were skilled in the use of bronze

 hmhsocialstudies.com TEST PRACTICE

For additional test practice, go online for:
- Diagnostic tests
- Strategies
- Tutorials

Interact *with* History

On page 188, you looked at a situation in which a government hired people to spy on each other. Now that you have read the chapter, reevaluate your decision about being a spy. What do you think are the best methods for a government to use to control large numbers of people? Consider the methods used by Chandragupta, Asoka, and the Han emperors.

FOCUS ON WRITING

Write a newspaper **editorial** either praising or criticizing Asoka and his methods of governing.

- In the first paragraph, introduce your opinion.
- In the middle paragraphs, give reasons and historical evidence to support your opinion.
- In the conclusion, restate your opinion in a forceful way.

MULTIMEDIA ACTIVITY

21ST CENTURY

Creating a Virtual Field Trip

Plan a two-week virtual field trip through China and India. Decide which cities you would visit from the Mauryan and Gupta empires in India and the Han Empire in China. Make sure also to include sites along the Silk Roads. Create an online or classroom presentation that includes the following:

- maps showing the route of your trip
- images of the major historic sites you would visit and why each site is historically significant
- images of the commercial goods and art objects you might see along the way

CHAPTER 8

African Civilizations,

1500 B.C.–A.D. 700

Essential Question

How did ancient African cultures adapt to their harsh environments and establish powerful kingdoms?

 What You Will Learn

In this chapter you will learn how African civilizations adapted to various environments and spread cultural ideas.

SECTION 1 Diverse Societies in Africa

Main Idea African peoples developed diverse societies as they adapted to varied environments.

SECTION 2 Migration Case Study: Bantu-Speaking Peoples

Main Idea Relocation of large numbers of Bantu-speaking people brings cultural diffusion and change to southern Africa.

SECTION 3 The Kingdom of Aksum

Main Idea The kingdom of Aksum became an international trading power and adopted Christianity.

Previewing Themes

INTERACTION WITH ENVIRONMENT The varied climates and natural resources of Africa offered opportunities for developing different lifestyles. By 500 B.C., the Nok people of West Africa had pioneered iron-making technology.

Geography *Look at the location of ironworking sites on the map. What might explain why ironworking took place at these sites?*

CULTURAL INTERACTION Massive migrations of Bantu-speaking people changed the culture of eastern and southern Africa. The migrating people brought new skills and ideas about society to people in the south and east.

Geography *Study the time line and the map. Where did ironworking spread from Nok, and which group probably brought the skills?*

POWER AND AUTHORITY The kingdom of Aksum became a major trading center for Indian Ocean and Arabian trade. It also became the center of Christianity in East Africa.

Geography *Why was Aksum better suited for trade than Nok or Djenné-Djeno?*

1500s B.C.
Africans south of the Sahara live in scattered farming communities, as pastoralists or hunter-gatherers.

751 B.C.
Kushite king, Pianki, conquers Memphis in Egypt.

AFRICA

1500 B.C.   1000 B.C.

WORLD

1200 B.C.
◄ Olmec culture rises in southern Mexico. (stone Olmec head)

461 B.C.
◄ Age of Pericles in Greece.

210

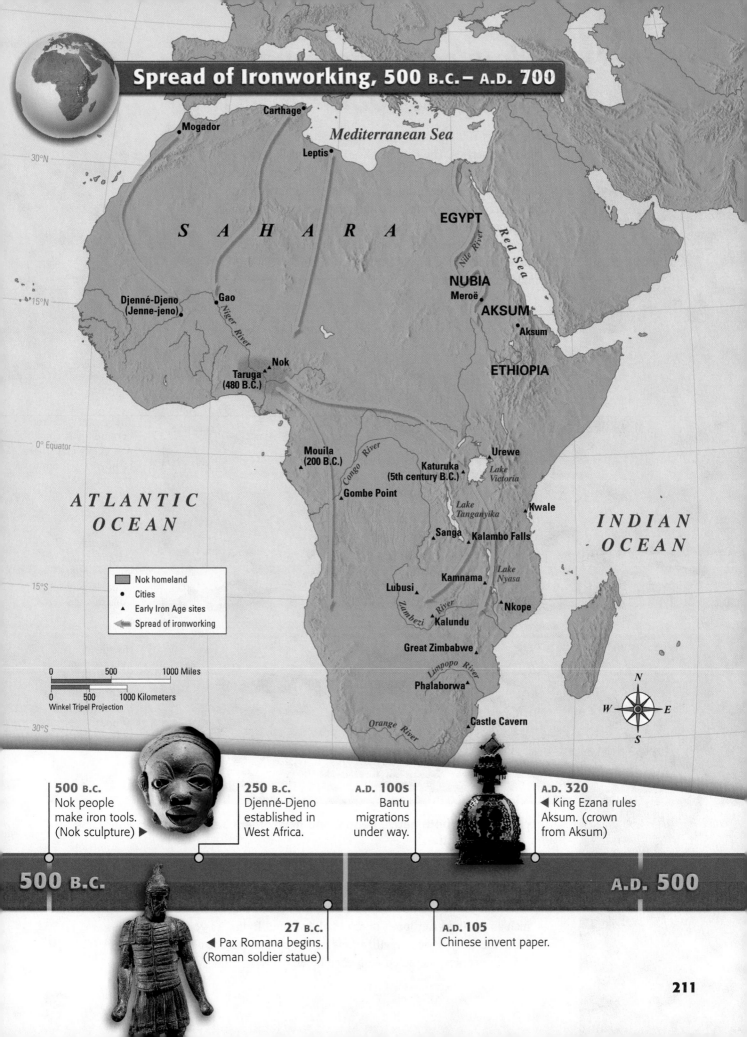

Spread of Ironworking, 500 B.C. – A.D. 700

Mediterranean Sea

Carthage
Mogador
Leptis

S A H A R A

EGYPT

Nile River

Red Sea

NUBIA
Meroë

AKSUM
Aksum

ETHIOPIA

Djenné-Djeno
(Jenne-jeno)

Gao

Niger River

Nok
Taruga
(480 B.C.)

0° Equator

Mouila
(200 B.C.)

Congo River

Katuruka
(5th century B.C.)

Urewe

Lake
Victoria

Kwale

Gombe Point

ATLANTIC
OCEAN

Lake
Tanganyika

INDIAN
OCEAN

Sanga

Kalambo Falls

Kamnama

Lake
Nyasa

Lubusi

Nkope

Zambezi River

Kalundu

Great Zimbabwe

Limpopo River

Phalaborwa

Orange River

Castle Cavern

N
W E
S

Legend
- Nok homeland
- Cities
- ▲ Early Iron Age sites
- Spread of ironworking

0   500   1000 Miles
0   500   1000 Kilometers
Winkel Tripel Projection

Timeline

500 B.C.
Nok people make iron tools. (Nok sculpture) ▶

250 B.C.
Djenné-Djeno established in West Africa.

A.D. 100s
Bantu migrations under way.

A.D. 320
◀ King Ezana rules Aksum. (crown from Aksum)

500 B.C.

A.D. 500

27 B.C.
◀ Pax Romana begins. (Roman soldier statue)

A.D. 105
Chinese invent paper.

How can newcomers change a community?

The year is 100 B.C., and you've spent most of the day gathering berries. The hunters have brought back some small game to add to the simmering pot. Just then you see something out of the ordinary. A stranger is approaching. He is carrying a spear and leading cows—a type of animal that none of you has ever seen. Your first reaction is fear. But you are also curious. Who is he? What does he want? Where has he come from? The communal elders have similar concerns, yet they cautiously go forward to greet him.

1 The hunter-gatherer community is small and tightly knit. There is, however, room to accommodate newcomers.

2 Having traveled long distances, this stranger might have valuable survival skills to share.

3 His spears could indicate that he is a good hunter or that his group may be hostile invaders— or both.

EXAMINING *the* ISSUES

- **How might both native people and newcomers benefit from their interaction?**

- **How would such interaction change everyone involved?**

Discuss these questions as a class. In your discussion, remember what you've learned about other peoples who dealt with foreigners, such as the Indo-European invaders of Asia and India. As you read about the early African civilizations in this chapter, notice how African peoples interacted with each other.

Diverse Societies in Africa

MAIN IDEA	WHY IT MATTERS NOW	TERMS & NAMES
INTERACTION WITH ENVIRONMENT African peoples developed diverse societies as they adapted to varied environments.	Differences among modern societies are also based on people's interactions with their environments.	• Sahara • animism • Sahel • griot • savanna • Nok • Djenné-Djeno

SETTING THE STAGE Africa spreads across the equator. It includes a broad range of Earth's environments—from steamy coastal plains to snow-capped mountain peaks. Some parts of Africa suffer from constant drought, while others receive over 200 inches of rain a year. Vegetation varies from sand dunes and rocky wastes to dense green rain forests. Interaction with the African environment has created unique cultures and societies. Each group found ways to adapt to the land and the resources it offers.

A Land of Geographic Contrasts

Africa is the second largest continent in the world. It stretches 4,600 miles from east to west and 5,000 miles from north to south. With a total of 11.7 million square miles, it occupies about one-fifth of Earth's land surface. Narrow coastlines (50 to 100 miles) lie on either side of a central plateau. Waterfalls and rapids often form as rivers drop down to the coast from the plateau, making navigation impossible to or from the coast. Africa's coastline has few harbors, ports, or inlets. Because of this, the coastline is actually shorter than that of Europe, a land one-third Africa's size.

hmhsocialstudies.com
TAKING NOTES

Use the graphic organizer online to take notes on the section's ideas and details about Africa.

Challenging Environments Each African environment offers its own challenges. The deserts are largely unsuitable for human life and also hamper people's movement to more welcoming climates. The largest deserts are the **Sahara** in the north and the Kalahari (kahl•uh•HAHR•ee) in the south.

Stretching from the Atlantic Ocean to the Red Sea, the Sahara covers an area roughly the size of the United States. Only a small part of the Sahara consists of sand dunes. The rest is mostly a flat, gray wasteland of scattered rocks and gravel. Each year the desert takes over more and more of the land at the southern edge of the Sahara Desert, the **Sahel** (suh•HAYL).

Another very different—but also partly uninhabitable—African environment is the rain forest. Sometimes called "nature's greenhouse," it produces mahogany and teak trees up to 150 feet tall. Their leaves and branches form a dense canopy that keeps sunlight from reaching the forest floor. The tsetse (TSET•see) fly is found in the rain forest. Its presence prevented Africans from using cattle, donkeys, and horses to farm near the rain forests. This deadly insect also prevented invaders—especially Europeans—from colonizing fly-infested territories.

EUROPE

1 The deadliest creature lurking in rain forests is a small fly called the tsetse fly. Tsetse flies carry a disease that is deadly to livestock and can cause fatal sleeping sickness in humans.

Mediterranean Sea

ATLAS MOUNTAINS

LIBYAN DESERT

S A H A R A

Nile R.

Red Sea

2 Sahel means "coastline" in Arabic. African people may have named it this because the Sahara seemed like a vast ocean of sand.

ARABIAN PENINSULA

Senegal R.

S Niger R. **2** A H E L

Lake Chad

A F R I C A

Gulf of Aden

ATLANTIC OCEAN

0° Equator

Gulf of Guinea

1

4

Congo R.

3

Lake Turkana

GREAT RIFT VALLEY

Lake Victoria

Mt. Kenya

Mt. Kilimanjaro

Lake Tanganyika

Lake Nyasa

INDIAN OCEAN

⌐ hmhsocialstudies.com

INTERACTIVE MAP

Explore the varied environments of Africa.

4 The dense trees and lack of edible vegetation in the humid rain forest make it an unwelcoming environment for most people.

■	Rain forest
■	Savanna
■	Desert
■	Mediterranean

MADAGASCAR

Zambezi R.

NAMIB DESERT

Limpopo R.

KALAHARI DESERT

Orange R.

DRAKENSBERG MTS.

40°W

N

0   1,000 Miles

0   2,000 Kilometers

3 The savannas are home to herds of animals such as giraffes, wildebeest, and antelope. They also support grain crops of millet, wheat, and maize (corn).

GEOGRAPHY SKILLBUILDER: Interpreting Maps

1. **Place** *About what percent of Africa is desert? savanna?*
2. **Region** *If you were to fold a map of Africa in half along the equator, what do you notice about the similar vegetation zones above and below the fold?*

Welcoming Lands The northern coast and the southern tip of Africa have welcoming Mediterranean-type climates and fertile soil. Because these coastal areas are so fertile, they are densely populated with farmers and herders.

Most people in Africa live on the **savannas**, or grassy plains. Africa's savannas are not just endless plains. They include mountainous highlands and swampy tropical stretches. Covered with tall grasses and dotted with trees, the savannas cover over 40 percent of the continent. Dry seasons alternate with rainy seasons—often, two of each a year. Unfortunately, the topsoil throughout Africa is thin, and heavy rains strip away minerals. In most years, however, the savannas support abundant agricultural production.

Early Humans Adapt to Their Environments

The first humans appeared in the Great Rift Valley, a deep gash in Earth's crust that runs through the floor of the Red Sea and across eastern Africa. As you learned earlier, people moved outward from this area in the world's first migration. They developed technologies that helped them survive in—and then alter—their surroundings.

Nomadic Lifestyle Africa's earliest peoples were nomadic hunter-gatherers. Today, some of the San of the Kalahari Desert and the BaMbuti (bah•uhm•BOO•tee) of the rain forests of Congo are still hunter-gatherers. The San, for example, travel in small bands of a few related families. The men hunt with spears and bows and arrows, and the women and children gather roots and berries.

Other early Africans eventually learned to domesticate and raise a variety of animals for food. Called herders, or pastoralists, these people kept cattle, goats, or sheep. They were nomads who drove their animals to find water and good pastures for grazing during the dry season. Millions of modern Africans are pastoral herders as well. The Masai (mah•SEYE) of Tanzania and southern Kenya, for example, still measure their wealth by the size of their herds. **A**

Transition to a Settled Lifestyle Experts believe that agriculture in Africa probably began by 6000 B.C. Between 8000 and 6000 B.C., the Sahara received increased rainfall and turned into a savanna. But about 6000 B.C., the Sahara began to dry up again. To survive, many early farmers moved east into the Nile Valley and south into West Africa. Some settled on the savannas, which had the best agricultural land. Grain grew well in the savannas. In addition to growing grain, Africans began to raise cattle. In areas where the tsetse fly was found, it was not possible to keep cattle. However, south and east of the rain forests, cattle raising became an important part of agricultural life. Other Africans learned to farm in the rain forest, where they planted root crops, such as yams, that needed little sun.

Agriculture drastically changed the way Africans lived. Growing their own food enabled them to build permanent shelters in one location. Settlements expanded because reliable food supplies led to longer, healthier lives and an increased birthrate. The increased food supply also freed

MAIN IDEA

Making Inferences
A Why might Africans continue living in a nomadic lifestyle?

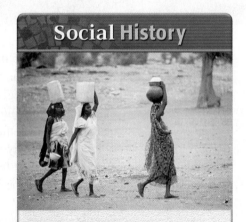

Social History

Collecting Water
Finding and collecting water traditionally has been the job of women, whether they have a settled lifestyle or a nomadic one.

Each day they set out to find clean water for their families. Drought in Africa, which has lasted for many years, has increased the difficulty of finding clean water. In the past, it was estimated that women spent about nine minutes a day collecting water. In 2003, that time increased to 21 minutes, and women had to walk as far as six miles (about 10 kilometers) to find the water.

Obtaining clean water will continue to be a challenging daily task, even for people who have made the transition to a settled lifestyle on small plots of land.

hmhsocialstudies.com

INTERNET ACTIVITY Go online to create a photographic report outlining Africa's clean water problems and solutions.

▲ This rock painting in northwestern Africa shows a line of calves tied to a rope in a pastoralist camp.

some members of the community to practice activities such as working metal, making pottery, and crafting jewelry.

These increasingly complex settlements of people required more organization than smaller communities. Various types of governing bodies developed to fill this need. Some governments consisted of a village chief and a council of the leaders of individual family groups. As strong groups moved to extend their land and conquered weaker settlements, they centralized their power and their governments. Some of these societies eventually developed into great kingdoms.

Early Societies in Africa

The societies south of the Sahara—like all human cultures—shared common elements. One of these elements was the importance of the basic social unit, the family. Besides parents and children, this primary group often included grandparents, aunts, uncles, and cousins in an extended family. Families that shared common ancestors sometimes formed groups known as clans.

Local Religions African peoples organized themselves into family groups. They also developed belief systems that helped them understand and organize information about their world. Nearly all of these local religions involved a belief in one creator, or god. They generally also included elements of **animism**, a religion in which spirits play an important role in regulating daily life. Animists believe that spirits are present in animals, plants, and other natural forces, and also take the form of the souls of their ancestors.

Keeping a History Few African societies had written languages. Instead, storytellers shared orally the history and literature of a culture. In West Africa, for example, these storytellers, or **griots** (gree•OHZ), kept this history alive, passing it from parent to child:

PRIMARY SOURCE B

I am a griot . . . master in the art of eloquence. . . . We are vessels of speech, we are the repositories [storehouses] which harbor secrets many centuries old. . . . Without us the names of kings would vanish. . . . We are the memory of mankind; by the spoken word we bring to life the deeds . . . of kings for younger generations. . . . For the world is old, but the future springs from the past.

DJELI MAMOUDOU KOUYATE, from *Sundiata, an Epic of Old Mali*

MAIN IDEA

Analyzing Primary Sources

B Why were griots important to African societies?

Recent discoveries in West Africa have proved how old and extensive the history of this part of Africa is. Archaeologists believe that early peoples from the north moved into West Africa as desertification forced them south to find better farmland. Discoveries in the areas of modern Mali and Nigeria reveal that West Africans developed advanced societies and cities long before outsiders came to the continent.

West African Iron Age

Archaeologists' main source of information about early West African cultures has been from artifacts such as pottery, charcoal, and slag—a waste product of iron smelting. By dating these artifacts, scientists can piece together a picture of life in West Africa as early as 500 B.C.

Unlike cultures to the north, the peoples of Africa south of the Sahara seem to have skipped the Copper and Bronze Ages and moved directly into the Iron Age. Evidence of iron production dating to around 500 B.C. has been found in the area just north of the Niger and Benue rivers. The ability to smelt iron was a major technological achievement of the ancient Nok of sub-Saharan Africa.

The Nok Culture West Africa's earliest known culture was that of the <u>Nok</u> (nahk) people. They lived in what is now Nigeria between 500 B.C. and A.D. 200. Their name came from the village where the first artifacts from their culture were discovered. Nok artifacts have been found in an area stretching for 300 miles between the Niger and Benue rivers. They were the first West African people known to smelt iron. The iron was fashioned into tools for farming and weapons for hunting. Some of the tools and weapons made their way into overland trade routes.

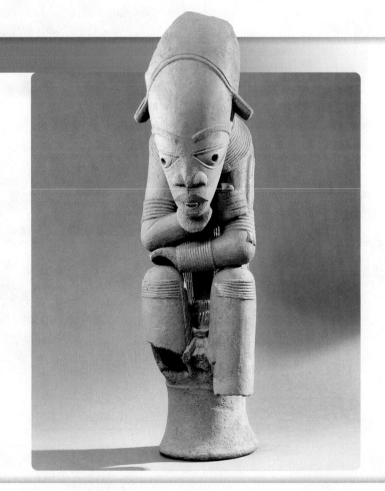

> ## Analyzing Art

Nok Sculpture

Nok artifacts show evidence of a sophisticated culture. Their sculptures are made of terra cotta, a reddish-brown baked clay. Sculptures include animals as well as people. This Nok figure features a classical look called "elongated" style.

Most Nok figurines have these characteristics:

• distinctive features such as bulging eyes, flaring nostrils, and protruding lips
• an elongated style, especially used for the head
• the hand or chin on the knee in some figures
• hairstyle still common in Nigeria

SKILLBUILDER: Interpreting Visual Sources
Formulating Historical Questions *What questions would you ask if you could speak with the creator of this sculpture?*

African Ironworking

Refining metal was an important technological advance in every civilization. Africa was no exception. Iron tools were stronger than copper or bronze tools, so iron tools and the technology to produce them were very valuable.

Producing iron began by mining the iron ore. The iron itself was bound up with other minerals in rocks. The trick was separating the iron from the unwanted minerals. That was the function of the furnace shown below. This process is known as smelting.

⤢ hmhsocialstudies.com

RESEARCH WEB LINKS Go online for more on ironworking.

① Layers of iron ore were alternated with layers of charcoal fuel inside the furnace. Temperatures inside the furnace would reach about 2000° F.

② A tuyère (twee·YAIR) was a clay pipe that allowed air to flow through the furnace.

③ The bellows—usually made out of an animal skin with a wooden plunger attached— increased air flow in the furnace, thus raising the temperature.

④ The intense heat would cause a chemical reaction, separating the iron from the impurities.

⑤ The iron would collect and form what is called a bloom. After cooling, the bloom was removed. An ironsmith then worked the bloom into the desired tool or weapon.

Connect *to* Today

1. **Hypothesizing** What advantages would iron tools give a civilization?

   See Skillbuilder Handbook, Page R15.

2. **Comparing and Contrasting** Use the Internet to research the history of modern ironworking techniques. What improvements have been made, and how do they benefit our life today?

Djenné-Djeno In the region south of the Sahel, most Africans lived in small villages. However, cities began to develop sometime between 600 B.C. and 200 B.C. Usually they were in areas along rivers or at an oasis. One of these cities was Djenné-Djeno.

<u>Djenné-Djeno</u> (jeh•NAY jeh•NOH), or ancient Djenné, was uncovered by archaeologists in 1977. Djenné-Djeno is located on a tributary of the Niger River in West Africa. There, scientists discovered hundreds of thousands of artifacts. These objects included pottery, copper hair ornaments, clay toys, glass beads, stone bracelets, and iron knives.

The oldest objects found there dated from 250 B.C., making Djenné-Djeno the oldest known city in Africa south of the Sahara. The city was abandoned sometime after A.D. 1400.

At its height, Djenné-Djeno had some 50,000 residents. They lived in round reed huts plastered with mud. Later, they built enclosed houses made of mud bricks. They fished in the Niger River, herded cattle, and raised rice on the river's fertile floodplains. By the third century B.C., they had learned how to smelt iron. They exchanged their rice, fish, and pottery for copper, gold, and salt from other peoples who lived along the river. Djenné-Djeno became a bustling trading center linked to other towns not only by the Niger, but also by overland camel routes. **C**

The early inhabitants of West Africa were developing cities, cultures, and technologies that would make their mark on history. Meanwhile, other groups in West Africa were beginning to make an historic move out of West Africa. The Bantu-speaking people would take their culture and ironworking techniques with them to parts of eastern and southern Africa.

▲ A modern artist, Charles Santore, has pictured life in Djenné-Djeno around A.D. 1000.

MAIN IDEA

Comparing-
C In what ways were the cultures of Djenné-Djeno and the Nok alike?

SECTION ① **ASSESSMENT**

TERMS & NAMES 1. For each term or name, write a sentence explaining its significance.
• Sahara   • Sahel   • savanna   • animism   • griot   • Nok   • Djenné-Djeno

USING YOUR NOTES	MAIN IDEAS	CRITICAL THINKING & WRITING

2. How were history and culture preserved in African societies?
 	
Africa
  I. A Land of Geographic Contrasts
    A.
    B.
  II. Early Humans Adapt to Their Environments
	3. What are four general vegetation types found in Africa?
	
	4. What is the main source of information about early African cultures?
	
	5. How is the African Iron Age different from that in other regions?
		6. **ANALYZING CAUSES** Why did diverse cultures develop in Africa?
		
		7. **RECOGNIZING EFFECTS** How did agriculture change the way Africans lived?
		
		8. **DRAWING CONCLUSIONS** What evidence shows that Djenné-Djeno was a major trading city in West Africa?
		
		9. **WRITING ACTIVITY** INTERACTION WITH ENVIRONMENT Choose one of the climate or vegetation zones of Africa. Write a **poem** from the perspective of a person living in the zone and interacting with the environment.

CONNECT TO TODAY **CREATING A MAP**
Create a three-dimensional **map** of Africa that illustrates both vegetation zones and geographic features. Use your map to demonstrate the geographic challenges to people living on the continent.

Migration

CASE STUDY: Bantu–Speaking Peoples

MAIN IDEA	WHY IT MATTERS NOW	TERMS & NAMES
CULTURAL INTERACTION Relocation of large numbers of Bantu-speaking people brings cultural diffusion and change to southern Africa.	Migration continues to shape the modern world.	• migration • push-pull factors • Bantu-speaking peoples

SETTING THE STAGE Human history is a constantly recurring set of movement, collision, settlement, and more movement. Throughout history, people have chosen to uproot themselves and move to explore their world. Sometimes they migrate in search of new opportunities. Other times, migration is a desperate attempt to find a place to survive or to live in peace.

People on the Move

hmhsocialstudies.com
TAKING NOTES
Use the graphic organizer online to take notes on the causes and effects of specific events related to Bantu migration.

As an important pattern in human culture, migrations have influenced world history from its outset. **Migration** is a permanent move from one country or region to another.

Causes of Migration Aside from the general human desire for change, the causes of migrations fall into three categories: environmental, economic, and political. In the early history of human life, environmental factors were most likely the strongest. Later, economic and political causes played a greater role. For example, in the 15th century, the Ottomans' drive for power pushed them to move all over the ancient world to create a massive empire. As the world became more industrialized, more people moved to cities where work in factories was available. Elsewhere, religious or ethnic persecution supported by governments often drove groups of people to flee in order to survive. Seventeenth-century European settlers were pulled to America by the hope of religious tolerance, land for farming, or better economic conditions.

▼ A mask of the Kuba, a Bantu-speaking people, from Congo and Zaire

When looking at migration, historians and geographers speak of **push-pull factors**. These factors can either push people out of an area or pull them into an area. An example of an environmental pull factor might be abundant land that attracts people. On the other hand, the depletion of natural resources forces people away from a location—a push factor. Employment or the lack of it is an economic push or pull factor. Political conditions such as freedom or persecution can encourage people to move or to stay where they are. Urbanization also causes migration because job opportunities and other

Migration: Push-Pull Factors		
Push Examples	**Migration Factors**	**Pull Examples**
Climate changes, exhausted resources, earthquakes, volcanoes, drought/famine	Environmental	Abundant land, new resources, good climate
Unemployment, slavery	Economic	Employment opportunities
Religious, ethnic, or political persecution, war	Political	Political and/or religious freedom

SKILLBUILDER: Interpreting Charts
1. **Developing Historical Perspective** *Are environmental factors still a cause of migration in the modern world? Explain.*
2. **Analyzing Causes** *Which cause do you think is most important in modern migrations? Why?*

benefits attract people. The chart above shows how causes of migration are related to push-pull factors.

Effects of Migration Life in a newly populated area changes because of the influx of new people. The results of migration may be positive or negative.

- Redistribution of the population may change population density.
- Cultural blending of languages or ways of life may occur.
- Ideas and technologies may be shared.
- People's quality of life may be improved as a result of moving.
- Clashes between groups may create unrest, persecution, or even war.
- Environmental conditions may change, causing famine or depleted natural resources.
- Employment opportunities may dry up, creating unemployment and poverty.

Migration changes the lives of those who migrate and also of the people in communities where they settle. Both groups may need to make adjustments in the way they live. Some adjustments may be relatively easy to make. For example, more advanced technology may improve living conditions. Other adjustments may be more difficult and may occur over a longer period of time. One of these adjustments may include language. **A**

MAIN IDEA

Forming Opinions

A Which of the effects of migration do you think are most negative? Explain.

Tracing Migration Through Language One way experts can trace the patterns of movement of people over time is by studying the spread of languages. People bring their languages with them when they move to new places. And languages, like the people who speak them, are living things that evolve and change in predictable ways. If two languages have similar words for a particular object or idea, for example, it is likely that the people who spoke those languages probably had close contact at one time.

Experts have studied languages in Africa. One group of African languages, the Niger-Congo, includes over 900 individual languages. A family of languages in this group developed from a single parent tongue, Proto-Bantu. Many anthropologists believe that the language spread across Africa as a result of migration. Today in Africa, Bantu speakers live in a region from south of the Sahara to the tip of Africa. A Bantu language is the first language of nearly one-third of all Africans.

African Civilizations **221**

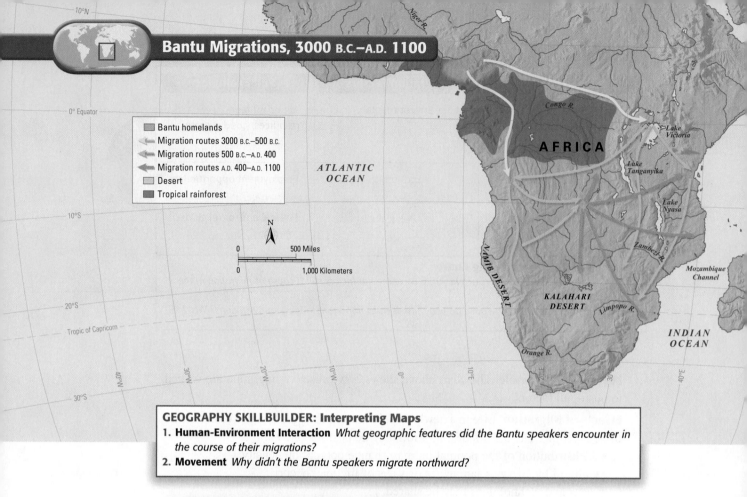

Bantu homelands
Migration routes 3000 B.C.–500 B.C.
Migration routes 500 B.C.–A.D. 400
Migration routes A.D. 400–A.D. 1100
Desert
Tropical rainforest

ATLANTIC
OCEAN

AFRICA

Congo R.

Lake
Victoria

Lake
Tanganyika

Lake
Nyasa

Zambezi R.

Mozambique
Channel

NAMIB DESERT

KALAHARI
DESERT

Limpopo R.

Orange R.

INDIAN
OCEAN

N

0   500 Miles

0   1,000 Kilometers

0° Equator

10°S

Tropic of Capricorn

20°S

30°S

GEOGRAPHY SKILLBUILDER: Interpreting Maps
1. **Human-Environment Interaction** *What geographic features did the Bantu speakers encounter in the course of their migrations?*
2. **Movement** *Why didn't the Bantu speakers migrate northward?*

CASE STUDY: Bantu-speaking Peoples

Massive Migrations

Early Africans made some of the greatest migrations in history. When the migrations were over they or their descendants populated the southern third of the continent. Starting in the first few centuries A.D. and continuing over 1,500 years, small groups moved southward throughout Africa, spreading their language and culture. Historians refer to these people as the **Bantu-speaking peoples**. (The word Bantu itself means "the people.") The Bantu-speaking peoples originally lived in the savanna south of the Sahara, in the area that is now southeastern Nigeria.

Migration Begins Bantu speakers were not one people, but rather a group of peoples who shared certain cultural characteristics. They were farmers and nomadic herders who developed and passed along the skill of ironworking. Many experts believe they were related to the Nok peoples.

Beginning at least 2,000 years ago or earlier, small groups of Bantu speakers began moving to the south and east. The farming techniques used by these people forced them to move every few years. The technique is called slash and burn. A patch of the forest is cut down and burned. The ashes are mixed into the soil creating a fertile garden area. However, the land loses its fertility quickly and is abandoned for another plot in a new location. When they moved, the Bantu speakers shared their skills with the people they met, adapted their methods to suit each new environment, and learned new customs. They followed the Congo River through the rain forests. There they farmed the riverbanks—the only place that received enough sunlight to support agriculture.

As they moved eastward into the savannas, they adapted their techniques for herding goats and sheep to raising cattle. Passing through what is now Kenya and

Tanzania, they learned to cultivate new crops. One such crop was the banana, which came from Southeast Asia via Indonesian travelers.

Causes of Migration Although it is impossible to know exactly what caused the Bantu-speaking peoples to migrate, anthropologists have proposed a logical explanation. These experts suggest that once these peoples developed agriculture, they were able to produce more food than they could obtain by hunting and gathering. As a result, the population of West Africa increased. Because this enlarged population required more food, the earliest Bantu speakers planted more land. Soon there wasn't enough land to go around. They couldn't go north in search of land, because the area was densely populated. The areas that once had been savanna were becoming more desertlike. The Sahara was slowly advancing toward them. So the people moved southward.

The Bantu people probably brought with them the technology of iron smelting. As they moved southward, they were searching for locations with iron ore resources and hardwood forests. They needed the hardwood to make charcoal to fuel the smelting furnaces. (See the Science & Technology feature on page 218.)

As you can see from the map, the migrations split into eastern and western streams. Eventually, the Bantu speakers worked their way around the geographical barriers of the Kalahari and Namib deserts. Within 1,500 years or so—a short time in the span of history—they reached the southern tip of Africa. The Bantu speakers now populated much of the southern half of Africa. **B**

Effects of the Migration When the Bantu speakers settled into an area, changes occurred. The lands they occupied were not always unpopulated. Some areas into

MAIN IDEA

Clarifying

B How did the Bantu deal with the problems they encountered in their migrations?

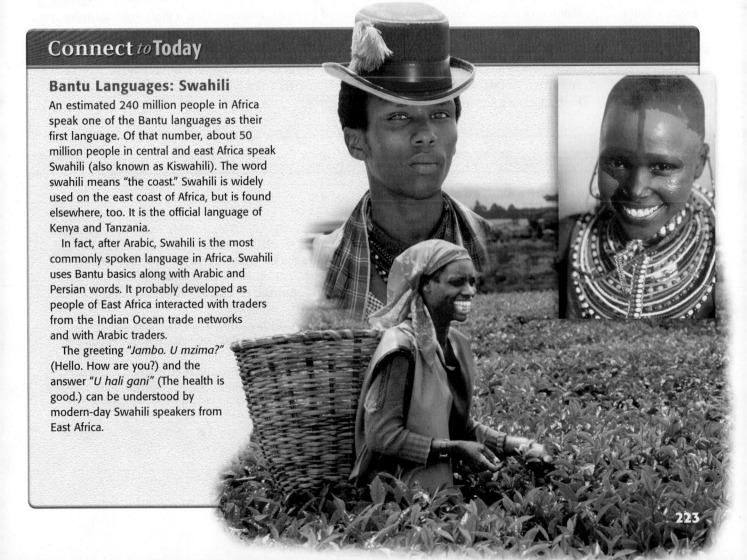

Connect *to* Today

Bantu Languages: Swahili

An estimated 240 million people in Africa speak one of the Bantu languages as their first language. Of that number, about 50 million people in central and east Africa speak Swahili (also known as Kiswahili). The word swahili means "the coast." Swahili is widely used on the east coast of Africa, but is found elsewhere, too. It is the official language of Kenya and Tanzania.

In fact, after Arabic, Swahili is the most commonly spoken language in Africa. Swahili uses Bantu basics along with Arabic and Persian words. It probably developed as people of East Africa interacted with traders from the Indian Ocean trade networks and with Arabic traders.

The greeting *"Jambo. U mzima?"* (Hello. How are you?) and the answer *"U hali gani"* (The health is good.) can be understood by modern-day Swahili speakers from East Africa.

▲ This Kuba mask represents the sister of the founding ancestor of the Kuba culture group, a Bantu-speaking people.

which the Bantu moved were sparsely populated with peoples like the BaMbuti and the San. These Africans were not Bantu speakers. They were not engaged in agriculture but were instead hunter-gatherers. They had to find ways to get along with the Bantu, get out of their way, or defend their lands and way of life.

As the Bantu speakers spread south into hunter-gatherers' lands, territorial wars often broke out. Fighting with iron-tipped spears, the newcomers easily drove off the BaMbuti and the San, who were armed only with stone weapons. Today, the BaMbuti are confined to a corner of the Congo Basin. The San live only around the Kalahari Desert in northwestern South Africa, Namibia, and Botswana. Both groups live a very simple life. They do not speak a Bantu language, and their culture does not reflect the influence of the Bantu-speaking peoples.

The Bantu speakers exchanged ideas and intermarried with the people they joined. This intermingling created new cultures with unique customs and traditions. The Bantu speakers brought new techniques of agriculture to the lands they occupied. They passed on the technology of ironworking to forge tools and weapons from copper, bronze, and iron. They also shared ideas about social and political organization. Some of these ideas still influence the political scene in eastern and southern Africa. Although the Bantu migrations produced a great diversity of cultures, language had a unifying influence on the continent. **C**

In the next section, you will see how cultures on the east coast of Africa experienced growth and change. These changes came about as a result of human migrations from Arabia and cultural interaction with traders from North Africa and the Indian Ocean trade routes.

MAIN IDEA

Analyzing Effects
C How did the Bantu migrations change the history of Africa?

SECTION 2 ASSESSMENT

TERMS & NAMES 1. For each term or name, write a sentence explaining its significance.
• migration   • push-pull factors   • Bantu-speaking peoples

USING YOUR NOTES
2. Which effects of the Bantu-speaking migrations do you think had the most long-term impact? Explain.

Bantu Migrations
Effect   Effect
Effect

MAIN IDEAS
3. What are push-pull factors in migration?
4. What are three effects of migration?
5. Into which regions of Africa did the Bantu-speaking migration move?

CRITICAL THINKING & WRITING
6. **MAKING INFERENCES** How can the effects of one migration become a cause of another migration?
7. **RECOGNIZING EFFECTS** How does migration shape the modern world?
8. **HYPOTHESIZING** How might the population of Africa be different today if the Bantu-speaking migrations had not taken place?
9. **WRITING ACTIVITY** CULTURAL INTERACTION Write a **compare-and-contrast essay** addressing how migrating Bantu speakers and the peoples they encountered may have reacted to each other.

CONNECT TO TODAY CREATING A DATABASE
Use online or library resources to find information on Bantu languages and the countries in which they are spoken. Build a **database** using the information.

The Kingdom of Aksum

MAIN IDEA	WHY IT MATTERS NOW	TERMS & NAMES
POWER AND AUTHORITY The kingdom of Aksum became an international trading power and adopted Christianity.	Ancient Aksum, which is now Ethiopia, is still a center of the Ethiopian Orthodox Christian Church.	• Aksum • Ezana • Adulis • terraces

SETTING THE STAGE While migrations were taking place in the southern half of Africa, they were also taking place along the east coast. Arab peoples crossed the Red Sea into Africa perhaps as early as 1000 B.C. There they intermarried with Kushite herders and farmers and passed along their written language, Ge'ez (GEE•ehz). The Arabs also shared their skills of working stone and building dams and aqueducts. This blended group of Africans and Arabs would form the basis of a new and powerful trading kingdom.

The Rise of the Kingdom of Aksum

You learned in Chapter 4 that the East African kingdom of Kush became powerful enough to push north and conquer Egypt. During the next century, fierce Assyrians swept into Egypt and drove the Kushite pharaohs south. However, Kush remained a powerful kingdom for over 1,000 years. Finally, a more powerful kingdom arose and conquered Kush. That kingdom was **Aksum** (AHK•soom). It was located south of Kush on a rugged plateau on the Red Sea, in what are now the countries of Eritrea and Ethiopia. (See map on page 226.)

hmhsocialstudies.com
TAKING NOTES
Use the graphic organizer online to take notes on the achievements of Aksum.

In this area of Africa, sometimes called the Horn of Africa, Arab traders from across the Red Sea established trading settlements. These traders were seeking ivory to trade in Persia and farther east in the Indian Ocean trade. They brought silks, textiles, and spices from eastern trade routes. Eventually, the trading settlements became colonies of farmers and traders. Trade with Mediterranean countries also flowed into seaports located here.

The Origins of Aksum A legend traces the founding of the kingdom of Aksum and the Ethiopian royal dynasty to the son of King Solomon (of ancient Israel) and of the Queen of Sheba, (a country in southern Arabia). That dynasty lasted into the 20th century, until the last ruler, Haile Selassie, died in 1975.

The first mention of Aksum was in a Greek guidebook written around A.D. 100, *Periplus of the Erythraean Sea*. It describes Zoskales (ZAHS•kuh•leez), thought to be the first king of Aksum. He was "a stickler about his possessions and always [greedy] for getting more, but in other respects a fine person and well versed in reading and writing Greek." Under Zoskales and other rulers, Aksum seized areas along the Red Sea and the Blue Nile in Africa. The rulers also

Aksum, A.D. 300–700

Legend:
- Aksum kingdom
- ← Trade routes

GEOGRAPHY SKILLBUILDER: Interpreting Maps
1. **Location** What nearby waterways enabled Aksum to become a major trading center?
2. **Movement** To which continents or countries did Aksum's trade routes give it access?

crossed the Red Sea and took control of lands on the southwestern Arabian Peninsula.

Aksum Controls International Trade Aksum's location and expansion made it a hub for caravan routes to Egypt and Meroë. Access to sea trade on the Mediterranean Sea and Indian Ocean helped Aksum become an international trading power. Traders from Egypt, Arabia, Persia, India, and the Roman Empire crowded Aksum's chief seaport, **Adulis** (AHD•uh•luhs), near present-day Massawa. **A**

Aksumite merchants traded necessities such as salt and luxuries such as rhinoceros horns, tortoise shells, ivory, emeralds, and gold. In return, they chose from items such as imported cloth, glass, olive oil, wine, brass, iron, and copper. Around A.D. 550, an Egyptian merchant named Cosmas described how Aksumite agents bargained for gold from the people in southern Ethiopia:

MAIN IDEA

Recognizing Effects

A How did Aksum's location and interactions with other regions affect its development?

PRIMARY SOURCE B
They take along with them to the mining district oxen, lumps of salt, and iron, and when they reach its neighborhood they . . . halt . . . and form an encampment, which they fence round with a great hedge of thorns. Within this they live, and having slaughtered the oxen, cut them in pieces and lay the pieces on top of the thorns along with the lumps of salt and the iron. Then come the natives bringing gold in nuggets like peas . . . and lay one or two or more of these upon what pleases them. . . . Then the owner of the meat approaches, and if he is satisfied he takes the gold away, and upon seeing this its owner comes and takes the flesh or the salt or the iron.

COSMAS quoted in *Travellers in Ethiopia*

MAIN IDEA

Analyzing Primary Sources

B Why don't the traders speak to each other instead of laying down goods or gold?

A Strong Ruler Expands the Kingdom The kingdom of Aksum reached its height between A.D. 325 and 360, when an exceptionally strong ruler, **Ezana** (AY•zah•nah), occupied the throne. Determined to establish and expand his authority, Ezana first conquered the part of the Arabian peninsula that is now Yemen. Then, in 330, Ezana turned his attention to Kush, which already had begun to decline. In 350, he conquered the Kushites and burned Meroë to the ground:

PRIMARY SOURCE
I carried war against [them] when they had rebelled. . . . I burnt their towns of stone and their towns of straw. At the same time, my men plundered [stole] their grain, their bronze, their iron and their copper, destroyed the idols in their homes, their stocks of corn and of cotton; and they threw themselves into the river.

KING EZANA OF AKSUM, quoted in *Africa: Past and Present*

An International Culture Develops

From the beginning, Aksumites had a diverse cultural heritage. This blend included traditions of the Arab peoples who crossed the Red Sea into Africa and those of the Kushite peoples they settled among. As the kingdom expanded and became a powerful trading center, it attracted people from all over the ancient world.

The port city of Adulis was particularly cosmopolitan. It included people from Aksum's widespread trading partners, such as Egypt, Arabia, Greece, Rome, Persia, India, and even Byzantium. In the babble of tongues heard in Aksum, Greek stood out as the international language of the time, much as English does in the world today.

Aksumite Religion The Aksumites, like other ancient Africans, traditionally believed in one god. They called their god Mahrem and believed that their king was directly descended from him. They were also animists, however, and worshiped the spirits of nature and honored their dead ancestors. They offered sacrifices—often as many as a dozen oxen at a time—to those spirits, to Mahrem, and often to the Greek god of war, Ares.

Merchants exchanged more than raw materials and finished goods in Aksum. They shared ideas as well. One of these ideas was a new religion, Christianity, which you learned about in Chapter 6. Based on the teachings of Jesus and a belief in one God—monotheism—Christianity began in Judea about A.D. 30. It spread throughout the Roman Empire and then to Africa, and eventually to Aksum.

Aksum Becomes Christian Ezana succeeded to the throne as an infant after the death of his father. While his mother ruled the kingdom, a young Christian man from Syria who had been captured and taken into the court educated him.

Global Impact

A Road Paved with Gold: Aksum to Rome

The kingdom of Aksum had a tremendous impact on the ancient Mediterranean world. It particularly influenced one of the most important powers of the time, the Roman Empire. Roman ships came to Adulis weekly to trade with the Aksumites. Many Roman merchants lived in Adulis and in the capital city, Aksum.

One of the chief commodities that linked the two powers was gold. The Aksumites had access to it from inland gold mines, and the Romans needed it to support the monetary system of their growing empire. Rome and Aksum were linked not only by gold, however. They also shared a spiritual link in their commitment to Christianity.

▼ This mural depicting Bible stories is located on the wall of one of the oldest Christian churches in Aksum.

When Ezana finally became ruler of Aksum, he converted to Christianity and established it as the kingdom's official religion. He vowed, "I will rule the people with righteousness and justice and will not oppress them, and may they preserve this Throne which I have set up for the Lord of Heaven." King Ezana's conversion and his devout practice of Christianity strengthened its hold in Aksum. The establishment of Christianity was the longest lasting achievement of the Aksumites. Today, the land of Ethiopia, where Aksum was located, is home to millions of Christians. **C**

MAIN IDEA

Analyzing Causes
C What conditions led to Aksum's becoming Christian?

Aksumite Innovations The inscription on Ezana's stele is written in Ge'ez, the language brought to Aksum by its early Arab inhabitants. Aside from Egypt and Meroë, Aksum was the only ancient African kingdom known to have developed a written language. It was also the first state south of the Sahara to mint its own coins. Made of bronze, silver, and gold, these coins were imprinted with the saying, "May the country be satisfied." Ezana apparently hoped that this inscription would make him popular with the people. Every time they used a coin, it would remind them that he had their interests at heart.

In addition to these cultural achievements, the Aksumites adapted creatively to their rugged, hilly environment. They created a new method of agriculture, terrace farming. This enabled them to greatly increase the productivity of their land. Terraces, or steplike ridges constructed on mountain slopes, helped the soil retain water and prevented its being washed downhill in heavy rains. The Aksumites dug canals to channel water from mountain streams into the fields. They also built dams and cisterns, or holding tanks, to store water.

> Analyzing Architecture

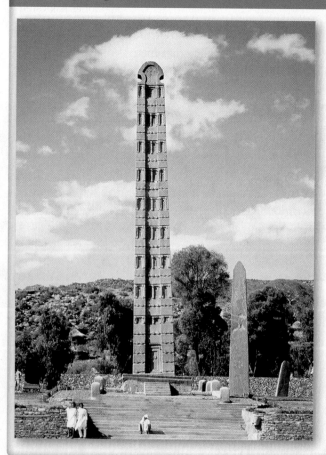

Pillars of Aksum

Aksumites developed a unique architecture. They put no mortar on the stones used to construct vast royal palaces and public buildings. Instead, they carved stones to fit together tightly. Huge stone pillars were erected as monuments or tomb markers. The carvings on the pillars are representations of the architecture of the time.

To the left, the towering stone pillar, or stele, was built to celebrate Aksum's achievements. Still standing today, its size and elaborate inscriptions make it an achievement in its own right. It has many unique features:

- False doors, windows, and timber beams are carved into the stone.
- Typically, the top of the pillar is a rounded peak.
- The tallest stele was about 100 feet high. Of those steles left standing, one is 60 feet tall and is among the largest structures in the ancient world.
- The stone for the pillar was quarried and carved two to three miles away and then brought to the site.
- Ezana dedicated one soaring stone pillar to the Christian God, "the Lord of heaven, who in heaven and upon earth is mightier than everything that exists."

SKILLBUILDER: Interpreting Visual Sources
Comparing *How would constructing these pillars be similar to constructing the pyramids in Egypt?*

The Fall of Aksum

Aksum's cultural and technological achievements enabled it to last for 800 years. The kingdom finally declined, however, under invaders who practiced the religion called Islam (ihs•LAHM). Its founder was Muhammad; by his death in 632, his followers had conquered all of Arabia. In Chapter 10, you will learn more about Islam and Muhammad. This territory included Aksum's lands on the Arabian coast of the Red Sea.

Islamic Invaders Between 632 and 750 Islamic invaders conquered vast territories in the Mediterranean world, spreading their religion as they went. (See the map on page 261.) Aksum protected Muhammad's family and followers during their rise to power. As a result, initially they did not invade Aksum's territories on the African coast of the Red Sea. Retaining control of that coastline enabled Aksum to remain a trading power.

Before long, though, the invaders seized footholds on the African coast as well. In 710 they destroyed Adulis. This conquest cut Aksum off from the major ports along both the Red Sea and the Mediterranean. As a result, the kingdom declined as an international trading power. But it was not only Aksum's political power that weakened. Its spiritual identity and environment were also endangered.

MAIN IDEA

Recognizing Effects

D How did the Muslim conquest of Africa affect the kingdom of Aksum?

Aksum Isolated As the invaders spread Islam to the lands they conquered, Aksum became isolated from other Christian settlements. To escape the advancing wave of Islam, Aksum's rulers moved their capital over the mountains into what is now northern Ethiopia. Aksum's new geographic isolation—along with depletion of the forests and soil erosion—led to its decline as a world power. **D**

Although the kingdom of Aksum reached tremendous heights and left a lasting legacy in its religion, architecture, and agriculture, it never expanded outside a fairly small area. This is a pattern found in other cultures, both in Africa and around the world. In the next chapter, you will study the pattern as it played out among the native peoples of North and South America.

SECTION 3 ASSESSMENT

TERMS & NAMES 1. For each term or name, write a sentence explaining its significance.
• Aksum   • Adulis   • Ezana   • terraces

USING YOUR NOTES

2. Which of Aksum's achievements has continued into modern times?

Aksum's Achievements

MAIN IDEAS

3. How did Aksum's location help make it a trade city?

4. Why did the people of Aksum become Christians?

5. Why did Aksum's leaders move their capital?

CRITICAL THINKING & WRITING

6. **DRAWING CONCLUSIONS** How did Aksum's location and interaction with other regions affect its development?

7. **ANALYZING CAUSES** Why did the kingdom of Aksum decline?

8. **EVALUATING DECISIONS** What impact did Ezana's decision to become a Christian have on the kingdom of Aksum?

9. **WRITING ACTIVITY** | POWER AND AUTHORITY | Write an **opinion paper** on the following statement: The kingdom of Aksum would have reached the same heights even if Ezana had not become king.

MULTIMEDIA ACTIVITY CREATING A FAMILY TREE

Use the Internet to trace the beginnings of the Ethiopian dynasties to the Aksum kings. Then create an Ethiopian dynasty **family tree** showing the dynasty in power until late in the 20th century.

INTERNET KEYWORD
Ethiopian dynasty

VISUAL SUMMARY

African Civilizations

1. Diverse Societies in Africa

- Savanna and Mediterranean areas are most hospitable.
- Nomadic lifestyles are replaced with settled life.
- Djenné-Djeno becomes a major trade center.
- Nok people develop ironworking.

2. Migration

- Environmental, economic, or political reasons cause migration.
- Push-pull factors influence migration.
- Bantu-speaker migrations influence most of Africa south of the Sahara.

3. The Kingdom of Aksum

- Aksum is a major trade center on the Indian Ocean trade routes.
- King Ezana converts to Christianity.
- Islamic invaders isolate Aksum.

TERMS & NAMES

Briefly explain the importance of each of the following to African civilizations in the period from 1500 B.C. to A.D. 700.

1. Sahara
2. animism
3. griot
4. Nok
5. Djenné-Djeno
6. push-pull factors
7. Bantu-speaking peoples
8. Aksum

MAIN IDEAS

Diverse Societies in Africa Section 1 (pages 213–219)

9. How did geographic features affect the settlement of Africa?
10. What technology did the Nok introduce to West Africa?
11. What circumstances enabled Djenné-Djeno to become a bustling trade center?

Case Study: Migration Section 2 (pages 220–224)

12. What are three general causes of migration?
13. How are push-pull factors related to migration?
14. What caused the Bantu-speaking peoples to migrate?
15. Why were the migrations of Bantu speakers so extensive and successful?

The Kingdom of Aksum Section 3 (pages 225–229)

16. Why was Aksum able to control international trade?
17. In what ways did Ezana contribute to the rise of his kingdom?
18. Why did Aksum fall?

CRITICAL THINKING

1. USING YOUR NOTES

INTERACTION WITH ENVIRONMENT Use a flow chart to trace the main events that followed the development of agriculture on the African savannas.

2. MAKING INFERENCES

How are the spread of ironmaking technology to east and south Africa and the Bantu migrations related?

3. EVALUATING DECISIONS

POWER AND AUTHORITY What were some of Ezana's most crucial leadership decisions?

4. FORMING OPINIONS

CULTURAL INTERACTION Do you think cultural characteristics or personal qualities determine how individuals act toward migrating people who settle among them? Explain.

5. COMPARING AND CONTRASTING

What are some positive and negative effects of migration?

Use the quotation about trade goods coming to Aksum and your knowledge of world history to answer questions 1 and 2.

PRIMARY SOURCE

Small axes are imported, and adzes and swords; copper drinking-cups, round and large; a little coin for those coming to the market; wine of Laodicea [on the Syrian coast] and Italy, not much; olive oil, not much; . . . there are imported Indian cloth called monaché [fine quality cotton] and that called sagmotogene [probably tree cotton].

Adapted from *Travellers in Ethiopia* edited by **RICHARD PANKHURST**

1. According to this passage, trade goods came to Aksum from which continents?

   A. Africa, Asia, and South America

   B. Asia and Europe

   C. Europe and Africa

   D. Africa, Asia, and Europe

2. What reason might be cited for the importing of cotton cloth?

   A. Cotton cloth was cheap and plentiful.

   B. Cotton cloth was popular with Aksumites.

   C. There was little or no cotton production in the country of Aksum.

   D. It is not possible to determine a reason from the passage.

Use the diagram and your knowledge of world history to answer question 3.

Land Area of Africa

3. Based on the diagram above, what conclusions can you draw about the land area of the continent of Africa?

   A. It is the largest continent on Earth.

   B. It is smaller than India.

   C. It is larger than Europe.

   D. The Sahara is larger than the United States.

hmhsocialstudies.com **TEST PRACTICE**

For additional test practice, go online for:

• Diagnostic tests

• Strategies

• Tutorials

Interact *with* History

On page 212, you considered the effects newcomers would have on a community. Now that you've read the chapter and learned about people's interactions with their environments and with other cultures, how would you modify your answer? Discuss your ideas with a small group.

FOCUS ON WRITING

Look at the causes for migration shown in the chart on page 221. Think about which of the causes might have an impact on you personally. Write a **paragraph** describing a cause that would force you to migrate to another part of the country or the world. Be sure to identify either the push or pull factor that might influence your decision. Consider the following:

• environmental conditions in the area in which you live

• economic or political factors that might have a direct effect on your life

MULTIMEDIA ACTIVITY

Creating a Documentary Film Script

Create a documentary film script on a current African ethnic group or country struggling to survive in its environment. Consider the following:

• current locations of drought, desertification, or overuse of land

• how the people are trying to deal with the problem

• what actions are needed to prevent a recurrence of the problem

• images, sounds, and interviews to tell the story

CHAPTER

9

The Americas: A Separate World, 40,000 B.C.–A.D. 700

Essential Question

How did early American civilizations influence future societies and cultures?

? What You Will Learn

In this chapter you will learn about the complex cultures that arose in Mesoamerica and the Andes.

SECTION 1 The Earliest Americans
Main Idea The cultures of the first Americans, including social organization, developed in ways similar to other early cultures.

SECTION 2 Early Mesoamerican Civilizations
Main Idea The Olmec created the Americas' first civilization, which in turn influenced later civilizations.

SECTION 3 Early Civilizations of the Andes
Main Idea In the Andes Mountains, various groups created flourishing civilizations.

Previewing Themes

POWER AND AUTHORITY The first civilizations in the Americas arose as people came together to create more powerful and structured societies.
Geography *What geographical feature do most of these early American civilizations share?*

CULTURAL INTERACTION From their art to their technology, the early Mesoamerican and South American civilizations influenced the better-known empires that followed them.
Geography *Why is it likely that the Nazca and Moche civilizations were aware of each other?*

INTERACTION WITH ENVIRONMENT The Olmec in Mesoamerica took advantage of their surroundings, while the groups in South America carved societies out of rough terrain.
Geography *How were geographic conditions different for the Olmec and Chavín peoples?*

AMERICAS

10,000 B.C.
Last Ice Age ends; land bridge to Asia disappears.

7000 B.C.
Agriculture begins in central Mexico.

1200 B.C.
Olmec civilization emerges in southeast Mexico. (figure of Olmec wrestler or ball player) ▶

10,000 B.C.

1200 B.C.

WORLD

1200 B.C.
◀ Egyptian Empire begins to decline. (Egyptian sphinx and pyramid)

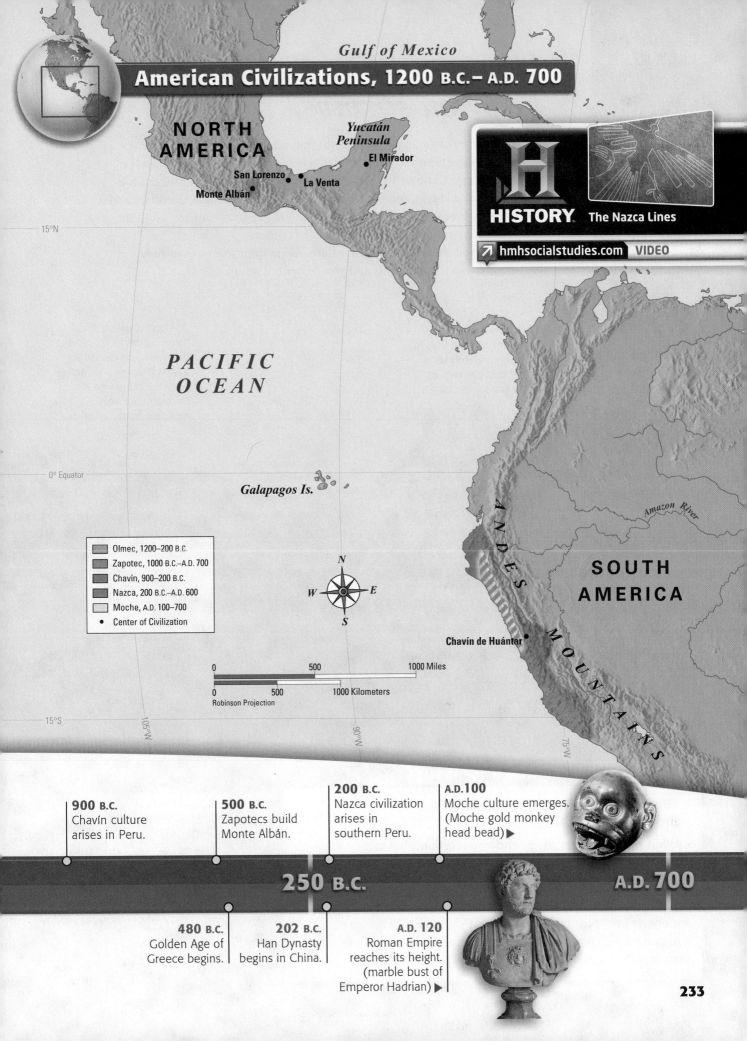

American Civilizations, 1200 B.C. – A.D. 700

Gulf of Mexico

NORTH AMERICA

Yucatán Peninsula

El Mirador

San Lorenzo
La Venta
Monte Albán

HISTORY. The Nazca Lines

hmhsocialstudies.com VIDEO

15°N

PACIFIC OCEAN

0° Equator

Galapagos Is.

Amazon River

A N D E S   M O U N T A I N S

SOUTH AMERICA

Chavín de Huántar

Olmec, 1200–200 B.C.
Zapotec, 1000 B.C.–A.D. 700
Chavín, 900–200 B.C.
Nazca, 200 B.C.–A.D. 600
Moche, A.D. 100–700
• Center of Civilization

N
W E
S

0   500   1000 Miles
0   500   1000 Kilometers
Robinson Projection

15°S

105°W   90°W   75°W

900 B.C.
Chavín culture arises in Peru.

500 B.C.
Zapotecs build Monte Albán.

200 B.C.
Nazca civilization arises in southern Peru.

A.D. 100
Moche culture emerges. (Moche gold monkey head bead) ▶

250 B.C.

A.D. 700

480 B.C.
Golden Age of Greece begins.

202 B.C.
Han Dynasty begins in China.

A.D. 120
Roman Empire reaches its height. (marble bust of Emperor Hadrian) ▶

How can killing a mammoth help you survive?

You are a hunter living in ancient North America. Along with several other hunters, you have been tracking the mammoth for days. This giant beast is a challenging prey. Close to 14 feet high at the shoulders, it can easily crush a human. Its curved tusks, measuring more than 15 feet in length, are sharp and therefore dangerous. Yet the rewards of killing the huge animal are worth the risks for you, your fellow hunters, and your families.

Suddenly you spot the massive creature. Aside from spears, your only weapons are some simple tools and your superior intelligence.

Should a hunter get too close, the mammoth might crush him under its large feet, or stab him with its deadly tusks.

The hunter uses a spear-throwing device to steady the spear and extend the length it travels. The device gives the hunter greater force and accuracy in hurling his spear from a distance.

Other hunters close in for the kill.

EXAMINING *the* ISSUES

- What uses might hunters and their families make of the slain mammoth?
- What roles might strategy and cooperation play in the hunt?

As a class, discuss these questions. In your discussion, consider how this situation speaks to the difficulties of life in a hunter-gatherer society. As you read about the growth of civilization in the Americas, notice how the old hunting and gathering way of life dramatically changed with the development of agriculture.

The Earliest Americans

MAIN IDEA	WHY IT MATTERS NOW	TERMS & NAMES
POWER AND AUTHORITY The cultures of the first Americans, including social organization, developed in ways similar to other early cultures.	The Americas' first inhabitants developed the basis for later American civilizations.	• Beringia • Ice Age • maize

SETTING THE STAGE While civilizations were developing in Africa, Asia, and Europe, they were also emerging in the Americas. Human settlement in the Americas is relatively recent compared to that in other parts of the world. However, it followed a similar pattern. At first the ancient people of the Americas survived mainly by hunting. Over time, they developed farming methods that ensured a more reliable supply of food. This in turn led to the growth of the first civilizations in the Americas.

A Land Bridge

The American continents include North and South America. They are connected and span two hemispheres, from the frigid Arctic Circle in the north to the icy waters around Antarctica in the south. Although this land mass narrows greatly around modern-day Panama, it stretches unbroken for about 9,000 miles. This large and rugged land is isolated from the rest of the world by vast oceans. Yet, thousands of years ago, the Americas were connected by a land bridge to Asia. Most experts believe that some of the first people came to the Americas from Asia over this land bridge. The land bridge is known as **Beringia**. Other people may have arrived by boat.

Peopling the Americas The first Americans arrived sometime toward the end of the last **Ice Age**, which lasted from roughly 1.9 million to about 10,000 B.C. Huge sheets of moving ice, called glaciers, spread southward from the Arctic Circle. They covered large portions of North America. The buildup of glaciers locked up huge amounts of the earth's water. It lowered sea levels and created a land corridor between Asia and Alaska across what is now the Bering Strait.

Herds of wild animals from Siberia, including the mammoth, migrated across the plains of the Beringia land bridge. Gradually, Siberian hunters followed these animals into North America. They most likely were unaware that they were entering a new continent. These migrants became the first Americans.

Thomas Canby, a writer for *National Geographic* magazine, spent a year with archaeologists as they searched for ancient burial sites throughout the Americas. From his experience, Canby described the type of world that might have greeted these hunters and migrants as they entered the Americas:

> hmhsocialstudies.com
> **TAKING NOTES**
>
> Use the graphic organizer online to take notes on the causes and effects of the development of the Americas.

MAIN IDEA

Analyzing Primary Sources

A What might account for the abundance of animal life that Canby describes?

PRIMARY SOURCE A

What a wild world it was! To see it properly, we must board a time machine and travel back into the Ice Age. The northern half of North America has vanished, buried beneath ice sheets two miles thick. Stretching south to Kentucky, they buckle the earth's crust with their weight. . . . Animals grow oversize. . . . Elephant-eating jaguars stand tall as lions, beavers grow as big as bears, South American sloths as tall as giraffes. With arctic cold pushing so far southward, walrus bask on Virginia beaches, and musk-oxen graze from Maryland to California.

THOMAS CANBY, "The Search for the First Americans," *National Geographic*

No one knows for sure when the first Americans arrived. Some scholars contend that the migration across the land bridge began as early as 40,000 B.C. Others argue it occurred as late as 10,000 B.C. For years, many researchers have regarded the discovery of spearheads dating back to 9500 B.C. near Clovis, New Mexico, to be the earliest evidence of humankind in the Americas.

However, recent discoveries of possible pre-Clovis sites have challenged this theory. One such discovery was made at Monte Verde, Chile, near the southern tip of the Americas. Researchers there have found evidence of human life dating back to 10,500 B.C. Underneath this site—a sandy bank near a creek—archaeologists discovered pieces of animal hide and various tools. They also found a preserved chunk of meat and a child's single footprint. The evidence at Monte Verde suggests that the first Americans arrived well before the Clovis era. To reach southern Chile at such an early date, some experts believe, humans would have had to cross the land bridge at least 20,000 years ago.

Most experts believe the earliest Americans traveled by foot across the land bridge. However, some scholars think they also may have paddled from Asia to the Pacific Coast in small boats. A skull discovered near Mexico City has recently been dated to about 11,000 B.C., making it the oldest skull ever found in the Americas. Some scientists studying the skull believe that it is related to the Ainu people of Japan and that these descendants of the Ainu reached the Americas by island-hopping on boats.

Hunters and Gatherers

Questions remain about how and when the first Americans arrived. What appears more certain—from the discovery of chiseled spearheads and charred bones at ancient sites—is that the earliest Americans lived as hunters. Perhaps their most challenging and rewarding prey was the mammoth. Weighing more than seven tons, this animal provided meat, hide, and bones for food, clothing, shelters, and tools.

Following the Game Eventually, large animals like the mammoth were over-hunted and became extinct. Hunters soon turned to smaller prey, such as deer and rabbits, for their survival. They also fished and gathered edible plants and fruits. Because they were hunters, the earliest Americans found it necessary to move regularly in search of food. Whenever they did settle in one place for a short time, pre-historic Americans lived in caves or temporary shelters in the open air. **B**

MAIN IDEA

Recognizing Effects

B How did the earliest Americans adapt to the loss of large animals?

With the end of the Ice Age, around 12,000 to 10,000 years ago, came the end of land travel across Beringia. As the great glaciers melted, sea levels rose. The ancient land bridge disappeared under the Bering Strait. By this time, however, humans inhabited most regions of the Americas. Wherever they roamed, from the grassy plains of the modern-day United States to the steamy tropical forests of Central America, the first Americans adapted to the variety of environments they inhabited. In doing so, they carved out unique ways of life.

Migration Routes, 40,000–10,000 B.C.

hmhsocialstudies.com
INTERACTIVE MAP

ARCTIC OCEAN

ASIA

Beringia

Broken Mammoth, Alaska
11,800 B.C.

NORTH AMERICA

ROCKY MOUNTAINS

Mississippi R.

Meadowcroft Rockshelter, Pennsylvania
17,000 B.C.

Clovis, New Mexico
9500 B.C.

40°N

Tropic of Cancer

0° Equator

Amazon R.

ATLANTIC OCEAN

PACIFIC OCEAN

SOUTH AMERICA

ANDES MOUNTAINS

Tropic of Capricorn

Monte Verde, Chile
10,500 B.C.

40°S

160°E   180°   160°W   140°W   120°W   100°W   80°W   60°W   40°W   0°

Travelers across Beringia might have encountered landscapes such as this in Alaska.

At the Meadowcroft Rockshelter site in Pennsylvania, pre-Clovis blades have been found that date back many thousands of years.

Spearheads similar to these were first discovered near Clovis, New Mexico, and later throughout North America. Many of these artifacts date back to around 9500 B.C.

Recent findings at Monte Verde, Chile, have provided evidence of human life in the Americas as early as 10,500 B.C.

☐ Glacier ice, 12,000 B.C.
☐ Beringia
← Possible land migration routes
◄- - Possible water migration route
☐ Fossil site

N

0   2,000 Miles
0   4,000 Kilometers

GEOGRAPHY SKILLBUILDER: Interpreting Maps
1. **Location**-*What two continents does the Beringia land bridge connect?*
2. **Movement** *From where do scholars believe the first Americans came? How did they come?*

A Bison Kill Site

The first hunters roaming North America hunted mammoths, deer, and bison. Researchers found the bones of bison at a kill site near Calgary, Alberta, in Canada. This kill site is believed to have been in use for more than 8,000 years.

Different layers of remains and artifacts have been found at the kill site, with different kinds of points—spears, arrows, knives, and so forth. The different styles of points can tell archaeologists about the age of a site and its various layers. Weapons and tools such as those shown here were used to kill and butcher animals for the hunters and their families to consume.

SKILLBUILDER:
Interpreting Visual Sources
1. **Drawing Conclusions** *What resources besides food might animals have provided to early hunters and their families?*
2. **Making Inferences** *What might have been the effect of the weapons and tools of early hunters on the big-game animals of the Americas?*

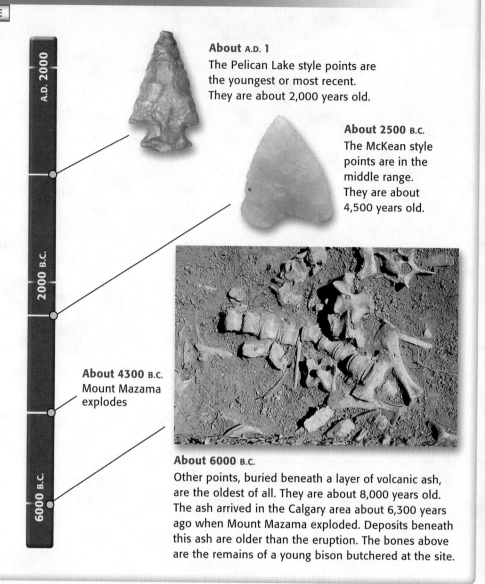

About A.D. 1
The Pelican Lake style points are the youngest or most recent. They are about 2,000 years old.

About 2500 B.C.
The McKean style points are in the middle range. They are about 4,500 years old.

About 4300 B.C.
Mount Mazama explodes

About 6000 B.C.
Other points, buried beneath a layer of volcanic ash, are the oldest of all. They are about 8,000 years old. The ash arrived in the Calgary area about 6,300 years ago when Mount Mazama exploded. Deposits beneath this ash are older than the eruption. The bones above are the remains of a young bison butchered at the site.

Agriculture Creates a New Way of Life

Gradually, the earliest Americans became more familiar with plant foods. They began to experiment with simple methods of farming. Their efforts at planting and harvesting led to agriculture. This dramatically changed their way of life.

The Development of Farming Around 7000 B.C., a revolution quietly began in what is now central Mexico. There, people began to rely more on wild edible plants, raising some of them from seeds. By 5000 B.C., many had begun to grow these preferred plants. They included squashes, gourds, beans, avocados, and chilies. By 3400 B.C., these early farmers grew **maize**, or corn. Maize soon became the most important crop. This highly nourishing crop flourished in the tropical climate of Mexico. There, a family of three could raise enough corn in four months to feed themselves for a long time.

Gradually, people settled in permanent villages in the Tehuacan (TAY•wuh•KAHN) Valley, south of present-day Mexico City. These people raised corn and other crops. The techniques of agriculture spread over North and South America. However, it is believed that people in some areas, such as Peru and eastern North America, may have discovered the secrets of cultivating local edible plants independently.

The Effects of Agriculture

Before Agriculture	After Agriculture
• People hunted or gathered what they ate. • Families continually moved in search of big game. • Groups remained small due to the scarcity of reliable sources of food. • Humans devoted much of their time to obtaining food.	• People enjoyed a more reliable and steady source of food. • Families settled down and formed larger communities. • Humans concentrated on new skills: arts and crafts, architecture, social organization. • Complex societies eventually arose.

SKILLBUILDER: Interpreting Charts
1. **Recognizing Effects** *How did life change after the development of agriculture?*
2. **Making Inferences** *How might the establishment of agriculture have helped humans to develop new skills and interests?*

Over the next several centuries, farming methods became more advanced. In central Mexico native farmers created small islands in swamps and shallow lakes by stacking layers of vegetation, dirt, and mud. They then planted crops on top of the island soil. The surrounding water provided irrigation. These floating gardens were very productive, yielding up to three harvests a year.

Farming Brings Great Change In the Americas, as in other regions of the world, agriculture brought great and lasting change to people's way of life. The cultivation of corn and other crops provided a more reliable and expanding food supply. This encouraged population growth and the establishment of large, settled communities. As the population grew, and as farming became more efficient and productive, more people turned their attention to nonagricultural pursuits. They developed specialized skills in arts and crafts, building trades, and other fields. Differences between social classes—between rich and poor, ruler and subject—began to emerge. With the development of agriculture, society became more complex. The stage was set for the rise of more advanced civilizations. **C**

MAIN IDEA

Making Inferences

C Why might the development of agriculture be characterized by some as a turning point in human history?

SECTION 1 ASSESSMENT

TERMS & NAMES 1. For each term or name, write a sentence explaining its significance.
• Beringia   • Ice Age   • maize

USING YOUR NOTES	MAIN IDEAS	CRITICAL THINKING & WRITING
2. Which effect do you think had the most significant impact on the Americas? Explain. 	Cause	Effect
---	---
1.	1.
2.	2.		3. How did human beings come to the Americas? 4. How did humans get food before the development of farming? 5. What sorts of changes did farming bring?	6. **FORMING OPINIONS** Why do you think early Americans, isolated from the rest of the world, developed in ways similar to other early humans? 7. **HYPOTHESIZING** What sailing routes might early humans have traveled to the Americas? 8. **COMPARING** What sorts of problems might the earliest Americans have encountered in their travels? 9. **WRITING ACTIVITY** `POWER AND AUTHORITY` What type of person might hold power in a hunter-gatherer society? in a settled, agricultural society? Support your opinions in a two-paragraph **essay**.

MULTIMEDIA ACTIVITY CREATING AN OUTLINE MAP

Use the Internet to find information on early archaeological sites in the Americas. Locate these sites on an **outline map** and show the dates that scientists have assigned to these sites.

INTERNET KEYWORD
Clovis, Meadowcroft Rockshelter

Early Mesoamerican Civilizations

MAIN IDEA	WHY IT MATTERS NOW	TERMS & NAMES
CULTURAL INTERACTION The Olmec created the Americas' first civilization, which in turn influenced later civilizations.	Later American civilizations relied on the technology and achievements of earlier cultures to make advances.	• Mesoamerica • Zapotec • Olmec • Monte Albán

SETTING THE STAGE The story of developed civilizations in the Americas begins in a region called **Mesoamerica**. (See map on opposite page.) This area stretches south from central Mexico to northern Honduras. It was here, more than 3,000 years ago, that the first complex societies in the Americas arose.

The Olmec

hmhsocialstudies.com
TAKING NOTES

Use the graphic organizer online to take notes on Olmec and Zapotec cultures.

Mesoamerica's first known civilization builders were a people known as the **Olmec**. They began carving out a society around 1200 B.C. in the jungles of southern Mexico. The Olmec influenced neighboring groups, as well as the later civilizations of the region. They often are called Mesoamerica's "mother culture."

The Rise of Olmec Civilization Around 1860, a worker clearing a field in the hot coastal plain of southeastern Mexico uncovered an extraordinary stone sculpture. It stood five feet tall and weighed an estimated eight tons. The sculpture was of an enormous head, wearing a headpiece. (See History Through Art, pages-244–245.) The head was carved in a strikingly realistic style, with thick lips, a flat nose, and large oval eyes. Archaeologists had never seen anything like it in the Americas.

This head, along with others that were discovered later, was a remnant of the Olmec civilization. The Olmec emerged about 1200 B.C. and thrived from approximately 800–400 B.C. They lived along the Gulf Coast of Mexico, in the modern-day Mexican states of Veracruz and Tabasco.

Gulf Coast Geography On the surface, the Gulf Coast seemed an unlikely site for a high culture to take root. The region was hot and humid and covered with swamps and jungle. In some places, giant trees formed a thick cover that prevented most sunlight from reaching the ground. Up to 100 inches of rain fell every year. The rainfall swelled rivers and caused severe flooding.

However, the region also had certain advantages. There were abundant deposits of salt and tar, as well as fine clay used in making pottery. There was also wood and rubber from the rain forest. The hills to the north provided hard stone from which the Olmec could make tools and monuments. The rivers that laced the region provided a means of transport. Most important, the flood plains of these rivers provided fertile land for farming.

The Olmec used their resources to build thriving communities. The oldest site, San Lorenzo, dates back to around 1150 B.C. Here archaeologists uncovered important clues that offered a glimpse into the Olmec world. **A**

MAIN IDEA

Making Inferences

A In what ways did the Olmec's environment help in the creation of its civilization?

Olmec Society At San Lorenzo archaeologists discovered earthen mounds, courtyards, and pyramids. Set among these earthworks were large stone monuments. They included columns, altars, and more colossal, sculpted heads, which may have represented particular Olmec rulers. These giant monuments weigh as much as 44 tons. Some scholars think that Olmec workers may have moved these sculptures over land on rolling logs to the river banks. From there, they may have rafted the monuments along waterways to various sites.

To the east of San Lorenzo, another significant Olmec site, La Venta, rose around 900 B.C. Here, researchers discovered a 100-foot-high mound of earth and clay. This structure may have served as the tomb of a great Olmec ruler. Known as the Great Pyramid, the mound also may have been the center of the Olmec religion. Experts believe the Olmec prayed to a variety of nature gods.

Most of all, they probably worshiped the jaguar spirit. Numerous Olmec sculptures and carvings depict a half-human, half-jaguar creature. Some scholars believe that the jaguar represented a powerful rain god. Others contend that there were several jaguar gods, representing the earth, fertility, and maize.

Trade and Commerce Archaeologists once believed that sites such as La Venta were ceremonial centers where important rituals were performed but few people lived. In recent years, however, experts have begun to revise that view. The Olmec appear to have been a prosperous people who directed a large trading network throughout Mesoamerica. Olmec goods traveled as far as Mexico City to the north and Honduras to the south. In addition, raw materials—including iron ore and various stones—reached San Lorenzo from faraway regions. This trade network helped boost the Olmec economy and spread Olmec influence.

Decline of the Olmec For reasons that are not fully understood, Olmec civilization eventually collapsed. Scholars believe San Lorenzo was destroyed around 900 B.C. La Venta may have fallen sometime around 400 B.C. Some experts speculate that outside invaders caused the destruction. Others believe the Olmec may have destroyed their own monuments upon the death of their rulers. **B**

MAIN IDEA

Hypothesizing

B What might lead to the disappearance of an entire civilization?

Olmec Civilization, 900 B.C.

Olmec homeland
Oaxaca Valley
Possible trade routes
Centers of Olmec civilization
Other Olmec sites
Limit of Mesoamerica

EASTERN SIERRA MADRE

Tropic of Cancer

Gulf of Mexico

Yucatán Peninsula

20°N

Bay of Campeche

San Lorenzo   La Venta

Oaxaca Valley

N

250 Miles

500 Kilometers

PACIFIC OCEAN

GEOGRAPHY SKILLBUILDER: Interpreting Maps

1. **Movement** *Judging from the map, what was one way in which the Olmec spread their influence?*
2. **Movement** *What difficulties might the Olmec have encountered in developing their trade routes?*

Zapotec Civilization Arises

By the time Olmec civilization had collapsed, another people—the **Zapotec**—were developing an advanced society to the southwest, in what is now the Mexican state of Oaxaca (wuh•HAH•kah). Though they showed traces of Olmec influence, the Zapotec built a unique civilization.

Peoples of the Oaxaca Valley Oaxaca is a rugged region of mountains and valleys in southern Mexico. In the center of the state, three valleys meet to form a large open area known as the Oaxaca Valley. This valley has fertile soil, a mild climate, and enough rainfall to support agriculture. As a result, various peoples have made the Oaxaca Valley their home, including the ancient Zapotec.

For centuries the Zapotec lived in scattered villages throughout the valley. By 1000 B.C., however, one site—San José Mogote—was emerging as the main power in the region. At this site, the Zapotec constructed stone platforms. They also built temples and began work on monumental sculptures. By 500 B.C. they had developed early forms of writing and a calendar system.

The Zapotec Flourish at Monte Albán Around 500 B.C., Zapotec civilization took a major leap forward. High atop a mountain at the center of the Oaxaca Valley, the Zapotec built the first real urban center in the Americas, **Monte Albán**. This city, with its commanding view of the entire valley, grew and prospered over the next several centuries. By 200 B.C., Monte Albán was home to around 15,000 people. The city eventually would reach a peak population of almost 25,000. **C**

From A.D. 250 to A.D. 700, Monte Albán was truly impressive. At the heart of the city was a giant plaza paved with stones. Towering pyramids, temples, and

MAIN IDEA

Comparing
C How does Monte Albán's population compare to the populations of today's major cities?

Global Patterns

Pyramids

A number of ancient peoples used pyramids for temples, tombs, and observatories. The Egyptians built pyramids as tombs. Their pyramids had smooth sides and came to a point. In contrast, the pyramids built by the Zapotec at Monte Albán (shown below) have stepped sides, with flat tops that served as platforms for temples.

⬈ **hmhsocialstudies.com**

INTERNET ACTIVITY Go online to research and make a poster about the different kinds of pyramids in Egypt and Mesoamerica.

palaces, all made out of stone, surrounded this plaza. There was even an observatory for observing the stars to establish a calendar. Nearby was a series of stone carvings of corpses. Their facial features show an Olmec influence.

For more than a thousand years the Zapotec controlled the Oaxaca Valley and the surrounding region. Sometime after A.D. 600, the Zapotec began to decline. Some scholars believe they may have suffered a loss of trade or other economic difficulties. As with the Olmec, the fall of Zapotec civilization remains a puzzle.

The Early Mesoamericans' Legacy

Although both the Zapotec and Olmec civilizations eventually collapsed, each culture influenced the Mesoamerican civilizations that followed.

The Olmec Leave Their Mark The Olmec contributed much to later Mesoamerican civilizations. They influenced the powerful Maya, who will be discussed in Chapter 16. Olmec art styles, especially the use of the jaguar motif, can be seen in the pottery and sculpture of later peoples in the region. In addition, future Mesoamerican societies copied the Olmec pattern of urban design.

The Olmec also left behind the notions of planned ceremonial centers, ritual ball games, and an elite ruling class. And while there is no clear evidence that the Olmec used a written language, their descendants or a related people carved out stone symbols that may have influenced later glyph writing. **D**

Zapotec Contributions The Zapotec left behind their own legacy. It included a hieroglyphic writing system and a calendar system based on the movement of the sun. In addition, the Zapotec are noted as the Americas' first city builders. Monte Albán combined ceremonial grandeur with residential living space. This style influenced the development of future urban centers and became a hallmark of Mesoamerican civilizations.

As the Zapotec and Olmec flourished and then declined, civilizations were also taking shape in South America. Along the rough and mountainous terrain in what is now Peru, ancient peoples came together. There, they created more advanced and complex societies.

MAIN IDEA
Forming Opinions
D What do you consider to be the Olmec's most important contributions to later cultures?

SECTION 2 ASSESSMENT

TERMS & NAMES 1. For each term or name, write a sentence explaining its significance.
• Mesoamerica   • Olmec   • Zapotec   • Monte Albán

USING YOUR NOTES	MAIN IDEAS	CRITICAL THINKING & WRITING
2. What was one characteristic unique to Olmec culture?	3. Why did Olmec civilization collapse? 4. What was the role of trade in Olmec civilization? 5. What were some important Zapotec contributions to later cultures?	6. **DRAWING CONCLUSIONS** Why do you think the Olmec are called Mesoamerica's "mother culture"? 7. **ANALYZING CAUSES** What factors made the Oaxaca Valley a likely place for civilization to develop? 8. **COMPARING** What were some similarities between the Olmec and Zapotec cultures? 9. **WRITING ACTIVITY** CULTURAL INTERACTION As a trader from a small Mesoamerican village, you have just returned from your first visit to the Olmec site at La Venta. Write a **description** of what you might tell your family about the things you saw at the site.

CONNECT TO TODAY DRAWING A MASK

What are some events or holidays in North America where participants wear masks? Draw a picture of a jaguar **mask** that you would like to wear for such a festival.

Olmec Sculpture

Around 1200 B.C., the Olmec civilization appeared in southeastern Mexico. Over the next several hundred years, its culture spread into the Valley of Mexico and into parts of Central America. The Olmec are especially known for their huge sculptures of heads and their small, finely crafted stone carvings. Much of their art reflects a fascination with the jaguar.

🡥 **hmhsocialstudies.com**

RESEARCH WEB LINKS Go online for more on Olmec art.

Olmec Head ▶

The Olmec Center at San Lorenzo, Honduras, contains several huge carved heads. Some of them are 9 feet high and weigh about 40 tons. The heads may be portraits of Olmec leaders or of players in a sacred ball game. The stone used for the sculptures came from a site more than 250 miles away. The Olmec transported this stone over mountain ranges, rivers, and swamps.

◀ Jaguar Figure

The Olmec created many carvings of beings that were part human, part jaguar. Peter Furst, in "New Light on the Olmec" in *National Geographic*, explains why: "You can almost call the Olmec the people of the jaguar. In tropical America, jaguars were the shamans [medicine men] of the animal world, the alter ego [other identity] of the shaman." Olmec jaguar art greatly influenced later Mesoamerican cultures.

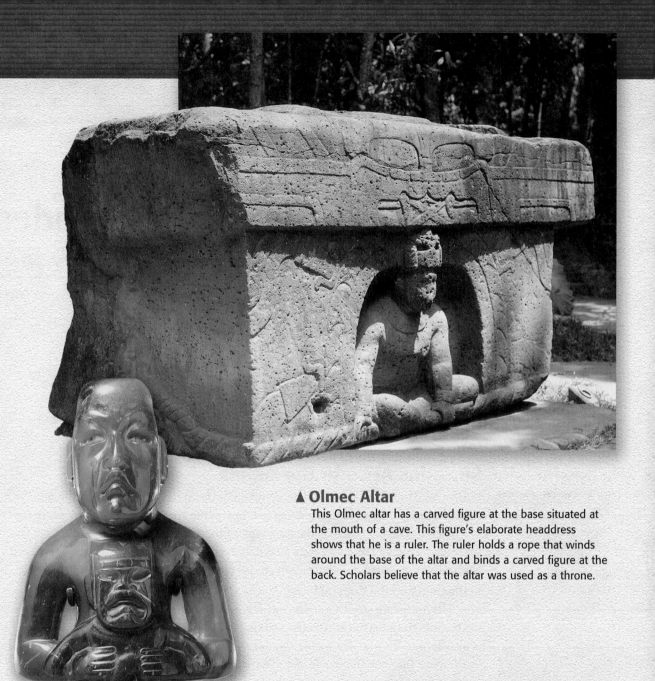

▲ Olmec Altar

This Olmec altar has a carved figure at the base situated at the mouth of a cave. This figure's elaborate headdress shows that he is a ruler. The ruler holds a rope that winds around the base of the altar and binds a carved figure at the back. Scholars believe that the altar was used as a throne.

▲ Jade Figure

Many Olmec figurines, such as this adult holding a baby, are made of this beautiful blue-green stone, a fact that puzzled scientists for decades because they believed that no jade deposits existed in the Americas. However, in May 2002, a scientist discovered what he believes to be an ancient Olmec jade mine in Guatemala.

Connect *to* Today

1. **Hypothesizing** The Olmec probably did not use the wheel. How do you think the Olmec transported the stone for the huge head sculptures?
   See Skillbuilder Handbook, Page R15.

2. **Comparing and Contrasting** Mount Rushmore in the United States also shows giant stone heads of leaders. Find out how it was made by using an encyclopedia or the Internet. What are similarities and differences between the way Mount Rushmore was made and the way the Olmec heads were made?

245

Early Civilizations of the Andes

MAIN IDEA	WHY IT MATTERS NOW	TERMS & NAMES
INTERACTION WITH ENVIRONMENT In the Andes Mountains, various groups created flourishing civilizations.	Like the early Andean civilizations, people today must adapt to their environment in order to survive.	• Chavín • Moche • Nazca

SETTING THE STAGE While civilizations were emerging in Mesoamerica, advanced societies were independently developing in South America. The early cultures of South America arose in a difficult environment, the rugged terrain of the Andes Mountains.

Societies Arise in the Andes

Use the graphic organizer online to take notes on important information about early Andean civilizations.

The Andes Mountains stretch about 4,500 miles down the western edge of South America, from Colombia in the north to Chile in the south. After the Himalayas in southern Asia, the Andes is the next highest mountain range in the world. The Andes has a number of peaks over 20,000 feet in elevation. South America's first civilizations emerged in the northern Andes region, in Peru.

Settlements on the Coastal Plain Peru was a harsh place to develop a civilization. The Andes are steep and rocky, with generally poor soil. Ice and snow cover the highest elevations year-round. Overland travel often is difficult. The climate is also severe: hot and dry during the day, and often freezing at night.

Between the mountains and the Pacific Ocean lies a narrow coastal plain. Most of this plain is harsh desert where rain seldom falls. In some places, however, rivers cross the desert on their path from the mountains to the sea. It was in these river valleys that the first settlements occurred.

Between 3600 and 2500 B.C., people began to establish villages along the Pacific coast. These first inhabitants were hunter-gatherers who relied on seafood and small game for their survival. Around 3000 B.C., these people began to farm. By 1800 B.C., a number of thriving communities existed along the coast.

The Chavín Period The first influential civilization in South America arose not on the coast, however, but in the mountains. This culture, known as the **Chavín** (chah•VEEN), flourished from around 900 B.C. to 200 B.C. Archaeologists named the culture after a major ruin, Chavín de Huántar, in the northern highlands of Peru. This site features pyramids, plazas, and massive earthen mounds.

Chavín culture spread quickly across much of northern and central Peru. Archaeologists have found no evidence of political or economic organization within the culture. Thus, they conclude that the Chavín were primarily a religious civilization. Nevertheless, the spread of Chavín art styles and religious images— as seen in stone carving, pottery, and textiles—shows the powerful influence of this culture. Ancient Peruvians may have visited Chavín temples to pay their respects. They then carried ideas back to their communities. The Chavín are believed to have established certain patterns that helped unify Andean culture and lay the foundation for later civilizations in Peru. Thus, like the Olmec in Mesoamerica, the Chavín may have acted as a "mother culture" in South America.

Other Andean Civilizations Flourish

Around the time Chavín culture declined, other civilizations were emerging in Peru. First the Nazca and then the Moche (MOH•chay) built societies that flourished in the Andes.

Nazca Achievements The <u>Nazca</u> culture flourished along the southern coast of Peru from around 200 B.C. to A.D. 600. This area is extremely dry. The Nazca developed extensive irrigation systems, including underground canals, that allowed them to farm the land. The Nazca are known for their beautiful textiles and pottery. Both feature images of animals and mythological beings. They are even more famous, however, for an extraordinary but puzzling set of creations known as the Nazca Lines. (See History in Depth on the next page.) **A**

Moche Culture Meanwhile, on the northern coast of Peru, another civilization was reaching great heights. This was the <u>Moche</u> culture, which lasted from about A.D. 100 to A.D. 700.

MAIN IDEA

Contrasting
A How did the environment of the Andes region differ from that of much of Mesoamerica?

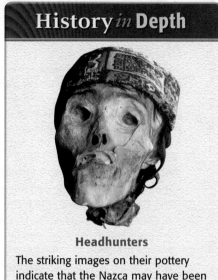

History *in* Depth

Headhunters

The striking images on their pottery indicate that the Nazca may have been headhunters. In numerous ceramic and textile designs, Nazca artisans depict the taking of human heads, probably from enemies in combat. Shown above is a shrunken head. Taking and displaying the head of an enemy was considered a way of increasing the strength and well-being of a community.

Early Civilizations, 1200 B.C.–A.D. 700

The region in which the Olmec arose included lush forests. Numerous rivers in the region provided fertile farming land.

The environment of the Andes region was harsh. Its dry terrain made farming difficult, which the Nazca overcame through irrigation.

- Chavín
- Moche
- Nazca
- Olmec

Gulf of Mexico

MESO-AMERICA

Tropic of Cancer

ATLANTIC OCEAN

Caribbean Sea

0° Equator

PACIFIC OCEAN

Amazon R.

SOUTH AMERICA

ANDES MOUNTAINS

N

0   1,000 Miles

0   2,000 Kilometers

Tropic of Capricorn

GEOGRAPHY SKILLBUILDER: Interpreting Maps
1. **Place** *Along what mountain range did the early South American civilizations arise?*
2. **Human Environment Interaction** *What advantages did the Olmec have over the early civilizations of the Andes?*

247

Nazca Lines

Etched on the plains of southeastern Peru are more than 1,000 drawings of animals, plants, humans, and geometric shapes. Most of them are so large that they can be recognized only from the air. Scientists believe that the Nazca people made the drawings between 200 B.C. and A.D. 600. Since the lines were discovered in 1927, people have proposed many theories about their purpose, including the following:

• The Nazca people worshiped mountain or sky gods and created the drawings to please them.

• The lines indicated where surface water entered the plain and marked elevated land between ancient riverbeds.

• The lines are a huge map that marks the course of underground aquifers, or water sources. (This is the most recent theory.)

Durability of the Nazca Lines

This spider was created more than 1,000 years ago. It survived because the region has little erosion. The plains are one of the driest regions on earth with only 20 minutes of rain a year. Also, the ground is flat and stony, so wind rarely carries away the soil.

Size of the Nazca Lines

Many of the Nazca drawings are huge. Some of the wedges (below) are more than 2,500 feet long. The hummingbird (right) is 165 feet long. The Nazca people probably created small model drawings and used math to reproduce them at such a vast scale.

Nazca Water Cult

Some scholars think the lines were linked to a Nazca water cult, or religion. The straight lines may have led to ceremonial sites. The animals may have been symbols. For example, according to traditional beliefs, the hummingbird (above) represents the mountain gods. The mountains were a main source of water.

VIDEO
HISTORY The Nasca Lines

↗ hmhsocialstudies.com

SKILLBUILDER: Interpreting Visual Sources

1. **Forming and Supporting Opinions** *Do you think the purpose of the Nazca lines had something to do with water? Why or why not?*

2. **Evaluating Courses of Action** *What might be the next step for researchers who wish to prove or disprove the aquifer theory? What are potential positive and negative consequences of such an action?*

The Moche took advantage of the rivers that flowed from the Andes Mountains. They built impressive irrigation systems to water their wide range of crops, which included corn, beans, potatoes, squash, and peanuts. According to Peruvian archaeologist Walter Alva, the Moche enjoyed a variety of foods. These included both fish and game:

PRIMARY SOURCE

The Moche enjoyed a diet rich in protein and probably better balanced than that of many modern Peruvians. Fish from the nearby Pacific were eaten fresh or sun dried. They ate Muscovy ducks and guinea pigs. To drink, there was potent *chicha,* a cloudy beverage fermented from corn that had been ground and boiled. Deer, now rare, were abundant. . . . Crayfish in irrigation ditches supplemented seafood from the coast.

WALTER ALVA, "Richest Unlooted Tomb of a Moche Lord," *National Geographic*

Moche tombs uncovered in the recent past have revealed a civilization with enormous wealth. Archaeologists have found beautiful jewelry crafted from gold, silver, and semiprecious stones. The Moche were also brilliant ceramic artists. They created pottery that depicted scenes from everyday life. Moche pots show doctors healing patients, women weaving cloth, and musicians playing instruments. They also show fierce soldiers armed with spears, leading enemy captives. Although the Moche never developed a written language, their pottery provides a wealth of detail about Moche life. **B**

Nevertheless, many questions about the Moche remain. Experts still do not fully understand Moche religious beliefs. Nor do they know why the Moche fell. Like many early cultures of the Americas, the Moche remain something of a mystery awaiting further archaeological discoveries.

Unlike the lands you will read about in the next chapter—which were unified by the spread of Islam—the Americas would remain a patchwork of separate civilizations until the early 16th century. Around that time, as you will read in Chapter 20, the Europeans would begin to arrive and bring dramatic and lasting changes to the American continents.

MAIN IDEA

Analyzing Issues

B How were archaeologists able to gain so much information about the Moche without the help of a written language?

SECTION 3 ASSESSMENT

TERMS & NAMES 1. For each term or name, write a sentence explaining its significance.
• Chavín • Nazca • Moche

USING YOUR NOTES

2. What achievements, if any, did all three cultures share? Explain.

Culture	Time Span	Location	Achievements
Chavín			
Nazca			
Moche			

MAIN IDEAS

3. Why was Peru a difficult place for a civilization to develop?

4. How was the Chavín culture like the Olmec culture?

5. How did the Nazca deal with their dry environment?

CRITICAL THINKING & WRITING

6. **HYPOTHESIZING** Would the Chavín culture have been more influential if it had arisen along the Peruvian coast?

7. **COMPARING** In which civilization did religion seem to play the most central role? Explain.

8. **DRAWING CONCLUSIONS** How did the Nazca and the Moche adapt to their environment in order to build flourishing societies? Give evidence.

9. **WRITING ACTIVITY** INTERACTION WITH ENVIRONMENT How did the Nazca change their environment to make it suitable for agriculture? Write an **expository essay** explaining their methods.

CONNECT TO TODAY MAKING A POSTER

Research recent findings on one of the three Andean cultures discussed in this section: Chavín, Nazca, or Moche. Then present your findings in a **poster** that will be displayed in the classroom.

TERMS & NAMES

For each term or name below, briefly explain its connection to the early peoples and civilizations of the Americas.

1. Beringia
2. maize
3. Olmec
4. Zapotec
5. Monte Albán
6. Chavín
7. Nazca
8. Moche

MAIN IDEAS

The Earliest Americans Section 1 (pages 235–239)

9. How do scientists know the first Americans were hunters?

10. Why was corn an important crop to early peoples?

11. What were the main differences between hunter-gatherer societies and those based primarily on agriculture?

Early Mesoamerican Civilizations Section 2
(pages 240–245)

12. Where did the Olmec arise?

13. How did the Olmec's location contribute to the development of their civilization?

14. How did the Olmec influence the Zapotec civilization?

15. How do archaeologists know that the Zapotec city of Monte Albán was more than just a ceremonial center?

Early Civilizations of the Andes Section 3 (pages 246–249)

16. In what ways did the Chavín influence other peoples?

17. What do scholars believe the Nazca lines represent?

18. How did the Nazca and Moche develop rich farmland?

CRITICAL THINKING

1. USING YOUR NOTES

In a sequence diagram, show how the early Americans' way of life developed through several stages.

2. SUMMARIZING

INTERACTION WITH ENVIRONMENT What environmental challenges did the first Americans face?

3. SUPPORTING OPINIONS

Would you rather have lived in a hunting or farming society?

4. DRAWING CONCLUSIONS

POWER AND AUTHORITY Why do you think the Olmec or Zapotec civilizations might have declined?

5. MAKING INFERENCES

CULTURAL INTERACTION What geographic factors would have made interactions between early Mesoamerican and Andean civilizations difficult?

VISUAL SUMMARY

The Americas: A Separate World

The Earliest Americans

- Hunted big game and later fished and gathered berries and plants
- Lived in small groups, as they had to move continually in search of food
- Eventually developed farming and settled down into large communities
- Developed various new skills, including arts and crafts, architecture, and social and political organization
- Gradually forged more complex societies

Early South American Societies

The Chavín

- Established powerful religious worship centers
- Created influential artistic styles

The Nazca and Moche

- Developed extensive irrigation systems for farming
- Crafted intricate ceramics and textiles and other decorative art

Early Mesoamerican Societies

The Olmec

- Designed and built pyramids, plazas, and monumental sculptures
- Developed ceremonial centers, ritual ball games, and a ruling class
- Directed a large trade network throughout Mesoamerica

The Zapotec

- Built a magnificent urban center at Monte Albán
- Developed early forms of hieroglyphic writing and a calendar system

Use the quotation and your knowledge of world history to answer questions 1 and 2 about a Chavín shrine.

PRIMARY SOURCE

Its U-shaped temple opens east toward the nearby Mosna River and the rising sun. The sacred precinct faces away from the nearby prehistoric settlement, presenting a high, almost menacing, wall to the outside world. The entire effect is one of mystery and hidden power. . . . Worshippers entered the sacred precincts by a roundabout route, passing along the temple pyramid to the river, then up some low terraces that led into the heart of the shrine. Here they found themselves in a sacred landscape set against a backdrop of mountains. Ahead of them lay the hidden place where the axis of the world passed from the sky into the underworld, an oracle famous for miles around.

BRIAN FAGAN, *quoted in* The Peru Reader

1. How might visitors have felt upon entering this shrine for the first time?

A. amused

B. awestruck

C. arrogant

D. angry

2. What effect might this shrine have had on the influence of the Chavín culture in the region?

A. helped spread culture's influence

B. limited its influence

C. shrine had no effect on spread of culture

D. undermined importance of the culture

Use the map and your knowledge of world history to answer question 3.

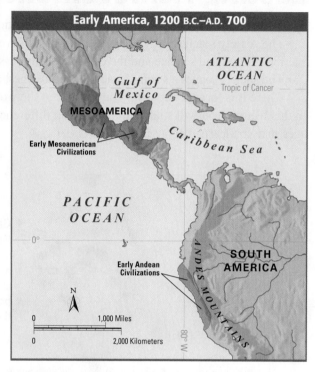

3. About how many miles apart by land do the early Mesoamerican and Andean civilizations appear to be?

A. 1,500 **C.** 3,500

B. 2,500 **D.** 4,500

 hmhsocialstudies.com | **TEST PRACTICE**

For additional test practice, go online for:
- Diagnostic tests
- Strategies
- Tutorials

Interact *with* History

On page 234 you examined how killing a mammoth would help you survive and discussed the difficulties of living in a hunter-gatherer society. Now that you have read the chapter, discuss why the early Americans moved from a hunting to a farming existence. In what ways was food gathering easier in an agricultural society?

FOCUS ON WRITING

Write a two-paragraph **essay** explaining why it might have taken many years to travel from the land bridge in upper North America to the southern tip of South America.

As you plan your essay, consider the following:
- means of transportation
- distances traveled
- nature of the terrain

MULTIMEDIA ACTIVITY

Writing a Documentary Film Script

Write a documentary film script on the spread of American culture. Contrast the spread of culture today with the modes of transmission among the earliest known inhabitants of the Americas. Consider the role, then and now, of factors such as climate change, war, trade, and technology. Provide a definition of culture in your script, and include examples of the following:

- ways in which culture was spread among the earliest peoples of the Americas
- agents and barriers to the spread of culture
- the role of trade in spreading culture today

Lasting Achievements

A classical age usually has two important characteristics:

• The society reaches a high level of cultural achievement, with advances in technology and science and the creation of impressive works of art.

• The society leaves a strong legacy for future ages, not only in the region where it is located but also in other parts of the world.

In this feature, you will study similarities and differences among five classical ages that you learned about in Unit 2.

◄ **Greece**
Pericles, shown at left, led the city-state of Athens during its golden age. The ancient Greeks of Athens and other cities created art, literature, philosophy, and political institutions that have influenced the world for thousands of years.

Greece
750–300 B.C.

Rome
500 B.C.–A.D 476

| 1200 B.C. | 1000 | 800 | 600 | 400 | 200 |

Olmec
1200–400 B.C.

Han China
202 B.C.–A.D. 220

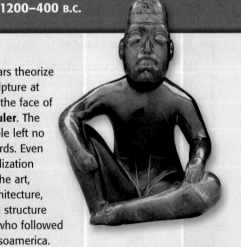

Olmec ►
Some scholars theorize that the sculpture at right shows the face of an **Olmec ruler.** The Olmec people left no written records. Even so, their civilization influenced the art, religion, architecture, and political structure of peoples who followed them in Mesoamerica.

Han China ►
Liu Bang, shown at right, seized control of China and founded the Han Dynasty. He and his successors ruled a vast empire, which saw the growth and spread of Chinese culture. Even today, many Chinese call themselves "the people of Han," a tribute to the lasting cultural impact of this period.

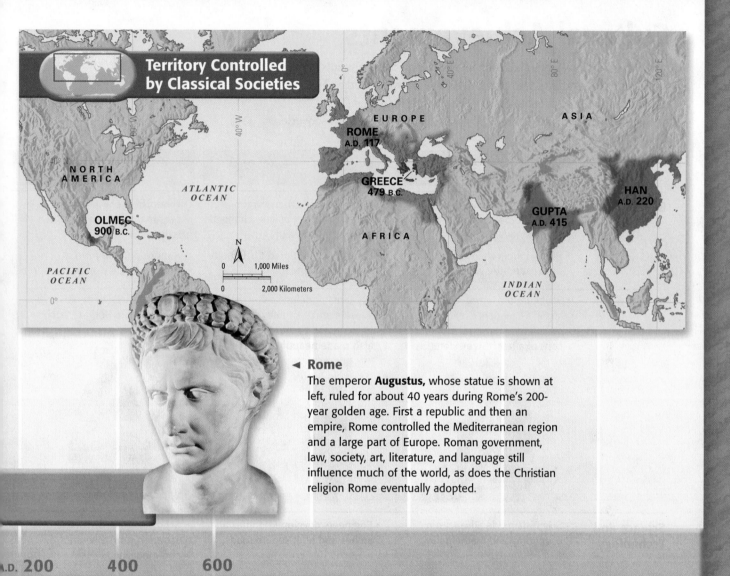

Territory Controlled by Classical Societies

EUROPE

ASIA

ROME
A.D. 117

NORTH AMERICA

ATLANTIC OCEAN

GREECE
479 B.C.

HAN
A.D. 220

OLMEC
900 B.C.

GUPTA
A.D. 415

AFRICA

PACIFIC OCEAN

N

0   1,000 Miles

0   2,000 Kilometers

INDIAN OCEAN

◄ **Rome**

The emperor **Augustus,** whose statue is shown at left, ruled for about 40 years during Rome's 200-year golden age. First a republic and then an empire, Rome controlled the Mediterranean region and a large part of Europe. Roman government, law, society, art, literature, and language still influence much of the world, as does the Christian religion Rome eventually adopted.

A.D. 200   400   600

Gupta India
A.D. 320–535

◄ **Gupta India**

Chandragupta II, shown on this coin, was one of the rulers of India's Gupta Empire. They oversaw an age of peace, prosperity, and artistic creativity. During this time, Hinduism and Buddhism took full form in India and spread through trade to other regions.

Comparing & Contrasting

1. Which of these societies controlled the most territory? the least? Explain how the size of a society's territory might affect its ability to leave a legacy.

2. Which classical ages had religion as an important part of their legacy? Why does religion have such an impact on societies?

Cultural Achievements

These five classical ages had impressive cultural achievements. Their beliefs are still studied—and in some cases followed—today. Their art and architecture are counted among the world's treasures. Their advances in science and technology paved the way for later discoveries.

	Greece	Rome	Gupta India
Beliefs	• The Greeks worshiped many gods who behaved in very human ways. • Philosophers used reason to understand the world.	• Rome adopted many of the Greek gods, but usually changed and added to them. • Later, Rome adopted Christianity and helped spread it.	• Hinduism became a more personal religion and gained followers. • A more popular form of Buddhism developed and spread.
Art	• Sculpture portrayed ideal beauty, and at a later period, moved toward realism—as shown by this Roman copy of a later Greek statue.	• Romans modeled sculpture after Greek statues and developed more realistic sculpture. They also made beautiful mosaics.	• Gupta statues were of Hindu gods and the Buddha, such as this figure.
Science and Technology	• Scientists made advances in astronomy and mathematics.	• Engineers developed domes and arches and built superb roads.	• Scholars made discoveries in astronomy, mathematics, and medicine.
Architecture	• Greek buildings show balance and symmetry; columns and pedestals were often used.	• Roman advances include domes and arches, such as those in the Colosseum.	• Hindu temples like this temple of Vishnu at Deogarh began to have pyramidal roofs.

Han China	Olmec
• The Han adopted the ethical system of Confucius as the basis for government.	• The Olmec worshiped a jaguar spirit. • They built religious centers with pyramids.
• The Han made intricate bronzes like this figure of a galloping horse. 	• The Olmec carved giant stone heads and small figurines like this ceremonial object.
• The Han invented paper, various farming tools, and watermills.	• The Olmec moved heavy stone for monuments without use of the wheel.
• Han buildings were wooden and none survive. This ceramic model of a three-story wooden tower shows Han styles. 	• This step pyramid at the Zapotec site in Monte Albán reflects Olmec architectural influence.

> " . . . to the glory that was Greece and the grandeur that was Rome"
>
> Edgar Allan Poe, from "To Helen"

> "The inhabitants [of the Gupta Empire] are rich and prosperous, and vie with one another in the practice of benevolence and righteousness."
>
> Fa Xian, from *The Travels of Fa Xian*

SKILLBUILDER: Interpreting Charts

1. **Drawing Conclusions** *Which of the art pieces shown here are religious in subject and which are not?*
2. **Contrasting** *How were the beliefs of Han China different from the other societies that had classical ages?*

Comparing & Contrasting

1. Which of the societies seemed to be more interested in mathematical and scientific theories? Which seemed to be more interested in practical technology?

2. What functions did monumental buildings fill for these societies? Explain whether the functions were similar or different.

Legacy of Classical Ages

The societies of the classical ages lasted for many centuries. In the end, though, they faded from the world scene. Still, some of their achievements have had an enduring impact on later societies.

Architecture

The Smolny Institute (below left) built in the early 1800s in St. Petersburg, Russia, reflects Greek and Roman architectural ideas. A modern hotel in South Africa (below right) recalls Olmec style.

DOCUMENT-BASED QUESTION
Compare these buildings to the Greek, Roman, and Olmec structures on pages 254–255. What similarities do you see?

Religion

Buddhism and Roman Catholicism are still widely practiced today, with millions of followers in countries far from the lands where the religions originated. The Buddhist monks (below left) are praying in Seoul, South Korea. Pope John Paul II (below right), former head of the Catholic Church, greets nuns and other believers who visit Rome from around the world.

DOCUMENT-BASED QUESTION
What similarity do you see in the religious legacies of Rome and Gupta India?

Government

The classical ages studied in Unit 2 laid foundations for government that influenced later times—even today. Read about three examples of their contributions.

PRIMARY SOURCE

Pericles

In a famous speech known as the Funeral Oration, the Athenian leader Pericles described the advantages of democracy.

[Our government] favors the many instead of the few; this is why it is called a democracy. If we look to the laws, they afford equal justice to all; . . . if no social standing, advancement in public life falls to reputation for capacity [ability], class considerations not being allowed to interfere with merit; nor again does poverty bar the way, if a man is able to serve the state, he is not hindered by the obscurity of his condition.

DOCUMENT-BASED QUESTION
According to Pericles, what values did Athens stand for?

SECONDARY SOURCE

Rhoads Murphey

In this passage from *A History of Asia*, historian Rhoads Murphey examines the lasting impact of the government of Han China.

Confucianism was more firmly established as the official orthodoxy and state ideology, and the famous Chinese imperial civil service system recruited men of talent, schooled in classical Confucian learning, to hold office through competitive examination regardless of their birth. . . . In China, the original Han ideal endured through the rise and fall of successive dynasties and, with all its imperfections, built a long and proud tradition of power combined with service that is still very much alive in China.

DOCUMENT-BASED QUESTION
What qualities of Han government still influence China today?

SECONDARY SOURCE

Henry C. Boren

In this excerpt from his book *Roman Society*, historian Henry C. Boren discusses the permanent legacy of Roman law.

The most imitated and studied code of law in history is the formulation by a group of lawyers . . . under the eastern Roman emperor Justinian. . . . This code served as a model for many of the nations of western Europe in the modern age and also for South Africa, Japan, and portions of Canada and the United States. Indirectly the principles of the Roman law, though perhaps not the procedures, have also strongly affected the development of the Anglo-Saxon common law, which is the basis of the legal systems in most English-speaking nations.

DOCUMENT-BASED QUESTION
According to this historian, how has Roman law affected the world?

Comparing & Contrasting

1. How did the idea of merit play a part in the governments of both Athens and Han China?

2. How is the U.S. government similar to each of the governments described in the excerpts?

3. What were some of the different forces that spread the ideas of these classical ages to many regions of the world?

EXTENSION ACTIVITY
Another Mesoamerican society that had a classical age was the Maya, which you will study in Chapter 16. Read about the Classic Age of the Maya either in this textbook or an encyclopedia. Then create a chart or a poster listing Maya beliefs and their achievements in the arts, science, technology, and architecture.

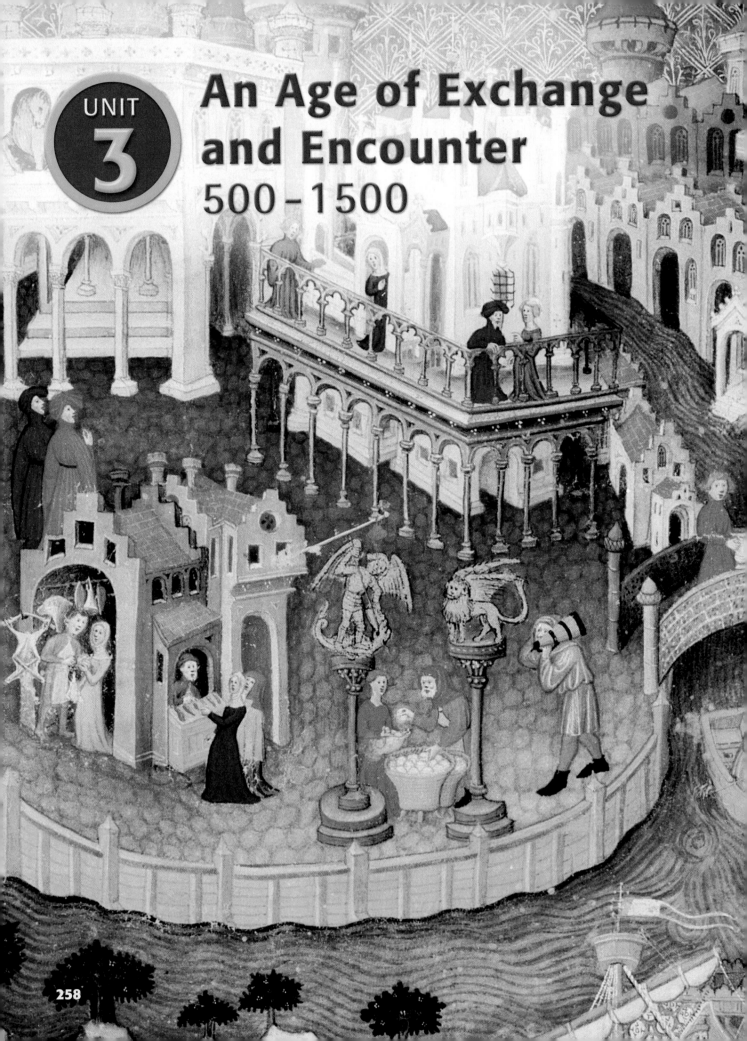

An Age of Exchange and Encounter
500–1500

Venice at the time of Marco Polo was a vibrant, bustling city. This depiction of the city comes from the *Romance of Alexander*, a 14th-century illuminated manuscript that included a French account of Polo's travels.

Comparing & Contrasting

Trade Networks

In Unit 3, you will learn how trade began to connect regions of the world and how it made the exchange of goods and ideas easier. At the end of the unit, you will have a chance to compare and contrast five different trade networks. (See pages 430–435.)

The Muslim World,
600–1250

Essential Question

How did Islam and the achievements of the Muslim world spread between 600 and 1250?

❓ What You Will Learn

In this chapter you will follow the amazing rise and spread of Islam, whose followers conquered lands on three continents while also preserving and furthering learning in many areas.

SECTION 1 The Rise of Islam
Main Idea Muhammad unified the Arab people both politically and through the religion of Islam.

SECTION 2 Islam Expands
Main Idea In spite of internal conflicts, the Muslims created a huge empire that included lands on three continents.

SECTION 3 Muslim Culture
Main Idea Muslims combined and preserved the traditions of many peoples and also advanced learning in a variety of areas.

Previewing Themes

RELIGIOUS AND ETHICAL SYSTEMS Islam, a monotheistic religion begun by Muhammad, developed during the 600s. Its followers, called Muslims, spread Islam through Southwest and Central Asia, parts of Africa, and Europe.
Geography *Study the time line and the map. What were some of the major cities of the Muslim world? Locate them on the map.*

EMPIRE BUILDING The leaders following Muhammad built a huge empire that by A.D. 750 included millions of people from diverse ethnic, language, and religious groups.
Geography *How did the location of the Arabian Peninsula—the origin of the Muslim world—promote empire building?*

CULTURAL INTERACTION Tolerance of conquered peoples and an emphasis on learning helped to blend the cultural traits of people under Muslim rule.
Geography *How far might cultural interaction have spread if the Muslims had won a key battle at Tours in 732?*

MUSLIM WORLD

630
Muhammad returns to Mecca after making the Hijrah to Medina.

732
◄ Charles Martel defeats the Muslims at Tours.

800s
Al-Khwarizmi writes the first algebra textbook.

600

800

WORLD

800
◄ Pope crowns Charlemagne (shown) emperor of the Romans.

850
Chinese invent gunpowder.

Muslim World, 1200

↗ hmhsocialstudies.com INTERACTIVE MAP

EUROPE

ATLANTIC
OCEAN

ASIA

Baltic Sea

Dnieper River

Don River

Volga River

Ural River

HOLY
ROMAN
EMPIRE

Tours

FRANCE

Venice

Danube River

BYZANTINE EMPIRE

Black Sea

Constantinople

Caspian Sea

Rome

Corsica

SPAIN

Córdoba

Granada

Balearic Is.

Sardinia

Sicily

Mediterranean Sea

Crete

Cyprus

Damascus

Tigris R.

Baghdad

PERSIA

Euphrates River

Tangier

Alexandria

Jerusalem

Persian Gulf

Indus River

30°N

Cairo

EGYPT

Nile River

Red Sea

Medina

Mecca

ARABIAN
PENINSULA

INDIA

S A H A R A

Arabian
Sea

Timbuktu

A F R I C A

N

W   E

S

INDIAN
OCEAN

0° Equator

Mogadishu

0   500   1000 Miles

0   500   1000 Kilometers

Winkel II Projection

Mombasa

Zanzibar

Kilwa

■	Muslim lands at the death of Abu Bakr, 634
■	Lands conquered by Muslims under first four caliphs by 661
■	Lands conquered by Muslims by 750
—	Extent of Muslim influence, 1200

1000s
◀ Muslim scholars, who pre-served Greek medical works, share them with Europeans.

1100s
Muslim literature flourishes.

1000

1250

960
Song Dynasty is established in China.

1054
Christian Church divides.

1209
◀ Genghis Khan begins the Mongol conquest.

How does a culture bloom in the desert?

In 642, Alexandria and the rest of Egypt fell to the Muslim army. Alexandria had been part of the Byzantine Empire. By 646, however, the city was firmly under Muslim rule.

You are a Muslim trader from Mecca. You admire Alexandria (shown below), with its cultural blend of ancient Egypt, Greece, and Rome. Now, as Islam spreads, the Muslim Empire is borrowing from conquered cultures and enriching its desert culture. As you look around Alexandria, you consider the cultural elements you might bring to your desert home in Mecca.

The Pharos, the great lighthouse of Alexandria, is said by some scholars to have inspired the minaret, the tower from which Muslims are called to prayer.

Because the Christian Church believed ancient Greek texts were not religious, these books lay neglected in Alexandrian libraries. Muslim scholars, however, would revive the Greek ideas and advance them.

The port of Alexandria thrived for many centuries. As a Muslim trader, you will bring your goods to Alexandria. You will also bring your language, your holy book, and your faith.

EXAMINING *the* ISSUES

- **What cultural elements of Alexandria do you want to adopt? What elements won't you accept?**

- **How might the desert affect a culture's architectural style?**

As a class, discuss which cultural element in Alexandria you think will be the most useful in the Muslim world. As you read this chapter, find out how the Muslim Empire adopted and adapted new ideas and developed a unique culture.

For the desert-dwelling Arab, water was scarce—and sacred. Fountains in Alexandria would have seemed a great gift.

The Rise of Islam

MAIN IDEA	WHY IT MATTERS NOW	TERMS & NAMES
RELIGIOUS AND ETHICAL SYSTEMS Muhammad unified the Arab people both politically and through the religion of Islam.	As the world's fastest-growing major religion, Islam has a strong impact on the lives of millions today.	• Allah • Muhammad • Islam • Muslim • Hijrah	• mosque • hajj • Qur'an • Sunna • shari'a

SETTING THE STAGE The cultures of the Arabian Peninsula were in constant contact with one another for centuries. Southwest Asia (often referred to as the Middle East) was a bridge between Africa, Asia, and Europe, where goods were traded and new ideas were shared. One set of shared ideas would become a powerful force for change in the world—the religion of Islam.

Deserts, Towns, and Trade Routes

The Arabian Peninsula is a crossroads of three continents—Africa, Europe, and Asia. At its longest and widest points, the peninsula is about 1,200 miles from north to south and 1,300 miles from east to west. Only a tiny strip of fertile land in south Arabia and Oman and a few oases can support agriculture. The remainder of the land is desert, which in the past was inhabited by nomadic Arab herders.

hmhsocialstudies.com
TAKING NOTES
Use the graphic organizer online to take notes on important aspects of Islam.

Desert and Town Life On this desert, the Arab nomads, called Bedouins (BEHD•oo•ihnz), were organized into tribes and groups called clans. These clans provided security and support for a life made difficult by the extreme conditions of the desert. The Bedouin ideals of courage and loyalty to family, along with their warrior skills, would become part of the Islamic way of life.

The areas with more fertile soil and the larger oases had enough water to support farming communities. By the early 600s, many Arabs had chosen to settle in an oasis or in a market town. Larger towns near the western coast of Arabia became market towns for local, regional, and long-distance trade goods.

Crossroads of Trade and Ideas By the early 600s, trade routes connected Arabia to the major ocean and land trade routes, as you can see on the map on the next page. Trade routes through Arabia ran from the extreme south of the peninsula to the Byzantine and Sassanid (Persian) empires to the north. Merchants from these two empires moved along the caravan routes, trading for goods from the Silk Roads of the east. They transported spices and incense from Yemen and other products to the west. They also carried information and ideas from the world outside Arabia.

Mecca During certain holy months, caravans stopped in Mecca, a city in western Arabia. They brought religious pilgrims who came to worship at an ancient shrine in the city called the Ka'aba (KAH•buh). Over the years, the Arabs had

Trade Goods Brought to Arabia

- spices
- incense
- perfumes
- precious metals
- ivory
- silk

Land route
Sea route
Hijrah
Byzantine Empire
Sassanid Empire

GEOGRAPHY SKILLBUILDER: Interpreting Maps
1. **Location** *Why is Arabia's location a good one for trade?*
2. **Movement** *Why was the location of Mecca ideal for the spread of ideas?*

introduced the worship of many gods and spirits to this place. The Ka'aba contained over 360 idols brought by many tribes. The Qur'an associated this house of worship with Abraham, a believer in one God and considered a prophet.

The concept of belief in one God, called <u>**Allah**</u> (AL•uh) in Arabic, was known on the Arabian Peninsula. Many Christians and Jews lived there and practiced monotheism. Into this mixed religious environment of Mecca, around A.D. 570, Muhammad was born.

Muhammad, Prophet of Islam

<u>**Muhammad**</u> (mu•HAM•id) was born into the clan of a powerful Meccan family. Orphaned at the age of six, Muhammad was raised by his grandfather and his uncle. He received little schooling and began working in the caravan trade as a very young man. At the age of 25, Muhammad became a trader and business manager for Khadijah (kah•DEE•juh), a wealthy businesswoman of about 40. Later, Muhammad and Khadijah married. Theirs was both a good marriage and a good business partnership.

Revelations Muhammad took great interest in religion and often spent time alone in prayer and meditation. At about the age of 40, Muhammad's life was changed overnight when he believed a voice called to him while he meditated in a cave outside Mecca. According to Muslim belief, the voice was that of the angel Gabriel, who told Muhammad that he was a messenger of Allah. "What shall I proclaim?" asked Muhammad. The voice answered:

MAIN IDEA

Analyzing Primary Sources

Ⓐ What kind of teaching does the phrase "the use of the pen" refer to?

PRIMARY SOURCE Ⓐ

Proclaim! In the name of thy Lord and Cherisher, who created man out of a (mere) clot of congealed blood. Proclaim! And thy Lord is most bountiful. He who taught (the use of) the pen taught man that which he knew not.

QUR'AN, sura 96:1–5

After much soul-searching, Muhammad came to believe that the Lord who spoke to him through Gabriel was Allah. Muhammad became convinced that he was the last of the prophets. He began to teach that Allah was the one and only God and that all other gods must be abandoned. People who agreed to this basic principle of Islam were called Muslims. In Arabic, **Islam** (ihs•LAHM) means "submission to the will of Allah." **Muslim** (MUHZ•lihm) means "one who has submitted." Muhammad's wife, Khadijah, and several close friends and relatives were his first followers.

By 613, Muhammad had begun to preach publicly in Mecca, but he met with some hostility. Many Meccans believed his revolutionary ideas would lead to neglect of the traditional Arab gods. They feared that Mecca would lose its position as a pilgrimage center if people accepted Muhammad's monotheistic beliefs.

The Hijrah After some of his followers had been attacked, Muhammad decided to leave Mecca in 622. Following a small band of supporters he sent ahead, Muhammad moved to the town of Yathrib, over 200 miles to the north of Mecca. This migration became known as the **Hijrah** (HIHJ•ruh). The Hijrah to Yathrib marked a turning point for Muhammad. He attracted many devoted followers. Later, Yathrib was renamed Medina.

In Medina, Muhammad displayed impressive leadership skills. He fashioned an agreement that joined his own people with the Arabs and Jews of Medina as a single community. These groups accepted Muhammad as a political leader. As a religious leader, he drew many more converts who found his message appealing. Finally, Muhammad also became a military leader in the growing hostilities between Mecca and Medina.

Returning to Mecca In 630, Muhammad and 10,000 of his followers marched to the outskirts of Mecca. Facing sure defeat, Mecca's leaders surrendered. Muhammad entered the city in triumph. He destroyed the idols in the Ka'aba and had the call to prayer made from its roof.

Most Meccans pledged their loyalty to Muhammad, and many converted to Islam. By doing so, they joined the *umma,* or Muslim religious community. Muhammad died two years later, at about the age of 62. However, he had taken great strides toward unifying the entire Arabian Peninsula under Islam.

▼ The Abyssinian army set out to destroy the Ka'aba. Their elephants, however, refused to attack.

The Dome of the Rock

The Dome of the Rock, located in Jerusalem, is the earliest surviving Islamic monument. It was completed in 691 and is part of a larger complex, which is the third most holy place in Islam. It is situated on Mount Moriah, the site of the Jewish Temple destroyed by the Romans in A.D. 70, Judaism's holiest place.

   The rock on the site (see photograph below, left) is the spot from which Muslims say Muhammad ascended to heaven to learn of Allah's will. With Allah's blessing, Muslims believe Muhammad returned to earth to bring God's message to all people.

▼ This interior view shows the point at which the dome meets the circular walls, or drum. The dome is about 100 feet tall and 60 feet in diameter. It is supported by 16 pillars and columns. The drum is covered with colored glass mosaics that date back to the 7th century. The dome was redecorated later.

▼ The ornate decorations of the exterior are also found on the interior of the building. Notice the geometric designs, a feature often found in Muslim art.

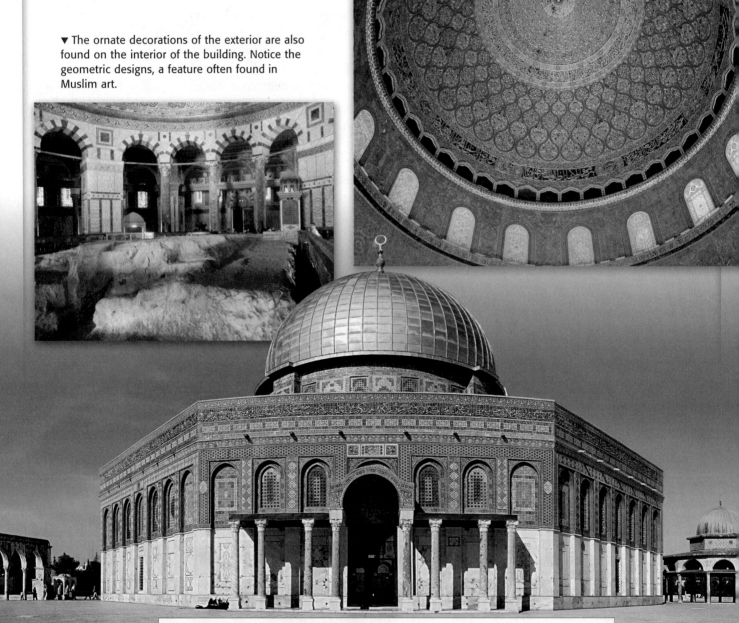

SKILLBUILDER: Interpreting Visual Sources
1. **Making Inferences** If you knew nothing about this building, what elements of the building might give you the impression that it is a religious structure?
2. **Comparing and Contrasting** How is the Dome of the Rock similar to or different from other religious buildings you have seen?

Beliefs and Practices of Islam

The main teaching of Islam is that there is only one God, Allah. All other beliefs and practices follow from this teaching. Islam teaches that there is good and evil, and that each individual is responsible for the actions of his or her life.

The Five Pillars To be a Muslim, all believers have to carry out five duties. These duties are known as the Five Pillars of Islam.

- **Faith** To become a Muslim, a person has to testify to the following statement of faith: "There is no God but Allah, and Muhammad is the Messenger of Allah." This simple statement is heard again and again in Islamic rituals and in Muslim daily life.
- **Prayer** Five times a day, Muslims face toward Mecca to pray. They may assemble at a **mosque** (mahsk), an Islamic house of worship, or wherever they find themselves.
- **Alms** Muhammad taught that all Muslims have a responsibility to support the less fortunate. Muslims meet that social responsibility by giving alms, or money for the poor, through a special religious tax.
- **Fasting** During the Islamic holy month of Ramadan, Muslims fast between dawn and sunset. A simple meal is eaten at the end of the day. Fasting serves to remind Muslims that their spiritual needs are greater than their physical needs.
- **Pilgrimage** All Muslims who are physically and financially able perform the **hajj** (haj), or pilgrimage to Mecca, at least once. Pilgrims wear identical garments so that all stand as equals before Allah.

A Way of Life Carrying out the Five Pillars of Islam ensures that Muslims live their religion while serving in their community. Along with the Five Pillars, there are other customs, morals, and laws for Islamic society that affect Muslims' daily lives. Believers are forbidden to eat pork or to drink intoxicating beverages. Friday afternoons are set aside for communal worship. Unlike many other religions, Islam has no priests or central religious authority. Every Muslim is expected to worship Allah directly. Islam does, however, have a scholar class called the *ulama*. The *ulama* includes religious teachers who apply the words and deeds of Muhammad to everyday life.

Sources of Authority The original source of authority for Muslims is Allah. According to Islamic belief, Allah expressed his will through the angel Gabriel, who revealed it to Muhammad. While Muhammad lived, his followers memorized and recited the revelations he received from Gabriel. Soon after Muhammad's death, it was suggested that the revelations be collected in a book. This book is the **Qur'an** (kuh•RAN), the holy book of the Muslims.

The Qur'an is written in Arabic, and Muslims consider only the Arabic version to be the true word of Allah. Only Arabic can be used in worship. Wherever Muslims carried the Qur'an, Arabic became the language of worshipers and scholars. Thus, the

▼ Artists decorate the Qur'an as a holy act. The geometric design often repeats to show the infinite quality of Allah.

Social History

Muslim Prayer

Five times a day—dawn, noon, mid-afternoon, sunset, and evening—Muslims face toward Mecca to pray. Worshipers are called to prayer by a *muezzin*. The call to prayer sometimes is given from a minaret and even over public address systems or the radio in large cities.

Because they believe that standing before Allah places them on holy ground, Muslims perform a ritual cleansing before praying. They also remove their shoes.

Arabic language helped unite conquered peoples as Muslim control expanded.

Muslims believe that Muhammad's mission as a prophet was to receive the Qur'an and to demonstrate how to apply it in life. To them, the **Sunna** (SOON•uh), or Muhammad's example, is the best model for proper living. The guidance of the Qur'an and Sunna was assembled in a body of law known as **shari'a** (shah•REE•ah). This system of law regulates the family life, moral conduct, and business and community life of Muslims. **B**

Links to Judaism and Christianity To Muslims, Allah is the same God that is worshiped in Christianity and Judaism. However, Muslims view Jesus as a prophet, not as the Son of God. They regard the Qur'an as the word of Allah as revealed to Muhammad, in a similar way to the beliefs of Jews and Christians in their holy scriptures. Muslims believe that the Qur'an perfects the earlier revelations. To them, it is the final book, and Muhammad was the final prophet. All three religions believe in heaven and hell and a day of judgment. The Muslims trace their ancestry to Abraham, as do the Jews and Christians.

Muslims refer to Christians and Jews as "people of the book" because each religion has a holy book with teachings similar to those of the Qur'an. Shari'a law requires Muslim leaders to extend religious tolerance to Christians and Jews. A huge Muslim empire, as you will learn in Section 2, grew to include people of many different cultures and religions.

MAIN IDEA

Clarifying

B What are the sources of authority for Muslims?

SECTION 1 ASSESSMENT

TERMS & NAMES 1. For each term or name, write a sentence explaining its significance.
• Allah • Muhammad • Islam • Muslim • Hijrah • mosque • hajj • Qur'an • Sunna • shari'a

USING YOUR NOTES

2. What event in the life of Muhammad signaled the beginning of Islam?

MAIN IDEAS

3. Why was Mecca an important city in western Arabia?

4. What are the Five Pillars of Islam?

5. Why did Muslims consider Christians and Jews "people of the book"?

CRITICAL THINKING & WRITING

6. **RECOGNIZING EFFECTS** How did the beliefs and practices of Islam create unity and strength among Muslims in the 600s?

7. **COMPARING** In what ways are the teachings of the Muslims similar to those of Christians and Jews?

8. **DRAWING CONCLUSIONS** How did Islam help spread Arabic culture?

9. **WRITING ACTIVITY** | RELIGIOUS AND ETHICAL SYSTEMS |
Write a **letter** to Muhammad, describing his legacy and that of Islam today.

CONNECT TO TODAY PREPARING AN ORAL REPORT

Today, tensions run high between Muslims, Christians, and Jews in the Middle East. Research to find out the causes of this tension. Present your findings in an **oral report.**

2

Islam Expands

MAIN IDEA	WHY IT MATTERS NOW	TERMS & NAMES
EMPIRE BUILDING In spite of internal conflicts, the Muslims created a huge empire that included lands on three continents.	Muslims' influence on three continents produced cultural blending that has continued into the modern world.	• caliph • Sufi • Umayyads • Abbasids • Shi'a • al-Andalus • Sunni • Fatimid

SETTING THE STAGE When Muhammad died in 632, the community faced a crisis. Muslims, inspired by the message of Allah, believed they had a duty to carry his word to the world. However, they lacked a clear way to choose a new leader. Eventually, the issue of leadership would divide the Muslim world.

Muhammad's Successors Spread Islam

Muhammad had not named a successor or instructed his followers how to choose one. Relying on ancient tribal custom, the Muslim community elected as their leader Abu-Bakr, a loyal friend of Muhammad. In 632, Abu-Bakr became the first **caliph** (KAY•lihf), a title that means "successor" or "deputy."

hmhsocialstudies.com
TAKING NOTES

Use the graphic organizer online to take notes on developments in Islam during each ruler's period in power.

"Rightly Guided" Caliphs Abu-Bakr and the next three elected caliphs—Umar, Uthman, and Ali—all had known Muhammad. They used the Qur'an and Muhammad's actions as guides to leadership. For this, they are known as the "rightly guided" caliphs. Their rule was called a caliphate (KAY•lih•FAYT).

Abu-Bakr had promised the Muslim community he would uphold what Muhammad stood for. Shortly after Muhammad's death, some tribes on the Arabian Peninsula abandoned Islam. Others refused to pay taxes, and a few individuals even declared themselves prophets. For the sake of Islam, Abu-Bakr invoked *jihad*. The word *jihad* means "striving" and can refer to the inner struggle against evil. However, the word is also used in the Qur'an to mean an armed struggle against unbelievers. For the next two years, Abu-Bakr applied this meaning of *jihad* to encourage and justify the expansion of Islam.

When Abu-Bakr died in 634, the Muslim state controlled all of Arabia. Under Umar, the second caliph, Muslim armies conquered Syria and lower Egypt, which were part of the Byzantine Empire. They also took parts of the Sassanid Empire. The next two caliphs, Uthman and Ali, continued to expand Muslim territory. By 750, the Muslim Empire stretched 6,000 miles from the Atlantic Ocean to the Indus River. (See the map on page 261.)

Reasons for Success The four "rightly guided" caliphs made great progress in their quest to spread Islam. Before his death, Muhammad had expressed a desire to spread the faith to the peoples of the north. Muslims of the day saw their victories as a sign of Allah's support and drew energy and inspiration from their faith. They fought to defend Islam and were willing to struggle to extend its word.

The Muslim armies were well disciplined and expertly commanded. However, the success of the armies was also due to weakness in the two empires north of Arabia. The Byzantine and Sassanid empires had been in conflict for a long period of time and were exhausted militarily.

Another reason for Muslim success was the persecution suffered by people under Byzantine or Sassanid rule because they did not support the official state religions, Christianity or Zoroastrianism. The persecuted people often welcomed the invaders and their cause and chose to accept Islam. They were attracted by the appeal of the message of Islam, which offered equality and hope in this world. They were also attracted by the economic benefit for Muslims of not having to pay a poll tax. **A**

MAIN IDEA

Analyzing Causes

A Why were Muslims successful conquerers?

Treatment of Conquered Peoples

Because the Qur'an forbade forced conversion, Muslims allowed conquered peoples to follow their own religion. Christians and Jews, as "people of the book," received special consideration. They paid a poll tax each year in exchange for exemption from military duties. However, they were also subject to various restrictions on their lives. Before entering the newly conquered city of Damascus in the northern Arabian province of Syria, Khalid ibn al-Walid, one of Abu-Bakr's chief generals, detailed the terms of surrender:

▲ From 632 to 750, highly mobile troops mounted on camels were successful in conquering lands in the name of Allah.

PRIMARY SOURCE

In the name of Allah, the compassionate, the merciful, this is what Khalid ibn al-Walid would grant to the inhabitants of Damascus. . . . He promises to give them security for their lives, property and churches. Their city wall shall not be demolished, neither shall any Muslim be quartered in their houses. Thereunto we give to them the pact of Allah and the protection of His Prophet, the Caliphs and the believers. So long as they pay the tax, nothing but good shall befall them.

KHALID IBN AL-WALID, quoted in *Early Islam*

Tolerance like this continued after the Muslim state was established. Though Christians and Jews were not allowed to spread their religion, they could be officials, scholars, and bureaucrats.

Internal Conflict Creates a Crisis

Despite spectacular gains on the battlefield, the Muslim community had difficulty maintaining a unified rule. In 656, Uthman was murdered, starting a civil war in which various groups struggled for power. Ali, as Muhammad's cousin and son-in-law, was the natural choice as a successor to Uthman. However, his right to rule was challenged by Muawiya, a governor of Syria. Then, in 661, Ali, too, was assassinated. The elective system of choosing a caliph died with him.

A family known as the **Umayyads** (oo•MY•adz) then came to power. The Umayyads moved the Muslim capital to Damascus. This location, away from Mecca, made controlling conquered territories easier. However, the Arab Muslims felt it was too far away from their lands. In addition, the Umayyads abandoned the simple life of previous caliphs and began to surround themselves with wealth and ceremony similar to that of non-Muslim rulers. These actions, along with the leadership issue, gave rise to a fundamental division in the Muslim community.

Sunni–Shi'a Split In the interest of peace, the majority of Muslims accepted the Umayyads' rule. However, a minority continued to resist. This group developed an alternate view of the office of caliph. In this view, the caliph needed to be a descendant of Muhammad. This group was called **Shi'a**, meaning the "party" of Ali. Members of this group are called Shi'ites. Those who did not outwardly resist the rule of the Umayyads later became known as **Sunni**, meaning followers of Muhammad's example. Another group, the **Sufi** (SOO•fee), rejected the luxurious life of the Umayyads. They pursued a life of poverty and devotion to a spiritual path.

Vigorous religious and political opposition to the Umayyad caliphate led to its downfall. Rebel groups overthrew the Umayyads in the year 750. The most powerful of those groups, the **Abbasids** (uh•BAS•IHDZ), took control of the empire. **B**

MAIN IDEA

Summarizing

B What are three groups within Islam and how do they differ?

Basic Differences Between Sunni and Shi'a Muslims

Sunni	Shi'a
• Believe that the first four caliphs were "rightly guided"	• Believe that Ali, Muhammad's son-in-law, should have succeeded him
• Believe that Muslim rulers should follow the Sunna, or Muhammad's example	• Believe that all Muslim rulers should be descended from Muhammad; do not recognize the authority of the Sunna
• Claim that the Shi'a have distorted the meaning of various passages in the Qur'an	• Claim that the Sunni have distorted the meaning of various passages in the Qur'an

Percentage Today of Sunni and Shi'a Muslims Worldwide

Sunni 83%
Shi'a 16%
Other 1%

Control Extends Over Three Continents

When the Abbasids came to power in 750, they ruthlessly murdered the remaining members of the Umayyad family. One prince named Abd al-Rahman escaped the slaughter and fled to Spain. There he set up an Umayyad caliphate. Spain had already been conquered and settled by Muslims from North Africa, who were known as Berbers. The Berber armies advanced north to within 200 miles of Paris before being halted at the Battle of Tours in 732. They then settled in southern Spain, where they helped form an extraordinary Muslim state in **al-Andalus** (al•AN•duh•LUS).

Abbasids Consolidate Power To solidify power, the Abbasids moved the capital of the empire in 762 to a newly created city, Baghdad, in central Iraq. The location on key trade routes gave the caliph access to trade goods, gold, and information about the far-flung empire.

The Abbasids developed a strong bureaucracy to conduct the huge empire's affairs. A treasury kept track of the money flow. A special department managed the business of the army. Diplomats from the empire were sent to courts in Europe,

Africa, and Asia to conduct imperial business. To support this bureaucracy, the Abbasids taxed land, imports and exports, and non-Muslims' wealth.

Rival Groups Divide Muslim Lands The Abbasid caliphate lasted from 750 to 1258. During that time, the Abbasids increased their authority by consulting religious leaders. But they failed to keep complete political control of the immense territory. Independent Muslim states sprang up, and local leaders dominated many smaller regions. The **Fatimid** (FAT•uh•MIHD) caliphate was formed by Shi'a Muslims who claimed descent from Muhammad's daughter Fatima. The caliphate began in North Africa and spread across the Red Sea to western Arabia and Syria. However, the Fatimids and other smaller states were still connected to the Abbasid caliphate through religion, language, trade, and the economy.

▼ This 13th-century miniature shows Arab traders navigating the Indian Ocean.

Muslim Trade Network At this time, two major sea-trading networks existed—the Mediterranean Sea and the Indian Ocean. Through these networks, the Muslim Empire could engage in sea trade with the rest of the world. The land network connected the Silk Roads of China and India with Europe and Africa. Muslim merchants needed only a single language, Arabic, and a single currency, the Abbasid dinar, to travel in the empire. **C**

To encourage the flow of trade, Muslim money changers set up banks in cities throughout the empire. Banks offered letters of credit, called *sakks,* to merchants. A merchant with a *sakk* from a bank in Baghdad could exchange it for cash at a bank in any other city in the empire. In Europe, *sakk* was pronounced "check." Thus, using checks dates back to the Muslim Empire.

At one end of the Muslim Empire was the city of Córdoba in al-Andalus. In the tenth century, this city had a population of 200,000; Paris, in contrast, had 38,000. The city attracted poets, philosophers, and scientists. Many non-Muslims adopted Muslim customs, and Córdoba became a dazzling center of Muslim culture.

In Córdoba, Damascus, Cairo, and Baghdad, a cultural blending of people fueled a period of immense achievements in the arts and the sciences.

MAIN IDEA

Recognizing Effects

C Why would a single language and a single currency be such an advantage to a trader?

SECTION 2 ASSESSMENT

TERMS & NAMES 1. For each term or name, write a sentence explaining its significance.
• caliph   • Umayyads   • Shi'a   • Sunni   • Sufi   • Abbasids   • al-Andalus   • Fatimid

USING YOUR NOTES	MAIN IDEAS	CRITICAL THINKING & WRITING
2. Which period of rule do you think was most effective?	**3.** How did Muslims under the "rightly guided" caliphs treat conquered peoples?	**6. EVALUATING COURSES OF ACTION** Do you think Muhammad should have appointed a successor? Why or why not?

USING YOUR NOTES

2. Which period of rule do you think was most effective?

Rulers	Period of Rule	Developments in Islam
Rightly guided caliphs		
Umayyads		
Abbasids		

MAIN IDEAS

3. How did Muslims under the "rightly guided" caliphs treat conquered peoples?

4. Why did the Shi'a oppose the rule of the Umayyads?

5. What tied the Abbasid caliphate and the independent Muslim states together?

CRITICAL THINKING & WRITING

6. **EVALUATING COURSES OF ACTION** Do you think Muhammad should have appointed a successor? Why or why not?

7. **DRAWING CONCLUSIONS** What attracted non-Muslims to Islam and Islamic culture?

8. **MAKING INFERENCES** What does opposition to the luxurious life of the Umayyads suggest about what is important to most Muslims?

9. **WRITING ACTIVITY** EMPIRE BUILDING Write a one-paragraph **summary** in which you determine whether or not the Muslim Empire was well run.

MULTIMEDIA ACTIVITY CREATING A PIE CHART

Use the Internet to find out the number of Sunni and Shi'a Muslims today in Iran, Iraq, Saudi Arabia, and Syria. Create a **pie chart** showing the results of your research.

INTERNET KEYWORD
country studies, Sunni, Shi'a

Muscle Culture

Muslim Culture

MAIN IDEA	WHY IT MATTERS NOW	TERMS & NAMES
CULTURAL INTERACTION Muslims combined and preserved the traditions of many peoples and also advanced learning in a variety of areas.	Many of the ideas developed during this time became the basis of today's scientific and academic disciplines.	• House of Wisdom • calligraphy

SETTING THE STAGE The Abbasids governed during a prosperous period of Muslim history. Riches flowed into the empire from all over Europe, Asia, and Africa. Rulers could afford to build luxurious cities. They supported the scientists, mathematicians, and philosophers that those cities attracted. In the special atmosphere created by Islam, the scholars preserved existing knowledge and produced an enormous body of original learning.

Muslim Society

Over time, the influence of Muslims grew as the empire attracted people from a variety of lands. The many cultural traditions combined with the Arabic culture to create an international flavor. Muslim society had a sophistication matched at that time only by the Tang Empire of China. That cosmopolitan character was most evident in urban centers.

hmhsocialstudies.com
TAKING NOTES
Use the graphic organizer online to take notes on key elements of Muslim culture.

The Rise of Muslim Cities Until the construction of Baghdad, Damascus was the leading city. It was also the cultural center of Islamic learning. Other cities grew up around power centers, such as Córdoba (the Umayyad capital), Cairo (the Fatimid capital), and Jerusalem. (See the map on page 261.) Cities, which symbolized the strength of the caliphate, were very impressive.

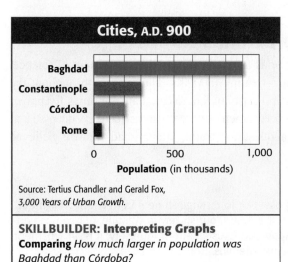

Cities, A.D. 900

Baghdad
Constantinople
Córdoba
Rome

0   500   1,000
Population (in thousands)

Source: Tertius Chandler and Gerald Fox, *3,000 Years of Urban Growth.*

SKILLBUILDER: Interpreting Graphs
Comparing *How much larger in population was Baghdad than Córdoba?*

The Abbasid capital city, Baghdad, impressed all who saw it. Caliph al-Mansur chose the site for his capital on the west bank of the Tigris River in 762. Extensive planning went into the city's distinctive circular design, formed by three circular protective walls. The caliph's palace of marble and stone sat in the innermost circle, along with the grand mosque. Originally, the main streets between the middle wall and

▲ In a miniature painting from Persia, women are shown having a picnic in a garden. Gardens were seen as earthly representations of paradise.

the palace were lined with shops. Later, the marketplace moved to a district outside the walls. Baghdad's population approached one million at its peak.

Four Social Classes Baghdad's population, made up of different cultures and social classes, was typical for a large Muslim city in the eighth and ninth centuries. Muslim society was made up of four classes. The upper class included those who were Muslims at birth. Converts to Islam were in the second class. The third class consisted of the "protected people" and included Christians, Jews, and Zoroastrians. The lowest class was composed of slaves. Many slaves were prisoners of war, and all were non-Muslim. Slaves most frequently performed household work or fought in the military.

Role of Women The Qur'an says, "Men are the managers of the affairs of women," and "Righteous women are therefore obedient." However, the Qur'an also declares that men and women, as believers, are equal. The shari'a gave Muslim women specific legal rights concerning marriage, family, and property. Thus, Muslim women had more economic and property rights than European, Indian, and Chinese women of the same time period. Nonetheless, Muslim women were still expected to submit to men. When a husband wanted to divorce his wife, all he had to do was repeat three times, "I dismiss thee." The divorce became final in three months.

Responsibilities of Muslim women varied with the income of their husbands. The wife of a poor man would often work in the fields with her husband. Wealthier women supervised the household and its servants. They had access to education, and among them were poets and scholars. Rich or poor, women were responsible for the raising of the children. In the early days of Islam, women could also participate in public life and gain an education. However, over time, Muslim women were forced to live increasingly isolated lives. When they did go out in public, they were expected to be veiled.

Muslim Scholarship Extends Knowledge

Muslims had several practical reasons for supporting the advancement of science. Rulers wanted qualified physicians treating their ills. The faithful throughout the empire relied on mathematicians and astronomers to calculate the times for prayer and the direction of Mecca. However, their attitude also reflected a deep-seated curiosity about the world and a quest for truth. Muhammad himself believed strongly in the power of learning:

PRIMARY SOURCE Ⓐ

Acquire knowledge. It enableth its possessor to distinguish right from wrong; it lighteth the way to Heaven; it is our friend in the desert, our society in solitude, our companion when friendless; it guideth us to happiness; it sustaineth us in misery; it is an ornament amongst friends, and an armour against enemies.

MUHAMMAD, quoted in *The Sayings of Muhammad*

MAIN IDEA

Analyzing Primary Sources

Ⓐ According to Muhammad, what are the nine valuable results of knowledge?

Science & *Technology*

Astronomy

Muslim interest in astronomy developed from the need to fulfill three of the Five Pillars of Islam—fasting during Ramadan, performing the hajj, and praying toward Mecca. A correct lunar calendar was needed to mark religious periods such as the month of Ramadan and the month of the hajj. Studying the skies helped fix the locations of cities so that worshipers could face toward Mecca as they prayed. Extensive knowledge of the stars also helped guide Muslim traders to the many trading cities of the ancient world.

↗ **hmhsocialstudies.com**

RESEARCH WEB LINKS Go online for more on astronomy.

▲ The device shown here is called an **armillary sphere.** The man standing in the center is aligning the sphere, while the seated man records the observations. Astronomers calculated the time of day or year by aligning the rings with various stars. This helped Muslims set their religious calendar.

◀ **Muslim observatories** were great centers of learning. This scene depicts astronomers working at the observatory in Istanbul. They are using many instruments including an astrolabe like the one shown on this page.

◀ **The astrolabe** was an early scientific instrument. It had a fixed "plate" and a rotating "rete." The plate was a map of the sky and the rete simulated the daily movement of the earth in relation to the stars. Using this tool, one could calculate time, celestial events, and relative position. For Muslims, the astrolabe helped determine where they were in relation to Mecca.

These pointers on the rete represented different stars. At night, observers could look at the sky, position the pointers, and make their calculations.

This is the plate. The plate was etched with a map of the sky for a certain latitude.

This is the rete—it rotated over the plate. The rete was mostly cut away so the map beneath was visible.

Connect *to* Today

1. **Recognizing Effects** How did fulfilling religious duties lead Muslims to astronomy and a better understanding of the physical world?

   📁 See Skillbuilder Handbook, page R6.

2. **Comparing and Contrasting** Muslim astronomers developed instruments to improve their observations of the sky. We do the same thing today. Research how modern astronomers make their observations and compare their methods with early Muslim astronomers. Write two paragraphs on how their methods are similar to and different from each other.

Muhammad's emphasis on study and scholarship led to strong support of places of learning by Muslim leaders. After the fall of Rome in A.D. 476, Europe entered a period of upheaval and chaos, an era in which scholarship suffered. The scientific knowledge gained up to that time might have been lost. However, Muslim leaders and scholars preserved and expanded much of that knowledge. Both Umayyads and Abbasids encouraged scholars to collect and translate scientific and philosophical texts. In the early 800s, Caliph al-Ma'mun opened in Baghdad a combination library, academy, and translation center called the **House of Wisdom**. There, scholars of different cultures and beliefs worked side by side translating texts from Greece, India, Persia, and elsewhere into Arabic.

Art and Sciences Flourish

Scholars at the House of Wisdom included researchers, editors, linguists, and technical advisers. These scholars developed standards and techniques for research that are a part of the basic methods of today's research. Some Muslim scholars used Greek ideas in fresh new ways. Others created original work of the highest quality. In these ways, Muslims in the Abbasid lands, especially in Córdoba and Baghdad, set the stage for a later revival of European learning.

Muslim Literature Literature had been a strong tradition in Arabia even before Islam. Bedouin poets, reflecting the spirit of desert life, composed poems celebrating ideals such as bravery, love, generosity, and hospitality. Those themes continued to appear in poetry written after the rise of Islam.

The Qur'an is the standard for all Arabic literature and poetry. Early Muslim poets sang the praises of Muhammad and of Islam and, later, of the caliphs and other patrons who supported them. During the age of the Abbasid caliphate, literary tastes expanded to include poems about nature and the pleasures of life and love.

Popular literature included *The Thousand and One Nights,* a collection of fairy tales, parables, and legends. The core of the collection has been linked to India and Persia, but peoples of the Muslim Empire added stories and arranged them, beginning around the tenth century.

Muslim Art and Architecture As the Muslim Empire expanded, the Arabs entered regions that had rich artistic traditions. Muslims continued these traditions but often adapted them to suit Islamic beliefs and practices. For example, since Muslims believed that only Allah can create life, images of living beings were discouraged. Thus, many artists turned to **calligraphy**, or the art of beautiful handwriting. Others expressed themselves through the decorative arts, such as woodwork, glass, ceramics, and textiles.

It is in architecture that the greatest cultural blending of the Muslim world can be seen. To some extent, a building reflected the culture of people of the area. For example, the Great Mosque of Damascus was built on the site of a Christian church. In many ways, the huge dome and vaulted ceiling of the mosque blended Byzantine architecture with Muslim ideas. In Syrian areas, the architecture included features that were very Roman, including baths using Roman heating systems. In Córdoba, the Great

Global Impact

The Thousand and One Nights

The Thousand and One Nights is a collection of stories tied together using a frame story. The frame story tells of King Shahryar, who marries a new wife each day and has her killed the next. When Scheherezade marries the king, however, she tells him fascinating tales for a thousand and one nights, until the king realizes that he loves her.

The tradition of using a frame story dates back to at least 200 B.C., when the ancient Indian fables of the *Panchatantra* were collected. Italian writer Giovanni Boccaccio also set his great work, *The Decameron,* within a frame story in 1335.

Muslim Art

Muslim art is intricate and colorful but often does not contain images of living beings. Muslim leaders feared that people might worship the images rather than Allah. Thus, Muslim artists found different ways to express their creativity, as shown on this page.

◄ **Calligraphy**

Calligraphy, or ornamental writing, is important to Muslims because it is considered a way to reflect the glory of Allah. In pictorial calligraphy, pictures are formed using the letters of the alphabet. This picture of a man praying is made up of the words of the Muslim declaration of faith.

◄ **Geometric Patterns**

Muslim artwork sometimes focuses on strictly geometric patterns. Geometric designs can be found in everything from pottery to architecture. This mosaic is from the Jami Masjid Mosque in India (shown below) and uses intricate patterns radiating out from the central shape.

▲ **Arabesque**

Arabesque decoration is a complex, ornate design. It usually incorporates flowers, leaves, and geometric patterns. These arabesque tiles are from the Jami Masjid Mosque. Arabesque designs are also found in Muslim mosaics, textiles, and sculptures.

SKILLBUILDER: Interpreting Visual Sources
Drawing Conclusions *What do these three artistic techniques suggest about Muslim art?*

This interior view of the Great Mosque of Córdoba showed a new architectural style. Two tiers of arches support the ceiling.

Mosque used two levels of arches in a style unknown before. The style was based on principles used in earlier mosques. These blended styles appeared in all the lands occupied by the Muslims.

Medical Advances Muslim contributions in the sciences were most recognizable in medicine, mathematics, and astronomy. A Persian scholar named al-Razi (Rhazes, according to the European pronunciation) was the greatest physician of the Muslim world and, more than likely, of world civilization between A.D. 500 and 1500. He wrote an encyclopedia called the *Comprehensive Book* that drew on knowledge from Greek, Syrian, Arabic, and Indian sources as well as on his own experience. Al-Razi also wrote *Treatise on Smallpox and Measles,* which was translated into several languages. He believed patients would recover more quickly if they breathed cleaner air.

Math and Science Stretch Horizons Among the ideas that Muslim scholars introduced to modern math and science, two especially stand out. They are the reliance on scientific observation and experimentation, and the ability to find mathematical solutions to old problems. As for science, Muslims translated and studied Greek texts. But they did not follow the Greek method of solving problems. Aristotle, Pythagoras, and other Greek thinkers preferred logical reasoning over uncovering facts through observation. Muslim scientists preferred to solve problems by conducting experiments in laboratory settings.

Muslim scholars believed that mathematics was the basis of all knowledge. Al-Khwarizmi, a mathematician born in Baghdad in the late 700s, studied Indian rather than Greek sources. He wrote a textbook in the 800s explaining "the art of bringing together unknowns to match a known quantity." He called this technique *al-jabr*—today called algebra.

Many of the advances in mathematics were related to the study of astronomy. Muslim observatories charted stars, comets, and planets. Ibn al-Haytham (Alhazen), a brilliant mathematician, produced a book called *Optics* that revolutionized ideas about vision. He showed that people see objects because rays pass from the objects to the eyes, not from the eyes to the objects as was commonly believed. His studies about optics were used in developing lenses for telescopes and microscopes.

Philosophy and Religion Blend Views

In addition to scientific works, scholars at the House of Wisdom in Baghdad translated works of Greek philosophers like Aristotle and Plato into Arabic. In the 1100s, Muslim philosopher Ibn Rushd (also known as Averroës), who lived in

Córdoba, was criticized for trying to blend Aristotle's and Plato's views with those of Islam. However, Ibn Rushd argued that Greek philosophy and Islam both had the same goal: to find the truth.

Moses Ben Maimon (Maimonides), a Jewish physician and philosopher, was born in Córdoba and lived in Egypt. Like Ibn Rushd, he faced strong opposition for his ideas, but he came to be recognized as the greatest Jewish philosopher in history. Writing during the same time as Ibn Rushd, Maimonides produced a book, *The Guide for the Perplexed*, that blended philosophy, religion, and science.

The "Ideal Man" The values of many cultures were recognized by the Muslims. A ninth-century Muslim philosophical society showed that it recognized the empire's diverse nature when it described its "ideal man":

PRIMARY SOURCE

The ideal and morally perfect man should be of East Persian derivation, Arabic in faith, of Iraqi education, a Hebrew in astuteness, a disciple of Christ in conduct, as pious as a Greek monk, a Greek in the individual sciences, an Indian in the interpretation of all mysteries, but lastly and especially a Sufi in his whole spiritual life.

IKHWAN AS-SAFA, quoted in *The World of Islam*

MAIN IDEA

Drawing Conclusions

B What is the advantage of blending various traditions within a culture?

Though the unified Muslim state broke up, Muslim culture continued. Three Muslim empires—the Ottoman, the Safavid, and the Mughal—would emerge that would reflect the blended nature of the culture of this time. The knowledge developed and preserved by the Muslim scholars would be drawn upon by European scholars in the Renaissance, beginning in the 14th century. **B**

History Makers

Ibn Rushd
1126–1198

Today Ibn Rushd is considered by many to be the most important of all Muslim philosophers. Yet his views were so offensive to Islamic conservatives that he was once stoned in the Great Mosque of Córdoba. In 1184, the philosopher began serving as physician to Caliph al-Mansur in Marrakech. Under pressure by conservatives, however, the caliph accused Ibn Rushd of heresy and ordered some of his books to be burned.

Fortunately, all of his work was not lost. Ibn Rushd's writings had a great impact on Europe in the 13th century and played a major role in the revival of Christian scholarship. In the 16th century, Italian painter Raphael placed Ibn Rushd among the ancient Greek philosophers in *School of Athens*.

↗ **hmhsocialstudies.com**

RESEARCH WEB LINKS Go online for more on Ibn Rushd.

SECTION **3** **ASSESSMENT**

TERMS & NAMES **1.** For each term or name, write a sentence explaining its significance.
• House of Wisdom   • calligraphy

USING YOUR NOTES

2. Which of these elements most strengthened the Abbasid rule? Explain.

Science and Math   City Life

Muslim Culture

Society   Arts and Literature

MAIN IDEAS

3. What was the role of women in Muslim society?

4. How did Muslim scholars help preserve the knowledge of the ancient Greeks and Romans?

5. What were some of the Muslim contributions in medicine, mathematics, and astronomy?

CRITICAL THINKING & WRITING

6. EVALUATING What do you consider to be the five most significant developments in scholarship and the arts during the reign of the Abbasids?

7. MAKING INFERENCES What united the scholars of different cultures who worked in the House of Wisdom?

8. SYNTHESIZING What role did cities play in the advancement of Muslim culture?

9. WRITING ACTIVITY CULTURAL INTERACTION Write a one-paragraph **analysis** explaining how the primary source quotation on this page reflects the Muslim Empire's diversity.

CONNECT TO TODAY CREATING A POSTER

Research to find out how the discoveries of Muslim physician al-Razi have influenced medicine today. Present your findings in a **poster**.

Chapter **10** Assessment

TERMS & NAMES

For each term or name below, briefly explain its connection to the Muslim world between 600 and 1250.

1. Allah
2. Muhammad
3. Islam
4. Hijrah
5. hajj
6. Shi'a
7. Sufi
8. House of Wisdom

MAIN IDEAS

The Rise of Islam Section 1 (pages 263–268)

9. Describe the religious environment into which Muhammad was born.

10. Why did many people in Mecca reject Muhammad's ideas at first?

11. How did early Muslims view and treat Jews and Christians?

Islam Expands Section 2 (pages 269–272)

12. Why were the "rightly guided" caliphs so successful in spreading Islam?

13. What were the main reasons for the split between the Sunni and the Shi'a?

14. Why did trade flourish under the Abbasids?

Muslim Culture Section 3 (pages 273–279)

15. How was Muslim society structured?

16. What were some of the practical reasons Muslims had for supporting the advancement of science?

17. In which fields of learning did Muslims excel?

18. How did the art and architecture of the Muslims reflect cultural blending?

CRITICAL THINKING

1. USING YOUR NOTES

In a time line, list the five most important events in the development and expansion of Islam between 550 and 1250.

2. SYNTHESIZING

CULTURAL INTERACTION How did the development of Islam influence the blending of cultures in the region where Europe, Africa, and Asia come together?

3. MAKING INFERENCES

RELIGIOUS AND ETHICAL SYSTEMS In what ways did the religious duties of Islam affect the everyday lives of Muslims?

4. SUMMARIZING

EMPIRE BUILDING How did the Abbasids keep the affairs of their empire under control?

5. DEVELOPING HISTORICAL PERSPECTIVE

What rebirth of learning in Europe was influenced by Muhammad's encouragement of the pursuit of knowledge?

VISUAL SUMMARY

The Muslim World

ISLAM

Empire Building

Four major Muslim caliphates build empires on parts of three continents.

- 661–750: Umayyad caliphate
- 750–1258: Abbasid caliphate
- 756–976: Umayyads of al-Andalus (Spain)
- 909–1171: Fatimid caliphate (North Africa, Egypt, Western Arabia, and Syria)

Culture

Muslim scholars preserve, blend, and expand knowledge, especially in mathematics, astronomy, architecture, and medical science.

Religion

- Muhammad receives revelations from Allah.
- The Five Pillars of Islam are Muslims' basic religious duties.
- The sources of authority— the Qur'an and the Sunna— guide daily life.
- Islam divides into several branches, including Sunni and Shi'a.

Use the quotation and your knowledge of world history to answer questions 1 and 2.

PRIMARY SOURCE

One should read histories, study biographies and the experiences of nations. By doing this, it will be as though, in his short life space, he lived contemporaneously with peoples of the past, was on intimate terms with them, and knew the good and the bad among them. . . . You should model your conduct on that of the early Muslims. Therefore, read the biography of the Prophet, study his deeds and concerns, follow in his footsteps, and try your utmost to imitate him.

ABD AL-LATIF quoted in *A History of the Arab Peoples*

1. Why does al-Latif advocate studying history?

 A. because history repeats itself

 B. because history provides insight into the lives of past peoples

 C. because studying history is a good intellectual exercise

 D. because studying history is required of all Muslims

2. Why does he want people to study the life of Muhammad?

 A. because Muhammad is a great historical figure

 B. because Muslim law requires it

 C. to learn to be like Muhammad

 D. to learn about cultural blending

Use the chart and your knowledge of world history to answer question 3.

Muslim Population, 2005

Country	Population	% of Total Population
India	155,115,142	13.7
Pakistan	151,467,325	95.8
Bangladesh	135,690,886	88.5
Indonesia	127,091,000	56.2
Turkey	71,054,050	97.4
Iran	68,227,726	98.3
Nigeria	62,390,860	44.1
Egypt	61,769,113	84.8
Algeria	32,198,881	98.0
Morocco	29,991,256	98.8
Iraq	27,187,493	97.1
Ethiopia	26,732,010	33.8

Source: *The World Almanac and Book of Facts, 2009*

3. In which nations do Muslims account for the highest percentage of the total population?

 A. India and Pakistan

 B. Pakistan and Bangladesh

 C. Indonesia and India

 D. Morocco and Iran

 hmhsocialstudies.com **TEST PRACTICE**

For additional test practice, go online for:

• Diagnostic tests

• Strategies

• Tutorials

Interact *with* History

In this chapter, you learned that a culture blooms by spreading ideas through trade, war and conquest, and through scholarly exchange. With a partner, make a list of at least five ways to spread an idea in today's world—ways that were not available to Muslims in A.D. 600–1250.

FOCUS ON WRITING

Imagine that your are a newspaper reporter investigating the newly opened House of Wisdom. Write a brief **newspaper article** about the new center in Baghdad and the work being undertaken there. In the article, be sure to

• describe the center and the scholars who work there

• include quotations from the scholars

• summarize some of the center's accomplishments and goals

MULTIMEDIA ACTIVITY

21ST CENTURY

Creating a Multimedia Presentation

Use the Internet, books, and other reference sources to create a multimedia presentation on the rise, growth, and culture of Islam. Write brief summaries on each topic. Use maps, pictures, and quotations to accompany your text and illustrate and enhance your presentation. Be sure to include information on the following:

• the life of Muhammad

• a time line of major events in the development of Islam

• the key beliefs and practices of Islam

• the impact of the Muslim Empire on other cultures

• the impact of Muslim learning in science and the arts

A Global View

Religion is defined as an organized system of beliefs, ceremonies, practices, and worship that centers on one or more gods. As many chapters in this book explain, religion has had a significant impact on world history. Throughout the centuries, religion has guided the beliefs and actions of millions around the globe. It has brought people together. But it has also torn them apart.

Religion continues to be a dominant force throughout the world, affecting everything from what people wear to how they behave. There are thousands of religions in the world. The following pages concentrate on five major religions and on Confucianism, an ethical system. They examine some of the characteristics and rituals that make these religions and systems similar as well as unique. They also present some of each religion's sects and denominations.

North America

2%
2%
12%
84%

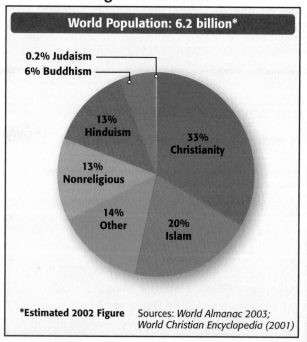

World Population's Religious Affiliations

World Population: 6.2 billion*

0.2% Judaism
6% Buddhism

13% Hinduism

33% Christianity

13% Nonreligious

14% Other

20% Islam

*Estimated 2002 Figure   Sources: *World Almanac 2003; World Christian Encyclopedia (2001)*

Latin America

3%
9%
88%

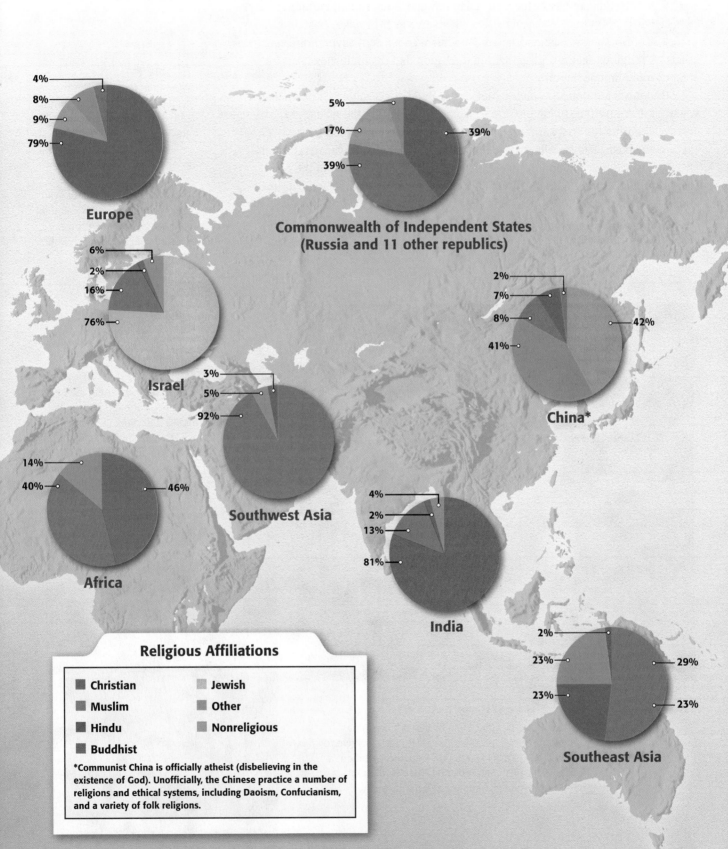

Europe
4%
8%
9%
79%

**Commonwealth of Independent States
(Russia and 11 other republics)**
5%
17%
39%
39%

Israel
6%
2%
16%
76%

China*
2%
7%
8%
41%
42%

Southwest Asia
3%
5%
92%

Africa
14%
40%
46%

India
4%
2%
13%
81%

Southeast Asia
2%
23%
23%
23%
29%

Religious Affiliations

- Christian
- Muslim
- Hindu
- Buddhist
- Jewish
- Other
- Nonreligious

*Communist China is officially atheist (disbelieving in the existence of God). Unofficially, the Chinese practice a number of religions and ethical systems, including Daoism, Confucianism, and a variety of folk religions.

Buddhism

Buddhism has influenced Asian religion, society, and culture for over 2,500 years. Today, most Buddhists live in Sri Lanka, East and Southeast Asia, and Japan. Buddhism consists of several different sects. A religious sect is a group within a religion that distinguishes itself by one or more unique beliefs.

Buddhists are united in their belief in the Buddha's teachings, known as the dharma. Because the Buddha is said to have "set in motion the wheel of the dharma" during his first sermon, his teaching is often symbolized by a wheel, as shown above. The Buddha taught that the key to happiness was detachment from all worldly goods and desires. This was achieved by following the Noble Eightfold Path, or the Middle Way, a life between earthly desires and extreme forms of self-denial.

 hmhsocialstudies.com

RESEARCH WEB LINKS Go online for more on Buddhism.

Ritual ►

Women in Rangoon, Myanmar, sweep the ground so that monks can avoid stepping on and killing any insects. Many Buddhists believe in rebirth, the idea that living beings, after death, are reborn and continue to exist. Buddhists believe that all living beings possess the potential for spiritual growth—and the possibility of rebirth as humans.

▼ Leadership

Those who dedicate their entire life to the teachings of the Buddha are known as Buddhist monks and nuns. In many Buddhist sects, monks are expected to lead a life of poverty, meditation, and study. Here, Buddhist monks file past shrines in Thailand. To learn humility, monks must beg for food and money.

▲ Worship Practices

Statues of the Buddha, such as this one in China, appear in shrines throughout Asia. Buddhists strive to follow the Buddha's teachings through meditation, a form of religious contemplation. They also make offerings at shrines, temples, and monasteries.

Learn More About Buddhism

Major Buddhist Sects

Theravada   Mahayana

Buddhism

Mantrayana

The Three Cardinal Faults

This image depicts what Buddhists consider the three cardinal faults of humanity: greed (the pig); hatred (the snake); and delusion (the rooster).

Dhammapada

PRIMARY SOURCE

One of the most well-known Buddhist scriptures is the *Dhammapada,* or *Verses of Righteousness.* The book is a collection of sayings on Buddhist practices. In this verse, Buddhists are instructed to avoid envying others:

> *Let him not despise what he has received, nor should he live envying the gains of others. The disciple who envies the gains of others does not attain concentration.*

Dhammapada 365

Chapter Connection

For a more in-depth examination of Buddhism, see pages 68–71 of Chapter 3, and page 193 of Chapter 7.

Christianity

Christianity is the largest religion in the world, with about 2 billion followers. It is based on the life and teachings of Jesus, whom Christians call Christ, or savior. Most Christians are members of one of three major groups: Roman Catholic, Protestant, or Eastern Orthodox. Christianity teaches the existence of only one God. Christians regard Jesus as the son of God. They believe that Jesus entered the world and died to save humanity from sin. The cross shown above, a symbol of the crucifixion of Jesus, represents Jesus' love for humanity by dying for its sins. Christians believe that they reach salvation by following the teachings of Jesus.

↗ hmhsocialstudies.com

RESEARCH WEB LINKS Go online for more on Christianity.

Ritual ▶

Each year, hundreds of thousands of Christians from all over the world visit the Basilica of Guadalupe in northern Mexico City. The church is considered the holiest in Mexico. It is near the site where Mary, the mother of Jesus, is said to have appeared twice in 1531. Out of deep respect for Mary, some pilgrims approach the holy cathedral on their knees.

Worship Practices ▶

Worshiping as a group is an important part of Christian life. Most Protestant services include praying, singing, and a sermon. Some services include baptism and communion, in which bread and wine are consumed in remembrance of Jesus' death.

Communion celebrates the last meal Jesus took with his disciples, as illustrated here in *The Last Supper* by Leonardo da Vinci.

▲ Leadership

In some Christian churches, the person who performs services in the local church is known as a priest. Shown here is a priest of the Ethiopian Orthodox Church. These priests, like the ministers and clergy in other Christian sects, conduct worship services and preside over marriages and funerals. Monks and nuns also provide leadership and guidance in the Christian church.

Learn More About Christianity

Major Christian Sects

Eastern Orthodox   Roman Catholic

Christianity

AME**   Protestant*   Baptist
Lutheran   Methodist
Episcopal   Pentecostal
Congregationalist   Church of God
Presbyterian

*In the United States alone, there are 30 Protestant denominations with over 400,000 members in each.
**African Methodist Episcopal

Fish Symbol

The fish is an early symbol of Christianity. There are many theories about the origin of the symbol, but some Christians believe that it derives from the fact that Jesus called his disciples, or followers, "fishers of men."

The Christian Bible

PRIMARY SOURCE

The Bible is the most sacred book of the Christian religion. It is divided into two major parts: the Old Testament, which is much the same as the Hebrew Bible, and the New Testament, which describes the teachings of Jesus. The following verses from the New Testament reveal the fundamental teaching about Jesus:

"Men, what must I do to be saved?" And they said, "Believe in the Lord Jesus, and you will be saved, you and your household."

Acts 16:30–31

Chapter Connection

For more about Christianity, see pages 168–172 of Chapter 6. To learn about the Protestant and Catholic Reformations, see sections 3 and 4 of Chapter 17.

Hinduism

Hinduism, one of the world's oldest surviving religions, is the major religion of India. It also has followers in Indonesia, as well as in parts of Africa, Europe, and the Western Hemisphere. Hinduism is a collection of religious beliefs that developed over thousands of years. Hindus worship several gods, which represent different forms of Brahman. Brahman is the most divine spirit in the Hindu religion. Hinduism, like Buddhism, stresses that persons reach true enlightenment and happiness only after they free themselves from their earthly desires. Followers of Hinduism achieve this goal through worship, the attainment of knowledge, and a lifetime of virtuous acts. The sound "Om," or "Aum," shown above, is the most sacred syllable for Hindus. It often is used in prayers.

�

hmhsocialstudies.com

RESEARCH WEB LINKS Go online for more on Hinduism.

▼ Ritual

Each year, thousands of Hindus make a pilgrimage to India's Ganges River. The Ganges is considered a sacred site in the Hindu religion. Most Hindus come to bathe in the water, an act they believe will cleanse and purify them. The sick and disabled come in the belief that the holy water might cure their ailments.

▲ Leadership

Gurus, or spiritual teachers, play a major role in spreading Hindu beliefs. These holy men are believed to have had the gods' words revealed to them. Brahmin priests, like the one shown here, are also religious leaders. They take care of the divine images in the temples and read from the sacred books.

▲ Celebration

Each spring, Hindus in India celebrate the festival of Holi. Originally a harvest festival, Holi also symbolizes the triumph of good over evil. The festival recalls the story of Prince Prahlada, who faced death rather than cease worshiping Vishnu. During this joyous celebration, people dance in the streets and shower each other with colored powder and dyed water.

Learn More About Hinduism

Major Hindu Sects

Shaktism   Reform Hinduism

Hinduism

Vaishnavites   Shaivites

Three Main Gods

This statue represents Brahma, creator of the universe. Brahma, Vishnu, and Shiva are the three main gods of Hinduism. Vishnu is the preserver of the universe, while Shiva is its destroyer.

Rig Veda

PRIMARY SOURCE

The Vedas are the oldest Hindu scriptures—and they are older than the sacred writings of any other major religion. The following is a verse from the Rig Veda, the oldest of the four Vedas:

He who gives liberally goes straight to the gods; on the high ridge of heaven he stands exalted.

Rig Veda 1.125.5

Chapter Connection

For a closer look at the origins and beliefs of Hinduism, see pages 66–67 of Chapter 3, and pages 193–194 of Chapter 7.

Islam

Islam is a religion based on the teachings of Muhammad, revered by his followers as the Prophet. Followers of Islam, known as Muslims, believe that God revealed these teachings to Muhammad through the angel Gabriel. Muslims are concentrated from southwest to central Asia and parts of Africa. Islam also has many followers in Southeast Asia. Sunni Muslims believe that their leaders should follow Muhammad's example. Shi'a Muslims believe that their leaders should be Muhammad's descendants.

Islam teaches the existence of only one God, called Allah in the Arabic language. Muslims believe in all prophets of Judaism and Christianity. They show their devotion by performing lifelong acts of worship known as the Five Pillars of Islam. These include faith, prayer, almsgiving (charity), fasting, and a pilgrimage to Mecca. The crescent moon (shown above) has become a familiar symbol for Islam. It may be related to the new moon that begins each month in the Islamic lunar calendar, which orders religious life for Muslims. The five points of the star may represent the Five Pillars of Islam.

⬈ hmhsocialstudies.com

RESEARCH WEB LINKS Go online for more on Islam.

▼ Ritual

At least once in their lifetime, all Muslims who are physically and financially able go on hajj, or pilgrimage, to the holy city of Mecca in Saudi Arabia. There, pilgrims perform several rites, or acts of worship. One rite, shown here, is walking seven times around the Ka'aba—the house of worship that Muslims face in prayer.

▲ Celebration

During the sacred month known as Ramadan, Muslims fast, or abstain from food and drink, from dawn to sunset. The family shown here is ending their fast. The most important night of Ramadan is called the Night of Power. This is believed to be the night the angel Gabriel first spoke to Muhammad.

▲ Worship Practices

Five times a day Muslims throughout the world face Mecca and pray to Allah. Pictured here are Muslims praying at a mosque in Turkey.

There are no priests or other clergy in Islam. However, a Muslim community leader known as the imam conducts the prayers in a mosque. Islam also has a scholar class called the ulama, which includes religious teachers.

Learn More About Islam

Major Islamic Sects

Sunni

⬆

Islam

⬇

Shi'a

Prayer Rug

Muslims often pray by kneeling on a rug. The design of the rug includes a pointed or arch-shaped pattern. The rug must be placed so that the arch points toward Mecca.

The Qur'an

PRIMARY SOURCE

The Qur'an, the sacred book of Muslims, consists of verses grouped into 114 chapters, or suras. The book is the spiritual guide on matters of Muslim faith. It also contains teachings for Muslim daily life. In the following verse, Muslims are instructed to appreciate the world's physical and spiritual riches:

> Do you not see that God has subjected to your use all things in the heavens and on earth, and has made His bounties flow to you in exceeding measure, both seen and unseen?

Qur'an, sura 31:20

Chapter Connection

For a closer look at Islam, including the rise and spread of Islam and Muslim culture, see Chapter 10.

Judaism

Judaism is the religion of the more than 14 million Jews throughout the world. Judaism was the first major religion to teach the existence of only one God. The basic laws and teachings of Judaism come from the Torah, the first five books of the Hebrew Bible. Judaism teaches that a person serves God by studying the Torah and living by its teachings. Orthodox Jews closely observe the laws of the Torah. Conservative and Reform Jews interpret the Torah less strictly and literally. The Star of David (shown above), also called the Shield of David, is the universal symbol of Judaism. The emblem refers to King David, who ruled the kingdom of Israel from about 1000–962 B.C.

↗ hmhsocialstudies.com

RESEARCH WEB LINKS Go online for more on Judaism.

Ritual ►

Major events in a Jew's life are marked by special rites and ceremonies. When Jewish children reach the age of 12 (girls) or 13 (boys), for example, they enter the adult religious community. The event is marked in the synagogue with a ceremony called a bar mitzvah for a boy and a bat mitzvah for a girl, shown here.

▲ Worship Practices

The synagogue is the Jewish house of worship and the center of Jewish community life. Services in the synagogue are usually conducted by a rabbi, the congregation's teacher and spiritual leader. Many Jews make the pilgrimage to the Western Wall, shown here. The sacred structure, built in the second century B.C., formed the western wall of the courtyard of the Second Temple of Jerusalem. The Romans destroyed the Temple in A.D. 70.

▼ Celebration

Jews celebrate a number of holidays that honor their history as well as God. Pictured here are Jews celebrating the holiday of Purim. Purim is a festival honoring the survival of the Jews who, in the fifth century B.C., were marked for death by their Persian rulers.

Jews celebrate Purim by sending food and gifts. They also dress in costumes and hold carnivals and dances.

Learn More About Judaism

Major Jewish Sects

Reform   Orthodox

Judaism

Conservative

Yarmulke

Out of respect for God, Jewish men are not supposed to leave their head uncovered. Therefore, many Orthodox and Conservative Jews wear a skullcap known as a yarmulke, or kippah.

The Torah

PRIMARY SOURCE

During a synagogue service, the Torah scroll is lifted, while the congregation declares: "This is the Law which Moses set before the children of Israel." The following verse from the Torah makes clear Moses's law regarding belief in one God:

Hear O Israel: the Lord our God, the Lord is One.

Deuteronomy 6:4

Chapter Connection

For a historical examination of Judaism, as well as the development of the Kingdom of Israel, see pages 77–82 of Chapter 3.

Confucianism

With no clergy and with no gods to worship, Confucianism is not a religion in the traditional sense. Rather, it is an ethical system that provides direction for personal behavior and good government. However, this ancient philosophy guides the actions and beliefs of millions of Chinese and other peoples of the East. Thus, many view it as a religion.

Confucianism is a way of life based on the teachings of the Chinese scholar Confucius. It stresses social and civic responsibility. Over the centuries, however, Confucianism has greatly influenced people's spiritual beliefs as well. While East Asians declare themselves to follow any one of a number of religions, many also claim to be Confucian. The yin and yang symbol shown above represents opposite forces in the world working together. It symbolizes the social order and harmony that Confucianism stresses.

↗ hmhsocialstudies.com

RESEARCH WEB LINKS Go online for more on Confucianism.

▼ Celebration

While scholars remain uncertain of Confucius's date of birth, people throughout East Asia celebrate it on September 28. In Taiwan, it is an official holiday, known as Teachers' Day. The holiday also pays tribute to teachers. Confucius himself was a teacher, and he believed that education was an important part of a fulfilled life. Here, dancers take part in a ceremony honoring Confucius.

Leadership ►

Confucius was born at a time of crisis and violence in China. He hoped his ideas and teachings would restore the order of earlier times to his society. But although he was active in politics, he never had enough political power to put his ideas into practice. Nonetheless, his ideas would become the foundation of Chinese thought for more than 2,000 years.

▲ Ritual

A key aspect of Confucianism is filial piety, the respect children owe their parents. Traditionally, filial piety meant complete obedience to one's parents during their lifetime. It also required the performance of certain rituals after their death. In this 12th-century Chinese painting, a sage instructs a pupil on the virtue of filial piety.

The Five Relationships

Confucius believed society should be organized around five basic relationships between the following:

1. ruler ⟷ subject
2. father ⟷ son
3. husband ⟷ wife
4. older brother ⟷ younger brother
5. friend ⟷ friend

Confucius's Golden Rule

"Do not do unto others what you would not want others to do unto you."

The *Analects*

PRIMARY SOURCE

The earliest and most authentic record of Confucius's ideas was collected by his students. Around 400 B.C., they compiled Confucius's thoughts in a book called the *Analects*. In the following selections from the *Analects*, Confucius (the Master) gives advice regarding virtue and pride:

> *The Master said: "Don't worry if people don't recognize your merits; worry that you may not recognize theirs."*

Analects 1.16

> *The Master said: "Do not be concerned that others do not recognize you; be concerned about what you are yet unable to do."*

Analects 14.30

Chapter Connection
For a closer look at the life and teachings of Confucius, see pages 104–105 of Chapter 4.

World Religions *and* Ethical Systems

	Buddhism	Christianity	Hinduism	Islam	Judaism	Confucianism
Followers Worldwide (estimated 2005 figures)	379 million	2.1 billion	860 million	1.3 billion	15.1 million	6.5 million
Name of Deity	no god	God	Brahman	Allah	God	no god
Founder	The Buddha	Jesus	No one founder	Muhammad	Abraham, Moses	Confucius
Holy Book	Many sacred texts, including the *Dhammapada*	Christian Bible	Many sacred texts, including the Upanishads	Qur'an	Hebrew Bible, including the Torah	the *Analects*, the Five Classics
Leadership	Buddhist monks and nuns	Priests, ministers, monks, and nuns	Brahmin priests, monks, and gurus	No clergy but a scholar class called the ulama, and the imams, who may lead prayers	Rabbis	No clergy
Basic Beliefs	• Persons achieve complete peace and happiness (nirvana) by eliminating their attachment to worldly things. • Nirvana is reached by following the Noble Eightfold Path: Right views; Right resolve; Right speech; Right conduct; Right livelihood; Right effort; Right mindfulness; Right concentration.	• There is only one God, who watches over and cares for his people. • Jesus is the Christ, the son of God. He died to save humanity from sin. His death and resurrection made eternal life possible for others.	• The soul never dies, but is continually reborn. • Persons achieve happiness and enlightenment after they free themselves from their earthly desires. • Freedom from earthly desires comes from a life-time of worship, knowledge, and virtuous acts.	• Persons achieve salvation by following the Five Pillars of Islam and living a just life. These pillars are: faith; prayer; almsgiving, or charity to the poor; fasting, which Muslims perform during Ramadan; pilgrimage to Mecca.	• There is only one God, who watches over and cares for all people. • God loves and protects his people, but also holds people accountable for their sins and shortcomings. • Persons serve God by studying the Torah and living by its teachings.	• Social order, harmony, and good government should be based on strong family relationships. • Respect for parents and elders is important to a well-ordered society. • Education is important both to the welfare of the individual and to society.

Assessment

MAIN IDEAS

Buddhism (pages 284–285)

1. According to the Buddha, how does one achieve happiness and fulfillment?

2. Why do Buddhists take special care to avoid killing any living being?

Christianity (pages 286–287)

3. Why is Jesus central to the Christian religion?

4. What do Christians hope to achieve by following the teachings of Jesus?

Hinduism (pages 288–289)

5. What is the importance of the Ganges River in Hinduism?

6. Who are the three main gods of Hinduism?

Islam (pages 290–291)

7. What is the most important night of Ramadan? Why?

8. What are the Five Pillars of Islam?

Judaism (pages 292–293)

9. Why do Jews consider the Western Wall to be sacred?

10. In the Jewish tradition, how do people serve God?

Confucianism (pages 294–295)

11. Around what five relationships did Confucius believe society should be organized?

12. According to tradition, what does filial piety require of children?

CRITICAL THINKING

1. SYNTHESIZING

What basic principles do all of the religions have in common?

2. DRAWING CONCLUSIONS

What role does religion play in people's everyday lives?

3. MAKING INFERENCES

Why do you think ritual and celebrations are an important part of all religions?

4. FORMING OPINIONS

What do you think people hope to gain from their religion?

STANDARDS-BASED ASSESSMENT

Use the quotation and your knowledge of world history to answer questions 1 and 2.

PRIMARY SOURCE

Human beings are spiritual animals. Indeed, there is a case for arguing that *Homo sapiens* is also *Homo religiosus*. Men and women started to worship gods as soon as they became recognizably human; they created religions at the same time they created works of art. . . . These early faiths expressed the wonder and mystery that seem always to have been an essential component of the human experience of this beautiful yet terrifying world. Like art, religion has been an attempt to find meaning and value in life, despite the suffering that flesh is heir to.

KAREN ARMSTRONG, *A History of God*

1. With which of the following opinions would Armstrong probably agree?

   A. People are naturally religious.

   B. People have no need of religion.

   C. People only believe in what they can see.

   D. People created religion out of fear.

2. According to Armstrong, what is the main similarity between art and religion?

   A. They both express the suffering human beings must endure.

   B. They first appeared at around the same time.

   C. They both place value on beauty.

   D. They are both used to find life's meaning.

hmhsocialstudies.com TEST PRACTICE

For additional test practice, go online for:

- Diagnostic tests
- Tutorials
- Strategies

Interact *with* History

Imagine that you could meet one of the founders listed in the chart on page 296. What questions would you ask about his life and beliefs? What views of your own would you share? Take turns role-playing your conversation with a partner.

FOCUS ON WRITING

Research to learn more about one of the celebrations you read about in this section. Then write a three-paragraph **essay** about its origins. Discuss the celebration's history, symbolism, and meaning.

CHAPTER 11

Byzantines, Russians, and Turks Interact, 500–1500

Essential Question

What characterized the rise and interaction of Byzantine, Russian, and Turkish civilizations in Eastern Europe and Central Asia?

 What You Will Learn

In this chapter you will follow the individual achievements and shared histories of three great empires that existed on the margin between Europe and Asia.

SECTION 1 The Byzantine Empire
Main Idea After Rome split, the Eastern Empire, known as Byzantium, flourished for a thousand years.

SECTION 2 The Russian Empire
Main Idea Russia grew out of a blending of Slavic and Byzantine cultures and adopted Eastern Orthodox traditions.

SECTION 3 Turkish Empires Rise in Anatolia
Main Idea Turkish people converted to Islam and founded new empires that would renew Muslim civilization.

Previewing Themes

RELIGIOUS AND ETHICAL SYSTEMS Two world religions, Islam and Christianity, met head-to-head as Arabs and Turks battled Byzantines and then Crusaders. At the same time, disputes over doctrine split Christianity into competing branches.
Geography *What land did the Seljuk Turks occupy?*

CULTURAL INTERACTION Byzantine influence inspired the growth of a unique Russian culture. The Turks meanwhile adopted Islam and sponsored a rebirth of Persian ways to create a dynamic cultural blend.
Geography *Why might the Dnieper River have been important to Kievan Russia?*

EMPIRE BUILDING The Byzantines, Slavs, Arabs, Turks, and Mongols waged bloody wars to expand their territories. However, each empire also brought together people of diverse traditions.
Geography *How does the map indicate that there was probably conflict between the Byzantine and Seljuk empires?*

CENTRAL ASIA

527
Justinian becomes ruler of Byzantine Empire. ▶

850s
Byzantine culture spreads to Russia.

500   **700**   **900**

WORLD

690
Empress Wu Zhao assumes throne in China.

771
Charlemagne becomes ruler of Frankish Kingdom in Europe.

Three Empires: Byzantine, Russian, Seljuk, c. 1100

SCANDINAVIA

SWEDEN

Novgorod

EUROPE

Baltic Sea

ENGLAND

Volga River

Dnieper River

Don River

Ural River

ASIA

GERMANY

Kiev

FRANCE

ATLANTIC OCEAN

Venice

Danube River

Black Sea

Caspian Sea

SPAIN

Corsica

Rome

Bukhara

Toledo

Sardinia

Constantinople

Córdoba

Balearic Is.

Tigris River

Sicily

Baghdad

PERSIA

Crete

Cyprus

Euphrates River

Mediterranean Sea

Damascus

Alexandria

Jerusalem

Cairo

Persian Gulf

Indus River

EGYPT

ARABIA

INDIA

AFRICA

Medina

Nile River

Red Sea

Mecca

Byzantine Empire
Kievan Russia
Seljuk Empire

0   500   1,000 Miles

0   500   1,000 Kilometers

Winkel II Projection

HISTORY

Byzantium's Call for Help

hmhsocialstudies.com VIDEO

1240
◀ Mongols destroy Kiev. (Mongolian archer on horseback)

1453
◀ Constantinople falls to Ottoman Turks.

1100

1300

1500

1095
◀ Pope Urban II (shown addressing the bishops of France) launches the first Crusade.

1347
Bubonic plague devastates Europe.

1502
Montezuma II takes charge of the Aztec Empire in modern-day Mexico.

How will you expand your empire?

You are the new ruler of the Byzantine Empire. Through expansion, you hope to make the empire even greater. Military conquest is an option, as shown here in a painting of a Turkish invasion of India. Your diplomats might persuade other groups to join you. You also know that rulers of several countries outside your empire would like to see their sons or daughters marry into your family. Now you must consider the best way to enlarge your empire.

EXAMINING *the* ISSUES

- **What are the benefits and drawbacks of a military conquest?**

- **Why might you choose diplomacy, or intermarriage with an outside ruling family?**

As a class, discuss the various ways to expand an empire. What option or options will you choose? Explain your decision. As you read the chapter, think about how empires expand.

The Byzantine Empire

MAIN IDEA	WHY IT MATTERS NOW	TERMS & NAMES
RELIGIOUS AND ETHICAL SYSTEMS After Rome split, the Eastern Empire, known as Byzantium, flourished for a thousand years.	Byzantine culture deeply influenced Orthodox Christianity, a major branch of modern Christianity.	• Justinian • Justinian Code • Hagia Sophia • patriarch • icon • excommunication • Cyrillic alphabet

SETTING THE STAGE As you learned in Chapter 6, the Western Roman Empire crumbled in the fifth century as it was overrun by invading Germanic tribes. By this time, however, the once great empire had already undergone significant changes. It had been divided into western and eastern empires, and its capital had moved east from Rome to the Greek city of Byzantium. The city would become known as Constantinople after the emperor Constantine, who made it the new capital in A.D.-330. (Byzantium would remain as the name of the entire Eastern Empire.) For nearly a thousand years after the collapse of the Western Empire, Byzantium and its flourishing capital would carry on the glory of Rome.

A New Rome in a New Setting

Roman leaders had divided the empire in 395, largely due to difficulties in communications between the eastern and the troubled western parts of the empire. Still, rulers in the East continued to see themselves as emperors for all of Rome.

▼ A glittering cross from the 11th century, Byzantine Empire

In 527, a high-ranking Byzantine nobleman named **Justinian** succeeded his uncle to the throne of the Eastern Empire. In an effort to regain Rome's fading glory, Justinian in 533 sent his best general, Belisarius (behl•uh•SAIR•ee•uhs), to recover North Africa from the invading Germanic tribes. Belisarius and his forces quickly succeeded.

Two years later, Belisarius attacked Rome and seized it from a group known as the Ostrogoths. But the city faced repeated attacks by other Germanic tribes. Over the next 16 years, Rome changed hands six times. After numerous campaigns, Justinian's armies won nearly all of Italy and parts of Spain. Justinian now ruled almost all the territory that Rome had ever ruled. He could honestly call himself a new Caesar.

Like the last of the old Caesars, the Byzantine emperors ruled with absolute power. They headed not just the state but the church as well. They appointed and dismissed bishops at will. Their politics were brutal—and often deadly. Emperors lived under constant risk of assassination. Of the 88 Byzantine emperors, 29 died violently, and 13 abandoned the throne to live in monasteries.

hmhsocialstudies.com
TAKING NOTES
Use the graphic organizer online to take notes on Justinian's accomplishments as emperor of the New Rome.

Life in the New Rome

A separate government and difficult communications with the West gave the Byzantine Empire its own character, different from that of the Western Empire. The citizens thought of themselves as sharing in the Roman tradition, but few spoke Latin anymore. Most Byzantines spoke Greek.

Having unified the two empires, Justinian set up a panel of legal experts to regulate Byzantium's increasingly complex society. The panel combed through 400 years of Roman law. It found a number of laws that were outdated and contradictory. The panel created a single, uniform code known as the **Justinian Code**. After its completion, the code consisted of four works.

1. The *Code* contained nearly 5,000 Roman laws that were still considered useful for the Byzantine Empire.
2. The *Digest* quoted and summarized the opinions of Rome's greatest legal thinkers about the laws. This massive work ran to a total of 50 volumes.
3. The *Institutes* was a textbook that told law students how to use the laws.
4. The *Novellae* (New Laws) presented legislation passed after 534.

Vocabulary
A *code* is a general system of laws, and it stems from the Latin word *codex*, meaning "book."

The Justinian Code decided legal questions that regulated whole areas of Byzantine life. Marriage, slavery, property, inheritance, women's rights, and criminal justice were just some of those areas. Although Justinian himself died in 565, his code served the Byzantine Empire for 900 years.

Creating the Imperial Capital While his scholars were creating the legal code, Justinian launched the most ambitious public building program ever seen in the Roman world. He rebuilt the crumbling fortifications of Constantinople, as workers constructed a 14-mile stone wall along the city's coastline and repaired the massive fortifications along its western land border.

⤤ hmhsocialstudies.com
INTERACTIVE HISTORY
Explore Constantinople—a city at a crossroads.

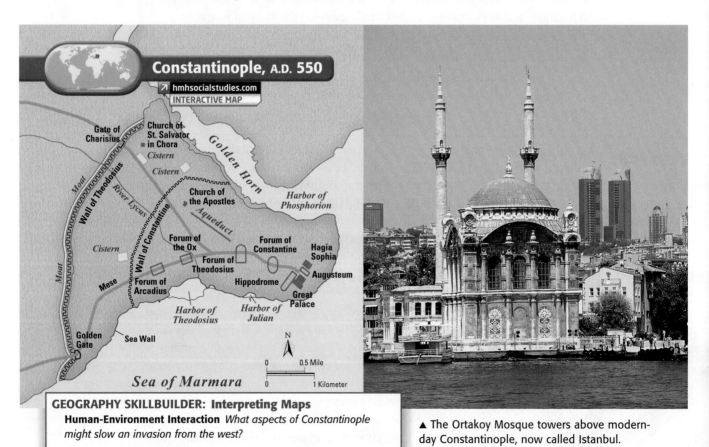

Constantinople, A.D. 550

⤤ hmhsocialstudies.com
INTERACTIVE MAP

Gate of Charisius
Church of St. Salvator in Chora
Cistern
Cistern
Golden Horn
Moat
Wall of Theodosius
River Lycus
Church of the Apostles
Harbor of Phosphorion
Aqueduct
Wall of Constantine
Forum of the Ox
Forum of Constantine
Hagia Sophia
Cistern
Forum of Theodosius
Augusteum
Moat
Mese
Forum of Arcadius
Hippodrome
Great Palace
Harbor of Theodosius
Harbor of Julian
Golden Gate
Sea Wall
Sea of Marmara

0   0.5 Mile
0   1 Kilometer

GEOGRAPHY SKILLBUILDER: Interpreting Maps
Human-Environment Interaction *What aspects of Constantinople might slow an invasion from the west?*

▲ The Ortakoy Mosque towers above modern-day Constantinople, now called Istanbul.

Church building, however, was the emperor's greatest passion. Justinian viewed churches as the most visible sign of the close connection between church and state in his empire. The crowning glory of his reign was **Hagia Sophia** (HAY•ee•uh-soh•FEE•uh), which means "Holy Wisdom" in Greek. A church of the same name had been destroyed in riots that swept Constantinople in 532. When Justinian rebuilt Hagia Sophia, many visitors hailed it as the most splendid church in the Christian world. **A**

MAIN IDEA

Analyzing Motives

A Why do you think governments so often build magnificent buildings like Hagia Sophia?

As part of his building program, Justinian enlarged his palace into a vast complex. He also built baths, aqueducts, law courts, schools, and hospitals. By the time the emperor was finished, the city teemed with an almost visible excitement.

Beneath such excitement, a less obvious but vitally important activity took place: the preservation of Greco-Roman culture. Byzantine families valued education—specifically classical learning. Basic courses for Byzantine students focused on Greek and Latin grammar, and philosophy. The classics of Greek and Roman literature served as textbooks. Students memorized Homer. They learned geometry from Euclid, history from Herodotus, and medicine from Galen. The modern world owes Byzantine scholars a huge debt for preserving many of the great works of Greece and Rome.

Constantinople's Hectic Pace The main street running through Constantinople was the Mese (MEHS•ee), or "Middle Way." Merchant stalls lined the main street and filled the side streets. Products from the most distant corners of Asia, Africa, and Europe passed through these stalls. Everywhere, food stands filled the air with the smell of their delicacies, while acrobats and street musicians performed.

Meanwhile, citizens could enjoy free entertainment at the Hippodrome, which offered wild chariot races and performance acts. The Hippodrome (from Greek words meaning "horse" and "racecourse") held 60,000 spectators. Fans of the different teams formed rowdy gangs named for the colors worn by their heroes.

In 532, two such fan groups sparked citywide riots called the Nika Rebellion (because the mob cried "Nika!" or "Victory!"). Both sides were angry with the government. They felt that city officials had been too severe in putting down a previous riot of Hippodrome fans. They packed the Hippodrome and demanded the overthrow of Justinian. Belisarius, however, broke in with his troops and slaughtered about 30,000 rebels.

Justinian had considered fleeing during the Nika Rebellion, but his wife, Theodora, urged him to stay. As her husband's steely adviser, Theodora had immense power. She rallied Justinian to remain in the capital with a fiery speech:

PRIMARY SOURCE

My opinion is that now is a poor time for flight, even though it bring safety. For any man who has seen the light of day will also die, but one who has been an emperor cannot endure to be a fugitive. If now you wish to go, Emperor, nothing prevents you. There is the sea, there are the steps to the boats. But take care that after you are safe, you do not find that you would gladly exchange that safety for death.

THEODORA, quoted by Procopius in *History of the Wars*

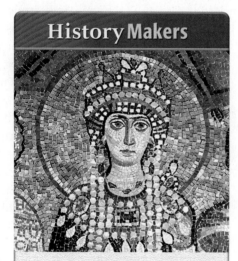

History Makers

Empress Theodora
500–548

The most powerful woman in Byzantine history rose from deep poverty. Early in life, Theodora was an actress. Eventually, she met Justinian, and in 525, they married.

As empress, Theodora met with foreign envoys, wrote to foreign leaders, passed laws, and built churches. During one political crisis, Theodora even confiscated the property of the general Belisarius. After she died in 548, Justinian was so depressed that he passed no major laws for the rest of his reign.

hmhsocialstudies.com

RESEARCH WEB LINKS Go online for more on Empress Theodora.

The Empire Falls

After Justinian's death in 565, the empire suffered countless setbacks. There were street riots, religious quarrels, palace intrigues, and foreign dangers. Each time the empire moved to the edge of collapse, it found some way to revive—only to face another crisis.

The Plague of Justinian The first crisis actually began before Justinian's death. It was a disease that resembled what we now know as the bubonic plague. This horrifying illness hit Constantinople in the later years of Justinian's reign. The plague probably arrived from India on ships infested with rats. Historians estimate that in 542, the worst year of the plague, 10,000 people were dying every day. The illness broke out repeatedly until around 700, when it finally faded. By that time, it had destroyed a huge percentage of the Byzantine population. **B**

Attacks from East and West From the very start of its rise to power, Byzantium faced constant challenges from foreign enemies. Lombards overran Justinian's conquests in the west. Avars, Slavs, and Bulgars made frequent raids on the northern borders. The powerful Sassanid Persians attacked relentlessly in the east. The Persians and Avars struck against Constantinople itself in 626. With the rise of Islam, Arab armies attacked the city in 674 and once again in 717. Russians attempted invasions of the city three times between 860 and 1043. In the 11th century, the Turks took over the Muslim world and fought their way slowly into Byzantine territory.

The Byzantines used bribes, diplomacy, political marriages, and military power to keep their enemies at bay. In the seventh century, Emperor Heraclius reorganized the empire along military lines. Provinces became themes, or military districts. Each theme was run by a general who reported directly to the emperor. These strategies, however, could not work forever. Slowly, the Byzantine Empire shrank under the impact of foreign attacks. By 1350, it was reduced to the tip of Anatolia and a strip of the Balkans. Yet thanks to its walls, its fleet, and its strategic location, Constantinople held out for another 100 years. Finally, the city fell to the Ottoman Turks in 1453.

The Church Divides

During the Byzantine Empire, Christianity underwent a dramatic development. Christianity had begun to develop differently in the Western and Eastern Roman Empires, due largely to the distance and lack of contact between the two regions. As the Eastern Empire became Byzantium and flourished, those differences grew and ultimately split apart the Church.

A Religious Split Eastern Christianity built its heritage on the works of early Church fathers. One was Saint Basil, who, around 357, wrote rules for the life of monks. Here, Saint Basil describes how monks and Christians should behave:

▼ Saint Basil

PRIMARY SOURCE C
The Christian should not be ostentatious [showy] in clothing or sandals, for all this is idle boasting. He should wear cheap clothes according to the need of the body. He should consume nothing beyond what is necessary or which tends to extravagance, for all this is abuse. He should not strive for honour nor always seek the first place. Each one should hold all men above himself. He should not be disobedient. . . . He should not be desirous of money, nor treasure up unnecessary things to no avail. He who approaches God ought to embrace poverty in all things, and be pierced with the fear of God.

SAINT BASIL, quoted in *The Letters*

MAIN IDEA

Making Inferences

B How might the plague have helped make Byzantium more vulnerable to foreign attack?

MAIN IDEA

Analyzing Primary Sources

C How might Saint Basil view a lavish and extravagant lifestyle?

Roman Catholicism and Eastern Orthodoxy

Originally, Christianity had one church. Because of political conflicts and differences in belief, the western and eastern parts of the Christian Church split apart in 1054. The western church became the Roman Catholic Church, and the eastern church became the Eastern Orthodox Church.

Both churches believe in the gospel of Jesus and in the Bible as interpreted by their church. They also believe that God uses sacraments to convey his love to humans. Sacraments are visible signs of something sacred; for instance, the water used in baptism is a sign of God's power to cleanse people of sin. The Venn diagram below shows other similarities and differences.

The 11th Century: Comparing Two Churches

Roman Catholic

Services are conducted in Latin.

The pope has authority over all other bishops.

The pope claims authority over all kings and emperors.

Priests may not marry.

Divorce is not permitted.

Similarities

They base their faith on the gospel of Jesus and the Bible.

They use sacraments such as baptism.

Their religious leaders are priests and bishops.

They seek to convert people.

Eastern Orthodox

Services are conducted in Greek or local languages.

The patriarch and other bishops head the Church as a group.

The emperor claims authority over the patriarch and other bishops of the empire.

Priests may be married.

Divorce is allowed under certain conditions.

Leaders of the Two Churches

Pope Benedict XVI (right) is the supreme head of the Roman Catholic Church. Ecumenical Patriarch Bartholomew (left) holds a slightly different position in the Orthodox Church. Eastern Orthodox churches pay him their highest honors because he heads the ancient Church of Constantinople, but they do not consider him their supreme authority.

hmhsocialstudies.com

RESEARCH WEB LINKS Go online for more on Roman Catholicism and Eastern Orthodoxy.

> **DATA FILE**

ROMAN CATHOLIC AND EASTERN ORTHODOX DATA

- U.S. state with highest percentage of Roman Catholics: Rhode Island, 51 percent.
  2001 American Religious Identification Survey by Graduate Center of City University of New York

- U.S. states with highest percentage of Eastern Orthodox: New Hampshire and New Jersey, 0.90 percent each.
  1990 National Survey of Religious Identification

- Vatican City is an independent state located in Rome, Italy. The Roman Catholic Church claims more than a billion members worldwide.
  Concise Columbia Encyclopedia, third edition; www.adherents.com

- The largest of the Eastern Orthodox churches is the Russian Orthodox Church. It claims 90 million members worldwide.
  www.adherents.com

- In 2003, the world region with the largest population of Roman Catholics: Latin America, 473,000,000
  Encyclopaedia Britannica Book of the Year 2004

- In 2003, the world region with the largest population of Eastern Orthodox members: Europe, 158,450,000
  Encyclopaedia Britannica Book of the Year 2004

Connect *to* Today

1. **Forming and Supporting Opinions** What do you think was the most important issue dividing the two churches? Explain your answer.
   See Skillbuilder Handbook, page R20.

2. **Making Predictions** Do you think the schism between the Roman Catholic Church and the Eastern Orthodox Church will ever be healed and the two churches reunited? Why or why not?

Another significant figure was Saint John Chrysostom (KRIHS•uhs•tuhm). As bishop of Constantinople from 398 to 404, Chrysostom was the **patriarch** (PAY•tree•AHRK), or leading bishop of the East. But even the patriarch bowed to the emperor.

A controversy that tested the emperor's authority over religious matters broke out in the eighth century. In 730, Emperor Leo III banned the use of **icons**, religious images used by Eastern Christians to aid their devotions. The emperor viewed the use of icons as idol worship. People responded with riots, and the clergy rebelled.

In the West, the pope became involved in this eastern dispute and supported the use of icons. One pope even ordered the **excommunication** of a Byzantine emperor—that is, he declared the emperor to be an outcast from the Church. In 843, more than 100 years after the controversy began, Empress Theodora restored icons to Eastern churches.

Differences between the Eastern and Western churches, continued to grow. In 1054, matters came to a head when the pope and the patriarch excommunicated each other in a dispute over religious doctrine. Shortly afterward, Christianity officially split between the Roman Catholic Church in the West and the Orthodox Church in the East.

Byzantine Missionaries Convert the Slavs As West and East grew apart, the two traditions of Christianity competed for converts. Missionaries from the Orthodox Church, for example, took their form of Christianity to the Slavs, groups that inhabited the forests north of the Black Sea. Two of the most successful Eastern missionaries, Saint Methodius and Saint Cyril (SEER•uhl), worked among the Slavs in the ninth century. Cyril and Methodius invented an alphabet for the Slavic languages. With an alphabet, Slavs would be able to read the Bible in their own tongues. Many Slavic languages, including Russian, are now written in what is called the **Cyrillic** (suh•RIHL•ihk) **alphabet**.

As these missionaries carried out their work, the Slavs themselves were creating a culture that would form one of history's most influential countries: Russia.

▲ (top) An 11th-century silver chalice displays the Cyrillic alphabet. (bottom) A closeup of the alphabet reveals its likeness to English.

SECTION 1 ASSESSMENT

TERMS & NAMES 1. For each term or name, write a sentence explaining its significance.
• Justinian • Justinian Code • Hagia Sophia • patriarch • icon • excommunication • Cyrillic alphabet

USING YOUR NOTES	MAIN IDEAS	CRITICAL THINKING & WRITING
2. In your opinion, was Justinian a great leader? Why or why not?	3. How did the Byzantines help to preserve Greco-Roman culture? 4. What various methods did the Byzantines use to hold off their enemies? 5. Why did Eastern Christians rebel against Emperor Leo III in 730?	6. **FORMING AND SUPPORTING OPINIONS** Do you agree or disagree with the characterization of Justinian as a new Caesar? Why? 7. **ANALYZING MOTIVES** Why do you think Justinian decided the time had come to reform Roman law? 8. **DRAWING CONCLUSIONS** Why do you think the Justinian Code lasted so long? 9. **WRITING ACTIVITY** RELIGIOUS AND ETHICAL SYSTEMS Imagine you are a Byzantine missionary attempting to convert a group of Slavs. Write a **speech** that you would give to the group in order to sway them.

Justinian

CONNECT TO TODAY CREATING A LIST

Locate the Cyrillic alphabet and make a **list** of what, if any, letters resemble their English counterparts. Discuss with the class why this might be.

The Russian Empire

MAIN IDEA	WHY IT MATTERS NOW	TERMS & NAMES
EMPIRE BUILDING Russia grew out of a blending of Slavic and Byzantine cultures and adopted Eastern Orthodox traditions.	Early Russia was separated from the West, leading to a difference in culture that still exists today.	• Slavs • Vladimir • Yaroslav the Wise	• Alexander Nevsky • Ivan III • czar

SETTING THE STAGE In addition to sending its missionaries to the land of the Slavs during the ninth century, Byzantium actively traded with its neighbors to the north. Because of this increased interaction, the Slavs began absorbing many Greek Byzantine ways. It was this blending of Slavic and Greek traditions that eventually produced Russian culture.

Russia's Birth

Russia's first unified territory originated west of the Ural Mountains in the region that runs from the Black Sea to the Baltic Sea. Hilly grasslands are found in the extreme south of that area. The north, however, is densely forested, flat, and swampy. Slow-moving, interconnecting rivers allow boat travel across these plains in almost any direction. Three great rivers, the Dnieper (NEE•puhr), the Don, and the Volga, run from the heart of the forests to the Black Sea or the Caspian Sea. (See the map on page 308.)

In the early days of the Byzantine Empire, these forests were inhabited by tribes of Slavic farmers and traders. They spoke similar languages but had no political unity. Sometime in the 800s, small bands of adventurers came down among them from the north. These Varangians, or Rus as they were also called, were most likely Vikings. (The name "Russia" is taken from this group.) Eventually, these Vikings built forts along the rivers and settled among the Slavs.

Slavs and Vikings Russian legends say the Slavs invited the Viking chief Rurik to be their king. So in 862, he founded Novgorod (NAHV•guh•rahd), Russia's first important city. That account is given in *The Primary Chronicle,* a history of Russia written by monks in the early 1100s. Around 880, a nobleman from Novgorod named Oleg moved south to Kiev (KEE•ehf), a city on the Dnieper River. From Kiev, the Vikings could sail by river and sea to Constantinople. There they could trade for products from distant lands.

Kiev grew into a principality, a small state ruled by a prince. As it did, the Viking nobles intermarried with their Slavic subjects and adopted many aspects of Slavic culture. Gradually, the line between Slavs and Vikings vanished.

Kiev Becomes Orthodox In 957, a member of the Kievan nobility, Princess Olga, paid a visit to Constantinople and publicly converted to Christianity. From 945 to 964, she governed Kiev until her son was old enough to rule. Her son

hmhsocialstudies.com
TAKING NOTES

Use the graphic organizer online to take notes on how Mongol rule affected different parts of Russian society.

Byzantines, Russians, and Turks Interact **307**

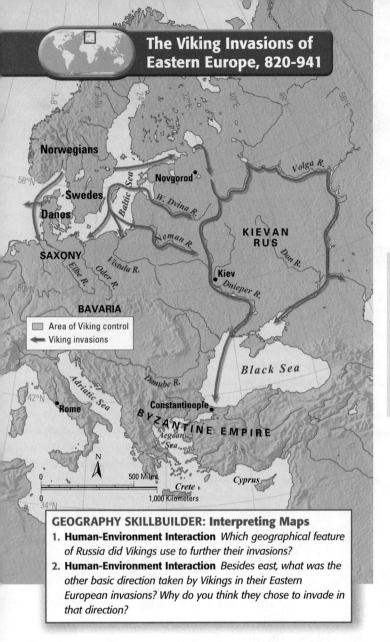

The Viking Invasions of Eastern Europe, 820–941

Norwegians

Swedes

Danes

SAXONY

BAVARIA

Novgorod

Baltic Sea

W. Dvina R.

Neman R.

Vistula R.

Oder R.

Elbe R.

Volga R.

KIEVAN RUS

Don R.

Kiev

Dnieper R.

Legend:
- Area of Viking control
- Viking invasions

Adriatic Sea

Rome

Danube R.

Constantinople

BYZANTINE EMPIRE

Aegean Sea

N

Black Sea

0   500 Miles
0   1,000 Kilometers

Crete

Cyprus

GEOGRAPHY SKILLBUILDER: Interpreting Maps
1. **Human-Environment Interaction** Which geographical feature of Russia did Vikings use to further their invasions?
2. **Human-Environment Interaction** Besides east, what was the other basic direction taken by Vikings in their Eastern European invasions? Why do you think they chose to invade in that direction?

resisted Christianity. However, soon after Olga's grandson **Vladimir** (VLAD•uh•meer) came to the throne about 980, he considered conversion to Christianity. *The Primary Chronicle* reports that Vladimir sent out teams to observe the major religions of the times. Three of the teams returned with lukewarm accounts of Islam, Judaism, and Western Christianity. But the team from Byzantium told quite a different story:

PRIMARY SOURCE

The Greeks led us to the [buildings] where they worship their God, and we knew not whether we were in heaven or on earth. For on earth there is no such splendor or such beauty, and we are at a loss how to describe it. We only know that God dwells there among men, and . . . we cannot forget that beauty.

from The Primary Chronicle

This report convinced Vladimir to convert to Byzantine Christianity and to make all his subjects convert, too. In 989, a baptism of all the citizens of Kiev was held in the Dnieper River. Kiev, already linked to Byzantium by trade, now looked to the empire for religious guidance. Vladimir imported teachers to instruct the people in the new faith. All the beliefs and traditions of Orthodox Christianity flourished in Kiev. Vladimir appreciated the Byzantine idea of the emperor as supreme ruler of the Church. So the close link between Church and state took root in Russia as well. **A**

MAIN IDEA

Analyzing Motives
A Why might Vladimir think it important that all his subjects become Christian?

Kiev's Power and Decline

Thanks to its Byzantine ties, Kiev grew from a cluster of crude wooden forts to the glittering capital of a prosperous and educated people. The rise of Kiev marked the appearance of Russia's first important unified territory.

Kievan Russia Vladimir led the way in establishing Kiev's power. He expanded his state west into Poland and north almost to the Baltic Sea. He also fought off troublesome nomads from the steppes to the south.

In 1019, Vladimir's son **Yaroslav the Wise** came to the throne and led Kiev to even greater glory. Like the rulers of Byzantium, Yaroslav skillfully married off his daughters and sisters to the kings and princes of Western Europe. Those marriages helped him to forge important trading alliances. At the same time, he created a legal code tailored to Kiev's commercial culture. Many of its rules dealt with crimes against property. Yaroslav also built the first library in Kiev. Under his rule, Christianity prospered. By the 12th century, Kiev was home to some 400 churches.

Kiev's Decline The decline of the Kievan state started with the death of Yaroslav in 1054. During his reign, Yaroslav had made what turned out to be a crucial error. He had divided his realm among his sons, instead of following the custom of passing on the throne to the eldest son. Upon their father's death, the sons tore the state apart fighting for the choicest territories. And because this system of dividing the kingdom among sons continued, each generation saw new struggles. The Crusades—the numerous clashes between Christians and Muslims for control of the Holy Lands of the Middle East that began in 1095—added to Kiev's troubles by disrupting trade. Then, just when it seemed that things could not get worse, a new threat emerged.

The Mongol Invasions

Vocabulary
Khan is the Mongol word for "ruler."

In the middle 1200s, a ferocious group of horsemen from central Asia slashed their way into Russia. These nomads were the Mongols. (See Chapter 12.) They had exploded onto the world scene at the beginning of the 1200s under Genghis Khan (JEHNG•gihs KAHN), one of the most feared warriors of all time.

VIDEO
Genghis Khan

hmhsocialstudies.com

The Mongols may have been forced to move out by economic or military pressures. They may have been lured by the wealth of cities to the west. Whatever their reasons for leaving, they rode their swift horses across the steppes of Asia and on into Europe. Their savage killing and burning won them a reputation for ruthless brutality. When Genghis Khan died in 1227, his successors continued the conquering that he had begun. At its fullest extent, the Mongol Empire stretched from the Yellow Sea to the Baltic Sea and from the Himalayas to northern Russia.

In 1240, the Mongols attacked and demolished Kiev. They rode under the leadership of Batu Khan, Genghis's grandson. So many inhabitants were slaughtered, a Russian historian reported, that "no eye remained to weep." A Roman Catholic bishop traveling through Kiev five years later wrote, "When we passed through that land, we found lying in the field countless heads and bones of dead people." After the fall of Kiev, Mongols ruled all of southern Russia for 200 years. The empire's official name was the "Khanate of the Golden Horde": *Khanate,* from the Mongol word for "kingdom"; *Golden,* because gold was the royal color of the Mongols; and *Horde,* from the Mongol word for "camp."

Mongol Rule in Russia Under Mongol rule, the Russians could follow all their usual customs, as long as they made no attempts to rebel. As fierce as they were, the Mongols tolerated all the religions in their realms. The Church, in fact, often acted as a mediator between the Russian people and their Mongol rulers.

The Khanate of the Golden Horde, 1294

Novgorod
Moscow
Vladimir
Kiev
RUSSIAN PRINCIPALITIES
Black Sea
Constantinople
Sarai
Seljuk Turks
Caspian Sea
Aral Sea
Lake Balkhash
KHANATE OF THE GOLDEN HORDE
Ob R.
Irtysh R.
URAL MOUNTAINS
Arctic Circle
CAUCASUS MOUNTAINS
Tabriz
Maragheh
Jerusalem
Baghdad
ILKHANATE (PERSIA)
CHAGATAI KHANATE
HIMALAYAS
DELHI SULTANATE
Indus R.
Dnieper R.
Don R.
Volga R.
Euphrates R.
Tigris R.
Syr Darya
60° N
40° N
70° E
60° E
80° E

■ Khanate of the Golden Horde at its greatest extent
□ Other land controlled by Mongols
⊙ Capital

0   500 Miles
0   1,000 Kilometers

GEOGRAPHY SKILLBUILDER: Interpreting Maps
1. **Location** *About how many miles did the Khanate of the Golden Horde stretch from east to west?*
2. **Region** *What role might geography have played in the Delhi Sultanate's escape from Mongol rule?*

Resisting Mongol Rule

Although Russians by and large obeyed their Mongol rulers, pockets of resistance existed, shown by this 1259 diary entry of a resident of Novgorod.

PRIMARY SOURCE

The same winter the accursed raw-eating Tartars [Mongols], Berkai and Kasachik, came with their wives, and many others, and there was great tumult in Novgorod, and they did much evil in the province, taking contribution for the accursed Tartars. And the accursed ones began to fear death; they said to [Prince] Alexander: 'Give us guards, lest they kill us.' And the Knayz ordered the son of Posadnik and all the sons of the Boyars to protect them by night. The Tartars said: 'Give us your numbers for tribute or we will run away and return in greater strength.' And the common people would not give their numbers for tribute but said: 'Let us die honourably for St. Sophia and for the angelic houses.'

Resident of Novgorod, from Medieval Russia

Rebelling Against the Mongols

Resistance against Mongol rule occasionally broke out into open rebellion, as this account from an anti-Mongol uprising in Tver in 1327 indicates.

PRIMARY SOURCE

The lawless Shevkal, the destroyer of Christianity, . . . came to Tver, drove the Grand Prince from his court and entrenched himself there with great haughtiness and violence. . . . The entire city assembled and the uprising was in the making. The Tverians cried out and began to kill the Tartars wherever they found them until they killed Shevkal and the rest [of his men]. They missed killing the messengers who were with the horses that grazed in the meadow [outside the city]. They [the messengers] saddled their best horses and swiftly galloped to Moscow and from there to the [Golden] Horde, where they brought the news of the death of Shevkal.

Tver Eyewitness Account, from Medieval Russia

DOCUMENT-BASED QUESTIONS

1. **Comparing** *In what way did the reasons for the uprisings in Novgorod and Tver differ?*
2. **Making Predictions** *Based on what you have read about the Mongols, what do you think their response was to the above events of resistance and rebellion?*

The Mongols demanded just two things from Russians: absolute obedience and massive amounts of tribute, or payments. By and large, the Russian nobles agreed. Novgorod's prince and military hero **Alexander Nevsky**, for example, advised his fellow princes to cooperate with the Mongols. The Russian nobles often crushed revolts against the Mongols and collected oppressive taxes for the foreign rulers.

Mongol rule isolated the Russians more than ever from their neighbors in Western Europe. This meant that among other things, the Russians had little access to many new ideas and inventions. During this period, however, forces were at work that eventually would lead to the rise of a new center of power in the country, and to Russia's liberation.

Russia Breaks Free

The city of Moscow was first founded in the 1100s. By 1156, it was a crude village protected by a log wall. Nonetheless, it was located near three major rivers: the Volga, Dnieper, and Don. From that strategic position, a prince of Moscow who could gain control of the three rivers could control nearly all of European Russia— and perhaps successfully challenge the Mongols. **B**

MAIN IDEA

Analyzing Issues
B What about Moscow's location was significant?

Moscow's Powerful Princes A line of Russian princes eventually emerged on the scene who would do just that. During the late 1320s, Moscow's Prince Ivan I had earned the gratitude of the Mongols by helping to crush a Russian revolt against Mongol rule. For his services, the Mongols appointed Ivan I as tax collector of all the Slavic lands they had conquered. They also gave him the title of "Grand Prince." Ivan had now become without any doubt the most powerful of all Russian princes. He also became the wealthiest and was known as "Ivan Moneybag."

Ivan convinced the Patriarch of Kiev, the leading bishop of Eastern Europe, to move to Moscow. The move improved the city's prestige and gave Moscow's princes a powerful ally: the Church. Ivan I and his successors used numerous strategies to enlarge their territory: land purchases, wars, trickery, and shrewd marriages. From generation to generation, they schemed to gain greater control over the small states around Moscow.

An Empire Emerges The Russian state would become a genuine empire during the long, 43-year reign of **Ivan III**. Upon becoming the prince of Moscow, Ivan openly challenged Mongol rule. He took the name **czar** (zahr), the Russian version of Caesar, and publicly claimed his intent to make Russia the "Third Rome." (The title "czar" became official only during the reign of Ivan IV.)

In 1480, Ivan made a final break with the Mongols. After he refused to pay his rulers further tribute, Russian and Mongol armies faced each other at the Ugra River, about 150 miles southwest of Moscow. However, neither side advanced to fight. So, after a time, both armies turned around and marched home. Russians have traditionally marked this bloodless standoff as their liberation from Mongol rule. After this liberation, the czars could openly pursue an empire.

Such a defeat for the Mongols would have seemed impossible nearly two centuries earlier, as they pushed west from present-day China and crushed nearly everything in their path. One of the peoples whom they conquered back then was a new group that had risen to power in Central Asia—the Turks.

History Makers

Ivan III
1440–1505

Those around him often viewed Ivan as cold, calculating, and ruthless. This may have been due in part to a difficult upbringing. Ivan came of age during a time of great civil strife in Russia. His father, Grand Prince Vasali II, was at one point imprisoned and blinded by opposition forces.

Ivan's cautious and calculating style drew criticism from Russians eager for more bold and swift action against the Mongols. Even a close aide questioned his tactics. "Would you surrender Russia to fire and sword?" he asked the prince. After Russian forces won the standoff at the Ugra River, however, such criticism turned to praise.

SECTION 2 ASSESSMENT

TERMS & NAMES 1. For each term or name, write a sentence explaining its significance.
• Slavs • Vladimir • Yaroslav the Wise • Alexander Nevsky • Ivan III • czar

USING YOUR NOTES
2. Which group fared the worst under Mongol rule?

Nobles	Church
People	Moscow Princes

MAIN IDEAS
3. How did Yaroslav's decision to divide his realm among his sons help cause Kiev's decline?

4. What main demands did the Mongols make on their Russian subjects?

5. How did Ivan III lead the Russians to their independence from the Mongols?

CRITICAL THINKING & WRITING
6. **RECOGNIZING EFFECTS** How did Vladimir's conversion to Christianity affect Kiev?

7. **FORMING AND SUPPORTING OPINIONS** Do you approve of Nevsky's cooperation with the Mongols? Was his policy practical or cowardly? Explain.

8. **ANALYZING ISSUES** How was Ivan I both friend and foe to the Mongol rulers?

9. **WRITING ACTIVITY** EMPIRE BUILDING Imagine you are a reporter for a major Russian newspaper. Write a **headline** and lead **paragraph** about Ivan III's standoff with Mongol forces at the Ugra River and its aftermath.

MULTIMEDIA ACTIVITY CREATING A PHOTO GALLERY

Use the Internet to create a **photo gallery** of modern-day Moscow. Possible subjects include the city's architecture, street scenes, and people.

INTERNET KEYWORD
Moscow photos

Russian Religious Art and Architecture

Russian religious art follows an ancient tradition dating back to the early Church. At first, Christians feared that artwork showing people might lead to idol worship. Gradually, however, the Church came to accept the use of icons, or depictions of holy people. In the West, other types of art eventually replaced the icon, but the Eastern Orthodox Church still uses icons today.

Icons are painted according to strict rules. This approach also shaped other religious art in Russia. To construct a church or create a religious artifact was a sacred task, performed according to rigid guidelines. Art was not a form of self-expression.

↗ **hmhsocialstudies.com**

RESEARCH WEB LINKS Go online for more on religious art.

Icon ▶
This 12th-century Russian icon is of the Archangel Gabriel. According to the Bible, Gabriel was the messenger who told the Virgin Mary that she would give birth to Jesus. In Orthodox churches, artists must follow certain rules when making icons. For example, icons are always two-dimensional because they are seen as windows through which worshipers can view heaven.

▲ Cross and Illuminated Manuscript ▶
The cross above was carved from ivory and shows the Archangel Michael. In Christian belief, Michael is the leader of the heavenly hosts and a spiritual warrior who helped the Israelites. That is why he is often shown with a sword, as he is here.

The illuminated manuscript was made during the 15th century and shows a scribe writing out the Gospel. Illuminated manuscripts were handwritten books decorated with gold or silver, vivid colors, elaborate designs, and small pictures. The word *illumination* originally referred to the gold or silver decoration, which made the pages seem as if light were shining on them.

▲ Reliquary

This elaborately decorated silver chest is a Russian cathedral reliquary. Reliquaries are containers that hold sacred relics, such as the bones of a saint. Most reliquaries are portable, allowing them to be carried in processions.

◄ Wooden Churches

Located in Varzuga, Russia, the Church of the Dormition was built in 1674. It is just one of many churches in Russia made out of wood. These churches were often built on a hilltop overlooking forests and villages. Roughly cut logs were used for the walls. However, the designs of the ceilings were complex and included the use of onion domes, as shown here. In the Russian Orthodox Church, onion domes represent heaven.

Connect *to* Today

1. **Making Inferences** Why do you think the archangels Michael and Gabriel were popular subjects for Russian religious art?

   See Skillbuilder Handbook, Page R10.

2. **Comparing and Contrasting** What types of religious art are common in our society today? How are they similar to or different from the art on these two pages?

313

Turkish Empires Rise in Anatolia

MAIN IDEA	WHY IT MATTERS NOW	TERMS & NAMES
CULTURAL INTERACTION Turkish people converted to Islam and founded new empires that would renew Muslim civilization.	In the 20th century, the collapse of the Turkish empire left ethnic and religious hostilities that still affect the world.	• Seljuks • Malik Shah • vizier

SETTING THE STAGE To the east of Constantinople and south of Russia, the mighty Muslim empire of the Abbasids had ruled since the eighth century. (See Chapter 10.) By the mid-tenth century, however, their control of the region would end as a powerful group known as the Turks emerged.

The Rise of the Turks

hmhsocialstudies.com
TAKING NOTES

Use the graphic organizer online to take notes on important events and features of the various occupations of Baghdad.

As powerful as the Abbasids were, they constantly struggled to maintain control of their empire. Spain broke away in 756, six years after the Abbasids came to power. After setting up their capital in Baghdad, the Abbasids lost their grip on other parts of the empire as well: Morocco in 788 and Tunisia in 800. In 809, they lost some regions of Persia. Then, in 868, the Abbasids lost control of Egypt.

Finally, in 945, Persian armies moved into Baghdad and put an end to the power of the caliph, an Islamic religious or political leader. Even though the caliph continued as the religious leader of Islam, he gave up all political power to the new Persian ruler. It wasn't long, however, before the Persians themselves fell to a powerful group in the region.

The Conquering Seljuks As early as 1300 B.C., Chinese records mention a people called the Tu-Kiu living west of their borders. The Tu-Kiu may well have been the Turks. For centuries, these nomads rode their horses over the vast plains. They herded goats and sheep, lived in tents, and used two-humped camels to carry their goods. The Islamic world first met them as raiders and traders along their northeastern frontiers.

The Abbasids took note of the Turks for their military skills. They began buying Turkish children to raise as slaves, train as soldiers, and employ as bodyguards. The Abbasids came to prize the slaves for their skill and loyalty. On the subject, one author wrote, "One obedient slave is better than 300 sons; for the latter desire their father's death, the former [desires] long life for his master." Over time, Turkish military slaves, or mamelukes, became a powerful force in the Abbasid Empire.

In the tenth century, a growing number of Turks began converting to Islam and slowly migrating into the weakened Abbasid Empire. One of the first of these migrating Turkish groups was known as the **Seljuks** (SEHL•JOOKS), after the family that led them. The Seljuks gradually grew in number and strength. In 1055, they attacked and captured Baghdad from the Persians.

Nearly 20 years later, the Seljuk sultans marched on the Byzantine Empire. At the Battle of Manzikert in 1071, Turkish forces crushed the Byzantine defenders. Within ten years, the Seljuks occupied most of Anatolia, the eastern flank of Byzantium. This brought the Turks closer to the Byzantine capital, Constantinople, than the Arabs or Persians had ever come. This near conquest of the New Rome also inspired the name of the Seljuk sultanate of Rum (from "Rome"). Rum survived in Anatolia after the rest of the Seljuk Empire had crumbled. **A**

The Turks Secure Persian Support Back in Baghdad and its surrounding region, Seljuk rulers wisely courted the support of their newly conquered Persian subjects. In fact, the founder of the Seljuk Dynasty, Toghril Beg, chose the Persian city of Isfahan (IHS•fuh•HAHN) as the capital of his kingdom. This favorable treatment made the Persians loyal supporters of the Seljuks, and the Turks often appointed them as government officials. The brilliant Nizam al-Mulk, for example, was a Persian who served as the **vizier**, or prime minister, of the most famous of Seljuk sultans, **Malik Shah**.

The Turks also showed a great admiration of Persian learning. The nomadic Seljuks had arrived in Southwest Asia basically illiterate. They were unfamiliar with the traditions of Islam, which they had just adopted. As a result, they looked to their Persian subjects for both cultural and religious guidance. The Turks adopted Persian as the language of culture and adopted features of the Persian way of life that they so admired. Seljuk rulers were called *shahs,* from the Persian word for a king. They also promoted Persian writers like the mystical Islamic poet Jalaludin Rumi, whose poetry is widely read today. Rumi often wrote of his desire to achieve a personal experience of God.

MAIN IDEA

Contrasting

A What advantages would a nomadic people like the Turks have in fighting settled people like the Persians or Byzantines?

PRIMARY SOURCE
Burning with longing-fire,
wanting to sleep with my head on your doorsill,
my living is composed only of this trying
to be in your presence.

JALALUDIN RUMI, quoted in *Unseen Rain*

Seljuk shahs like the great Malik Shah took pride in supporting Persian artists and architects. Malik beautified the city of Isfahan, for example, by building many splendid mosques. The Turks' political and cultural preference for the Persians caused the almost complete disappearance of the Arabic language from Persia. Arabic was kept alive mainly by religious scholars studying the Qur'an.

As a result of their policies, the Seljuks won strong support from the Persians, who were proud of their long heritage and eager to pass it on. Like other conquering peoples throughout history, the Seljuk Turks found that they had much to learn from those whom they had defeated.

History Makers

Malik Shah
1055–1092

Malik Shah is thought to be the greatest of the Seljuk sultans. Among his achievements, he built the great mosque Masjid-i-Jame (shown above) in Isfahan. Malik also patronized intellectuals and artists like Omar Khayyam (OH•mahr ky•YAHM), who is most famous today for the *Rubaiyat* (ROO•bee•AHT). The *Rubaiyat* is a collection of poems describing the poet's love of life's pleasures. Omar also created a more accurate calendar for Malik.

Malik Shah was also capable of great cruelty. When his brother Takash revolted against him, Malik punished Takash by blinding him. Malik Shah died suddenly at the age of 37, possibly poisoned by his wife.

hmhsocialstudies.com

RESEARCH WEB LINKS Go online for more on Malik Shah.

▲ This drawing from an early 13th-century manuscript illustrates the Turkish siege of a city.

Seljuks Confront Crusaders and Mongols

Malik Shah ruled as the last of the strong Seljuk leaders. After his unexpected death in 1092, no capable shah appeared to replace him. So, the Seljuk Empire quickly disintegrated into a loose collection of minor kingdoms. Just at that point, the West launched a counterattack against the Turks and other Muslims for control of the Holy Land of the Middle East. This series of military campaigns was known as the Crusades.

The Seljuks and the Crusaders Pope Urban II launched the First Crusade in 1095. He called on Christians to drive the Turks out of Anatolia and recover Jerusalem from Muslim rule. Armies from Western Europe soon poured through Constantinople and proceeded on to Palestine. In 1099, the Crusaders captured Jerusalem and massacred its Jewish and Muslim inhabitants. They established a Latin Christian kingdom that lasted about a century. **B**

Eventually, a fragment of the former Seljuk Empire gathered enough strength to fight back. Under their famous Kurdish captain Saladin, the Muslims recovered Jerusalem in 1187. Eventually, Saladin and his Western opponent King Richard I of England signed a truce. Their agreement gave Jerusalem to the Muslims but granted Western pilgrims access to Christian holy places.

Subsequent popes called for further Crusades. But each new military expedition proved weaker than the last. By the 13th century, the Western powers seemed to pose little problem for the Turks. It was around this time, however, that a new threat emerged from the east—the mighty and brutal Mongols.

Seljuks Face the Mongols As you have read previously, the Mongols were a group of nomadic clans along the Asian steppes. In the early 1200s, they grew into a unified force under the ruler Genghis Khan and swiftly conquered China.

The Mongol armies eventually turned to the west and leveled any cities that dared to resist them. They slaughtered whole populations. In 1258, Genghis's grandson Hulagu led his troops to the outskirts of Baghdad, which by this time was surrounded by a defensive wall. The account of what followed by Persian historian

MAIN IDEA

Summarizing
B Why did the Crusades take place?

Wassaf speaks to the Mongols' fierce and overwhelming fighting methods:

PRIMARY SOURCE
The arrows and bolts, the lances and spears, the stones from the slings and catapults of both sides shot swiftly up to heaven, like the messengers of the prayers of the just, then fell as swiftly, like the judgements of fate. . . . In this way, Baghdad was besieged and terrorized for fifty days. But since the city still held out the order was given for baked bricks lying outside the walls to be collected, and with them high towers were built in every direction, overlooking the streets and alleys of Baghdad. On top of these they set up the catapults. Now the city was filled with the thunder and lightning of striking stones and flaring naphtha pots. A dew of arrows rained from a cloud of bows and the population was trampled underfoot. . . . The cry went up, 'Today we have no strength against Goliath and his army!'

WASSAF, quoted in *The Mongol Empire*

When Hulagu finally took Baghdad, he burned down the caliph's palace and had tens of thousands of people killed. Mongol belief forbade the spilling of sacred blood. So Hulagu executed the last Abbasid caliph by having him wrapped in a carpet and trampled to death by horses.

With untold brutality, Genghis Khan and his successors shaped the biggest land empire in history. (See Chapter 12 for more about the Mongol Empire.) The warrior Mongols, however, knew little about administering their territory. As a result, their vast empire crumbled in just a few generations. And out of the rubble of the Mongol Empire rose another group of Turks—the Ottomans. They would build an empire that lasted into the 20th century. You will learn more about the Ottoman Empire in Chapter 18.

Connect *to* Today

Turkey
Today, Turkey is a nation located between Europe and Asia just north of the Mediterranean Sea. About 80 percent of its residents are descendants of the Seljuks and other Turkish groups.

Turkey became a republic in 1923. Many of today's Turks, like their ancestors, practice Islam, as evidenced by the nation's flag (shown above). It depicts the crescent and the five-pointed star, the symbols of the Islamic faith.

🔼 **hmhsocialstudies.com**

INTERNET ACTIVITY Go online to research and write about a cultural practice in Turkey.

SECTION 3 ASSESSMENT

TERMS & NAMES 1. For each term or name, write a sentence explaining its significance.
• Seljuks • vizier • Malik Shah

USING YOUR NOTES
2. Which occupier proved to be the worst for Baghdad?

Occupiers	Events
Abbasids	
Persians	
Seljuks	
Mongols	

MAIN IDEAS
3. Why did the Seljuks need to seek religious guidance from the Persian peoples they had conquered?

4. How did the death of Malik Shah affect the Seljuk Empire?

5. What agreement did Saladin and England's King Richard I reach about Jerusalem?

CRITICAL THINKING & WRITING
6. **ANALYZING ISSUES** In what ways would it be accurate to say that the Persians actually won over the Turks?

7. **FORMING AND SUPPORTING OPINIONS** Do you think it is wise for rulers to place members of conquered peoples in positions of government? Why or why not?

8. **MAKING INFERENCES** Based on the observations by the Persian historian Wassaf, why do you think the Mongols were such successful conquerors?

9. **WRITING ACTIVITY** CULTURAL INTERACTION Write several **paragraphs** comparing the ways in which the different groups in this section interacted.

CONNECT TO TODAY CREATING A SUMMARY
Identify a modern-day Arab poet. Then analyze one of his or her works and write a brief **summary** that expresses its main idea.

TERMS & NAMES

For each term or name below, briefly explain its connection to the Byzantine, Russian, and Turkish empires between 500 and 1500.

1. Justinian Code
2. Hagia Sophia
3. patriarch
4. icon
5. Slavs
6. Alexander Nevsky
7. Seljuks
8. Malik Shah

MAIN IDEAS

The Byzantine Empire Section 1 (pages 301–306)

9. What were the names and characteristics of the four parts of the Justinian Code?
10. What were some important features of life in Constantinople?
11. Which peoples attacked the Byzantine Empire? What part of the empire did they invade?
12. What two main religions emerged out of the split in the Christian Church?

The Russian Empire Section 2 (pages 307–313)

13. What does *The Primary Chronicle* say about Rurik and the origin of Novgorod?
14. According to *The Primary Chronicle,* how did Vladimir choose Byzantine Christianity?
15. How did Moscow's location contribute to its growth?
16. What event marked Russia's liberation from Mongol rule?

Turkish Empires Rise in Anatolia Section 3 (pages 314–317)

17. In what ways did the Turks show respect for their Persian subjects?
18. What group eventually conquered the empire established by the Seljuk Turks?

CRITICAL THINKING

1. USING YOUR NOTES

On a chart, describe several key characteristics about the Vikings, Turks, and Mongols—all of whom moved into foreign lands.

	Where from?	Where settled?	Interactions with people
Vikings			
Turks			
Mongols			

2. ANALYZING ISSUES

EMPIRE BUILDING   What were Justinian's goals in creating his law code? Why might a leader want to organize the laws?

3. FOLLOWING CHRONOLOGICAL ORDER

Examine the time lines on this page. How many years did the Byzantine Empire last? How long did it take the Seljuk Empire to decline after the Seljuks took Baghdad?

4. COMPARING AND CONTRASTING

CULTURAL INTERACTION   What was different about the way in which the Seljuk Turks and Mongols interacted with their subjects?

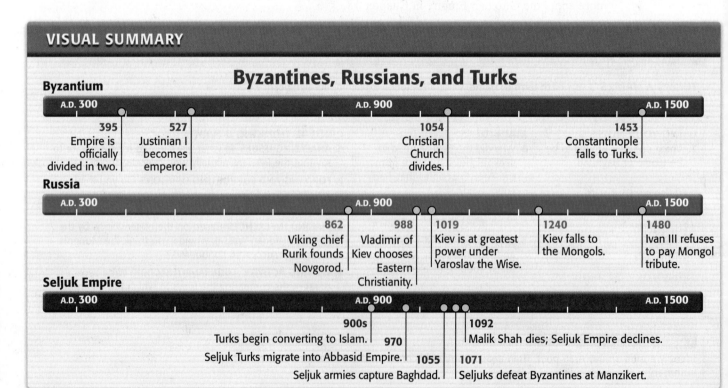

VISUAL SUMMARY

Byzantines, Russians, and Turks

Byzantium

A.D. 300 — A.D. 900 — A.D. 1500

395 Empire is officially divided in two.
527 Justinian I becomes emperor.
1054 Christian Church divides.
1453 Constantinople falls to Turks.

Russia

A.D. 300 — A.D. 900 — A.D. 1500

862 Viking chief Rurik founds Novgorod.
988 Vladimir of Kiev chooses Eastern Christianity.
1019 Kiev is at greatest power under Yaroslav the Wise.
1240 Kiev falls to the Mongols.
1480 Ivan III refuses to pay Mongol tribute.

Seljuk Empire

A.D. 300 — A.D. 900 — A.D. 1500

900s Turks begin converting to Islam.
970 Seljuk Turks migrate into Abbasid Empire.
1055 Seljuk armies capture Baghdad.
1092 Malik Shah dies; Seljuk Empire declines.
1071 Seljuks defeat Byzantines at Manzikert.

Use this comparison chart of various empires and your knowledge of world history to answer questions 1 and 2.

Five Empires			
	Dates	Greatest Territory*	Greatest Population**
Persian	550 B.C.–330 B.C.	2.0	14.0
Roman	27 B.C.–A.D. 476	3.4	54.8
Byzantine	A.D. 395–A.D.1453	1.4	30.0
Mongol	A.D. 1206–A.D. 1380	11.7	125.0
Aztec	A.D. 1325–A.D. 1521	0.2	6.0

* Estimated in millions of square miles
** Estimated in millions of people

1. Which of the empires shown here lasted the longest?

   A. Mongol

   B. Roman

   C. Persian

   D. Byzantine

2. The population of Byzantium was five times the size of which empire?

   A. Aztec

   B. Persian

   C. Roman

   D. Mongol

Use the quotation and your knowledge of world history to answer question 3.

PRIMARY SOURCE

On the dawn of the sixth day the pagan warriors began to storm the city. . . . And the Tartars [Mongols] cut down many people, including women and children. Still others were drowned in the river. And they killed without exception all monks and priests. And they burned this holy city with all its beauty and wealth. . . . And churches of God were destroyed, and much blood was spilled on the holy altars. And not one man remained alive in the city. All were dead. . . . And this happened for our sins.

ZENKOVSKY, *Medieval Russia's Epics, Chronicles, and Tales*

3. According to the author, why did the Mongols destroy the city?

   A. It was located along a strategic river.

   B. The Mongols wanted to make it their new capital.

   C. The city's residents had to be punished for their sins.

   D. The Mongols sought to wipe out all who opposed their religion.

 hmhsocialstudies.com **TEST PRACTICE**

For additional test practice, go online for:

- Diagnostic tests
- Tutorials
- Strategies

Interact *with* History

On page 300, you considered ways of expanding the Byzantine Empire. Which approach did you choose and why? Now that you've read about the Byzantine Empire, do you think that you chose the right strategy? Discuss your present ideas on enlarging an empire.

FOCUS ON WRITING

RELIGIOUS AND ETHICAL SYSTEMS Find a photograph of a holy place connected with the Byzantine, Russian, or Turkish empire. Write a two-minute **documentary script** about the site. Make an audio or video recording of your documentary and present it to the class. Provide the following:

- the meaning or importance of the site
- a brief history of the site
- the beliefs associated with the site

MULTIMEDIA ACTIVITY

Writing an Internet-Based Research Paper

Go to the *Web Research Guide* at **hmhsocialstudies.com** to learn about conducting research on the Internet. Then, working with a partner, use the Internet to find examples of how two peoples today have influenced each other. Focus on such characteristics as language, food, clothing, music, social customs, religion, and systems of government. Present the results of your research in a well-organized paper. Be sure to:

- apply a search strategy when using directories and search engines to locate Web resources
- judge the usefulness and reliability of each Web site
- correctly cite your Web sources
- peer edit for organization and correct use of language

CHAPTER 12

Empires in East Asia,
600-1350

Essential Question

How did the development of kingdoms and empires in East Asia help spread religions, culture, trade, and technological innovations?

 What You Will Learn

In this chapter you will learn how the cultures of East Asia influenced one another, as belief systems and ideas spread through both peaceful and violent means.

SECTION 1 Tang and Song China
Main Idea During the Tang and Song dynasties, China experienced an era of prosperity and technological innovation.

SECTION 2 The Mongol Conquests
Main Idea The Mongols, a nomadic people from the steppe, conquered settled societies across much of Asia.

SECTION 3 The Mongol Empire
Main Idea As emperor of China, Kublai Khan encouraged foreign trade.

SECTION 4 Feudal Powers in Japan
Main Idea Japanese civilization was shaped by cultural borrowing from China and the rise of feudalism and military rulers.

SECTION 5 Kingdoms of Southeast Asia and Korea
Main Idea Several smaller kingdoms prospered in East and Southeast Asia, a region influenced by China and India.

Previewing Themes

RELIGIOUS AND ETHICAL SYSTEMS Buddhism, which had reached China from India, spread from China to Japan. Both Hindu and Buddhist missionaries from India spread their religions across Southeast Asia.

Geography *Why might the Khmer Empire, rather than Korea or Japan, be more open to influence from India?*

EMPIRE BUILDING The Tang Dynasty built China into the most powerful and advanced empire in the world. Later, China fell to another group of empire builders, the Mongols.

Geography *Locate the Great Wall on the map. Why do you think the Chinese constructed the wall along their northern border?*

CULTURAL INTERACTION Chinese culture spread across East Asia, influencing Korea, Japan, and much of mainland Southeast Asia. The Mongol conquests led to interaction between settled and nomadic peoples across Asia.

Geography *Why would China tend to exert a strong influence over other parts of East Asia?*

EAST AND SOUTHEAST ASIA

618
Tang Dynasty begins 289-year rule in China. (Tang statuette) ▶

794
Heian period begins in Japan.

935
Koryu Dynasty controls Korea.

600

800

WORLD

630s
Muhammad unifies Arabian Peninsula under Islam.

800
Charlemagne crowned Holy Roman Emperor by pope.

900s
◀ Maya civilization goes into decline. (Maya stone sculpture)

East and Southeast Asia, 900–1200

Karakorum

ASIA

GOBI DESERT

TAKLIMAKAN DESERT

Huang He   Kaifeng   Yellow Sea

Yangzhou

Chang Jiang   Hangzhou   East China Sea

TIBET

HIMALAYAS

Indus River

Ganges River

INDIA

30°N

Guangzhou

Hanoi

Hainan

PACIFIC OCEAN

Bay of Bengal

Angkor   South China Sea   Philippines

N
W   E
S

Sumatra

Borneo

INDIAN OCEAN   Palembang

Heian (Kyoto)

Legend
- Japan, 1100
- Khmer, 1100
- Koryu Dynasty (Korea), 1100
- Mongol homeland, 1200
- Song (China), 1100
- Srivijaya, 1200
- Vietnam, 1200
- Grand Canal
- Great Wall

0   300   600 Miles
0   300   600 Kilometers
Robinson Projection

Borobudur
Java

90°E

120°E

HISTORY.   A Mongol Empire in China

hmhsocialstudies.com   VIDEO

960
Song Dynasty established in China.

1192
Kamakura Shogunate rules Japan. (Kamakura period painting) ▶

1279
Kublai Khan conquers China.

1000

1200

1400

1054
◀ The pope expels the patriarch of Constantinople, splitting Christianity into Roman Catholic and Orthodox branches.

1324
Mali king Mansa Musa makes hajj to Mecca.

1347
Bubonic plague strikes Europe.

Which Chinese invention would be most useful to your society?

Imagine yourself in the year 1292. You have spent the last 17 years traveling in China—the world's most advanced country. Your own civilization is on the other side of the world. It, too, is very sophisticated, but it lacks many of the innovations you have seen on your travels.

During your stay in China, you were of great assistance to the emperor. As a going-away present, he asks you to choose one of the inventions shown here to take back to your own society. He also will provide you with the knowledge of how to create the invention of your choice.

Silk makes a luxurious cloth—soft to the touch but also amazingly strong and warm.

The magnetic compass can help sailors navigate the open sea.

Gunpowder can be used for fireworks or made into explosive weapons.

Paper is a relatively inexpensive and easy-to-produce surface for writing and printing.

EXAMINING *the* ISSUES

- Which invention would most improve the quality of life?
- Which might be the most profitable?
- What benefits and drawbacks might there be to introducing the item into your society?

Discuss these questions with your classmates. In your discussion, remember what you have learned about the spread of new ideas. As you read about China in this chapter, see how its ideas spread from the East to the West.

Tang and Song China

MAIN IDEA	WHY IT MATTERS NOW	TERMS & NAMES
EMPIRE BUILDING During the Tang and Song dynasties, China experienced an era of prosperity and technological innovation.	Chinese inventions from this period, such as printing, gunpowder, and the compass, changed history.	• Tang Taizong · movable type • Wu Zhao · gentry

SETTING THE STAGE After the Han Dynasty collapsed in A.D. 220, no emperor was strong enough to hold China together. Over the next 350 years, more than 30 local dynasties rose and fell. Finally, by 589, an emperor named Wendi had united northern and southern China once again. He restored a strong central government. Under the next two dynasties, the Tang and the Song, China experienced a prolonged golden age. It became the richest, most powerful, and most advanced country in the world.

The Tang Dynasty Expands China

Wendi declared himself the first emperor of the Sui (sway) Dynasty. The dynasty lasted through only two emperors, from 581 to 618. The Sui emperors' greatest accomplishment was the completion of the Grand Canal. This waterway connected the Huang He and the Chang Jiang. The canal provided a vital route for trade between the northern cities and the southern rice-producing region of the Chang delta.

hmhsocialstudies.com
TAKING NOTES
Use the graphic organizer online to take notes on the similarities and differences between the Tang and Song dynasties.

About a million peasant men and women toiled five years to dig the more than 1,000-mile waterway. Perhaps as many as half of the workers died on this project. Thousands more toiled and died rebuilding the Great Wall. The endless labor on state projects turned the people against the Sui Dynasty. Overworked and overtaxed, they finally revolted. In 618, a member of the imperial court assassinated the second Sui emperor.

Tang Rulers Create a Powerful Empire While short-lived, the Sui Dynasty built a strong foundation for the great achievements of the next dynasty, the Tang (tahng). The Tang Dynasty ruled for nearly 300 years (618–907). The Tang emperor who began these achievements was **Tang Taizong**. His brilliant reign lasted from 626 to 649.

Under the Tang rulers, the empire expanded. Taizong's armies reconquered the northern and western lands that China had lost since the decline of the Han Dynasty. By 668, China had extended its influence over Korea as well. The ruler during the campaign in Korea was the empress **Wu Zhao** (woo-jow). From about 660 on, she held the real power while weak emperors sat on the throne. Finally, in 690, Empress Wu assumed the title of emperor for herself—the only woman ever to do so in China.

History Makers

Tang Taizong 600–649

The man who restored China to its glory was a distinguished general named Li Shimin. He seized the imperial throne in 626 after killing his brothers and forcing his father, the first Tang emperor, to step aside. As emperor, Li Shimin took the title Taizong, meaning "Great Ancestor."

Taizong's military campaigns extended China's borders north to Manchuria, south to Vietnam, and west to the Aral Sea. At home, aided by his gifted advisers, Taizong reformed the government organization and law code. These became models for all of East Asia.

Wu Zhao 625–705

At the age of 13, the beautiful Wu Zhao arrived at the court of Tang Taizong to become one of the emperor's secondary wives. After Taizong's death, she became a favored wife of his son and successor. Wu Zhao soon rose above rival wives and became the emperor's chief wife, or empress.

For many years, Empress Wu virtually ruled China on behalf of her sickly husband. After his death, two of their sons briefly held the throne. Frustrated by their lack of ability, she took the throne herself at the age of 65. She was 80 when she finally lost power. A strong leader, Wu Zhao continued the work begun by Taizong to build and expand China.

Tang rulers further strengthened the central government of China. They expanded the network of roads and canals begun by the Sui. This helped to pull the empire together. They also promoted foreign trade and improvements in agriculture.

Scholar-Officials To manage their large empire, the Tang rulers needed to restore China's vast bureaucracy. They did this by reviving and expanding the civil service examination system begun by the Han Dynasty. The relatively few candidates who passed the tough exams became part of an elite group of scholar-officials.

In theory, the exams were open to all men, even commoners. However, only the wealthy could afford the necessary years of education. Also, men with political connections could obtain high positions without taking the exams. Despite these flaws, the system created a remarkably intelligent and capable governing class in China. Before the Tang Dynasty, a few noble families dominated the country. As the examination system grew in importance, talent and education became more important than noble birth in winning power. As a result, many moderately wealthy families shared in China's government. **A**

The Tang Lose Power To meet the rising costs of government, Tang rulers imposed crushing taxes in the mid-700s. These brought hardship to the people but failed to cover the costs of military expansion and new building programs.

Moreover, the Tang struggled to control the vast empire they had built. In 751, Muslim armies soundly defeated the Chinese at the Battle of Talas. As a result, Central Asia passed out of Chinese control and into foreign hands. After this time, border attacks and internal rebellions steadily chipped away at the power of the imperial government. Finally, in 907, Chinese rebels sacked and burned the Tang capital at Ch'ang-an and murdered the last Tang emperor, a child.

MAIN IDEA

Recognizing Effects

A What resulted from the revival and expansion of the civil service system?

The Song Dynasty Restores China

After the fall of the Tang Dynasty, rival warlords divided China into separate kingdoms. Then, in 960, an able general named Taizu reunited China and proclaimed himself the first Song (sung) emperor. The Song Dynasty, like the Tang, lasted about three centuries (960–1279). Although the Song ruled a smaller empire than either the Han or the Tang, China remained stable, powerful, and prosperous.

Song armies never regained the western lands lost after 751. Nor did they regain northern lands that had been lost to nomadic tribes during the Tang decline. For a time, Song emperors tried to buy peace with their northern enemies. They paid hefty annual tributes of silver, silk, and tea. This policy, however, ultimately failed to stop the threat from the north. In the early 1100s, a Manchurian people called the Jurchen conquered northern China and established the Jin Empire. The Jurchen forced the Song to retreat south across the Huang He. After 1127, the Song emperors ruled only southern China.

The Song rulers established a grand new capital at Hangzhou, a coastal city south of the Chang Jiang. Despite its military troubles, the dynasty of the Southern Song (1127–1279) saw rapid economic growth. The south had become the economic heartland of China. Merchants in southern cities grew rich from trade with Chinese in the north, nomads of Central Asia, and people of western Asia and Europe.

An Era of Prosperity and Innovation

During the Tang and Song dynasties, China's population nearly doubled, soaring to 100 million. By the Song era, China had at least ten cities with a population of 1 million each. China had become the most populous country in the world. It also had become the most advanced.

Science and Technology Artisans and scholars made important technological advances during the Tang and Song eras. Among the most important inventions were movable type and gunpowder. With **movable type**, a printer could arrange blocks of individual characters in a frame to make up a page for printing. Previously, printers had carved the words of a whole page into one large block. The development of gunpowder, in time, led to the creation of explosive weapons such as bombs, grenades, small rockets, and cannons. Other important inventions of this period include porcelain, the mechanical clock, paper money, and the use of the magnetic compass for sailing. (See the Social History feature on pages 328–329.)

The 1000s to the 1200s was a rich period for Chinese mathematics. The Chinese made advances in arithmetic and algebra. Many mathematical ideas, such as using negative numbers, spread from China southward and westward. **B**

Agriculture The rapid growth of China resulted in part from advances in farming. Farmers especially improved the cultivation of rice. In about the year 1000, China imported a new variety of fast-ripening rice from Vietnam. This allowed the farmers to harvest two rice crops each year rather than one. To make sure that farmers knew about this improved variety, Chinese officials distributed seedlings throughout the country. The agricultural improvements enabled China's farmers to produce more food. This was necessary to feed the rapidly expanding population in the cities.

Trade and Foreign Contacts Under the Tang and Song emperors, foreign trade flourished. Tang imperial armies guarded the great Silk Roads, which linked China to the West. Eventually, however, China lost control over these routes during the long Tang decline. After this time, Chinese merchants relied increasingly on ocean trade. Chinese advances in sailing technology, including use of the magnetic compass, made it possible for sea trade to expand. Up and down China's long coastline, the largest port cities in the

MAIN IDEA

Making Inferences

B How might the spread of mathematical ideas from China affect other countries?

Connect to Today

hmhsocialstudies.com **INTERACTIVE**

Acupuncture

During the Song Dynasty, the Chinese carefully studied human anatomy and created charts and models of the body. These helped to improve the practice of acupuncture, a system of treatment that involves inserting slender needles into the body at specific points, depending on the nature of the problem.

In recent years, this ancient practice has gained some acceptance in mainstream Western medicine. More and more practicing doctors are seeking training in acupuncture methods. And mainstream doctors are increasing their referrals to acupuncture specialists. In 2001 alone, Americans made about 20 million visits to acupuncturists, seeking treatment for everything from migraine headaches to drug dependency.

world bustled with international trade. Merchant ships carried trade goods to Korea and Japan. They sailed across the Indian Ocean to India, the Persian Gulf, and even the coast of Africa. Chinese merchants established trading colonies around Southeast Asia. Many foreign traders, mostly Arabs, resided in Chinese cities. Through trade and travel, Chinese culture spread throughout East Asia. One major cultural export was Buddhism. This religion spread from China to Vietnam, Korea, and Japan. The exchange of goods and ideas was two-way. For example, foreign religions, including Islam and some Eastern sects of Christianity, spread to China and won followers.

A Golden Age of Poetry and Art The prosperity of the Tang and Song dynasties nourished an age of artistic brilliance. The Tang period produced great poetry. Two of its most celebrated poets were Li Bo, who wrote about life's pleasures, and Tu Fu, who praised orderliness and Confucian virtues. Tu Fu also wrote critically about war and the hardships of soldiers. Once he himself was captured by rebels and taken to Ch'ang-an, the capital city. He had sent his family to the village of Fuzhou for safety. Here he describes their separation:

PRIMARY SOURCE C

The same moon is above Fuzhou tonight;

From the open window she will be watching it alone,

The poor children are too little to be able to remember Ch'ang-an.

Her perfumed hair will be dampened by the dew, the air may be too chilly on her delicate arms.

When can we both lean by the wind-blown curtains and see the tears dry on each other's face?

TU FU, "Moonlight Night"

MAIN IDEA

Analyzing Primary Sources

C What themes does Tu Fu explore in this poem?

Chinese painting reached new heights of beauty during the Song Dynasty. Painting of this era shows Daoist influence. Artists emphasized the beauty of natural landscapes and objects such as a single branch or flower. The artists did not use bright colors. Black ink was their favorite paint. Said one Song artist, "Black is ten colors."

Birds and flowers were favorite subjects for Song painters. ▼

Changes in Chinese Society

China's prosperity produced many social changes during the Tang and Song periods. Chinese society became increasingly mobile. People moved to the cities in growing numbers. The Chinese also experienced greater social mobility than ever before. The most important avenue for social advancement was the civil service system.

Levels of Society During Tang and Song times, the power of the old aristocratic families began to fade. A new, much larger upper class emerged, made up of scholar-officials and their families. Such a class of powerful, well-to-do people is called the **gentry**. The gentry attained their status through education and civil service positions rather than through land ownership. Below the gentry was an urban middle class. It included merchants, shopkeepers, skilled artisans, minor officials, and others. At the bottom of urban society were laborers, soldiers, and servants. In the countryside lived the largest class by far, the peasants. They toiled for wealthy landowners as they had for centuries.

The Status of Women Women had always been subservient to men in Chinese society. Their status further declined during the Tang and Song periods. This was especially true among the upper classes in cities. There a woman's work was deemed less important to the family's prosperity and status. Changing attitudes affected peasant families less, however. Peasant women worked in the fields and helped produce their family's food and income.

One sign of the changing status of women was the new custom of binding the feet of upper-class girls. When a girl was very young, her feet were bound tightly with cloth, which eventually broke the arch and curled all but the big toe under. This produced what was admiringly called a "lily-foot." Women with bound feet were crippled for life. To others in society, such a woman reflected the wealth and prestige of her husband, who could afford such a beautiful but impractical wife. **D**

The social, economic, and technological transformations of the Tang and Song periods permanently shaped Chinese civilization. They endured even as China fell to a group of nomadic outsiders, the Mongols, whom you will learn about in Section 2.

MAIN IDEA

Making Inferences
D How did the practice of foot binding reflect the changing status of Chinese women?

SECTION ① **ASSESSMENT**

TERMS & NAMES 1. For each term or name, write a sentence explaining its significance.
- Tang Taizong
- Wu Zhao
- movable type
- gentry

USING YOUR NOTES

2. How are the accomplishments of the two dynasties similar?

Tang only
Both
Song only

MAIN IDEAS

3. How did the Tang Dynasty benefit from the accomplishments of the Sui?

4. What steps did the Tang take to restore China's bureaucracy?

5. Describe the urban social classes that emerged during the Tang and Song periods.

CRITICAL THINKING & WRITING

6. **RECOGNIZING EFFECTS** What impact did improvements in transportation have on Tang and Song China?

7. **FORMING AND SUPPORTING OPINIONS** "Gaining power depends on merit, not birth." Do you agree with this view of China under the Tang and Song? Explain.

8. **PRIMARY SOURCES** How do the feelings expressed in Tu Fu's poem on page 326 still relate to life today?

9. **WRITING ACTIVITY** EMPIRE BUILDING Write two short **paragraphs,** one discussing how Tang and Song emperors strengthened China's empire, and the other discussing how they weakened it.

CONNECT TO TODAY CREATING A LIST

Gunpowder is used in the making of fireworks. Conduct research to find interesting facts about fireworks in the United States—the number produced in a year, the amount of gunpowder in a typical firework, and so on. Present your findings in a **list** titled "Fun Facts About Fireworks."

Tang and Song China: People and Technology

The Tang and Song dynasties were eras of major technological advancement in China. The technologies improved China as a country and, in turn, helped people conduct their daily business.

Much of China's technology spread to other parts of the world where it improved the lives of the people living there. The table on this page identifies some of that movement.

↗ hmhsocialstudies.com

RESEARCH WEB LINKS Go online for more on Tang and Song China.

Porcelain ▶

Marco Polo was the first to describe the pottery found in China as porcelain. The plain piece shown here is an early example of porcelain work from the Song Dynasty. A piece like this might be used daily. Later porcelain work, such as the distinctive blue and white porcelain of the Ming Dynasty, became more decorative. Porcelain, however, was a luxury reserved for the middle and upper classes of Chinese society.

Inventions of Tang and Song China		
	Description	**Impact**
Porcelain Late 700s	Bone-hard, white ceramic made of a special clay and a mineral found only in China	Became a valuable export—so associated with Chinese culture that it is now called china; technology remained a Chinese secret for centuries
Mechanical clock 700s	Clock in which machinery (driven by running water) regulated the movements	Early Chinese clocks short-lived; idea for mechanical clock carried by traders to medieval Europe
Printing Block printing: 700s Movable type: 1040	Block printing: one block on which a whole page is cut; movable type: individual characters arranged in frames, used over and over	Printing technology spread to Korea and Japan; movable type also developed later in Europe
Explosive powder 800s	Made from mixture of saltpeter, sulfur, and charcoal	First used for fireworks, then weapons; technology spread west within 300 years
Paper money 1020s	Paper currency issued by Song government to replace cumbersome strings of metal cash used by merchants	Contributed to development of large-scale commercial economy in China
Magnetic compass (for navigation) 1100s	Floating magnetized needle that always points north-south; device had existed in China for centuries before it was adapted by sailors for use at sea	Helped China become a sea power; technology quickly spread west

SKILLBUILDER: Interpreting Charts

1. **Making Inferences** *Which inventions eventually affected warfare and exploration?*
2. **Forming and Supporting Opinions** *Which of these inventions do you think had the greatest impact on history? Why?*

Movable Type ▼

Traditionally, an entire page of characters was carved into a block of wood from which prints were made. Pi Sheng, a Chinese alchemist, came up with the idea of creating individual characters that could be reused whenever needed. Later, a government official created rotating storage trays for the characters.

As you have read, Tang rulers restored China's system of scholar-officials. Thus, education and printed materials became important to a larger part of Chinese society.

The trays allowed the typesetter to quickly find the characters. The typesetter would then order the characters in a tray that would be used to produce the printed pages. The two wheels held about 60,000 characters.

LEGACY OF TANG AND SONG CHINA

Printing
- U.S. publishers produced 122,108 books in 2000.
- The Library of Congress, the largest library in the world, has over 18 million books.
- The world's best-selling book is the Bible. Since 1815, around 2.5 billion copies of the Bible have been sold.

Porcelain
- The United States imported 423,041 one-piece toilet bowls and tanks in 2002. Of those, 302,489 came from China.
- In 2001, a Chinese newspaper reported the production of possibly the world's largest porcelain kettle—just under 10 feet tall, about 6 feet in diameter, and weighing 1.5 tons.

Explosive Powder
- In 2002, the United States imported over 90 percent of its fireworks from China.
- The largest single firework was used at a Japanese festival in 1988. It weighed over 1,000 pounds, and its burst was over half a mile wide.

Explosive Powder ▶

Around A.D. 900, Chinese alchemists first discovered that the right mixture of saltpeter, sulfur, and charcoal could be explosive. The Chinese initially used the powder for fireworks, then for military applications. It is now commonly referred to as gunpowder.

The device shown here is a modern reproduction of an ancient rocket launcher. The Chinese tied gunpowder charges to arrows, balanced them, and placed them in a holder. The holder helped aim the rockets, and its flared shape spread the rockets over a large area.

Connect *to* Today

1. **Forming and Supporting Opinions** Of all the inventions listed on these pages, which do you think had the most lasting impact? Why?

   See Skillbuilder Handbook, page R20.

2. **Hypothesizing** What are some modern inventions that you believe will still have an impact 1,000 years from now?

329

The Mongol Conquests

MAIN IDEA	WHY IT MATTERS NOW	TERMS & NAMES
EMPIRE BUILDING The Mongols, a nomadic people from the steppe, conquered settled societies across much of Asia.	The Mongols built the largest unified land empire in world history.	• pastoralist • Pax • clan Mongolica • Genghis Khan

SETTING THE STAGE While the Chinese prospered during the Song Dynasty, a great people far to the north were also gaining strength. The Mongols of the Asian steppe lived their lives on the move. They prided themselves on their skill on horseback, their discipline, their ruthlessness, and their courage in battle. They also wanted the wealth and glory that came with conquering mighty empires. This desire soon exploded into violent conflict that transformed Asia and Europe forever.

Nomads of the Asian Steppe

hmhsocialstudies.com
TAKING NOTES

Use the graphic organizer online to take notes on the series of events leading to the creation of the Mongol Empire.

A vast belt of dry grassland, called the steppe, stretches across the landmass of Eurasia. The significance of the steppe to neighboring civilizations was twofold. First, it served as a land trade route connecting the East and the West. Second, it was home to nomadic peoples who frequently swept down on their neighbors to plunder, loot, and conquer.

Geography of the Steppe There are two main expanses of the Eurasian steppe. The western steppe runs from Central Asia to eastern Europe. It was the original home of some of the ancient invaders you have read about, including the Hittites. The eastern steppe, covering the area of present-day Mongolia, was the first home of the Huns, the Turks, and the Mongols.

Very little rain falls on the steppe, but the dry, windswept plain supports short, hardy grasses. Seasonal temperature changes can be dramatic. Temperatures in Mongolia, for example, range from −57°F in winter to 96°F in the summer. Rainfall is somewhat more plentiful and the climate milder in the west than in the east. For this reason, movements of people have historically tended to be toward the west and the south.

The Nomadic Way of Life Nomadic peoples were <u>pastoralists</u>—that is, they herded domesticated animals. They were constantly on the move, searching for good pasture to feed their herds. But they did not wander. Rather, they followed a familiar

The Steppe

SIBERIA

Moscow

EUROPE   ASIA

Kiev   WESTERN STEPPE

Aral   EASTERN
Sea   Karakorum   STEPPE
Constantinople   GOBI DESERT
Tashkent
Samarkand   Kashgar   Beijing
CHINA
Kaifeng

INDIA

0   1,000 Miles
0   2,000 Kilometers

seasonal pattern and returned on a regular basis to the same campsites. Keeping claim to land that was not permanently occupied was difficult. Battles frequently arose among nomadic groups over grassland and water rights.

Asian nomads practically lived on horseback as they followed their huge herds over the steppe. They depended on their animals for food, clothing, and housing. Their diet consisted of meat and mare's milk. They wore clothing made of skins and wool, and they lived in portable felt tents called yurts.

Steppe nomads traveled together in kinship groups called **clans**. The members of each clan claimed to be descended from a common ancestor. Different clans sometimes came together when they needed a large force to attack a common enemy or raid their settled neighbors.

Steppe Nomads and Settled Societies The differing ways of life of nomadic and settled peoples resulted in constant interaction between them. Often, they engaged in peaceful trade. The nomads exchanged horses, for example, for basic items they lacked, such as grain, metal, cloth, and tea. Nomads were accustomed to scarcity and hardship. They prided themselves on their toughness. However, they were sometimes tempted by the rich land and relative wealth of townspeople and took what they wanted by force. As a result, settled peoples lived in constant fear of raids.

Time and again in history, nomadic peoples rode out of the steppe to invade border towns and villages. When a state or empire was strong and organized, it could protect its frontier. If the state or empire became divided and weak, the nomads could increase their attacks and gain more plunder. Occasionally, a powerful nomadic group was able to conquer a whole empire and become its rulers. Over generations, these nomadic rulers often became part of the civilization they conquered. **Ⓐ**

MAIN IDEA

Making Inferences
Ⓐ How might a strong, organized empire defend its frontier?

The Rise of the Mongols

For centuries, the Mongol people had roamed the eastern steppe in loosely organized clans. It took a military and political genius to unite the Mongols into a force with a single purpose—conquest.

Genghis Khan Unites the Mongols Around 1200, a Mongol clan leader named Temujin sought to unify the Mongols under his leadership. He fought and defeated his rivals one by one. In 1206, Temujin accepted the title **Genghis Khan**, or "universal ruler" of the Mongol clans.

Over the next 21 years, Genghis led the Mongols in conquering much of Asia. His first goal was China. After invading the northern Jin Empire in 1211, however, his attention turned to the Islamic region west of Mongolia. Angered by the murder of Mongol traders and an ambassador at the hands of the Muslims, Genghis launched a campaign of terror across Central Asia. The Mongols destroyed one city after another—Utrar, Samarkand, Bukhara—and slaughtered many inhabitants. By 1225, Central Asia was under Mongol control.

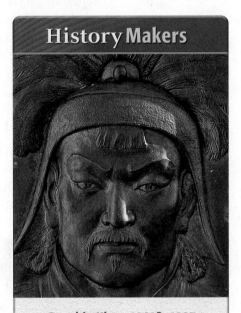

History Makers

Genghis Khan 1162?–1227
Temujin, according to legend, was born with a blood clot in his fist. In his lifetime, his hands were often covered with the blood of others.

When Temujin was about nine, the Tatars, a rival people, poisoned his father. For a time, he and his family lived in extreme poverty, abandoned by their clan. When in manhood he fought and defeated the Tatars, he slaughtered every male taller than a cart axle.

While driven by revenge, Genghis also loved conquest. He once remarked to his personal historian:

Man's greatest good fortune is to chase and defeat his enemy, seize his total possessions, leave his married women weeping and wailing, [and] ride his [horse].

🔗 hmhsocialstudies.com

RESEARCH WEB LINKS Go online for more on Genghis Khan.

Genghis the Conqueror Several characteristics lay behind Genghis Khan's stunning success as a conqueror. First, he was a brilliant organizer. He assembled his Mongol warriors into a mighty fighting force (see below). Following the model of the Chinese military, Genghis grouped his warriors in armies of 10,000. These in turn were organized into 1,000-man brigades, 100-man companies, and 10-man squads. He put his most battle-proven and loyal men in command of these units.

Second, Genghis was a gifted strategist. He used various tricks to confuse his enemy. Sometimes, a small Mongol cavalry unit would attack, then pretend to gallop away in flight. The enemy usually gave chase. Then the rest of the Mongol army would appear suddenly and slaughter the surprised enemy forces.

Finally, Genghis Khan used cruelty as a weapon. He believed in terrifying his enemies into surrender. If a city refused to open its gates to him, he might kill the entire population when he finally captured the place. The terror the Mongols inspired spread ahead of their armies, which led many towns to surrender without a fight. As one Arab historian wrote, "In the countries that have not yet been overrun by them, everyone spends the night afraid that they may appear there too." **B**

The Mongol Empire

Genghis Khan died in 1227—not from violence, but from illness. His successors continued to expand his empire. In less than 50 years, the Mongols conquered territory from China to Poland. In so doing, they created the largest unified land empire in history. (See the map on page 334.)

MAIN IDEA

Summarizing
B What were some of the tactics Genghis Khan used in war?

History *in* Depth

hmhsocialstudies.com INTERACTIVE

A Mighty Fighting Force

Mongol soldiers were superb horsemen, having spent all their lives in the saddle. Annual game roundups gave young men the chance to practice skills they would use in battle and gave their leaders the opportunity to spot promising warriors. When on the move, each soldier was accompanied by three extra horses. By changing mounts, soldiers could stay in the saddle for up to ten days and nights at a time. When charging toward a target, they covered as much as 120 miles a day. If food was scarce, a Mongol soldier might make a small gash in the neck of one of his horses and sustain himself by drinking the blood.

A key to Mongol horsemanship was the stirrup, which was invented on the steppe in the second century B.C. Stirrups enabled a mounted warrior to stand, turn, and shoot arrows behind him.

Under his armor, each cavalry warrior wore silk underwear, which arrows often did not pierce. The warriors could use the silk to help pull the arrow cleanly out of a wound.

The cavalry warrior's weapons included leather armor, a lance, a dagger, a bow and arrows, and his stout, sturdy horse.

The Khanates After Genghis's death, his sons and grandsons continued the campaign of conquest. Armies under their leadership drove south, east, and west out of inner Asia. They completed their conquest of northern China and invaded Korea. They leveled the Russian city of Kiev and reached the banks of the Adriatic Sea. The cities of Venice and Vienna were within their grasp. However, in the 1250s the Mongols halted their westward campaign and turned their attention to Persia. By 1260, the Mongols had divided their huge empire into four regions, or khanates. (See the map on page 334.) These were the Khanate of the Great Khan (Mongolia and China), the Khanate of Chagatai (Central Asia), the Ilkhanate (Persia), and the Khanate of the Golden Horde (Russia). A descendant of Genghis ruled each khanate.

The Mongols as Rulers Many of the areas invaded by the Mongols never recovered. The populations of some cities were wiped out. In addition, the Mongols destroyed ancient irrigation systems in areas such as the Tigris and Euphrates valleys. Thus, the land could no longer support resettlement. While ferocious in war, the Mongols were quite tolerant in peace. They rarely imposed their beliefs or way of life on those they conquered. Over time, some Mongol rulers even adopted aspects of the culture of the people they ruled. The Ilkhans and the Golden Horde, for example, became Muslims. Growing cultural differences among the khanates contributed to the eventual splitting up of the empire.

The Mongol Peace From the mid-1200s to the mid-1300s, the Mongols imposed stability and law and order across much of Eurasia. This period is sometimes called the <u>Pax Mongolica</u>, or Mongol Peace. The Mongols guaranteed safe passage for trade caravans, travelers, and missionaries from one end of the empire to another.

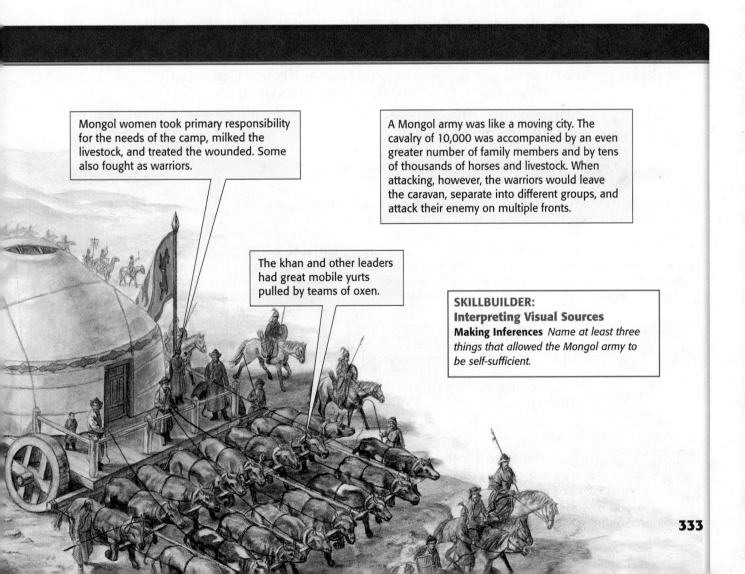

Mongol women took primary responsibility for the needs of the camp, milked the livestock, and treated the wounded. Some also fought as warriors.

A Mongol army was like a moving city. The cavalry of 10,000 was accompanied by an even greater number of family members and by tens of thousands of horses and livestock. When attacking, however, the warriors would leave the caravan, separate into different groups, and attack their enemy on multiple fronts.

The khan and other leaders had great mobile yurts pulled by teams of oxen.

SKILLBUILDER:
Interpreting Visual Sources
Making Inferences *Name at least three things that allowed the Mongol army to be self-sufficient.*

333

The Mongol Empire, 1294

hmhsocialstudies.com
INTERACTIVE MAP

Legend:
— Border of Mongol Empire
→ Campaigns of Genghis Khan
→ Campaigns of his successors
→ Route of Marco Polo
ᴖᴖ Great Wall

GEOGRAPHY SKILLBUILDER: Interpreting Maps
1. **Region** What khanate controlled Russia? Persia? Korea?
2. **Region** What parts of Asia did the Mongols fail to control?

Trade between Europe and Asia had never been more active. Ideas and inventions traveled along with the trade goods. Many Chinese innovations, such as gunpowder, reached Europe during this period.

Other things spread along with the goods and the ideas. Some historians speculate that the epidemic of bubonic plague that devastated Europe during the 1300s was first spread by the Mongols. (See Chapter 14.) The disease might have traveled along trade routes or have been passed to others by infected Mongol troops.

For a brief period of history, the nomadic Mongols were the lords of city-based civilizations across Asia, including China. As you will read in Section 3, China continued to thrive under Mongol rule.

SECTION 2 ASSESSMENT

TERMS & NAMES 1. For each term or name, write a sentence explaining its significance.
• pastoralist   • clan   • Genghis Khan   • Pax Mongolica

USING YOUR NOTES
2. Which of the listed events do you think is the most important? Why?

MAIN IDEAS
3. In what ways did steppe nomads and the people of neighboring settled societies interact?
4. Why was terror an important weapon for Genghis Khan?
5. What happened to the Mongol Empire in the years after Genghis Khan's death?

CRITICAL THINKING & WRITING
6. **MAKING INFERENCES** What characteristics of their culture do you think contributed to the Mongols' military success? Explain your response.
7. **ANALYZING MOTIVES** What do you think drove Genghis Khan to conquer a great empire? Explain your answer.
8. **FORMING AND SUPPORTING OPINIONS** "The Mongols were great conquerors but poor rulers." Do you agree with this statement? Why or why not?
9. **WRITING ACTIVITY** CULTURAL INTERACTION Write a brief **essay** discussing the impact of interaction between the Mongols and the various cultures that they conquered.

MULTIMEDIA ACTIVITY CREATING AN ILLUSTRATED REPORT

Today, most Mongols live in the country of Mongolia. Use the Internet to find information on Mongolian ways of life. Then create an **illustrated report** comparing ways of life today and in Genghis Khan's time.

INTERNET KEYWORD
Mongolia

The Mongol Empire

MAIN IDEA	WHY IT MATTERS NOW	TERMS & NAMES
CULTURAL INTERACTION As emperor of China, Kublai Khan encouraged foreign trade.	The influence of Chinese ideas on Western civilization began with the Mongols' encouragement of trade.	• Kublai Khan • Marco Polo

SETTING THE STAGE Kublai Khan, the grandson of Genghis Khan, assumed the title Great Khan in 1260. In theory, the Great Khan ruled the entire Mongol Empire. In reality, the empire had split into four khanates. Other descendants of Genghis ruled Central Asia, Persia, and Russia as semi-independent states. So, Kublai focused instead on extending the power and range of his own khanate, which already included Mongolia, Korea, Tibet, and northern China. To begin, however, he had to fulfill the goal of his grandfather to conquer all of China.

Kublai Khan Becomes Emperor

The Chinese held off Kublai's attacks for several years. However, his armies finally overwhelmed them in 1279. Throughout China's long history, the Chinese feared and fought off invasions by northern nomads. China sometimes lost territory to nomadic groups, but no foreigner had ever ruled the whole country. With Kublai's victory, that changed.

Beginning a New Dynasty As China's new emperor, Kublai Khan founded a new dynasty called the Yuan (yoo•AHN) Dynasty. It lasted less than a century, until 1368, when it was overthrown. However, the Yuan era was an important period in Chinese history for several reasons. First, Kublai Khan united China for the first time in more than 300 years. For this he is considered one of China's great emperors. Second, the control imposed by the Mongols across all of Asia opened China to greater foreign contacts and trade. Finally, Kublai and his successors tolerated Chinese culture and made few changes to the system of government.

Unlike his Mongol ancestors, Kublai abandoned the Mongolian steppes for China. He did not share his ancestors' dislike of the settled life. On the contrary, he rather enjoyed living in the luxurious manner of a Chinese emperor. He maintained a beautiful summer palace at Shangdu, on the border between Mongolia and China. He also built a new square-walled capital at the site of modern Beijing. Kublai built this palace to enhance his prestige, but his new capital meant something more. Previously, the Great Khans had ruled their empire from Mongolia. Moving the capital from Mongolia to China was a sign that Kublai intended to make his mark as emperor of China.

Failure to Conquer Japan After conquering China, Kublai Khan tried to extend his rule to Japan. In 1274 and again in 1281, the Great Khan sent huge fleets

hmhsocialstudies.com
TAKING NOTES

Use the graphic organizer online to take notes on the impact of Kublai Khan on East Asia.

▲ This detail from a 13th-century Japanese scroll depicts Japanese warriors fighting off a Mongol warship.

against Japan. The Mongols forced Koreans to build, sail, and provide provisions for the boats, a costly task that almost ruined Korea. Both times the Japanese turned back the Mongol fleets.

The second fleet carried 150,000 Mongol, Chinese, and Korean warriors—the largest seaborne invasion force in history until World War II. After 53 days, Japanese warriors had fought the invaders to a standstill. Then, on the following day, the sky darkened and a typhoon swept furiously across the Sea of Japan. Mongol ships were upended, swamped, and dashed to bits against the rocky shore, despite their sailors' attempts to escape onto the open sea. For centuries afterward, the Japanese spoke reverently of the *kamikaze,* or "divine wind," that had saved Japan.

Mongol Rule in China

Early in Kublai Khan's reign, one of his Chinese advisers told him, "I have heard that one can conquer the empire on horseback, but one cannot govern it on horseback." This advice illustrates the problems Kublai faced as emperor. Mongol ways would not work in a sophisticated civilization like China's. Besides, the number of Mongols in China was few compared to the huge native population. Kublai would need to make use of non-Mongol officials to help him rule successfully.

The Mongols and the Chinese The Mongol rulers had little in common with their Chinese subjects. Because of their differences, the Mongols kept their separate identity. Mongols lived apart from the Chinese and obeyed different laws. They kept the Chinese out of high government offices, although they retained as many Chinese officials as possible to serve on the local level. Most of the highest government posts went to Mongols or to foreigners. The Mongols believed that foreigners were more trustworthy since they had no local loyalties. **A**

Despite his differences with the Chinese, Kublai Khan was an able leader. He restored the Grand Canal and extended it 135 miles north to Beijing. Along its banks he built a paved highway that ran some 1,100 miles, from Hangzhou to Beijing. These land and water routes ensured the north a steady supply of grain and other goods from the southern heartland.

Foreign Trade Foreign trade increased under Kublai Khan. This was largely due to the Mongol Peace, which made the caravan routes across Central Asia safe for trade and travel. Traders transported Chinese silk and porcelain, which were greatly valued in Europe and western Asia, over the Silk Roads and other routes. These traders also carried with them such Chinese products and inventions as printing, gunpowder, the compass, paper currency, and playing cards.

MAIN IDEA

Making Inferences
A How might the Chinese have felt about their lack of power in Kublai's government?

Kublai further encouraged trade by inviting foreign merchants to visit China. Most of them were Muslims from India, Central Asia, and Persia. Many European traders and travelers, including Christian missionaries, also reached China.

Marco Polo at the Mongol Court The most famous European to visit China in these years was a young Venetian trader, <u>Marco Polo</u>. He traveled by caravan on the Silk Roads with his father and uncle, arriving at Kublai Khan's court around 1275. Polo had learned several Asian languages in his travels, and Kublai Khan sent him to various Chinese cities on government missions. Polo served the Great Khan well for 17 years. In 1292, the Polos left China and made the long journey back to Venice. **B**

Later, during a war against Venice's rival city, Genoa, Marco Polo was captured and imprisoned. In prison he had time to tell the full story of his travels and adventures. To his awed listeners, he spoke of China's fabulous cities, its fantastic wealth, and the strange things he had seen there. He mentioned the burning of "black stones" (coal) in Chinese homes. (Coal as a fuel was little known in Europe.) He also recorded the practical workings of Kublai's government and aspects of Chinese life. Here is his description of trade in Beijing:

> **PRIMARY SOURCE**
> [M]ore precious and costly wares are imported into Khan-balik [Beijing] than into any other city in the world. . . . All the treasures that come from India— precious stones, pearls, and other rarities—are brought here. So too are the choicest and costliest products of Cathay [China] itself and every other province.
> **MARCO POLO,** *The Travels of Marco Polo*

A fellow prisoner gathered Polo's stories into a book. It was an instant success in Europe, but most readers did not believe a word of it. They thought Polo's account was a marvelous collection of tall tales. It was clear to Marco Polo, however, that the civilization he had visited was the greatest in the world.

MAIN IDEA

Analyzing Motives

B Why do you think Kublai Khan employed Marco Polo?

History Makers

Kublai Khan 1215–1294
As ruler of both China and the Mongol Empire, Kublai Khan straddled two worlds. He built luxurious palaces, dressed as a Chinese emperor, and supported the work of Chinese artists. However, he remained a Mongol warrior at heart. The Great Khan is said to have planted a plot of grass from the steppe in the gardens at Beijing to remind himself of his home. He also loved to hunt and enclosed a large hunting ground at his palace at Shangdu.

Marco Polo 1254?–1324
The man who described Kublai Khan to Europeans left behind very little information about himself. According to Polo, Kublai recognized his "merit and worth" and sent him on special missions around the empire. His impressions of China became the basis of his book, but he described few actual events about his life.

Since his book first appeared, people have debated whether Polo even visited China. He is not mentioned in Chinese accounts of this time. His tales also fail to mention such common features of China as tea, acupuncture, or foot binding. On his deathbed, Polo was asked if his travel stories were true. He replied that he had told barely half of what he had seen.

hmhsocialstudies.com

RESEARCH WEB LINKS Go online for more on Kublai Khan and Marco Polo.

VIDEO
Marco Polo
hmhsocialstudies.com

The End of Mongol Rule

During the last years of Kublai Khan's reign, weaknesses began to appear in Mongol rule. In an attempt to further expand his empire, Kublai sent several expeditions into Southeast Asia. His armies and navies suffered many humiliating defeats at a huge expense of lives and equipment. Heavy spending on fruitless wars, on public works, and on the luxuries of the Yuan court burdened the treasury and created resentment among the overtaxed Chinese. This presented problems that Kublai's less able successors could not resolve.

Dynasties of China, 500–1400

850 Gunpowder invented	**1215** Genghis Kahn invades northern China.	**1275** Marco Polo reaches China.

SUI   TANG   SONG   SOUTHERN SONG   YUAN

WARFARE AND REVOLT

500 A.D.   800 A.D.   1100 A.D.   1400 A.D.

627 Tang Taizong becomes emperor.

690 Empress Wu Zhao assumes throne.

751 Chinese lose Battle of Talas.

1024 Government issues paper money.

1040 Movable type invented

1126 Song Dynasty retreats to south.

1260 Kublai becomes Great Kahn.

Yuan Dynasty Overthrown Kublai Khan died in 1294. After his death, the Yuan Dynasty began to fade. Family members continually argued over who would rule. In one eight-year period, four different khans took the throne.

Rebellions broke out in many parts of China in the 1300s. The Chinese had long resented their Mongol rulers, and the Mongol humiliation of the Chinese only increased under Kublai Khan's successors. The rebellions were also fueled by years of famine, flood, and disease, along with growing economic problems and official corruption. In 1368, Chinese rebels finally overthrew the Mongols. The rebel leader founded a new dynasty, the Ming, which you will read about in Chapter 19. **C**

Decline of the Mongol Empire By the time of the collapse of the Yuan Dynasty, the entire Mongol Empire had disintegrated. The government of the Ilkhanate in Persia fell apart in the 1330s. The Chagatai khans ruled Central Asia until the 1370s. Only the Golden Horde in Russia stayed in power. The Golden Horde ruled Russia for 250 years. As you read in Chapter 11, Ivan III finally led Russia to independence from Mongol rule in 1480.

The rise and fall of Mongol rule affected civilizations from eastern Europe to China. Kublai Khan had tried to extend this influence to Japan but had failed. However, several centuries earlier, the Japanese had embraced the influence of an outside culture—China. This development is described in Section 4.

> **MAIN IDEA**
>
> **Analyzing Causes**
> **C** What factors contributed to the decline and fall of the Yuan Dynasty?

SECTION 3 ASSESSMENT

TERMS & NAMES 1. For each term or name, write a sentence explaining its significance.
• Kublai Khan   • Marco Polo

USING YOUR NOTES

2. Select one of the entries. Did this event make China stronger or weaker?

Kublai Khan

MAIN IDEAS

3. Why did the Mongols employ foreigners rather than Chinese in high government offices?

4. How did Europeans view Marco Polo's account of his time in China?

5. What happened to the Yuan Dynasty after Kublai Khan's death?

CRITICAL THINKING & WRITING

6. **EVALUATING DECISIONS** Judging from the events of the Yuan Dynasty, do you think the Mongol policies toward the Chinese were effective? Explain your answer.

7. **RECOGNIZING EFFECTS** What impact did the Mongol Peace have on interaction between East and West?

8. **FORMING AND SUPPORTING OPINIONS** Do you think that Kublai Khan was a successful ruler? Why or why not?

9. **WRITING ACTIVITY** CULTURAL INTERACTION Adopt the role of a traveler in Mongol China. Write a **letter** to friends explaining how the Chinese way of life has influenced the Mongol conquerors.

CONNECT TO TODAY WRITING A SUMMARY

Some people consider Marco Polo to be the first travel writer. Locate modern travel writing on China. Select and read descriptions of major cities, such as Beijing. Using photographs and sketches, create an **illustrated summary** of the main points included in the descriptions.

Feudal Powers in Japan

MAIN IDEA	WHY IT MATTERS NOW	TERMS & NAMES
RELIGIOUS AND ETHICAL SYSTEMS Japanese civilization was shaped by cultural borrowing from China and the rise of feudalism and military rulers.	An openness to adapting innovations from other cultures is still a hallmark of Japanese society.	• Shinto • Bushido • samurai • shogun

SETTING THE STAGE Japan lies east of China, in the direction of the sunrise. In fact, the name Japan comes from the Chinese word *ri-ben,* which means "origin of the sun" or "land of the rising sun." From ancient times, Japan had borrowed ideas, institutions, and culture from the Chinese people. Japan's genius was its ability to take in new ideas and make them uniquely its own.

The Growth of Japanese Civilization

Japan's island location shaped the growth of its civilization. About 120 miles of water separates Japan from its closest neighbor, Korea, and 500 miles of water separates Japan from China. The Japanese were close enough to feel the civilizing effect of China. Yet they were far enough away to be reasonably safe from invasion.

The Geography of Japan About 4,000 islands make up the Japanese archipelago (AHR•kuh•PEHL•uh•GOH), or island group, that extends in an arc more than 1,200 miles long. Historically, most Japanese people have lived on the four largest islands: Hokkaido (hah•KY•doh), Honshu (HAHN•shoo), Shikoku (shee•KAW•koo), and Kyushu (kee•OO•shoo).

Japan's geography has both advantages and disadvantages. Southern Japan enjoys a mild climate with plenty of rainfall. The country is so mountainous, however, that only about 12 percent of the land is suitable for farming. Natural resources such as coal, oil, and iron are in short supply. During the late summer and early fall, strong tropical storms called typhoons occur. Earthquakes and tidal waves are also threats.

Early Japan The first historic mention of Japan comes from Chinese writings of the first century B.C. Japan at this time was not a united country. Instead, hundreds of clans controlled their own territories. Each clan worshiped its own nature gods and goddesses. In different parts of Japan, people honored thousands of local gods. Their varied customs and beliefs eventually combined to form Japan's earliest religion. In later times, this religion was called **Shinto** (SHIHN•toh), meaning "way of the gods."

Shinto was based on respect for the forces of nature and on the worship of ancestors. Shinto worshipers believed in *kami,* divine spirits that dwelled in nature. Any unusual or especially beautiful tree, rock, waterfall, or mountain was considered the home of a *kami.*

hmhsocialstudies.com
TAKING NOTES
Use the graphic organizer online to take notes on the main periods and events in Japanese history from 300 to 1300.

Japan to 1300

Hokkaido

PACIFIC
OCEAN

Sea of
Japan
(East Sea)

JAPAN

KOREA

Honshu

Mt. Fuji

Edo (Tokyo)

Heian (Kyoto)

Kamakura

Yellow
Sea

Nara

CHINA

Shikoku

Kyushu

Under Mongol control
City
Mountain
Mongol invasion, 1274
Mongol invasion, 1281

GEOGRAPHY SKILLBUILDER: Interpreting Maps
1. **Location** How far is the southern end of the Japanese island of Kyushu from China?
2. **Location** On what island did Japan's major cities develop?

The Yamato Emperors By the A.D. 400s, the Yamato clan had established itself as the leading clan. The Yamato claimed to be descended from the sun goddess Amaterasu. By the seventh century, the Yamato chiefs called themselves the emperors of Japan. The early emperors did not control the entire country, or even much of it, but the Japanese gradually accepted the idea of an emperor.

Although many of the Yamato rulers lacked real power, the dynasty was never overthrown. When rival clans fought for power, the winning clan claimed control of the emperor and then ruled in the emperor's name. Japan had both an emperor who served as a figurehead and a ruling power who reigned behind the throne. This dual structure became an enduring characteristic of Japanese government.

Japanese Culture

During the 400s, the Japanese began to have more and more contact with mainland Asia. They soon came under the influence of Chinese ideas and customs, which they first learned about from Korean travelers.

Buddhism in Japan One of the most important influences brought by Korean travelers was Buddhism. In the mid-700s, the Japanese imperial court officially accepted Buddhism in Japan. By the eighth or ninth century, Buddhist ideas and worship had spread through Japanese society. The Japanese, however, did not give up their Shinto beliefs. Some Buddhist rituals became Shinto rituals, and some Shinto gods and goddesses were worshiped in Buddhist temples.

Cultural Borrowing from China Interest in Buddhist ideas at the Japanese court soon grew into an enthusiasm for all things Chinese. The most influential convert to Buddhism was Prince Shotoku (shoh•toh•ku), who served as regent for his aunt, the empress Suiko. (A regent is someone who rules when a monarch is absent, ill, or too young to rule.) In 607, Prince Shotoku sent the first of three missions to China. His people studied Chinese civilization firsthand. Over the next 200 years, the Japanese sent many such groups to learn about Chinese ways. **A**

The Japanese adopted the Chinese system of writing. Japanese artists painted landscapes in the Chinese manner. The Japanese also followed Chinese styles in the simple arts of everyday living, such as cooking, gardening, drinking tea, and hairdressing. For a time, Japan even modeled its government on China's. Prince Shotoku planned a strong central government like that of the Tang rulers. He also tried to introduce China's civil-service system. However, this attempt failed. In Japan, noble birth remained the key to winning a powerful position. Unlike China, Japan continued to be a country where a few great families held power.

The Japanese adapted Chinese ways to suit their own needs. While they learned much, they still retained their own traditions. Eventually, the Japanese imperial court decided it had learned enough from Tang China. In the late ninth century, it ended formal missions to the Tang Empire, which had fallen into decline. Although Chinese cultural influence would remain strong in Japan, Japan's own culture was about to bloom.

MAIN IDEA

Synthesizing
A How did Chinese culture spread to Japan?

Life in the Heian Period

In the late 700s, the imperial court moved its capital from Nara to Heian (HAY•ahn), the modern Kyoto (kee•OH•toh). Many of Japan's noble families also moved to Heian. Among the upper class in Heian, a highly refined court society arose. This era in Japanese history, from 794 to 1185, is called the Heian period.

Gentlemen and ladies of the court filled their days with elaborate ritual and artistic pursuits. Rules dictated every aspect of court life—the length of swords, the color of official robes, forms of address, even the number of skirts a woman wore. Etiquette was also extremely important. Laughing aloud in public, for example, was frowned upon. And everyone at court was expected to write poetry and to paint.

The best accounts of Heian society come from the diaries, essays, and novels written by the women of the court. One of the finest writers of the period was Lady Murasaki Shikibu. Lady Murasaki's 11th-century masterpiece, *The Tale of Genji,* is an account of the life of a prince in the imperial court. This long prose narrative is considered the world's first novel.

Vocabulary
etiquette: the code governing correct behavior and appearance

Feudalism Erodes Imperial Authority

During the Heian period, Japan's central government was relatively strong. However, this strength was soon to be challenged by great landowners and clan chiefs who acted more and more as independent local rulers.

Decline of Central Power For most of the Heian period, the rich Fujiwara family held the real power in Japan. By about the middle of the 11th century, however, the power of the central government and the Fujiwaras began to slip.

Large landowners living away from the capital set up private armies. The countryside became lawless and dangerous. Armed soldiers on horseback preyed on farmers and travelers, and pirates took control of the seas. For safety, farmers and

> ## Analyzing Art

Women of the Heian Court

The Tale of Genji picture scroll—an illustrated version of the story—provides insights into the life of women at the Heian court. Since servants did almost all domestic chores, upper class women had much leisure time. How did they spend this time?

1. Because women were expected to look attractive, they spent time on personal grooming, such as hair care.
2. Women spent much time reading, usually the *monogatari,* or prose fiction, popular at the time. As the prince notes in *The Tale of Genji,* "Without these monogatari how on earth would [women entertain themselves] during these tedious hours?"

SKILLBUILDER: Interpreting Visual Sources
1. **Drawing Conclusions** *From what you have read about Heian court life, why do you think women spent so much time in personal grooming?*
2. **Making Inferences** *Based on what you have read, in what other ways might the women of the Heian court have spent their time?*

Japanese Samurai

Samurai were members of Japan's warrior class. Early samurai protected local aristocratic landowners. In the late 1100s, however, the warrior class secured national power and dominated Japanese government until 1868.

Samurai warriors followed an unwritten code that emphasized honor, bravery, and loyalty. This code came to be known as Bushido. Their reputation as fearsome warriors has become legendary.

▲ Female Samurai
Samurai were not always men. Here, Lady Tomoe Gozen, a famous female warrior of the 1180s, enters bravely into battle.

Helmets were made from iron plates to repel sword blows.

An iron mask was sometimes worn not only to protect the face, but to frighten the samurai's enemy as well.

Samurai swords were made by skilled artisans. The curvature of the blade makes the weapon more effective when slashing.

Individual iron plates provided protection and freedom of movement when in combat. As you can see, a samurai's armor was often richly decorated.

HISTORY

VIDEO
Samurai

↗ hmhsocialstudies.com

◄ Samurai Warrior
In combat, a samurai's life depended on his skill and his equipment. Here you can see how the samurai's weapons and armor aided him or her in battle.

SKILLBUILDER:
Interpreting Visual Sources
1. **Comparing and Contrasting** *What are some similarities or differences between Japanese samurai and European knights?*
2. **Hypothesizing** *How might the code of the Samurai help them in battle?*

small landowners traded parts of their land to strong warlords in exchange for protection. With more land, the lords gained more power. This marked the beginning of a feudal system of localized rule like that of ancient China and medieval Europe.

Samurai Warriors Since wars between rival lords were commonplace, each lord surrounded himself with a bodyguard of loyal warriors called <u>samurai</u> (SAM•uh•RY). (*Samurai* means "one who serves.") Samurai lived according to a demanding code of behavior called <u>Bushido</u> (BUSH•ih•DOH), or "the way of the warrior." A samurai was expected to show reckless courage, reverence for the gods, fairness, and generosity toward those weaker than himself. Dying an honorable death was judged more important than living a long life.

The Kamakura Shogunate During the late 1100s, Japan's two most powerful clans fought for power. After almost 30 years of war, the Minamoto family emerged victorious. In 1192, the emperor gave a Minamoto leader named Yoritomo the title of <u>shogun</u>, or "supreme general of the emperor's army." In effect, the shogun had the powers of a military dictator.

Following tradition, the emperor still reigned from Kyoto. (Kyoto was rebuilt on the ruins of Heian, which had been destroyed in war.) However, the real center of power was at the shogun's military headquarters at Kamakura (KAHM•uh•KUR•uh). The 1200s are known in Japanese history as the Kamakura shogunate. The pattern of government in which shoguns ruled through puppet emperors lasted in Japan until 1868. **B**

The Kamakura shoguns were strong enough to turn back the two naval invasions sent by the great Mongol ruler Kublai Khan in 1274 and 1281. However, the Japanese victory over the Mongols drained the shoguns' treasury. Loyal samurai were bitter when the government failed to pay them. The Kamakura shoguns lost prestige and power. Samurai attached themselves more closely to their local lords, who soon fought one another as fiercely as they had fought the Mongols.

Although feudal Japan no longer courted contact with China, it would continue to absorb Chinese ideas and shape them into the Japanese way. As you will read in Section 5, China's culture also influenced Korea and kingdoms of Southeast Asia.

MAIN IDEA

Drawing Conclusions

B What advantages were there to preserving the imperial dynasty, even if it lacked real power?

SECTION 4 ASSESSMENT

TERMS & NAMES 1. For each term or name, write a sentence explaining its significance.
• Shinto   • samurai   • Bushido   • shogun

USING YOUR NOTES

2. What event would you consider the most important turning point in Japan's early history? Why?

MAIN IDEAS

3. Why were Japanese missions to Tang China so important?

4. What was life like in the Heian court?

5. What purpose did the samurai serve?

CRITICAL THINKING & WRITING

6. **FORMING AND SUPPORTING OPINIONS** "The Japanese selectively borrowed from Chinese culture." Use information from the text to support this statement.

7. **EVALUATING COURSES OF ACTION** Why do you think the shoguns chose to rule through puppet emperors rather than simply seizing the imperial throne themselves?

8. **DRAWING CONCLUSIONS** Was the rise of the shogun beneficial for Japan overall? Explain.

9. **WRITING ACTIVITY** RELIGIOUS AND ETHICAL SYSTEMS Write a **dialogue** between two members of a Japanese family on why they have decided to convert to Buddhism.

CONNECT TO TODAY PREPARING AN ORAL REPORT

After World War II, the Japanese adopted aspects of American culture such as baseball. Find information about baseball in Japan, noting how the Japanese have adapted the game to suit their own traditions. Present your findings in a brief **oral report.**

Kingdoms of Southeast Asia and Korea

MAIN IDEA	WHY IT MATTERS NOW	TERMS & NAMES
CULTURAL INTERACTION Several smaller kingdoms prospered in East and Southeast Asia, a region culturally influenced by China and India.	Chinese cultural influences still affect East and Southeast Asia today.	• Khmer Empire • Koryu Dynasty • Angkor Wat

SETTING THE STAGE To the south of China lies the region called Southeast Asia. It includes the modern countries of Myanmar (Burma), Laos, Cambodia, Vietnam, Malaysia, Indonesia, Thailand, Singapore, Brunei, and the Philippines. Thousands of miles from this region, to China's northeast, lies the Korean peninsula. This peninsula is currently divided between North Korea and South Korea. In the shadow of powerful China, many small but prosperous kingdoms rose and fell in Southeast Asia and Korea.

Kingdoms of Southeast Asia

Use the graphic organizer online to take notes on the kingdoms discussed in this section.

In Southeast Asia's river valleys and deltas and on its islands, many kingdoms had centuries of glory and left monuments of lasting beauty.

Geography of Southeast Asia Southeast Asia lies between the Indian and Pacific oceans and stretches from Asia almost to Australia. It consists of two main parts: (1) Indochina, the mainland peninsula that borders China to the north and India to the west, and (2) the islands, the largest of which include Sumatra, Borneo, and Java. All of Southeast Asia lies within the warm, humid tropics. Monsoon winds bring the region heavy seasonal rains.

Seas and straits separate the islands of Southeast Asia. On the mainland, five great rivers flow from the north and cut valleys to the sea. Between the valleys rise hills and mountains, making travel and communication difficult. Over time, many different peoples settled the region, so it was home to many cultures.

Throughout Southeast Asia's history, the key to political power often has been control of trade routes and harbors. This is because Southeast Asia lies on the most direct sea route between the Indian Ocean and the South China Sea. Two important waterways connect the two seas: the Strait of Malacca, between the Malay Peninsula and Sumatra, and the Sunda Strait, between Sumatra and Java.

Influence of India and China Indian merchant ships, taking advantage of the monsoon winds, began arriving in Southeast Asia by the first century A.D. In the period that followed, Hindu and Buddhist missionaries spread their faiths to the region. In time, kingdoms arose that followed these religions and were modeled on Indian political ideas. Gradually, Indian influence shaped many aspects of the region's culture. This early Indian influence on Southeast Asia is evident today in the region's religions, languages, and art forms.

Chinese ideas and culture spread southward in the region through migration and trade. At different times, the Chinese also exerted political influence over parts of mainland Southeast Asia, either through direct rule or by demanding tribute from local rulers.

The Khmer Empire The <u>Khmer</u> (kmair) <u>Empire</u>, in what is now Cambodia, was for centuries the main power on the Southeast Asian mainland. By the 800s, the Khmer had conquered neighboring kingdoms and created an empire. This empire reached the peak of its power around 1200.

Improved rice cultivation helped the Khmer become prosperous. The Khmer built elaborate irrigation systems and waterways. These advances made it possible to grow three or four crops of rice a year in an area that had previously produced only one.

MAIN IDEA

Making Inferences

A What does the size and splendor of Angkor Wat suggest about the empire that constructed it?

At their capital, Angkor, Khmer rulers built extensive city-and-temple complexes. One of these, called <u>**Angkor Wat**</u>, is one of the world's greatest architectural achievements. The complex, which covers nearly a square mile, was built as a symbolic mountain dedicated to the Hindu god Vishnu. The Khmer also used it as an observatory. **A**

Island Trading Kingdoms Powerful kingdoms also developed on Southeast Asia's islands. For example, a dynasty called Sailendra ruled an agricultural kingdom on the island of Java. The Sailendra kings left behind another of the world's great architectural monuments, the Buddhist temple at Borobudur. Built around 800, this temple—like Angkor Wat—reflects strong Indian influence. The massive complex has nine terraced levels like a stepped pyramid.

The Sailendra Dynasty eventually fell under the domination of the powerful island empire of Srivijaya. At its height from the 7th to the 13th centuries, Srivijaya ruled the Strait of Malacca and other waters around the islands of Sumatra, Borneo, and Java. It grew wealthy by taxing the trade that passed through its waters. The

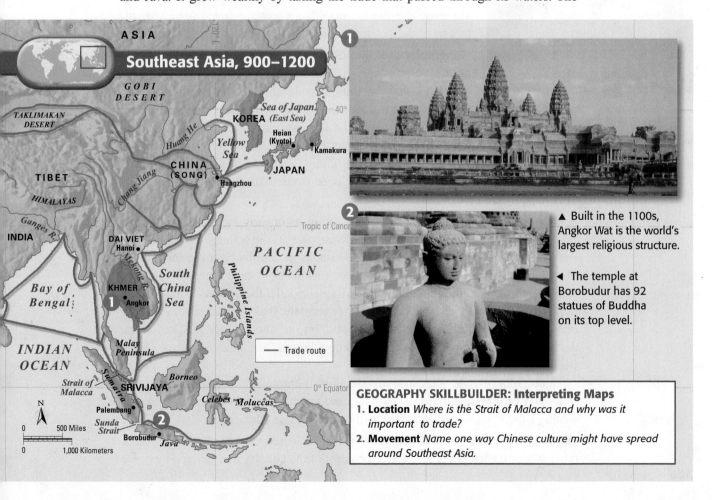

▲ Built in the 1100s, Angkor Wat is the world's largest religious structure.

◄ The temple at Borobudur has 92 statues of Buddha on its top level.

GEOGRAPHY SKILLBUILDER: Interpreting Maps

1. **Location** Where is the Strait of Malacca and why was it important to trade?
2. **Movement** Name one way Chinese culture might have spread around Southeast Asia.

Srivijayas established their capital, Palembang, on Sumatra. Palembang became a great center of Buddhist learning, where Chinese monks could study instead of traveling to India.

Dai Viet The people of Southeast Asia least influenced by India were the Vietnamese. Located in the coastal region just south of China, Vietnam fell under Chinese domination. Around 100 B.C., during the mighty Han Dynasty, China took northern Vietnam. When China's Tang Dynasty weakened in the early A.D. 900s, Vietnam managed to break away. It became an independent kingdom, known as Dai Viet, in 939.

The Vietnamese absorbed many Chinese cultural influences, including Buddhism and ideas about government. However, they also preserved a strong spirit of independence and kept their own cultural identity. Vietnamese women, for example, traditionally had more freedom and influence than their Chinese counterparts. **B**

Rulers of the Ly Dynasty (1009–1225) located their capital at Hanoi, on the Red River delta. They established a strong central government, encouraged agriculture and trade, and greatly improved road and river transportation. The changes made by the Ly continued to influence life in Vietnam long after they fell from power.

MAIN IDEA

Comparing
B How was Vietnam's culture influenced by Chinese culture?

Korean Dynasties

According to a Korean legend, the first Korean state was founded by the hero Tan'gun, whose father was a god and whose mother was a bear. Another legend relates that it was founded by a royal descendant of the Chinese Shang Dynasty. These legends reflect two sides of Korean culture. On one hand, the Koreans were a distinct people who developed their own native traditions. On the other hand, their culture was shaped by Chinese influences from early dynastic times. However, like the Japanese, the Koreans adapted borrowed culture to fit their own needs and maintained a distinct way of life.

▼ Tan'gun (or Dangun) is said to have founded Korea in Pyongyang in 2333 B.C.

Geography of Korea Korea is located on a peninsula that juts out from the Asian mainland toward Japan. It is about the same size as the state of Utah. Korea's climate is hot in the summer and very cold in the winter. Like Japan, Korea is a mountainous land, and only a limited portion of the peninsula can be farmed. A mountainous barrier lies between Korea and its northern neighbor, Manchuria. Because of the mountains and the seas, Korea developed somewhat in isolation from its neighbors.

Early History In early Korea, as in early Japan, different clans or tribes controlled different parts of the country. In 108 B.C., the Han empire conquered much of Korea and established a military government there. Through the Chinese, Koreans learned about such ideas as centralized government, Confucianism, Buddhism, and writing. During Han rule, the various Korean tribes began to gather together into federations. Eventually, these federations developed into three rival kingdoms. In the mid-600s, one of these kingdoms, the Silla, defeated the other kingdoms, drove out the Chinese, and gained control of the whole Korean peninsula.

Under Silla rule, the Koreans built Buddhist monasteries and produced elegant stone and bronze sculptures. They also developed a writing system suitable for writing Korean phonetically though still using Chinese characters.

The Koryu Dynasty By the tenth century, Silla rule had weakened. Around 935, a rebel officer named Wang Kon gained control of the country and became king. He named his new dynasty Koryu. The **Koryu Dynasty** lasted four and a half centuries, from 935 to 1392.

The Koryu Dynasty modeled its central government after China's. It also established a civil service system. However, this system did not provide the social mobility for Koreans that it did for the Chinese. Koryu society was sharply divided between a landed aristocracy and the rest of the population, including the military, commoners, and slaves. Despite the examination system, the sons of nobles received the best positions, and these positions became hereditary. **C**

The Koryu Dynasty faced a major threat in 1231, when the Mongols swept into Korea. They demanded a crushing tribute including 20,000 horses, clothing for 1 million soldiers, and many children and artisans, who were to be taken away as slaves. The harsh period of Mongol occupation lasted until the 1360s, when the Mongol Empire collapsed.

In 1392, a group of scholar-officials and military leaders overthrew the Koryu Dynasty and instituted land reforms. They established a new dynasty, called the Choson (or Yi) Dynasty, which would rule for 518 years.

Koryu Culture The Koryu period produced great achievements in Korean culture. Inspired by Song porcelain artists, Korean potters produced the much-admired celadon pottery, famous for its milky green glaze. Korean artisans produced one of the great treasures of the Buddhist world—many thousands of large wooden blocks for printing all the Buddhist scriptures. This set of blocks was destroyed by the Mongols, but the disaster sparked a national effort to re-create them. The more than 80,000 blocks in the new set remain in Korea today.

MAIN IDEA

Comparing

C How did the Koryu government compare with the early imperial government of Japan (page 340)?

Connect to Today

Two Koreas

Since the end of World War II, Korea has been arbitrarily divided into two countries—communist North Korea and democratic South Korea. For years, many Koreans longed for their country to be reunited. Hopes for such a day rose in 2000 when the presidents of the two nations sat down to discuss reunification. In 2002, however, North Korea announced that it was developing nuclear weapons and would use them against South Korea if necessary. This greatly dimmed people's hopes for one Korea.

hmhsocialstudies.com

INTERNET ACTIVITY Go online to research and write a news story on the latest developments in relations between the two Koreas.

SECTION 5 ASSESSMENT

TERMS & NAMES 1. For each term or name, write a sentence explaining its significance.
• Khmer Empire   • Angkor Wat   • Koryu Dynasty

USING YOUR NOTES

2. What common themes do you notice about the mainland kingdoms? about the island kingdoms?

Kingdom	Notes
Khmer	
Dai Viet	
Korea	
Sailendra	
Srivijaya	

MAIN IDEAS

3. On what was Khmer prosperity based?

4. How did Srivijaya become wealthy and powerful?

5. Why are there two sides to the development of Korean culture?

CRITICAL THINKING & WRITING

6. **RECOGNIZING EFFECTS** How did geography influence the history and culture of Southeast Asia and of Korea? Illustrate your answer with examples.

7. **COMPARING** In what ways did the cultural development of Vietnam resemble that of Korea?

8. **DRAWING CONCLUSIONS** Why do you think that of all the cultures of Southeast Asia, Vietnam was the least influenced by India?

9. **WRITING ACTIVITY** RELIGIOUS AND ETHICAL SYSTEMS Create an **annotated map** showing how Hinduism and Buddhism entered Southeast Asia from China and India.

CONNECT TO TODAY CREATING A TRAVEL BROCHURE

Conduct research to find information about Angkor Wat or the Buddhist temple at Borobudur. Use your findings to create a one-page **illustrated travel brochure**.

TERMS & NAMES

For each term or name below, briefly explain its connection to East Asia between 600 and 1350.

1. Tang Taizong
2. Wu Zhao
3. Genghis Khan
4. Kublai Khan
5. Marco Polo
6. Shinto
7. Angkor Wat
8. Koryu Dynasty

MAIN IDEAS

Tang and Song China Section 1 (pages 323–329)

9. Why was the reform of the civil service under the Tang so significant?

10. How did changes in agriculture support other developments during the Song Dynasty?

The Mongol Conquests Section 2 (pages 330–334)

11. Why were nomads and settled peoples sometimes in conflict?

12. What were the most important accomplishments of the Mongol Empire?

The Mongol Empire Section 3 (pages 335–338)

13. Explain how Kublai Khan treated his Chinese subjects.

14. How did Kublai Khan encourage trade?

Feudal Powers in Japan Section 4 (pages 339–343)

15. Describe the impact of Chinese culture on Japan.

16. How did feudalism develop in Japan?

Kingdoms of Southeast Asia and Korea Section 5 (pages 344–347)

17. Describe the two sources of prosperity for Southeast Asian empires.

18. What were the major accomplishments of the Koryu Dynasty?

CRITICAL THINKING

1. USING YOUR NOTES

Create diagrams to identify two results from these developments: (a) completion of the Grand Canal under the Sui, and (b) use of the compass at sea.

2. HYPOTHESIZING

EMPIRE BUILDING How might history have been different if the Mongols had conquered all or most of Europe? Discuss the possible immediate and long-term consequences for Europe and the rest of the Mongol Empire.

3. IDENTIFYING PROBLEMS AND SOLUTIONS

This chapter describes the rise and fall of three Chinese dynasties. What recurring patterns appear in the decline of these dynasties? What advice, based on those patterns, might you give a Chinese emperor?

4. DRAWING CONCLUSIONS

CULTURAL INTERACTION How does Japanese adaptation of Buddhism illustrate the process of selective cultural borrowing?

VISUAL SUMMARY

East Asian Interaction with China

CHINA

Japan
- Buddhism
- Writing system
- Civil service

Mongols
- Conquest of China
- Spread of Chinese ideas through Mongol Empire across Eurasia

Korea
- Buddhism
- Writing system
- Civil service
- Printing
- Porcelain

Southeast Asia
- Dai Viet: Buddhism, strong central government
- Other areas: spread of ideas through migration and trade

Use the quotation—part of a message sent by Kublai Khan to Japan's imperial court—and your knowledge of world history to answer questions 1 and 2.

PRIMARY SOURCE

The Emperor of the Great Mongols addresses the King of Japan as follows: . . . I am sending you my envoys bearing my personal message. It is my hope that the communication between our two countries be opened and maintained and that our mutual friendship be established. A sage regards the whole world as one family; how can different countries be considered one family if there is not friendly communication between them? Is force really necessary to establish friendly relations? I hope that you will give this matter your most careful attention.

SUNG LIEN, quoted in *The Essence of Chinese Civilization*

1. What is Kublai Khan asking of the Japanese?

   A. to surrender without a fight

   B. to exchange prisoners of war

   C. to establish diplomatic relations with the Mongols

   D. to join the Mongols in a war against Europe

2. Which of the following best describes the tone of the message?

   A. mildly threatening

   B. funny

   C. extremely violent

   D. pleading

Use the map and your knowledge of world history to answer question 3.

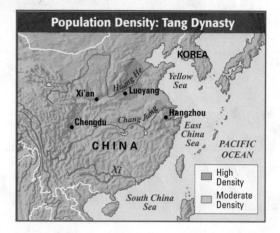

Population Density: Tang Dynasty

3. During the Tang Dynasty, which areas of China were most densely populated?

   A. east and north

   B. west and south

   C. central China

   D. far west

hmhsocialstudies.com | **TEST PRACTICE**

For additional test practice, go online for:

- Diagnostic tests
- Tutorials
- Strategies

Interact *with* History

Through the activity on page 322, you looked at the importance of Chinese inventions in world history. (After reading the chapter, you may have recognized that this imaginary situation was inspired by the travels of Marco Polo.) Now that you have read the chapter, consider the impact of Chinese inventions and how they spread. Would you now choose a different invention? Is there any other invention you would choose instead of those on page 322? Discuss these questions with a small group.

FOCUS ON WRITING

RELIGIOUS AND ETHICAL SYSTEMS Write a **report** on the Japanese religion of Shinto. Illustrate your report with photographs and sketches. In your report, consider the following:

- essential Shinto beliefs
- development of Shinto, especially the influence of Buddhism and Confucianism
- Shinto rituals and shrines

MULTIMEDIA ACTIVITY

NetExplorations: **Chinese Healing Arts**

Go to *NetExplorations* at **hmhsocialstudies.com** to learn more about Chinese healing arts. Use the Internet to learn how Chinese and Western doctors treat a variety of common illnesses and how long these treatments have been common practice. You may want to include the following illnesses in your research:

- the common cold
- influenza
- asthma
- arthritis

Create a table comparing Chinese and Western treatments for these illnesses. Display the table online or in the classroom.

Japan and the Samurai Warrior

For over a thousand years, the samurai—an elite warrior class—were a powerful force in Japanese society. The way of life of the samurai lords and warriors was, in many ways, like those of the medieval lords and knights of Europe. The great samurai warlords ruled large territories and relied on the fighting skills of their fierce samurai warriors to battle their enemies. But samurai warriors were more than just soldiers. Samurai were expected to embrace beauty and culture, and many were skilled artists. They also had a strict personal code that valued personal honor above all things—even life itself.

Explore the fascinating world of the samurai warrior online. You can find a wealth of information, video clips, primary sources, activities, and more at ⬈ hmhsocialstudies.com .

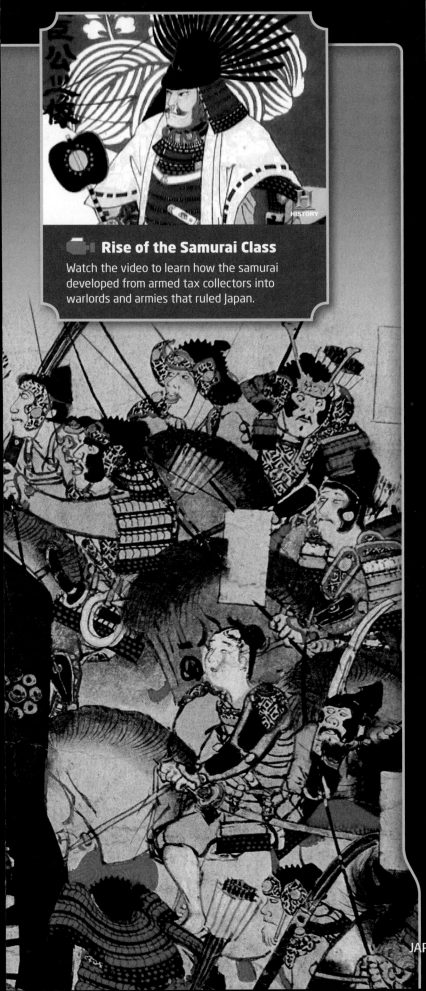

▶ Rise of the Samurai Class

Watch the video to learn how the samurai developed from armed tax collectors into warlords and armies that ruled Japan.

▶ A New Way of Life in Japan

Watch the video to learn how peace and isolation took hold in Japan and changed the role of the samurai in society.

> *I have no eyes;*
>   *I make the Flash of Lightning my Eyes.*
> *I have no ears; I make Sensibility my Ears.*
> *I have no limbs;*
>   *I make Promptitude my Limbs.*
> *I have no laws;*
>   *I make Self-Protection my Laws.*

📜 A Code for Samurai Living

Read the document to learn about the strict but lyrical code of the samurai warrior.

▶ Death of the Samurai Class

Watch the video to see how the end of Japan's isolation from the outside world signaled the beginning of the end of the samurai class.

European Middle Ages, 500-1200

Essential Question

What political and economic systems emerged in the Middle Ages and how was the Church a unifying force?

❓ What You Will Learn

In this chapter you will follow the changing political, religious, and cultural landscape of medieval Europe.

SECTION 1 Charlemagne Unites Germanic Kingdoms

Main Idea Many Germanic kingdoms that succeeded the Roman Empire were reunited under Charlemagne's empire.

SECTION 2 Feudalism in Europe

Main Idea Feudalism, a political and economic system based on land-holding and protective alliances, emerges in Europe.

SECTION 3 The Age of Chivalry

Main Idea The code of chivalry for knights glorified both combat and romantic love.

SECTION 4 The Power of the Church

Main Idea Church leaders and political leaders competed for power and authority.

Previewing Themes

EMPIRE BUILDING In western Europe, the Roman Empire had broken into many small kingdoms. During the Middle Ages, Charlemagne and Otto the Great tried to revive the idea of empire. Both allied with the Church.
Geography *Study the maps. What were the six major kingdoms in western Europe about A.D. 500?*

POWER AND AUTHORITY Weak rulers and the decline of central authority led to a feudal system in which local lords with large estates assumed power. This led to struggles over power with the Church.
Geography *Study the time line and the map. The ruler of what kingdom was crowned emperor by Pope Leo III?*

RELIGIOUS AND ETHICAL SYSTEMS During the Middle Ages, the Church was a unifying force. It shaped people's beliefs and guided their daily lives. Most Europeans at this time shared a common bond of faith.
Geography *Find Rome, the seat of the Roman Catholic Church, on the map. In what kingdom was it located after the fall of the Roman Empire in A.D. 476?*

EUROPE

500

700

511
Clovis unites Franks under Christian rule.

732
◄ Charles Martel stops Muslim invasion. (Charles Martel and advisers)

800
Pope Leo III crowns the Frankish king Charlemagne emperor.

WORLD

527
Justinian becomes Byzantine emperor.

750
Abbasids in Persia take control of the Muslim Empire.

800
Empire of Ghana thrives in West Africa.

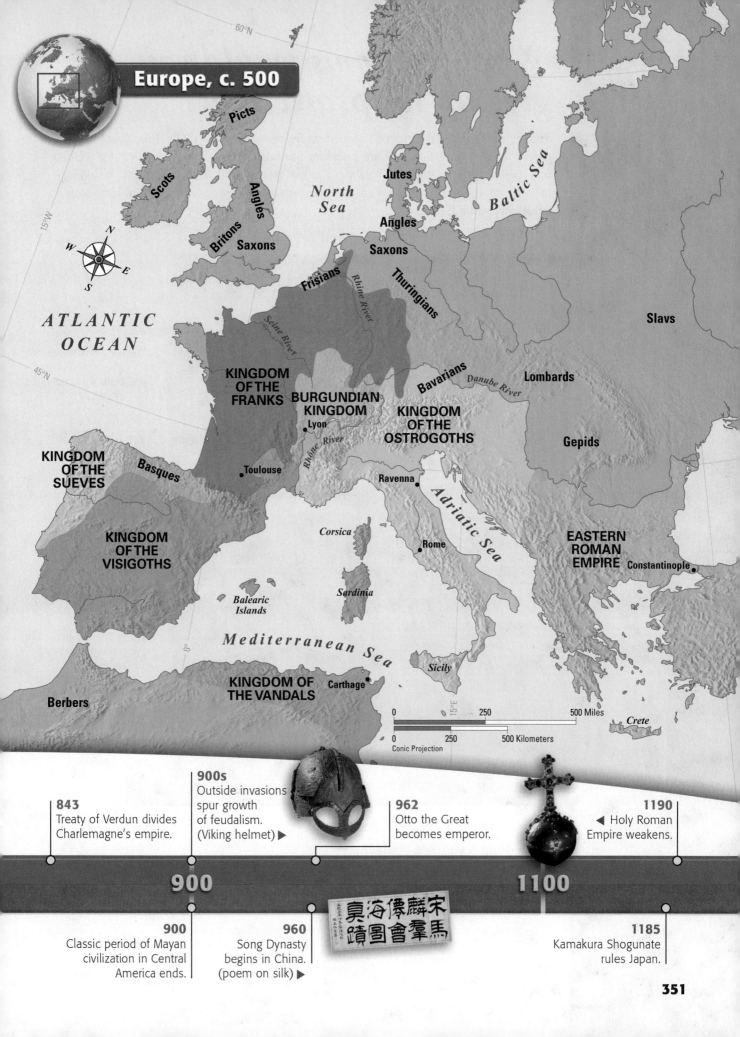

Europe, c. 500

Picts
Scots
Angles
Britons
Saxons
Jutes
Angles
Saxons
Frisians
Thuringians
Slavs

North Sea
Baltic Sea

Rhine River
Seine River

ATLANTIC OCEAN

60°N
15°W
45°N

KINGDOM OF THE FRANKS

BURGUNDIAN KINGDOM
Lyon

Bavarians
Danube River
Lombards

KINGDOM OF THE OSTROGOTHS

Gepids

KINGDOM OF THE SUEVES

Basques

Rhine River

Toulouse

Ravenna

KINGDOM OF THE VISIGOTHS

Corsica
Rome

Adriatic Sea

EASTERN ROMAN EMPIRE
Constantinople

Balearic Islands

Sardinia

Mediterranean Sea

Sicily

Carthage

KINGDOM OF THE VANDALS

Crete

Berbers

15°E

0   250   500 Miles
0   250   500 Kilometers
Conic Projection

843
Treaty of Verdun divides Charlemagne's empire.

900s
Outside invasions spur growth of feudalism. (Viking helmet) ▶

962
Otto the Great becomes emperor.

1190
◀ Holy Roman Empire weakens.

900

1100

900
Classic period of Mayan civilization in Central America ends.

960
Song Dynasty begins in China. (poem on silk) ▶

1185
Kamakura Shogunate rules Japan.

351

What freedoms would you give up for protection?

You are living in the countryside of western Europe during the 1100s. Like about 90 percent of the population, you are a peasant working the land. Your family's hut is located in a small village on your lord's estate. The lord provides all your basic needs, including housing, food, and protection. Especially important is his protection from invaders who repeatedly strike Europe.

❶ For safety, peasants retreat behind the castle walls during attacks.

❷ Peasants owe their lord two or three days' labor every week farming his land.

❸ This peasant feels that the right to stay on his lord's land is more important than his freedom to leave.

❹ Peasants cannot marry without their lord's consent.

EXAMINING *the* ISSUES

- **What is secure about your world?**

- **How is your life limited?**

As a class, discuss these questions. In your discussion, think about other people who have limited power over their lives. As you read about the lot of European peasants in this chapter, see how their living arrangements determine their role in society and shape their beliefs.

Charlemagne Unites Germanic Kingdoms

MAIN IDEA	WHY IT MATTERS NOW	TERMS & NAMES
EMPIRE BUILDING Many Germanic kingdoms that succeeded the Roman Empire were reunited under Charlemagne's empire.	Charlemagne spread Christian civilization through Northern Europe, where it had a permanent impact.	• Middle Ages • Franks • monastery • secular	• Carolingian Dynasty • Charlemagne

SETTING THE STAGE The gradual decline of the Roman Empire ushered in an era of European history called the **Middle Ages**, or the medieval period. It spanned the years from about 500 to 1500. During these centuries, a new society slowly emerged. It had roots in: (1) the classical heritage of Rome, (2) the beliefs of the Roman Catholic Church, and (3) the customs of various Germanic tribes.

Invasions of Western Europe

In the fifth century, Germanic invaders overran the western half of the Roman Empire (see map on page 351). Repeated invasions and constant warfare caused a series of changes that altered the economy, government, and culture:

- **Disruption of Trade** Merchants faced invasions from both land and sea. Their businesses collapsed. The breakdown of trade destroyed Europe's cities as economic centers. Money became scarce.
- **Downfall of Cities** With the fall of the Roman Empire, cities were abandoned as centers of administration.
- **Population Shifts** As Roman centers of trade and government collapsed, nobles retreated to the rural areas. Roman cities were left without strong leadership. Other city dwellers also fled to the countryside, where they grew their own food. The population of western Europe became mostly rural.

The Decline of Learning The Germanic invaders who stormed Rome could not read or write. Among Romans themselves, the level of learning sank sharply as more and more families left for rural areas. Few people except priests and other church officials were literate. Knowledge of Greek, long important in Roman culture, was almost lost. Few people could read Greek works of literature, science, and philosophy. The Germanic tribes, though, had a rich oral tradition of songs and legends. But they had no written language.

Loss of a Common Language As German-speaking peoples mixed with the Roman population, Latin changed. While it was still an official language, it was no longer understood. Different dialects developed as new words and phrases became part of everyday speech. By the 800s, French, Spanish, and other Roman-based languages had evolved from Latin. The development of various languages mirrored the continued breakup of a once-unified empire.

hmhsocialstudies.com
TAKING NOTES

Use the graphic organizer online to take notes on the unification of the Germanic kingdoms.

Germanic Kingdoms Emerge

In the years of upheaval between 400 and 600, small Germanic kingdoms replaced Roman provinces. The borders of those kingdoms changed constantly with the fortunes of war. But the Church as an institution survived the fall of the Roman Empire. During this time of political chaos, the Church provided order and security.

The Concept of Government Changes Along with shifting boundaries, the entire concept of government changed. Loyalty to public government and written law had unified Roman society. Family ties and personal loyalty, rather than citizenship in a public state, held Germanic society together. Unlike Romans, Germanic peoples lived in small communities that were governed by unwritten rules and traditions.

Every Germanic chief led a band of warriors who had pledged their loyalty to him. In peacetime, these followers lived in their lord's hall. He gave them food, weapons, and treasure. In battle, warriors fought to the death at their lord's side. They considered it a disgrace to outlive him. But Germanic warriors felt no obligation to obey a king they did not even know. Nor would they obey an official sent to collect taxes or administer justice in the name of an emperor they had never met. The Germanic stress on personal ties made it impossible to establish orderly government for large territories.

Clovis Rules the Franks In the Roman province of Gaul (mainly what is now France and Switzerland), a Germanic people called the **Franks** held power. Their leader was Clovis (KLOH•vihs). He would bring Christianity to the region. According to legend, his wife, Clothilde, had urged him to convert to her faith, Christianity. In 496, Clovis led his warriors against another Germanic army. Fearing defeat, he appealed to the Christian God. "For I have called on my gods," he prayed, "but I find they are far from my aid. . . . Now I call on Thee. I long to believe in Thee. Only, please deliver me from my enemies." The tide of the battle shifted and the Franks won. Afterward, Clovis and 3,000 of his warriors asked a bishop to baptize them.

The Church in Rome welcomed Clovis's conversion and supported his military campaigns against other Germanic peoples. By 511, Clovis had united the Franks into one kingdom. The strategic alliance between Clovis's Frankish kingdom and the Church marked the start of a partnership between two powerful forces.

▼ Illuminated manuscripts, such as the one below, were usually the work of monks.

Germans Adopt Christianity

Politics played a key role in spreading Christianity. By 600, the Church, with the help of Frankish rulers, had converted many Germanic peoples. These new converts had settled in Rome's former lands. Missionaries also spread Christianity. These religious travelers often risked their lives to bring religious beliefs to other lands. During the 300s and 400s, they worked among the Germanic and Celtic groups that bordered the Roman Empire. In southern Europe, the fear of coastal attacks by Muslims also spurred many people to become Christians in the 600s.

Monasteries, Convents, and Manuscripts To adapt to rural conditions, the Church built religious communities called **monasteries**. There, Christian men called monks gave up their private possessions and devoted their lives to serving God. Women who followed this way of life were called nuns and lived in convents.

Benedict
480?–543

At 15, Benedict left school and hiked up to the Sabine Hills, where he lived in a cave as a hermit. After learning about Benedict's deep religious conviction, a group of monks persuaded him to lead their monastery. Benedict declared:

We must prepare our hearts and bodies for combat under holy obedience to the divine commandments. . . . We are therefore going to establish a school in which one may learn the service of the Lord.

In his book describing the rules for monastic life, Benedict emphasized a balance between work and study. Such guidelines turned monasteries into centers of stability and learning.

Scholastica
480?–543

Scholastica is thought to be the twin sister of Benedict. She was born into a wealthy Italian family in the late Roman Empire. Little is known of her early life, except that she and Benedict were inseparable.

Like her brother, Scholastica devoted her life to the Church. She is thought to have been the abbess of a convent near the monastery founded by Benedict and is considered the first nun of the Benedictine order. She was a strong influence on her brother as he developed rules that guide Benedictine monasteries to this day. They died in the same year and are buried in one grave.

⤢ **hmhsocialstudies.com**

RESEARCH WEB LINKS Go online for more on Benedict and Scholastica.

Around 520, an Italian monk named Benedict began writing a book describing a strict yet practical set of rules for monasteries. Benedict's sister, Scholastica (skuh•LAS•tik•uh), headed a convent and adapted the same rules for women. These guidelines became a model for many other religious communities in western Europe. Monks and nuns devoted their lives to prayer and good works.

MAIN IDEA

Making Inferences
A What role did monasteries play during this time of chaos?

Monasteries also became Europe's best-educated communities. Monks opened schools, maintained libraries, and copied books. In 731, the Venerable Bede, an English monk, wrote a history of England. Scholars still consider it the best historical work of the early Middle Ages. In the 600s and 700s, monks made beautiful copies of religious writings, decorated with ornate letters and brilliant pictures. These illuminated manuscripts preserved at least part of Rome's intellectual heritage.

Papal Power Expands Under Gregory I In 590, Gregory I, also called Gregory the Great, became pope. As head of the Church in Rome, Gregory broadened the authority of the papacy, or pope's office, beyond its spiritual role. Under Gregory, the papacy also became a **secular**, or worldly, power involved in politics. The pope's palace was the center of Roman government. Gregory used church revenues to raise armies, repair roads, and help the poor. He also negotiated peace treaties with invaders such as the Lombards.

According to Gregory, the region from Italy to England and from Spain to Germany fell under his responsibility. Gregory strengthened the vision of Christendom. It was a spiritual kingdom fanning out from Rome to the most distant churches. This idea of a churchly kingdom, ruled by a pope, would be a central theme of the Middle Ages. Meanwhile, secular rulers expanded their political kingdoms.

An Empire Evolves

After the Roman Empire dissolved, small kingdoms sprang up all over Europe. For example, England splintered into seven tiny kingdoms. Some of them were no

hmhsocialstudies.com
INTERACTIVE MAP

Frankish Kingdom before
Charlemagne, 768

Areas conquered by
Charlemagne, 814

Papal States

Division by Treaty
of Verdun, 843

North
Sea

0 ⎯⎯⎯ 250 Miles

0 ⎯⎯⎯ 500 Kilometers

ENGLAND

Aachen

Paris

Tours

EAST
FRANKISH
KINGDOM
(Louis
the German)

SLAVIC
STATES

Rhine R.

Elbe R.

Danube R.

ATLANTIC
OCEAN

WEST
FRANKISH
KINGDOM
(Charles
the Bald)

CENTRAL
KINGDOM
(Lothair)

Pavia

Ebro R.

SPAIN

Corsica

PAPAL
STATES

Rome

Mediterranean
Sea

GEOGRAPHY SKILLBUILDER: Interpreting Maps
1. **Region** *By 814, what was the extent of Charlemagne's empire (north to south, east to west)?*
2. **Region** *Based on the map, why did the Treaty of Verdun signal the decline of Charlemagne's empire?*

larger than the state of Connecticut. The Franks controlled the largest and strongest of Europe's kingdoms, the area that was formerly the Roman province of Gaul. When the Franks' first Christian king, Clovis, died in 511, he had extended Frankish rule over most of what is now France.

Charles Martel Emerges By 700, an official known as the *major domo,* or mayor of the palace, had become the most powerful person in the Frankish kingdom. Officially, he had charge of the royal household and estates. Unofficially, he led armies and made policy. In effect, he ruled the kingdom.

The mayor of the palace in 719, Charles Martel (Charles the Hammer), held more power than the king. Charles Martel extended the Franks' reign to the north, south, and east. He also defeated Muslim raiders from Spain at the Battle of Tours in 732. This battle was highly significant for Christian Europeans. If the Muslims had won, western Europe might have become part of the Muslim Empire. Charles Martel's victory at Tours made him a Christian hero.

At his death, Charles Martel passed on his power to his son, Pepin the Short. Pepin wanted to be king. He shrewdly cooperated with the pope. On behalf of the Church, Pepin agreed to fight the Lombards, who had invaded central Italy and threatened Rome. In exchange, the pope anointed Pepin "king by the grace of God." Thus began the **Carolingian** (KAR•uh•LIHN•juhn) **Dynasty**, the family that would rule the Franks from 751 to 987.

Charlemagne Becomes Emperor

Pepin the Short died in 768. He left a greatly strengthened Frankish kingdom to his two sons, Carloman and Charles. After Carloman's death in 771, Charles, who was known as **Charlemagne** (SHAHR•luh•MAYN), or Charles the Great, ruled the kingdom. An imposing figure, he stood six feet four inches tall. His admiring secretary, a monk named Einhard, described Charlemagne's achievements:

PRIMARY SOURCE
[Charlemagne] was the most potent prince with the greatest skill and success in different countries during the forty-seven years of his reign. Great and powerful as was the realm of Franks, Karl [Charlemagne] received from his father Pippin, he nevertheless so splendidly enlarged it . . . that he almost doubled it.

EINHARD, *Life of Charlemagne*

Charlemagne Extends Frankish Rule Charlemagne built an empire greater than any known since ancient Rome. Each summer he led his armies against enemies that surrounded his kingdom. He fought Muslims in Spain and tribes from other

Germanic kingdoms. He conquered new lands to both the south and the east. Through these conquests, Charlemagne spread Christianity. He reunited western Europe for the first time since the Roman Empire. By 800, Charlemagne's empire was larger than the Byzantine Empire. He had become the most powerful king in western Europe.

In 800, Charlemagne traveled to Rome to crush an unruly mob that had attacked the pope. In gratitude, Pope Leo III crowned him emperor. The coronation was historic. A pope had claimed the political right to confer the title "Roman Emperor" on a European king. This event signaled the joining of Germanic power, the Church, and the heritage of the Roman Empire.

Charlemagne Leads a Revival Charlemagne strengthened his royal power by limiting the authority of the nobles. To govern his empire, he sent out royal agents. They made sure that the powerful landholders, called counts, governed their counties justly. Charlemagne regularly visited every part of his kingdom. He also kept a close watch on the management of his huge estates—the source of Carolingian wealth and power. One of his greatest accomplishments was the encouragement of learning. He surrounded himself with English, German, Italian, and Spanish scholars. For his many sons and daughters and other children at the court, Charlemagne opened a palace school. He also ordered monasteries to open schools to train future monks and priests. **B**

MAIN IDEA

Drawing Conclusions

B What were Charlemagne's most notable achievements?

Charlemagne's Heirs A year before Charlemagne died in 814, he crowned his only surviving son, Louis the Pious, as emperor. Louis was a devoutly religious man but an ineffective ruler. He left three sons: Lothair (loh•THAIR), Charles the Bald, and Louis the German. They fought one another for control of the Empire. In 843, the brothers signed the Treaty of Verdun, dividing the empire into three kingdoms. As a result, Carolingian kings lost power and central authority broke down. The lack of strong rulers led to a new system of governing and landholding—feudalism.

▲ Emperor Charlemagne

SECTION 1 ASSESSMENT

TERMS & NAMES 1. For each term or name, write a sentence explaining its significance.
• Middle Ages   • Franks   • monastery   • secular   • Carolingian Dynasty   • Charlemagne

USING YOUR NOTES

2. What was the most important event in the unification of the Germanic kingdoms? Why?

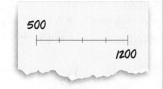

500

1200

MAIN IDEAS

3. What were three roots of medieval culture in western Europe?

4. What are three ways that civilization in western Europe declined after the Roman Empire fell?

5. What was the most important achievement of Pope Gregory I?

CRITICAL THINKING & WRITING

6. **DRAWING CONCLUSIONS** How was the relationship between a Frankish king and the pope beneficial to both?

7. **RECOGNIZING EFFECTS** Why was Charles Martel's victory at the Battle of Tours so important for Christianity?

8. **EVALUATING** What was Charlemagne's greatest achievement? Give reasons for your answer.

9. **WRITING ACTIVITY** EMPIRE BUILDING How does Charlemagne's empire in medieval Europe compare with the Roman Empire? Support your opinions in a three-paragraph **expository essay**.

MULTIMEDIA ACTIVITY WRITING A HISTORY

Use the Internet to locate a medieval monastery that remains today in western Europe. Write a two-paragraph **history** of the monastery and include an illustration.

INTERNET KEYWORD
Medieval monasteries

Feudalism in Europe

MAIN IDEA	WHY IT MATTERS NOW	TERMS & NAMES
POWER AND AUTHORITY Feudalism, a political and economic system based on land-holding and protective alliances, emerges in Europe.	The rights and duties of feudal relationships helped shape today's forms of representative government.	• lord • serf • fief • manor • vassal • tithe • knight

SETTING THE STAGE After the Treaty of Verdun, Charlemagne's three feuding grandsons broke up the kingdom even further. Part of this territory also became a battleground as new waves of invaders attacked Europe. The political turmoil and constant warfare led to the rise of European feudalism, which, as you read in Chapter 2, is a political and economic system based on land ownership and personal loyalty.

Invaders Attack Western Europe

hmhsocialstudies.com
TAKING NOTES

Use the graphic organizer online to take notes on important events in the history of European invasions.

From about 800 to 1000, invasions destroyed the Carolingian Empire. Muslim invaders from the south seized Sicily and raided Italy. In 846, they sacked Rome. Magyar invaders struck from the east. Like the earlier Huns and Avars, they terrorized Germany and Italy. And from the north came the fearsome Vikings.

The Vikings Invade from the North The Vikings set sail from Scandinavia (SKAN•duh•NAY•vee•uh), a wintry, wooded region in Northern Europe. (The region is now the countries of Denmark, Norway, and Sweden.) The Vikings, also called Northmen or Norsemen, were a Germanic people. They worshiped warlike gods and took pride in nicknames like Eric Bloodaxe and Thorfinn Skullsplitter.

The Vikings carried out their raids with terrifying speed. Clutching swords and heavy wooden shields, these helmeted seafarers beached their ships, struck quickly, and then moved out to sea again. They were gone before locals could mount a defense. Viking warships were awe-inspiring. The largest of these long ships held 300 warriors, who took turns rowing the ship's 72 oars. The prow of each ship swept grandly upward, often ending with the carved head of a sea monster. A ship might weigh 20 tons when fully loaded. Yet, it could sail in a mere three feet of water. Rowing up shallow creeks, the Vikings looted inland villages and monasteries.

▼ A sketch of a Viking longboat

0   500 Miles

0   1,000 Kilometers

Viking invasion routes
Viking areas
Muslim invasion routes
Muslim areas
Magyar invasion routes
Magyar areas

GEOGRAPHY SKILLBUILDER: Interpreting Maps
1. **Location**-*What lands did the Vikings raid?*
2. **Movement**-*Why were the Viking, Magyar, and Muslim invasions so threatening to Europe?*

The Vikings were not only warriors but also traders, farmers, and explorers. They ventured far beyond western Europe. Vikings journeyed down rivers into the heart of Russia, to Constantinople, and even across the icy waters of the North Atlantic. A Viking explorer named Leif (leef) Ericson reached North America around 1000, almost 500 years before Columbus. About the same time, the Viking reign of terror in Europe faded away. As Vikings gradually accepted Christianity, they stopped raiding monasteries. Also, a warming trend in Europe's climate made farming easier in Scandinavia. As a result, fewer Scandinavians adopted the seafaring life of Viking warriors.

Magyars and Muslims Attack from the East and South As Viking invasions declined, Europe became the target of new assaults. The Magyars, a group of nomadic people, attacked from the east, from what is now Hungary. Superb horsemen, the Magyars swept across the plains of the Danube River and invaded western Europe in the late 800s. They attacked isolated villages and monasteries. They overran northern Italy and reached as far west as the Rhineland and Burgundy. The Magyars did not settle conquered land. Instead, they took captives to sell as slaves.

The Muslims struck from the south. They began their encroachments from their strongholds in North Africa, invading through what are now Italy and Spain. In the 600s and 700s, the Muslim plan was to conquer and settle in Europe. By the 800s and 900s, their goal was also to plunder. Because the Muslims were expert sea farers, they were able to attack settlements on the Atlantic and Mediterranean coasts. They also struck as far inland as Switzerland.

The invasions by Vikings, Magyars, and Muslims caused widespread disorder and suffering. Most western Europeans lived in constant danger. Kings could not effectively defend their lands from invasion. As a result, people no longer looked to a central ruler for security. Instead, many turned to local rulers who had their own armies. Any leader who could fight the invaders gained followers and political strength. **Ⓐ**

MAIN IDEA

Recognizing Effects

Ⓐ What was the impact of Viking, Magyar, and Muslim invasions on medieval Europe?

A New Social Order: Feudalism

In 911, two former enemies faced each other in a peace ceremony. Rollo was the head of a Viking army. Rollo and his men had been plundering the rich Seine (sayn) River valley for years. Charles the Simple was the king of France but held little power. Charles granted the Viking leader a huge piece of French territory. It became known as Northmen's land, or Normandy. In return, Rollo swore a pledge of loyalty to the king.

Feudalism Structures Society The worst years of the invaders' attacks spanned roughly 850 to 950. During this time, rulers and warriors like Charles and Rollo made similar agreements in many parts of Europe. The system of governing and landholding, called feudalism, had emerged in Europe. A similar feudal system existed in China under the Zhou Dynasty, which ruled from around the 11th century B.C. until 256 B.C. Feudalism in Japan began in A.D. 1192 and ended in the 19th century.

The feudal system was based on rights and obligations. In exchange for military protection and other services, a **lord**, or landowner, granted land called a **fief**. The person receiving a fief was called a **vassal**. Charles the Simple, the lord, and Rollo, the vassal, showed how this two-sided bargain worked. Feudalism depended on the control of land.

The Feudal Pyramid The structure of feudal society was much like a pyramid. At the peak reigned the king. Next came the most powerful vassals—wealthy landowners such as nobles and bishops. Serving beneath these vassals were knights. **Knights** were mounted horsemen who pledged to defend their lords' lands in exchange for fiefs. At the base of the pyramid were landless peasants who toiled in the fields. (See Analyzing Key Concepts on next page.)

Social Classes Are Well Defined In the feudal system, status determined a person's prestige and power. Medieval writers classified people into three groups: those who fought (nobles and knights), those who prayed (men and women of the Church), and those who worked (the peasants). Social class was usually inherited.

Vocabulary
Status is social ranking.

In Europe in the Middle Ages, the vast majority of people were peasants. Most peasants were serfs. **Serfs** were people who could not lawfully leave the place where they were born. Though bound to the land, serfs were not slaves. Their lords could not sell or buy them. But what their labor produced belonged to the lord.

Manors: The Economic Side of Feudalism

The **manor** was the lord's estate. During the Middle Ages, the manor system was the basic economic arrangement. The manor system rested on a set of rights and obligations between a lord and his serfs. The lord provided the serfs with housing, farmland, and protection from bandits. In return, serfs tended the lord's lands, cared for his animals, and performed other tasks to maintain the estate. Peasant women shared in the farm work with their husbands. All peasants, whether free or serf, owed the lord certain duties. These included at least a few days of labor each week and a certain portion of their grain.

A Self-Contained World Peasants rarely traveled more than 25 miles from their own manor. By standing in the center of a plowed field, they could see their entire world at a glance. A manor usually covered only a few square miles of land. It

Feudalism

Feudalism was a political system in which nobles were granted the use of land that legally belonged to the king. In return, the nobles agreed to give their loyalty and military services to the king. Feudalism developed not only in Europe but also in countries like Japan.

European Feudalism

King

Church Official

Noble

Knights

Knights

Peasants

Peasants

Japanese Feudalism

Emperor

Daimyo

Daimyo

Samurai

Samurai

Artisans

Peasants

Merchants

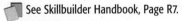

↗ hmhsocialstudies.com

RESEARCH WEB LINKS Go online for more on feudalism.

> ## DATA FILE

FEUDAL FACTS AND FIGURES

- In the 14th century, before the bubonic plague struck, the population of France was probably between 10 and 21 million people.

- In feudal times, the building of a cathedral took between 50 to 150 years.

- In feudal times, dukedoms were large estates ruled by a duke. In 1216, the Duke of Anjou had 34 knights, the Duke of Brittany had 36 knights, and the Count of Flanders had 47 knights.

- In the 14th century, the nobility in France made up about 1 percent of the population.

- The word *feudalism* comes from the Latin word *feudum*, meaning *fief*.

- The Japanese word *daimyo* comes from the words *dai*, meaning "large," and *myo* (shortened from *myoden*), meaning "name-land" or "private land."

* SOURCES: A Distant Mirror by Barbara Tuchman; Encyclopaedia Britannica

Connect *to* Today

1. **Comparing** What are the similarities between feudalism in Europe and feudalism in Japan?

   📖 See Skillbuilder Handbook, Page R7.

2. **Forming and Supporting Opinions** Today, does the United States have a system of social classes? Support your answer with evidence.

361

The Medieval Manor

The medieval manor varied in size. The illustration to the right is a plan of a typical English manor.

1 Manor House
The dwelling place of the lord and his family and their servants

2 Village Church
Site of both religious services and public meetings

3 Peasant Cottages
Where the peasants lived

4 Lord's Demesne
Fields owned by the lord and worked by the peasants

5 Peasant Crofts
Gardens that belonged to the peasants

6 Mill
Water-powered mill for grinding grain

7 Common Pasture
Common area for grazing animals

8 Woodland
Forests provided wood for fuel.

typically consisted of the lord's manor house, a church, and workshops. Generally, 15 to 30 families lived in the village on a manor. Fields, pastures, and woodlands surrounded the village. Sometimes a stream wound through the manor. Streams and ponds provided fish, which served as an important source of food. The mill for grinding the grain was often located on the stream.

The manor was largely a self-sufficient community. The serfs and peasants raised or produced nearly everything that they and their lord needed for daily life—crops, milk and cheese, fuel, cloth, leather goods, and lumber. The only outside purchases were salt, iron, and a few unusual objects such as millstones. These were huge stones used to grind flour. Crops grown on the manor usually included grains, such as wheat, rye, barley, and oats, and vegetables, such as peas, beans, onions, and beets. **B**

The Harshness of Manor Life For the privilege of living on the lord's land, peasants paid a high price. They paid a tax on all grain ground in the lord's mill. Any attempt to avoid taxes by baking bread elsewhere was treated as a crime. Peasants also paid a tax on marriage. Weddings could take place only with the lord's

MAIN IDEA

Analyzing Causes
B How might the decline of trade during the early Middle Ages have contributed to the self-sufficiency of the manor system?

consent. After all these payments to the lord, peasant families owed the village priest a **tithe**, or church tax. A tithe represented one-tenth of their income.

Serfs lived in crowded cottages, close to their neighbors. The cottages had only one or two rooms. If there were two rooms, the main room was used for cooking, eating, and household activities. The second was the family bedroom. Peasants warmed their dirt-floor houses by bringing pigs inside. At night, the family huddled on a pile of straw that often crawled with insects. Peasants' simple diet consisted mainly of vegetables, coarse brown bread, grain, cheese, and soup.

Piers Plowman, written by William Langland in 1362, reveals the hard life of English peasants:

MAIN IDEA
Analyzing Primary Sources
C What problems did peasant families face?

PRIMARY SOURCE C
What by spinning they save, they spend it in house-hire,
Both in milk and in meal to make a mess of porridge,
To cheer up their children who chafe for their food,
And they make themselves suffer surely much hunger
And woe in the winter, with waking at nights
And rising to rock an oft restless cradle.
WILLIAM LANGLAND, *Piers Plowman*

This 14th century drawing shows two men flailing corn.

For most serfs, both men and women, life was work and more work. Their days revolved around raising crops and livestock and taking care of home and family. As soon as children were old enough, they were put to work in the fields or in the home. Many children did not survive to adulthood. Illness and malnutrition were constant afflictions for medieval peasants. Average life expectancy was about 35 years. And during that short lifetime, most peasants never traveled more than 25 miles from their homes.

Yet, despite the hardships they endured, serfs accepted their lot in life as part of the Church's teachings. They, like most Christians during medieval times, believed that God determined a person's place in society.

SECTION 2 ASSESSMENT

TERMS & NAMES 1. For each term or name, write a sentence explaining its significance.
• lord   • fief   • vassal   • knight   • serf   • manor   • tithe

USING YOUR NOTES
2. What was the most important event during the period of European invasions?

300
1000

MAIN IDEAS
3. What groups invaded Europe in the 800s?
4. What obligations did a peasant have to the lord of the manor?
5. What were the three social classes of the feudal system?

CRITICAL THINKING & WRITING
6. **COMPARING** How were the Vikings different from earlier Germanic groups that invaded Europe?
7. **MAKING INFERENCES** How was a manor largely self-sufficient both militarily and economically during the early Middle Ages?
8. **DRAWING CONCLUSIONS** What benefits do you think a medieval manor provided to the serfs who lived there?
9. **WRITING ACTIVITY** POWER AND AUTHORITY Draw up a **contract** between a lord and a vassal, such as a knight, or between the lord of a manor and a serf. Include the responsibilities, obligations, and rights of each party.

CONNECT TO TODAY WRITING A NEWS ARTICLE
Research modern marauders, who, like the Vikings of history, are involved in piracy on the seas. Write a brief **news article** describing their activities.

The Age of Chivalry

MAIN IDEA	WHY IT MATTERS NOW	TERMS & NAMES
RELIGIOUS AND ETHICAL SYSTEMS The code of chivalry for knights glorified both combat and romantic love.	The code of chivalry has shaped modern ideas of romance in Western cultures.	• chivalry • troubadour • tournament

SETTING THE STAGE During the Middle Ages, nobles constantly fought one another. Their feuding kept Europe in a fragmented state for centuries. Through warfare, feudal lords defended their estates, seized new territories, and increased their wealth. Lords and their armies lived in a violent society that prized combat skills. By the 1100s, though, a code of behavior began to arise. High ideals guided warriors' actions and glorified their roles.

Knights: Warriors on Horseback

hmhsocialstudies.com
TAKING NOTES

Use the graphic organizer online to take notes on the ideas associated with chivalry.

Soldiers mounted on horseback became valuable in combat during the reign of Charlemagne's grandfather, Charles Martel, in the 700s. Charles Martel had observed that the Muslim cavalry often turned the tide of battles. As a result, he organized Frankish troops of armored horsemen, or knights.

The Technology of Warfare Changes Leather saddles and stirrups changed the way warfare was conducted in Europe during the 700s. Both had been developed in Asia around 200 B.C.

The saddle kept a warrior firmly seated on a moving horse. Stirrups enabled him to ride and handle heavier weapons. Without stirrups to brace him, a charging warrior was likely to topple off his own horse. Frankish knights, galloping full tilt, could knock over enemy foot soldiers and riders on horseback. Gradually, mounted knights became the most important part of an army. Their warhorses played a key military role.

The Warrior's Role in Feudal Society By the 11th century, western Europe was a battleground of warring nobles vying for power. To defend their territories, feudal lords raised private armies of knights. In exchange for military service,

◄ These two-inch iron spikes, called caltrops, were strewn on a battlefield to maim warhorses or enemy foot soldiers.

feudal lords used their most abundant resource—land. They rewarded knights, their most skilled warriors, with fiefs from their sprawling estates. Wealth from these fiefs allowed knights to devote their lives to war. Knights could afford to pay for costly weapons, armor, and warhorses.

As the lord's vassal, a knight's main obligation was to serve in battle. From his knights, a lord typically demanded about 40 days of combat a year. Knights' pastimes also often revolved around training for war. Wrestling and hunting helped them gain strength and practice the skills they would need on the battlefield.

Knighthood and the Code of Chivalry

Knights were expected to display courage in battle and loyalty to their lord. By the 1100s, the code of <u>chivalry</u> (SHIHV•uhl•ree), a complex set of ideals, demanded that a knight fight bravely in defense of three masters. He devoted himself to his earthly feudal lord, his heavenly Lord, and his chosen lady. The chivalrous knight also protected the weak and the poor. The ideal knight was loyal, brave, and courteous. Most knights, though, failed to meet all of these high standards. For example, they treated the lower classes brutally.

A Knight's Training Sons of nobles began training for knighthood at an early age and learned the code of chivalry. At age 7, a boy would be sent off to the castle of another lord. As a page, he waited on his hosts and began to practice fighting skills. At around age 14, the page reached the rank of squire. A squire acted as a servant to a knight. At around age 21, a squire became a full-fledged knight.

> **Analyzing Art**

Chivalry

The Italian painter Paolo Uccello captures the spirit of the age of chivalry in this painting, *St. George and the Dragon* (c. 1455–1460). According to myth, St. George rescues a captive princess by killing her captor, a dragon.

- **The Knight** St. George, mounted on a horse and dressed in armor, uses his lance to attack the dragon.
- **The Dragon** The fierce-looking dragon represents evil.
- **The Princess** The princess remains out of the action as her knight fights the dragon on her behalf.

SKILLBUILDER:
Interpreting Visual Sources
In what way does this painting show the knight's code of chivalry?

Castles and Siege Weapons

Attacking armies carefully planned how to capture a castle. Engineers would inspect the castle walls for weak points in the stone. Then, enemy soldiers would try to ram the walls, causing them to collapse. At the battle site, attackers often constructed the heavy and clumsy weapons shown here.

Siege Tower
- had a platform on top that lowered like a drawbridge
- could support weapons and soldiers

Mantlet
- shielded soldiers

Battering Ram
- made of heavy timber with a sharp metal tip
- swung like a pendulum to crack castle walls or to knock down drawbridge

Trebuchet
- worked like a giant slingshot
- propelled objects up to a distance of 980 feet

Tortoise
- moved slowly on wheels
- sheltered soldiers from falling arrows

Mangonel
- flung huge rocks that crashed into castle walls
- propelled objects up to a distance of 1,300 feet

An Array of High-Flying Missiles

Using the trebuchet, enemy soldiers launched a wide variety of missiles over the castle walls:
- pots of burning lime
- boulders
- severed human heads
- captured soldiers
- diseased cows
- dead horses

Connect *to* Today

1. **Making Inferences** How do these siege weapons show that their designers knew the architecture of a castle well?

   See Skillbuilder Handbook, Page R16.

2. **Drawing Conclusions** What are some examples of modern weapons of war? What do they indicate about the way war is conducted today?

↗ **hmhsocialstudies.com**

RESEARCH WEB LINKS Go online for more on medieval weapons.

After being dubbed a knight, most young men traveled for a year or two. The young knights gained experience fighting in local wars. Some took part in mock battles called **tournaments**. Tournaments combined recreation with combat training. Two armies of knights charged each other. Trumpets blared, and lords and ladies cheered. Like real battles, tournaments were fierce and bloody competitions. Winners could usually demand large ransoms from defeated knights. **A**

MAIN IDEA

Comparing

A How are tournaments like modern sports competitions?

Vocabulary

A *siege* is a military blockade staged by enemy armies trying to capture a fortress.

Brutal Reality of Warfare The small-scale violence of tournaments did not match the bloodshed of actual battles, especially those fought at castles. By the 1100s, massive walls and guard towers encircled stone castles. These castles dominated much of the countryside in western Europe. Lord and lady, their family, knights and other men-at-arms, and servants made their home in the castle. The castle also was a fortress, designed for defense.

A castle under siege was a gory sight. Attacking armies used a wide range of strategies and weapons to force castle residents to surrender. Defenders of a castle poured boiling water, hot oil, or molten lead on enemy soldiers. Expert archers were stationed on the roof of the castle. Armed with crossbows, they fired deadly bolts that could pierce full armor.

The Literature of Chivalry

In the 1100s, the themes of medieval literature downplayed the brutality of knighthood and feudal warfare. Many stories idealized castle life. They glorified knighthood and chivalry, tournaments and real battles. Songs and poems about a knight's undying love for a lady were also very popular.

Epic Poetry Feudal lords and their ladies enjoyed listening to epic poems. These poems recounted a hero's deeds and adventures. Many epics retold stories about legendary heroes such as King Arthur and Charlemagne.

The Song of Roland is one of the earliest and most famous medieval epic poems. It praises a band of French soldiers who perished in battle during Charlemagne's reign. The poem transforms the event into a struggle. A few brave French knights led by Roland battle an overwhelming army of Muslims from Spain. Roland's friend, Turpin the Archbishop, stands as a shining example of medieval ideals. Turpin represents courage, faith, and chivalry:

PRIMARY SOURCE
And now there comes the Archbishop.
He spurs his horse, goes up into a mountain,
summons the French; and he preached them a sermon:
"Barons, my lords, [Charlemagne] left us in this place.
We know our duty: to die like good men for our King.
Fight to defend the holy Christian faith."

from *The Song of Roland*

Love Poems and Songs Under the code of chivalry, a knight's duty to his lady became as important as his duty to his lord. In many medieval poems, the hero's difficulties resulted from a conflict between those two obligations.

Troubadours were traveling poet-musicians at the castles and courts of Europe. They composed short verses and

Connect *to* Today

Epic Films

The long, narrative epic poem has given way in modern times to the epic film. Epic films feature larger-than-life characters in powerful stories that deal with mythic and timeless themes. These films take their stories from history, legend, and fantasy. The first epic film was *Birth of a Nation*, released in 1915.

Some modern epic films are *Braveheart* (1995), pictured above; *Gladiator* (2000); and the *Star Wars* saga (six films, 1977–2005).

↗ **hmhsocialstudies.com**

INTERNET ACTIVITY Go online to research and write about the historical content of five epic films.

songs about the joys and sorrows of romantic love. Sometimes troubadours sang their own verses in the castles of their lady. They also sent roving minstrels to carry their songs to courts.

A troubadour might sing about love's disappointments: "My loving heart, my faithfulness, myself, my world she deigns to take. Then leave me bare and comfortless to longing thoughts that ever wake."

Other songs told of lovesick knights who adored ladies they would probably never win: "Love of a far-off land/For you my heart is aching/And I can find no relief." The code of chivalry promoted a false image of knights, making them seem more romantic than brutal. In turn, these love songs created an artificial image of women. In the troubadour's eyes, noblewomen were always beautiful and pure.

The most celebrated woman of the age was Eleanor of Aquitaine (1122–1204). Troubadours flocked to her court in the French duchy of Aquitaine. Later, as queen of England, Eleanor was the mother of two kings, Richard the Lion-Hearted and John. Richard himself composed romantic songs and poems.

Women's Role in Feudal Society

Most women in feudal society were powerless, just as most men were. But women had the added burden of being thought inferior to men. This was the view of the Church and was generally accepted in feudal society. Nonetheless, women

---

> Analyzing Primary Sources

Daily Life of a Noblewoman
This excerpt describes the daily life of an English noblewoman of the Middle Ages, Cicely Neville, Duchess of York. A typical noblewoman is pictured below.

PRIMARY SOURCE

She gets up at 7a.m., and her chaplain is waiting to say morning prayers . . . and when she has washed and dressed . . . she has breakfast, then she goes to the chapel, for another service, then has dinner. . . . After dinner, she discusses business . . . then has a short sleep, then drinks ale or wine. Then . . . she goes to the chapel for evening service, and has supper. After supper, she relaxes with her women attendants. . . . After that, she goes to her private room, and says nighttime prayers. By 8 p.m. she is in bed.

DAILY ROUTINE OF CICELY, DUCHESS OF YORK, quoted in *Women in Medieval Times* by Fiona Macdonald

Daily Life of a Peasant Woman
This excerpt describes the daily life of a typical medieval peasant woman as pictured below.

PRIMARY SOURCE

I get up early . . . milk our cows and turn them into the field. . . . Then I make butter. . . . Afterward I make cheese. . . . Then the children need looking after. . . . I give the chickens food . . . and look after the young geese. . . . I bake, I brew. . . . I twist rope. . . . I tease out wool, and card it, and spin it on a wheel. . . . I organize food for the cattle, and for ourselves. . . . I look after all the household.

FROM A BALLAD FIRST WRITTEN DOWN IN ABOUT 1500, quoted in *Women in Medieval Times* by Fiona Macdonald

DOCUMENT-BASED QUESTIONS
1. **Drawing Conclusions** *What seem to be the major concerns in the noblewoman's life? How do they compare with those of the peasant woman?*
2. **Making Inferences** *What qualities would you associate with the peasant woman and the life she lived?*

played important roles in the lives of both noble and peasant families.

Noblewomen Under the feudal system, a noblewoman could inherit an estate from her husband. Upon her lord's request, she could also send his knights to war. When her husband was off fighting, the lady of a medieval castle might act as military commander and a warrior. At times, noblewomen played a key role in defending castles. They hurled rocks and fired arrows at attackers. (See the illustration to the right.)

In reality, however, the lives of most noblewomen were limited. Whether young or old, females in noble families generally were confined to activities in the home or the convent. Also, noblewomen held little property because lords passed down their fiefs to sons and not to daughters. **B**

Peasant Women For the vast majority of women of the lower classes, life had remained unchanged for centuries. Peasant women performed endless labor around the home and often in the fields, bore children, and took care of their families. Young peasant girls learned practical household skills from their mother at an early age, unlike daughters in rich households who were educated by tutors. Females in peasant families were poor and powerless. Yet, the economic contribution they made was essential to the survival of the peasant household.

As you have read in this section, the Church significantly influenced the status of medieval women. In Section 4, you will read just how far-reaching was the influence of the Church in the Middle Ages.

MAIN IDEA

Summarizing

B What privileges did a noblewoman have in medieval society?

▲ The noblewomen depicted in this manuscript show their courage and combat skills in defending a castle against enemies.

SECTION 3 ASSESSMENT

TERMS & NAMES 1. For each term or name, write a sentence explaining its significance.
• chivalry   • tournament   • troubadour

USING YOUR NOTES	MAIN IDEAS	CRITICAL THINKING & WRITING
2. Which ideas associated with chivalry have remnants in today's society? Explain.	3. What were two inventions from Asia that changed the technology of warfare in western Europe? 4. Who were the occupants of a castle? 5. What were some of the themes of medieval literature?	6. **DEVELOPING HISTORICAL PERSPECTIVE** How important a role did knights play in the feudal system? 7. **MAKING INFERENCES** How was the code of chivalry like the idea of romantic love? 8. **COMPARING AND CONTRASTING** In what ways were the lives of a noblewoman and a peasant woman the same? different? 9. **WRITING ACTIVITY** RELIGIOUS AND ETHICAL SYSTEMS Write a **persuasive essay** in support of the adoption of a code of chivalry, listing the positive effects it might have on feudal society.

Chivalry

CONNECT TO TODAY WRITING AN ADVERTISEMENT

Conduct research to learn more about tournaments. Then, write a 50-word **advertisement** promoting a tournament to be held at a modern re-creation of a medieval fair.

The Power of the Church

MAIN IDEA	WHY IT MATTERS NOW	TERMS & NAMES
POWER AND AUTHORITY Church leaders and political leaders competed for power and authority.	Today, many religious leaders still voice their opinions on political issues.	• clergy • sacrament • canon law	• Holy Roman Empire • lay investiture

SETTING THE STAGE Amid the weak central governments in feudal Europe, the Church emerged as a powerful institution. It shaped the lives of people from all social classes. As the Church expanded its political role, strong rulers began to question the pope's authority. Dramatic power struggles unfolded in the Holy Roman Empire, the scene of mounting tensions between popes and emperors.

The Far-Reaching Authority of the Church

hmhsocialstudies.com
TAKING NOTES

Use the graphic organizer online to take notes on significant dates and events of the Holy Roman Empire.

In crowning Charlemagne as the Roman Emperor in 800, the Church sought to influence both spiritual and political matters. Three hundred years earlier, Pope Gelasius I recognized the conflicts that could arise between the two great forces—the Church and the state. He wrote, "There are two powers by which this world is chiefly ruled: the sacred authority of the priesthood and the authority of kings."

Gelasius suggested an analogy to solve such conflicts. God had created two symbolic swords. One sword was religious. The other was political. The pope held a spiritual sword. The emperor wielded a political one. Gelasius thought that the pope should bow to the emperor in political matters. In turn, the emperor should bow to the pope in religious matters. If each ruler kept the authority in his own realm, Gelasius suggested, the two leaders could share power in harmony. In reality, though, they disagreed on the boundaries of either realm. Throughout the Middle Ages, the Church and various European rulers competed for power.

The Structure of the Church Like the system of feudalism, the Church had its own organization. Power was based on status. Church structure consisted of different ranks of clergy, or religious officials. The pope in Rome headed the Church. All **clergy**, including bishops and priests, fell under his authority. Bishops supervised priests, the lowest ranking members of the clergy. Bishops also settled disputes over Church teachings and practices. For most people, local priests served as the main contact with the Church.

Religion as a Unifying Force Feudalism and the manor system created divisions among people. But the shared beliefs in the teachings of the Church bonded people together. The church was a stable force during an era of constant warfare and political turmoil. It provided Christians with a sense of security and of belonging to a religious community. In the Middle Ages, religion occupied center stage.

▼ A pope's tiara symbolized his power.

Medieval Christians' everyday lives were harsh. Still, they could all follow the same path to salvation—everlasting life in heaven. Priests and other clergy administered the **sacraments**, or important religious ceremonies. These rites paved the way for achieving salvation. For example, through the sacrament of baptism, people became part of the Christian community.

At the local level, the village church was a unifying force in the lives of most people. It served as a religious and social center. People worshiped together at the church. They also met with other villagers. Religious holidays, especially Christmas and Easter, were occasions for festive celebrations. Ⓐ

MAIN IDEA

Analyzing Motives
Ⓐ Why did medieval peasants support the Church?

The Law of the Church The Church's authority was both religious and political. It provided a unifying set of spiritual beliefs and rituals. The Church also created a system of justice to guide people's conduct. All medieval Christians, kings and peasants alike, were subject to **canon law**, or Church law, in matters such as marriage and religious practices. The Church also established courts to try people accused of violating canon law. Two of the harshest punishments that offenders faced were excommunication and interdict.

Popes used the threat of excommunication, or banishment from the Church, to wield power over political rulers. For example, a disobedient king's quarrel with a pope might result in excommunication. This meant the king would be denied salvation. Excommunication also freed all the king's vassals from their duties to him. If an excommunicated king continued to disobey the pope, the pope, in turn, could use an even more frightening weapon, the interdict.

Under an interdict, many sacraments and religious services could not be performed in the king's lands. As Christians, the king's subjects believed that without such sacraments they might be doomed to hell. In the 11th century, excommunication and the possible threat of an interdict would force a German emperor to submit to the pope's commands.

Social History

An Age of Superstition

Lacking knowledge of the laws of nature, many people during the Middle Ages were led to irrational beliefs. They expected the dead to reappear as ghosts. A friendly goblin might do a person a good deed, but an evil witch might cause great harm. Medieval people thought an evil witch had the power to exchange a healthy child for a sickly one.

The medieval Church frowned upon superstitions such as these:

- preparing a table with three knives to please good fairies
- making a vow by a tree, a pond, or any place but a church
- believing that a person could change into the shape of a wolf
- believing that the croak of a raven or meeting a priest would bring a person good or bad luck

The Church and the Holy Roman Empire

When Pope Leo III crowned Charlemagne emperor in 800, he unknowingly set the stage for future conflicts between popes and emperors. These clashes would go on for centuries.

Otto I Allies with the Church The most effective ruler of medieval Germany was Otto I, known as Otto the Great. Otto, crowned king in 936, followed the policies of his hero, Charlemagne. Otto formed a close alliance with the Church. To limit the nobles' strength, he sought help from the clergy. He built up his power base by gaining the support of the bishops and abbots, the heads of monasteries. He dominated the Church in Germany. He also used his power to defeat German princes. Following in Charlemagne's footsteps, Otto also invaded Italy on the pope's behalf. In 962, the pope rewarded Otto by crowning him emperor.

Signs of Future Conflicts The German-Italian empire Otto created was first called the Roman Empire of the German Nation. It later became the **Holy Roman Empire**. It remained the strongest state in Europe until about 1100. However,

Otto's attempt to revive Charlemagne's empire caused trouble for future German leaders. Popes and Italian nobles, too, resented German power over Italy.

The Emperor Clashes with the Pope

The Church was not happy that kings, such as Otto, had control over clergy and their offices. It especially resented the practice of **lay investiture**, a ceremony in which kings and nobles appointed church officials. Whoever controlled lay investiture held the real power in naming bishops, who were very influential clergy that kings sought to control. Church reformers felt that kings should not have that power. In 1075, Pope Gregory VII banned lay investiture.

The furious young German emperor, Henry IV, immediately called a meeting of the German bishops he had appointed. With their approval, the emperor ordered Gregory to step down from the papacy. Gregory then excommunicated Henry. Afterward, German bishops and princes sided with the pope. To save his throne, Henry tried to win the pope's forgiveness.

Showdown at Canossa In January 1077, Henry crossed the snowy Alps to the Italian town of Canossa (kuh•NAHS•uh). He approached the castle where Gregory was a guest. Gregory later described the scene:

PRIMARY SOURCE

There, having laid aside all the belongings of royalty, wretchedly, with bare feet and clad in wool, he [Henry IV] continued for three days to stand before the gate of the castle. Nor did he desist from imploring with many tears the aid and consolation of the apostolic mercy until he had moved all of those who were present there.

POPE GREGORY, in *Basic Documents in Medieval History*

The Holy Roman Empire, 1100

Friesland
Saxony
POLAND
Aachen
Lorraine
Franconia
Worms
Bohemia
FRANCE
Swabia
Bavaria
KINGDOM OF HUNGARY
Burgundy
Carinthia
Lombardy
Papal States
Tuscany
Mediterranean Sea
Adriatic Sea
Spoleto
Rome

Elbe R.
Rhine R.
Danube R.
Rhône R.
Po R.

0   200 Miles
0   400 Kilometers

The Holy Roman Empire
Papal States

GEOGRAPHY SKILLBUILDER: Interpreting Maps

1. **Region** How many states made up the Holy Roman Empire? What does this suggest about ruling it as an empire?
2. **Location** How did the location of the Papal States make them an easy target for frequent invasions by Germanic rulers?

The Pope was obligated to forgive any sinner who begged so humbly. Still, Gregory kept Henry waiting in the snow for three days before ending his excommunication. Their meeting actually solved nothing. The pope had humiliated Henry, the proudest ruler in Europe. Yet, Henry felt triumphant and rushed home to punish rebellious nobles. **B**

Concordat of Worms The successors of Gregory and Henry continued to fight over lay investiture until 1122. That year, representatives of the Church and the emperor met in the German city of Worms (wurms). They reached a compromise known as the Concordat of Worms. By its terms, the Church alone could appoint a bishop, but the emperor could veto the appointment. During Henry's struggle, German princes regained power lost under Otto. But a later king, Frederick I, would resume the battle to build royal authority.

MAIN IDEA

Making Inferences
B Why was Henry's journey to Canossa a political act?

Disorder in the Empire

By 1152, the seven princes who elected the German king realized that Germany needed a strong ruler to keep the peace. They chose Frederick I, nicknamed "Barbarossa" for his red beard.

Vocabulary
Barbarossa means "red beard" in Italian.

The Reign of Frederick I Frederick I was the first ruler to call his lands the Holy Roman Empire. However, this region was actually a patchwork of feudal territories. His forceful personality and military skills enabled him to dominate the German princes. Yet, whenever he left the country, disorder returned. Following Otto's example, Frederick repeatedly invaded the rich cities of Italy. His brutal tactics spurred Italian merchants to unite against him. He also angered the pope, who joined the merchants in an alliance called the Lombard League.

In 1176, the foot soldiers of the Lombard League faced Frederick's army of mounted knights at the Battle of Legnano (lay•NYAHN•oh). In an astonishing victory, the Italian foot soldiers used crossbows to defeat feudal knights for the first time in history. In 1177, Frederick made peace with the pope and returned to Germany. His defeat, though, had undermined his authority with the German princes. After he drowned in 1190, his empire fell to pieces.

▲ This manuscript shows Frederick I at the height of his imperial power.

German States Remain Separate German kings after Frederick, including his grandson Frederick II, continued their attempts to revive Charlemagne's empire and his alliance with the Church. This policy led to wars with Italian cities and to further clashes with the pope. These conflicts were one reason why the feudal states of Germany did not unify during the Middle Ages. Another reason was that the system of German princes electing the king weakened royal authority. German rulers controlled fewer royal lands to use as a base of power than French and English kings of the same period, who, as you will learn in Chapter 14, were establishing strong central authority. **C**

MAIN IDEA

Analyzing Causes
C What political trend kept German states separate during the Middle Ages?

SECTION 4 ASSESSMENT

TERMS & NAMES 1. For each term or name, write a sentence explaining its significance.
• clergy   • sacrament   • canon law   • Holy Roman Empire   • lay investiture

USING YOUR NOTES

2. Which of the events were power struggles between the Church and rulers? Explain.

MAIN IDEAS

3. What were some of the matters covered by canon law?

4. How did Otto the Great make the crown stronger than the German nobles?

5. Why did lay investiture cause a struggle between kings and popes?

CRITICAL THINKING & WRITING

6. **COMPARING** How was the structure of the Church like that of the feudal system?

7. **EVALUATING DECISIONS** Was the Concordat of Worms a fair compromise for both the emperor and the Church? Why or why not?

8. **DRAWING CONCLUSIONS** Why did German kings fail to unite their lands?

9. **WRITING ACTIVITY** POWER AND AUTHORITY Why did Henry IV go to Canossa to confront Pope Gregory VII? Write a brief **dialogue** that might have taken place between them at their first meeting.

CONNECT TO TODAY CREATING A CHART

Research the ruling structure of the modern Roman Catholic Church and then create a **chart** showing the structure, or hierarchy.

TERMS & NAMES

For each term or name below, briefly explain its connection to the Middle Ages from 500 to 1200.

1. monastery
2. Charlemagne
3. vassal
4. serf
5. manor
6. chivalry
7. clergy
8. Holy Roman Empire

MAIN IDEAS

Charlemagne Unites Germanic Kingdoms Section 1 (pages 353–357)

9. How did Gregory I increase the political power of the pope?

10. What was the outcome of the Battle of Tours?

11. What was the significance of the pope's declaring Charlemagne emperor?

Feudalism in Europe Section 2 (pages 358–363)

12. Which invading peoples caused turmoil in Europe during the 800s?

13. What exchange took place between lords and vassals under feudalism?

14. What duties did the lord of a manor and his serfs owe one another?

The Age of Chivalry Section 3 (pages 364–369)

15. What were the stages of becoming a knight?

16. What were common subjects of troubadours' songs?

17. What role did women play under feudalism?

The Power of the Church Section 4 (pages 370–373)

18. What was Gelasius's two-swords theory?

19. Why was Otto I the most effective ruler of Medieval Germany?

20. How was the conflict between Pope Gregory VII and Henry IV resolved?

CRITICAL THINKING

1. USING YOUR NOTES

In a chart, compare medieval Europe to an earlier civilization, such as Rome or Greece. Consider government, religion, and social roles.

Medieval Europe	
government	
religion	
social roles	

2. COMPARING AND CONTRASTING

EMPIRE BUILDING How did Otto I and Frederick I try to imitate Charlemagne's approach to empire building?

3. DRAWING CONCLUSIONS

POWER AND AUTHORITY Why do you think the ownership of land became an increasing source of power for feudal lords?

4. ANALYZING ISSUES

Why did the appointment of bishops become the issue in a struggle between kings and popes?

5. SYNTHESIZING

RELIGIOUS AND ETHICAL SYSTEMS What generalizations could you make about the relationship between politics and religion in the Middle Ages?

VISUAL SUMMARY

European Middle Ages

Economic System

Manors

- Lord's estate
- Set of rights and obligations between serfs and lords
- Self-sufficient community producing a variety of goods

Code of Behavior

Chivalry

- Displays of courage and valor in combat
- Respect toward women
- Devotion to a feudal lord and heavenly lord

Belief System

The Church

- Power over people's everyday lives
- Unifying force of Christian faith
- Involvement in political affairs

Political System

Feudalism

- Form of government based on landholding
- Alliances between lords and vassals
- Oaths of loyalty in exchange for land and military service
- Ranking of power and authority

MEDIEVAL SOCIETY

Use the quotation and your knowledge of world history to answer questions 1 and 2.

PRIMARY SOURCE

There was a knight, a most distinguished man,
Who from the day on which he first began
To ride abroad had followed chivalry,
Truth, honor, generous, and courtesy.
He had done nobly in sovereign's war
And ridden in battle, no man more,
As well as Christian in heathen places
And ever honored for his noble graces.

GEOFFREY CHAUCER, *The Canterbury Tales*

1. Which of these phrases does not characterize the knight Chaucer describes?

   A. a skilled fighter

   B. a devoted Christian

   C. a young man

   D. a well-traveled warrior

2. What qualities of knighthood do you think are missing from Chaucer's description?

   A. that a knight was of noble birth

   B. that a knight was a skilled warrior

   C. that a knight adored his chosen lady

   D. that a knight devoted himself to his heavenly Lord

Use the bar graph and your knowledge of world history to answer question 3.

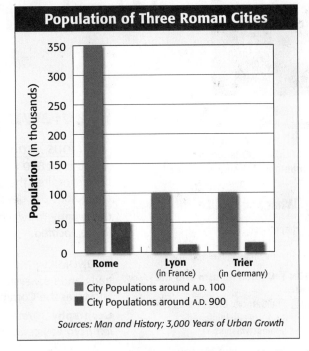

Population of Three Roman Cities

Sources: *Man and History; 3,000 Years of Urban Growth*

3. What is the most important point this chart is making?

   A. Trier and Lyon were not as large as Rome.

   B. Rome was the most populous city in the Roman Empire.

   C. All three cities lost significant population after the fall of the Roman Empire.

   D. Rome lost about 300,000 people from A.D. 100 to A.D. 200.

 hmhsocialstudies.com TEST PRACTICE

For additional test practice, go online for:
- Diagnostic tests
- Tutorials
- Strategies

Interact *with* History

On page 352, you considered the issue of what freedoms you would give up for protection. Now that you have read the chapter, reconsider your answer. How important was security? Was it worth not having certain basic freedoms? Discuss your ideas in a small group.

FOCUS ON WRITING

Refer to the text, and then write a three-paragraph **character sketch** of a religious or political figure described in this chapter. Consider the following:
- why the figure was important
- how the figure performed his or her role

MULTIMEDIA ACTIVITY 21ST CENTURY

Designing a Video Game

Use the Internet, books, and other reference materials to find out more about medieval tournaments. Then create a video game that imitates a medieval tournament between knights. Describe your ideas in a proposal that you might send to a video game company.

Think about video games that are based on contests. You might adapt some of the rules to your game. Consider the following:
- the rules of the game
- the system of keeping score of wins and losses
- weapons that should be used

CHAPTER 14

The Formation of Western Europe, 800–1500

Essential Question

What religious, economic, and political events led to the development of Western Europe?

What You Will Learn

In this chapter you will study the effects of the Crusades, the Hundred Years' War, and the Plague on medieval society.

SECTION 1 Church Reform and the Crusades

Main Idea The Catholic Church underwent reform and launched Crusades against Muslims.

SECTION 2 Changes in Medieval Society

Main Idea The feudal system declined as agriculture, trade, finance, towns, and universities developed.

SECTION 3 England and France Develop

Main Idea As the kingdoms of England and France began to develop into nations, certain democratic traditions evolved.

SECTION 4 The Hundred Years' War and the Plague

Main Idea In the 1300s, Europe was torn apart by religious strife, the bubonic plague, and the Hundred Years' War.

Previewing Themes

RELIGIOUS AND ETHICAL SYSTEMS In Western Europe the time period from 800 to 1500 is known as the Age of Faith. Christian beliefs inspired the Crusades and the building of great cathedrals, and guided the development of universities.

Geography *In which political unit was the capital of Christianity, Rome, located?*

ECONOMICS Medieval Europeans developed new methods of trade and new systems of finance and commerce. The changes are known as the Commercial Revolution.

Geography *Through which political units would a trader pass if he left from Venice and went to Calais using a land route?*

CULTURAL INTERACTION Although destructive in many ways, the Crusades resulted in a great deal of cultural exchange. Medieval Christian Europe learned and adopted much from the Muslim world.

Geography *A stopping place for Crusaders on their way to the Holy Land was the city of Constantinople. In what political unit is Constantinople located?*

EUROPE

800

1000

987
Capetian dynasty begins in France.

1066
Norman invasion of England

1095
First Crusade begins. ▶

WORLD

980
◀ Toltec Empire at its peak. (a Toltec warrior figurine)

1041
Movable type invented in China.

Europe, 14TH Century

NORWAY

North Sea

DENMARK

Baltic Sea

SCOTLAND

IRELAND

ENGLAND

London

Calais

Ghent

ATLANTIC OCEAN

45°N

HOLY ROMAN EMPIRE

LITHUANIA

POLAND

Kiev

Orléans

FRANCE

AQUITAINE

GASCONY

NAVARRE

Avignon

RUTHENIA

MOLDAVIA

Venice

HUNGARY

Genoa

WALLACHIA

PORTUGAL

ARAGON

Barcelona

Toledo

Corsica (Genoa)

PAPAL STATES

Rome

Adriatic Sea

BOSNIA

SERBIAN STATES

BULGARIAN STATES

Black Sea

Constantinople

CASTILE

Cordoba

Balearic Is.

Sardinia (Aragon)

Naples

KINGDOM OF NAPLES

BYZANTINE EMPIRE

GRANADA

0   250   500 Miles

0   250   500 Kilometers

Conic Projection

Sicily (Aragon)

Mediterranean Sea

15°E

Crete (Venice)

HISTORY

The Crusades: The Legacy

hmhsocialstudies.com VIDEO

1215
King John approves Magna Carta.

1347
◄ Bubonic plague strikes Europe.

1429
Joan of Arc leads the French to victory over the English at Orleans.

1453
Hundred Years' War ends with French victory.

1200

1500

1206
◄ Genghis Khan unites Mongols and is proclaimed the Great Khan.

1325
The Aztec establish Tenochtitlán.

What are the dangers and rewards of going on a Crusade?

You are a squire in England. The knight you serve has decided to join a Christian Crusade (a holy war) to capture the city of Jerusalem from the Muslims. He has given you the choice of joining or staying home to look after his family and manor. On an earlier Crusade, the knight and his friends looted towns and manors, taking jewels and precious objects. But some of the knights were also held for ransom, robbed, and murdered. You are torn between the desire for adventure and possible riches that you might find on the Crusade, and fear of the hazards that await you on such a dangerous journey.

1 Richard the Lion-Hearted leads a group of Crusaders on the Third Crusade to regain Jerusalem from the Muslims.

2 Servants and women sometimes accompanied the Crusaders as they made their way toward the Holy Land.

EXAMINING *the* ISSUES

- **What reasons might an individual have to join a Crusade?**

- **What might be the advantages and disadvantages of staying home to defend the knight's family and estate?**

As a class, discuss these questions. In your discussion, remember what you've learned about the power of religious beliefs to move people to action. As you read about the Crusades in this chapter, see how events turned out for the Crusaders.

Church Reform and the Crusades

MAIN IDEA	WHY IT MATTERS NOW	TERMS & NAMES
CULTURAL INTERACTION The Catholic Church underwent reform and launched Crusades against Muslims.	The Crusades left a legacy of distrust between Christians and Muslims that continues to the present.	• simony • Gothic • Urban II • Crusade • Saladin • Richard the Lion-Hearted • Reconquista • Inquisition

SETTING THE STAGE Some historians have called the period in Western Europe between 500 and 1000 a "dark age." Magyars seeking plunder pushed up from the Danube River region. Vikings raided western European church monasteries. These groups destroyed many of these centers of learning. Around the 900s, however, a new spirit invaded the church and brought about a spiritual revival in the clergy. Filled with new energy, the church began restructuring itself and started massive building programs to create new places of worship.

The Age of Faith

Monasteries led the spiritual revival. The monastery founded at Cluny in France in 910 was especially important. The reformers there wanted to return to the basic principles of the Christian religion. To do so, they established new religious orders. Influenced by the religious devotion and reverence for God shown by the new monasteries, the popes began to reform the Church. They restored and expanded its power and authority. A new age of religious feeling was born—the Age of Faith. Still, many problems troubled the Church.

hmhsocialstudies.com
TAKING NOTES

Use the graphic organizer online to take notes on important events in the Age of Faith.

Problems in the Church Some priests were nearly illiterate and could barely read their prayers. Some of the popes were men of questionable morals. Many bishops and abbots cared more about their positions as feudal lords than about their duties as spiritual leaders. Reformers were most distressed by three main issues.

- Many village priests married and had families. Such marriages were against Church rulings.
- Bishops sold positions in the Church, a practice called **simony** (SY•muh•nee).
- Using the practice of lay investiture, kings appointed church bishops. Church reformers believed the Church alone should appoint bishops.

Reform and Church Organization Pope Leo IX and Pope Gregory VII enforced Church laws against simony and the marriage of priests. The popes who followed Leo and Gregory reorganized the Church to continue the policy of reform. In the 1100s and 1200s, the Church was restructured to resemble a kingdom, with the pope at its head. The pope's group of advisers was called the papal Curia. The Curia also acted as a court. It developed canon law (the law of the Church) on matters such as marriage, divorce, and inheritance. The Curia also decided cases based on these laws. Diplomats for the pope traveled through Europe dealing with bishops and kings. In this way the popes established their authority throughout Europe.

The Church collected taxes in the form of tithes. These consumed one-tenth the yearly income from every Christian family. The Church used some of the money to perform social services such as caring for the sick and the poor. In fact, the Church operated most hospitals in medieval Europe. **A**

New Religious Orders In the early 1200s, wandering friars traveled from place to place preaching and spreading the Church's ideas. Like monks, friars took vows of chastity, poverty, and obedience. Unlike monks, friars did not live apart from the world in monasteries. Instead, they preached to the poor throughout Europe's towns and cities. Friars owned nothing and lived by begging.

Dominic, a Spanish priest, founded the Dominicans, one of the earliest orders of friars. Because Dominic emphasized the importance of study, many Dominicans were scholars. Francis of Assisi (uh•SEE•zee), an Italian, founded another order of friars, the Franciscans. Francis treated all creatures, including animals, as if they were his spiritual brothers and sisters.

Women played an important role in the spiritual revival. Women joined the Dominicans, Benedictines, and Franciscans. In 1212, a woman named Clare and her friend Francis of Assisi founded the Franciscan order for women. It was known as the Poor Clares. In Germany, Hildegard of Bingen, a mystic and musician, founded a Benedictine convent in 1147. Like friars, these women lived in poverty and worked to help the poor and sick. Unlike the friars, however, women were not allowed to travel from place to place as preachers.

Cathedrals—Cities of God

During the medieval period most people worshiped in small churches near their homes. Larger churches called cathedrals were built in city areas. The cathedral was viewed as the representation of the City of God. As such, it was decorated with all the richness that Christians could offer. Between about 800 and 1100, churches were built in the Romanesque (ROH•muh•NEHSK) style. The churches had round arches and a heavy roof held up by thick walls and pillars. The thick walls had tiny windows that let in little light.

A New Style of Church Architecture A new spirit in the church and access to more money from the growing wealth of towns and from trade helped fuel the building of churches in several European countries. In the early 1100s, a new style of architecture, known as **Gothic**, evolved throughout medieval Europe. The term *Gothic* comes from a Germanic tribe named the Goths. Unlike the heavy, gloomy Romanesque buildings, Gothic cathedrals thrust upward as if reaching toward heaven. Light streamed in through huge stained glass windows. Other arts of the medieval world were evident around or in the Gothic cathedral—sculpture, wood-carvings, and stained glass windows. All of these elements were meant to inspire the worshiper with the magnificence of God. See the diagram on the next page to learn more about Gothic cathedrals.

Soon Gothic cathedrals were built in many towns of France. In Paris, the vaulted ceiling of the Cathedral of Notre Dame (NOH•truh-DAHM) eventually rose to more than 100 feet. Then Chartres, Reims, Amiens, and Beauvais built even taller cathedrals. In all, nearly 500 Gothic churches were built between 1170 and 1270.

↗ hmhsocialstudies.com **INTERACTIVE**

Gothic Architecture

The master builders in France, where the Gothic style originated, developed techniques of structural engineering that were key to Gothic architecture: ❶ ribbed vaults that supported the roof's weight, ❷ flying buttresses that transferred weight to thick, exterior walls, ❸ pointed arches that framed huge stained glass windows, and ❹ tall spires that seemed to be pointing to heaven.

❶ ribbed vaults

❷ flying buttresses

❸ pointed arches

❹ tall spires

▲ Chartres Cathedral

The cathedral of Chartres (shahrt) is a masterpiece of Gothic architecture. The cathedral has hundreds of sculptures. The stone carvings that frame every door illustrate Bible stories. In this photograph, you can see the cathedral has not one, but two bell towers.

▲ Stained Glass

In addition to its sculpture and soaring towers, Chartres Cathedral has some of the most beautiful stained glass windows of any Gothic cathedral in Europe. The windows illustrate stories from the Bible. As illiterate peasants walked past the 176 windows, they could view those stories. The window above depicts the parable of the Good Samaritan.

SKILLBUILDER: Interpreting Visual Sources

1. **Drawing Conclusions** *Pose and answer three questions about elements in the style of Gothic architecture that might affect the sense of height and light inside.*
2. **Comparing and Contrasting** *Think about stained glass windows you have seen. Do they tell a story? What figures or events do they illustrate?*

The Crusades

The Age of Faith also inspired wars of conquest. In 1093, the Byzantine emperor Alexius Comnenus sent an appeal to Robert, Count of Flanders. The emperor asked for help against the Muslim Turks. They were threatening to conquer his capital, Constantinople:

PRIMARY SOURCE

Come then, with all your people and give battle with all your strength, so that all this treasure shall not fall into the hands of the Turks. . . . Therefore act while there is still time lest the kingdom of the Christians shall vanish from your sight and, what is more important, the Holy Sepulchre [the tomb where Jesus was buried] shall vanish. And in your coming you will find your reward in heaven, and if you do not come, God will condemn you.

EMPEROR ALEXIUS COMNENUS, quoted in *The Dream and the Tomb* by Robert Payne

Pope <u>Urban II</u> also read that letter. Shortly after this appeal, he issued a call for what he termed a "holy war," a <u>Crusade</u>, to gain control of the Holy Land. Over the next 300 years, a number of such Crusades were launched.

Goals of the Crusades The Crusades had economic, social, and political goals as well as religious motives. Muslims controlled Palestine (the Holy Land) and threatened Constantinople. The Byzantine emperor in Constantinople appealed to Christians to stop Muslim attacks. In addition, the pope wanted to reclaim Palestine and reunite Christendom, which had split into Eastern and Western branches in 1054.

▼ The red cross on his tunic identifies this knight as a crusader.

In addition, kings and the Church both saw the Crusades as an opportunity to get rid of quarrelsome knights who fought each other. These knights threatened the peace of the kingdoms, as well as Church property.

Others who participated in the Crusades were younger sons who, unlike eldest sons, did not stand to inherit their father's property. They were looking for land and a position in society, or for adventure.

In the later Crusades, merchants profited by making cash loans to finance the journey. They also leased their ships for a hefty fee to transport armies over the Mediterranean Sea. In addition, the merchants of Pisa, Genoa, and Venice hoped to win control of key trade routes to India, Southeast Asia, and China from Muslim traders.

The First and Second Crusades Pope Urban's call brought a tremendous outpouring of religious feeling and support for the Crusade. According to the pope, those who died on Crusade were assured of a place in heaven. With red crosses sewn on tunics worn over their armor and the battle cry of "God wills it!" on their lips, knights and commoners were fired by religious zeal and became Crusaders.

By early 1097, three armies of knights and people of all classes had gathered outside Constantinople. Most of the Crusaders were French, but Bohemians, Germans, Englishmen, Scots, Italians, and Spaniards came as well. The Crusaders were ill-prepared for war in this First Crusade. Many knew nothing of the geography, climate, or culture of the Holy Land. They had no grand strategy to capture Jerusalem. The nobles argued among themselves and couldn't agree on a leader. Finally an army of 12,000 (less than one-fourth of the original army) approached Jerusalem. The Crusaders besieged the city for over a month. On July-15, 1099, they captured the city.

Vocabulary
Holy Land: Palestine; the area where Jesus lived and preached

ENGLAND

HOLY ROMAN EMPIRE

POLAND

English Channel

Paris

Metz

Vezelay

Regensburg

Vienna

FRANCE

Venice

HUNGARY

Clermont

Genoa

Belgrade

Marseille

SERBIA

BULGARIA

ATLANTIC OCEAN

Corsica

Rome

Black Sea

SPAIN

Sardinia

KINGDOM OF SICILY

Adrianople

Constantinople

PORTUGAL

40°N

Lisbon

Mediterranean Sea

BYZANTINE EMPIRE

SELJUK TURKS

Crete

Cyprus

Edessa

Antioch

Tripoli

Acre

Jerusalem

N

0   500 Miles

0   1,000 Kilometers

☐	Christian lands
☐	Muslim lands
☐	Kingdoms established by the Crusaders
⇒	First Crusade, 1096–1099
⇒	Second Crusade, 1147–1149
⇒	Third Crusade, 1189–1191
⇒	Fourth Crusade, 1202–1204

GEOGRAPHY SKILLBUILDER: Interpreting Maps
1. **Place** *What Muslim power ruled lands close to the Christian city of Constantinople?*
2. **Movement** *Which Crusade did not make it to Jerusalem? Where did this Crusade end?*

All in all, the Crusaders had won a narrow strip of land. It stretched about 650 miles from Edessa in the north to Jerusalem in the south. Four feudal Crusader states were carved out of this territory, each ruled by a European noble.

The Crusaders' states were extremely vulnerable to Muslim counterattack. In 1144, Edessa was reconquered by the Turks. The Second Crusade was organized to recapture the city. But its armies straggled home in defeat. In 1187, Europeans were shocked to learn that Jerusalem itself had fallen to a Kurdish warrior and Muslim leader **Saladin** (SAL•uh•dihn). **B**

MAIN IDEA

Summarizing

B What, if anything, had the Crusaders gained by the end of the Second Crusade?

The Third Crusade The Third Crusade to recapture Jerusalem was led by three of Europe's most powerful monarchs. They were Philip II (Augustus) of France, German emperor Frederick I (Barbarossa), and the English king, **Richard the Lion-Hearted**. Philip argued with Richard and went home. Barbarossa drowned on the journey. So, Richard was left to lead the Crusaders in an attempt to regain the Holy Land from Saladin. Both Richard and Saladin were brilliant warriors. After many battles, the two agreed to a truce in 1192. Jerusalem remained under Muslim control. In return, Saladin promised that unarmed Christian pilgrims could freely visit the city's holy places.

VIDEO
Byzantine: The Appeal for a Third Crusade

⇗ hmhsocialstudies.com

The Crusading Spirit Dwindles

In 1204, the Fourth Crusade to capture Jerusalem failed. The knights did not reach the Holy Land. Instead, they ended up looting the city of Constantinople. In the 1200s, four more Crusades to free the holy land were also unsuccessful. The religious spirit of the First Crusade faded, and the search for personal gain grew. In two later Crusades, armies marched not to the Holy Land but to Egypt. The Crusaders intended to weaken Muslim forces there before going to the Holy Land. But none of these attempts conquered much land.

History Makers

Richard the Lion-Hearted
1157–1199

Richard was noted for his good looks, charm, courage, grace—and ruthlessness. When he heard that Jerusalem had fallen to the Muslims, he was filled with religious zeal. He joined the Third Crusade, leaving others to rule England in his place.

Richard mounted a siege on the city of Acre. Saladin's army was in the hills overlooking the city, but it was not strong enough to defeat the Crusaders. When finally the city fell, Richard had the Muslim survivors—some 3,000 men, women, and children—slaughtered. The Muslim army watched helplessly from the hills.

Saladin
1138–1193

Saladin was the most famous Muslim leader of the 1100s. His own people considered him a most devout man. Even the Christians regarded him as honest and brave.

He wished to chase the Crusaders back into their own territories. He said:

I think that when God grants me victory over the rest of Palestine, I shall divide my territories, make a will stating my wishes, then set sail on this sea for their far-off lands and pursue the Franks there, so as to free the earth from anyone who does not believe in Allah, or die in the attempt.

The Children's Crusade The Children's Crusade took place in 1212. In two different movements, thousands of children set out to conquer Jerusalem. One group in France was led by 12-year-old Stephen of Cloyes. An estimated 30,000 children under 18 joined him. They were armed only with the belief that God would give them Jerusalem. On their march south to the Mediterranean, many died from cold and starvation. The rest drowned at sea or were sold into slavery.

In Germany, Nicholas of Cologne gathered about 20,000 children and young adults. They began marching toward Rome. Thousands died in the cold and treacherous crossing of the Alps. Those who survived the trip to Italy finally did meet the pope. He told them to go home and wait until they were older. About 2,000 survived the return trip to Germany. A few boarded a ship for the Holy Land and were never heard of again. **C**

A Spanish Crusade In Spain, Muslims (called Moors) controlled most of the country until the 1100s. The **Reconquista** (reh•kawn•KEES•tah) was a long effort by the Spanish to drive the Muslims out of Spain. By the late 1400s, the Muslims held only the tiny kingdom of Granada. In 1492, Granada finally fell to the Christian army of Ferdinand and Isabella, the Spanish monarchs.

To unify their country under Christianity and to increase their power, Isabella and Ferdinand made use of the **Inquisition**. This was a court held by the Church to suppress heresy. Heretics were people whose religious beliefs differed from the teachings of the Church. Many Jews and Muslims in Spain converted to Christianity during the late 1400s. Even so, the inquisitors suspected these Jewish and Muslim converts of heresy. A person suspected of heresy might be questioned for weeks and even tortured. Once suspects confessed, they were often burned at the stake. In 1492,

MAIN IDEA

Making Inferences
C How does the Children's Crusade illustrate the power of the Church?

the monarchs expelled all practicing Jews and Muslims from Spain.

The Effects of the Crusades

The Crusades are a forceful example of the power of the Church during the medieval period. The call to go to the Holy Land encouraged thousands to leave their homes and travel to faraway lands. For those who stayed home, especially women, it meant a chance to manage affairs on the estates or to operate shops and inns.

European merchants who lived and traded in the Crusader states expanded trade between Europe and Southwest Asia. The goods imported from Southwest Asia included spices, fruits, and cloth. This trade with the West benefited both Christians and Muslims.

However, the failure of later Crusades also lessened the power of the pope. The Crusades weakened the feudal nobility and increased the power of kings. Thousands of knights and other participants lost their lives and fortunes. The fall of Constantinople weakened the Byzantine Empire.

For Muslims, the intolerance and prejudice displayed by Christians in the Holy Land left behind a legacy of bitterness and hatred. This legacy continues to the present. For Christians and Jews who remained in the Muslim controlled region after the fall of the Crusader states, relations with the Muslim leadership worsened. For Jews in Europe, the Crusades were a time of increased persecution.

The Crusades grew out of religious fervor, feudalism, and chivalry, which came together with explosive energy. This same energy led to the growth of trade, towns, and universities in medieval Europe.

▲ This scene reveals torture used in the Inquisition.

SECTION 1 ASSESSMENT

TERMS & NAMES 1. For each term or name, write a sentence explaining its significance.
• simony • Gothic • Urban II • Crusade • Saladin • Richard the Lion-Hearted • Reconquista • Inquisition

USING YOUR NOTES
2. Which of the events of the Age of Faith do you think was most important to the Church? Explain.

900

1500

MAIN IDEAS
3. What were three main causes of the need to reform the Church?
4. Which Crusade was the only successful one?
5. How did the goals of the Crusades change over the years?

CRITICAL THINKING & WRITING
6. **FORMING AND SUPPORTING OPINIONS** Which of the following do you think best represents the spirit of the Age of Faith—Church reform, the Crusades, or the Gothic cathedrals? Explain.
7. **MAKING INFERENCES** What evidence supports the idea that the Church functioned like a kingdom?
8. **RECOGNIZING EFFECTS** How did the Crusades change the history of Europe? Give reasons for your answer.
9. **WRITING ACTIVITY** [CULTURAL INTERACTION] Write a **script** about an encounter between a Crusader and a Muslim defender of Jerusalem.

MULTIMEDIA ACTIVITY PREPARING A MULTIMEDIA PRESENTATION

Review the information on page 381. Use the Internet to research the Washington National Cathedral. Prepare a **multimedia presentation** showing the Gothic characteristics of the Washington National Cathedral.

INTERNET KEYWORD
Washington National Cathedral

Different Perspectives: Using Primary and Secondary Sources

The Crusades

In the Crusades, both Christians and Muslims believed that God was on their side. They both felt justified in using violence to win or to keep the Holy Land. The following excerpts show their belief in the rightness of their deeds.

A PRIMARY SOURCE
Pope Urban II

In 1095, Pope Urban II issued a plea that resulted in the First Crusade. The pope assured his listeners that God was on their side.

Let the holy sepulcher of our Lord and Saviour, which is possessed by the unclean nations, especially arouse you. . . . This royal city [Jerusalem], situated at the center of the earth, is now held captive by the enemies of Christ and is subjected, by those who do not know God, to the worship of the heathen. Accordingly, undertake this journey eagerly for the remission of your sins, with the assurance of the reward of imperishable glory in the kingdom of heaven.

D PRIMARY SOURCE
Luttrell Psalter

The illustration below from a Latin text shows Richard the Lion-Hearted (left) unhorsing Saladin during the Third Crusade. However, the two men never actually met in personal combat.

B PRIMARY SOURCE
William of Tyre

A Christian bishop, William of Tyre, drew upon eyewitness accounts of the capture of Jerusalem by Crusaders.

It was impossible to look upon the vast numbers of the slain without horror; everywhere lay fragments of human bodies, and the very ground was covered with the blood of the slain. It was not alone the spectacle of headless bodies and mutilated limbs strewn in all directions that roused horror in all who looked upon them. Still more dreadful was it to gaze upon the victors themselves, dripping with blood from head to foot, an ominous sight which brought terror to all who met them. It is reported that within the Temple enclosure alone about ten thousand infidels perished, in addition to those who lay slain everywhere throughout the city in the streets and squares, the number of whom was estimated as no less.

C PRIMARY SOURCE
Saladin

This is an excerpt of Saladin's reply to a letter from Frederick I (Barbarossa) threatening Saladin. Saladin wrote the letter after he recaptured Jerusalem.

Whenever your armies are assembled . . . we will meet you in the power of God. We will not be satisfied with the land on the seacoast, but we will cross over with God's good pleasure and take from you all your lands in the strength of the Lord. . . . And when the Lord, by His power, shall have given us victory over you, nothing will remain for us to do but freely to take your lands by His power and with His good pleasure. . . . By the virtue and power of God we have taken possession of Jerusalem and its territories; and of the three cities that still remain in the hands of the Christians . . . we shall occupy them also.

Document-Based QUESTIONS

1. Using specific phrases or passages from Source A and Source C, demonstrate how their attitudes were similar.

2. What directive in Source A might have been at the root of the action described in Source B?

3. What evidence in Source D reveals the artist's bias about the confrontation between Islam and Christianity?

386

Changes in Medieval Society

MAIN IDEA	WHY IT MATTERS NOW	TERMS & NAMES
ECONOMICS The feudal system declined as agriculture, trade, finance, towns, and universities developed.	The changes in the Middle Ages laid the foundations for modern Europe.	• three-field system • guild • Commercial Revolution	• burgher • vernacular • Thomas Aquinas • scholastics

SETTING THE STAGE While Church reform, cathedral building, and the Crusades were taking place, other important changes were occurring in medieval society. Between 1000 and 1300, agriculture, trade, and finance made significant advances. Towns and cities grew. This was in part due to the growing population and to territorial expansion of western Europe. Cultural interaction with the Muslim and Byzantine worlds sparked the growth of learning and the birth of an institution new to Europe—the university.

A Growing Food Supply

Europe's great revival would have been impossible without better ways of farming. Expanding civilization required an increased food supply. A warmer climate, which lasted from about 800 to 1200, brought improved farm production. Farmers began to cultivate lands in regions once too cold to grow crops. They also developed new methods to take advantage of more available land.

Switch to Horsepower For hundreds of years, peasants had depended on oxen to pull their plows. Oxen lived on the poorest straw and stubble, so they were easy to keep. Horses needed better food, but a team of horses could plow three times as much land in a day as a team of oxen.

Before farmers could use horses, however, a better harness was needed. Sometime before 900, farmers in Europe began using a harness that fitted across the horse's chest, enabling it to pull a plow. As a result, horses gradually replaced oxen for plowing and for pulling wagons. All over Europe, axes rang as the great forests were cleared for new fields.

The Three-Field System Around A.D. 800, some villages began to organize their lands into three fields instead of two. Two of the fields were planted and the other lay fallow (resting) for a year. Under this new **three-field system**, farmers could grow crops on two-thirds of their land each year, not just on half of it. As a result, food production increased. Villagers had more to eat. Well-fed people, especially children, could better resist disease and live longer, and as a result the European population grew dramatically.

hmhsocialstudies.com
TAKING NOTES

Use the graphic organizer online to take notes on changes in medieval society.

Surnames

Many people can trace their last names, or surnames, back to a medieval occupation in Europe. The name Smith, for example, refers to someone who "smites," or works, metal. The surname Silversmith would belong to a person who works silver. In German-speaking areas, a smith was named Schmidt.

Someone who made goods out of wood was often surnamed Carpenter. In French-speaking areas, a carpenter was called Charpentier, while in German areas, the same person would be called Zimmerman.

The last name of Boulanger indicated a baker in France. A baker in Germany often had the surname Becker.

The Guilds

A second change in the European economy was the development of the guild. A **guild** was an organization of individuals in the same business or occupation working to improve the economic and social conditions of its members. The first guilds were merchant guilds. Merchants banded together to control the number of goods being traded and to keep prices up. They also provided security in trading and reduced losses.

About the same time, skilled artisans, such as wheelwrights, glassmakers, winemakers, tailors, and druggists, began craft guilds. In most crafts, both husband and wife worked at the family trade. In a few crafts, especially for cloth making, women formed the majority. The guilds set standards for quality of work, wages, and working conditions. For example, bakers were required to sell loaves of bread of a standard size and weight. The guilds also created plans for supervised training of new workers.

By the 1000s, artisans and craftspeople were manufacturing goods by hand for local and long-distance trade. More and better products were now available to buyers in small towns, in bigger cities, and at trade fairs. Guilds became powerful forces in the medieval economy. The wealth they accumulated helped them establish influence over the government and the economy of towns and cities. Ⓐ

MAIN IDEA

Summarizing

Ⓐ How did guilds change the way business was conducted and products made?

History *in* Depth

Craft Guilds

Craft guilds formed an important part of town life during the medieval period. They trained young people in a skilled job, regulated the quality of goods sold, and were major forces in community life.

Guild Services	
To members:	**To the community:**
• Set working conditions	• Built almshouses for victims of misfortune
• Covered members with a type of health insurance	• Guaranteed quality work
• Provided funeral expenses	• Took turns policing the streets
• Provided dowries for poor girls	• Donated windows to the Church

Apprentice

• Parents paid for training

• Lived with a master and his family

• Required to obey the master

• Trained 2–7 years

• Was not allowed to marry during training

• When trained progressed to journeyman

Journeyman
(Day Worker)

• Worked for a master to earn a salary

• Worked 6 days a week

• Needed to produce a masterpiece (his finest work) to become a master

• Had to be accepted by the guild to become a master

Master

• Owned his own shop

• Worked with other masters to protect their trade

• Sometimes served in civic government

hmhsocialstudies.com

INTERACTIVE
HISTORY

Explore the
colorful world
of a medieval
trade fair.

Commercial Revolution

Just as agriculture was expanding and craftsmanship changing, so were trade and finance. Increased availability of trade goods and new ways of doing business changed life in Europe. Taken together, this expansion of trade and business is called the **Commercial Revolution**.

Fairs and Trade Most trade took place in towns. Peasants from nearby manors traveled to town on fair days, hauling items to trade. Great fairs were held several times a year, usually during religious festivals, when many people would be in town. People visited the stalls set up by merchants from all parts of Europe.

Cloth was the most common trade item. Other items included bacon, salt, honey, cheese, wine, leather, dyes, knives, and ropes. Such local markets met all the needs of daily life for a small community. No longer was everything produced on a self-sufficient manor.

More goods from foreign lands became available. Trade routes spread across Europe from Flanders to Italy. Italian merchant ships traveled the Mediterranean to ports in Byzantium such as Constantinople. They also traveled to Muslim ports along the North African coast. Trade routes were opened to Asia, in part by the Crusades.

Increased business at markets and fairs made merchants willing to take chances on buying merchandise that they could sell at a profit. Merchants then reinvested the profits in more goods.

Vocabulary

Letters of credit: A letter issued by a bank allowing the bearer to withdraw a specific amount of money from the bank or its branches.

Business and Banking As traders moved from fair to fair, they needed large amounts of cash or credit and ways to exchange many types of currencies. Enterprising merchants found ways to solve these problems. For example, bills of exchange established exchange rates between different coinage systems. Letters of credit between merchants eliminated the need to carry large amounts of cash and made trading easier. Trading firms and associations formed to offer these services to their groups.

▼ This fish market expanded the variety of food available in a medieval town.

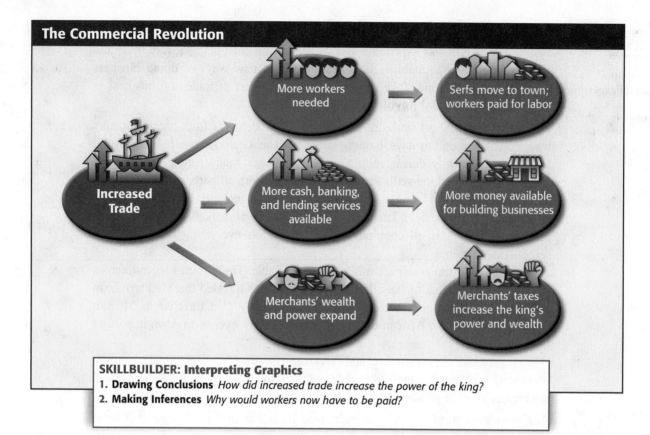

SKILLBUILDER: Interpreting Graphics
1. **Drawing Conclusions** *How did increased trade increase the power of the king?*
2. **Making Inferences** *Why would workers now have to be paid?*

Merchants looked for new markets and opportunities to make a profit. Merchants first had to purchase goods from distant places. To do so they had to borrow money, but the Church forbade Christians from lending money at interest, a sin called usury. Over time, the Church relaxed its rule on usury and Christians entered the banking business. Banking became an important business, especially in Italy. **B**

Society Changes The changes brought about by the Commercial Revolution were slow, yet they had a major effect on the lives of Europeans. As you can see in the diagram shown above, increased trade brought many changes to aspects of society. Two of the most important changes involved what people did to earn a living and where they lived. As towns attracted workers, the towns grew into cities. Life in the cities was different from life in the sleepy villages or on manors.

MAIN IDEA

Drawing Conclusions

B Why were changes in financial services necessary to expand trade?

Urban Life Flourishes

Scholars estimate that between 1000 and 1150, the population of western Europe rose from around 30 million to about 42 million. Towns grew and flourished. Compared to great cities like Constantinople, European towns were unsophisticated and tiny. Europe's largest city, Paris, probably had no more than 60,000 people by the year 1200. A typical town in medieval Europe had only about 1,500 to 2,500 people. Even so, these small communities became a powerful force for change in Europe.

Trade and Towns Grow Together By the later Middle Ages, trade was the very lifeblood of the new towns, which sprung up at ports and crossroads, on hilltops, and along rivers. As trade grew, towns all over Europe swelled with people. The excitement and bustle of towns drew many people. But there were some drawbacks to living in a medieval town. Streets were narrow, filled with animals and their waste. With no sewers, most people dumped household and human waste into the street in front of the house. Most people never bathed, and their houses lacked fresh air, light, and clean water. Because houses were built of wood with thatched roofs, they were a constant fire hazard. Nonetheless, many people chose to move to towns to pursue the economic and social opportunities they offered.

People were no longer content with their old feudal existence on manors or in tiny villages. Even though legally bound to their lord's manor, many serfs ran away. According to custom, a serf could now become free by living within a town for a year and a day. A saying of the time went, "Town air makes you free." Many of these runaway serfs, now free people, made better lives for themselves in towns.

Merchant Class Shifts the Social Order The merchants and craftspeople of medieval towns did not fit into the traditional medieval social order of noble, clergy, and peasant. At first, towns came under the authority of feudal lords, who used their authority to levy fees, taxes, and rents. As trade expanded, the **burghers**, or merchant-class town dwellers, resented this interference in their trade and commerce. They organized themselves and demanded privileges. These included freedom from certain kinds of tolls and the right to govern the town. At times they fought against their landlords and won these rights by force.

The Revival of Learning

MAIN IDEA

Recognizing Effects

C How did the Crusades contribute to the expansion of trade and learning?

During the Crusades, European contact with Muslims and Byzantines greatly expanded. This contact brought a new interest in learning, especially in the works of Greek philosophers. The Muslim and Byzantine libraries housed copies of these writings. Most had disappeared during the centuries following the fall of Rome and the invasions of western Europe. **C**

The Muslim Connection In the 1100s, Christian scholars from Europe began visiting Muslim libraries in Spain. Few Western scholars knew Greek but most did know Latin. So Jewish scholars living in Spain translated the Arabic versions of works by Aristotle and other Greek writers into Latin. All at once, Europeans acquired a huge new body of knowledge. This included science, philosophy, law, mathematics, and other fields. In addition, the Crusaders brought back to Europe superior Muslim technology in ships, navigation, and weapons.

Scholars and the University At the center of the growth of learning stood a new European institution—the university. The word *university* originally referred to a group of scholars meeting wherever they could. People, not buildings, made up the medieval university. Universities arose at Paris and at Bologna, Italy, by the end of the 1100s. Others followed at the English town of Oxford and at Salerno, Italy. Most students were the sons of burghers or well-to-do artisans. For most students, the goal was a job in government or the Church. Earning a bachelor's degree in theology might take five to seven years in school; becoming a master of theology took at least 12 years of study.

New ideas and forms of expression began to flow out of the universities. At a time when serious scholars and writers were writing in Latin, a few remarkable poets began using a lively **vernacular**, or the everyday language of their homeland. Some of these writers wrote masterpieces that are still

History *in* **Depth**

Muslim Scholars

A number of Islamic scholars had a great influence on European thought. The image above shows Ibn Sina, known in the West as Avicenna. He was a Persian philosopher, astronomer, poet, and physician. His book, *The Cure*, an interpretation of Aristotle's philosophy, greatly affected Western thought. This work, translated into Latin, influenced the scholastics.

↗ **hmhsocialstudies.com**

INTERNET ACTIVITY Go online to create a documentary film script on Muslim scholars.

▲ Thomas Aquinas's writings focused on questions of faith versus reason and logic.

read today. Dante Alighieri wrote *The Divine Comedy* (1308–1314) in Italian. Geoffrey Chaucer wrote *The Canterbury Tales* (about 1386–1400) in English. Christine de Pisan wrote *The Book of The City of Ladies* (1405) in French. Since most people couldn't read or understand Latin, these works written in the vernacular brought literature to many people.

Aquinas and Medieval Philosophy Christian scholars were excited by the ideas of Greek philosophers. They wondered if a Christian scholar could use Aristotle's logical approach to truth and still keep faith with the Bible.

In the mid-1200s, the scholar **Thomas Aquinas** (uh•KWY•nuhs) argued that the most basic religious truths could be proved by logical argument. Between 1267 and 1273, Aquinas wrote the *Summa Theologicae*. Aquinas's great work, influenced by Aristotle, combined ancient Greek thought with the Christian thought of his time. Aquinas and his fellow scholars who met at the great universities were known as schoolmen, or **scholastics**. The scholastics used their knowledge of Aristotle to debate many issues of their time. Their teachings on law and government influenced the thinking of western Europeans, particularly the English and French. Accordingly, they began to develop democratic institutions and traditions.

SECTION 2 ASSESSMENT

TERMS & NAMES 1. For each term or name, write a sentence explaining its significance.
• three-field system • guild • Commercial Revolution • burgher • vernacular • Thomas Aquinas • scholastics

USING YOUR NOTES	MAIN IDEAS	CRITICAL THINKING & WRITING
2. How did medieval society change between 1000 and 1500?	3. How did guilds influence business practices in medieval towns?	6. **RECOGNIZING EFFECTS** What was the effect of the development of towns on the feudal system?
Changes in Medieval Society	4. How were Muslim scholars linked to the revival of learning in Europe?	7. **ANALYZING MOTIVES** Why would writers choose to produce works in the vernacular instead of in Latin?
	5. In what ways did burghers expand their freedom from landlords?	8. **RECOGNIZING EFFECTS** How did the Commercial Revolution lay the foundation for the economy of modern Europe?
		9. **WRITING ACTIVITY** ECONOMICS Write a brief **news article** on the value of letters of credit and how they have changed commercial trade activities.

CONNECT TO TODAY WRITING AN INVESTIGATIVE REPORT
Contact a local bank and find out what services are available to its commercial clients. Write a brief **report** on the banking services. Identify which services seem to have had their beginnings in the late medieval period and which ones are modern.

England and France Develop

3

MAIN IDEA	WHY IT MATTERS NOW	TERMS & NAMES
POWER AND AUTHORITY As the kingdoms of England and France began to develop into nations, certain democratic traditions evolved.	Modern concepts of jury trials, common law, and legal rights developed during this period.	• William the Conqueror • Henry II • common law • Magna Carta • parliament • Hugh Capet • Philip II • Estates-General

SETTING THE STAGE By the early 800s, small Anglo-Saxon kingdoms covered the former Roman province of Britain. In Europe, the decline of the Carolingian Empire in the 900s left a patchwork of feudal states controlled by local lords. Gradually, the growth of towns and villages, and the breakup of the feudal system were leading to more centralized government and the development of nations. The earliest nations in Europe to develop a strong unified government were England and France. Both would take similar paths.

England Absorbs Waves of Invaders

For centuries, invaders from various regions in Europe landed on English shores. The Angles and the Saxons stayed, bringing their own ways and creating an Anglo-Saxon culture.

Early Invasions In the 800s, Britain was battered by fierce raids of Danish Vikings. These invaders were so feared that a special prayer was said in churches: "God, deliver us from the fury of the Northmen." Only Alfred the Great, Anglo-Saxon king from 871 to 899, managed to turn back the Viking invaders. Gradually he and his successors united the kingdom under one rule, calling it England, "land of the Angles." The Angles were one of the Germanic tribes that had invaded the island of Britain.

In 1016, the Danish king Canute (kuh•NOOT) conquered England, molding Anglo-Saxons and Vikings into one people. In 1042, King Edward the Confessor, a descendant of Alfred the Great, took the throne. Edward died in January 1066 without an heir. A great struggle for the throne erupted, leading to one last invasion.

The Norman Conquest The invader was William, duke of Normandy, who became known as <u>**William the Conqueror**</u>. Normandy is a region in the north of France that had been conquered by the Vikings. Its name comes from the French term for the Vikings—North men, or Norman. The Normans were descended from the Vikings, but they were French in language and in culture. As King Edward's cousin, William claimed the English crown and invaded England with a Norman army.

William's rival was Harold Godwinson, the Anglo-Saxon who claimed the throne. Harold was equally ambitious. On October 14, 1066, Normans and

hmhsocialstudies.com
TAKING NOTES

Use the graphic organizer online to take notes on major steps toward democratic government.

Eleanor of Aquitaine
1122–1204

Eleanor of Aquitaine was one of the most remarkable women in history. She was wife to two kings and mother to two kings. She married Louis VII of France when the Second Crusade began. In 1147, she accompanied him to the Holy Land. Shortly afterward their marriage was annulled. Eleanor then married Henry Plantagenet, who was to become Henry II of England. Their marriage produced eight children. Two became English kings, Richard the Lion-Hearted and John.

↗ hmhsocialstudies.com

RESEARCH WEB LINKS Go online for more on Eleanor of Aquitaine.

Anglo-Saxons fought the battle that changed the course of English history—the Battle of Hastings. After Harold was killed by an arrow that pierced his eye, the Normans won a decisive victory.

After his victory, William declared all England his personal property. William kept about one-fifth of England for himself. The English lords who supported Harold lost their lands. William then granted their lands to about 200 Norman lords who swore oaths of loyalty to him personally. By doing this, William unified control of the lands and laid the foundation for centralized government in England.

England's Evolving Government

Over the next centuries, English kings tried to achieve two goals. First, they wanted to hold and add to their French lands. Second, they wanted to strengthen their own power over the nobles and the Church.

William the Conqueror's descendants owned land both in Normandy and in England. The English king **Henry II** added to these holdings by marrying Eleanor of Aquitaine from France.

The marriage brought Henry a large territory in France called Aquitaine. He added Aquitaine to the lands in Normandy he had already inherited from William the Conqueror. Because Henry held lands in France, he was a vassal to the French king. But he was also a king in his own right.

Juries and Common Law Henry ruled England from 1154 to 1189. He strengthened the royal courts of justice by sending royal judges to every part of England at least once a year. They collected taxes, settled lawsuits, and punished crimes. Henry also introduced the use of the jury in English courts. A jury in medieval England was a group of loyal people—usually 12 neighbors of the accused—who answered a royal judge's questions about the facts of a case. Jury trials became a popular means of settling disputes. Only the king's courts were allowed to conduct them.

Over the centuries, case by case, the rulings of England's royal judges formed a unified body of law that became known as **common law**. Today the principles of English common law are the basis for law in many English-speaking countries, including the United States. Ⓐ

The Magna Carta Henry was succeeded first by his son Richard the Lion-Hearted, hero of the Third Crusade. When Richard died, his younger brother John took the throne. John ruled from 1199 to 1216. He failed as a military leader, earning the nickname John Softsword. John lost Normandy and all his lands in northern France to the French under Philip Augustus. This loss forced a confrontation with his own nobles.

Some of John's problems stemmed from his own personality. He was cruel to his subjects and tried to squeeze money out of them. He alienated the Church and threatened to take away town charters guaranteeing self-government. John raised taxes to an all-time high to finance his wars. His nobles revolted. On June 15, 1215, they forced John to agree to the most celebrated document in English history, the **Magna Carta** (Great Charter). This document, drawn up by English nobles and

MAIN IDEA

Recognizing Effects

Ⓐ What impact did the English common law have on the United States?

reluctantly approved by King John, guaranteed certain basic political rights. The nobles wanted to safeguard their own feudal rights and limit the king's powers. In later years, however, English people of all classes argued that certain clauses in the Magna Carta applied to every citizen. Guaranteed rights included no taxation without representation, a jury trial, and the protection of the law. The Magna Carta guaranteed what are now considered basic legal rights both in England and in the United States. **B**

MAIN IDEA

Summarizing

B What is the significance of the Magna Carta?

Vocabulary
borough: a self-governing town

The Model Parliament Another important step toward democratic government came during the rule of the next English king, Edward I. Edward needed to raise taxes for a war against the French, the Welsh, and the Scots. In 1295, Edward summoned two burgesses (citizens of wealth and property) from every borough and two knights from every county to serve as a **parliament**, or legislative group. In November 1295, knights, burgesses, bishops, and lords met together at Westminster in London. This is now called the Model Parliament because its new makeup (commoners, or non-nobles, as well as lords) served as a model for later kings.

Over the next century, from 1300 to 1400, the king called the knights and burgesses whenever a new tax was needed. In Parliament, these two groups gradually formed an assembly of their own called the House of Commons. Nobles and bishops met separately as the House of Lords. Under Edward I, Parliament was in part a royal tool that weakened the great lords. As time went by, Parliament became strong. Like the Magna Carta, it provided a check on royal power.

> Analyzing Primary Sources

The Magna Carta
The Magna Carta is considered one of the cornerstones of democratic government. The underlying principle of the document is the idea that all must obey the law, even the king. Its guaranteed rights are an important part of modern liberties and justice.

PRIMARY SOURCE

38. No bailiff [officer of the court] for the future shall, upon his own unsupported complaint, put anyone to his "law," without credible witnesses brought for this purposes.

39. No freeman shall be taken or imprisoned . . . or exiled or in any way destroyed, nor will we [the king] go upon him nor send upon him, except by the lawful judgement of his peers or by the law of the land.

40. To no one will we sell, to no one will we refuse or delay, right or justice.

45. We will appoint as justices, constables, sheriffs, or bailiffs only such as know the law of the realm and mean to observe it well.

DOCUMENT-BASED QUESTIONS
1. **Analyzing Motives** *Why might the English nobles have insisted on the right listed in number 45?*
2. **Making Inferences** *Which of the statements is a forerunner to the right to a speedy public trial guaranteed in the Sixth Amendment of the U.S. Constitution?*

▲ The coronation of Philip II in Reims Cathedral

Capetian Dynasty Rules France

The kings of France, like those of England, looked for ways to increase their power. After the breakup of Charlemagne's empire, French counts and dukes ruled their lands independently under the feudal system. By the year 1000, France was divided into about 47 feudal territories. In 987, the last member of the Carolingian family—Louis the Sluggard—died. **Hugh Capet** (kuh•PAY), an undistinguished duke from the middle of France, succeeded him. The Capet family ruled only a small territory, but at its heart stood Paris. Hugh Capet began the Capetian dynasty of French kings that ruled France from 987 to 1328.

France Becomes a Separate Kingdom Hugh Capet, his son, and his grandson all were weak rulers, but time and geography favored the Capetians. Their territory, though small, sat astride important trade routes in northern France. For 300 years, Capetian kings tightened their grip on this strategic area. The power of the king gradually spread outward from Paris. Eventually, the growth of royal power would unite France.

Philip II Expands His Power One of the most powerful Capetians was **Philip II**, called Philip Augustus, who ruled from 1180 to 1223. As a child, Philip had watched his father lose land to King Henry II of England. When Philip became king at the age of 15, he set out to weaken the power of the English kings in France. Philip was crafty, unprincipled, and willing to do whatever was necessary to achieve his goals.

Philip had little success against Henry II or Henry's son, Richard the Lion-Hearted. However, when King John, Richard's brother, gained the English throne, it was another matter. Philip earned the name Augustus (from the Latin word meaning "majestic"), probably because he greatly increased the territory of France. He seized Normandy from King John in 1204 and within two years had gained other territory. By the end of Philip's reign, he had tripled the lands under his direct control. For the first time, a French king had become more powerful than any of his vassals.

Philip II not only wanted more land, he also wanted a stronger central government. He established royal officials called bailiffs. They were sent from Paris to every district in the kingdom to preside over the king's courts and to collect the king's taxes.

Philip II's Heirs France's central government became even stronger during the reign of Philip's grandson, Louis IX, who ruled from 1226 to 1270. Unlike his grandfather, Louis was pious and saintly. He was known as the ideal king. After his death, he was made a saint by the Catholic Church. Louis created a French appeals court, which could overturn the decisions of local courts. These royal courts of France strengthened the monarchy while weakening feudal ties.

In 1302, Philip IV, who ruled France from 1285 to 1314, was involved in a quarrel with the pope. The pope refused to allow priests to pay taxes to the king. Philip disputed the right of the pope to control Church affairs in his kingdom. As in England, the French king usually called a meeting of his lords and bishops when he needed support for his policies. To win wider support against the pope, Philip IV decided to include commoners in the meeting.

The Development of England and France

England	France
• William the Conqueror invades England in 1066. • Henry II (1154–1189) introduces use of the jury in English courts. • John (1199–1216) agrees to the Magna Carta in 1215. • Edward I (1272–1307) calls the Model Parliament in 1295.	• Hugh Capet increases the territory of France. • Philip II (1180–1223) established bailiffs to preside over courts and collect taxes. • Louis IX (1226–1270) creates a French appeals court. • Philip IV (1285–1314) adds Third Estate to the Estates-General.

SKILLBUILDER: Interpreting Charts
1. **Clarifying** *What aspects of courts were developed during the rule of Henry II and Philip II?*
2. **Developing Historical Perspective** *Which aspect of centralized government developed about the same time in both England and France?*

MAIN IDEA

Summarizing
C What three estates made up the Estates-General?

Estates-General In France, the Church leaders were known as the First Estate, and the great lords as the Second Estate. The commoners, wealthy landholders or merchants, that Philip invited to participate in the council became known as the Third Estate. The whole meeting was called the **Estates-General**. **C**

Like the English Parliament in its early years, the Estates-General helped to increase royal power against the nobility. Unlike Parliament, however, the Estates-General never became an independent force that limited the king's power. However, centuries later, the Third Estate would play a key role in overthrowing the French monarchy during the French Revolution.

Beginnings of Democracy England and France were just beginning to establish a democratic tradition. This tradition rested on setting up a centralized government that would be able to govern widespread lands. The creation of common law and court systems was a first step toward increased central government power. Including commoners in the decision-making process of government was also an important step in the direction of democratic rule. Before England and France could move forward in this direction, however, they had to contend with a century of turmoil that included religious disputes, plague, and war.

SECTION 3 ASSESSMENT

TERMS & NAMES 1. For each term or name, write a sentence explaining its significance.
• William the Conqueror • Henry II • common law • Magna Carta • parliament • Hugh Capet • Philip II • Estates-General

USING YOUR NOTES
2. Which of the steps toward democratic government are similar to U.S. practices? Explain.

MAIN IDEAS
3. What two legal practices date back to Henry II?
4. What are some basic rights guaranteed by the Magna Carta?
5. Why did Philip II call the Estates-General together?

CRITICAL THINKING & WRITING
6. **COMPARING** Compare the way in which England and France began developing as nations.
7. **RECOGNIZING EFFECTS** Which of the changes in English government is reflected in the government of the United States today?
8. **EVALUATING COURSES OF ACTION** What steps were necessary to centralize governments in England and France?
9. **WRITING ACTIVITY** POWER AND AUTHORITY Imagine that you are an adviser to the English or French king. Write him a **letter** to argue for or against including commoners in the Parliament or Estates-General.

CONNECT TO TODAY COMPARING HISTORICAL DOCUMENTS
Find a copy of the Magna Carta and a copy of the Bill of Rights of the United States Constitution. Study both documents and create a **table** showing where the Constitution reflects the ideas of the Magna Carta.

The Hundred Years' War and the Plague

MAIN IDEA	WHY IT MATTERS NOW	TERMS & NAMES
RELIGIOUS AND ETHICAL SYSTEMS In the 1300s, Europe was torn apart by religious strife, the bubonic plague, and the Hundred Years' War.	Events of the 1300s led to a change in attitudes toward religion and the state, a change reflected in modern attitudes.	• Avignon • Great Schism • John Wycliffe • Jan Hus • bubonic plague • Hundred Years' War • Joan of Arc

SETTING THE STAGE The 1300s were filled with disasters, both natural and human-made. The Church seemed to be thriving but soon would face a huge division. A deadly epidemic claimed millions of lives. So many people died in the epidemic that the structure of the economy changed. Claims to thrones in France and England led to wars in those lands. The wars would result in changes in the governments of both France and England. By the end of the century, the medieval way of life was beginning to disappear.

A Church Divided

hmhsocialstudies.com
TAKING NOTES

Use the graphic organizer online to take notes on major events at the end of the Middle Ages.

At the beginning of the 1300s, the Age of Faith still seemed strong. Soon, however, both the pope and the Church were in desperate trouble.

Pope and King Collide In 1300, Pope Boniface VIII attempted to enforce papal authority on kings as previous popes had. When King Philip IV of France asserted his authority over French bishops, Boniface responded with an official document. It stated that kings must always obey popes.

Philip merely sneered at this statement. In fact, one of Philip's ministers is said to have remarked that "my master's sword is made of steel, the pope's is made of [words]." Instead of obeying the pope, Philip had him held prisoner in September 1303. The king planned to bring him to France for trial. The pope was rescued, but the elderly Boniface died a month later. Never again would a pope be able to force monarchs to obey him.

Avignon and the Great Schism In 1305, Philip IV persuaded the College of Cardinals to choose a French archbishop as the new pope. Clement V, the newly selected pope, moved from Rome to the city of **Avignon** (av•vee•NYAWN) in France. Popes would live there for the next 69 years.

The move to Avignon badly weakened the Church. When reformers finally tried to move the papacy back to Rome, however, the result was even worse. In 1378, Pope Gregory XI died while visiting Rome. The College of Cardinals then met in Rome to choose a successor. As they deliberated, they could hear a mob outside screaming, "A Roman, a Roman, we want a Roman for pope, or at least an Italian!" Finally, the cardinals announced to the crowd that an Italian had been chosen: Pope Urban VI. Many cardinals regretted their choice almost immediately. Urban VI's passion for reform and his arrogant personality caused the cardinals to elect a second pope a few months later. They chose Robert of Geneva, who spoke French. He took the name Clement VII.

Now there were two popes. Each declared the other to be a false pope, excommunicating his rival. The French pope lived in Avignon, while the Italian pope lived in Rome. This began the split in the Church known as the **Great Schism** (SIHZ•uhm), or division.

In 1414, the Council of Constance attempted to end the Great Schism by choosing a single pope. By now, there were a total of three popes: the Avignon pope, the Roman pope, and a third pope elected by an earlier council at Pisa. With the help of the Holy Roman Emperor, the council forced all three popes to resign. In 1417, the Council chose a new pope, Martin V, ending the Great Schism but leaving the papacy greatly weakened.

Scholars Challenge Church Authority The papacy was further challenged by an Englishman named **John Wycliffe** (WIHK•lihf). He preached that Jesus Christ, not the pope, was the true head of the Church. He was much offended by the worldliness and wealth many clergy displayed. Wycliffe believed that the clergy should own no land or wealth. Wycliffe also taught that the Bible alone—not the pope—was the final authority for Christian life. He helped spread this idea by inspiring an English translation of the New Testament of the Bible.

Influenced by Wycliffe's writings, **Jan Hus**, a professor in Bohemia (now part of the Czech Republic), taught that the authority of the Bible was higher than that of the pope. Hus was excommunicated in 1412. In 1414, he was seized by Church leaders, tried as a heretic, and then burned at the stake in 1415. **A**

MAIN IDEA

Contrasting

A According to the different beliefs of the time, what was the true source of religious authority?

The Bubonic Plague Strikes

During the 1300s an epidemic struck parts of Asia, North Africa, and Europe. Approximately one-third of the population of Europe died of the deadly disease known as the **bubonic plague**. Unlike catastrophes that pull communities together, this epidemic was so terrifying that it ripped apart the very fabric of society. Giovanni Boccaccio, an Italian writer of the time, described its effect:

> **PRIMARY SOURCE**
> This scourge had implanted so great a terror in the hearts of men and women that brothers abandoned brothers, uncles their nephews, sisters their brothers, and in many cases wives deserted their husbands. But even worse, . . . fathers and mothers refused to nurse and assist their own children.
> **GIOVANNI BOCCACCIO**, *The Decameron*

Origins and Impact of the Plague The plague began in Asia. Traveling trade routes, it infected parts of Asia, the Muslim world, and Europe. In 1347, a fleet of Genoese merchant ships arrived in Sicily carrying bubonic plague, also known as the Black Death. It got the name because of the purplish or blackish spots it produced on the skin. The disease swept through Italy. From there it followed trade routes to Spain, France, Germany, England, and other parts of Europe and North Africa.

▼ This painting, titled *The Triumph of Death*, depicts the effect of the plague.

The Bubonic Plague

The bubonic plague, or Black Death, was a killer disease that swept repeatedly through many areas of the world. It wiped out two-thirds of the population in some areas of China, destroyed populations of Muslim towns in Southwest Asia, and then decimated one-third of the European population.

Route of the Plague

① The horse-riding Mongols likely carried infected fleas and rats in their food supplies as they swooped into China.

② The disease came with merchants along the trade routes of Asia to southern Asia, southwest Asia, and Africa.

③ In 1345–1346, a Mongol army besieged Kaffa. A year later, Italian merchants returned to Italy, unknowingly bringing the plague with them.

Disease Spreads

Black rats carried fleas that were infested with a bacillus called *Yersinia pestis*. Because people did not bathe, almost all had fleas and lice. In addition, medieval people threw their garbage and sewage into the streets. These unsanitary streets became breeding grounds for more rats. The fleas carried by rats leapt from person to person, thus spreading the bubonic plague with incredible speed.

Symptoms of the Bubonic Plague

- Painful swellings called buboes (BOO•bohz) in the lymph nodes, particularly those in the armpits and groin
- Sometimes purplish or blackish spots on the skin
- Extremely high fever, chills, delirium, and in most cases, death

Death Tolls, 1300s

Western Europe	💀💀💀💀💀💀	20–25 million
China, India, other Asians	💀💀💀💀💀💀	25 million
	💀 = 4 million	

Connect *to* Today

1. **Hypothesizing** Had people known the cause of the bubonic plague, what might they have done to slow its spread?

   See Skillbuilder Handbook, page R15.

2. **Comparing** What diseases of today might be compared to the bubonic plague? Why?

The bubonic plague took about four years to reach almost every corner of Europe. Some communities escaped unharmed, but in others, approximately two-thirds to three-quarters of those who caught the disease died. Before the bubonic plague ran its course, it killed almost 25 million Europeans and many more millions in Asia and North Africa.

The plague returned every few years, though it never struck as severely as in the first outbreak. However, the periodic attacks further reduced the population.

Effects of the Plague The economic and social effects of the plague were enormous. The old manorial system began to crumble. Some of the changes that occurred included these:

- Town populations fell.
- Trade declined. Prices rose.
- The serfs left the manor in search of better wages.
- Nobles fiercely resisted peasant demands for higher wages, causing peasant revolts in England, France, Italy, and Belgium.
- Jews were falsely blamed for bringing on the plague. All over Europe, Jews were driven from their homes or, worse, massacred.
- The Church suffered a loss of prestige when its prayers failed to stop the onslaught of the bubonic plague and priests abandoned their duties. **B**

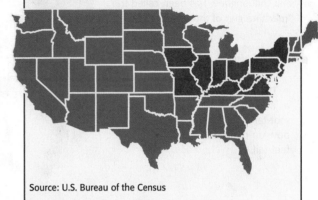

If the Plague Struck America Today

The bubonic plague reportedly wiped out about one-third of Europe's population in the 1300s. In the United States today, a one-third death toll would equal over 96 million people, or the number living in the states represented by the color ■.

Source: U.S. Bureau of the Census

SKILLBUILDER: Interpreting Charts
1. **Clarifying** How many states on the chart would have lost their entire population to the plague?
2. **Drawing Conclusions** How might the chart help explain why many Europeans thought the world was ending?

MAIN IDEA

Recognizing Effects

B Which of the effects of the plague do you think most changed life in the medieval period?

The bubonic plague and its aftermath disrupted medieval society, hastening changes that were already in the making. The society of the Middle Ages was collapsing. The century of war between England and France was that society's final death struggle.

The Hundred Years' War

Not only did the people in Europe during the 1300s have to deal with epidemic disease, but they also had to deal with war. England and France battled with each other on French soil for just over a century. The century of war between England and France marked the end of medieval Europe's society.

When the last Capetian king died without a successor, England's Edward III, as grandson of Philip IV, claimed the right to the French throne. The war that Edward III launched for that throne continued on and off from 1337 to 1453. It became known as the **Hundred Years' War**. Victory passed back and forth between the two countries. Finally, between 1421 and 1453, the French rallied and drove the English out of France entirely, except for the port city of Calais.

The Hundred Years' War brought a change in the style of warfare in Europe. At this time some combatants were still operating under medieval ideals of chivalry. They looked with contempt on the common foot soldiers and archers who fought alongside them. This contempt would change as the longbow changed warfare.

The Longbow

The longbow was cheap, easy to carry, and deadly. It was powerful enough to penetrate armor, thus reducing the impact of mounted cavalry. Bowmen could fire so fast that the longbow has been called the "machine gun of the Middle Ages."

▶ English archers usually carried a case with extra bowstrings and a sheaf of 24 arrows. The arrows were about 27 inches long and balanced in flight by feathers.

▶ The longbow was as tall as a man, or taller. A six-foot-tall man might have a bow up to six and a half feet tall.

▲ The arrows were absolutely fatal when shot within 100 yards. The average archer could fire 12 to 15 arrows per minute and hit a man at 200 yards away.

The Longbow Changes Warfare The English introduced the longbow and demonstrated its power in three significant battles: Crécy, Poitiers, and Agincourt. The first and most spectacular battle was the Battle of Crécy (KREHS•ee) on August 26, 1346. The English army, including longbowmen, was outnumbered by a French army three times its size. The French army included knights and archers with crossbows. French knights believed themselves invincible and attacked.

English longbowmen let fly thousands of arrows at the oncoming French. The crossbowmen, peppered with English arrows, retreated in panic. The knights trampled their own archers in an effort to cut a path through them. English longbowmen sent volley after volley of deadly arrows. They unhorsed knights who then lay helplessly on the ground in their heavy armor. Then, using long knives, the English foot soldiers attacked, slaughtering the French. At the end of the day, more than a third of the French force lay dead. Among them were some of the most honored in chivalry. The longbow, not chivalry, had won the day. The mounted, heavily armored medieval knight was soon to become extinct.

The English repeated their victory ten years later at the Battle of Poitiers (pwah•TYAY). The third English victory, the Battle of Agincourt (AJ•ihn•KAWRT), took place in 1415. The success of the longbow in these battles spelled doom for chivalric warfare.

Joan of Arc In 1420, the French and English signed a treaty stating that Henry V would inherit the French crown upon the death of the French king Charles VI. Then, in 1429, a teenage French peasant girl named **Joan of Arc** felt moved by God to rescue France from its English conquerors. When Joan was just 13 she began to have visions and hear what she believed were voices of the saints. They urged her to drive the English from France and give the French crown to France's true king, Charles VII, son of Charles VI.

On May 7, 1429, Joan led the French army into battle at a fort city near Orléans. The fort blocked the road to Orléans. It was a hard-fought battle for both sides. The French finally retreated in despair. Suddenly, Joan and a few soldiers charged back toward the fort. The entire French army stormed after her. The siege of Orléans was broken. Joan of Arc guided the French onto the path of victory.

After that victory, Joan persuaded Charles to go with her to Reims. There he was crowned king on July 17, 1429. In 1430, the Burgundians, England's allies, captured Joan in battle. They turned her over to the English. The English, in turn, handed her over to Church authorities to stand trial. Although the French king Charles VII owed his crown to Joan, he did nothing to rescue her. Condemned as a witch and a heretic because of her claim to hear voices, Joan was burned at the stake on May 30, 1431.

The Impact of the Hundred Years' War The long, exhausting war finally ended in 1453. Each side experienced major changes.

- A feeling of nationalism emerged in England and France. Now people thought of the king as a national leader, fighting for the glory of the country, not simply a feudal lord.
- The power and prestige of the French monarch increased.
- The English suffered a period of internal turmoil known as the War of the Roses, in which two noble houses fought for the throne.

Some historians consider the end of the Hundred Years' War in 1453 as the end of the Middle Ages. The twin pillars of the medieval world, religious devotion and the code of chivalry, both crumbled. The Age of Faith died a slow death. This death was caused by the Great Schism, the scandalous display of wealth by the Church, and the discrediting of the Church during the bubonic plague. The Age of Chivalry died on the battlefields of Crécy, Poitiers, and Agincourt.

MAIN IDEA

Drawing Conclusions

C How did the Hundred Years' War change the perception of people toward their king?

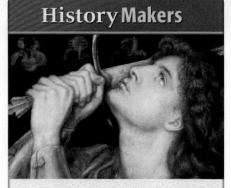

History Makers

Joan of Arc
1412?–1431

In the 1420s, rumors circulated among the French that a young woman would save France from the English. So when Joan arrived on the scene she was considered the fulfillment of that prophecy. Joan cut her hair short and wore a suit of armor and carried a sword.

Her unusual appearance and extraordinary confidence inspired French troops. Eventually she was given command of troops that broke the siege of Orléans. In 1430, she was turned over to a Church court for trial. In truth, her trial was more political than religious. The English were determined to prove her a fake and to weaken her image.

↗ **hmhsocialstudies.com**

RESEARCH WEB LINKS Go online for more on Joan of Arc.

SECTION **4** **ASSESSMENT**

TERMS & NAMES 1. For each term or name, write a sentence explaining its significance.
• Avignon • Great Schism • John Wycliffe • Jan Hus • bubonic plague • Hundred Years' War • Joan of Arc

USING YOUR NOTES	MAIN IDEAS	CRITICAL THINKING & WRITING
2. Which event had some economic effects? Explain.	3. What was the Great Schism?	6. **RECOGNIZING EFFECTS** Which event do you think diminished the power of the Church more—the Great Schism or the bubonic plague?
	4. What were three effects of the bubonic plague?	7. **IDENTIFYING PROBLEMS** What problems did survivors face after the bubonic plague swept through their town?
	5. What impact did Joan of Arc have on the Hundred Years' War?	8. **RECOGNIZING EFFECTS** How did the Hundred Years' War encourage a feeling of nationalism in both France and England?
		9. **WRITING ACTIVITY** RELIGIOUS AND ETHICAL SYSTEMS Write a **persuasive essay** supporting the right of the pope to appoint French bishops.

USING YOUR NOTES note table:

	Cause & Effect
Split in Church	
Plague	
100 Years' War	

CONNECT TO TODAY MAPPING AN EPIDEMIC

Research the number of AIDS victims in countries throughout the world. Then, create an annotated **world map** showing the numbers in each country. Be sure to list your sources.

TERMS & NAMES

Briefly explain the importance of each of the following to western Europe during the medieval period.

1. Crusade
2. Reconquista
3. Commercial Revolution
4. Magna Carta
5. parliament
6. Great Schism
7. bubonic plague
8. Hundred Years' War

MAIN IDEAS

Church Reform and the Crusades Section 1
(pages 379–386)

9. Explain the three main abuses that most distressed Church reformers.
10. What were the effects of the Crusades?

Changes in Medieval Society Section 2 (pages 387–392)

11. How did trade and finance change in the period from 1000 to 1500?
12. How did the growth of towns hurt the feudal system?
13. What role did Muslims play in Europe's revival of learning?

England and France Develop Section 3 (pages 393–397)

14. How did English kings increase their power and reduce the power of the nobles?
15. Why was Philip II called Augustus?

The Hundred Years' War and the Plague Section 4
(pages 398–403)

16. Summarize the main ideas of John Wycliffe.
17. Why did the bubonic plague cause people to turn away from the Church?
18. How did the Hundred Years' War change warfare in Europe?

CRITICAL THINKING

1. **USING YOUR NOTES**

   In a diagram, show how governments became more centralized in France and in England.

Centralized Government

2. **SUMMARIZING**

   CULTURAL INTERACTION What role did Jews and Muslims play in Christian Europe's financial revolution?

3. **ANALYZING CAUSES**

   RELIGIOUS AND ETHICAL SYSTEMS Identify and discuss the events that led to the decline of the power of the Church in the period from 1000 to 1500.

4. **CLARIFYING**

   ECONOMICS In what ways did the guilds change business and employment practices?

5. **HYPOTHESIZING**

   Using the visual summary and your notes, suggest how the history of Western Europe would have been different if one of the events shown on the visual summary had not occurred.

VISUAL SUMMARY

Europe in the Middle Ages

Economics	Politics/Government	Religion	Society
• Better farming methods increased food production. • Trade expanded. • Guilds formed for both merchants and artisans.	• England and France developed strong central governments. • Parliament and the Estates-General bring representation to commoners. • The Hundred Years' War further weakened feudal power.	• Kings and popes engaged in power struggles. • The Great Schism weakened the Church. • The First Crusade captured Jerusalem. • Later Crusades accomplished little.	• Population increased in the Middle Ages. • The bubonic plague killed millions and weakened the manorial economy. • Europe's first universities developed.•

Use the quotation and your knowledge of world history to answer questions 1 and 2.

PRIMARY SOURCE

The king to the sheriff of Northampton, greeting. Whereas we wish to have a conference and discussion with the earls, barons, and other nobles of our realm concerning the provision of remedies for the dangers that in these days threaten the same kingdom . . . we command and firmly enjoin you that without delay you cause two knights, of the more discreet and more capable of labor, to be elected from the aforesaid county, and two citizens from each city of the aforesaid county, and two burgesses from each borough, and that you have them come to us . . . to do whatever in the aforesaid matters may be ordained by common counsel.

KING EDWARD I in a letter to sheriffs in England

1. Why is the king calling a meeting of Parliament?

   A. He wants to raise taxes.

   B. He wants to select new knights.

   C. He wants to discuss threats to the kingdom.

   D. He wants to give advice to the leaders.

2. How will the representatives be chosen?

   A. They will be selected by the sheriff.

   B. They will be elected by the people.

   C. They will be selected by the lords.

   D. They will be elected by the knights.

Use the chart and your knowledge of world history to answer question 3.

Population in Europe, 1000–1340		
Area	Population Estimates in Millions, 1000	Population Estimates in Millions, 1340
Mediterranean	17	25
Western and Central Europe	12	35.5
Eastern Europe	9.5	13
Total	38.5	73.5

Source: J.C. Russell, *The Control of Late Ancient and Medieval Population*

3. What reason can be suggested for the dramatic increase in Western and Central Europe's population?

   A. Invading peoples settled in the area.

   B. Technical developments allowed people to live longer.

   C. Agricultural production increased.

   D. Trade expanded in Europe.

 hmhsocialstudies.com **TEST PRACTICE**

For additional test practice, go online for:

- Diagnostic tests
- Tutorials
- Strategies

Interact *with* History

On page 378, you thought about whether or not you would join a Crusade before completely understanding what the Crusades were and what sort of rewards and dangers they entailed. Now that you've read the chapter, reexamine whether or not you would join a Crusade. What might a Crusader bring home from his travels? What problems might a Crusader encounter on his adventures? Discuss your opinions with a small group.

FOCUS ON WRITING

Study the information on Joan of Arc in the chapter. Write a brief **biography** about her. Be sure to include information on her influence on Charles and on the nation of France. Consider the following:

- What are the major events in her life?
- Why did Charles value her advice?
- How is she viewed in France today?

MULTIMEDIA ACTIVITY

Writing an Internet-Based Research Paper

Go to the *Web Research Guide* at **hmhsocialstudies.com** to learn about conducting research on the Internet. Then, working with a partner, use the Internet to find examples of the impact of the bubonic plague and the Hundred Years' War on the economy of medieval Europe. Consider changes in population, working conditions, and the volume of trade. Present the results of your research in a well-organized paper. Be sure to

- apply a search strategy when using directories and search engines to locate Web resources
- judge the usefulness and reliability of each Web site
- correctly cite your Web sources
- peer-edit for organization and correct use of language

THE CRUSADES

CRESCENT & THE CROSS

Fought over nearly two centuries, the Crusades were a violent struggle between soldiers of two religions. In a series of nine wars, European Christians battled Turkish and Arabic Muslims for control of the city of Jerusalem and the surrounding areas, considered sacred by both religions. Thousands died in the fighting—both soldiers and civilians—and whole cities were destroyed. The brutality of the Crusades created strong feelings of resentment between Christians and Muslims. This resentment lingered for centuries after the wars themselves had ended.

Explore the causes, events, and results of the Crusades online. You can find a wealth of information, video clips, primary sources, activities, and more at ⟲ hmhsocialstudies.com .

📹 Siege of Jerusalem

Watch the video to learn how the Christian army captured Jerusalem from the Turks in 1099.

🌐 The First Four Crusades

Explore the map to see the different routes followed by Crusaders from Europe to the Holy Land.

📹 Defeat of the Crusaders

Watch the video to understand how Muslim leaders rallied after the Second Crusade to drive Christians out of the Holy Land.

Societies and Empires of Africa, 800–1500

Essential Question

How did early African societies develop from hunting-gathering groups into empires?

 What You Will Learn

In this chapter you will learn about the many, diverse societies that developed in all parts of the continent of Africa.

SECTION 1 North and Central African Societies

Main Idea North and central Africa developed hunting-gathering societies, stateless societies, and Muslim states.

SECTION 2 West African Civilizations

Main Idea West Africa contained several rich and powerful states, including Ghana, Mali, and Songhai.

SECTION 3 Eastern City-States and Southern Empires

Main Idea African city-states and empires gained wealth through developing and trading resources.

Previewing Themes

RELIGIOUS AND ETHICAL SYSTEMS Beginning about 640, Islam created two North African empires. Merchants and traders spread Islam into both West and East Africa, where it influenced rulers.

Geography *What empires developed in West Africa during this period?*

INTERACTION WITH ENVIRONMENT In parts of Africa, hunter-gatherers used up an area's food supply and then moved on. In some Saharan villages, workers built houses of salt. The location of gold determined trade routes.

Geography *What factors might have caused three empires to arise in the same area?*

ECONOMICS Trade networks developed in Africa because different regions had items that other regions wanted. African city-states and empires that were able to control and tax such trade became wealthy and powerful.

Geography *How were the locations of Timbuktu and Kilwa different and how might that have influenced trade?*

AFRICA

800
Empire of Ghana thrives on trade.

1000
◄ Hausa city-states begin to emerge. (bronze head)

1100
Yoruba kingdom of Ife is established.

800

1000

WORLD

850s
Byzantine culture spreads to Russia.

 1095
◄ First Crusade begins. (battle between Muslims and Crusaders)

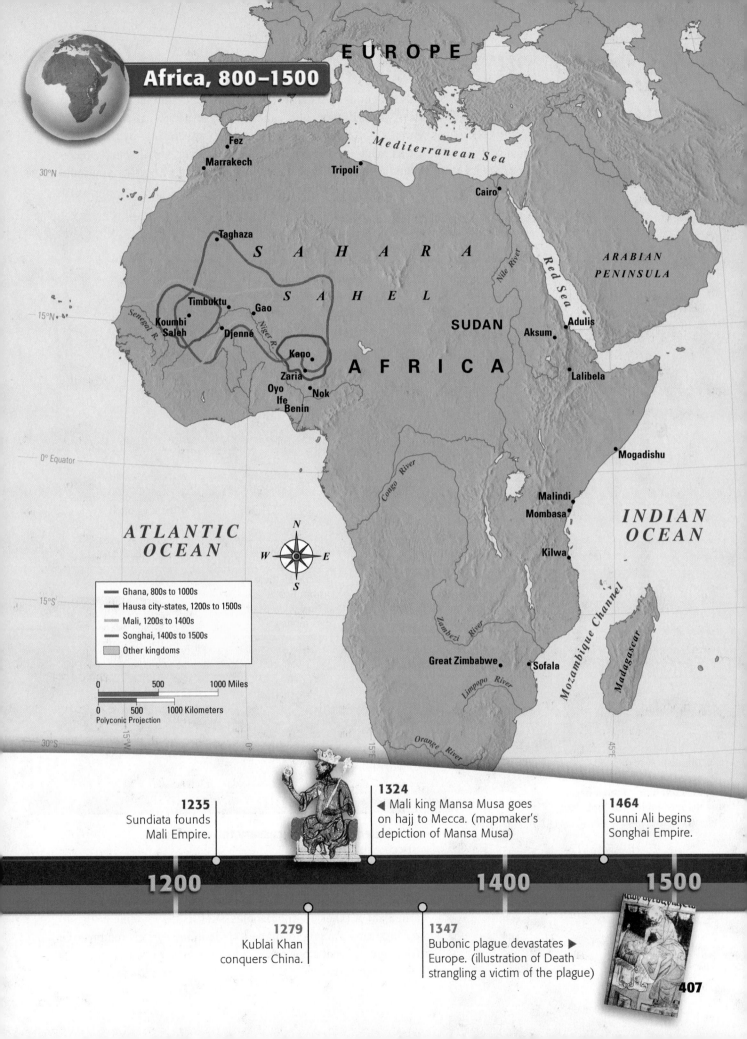

Africa, 800–1500

EUROPE

Mediterranean Sea

Fez

Marrakech

Tripoli

Cairo

30°N

SAHARA

SAHEL

Taghaza

Nile River

Red Sea

ARABIAN PENINSULA

Senegal R.

Timbuktu

Koumbi Saleh

Gao

Djenné

Niger R.

15°N

SUDAN

Adulis

Aksum

Kano

Zaria

Oyo

Ife

Nok

Benin

AFRICA

Lalibela

0° Equator

Congo River

Mogadishu

Malindi

Mombasa

INDIAN OCEAN

ATLANTIC OCEAN

N
W   E
S

Kilwa

15°S

Zambezi River

Mozambique Channel

Madagascar

Ghana, 800s to 1000s
Hausa city-states, 1200s to 1500s
Mali, 1200s to 1400s
Songhai, 1400s to 1500s
Other kingdoms

0   500   1000 Miles
0   500   1000 Kilometers
Polyconic Projection

Great Zimbabwe

Sofala

Limpopo River

30°S

Orange River

15°W   0°   15°E   45°E

1235
Sundiata founds Mali Empire.

1324
◄ Mali king Mansa Musa goes on hajj to Mecca. (mapmaker's depiction of Mansa Musa)

1464
Sunni Ali begins Songhai Empire.

1200   **1400**   **1500**

1279
Kublai Khan conquers China.

1347
Bubonic plague devastates ► Europe. (illustration of Death strangling a victim of the plague)

407

How might trade benefit both sides?

You are crossing the Sahara with goods to trade. Your destination is Timbuktu, the great trading center of Africa. There you will meet with other traders, especially those from the gold-mining regions to the south. You hope to make the journey worthwhile by trading salt and manufactured goods for as much gold as possible. The gold traders will want to receive as much of your salt and manufactured goods as they can in exchange. Together you must come to an agreement on what your trade items are worth.

To survive the trip across the Sahara, traders stopped at oases for water. However, it was 500 miles to Timbuktu from the nearest oasis! The journey was very hard.

The camel was the only animal that could go without water long enough to cross the Sahara.

Workers in the Sahara endured hardship to mine this salt. In a hot climate, salt helps the human body to retain water. Salt was scarce in the gold-mining region.

These beautiful cowrie shells came all the way from East Africa. They were used as money.

The king often demanded these gold nuggets as taxes.

This cloth was shipped across the Mediterranean Sea to North Africa. Then it began the long journey to Timbuktu.

EXAMINING *the* ISSUES

- **What elements are necessary for a mutually successful trade?**

- **How do scarcity and abundance affect trade?**

As you discuss these questions in class, think about what you have learned about other trading peoples, such as the Phoenicians and the Europeans. As you read about trade in the various regions of Africa, notice what steps rulers took to control trade moving through their territory.

North and Central African Societies

MAIN IDEA	WHY IT MATTERS NOW	TERMS & NAMES
RELIGIOUS AND ETHICAL SYSTEMS North and central Africa developed hunting-gathering societies, stateless societies, and Muslim states.	Modern African nations often must find ways to include these various peoples and traditions in one society.	• lineage • stateless societies • patrilineal • matrilineal • Maghrib • Almoravids • Almohads

SETTING THE STAGE Throughout history, different groups of Africans have found different ways to organize themselves to meet their political, economic, and social needs. In the varied regions of Africa, climate and topography, or landforms, influenced how each community developed.

Hunting-Gathering Societies

Hunting-gathering societies—the oldest form of social organization in the world—began in Africa. Hunting-gathering societies still exist in Africa today, though they form an extremely small percentage of the population. Scattered throughout Africa, these groups speak their own languages and often use their own hunting techniques. By studying these groups, scholars learn clues about how hunter-gatherers may have lived in the past.

hmhsocialstudies.com
TAKING NOTES

Use the graphic organizer online to take notes on characteristics of stateless societies.

Forest Dwellers The Efe (AY•fay) are just one of several hunting-gathering societies in Africa. They make their home in the Ituri Forest in the Democratic Republic of Congo (formerly Zaire). Like their ancestors, the modern-day Efe live in small groups of between 10 and 100 members, all of whom are related. Each family occupies its own grass-and-brush shelter within a camp, but their homes are rarely permanent. Their search for food causes them to be somewhat nomadic. As a result, the Efe collect few possessions and move to new camps as they use up the resources in the surrounding area.

In the Efe society, women are the gatherers. They walk through the forest searching for roots, yams, mushrooms, and wild seeds. Efe men and older boys do all the hunting. Sometimes they gather in groups to hunt small antelope called duikers. At other times, hunters go solo and use poison-tipped arrows to kill mammals such as monkeys. The Efe add to their diet by trading honey, wild game, and other forest products for crops grown by farmers in nearby villages.

Social Structure A respected older male, such as a father, uncle, or father-in-law, typically serves as group leader. Although members of the group listen to and value this man's opinion, he does not give orders or act as chief. Each family within the band makes its own decisions and is free to come and go. Group members settle arguments through long discussions. If conflicts cannot be settled by talking, a group member may decide to move to a different hunting band. Daily life for the Efe is not governed by formal written laws.

Stateless Societies

As in other parts of the world, family organization is central to African society. In many African societies, families are organized in groups called lineages. The members of a **lineage** (LIHN•ee•ihj) believe they are descendants of a common ancestor. Besides its living members, a lineage includes past generations (spirits of ancestors) and future generations (children not yet born). Within a lineage, members feel strong loyalties to one another.

South of the Sahara, many African groups developed systems of governing based on lineages. In some African societies, lineage groups took the place of rulers. These societies, known as **stateless societies**, did not have a centralized system of power. Instead, authority in a stateless society was balanced among lineages of equal power so that no one family had too much control. The Igbo (IHG•boh) people—also called Ibo—of southern Nigeria lived in a stateless society as early as the ninth century. (Although the Igbo lived in West Africa, their political structure was similar to stateless societies found in central Africa.) If a dispute arose within an Igbo village, respected elders from different lineages settled the problem. Igbos later encountered challenges from 19th-century European colonizers who expected one single leader to rule over society.

Social History

Negotiating Conflict in Stateless Societies

In a stateless society, the power to negotiate conflicts shifts from generation to generation as circumstances demand.

Look at the diagram of two lineages above. If **d** is in conflict with **f**, then **c** will side with his brother **d**, and **e** will side with his brother **f**. Therefore, the parents—**1** and **2**—will meet to negotiate.

If **f** is in conflict with **g**, both entire lineages will take sides in the dispute. Therefore, the members of the oldest surviving generation—**A** and **B**—must meet to negotiate.

hmhsocialstudies.com

INTERNET ACTIVITY Go online to prepare a poster on methods of conflict resolution.

Tracing Family Descent In African societies, the way a society traces lineage determines how possessions and property are passed on and what groups individuals belong to. Members of a **patrilineal** society trace their ancestors through their fathers. Inheritance passes from father to son. When a son marries, he, his wife, and their children remain part of his father's extended family.

In a **matrilineal** society, children trace their ancestors through their mothers. Young men from a matrilineal culture inherit land and wealth from their mother's family. However, even in a matrilineal society, men usually hold the positions of authority.

Age-Set System In many African societies, young people form close ties to individuals outside their lineage through the age-set system. An age set consists of young people within a region who are born during a certain time period. Each age set passes together through clearly identified life stages, such as warrior or elder. Ceremonies mark the passage to each new stage.

Men and women have different life stages, and each stage has its own duties and importance. Societies like the Igbo use the age-set system to teach discipline, community service, and leadership skills to their young. **Ⓐ**

Muslim States

While stateless societies developed south of the Sahara, Islam played a vital role in North Africa. After Muhammad's death in 632, Muslims swept across the northwest part of the continent. They converted many by the sword of conquest and others peacefully. By 670, Muslims ruled Egypt and had entered the **Maghrib**, the part of North Africa that is today the Mediterranean coast of Libya, Tunisia, Algeria, and Morocco.

MAIN IDEA

Making Inferences
Ⓐ What advantages might an age-set system have for a society?

Selected African Societies, 800–1500

hmhsocialstudies.com
INTERACTIVE MAP

Muslim rule

Fez • Maghrib
Marrakech • ALMOHAD EMPIRE

ALMORAVID EMPIRE

Mediterranean Sea

Nile R.

ASIA

SAHARA

Tropic of Cancer

AFRICA

Niger R.

Tiv

Igbo

Efe   Mbuti

Nuer

Pygmies   L. Victoria

Congo R.

Luba

0°

ATLANTIC OCEAN

INDIAN OCEAN

San

Tropic of Capricorn

40°E

Legend
- 0–500 meters
- 500–2,000 meters
- Over 2,000 meters
- – – – Almohad Empire
- • • • Almoravid Empire
- —— Hunter-gatherers
- —— Stateless society

N

0   1,500 Miles
0   3,000 Kilometers

Societies

Hunter-Gatherers

The seminomadic hunter-gatherers lived by gathering wild foods and hunting animals.

- The Efe were hunter-gatherers who traded with farming villages.
- The San (also called the Bushmen) lived in southern Africa and part of East Africa.

Stateless Societies

Stateless societies did not have centralized power. Instead, power was balanced among lineage groups, usually within villages.

- The Tiv had no formal government.
- The Igbo resolved disputes by having elders from different lineages meet.
- The Nuer organized over 250,000 people without an official ruler.

Muslim States

In North Africa, two groups of Muslim reformers founded empires.

- In the 11th century, the Almoravid Empire controlled Mauritania, Morocco, Algeria, and part of Spain.
- Beginning in the mid-1100s, the Almohad Empire controlled Morocco, much of the Maghrib, and part of Spain.

GEOGRAPHY SKILLBUILDER: Interpreting Maps
1. **Location** *Where were the Muslim states located?*
2. **Region** *Why would hunter-gatherers be spread across such a large region?*

As Islam spread, some African rulers converted to Islam. These African Muslim rulers then based their government upon Islamic law. Muslims believe that God's law is a higher authority than any human law. Therefore, Muslim rulers often relied on religious scholars as government advisers. (See World Religions, pages 290–291.)

Islamic Law In Islam, following the law is a religious obligation. Muslims do not separate their personal life from their religious life, and Islamic law regulates almost all areas of human life. Islamic law helped to bring order to Muslim states.

However, various Muslim states had ethnic and cultural differences. Further, these states sometimes had differing interpretations, and schools, of Islamic law. Nonetheless, Islamic law has been such a significant force in history that some states, especially in North Africa, are still influenced by it today.

Among those who converted to Islam were the Berbers. Fiercely independent desert and mountain dwellers, the Berbers were the original inhabitants of North Africa. While they accepted Islam as their faith, many maintained their Berber identities and loyalties. Two Berber groups, the Almoravids and the Almohads, founded empires that united the Maghrib under Muslim rule.

Almoravid Reformers In the 11th century, Muslim reformers founded the Almoravid (al•muh•RAHV•uhd) Empire. Its members came from a Berber group living in the western Sahara in what is today Mauritania. The movement began after devout Berber Muslims made a hajj, or pilgrimage, to Mecca. On their journey

▲ Carpets for sale in Marrakech, Morocco

home, they convinced a Muslim scholar from Morocco named Abd Allah Ibn Yasin to return with them to teach their people about Islam. Ibn Yasin's teachings soon attracted followers, and he founded a strict religious brotherhood, known as the **Almoravids**. According to one theory about the name's origin, the group lived in a *ribat,* or fortified monastery. They were therefore called the "people of the *ribat,*" or *al-Murabitun.* This eventually became "Almoravid."

In the 1050s, Ibn Yasin led the Almoravids in an effort to spread Islam through conquest. After Ibn Yasin's death in 1059, the Almoravids went on to take Morocco and found Marrakech. It became their capital. They overran the West African empire of Ghana by 1076. The Almoravids also captured parts of southern Spain, where they were called Moors.

Almohads Take Over In the mid-1100s, the **Almohads** (AL•moh•HADZ), another group of Berber Muslim reformers, seized power from the Almoravids. The Almohads began as a religious movement in the Atlas Mountains of Morocco.

The Almohads followed the teachings of Ibn Tumart. After a pilgrimage to Mecca, Ibn Tumart criticized the later Almoravid rulers for moving away from the traditional practice of Islam. He urged his followers to strictly obey the teachings of the Qur'an and Islamic law. The Almohads, led by Abd al-Mumin, fought to overthrow the Almoravids and remain true to their view of traditional Islamic beliefs.

By 1148 the Almohads controlled most of Morocco and ended Almoravid rule. The new Muslim reformers kept Marrakech as their capital. By the end of the 12th century, they had conquered much of southern Spain. In Africa, their territory stretched from Marrakech to Tripoli and Tunis on the Mediterranean. The Almohad Empire broke up into individual Muslim dynasties. While the Almohad Empire lasted just over 100 years, it united the Maghrib under one rule for the first time. **B**

Stronger empires were about to emerge. Societies in West Africa created empires that boasted economic and political power and strong links to trade routes.

MAIN IDEA

Recognizing Effects

B What was the main effect of Almohad rule on the Maghrib?

SECTION 1 ASSESSMENT

TERMS & NAMES 1. For each term or name, write a sentence explaining its significance.
• lineage • stateless societies • patrilineal • matrilineal • Maghrib • Almoravids • Almohads

USING YOUR NOTES

2. How might these characteristics have helped stateless societies to endure for many centuries? Explain.

Stateless Societies

MAIN IDEAS

3. What sorts of food do the Efe hunt and gather in the Ituri Forest?

4. What different purposes does the age-set system serve in African societies?

5. What role did Islam play in the political history of North Africa?

CRITICAL THINKING & WRITING

6. **ANALYZING ISSUES** What was the main disagreement that the Almohads had with the Almoravids?

7. **DRAWING CONCLUSIONS** How did the law help to unify Muslim society?

8. **COMPARING** In what ways are hunting-gathering societies and stateless societies similar?

9. **WRITING ACTIVITY** RELIGIOUS AND ETHICAL SYSTEMS
Working with a partner, prepare a **time line** showing the impact of Islam on North Africa. Include significant events for the period described in this section. Display your time line in the classroom.

CONNECT TO TODAY MAKING A CHART

Research hunting-gathering societies in Africa today. Find out their numbers and where they live and present your findings in a **chart.**

West African Civilizations

MAIN IDEA	WHY IT MATTERS NOW	TERMS & NAMES
ECONOMICS West Africa contained several rich and powerful states, including Ghana, Mali, and Songhai.	These civilizations demonstrate the richness of African culture before European colonization.	• Ghana • Songhai • Mali • Hausa • Sundiata • Yoruba • Mansa Musa • Benin • Ibn Battuta

SETTING THE STAGE While the Almohads and Almoravids were building empires in North Africa, three powerful empires flourished in West Africa. These ancient African empires arose in the Sahel, the savanna region just south of the Sahara. They grew strong by controlling trade. In this section you will learn about the West African empires of Ghana, Mali, and Songhai.

Empire of Ghana

By A.D. 200, trade across the Sahara had existed for centuries. However, this trade remained infrequent and irregular because of the harsh desert conditions. Most pack animals—oxen, donkeys, and horses—could not travel very far in the hot, dry Sahara without rest or water. Then, in the third century A.D., Berber nomads began using camels. The camel could plod steadily over much longer distances, covering as much as 60 miles in a day. In addition, it could travel more than ten days without water, twice as long as most pack animals. With the camel, nomads blazed new routes across the desert and trade increased.

hmhsocialstudies.com
TAKING NOTES

Use the graphic organizer online to take notes on the Mali and Songhai empires.

The trade routes crossed the savanna through the region farmed by the Soninke (soh•NIHN•keh) people. The Soninke people called their ruler *ghana,* or war chief. Muslim traders began to use the word to refer to the Soninke region. By the 700s, **Ghana** was a kingdom, and its rulers were growing rich by taxing the goods that traders carried through their territory.

Gold-Salt Trade The two most important trade items were gold and salt. Gold came from a forest region south of the savanna between the Niger (NY•juhr) and Senegal (SEHN•ih•GAWL) rivers. Miners dug gold from shafts as deep as 100 feet or sifted it from fast-moving streams. Some sources estimate that until about 1350, at least two-thirds of the world's supply of gold came from West Africa. Although rich in gold, West Africa's savanna and forests lacked salt, a material essential to human life. The Sahara contained deposits of salt. In fact, in the Saharan village of Taghaza, workers built their houses from salt blocks because it was the only material available.

Arab and Berber traders crossed the desert with camel caravans loaded down with salt. They also carried cloth, weapons, and manufactured goods from ports on the Mediterranean. After a long journey, they reached the market towns of the savanna. Meanwhile, African traders brought gold north from the forest regions.

Societies and Empires of Africa **413**

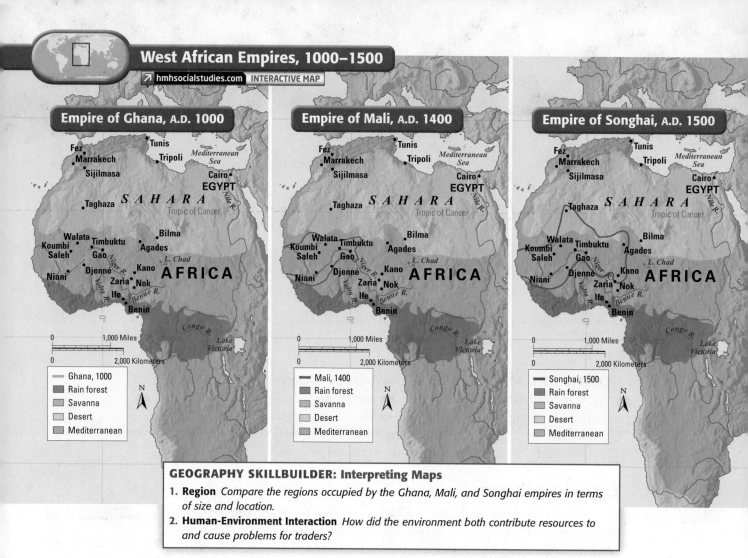

Empire of Ghana, A.D. 1000

Empire of Mali, A.D. 1400

Empire of Songhai, A.D. 1500

GEOGRAPHY SKILLBUILDER: Interpreting Maps

1. **Region** Compare the regions occupied by the Ghana, Mali, and Songhai empires in terms of size and location.
2. **Human-Environment Interaction** How did the environment both contribute resources to and cause problems for traders?

Merchants met in trading cities, where they exchanged goods under the watchful eye of the king's tax collector. In addition to taxing trade, royal officials made sure that all traders weighed goods fairly and did business according to law. Royal guards also provided protection from bandits.

Land of Gold By the year 800, Ghana had become an empire. Because Ghana's king controlled trade and commanded a large army, he could demand taxes and gifts from the chiefs of surrounding lands. As long as the chiefs made their payments, the king left them in peace to rule their own people.

In his royal palace, the king stored gold nuggets and slabs of salt (collected as taxes). Only the king had the right to own gold nuggets, although gold dust freely circulated in the marketplace. By this means, the king limited the supply of gold and kept its price from falling. Ghana's African ruler acted as a religious leader, chief judge, and military commander. He headed a large bureaucracy and could call up a huge army. In 1067, a Muslim geographer and scholar named al-Bakri wrote a description of Ghana's royal court:

PRIMARY SOURCE

The king adorns himself . . . wearing necklaces and bracelets. . . . The court of appeal is held in a domed pavilion around which stand ten horses with gold embroidered trappings. Behind the king stand ten pages holding shields and swords decorated with gold, and on his right are the sons of the subordinate [lower] kings of his country, all wearing splendid garments and with their hair mixed with gold.

AL-BAKRI, quoted in *Africa in the Days of Exploration*

Islamic Influences While Islam spread through North Africa by conquest, south of the Sahara, Islam spread through trade. Muslim merchants and teachers settled in the states south of the Sahara and introduced their faith there.

Eventually, Ghana's rulers converted to Islam. By the end of the 11th century, Muslim advisers were helping the king run his kingdom. While Ghana's African rulers accepted Islam, many people in the empire clung to their animistic beliefs and practices. Animism is the belief that spirits living in animals, plants, and natural forces play an important role in daily life. Much of the population never converted. Those who did kept many of their former beliefs, which they observed along with Islam. Among the upper class, Islam's growth encouraged the spread of literacy. To study the Qur'an, converts to Islam had to learn Arabic.

In 1076 the Muslim Almoravids of North Africa completed their conquest of Ghana. Although the Almoravids eventually withdrew from Ghana, the war had badly disrupted the gold-salt trade. As a result, Ghana never regained its power. **A**

MAIN IDEA

Analyzing Causes
A Why would the disruption of trade destroy Ghana's power?

Empire of Mali

By 1235 the kingdom of **Mali** had emerged. Its founders were Mande-speaking people, who lived south of Ghana. Mali's wealth, like Ghana's, was built on gold. As Ghana remained weak, people who had been under its control began to act independently. In addition, miners found new gold deposits farther east. This caused the most important trade routes to shift eastward, which made a new group of people—the people of Mali—wealthy. It also enabled them to seize power.

Sundiata Conquers an Empire Mali's first great leader, **Sundiata** (sun•JAHT•ah), came to power by crushing a cruel, unpopular leader. Then, in the words of a Mande oral tradition, "the world knew no other master but Sundiata." Sundiata became Mali's *mansa,* or emperor. Through a series of military victories, he took over the kingdom of Ghana and the trading cities of Kumbi and Walata. A period of peace and prosperity followed.

Sundiata proved to be as great a leader in peace as he had been in war. He put able administrators in charge of Mali's finances, defense, and foreign affairs. From his new capital at Niani, he promoted agriculture and reestablished the gold-salt trade. Niani became an important center of commerce and trade. People began to call Sundiata's empire Mali, meaning "where the king lives."

Mansa Musa Expands Mali Sundiata died in 1255. Some of Mali's next rulers became Muslims. These African Muslim rulers built mosques, attended public prayers, and supported the preaching of Muslim holy men. The most famous of them was **Mansa Musa** (MAHN•sah-moo•SAH), who may have been Sundiata's grandnephew. Mansa Musa ruled from about 1312 to 1332.

History Makers

Sundiata
?–1255
Sundiata came from the kingdom of Kangaba near the present-day Mali-Guinea border. According to tradition, he was one of 12 brothers who were heirs to the throne of Kangaba.

When Sumanguru, ruler of a neighboring state, overran Kangaba in the early 1200s, he wanted to eliminate rivals, so he murdered all of Sundiata's brothers. He spared Sundiata, who was sickly and seemed unlikely to survive.

However, as Sundiata grew up, he gained strength and became a popular leader of many warriors. In 1235, Sundiata's army defeated Sumanguru and his troops.

Mansa Musa
?–1332?
Mansa Musa, the strongest of Sundiata's successors, was a devout Muslim. On his hajj, Mansa Musa stopped in Cairo, Egypt. Five hundred slaves, each carrying a staff of gold, arrived first. They were followed by 80 camels, each carrying 300 pounds of gold dust. Hundreds of other camels brought supplies. Thousands of servants and officials completed the procession.

Mansa Musa gave away so much gold in Cairo that the value of this precious metal declined in Egypt for 12 years.

↗ **hmhsocialstudies.com**

RESEARCH WEB LINKS Go online for more on Sundiata and Mansa Musa.

Mansa Musa's Kingdom

In 1324, Mansa Musa left Mali for the hajj to Mecca. On the trip, he gave away enormous amounts of gold. Because of this, Europeans learned of Mali's wealth. In 1375, a Spanish mapmaker created an illustrated map showing Mansa Musa's kingdom in western Africa. Drawn on the map is Mansa Musa holding a gold nugget.

At the top of the map is Spain. At the bottom of Spain, the Mediterranean meets the Atlantic Ocean at the Strait of Gibraltar. South of Gibraltar is Africa. Filling most of the map is North Africa, with the Mediterranean extending east and the Atlantic west of Gibraltar.

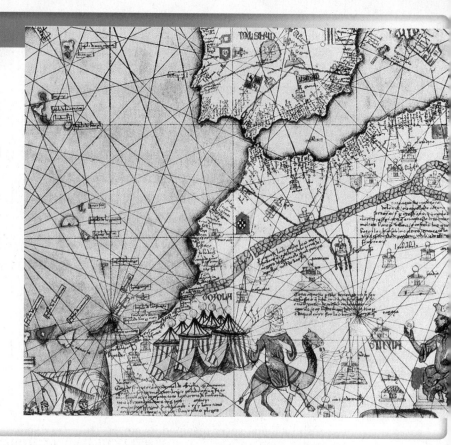

DOCUMENT-BASED QUESTIONS

1. **Determining Main Ideas** *What was a major source of wealth for the Empire of Mali?*
2. **Making Inferences** *How might Mali's (and Africa's) wealth have influenced interactions between Africans and Europeans?*

Between the reigns of Sundiata and Mansa Musa, Mali experienced turmoil. There had been seven different rulers in approximately 50 years. Like Sundiata, Mansa Musa was a skilled military leader who exercised royal control over the gold-salt trade and put down every rebellion. His 100,000-man army kept order and protected Mali from attack. Under Mansa Musa, the empire expanded to roughly twice the size of the empire of Ghana. To govern his far-reaching empire, Mansa Musa divided it into provinces and appointed governors, who ruled fairly and efficiently.

A devout Muslim, Mansa Musa went on a hajj to Mecca from 1324 to 1325. When he returned, he ordered the building of new mosques at the trading cities of Timbuktu (TIHM•buhk•TOO) and Gao. Timbuktu became one of the most important cities of the empire. It attracted Muslim judges, doctors, religious leaders, and scholars from far and wide. They attended Timbuktu's outstanding mosques and universities.

Travels of Ibn Battuta In 1352, one of Mansa Musa's successors prepared to receive a traveler and historian named **Ibn Battuta** (IHB•uhn-ba•TOO•tah). A native of Tangier in North Africa, Ibn Battuta had traveled for 27 years, visiting most of the countries in the Islamic world.

After leaving the royal palace, Ibn Battuta visited Timbuktu and other cities in Mali. He found he could travel without fear of crime. As a devout Muslim, he praised the people for their study of the Qur'an. However, he also criticized them for not strictly practicing Islam's moral code. Even so, Mali's justice system greatly impressed him:

PRIMARY SOURCE

They are seldom unjust, and have a greater abhorrence of injustice than any other people. Their sultan shows no mercy to anyone who is guilty of the least act of it. There is complete security in their country. Neither traveler nor inhabitant in it has anything to fear from robbers.

IBN BATTUTA, quoted in *Africa in the Days of Exploration*

hmhsocialstudies.com

INTERACTIVE HISTORY

Explore the splendor of Mansa Musa's pilgrimage.

Ibn Battuta left Mali in 1353. Within 50 years, the once-powerful empire began to weaken. Most of Mansa Musa's successors lacked his ability to govern well. In addition, the gold trade that had been the basis of Mali's wealth shifted eastward as new goldfields were developed elsewhere.

Empire of Songhai

As Mali declined in the 1400s, people who had been under its control began to break away. Among them were the **Songhai** (SAWNG•HY) people to the east. They built up an army and extended their territory to the large bend in the Niger River near Gao. They gained control of the all-important trade routes. Gao was the capital of their empire. **B**

MAIN IDEA

Making Inferences

B Why might the people who had been conquered by Mali want to break away?

Sunni Ali, a Conquering Hero The Songhai had two extraordinary rulers, both of whom were Muslims. One was Sunni Ali, who built a vast empire by military conquest. Sunni Ali's rule began in 1464 and lasted almost 30 years.

Sunni Ali built a professional army that had a riverboat fleet of war canoes and a mobile fighting force on horseback. He expanded Songhai into an empire through his skill as a military commander and his aggressive leadership. In 1468, Sunni Ali achieved his first major military triumph. He captured the city of Timbuktu, which had been an important part of Mali's empire.

Five years later, he took Djenné, also a trade city that had a university. To take Djenné, Sunni Ali surrounded the city with his army for seven years before it fell in 1473. Sunni Ali completed the takeover of Djenné by marrying its queen.

Askia Muhammad Governs Well After Sunni Ali's death in 1492, his son succeeded him as ruler. Almost at once, the son faced a major revolt by Muslims who were angry that he did not practice their religion faithfully. The leader of the revolt was a devout Muslim named Askia Muhammad. He drove Sunni Ali's son from power and replaced him.

During his 37-year rule, Askia Muhammad proved to be an excellent administrator. He set up an efficient tax system and chose able officials. Adding to the centralized government created by Sunni Ali, he appointed officials to serve as ministers of the treasury, army, navy, and agriculture. Under his rule, the well-governed empire thrived.

Despite its wealth and learning, the Songhai Empire lacked modern weapons. The Chinese had invented gunpowder in the ninth century. About 1304, Arabs developed the first gun, which shot arrows. In 1591, a Moroccan fighting force of several thousand men equipped with gunpowder and cannons crossed the Sahara and invaded Songhai. The Moroccan troops quickly defeated the Songhai warriors, who were armed only with swords and spears. The collapse of the Songhai Empire ended a 1,000-year period in which powerful kingdoms and empires ruled the central region of West Africa.

Other Peoples of West Africa

While empires rose and fell, city-states developed in other parts of West Africa. As in Ghana, Mali, and Songhai, Muslim traditions influenced some of these city-states. Other city-states held to their traditional African beliefs.

Hausa City-States Compete The **Hausa** (HOW•suh) were a group of people named after the language they spoke. The

Social History

Islam in West Africa

South of the Sahara, many converts to Islam also kept their African beliefs. They found ways to include their traditional rituals and customs in their new religion.

The status of women in West African societies demonstrates how local custom altered Muslim practice. In many 15th-century Muslim societies, women seldom left their homes. When they did, they veiled their faces. Muslim women in West Africa, however, did not wear veils. They also mingled freely with men in public, which shocked visiting Muslim religious leaders.

Queen Amina's Reign

In the 1500s, the Hausa city-state of Zazzau (later called Zaria) was governed by Queen Amina. She was remembered as the "headdress among the turbans." Her rule was distinguished for its military conquests.

The *Kano Chronicle*, a history of the city-state of Kano, records:

> *At this time Zaria, under Queen Amina, conquered all the towns as far as Kawarajara and Nupe. Every town paid tribute to her. . . . Her conquests extended over 34 years.*

Queen Amina's commitment to her Muslim faith also led her to encourage Muslim scholars, judges, and religious leaders from religious centers at Kano and Timbuktu to come to Zazzau.

▼ This Yoruba crown made of glass beads and grass cloth stands about 20 inches high.

city-states of the Hausa people first emerged between the years 1000 and 1200 in the savanna area east of Mali and Songhai in what is today northern Nigeria. Songhai briefly ruled the Hausa city-states, but they soon regained their independence. In such city-states as Kano, Katsina, and Zazzau (later Zaria), local rulers built walled cities for their capitals. From their capitals, Hausa rulers governed the farming villages outside the city walls.

Each ruler depended on the crops of the farmers and on a thriving trade in salt, grain, and cotton cloth made by urban weavers. Because they were located on trade routes that linked other West African states with the Mediterranean, Kano and Katsina became major trading states. They profited greatly from supplying the needs of caravans. Kano was noted for its woven and dyed cloth and for its leather goods.

Zazzau, the southernmost state, conducted a vigorous trade in enslaved persons. Zazzau's traders raided an area south of the city and sold their captives to traders in other Hausa states. These traders sold them to other North or West African societies in exchange for horses, harnesses, and guns. The Hausa kept some slaves to build and repair city walls and grow food for the cities.

All the Hausa city-states had similar forms of government. Rulers held great power over their subjects, but ministers and other officials acted to check this power. For protection, each city-state raised an army of mounted horsemen. Although rulers often schemed and fought to gain control over their neighbors, none succeeded for long. The constant fighting among city-states prevented any one of them from building a Hausa empire. **C**

Yoruba Kings and Artists Like the Hausa, the <u>Yoruba</u> (YAWR•uh•buh) people all spoke a common language. Originally the Yoruba-speaking people belonged to a number of small city-states in the forests on the southern edge of the savanna in what is today Benin and southwestern Nigeria. In these communities most people farmed. Over time, some of these smaller communities joined together under strong leaders. This led to the formation of several Yoruba kingdoms.

Considered divine, Yoruba kings served as the most important religious and political leaders in their kingdoms. All Yoruba chiefs traced their descent from the first ruler of Ife (EE•fay). According to legend, the creator sent this first ruler down to earth at Ife, where he founded the first Yoruba state. His many sons became the heads of other Yoruba kingdoms. All Yoruba chiefs regarded the king of Ife as their highest spiritual authority. A secret society of religious and political leaders limited the king's rule by reviewing the decisions he made.

Ife and Oyo were the two largest Yoruba kingdoms. Ife, developed by 1100, was the most powerful Yoruba kingdom until the late 1600s, when Oyo became more prosperous. As large urban centers, both Ife and Oyo had high walls surrounding them. Most rural farms in the surrounding areas produced surplus

MAIN IDEA

Analyzing Causes
C What was the main reason that the Hausa did not develop an empire?

food, which was sent to the cities. This enabled city dwellers to become both traders and craftspeople.

The Ife were gifted artists who carved in wood and ivory. They produced terra cotta sculptures and cast in metal. Some scholars believe that the rulers supported artists. Many clay and metal casts portray Ife rulers in an idealistic way.

Vocabulary
terra cotta: a reddish-brown clay, hard ceramic

Kingdom of Benin To the south and west of Ife, near the delta of the Niger River, lay the kingdom of <u>Benin</u> (buh•NIHN). Like the Yoruba people of Ife and Oyo, the people of Benin made their homes in the forest. The first kings of Benin date from the 1200s. Like the Yoruba kings, the oba, or ruler, of Benin based his right to rule on claims of descent from the first king of Ife.

In the 1400s, the oba named Ewuare made Benin into a major West African state. He did so by building a powerful army. He used it to control an area that by 1500 stretched from the Niger River delta in the east to what is today Lagos, Nigeria. Ewuare also strengthened Benin City by building walls around it. Inside the city, broad streets were lined by neat rows of houses.

The huge palace contained many courtyards and works of art. Artists working for the oba created magnificent brass heads of the royal family and copper figurines. Brass plaques on the walls and columns of the royal palace of the oba showed legends, historical scenes, and the deeds of the oba and his nobles. According to tradition, Benin artists learned their craft from an Ife artist brought to Benin by the oba to teach them.

In the 1480s, Portuguese trading ships began to sail into Benin's port at Gwatto. The Portuguese traded with Benin merchants for pepper, leopard skins, ivory, and enslaved persons. This began several centuries of European interference in Africa, during which they enslaved Africans and seized African territories for colonies. Meanwhile, East Africans—discussed in Section 3—prospered from trade and developed thriving cities and empires.

▲ This ivory mask is one of four taken from the king of Benin in 1897. It was worn on the belt of a ceremonial costume.

SECTION 2 ASSESSMENT

TERMS & NAMES 1. For each term or name, write a sentence explaining its significance.
• Ghana   • Mali   • Sundiata   • Mansa Musa   • Ibn Battuta   • Songhai   • Hausa   • Yoruba   • Benin

USING YOUR NOTES

2. What are some similarities between the two empires? Explain.

Mali

both

Songhai

MAIN IDEAS

3. How did Ghana's gold-salt trade work?

4. How did Sunni Ali build an empire?

5. What form of government was typical of Hausa city-states?

CRITICAL THINKING & WRITING

6. **DRAWING CONCLUSIONS** Which of the two—the Yoruba or the people of Benin—had more influence on the other?

7. **COMPARING** What are some of the similarities between the Hausa city-states and other city-states you have read about?

8. **COMPARING** What are some of the similarities between Sundiata and Mansa Musa?

9. **WRITING ACTIVITY** [ECONOMICS] What do you think was the most effective method Ghana used to regulate its economy? Explain your answer in a short **paragraph** in which you touch upon trade routes, gold, and taxes.

CONNECT TO TODAY CREATING A POSTER

Learn more about the mining and production of salt today. Present your findings in a **poster**, with illustrations and captions.

Societies and Empires of Africa **419**

Benin Bronzes

Benin is famous for its bronze and brass sculptures. Benin sculpture was made by guilds controlled by the king. One of the main functions of Benin art was to please the ruler by recording his history or by displaying his power. For instance, brass plaques commemorating the ruler's great achievements adorned the palace walls. Busts of the ruler and his family showed them as idealized figures.

↗ **hmhsocialstudies.com**

RESEARCH WEB LINKS Go online for more on the art of Benin.

Queen Mother ▶
Perhaps the most widely known type of Benin sculpture was the royal head, such as this one. In Benin, the Queen Mother held a lot of power. To symbolize that power, she wore a woven crown called a "chicken's beak."

◀ **Plaque**
Plaques such as this decorated the palace of the Oba, or ruler, of Benin

The Lost-Wax Process

Many of the Benin sculptures were made using the lost-wax process.

1. The artist forms a core of clay that is roughly the shape of the planned sculpture.

2. The artist applies a layer of wax over the core, then carves fine details into the surface of the wax.

3. A layer of fine clay is spread over the wax surface. This creates a smooth finish and captures the small details.

4. Several layers of coarse clay are applied to create the mold.

5. The entire object is fired in a kiln (oven). The clay hardens, and the wax melts away, leaving a clay mold. (The melted wax is the origin of the name "lost-wax.")

6. Melted bronze is poured into the mold and left to harden.

7. The clay mold is broken off, revealing the finished bronze sculpture.

Leopard ▶
Admired for its power, fierceness, and intelligence, the leopard was depicted on many royal objects. This snarling leopard is a symbol of the king's power. It is also a water vessel that was used on ceremonial occasions.

◀ Musician
This figure was probably made in the late 16th or early 17th century. It shows an attendant of the king blowing a horn or flute. This type of figure was often found on altars.

Connect *to* Today

1. **Making Inferences** Why do you think the figure of a servant blowing a horn was found on an altar?

   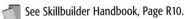 See Skillbuilder Handbook, Page R10.

2. **Comparing and Contrasting** Use library resources to identify a sculpture of a U.S. leader. What quality about that leader does the sculpture portray? How is it similar to or different from Benin's royal sculptures?

421

Eastern City-States and Southern Empires

MAIN IDEA	WHY IT MATTERS NOW	TERMS & NAMES
INTERACTION WITH ENVIRONMENT African city-states and empires gained wealth through developing and-trading resources.	The country of Zimbabwe and cities such as Mogadishu and Mombasa have their roots in this time period.	• Swahili • Great Zimbabwe • Mutapa

SETTING THE STAGE As early as the third century A.D., the kingdom of Aksum had taken part in an extensive trade network. From its Red Sea port, Aksum traded with Arabia, Persia, India, and Rome. In the 600s, Muslim forces gained control of Arabia, the Red Sea, and North Africa. The Muslims cut off the Aksumites from their port. The Aksumites moved their capital south from Aksum to Roha (later called Lalibela) shortly before 1100. In the meantime, other cities on the east coast were thriving because of Indian Ocean trade. In this section, you will learn about East African trade, Islamic influences in East Africa, and the peoples of southern Africa.

East Coast Trade Cities

Use the graphic organizer online to take notes on cultural interaction resulting from trade.

Villages along the east coast began to develop into important trade cities. By 1100, waves of Bantu-speaking people had migrated across central Africa to the east coast. There they established farming and fishing villages. Slowly, the existing coastal villages grew into bustling seaports, built on trade between East African merchants and traders from Arabia, Persia, and India. As trade increased, many Muslim Arab and Persian traders settled in these port cities. Arabic blended with the Bantu language to create the **Swahili** (swah•HEE•lee) language.

Persian traders moved south from the Horn of Africa, a triangular peninsula near Arabia. They brought Asian manufactured goods to Africa and African raw materials to Asia. In the coastal markets, Arab traders sold porcelain bowls from China and jewels and cotton cloth from India. They bought African ivory, gold, tortoiseshell, ambergris, leopard skins, and rhinoceros horns to carry to Arabia.

By 1300, more than 35 trading cities dotted the coast from Mogadishu in the north to Kilwa and Sofala in the south. Like the empires of West Africa, these seaports grew wealthy by controlling all incoming and outgoing trade. Some cities also manufactured trade goods for export. For example, weavers in Mogadishu and Sofala made cloth. Workers in Mombasa and Malindi made iron tools.

The City-State of Kilwa In 1331, Ibn Battuta visited Kilwa. He admired the way that its Muslim rulers and merchants lived. Rich families lived in fine houses of coral and stone. They slept in beds inlaid with ivory and their meals were served on porcelain. Wealthy Muslim women wore silk robes and gold and silver bracelets.

Trade Goods

Origin	Raw Materials	Products Made
Savanna region	leopard skins	saddles
Coastal region	tortoiseshells	combs
Southern African	gold from mines	coins, jewelry
Savanna region	ivory from elephants	chess pieces, sword hilts

40°N

40°E

80°E

Nile R.

EGYPT

Tropic of Cancer

SAHARA

Jiddah

Muscat

ARABIA

Red Sea

Dhofar

INDIA

Aksum

Aden

Gulf of Aden

AFRICA

Lalibela

Zeila

Arabian
Sea

Calicut

Congo R.

Mogadishu

INDIAN OCEAN

Equator 0°

L. Victoria

Malindi

Mombasa

Zanzibar I.

N

Kilwa

0   1,000 Miles

0   2,000 Kilometers

Zambezi R.

Madagascar

Zimbabwe   Sofala

Limpopo R.

Tropic of Capricorn

	Land route
	Sea route
→	Summer monsoon
→	Winter monsoon
	Rain forest
	Savanna
	Desert

GEOGRAPHY SKILLBUILDER: Interpreting Maps

1. **Movement** *How far did a trader have to travel to make a round trip from Calicut in India to Kilwa in Africa and back again?*
2. **Human-Environment Interaction** *Which monsoon would a trader rely on to sail from India to Africa?*
3. **Region** *Which raw materials came from the savanna region?*

Kilwa grew rich because it was as far south on the coast as a ship from India could sail in one monsoon season. Therefore, trade goods from southerly regions had to funnel into Kilwa, so Asian merchants could buy them.

In addition, in the late 1200s Kilwa had seized the port of Sofala, which was a trading center for gold mined inland. By controlling Sofala, Kilwa was able to control the overseas trade of gold from southern Africa. As a result, Kilwa became the wealthiest, most powerful coastal city-state. **A**

Portuguese Conquest In 1488, the first Portuguese ships rounded the southern tip of Africa and sailed north, looking for a sea route to India. They wanted to gain profits from the Asian trade in spices, perfumes, and silks. When the Portuguese saw the wealth of the East African city-states, they decided to conquer those cities and take over the trade themselves.

Using their shipboard cannon, the Portuguese took Sofala, Kilwa, and Mombasa. They burned parts of Kilwa and built forts on the sites of Kilwa and Mombasa. The Portuguese kept their ports and cities on the East African coast for the next two centuries.

MAIN IDEA

Analyzing Causes
A What were the two main reasons Kilwa became so wealthy?

Islamic Influences

Muslim traders introduced Islam to the East African coast, and the growth of commerce caused the religion to spread. Even the smallest towns had a mosque for the faithful. A Muslim sultan, or ruler, governed most cities. In addition, most government officials and wealthy merchants were Muslims. However, the vast majority of people along the East African coast held on to their traditional religious beliefs.

> **Analyzing Primary Sources**

Islamic Law in Mogadishu

In 1331, Ibn Battuta, traveling by caravan similar to the one at right, visited the African city of Mogadishu. He described how Muslim officials decided legal matters.

PRIMARY SOURCE

The Shaikh [sultan] takes his place in his hall of audience and sends for the Qadi [judge]. He takes his place on the Shaikh's left and then the lawyers come in and the chief of them sit in front of the Shaikh. . . . Then food is brought and . . . those who are in the audience chamber eat in the presence of the Shaikh. . . . After this the Shaikh retires to his private apartments and the Qadi, the wazirs [government ministers] . . . and . . . chief amirs [military commanders] sit to hear causes and complaints. Questions of religious law are decided by the Qadi, other cases are judged by the . . . wazirs and amirs. If a case requires the views of the [Shaikh], it is put in writing for him. He sends back an immediate reply.

IBN BATTUTA, *Travels of Ibn Battuta*

DOCUMENT-BASED QUESTIONS
1. **Summarizing** *Who were the four types of people who decided legal matters?*
2. **Clarifying** *What types of cases did they judge?*

This was also true of the people who lived in inland villages.

Enslavement of Africans Along with luxury goods, Arab Muslim traders exported enslaved persons from the East African coast. Traders sent Africans acquired through kidnapping to markets in Arabia, Persia, and Iraq. Wealthy people in these countries often bought slaves to do domestic tasks. Muslim traders shipped enslaved Africans across the Indian Ocean to India, where Indian rulers employed them as soldiers. Enslaved Africans also worked on docks and ships at Muslim-controlled ports and as household servants in China.

Although Muslim traders had been enslaving East Africans and selling them overseas since about the ninth century, the numbers remained small—perhaps about 1,000 a year. The trade in slaves did not increase dramatically until the 1700s. At that time, Europeans started to buy captured Africans for their colonial plantations. **B**

MAIN IDEA

Summarizing
B How extensive was the trade in enslaved persons from East Africa before 1700?

▲ An Arab slave market in Yemen, A.D. 1237

Southern Africa and Great Zimbabwe

The gold and ivory that helped the coastal city-states grow rich came from the interior of southern Africa. In southeastern Africa the Shona people established a city called **Great Zimbabwe** (zihm•BAHB•way), which grew into an empire built on the gold trade.

Great Zimbabwe By 1000, the Shona people had settled the fertile, well-watered plateau between the Zambezi and Limpopo rivers in modern Zimbabwe. The area was well suited to farming and cattle raising. Its location also had economic advantages. The city of Great Zimbabwe stood near an important trade route linking the goldfields with the coastal trading city of Sofala. Sometime after 1000, Great Zimbabwe gained control of these trade routes. From the 1200s through the 1400s, it became the capital of a thriving state. Its leaders taxed the traders who traveled these routes. They also demanded payments from less powerful chiefs. Because of this growing wealth, Great Zimbabwe became the economic, political, and religious center of its empire.

But by 1450, Great Zimbabwe was abandoned. No one knows for sure why it happened. According to one theory, cattle grazing had worn out the grasslands. In addition, farming had worn out the soil, and people had used up the salt and timber. The area could no longer support a large population.

Almost everything that is known about Great Zimbabwe comes from its impressive ruins. Portuguese explorers knew about the site in the 1500s. Karl Mauch, a German explorer, was one of the first Europeans to discover the remains of these stone dwellings in 1871.

Great Zimbabwe

Great Zimbabwe was an important city in southern Africa. The word *zimbabwe* comes from a Shona phrase meaning "stone houses." The ruins consist of two complexes of stone buildings that once housed the royal palace of Great Zimbabwe's rulers. There are great curving walls around the ruins. Because there was no way for soldiers to climb to the top of the walls, archaeologists theorize that they were not used primarily as defenses.

The massive walls were probably built to impress visitors with the strength of Zimbabwe and its ruler. Inside the walls stands a cone-shaped tower. Among the ruins were found tall figures of birds, carved from soapstone. Archaeologists believe the construction of Great Zimbabwe may have taken about 400 years.

City of Great Zimbabwe

The Shona people built this impressive city as the center of their empire.

- It covered many acres.
- Its population was more than 10,000.
- The walls contain approximately 900,000 stone blocks. They were so well built that the blocks hold together without mortar.
- The Great Enclosure is a curving wall up to 36 feet high and 15 feet thick.

This photograph shows part of the Great Enclosure.

This picture shows how very high the enclosing walls are.

SKILLBUILDER: Interpreting Visual Sources

1. **Drawing Conclusions** *If the walls were not built for defense, what does this suggest about the safety and security of Great Zimbabwe?*
2. **Making Inferences** *If military assault did not account for the fall of Zimbabwe, what other factors might have played a part?*

The Mutapa Empire

According to Shona oral tradition, a man named Mutota left Great Zimbabwe about 1420 to find a new source of salt. Traveling north, he settled in a valley with fertile soil, good rainfall, and ample wood. There he founded a new state to replace Great Zimbabwe. As the state grew, its leader Mutota used his army to dominate the northern Shona people living in the area. He forced them to make payments to support him and his army.

Mutapa Rulers These conquered people called Mutota and his successors *mwene mutapa,* meaning "conqueror" or "master pillager." The Portuguese who arrived on the East African coast in the early 1500s believed *mwene mutapa* to be a title of respect for the ruler. The term is also the origin of the name of the **Mutapa** Empire. By the time of Mutota's death, the Mutapa Empire had conquered all of what is now Zimbabwe except the eastern portion. By 1480 Mutota's son Matope claimed control of the area along the Zambezi River to the Indian Ocean coast.

The Mutapa Empire was able to mine gold deposited in nearby rivers and streams. In addition, Mutapa rulers forced people in conquered areas to mine gold for them. The rulers sent gold to the coastal city-states in exchange for luxuries. Even before the death of Matope, the southern part of his empire broke away. However, the Mutapa Dynasty remained in control of the smaller empire.

In the 1500s, the Portuguese tried to conquer the empire. When they failed to do so, they resorted to interfering in Mutapa politics. They helped to overthrow one ruler and replace him with one they could control. This signaled increasing European interference in Africa in centuries to come. **C**

> **MAIN IDEA**
>
> **Making Inferences**
> **C** Why do you think the Portuguese wanted to conquer the Mutapa Empire?

Global Impact

Swahili

Over the centuries, contacts between two peoples—Bantu speakers and Arabs—led to the creation of a new people and a new language. Many Arab traders married African women. People of mixed Arab and African ancestry came to be called Swahili. The word comes from an Arabic term meaning "people of the coast" and refers to the East African coast.

Although Swahili peoples do not share a single culture, they do speak a common language. Swahili is a Bantu language with many words borrowed from Arabic. The Swahili peoples traded the gold and ivory of Africa for goods from India and China. During the 1500s and 1600s, the Portuguese looted Swahili cities and damaged Swahili trade.

SECTION 3 ASSESSMENT

TERMS & NAMES 1. For each term or name, write a sentence explaining its significance.
- Swahili
- Great Zimbabwe
- Mutapa

USING YOUR NOTES

2. Do you think this interaction had a positive or negative effect? Explain.

MAIN IDEAS

3. How did the Swahili language develop?

4. How was Islam introduced to East Africa?

5. How did the people of Great Zimbabwe positively interact with their environment?

CRITICAL THINKING & WRITING

6. **COMPARING** Compare the Portuguese who arrived in East Africa with the rulers of the Mutapa Empire.

7. **SYNTHESIZING** What were some of the effects of East African trade on different cultural groups?

8. **DRAWING CONCLUSIONS** How is Swahili an example of cultural interaction?

9. **WRITING ACTIVITY** INTERACTION WITH ENVIRONMENT How did the people of Great Zimbabwe negatively interact with their environment? Write a one-paragraph **essay** explaining your answer.

MULTIMEDIA ACTIVITY CREATING AN OUTLINE MAP

 Use the Internet to research the modern African country of Zimbabwe. Find out where it is located in Africa, its capital, and other information. Enter your findings on an **outline map** of Africa.

INTERNET KEYWORD
Zimbabwe

Chapter 15 Assessment

TERMS & NAMES

For each term or name below, briefly explain its connection to African history from 800 to 1500.

1. lineage
2. stateless society
3. matrilineal
4. Ghana
5. Mali
6. Songhai
7. Swahili
8. Great Zimbabwe

MAIN IDEAS

North and Central African Societies
Section 1 (pages 409–412)

9. How is a dispute settled in Efe society?
10. What is an age-set system?
11. How were the beginnings of the Almoravid and Almohad empires similar?

West African Civilizations
Section 2 (pages 413–421)

12. What accounted for Ghana's financial success?
13. What were two ways that Islam spread through Africa?
14. What was the economy of the Hausa city-states like?

Eastern City-States and Southern Empires
Section 3 (pages 422–427)

15. How did the Swahili language evolve?
16. Why was it important for Kilwa to control Sofala?

17. Who was most affected by the introduction of Islam to East Africa?
18. What was the relationship of Great Zimbabwe to the Mutapa Empire?

CRITICAL THINKING

1. USING YOUR NOTES
In a chart like the one shown, list for each leader what group of people he led and one of his achievements.

Leader	Group	Achievement
Ibn Yasin		
Askia Muhammad		
Ewuare		

2. RECOGNIZING EFFECTS
RELIGIOUS AND ETHICAL SYSTEMS In what way did Islam encourage the spread of literacy?

3. RECOGNIZING EFFECTS
INTERACTION WITH ENVIRONMENT How did people adapt to the harsh conditions of the Sahara? Discuss traders who crossed the Sahara and people who lived in the Saharan village of Taghaza.

4. SUMMARIZING
How are group membership, inheritance rights, and positions of authority usually decided in a matrilineal society?

5. CLARIFYING
Why was the location of Great Zimbabwe advantageous?

VISUAL SUMMARY

Societies and Empires of Africa

	Organization & Time Period	Important Facts
Igbo People	Existed as a stateless society from **9th to 19th centuries**	Elders resolved conflicts
Almoravids	Muslim state from **mid-1000s to mid-1100s**	Founded city of Marrakech
Almohads	Muslim state from **mid-1100s to mid-1200s**	Unified the Maghrib under one authority for first time in history
Ghana	West African empire from **700s to 1076**	Grew wealthy and powerful by controlling gold-salt trade
Mali	West African empire from **1235 to 1400s**	Mansa Musa's hajj made Mali's wealth famous
Songhai	West African empire that flourished in the **1400s and 1500s**	Conquered Mali and gained control of trade routes
Benin	West African trading kingdom strong in **1400s and 1500s**	Famous for bronze and brass works of art
Kilwa	East African city-state flourished from **1200s to 1400s**	Grew wealthy from trade
Great Zimbabwe	Capital of trade-based empire from **1200s until about 1450**	City abandoned, perhaps because natural resources were used up
Mutapa Empire	Founded about **1420** by man from Great Zimbabwe	Remained independent in spite of Portuguese attempts

Use the map and your knowledge of world history to answer the questions.

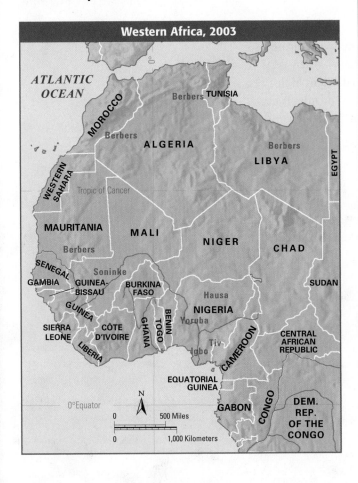

Western Africa, 2003

ATLANTIC OCEAN

MOROCCO
Berbers TUNISIA
Berbers
ALGERIA
Berbers
LIBYA
EGYPT
WESTERN SAHARA
Tropic of Cancer
MAURITANIA
MALI
NIGER
CHAD
Berbers
SENEGAL Soninke
GAMBIA GUINEA-BISSAU BURKINA FASO
SUDAN
GUINEA
Hausa
NIGERIA
SIERRA LEONE CÔTE D'IVOIRE GHANA TOGO BENIN Yoruba
Tiv
CENTRAL AFRICAN REPUBLIC
LIBERIA
Igbo
CAMEROON
EQUATORIAL GUINEA
0° Equator
N
GABON CONGO
DEM. REP. OF THE CONGO
0   500 Miles
0   1,000 Kilometers

1. Which is the most widespread ethnic group?
   A. Soninke
   B. Berbers
   C. Hausa
   D. Igbo

2. In which nation does that group *not* live?
   A. Algeria
   B. Mauritania
   C. Niger
   D. Libya

3. Which group does *not* live in modern Nigeria?
   A. Soninke
   B. Hausa
   C. Yoruba
   D. Igbo

4. What geographical feature might explain why there are no ethnic groups shown in the center of the map?
   A. Atlantic Ocean
   B. equator
   C. the Sahara
   D. Tropic of Cancer

 hmhsocialstudies.com TEST PRACTICE

For additional test practice, go online for:
- Diagnostic tests
- Tutorials
- Strategies

Interact *with* History

Recall your discussion of the question on page 408: How might trade benefit both sides? Now that you've read the chapter, reevaluate what makes trade beneficial. How did environmental conditions affect what items had value in Africa? Did government policies have any effect on value? Consider what you learned about trading states in both West and East Africa.

FOCUS ON WRITING

ECONOMICS Do you think Africa was connected to most of the world through trade, or was it relatively isolated from the rest of the world? Write an **essay** in which you support your answer with evidence from the chapter.

Consider the following:
- Muslim states of North Africa
- gold-salt trade
- empires and kingdoms of West Africa
- east coast trade cities

MULTIMEDIA ACTIVITY
21ST CENTURY

Participating in a WebQuest

Introduction Today, much of eastern Africa still relies heavily on trade. With a group of students, have each member choose one East African country to research in terms of its trade and culture. Issues to investigate might include what goods present-day East African nations trade and who their trading partners are.

Task Create an electronic presentation of information on exports and imports, quantities shipped, where the goods are going, and how they are being transported.

Process and Resources Have each member of the group bring his or her information on East African trade and culture to the group to create a presentation. Use this chapter and the Internet as resources for your research.

Evaluation and Conclusion East African trade has been important to the economies of the region. How did this project contribute to your understanding of the interrelationship between prosperity and trade?

Trade Creates Links

A trade network exists when a group of people or countries buys from or sells to each other on a regular basis. Historically, trade networks arose as merchants traded local products for those from other places—often very distant places. Trade is a good way to spread products that are in high demand. Unit 3 discussed trade networks in the Arabian Peninsula, Asia, the Mediterranean Sea, the Sahara, and the Indian Ocean. In the next six pages, you will see how these networks worked.

Trade Routes: Africa, Asia, Europe 1500

Trade Routes
- Indian Ocean
- Mediterranean Sea
- Silk Roads
- Trans-Arabia
- Trans-Sahara

Components of Trade Networks

Trading Partners

Merchants could grow rich selling highly desired goods that were not produced locally. To obtain such goods, merchants traded with people in other regions. When two regions trade regularly, they become trading partners.

Trade Goods

Products become trade goods when one region lacks them and another has a surplus to sell. Trade goods may be valuable because they are rare (such as ivory), useful (such as salt to preserve meat), or beautiful (such as silk).

Modes of Transport

Caravans of camels, mules, or other animals carried trade goods over land. Vessels that relied on wind power (such as the dhow) or the strength of human rowers shipped trade goods across the seas.

Currency

Merchants do not always exchange one product directly for another. They may buy goods with money. Currency is any item that is accepted as money in a region. Besides paper money, cowrie shells, salt, and metals served as currency.

Middlemen

Because some trade goods traveled very long distances, merchants did not always buy products directly from their places of origin. Middlemen acted as go-betweens, buying goods from merchants in one region to sell to merchants in another.

Types of Trade Networks

Trade networks frequently include more than two partners. Merchants from one area might sell their goods to several different regions. Middlemen might also do business with various different partners. The diagrams below show three basic types of trade networks.

Comparing & Contrasting

1. Judging from the map, which region had the best location for establishing itself as a middleman between the others? Explain why.

2. What are the advantages and disadvantages of using currency rather than trading products directly?

431

Major Trade Networks

The five major trade networks that you studied in Unit 3 are listed on the chart. Notice who the different trading partners were in each network and the products that they sold each other. Consider why the dhow and the camel described on the next page were particularly useful as modes of transport.

	Trading Partners	Trade Goods	Modes of Transport
Trans-Arabia	• Sassanid Empire • Arabia • Byzantine Empire	• East Asia: silk, gems, dyes, cotton cloth • Arabia: incense, spices • Southwest Asia: wool, gold, silver	• camel caravans
Silk Roads	• China • India • Persia and Central Asia • Europe	• Asia: silk, porcelain, spices, precious woods, gems • Europe: wool cloth, gold, silver	• caravans of camels and other pack animals
Mediterranean	• Europe • North Africa • Southwest Asia	• Europe: wool and linen cloth, wine, metal • North Africa: wool • Asia: spices, fruit, cloth	• by sea, galleys with numerous rowers • overland, caravans of pack animals
Trans-Sahara	• North Africa • West Africa	• North Africa: cloth, salt, horses, guns • West Africa: gold, dyed cloth, leather goods, slaves	• camel caravans
Indian Ocean	• China • India • Arabia • East Africa	• Asia: porcelain, silk, jewelry, cotton • East Africa: ivory, gold, tortoiseshell, leopard skins, slaves	• Arab dhows • Chinese junks

SKILLBUILDER: Interpreting Charts

1. **Making Generalizations** *How would you characterize most of the products that came from Asia?*
2. **Making Inferences** *What role did Arabian traders probably play in the Indian Ocean trade network? Explain.*

By Land or by Sea?

The different modes of transport used were well suited to their environments.

Advantages of Dhow Ocean Travel

- Stern rudders made dhows (shown in photograph) easy to maneuver.
- Lateen, or triangular, sails enabled sailors to sail against the wind.

Advantages of Land Travel by Camel

- Camels can carry heavy burdens over long distances.
- Fat reserves in their humps enable them to go without food or water for many days.
- Double sets of eyelashes, hairy ears, and nostrils that close protect camels from sand.
- Soft feet that stretch out make camels sure-footed on sand or snow.

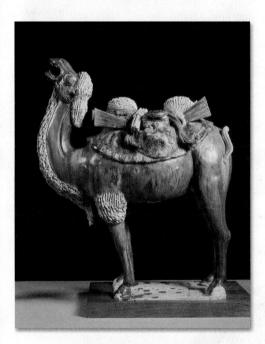

Astrolabe ▶
Sailors used astrolabes to measure the height of the sun or a star above the horizon. With that information, they could determine both the time of day and the latitude where they were located.

◀ Chinese Compass
Although the floating compass needle actually points to magnetic north, sailors could calculate true north and use that information to navigate. Knowing which way was north also enabled them to figure out in what direction the wind was blowing their ship.

Comparing & Contrasting

1. Read the information about the camel above. Then notice which trade networks on the chart on page 432 relied on camel caravans. What geographic information can you infer about those trade routes?

2. Which of the two navigation instruments do you think would be most useful for land travelers, such as those who traveled the Silk Roads or the trans-Saharan routes? Why?

Trade Goods

As trade networks developed, trading partners began to manufacture goods specifically for sale in other places. The more they learned about other cultures, the better they were able to design products that would suit foreign tastes. Consider how the items below were appropriate for sale in foreign places.

PRIMARY SOURCE

Moon Flask

This porcelain object is known as a moon flask for its round shape. During the Yuan Dynasty (1279–1368), China produced delicate porcelains with elaborate painted decorations such as this. Like silk, porcelain originated in China. It was several centuries before Europe learned how to produce porcelain of such a high quality.

DOCUMENT-BASED QUESTION
A trade good may be valued for its usefulness, rarity, or beauty. For which of those reasons do you think people wanted this porcelain flask? Explain.

PRIMARY SOURCE

African Ivory Spoon

Ivory, which usually comes from elephant tusks, was one of Africa's most common trade goods. Frequently, it was carved into utensils or decorative objects. This carved spoon came from Benin.

DOCUMENT-BASED QUESTION
Why would people in Europe or China need to trade to obtain ivory?

PRIMARY SOURCE

Silk Cloth

The Chinese began manufacturing silk by about 2500 B.C. and trading it to foreign lands by the time of the Han Dynasty (202 B.C. to A.D. 220). Many people desired silk because it was shiny and could be dyed many beautiful colors. It was also extremely strong yet lightweight.

DOCUMENT-BASED QUESTION
What class of people do you think were most likely to wear clothes made of silk?

Trade Narratives

The following excerpts describe life in towns and countries along the different trade routes that merchants traveled.

↗ hmhsocialstudies.com **INTERACTIVE**
Go online to listen to selected audio excerpts.

PRIMARY SOURCE

Francesco Balducci Pegolotti

An Italian commercial agent, Pegolotti wrote a guidebook around 1340 for European merchants traveling overland to China.

Whatever silver the merchants may carry with them as far as Cathay [China] the lord of Cathay will take from them and put into his treasury. And to merchants who thus bring silver they give that paper money of theirs in exchange . . . With this money you can readily buy silk and other [merchandise] . . . And all the people of the country are bound to receive it. And yet you shall not pay a higher price for your goods because your money is of paper.

DOCUMENT-BASED QUESTION
Judging from this excerpt, were Pegolotti's European readers familiar with paper money? How can you tell?

PRIMARY SOURCE

Fernão Lopes de Castanheda

The following description of the goods available in Calicut is from *History of the Discovery and Conquest of India*, published in 1552.

[Calicut is] the richest mart [market] of all India; in which is to be found all the spices, drugs, nutmegs, . . . pearls and seed-pearls, musk, sanders [sandalwood], fine dishes of earthenware, lacquer, gilded coffers, and all the fine things of China, gold, amber, wax, ivory, fine and coarse cotton goods, both white and dyed of many colours, much raw and twisted silk, . . . cloth of gold, cloth of tissue, grain, scarlets, silk carpets, copper, . . . and all kinds of conserves.

DOCUMENT-BASED QUESTION
How does Lopes de Castanheda support his point that Calicut is the richest market in India?

PRIMARY SOURCE

Ibn Battuta

The following excerpt was written by the Muslim traveler Ibn Battuta. In it, he describes the the Egyptian city of Cairo.

I arrived at length at Cairo, mother of cities and seat of Pharaoh the tyrant, mistress of broad regions and fruitful lands, boundless in multitude of buildings, peerless in beauty and splendour . . . It is said that in Cairo there are . . . thirty thousand hirers of mules and donkeys, and that on the Nile there are thirty-six thousand boats belonging to the Sultan and his subjects which sail upstream to Upper Egypt and downstream to Alexandria and Damietta, laden with goods and profitable merchandise of all kinds.

DOCUMENT-BASED QUESTION
How were goods transported within Cairo?

Travels in Asia and Africa, 1325–1354 by Ibn Battuta, translated by H.A.R. Gibb.

Comparing & Contrasting

1. Judging from the information in the sources, who besides the merchants profited from trade in Cathay and Cairo?
2. Which of the trade goods shown on the opposite page are mentioned in the description of Calicut? What does this tell you about the reason for Calicut's riches?

EXTENSION ACTIVITY
Go to a supermarket or produce store and write down what fruits and vegetables are being sold that are out of season or not native to your area. Then find out where they come from. Start by looking at signs and boxes where foods are packed. Interview the produce manager to find out what countries supplied the produce. Then create a chart or map that conveys the information you have learned.

Connecting Hemispheres
900–1800

Seeking new land and new markets, European explorers sailed around the world. This painting by Theodore Gudin depicts French explorer La Salle's Louisiana expedition of 1684.

Comparing & Contrasting

Methods of Government
In Unit 4, you will learn about different methods of ruling a nation or empire. At the end of the unit, you will have a chance to compare and contrast the governments you have studied. (See pages 578–583.)

CHAPTER 16

People and Empires in the Americas, 500–1500

Essential Question

What empires and peoples existed in the Americas before the arrival of Europeans?

❓ What You Will Learn

In this chapter, you follow the development of complex societies in North America, Mesoamerica, and South America in the period before contact with Europeans.

SECTION 1 North American Societies

Main Idea Complex North American societies were linked to each other through culture and economics.

SECTION 2 Maya Kings and Cities

Main Idea The Maya developed a highly complex civilization based on city-states and elaborate religious practices.

SECTION 3 The Aztecs Control Central Mexico

Main Idea Through alliances and conquest, the Aztecs created a powerful empire in what is today Mexico.

SECTION 4 The Inca Create a Mountain Empire

Main Idea The Inca built a vast empire supported by taxes, governed by a bureaucracy, and linked by extensive road systems.

Previewing Themes

CULTURAL INTERACTION Cultures in the Americas had frequent contact across distance and time. Both conquest and trade brought different cultures together.

Geography *In which part of the Americas do you think the greatest cultural interaction occurred? Why?*

POWER AND AUTHORITY Societies in the Americas ranged from small tribal bands to immense empires. Warrior-kings or priest-kings ruled most of these empires.

Geography *Which empire covered the greatest geographic area?*

RELIGIOUS AND ETHICAL SYSTEMS Religion was a powerful force in the Americas. Many societies combined religious and state rule. Much of their art and architecture concerned the gods and the need to please them.

Geography *The Aztecs adopted the gods of other Mesoamerican cultures. Why do you think this happened?*

THE AMERICAS

500s
Teotihuacán reaches population peak in central Mexico. (mask from Teotihuacán) ▶

800
Anasazi culture develops in the Southwest.

900
Classic period of Maya civilization ends.

500   750

WORLD

618
Tang Dynasty begins 289-year rule in China.

800
Charlemagne crowned Holy Roman Emperor by the pope. (crown of the Holy Roman Empire) ▶

The Americas, 800 B.C. – A.D. 1535

NORTH AMERICA

Pueblo Bonito
Chaco Canyon
Cahokia
Great Serpent Mound

Gulf of Mexico

MESOAMERICA

Tenochtitlán
Chichén Itzá

ATLANTIC OCEAN

HISTORY

Ancient Maya: Power Centers

hmhsocialstudies.com **VIDEO**

PACIFIC OCEAN

0° Equator

SOUTH AMERICA

Cuzco

30°N

30°S

120°W 90°W 60°W

Major Empires and Culture Areas

Mound Builder cultures (Adena, Hopewell, Mississippian), 800 B.C.–A.D. 1500

Maya, 250 B.C.–A.D. 900

Southwest cultures (Hohokam, Anasazi), A.D. 300–1400

Aztec, A.D. 1200–1521

Inca, A.D. 1438–1535

■ Archaeological site

0   500   1000 Miles

0   500   1000 Kilometers
Lambert Azimuthal Projection

N W E S

1100
Mississippian culture thrives at Cahokia.

1325
◄ Aztecs build Tenochtitlán. (figure of an Aztec goddess)

1438
Pachacuti becomes Incan emperor.

1502
Montezuma II crowned Aztec emperor.

1000   **1250**   **1500**

1066
Normans invade England.

1300
◄ Renaissance begins in Italy. (Michelangelo's *David*)

1324
Mansa Musa, king of Mali, goes on hajj to Mecca.

1492
Columbus makes first voyage to the Americas.

What does this headdress tell you about the people who made it?

You are preparing an exhibit for your local history museum on an early Native American society—one with no written language. In many ways, you must act like a detective. You sift through the evidence for clues and then draw conclusions based on your findings. Imagine you want to include this headdress in the exhibit. Study the headdress carefully to see how much you can learn about the Kwakiutl, the people who made it.

▲ This headdress was used by the Kwakiutl in religious ceremonies. Carved of red cedar and painted, it shows a thunderbird, the highest of the spirits in the Kwakiutl religion. Like a huge eagle, the thunderbird flew high in the sky. When it was hungry, it swooped down to catch and eat killer whales.

EXAMINING *the* ISSUES

- **What does the figure represented by the headdress and the materials used to make it tell you about Kwakiutl culture?**

- **How else might you find out information about this culture?**

Discuss these questions with your classmates. Think about the kinds of information you have learned about other cultures that did not have a written language. As you read this chapter, examine the symbolic objects made by different peoples of the Americas. Think about what these objects reveal about the various cultures.

North American Societies

MAIN IDEA	WHY IT MATTERS NOW	TERMS & NAMES
CULTURAL INTERACTION Complex North American societies were linked to each other through culture and economics.	Traditions and ideas from these cultures became part of the cultures of North America.	• potlatch • Mississippian • Anasazi • Iroquois • pueblo • totem

SETTING THE STAGE Between 40,000 and 12,000 years ago, hunter-gatherers migrated across the Bering Strait land bridge from Asia and began to populate the Americas. Migrating southward, those first Americans reached the southern tip of South America by somewhere between 12,000 and 7000 B.C. At the same time, they began to spread out east and west across North America. Over the centuries, the early North American peoples adapted to their environment, creating a very diverse set of cultures.

Complex Societies in the West

In some ways, the early North American cultures were less developed than those of South America and Mesoamerica. The North American groups created no great empires. They left few ruins as spectacular as those of ancient Mexico or Peru. Nevertheless, the first peoples of North America did create complex societies. These societies were able to conduct long-distance trade and construct magnificent buildings.

hmhsocialstudies.com
TAKING NOTES
Use the graphic organizer online to take notes on the Native Americans of the Northwest and the Southwest.

Cultures of Abundance The Pacific Northwest—from Oregon to Alaska—was rich in resources and supported a sizable population. To the Kwakiutl, Nootka, and Haida peoples, the most important resource was the sea. (See the map on page 442.) They hunted whales in canoes. Some canoes were large enough to carry at least 15 people. In addition to the many resources of the sea, the coastal forest provided plentiful food. In this abundant environment, the Northwest Coast tribes developed societies in which differences in wealth created social classes. Families displayed their rank and prosperity in an elaborate ceremony called the **potlatch** (PAHT•LACH). In this ceremony, they gave food, drink, and gifts to the community.

Accomplished Builders The dry, desert lands of the Southwest were a much harsher environment than the temperate Pacific coastlands. However, as early as 1500 B.C., the peoples of the Southwest were beginning to farm the land. Among the most successful of these early farmers were the Hohokam (huh•HOH•kuhm) of central Arizona. (See the map on page 439.) They used irrigation to produce harvests of corn, beans, and squash. Their use of pottery rather than baskets, as well as certain religious rituals, showed contact with Mesoamerican peoples to the south.

Inuit

Arctic Circle

Kutchin

Dogrib

Inuit

Aleut

Slave

Tlingit

Hudson Bay

Inuit

Haida

Cree

Montagnais

Kwakiutl

Nootka

Salish

Blackfeet

Ojibwa

Algonquin

Chinook

Nez Perce

Mandan

Huron

Abenaki

Coos

Crow

Lakota

Cheyenne

Mississippi R.

Iroquois

Shoshone

Illinois

Miami

Delaware

Cayuga, Mohawk, Oneida, Onondaga, Seneca

40°N

Pomo

Arapaho

Kiowa

Shawnee

Miwok

Ute

Apache

Cherokee

Chumash

Hopi

Navajo

Comanche

Muskogee (Creek)

PACIFIC OCEAN

Tohono O'odham

Zuni

Natchez

Timucua

ATLANTIC OCEAN

Cochimi

Rio Grande

Gulf of Mexico

Tropic of Cancer

160°W

120°W

80°W

Aztec

Maya

Mixtec

Caribbean Sea

0°

N

0   1,000 Miles

0   2,000 Kilometers

Native American Cultures

- Arctic
- Subarctic
- Northwest Coast
- Plateau
- Great Basin
- California
- Southwest
- Great Plains
- Northeast
- Southeast
- Mesoamerica

Kiowa Tribe name

GEOGRAPHY SKILLBUILDER: Interpreting Maps

1. **Region** Which Native American culture groups had the largest number of tribes?
2. **Human-Environment Interaction** In which culture areas would movement of trade goods be made easier by river and lake connections?

A people to the north—the **Anasazi** (AH•nuh•SAH•zee)—also influenced the Hohokam. They lived in the Four Corners region, where the present-day states of Utah, Arizona, Colorado, and New Mexico meet. The Anasazi built impressive cliff dwellings, such as the ones at Mesa Verde, Colorado. These large houses were built on top of mesas—flat-topped hills—or in shallow caves in the sheer walls of deep canyons. By the A.D. 900s, the Anasazi were living in **pueblos** (PWEHB•lohs), villages of large, apartment-style compounds made of stone and adobe, or sun-baked clay.

The largest Anasazi pueblo, begun around A.D. 900, was Pueblo Bonito, a Spanish name meaning "beautiful village." Its construction required a high degree of social organization and inventiveness. The Anasazi relied on human labor to quarry sandstone from the canyon walls and move it to the site. Skilled builders then used a mudlike mortar to construct walls up to five stories high. Windows were small to keep

▲ Cliff Palace, Mesa Verde, had 217 rooms and 23 kivas.

out the burning sun. When completed, Pueblo Bonito probably housed about 1,000 people and contained more than 600 rooms. In addition, a number of underground or partly underground ceremonial chambers called kivas (KEE•vuhs) were used for a variety of religious practices.

Many Anasazi pueblos were abandoned around 1200, possibly because of a prolonged drought. The descendants of the Anasazi, the Pueblo peoples, continued many of their customs. Pueblo groups like the Hopi and Zuni used kivas for religious ceremonies. They also created beautiful pottery and woven blankets. They traded these, along with corn and other farm products, with Plains Indians to the east, who supplied bison meat and hides. These nomadic Plains tribes eventually became known by such names as the Comanche, Kiowa, and Apache.

Mound Builders and Other Woodland Cultures

Beyond the Great Plains, in the woodlands east of the Mississippi River, other ancient peoples—the Mound Builders—were creating their own unique traditions. (See the map on page 439.) Beginning around 700 B.C., a culture known as the Adena began to build huge earthen mounds in which they buried their dead. Mounds that held the bodies of tribal leaders often were filled with gifts, such as finely crafted copper and stone objects.

Some 500 years later, the Hopewell culture also began building burial mounds. Their mounds were much larger and more plentiful than those of the Adena. Some of the Hopewell mounds may have been used for purposes other than burials. For example, the Great Serpent Mound, near Hillsboro, Ohio, may have played a part in Hopewell religious ceremonies.

The last Mound Builder culture, the **Mississippian**, lasted from around A.D. 800 until the arrival of Europeans in the 1500s. These people created thriving villages based on farming and trade. Between 1000 and 1200, perhaps as many as 30,000

▲ Great Serpent Mound runs some 1,300 feet along its coils and is between 4 and 5 feet high.

people lived at Cahokia (kuh•HOH•kee•uh), the leading site of Mississippian culture. Cahokia was led by priest-rulers, who regulated farming activities. The heart of the community was a 100-foot-high, flat-topped earthen pyramid, which was crowned by a wooden temple.

These Mississippian lands were located in a crossroads region between east and west. They enjoyed easy transportation on the Mississippi and Ohio rivers. Items found in burial mounds show that the Mississippians had traded with peoples in the West and, possibly, Mesoamerica. Similar evidence shows that they also came into contact with peoples from the Northeast.

Northeastern Tribes Build Alliances The northeastern woodlands tribes developed a variety of cultures. The woodlands peoples often clashed with each other over land. In some areas, tribes formed political alliances to ensure protection of tribal lands. The best example of a political alliance was the **Iroquois** (IHR•uh•KWOY), a group of tribes speaking related languages living in the eastern Great Lakes region. In the late 1500s, five of these tribes in upper New York—the Mohawk, Oneida, Onondaga, Cayuga, and Seneca—formed the Iroquois League. According to legend, Chief Hiawatha helped to create this league. His goal was to promote joint defense and cooperation among the tribes. **A**

Cultural Connections

The Iroquois alliance was a notable example of a political link among early North American peoples. For the most part, however, the connections between native North Americans were economic and cultural. They traded, had similar religious beliefs, and shared social patterns.

Trading Networks Tie Tribes Together Trade was a major factor linking the peoples of North America. Along the Columbia River in Oregon, the Chinook people established a lively marketplace that brought together trade goods from all over the West. And the Mississippian trade network stretched from the Rocky Mountains to the Atlantic coast and from the Great Lakes to the Gulf of Mexico.

Religion Shapes Views of Life Another feature that linked early Americans was their religious beliefs. Nearly all native North Americans believed that the world around them was filled with nature spirits. Most Native Americans recognized a number of sacred spirits. Some groups held up one supreme being, or Great Spirit, above all others. North American peoples believed that the spirits gave them rituals and customs to guide them in their lives and to satisfy their basic needs. If people practiced these rituals, they would live in peace and harmony.

MAIN IDEA

Drawing Conclusions

A Of what value would a political alliance be to an individual tribe?

Native American religious beliefs also included great respect for the land as the source of life. Native Americans used the land but tried to alter it as little as possible. The land was sacred, not something that could be bought and sold. Later, when Europeans claimed land in North America, the issue of land ownership created conflict.

Shared Social Patterns The family was the basis for social organization for Native Americans. Generally, the family unit was the extended family, including parents, children, grandparents, and other close relatives. Some tribes further organized families into clans, groups of families descended from a common ancestor. In some tribes, clan members lived together in large houses or groups of houses.

Common among Native American clans was the use of **totems** (TOH•tuhmz). The term refers to a natural object with which an individual, clan, or group identifies itself. The totem was used as a symbol of the unity of a group or clan. It also helped define certain behaviors and the social relationships of a group. The term comes from an Ojibwa word, but refers to a cultural practice found throughout the Americas. For example, Northwestern peoples displayed totem symbols on masks, boats, and huge poles set in front of their houses. Others used totem symbols in rituals or dances associated with important group events such as marriages, the naming of children, or the planting or harvesting of crops. **B**

There were hundreds of different patterns of Native American life in North America. Some societies were small and dealt with life in a limited region of the vast North American continent. Other groups were much larger, and were linked by trade and culture to other groups in North America and Mesoamerica. As you will learn in Section 2, peoples in Mesoamerica and South America also lived in societies that varied from simple to complex. Three of these cultures—the Maya, the Aztec, and the Incan—would develop very sophisticated ways of life.

MAIN IDEA

Making Inferences

B What artificial symbols are used by nations or organizations in a way similar to totems?

Social History

Iroquois Women

Iroquois society was matrilineal. This means that all Iroquois traced their descent through their female ancestors. Clans of the mother controlled property, held ceremonies, and determined official titles.

The ability to grant titles to men was handed down from mother to daughter. The most important title given to men was that of "sachem," the peace, or civil, chief.

A council of sachems met once a year to decide on war and peace and other important matters. Since sachems could not go to war, they appointed warriors to lead a war party. Thus, in a way women had a say in warfare in the Iroquois tribes.

SECTION 1 ASSESSMENT

TERMS & NAMES 1. For each term or name, write a sentence explaining its significance.
- potlatch
- Anasazi
- pueblo
- Mississippian
- Iroquois
- totem

USING YOUR NOTES

2. How did environment affect the development of the cultures of the Northwest Coast and the Southwest?

Northwest Coast

Both

Southwest

MAIN IDEAS

3. What was the most important resource for the peoples of the Northwest? Why?

4. For what purpose did the Mound Builder cultures use earthen mounds?

5. Why did the tribes of upper New York form a political alliance?

CRITICAL THINKING & WRITING

6. **ANALYZING MOTIVES** Why might the people of the Northwest consider the potlatch to be a good way to signal social standing and wealth?

7. **ANALYZING CAUSES** Why might location have been important to the power and wealth of the Mississippian culture?

8. **COMPARING** In what ways did the peoples of North America share similar cultural patterns?

9. **WRITING ACTIVITY** CULTURAL INTERACTION Write a brief **essay** detailing the evidence that shows how societies in North America interacted with each other.

MULTIMEDIA ACTIVITY WRITING AN ILLUSTRATED REPORT

Use the Internet to research one of the Native American groups discussed in this section. Use your findings to write an **illustrated report.** Focus your report on how the group lives today.

INTERNET KEYWORD
Native American Nations

Maya Kings and Cities

MAIN IDEA	WHY IT MATTERS NOW	TERMS & NAMES
RELIGIOUS AND ETHICAL SYSTEMS The Maya developed a highly complex civilization based on city-states and elaborate religious practices.	Descendants of the Maya still occupy the same territory.	• Tikal • codex • glyph • *Popol Vuh*

SETTING THE STAGE In the early centuries A.D., most North American peoples were beginning to develop complex societies. Further south, the peoples of Mexico and Central America were entering into the full flower of civilization. A prime example of this cultural flowering were the Maya, who built an extraordinary civilization in the heart of Mesoamerica.

Maya Create City-States

hmhsocialstudies.com
TAKING NOTES

Use the graphic organizer online to take notes on the major features of the Maya civilization.

The homeland of the Maya stretched from southern Mexico into northern Central America. This area includes a highland region and a lowland region. The lowlands lie to the north. They include the dry scrub forest of the Yucatán (YOO•kuh•TAN) Peninsula and the dense, steamy jungles of southeastern Mexico and northern Guatemala. The highlands are further south—a range of cool, cloud-wreathed mountains that stretch from southern Mexico to El Salvador.

While the Olmec were building their civilization along the Gulf Coast in the period from 1200 B.C. to 400 B.C., the Maya were also evolving. (See Chapter 9.) They took on Olmec influences, blending these with local customs. By A.D. 250, Maya culture had burst forth in a flourishing civilization.

Urban Centers The period from A.D. 250 to 900 is known as the Classic Period of Maya civilization. During this time, the Maya built spectacular cities such as **Tikal** (tee•KAHL), a major center in northern Guatemala. Other important sites included Copán, Palenque, Uxmal, and Chichén Itzá (chee•CHEHN ee•TSAH). (See the map on page 447.) Each of these was an independent city-state, ruled by a god-king and serving as a center for religious ceremonies and trade. Maya cities featured giant pyramids, temples, palaces, and elaborate stone carvings dedicated to the gods and to important rulers. Tens of thousands of people lived in residential areas surrounding the city center, which bustled with activity.

Archaeologists have identified at least 50 major Maya sites, all with monumental architecture. For example, Temple IV pyramid at Tikal stretched 212 feet into the jungle sky. In addition to temples and pyramids, each

▼ Maya jade death mask, seventh century A.D.

Maya city featured a ball court. In this stone-sided playing field, the Maya played a game that had religious and political significance. The Maya believed the playing of this game would maintain the cycles of the sun and moon and bring life-giving rains. **A**

MAIN IDEA

Drawing Conclusions

A What does the ability to construct complex buildings reveal about a society?

Agriculture and Trade Support Cities

Although the Maya city-states were independent of each other, they were linked through alliances and trade. Cities exchanged their local products such as salt, flint, feathers, shells, and honey. They also traded craft goods like cotton textiles and jade ornaments. While the Maya did not have a uniform currency, cacao (chocolate) beans sometimes served as one.

As in the rest of Mesoamerica, agriculture—particularly the growing of maize, beans, and squash—provided the basis for Maya life. For years, experts assumed that the Maya practiced slash-and-burn agriculture. This method involves farmers clearing the land by burning existing vegetation and planting crops in the ashes. Evidence now shows, however, that the Maya also developed more sophisticated methods, including planting on raised beds above swamps and on hillside terraces.

Kingdoms Built on Dynasties Successful farming methods led to the accumulation of wealth and the development of social classes. The noble class, which included priests and the leading warriors, occupied the top rung of Maya society. Below them came merchants and those with specialized knowledge, such as skilled artisans. Finally, at the bottom, came the peasant majority.

The Maya king sat at the top of this class structure. He was regarded as a holy figure, and his position was hereditary. When he died, he passed the throne on to his eldest son. Other sons of the ruler might expect to join the priesthood.

Religion Shapes Maya Life

Religion influenced most aspects of Maya life. The Maya believed in many gods. There were gods of corn, of death, of rain, and of war. Gods could be good or evil, and sometimes both. Gods also were associated with the four directions and with different colors: white for north, black for west, yellow for south, red for east, and green in the center. The Maya believed that each day was a living god whose behavior could be predicted with the help of a system of calendars.

Religious Practices The Maya worshiped their gods in various ways. They prayed and made offerings of food, flowers, and incense. They also pierced and cut their bodies and offered their blood, believing that this would nourish the gods. Sometimes the Maya even carried out human sacrifice, usually of captured enemies. At Chichén Itzá, they threw captives into a deep sinkhole lake, called a *cenote* (say•NO•tay), along with gold, jade, and other offerings. The Maya believed

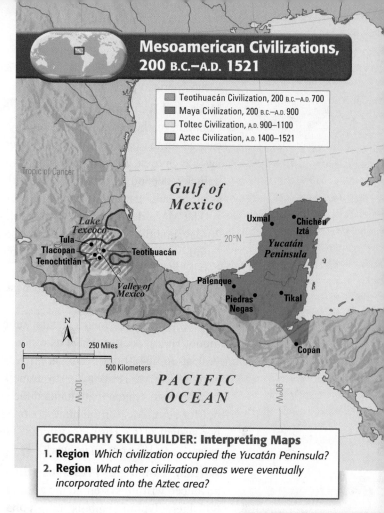

Mesoamerican Civilizations, 200 B.C.–A.D. 1521

- Teotihuacán Civilization, 200 B.C.–A.D. 700
- Maya Civilization, 200 B.C.–A.D. 900
- Toltec Civilization, A.D. 900–1100
- Aztec Civilization, A.D. 1400–1521

GEOGRAPHY SKILLBUILDER: Interpreting Maps
1. **Region** Which civilization occupied the Yucatán Peninsula?
2. **Region** What other civilization areas were eventually incorporated into the Aztec area?

VIDEO
Mexico's Ancient Civilizations

hmhsocialstudies.com

that human sacrifice pleased the gods and kept the world in balance. Nevertheless, the Maya's use of sacrifice never reached the extremes of some other Mesoamerican peoples.

Math and Religion Maya religious beliefs also led to the development of the calendar, mathematics, and astronomy. The Maya believed that time was a burden carried on the back of a god. At the end of a day, month, or year, one god would lay the burden down and another would pick it up. A day would be lucky or unlucky, depending on the nature of the god. So it was very important to have an accurate calendar to know which god was in charge of the day.

The Maya developed a 260-day religious calendar, which consisted of thirteen 20-day months. A second 365-day solar calendar consisted of eighteen 20-day months, with a separate period of 5 days at the end. The two calendars were linked together like meshed gears so that any given day could be identified in both cycles. The calendar helped identify the best times to plant crops, attack enemies, and crown new rulers.

The Maya based their calendar on careful observation of the planets, sun, and moon. Highly skilled Maya astronomers and mathematicians calculated the solar year at 365.2420 days. This is only .0002 of a day short of the figure generally accepted today! The Maya astronomers were able to attain such great precision by using a math system that included the concept of zero. The Maya used a shell symbol for zero, dots for the numbers one to four, and a bar for five. The Maya number system was a base-20 system. They used the numerical system primarily for calendar and astronomical work. **B**

MAIN IDEA

Making Inferences

B How are math, astronomy, and calendars related?

Written Language Preserves History The Maya also developed the most advanced writing system in the ancient Americas. Maya writing consisted of about 800 hieroglyphic symbols, or **glyphs** (glihfs). Some of these glyphs stood for whole words, and others represented syllables. The Maya used their writing system to record important historical events, carving their glyphs in stone or recording them in a bark-paper book known as a **codex** (KOH•DEHKS). Only three of these ancient books have survived.

Other original books telling of Maya history and customs do exist, however. Maya peoples wrote down their history after the arrival of the Spanish. The most famous of these books, the ***Popol Vuh*** (POH•pohl VOO), recounts the Highland Maya's version of the story of creation. "Before the world was created, Calm and Silence were the great kings that ruled," reads the first sentence in the book. "Nothing existed, there was nothing."

▼ A detail from the Maya *Codex Troano*

PRIMARY SOURCE
Then let the emptiness fill! they said. Let the water weave its way downward so the earth can show its face! Let the light break on the ridges, let the sky fill up with the yellow light of dawn! Let our glory be a man walking on a path through the trees! "Earth!" the Creators called. They called only once, and it was there, from a mist, from a cloud of dust, the mountains appeared instantly.

From the Popol Vuh

Rise and Fall of the Maya

Traits of Civilization	Strength Leading to Power	Weakness Leading to Decline
Religious beliefs and theocracy	United culture that is loyal to the king	Many physical and human resources funneled into religious activities
Independent city-states	Wealthy and prosperous urban centers	Frequent warfare occurs between city-states
Intensive agriculture	Production of more food feeds a larger population	Population growth creates need for more land

SKILLBUILDER: Interpreting Charts
1. **Recognizing Effects** *Which trait aids in building a sense of loyalty to the ruler?*
2. **Drawing Conclusions** *How can intensive agriculture be both a strength and a weakness?*

HISTORY

VIDEO
A Civilization Abandoned

↗ hmhsocialstudies.com

Mysterious Maya Decline

The remarkable history of the Maya ended in mystery. In the late 800s, the Maya suddenly abandoned many of their cities. Invaders from the north, the Toltec, moved into the lands occupied by the Maya. These warlike peoples from central Mexico changed the culture. The high civilization of Maya cities like Tikal and Copán disappeared.

No one knows exactly why this happened, though experts offer several overlapping theories. By the 700s, warfare had broken out among the various Maya city-states. Increased warfare disrupted trade and produced economic hardship. In addition, population growth and over-farming may have damaged the environment, and this led to food shortages, famine, and disease. By the time the Spanish arrived in the early 1500s, the Maya were divided into small, weak city-states that gave little hint of their former glory. **C**

As the Maya civilization faded, other peoples of Mesoamerica were growing in strength and sophistication. Like the Maya, these peoples would trace some of their ancestry to the Olmec. Eventually, these people would dominate the Valley of Mexico and lands beyond it, as you will learn in Section 3.

MAIN IDEA

Analyzing Causes
C Why did the Maya civilization go into decline?

SECTION 2 ASSESSMENT

TERMS & NAMES 1. For each term or name, write a sentence explaining its significance.
- Tikal   • glyph   • codex   • *Popol Vuh*

USING YOUR NOTES	MAIN IDEAS	CRITICAL THINKING & WRITING
2. How do the characteristics of Maya civilization compare with the characteristics of a typical civilization?	3. What was the basis of Maya life? 4. Why was the calendar important for the Maya religion? 5. What three explanations have been given for the collapse of the Maya civilization?	6. **RECOGNIZING EFFECTS** Why was trade important to the Maya civilization? 7. **DRAWING CONCLUSIONS** How important do you think the development of advanced mathematics was in the creation of the Maya calendar? 8. **ANALYZING CAUSES** Which of the causes for the fall of the Maya do you think was most important? Explain. 9. **WRITING ACTIVITY** RELIGIOUS AND ETHICAL SYSTEMS Imagine that you are a reporter visiting Maya city-states. Write a one-page **news article** that describes various aspects of the Maya religion.

The Maya Civilization in Mesoamerica
Supporting detail
Supporting detail

CONNECT TO TODAY **CREATING A MAP**

Conduct research to discover the countries in which the modern Maya live. Use your findings to create a **map** showing the areas within these countries occupied by the Maya.

Maya Architecture

Maya architects created beautiful and monumental structures. The buildings are artistic in structure, as well as in ornamentation. The style and complexity of the ornamentation varies by region, but narrative, ceremonial, and celestial themes are common. Archaeologists and tourists alike are still awed by Maya architecture.

These large structures seem to be designed for ceremonial or religious purposes and dominate the landscapes of the cities. The most recognizable structures are the pyramids, but there is much more to the artful Maya architecture.

↗ hmhsocialstudies.com

RESEARCH WEB LINKS Go online for more on Maya architecture.

▲ **Detailing**
One characteristic of Maya architecture is the exterior and interior ornamental detailing. This two-headed jaguar throne was found at Uxmal. It represents the jaguar god of the underworld, one of the many Maya gods. An ancient Maya manuscript lists over 160 gods.

◄ **Stele**
A stele (STEE•lee) is an inscribed or carved marker that is often used to mark special dates or as a building marker. This stele is in the Maya city of Copán and is part of a series of finely carved commemorative steles in the great plaza. The 13th king is represented on most of the steles in ceremonial clothing.

▲ **Ball Court**

Ball courts were a feature of ancient Maya cities. The games held deep religious significance, and the same artistic detail is found in the ball courts as in other religious structures. The court shown here is at Chichén Itzá in modern Mexico. It is 545 feet long and 223 feet wide, and is the largest in the Americas. The ornate hoop (above left) is 20 feet off the ground.

The exact rules and method of scoring the game are unknown. However, inscriptions indicate that players could not use their hands or feet to move a solid rubber ball, and that members of the losing team might be sacrificed by beheading.

◀ **Pyramid**

Archaeologists have found pyramids at many Maya cities. Pyramids were religious structures and, as in Egypt, could be used as tombs. The pyramid shown here is known as Temple I in the Maya city of Tikal. It is the tomb of Ha Sawa Chaan K'awil, a Tikal ruler. The pyramid is about 160 feet tall. Another pyramid in the city is 212 feet tall. In fact, the Tikal pyramids were the tallest structures in the Americas until 1903, when the Flatiron Building was built in New York City.

Connect *to* Today

1. **Making Inferences** What does the size and ornamentation of Maya architecture indicate about their society?

   See Skillbuilder Handbook, Page R10.

2. **Comparing and Contrasting** What are some examples of large-scale architecture in the United States? What do they indicate about our culture?

451

The Aztecs Control Central Mexico

MAIN IDEA	WHY IT MATTERS NOW	TERMS & NAMES
POWER AND AUTHORITY Through alliances and conquest, the Aztecs created a powerful empire in Mexico.	This time period saw the origins of one of the 20th century's most populous cities, Mexico City.	• obsidian • Quetzalcoatl • Triple Alliance • Montezuma II

SETTING THE STAGE While the Maya were developing their civilization to the south, other high cultures were evolving in central Mexico. Some of the most important developments took place in and around the Valley of Mexico. This valley, where modern Mexico City is located, eventually became the site of the greatest empire of Mesoamerica, the Aztec. The Aztecs were preceded by two other important civilizations that traced their ancestry to the Olmec and Zapotec. You learned about the Olmec and Zapotec in Chapter 9.

The Valley of Mexico

TAKING NOTES
Use the graphic organizer online to take notes on the establishment and growth of the Aztec Empire.

The Valley of Mexico, a mountain basin about 7,500 feet above sea level, served as the home base of several powerful cultures. The valley had several large, shallow lakes at its center, accessible resources, and fertile soil. These advantages attracted the people of Teotihuacán (TAY•oh•TEE•wah•KAHN) and the Toltecs. They settled in the valley and developed advanced civilizations that controlled much of the area. (See the map on page 447.)

An Early City-State The first major civilization of central Mexico was Teotihuacán, a city-state whose ruins lie just outside Mexico City. In the first century A.D., villagers at this site began to plan and construct a monumental city, even larger than Monte Albán, in Oaxaca.

At its peak in the sixth century, Teotihuacán had a population of between 150,000 and 200,000 people, making it one of the largest cities in the world at the time. The heart of the city was a central avenue lined with more than 20 pyramids dedicated to various gods. The biggest of these was the giant Pyramid of the Sun. This imposing building stood more than 200 feet tall and measured close to 3,000 feet around its base. The people of Teotihuacán lived in apartment-block buildings in the area around the central avenue.

Teotihuacán became the center of a thriving trade network that extended far into Central America. The

▼ Quetzalcoatl was a god for many ancient Mexican civilizations.

city's most valuable trade item was **obsidian** (ahb•SIHD•ee•uhn), a green or black volcanic glass found in the Valley of Mexico and used to make razor-sharp weapons. There is no evidence that Teotihuacán conquered its neighbors or tried to create an empire. However, evidence of art styles and religious beliefs from Teotihuacán have been found throughout Mesoamerica.

After centuries of growth, the city abruptly declined. Historians believe this decline was due either to an invasion by outside forces or conflict among the city's ruling classes. Regardless of the causes, the city was virtually abandoned by 750. The vast ruins astonished later settlers in the area, who named the site Teotihuacán, which means "City of the Gods."

Toltecs Take Over After the fall of Teotihuacán, no single culture dominated central Mexico for decades. Then around 900, a new people—the Toltecs—rose to power. For the next three centuries, the Toltecs ruled over the heart of Mexico from their capital at Tula. (See the map on page 447.) Like other Mesoamericans, they built pyramids and temples. They also carved tall pillars in the shape of armed warriors.

In fact, the Toltecs were an extremely warlike people whose empire was based on conquest. They worshiped a fierce war god who demanded blood and human sacrifice from his followers. Sometime after 1000, a Toltec ruler named Topiltzin (toh•PEELT•zeen) tried to change the Toltec religion. He called on the Toltec people to end the practice of human sacrifice. He also encouraged them to worship a different god, **Quetzalcoatl** (keht•SAHL•koh•AHT•uhl), or the Feathered Serpent. Followers of the war god rebelled, however, forcing Topiltzin and his followers into exile on the Yucatán Peninsula. There, they greatly influenced late-Mayan culture. After Topiltzin's exile, Toltec power began to decline. By the early 1200s, their reign over the Valley of Mexico had ended. **(A)**

In time, Topiltzin and Quetzalcoatl became one in the legends of the people of the Valley of Mexico. According to these legends, after his exile from Tula, the god traveled east, crossing the sea on a raft of snakes. He would return one day, bringing a new reign of light and peace. The story of Quetzalcoatl would come back to haunt the greatest empire of Mexico, the Aztecs.

The Aztec Empire

The Aztecs arrived in the Valley of Mexico around A.D. 1200. The valley contained a number of small city-states that had survived the collapse of Toltec rule. The Aztecs, who were then called the Mexica, were a poor, nomadic people from the harsh deserts of northern Mexico. Fierce and ambitious, they soon adapted to local ways, finding work as soldiers-for-hire to local rulers.

▲ The Pyramid of the Sun (left background) dominates Teotihuacán's main highway, the Avenue of the Dead.

MAIN IDEA

Making Inferences

A) Why might the followers of the war god rebel against Topiltzin?

People and Empires in the Americas **453**

According to one of the Aztec legends, the god of the sun and warfare, Huitzilopochtli (wee•tsee•loh•POHCH•tlee), told them to found a city of their own. He said to look for a place where an eagle perched on a cactus, holding a snake in its mouth. These words capture part of the legend:

PRIMARY SOURCE
The place where the eagle screams,
where he spreads his wings;
the place where he feeds,
where the fish jump,
where the serpents
coil up and hiss!
This shall be Mexico Tenochtitlán
and many things shall happen!

Crónica Mexicayotl

They found such a place on a small island in Lake Texcoco, at the center of the valley. There, in 1325, they founded their city, which they named Tenochtitlán (teh•NOCH•tee•TLAHN).

Aztecs Grow Stronger Over the years, the Aztecs gradually increased in strength and number. In 1428, they joined with two other city-states—Texcoco and Tlacopan—to form the **Triple Alliance**. This alliance became the leading power in the Valley of Mexico and soon gained control over neighboring regions. By the early 1500s, they controlled a vast empire that covered some 80,000 square miles stretching from central Mexico to the Atlantic and Pacific coasts and south into Oaxaca. This empire was divided into 38 provinces. It had an estimated population of between 5 and 15 million people.

The Aztecs based their power on military conquest and the tribute they gained from their conquered subjects. The Aztecs generally exercised loose control over the empire, often letting local rulers govern their own regions. The Aztecs did demand tribute, however, in the form of gold, maize, cacao beans, cotton, jade, and other products. If local rulers failed to pay tribute, or offered any other kind of resistance, the Aztecs responded brutally. They destroyed the rebellious villages and captured or slaughtered the inhabitants. **B**

Nobles Rule Aztec Society At the height of the Aztec Empire, military leaders held great power in Aztec society. Along with government officials and priests, these military leaders made up the noble class. Many nobles owned vast estates, which they ruled over like lords, living a life of great wealth and luxury.

There were two other broad classes in Aztec society, commoners and enslaved persons. Commoners included merchants, artisans, soldiers, and farmers who owned their own land. The merchants formed a special type of elite. They often traveled widely, acting as spies for the emperor and gaining great wealth for themselves. The lowest class, enslaved persons, were captives who did many different jobs.

The emperor sat atop the Aztec social pyramid. Although he sometimes consulted with top generals or officials, his power was absolute. The emperor lived in a magnificent

MAIN IDEA

Comparing

B How were the Aztecs' methods of controlling the empire like those of other empires you have read about?

Global Patterns

Warriors and Animal Symbols
Some of the highest-ranking Aztec leaders were eagle warriors. (A statue of an eagle warrior is shown above.) In battle, they wore eagle costumes in honor of the sun god, Huitzilopochtli, who often took the form of an eagle.

The use of animal symbols by warriors was a widespread practice in ancient times. The eagle was a favorite among Roman soldiers because they thought it symbolized victory. In many cultures, warriors adopted an animal so that they would inherit the animal's qualities. Celtic fighters, for example, wore boars' heads on their helmets so that they, like the boar, would be strong and fearless. Similarly, many African warriors adopted the lion for its fighting ferocity.

↗ hmhsocialstudies.com

INTERNET ACTIVITY Go online to plan a Web page on animal symbols used by ancient warriors.

palace, surrounded by servants and his wives. Visitors—even nobles—entered his presence in bare feet and cast their eyes down so as not to look at him.

Tenochtitlán: A Planned City

By the early 1500s, Tenochtitlán had become an extraordinary urban center. With a population of between 200,000 and 400,000 people, it was larger than London or any other European capital of the time. Tenochtitlán remained on its original island site. To connect the island to the mainland, Aztec engineers built three raised roads, called causeways, over the water and marshland. Other smaller cities ringed the lake, creating a dense concentration of people in the Valley of Mexico.

Streets and broad avenues connected the city center with outlying residential districts. The canals that intersected with these roadways allowed canoes to bring people directly into the city center. Canoes also brought goods from the farthest reaches of the empire to the economic heart of the city, the huge market of Tlatelolco (TLAH•tehl•AWL•koh). Visitors to the market also found a great deal of local agricultural produce on display, including avocados, beans, chili peppers, corn, squash, and tomatoes. Most of the fruits and vegetables sold at the market were grown on *chinampas,* farm plots built on the marshy fringes of the lake. These plots, sometimes called "floating gardens," were extremely productive, providing the food needed for a huge urban population.

At the center of the city was a massive, walled complex, filled with palaces, temples, and government buildings. The main structure in the complex was the Great Temple. This giant pyramid with twin temples at the top, one dedicated to the sun god and the other to the rain god, served as the center of Aztec religious life.

> Analyzing Primary Sources

The Market at Tlatelolco

Hernando Cortés, the Spanish conqueror of Mexico, noted that the market at Tlatelolco was twice the size of the market at Salamanca, the Spanish city where he had attended university.

PRIMARY SOURCE

Day after day 60,000 people congregate here to buy and sell. Every imaginable kind of merchandise is available from all parts of the Empire, foodstuffs and dress, . . . gold, silver, copper, . . . precious stones, leather, bone, mussels, coral, cotton, feathers. . . . Everything is sold by the piece or by measurement, never by weight. In the main market there is a law court in which there are always ten or twelve judges performing their office and taking decisions on all marketing controversies.

HERNANDO CORTÉS, *Letters of Information*

Tenochtitlán—A Bustling City

Bernal Díaz, one of Cortés's soldiers, was amazed to find a bustling urban center in the heart of Mexico.

PRIMARY SOURCE

When we saw all those cities and villages built in the water, and other great towns on dry land, and that straight and level causeway leading to Mexico, we were astounded. These great towns and cues [pyramids] and buildings rising from the water, all made of stone, seemed like an enchanted vision. . . . Indeed, some of our soldiers asked whether it was not all a dream.

BERNAL DÍAZ, *The Conquest of New Spain*

DOCUMENT-BASED QUESTIONS

1. **Contrasting** *How do the descriptions of Cortés and Díaz differ?*
2. **Making Inferences** *How do you think Cortés and Díaz feel about Aztec accomplishments?*

Religion Rules Aztec Life

Religion played a major role in Aztec society. Tenochtitlán contained hundreds of temples and religious structures dedicated to the approximately 1,000 gods that the Aztecs worshiped. The Aztecs adopted many of these gods, and religious practices related to them, from other Mesoamerican peoples. For example, the Aztecs worshiped the Toltec god Quetzalcoatl in many forms. They saw him as the god of learning and books, the god of the wind, and a symbol of death and rebirth. The Aztecs pictured Quetzalcoatl not only as a feathered serpent, but also as a pale-skinned man with a beard.

▲ This mural, in the National Palace in Mexico City, shows Quetzalcoatl in many forms.

Religious Practices Aztec religious practices centered on elaborate public ceremonies designed to communicate with the gods and win their favor. At these ceremonies, priests made offerings to the gods and presented ritual dramas, songs, and dances featuring masked performers. The Aztec ceremonial calendar was full of religious festivals, which varied according to the god being honored.

Sacrifices for the Sun God The most important rituals involved a sun god, Huitzilopochtli. According to Aztec belief, Huitzilopochtli made the sun rise every day. When the sun set, he had to battle the forces of evil to get to the next day. To make sure that he was strong enough for this ordeal, he needed the nourishment of human blood. Without regular offerings of human blood, Huitzilopochtli would be too weak to fight. The sun would not rise, the world would be plunged into darkness, and all life would perish. For this reason, Aztec priests practiced human sacrifice on a massive scale. Each year, thousands of victims were led to the altar atop the Great Temple, where priests carved out their hearts using obsidian knives.

Sacrificial victims included enslaved persons, criminals, and people offered as tribute by conquered provinces. Prisoners of war, however, were the preferred victims. As a result, the priests required a steady supply of war captives. This in turn pushed the Aztec military to carry out new conquests. In fact, the Aztecs often went to war not to conquer new lands, but simply to capture prisoners for sacrifice. They even adapted their battle tactics to ensure that they took their opponents alive. **C**

MAIN IDEA

Clarifying

C Why did the Aztecs take so many war captives?

Problems in the Aztec Empire

In 1502, a new ruler, **Montezuma II** (MAHN•tih•ZOO•muh), was crowned emperor. Under Montezuma, the Aztec Empire began to weaken. For nearly a century, the Aztecs had been demanding tribute and sacrificial victims from the provinces under their control. Now, with the population of Tenochtitlán growing ever greater, Montezuma called for even more tribute and sacrifice. A number of provinces rose

The Aztec Calendar

The Aztec system of tracking the days was very intricate. Archaeologists believe that the Aztec calendar system was derived from the Maya system. The Aztecs followed two main calendars: a sacred one with 13 months of 20 days and an agricultural or solar one with 18 months of 20 days. (Notice that this comes to 360 days. The Aztecs then had an unlucky five-day period known as *nemontemi*, making their solar calendar 365 days long.) Every 52 years, the two calendars would start on the same day, and a great ceremony of fire marked the occasion.

▲ Aztec Gods

The Aztecs worshiped many different gods. They were a vital part of the Aztec calendar and daily life. The Aztecs paid tribute to different gods depending, in part, on the day, week, month, year, and religious cycle of the Aztec calendars. The god shown here is a sun god, Tonatiuh.

◄ Aztec Sunstone

Originally located in the main ceremonial plaza of Tenochtitlán, the Aztec calendar stone measures 13 feet in diameter and weighs 24 tons. It was uncovered in Mexico City in 1790. The Sunstone, as it is called, contains a wealth of information about the days that began and ended the Aztec months, the gods associated with the days, and many other details.

This is an artist's rendition of the inner circle of the Sunstone. In the center is the god Tonatiuh.

The four squares that surround Tonatiuh are glyphs or symbols of the four ages preceding the time of the Aztecs: Tiger, Water, Wind, and Rain.

In the ring just outside the symbols of the previous ages, 20 segments represent the 20 days that made up an Aztec month. Each day had its own symbol and a god who watched over the day. The symbol pointed to here is Ocelotl, the jaguar.

SKILLBUILDER: Interpreting Visual Sources

1. **Hypothesizing** *Why do you think the Aztecs put Tonatiuh, a sun god, in the center of the Sunstone? Explain your reasons.*
2. **Comparing and Contrasting** *How is the Aztec calendar different from the calendar we use today? How is it similar?*

HISTORY

VIDEO
Aztecs: Culture of
Art and Death

hmhsocialstudies.com

Rise and Fall of the Aztecs		
Traits of Civilization	**Strength Leading to Power**	**Weakness Leading to Decline**
Religious beliefs and theocracy	United culture that is loyal to the emperor	Many physical and human resources funneled into religious activities
Powerful army	More land, power, and prisoners for religious sacrifices	Need for prisoners changes warfare style to less deadly and less aggressive
Empire of tribute states	Provides wealth and power and prisoners for religious sacrifice	Tribute states are rebellious and need to be controlled

SKILLBUILDER: Interpreting Charts
1. **Drawing Conclusions** *How was the tribute system both a strength and a weakness?*
2. **Clarifying** *How are the army and religious beliefs linked in the Aztec Empire?*

up against Aztec oppression. This began a period of unrest and rebellion, which the military struggled to put down.

Over time, Montezuma tried to lessen the pressure on the provinces. For example, he reduced the demand for tribute payment by cutting the number of officials in the Aztec government. But resentment continued to grow. Many Aztecs began to predict that terrible things were about to happen. They saw bad omens in every unusual occurrence—lightning striking a temple in Tenochtitlán, or a partial eclipse of the sun, for example. The most worrying event, however, was the arrival of the Spanish. For many Aztecs, these fair-skinned, bearded strangers from across the sea brought to mind the legend of the return of Quetzalcoatl. **D**

Further south in the high mountain valleys of the Andes, another empire was developing, one that would transcend the Aztec Empire in land area, power, and wealth. Like the Aztecs, the people of this Andean empire worshiped the sun and had large armies. However, the society they built was much different from that of the Aztecs, as you will see in Section 4.

MAIN IDEA

Making Inferences

D Why would cutting the number of government officials reduce the need for tribute money?

SECTION 3 ASSESSMENT

TERMS & NAMES 1. For each term or name, write a sentence explaining its significance.
• obsidian   • Quetzalcoatl   • Triple Alliance   • Montezuma II

USING YOUR NOTES	**MAIN IDEA**	**CRITICAL THINKING & WRITING**
2. How do you think the Aztecs were able to establish an extensive empire in such a relatively short period of time? Aztec Empire · main event	3. On what was Teotihuacán's power and wealth based? 4. How did the Aztecs rule their empire? 5. Why did the Aztecs think it was necessary to make blood sacrifices to the sun god, Huitzilopochtli?	6. **IDENTIFYING SOLUTIONS** How were the Aztecs able to overcome the problems associated with Tenochtitlán's island location? 7. **ANALYZING MOTIVES** Why do you think the Aztecs allowed some conquered peoples to govern themselves with relatively little interference? 8. **RECOGNIZING EFFECTS** How did the Aztec need for victims for sacrifice lead to problems controlling the empire? 9. **WRITING ACTIVITY** POWER AND AUTHORITY Write a short **play** in which Montezuma discusses with his advisers how to gain control of the empire's rebellious provinces.

CONNECT TO TODAY CREATING A MENU
Many of the foods eaten by Mexicans today date back to Aztec times. Conduct research to discover more about the Aztec origins of Mexican food. Use your findings to create a **menu** for a modern "Aztec" meal.

The Inca Create a Mountain Empire

MAIN IDEA	WHY IT MATTERS NOW	TERMS & NAMES
POWER AND AUTHORITY The Inca built a vast empire supported by taxes, governed by a bureaucracy, and linked by extensive road systems.	The Incan system of government was similar to some socialist governments in the 20th century.	• Pachacuti • ayllu • mita • quipu

SETTING THE STAGE While the Aztecs ruled in the Valley of Mexico, another people—the Inca—created an equally powerful state in South America. From Cuzco, their capital in southern Peru, the Inca spread outward in all directions. They brought various Andean peoples under their control and built an empire that stretched from Ecuador in the north to Chile in the south. It was the largest empire ever seen in the Americas.

The Inca Build an Empire

Like the Aztecs, the Inca built their empire on cultural foundations thousands of years old. (See Chapter 9.) Ancient civilizations such as Chavín, Moche, and Nazca had already established a tradition of high culture in Peru. They were followed by the Huari and Tiahuanaco cultures of southern Peru and Bolivia. The Chimú, an impressive civilization of the 1300s based in the northern coastal region once controlled by the Moche, came next. The Inca would create an even more powerful state, however, extending their rule over the entire Andean region.

Incan Beginnings The Inca originally lived in a high plateau of the Andes. After wandering the highlands for years, the Inca finally settled on fertile lands in the Valley of Cuzco. By the 1200s, they had established their own small kingdom in the valley.

During this early period, the Inca developed traditions and beliefs that helped launch and unify their empire. One of these traditions was the belief that the Incan ruler was descended from the sun god, Inti, who would bring prosperity and greatness to the Incan state. Only men from one of 11 noble lineages believed to be descendants of the sun god could be selected as Incan leaders.

Pachacuti Builds an Empire At first the Incan kingdom grew slowly. In 1438, however, a powerful and ambitious ruler, **Pachacuti** (PAH•chah•KOO•tee), took the throne. Under his leadership, the Inca conquered all of Peru and then moved into neighboring lands. By 1500, the Inca ruled an empire that stretched 2,500 miles along the western coast of South America. (See the map on page 461.) The Inca called this empire "Land of the Four Quarters." It included about 80 provinces and was home to as many as 16 million people.

Pachacuti and his successors accomplished this feat of conquest through a combination of diplomacy and military force. The Inca had a powerful military

hmhsocialstudies.com
TAKING NOTES

Use the graphic organizer online to take notes on the methods the Inca used to build their empire.

Pachacuti
c. 1391–c. 1473

As the second son of the Incan ruler Viracocha, Pachacuti did not expect to succeed to the throne. However, when Cuzco was attacked in 1438, Viracocha and Pachacuti's older brother fled the city. Pachacuti stayed and drove off the attackers. He then proclaimed himself the new Incan ruler.

Pachacuti, whose name means "World Transformer" or "Earthshaker," ruled for 33 years. During that time, he drew up the plans for the rebuilding of Cuzco and established the Incan system of government.

↗ **hmhsocialstudies.com**

RESEARCH WEB LINKS Go online for more on Pachacuti and other Incan rulers.

but used force only when necessary. They were also clever diplomats. Before attacking, they typically offered enemy states an honorable surrender. They would allow them to keep their own customs and rulers in exchange for loyalty to the Incan state. Because of this treatment, many states gave up without resisting. Even when force was used, the Inca took a similar approach. Once an area was defeated, they made every effort to gain the loyalty of the newly conquered people.

Incan Government Creates Unity

To control the huge empire, the rulers divided their territory and its people into manageable units, governed by a central bureaucracy. The Inca created an efficient economic system to support the empire and an extensive road system to tie it together. They also imposed a single official language, Quechua (KEHCH•wuh), and founded schools to teach Incan ways. Certain social groups were identified by officially dictated patterns on clothing. All of these actions were calculated to unify the variety of people controlled by the Inca. **A**

Incan Cities Show Government Presence To exercise control over their empire, the Inca built many cities in conquered areas. The architecture of government buildings was the same all over the empire, making the presence of the government apparent. As in Rome, all roads led to the capital, Cuzco. The heart of the Incan empire, Cuzco was a splendid city of temples, plazas, and palaces. "Cuzco was grand and stately," wrote Cieza de León. "It had fine streets, . . . and the houses were built of solid stones, beautifully joined." Like the Romans, the Inca were masterful engineers and stonemasons. Though they had no iron tools and did not use the wheel, Incan builders carved and transported huge blocks of stone, fitting them together perfectly without mortar. Many Incan walls still stand in Cuzco today, undisturbed by the region's frequent earthquakes.

MAIN IDEA

Forming Opinions
A Of all of the methods used to create unity, which do you think would be most successful? Why?

Incan Government The Incan state exercised almost total control over economic and social life. It controlled most economic activity, regulating the production and distribution of goods. Unlike the Maya and the Aztecs, the Inca allowed little private commerce or trade.

The Incan social system was based on an age-old form of community cooperation—the ayllu (EYE•loo). The **ayllu**, or extended family group, undertook tasks too big for a single family. These tasks included building irrigation canals or cutting agricultural terraces into steep hillsides. The ayllu also stored food and other supplies to distribute among members during hard times.

The Inca incorporated the ayllu structure into a governing system based on the decimal system. They divided families into groups of 10, 100, 1,000, and 10,000. A chief led each group. He was part of a chain of command. That chain stretched from the community and regional levels all the way to Cuzco, where the Incan ruler and his council of state held court. In general, local administration was left in the hands of local rulers, and villages were allowed to continue their traditional ways. If a community resisted Incan control, however, the Inca might relocate the whole group

MAIN IDEA

Identifying Solutions

B How would relocating troublesome people help government control of an area?

to a different territory. The resisters would be placed under the control of rulers appointed by the government in Cuzco. **B**

The main demand the Incan state placed on its subjects was for tribute, usually in the form of labor. The labor tribute was known as **mita** (MEE•tuh). It required all able-bodied citizens to work for the state a certain number of days every year. Mita workers might labor on state farmlands, produce craft goods for state warehouses, or help with public works projects.

Historians have compared the Incan system to a type of socialism or a modern welfare state. Citizens were expected to work for the state and were cared for in return. For example, the aged and disabled were often supported by the state. The state also made sure that the people did not go hungry when there were bad harvests. Freeze-dried potatoes, called *chuño*, were stored in huge government warehouses for distribution in times of food shortages.

Public Works Projects The Inca had an ambitious public works program. The most spectacular project was the Incan road system. A marvel of engineering, this road system symbolized the power of the Incan state. The 14,000-mile-long network of roads and bridges spanned the empire, traversing rugged mountains and harsh deserts. The roads ranged from paved stone to simple paths. Along the roads, the Inca built guesthouses to provide shelter for weary travelers. A system of runners, known as *chasquis* (SHAH•skeys), traveled these roads as a kind of postal service, carrying messages from one end of the empire to the other. The road system also allowed the easy movement of troops to bring control to areas of the empire where trouble might be brewing.

Government Record-Keeping Despite the sophistication of many aspects of Incan life, the Inca never developed a writing system. History and literature were memorized as part of an oral tradition. For numerical information, the Inca created an accounting device known as the **quipu**, a set of knotted strings that could be used to record data. (See the Global Patterns feature on page 20.) The knots and their position on the string indicated numbers. Additionally, the colors of the strings represented different categories of information important to the government. For example, red strings were used to count warriors; yellow strings were used to count gold. However, the meanings of the colors changed depending on the general purpose of the quipu. **C**

Some historians believe that the Inca also developed an elaborate calendar system with two types of calendars, one for night and one for day. They were used primarily for religious purposes. Like the calendars of the Maya and the Aztecs, the two calendars provided information about the gods whom the Inca believed ruled the day and time.

MAIN IDEA

Recognizing Effects

C How might the Incan system of record-keeping help support a strong government?

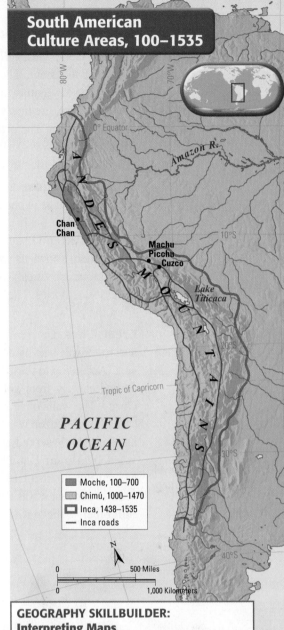

South American Culture Areas, 100–1535

Moche, 100–700
Chimú, 1000–1470
Inca, 1438–1535
— Inca roads

0   500 Miles
0   1,000 Kilometers

GEOGRAPHY SKILLBUILDER: Interpreting Maps

1. **Place** The lands of which earlier South American cultures were included in the Incan Empire?
2. **Human-Environment Interaction** Look at the shape and terrain of the Incan Empire. What problems related to geography might occur in controlling the land?

People and Empires in the Americas **461**

Religion Supports the State

As with the Aztecs, religion was important to the Inca and helped reinforce the power of the state. The Inca worshiped fewer gods than the Aztecs. The Inca focused on key nature spirits such as the moon, the stars, and thunder. In the balance of nature, the Inca saw patterns for the way humans should relate to each other and to the earth. The primary Incan god was a creator god called Viracocha. Next in importance was the sun god, Inti. Because the Incan ruler was considered a descendant of Inti, sun worship amounted to worship of the king.

Religious Practices Incan priests led the sun-worship services, assisted by young women known as *mamakuna,* or "virgins of the sun." These women, all unmarried, were drafted by the Inca for a lifetime of religious service. The young women were trained in religious activities, as teachers, spinners, weavers, and beer makers. Young men, known as *yamacuna,* also served as full-time workers for the state and in religious activities. Sacrifice of llamas and exchange of goods were a part of the religious activities. The goods were distributed by the priests to the people as gifts from the gods.

Great Cities The Temple of the Sun in Cuzco was the most sacred of all Incan shrines. It was heavily decorated in gold, a metal the Inca referred to as "sweat of the sun." According to some sources, the temple even had a garden with plants and animals crafted entirely from gold and silver. In fact, gold was a common sight throughout Cuzco. The walls of several buildings had a covering of thin gold sheeting.

Although Cuzco was the religious capital of the Incan Empire, other Incan cities also may have served a ceremonial purpose. For example, Machu Picchu, excavated by Hiram Bingham in 1912, was isolated and mysterious. Like Cuzco, Machu Picchu also had a sun temple, public buildings, and a central plaza. Some sources suggest it was a religious center. Others think it was an estate of Pachacuti. Still others believe it was a retreat for Incan rulers or the nobility.

▼ Machu Picchu lies some 8,000 feet above sea level on a ridge between two mountain peaks.

Rise and Fall of the Inca		
Traits of Civilization	**Strength Leading to Power**	**Weakness Leading to Decline**
Religious beliefs and theocracy	United culture that is loyal to the emperor	Many physical and human resources funneled into religious activities
Major road systems	An interconnected empire that is easier to control	Enemy could also use roads to move troops
Type of welfare state with huge bureaucracy	Able to care for entire population during good and bad times	People struggled to care for themselves with the elimination of the welfare state

SKILLBUILDER: Interpreting Charts
1. **Forming and Supporting Opinions** *In your opinion, which of the three traits leading to power was the most valuable? Briefly discuss your reasons.*
2. **Comparing** *Which trait did you find repeated in the Maya and Aztec empires?*

HISTORY.
VIDEO
Machu Picchu
↗ hmhsocialstudies.com

Discord in the Empire

The Incan Empire reached the height of its glory in the early 1500s during the reign of Huayna Capac. Trouble was brewing, however. In the 1520s, Huayna Capac undertook a tour of Ecuador, a newly conquered area of the empire. In the city of Quito, he received a gift box. When he opened it, out flew butterflies and moths, considered an evil omen. A few weeks later, while still in Quito, Huayna Capac died of disease—probably smallpox.

After his death, the empire was split between his sons, Atahualpa (ah•tah•WAHL•pah) and Huascar (WAHS•kahr). Atahualpa received Ecuador, about one-fifth of the empire. The rest went to Huascar. At first, this system of dual emperors worked. Soon, however, Atahualpa laid claim to the whole of the empire. A bitter civil war followed. Atahualpa eventually won, but the war tore apart the empire. As you will learn in Chapter 20, the Spanish arrived in the last days of this war. Taking advantage of Incan weakness, they would soon divide and conquer the empire.

SECTION 4 ASSESSMENT

TERMS & NAMES 1. For each term or name, write a sentence explaining its significance.
• Pachacuti   • ayllu   • mita   • quipu

USING YOUR NOTES
2. Which of these methods for unification were acceptable to the conquered people? Explain.

The Inca built a vast empire.

MAIN IDEAS
3. How were the Inca able to conquer such a vast empire?
4. What methods did the Inca use to create unity among the diverse peoples in their empire?
5. What role did the mita play in building the Incan Empire?

CRITICAL THINKING & WRITING
6. **IDENTIFYING SOLUTIONS** How did the Inca overcome geographical obstacles in building and ruling their empire?
7. **ANALYZING MOTIVES** Why do you think the Inca used the ayllu system as the basis for governing in the empire?
8. **COMPARING AND CONTRASTING** How were Incan and Aztec religious practices similar? How were they different?
9. **WRITING ACTIVITY** POWER AND AUTHORITY Write a short **description** of one of the great public works projects completed by the Inca.

CONNECT TO TODAY CREATING AN ORAL REPORT
The Incan Empire has been compared to a modern welfare state. Study the government of one such state—Sweden, for example. In an **oral report,** compare the Incan government with the government of the country you studied.

Incan Mummies

For the Inca, death was an important part of life. The Inca worshiped the spirits and the bodies of their ancestors. They believed in an afterlife, and tombs and the mummies they held were considered holy.

Like the Egyptians, the Inca embalmed their dead to preserve the body. The mummies were bundled with offerings of food, tools, and precious items to help them in the afterlife. These "mummy bundles" were then buried or put in an aboveground tomb to be worshiped. Mummies have been found from many different social classes, and, as you will read, not all of them died natural deaths.

 hmhsocialstudies.com

RESEARCH WEB LINKS Go online for more on mummies.

▶ Royal Treatment

The mummies of Incan rulers were among the holiest objects of Incan religion. The mummies were actually treated as if they were still alive. They had servants, maintained ownership of their property, were consulted as oracles, and were taken to major festivals or to visit other mummies. The mummy shown at right in a 16th-century Spanish codex is being transported in the same manner as the living royalty.

▼ Human Sacrifice

Some Incan mummies have been found on high mountain peaks in the Andes. These mummies were human sacrifices. Frozen for hundreds of years, the mummies allow researchers to examine the clothes, health, and sometimes even the internal organs of ancient humans. Scientists determined that this mummy was killed by a sharp blow to the head.

► Mummy Bundles

At a site known as Puruchuco, just outside of Lima, Peru, archaeologists discovered a huge Incan cemetery. Some of the mummies unearthed were wrapped in layers of cotton. The outside of the bundle might have a false head made of cloth like the one shown on the right. Inside the bundle were the mummy, religious offerings, and personal items. The illustration shown below re-creates the inside of an actual bundle that archaeologists unwrapped.

Corn, or maize, was the Inca's most important crop and is often found in Incan burials.

The Inca used gourds as bowls and containers. The gourds found in this bundle held food and cotton.

This man wears a feathered headdress that indicates high social standing.

AN INCAN GRAVEYARD

The Puruchuco graveyard lies beneath a shantytown in Peru called Tupac Amaru. In 1999, when archaeologists discovered the extent of the site, it was about to be bulldozed. Archaeologists began an emergency recovery effort.

- The remains of over 2,000 men, women, and children were recovered.
- The site may contain as many as 10,000 individuals.
- Some bundles contained up to seven bodies and weighed as much as 400 pounds.
- Between 50,000 and 60,000 artifacts were recovered.
- One of the mummy bundles became known as the "Cotton King." The mummy was wrapped in about 300 pounds of raw cotton.
- The Cotton King's bundle contained 170 artifacts, including food, pottery, animal skins, and sandals. Footwear was not common among the Inca, and sandals were a status symbol.

PERU

PACIFIC OCEAN

Lima

◄ Gifts for the Dead

The Inca sometimes placed mummies in aboveground tombs called *chullpas*. Descendants of the mummy would bring offerings of food and precious goods to honor their ancestor. This mummy is shown as it might have appeared in its tomb.

Connect *to* Today

1. **Making Inferences** What do Incan mummification practices suggest about Incan culture?

   See Skillbuilder Handbook, page R10.

2. **Forming and Supporting Opinions** Why do you think mummification is not a common practice in the United States today?

VISUAL SUMMARY

People and Empires in the Americas

North America: 600–late 1500s

- Government by a variety of small tribes to very complex societies
- Similar religious beliefs in the Great Spirit
- Economy influenced by the environment
- Trade links to other groups

Mesoamerica: Maya 250–900

- Government by city-state kings
- Religion plays a major role in society and rule
- Trade links between city-states and other Mesoamerican groups
- Math and astronomy develop to support religious beliefs
- Pyramid builders
- Written language using hieroglyphs

Mesoamerica: Aztec 1200–1521

- Government by warrior-kings
- Religion plays a major role in society and rule
- Trade links between tribute states and other Mesoamerican groups
- Human sacrifice practiced for religious offerings
- Pyramid builders
- Pictorial written language

South America: Inca 1400–1532

- Government by theocracy—sun-god king
- Religion plays a major role in society and rule
- Social welfare state cares for all people
- Extensive road system links the country together

TERMS & NAMES

For each term or name below, briefly explain its connection to the development of Native American cultures in North America, Mesoamerica, or South America.

1. pueblo
2. Mississippian
3. Iroquois
4. Tikal
5. glyph
6. Quetzalcoatl
7. Triple Alliance
8. Montezuma II
9. Pachacuti
10. mita

MAIN IDEAS

North American Societies Section 1 (pages 441–445)

11. Why were Native American societies in North America so diverse?
12. What were the three things that most Native Americans in North America had in common?

Maya Kings and Cities Section 2 (pages 446–451)

13. What role did religion play in Maya life?
14. What were three major achievements of the Maya civilization?

The Aztecs Control Central Mexico Section 3 (pages 452–458)

15. How did the Aztecs build and control their empire?
16. Why did the Aztecs sacrifice human beings to their gods?

The Inca Create a Mountain Empire Section 4 (pages 459–465)

17. List three ways in which the Incan government involved itself in people's lives.
18. How did Incan religion reinforce the power of the state?

CRITICAL THINKING

1. USING YOUR NOTES

On a double time line, place two dates for each of the major culture groups that controlled the Valley of Mexico from the beginning of the first century A.D. Write a brief description of the importance of each date.

2. FORMULATING HISTORICAL QUESTIONS

Study the information on the Mound Builders again. What questions might you ask to gain a better understanding of these cultures?

3. COMPARING AND CONTRASTING

RELIGIOUS AND ETHICAL SYSTEMS Compare the religious beliefs of the Maya, the Aztecs, and the Inca. How were they similar? How were they different?

4. MAKING INFERENCES

POWER AND AUTHORITY What can you infer about the values of the Inca from the fact that the government provided care for citizens who were aged or unable to care for themselves?

5. FORMING AND SUPPORTING OPINIONS

The Maya was the most advanced of the early American civilizations. Do you agree or disagree with this statement? Give reasons for your answer.

Use the excerpt and your knowledge of world history to answer questions 1 and 2.

PRIMARY SOURCE

We return thanks to our mother, the earth, which sustains us. We return thanks to the rivers and streams, which supply us with water. . . . We return thanks to the corn, and to her sisters, the beans and squashes, which give us life. . . . We return thanks to the sun, that he has looked upon the earth with a beneficent eye. . . . We return thanks to the Great Spirit . . . who directs all things for the good of his children.

Quoted in *In the Trail of the Wind*

1. How did the Iroquois feel about nature?

   A. They felt angry at nature.

   B. They felt grateful to nature.

   C. Nature was seen as a mere tool to the Iroquois.

   D. Nature played little part in the lives of the Iroquois.

2. Which statement best sums up the overall role that the Great Spirit played in Iroquois life?

   A. The Great Spirit ruled over all for the good of all.

   B. The Great Spirit provided food for the Iroquois.

   C. The Great Spirit ruled over the earth and the sun.

   D. The Great Spirit provided the Iroquois with water.

Use this map, which provides a bird's-eye view of the island city of Tenochtitlán, and your knowledge of world history to answer question 3.

3. What appears to be in the center of the city?

   A. an enormous lake   **C.** a temple complex

   B. a small harbor   **D.** an empty square

 hmhsocialstudies.com **TEST PRACTICE**

For additional test practice, go online for:

• Diagnostic tests

• Tutorials

• Strategies

Interact *with* History

From the headdress clues and detective thinking, you should have determined that the Kwakiutl lived in the forests by the Pacific Ocean. They probably used the headdress in a ceremony asking the gods to protect them. Using the guide questions on page 440, look back in the chapter at other artifacts in each section to see what you can determine about other cultures.

FOCUS ON WRITING

CULTURAL INTERACTION   In recent years, Aztec cultural ruins have been excavated in Mexico City. Using the Internet and library resources, conduct research into some of these archaeological finds, such as the Plaza of Three Cultures and the Great Temple. Then write an illustrated **magazine article** that describes these places and shows the heritage of the Mexican people.

MULTIMEDIA ACTIVITY

NetExplorations: Counting Calendars and Cords

Go to *NetExplorations* at **hmhsocialstudies.com** to learn more about the Aztec and Maya calendars. Use the Internet to learn about the calendars of other civilizations during the same period. Find out:

• how various calendars were organized

• what names were given to the various time periods on each calendar (for example, agricultural names or names of important gods)

• which calendars were most accurate

• how long each calendar was in use

Use the information and images you find to create a virtual museum where viewers can compare and contrast civilizations, their notions of time, and the calendars they used.

THE
Maya

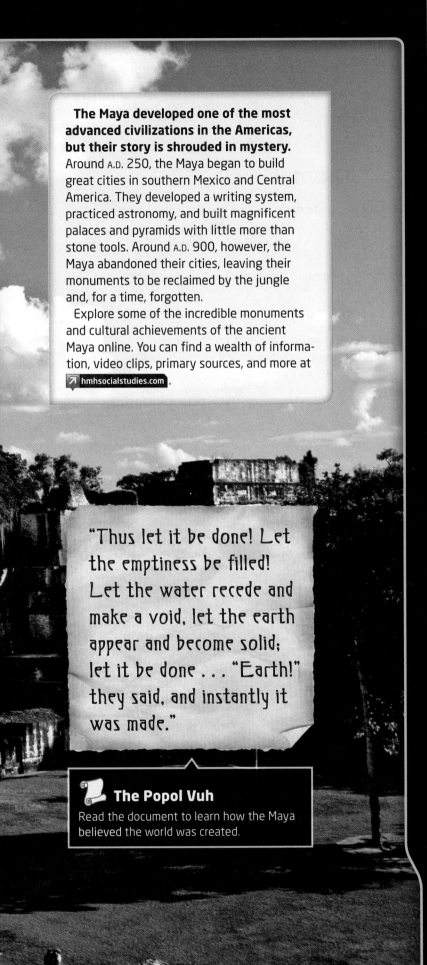

The Maya developed one of the most advanced civilizations in the Americas, but their story is shrouded in mystery. Around A.D. 250, the Maya began to build great cities in southern Mexico and Central America. They developed a writing system, practiced astronomy, and built magnificent palaces and pyramids with little more than stone tools. Around A.D. 900, however, the Maya abandoned their cities, leaving their monuments to be reclaimed by the jungle and, for a time, forgotten.

Explore some of the incredible monuments and cultural achievements of the ancient Maya online. You can find a wealth of information, video clips, primary sources, and more at ↗ hmhsocialstudies.com .

> "Thus let it be done! Let the emptiness be filled! Let the water recede and make a void, let the earth appear and become solid; let it be done . . . "Earth!" they said, and instantly it was made."

The Popol Vuh
Read the document to learn how the Maya believed the world was created.

Destroying the Maya's Past
Watch the video to learn how the actions of one Spanish missionary nearly destroyed the written record of the Maya world.

Finding the City of Palenque
Watch the video to learn about the great Maya city of Palenque and the European discovery of the site in the eighteenth century.

Pakal's Tomb
Watch the video to explore how the discovery of the tomb of a great king helped archaeologists piece together the Maya past.

CHAPTER 17

European Renaissance and Reformation, 1300–1600

Essential Question

What new ideas and values led to the Renaissance and the Reformation?

? What You Will Learn

In this chapter you will learn how European society was revitalized, as classical art and ideas were embraced and improved upon and the Catholic Church was openly challenged.

SECTION 1 Italy: Birthplace of the Renaissance

Main Idea The Italian Renaissance was a rebirth of learning that produced many great works of art and literature.

SECTION 2 The Northern Renaissance

Main Idea In the 1400s, the ideas of the Italian Renaissance began to spread to Northern Europe.

SECTION 3 Luther Leads the Reformation

Main Idea Martin Luther's protest over abuses in the Catholic Church led to the founding of Protestant churches.

SECTION 4 The Reformation Continues

Main Idea As Protestant reformers divided over beliefs, the Catholic Church made reforms.

Previewing Themes

CULTURAL INTERACTION Trade with the East and the rediscovery of ancient manuscripts caused Europeans to develop new ideas about culture and art. This period was called the "Renaissance," which means rebirth.

Geography *Study the time line and the map. In which countries did the Renaissance begin?*

RELIGIOUS AND ETHICAL SYSTEMS Martin Luther began a movement to reform practices in the Catholic Church that he believed were wrong. That movement, the Reformation, led to the founding of non-Catholic churches.

Geography *Locate Wittenberg, the city where the Reformation began. What geographical features helped the Reformation spread from there?*

REVOLUTION The invention of the printing press allowed books and pamphlets to be made faster and more cheaply. This new technology helped spread the revolutionary ideas of the Renaissance and Reformation.

Geography *Printing spread from Mainz to other parts of Europe. How might the location of Mainz have helped the spread of printing?*

EUROPE

1300
In the 1300s the Renaissance begins in Italian city-states such as Florence, Milan, and Mantua.

1434
◄ Medici family takes control of Florence. (bust of Lorenzo Medici)

1300

1400

WORLD

1324
Mali king Mansa Musa makes a pilgrimage to Mecca.

1368
◄ Hongwu founds Ming Dynasty in China. (vase from that period)

1405
Chinese explorer Zheng He begins exploration of Asia and Africa.

Europe, 1500

SCOTLAND

NORWAY-DENMARK

North Sea

58° N

IRELAND

ENGLAND

London

Rotterdam

FLANDERS

LITHUANIA

BRANDENBURG

Wittenberg

POLAND

HOLY ROMAN EMPIRE

Mainz

Worms

Prague

50° N

ATLANTIC OCEAN

Paris

Nantes

FRANCE

Augsburg

AUSTRIA

HUNGARY

SWISS CONFEDERATION

Trent

Geneva

Milan

Mantua

VENETIAN REPUBLIC

Adriatic Sea

OTTOMAN EMPIRE

— Boundary of the Holy Roman Empire

Florence

PAPAL STATES

MONTENEGRO

AVIGNON (Papal State)

CORSICA

Rome

KINGDOM OF NAPLES

PORTUGAL

Madrid

SPAIN

Naples

SARDINIA

Mediterranean Sea

KINGDOM OF SICILY

N
W E
S

0   150   300 Miles
0   300   600 Kilometers

Conic Projection

HISTORY
Humanism Triggers the Renaissance

↗ hmhsocialstudies.com   VIDEO

1455
Gutenberg Bible printed in Mainz. ▶

1517
Martin Luther begins the Reformation in Wittenberg.

1534
English king Henry VIII starts the Church of England.

1563
Council of Trent mandates reforms in Catholic Church.

1500

1600

1453
Ottoman Turks capture Constantinople.

1492
Columbus reaches the Americas.

1526
Babur establishes Mughal Empire in India. (Mughal noble) ▶

What can you learn from art?

You work at a museum that is considering buying this painting by Jan van Eyck. It is a portrait of Chancellor Rolin, a powerful government official in Burgundy (later part of France). Before deciding, the museum director wants to know what this painting can teach the public about the Renaissance.

↗ hmhsocialstudies.com INTERACTIVE

▲ *The Madonna of Chancellor Rolin* (about 1435), Jan van Eyck

1 Classical Art Renaissance artists admired classical art. The columns show classical style.

2 Perspective Van Eyck used the technique of perspective, which shows distant objects as smaller than close ones. He also used oil paints, a new invention.

3 Religion This painting portrays the infant Jesus and his mother Mary in 15th-century Europe. Such a depiction shows the continuing importance of religion during the Renaissance.

4 The Individual Renaissance artists portrayed the importance of individuals. Chancellor Rolin is wearing a fur-trimmed robe that shows his high status.

5 Beauty Van Eyck included many details simply to add beauty. These include the design on the floor, the folds of Mary's cloak, and the scenery outside.

EXAMINING *the* ISSUES

- What can you infer about the setting of the painting?
- What details in the painting give you an idea of the role of religion in society?

As a class, discuss these questions to see what you can learn about this art. Also recall what you know about art in such places as Egypt and India. As you read about the Renaissance, notice what the art of that time reveals about European society.

Italy: Birthplace of the Renaissance

MAIN IDEA	WHY IT MATTERS NOW	TERMS & NAMES
REVOLUTION The Italian Renaissance was a rebirth of learning that produced many great works of art and literature.	Renaissance art and literature still influence modern thought and modern art.	• Renaissance • patron • humanism • perspective • secular • vernacular

SETTING THE STAGE During the late Middle Ages, Europe suffered from both war and plague. Those who survived wanted to celebrate life and the human spirit. They began to question institutions of the Middle Ages, which had been unable to prevent war or to relieve suffering brought by the plague. Some people questioned the Church, which taught Christians to endure suffering while they awaited their rewards in heaven. In northern Italy, writers and artists began to express this new spirit and to experiment with different styles. These men and women would greatly change how Europeans saw themselves and their world.

Italy's Advantages

This movement that started in Italy caused an explosion of creativity in art, writing, and thought that lasted approximately from 1300 to 1600. Historians call this period the **Renaissance** (REHN•ih•SAHNS). The term means rebirth, and in this context, it refers to a revival of art and learning. The educated men and women of Italy hoped to bring back to life the culture of classical Greece and Rome. Yet in striving to revive the past, the people of the Renaissance created something new. The contributions made during this period led to innovative styles of art and literature. They also led to new values, such as the importance of the individual.

The Renaissance eventually spread from northern Italy to the rest of Europe. Italy had three advantages that made it the birthplace of the Renaissance: thriving cities, a wealthy merchant class, and the classical heritage of Greece and Rome.

City-States Overseas trade, spurred by the Crusades, had led to the growth of large city-states in northern Italy. The region also had many sizable towns. Thus, northern Italy was urban while the rest of Europe was still mostly rural. Since cities are often places where people exchange ideas, they were an ideal breeding ground for an intellectual revolution.

In the 1300s, the bubonic plague struck these cities hard, killing up to 60 percent of the population. This brought economic changes. Because there were fewer laborers, survivors could demand higher wages. With few opportunities to expand business, merchants began to pursue other interests, such as art.

Merchants and the Medici A wealthy merchant class developed in each Italian city-state. Because city-states like Milan and Florence were relatively small, a high percentage of citizens could be intensely involved in political life.

TAKING NOTES

Use the graphic organizer online to take notes on important events in the rise of Italian city-states.

History Makers

Medici Family

A rival family grew so jealous of the Medici that they plotted to kill Lorenzo (above) and his brother Giuliano. As the Medici attended Mass, assassins murdered Giuliano at the altar. Drawing his sword, Lorenzo escaped to a small room and held off his attackers until help arrived. Later, he had the killers brutally, publicly executed.

More positively, Lorenzo was a generous patron of the arts who collected many rare manuscripts. Eventually the Medici family made their library available to the public.

HISTORY

VIDEO
The Medici
Assassination

hmhsocialstudies.com

Merchants dominated politics. Unlike nobles, merchants did not inherit social rank. To succeed in business, they used their wits. As a result, many successful merchants believed they deserved power and wealth because of their individual merit. This belief in individual achievement became important during the Renaissance.

Since the late 1200s, the city-state of Florence had a republican form of government. But during the Renaissance, Florence came under the rule of one powerful banking family, the Medici (MEHD•ih•chee). The Medici family bank had branch offices throughout Italy and in the major cities of Europe. Cosimo de Medici was the wealthiest European of his time. In 1434, he won control of Florence's government. He did not seek political office for himself, but influenced members of the ruling council by giving them loans. For 30 years, he was dictator of Florence.

Cosimo de Medici died in 1464, but his family continued to control Florence. His grandson, Lorenzo de Medici, came to power in 1469. Known as Lorenzo the Magnificent, he ruled as a dictator yet kept up the appearance of having an elected government.

Looking to Greece and Rome Renaissance scholars looked down on the art and literature of the Middle Ages. Instead, they wanted to return to the learning of the Greeks and Romans. They achieved this in several ways. First, the artists and scholars of Italy drew inspiration from the ruins of Rome that surrounded them. Second, Western scholars studied ancient Latin manuscripts that had been preserved in monasteries. Third, Christian scholars in Constantinople fled to Rome with Greek manuscripts when the Turks conquered Constantinople in 1453. **A**

Classical and Worldly Values

As scholars studied these manuscripts, they became more influenced by classical ideas. These ideas helped them to develop a new outlook on life and art.

Classics Lead to Humanism The study of classical texts led to **humanism**, an intellectual movement that focused on human potential and achievements. Instead of trying to make classical texts agree with Christian teaching as medieval scholars had, humanists studied them to understand ancient Greek values. Humanists influenced artists and architects to carry on classical traditions. Also, humanists popularized the study of subjects common to classical education, such as history, literature, and philosophy. These subjects are called the humanities.

Worldly Pleasures In the Middle Ages, some people had demonstrated their piety by wearing rough clothing and eating plain foods. However, humanists suggested that a person might enjoy life without offending God. In Renaissance Italy, the wealthy enjoyed material luxuries, good music, and fine foods.

Most people remained devout Catholics. However, the basic spirit of Renaissance society was **secular**—worldly rather than spiritual and concerned with the here and now. Even church leaders became more worldly. Some lived in beautiful mansions, threw lavish banquets, and wore expensive clothes.

Patrons of the Arts Church leaders during the Renaissance beautified Rome and other cities by spending huge amounts of money for art. They became **patrons** of the

MAIN IDEA

Analyzing Causes
A What three advantages fostered the Renaissance in Italy?

Vocabulary
The words *humanist* and *humanities* come from the Latin word *humanitas,* which refers to the literary culture that every educated person should possess.

arts by financially supporting artists. Renaissance merchants and wealthy families also were patrons of the arts. By having their portraits painted or by donating art to the city to place in public squares, the wealthy demonstrated their own importance.

The Renaissance Man Renaissance writers introduced the idea that all educated people were expected to create art. In fact, the ideal individual strove to master almost every area of study. A man who excelled in many fields was praised as a "universal man." Later ages called such people "Renaissance men."

Baldassare Castiglione (KAHS•teel•YOH•nay) wrote a book called *The Courtier* (1528) that taught how to become such a person. A young man should be charming, witty, and well educated in the classics. He should dance, sing, play music, and write poetry. In addition, he should be a skilled rider, wrestler, and swordsman.

The Renaissance Woman According to *The Courtier,* upper-class women also should know the classics and be charming. Yet they were not expected to seek fame. They were expected to inspire art but rarely to create it. Upper-class Renaissance women were better educated than medieval women. However, most Renaissance women had little influence in politics.

A few women, such as Isabella d'Este, did exercise power. Born into the ruling family of the city-state of Ferrara, she married the ruler of another city-state, Mantua. She brought many Renaissance artists to her court and built a famous art collection. She was also skilled in politics. When her husband was taken captive in war, she defended Mantua and won his release. **B**

> **MAIN IDEA**
>
> **Comparing**
> **B** How were expectations for Renaissance men and Renaissance women similar?

> Analyzing Primary Sources

The Renaissance Man

In *The Courtier,* Baldassare Castiglione described the type of accomplished person who later came to be called the Renaissance man.

PRIMARY SOURCE

Let the man we are seeking be very bold, stern, and always among the first, where the enemy are to be seen; and in every other place, gentle, modest, reserved, above all things avoiding ostentation [showiness] and that impudent [bold] self-praise by which men ever excite hatred and disgust in all who hear them. . . .

I would have him more than passably accomplished in letters, at least in those studies that are called the humanities, and conversant not only with the Latin language but with Greek, for the sake of the many different things that have been admirably written therein. Let him be well versed in the poets, and not less in the orators and historians, and also proficient in writing verse and prose.

BALDASSARE CASTIGLIONE, *The Courtier*

The Renaissance Woman

Although Renaissance women were not expected to create art, wealthy women often were patrons of artists, as this letter by Isabella d'Este demonstrates.

PRIMARY SOURCE

To Master Leonardo da Vinci, the painter: Hearing that you are settled at Florence, we have begun to hope that our cherished desire to obtain a work by your hand might be at length realized. When you were in this city and drew our portrait in carbon, you promised us that you would some day paint it in colors. But because this would be almost impossible, since you are unable to come here, we beg you to keep your promise by converting our portrait into another figure, which would be still more acceptable to us; that is to say, a youthful Christ of about twelve years . . . executed with all that sweetness and charm of atmosphere which is the peculiar excellence of your art.
Mantua, May 14, 1504

ISABELLA D'ESTE, *Letters*

DOCUMENT-BASED QUESTIONS
1. **Drawing Conclusions** *Do the qualities called for in the ideal Renaissance man and woman seem to emphasize the individual or the group?*
2. **Making Inferences** *Isabella d'Este's portrait was painted by Titian, and Castiglione's by Raphael, two famous painters. What does this tell you about the subjects' social status?*

The Renaissance Revolutionizes Art

Supported by patrons like Isabella d'Este, dozens of artists worked in northern Italy. As the Renaissance advanced, artistic styles changed. Medieval artists had used religious subjects to convey a spiritual ideal. Renaissance artists often portrayed religious subjects, but they used a realistic style copied from classical models. Greek and Roman subjects also became popular. Renaissance painters used the technique of **perspective**, which shows three dimensions on a flat surface.

Realistic Painting and Sculpture Following the new emphasis on individuals, painters began to paint prominent citizens. These realistic portraits revealed what was distinctive about each person. In addition, artists such as the sculptor, poet, architect, and painter Michelangelo (MY•kuhl•AN•juh•LOH) Buonarroti used a realistic style when depicting the human body. **C**

Donatello (DAHN•uh•TEHL•oh) also made sculpture more realistic by carving natural postures and expressions that reveal personality. He revived a classical form in his statue of David, a boy who, according to the Bible, became a great king. Donatello's statue was created in the late 1460s. It was the first European sculpture of a large, free-standing nude since ancient times. For sculptors of the period, including Michelangelo, David (page 478) was a favorite subject.

MAIN IDEA

Synthesizing
C What major change did a belief in individual merit bring about in art?

> Analyzing Art

Perspective

Perspective creates the appearance of three dimensions. Classical artists had used perspective, but medieval artists abandoned the technique. In the 1400s, Italian artists rediscovered it.

Perspective is based on an optical illusion. As parallel lines stretch away from a viewer, they seem to draw together, until they meet at a spot on the-horizon called the vanishing point. The use of perspective was a feature of most Western painting for the next 450 years.

Marriage of the Virgin (1504), Raphael

SKILLBUILDER: Interpreting Visual Sources
Contrasting *What is the major difference between the figures in the background of the painting and the figures in the foreground? What is the effect of this difference?*

Vanishing Point

Horizon

Leonardo, Renaissance Man Leonardo da Vinci (LAY•uh•NAHR•doh-duh•VIHN•chee) was a painter, sculptor, inventor, and scientist. A true "Renaissance man," he was interested in how things worked. He studied how a muscle moves and how veins are arranged in a leaf. He filled his notebooks with observations and sketches. Then he incorporated his findings in his art.

Among his many masterpieces, Leonardo painted one of the best-known portraits in the world, the *Mona Lisa* (page 478). The woman in the portrait seems so real that many writers have tried to explain the thoughts behind her smile. Leonardo also produced a famous religious painting, *The Last Supper.* It shows the personalities of Jesus' disciples through facial expressions.

Raphael Advances Realism Raphael (RAHF•ee•uhl) Sanzio was younger than Michelangelo and Leonardo. He learned from studying their works. One of Raphael's favorite subjects was the Madonna and child. Raphael often portrayed their expressions as gentle and calm. He was famous for his use of perspective.

In his greatest achievement, Raphael filled the walls of Pope Julius II's library with paintings. One of these, *School of Athens* (page 479), conveys the classical influence on the Renaissance. Raphael painted famous Renaissance figures, such as Michelangelo, Leonardo, and himself, as classical philosophers and their students.

Anguissola and Gentileschi Renaissance society generally restricted women's roles. However, a few Italian women became notable painters. Sofonisba Anguissola (ahng•GWEES•soh•lah) was the first woman artist to gain an international reputation. She is known for her portraits of her sisters and of prominent people such as King Philip II of Spain. Artemisia Gentileschi (JAYN•tee•LEHS•kee) was another accomplished artist. She trained with her painter father and helped with his work. In her own paintings, Gentileschi painted pictures of strong, heroic women.

History Makers

Leonardo da Vinci
1452–1519
Leonardo da Vinci's notebooks—and life—are mysterious. Some 3,500 pages closely covered with writings and drawings survive. His-writing is clear and easy to read, but only if you look at it in a mirror. No one-knows why he wrote backwards.

Leonardo planned scholarly works and great feats of-engineering that were never completed. Only 17 of his paintings survive. And yet the-work that Leonardo did produce is so amazing that it confirms his genius.

Michelangelo Buonarroti
1475–1564
Like Leonardo, Michelangelo was a Renaissance man. He excelled as a painter, sculptor, architect, and poet.
Michelangelo is most famous for the way he portrayed the human body in painting and sculpture. Influenced by classical art, he created figures that are forceful and show heroic grandeur.

Among his achievements are the dome of St. Peter's, the paintings on the ceiling of the Sistine Chapel, and the statue of David.

hmhsocialstudies.com

INTERNET ACTIVITY Go online to plan a Web site on Renaissance leaders that showcases these two artists.

Renaissance Writers Change Literature

Renaissance writers produced works that reflected their time, but they also used techniques that writers rely on today. Some followed the example of the medieval writer Dante. He wrote in the **vernacular**, his native language, instead of Latin. Dante's native language was Italian. In addition, Renaissance writers wrote either for self-expression or to portray the individuality of their subjects. In these ways, writers of the Renaissance began trends that modern writers still follow.

Petrarch and Boccaccio Francesco Petrarch (PEE•trahrk) was one of the earliest and most influential humanists. Some have called him the father of Renaissance humanism. He was also a great poet. Petrarch wrote both in Italian and in Latin. In

HISTORY
VIDEO
Da Vinci Tech
hmhsocialstudies.com

Italian, he wrote sonnets—14-line poems. They were about a mysterious woman named Laura, who was his ideal. (Little is known of Laura except that she died of the plague in 1348.) In classical Latin, he wrote letters to many important friends.

The Italian writer Giovanni Boccaccio (boh•KAH•chee•oh) is best known for the *Decameron,* a series of realistic, sometimes off-color stories. The stories are supposedly told by a group of worldly young people waiting in a rural villa to avoid the plague sweeping through Florence:

PRIMARY SOURCE

In the year of Our Lord 1348 the deadly plague broke out in the great city of Florence, most beautiful of Italian cities. Whether through the operation of the heavenly bodies or because of our own iniquities [sins] which the just wrath of God sought to correct, the plague had arisen in the East some years before, causing the death of countless human beings. It spread without stop from one place to another, until, unfortunately, it swept over the West. Neither knowledge nor human foresight availed against it, though the city was cleansed of much filth by chosen officers in charge and sick persons were forbidden to enter it, while advice was broadcast for the preservation of health.

GIOVANNI BOCCACCIO, Preface, *Decameron*

The *Decameron* presents both tragic and comic views of life. In its stories, the author uses cutting humor to illustrate the human condition. Boccaccio presents his characters in all of their individuality and all their folly.

Machiavelli Advises Rulers *The Prince* (1513) by Niccolò Machiavelli (MAK•ee•uh•VEHL•ee) also examines the imperfect conduct of human beings. It does so by taking the form of a political guidebook. In *The Prince,* Machiavelli examines how a ruler can gain power and keep it in spite of his enemies. In answering this question, he began with the idea that most people are selfish, fickle, and corrupt.

To succeed in such a wicked world, Machiavelli said, a prince must be strong as a lion and shrewd as a fox. He might have to trick his enemies and even his own people for the good of the state. In *The Prince,* Machiavelli was not concerned with what was morally right, but with what was politically effective.

He pointed out that most people think it is praiseworthy in a prince to keep his word and live with integrity. Nevertheless, Machiavelli argued that in the real world of power and politics a prince must sometimes mislead the people and lie to his opponents. As a historian and political thinker, Machiavelli suggested that in order for a prince to accomplish great things, he must be crafty enough to not only overcome the suspicions but also gain the trust of others:

PRIMARY SOURCE

From this arises the question whether it is better to be loved more than feared, or feared more than loved. The reply is, that one ought to be both feared and loved, but as it is difficult for the two to go together, it is much safer to be feared than loved, if one of the two has to be wanting. For it may be said of men in general that they are ungrateful, voluble [changeable], dissemblers [liars], anxious to avoid danger, and covetous of gain; as long as you benefit them, they are entirely yours; they offer you their blood, their goods, their life, and their children, as I have before said, when the necessity is remote; but when it approaches, they revolt. And the prince who has relied solely on their words, without making preparations, is ruined.

NICCOLÒ MACHIAVELLI, *The Prince*

MAIN IDEA

Analyzing Primary Sources

D Does Machiavelli think that a prince should prefer to be loved or feared? Why?

Vittoria Colonna The women writers who gained fame during the Renaissance usually wrote about personal subjects, not politics. Yet, some of them had great influence. Vittoria Colonna (1492–1547) was born of a noble family. In 1509, she married the Marquis of Pescara. He spent most of his life away from home on military campaigns.

Vittoria Colonna exchanged sonnets with Michelangelo and helped Castiglione publish *The Courtier.* Her own poems express personal emotions. When her husband was away at the Battle of Ravenna in 1512, she wrote to him:

PRIMARY SOURCE
But now in this perilous assault,
in this horrible, pitiless battle
that has so hardened my mind and heart,
your great valor has shown you an equal
to Hector and Achilles. But what good is
this to me, sorrowful, abandoned? . . .
Your uncertain enterprises do not hurt you;
but we who wait, mournfully grieving,
are wounded by doubt and fear.
You men, driven by rage, considering nothing
but your honor, commonly go off, shouting,
with great fury, to confront danger.
We remain, with fear in our heart and
grief on our brow for you; sister longs for
brother, wife for husband, mother for son.

VITTORIA COLONNA, *Poems*

Toward the end of the 15th century, Renaissance ideas began to spread north from Italy. As you will read in Section 2, northern artists and thinkers adapted Renaissance ideals in their own ways.

Global Patterns

Other Renaissances

In addition to the Italian Renaissance, there have been rebirths and revivals in other places around the world. For example, the Tang (618–907) and Song (960–1279) dynasties in China saw periods of great artistic and technological advances.

Like the Italian Renaissance, the achievements of the Tang and the Song had roots in an earlier time, the Han Dynasty (202 B.C. to A.D. 220). After the Han collapsed, China experienced turmoil.

When order was restored, Chinese culture flourished. The Chinese invented gunpowder and printing. Chinese poets wrote literary masterpieces. Breakthroughs were made in architecture, painting, and pottery. The Song painting above, *Waiting for Guests by Lamplight,* was done with ink and color on silk.

SECTION 1 ASSESSMENT

TERMS & NAMES 1. For each term or name, write a sentence explaining its significance.
• Renaissance • humanism • secular • patron • perspective • vernacular

USING YOUR NOTES
2. Which event most affected the rise of Italian city-states?

1300
1500

MAIN IDEAS
3. What are some of the characteristics of the "Renaissance man" and "Renaissance woman"?

4. How did Italy's cities help to make it the birthplace of the Renaissance?

5. What was the attitude of Church leaders and the wealthy toward the arts? Why?

CRITICAL THINKING & WRITING
6. **DRAWING CONCLUSIONS** How did study of the classics influence branches of learning such as history, literature, and philosophy?

7. **MAKING INFERENCES** How is the humanism of the Renaissance reflected in its art? Explain with examples.

8. **COMPARING** What were the differences between the Middle Ages and the Renaissance in the attitude toward worldly pleasures?

9. **WRITING ACTIVITY** REVOLUTION How did the Renaissance revolutionize European art and thought? Support your opinions in a three-paragraph **essay.**

CONNECT TO TODAY WRITING A DESCRIPTION
In a book on modern art, find an artist who worked in more than one medium, such as painting and sculpture. Write a **description** of one of the artist's works in each medium.

Renaissance Ideas Influence Renaissance Art

The Renaissance in Italy produced extraordinary achievements in many different forms of art, including painting, architecture, sculpture, and drawing. These art forms were used by talented artists to express important ideas and attitudes of the age.

The value of humanism is shown in Raphael's *School of Athens*, a depiction of the greatest Greek philosophers. The realism of Renaissance art is seen in a portrait such as the *Mona Lisa*, which is an expression of the subject's unique features and personality. And Michelangelo's *David* shares stylistic qualities with ancient Greek and Roman sculpture.

↗ hmhsocialstudies.com

RESEARCH WEB LINKS Go online for more on Renaissance art.

▲ **Portraying Individuals**
Da Vinci The *Mona Lisa* (c. 1504–1506) is thought to be a portrait of Lisa Gherardini, who, at 16, married Francesco del Giocondo, a wealthy merchant of Florence who commissioned the portrait. Mona Lisa is a shortened form of Madonna Lisa (Madam, or My Lady, Lisa). Renaissance artists showed individuals as they really looked.

▼ **Classical and Renaissance Sculpture**
Michelangelo Influenced by classical statues, Michelangelo sculpted *David* from 1501 to 1504. Michelangelo portrayed the biblical hero in the moments just before battle. David's posture is graceful, yet his figure also displays strength. The statue, which is 18 feet tall, towers over the viewer.

▲ The Importance of Ancient Greece

Raphael The painting *School of Athens* (1508) for the pope's apartments in the Vatican shows that the scholars of ancient Greece were highly honored. Under the center arch stand Plato and Aristotle. To their right, Socrates argues with several young men. Toward the front, Pythagoras draws a lesson on a slate and Ptolemy holds a globe.

▲ Renaissance Science and Technology

Da Vinci Leonardo da Vinci filled his notebooks with observations and sketches of new inventions. This drawing from his notebooks shows a design for a spiral screw to achieve vertical flight. Leonardo's drawing anticipated the helicopter.

Connect *to* Today

1. **Clarifying** How do the works of Renaissance artists and architects reflect Renaissance ideas? Explain.

   See Skillbuilder Handbook, page R4.

2. **Synthesizing** Look through books on architecture to find examples of American architects who were influenced by the architects and buildings of the Italian Renaissance. Share your findings with the class.

479

The Northern Renaissance

MAIN IDEA	WHY IT MATTERS NOW	TERMS & NAMES
CULTURAL INTERACTION In the 1400s, the ideas of the Italian Renaissance began to spread to Northern Europe.	Renaissance ideas such as the importance of the individual are a-strong part of modern thought.	• utopia • William Shakespeare • Johann Gutenberg

SETTING THE STAGE The work of such artists as Leonardo da Vinci, Michelangelo, and Raphael showed the Renaissance spirit. All three artists demonstrated an interest in classical culture, a curiosity about the world, and a belief in human potential. Humanist writers expanded ideas about individuality. These ideas impressed scholars, students, and merchants who visited Italy. By the late 1400s, Renaissance ideas had spread to Northern Europe—especially England, France, Germany, and Flanders (now part of France and the Netherlands).

The Northern Renaissance Begins

hmhsocialstudies.com
TAKING NOTES

Use the graphic organizer online to take notes on important events of the Northern Resnaissance.

By 1450 the population of northern Europe, which had declined due to bubonic plague, was beginning to grow again. When the destructive Hundred Years' War between France and England ended in 1453, many cities grew rapidly. Urban merchants became wealthy enough to sponsor artists. This happened first in Flanders, which was rich from long-distance trade and the cloth industry. Then, as wealth increased in other parts of Northern Europe, patronage of artists increased as well.

As Section 1 explained, Italy was divided into city-states. In-contrast, England and France were unified under strong monarchs. These rulers often sponsored the arts by purchasing paintings and by supporting artists and writers. For example, Francis I of France invited Leonardo da Vinci to retire in France, and hired Italian artists and architects to rebuild and decorate his castle at Fontainebleau (FAHN•tihn•BLOH). The castle became a showcase for Renaissance art.

As Renaissance ideas spread out of Italy, they mingled with northern traditions. As a result, the northern Renaissance developed its own character. For example, the artists were especially interested in realism. The Renaissance ideal of human dignity inspired some northern humanists to develop plans for social reform based on Judeo-Christian values.

Artistic Ideas Spread

In 1494, a French king claimed the throne of Naples in southern Italy and launched an invasion through northern Italy. As the war dragged on, many Italian artists and writers left for a safer life in Northern Europe. They brought with them the styles and techniques of the Italian Renaissance. In addition, Northern European artists who studied in Italy carried Renaissance ideas back to their homelands.

German Painters Perhaps the most famous person to do this was the German artist Albrecht Dürer (DYUR•uhr). He traveled to Italy to study in 1494. After returning to Germany, Dürer produced woodcuts and engravings. Many of his prints portray religious subjects. Others portray classical myths or realistic landscapes. The popularity of Dürer's work helped to spread Renaissance styles.

Dürer's emphasis upon realism influenced the work of another German artist, Hans Holbein (HOHL•byn) the Younger. Holbein specialized in painting portraits that are almost photographic in detail. He emigrated to England where he painted portraits of King Henry VIII and other members of the English royal family.

Flemish Painters The support of wealthy merchant families in Flanders helped to make Flanders the artistic center of northern Europe. The first great Flemish Renaissance painter was Jan van Eyck (yahn van YK). Van Eyck used recently developed oil-based paints to develop techniques that painters still use. By applying layer upon layer of paint, van Eyck was able to create a variety of subtle colors in clothing and jewels. Oil painting became popular and spread to Italy.

In addition to new techniques, van Eyck's paintings display unusually realistic details and reveal the personality of their subjects. His work influenced later artists in Northern Europe.

Flemish painting reached its peak after 1550 with the work of Pieter Bruegel (BROY•guhl) the Elder. Bruegel was also interested in realistic details and individual people. He was very skillful in portraying large numbers of people. He captured scenes from everyday peasant life such as weddings, dances, and harvests. Bruegel's rich colors, vivid details, and balanced use of space give a sense of life and feeling. **A**

MAIN IDEA

Summarizing

A What techniques does Bruegel use to give life to his paintings?

> Analyzing Art

Peasant Life

The Flemish painter Pieter Bruegel's paintings provide information about peasant life in the 1500s. *Peasant Wedding* (1568) portrays a wedding feast.

- **The Bride** The bride sits under the paper crown hanging on the green cloth.
- **The Servers** Men who may be her brothers are passing out plates.
- **The Guests** Several children have come to the party.
- **The Musicians** They are carrying bagpipes. One glances hungrily at the food.

SKILLBUILDER:
Interpreting Visual Sources
Forming Generalizations
In what ways does this painting present a snapshot of peasant life?

Northern Writers Try to Reform Society

Italian humanists were very interested in reviving classical languages and classical texts. When the Italian humanist ideas reached the north, people used them to examine the traditional teachings of the Church. The northern humanists were critical of the failure of the Christian Church to inspire people to live a Christian life. This criticism produced a new movement known as Christian humanism. The focus of Christian humanism was the reform of society. Of particular importance to humanists was education. The humanists promoted the education of women and founded schools attended by both boys and girls.

Christian Humanists The best known of the Christian humanists were Desiderius Erasmus (DEHZ•ih•DEER•ee•uhs ih•RAZ•muhs) of Holland and Thomas More of England. The two were close friends.

In 1509, Erasmus wrote his most famous work, *The Praise of Folly.* This book poked fun at greedy merchants, heartsick lovers, quarrelsome scholars, and pompous priests. Erasmus believed in a Christianity of the heart, not one of ceremonies or rules. He thought that in order to improve society, all people should study the Bible.

Thomas More tried to show a better model of society. In 1516, he wrote the book *Utopia.* In Greek, **utopia** means "no place." In English it has come to mean an ideal place as depicted in More's book. The book is about an imaginary land where greed, corruption, and war have been weeded out. In Utopia, because there was little greed, Utopians had little use for money:

▼ Christian humanist Thomas More

PRIMARY SOURCE
Gold and silver, of which money is made, are so treated . . . that no one values them more highly than their true nature deserves. Who does not see that they are far inferior to iron in usefulness since without iron mortals cannot live any more than without fire and water?

THOMAS MORE, *Utopia*

More wrote in Latin. As his work became popular, More's works were translated into a variety of languages including French, German, English, Spanish, and Italian.

Women's Reforms During this period the vast majority of Europeans were unable to read or write. Those families who could afford formal schooling usually sent only their sons. One woman spoke out against this practice. Christine de Pizan was highly educated for the time and was one of the first women to earn a living as a writer. Writing in French, she produced many books, including short stories, biographies, novels, and manuals on military techniques. She frequently wrote about the objections men had to educating women. In one book, *The Book of The City of Ladies,* she wrote:

◄ Christine de Pizan is best known for her works defending women.

PRIMARY SOURCE B
I am amazed by the opinion of some men who claim that they do not want their daughters, wives, or kinswomen to be educated because their mores [morals] would be ruined as a result. . . . Here you can clearly see that not all opinions of men are based on reason and that these men are wrong.

CHRISTINE DE PIZAN, *The Book of The City of Ladies*

MAIN IDEA

Analyzing Primary Sources
B What does de Pizan argue for in this passage?

Christine de Pizan was one of the first European writers to question different treatment of boys and girls. However, her goal of formal education for children of both sexes would not be achieved for several centuries.

The Elizabethan Age

The Renaissance spread to England in the mid-1500s. The period was known as the Elizabethan Age, after Queen Elizabeth I. Elizabeth reigned from 1558 to 1603. She was well educated and spoke French, Italian, Latin, and Greek. She also wrote poetry and music. As queen she did much to support the development of English art and literature.

William Shakespeare The most famous writer of the Elizabethan Age was <u>William Shakespeare</u>. Many people regard him as the greatest playwright of all time. Shakespeare was born in 1564 in Stratford-upon-Avon, a small town about 90 miles northwest of London. By 1592 he was living in London and writing poems and plays, and soon he would be performing at the Globe Theater.

Like many Renaissance writers, Shakespeare revered the classics and drew on them for inspiration and plots. His works display a masterful command of the English language and a deep understanding of human beings. He revealed the souls of men and women through scenes of dramatic conflict. Many of these plays examine human flaws. However, Shakespeare also had one of his characters deliver a speech that expresses the Renaissance's high view of human nature:

PRIMARY SOURCE

What a piece of work is a man, how noble in reason, how infinite in faculties, in form and moving, how express and admirable; in action how like an angel, in apprehension [understanding] how like a god: the beauty of the world, the paragon of animals.

WILLIAM SHAKESPEARE, *Hamlet (Act 2, Scene 2)*

MAIN IDEA

Summarizing

C What are two ways in which Shakespeare's work-showed Renaissance influences?

Shakespeare's most famous plays include the tragedies *Macbeth, Hamlet, Othello, Romeo and Juliet,* and *King Lear,* and the comedies *A Midsummer Night's Dream* and *The Taming of the Shrew.* **C**

Connect *to* Today

Shakespeare's Popularity

Even though he has been dead for about 400 years, Shakespeare is one of the favorite writers of filmmakers. His works are produced both in period costumes and in modern attire. The themes or dialogue have been adapted for many films, including some in foreign languages. The posters at the right illustrate *Othello* (done in period costume); *Romeo and Juliet* in a modern setting; a Japanese film, *Ran,* an adaptation of *King Lear;.* and *10 Things I Hate About You,* an adaptation of *The Taming of the Shrew.*

Printing Spreads Renaissance Ideas

The Chinese invented block printing, in which a printer carved words or letters on a wooden block, inked the block, and then used it to print on paper. Around 1045, Bi Sheng invented movable type, or a separate piece of type for each character in the language. The Chinese writing system contains thousands of different characters, so most Chinese printers found movable type impractical. However, the method would prove practical for Europeans because their languages have a very small number of letters in their alphabets.

Gutenberg Improves the Printing Process During the 13th century, block-printed items reached Europe from China. European printers began to use block printing to create whole pages to bind into books. However, this process was too slow to satisfy the Renaissance demand for knowledge, information, and books.

Around 1440 **Johann Gutenberg**, a craftsman from Mainz, Germany, developed a printing press that incorporated a number of technologies in a new way. The process made it possible to produce books quickly and cheaply. Using this improved process, Gutenberg printed a complete Bible, the Gutenberg Bible, in about 1455. It was the first full-sized book printed with movable type. **D**

The printing press enabled a printer to produce hundreds of copies of a single work. For the first time, books were cheap enough that many people could buy them. At first printers produced mainly religious works. Soon they began to provide books on other subjects such as travel guides and medical manuals.

MAIN IDEA

Recognizing Effects

D What were the major effects of the invention of the printing press?

Global Impact

The Printing Press

Many inventions are creative combinations of known technologies. In 1452, Johann Gutenberg combined known technologies from Europe and Asia with his idea for molding movable type to create a printing press that changed the world.

Screw-type Press An adaptation of Asian olive-oil presses made a workable printing press.

Movable Type Letters that could be put together in any fashion and reused was a Chinese idea.

Paper Using paper mass-produced by Chinese techniques, rather than vellum (calf or lambskin), made printing books possible.

Ink Oil-based inks from 10th-century Europe worked better on type than tempera ink.

A copyist took five months to produce a single book.

5 months → 1 book

One man and a printing press could produce 500 books in the same amount of time.

5 months → 500 books

SKILLBUILDER: Interpreting Graphics
1. **Drawing Conclusions** *About how many books could a printing press produce in a month?*
2. **Making Inferences** *Which areas of the world contributed technologies to Gutenberg's printing press?*

The Legacy of the Renaissance

The European Renaissance was a period of great artistic and social change. It marked a break with the medieval-period ideals focused around the Church. The Renaissance belief in the dignity of the individual played a key role in the gradual rise of democratic ideas. Furthermore, the impact of the movable-type printing press was tremendous. Some historians have suggested that its effects were even more dramatic than the arrival of personal computers in the 20th century. Below is a summary of the changes that resulted from the Renaissance.

Changes in the Arts

- Art drew on techniques and styles of classical Greece and Rome.
- Paintings and sculptures portrayed individuals and nature in more realistic and lifelike ways.
- Artists created works that were secular as well as those that were religious.
- Writers began to use vernacular languages to express their ideas.
- The arts praised individual achievement.

Changes in Society

- Printing changed society by making more information available and inexpensive enough for society at large.
- A greater availability of books prompted an increased desire for learning and a rise in literacy throughout Europe.
- Published accounts of new discoveries, maps, and charts led to further discoveries in a variety of fields.
- Published legal proceedings made the laws clear so that people were more likely to understand their rights.
- Christian humanists' attempts to reform society changed views about how life should be lived.
- People began to question political structures and religious practices.

Renaissance ideas continued to influence European thought—including religious thought—as you will see in Section 3.

SECTION 2 ASSESSMENT

TERMS & NAMES 1. For each term or name, write a sentence explaining its significance.
- utopia   • William Shakespeare   • Johann Gutenberg

USING YOUR NOTES

2. Which of the events listed do you think was most important? Explain.

MAIN IDEAS

3. How did Albrecht Dürer's work reflect the influence of the Italian Renaissance?

4. What was one way the Renaissance changed society?

5. Why was the invention of the printing press so important?

CRITICAL THINKING & WRITING

6. **COMPARING** How were the works of German painters different from those of the Flemish painters? Give examples.

7. **ANALYZING MOTIVES** What reasons did humanists give for wanting to reform society? Explain.

8. **RECOGNIZING EFFECTS** How did the availability of cheap books spread learning?

9. **WRITING ACTIVITY** [CULTURAL INTERACTION] Reread the primary source quotation from Christine de Pizan on page 482. Write a one paragraph **opinion piece** about the ideas expressed there.

MULTIMEDIA ACTIVITY CREATING A PIE GRAPH

Use the Internet to find information on the number of books published in print and those published electronically last year. Create a **pie graph** showing the results of your research.

INTERNET KEYWORD
book publishing statistics

Social History

City Life in Renaissance Europe

Throughout the 1500s, the vast majority of Europeans—more than 75 percent—lived in rural areas. However, the capital and port cities of most European countries experienced remarkable growth during this time. The population of London, for example, stood at about 200,000 in 1600, making it perhaps the largest city in Europe. In London, and in other large European cities, a distinctively urban way of life developed in the Renaissance era.

↗ **hmhsocialstudies.com**

RESEARCH WEB LINKS Go online for more on life in Renaissance Europe.

▼ Joblessness

Many newcomers to London struggled to find jobs and shelter. Some turned to crime to make a living. Others became beggars. However, it was illegal for able-bodied people to beg. To avoid a whipping or prison time, beggars had to be sick or disabled.

▲ Entertainment

In Renaissance England, performances at playhouses often were wild affairs. If audiences did not like the play, they booed loudly, pelted the stage with garbage, and sometimes attacked the actors.

▼ Sanitation

This small pomander (POH•man•durh), a metal container filled with spices, was crafted in the shape of orange segments. Well-to-do Londoners held pomanders to their noses to shield themselves from the stench of the rotting garbage that littered the streets.

▼ Food

A typical meal for wealthy Londoners might include fish, several kinds of meat, bread, and a variety of vegetables, served on silver or pewter tableware. The diet of the poor was simpler. They rarely ate fish, meat, or cheese. Usually, their meals consisted of a pottage—a kind of soup—of vegetables. And the poor ate their meals from a trencher, a hollowed-out slab of stale bread or wood.

▼ Transportation

Many of London's streets were so narrow that walking was the only practical means of transportation. Often, however, the quickest way to get from here to there in the city was to take the river. Boat traffic was especially heavy when the playhouses were open. On those days, as many as 4,000 people crossed the Thames from the city to Southwark, where most of the theaters were located.

> DATA FILE

COST OF LIVING IN RENAISSANCE LONDON

These tables show what typical Londoners earned and spent in the late 1500s. The basic denominations in English currency at the time were the pound (£), the shilling, and the penny (12 pence equaled 1 shilling, and 20 shillings equaled 1 pound). The pound of the late 1500s is roughly equivalent to $400 in today's U.S. currency.

Typical Earnings

Merchant	£100 per year
Skilled Worker	£13 per year (about 5 shillings/week)
Unskilled Worker	£5 per year (about 4 pence/day)
Servant	£1 to £2 per year (plus food and lodging)

Typical Prices

Lodging	4 to 8 pence a week
Beef	3 pence per lb
Chickens	1 penny each
Eggs	2 pence per dozen
Apples	1 penny per dozen
Onions	1/2 penny a sack
Various Spices	10 to 11 shillings per lb

Connect *to* Today

1. **Making Inferences** Study the images and captions as well as the information in the Data File. What inferences about the standard of living of London's wealthy citizens can you make from this information? How did it compare to the standard of living of London's common people?

   See Skillbuilder Handbook, page R9.

2. **Comparing** How does diet in the United States today compare to the diet of Renaissance Europeans? Cite specific examples in your answer.

Luther Leads the Reformation

MAIN IDEA	WHY IT MATTERS NOW	TERMS & NAMES
REVOLUTION Martin Luther's protest over abuses in the Catholic Church led to the founding of Protestant churches.	Nearly one-fifth of the Christians in today's world are Protestants.	• indulgence • Reformation • Lutheran • Protestant	• Peace of Augsburg • annul • Anglican

SETTING THE STAGE By the tenth century, the Roman Catholic Church had come to dominate religious life in Northern and Western Europe. However, the Church had not won universal approval. Over the centuries, many people criticized its practices. They felt that Church leaders were too interested in worldly pursuits, such as gaining wealth and political power. Even though the Church made some reforms during the Middle Ages, people continued to criticize it. Prompted by the actions of one man, that criticism would lead to rebellion.

Causes of the Reformation

TAKING NOTES

Use the graphic organizer online to take notes on the effects of Martin Luther's protests.

By 1500, additional forces weakened the Church. The Renaissance emphasis on the secular and the individual challenged Church authority. The printing press spread these secular ideas. In addition, some rulers began to challenge the Church's political power. In Germany, which was divided into many competing states, it was difficult for the pope or the emperor to impose central authority. Finally, northern merchants resented paying church taxes to Rome. Spurred by these social, political, and economic forces, a new movement for religious reform began in Germany. It then swept much of Europe.

Criticisms of the Catholic Church Critics of the Church claimed that its leaders were corrupt. The popes who ruled during the Renaissance patronized the arts, spent extravagantly on personal pleasure, and fought wars. Pope Alexander VI,

Causes of the Reformation

Social	Political	Economic	Religious
• The Renaissance values of humanism and secularism led people to question the Church. • The printing press helped to spread ideas critical of the Church.	• Powerful monarchs challenged the Church as the supreme power in Europe. • Many leaders viewed the pope as a foreign ruler and challenged his authority.	• European princes and kings were jealous of the Church's wealth. • Merchants and others resented having to pay taxes to the Church.	• Some Church leaders had become worldly and corrupt. • Many people found Church practices such as the sale of indulgences unacceptable.

for example, admitted that he had fathered several children. Many popes were too busy pursuing worldly affairs to have much time for spiritual duties.

The lower clergy had problems as well. Many priests and monks were so poorly educated that they could scarcely read, let alone teach people. Others broke their priestly vows by marrying, and some drank to excess or gambled.

Early Calls for Reform Influenced by reformers, people had come to expect higher standards of conduct from priests and church leaders. In the late 1300s and early 1400s, John Wycliffe of England and Jan Hus of Bohemia had advocated Church reform. They denied that the pope had the right to worldly power. They also taught that the Bible had more authority than Church leaders did. In the 1500s, Christian humanists like Desiderius Erasmus and Thomas More added their voices to the chorus of criticism. In addition, many Europeans were reading religious works and forming their own opinions about the Church. The atmosphere in Europe was ripe for reform by the early 1500s.

Luther Challenges the Church

Martin Luther's parents wanted him to be a lawyer. Instead, he became a monk and a teacher. From 1512 until his death, he taught scripture at the University of Wittenberg in the German state of Saxony. All he wanted was to be a good Christian, not to lead a religious revolution.

The 95 Theses In 1517, Luther decided to take a public stand against the actions of a friar named Johann Tetzel. Tetzel was raising money to rebuild St. Peter's Cathedral in Rome. He did this by selling indulgences. An **indulgence** was a pardon. It released a sinner from performing the penalty that a priest imposed for sins. Indulgences were not supposed to affect God's right to judge. Unfortunately, Tetzel gave people the impression that by buying indulgences, they could buy their way into heaven.

Luther was troubled by Tetzel's tactics. In response, he wrote 95 Theses, or formal statements, attacking the "pardon-merchants." On October 31, 1517, he posted these statements on the door of the castle church in Wittenberg and invited other scholars to debate him. Someone copied Luther's words and took them to a printer. Quickly, Luther's name became known all over Germany. His actions began the **Reformation**, a movement for religious reform. It led to the founding of Christian churches that did not accept the pope's authority.

Luther's Teachings Soon Luther went beyond criticizing indulgences. He wanted full reform of the Church. His teachings rested on three main ideas:

MAIN IDEA

Summarizing

A What were the main points of Luther's teachings?

- People could win salvation only by faith in God's gift of forgiveness. The Church taught that faith and "good works" were needed for salvation.
- All Church teachings should be clearly based on the words of the Bible. Both the pope and Church traditions were false authorities.
- All people with faith were equal. Therefore, people did not need priests to interpret the Bible for them. **A**

History Makers

Martin Luther
1483–1546

In one way, fear led Luther to become a monk. At the age of 21, Luther was caught in a terrible thunderstorm. Convinced he would die, he cried out, "Saint Anne, help me! I will become a monk."

Even after entering the monastery, Luther felt fearful, lost, sinful, and rejected by God. He confessed his sins regularly, fasted, and did penance. However, by studying the Bible, Luther came to the conclusion that faith alone was the key to salvation. Only then did he experience peace.

↗ hmhsocialstudies.com

RESEARCH WEB LINKS Go online for more on Martin Luther.

The Response to Luther

Luther was astonished at how rapidly his ideas spread and attracted followers. Many people had been unhappy with the Church for political and economic reasons. They saw Luther's protests as a way to challenge Church control.

The Pope's Threat Initially, Church officials in Rome viewed Luther simply as a rebellious monk who needed to be punished by his superiors. However, as Luther's ideas became more popular, the pope realized that this monk was a serious threat. In one angry reply to Church criticism, Luther actually suggested that Christians drive the pope from the Church by force.

In 1520, Pope Leo X issued a decree threatening Luther with excommunication unless he took back his statements. Luther did not take back a word. Instead, his students at Wittenberg gathered around a bonfire and cheered as he threw the pope's decree into the flames. Leo excommunicated Luther.

The Emperor's Opposition Holy Roman Emperor Charles V, a devout Catholic, also opposed Luther's teaching. Charles controlled a vast empire, including the German states. He summoned Luther to the town of Worms (vawrmz) in 1521 to stand trial. Told to recant, or take back his statements, Luther refused:

Vocabulary
Excommunication is the taking away of a person's right to membership in the Church.

PRIMARY SOURCE

I am bound by the Scriptures I have quoted and my conscience is captive to the Word of God. I cannot and I will not retract anything, since it is neither safe nor right to go against conscience. I cannot do otherwise, here I stand, may God help me. Amen.

MARTIN LUTHER, quoted in *The Protestant Reformation* by Lewis W. Spitz

A month after Luther made that speech, Charles issued an imperial order, the Edict of Worms. It declared Luther an outlaw and a heretic. According to this edict, no one in the empire was to give Luther food or shelter. All his books were to be burned. However, Prince Frederick the Wise of Saxony disobeyed the emperor. For almost a year after the trial, he sheltered Luther in one of his castles. While there, Luther translated the New Testament into German.

Luther returned to Wittenberg in 1522. There he discovered that many of his ideas were already being put into practice. Instead of continuing to seek reforms in the Catholic Church, Luther and his followers had become a separate religious group, called **Lutherans**.

The Peasants' Revolt Some people began to apply Luther's revolutionary ideas to society. In 1524, German peasants, excited by reformers' talk of Christian freedom, demanded an end to serfdom. Bands of angry peasants went about the countryside raiding monasteries, pillaging, and burning. The revolt horrified Luther. He wrote a pamphlet urging the German princes to show the peasants no mercy. The princes' armies crushed the revolt, killing as many as 100,000 people. Feeling betrayed, many peasants rejected Luther's religious leadership. **B**

Germany at War In contrast to the bitter peasants, many northern German princes supported Lutheranism. While some princes genuinely shared Luther's beliefs, others liked Luther's ideas for selfish reasons. They saw his teachings as a good excuse to seize Church property and to assert their independence from Charles V.

In 1529, German princes who remained loyal to the pope agreed to join forces against Luther's ideas. Those princes who supported Luther signed a protest against that agreement. These protesting princes came to be known as Protestants. Eventually, the term **Protestant** was applied to Christians who belonged to non-Catholic churches.

Vocabulary
A *heretic* is a person who holds beliefs that differ from official Church teachings.

MAIN IDEA

Analyzing Causes

B Why did Luther's ideas encourage the German peasants to revolt?

Protestantism

Protestantism is a branch of Christianity. It developed out of the Reformation, the 16th-century protest in Europe against beliefs and practices of the Catholic Church. Three distinct branches of Protestantism emerged at first. They were Lutheranism, based on the teachings of Martin Luther in Germany; Calvinism, based on the teachings of John Calvin in Switzerland; and Anglicanism, which was established by King Henry VIII in England. Protestantism spread throughout Europe in the 16th century, and later, the world. As differences in beliefs developed, new denominations formed.

The Division of Christianity

Religious Beliefs and Practices in the 16th Century

	Roman Catholicism	Lutheranism	Calvinism	Anglicanism
Leadership	Pope is head of the Church	Ministers lead congregations	Council of elders govern each church	English monarch is head of the Church
Salvation	Salvation by faith and good works	Salvation by faith alone	God has predetermined who will be saved	Salvation by faith alone
Bible	Church and Bible tradition are sources of revealed truth	Bible is sole source of revealed truth	Bible is sole source of revealed truth	Bible is sole source of revealed truth
Worship Service	Worship service based on ritual	Worship service focused on preaching and ritual	Worship service focused on preaching	Worship service based on ritual and preaching
Interpretation of Beliefs	Priests interpret Bible and Church teachings for believers	Believers interpret the Bible for themselves	Believers interpret the Bible for themselves	Believers interpret the Bible using tradition and reason

 hmhsocialstudies.com

RESEARCH WEB LINKS Go online for more on Protestantism.

> DATA FILE

PROTESTANTISM TODAY

Membership:
- Nearly 400 million Protestants worldwide
- About 65 million Protestants in the United States

Branches:
- More than 465 major Protestant denominations worldwide
- Major denominational families worldwide: Anglican, Assemblies of God, Baptist, Methodist, Lutheran, and Presbyterian
- More than 250 denominations in the United States
- About 40 denominations with more than 400,000 members each in the United States

Religious Adherents in the United States:

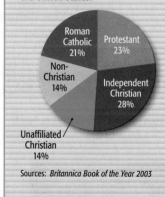

Sources: *Britannica Book of the Year 2003*

Connect *to* Today

1. **Comparing** Which of the branches on the chart at left are most different and which are most similar?

   See Skillbuilder Handbook, page R7.

2. **Developing Historical Perspective** Do research on Protestantism. Select a denomination not shown on this page and write a paragraph tracing its roots to Reformation Protestantism.

Still determined that his subjects should remain Catholic, Charles V went to war against the Protestant princes. Even though he defeated them in 1547, he failed to force them back into the Catholic Church. In 1555, Charles, weary of fighting, ordered all German princes, both Protestant and Catholic, to assemble in the city of Augsburg. There the princes agreed that each ruler would decide the religion of his state. This famous religious settlement was known as the **Peace of Augsburg**.

England Becomes Protestant

The Catholic Church soon faced another great challenge to its authority, this time in England. Unlike Luther, the man who broke England's ties to the Roman Catholic Church did so for political and personal, not religious, reasons.

Henry VIII Wants a Son When Henry VIII became king of England in 1509, he was a devout Catholic. Indeed, in 1521, Henry wrote a stinging attack on Luther's ideas. In recognition of Henry's support, the pope gave him the title "Defender of the Faith." Political needs, however, soon tested his religious loyalty. He needed a male heir. Henry's father had become king after a long civil war. Henry feared that a similar war would start if he died without a son as his heir. He and his wife, Catherine of Aragon, had one living child—a daughter, Mary—but no woman had ever successfully claimed the English throne.

By 1527, Henry was convinced that the 42-year-old Catherine would have no more children. He wanted to divorce her and take a younger queen. Church law did not allow divorce. However, the pope could **annul**, or set aside, Henry's marriage if proof could be found that it had never been legal in the first place. In 1527, Henry asked the pope to annul his marriage, but the pope turned him down. The pope did not want to offend Catherine's powerful nephew, the Holy Roman Emperor Charles V.

The Reformation Parliament Henry took steps to solve his marriage problem himself. In 1529, he called Parliament into session and asked it to pass a set of laws

Henry VIII Causes Religious Turmoil

Henry's many marriages led to conflict with the Catholic Church and the founding of the Church of England.

1509 Henry VIII becomes king; marries Catherine of Aragon.

1516 Daughter Mary is born.

1527 Henry asks the pope to end his first marriage; the pope refuses.

1529 Henry summons the Reformation Parliament; dismantling of pope's power in England begins.

1534 Act of Supremacy names Henry and his successors supreme head of the English Church.

1531 Parliament recognizes Henry as head of the Church.

1533 Parliament places clergy under Henry's control; Henry divorces Catherine, marries Anne Boleyn (at left); daughter Elizabeth born.

1510 — 1520 — 1530

that ended the pope's power in England. This Parliament is known as the Reformation Parliament.

In 1533, Henry secretly married Anne Boleyn (BUL•ihn), who was in her twenties. Shortly after, Parliament legalized Henry's divorce from Catherine. In 1534, Henry's break with the pope was completed when Parliament voted to approve the Act of Supremacy. This called on people to take an oath recognizing the divorce and accepting Henry, not the pope, as the official head of England's Church.

The Act of Supremacy met some opposition. Thomas More, even though he had strongly criticized the Church, remained a devout Catholic. His faith, he said, would not allow him to accept the terms of the act and he refused to take the oath. In response, Henry had him arrested and imprisoned in the Tower of London. In 1535, More was found guilty of high treason and executed.

Consequences of Henry's Changes Henry did not immediately get the male heir he sought. After Anne Boleyn gave birth to a daughter, Elizabeth, she fell out of Henry's favor. Eventually, she was charged with treason. Like Thomas More, she was imprisoned in the Tower of London. She was found guilty and beheaded in 1536. Almost at once, Henry took a third wife, Jane Seymour. In 1537, she gave him a son named Edward. Henry's happiness was tempered by his wife's death just two weeks later. Henry married three more times. None of these marriages, however, produced children.

After Henry's death in 1547, each of his three children ruled England in turn. This created religious turmoil. Henry's son, Edward, became king when he was just nine years old. Too young to rule alone, Edward VI was guided by adult advisers. These men were devout Protestants, and they introduced Protestant reforms to the English Church. Almost constantly in ill health, Edward reigned for just six years. Mary, the daughter of Catherine of Aragon, took the throne in 1553. She was a Catholic who returned the English Church to the rule of the pope. Her efforts met with considerable resistance, and she had many Protestants executed. When Mary died in 1558, Elizabeth, Anne Boleyn's daughter, inherited the throne.

1536
Anne Boleyn is beheaded.

1537
Henry's third wife, Jane Seymour, has son, Edward. She dies from complications.

1547
Henry dies; Catherine Parr, his sixth wife, outlives him; Edward VI begins six-year rule; Protestants are strong.

1558
Elizabeth I (at right) begins rule; she restores the Protestant Church.

1540

1550

1560

1540-1542
Henry divorces Anne of Cleves, his fourth wife, and executes Catherine Howard (above), his fifth wife.

1553
Mary I (at left) begins rule and restores the Catholic Church.

History Makers

Elizabeth I
1533–1603

Elizabeth I, like her father, had a robust nature and loved physical activity. She had a particular passion for dancing. Her fondness for exercise diminished little with age, and she showed amazing energy and strength well into her sixties.

Elizabeth also resembled her father in character and temperament. She was stubborn, strong-willed, and arrogant, and she expected to be obeyed without question. And Elizabeth had a fierce and unpredictable temper. To her subjects, Elizabeth was an object of both fear and love. She was their "most dread sovereign lady."

Elizabeth Restores Protestantism Elizabeth I was determined to return her kingdom to Protestantism. In 1559, Parliament followed Elizabeth's wishes and set up the Church of England, or **Anglican** Church, with Elizabeth as its head. This was to be the only legal church in England.

Elizabeth decided to establish a state church that moderate Catholics and moderate Protestants might both accept. To please Protestants, priests in the Church of England were allowed to marry. They could deliver sermons in English, not Latin. To please Catholics, the Church of England kept some of the trappings of the Catholic service such as rich robes. In addition, church services were revised to be somewhat more acceptable to Catholics. **C**

Elizabeth Faces Other Challenges By taking this moderate approach, Elizabeth brought a level of religious peace to England. Religion, however, remained a problem. Some Protestants pushed for Elizabeth to make more far-reaching church reforms. At the same time, some Catholics tried to overthrow Elizabeth and replace her with her cousin, the Catholic Mary Queen of Scots. Elizabeth also faced threats from Philip II, the Catholic king of Spain.

Elizabeth faced other difficulties. Money was one problem. In the late 1500s, the English began to think about building an American empire as a new source of income. While colonies strengthened England economically, they did not enrich the queen directly. Elizabeth's constant need for money would carry over into the next reign and lead to bitter conflict between the monarch and Parliament. You will read more about Elizabeth's reign in Chapter 21. In the meantime, the Reformation gained ground in other European countries.

MAIN IDEA

Recognizing Effects

C How did Henry VIII's marriages and divorces cause religious turmoil in England?

SECTION 3 ASSESSMENT

TERMS & NAMES **1.** For each term or name, write a sentence explaining its significance.
• indulgence   • Reformation   • Lutheran   • Protestant   • Peace of Augsburg   • annul   • Anglican

USING YOUR NOTES	MAIN IDEAS	CRITICAL THINKING & WRITING
2. Which effect do you think had the most permanent impact? Explain.	**3.** What political, economic, and social factors helped bring about the Reformation?	**6. DRAWING CONCLUSIONS** Explain how Elizabeth I was able to bring a level of religious peace to England.
	4. From where did the term *Protestantism* originate?	**7. COMPARING** Do you think Luther or Henry VIII had a better reason to break with the Church? Provide details to support your answer.
	5. What impact did Henry VIII's actions have on England in the second half of the 1500s?	**8. ANALYZING MOTIVES** How did the Catholic Church respond to Luther's teachings? Why do you think this was so?
		9. WRITING ACTIVITY REVOLUTION Imagine Martin Luther and a leader of the Catholic Church are squaring off in a public debate. Write a brief **dialogue** between the two.

cause:
Luther protests abuses

effect 1
effect 2
effect 3

CONNECT TO TODAY CREATING A GRAPHIC

Use library resources to find information on the countries in which Protestantism is a major religion. Use your findings to create a **graphic** that makes a comparison among those countries.

The Reformation Continues

MAIN IDEA	WHY IT MATTERS NOW	TERMS & NAMES
RELIGIOUS AND ETHICAL SYSTEMS As Protestant reformers divided over beliefs, the Catholic Church made reforms.	Many Protestant churches began during this period, and many Catholic schools are the result of reforms in the Church.	• predestination • Catholic • Calvinism Reformation • theocracy • Jesuits • Presbyterian • Council of • Anabaptist Trent

SETTING THE STAGE Under the leadership of Queen Elizabeth I, the Anglican Church, though Protestant, remained similar to the Catholic Church in many of its doctrines and ceremonies. Meanwhile, other forms of Protestantism were developing elsewhere in Europe. Martin Luther had launched the Reformation in northern Germany, but reformers were at work in other countries. In Switzerland, another major branch of Protestantism emerged. Based mainly on the teachings of John Calvin, a French follower of Luther, it promoted unique ideas about the relationship between people and God.

Calvin Continues the Reformation

Religious reform in Switzerland was begun by Huldrych Zwingli (HUL•drykh ZWIHNG•lee), a Catholic priest in Zurich. He was influenced both by the Christian humanism of Erasmus and by the reforms of Luther. In 1520, Zwingli openly attacked abuses in the Catholic Church. He called for a return to the more personal faith of early Christianity. He also wanted believers to have more control over the Church.

hmhsocialstudies.com
TAKING NOTES

Use the graphic organizer online to take notes on the ideas of the reformers who came after Luther.

Zwingli's reforms were adopted in Zurich and other cities. In 1531, a bitter war between Swiss Protestants and Catholics broke out. During the fighting, Zwingli met his death. Meanwhile, John Calvin, then a young law student in France with a growing interest in Church doctrine, was beginning to clarify his religious beliefs.

Calvin Formalizes Protestant Ideas When Martin Luther posted his 95 Theses in 1517, John Calvin had been only eight years old. But Calvin grew up to have as much influence in the spread of Protestantism as Luther did. He would give order to the faith Luther had begun.

In 1536, Calvin published *Institutes of the Christian Religion*. This book expressed ideas about God, salvation, and human nature. It was a summary of Protestant theology, or religious beliefs. Calvin wrote that men and women are sinful by nature. Taking Luther's idea that humans cannot earn salvation, Calvin went on to say that God chooses a very few people to save. Calvin called these few the "elect." He believed that God has known since the beginning of time who will be saved. This doctrine is called **predestination**. The religion based on Calvin's teachings is called **Calvinism**.

John Calvin
1509–1564

A quiet boy, Calvin grew up to study law and philosophy at the University of Paris. In the 1530s, he was influenced by French followers of Luther. When King Francis I ordered Protestants arrested, Calvin fled. Eventually, he moved to Geneva.

Because Calvin and his followers rigidly regulated morality in Geneva, Calvinism is often described as strict and grim. But Calvin taught that people should enjoy God's gifts. He wrote that it should not be "forbidden to laugh, or to enjoy food, or to add new possessions to old."

Calvin Leads the Reformation in Switzerland Calvin believed that the ideal government was a **theocracy**, a government controlled by religious leaders. In 1541, Protestants in Geneva, Switzerland, asked Calvin to lead their city.

When Calvin arrived there in the 1540s, Geneva was a self-governing city of about 20,000 people. He and his followers ran the city according to strict rules. Everyone attended religion class. No one wore bright clothing or played card games. Authorities would imprison, excommunicate, or banish those who broke such rules. Anyone who preached different doctrines might be burned at the stake. Yet, to many Protestants, Calvin's Geneva was a model city of highly moral citizens.

Calvinism Spreads One admiring visitor to Geneva was a Scottish preacher named John Knox. When he returned to Scotland in 1559, Knox put Calvin's ideas to work. Each community church was governed by a group of laymen called elders or presbyters (PREHZ•buh•tuhrs). Followers of Knox became known as **Presbyterians**. In the 1560s, Protestant nobles led by Knox made Calvinism Scotland's official religion. They also deposed their Catholic ruler, Mary Queen of Scots, in favor of her infant son, James.

Elsewhere, Swiss, Dutch, and French reformers adopted the Calvinist form of church organization. One reason Calvin is considered so influential is that many Protestant churches today trace their roots to Calvin. Over the years, however, many of them have softened Calvin's strict teachings.

In France, Calvin's followers were called Huguenots. Hatred between Catholics and Huguenots frequently led to violence. The most violent clash occurred in Paris on August 24, 1572—the Catholic feast of St. Bartholomew's Day. At dawn, Catholic mobs began hunting for Protestants and murdering them. The massacres spread to other cities and lasted six months. Scholars believe that as many as 12,000 Huguenots were killed.

Other Protestant Reformers

Protestants taught that the Bible is the source of all religious truth and that people should read it to discover those truths. As Christians interpreted the Bible for themselves, new Protestant groups formed over differences in belief. **A**

The Anabaptists One such group baptized only those persons who were old enough to decide to be Christian. They said that persons who had been baptized as children should be rebaptized as adults. These believers were called **Anabaptists**, from a Greek word meaning "baptize again." The Anabaptists also taught that church and state should be separate, and they refused to fight in wars. They shared their possessions.

Viewing Anabaptists as radicals who threatened society, both Catholics and Protestants persecuted them. But the Anabaptists survived and became the forerunners of the Mennonites and the Amish. Their teaching influenced the later Quakers and Baptists, groups who split from the Anglican Church.

Women's Role in the Reformation Many women played prominent roles in the Reformation, especially during the early years. For example, the sister of King

MAIN IDEA

Analyzing Causes
A How did Protestant teaching lead to the forming of new groups?

SCOTLAND
Edinburgh

IRELAND

North Sea

DENMARK–NORWAY

SWEDEN

Baltic Sea

ENGLAND
London

ATLANTIC OCEAN

NETHERLANDS

Munster

GERMAN STATES

Wittenburg

POLAND-LITHUANIA

N

0   200 Miles
0   400 Kilometers

Paris

Worms

AUSTRIA

FRANCE

Augsburg

SWISS CONFEDERATION

Geneva

Vienna

HUNGARY

PORTUGAL

Avignon

ITALIAN STATES

Venice

Madrid

SPAIN

Barcelona

42° N

PAPAL STATES

OTTOMAN EMPIRE

Seville

Rome

Mediterranean Sea

NAPLES

Naples

Constantinople

Spread of Protestantism

NORWAY   SWEDEN

58° N

SCOTLAND

IRELAND

DENMARK

PRUSSIA

ENGLAND

London

BRANDENBURG

Wittenberg

POLAND-LITHUANIA

FLANDERS

HOLY ROMAN EMPIRE

AUSTRIA

FRANCE

SWISS CONFEDERATION

Geneva

Spread of Religion
← Lutheran
← Anglican
← Calvinist

42° N

VENETIAN REPUBLIC

PAPAL STATES

OTTOMAN EMPIRE

CORSICA

KINGDOM OF NAPLES

PORTUGAL

SPAIN

SARDINIA

KINGDOM OF SICILY

N

34° N

0   400 Miles
0   800 Kilometers

Dominant Religion

Roman Catholic   Eastern Orthodox
Lutheran   Islam
Anglican   Mixture of Calvinist,
Calvinist   Lutheran, and Roman Catholic

Minority Religion
Roman Catholic   Islam
Lutheran   Anabaptist
Calvinist

GEOGRAPHY SKILLBUILDER: Interpreting Maps

1. **Region** *Which European countries became mostly Protestant and which remained mostly Roman Catholic?*
2. **Location** *Judging from the way the religions were distributed, where would you expect religious conflicts to take place? Explain.*

▲ Although Catholic, Marguerite of Navarre supported the call for reform in the Church.

Francis I, Marguerite of Navarre, protected John Calvin from being executed for his beliefs while he lived in France. Other noblewomen also protected reformers. The wives of some reformers, too, had influence. Katherina Zell, married to Matthew Zell of Strasbourg, once scolded a minister for speaking harshly of another reformer. The minister responded by saying that she had "disturbed the peace." She answered his criticism sharply:

PRIMARY SOURCE
Do you call this disturbing the peace that instead of spending my time in frivolous amusements I have visited the plague-infested and carried out the dead? I have visited those in prison and under sentence of death. Often for three days and three nights I have neither eaten nor slept. I have never mounted the pulpit, but I have done more than any minister in visiting those in misery.

KATHERINA ZELL, quoted in *Women of the Reformation*

Katherina von Bora played a more typical, behind-the-scenes role as Luther's wife. Katherina was sent to a convent at about age ten, and had become a nun. Inspired by Luther's teaching, she fled the convent. After marrying Luther, Katherina had six children. She also managed the family finances, fed all who visited their house, and supported her husband's work. She respected Luther's position but argued with him about woman's equal role in marriage.

As Protestant religions became more firmly established, their organization became more formal. Male religious leaders narrowly limited women's activities to the home and discouraged them from being leaders in the church. In fact, it was Luther who said, "God's highest gift on earth is a pious, cheerful, God-fearing, home-keeping wife." **B**

MAIN IDEA
Making Inferences
B Why was it easier for women to take part in the earlier stages of the Reformation than in the later stages?

The Catholic Reformation

While Protestant churches won many followers, millions remained true to Catholicism. Helping Catholics to remain loyal was a movement within the Catholic Church to reform itself. This movement is now known as the **Catholic Reformation**. Historians once referred to it as the Counter Reformation. Important leaders in this movement were reformers, such as Ignatius (ihg•NAY•shuhs) of Loyola, who founded new religious orders, and two popes—Paul III and Paul IV—who took actions to reform and renew the Church from within.

Ignatius of Loyola Ignatius grew up in his father's castle in Loyola, Spain. The great turning point in his life came in 1521 when he was injured in a war. While recovering, he thought about his past sins and about the life of Jesus. His daily devotions, he believed, cleansed his soul. In 1522, Ignatius began writing a book called *Spiritual Exercises* that laid out a day-by-day plan of meditation, prayer, and study. In it, he compared spiritual and physical exercise:

PRIMARY SOURCE
Just as walking, traveling, and running are bodily exercises, preparing the soul to remove ill-ordered affections, and after their removal seeking and finding the will of God with respect to the ordering of one's own life and the salvation of one's soul, are Spiritual Exercises.

IGNATIUS OF LOYOLA, *Spiritual Exercises*

▲ Church leaders consult on reforms at the Council of Trent in this 16th-century painting.

For the next 18 years, Ignatius gathered followers. In 1540, the pope created a religious order for his followers called the Society of Jesus. Members were called **Jesuits** (JEHZH•oo•ihts). The Jesuits focused on three activities. First, they founded schools throughout Europe. Jesuit teachers were well-trained in both classical studies and theology. The Jesuits' second mission was to convert non-Christians to Catholicism. So they sent out missionaries around the world. Their third goal was to stop the spread of Protestantism. The zeal of the Jesuits overcame the drift toward Protestantism in Poland and southern Germany.

Reforming Popes Two popes took the lead in reforming the Catholic Church. Paul III, pope from 1534 to 1549, took four important steps. First, he directed a council of cardinals to investigate indulgence selling and other abuses in the Church. Second, he approved the Jesuit order. Third, he used the Inquisition to seek out heresy in papal territory. Fourth, and most important, he called a council of Church leaders to meet in Trent, in northern Italy.

Vocabulary
The *Inquisition* was a papal judicial process established to try and punish those thought to be heretics.

From 1545 to 1563, at the **Council of Trent**, Catholic bishops and cardinals agreed on several doctrines:

• The Church's interpretation of the Bible was final. Any Christian who substituted his or her own interpretation was a heretic.
• Christians needed faith and good works for salvation. They were not saved by faith alone, as Luther argued.
• The Bible and Church tradition were equally powerful authorities for guiding Christian life.
• Indulgences were valid expressions of faith. But the selling of indulgences was banned.

The next pope, Paul IV, vigorously carried out the council's decrees. In 1559, he had officials draw up a list of books considered dangerous to the Catholic faith. This list was known as the Index of Forbidden Books. Catholic bishops throughout Europe were ordered to gather up the offensive books (including Protestant Bibles) and burn them in bonfires. In Venice alone, followers burned 10,000 books in one day.

European Renaissance and Reformation **499**

Global Impact

Jesuit Missionaries

The work of Jesuit missionaries has had a lasting impact around the globe. By the time Ignatius died in 1556, about a thousand Jesuits had brought his ministry to Europe, Africa, Asia, and the Americas. Two of the most famous Jesuit missionaries of the 1500s were Francis Xavier, who worked in India and Japan, and Matteo Ricci, who worked in China.

One reason the Jesuits had such an impact is that they founded schools throughout the world. For example, the Jesuits today run about 45 high schools and 28 colleges and universities in the United States. Four of these are Georgetown University (shown above), Boston College, Marquette University, and Loyola University of Chicago.

The Legacy of the Reformation

The Reformation had an enduring impact. Through its religious, social, and political effects, the Reformation set the stage for the modern world. It also ended the Christian unity of Europe and left it culturally divided.

Religious and Social Effects of the Reformation Despite religious wars and persecutions, Protestant churches flourished and new denominations developed. The Roman Catholic Church itself became more unified as a result of the reforms started at the Council of Trent. Both Catholics and Protestants gave more emphasis to the role of education in promoting their beliefs. This led to the founding of parish schools and new colleges and universities throughout Europe.

Some women reformers had hoped to see the status of women in the church and society improve as a result of the Reformation. But it remained much the same both under Protestantism and Roman Catholicism. Women were still mainly limited to the concerns of home and family.

Political Effects of the Reformation As the Catholic Church's moral and political authority declined, individual monarchs and states gained power. This led to the development of modern nation-states. In the 1600s, rulers of nation-states would seek more power for themselves and their countries through warfare, exploration, and expansion.

The Reformation's questioning of beliefs and authority also laid the groundwork for the Enlightenment. As you will read in Chapter 22, this intellectual movement would sweep Europe in the late 18th century. It led some to reject all religions and others to call for the overthrow of existing governments.

SECTION 4 ASSESSMENT

TERMS & NAMES 1. For each term or name, write a sentence explaining its significance.
• predestination   • Calvinism   • theocracy   • Presbyterian   • Anabaptist   • Catholic Reformation   • Jesuits   • Council of Trent

USING YOUR NOTES

2. Which Catholic reform do you think had the most impact?

Reformers	Ideas
Zwingli	
Calvin	
Anabaptists	
Catholic Reformers	

MAIN IDEAS

3. What was Calvin's idea of the "elect" and their place in society?

4. What role did noblewomen play in the Reformation?

5. What were the goals of the Jesuits?

CRITICAL THINKING & WRITING

6. **DRAWING CONCLUSIONS** How did the Reformation set the stage for the modern world? Give examples.

7. **MAKING INFERENCES** Why do you think the Church wanted to forbid people to read certain books?

8. **COMPARING** How did steps taken by Paul III and Paul IV to reform the Catholic Church differ from Protestant reforms? Support your answer with details from the text.

9. **WRITING ACTIVITY** RELIGIOUS AND ETHICAL SYSTEMS Write a two-paragraph **essay** on whether church leaders should be political rulers.

CONNECT TO TODAY PRESENTING AN ORAL REPORT

Research the religious origins of a university in the United States. Then present your findings to the class in an **oral report.**

↗ hmhsocialstudies.com INTERACTIVE

The Reformation

Martin Luther's criticisms of the Catholic Church grew sharper over time. Some Catholics, in turn, responded with personal attacks on Luther. In recent times, historians have focused less on the theological and personal issues connected with the Reformation. Instead, many modern scholars analyze the political, social, and economic conditions that contributed to the Reformation.

A PRIMARY SOURCE

Martin Luther

In 1520, Martin Luther attacked the whole system of Church government and sent the pope the following criticism of the Church leaders who served under him in Rome.

———

The Roman Church has become the most licentious [sinful] den of thieves. . . . They err who ascribe to thee the right of interpreting Scripture, for under cover of thy name they seek to set up their own wickedness in the Church, and, alas, through them Satan has already made much headway under thy predecessors. In short, believe none who exalt thee, believe those who humble thee.

B SECONDARY SOURCE

Steven Ozment

In 1992, historian Steven Ozment published *Protestants: The Birth of a Revolution.* Here, he comments on some of the political aspects of the Reformation.

———

Beginning as a protest against arbitrary, self-aggrandizing, hierarchical authority in the person of the pope, the Reformation came to be closely identified in the minds of contemporaries with what we today might call states' rights or local control. To many townspeople and villagers, Luther seemed a godsend for their struggle to remain politically free and independent; they embraced his Reformation as a conserving political force, even though they knew it threatened to undo traditional religious beliefs and practices.

C SECONDARY SOURCE

G. R. Elton

In *Reformation Europe,* published in 1963, historian G. R. Elton notes the role of geography and trade in the spread of Reformation ideas.

———

Could the Reformation have spread so far and so fast if it had started anywhere but in Germany? The fact that it had its beginnings in the middle of Europe made possible a very rapid radiation in all directions. . . . Germany's position at the center of European trade also helped greatly. German merchants carried not only goods but Lutheran ideas and books to Venice and France; the north German Hanse [a trade league] transported the Reformation to the Scandinavian countries.

D PRIMARY SOURCE

Hans Brosamer

"Seven-Headed Martin Luther" (1529) The invention of the printing press enabled both Protestants and Catholics to engage in a war of words and images. This anti-Luther illustration by German painter Hans Brosamer depicted Martin Luther as a seven-headed monster—doctor, monk, infidel, preacher, fanatic swarmed by bees, self-appointed pope, and thief Barabbas from the Bible.

Sieben Köpffe Martini Luthers
Vom Hochwürdigen Sacrament des Altars / Durch Doctor Jo. Cocleus.

Martinus Luther Siebenkopff.

Document-Based QUESTIONS

1. In what way does Luther's letter (Source A) support the point of view of the historian in Source B?

2. Based on Source C, why was Germany's location important to the spread of Reformation ideas?

3. Why might Hans Brosamer's woodcut (Source D) be an effective propaganda weapon against Martin Luther?

VISUAL SUMMARY

European Renaissance and Reformation

The Renaissance and the Reformation bring dramatic changes to social and cultural life in Europe.

1. Italy: Birthplace of the Renaissance

- A period of intellectual and artistic creativity begins in Italy around the 1300s.
- Artists and writers revive techniques, styles, and subjects from classical Greece and Rome and celebrate human achievements.

2. The Northern Renaissance

- Renaissance ideas spread to Northern Europe, where German and Flemish artists create distinctive works of art.
- Thousands of books and pamphlets created on printing presses spread political, social, and artistic ideas.

3. Luther Leads the Reformation

- Martin Luther starts a movement for religious reform and challenges the authority of the Catholic Church.
- King Henry VIII breaks ties with the Catholic Church and starts the Church of England.

4. The Reformation Continues

- Protestant groups divide into several denominations, including the Calvinists and the Anabaptists.
- The Catholic Church introduces its own reforms.

TERMS & NAMES

For each term or name below, briefly explain its connection to European history from 1300 to 1600.

1. Renaissance
2. vernacular
3. utopia
4. Reformation
5. Protestant
6. Peace of Augsburg
7. Catholic Reformation
8. Council of Trent

MAIN IDEAS

Italy: Birthplace of the Renaissance Section 1 (pages-471–479)

9. How did the merchant class in northern Italy influence the Renaissance?
10. In what ways did literature and the arts change during the Renaissance?

The Northern Renaissance Section 2 (pages 480–487)

11. What did northern European rulers do to encourage the spread of Renaissance ideas?
12. How were the Christian humanists different from the humanists of the Italian Renaissance?

Luther Leads the Reformation Section 3 (pages 488–494)

13. On what three teachings did Martin Luther rest his Reformation movement?
14. Why did the Holy Roman emperor go to war against Protestant German princes?
15. Why did Henry VIII create his own church? Refer to the time line on pages 492–493.

The Reformation Continues Section 4 (pages 495–501)

16. In what ways was John Calvin's church different from the Lutheran Church?
17. What was the goal of the Catholic Reformation?
18. What are three legacies of the Reformation?

CRITICAL THINKING

1. **USING YOUR NOTES**

   In a diagram, show how the Reformation led to great changes in European ideas and institutions.

Effects of the Reformation		
Religious	Political	Social

2. **ANALYZING ISSUES**

   REVOLUTION What role did the printing press play in the spread of the Reformation and the spread of democracy?

3. **RECOGNIZING EFFECTS**

   CULTURAL INTERACTION How did the Renaissance and Reformation expand cultural interaction both within Europe and outside of it?

4. **DEVELOPING HISTORICAL PERSPECTIVE**

   What conditions needed to exist before the Renaissance could occur?

5. **SYNTHESIZING**

   How did views of the role of women change in the Renaissance period?

Use the quotation and your knowledge of world history to answer questions 1 and 2.

PRIMARY SOURCE

A prince must also show himself a lover of merit [excellence], give preferment [promotion] to the able, and honour those who excel in every art. Moreover he must encourage his citizens to follow their callings [professions] quietly, whether in commerce, or agriculture, or any other trade that men follow. . . . [The prince] should offer rewards to whoever does these things, and to whoever seeks in any way to improve his city or state.

NICCOLÒ MACHIAVELLI, *The Prince*

1. Which phrase best describes the advice given by Machiavelli?

   A. Rule with an iron hand in a velvet glove.

   B. Do not give your subjects any freedoms.

   C. Reward hard work and patriotism.

   D. To retain your rule, you must interfere in the lives of your subjects.

2. In his book *The Prince,* the writer of this advice also suggested

   A. the pope should listen to the calls for reform of the Church.

   B. a prince might have to trick his people for the good of the state.

   C. merchants should try to take control of the cities away from the prince.

   D. the prince should reform society by establishing a utopia.

Use this drawing of a machine from the notebooks of Leonardo da Vinci and your knowledge of world history to answer question 3.

3. The principles upon which this machine is based evolved into what modern machine?

   A. food blender

   B. a fan

   C. a well-digging machine

   D. helicopter

hmhsocialstudies.com **TEST PRACTICE**

For additional test practice, go online for:

• Diagnostic tests

• Tutorials

• Strategies

Interact *with* History

On page 470, you looked at a painting and discussed what you learned about Renaissance society from that painting. Now choose one other piece of art from the chapter. Explain what you can learn about Renaissance or Reformation society from that piece of art.

FOCUS ON WRITING

RELIGIOUS AND ETHICAL SYSTEMS Study the information about Protestantism in the Analyzing Key Concepts on page 491. Write a three-page **essay** analyzing the effects Protestantism had on the Christian Church.

• Examine its impact on the number of denominations.

• Explain the different beliefs and practices it promoted.

MULTIMEDIA ACTIVITY

Writing an Internet-Based Research Paper

Go to the *Web Research Guide* at **hmhsocialstudies.com** to learn about conducting research on the Internet. Then, working with a partner, use the Internet to research major religious reforms of the 20th century. You might search for information on changes in the Catholic Church as a result of Vatican II, or major shifts in the practices or doctrines of a branch of Hinduism, Islam, Judaism, or Protestantism. Compare the 20th-century reforms with those of the Protestant Reformation. Present the results of your research in a well-organized paper. Be sure to

• apply a search strategy when using directories and search engines to locate Web resources.

• judge the usefulness and reliability of each Web site.

• correctly cite your Web sources.

• peer-edit for organization and correct use of language.

CHAPTER 18

The Muslim World Expands, 1300–1700

Essential Question

What were the causes of the rise and decline of Muslim empires between 1300 and 1700?

 What You Will Learn

In this chapter, you will trace the development of empires in Turkey and India and another in Persia that mixed domestic and foreign Islamic cultures.

SECTION 1 The Ottomans Build a Vast Empire

Main Idea The Ottomans established a Muslim empire that combined many cultures and lasted more than 600 years.

SECTION 2 Cultural Blending Case Study: The Safavid Empire

Main Idea The Safavid Empire produced a rich and complex blended culture in Persia.

SECTION 3 The Mughal Empire in India

Main Idea The Mughal Empire brought Turks, Persians, and Indians together in a vast empire.

Previewing Themes

EMPIRE BUILDING Three of the great empires of history—the Ottomans in Turkey, the Safavids in Persia, and the Mughals in India—emerged in the Muslim world between the 14th and the 18th centuries.

Geography *Locate the empires on the map. Which of the empires was the largest? Where was it located?*

CULTURAL INTERACTION As powerful societies moved to expand their empires, Turkish, Persian, Mongol, and Arab ways of life blended. The result was a flowering of Islamic culture that peaked in the 16th century.

Geography *The Ottoman Empire included cultures from which continents?*

POWER AND AUTHORITY The rulers of all three great Muslim empires of this era based their authority on Islam. They based their power on strong armies, advanced technology, and loyal administrative officers.

Geography *Study the time line and the map. When was the Mughal Empire founded? Where was Babur's empire located?*

MUSLIM WORLD

1300
Osman founds Ottoman state. ▶

1300

1398
Timur the Lame destroys Delhi.

1400

1453
Ottomans capture Constantinople.

WORLD

1325
Aztecs build Tenochtitlán. (ornament of an Aztec snake god) ▶

1455
◀ Gutenberg prints the Bible.

Empire Builders, 1683

HISTORY. Hagia Sophia

hmhsocialstudies.com VIDEO

EUROPE

ASIA

AFRICA

Mughal Empire
Ottoman Empire
Safavid Empire

0   500   1,000 Miles

0   500   1,000 Kilometers
Polyconic Projection

ATLAS MOUNTAINS

Mediterranean Sea

Black Sea

Baltic Sea

ALPS

Danube R.

CAUCASUS MTS.

Caspian Sea

Aral Sea

ZAGROS MTS.

Persian Gulf

HIMALAYAS

Ganges R.

Indus R.

Tigris R.

Euphrates R.

Nile R.

Red Sea

Arabian Sea

Bay of Bengal

INDIAN OCEAN

Vienna
Rome
Constantinople
Algiers
Tunis
Tripoli
Alexandria
Aleppo
Damascus
Jerusalem
Baghdad
Tehran
Esfahan
Ormuz (Hormuz)
Medina
Mecca
Kabul
Delhi
Agra
Benares

45°N
0° Equator

15°W   0°   15°E   30°E   45°E   60°E   75°E   90°E

N W E S

1501
Safavids conquer Persia.

1526
Babur founds Mughal Empire.

1587
Shah Abbas I rules Safavid Empire.

1632
◄ Shah Jahan orders construction of Taj Mahal at Agra.

1500   **1600**   **1700**

1522
Magellan's crew sails around the world.

1603
Tokugawa regime begins in Japan.

1607
British settle in North America at Jamestown.

How do you govern a diverse empire?

Your father is a Safavid shah, the ruler of a growing empire. With a well-trained army and modern weapons, he has easily conquered most of the surrounding area. Because you are likely to become the next ruler, you are learning all you can about how to rule. You wonder what is best for the empire. Should conquered people be given the freedom to practice a religion that is different from your own and to follow their own traditions? Or would it be better to try and force them to accept your beliefs and way of life—or even to enslave them?

hmhsocialstudies.com INTERACTIVE

1 The shah entertains the emperor of a neighboring land. Both lands have great diversity of people and cultures.

2 Distinctive headgear marks the status of military leaders and scholars gathered from all parts of the empire.

3 Clothing, music, dancing, and food reflect the customs of several groups within the empire.

4 People in the court, from the servants to the members of the court, mirror the empire's diversity.

EXAMINING *the* ISSUES

- **What problems might conquered people present for their conqueror?**

- **In what ways might a conqueror integrate conquered people into the society?**

As a class, discuss the ways other empires—such as those of Rome, Assyria, and Persia—treated their conquered peoples. As you read about the three empires featured in this chapter, notice how the rulers dealt with empires made up of different cultures.

The Ottomans Build a Vast Empire

MAIN IDEA	WHY IT MATTERS NOW	TERMS & NAMES
EMPIRE BUILDING The Ottomans established a Muslim empire that combined many cultures and lasted for more than 600 years.	Many modern societies, from Algeria to Turkey, had their origins under Ottoman rule.	• ghazi • Ottoman • sultan • Timur the Lame • Mehmed II • Suleyman the Lawgiver • *devshirme* • janissary

SETTING THE STAGE By 1300, the Byzantine Empire was declining, and the Mongols had destroyed the Turkish Seljuk kingdom of Rum. Anatolia was inhabited mostly by the descendants of nomadic Turks. These militaristic people had a long history of invading other countries. Loyal to their own groups, they were not united by a strong central power. A small Turkish state occupied land between the Byzantine Empire and that of the Muslims. From this place, a strong leader would emerge to unite the Turks into what eventually would become an immense empire stretching across three continents.

Turks Move into Byzantium

Many Anatolian Turks saw themselves as **ghazis** (GAH•zees), or warriors for Islam. They formed military societies under the leadership of an emir, a chief commander, and followed a strict Islamic code of conduct. They raided the territories of people who lived on the frontiers of the Byzantine Empire.

Osman Establishes a State The most successful ghazi was Osman. People in the West called him Othman and named his followers **Ottomans**. Osman built a small Muslim state in Anatolia between 1300 and 1326. His successors expanded it by buying land, forming alliances with some emirs, and conquering others.

The Ottomans' military success was largely based on the use of gunpowder. They replaced their archers on horseback with musket-carrying foot soldiers. They also were among the first people to use cannons as weapons of attack. Even heavily walled cities fell to an all-out attack by the Turks.

The second Ottoman leader, Orkhan I, was Osman's son. He felt strong enough to declare himself **sultan**, meaning "overlord" or "one with power." And in 1361, the Ottomans captured Adrianople (ay•dree•uh•NOH•puhl), the second most important city in the Byzantine Empire. A new Turkish empire was on the rise.

The Ottomans acted wisely toward the people they conquered. They ruled through local officials appointed by the sultan and often improved the lives of the peasants. Most Muslims had to serve in Turkish armies and make contributions required by their faith. Non-Muslims did not have to serve in the army but had to pay for their exemption with a small tax.

hmhsocialstudies.com
TAKING NOTES
Use the graphic organizer online to take notes on rulers of the Ottoman Empire and their successes.

Timur the Lame Halts Expansion The rise of the Ottoman Empire was briefly interrupted in the early 1400s by a rebellious warrior and conqueror from Samarkand in Central Asia. Permanently injured by an arrow in the leg, he was called Timur-i-Lang, or **Timur the Lame**. Europeans called him Tamerlane. Timur burned the powerful city of Baghdad in present-day Iraq to the ground. He crushed the Ottoman forces at the Battle of Ankara in 1402. This defeat halted the expansion of their empire.

Powerful Sultans Spur Dramatic Expansion

Soon Timur turned his attention to China. When he did, war broke out among the four sons of the Ottoman sultan. Mehmed I defeated his brothers and took the throne. His son, Murad II, defeated the Venetians, invaded Hungary, and overcame an army of Italian crusaders in the Balkans. He was the first of four powerful sultans who led the expansion of the Ottoman Empire through 1566.

Mehmed II Conquers Constantinople Murad's son **Mehmed II**, or Mehmed the Conqueror, achieved the most dramatic feat in Ottoman history. By the time Mehmed took power in 1451, the ancient city of Constantinople had shrunk from a population of a million to a mere 50,000. Although it controlled no territory outside its walls, it still dominated the Bosporus Strait. Controlling this waterway meant that it could choke off traffic between the Ottomans' territories in Asia and in the Balkans.

Mehmed II decided to face this situation head-on. "Give me Constantinople!" he thundered, shortly after taking power at age 21. Then, in 1453, he launched his attack.

Ottoman Empire, 1451–1566

hmhsocialstudies.com
INTERACTIVE MAP

Ottoman Empire, 1451
Acquisitions to 1481
Acquisitions to 1521
Acquisitions to 1566

GEOGRAPHY SKILLBUILDER: Interpreting Maps
1. **Location** To which waterways did the Ottoman Empire have access?
2. **Movement** In which time period did the Ottoman Empire gain the most land?

The Conquest of Constantinople

Kritovoulos, a Greek who served in the Ottoman administration, recorded the following about the Ottoman takeover of Constantinople. The second source, the French miniature at the right, shows a view of the siege of Constantinople.

PRIMARY SOURCE

After this the Sultan entered the City and looked about to see its great size, its situation, its grandeur and beauty, its teeming population, its loveliness, and the costliness of its churches and public buildings and of the private houses and community houses and those of the officials. . . .

When he saw what a large number had been killed and the ruin of the buildings, and the wholesale ruin and destruction of the City, he was filled with compassion and repented not a little at the destruction and plundering. Tears fell from his eyes as he groaned deeply and passionately: "What a city we have given over to plunder and destruction."

KRITOVOULOS, *History of Mehmed the Conqueror*

DOCUMENT-BASED QUESTIONS

1. **Comparing and Contrasting** *In what details do the two sources agree? disagree?*
2. **Making Inferences** *Why do you think the sultan wept over the destruction?*

Mehmed's Turkish forces began firing on the city walls with mighty cannons. One of these was a 26-foot gun that fired 1,200-pound boulders. A chain across the Golden Horn between the Bosporus Strait and the Sea of Marmara kept the Turkish fleet out of the city's harbor. Finally, one night Mehmed's army tried a daring tactic. They dragged 70 ships over a hill on greased runners from the Bosporus to the harbor. Now Mehmed's army was attacking Constantinople from two sides. The city held out for over seven weeks, but the Turks finally found a break in the wall and entered the city.

Mehmed the Conqueror, as he was now called, proved to be an able ruler as well as a magnificent warrior. He opened Constantinople to new citizens of many religions and backgrounds. Jews, Christians, and Muslims, Turks and non-Turks all flowed in. They helped rebuild the city, which was now called Istanbul. **A**

Ottomans Take Islam's Holy Cities Mehmed's grandson, Selim the Grim, came to power in 1512. He was an effective sultan and a great general. In 1514, he defeated the Safavids (suh•FAH•vihdz) of Persia at the Battle of Chaldiran. Then he swept south through Syria and Palestine and into North Africa. At the same time that Cortez was toppling the Aztec Empire in the Americas, Selim's empire took responsibility for Mecca and Medina. Finally he took Cairo, the intellectual center of the Muslim world. The once-great civilization of Egypt had become just another province in the growing Ottoman Empire.

MAIN IDEA

Analyzing Motives

A Why was taking Constantinople so important to Mehmed II?

The Muslim World Expands **509**

History Makers

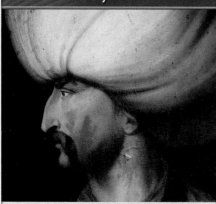

**Suleyman the Lawgiver
1494–1566**

In the halls of the U.S. Congress are images of some of the greatest lawgivers of all time. Included in that group are such persons as Thomas Jefferson, Moses, and Suleyman.

Suleyman's law code prescribed penalties for various criminal acts and for bureaucratic and financial corruption. He also sought to reduce bribes, did not allow imprisonment without a trial, and rejected promotions that were not based on merit. He also introduced the idea of a balanced budget for governments.

↗ **hmhsocialstudies.com**

RESEARCH WEB LINKS Go online for more on Suleyman the Lawgiver.

Suleyman the Lawgiver

The Ottoman Empire didn't reach its peak size and grandeur until the reign of Selim's son, Suleyman I (SOO•lay•mahn). Suleyman came to the throne in 1520 and ruled for 46 years. His own people called him <u>Suleyman the Lawgiver</u>. He was known in the West, though, as Suleyman the Magnificent. This title was a tribute to the splendor of his court and to his cultural achievements.

The Empire Reaches Its Limits Suleyman was a superb military leader. He conquered the important European city of Belgrade in 1521. The next year, Turkish forces captured the island of Rhodes in the Mediterranean and now dominated the whole eastern Mediterranean.

Applying their immense naval power, the Ottomans captured Tripoli on the coast of North Africa. They continued conquering peoples along the North African coastline. Although the Ottomans occupied only the coastal cities of North Africa, they managed to control trade routes to the interior of the continent.

In 1526, Suleyman advanced into Hungary and Austria, throwing central Europe into a panic. Suleyman's armies then pushed to the outskirts of Vienna, Austria. Reigning from Istanbul, Suleyman had waged war with central Europeans, North Africans, and Central Asians. He had become the most powerful monarch on earth. Only Charles V, head of the Hapsburg Empire in Europe, came close to rivaling his power.

Highly Structured Social Organization Binding the Ottoman Empire together in a workable social structure was Suleyman's crowning achievement. The massive empire required an efficient government structure and social organization. Suleyman created a law code to handle both criminal and civil actions. He also simplified and limited taxes, and systematized and reduced government bureaucracy. These changes improved the lives of most citizens and helped earn Suleyman the title of Lawgiver.

The sultan's 20,000 personal slaves staffed the palace bureaucracy. The slaves were acquired as part of a policy called *devshirme* (dehv•SHEER•meh). Under the <u>*devshirme*</u> system, the sultan's army drafted boys from the peoples of conquered Christian territories. The army educated them, converted them to Islam, and trained them as soldiers. An elite force of 30,000 soldiers known as <u>janissaries</u> was trained to be loyal to the sultan only. Their superb discipline made them the heart of the Ottoman war machine. In fact, Christian families sometimes bribed officials to take their children into the sultan's service, because the brightest ones could rise to high government posts or military positions. **B**

As a Muslim, Suleyman was required to follow Islamic law. In accordance with Islamic law, the Ottomans granted freedom of worship to other religious communities, particularly to Christians and Jews. They treated these communities as *millets,* or nations. They allowed each *millet* to follow its own religious laws and practices. The head of the *millets* reported to the sultan and his staff. This system kept conflict among people of the various religions to a minimum.

MAIN IDEA

Making Inferences

B What were the advantages of the *devshirme* system to the sultan?

Cultural Flowering Suleyman had broad interests, which contributed to the cultural achievements of the empire. He found time to study poetry, history, geography, astronomy, mathematics, and architecture. He employed one of the world's finest architects, Sinan, who was probably from Albania. Sinan's masterpiece, the Mosque of Suleyman, is an immense complex topped with domes and half domes. It includes four schools, a library, a bath, and a hospital.

MAIN IDEA

Comparing

C Which cultural achievements of Suleyman's reign were similar to the European Renaissance?

Art and literature also flourished under Suleyman's rule. This creative period was similar to the European Renaissance. Painters and poets looked to Persia and Arabia for models. The works that they produced used these foreign influences to express original Ottoman ideas in the Turkish style. They are excellent examples of cultural blending. **C**

▲ Sinan's Mosque of Suleyman in Istanbul is the largest mosque in the Ottoman Empire.

The Empire Declines Slowly

Despite Suleyman's magnificent social and cultural achievements, the Ottoman Empire was losing ground. Suleyman killed his ablest son and drove another into exile. His third son, the incompetent Selim II, inherited the throne.

Suleyman set the pattern for later sultans to gain and hold power. It became customary for each new sultan to have his brothers strangled. The sultan would then keep his sons prisoner in the harem, cutting them off from education or contact with the world. This practice produced a long line of weak sultans who eventually brought ruin on the empire. However, the Ottoman Empire continued to influence the world into the early 20th century.

SECTION 1 ASSESSMENT

TERMS & NAMES 1. For each term or name, write a sentence explaining its significance.
• ghazi   • Ottoman   • sultan   • Timur the Lame   • Mehmed II   • Suleyman the Lawgiver   • *devshirme*   • janissary

USING YOUR NOTES

2. Which do you consider more significant to the Ottoman Empire, the accomplishments of Mehmed II or those of Selim the Grim? Explain.

Rulers	Successes

MAIN IDEAS

3. By what means did the early Ottomans expand their empire?

4. Why was Suleyman called the Lawgiver?

5. How powerful was the Ottoman Empire compared to other empires of the time?

CRITICAL THINKING & WRITING

6. EVALUATING DECISIONS Do you think that the Ottomans were wise in staffing their military and government with slaves? Explain.

7. EVALUATING COURSES OF ACTION How did Suleyman's selection of a successor eventually spell disaster for the Ottoman Empire?

8. ANALYZING MOTIVES Do you think that Suleyman's religious tolerance helped or hurt the Ottoman Empire?

9. WRITING ACTIVITY EMPIRE BUILDING Using the description of Mehmed II's forces taking Constantinople, write a **newspaper article** describing the action.

CONNECT TO TODAY CREATING A TIME LINE
Create a **time line** showing events in the decline of the Ottoman Empire and the creation of the modern nation of Turkey.

Cultural Blending

CASE STUDY: The Safavid Empire

MAIN IDEA	WHY IT MATTERS NOW	TERMS & NAMES
CULTURAL INTERACTION The Safavid Empire produced a rich and complex blended culture in Persia.	Modern Iran, which plays a key role in global politics, descended from the culturally diverse Safavid Empire.	• Safavid • Shah Abbas • Isma'il • Esfahan • shah

SETTING THE STAGE Throughout the course of world history, cultures have interacted with each other. Often such interaction has resulted in the mixing of different cultures in new and exciting ways. This process is referred to as cultural blending. The **Safavid** Empire, a Shi'ite Muslim dynasty that ruled in Persia between the 16th and 18th centuries, provides a striking example of how interaction among peoples can produce a blending of cultures. This culturally diverse empire drew from the traditions of Persians, Ottomans, and Arabs.

Patterns of Cultural Blending

hmhsocialstudies.com
TAKING NOTES

Use the graphic organizer online to take notes on cultural blending in the Safavid Empire.

Each time a culture interacts with another, it is exposed to ideas, technologies, foods, and ways of life not exactly like its own. Continental crossroads, trade routes, ports, and the borders of countries are places where cultural blending commonly begins. Societies that are able to benefit from cultural blending are those that are open to new ways and are willing to adapt and change. The blended ideas spread throughout the culture and produce a new pattern of behavior. Cultural blending has several basic causes.

Causes of Cultural Blending Cultural change is most often prompted by one or more of the following four activities:

- migration
- pursuit of religious freedom or conversion
- trade
- conquest

The blending that contributed to the culture of the Ottomans, which you just read about in Section 1, depended on some of these activities. Surrounded by the peoples of Byzantium, the Turks were motivated to win territory for their empire. The Ottoman Empire's location on a major trading route created many opportunities for contact with different cultures. Suleyman's interest in learning and culture prompted him to bring the best foreign artists and scholars to his court. They brought new ideas about art, literature, and learning to the empire.

Results of Cultural Blending Cultural blending may lead to changes in language, religion, styles of government, the use of technology, and military tactics.

Cultural Blending			
Location	**Interacting Cultures**	**Reason for Interaction**	**Some Results of Interaction**
India—1000 B.C.	Aryan and Dravidian Indian Arab, African, Indian	Migration	Vedic culture, forerunner of Hinduism
East Africa—A.D. 700	Islamic, Christian	Trade, religious conversion	New trade language, Swahili
Russia—A.D. 1000	Christian and Slavic	Religious conversion	Eastern Christianity, Russian identity
Mexico—A.D. 1500	Spanish and Aztec	Conquest	Mestizo culture, Mexican Catholicism
United States—A.D. 1900	European, Asian, Caribbean	Migration, religious freedom	Cultural diversity

SKILLBUILDER: Interpreting Charts
1. **Determining Main Ideas** *What are the reasons for interaction in the Americas?*
2. **Hypothesizing** *What are some aspects of cultural diversity?*

These changes often reflect unique aspects of several cultures. For example:
- **Language** Sometimes the written characters of one language are used in another, as in the case of written Chinese characters used in the Japanese language. In the Safavid Empire, the language spoken was Persian. But after the area converted to Islam, a significant number of Arabic words appeared in the Persian language.
- **Religion and ethical systems** Buddhism spread throughout Asia. Yet the Buddhism practiced by Tibetans is different from Japanese Zen Buddhism.
- **Styles of government** The concept of a democratic government spread to many areas of the globe. Although the basic principles are similar, it is not practiced exactly the same way in each country.
- **Racial or ethnic blending** One example is the mestizo, people of mixed European and Indian ancestry who live in Mexico.
- **Arts and architecture** Cultural styles may be incorporated or adapted into art or architecture. For example, Chinese artistic elements are found in Safavid Empire tiles and carpets as well as in European paintings.

The chart above shows other examples of cultural blending that have occurred over time in various areas of the world. **A**

MAIN IDEA

Recognizing Effects

A Which of the effects of cultural blending do you think is the most significant? Explain.

CASE STUDY: The Safavid Empire

The Safavids Build an Empire

Conquest and ongoing cultural interaction fueled the development of the Safavid Empire. Originally, the Safavids were members of an Islamic religious brotherhood named after their founder, Safi al-Din. In the 15th century, the Safavids aligned themselves with the Shi'a branch of Islam.

The Safavids were also squeezed geographically between the Ottomans and Uzbek tribespeople and the Mughal Empire. (See the map on page 514.) To protect themselves from these potential enemies, the Safavids concentrated on building a powerful army.

Isma'il Conquers Persia The Safavid military became a force to reckon with. In 1499, a 12-year-old named **Isma'il** (ihs•MAH•eel) began to seize most of what is now Iran. Two years later he completed the task.

▼ Grandson of Isma'il, Shah Abbas led the Safavid Empire during its Golden Age.

RUSSIA

Azov

CAUCASUS MTS.

Aral
Sea

Caspian Sea

Trabzon

Chaldiran

Tabriz

Mosul

Euphrates R.

Tigris R.

Tehran

MESOPOTAMIA

Baghdad

Esfahan

Herat

ARABIA

Basra

PERSIA

Persian Gulf

Shiraz

Ormuz (Hormuz)

40° N

UZBEKS

Amu Darya

Ottoman Empire
Safavid Empire
Mughal Empire

N

0   500 Miles

0   1,000 Kilometers

Tropic of Cancer

GEOGRAPHY SKILLBUILDER: Interpreting Maps
1. **Movement** *What waterways might have enabled the Safavids to interact with other cultures?*
2. **Location** *Why might the Safavids not have expanded further?*

To celebrate his achievement, he took the ancient Persian title of <u>shah</u>, or king. He also established Shi'a Islam as the state religion.

Isma'il became a religious tyrant. Any citizen who did not convert to Shi'ism was put to death. Isma'il destroyed the Sunni population of Baghdad in his confrontation with the Ottomans. Their leader, Selim the Grim, later ordered the execution of all Shi'a in the Ottoman Empire. As many as 40,000 died. Their final face-off took place at the Battle of Chaldiran in 1514. Using artillery, the Ottomans pounded the Safavids into defeat. Another outcome of the battle was to set the border between the two empires. It remains the border today between Iran and Iraq.

Isma'il's son Tahmasp learned from the Safavids' defeat at Chaldiran. He adopted the use of artillery with his military forces. He expanded the Safavid Empire up to the Caucasus Mountains, northeast of Turkey, and brought Christians under Safavid rule. Tahmasp laid the groundwork for the golden age of the Safavids. **B**

MAIN IDEA

Drawing Conclusions
B How did Tahmasp's cultural borrowing lead to the expansion of the Safavid Empire?

A Safavid Golden Age

<u>Shah Abbas</u>, or Abbas the Great, took the throne in 1587. He helped create a Safavid culture and golden age that drew from the best of the Ottoman, Persian, and Arab worlds.

Reforms Shah Abbas reformed aspects of both military and civilian life. He limited the power of the military and created two new armies that would be loyal to him alone. One of these was an army of Persians. The other was a force that Abbas recruited from the Christian north and modeled after the Ottoman janissaries. He equipped both of these armies with modern artillery.

Abbas also reformed his government. He punished corruption severely and promoted only officials who proved their competence and loyalty. He hired foreigners from neighboring countries to fill positions in the government.

To convince European merchants that his empire was tolerant of other religions, Abbas brought members of Christian religious orders into the empire. As a result, Europeans moved into the land. Then industry, trade, and art exchanges grew between the empire and European nations.

A New Capital The Shah built a new capital at <u>Esfahan</u>. With a design that covered four and a half miles, the city was considered one of the most beautiful in the world. It was a showplace for the many artisans, both foreign and Safavid, who worked on the buildings and the objects in them. For example, 300 Chinese potters produced glazed building tiles for the buildings in the city, and Armenians wove carpets.

Art Works Shah Abbas brought hundreds of Chinese artisans to Esfahan. Working with Safavid artists, they produced intricate metalwork, miniature paintings, calligraphy, glasswork, tile work, and pottery. This collaboration gave rise to artwork that blended Chinese and Persian ideas. These decorations beautified the many mosques, palaces, and marketplaces.

Carpets The most important result of Western influence on the Safavids, however, may have been the demand for Persian carpets. This demand helped change carpet weaving from a local craft to a national industry. In the beginning, the carpets reflected traditional Persian themes. As the empire became more culturally blended, the designs incorporated new themes. In the 16th century, Shah Abbas sent artists to Italy to study under the Renaissance artist Raphael. Rugs then began to reflect European designs. **C**

▲ The Masjid-e-Imam mosque in Esfahan is a beautiful example of the flowering of the arts in the Safavid Empire.

MAIN IDEA

Comparing

C In what ways were Shah Abbas and Suleyman the Lawgiver similar?

The Dynasty Declines Quickly

In finding a successor, Shah Abbas made the same mistake the Ottoman monarch Suleyman made. He killed or blinded his ablest sons. His incompetent grandson, Safi, succeeded Abbas. This pampered young prince led the Safavids down the same road to decline that the Ottomans had taken, only more quickly.

In 1736, however, Nadir Shah Afshar conquered land all the way to India and created an expanded empire. But Nadir Shah was so cruel that one of his own troops assassinated him. With Nadir Shah's death in 1747, the Safavid Empire fell apart.

At the same time that the Safavids flourished, cultural blending and conquest led to the growth of a new empire in India, as you will learn in Section 3.

SECTION **2** **ASSESSMENT**

TERMS & NAMES 1. For each term or name, write a sentence explaining its significance.
• Safavid   • Isma'il   • shah   • Shah Abbas   • Esfahan

USING YOUR NOTES	**MAIN IDEAS**	**CRITICAL THINKING & WRITING**
2. What are some examples of cultural blending in the Safavid Empire? *Cultural Blending*	3. What are the four causes of cultural blending? 4. What reforms took place in the Safavid Empire under Shah Abbas? 5. Why did the Safavid Empire decline so quickly?	6. **FORMING OPINIONS** Which of the results of cultural blending do you think has the most lasting effect on a country? Explain. 7. **DRAWING CONCLUSIONS** How did the location of the Safavid Empire contribute to the cultural blending in the empire? 8. **ANALYZING MOTIVES** Why might Isma'il have become so intolerant of the Sunni Muslims? 9. **WRITING ACTIVITY** CULTURAL INTERACTION Write a **letter** from Shah Abbas to a Chinese artist persuading him to come teach and work in the Safavid Empire.

MULTIMEDIA ACTIVITY WRITING A DOCUMENTARY SCRIPT

 Use the Internet to research the charge that Persian rugs are largely made by children under the age of 14. Write a television **documentary script** detailing your research results.

INTERNET KEYWORD
child labor rug making

The Mughal Empire in India

MAIN IDEA	WHY IT MATTERS NOW	TERMS & NAMES
POWER AND AUTHORITY The Mughal Empire brought Turks, Persians, and Indians together in a vast empire.	The legacy of great art and deep social division left by the Mughal Empire still influences southern Asia.	• Mughal • Sikh • Babur • Shah Jahan • Akbar • Taj Mahal • Aurangzeb

SETTING THE STAGE The Gupta Empire, which you read about in Chapter 7, crumbled in the late 400s. First, Huns from Central Asia invaded. Then, beginning in the 700's, warlike Muslim tribes from Central Asia carved northwestern India into many small kingdoms. The people who invaded descended from Muslim Turks and Afghans. Their leader was a descendant of Timur the Lame and of the Mongol conqueror Genghis Khan. They called themselves **Mughals**, which means "Mongols." The land they invaded had been through a long period of turmoil.

Early History of the Mughals

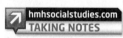

TAKING NOTES

Use the graphic organizer online to take notes on Mughal emperors and their successes.

The 8th century began with a long clash between Hindus and Muslims in this land of many kingdoms. For almost 300 years, the Muslims were able to advance only as far as the Indus River valley. Starting around the year 1000, however, well-trained Turkish armies swept into India. Led by Sultan Mahmud (muh•MOOD) of Ghazni, they devastated Indian cities and temples in 17 brutal campaigns. These attacks left the region weakened and vulnerable to other conquerors. Delhi eventually became the capital of a loose empire of Turkish warlords called the Delhi Sultanate. These sultans treated the Hindus as conquered people.

Delhi Sultanate Between the 13th and 16th centuries, 33 different sultans ruled this divided territory from their seat in Delhi. In 1398, Timur the Lame destroyed Delhi. The city was so completely devastated that according to one witness, "for months, not a bird moved in the city." Delhi eventually was rebuilt. But it was not until the 16th century that a leader arose who would unify the empire.

Babur Founds an Empire In 1494, an 11-year-old boy named **Babur** inherited a kingdom in the area that is now Uzbekistan and Tajikistan. It was only a tiny kingdom, and his elders soon took it away and drove him south. But Babur built up an army. In the years that followed, he swept down into India and laid the foundation for the vast Mughal Empire.

Babur was a brilliant general. In 1526, for example, he led 12,000 troops to victory against an army of 100,000 commanded by a sultan of Delhi. A year later, Babur also defeated a massive rajput army. After Babur's death, his incompetent son, Humayun, lost most of the territory Babur had gained. Babur's 13-year-old grandson took over the throne after Humayun's death.

Akbar's Golden Age

Babur's grandson was called **Akbar**, which means "Great." Akbar certainly lived up to his name, ruling India with wisdom and tolerance from 1556 to 1605.

A Military Conqueror Akbar recognized military power as the root of his strength. In his opinion, a King must always be aggresive so that his neighbors will not try to conquer him.

Like the Safavids and the Ottomans, Akbar equipped his armies with heavy artillery. Cannons enabled him to break into walled cities and extend his rule into much of the Deccan plateau. In a brilliant move, he appointed some rajputs as officers. In this way he turned potential enemies into allies. This combination of military power and political wisdom enabled Akbar to unify a land of at least 100 million people—more than in all of Europe put together.

A Liberal Ruler Akbar was a genius at cultural blending. A Muslim, he continued the Islamic tradition of religious freedom. He permitted people of other religions to practice their faiths. He proved his tolerance by marrying Hindu princesses without forcing them to convert. He

Growth of the Mughal Empire, 1526–1707

- ■ Mughal Empire, 1526 (Babur)
- ■ Added by 1605 (Akbar)
- ■ Added by 1707 (Aurangzeb)

GEOGRAPHY SKILLBUILDER: Interpreting Maps
1. **Movement** *During which time period was the most territory added to the Mughal Empire?*
2. **Human-Environment Interaction** *What landform might have prevented the empire from expanding farther east?*

allowed his wives to practice their religious rituals in the palace. He proved his tolerance again by abolishing both the tax on Hindu pilgrims and the hated *jizya*, or tax on non-Muslims. He even appointed a Spanish Jesuit to tutor his second son.

Akbar governed through a bureaucracy of officials. Natives and foreigners, Hindus and Muslims, could all rise to high office. This approach contributed to the quality of his government. Akbar's chief finance minister, Todar Mal, a Hindu, created a clever—and effective—taxation policy. He levied a tax similar to the present-day U.S. graduated income tax, calculating it as a percentage of the value of the peasants' crops. Because this tax was fair and affordable, the number of peasants who paid it increased. This payment brought in much needed money for the empire. **A**

Akbar's land policies had more mixed results. He gave generous land grants to his bureaucrats. After they died, however, he reclaimed the lands and distributed them as he saw fit. On the positive side, this policy prevented the growth of feudal aristocracies. On the other hand, it did not encourage dedication and hard work by the Mughal officials. Their children would not inherit the land or benefit from their parents' work. So the officials apparently saw no point in devoting themselves to their property.

MAIN IDEA

Comparing

A In what ways were Akbar's attitudes toward religion similar to those of Suleyman the Lawgiver?

History Makers

Akbar
1542–1605

Akbar was brilliant and curious, especially about religion. He even invented a religion of his own—the "Divine Faith"—after learning about Hinduism, Jainism, Christianity, and Sufism. The religion attracted few followers, however, and offended Muslims so much that they attempted a brief revolt against Akbar in 1581. When he died, so did the "Divine Faith."

Surprisingly, despite his wisdom and his achievements, Akbar could not read. He hired others to read to him from his library of 24,000 books.

↗ hmhsocialstudies.com

RESEARCH WEB LINKS Go online for more on Akbar.

Blended Cultures As Akbar extended the Mughal Empire, he welcomed influences from the many cultures in the empire. This cultural blending affected art, education, politics, and language. Persian was the language of Akbar's court and of high culture. The common people, however, spoke Hindi, a language derived from Sanskrit. Hindi remains one of the most widely spoken languages in India today. Out of the Mughal armies, where soldiers of many backgrounds rubbed shoulders, came yet another new language. This language was Urdu, which means "from the soldier's camp." A blend of Arabic, Persian, and Hindi, Urdu is today the official language of Pakistan.

The Arts and Literature The arts flourished at the Mughal court, especially in the form of book illustrations. These small, highly detailed, and colorful paintings were called miniatures. They were brought to a peak of perfection in the Safavid Empire. (See Section 2.) Babur's son, Humayun, brought two masters of this art to his court to teach it to the Mughals. Some of the most famous Mughal miniatures adorned the *Akbarnamah* ("Book of Akbar"), the story of the great emperor's campaigns and deeds. Indian art drew from traditions developed earlier in Rajput kingdoms.

Hindu literature also enjoyed a revival in Akbar's time. The poet Tulsi Das, for example, was a contemporary of Akbar's. He retold the epic love story of Rama and Sita from the fourth century B.C. Indian poem the *Ramayana* (rah•MAH•yuh•nuh) in Hindi. This retelling, the *Ramcaritmanas,* is now even more popular than the original.

Architecture Akbar devoted himself to architecture too. The style developed under his reign is still known as Akbar period architecture. Its massive but graceful structures are decorated with intricate stonework that portrays Hindu themes. The capital city of Fatehpur Sikri is one of the most important examples of this type of architecture. Akbar had this red-sandstone city built to thank a Sufi saint, Sheik Salim Chisti, who had predicted the birth of his first son. **B**

MAIN IDEA

Drawing Conclusions
B How was Akbar able to build such an immense empire?

Akbar's Successors

With Akbar's death in 1605, the Mughal court changed to deal with the changing times. The next three emperors each left his mark on the Mughal Empire.

Jahangir and Nur Jahan Akbar's son called himself Jahangir (juh•hahn•GEER), or "Grasper of the World." However, for most of his reign, he left the affairs of state to his wife, who ruled with an iron hand.

Jahangir's wife was the Persian princess Nur Jahan. She was a brilliant politician who perfectly understood the use of power. As the real ruler of India, she installed her father as prime minister in the Mughal court. She saw Jahangir's son Khusrau as her ticket to future power. But when Khusrau rebelled against his father, Nur Jahan removed him. She then shifted her favor to another son.

This rejection of Khusrau affected more than the political future of the empire. It was also the basis of a long and bitter religious conflict. Jahangir tried to promote Islam in the Mughal state, but was tolerant of other religions. When Khusrau

Women Leaders of the Indian Subcontinent

Since World War II, the subcontinent of India has seen the rise of several powerful women. Unlike Nur Jahan, however, they achieved power on their own—not through their husbands.

Indira Gandhi headed the Congress Party and dominated Indian politics for almost 30 years. She was elected prime minister in 1966 and again in 1980. Gandhi was assassinated in 1984 by Sikh separatists.

Benazir Bhutto took charge of the Pakistan People's Party after her father was assassinated. She became prime minister in 1988, the first woman to run a modern Muslim state. Reelected in 1993, she was dismissed from office in 1996 and went into exile. She returned from exile in 2007 but was killed by a suicide bomb attack just months later.

Chandrika Bandaranaike Kumaratunga is the president of Sri Lanka. She was elected in 1994. She survived an assassination attempt in 1999 and was reelected.

Khaleda Zia became Bangladesh's first woman prime minister in 1991. She was reelected several times, the last time in 2001.

Pratibha Patil, elected in 2007, is India's first female president.

Indira Gandhi

Chandrika Bandaranaike Kumaratunga

Khaleda Zia

Pratibha Patil

---

rebelled, he turned to the **Sikhs**. This was a nonviolent religious group whose doctrines contained elements similar to Hinduism and Sufism (Islamic mysticism). However, the Sikhs see themselves as an independent tradition and not an offshoot of another religion. Their leader, Guru Arjun, sheltered Khusrau and defended him. In response, the Mughal rulers had Arjun arrested and tortured to death. The Sikhs became the target of the Mughals' particular hatred. **C**

MAIN IDEA

Analyzing Causes
C How did the Mughals' dislike of the Sikhs develop?

Shah Jahan Jahangir's son and successor, **Shah Jahan**, could not tolerate competition and secured his throne by assassinating all his possible rivals. He had a great passion for two things: beautiful buildings and his wife Mumtaz Mahal (moom•TAHZ mah•HAHL). Nur Jahan had arranged this marriage between Jahangir's son and her niece for political reasons. Shah Jahan, however, fell genuinely in love with his Persian princess.

In 1631, Mumtaz Mahal died at age 39 while giving birth to her 14th child. To enshrine his wife's memory, he ordered that a tomb be built "as beautiful as she was beautiful." Fine white marble and fabulous jewels were gathered from many parts of Asia. This memorial, the **Taj Mahal**, has been called one of the most beautiful buildings in the world. Its towering marble dome and slender minaret towers look like lace and seem to change color as the sun moves across the sky.

The People Suffer But while Shah Jahan was building gardens, monuments, and forts, his country was suffering. There was famine in the land. Furthermore, farmers needed tools, roads, and ways of irrigating their crops and dealing with India's harsh environment. What they got instead were taxes and more taxes to support the building of monuments, their rulers' extravagant living, and war.

▲ Mirrored in a reflecting pool is the Taj Mahal, a monument to love and the Mughal Empire.

History *in* Depth

Building the Taj Mahal

Some 20,000 workers labored for 22 years to build the famous tomb. It is made of white marble brought from 250 miles away. The minaret towers are about 130 feet high. The building itself is 186 feet square.

The design of the building is a blend of Hindu and Muslim styles. The pointed arches are of Muslim design, and the perforated marble windows and doors are typical of a style found in Hindu temples.

The inside of the building is a glittering garden of thousands of carved marble flowers inlaid with tiny precious stones. One tiny flower, one inch square, had 60 different inlays.

 hmhsocialstudies.com

INTERNET ACTIVITY Go online to create a brochure about the Taj Mahal.

All was not well in the royal court either. When Shah Jahan became ill in 1657, his four sons scrambled for the throne. The third son, **Aurangzeb** (AWR•uhng•zehb), moved first and most decisively. In a bitter civil war, he executed his older brother, who was his most serious rival. Then he arrested his father and put him in prison, where he died several years later. After Shah Jahan's death, a mirror was found in his room, angled so that he could look out at the reflection of the Taj Mahal.

Aurangzeb's Reign A master at military strategy and an aggressive empire builder, Aurangzeb ruled from 1658 to 1707. He expanded the Mughal holdings to their greatest size. However, the power of the empire weakened during his reign.

This loss of power was due largely to Aurangzeb's oppression of the people. He rigidly enforced Islamic laws, outlawing drinking, gambling, and other activities viewed as vices. He appointed censors to police his subjects' morals and make sure they prayed at the appointed times. He also tried to erase all the gains Hindus had made under Akbar. For example, he brought back the hated tax on non-Muslims and dismissed Hindus from high positions in his government. He banned the construction of new temples and had Hindu monuments destroyed. Not surprisingly, these actions outraged the Hindus.

The Hindu rajputs, whom Akbar had converted from potential enemies to allies, rebelled. Aurangzeb defeated them repeatedly, but never completely. In the southwest, a Hindu warrior community called Marathas founded their own state. Aurangzeb captured their leader but could never conquer them. Meanwhile, the Sikhs transformed themselves into a brotherhood of warriors. They began building a state in the Punjab, an area in northwest India.

MAIN IDEA

Recognizing Effects

D How did Aurangzeb's personal qualities and political policies affect the Mughal Empire?

Aurangzeb levied oppressive taxes to pay for the wars against the increasing numbers of enemies. He had done away with all taxes not authorized by Islamic law, so he doubled the taxes on Hindu merchants. This increased tax burden deepened the Hindus' bitterness and led to further rebellion. As a result, Aurangzeb needed to raise more money to increase his army. The more territory he conquered, the more desperate his situation became. **D**

The Empire's Decline and Decay

By the end of Aurangzeb's reign, he had drained the empire of its resources. Over 2 million people died in a famine while Aurangzeb was away waging war. Most of his subjects felt little or no loyalty to him.

As the power of the central state weakened, the power of local lords grew. After Aurangzeb's death, his sons fought a war of succession. In fact, three emperors reigned in the first 12 years after Aurangzeb died. By the end of this period, the Mughal emperor was nothing but a wealthy figurehead. He ruled not a united empire but a patchwork of independent states.

As the Mughal Empire rose and fell, Western traders slowly built their own power in the region. The Portuguese were the first Europeans to reach India. In fact, they arrived just before Babur did. Next came the Dutch, who in turn gave way to the French and the English. However, the great Mughal emperors did not feel threatened by the European traders. In 1661, Aurangzeb casually handed them the port of Bombay. Aurangzeb had no idea that he had given India's next conquerors their first foothold in a future empire.

SECTION 3 ASSESSMENT

TERMS & NAMES 1. For each term or name, write a sentence explaining its significance.
• Mughal   • Babur   • Akbar   • Sikh   • Shah Jahan   • Taj Mahal   • Aurangzeb

USING YOUR NOTES	**MAIN IDEAS**	**CRITICAL THINKING & WRITING**
2. Which of the Mughal emperors on your time line had a positive effect on the empire? Which had negative effects? 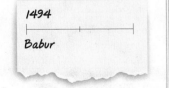	3. How did Akbar demonstrate tolerance in his empire? 4. What pattern is seen in the ways individuals came to power in the Mughal Empire? 5. Why did the empire weaken under the rule of Aurangzeb?	6. **CLARIFYING** Why were Akbar's tax policies so successful? 7. **MAKING INFERENCES** Why was Nur Jahan able to hold so much power in Jahangir's court? 8. **EVALUATING COURSES OF ACTION** Why were the policies of Aurangzeb so destructive to the Mughal Empire? 9. **WRITING ACTIVITY** POWER AND AUTHORITY Write a **compare-and-contrast essay** on the policies of Akbar and Aurangzeb. Use references from the text in your response.

1494
Babur

CONNECT TO TODAY CREATING A BIOGRAPHY

Select one of the women leaders in Connect to Today on page 519. Research her life and write a short **biography** of her.

Cultural Blending in Mughal India

As you have read, Mughal India enjoyed a golden age under Akbar. Part of Akbar's success—indeed, the success of the Mughals—came from his religious tolerance. India's population was largely Hindu, and the incoming Mughal rulers were Muslim. The Mughal emperors encouraged the blending of cultures to create a united India.

This cultural integration can be seen in the art of Mughal India. Muslim artists focused heavily on art with ornate patterns of flowers and leaves, called arabesque or geometric patterns. Hindu artists created naturalistic and often ornate artworks. These two artistic traditions came together and created a style unique to Mughal India. As you can see, the artistic collaboration covered a wide range of art forms.

↗ hmhsocialstudies.com

RESEARCH WEB LINKS Go online for more on art in Mughal India.

▼ Decorative Arts

Decorative work on items from dagger handles to pottery exhibits the same cultural blending as other Mughal art forms. This dagger handle shows some of the floral and geometric elements common in Muslim art, but the realistic depiction of the horse comes out of the Hindu tradition.

▼ Architecture

Mughal emperors brought to India a strong Muslim architectural tradition. Indian artisans were extremely talented with local building materials—specifically, marble and sandstone. Together, they created some of the most striking and enduring architecture in the world, like Humayun's Tomb shown here.

▼ Painting

Mughal painting was largely a product of the royal court. Persian artists brought to court by Mughal emperors had a strong influence, but Mughal artists quickly developed their own characteristics. The Mughal style kept aspects of the Persian influence—particularly the flat aerial perspective. But, as seen in this colorful painting, the Indian artists incorporated more naturalism and detail from the world around them.

▲ Fabrics

Mughal fabrics included geometric patterns found in Persian designs, but Mughal weavers, like other Mughal artisans, also produced original designs. Themes that were common in Mughal fabrics were landscapes, animal chases, floral latticeworks, and central flowering plants like the one on this tent hanging.

Connect *to* Today

1. **Clarifying** What does the art suggest about the culture of Mughal India?

    See Skillbuilder Handbook, page R4.

2. **Forming and Supporting Opinions**
    What are some modern examples of cultural blending in art? What elements of each culture are represented in the artwork? Consider other art forms, such as music and literature, as well.

TERMS & NAMES

Briefly explain the importance of each of the following to the Ottoman, Safavid, or Mughal empires.

1. Suleyman the Lawgiver
2. *devshirme*
3. janissary
4. shah
5. Shah Abbas
6. Akbar
7. Sikh
8. Taj Mahal

MAIN IDEAS

The Ottomans Build a Vast Empire
Section 1 (pages 507–511)

9. Why were the Ottomans such successful conquerors?
10. How did Mehmed the Conqueror show his tolerance of other cultures?
11. Why was Selim's capture of Mecca, Medina, and Cairo so significant?

Case Study: Cultural Blending Section 2 (pages 512–515)

12. What were some of the causes of cultural blending in the Safavid Empire?
13. In what ways did the Safavids weave foreign ideas into their culture?

The Mughal Empire in India Section 3 (pages 516–523)

14. In what ways did Akbar defend religious freedom during his reign?
15. How did Akbar's successors promote religious conflict in the empire?

CRITICAL THINKING

1. USING YOUR NOTES

In a chart, compare and contrast the Mughal Empire under Akbar, the Safavid Empire under Shah Abbas, and the Ottoman Empire under Suleyman I.

	Government Reforms	Cultural Blending
Akbar		
Abbas		
Suleyman		

2. EVALUATING COURSES OF ACTION

POWER AND AUTHORITY How did the use of artillery change the way empires in this chapter and lands that bordered them reacted to each other?

3. RECOGNIZING EFFECTS

CULTURAL INTERACTION What impact did religion have on governing each of the three empires in this chapter?

4. EVALUATING DECISIONS

EMPIRE BUILDING What was the value of treating conquered peoples in a way that did not oppress them?

5. MAKING INFERENCES

Why do you think the three empires in this chapter did not unite into one huge empire? Give reasons for your answer.

6. MAKING INFERENCES

Conquest of new territories contributed to the growth of the Muslim empires you read about in this chapter. How might it have also hindered this growth?

VISUAL SUMMARY

The Muslim World Expands

Muslims control Middle East, India, North Africa, and parts of Europe.

Ottoman Empire

- Move into Byzantium
- Take Constantinople
- Add Syria and Palestine
- Use janissaries and *devshirme* to control the empire

Safavid Empire

- Take old Persian Empire
- Expand to Caucasus Mountains
- Build a new capital
- Use janissary-style army to control the empire

Mughal Empire

- Delhi Sultanate loosely controls Indian subcontinent
- Babur lays groundwork for an empire
- Akbar controls most of sub-continent in empire
- Aurangzeb expands empire to its largest size

Use the graphs and your knowledge of world history to answer questions 1 and 2.

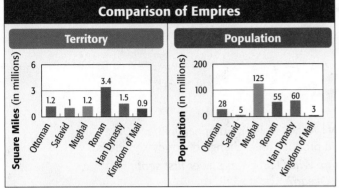

Source: Atlas of World Population History

1. Which empire was most densely populated?

   A. Han

   B. Roman

   C. Mughal

   D. Mali

2. Of the three Asian Muslim empires shown on the graph, which one had the smallest territory?

   A. Ottoman

   B. Safavid

   C. Mughal

   D. Mali

Use the quotation from Kritovoulos, a Greek historian and a governor in the court of Mehmed II, and your knowledge of world history to answer question 3.

PRIMARY SOURCE

When the Sultan [Mehmed] had captured the City of Constantinople, almost his very first care was to have the City repopulated. He also undertook the further care and repairs of it. He sent an order in the form of an imperial command to every part of his realm, that as many inhabitants as possible be transferred to the City, not only Christians but also his own people and many of the Hebrews.

KRITOVOULOS, *History of Mehmed the Conqueror*

3. What groups of people were to be sent to Constantinople?

   A. Hebrews and Christians

   B. Christians and Turks

   C. Christians, Hebrews, and Turkish Muslims

   D. Imperial armies

 hmhsocialstudies.com **TEST PRACTICE**

For additional test practice, go online for:

• Diagnostic tests

• Tutorials

• Strategies

Interact *with* History

On page 506, you considered how you might treat the people you conquered. Now that you have learned more about three Muslim empires, in what ways do you think you would change your policies? Discuss your thoughts with a small group of classmates.

FOCUS ON WRITING

Think about the experience of being a janissary in the court of Suleyman the Lawgiver. Write a **journal entry** about your daily activities. Consider the following:

• how a janissary was recruited

• what jobs or activities a janissary may have done

• the grandeur of the court of Suleyman

MULTIMEDIA ACTIVITY

Creating a Database

The three empires discussed in this chapter governed many religious and ethnic groups. Gather information on the religious and ethnic makeup of the modern nations of the former Ottoman, Safavid, and Mughal empires. Organize the information in a population database.

• Create one table for each empire.

• Make row headings for each modern nation occupying the lands of that empire.

• Make column headings for each ethnic group and each religious group.

• Insert the most recent population figures or percentages for each group.

• Use the final column to record the population total for each modern nation.

CHAPTER
19

An Age of Explorations and Isolation, 1400–1800

Essential Question

What fueled the age of exploration and why did China and Japan withdraw into isolation?

 What You Will Learn

In this chapter you will examine the era of European and Chinese exploration and the events that led the Chinese and Japanese to isolate themselves from Europeans.

SECTION 1 Europeans Explore the East

Main Idea Advances in sailing technology enabled Europeans to explore other parts of the world.

SECTION 2 China Limits European Contact

Main Idea Advances under the Ming and Qing dynasties left China uninterested in European contact.

SECTION 3 Japan Returns to Isolation

Main Idea The Tokugawa regime unified Japan and began 250 years of isolation, autocracy, and economic growth.

Previewing Themes

CULTURAL INTERACTION Asians resisted European influence, but this cultural interaction did produce an exchange of goods and ideas.

Geography *Study the map. What European power first sent explorers into the Indian Ocean?*

ECONOMICS The desire for wealth was a driving force behind the European exploration of the East. Europeans wanted to control trade with Asian countries.

Geography *How did the voyages of Bartolomeu Dias and Vasco da Gama compare in length?*

SCIENCE AND TECHNOLOGY Europeans were able to explore faraway lands after they improved their sailing technology.

Geography *Look at the map and time line. What country sent the first expedition to explore the Indian Ocean in the 15th century?*

EUROPE AND ASIA

1405 Zheng He takes first voyage.

1419 Prince Henry ▶ founds navigation school.

1494 Spain and Portugal sign Treaty of Tordesillas.

1400

1500

WORLD

1453 ◀ Ottomans capture Constantinople.

1464 Songhai Empire begins in West Africa.

1511 First enslaved Africans arrive in the Americas.

Early Explorations, 1400s

HISTORY
Ming Dynasty
Wall Building

hmhsocialstudies.com VIDEO

ATLANTIC
OCEAN

EUROPE

ENGLAND
NETHERLANDS
London Amsterdam
Paris
FRANCE Venice
PORTUGAL Madrid
Lisbon SPAIN
Seville
Ceuta
Madeira

A S I A

Beijing

Nanjing

CHINA

30°N

Canary
Is.

Mediterranean Sea

Cairo

Hormuz

Cape
Verde
Is.

A F R I C A

Jiddah

Bombay

Goa

Aden

Calicut

Arabian
Sea

0° Equator

Mogadishu

Malindi
Mombasa
Kilwa

INDIAN
OCEAN

Malacca

Mozambique

Sofala

ATLANTIC
OCEAN

30°S

Cape of
Good Hope

N
W   E
S

- - - Dias, 1487–1488
——— da Gama, (1st voyage) 1497–1498
——— Zheng He, (7 voyages) 1405–1433

0   500   1000 Miles
0   500   1000 Kilometers
Winkel II Projection

1603
Tokugawa
shoguns rule Japan.

1619
Dutch open
trade with Java.

1644
Manchus establish
Qing Dynasty in China.

1793
Britain seeks to trade
with China.

1600   **1700**   **1800**

1608
◀ Samuel de Champlain
founds Quebec. (French flag)

1776
◀ American colonies declare
independence from Britain.
(George Washington)

Would you sail into the unknown?

It is a gray morning in 1430. You are standing on a dock in the European country of Portugal, staring out at the mysterious Atlantic Ocean. You have been asked to go on a voyage of exploration. Yet, like most people at the time, you have no idea what lies beyond the horizon. The maps that have been drawn show some of the dangers you might face. And you've heard the terrifying stories of sea monsters and shipwrecks (see map below). You also have heard that riches await those who help explore and claim new lands. Now, you must decide whether to go.

EXAMINING *the* ISSUES

- **What possible rewards might come from exploring the seas for new lands?**

- **What are the risks involved in embarking on a voyage into the unknown?**

Discuss these questions with your classmates. In your discussion, recall what you have learned about the lands beyond Europe and what they have to offer. As you read about the age of explorations and isolation, see why Europeans explored and what they achieved.

Europeans Explore the East

MAIN IDEA	WHY IT MATTERS NOW	TERMS & NAMES
SCIENCE AND TECHNOLOGY Advances in sailing technology enabled Europeans to explore other parts of the world.	European exploration was an important step toward the global interaction existing in the world today.	• Prince Henry • Bartolomeu Dias • Vasco da Gama • Treaty of Tordesillas • Dutch East India Company

SETTING THE STAGE By the early 1400s, Europeans were ready to venture beyond their borders. As Chapter 17 explained, the Renaissance encouraged, among other things, a new spirit of adventure and curiosity. This spirit of adventure, along with several other important reasons, prompted Europeans to explore the world around them. This chapter and the next one describe how these explorations began a long process that would bring together the peoples of many different lands and permanently change the world.

For "God, Glory, and Gold"

Europeans had not been completely isolated from the rest of the world before the 1400s. Beginning around 1100, European crusaders battled Muslims for control of the Holy Lands in Southwest Asia. In 1275, the Italian trader Marco Polo reached the court of Kublai Khan in China. For the most part, however, Europeans had neither the interest nor the ability to explore foreign lands. That changed by the early 1400s. The desire to grow rich and to spread Christianity, coupled with advances in sailing technology, spurred an age of European exploration.

Europeans Seek New Trade Routes The desire for new sources of wealth was the main reason for European exploration. Through overseas exploration, merchants and traders hoped ultimately to benefit from what had become a profitable business in Europe: the trade of spices and other luxury goods from Asia. The people of Europe had been introduced to these items during the Crusades, the wars fought between Christians and Muslims from 1096 to 1270 (see Chapter 14). After the Crusades ended, Europeans continued to demand such spices as nutmeg, ginger, cinnamon, and pepper, all of which added flavor to the bland foods of Europe. Because demand for these goods was greater than the supply, merchants could charge high prices and thus make great profits.

The Muslims and the Italians controlled trade from East to West. Muslims sold Asian goods to Italian merchants, who controlled trade across the land routes of the Mediterranean region. The Italians resold the items at increased prices to merchants throughout Europe.

hmhsocialstudies.com
TAKING NOTES
Use the graphic organizer online to take notes on important events in the European exploration of the East.

▼ This early globe depicts the Europeans' view of Europe and Africa around 1492.

Other European traders did not like this arrangement. Paying such high prices to the Italians severely cut into their own profits. By the 1400s, European merchants—as well as the new monarchs of England, Spain, Portugal, and France—sought to bypass the Italian merchants. This meant finding a sea route directly to Asia.

The Spread of Christianity The desire to spread Christianity also motivated Europeans to explore. The Crusades had left Europeans with a taste for spices, but more significantly with feelings of hostility between Christians and Muslims. European countries believed that they had a sacred duty not only to continue fighting Muslims, but also to convert non-Christians throughout the world.

Europeans hoped to obtain popular goods directly from the peoples of Asia. They also hoped to Christianize them. Bernal Díaz del Castillo, an early Spanish explorer, explained his motives: "To serve God and His Majesty, to give light to those who were in darkness and to grow rich as all men desire to do." **A**

Technology Makes Exploration Possible While "God, glory, and gold" were the primary motives for exploration, advances in technology made the voyages of discovery possible. During the 1200s, it would have been nearly impossible for a European sea captain to cross 3,000 miles of ocean and return again. The main problem was that European ships could not sail against the wind. In the 1400s, shipbuilders designed a new vessel, the caravel. The caravel was sturdier than earlier vessels. In addition, triangular sails adopted from the Arabs allowed it to sail effectively against the wind.

Europeans also improved their navigational techniques. To better determine their location at sea, sailors used the astrolabe, which the Muslims had perfected. The astrolabe was a brass circle with carefully adjusted rings marked off in degrees. Using the rings to sight the stars, a sea captain could calculate latitude, or how far north or south of the equator the ship was. Explorers were also able to more accurately track direction by using a magnetic compass, a Chinese invention.

Portugal Leads the Way

The leader in developing and applying these sailing innovations was Portugal. Located on the Atlantic Ocean at the southwest corner of Europe, Portugal was the first European country to establish trading outposts along the west coast of Africa. Eventually, Portuguese explorers pushed farther east into the Indian Ocean.

The Portuguese Explore Africa Portugal took the lead in overseas exploration in part due to strong government support. The nation's most enthusiastic supporter of exploration was **Prince Henry**, the son of Portugal's king. Henry's dreams of overseas exploration began in 1415 when he helped conquer the Muslim city of Ceuta in North Africa. There, he had his first glimpse of the dazzling wealth that lay beyond Europe. In Ceuta, the Portuguese invaders found exotic stores filled with pepper, cinnamon, cloves, and other spices. In addition, they encountered large supplies of gold, silver, and jewels.

MAIN IDEA

Summarizing

A How might the phrase "God, glory, and gold" summarize the Europeans' motives for exploration?

History Makers

Prince Henry
1394–1460

For his role in promoting Portuguese exploration, historians call Prince Henry "the Navigator." Although he never went on voyages of discovery, Henry was consumed by the quest to find new lands and to spread Christianity. A devout Catholic, he wanted "to make increase in the faith of our lord Jesus Christ and bring to him all the souls that should be saved."

To that end, Henry used his own fortune to organize more than 14 voyages along the western coast of Africa, which was previously unexplored by Europeans. As a result, Henry died in debt. The Portuguese crown spent more than 60 years paying off his debts.

↗ hmhsocialstudies.com

RESEARCH WEB LINKS Go online for more on Prince Henry.

↗ hmhsocialstudies.com INTERACTIVE

The Tools of Exploration

Out on the open seas, winds easily blew ships off course. With only the sun, moon, and stars to guide them, few sailors willingly ventured beyond the sight of land. In order to travel to distant places, European inventors and sailors experimented with new tools for navigation and new designs for sailing ships, often borrowing from other cultures.

↗ hmhsocialstudies.com

RESEARCH WEB LINKS Go online for more on the tools of exploration.

▲ Here, a French mariner uses an early navigation instrument that he has brought ashore to fix his ship's position. It was difficult to make accurate calculations aboard wave-tossed vessels.

❶ The average caravel was 65 feet long. This versatile ship had triangular sails for maneuverability and square sails for power.

❷ The large cargo area could hold the numerous supplies needed for long voyages.

❸ Its shallow draft (depth of the ship's keel below the water) allowed it to explore close to the shore.

◄ The sextant replaced the astrolabe in the mid-1700s as the instrument for measuring the height of the stars above the horizon—to determine latitude and longitude.

▲ This 17th-century compass is typical of those taken by navigators on voyages of exploration. The compass was invented by the Chinese.

Connect *to* Today

1. **Analyzing Motives** Why did inventors and sailors develop better tools for navigation?
   See Skillbuilder Handbook, page R16.

2. **Summarizing** What types of navigational or other tools do sailors use today? Choose one type of tool and write a brief explanation of what it does.

A Ship's Rations

The captain of a 17th-century sailing vessel, with a crew of 190 sailors, would normally order the following food items for a three-month trip:

- 8,000 pounds of salt beef; 2,800 pounds of salt pork; 600 pounds of salt cod; a few beef tongues
- 15,000 brown biscuits; 5,000 white biscuits
- 30 bushels of oatmeal; 40 bushels of dried peas; 1 1/2 bushels of mustard seed
- 1 barrel of salt; 1 barrel of flour
- 11 small wooden casks of butter; 1 large cask of vinegar
- 10,500 gallons of beer; 3,500 gallons of water; 2 large casks of cider

↗ hmhsocialstudies.com

INTERNET ACTIVITY Go online to research food services aboard a modern U.S. warship and prepare a menu for a typical meal.

Henry returned to Portugal determined to reach the source of these treasures in the East. The prince also wished to spread the Christian faith. In 1419, Henry founded a navigation school on the southwestern coast of Portugal. Mapmakers, instrument makers, shipbuilders, scientists, and sea captains gathered there to perfect their trade.

Within several years, Portuguese ships began sailing down the western coast of Africa. By the time Henry died in 1460, the Portuguese had established a series of trading posts along western Africa's shores. There, they traded with Africans for such profitable items as gold and ivory. Eventually, they traded for African captives to be used as slaves. Having established their presence along the African coast, Portuguese explorers plotted their next move. They would attempt to find a sea route to Asia.

Portuguese Sailors Reach Asia The Portuguese believed that to reach Asia by sea, they would have to sail around the southern tip of Africa. In 1488, Portuguese captain **Bartolomeu Dias** ventured far down the coast of Africa until he and his crew reached the tip. As they arrived, a huge storm rose and battered the fleet for days. When the storm ended, Dias realized his ships had been blown around the tip to the other side. Dias explored the southeast coast of Africa and then considered sailing to India. However, his crew was exhausted and food supplies were low. As a result, the captain returned home.

With the tip of Africa finally rounded, the Portuguese continued pushing east. In 1497, Portuguese explorer **Vasco da Gama** began exploring the east African coast. In 1498, he reached the port of Calicut, on the southwestern coast of India. Da Gama and his crew were amazed by the spices, rare silks, and precious gems that filled Calicut's shops. The Portuguese sailors filled their ships with such spices as pepper and cinnamon and returned to Portugal in 1499. Their cargo was worth 60 times the cost of the voyage. Da Gama's remarkable voyage of 27,000 miles had given Portugal a direct sea route to India.

Spain Also Makes Claims

As the Portuguese were establishing trading posts along the west coast of Africa, Spain watched with increasing envy. The Spanish monarchs also desired a direct sea route to Asia.

In 1492, an Italian sea captain, Christopher Columbus, convinced Spain to finance a bold plan: finding a route to Asia by sailing west across the Atlantic Ocean. In October of that year, Columbus reached an island in the Caribbean. He was mistaken in his thought that he had reached the East Indies. But his voyage would open the way for European colonization of the Americas—a process that would forever change the world. The immediate impact of Columbus's voyage, however, was to increase tensions between Spain and Portugal.

The Portuguese believed that Columbus had indeed reached Asia. Portugal suspected that Columbus had claimed for Spain lands that Portuguese sailors might have reached first. The rivalry between Spain and Portugal grew more tense. In 1493, Pope Alexander VI stepped in to keep peace between the two nations. He suggested an imaginary dividing line, drawn north to south, through the Atlantic Ocean. All lands to the west of the line, known as the Line of Demarcation, would be Spain's. These lands included most of the Americas. All lands to the east of the line would belong to Portugal.

MAIN IDEA

Analyzing Issues

B How did the Treaty of Tordesillas ease tensions between Spain and Portugal?

Portugal complained that the line gave too much to Spain. So it was moved farther west to include parts of modern-day Brazil for the Portuguese. In 1494, Spain and Portugal signed the **Treaty of Tordesillas**, in which they agreed to honor the line. The era of exploration and colonization was about to begin in earnest. **B**

Trading Empires in the Indian Ocean

With da Gama's voyage, Europeans had finally opened direct sea trade with Asia. They also opened an era of violent conflict in the East. European nations scrambled to establish profitable trading outposts along the shores of South and Southeast Asia. And all the while they battled the region's inhabitants, as well as each other.

Portugal's Trading Empire In the years following da Gama's voyage, Portugal built a bustling trading empire throughout the Indian Ocean. As the Portuguese moved into the region, they took control of the spice trade from Muslim merchants. In 1509, Portugal extended its control over the area when it defeated a Muslim fleet off the coast of India, a victory made possible by the cannons they had added aboard their ships.

Portugal strengthened its hold on the region by building a fort at Hormuz in 1514. It established control of the Straits of Hormuz, connecting the Persian Gulf and Arabian Sea, and helped stop Muslim traders from reaching India.

In 1510, the Portuguese captured Goa, a port city on India's west coast. They made it the capital of their trading empire. They then sailed farther east to Indonesia, also known as the East Indies. In 1511, a Portuguese fleet attacked the city of Malacca on the west coast of the Malay Peninsula. In capturing the town, the Portuguese seized control of the Strait of Malacca. Seizing this waterway gave them control of the Moluccas. These were islands so rich in spices that they became known as the Spice Islands.

In convincing his crew to attack Malacca, Portuguese sea captain Afonso de Albuquerque stressed his country's intense desire to crush the Muslim-Italian domination over Asian trade:

MAIN IDEA

Analyzing Primary Sources

C What did de Albuquerque see as the outcome of a Portuguese victory at Malacca?

PRIMARY SOURCE C
If we deprive them [Muslims] of this their ancient market there, there does not remain for them a single port in the whole of these parts, where they can carry on their trade in these things. . . . I hold it as very certain that if we take this trade of Malacca away out of their hands, Cairo and Mecca are entirely ruined, and to Venice will no spiceries . . . [be] . . . conveyed except that which her merchants go and buy in Portugal.

AFONSO DE ALBUQUERQUE, from *The Commentaries of the Great Afonso Dalbuquerque*

Portugal did break the old Muslim-Italian domination on trade from the East, much to the delight of European consumers. Portuguese merchants brought back goods from Asia at about one-fifth of what they cost when purchased through the Arabs and Italians. As a result, more Europeans could afford these items.

European territories
- Dutch
- English
- French
- Portuguese
- Spanish

European trading posts
- Dutch
- English
- French
- Portuguese
- Spanish

◄••• Dias's route
Aug. 1487– Feb. 1488

◄— Da Gama's route
July 1497–May 1498

GEOGRAPHY SKILLBUILDER: Interpreting Maps

1. **Place** Why would a fort at Hormuz help the Portuguese to stop trade between the Arabian Peninsula and India?
2. **Region** Where was the Dutch influence the greatest?

In time, Portugal's success in Asia attracted the attention of other European nations. As early as 1521, a Spanish expedition led by Ferdinand Magellan arrived in the Philippines. Spain claimed the islands and began settling them in 1565. By the early 1600s, the rest of Europe had begun to descend upon Asia. They wanted to establish their own trade empires in the East.

Other Nations Challenge the Portuguese Beginning around 1600, the English and Dutch began to challenge Portugal's dominance over the Indian Ocean trade. The Dutch Republic, also known as the Netherlands, was a small country situated along the North Sea in northwestern Europe. Since the early 1500s, Spain had ruled the area. In 1581, the people of the region declared their independence from Spain and established the Dutch Republic.

In a short time, the Netherlands became a leading sea power. By 1600, the Dutch owned the largest fleet of ships in the world—20,000 vessels. Pressure from Dutch and also English fleets eroded Portuguese control of the Asian region. The Dutch and English then battled one another for dominance of the area.

Both countries had formed an East India Company to establish and direct trade throughout Asia. These companies had the power to mint money, make treaties, and even raise their own armies. The **Dutch East India Company** was richer and more powerful than England's company. As a result, the Dutch eventually drove out the English and established their dominance over the region. **D**

Dutch Trade Outposts In 1619, the Dutch established their trading headquarters at Batavia on the island of Java. From there, they expanded west to

MAIN IDEA

Analyzing Issues

D How were the Dutch able to dominate the Indian Ocean trade?

conquer several nearby islands. In addition, the Dutch seized both the port of Malacca and the valuable Spice Islands from Portugal. Throughout the 1600s, the Netherlands increased its control over the Indian Ocean trade. With so many goods from the East traveling to the Netherlands, the nation's capital, Amsterdam, became a leading commercial center. By 1700, the Dutch ruled much of Indonesia and had trading posts in several Asian countries. They also controlled the Cape of Good Hope on the southern tip of Africa, which was used as a resupply stop.

British and French Traders By 1700 also, Britain and France had gained a foothold in the region. Having failed to win control of the larger area, the English East India Company focused much of its energy on establishing outposts in India. There, the English developed a successful business trading Indian cloth in Europe. In 1664, France also entered the Asia trade with its own East India Company. It struggled at first, as it faced continual attacks by the Dutch. Eventually, the French company established an outpost in India in the 1720s. However, it never showed much of a profit.

As the Europeans battled for a share of the profitable Indian Ocean trade, their influence inland in Southeast Asia remained limited. European traders did take control of many port cities in the region. But their impact rarely spread beyond the ports. From 1500 to about 1800, when Europeans began to conquer much of the region, the peoples of Asia remained largely unaffected by European contact. As the next two sections explain, European traders who sailed farther east to seek riches in China and Japan had even less success in spreading Western culture. **E**

MAIN IDEA

Recognizing Effects

E How did the arrival of Europeans affect the peoples of the East in general?

Connect *to* Today

Trading Partners

Global trade is important to the economies of Asian countries now just as it was when the region first began to export spices, silks, and gems centuries ago. Today, a variety of products, including automobiles and electronic goods, as well as tea and textiles, are shipped around the world. (Hong Kong harbor is pictured.)

Regional trade organizations help to strengthen economic cooperation among Asian nations and promote international trade. They include the Association of Southeast Asian Nations (ASEAN) and the South Asian Association for Regional Cooperation (SAARC).

SECTION 1 ASSESSMENT

TERMS & NAMES 1. For each term or name, write a sentence explaining its significance.
• Prince Henry • Bartolomeu Dias • Vasco da Gama • Treaty of Tordesillas • Dutch East India Company

USING YOUR NOTES

2. Which event in the European exploration of the East is the most significant? Explain with references from the text.

MAIN IDEAS

3. What role did the Renaissance play in launching an age of exploration?

4. What was Prince Henry's goal and who actually achieved it?

5. What European countries were competing for Asian trade during the age of exploration?

CRITICAL THINKING & WRITING

6. **MAKING INFERENCES** What did the Treaty of Tordesillas reveal about Europeans' attitudes toward non-European lands and peoples?

7. **ANALYZING MOTIVES** What were the motives behind European exploration in the 1400s? Explain.

8. **RECOGNIZING EFFECTS** In what ways did Europeans owe some of their sailing technology to other peoples?

9. **WRITING ACTIVITY** | SCIENCE AND TECHNOLOGY | Review "The Tools of Exploration" on page 531. Write a one-paragraph **opinion piece** on which technological advancement was the most important for European exploration.

CONNECT TO TODAY **WRITING A DESCRIPTION**

Research the Global Positioning System (GPS). Then write a brief **description** of this modern navigation system.

China Limits European Contacts

MAIN IDEA	WHY IT MATTERS NOW	TERMS & NAMES
CULTURAL INTERACTION Advances under the Ming and Qing dynasties left China uninterested in European contact.	China's independence from the West continues today, even as it forges new economic ties with the outside world.	• Ming Dynasty • Hongwu • Yonglo • Zheng He • Manchus • Qing Dynasty • Kangxi

SETTING THE STAGE The European voyages of exploration had led to opportunities for trade. Europeans made healthy profits from trade in the Indian Ocean region. They began looking for additional sources of wealth. Soon, European countries were seeking trade relationships in East Asia, first with China and later with Japan. By the time Portuguese ships dropped anchor off the Chinese coast in 1514, the Chinese had driven out their Mongol rulers and had united under a new dynasty.

China Under the Powerful Ming Dynasty

Use the graphic organizer online to take notes on relevant facts about each emperor.

China had become the dominant power in Asia under the **Ming Dynasty** (1368–1644). In recognition of China's power, vassal states from Korea to Southeast Asia paid their Ming overlords regular tribute, which is a payment by one country to another to acknowledge its submission. China expected Europeans to do the same. Ming rulers were not going to allow outsiders from distant lands to threaten the peace and prosperity the Ming had brought to China when they ended Mongol rule.

The Rise of the Ming A peasant's son, **Hongwu**, commanded the rebel army that drove the Mongols out of China in 1368. That year, he became the first Ming emperor. Hongwu continued to rule from the former Yuan capital of Nanjing in the south. (See the map on page 527.) He began reforms designed to restore agricultural lands devastated by war, erase all traces of the Mongol past, and promote China's power and prosperity. Hongwu's agricultural reforms increased rice production and improved irrigation. He also encouraged fish farming and growing commercial crops, such as cotton and sugar cane.

Hongwu used respected traditions and institutions to bring stability to China. For example, he encouraged a return to Confucian moral standards. He improved imperial administration by restoring the merit-based civil service examination system. Later in his rule, however, when problems developed, Hongwu became a ruthless tyrant. Suspecting plots against his rule everywhere, he conducted purges of the government, killing thousands of officials.

Hongwu's death in 1398 led to a power struggle. His son **Yonglo** (yung•lu) emerged victorious. Yonglo continued many of his father's policies, although he moved the royal court to Beijing. (See the Forbidden City feature on page 538.)

▼ Porcelain vase from the Ming Dynasty

Zheng He's Treasure Ship

85 FEET 400 FEET

◀ Zheng He's treasure ship compared with Christopher Columbus's *Santa Maria*

Yonglo also had a far-ranging curiosity about the outside world. In 1405, before Europeans began to sail beyond their borders, he launched the first of seven voyages of exploration. He hoped they would impress the world with the power and splendor of Ming China. He also wanted to expand China's tribute system.

The Voyages of Zheng He A Chinese Muslim admiral named <u>Zheng He</u> (jung huh) led all of the seven voyages. His expeditions were remarkable for their size. Everything about them was large—distances traveled, fleet size, and ship measurements. The voyages ranged from Southeast Asia to eastern Africa. From 40 to 300 ships sailed in each expedition. Among them were fighting ships, storage vessels, and huge "treasure" ships measuring more than 400 feet long. The fleet's crews numbered over 27,000 on some voyages. They included sailors, soldiers, carpenters, interpreters, accountants, doctors, and religious leaders. Like a huge floating city, the fleet sailed from port to port along the Indian Ocean.

Everywhere Zheng He went, he distributed gifts including silver and silk to show Chinese superiority. As a result, more than 16 countries sent tribute to the Ming court. Even so, Chinese scholar-officials complained that the voyages wasted valuable resources that could be used to defend against barbarians' attacks on the northern frontier. After the seventh voyage, in 1433, China withdrew into isolation. **A**

Ming Relations with Foreign Countries China's official trade policies in the 1500s reflected its isolation. To keep the influence of outsiders to a minimum, only the government was to conduct foreign trade, and only through three coastal ports, Canton, Macao, and Ningbo. In reality, trade flourished up and down the coast. Profit-minded merchants smuggled cargoes of silk, porcelain, and other valuable goods out of the country into the eager hands of European merchants. Usually, Europeans paid for purchases with silver, much of it from mines in the Americas.

Demand for Chinese goods had a ripple effect on the economy. Industries such as silk-making and ceramics grew rapidly. Manufacturing and commerce increased. But China did not become highly industrialized for two main reasons. First, the idea of commerce offended China's Confucian beliefs. Merchants, it was said, made their money "supporting foreigners and robbery." Second, Chinese economic policies traditionally favored agriculture. Taxes on agriculture stayed low. Taxes on manufacturing and trade skyrocketed.

Christian missionaries accompanied European traders into China. They brought Christianity and knowledge of European science and technology, such as the clock. The first missionary to have an impact was an Italian Jesuit named Matteo Ricci. He

MAIN IDEA

Making Inferences

A What do you think the people of other countries thought about China after one of Zheng He's visits?

↗ hmhsocialstudies.com

INTERACTIVE MAP

Accompany Zheng He on his voyages throughout the Indian Ocean.

An Age of Explorations and Isolation **537**

The Forbidden City

When Yonglo moved the Chinese capital to Beijing, he ordered the building of a great palace complex to symbolize his power and might. Construction took 14 years, from 1406 to 1420. Red walls 35 feet in height surrounded the complex, which had dozens of buildings, including palaces and temples. The complex became known as the Forbidden City because commoners and foreigners were not allowed to enter.

.75 mi (1207 m)

.5 mi (804.7 m)

The Moat • The Moat
Corner Tower • Shenwu Gate • Corner Tower
Qin'an Hall
Imperial Garden
Kunning Hall
Jiactal Hall
Huangji Hall
Qianqing Hall
Yangxin Hall
Fenngxian Hall
Qianqing Gate
❸
Bache Hall
Nine-Dragon Wall
❷ Zhonghe Hall
Cining Garden
❶ Taihe Hall
Imperial Kitchen
Taihe Gate
Golden River Bridge
Corner Tower • Wumen Gate • Corner Tower
The Moat • The Moat

▲ Hall of Supreme Harmony
Taihe Hall, or the Hall of Supreme Harmony, is the largest building in the compound. It measures 201 by 122 feet and stands about 125 feet high. This hall was used for important ceremonies, such as those marking the emperor's birthday or the day the crown prince took the throne.

▲ Hall of Central Harmony
Zhonge Hall, or the Hall of Central Harmony, was a smaller square building between the two main halls. It was a sort of private office where the emperor could stop to rest on his way to ceremonies.

▼ Nine-Dragon Wall
This wall, or screen, of glazed tiles shows nine dragons playing with pearls against a background of sea and sky. From ancient times, the dragon was the symbol of the imperial family. This is the largest of three famous nine-dragon screens that exist in China.

SKILLBUILDER: Interpreting Visuals
1. **Analyzing Motives** *Why do you think the emperor wanted to keep common people out of the Forbidden City?*
2. **Drawing Conclusions** *What aspects of the Forbidden City helped to convey the power of the emperor?*

gained special favor at the Ming court through his intelligence and fluency in Chinese. Still, many educated Chinese opposed the European and Christian presence.

Manchus Found the Qing Dynasty

By 1600, the Ming had ruled for more than 200 years, and the dynasty was weakening. Its problems grew—ineffective rulers, corrupt officials, and a government that was out of money. Higher taxes and bad harvests pushed millions of peasants toward starvation. Civil strife and rebellion followed.

Northeast of the Great Wall lay Manchuria. In 1644, the **Manchus** (MAN•chooz), the people of that region, invaded China and the Ming Dynasty collapsed. The Manchus seized Beijing, and their leader became China's new emperor. As the Mongols had done in the 1300s, the Manchus took a Chinese name for their dynasty, the **Qing** (chihng) **Dynasty**. They would rule for more than 260 years and expand China's borders to include Taiwan, Chinese Central Asia, Mongolia, and Tibet.

China Under the Qing Many Chinese resisted rule by the non-Chinese Manchus. Rebellions flared up periodically for decades. The Manchus, however, slowly earned the people's respect. They upheld China's traditional Confucian beliefs and social structures. They made the country's frontiers safe and restored China's prosperity. Two powerful Manchu rulers contributed greatly to the acceptance of the new dynasty.

The first, **Kangxi** (kahng•shee), became emperor in 1661 and ruled for some 60 years. He reduced government expenses and lowered taxes. A scholar and patron of the arts, Kangxi gained the support of intellectuals by offering them government positions. He also enjoyed the company of the Jesuits at court. They told him about developments in science, medicine, and mathematics in Europe. Under his grandson Qian-long (chyahn•lung), who ruled from 1736 to 1795, China reached its greatest size and prosperity. An industrious emperor like his grandfather, Qian-long often rose at dawn to work on the empire's problems. These included armed nomads on its borders and the expanding presence of European missionaries and merchants in China.

Manchus Continue Chinese Isolation To the Chinese, their country—called the Middle Kingdom—had been the cultural center of the universe for 2,000 years. If foreign states wished to trade with China, they would have to follow Chinese rules. These rules included trading only at special ports and paying tribute.

The Dutch were masters of the Indian Ocean trade by the time of Qian-long. They accepted China's restrictions. Their diplomats paid tribute to the emperor through gifts and by performing the required "kowtow" ritual. This ritual involved kneeling in front of the emperor and touching one's head to the ground nine times. As a result, the Chinese accepted the Dutch as trading partners. The Dutch returned home with traditional porcelains and silk, as well as a new trade item, tea. By 1800, tea would make up 80 percent of shipments to Europe. **B**

Great Britain also wanted to increase trade with China. But the British did not like China's trade restrictions. In 1793, Lord George Macartney delivered a letter from King George III to Qian-long. It asked for a better trade arrangement,

History Makers

Kangxi
1654–1722

The emperor Kangxi had too much curiosity to remain isolated in the Forbidden City. To calm the Chinese in areas devastated by the Manchu conquest, Kangxi set out on a series of "tours."

On tours I learned about the common people's grievances by talking with them. . . . I asked peasants about their officials, looked at their houses, and discussed their crops.

In 1696, with Mongols threatening the northern border, Kangxi exhibited leadership unheard of in later Ming times. Instead of waiting in the palace for reports, he personally led 80,000 troops to victory over the Mongols.

MAIN IDEA

Making Inferences

B Why do you think the kowtow ritual was so important to the Chinese emperor?

including Chinese acceptance of British manufactured goods. Macartney refused to kowtow, and Qian-long denied Britain's request. As the emperor made clear in a letter to the king, China was self-sufficient and did not need the British:

PRIMARY SOURCE
There is nothing we lack, as your principal envoy and others have themselves observed. We have never set much store on strange or ingenious objects, nor do we need any more of your country's manufactures.

QIAN-LONG, from a letter to King George III of Great Britain

In the 1800s, the British, Dutch, and others would attempt to chip away at China's trade restrictions until the empire itself began to crack, as Chapter 28 will describe.

Korea Under the Manchus In 1636, even before they came to power in China, the Manchus conquered nearby Korea and made it a vassal state. Although Korea remained independent it existed in China's shadow. Koreans organized their government according to Confucian principles. They also adopted China's technology, its culture, and especially its policy of isolation.

When the Manchus established the Qing dynasty, Korea's political relationship with China did not change. But Korea's attitude did. The Manchu invasion, combined with a Japanese attack in the 1590s, provoked strong feelings of nationalism in the Korean people. This sentiment was most evident in their art. Instead of traditional Chinese subjects, many artists chose to show popular Korean scenes.

Social History

China's Population Boom

China's population grew dramatically from 1650 to 1900. General peace and increased agricultural productivity were the causes.

The Growth of Early Modern China

Population (in millions)

500
400
300
200
100

1650 1700 1750 1800 1850 1900

▲ A Chinese family prepares for a wedding in the 1800s.

SKILLBUILDER: Interpreting Graphs
Comparing *By what percentage did China's population increase between 1650 and 1900?*

Life in Ming and Qing China

In the 1600s and 1700s, there was general peace and prosperity in China. Life improved for most Chinese.

Families and the Role of Women Most Chinese families had farmed the land the same way their ancestors had. However, during the Qing Dynasty, irrigation and fertilizer use increased. Farmers grew rice and new crops, such as corn and sweet potatoes, brought by Europeans from the Americas. As food production increased, nutrition improved and families expanded. A population explosion followed.

These expanded Chinese families favored sons over daughters. Only a son was allowed to perform vital religious rituals. A son also would raise his own family under his parents' roof, assuring aging parents of help with the farming. As a result, females were not valued, and many female infants were killed. Although men dominated the household and their wives, women had significant responsibilities. Besides working in the fields, they supervised the children's education and managed the family's finances. While most women were forced to remain secluded in their homes, some found outside jobs such as working as midwives or textile workers.

Cultural Developments The culture of early modern China was based mainly on traditional forms. The great masterpiece of traditional Chinese fiction was written during this period. *Dream of the Red Chamber* by Cao Zhan examines upper class Manchu society in the 1700s. Most artists of the time painted in traditional styles, which valued technique over creativity. In pottery, technical skill as well as experimentation led to the production of high-quality ceramics, including porcelain. Drama was a popular entertainment, especially in rural China where literacy rates were low. Plays that presented Chinese history and cultural heroes entertained and also helped unify Chinese society by creating a national culture. **C**

While China preserved its traditions in isolation, another civilization that developed in seclusion—the Japanese—was in conflict, as you will read in Section 3.

Vocabulary
A *midwife* is a woman trained to assist women in childbirth.

MAIN IDEA

Making Inferences
C What was the effect of the emphasis on tradition in early modern China?

▲ These 12th-century Chinese women work outside the home making silk.

SECTION **2** ASSESSMENT

TERMS & NAMES 1. For each term or name, write a sentence explaining its significance.
• Ming Dynasty • Hongwu • Yonglo • Zheng He • Manchus • Qing Dynasty • Kangxi

USING YOUR NOTES

2. Which of these emperors was most influential? Explain with text references.

Emperor	Facts
1.	1.
2.	2.
3.	3.

MAIN IDEAS

3. How did Beijing become the capital of China?

4. What evidence indicates that China lost interest in contacts abroad after 1433?

5. What did Christian missionaries bring to China?

CRITICAL THINKING & WRITING

6. **MAKING DECISIONS** Do you think Lord George Macartney should have kowtowed to Emperor Qian-long? Why?

7. **ANALYZING CAUSES** What factors, both within China and outside its borders, contributed to the downfall of the Ming Dynasty?

8. **DRAWING CONCLUSIONS** What was Korea's relationship with China under the Qing Dynasty?

9. **WRITING ACTIVITY** CULTURAL INTERACTION Choose one emperor of China and write a one-paragraph **biography** using the information you listed in your Taking Notes chart and from the text.

CONNECT TO TODAY WRITING AN ESSAY

Learn more about popular culture in China today. Then write a two-paragraph **expository essay** on some form of popular entertainment in the arts or sports.

Japan Returns to Isolation

MAIN IDEA	WHY IT MATTERS NOW	TERMS & NAMES
ECONOMICS The Tokugawa regime unified Japan and began 250 years of isolation, autocracy, and economic growth.	Even now, Japan continues to limit and control dealings with foreigners, especially in the area of trade.	• daimyo • Oda Nobunaga • Toyotomi Hideyoshi • Tokugawa Shogunate • haiku • kabuki

SETTING THE STAGE In the 1300s, the unity that had been achieved in Japan in the previous century broke down. Shoguns, or military leaders, in the north and south fiercely fought one another for power. Although these two rival courts later came back together at the end of the century, a series of politically weak shoguns let control of the country slip from their grasp. The whole land was torn by factional strife and economic unrest. It would be centuries before Japan would again be unified.

A New Feudalism Under Strong Leaders

hmhsocialstudies.com
TAKING NOTES

Use the graphic organizer online to take notes on the achievements of the daimyos who unified Japan.

In 1467, civil war shattered Japan's old feudal system. The country collapsed into chaos. Centralized rule ended. Power drained away from the shogun to territorial lords in hundreds of separate domains.

Local Lords Rule A violent era of disorder followed. This time in Japanese history, which lasted from 1467 to 1568, is known as the Sengoku, or "Warring States," period. Powerful samurai seized control of old feudal estates. They offered peasants and others protection in return for their loyalty. These warrior-chieftains, called **daimyo** (DY•mee•OH), became lords in a new kind of Japanese feudalism. Daimyo meant "great name." Under this system, security came from this group of powerful warlords. The emperor at Kyoto became a figurehead, having a leadership title but no actual power.

The new Japanese feudalism resembled European feudalism in many ways. The daimyo built fortified castles and created small armies of samurai on horses. Later they added foot soldiers with muskets (guns) to their ranks. Rival daimyo often fought each other for territory. This led to disorder throughout the land.

New Leaders Restore Order A number of ambitious daimyo hoped to gather enough power to take control of the entire country. One, the brutal and ambitious **Oda Nobunaga** (oh•dah-noh•boo•nah•gah), defeated his rivals and seized the imperial capital Kyoto in 1568.

Following his own motto "Rule the empire by force," Nobunaga sought to eliminate his remaining enemies. These included rival daimyo as well as wealthy Buddhist monasteries aligned with them. In 1575, Nobunaga's 3,000 soldiers armed with muskets crushed an enemy force of samurai cavalry. This was the first time firearms had been used effectively in battle in Japan. However,

A samurai warrior ▼

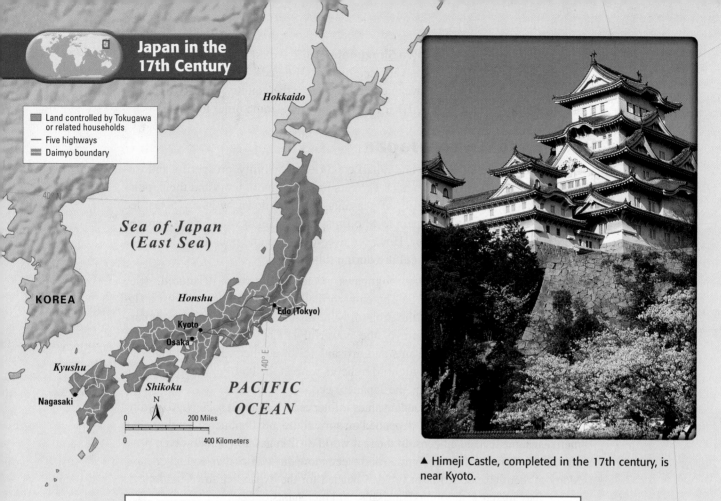

Land controlled by Tokugawa
or related households
— Five highways
═ Daimyo boundary

Hokkaido

Sea of Japan
(East Sea)

KOREA

Honshu

Edo (Tokyo)

Kyoto

Osaka

Kyushu

Shikoku

PACIFIC
OCEAN

N

Nagasaki

0   200 Miles
0   400 Kilometers

▲ Himeji Castle, completed in the 17th century, is
near Kyoto.

GEOGRAPHY SKILLBUILDER: Interpreting Maps
1. **Place** *Why might Edo have been a better site for a capital in the 17th century than Kyoto?*
2. **Region** *About what percentage of Japan was controlled by Tokugawa or related
households when Tokugawa Ieyasu took power in the early 1600s?*

Nobunaga was not able to unify Japan. He committed *seppuku,* the ritual suicide
of a samurai, in 1582, when one of his own generals turned on him.

Nobunaga's best general, <u>**Toyotomi Hideyoshi**</u> (toh•you•toh•mee hee•deh•yoh•
shee), continued his fallen leader's mission. Hideyoshi set out to destroy the
daimyo that remained hostile. By 1590, by combining brute force with shrewd
political alliances, he controlled most of the country. Hideyoshi did not stop with
Japan. With the idea of eventually conquering China, he invaded Korea in 1592 and
began a long campaign against the Koreans and their Ming Chinese allies. When
Hideyoshi died in 1598, his troops withdrew from Korea.

Tokugawa Shogunate Unites Japan One of Hideyoshi's strongest daimyo allies,
Tokugawa Ieyasu (toh•koo•gah•wah ee•yeh•yah•soo), completed the unification of
Japan. In 1600, Ieyasu defeated his rivals at the Battle of Sekigahara. His victory earned
him the loyalty of daimyo throughout Japan. Three years later, Ieyasu became the sole
ruler, or shogun. He then moved Japan's capital to his power base at Edo, a small fishing village that would later become the city of Tokyo.

Japan was unified, but the daimyo still governed at the local level. To keep them
from rebelling, Ieyasu required that they spend every other year in the capital. Even
when they returned to their lands, they had to leave their families behind as
hostages in Edo. Through this "alternate attendance policy" and other restrictions,
Ieyasu tamed the daimyo. This was a major step toward restoring centralized government to Japan. As a result, the rule of law overcame the rule of the sword. **A**

MAIN IDEA

**Drawing
Conclusions**

A) How would the
"alternate atten-
dance policy"
restrict the daimyo?

An Age of Explorations and Isolation **543**

Ieyasu founded the <u>Tokugawa Shogunate</u>, which would hold power until 1867. On his deathbed in 1616, Ieyasu advised his son, Hidetada, "Take care of the people. Strive to be virtuous. Never neglect to protect the country." Most Tokugawa shoguns followed that advice. Their rule brought a welcome order to Japan.

Vocabulary
A *shogunate* is the administration or rule of a shogun.

Life in Tokugawa Japan

Japan enjoyed more than two and a half centuries of stability, prosperity, and isolation under the Tokugawa shoguns. Farmers produced more food, and the population rose. Still, the vast majority of peasants, weighed down by heavy taxes, led lives filled with misery. The people who prospered in Tokugawa society were the merchant class and the wealthy. However, everyone, rich and poor alike, benefited from a flowering of Japanese culture during this era.

Society in Tokugawa Japan Tokugawa society was very structured. (See Feudalism feature on page 361.) The emperor had the top rank but was just a figurehead. The actual ruler was the shogun, who was the supreme military commander. Below him were the daimyo, the powerful landholding samurai. Samurai warriors came next. The peasants and artisans followed them. Peasants made up about four-fifths of the population. Merchants were at the bottom, but they gradually became more important as the Japanese economy expanded.

In Japan, as in China, Confucian values influenced ideas about society. According to Confucius, the ideal society depended on agriculture, not commerce. Farmers, not merchants, made ideal citizens. In the real world of Tokugawa Japan, however, peasant farmers bore the main tax burden and faced more difficulties than any other class. Many of them abandoned farm life and headed for the expanding towns and cities. There, they mixed with samurai, artisans, and merchants.

By the mid-1700s, Japan began to shift from a rural to an urban society. Edo had grown from a small village in 1600 to perhaps the largest city in the world. Its population was more than 1 million. The rise of large commercial centers also increased employment opportunities for women. Women found jobs in entertainment, textile manufacturing, and publishing. Still, the majority of Japanese women led sheltered and restricted lives as peasant wives. They worked in the fields, managed the household, cared for the children, and each woman obeyed her husband without question.

Culture Under the Tokugawa Shogunate Traditional culture continued to thrive. Samurai attended ceremonial *noh* dramas, which were based on tragic themes. They read tales of ancient warriors and their courage in battle. In their homes, they hung paintings that showed scenes from classical literature. But traditional entertainment faced competition in the cities from new styles of literature, drama, and art.

Townspeople read a new type of fiction, realistic stories about self-made merchants or the hardships of life. The people also read <u>haiku</u> (HY•koo), 5-7-5-syllable, 3-line verse poetry. This poetry presents images rather than ideas. For example, Matsuo Basho, the greatest haiku poet, wrote before his death in 1694:

PRIMARY SOURCE B

On a journey, ailing—
My dreams roam about
Over a withered moor.

MATSUO BASHO, from *Matsuo Basho*

Tabi ni yande
Yume wa Kareno o
Kakemeguru

MATSUO BASHO, in Japanese

MAIN IDEA

Analyzing Primary Sources

B How is Matsuo Basho's haiku a poem about death?

Townspeople also attended <u>kabuki</u> theater. Actors in elaborate costumes, using music, dance, and mime, performed skits about modern life. The paintings the people enjoyed were often woodblock prints showing city life.

Kabuki Theater

Kabuki is a traditional form of Japanese theater. It makes use of extravagant costumes, masklike makeup, and exaggerated postures and gestures. The illustrations to the right show a contemporary actor and a 19th-century performer playing warriors.

Although kabuki was created by a woman, all roles, both male and female, are performed by men. Kabuki plays are about grand historical events or the everyday life of people in Tokugawa Japan.

For 400 years, kabuki has provided entertainment for the Japanese people. And more recently, kabuki has been performed for audiences around the world, including the United States. Major centers for kabuki theater in Japan are Tokyo, Kyoto, and Osaka.

Contact Between Europe and Japan

Europeans began coming to Japan in the 16th century, during the Warring States period. Despite the severe disorder in the country, the Japanese welcomed traders and missionaries, from Portugal and, later, other European countries. These newcomers introduced fascinating new technologies and ideas. Within a century, however, the aggressive Europeans had worn out their welcome.

Portugal Sends Ships, Merchants, and Technology to Japan The Japanese first encountered Europeans in 1543, when shipwrecked Portuguese sailors washed up on the shores of southern Japan. Portuguese merchants soon followed. They hoped to involve themselves in Japan's trade with China and Southeast Asia. The Portuguese brought clocks, eyeglasses, tobacco, firearms, and other unfamiliar items from Europe. Japanese merchants, eager to expand their markets, were happy to receive the newcomers and their goods. **C**

MAIN IDEA

Analyzing Motives

C Why did Europeans want to open trade with Japan?

The daimyo, too, welcomed the strangers. They were particularly interested in the Portuguese muskets and cannons, because every daimyo sought an advantage over his rivals. One of these warlords listened intently to a Japanese observer's description of a musket:

PRIMARY SOURCE
In their hands they carried something two or three feet long, straight on the outside with a passage inside, and made of a heavy substance. . . . This thing with one blow can smash a mountain of silver and a wall of iron. If one sought to do mischief in another man's domain and he was touched by it, he would lose his life instantly.
ANONYMOUS JAPANESE WRITER, quoted in *Sources of Japanese Tradition* (1958)

The Japanese purchased weapons from the Portuguese and soon began their own production. Firearms forever changed the time-honored tradition of the Japanese warrior, whose principal weapon had been the sword. Some daimyo recruited and trained corps of peasants to use muskets. Many samurai, who retained the sword as their principal weapon, would lose their lives to musket fire in future combat.

The cannon also had a huge impact on warfare and life in Japan. Daimyo had to build fortified castles to withstand the destructive force of cannonballs. (See the photograph of Himeji Castle on page 543.) The castles attracted merchants, artisans, and others to surrounding lands. Many of these lands were to grow into the towns and cities of modern Japan, including Edo (Tokyo), Osaka, Himeji, and Nagoya.

Christian Missionaries in Japan In 1549, Christian missionaries began arriving in Japan. The Japanese accepted the missionaries in part because they associated them with the muskets and other European goods that they wanted to purchase. However, the religious orders of Jesuits, Franciscans, and Dominicans came to convert the Japanese.

Francis Xavier, a Jesuit, led the first mission to Japan. He wrote that the Japanese were "very sociable. . . and much concerned with their honor, which they prize above everything else." Francis Xavier baptized about a hundred converts before he left Japan. By the year 1600, other European missionaries had converted about 300,000 Japanese to Christianity.

The success of the missionaries upset Tokugawa Ieyasu. He found aspects of the Christian invasion troublesome. Missionaries, actively seeking converts, scorned traditional Japanese beliefs and sometimes involved themselves in local politics. At first, Ieyasu did not take any action. He feared driving off the Portuguese, English, Spanish, and Dutch traders who spurred Japan's economy. By 1612, however, the shogun had come to fear religious uprisings more. He banned Christianity and focused on ridding his country of all Christians.

Ieyasu died in 1616, but repression of Christianity continued off and on for the next two decades under his successors. In 1637, the issue came to a head. An uprising in southern Japan of some 30,000 peasants, led by dissatisfied samurai, shook the Tokugawa shogunate. Because so many of the rebels were Christian, the shogun decided that Christianity was at the root of the rebellion. After that, the shoguns ruthlessly persecuted Christians. European missionaries were killed or driven out of Japan. All Japanese were forced to demonstrate faithfulness to some branch of Buddhism. These policies eventually eliminated Christianity in Japan and led to the formation of an exclusion policy. **D**

MAIN IDEA

Comparing
D How was the treatment of Europeans different in Japan and China? How was it similar?

▼ Japanese merchants and Jesuit missionaries await the arrival of a Portuguese ship at Nagasaki in the 1500s in this painting on wood panels.

The Closed Country Policy

The persecution of Christians was part of an attempt to control foreign ideas. When Europeans first arrived, no central authority existed to contain them. The strong leaders who later took power did not like the introduction of European ideas and ways, but they valued European trade. As time passed, the Tokugawa shoguns realized that they could safely exclude both the missionaries and the merchants. By 1639, they had sealed Japan's borders and instituted a "closed country policy."

Japan in Isolation Most commercial contacts with Europeans ended. One port, Nagasaki, remained open to foreign traders. But only Dutch and Chinese merchants were allowed into the port. Earlier, the English had left Japan voluntarily; the Spanish and the Portuguese had been expelled. Since the Tokugawa shoguns controlled Nagasaki, they now had a monopoly on foreign trade, which continued to be profitable.

For more than 200 years, Japan remained basically closed to Europeans. In addition, the Japanese were forbidden to leave, so as not to bring back foreign ideas. Japan would continue to develop, but as a self-sufficient country, free from European attempts to colonize or to establish their presence.

Europeans had met with much resistance in their efforts to open the East to trade. But expansion to the West, in the Americas, as you will learn in Chapter 20, would prove much more successful for European traders, missionaries, and colonizers.

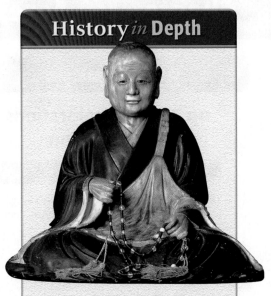

History in Depth

Zen Buddhism

The form of Buddhism that had the greatest impact on Japanese culture was Zen Buddhism. It especially influenced the samurai.

Zen Buddhists sought spiritual enlightenment through meditation. Strict discipline of mind and body was the Zen path to wisdom. Zen monks would sit in meditation for hours, as shown in the sculpture above. If they showed signs of losing concentration, a Zen master might shout at them or hit them with a stick.

SECTION 3 ASSESSMENT

TERMS & NAMES 1. For each term or name, write a sentence explaining its significance.
• daimyo   • Oda Nobunaga   • Toyotomi Hideyoshi   • Tokugawa Shogunate   • haiku   • kabuki

USING YOUR NOTES

2. Which contribution by a daimyo was the most significant? Why?

Daimyo	Achievements

MAIN IDEAS

3. What happened during the period of the "Warring States"?

4. What was the structure of society in Tokugawa Japan?

5. What were the new styles of drama, art, and literature in Tokugawa Japan?

CRITICAL THINKING & WRITING

6. **DRAWING CONCLUSIONS** Why do you think that the emperor had less power than a shogun?

7. **ANALYZING CAUSES** Why did the Japanese policy toward Christians change from acceptance to repression?

8. **FORMING OPINIONS** Do you think Japan's closed country policy effectively kept Western ideas and customs out of Japan?

9. **WRITING ACTIVITY** CULTURAL INTERACTION Write a two-paragraph **comparison** of the similarities and differences between the roles of women in China (discussed on page 541) and in Japan (page 544).

MULTIMEDIA ACTIVITY CREATING AN ORGANIZATIONAL CHART

Use the Internet to find information on the Japanese government today. Then create an **organizational chart** showing the structure of the government.

INTERNET KEYWORD
country profiles

VISUAL SUMMARY

An Age of Explorations and Isolation

Explorations

1405 **Zheng He of China** launches voyages of exploration to Southeast Asia, India, Arabia, and eastern Africa.

1500s **The Portuguese** establish trading outposts throughout Asia and gain control of the spice trade.

1600s **The Dutch** drive out the Portuguese and establish their own trading empire in the East. (Below, a Dutch ship is pictured on a plate made in China for European trade.)

Europeans sail farther east to China and Japan in search of more trade; both nations ultimately reject European advances.

Isolation

1433 **China** abandons its voyages of exploration.

1500s **The Chinese** severely restrict trade with foreigners.

1612 **Japan** outlaws Christianity and drives out Christian missionaries.

1630s **The Japanese** institute a "closed country policy" and remain isolated from Europe for 200 years.

TERMS & NAMES

For each term or name below, briefly explain its importance to European exploration and the development of China and Japan.

1. Bartolomeu Dias
2. Vasco da Gama
3. Treaty of Tordesillas
4. Dutch East India Company
5. Ming dynasty
6. Manchus
7. Qing dynasty
8. Oda Nobunaga
9. Toyotomi Hideyoshi
10. Tokugawa Shogunate

MAIN IDEAS

Europeans Explore the East Section 1 (pages 529–535)

11. What factors helped spur European exploration?
12. What role did Portugal's Prince Henry play in overseas exploration?
13. What was the significance of Dias's voyage? da Gama's voyage?
14. Why were the Dutch so successful in establishing a trading empire in the Indian Ocean?

China Limits European Contacts Section 2 (pages 536–541)

15. Why did China not undergo widespread industrialization?
16. What did Christian missionaries bring to China?
17. What are five reasons the Ming Dynasty fell to civil disorder?

Japan Returns to Isolation Section 3 (pages 542–547)

18. Why was the time between 1467 and 1568 called the period of the "Warring States"?
19. What was the difference between the Confucian ideal of society and the real society of Japan?
20. How did the Japanese express themselves culturally under the Tokugawa shoguns?

CRITICAL THINKING

1. USING YOUR NOTES

In a time line, trace the events that led to Japan's expulsion of European Christians.

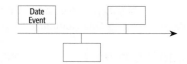

2. RECOGNIZING EFFECTS

How might a Chinese emperor's leadership be affected by living in the Forbidden City? Explain and support your opinion.

3. ANALYZING ISSUES

SCIENCE AND TECHNOLOGY Of the technological advances that helped spur European exploration, which do you think was the most important? Why?

4. ANALYZING CAUSES

CULTURAL INTERACTION What caused Japan to institute a policy of isolation? Defend your viewpoint with text references.

5. SUMMARIZING

ECONOMICS How did the Manchus earn the respect of the Chinese? Support your answer with details from the chapter.

Use the quotation and your knowledge of world history to answer questions 1 and 2.

PRIMARY SOURCE

But I was careful not to refer to these Westerners as "Great Officials," and corrected Governor Liu Yin-shu when he referred to the Jesuits Regis and Fridelli . . . as if they were honored imperial commissioners. For even though some of the Western methods are different from our own, and may even be an improvement, there is little about them that is new. The principles of mathematics all derive from the Book of Changes, and the Western methods are Chinese in origin: this algebra—"A-erh-chu-pa-erh"—springs from an Eastern word. And though it was indeed the Westerners who showed us something our ancient calendar experts did not know—namely how to calculate the angles of the northern pole—this but shows the truth of what Chu Hsi arrived at through his investigation of things: the earth is like the yolk within an egg.

KANGXI, quoted in *Emperor of China: Self-Portrait of K'Ang-Hsi*

1. Which phrase best describes Kangxi's thoughts about Europeans, or "Westerners"?

   A. Westerners use methods that are inferior to Chinese methods.

   B. Westerners would make good trading partners.

   C. Westerners use methods that are based on Chinese methods.

   D. There are too many Westerners in China.

2. What can be inferred about Kangxi's beliefs about China?

   A. China needs the assistance of Westerners.

   B. China is superior to countries of the West.

   C. China has many problems.

   D. China is destined to rule the world.

Use this map produced by German cartographer Henricus Martellus in about 1490 and your knowledge of world history to answer question 3.

3. Which of these statements about Martellus's map is not accurate?

   A. Martellus shows Europe, Africa, and Asia.

   B. Martellus's map includes the oceans.

   C. Martellus shows North America.

   D. Martellus's map has many ports marked on the western coast of Africa.

 hmhsocialstudies.com TEST PRACTICE

For additional test practice, go online for:

• Diagnostic tests

• Strategies

• Tutorials

Interact *with* History

On page 528, you decided whether or not you would sail into the unknown. Now that you have read the chapter, reevaluate your decision. If you decided to go, did what you read reaffirm your decision? Why or why not? If you chose not to go, explain what your feelings are now. Discuss your answers within a small group.

FOCUS ON WRITING

Imagine you are the Jesuit missionary Matteo Ricci. Write an **expository essay** describing your impressions of Chinese rule and culture. Consider the following in the essay:

• Matteo Ricci's values

• Chinese culture as compared with Western Christian culture

MULTIMEDIA ACTIVITY

21ST CENTURY

Planning a Television Special

Use the Internet, books, and other reference materials to create a script for a television special "The Voyages of Zheng He." The script should address the historical context of Zheng He's voyages and their impact on China and the lands visited. The script should include narration, sound, re-creations, and locations. In researching, consider the following:

• biographical data on Zheng He

• information on the ships, crews, and cargo

• descriptions of the voyages

• music and visuals

The Atlantic World,
1492–1800

Essential Question

What was the impact of European exploration and colonization of the Americas?

 What You Will Learn

In this chapter you will learn about the exploration and colonization of the Americas, which strongly affected both the Eastern and Western hemispheres.

SECTION 1 Spain Builds an American Empire

Main Idea The voyages of Columbus prompted the Spanish to establish colonies in the Americas.

SECTION 2 European Nations Settle North America

Main Idea Several European nations fought for control of North America, and England emerged victorious.

SECTION 3 The Atlantic Slave Trade

Main Idea To meet their growing labor needs, Europeans enslaved millions of Africans in the Americas.

SECTION 4 The Columbian Exchange and Global Trade

Main Idea The colonization of the Americas introduced new items into the Eastern and Western hemispheres.

Previewing Themes

CULTURAL INTERACTION The voyages of Columbus prompted a worldwide exchange of everything from religious and political ideas to new foods and plants.
Geography *According to the map, what lands were included in the viceroyalty of New Spain in 1700?*

ECONOMICS The vast wealth to be had from colonizing the Americas sealed the fate of millions of Native Americans and Africans who were forced to work in mines and on plantations.
Geography *On which coast of the Americas would enslaved persons from Africa have arrived?*

EMPIRE BUILDING Over the span of several centuries, Europeans conquered the Americas' native inhabitants and built powerful American empires.
Geography *What two major Native American empires did the Spanish conquer in the sixteenth century?*

AMERICAS

1492 Columbus makes first voyage.

1521 Cortés conquers Aztec Empire. ▶

1533 Pizarro conquers Incan Empire.

1607 English found Jamestown.

1500

1600

WORLD

1494 Spain and Portugal sign Treaty of Tordesillas.

1547 Ivan the Terrible assumes throne of Russia.

1603 ◀ Tokugawa shoguns rule Japan.

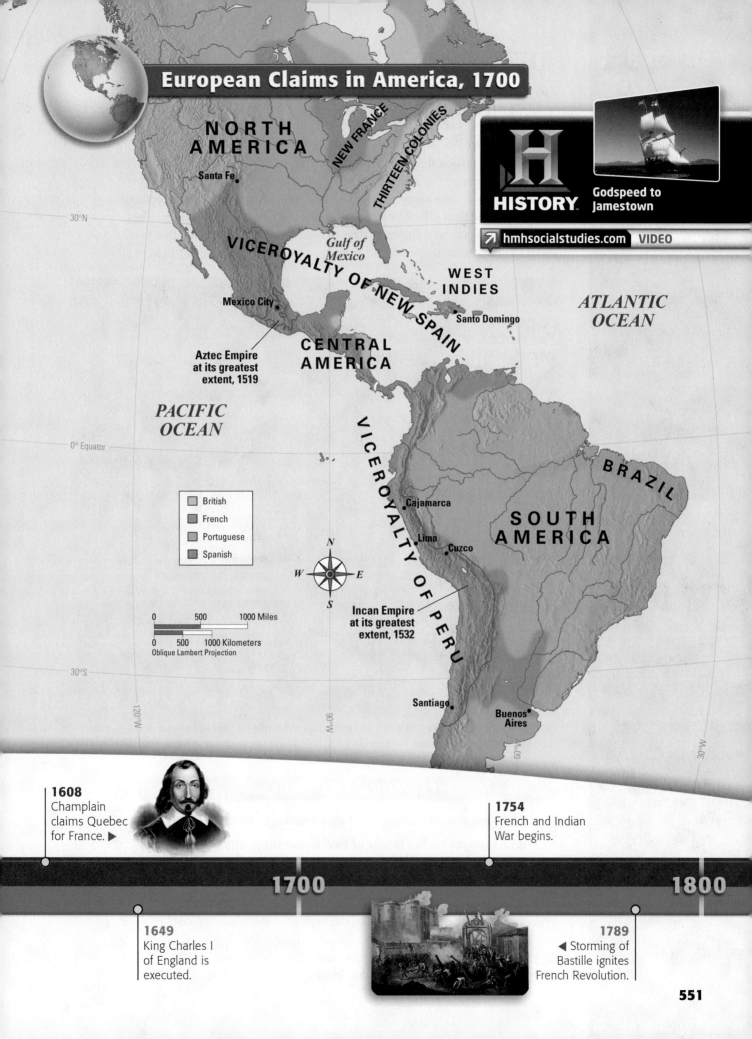

European Claims in America, 1700

NORTH AMERICA

NEW FRANCE

THIRTEEN COLONIES

Santa Fe

30°N

VICEROYALTY OF NEW SPAIN

Gulf of Mexico

Mexico City

Aztec Empire at its greatest extent, 1519

CENTRAL AMERICA

WEST INDIES

Santo Domingo

ATLANTIC OCEAN

PACIFIC OCEAN

0° Equator

VICEROYALTY OF PERU

Cajamarca

Lima

Cuzco

SOUTH AMERICA

B R A Z I L

Incan Empire at its greatest extent, 1532

Santiago

Buenos Aires

120°W

90°W

60°W

30°S

HISTORY™

Godspeed to Jamestown

↗ hmhsocialstudies.com **VIDEO**

British	
French	
Portuguese	
Spanish	

N / W / E / S

0   500   1000 Miles

0   500   1000 Kilometers

Oblique Lambert Projection

1608
Champlain claims Quebec for France. ▶

1754
French and Indian War begins.

1700

1800

1649
King Charles I of England is executed.

1789
◀ Storming of Bastille ignites French Revolution.

What might you gain or lose by joining the fight?

You are a Native American living in central Mexico in 1520. Suddenly you are faced with a decision that may change your life forever. Invaders, known as the Spanish, are engaged in a fierce battle with the nearby Aztecs, who are cruel and harsh rulers. Like many of your people, you hate the powerful Aztecs and hope for their defeat. The newcomers, however, are equally frightening. They ride on large beasts and fire loud, deadly weapons. You wonder whether you should follow the example of your friends and join the fight, or not fight at all.

▲ This 16th-century painting by an Indian artist depicts a battle on the left between the Aztecs and Spanish. The right side shows the Spanish with their main Indian allies, the Tlaxcalans.

EXAMINING *the* ISSUES

- **What are the advantages and disadvantages of not fighting?**

- **Which might be the lesser of two evils—supporting the Aztecs, whom you know as oppressors, or the fierce invaders, about whom you know almost nothing?**

Discuss these questions with your classmates. In your discussion, examine whether invading armies throughout history have made life better or worse for people in the areas they conquer. As you read about colonization in the Americas, learn the outcome of the battle between the Aztecs and the Spanish.

Spain Builds an American Empire

MAIN IDEA	WHY IT MATTERS NOW	TERMS & NAMES
EMPIRE BUILDING The voyages of Columbus prompted the Spanish to establish colonies in the Americas.	Throughout the Americas, Spanish culture, language, and descendants are the legacy of this period.	• Christopher Columbus • colony • Hernando Cortés • conquistador • Francisco Pizarro • Atahualpa • mestizo • *encomienda*

SETTING THE STAGE Competition for wealth in Asia among European nations was fierce. This competition prompted a Genoese sea captain named <u>Christopher Columbus</u> to make a daring voyage from Spain in 1492. Instead of sailing south around Africa and then east, Columbus sailed west across the Atlantic in search of an alternate trade route to Asia and its riches. Columbus never reached Asia. Instead, he stepped onto an island in the Caribbean. That event would bring together the peoples of Europe, Africa, and the Americas.

The Voyages of Columbus

The *Niña, Pinta,* and *Santa María* sailed out of a Spanish port around dawn on August 3, 1492. In a matter of months, Columbus's fleet would reach the shores of what Europeans saw as an astonishing new world.

First Encounters In the early hours of October 12, 1492, the long-awaited cry came. A lookout aboard the *Pinta* caught sight of a shoreline in the distance. *"Tierra! Tierra!"* he shouted. "Land! Land!" By dawn, Columbus and his crew were ashore. Thinking he had successfully reached the East Indies, Columbus called the surprised inhabitants who greeted him, *los indios.* The term translated into "Indian," a word mistakenly applied to all the native peoples of the Americas. In his journal, Columbus recounted his first meeting with the native peoples:

> **PRIMARY SOURCE**
>
> I presented them with some red caps, and strings of glass beads to wear upon the neck, and many other trifles of small value, wherewith they were much delighted, and became wonderfully attached to us. Afterwards they came swimming to the boats where we were, bringing parrots, balls of cotton thread, javelins, and many other things which they exchanged for articles we gave them . . . in fact they accepted anything and gave what they had with the utmost good will.
>
> **CHRISTOPHER COLUMBUS,** *Journal of Columbus*

Columbus had miscalculated where he was. He had not reached the East Indies. Scholars believe he landed instead on an island in the Bahamas in the Caribbean Sea. The natives there were not Indians, but a group who called themselves the Taino. Nonetheless, Columbus claimed the island for Spain. He named it San Salvador, or "Holy Savior."

hmhsocialstudies.com
TAKING NOTES

Use the graphic organizer online to take notes on major events in the establishment of Spain's empire in the Americas.

▲ *Portrait of a Man Called Christopher Columbus* (1519) by Sebastiano del Piombo

Columbus, like other explorers, was interested in gold. Finding none on San Salvador, he explored other islands, staking his claim to each one. "It was my wish to bypass no island without taking possession," he wrote.

In early 1493, Columbus returned to Spain. The reports he relayed about his journey delighted the Spanish monarchs. Spain's rulers, who had funded his first voyage, agreed to finance three more trips. Columbus embarked on his second voyage to the Americas in September of 1493. He journeyed no longer as an explorer, but as an empire builder. He commanded a fleet of some 17 ships that carried over 1,000 soldiers, crewmen, and colonists. The Spanish intended to transform the islands of the Caribbean into **colonies**, or lands that are controlled by another nation. Over the next two centuries, other European explorers began sailing across the Atlantic in search of new lands to claim.

Other Explorers Take to the Seas In 1500, the Portuguese explorer Pedro Álvares Cabral reached the shores of modern-day Brazil and claimed the land for his country. A year later, Amerigo Vespucci (vehs•POO•chee), an Italian in the service of Portugal, also traveled along the eastern coast of South America. Upon his return to Europe, he claimed that the land was not part of Asia, but a "new" world. In 1507, a German mapmaker named the new continent "America" in honor of Amerigo Vespucci.

In 1519, Portuguese explorer Ferdinand Magellan led the boldest exploration yet. Several years earlier, Spanish explorer Vasco Núñez de Balboa had marched through modern-day Panama and had become the first European to gaze upon the Pacific Ocean. Soon after, Magellan convinced the king of Spain to fund his voyage into the newly discovered ocean.

With about 250 men and five ships, Magellan sailed around the southern end of South America and into the waters of the Pacific. The fleet sailed for months without seeing land, except for some small islands. Food supplies soon ran out.

After exploring the island of Guam, Magellan and his crew eventually reached the Philippines. Unfortunately, Magellan became involved in a local war there and was killed. His crew, greatly reduced by disease and starvation, continued sailing west toward home. Out of Magellan's original crew, only 18 men and one ship arrived back in Spain in 1522, nearly three years after they had left. They were the first persons to circumnavigate, or sail around, the world. **A**

Spanish Conquests in Mexico

In 1519, as Magellan embarked on his historic voyage, a Spaniard named **Hernando Cortés** landed on the shores of Mexico. After colonizing several Caribbean islands, the Spanish had turned their attention to the American mainland. Cortés marched inland, looking to claim new lands for Spain. Cortés and the many other Spanish explorers who followed him were known as **conquistadors** (conquerors). Lured by rumors of vast lands filled with gold and silver, conquistadors carved out colonies in regions that would become Mexico, South America, and the United States. The Spanish were the first European settlers in the Americas. As a result of their colonization, the Spanish greatly enriched their empire and left a mark on the cultures of North and South America that exists today.

MAIN IDEA

Making Inferences
A What was the significance of Magellan's voyage?

GREENLAND

ICELAND

Hudson 1610

Hudson 1609

Cabot 1497

ENGLAND

Cartier 1534–35

EUROPE

FRANCE

Hudson Bay

Marquette 1673

NORTH AMERICA

Smith 1606–07, Mayflower 1620

PORTUGAL

SPAIN

Plymouth

LaSalle 1682

40° N

Coronado 1540–42

De Soto 1539–42

Jamestown

ATLANTIC OCEAN

Santa Fe

Cabrillo 1542–43

St. Augustine

Ponce de León 1512–13

CANARY ISLANDS

MADEIRA

Verrazzano 1524

HISPANIOLA

Columbus 1492

AFRICA

Cabeza de Vaca 1535–36

Gulf of Mexico

CUBA

Cortés 1519

Santo Domingo

Columbus 1493–95

Tenochtitlán (Mexico City)

Veracruz

Caribbean Sea

Columbus 1502–03

Cabral 1500

Magellan 1519

PACIFIC OCEAN

Balboa 1510–13

Columbus 1498

Magellan's Crew 1522

Pizarro 1530–33

Vespucci 1499

0° Equator

N

| 0 | 1,000 Miles |
| 0 | 2,000 Kilometers |

Explorers' Routes
- Spanish
- Portuguese
- French
- English
- Dutch

SOUTH AMERICA

Magellan 1519

120° W

80° W

40° W

0°

40° S

VIDEO
Christopher Columbus: Explorer of the New World

HISTORY

hmhsocialstudies.com

GEOGRAPHY SKILLBUILDER: Interpreting Maps

1. **Movement** How many different voyages did Columbus make to the Americas?
2. **Region** Which general region did the Spanish and Portuguese explore? Where did the English, Dutch, and French explore?

The Atlantic World **555**

Native Population of Central Mexico, 1500–1620

1519: 25.3 million

1523: 16.8 million

1548: 6.3 million

1605: 1.0 million

Year

Source: *The Population of Latin America: A History*

SKILLBUILDER: Interpreting Graphs

1. **Drawing Conclusions** *By what percentage did the native population decrease between 1519 and 1605?*
2. **Making Inferences** *How did the sharp decline in the native population, due greatly to disease, affect the Spaniards' attempts to conquer the region?*

VIDEO
The Arrival of the Spanish

hmhsocialstudies.com

Cortés Conquers the Aztecs Soon after landing in Mexico, Cortés learned of the vast and wealthy Aztec Empire in the region's interior. (See Chapter 16.) After marching for weeks through difficult mountain passes, Cortés and his force of roughly 600 men finally reached the magnificent Aztec capital of Tenochtitlán (teh•NAWCH•tee•TLAHN). The Aztec emperor, Montezuma II, was convinced at first that Cortés was a god wearing armor. He agreed to give the Spanish explorer a share of the empire's existing gold supply. The conquistador was not satisfied. Cortés admitted that he and his comrades had a "disease of the heart that only gold can cure."

In the late spring of 1520, some of Cortés's men killed many Aztec warriors and chiefs while they were celebrating a religious festival. In June of 1520, the Aztecs rebelled against the Spanish intruders and drove out Cortés's forces.

The Spaniards, however, struck back. Despite being greatly outnumbered, Cortés and his men conquered the Aztecs in 1521. Several factors played a key role in the stunning victory. First, the Spanish had the advantage of superior weaponry. Aztec arrows were no match for the Spaniards' muskets and cannons.

Second, Cortés was able to enlist the help of various native groups. With the aid of a native woman translator named Malinche, Cortés learned that some natives resented the Aztecs. They hated their harsh practices, including human sacrifice. Through Malinche, Cortés convinced these natives to fight on his side.

Finally, and most important, the natives could do little to stop the invisible warrior that marched alongside the Spaniards—disease. Measles, mumps, smallpox, and typhus were just some of the diseases Europeans were to bring with them to the Americas. Native Americans had never been exposed to these diseases. Thus, they had developed no natural immunity to them. As a result, they died by the hundreds of thousands. By the time Cortés launched his counterattack, the Aztec population had been greatly reduced by smallpox and measles. In time, European disease would truly devastate the natives of central Mexico, killing millions of them. **B**

Spanish Conquests in Peru

In 1532, another conquistador, <u>Francisco Pizarro</u>, marched a small force into South America. He conquered the Incan Empire, as you learned in Chapter 16.

Pizarro Subdues the Inca Pizarro and his army of about 200 met the Incan ruler, <u>Atahualpa</u> (Ah•tuh•WAHL•puh), near the city of Cajamarca. Atahualpa, who commanded a force of about 30,000, brought several thousand mostly unarmed men for the meeting. The Spaniards waited in ambush, crushed the Incan force, and kidnapped Atahualpa.

Atahualpa offered to fill a room once with gold and twice with silver in exchange for his release. However, after receiving the ransom, the Spanish strangled the Incan king. Demoralized by their leader's death, the remaining Incan force retreated from Cajamarca. Pizarro then marched on the Incan capital, Cuzco. He captured it without a struggle in 1533.

MAIN IDEA

Summarizing
B What factors enabled the Spanish to defeat the Aztecs?

As Cortés and Pizarro conquered the civilizations of the Americas, fellow conquistadors defeated other native peoples. Spanish explorers also conquered the Maya in Yucatan and Guatemala. By the middle of the 16th century, Spain had created an American empire. It included New Spain (Mexico and parts of Guatemala), as well as other lands in Central and South America and the Caribbean.

Spain's Pattern of Conquest In building their new American empire, the Spaniards drew from techniques used during the *reconquista* of Spain. When conquering the Muslims, the Spanish lived among them and imposed their Spanish culture upon them. The Spanish settlers to the Americas, known as *peninsulares,* were mostly men. As a result, relationships between Spanish settlers and native women were common. These relationships created a large **mestizo**—or mixed Spanish and Native American—population.

Although the Spanish conquerors lived among the native people, they also oppressed them. In their effort to exploit the land for its precious resources, the Spanish forced Native Americans to work within a system known as **_encomienda_**. Under this system, natives farmed, ranched, or mined for Spanish landlords. These landlords had received the rights to the natives' labor from Spanish authorities. The holders of *encomiendas* promised the Spanish rulers that they would act fairly and respect the workers. However, many abused the natives and worked many laborers to death, especially inside dangerous mines.

The Portuguese in Brazil One area of South America that remained outside of Spanish control was Brazil. In 1500, Cabral claimed the land for Portugal. During the 1530s, colonists began settling Brazil's coastal region. Finding little gold or silver, the settlers began growing sugar. Clearing out huge swaths of forest land, the Portuguese built giant sugar plantations. The demand for sugar in Europe was great, and the colony soon enriched Portugal. In time, the colonists pushed farther west into Brazil. They settled even more land for the production of sugar.

History Makers

Francisco Pizarro
1475?–1541
Pizarro was the son of an infantry captain and a young peasant woman. His parents never married. Raised by his mother's poor family, he never learned to read. Ambitious, brave, and ruthless, he determined to make his fortune as an explorer and conqueror.

Embarked on a voyage of conquest down the west coast of South America, Pizarro was ordered by the governor of Panama to abandon the expedition to prevent the loss of lives. Pizarro took his sword and drew a line in the dust, inviting those of his followers who desired wealth and fame to cross the line and follow him. Thus began the conquest of Peru.

Pizarro founded the city of Lima, Peru's capital, in 1535. He became governor of Peru and encouraged settlers from Spain.

Atahualpa
1502?–1533
Atahualpa was the last ruler of the Incan empire in Peru. After Atahualpa was captured and held for ransom by the Spanish, the Incan people throughout the empire brought gold and silver that the Spanish then had melted down into bullion and ingots. They accumulated 24 tons of gold and silver, the richest ransom in history.

The Spanish executed Atahualpa despite the ransom paid by his people. As he was about to be burned at the stake, the Spanish offered him a more merciful death by strangulation if he agreed to convert to Christianity, which he did. Thus died the last emperor of the Inca.

↗ hmhsocialstudies.com

INTERNET ACTIVITY Go online to create a poster about the ransom paid by the Incan people to rescue Atahualpa.

This U.S. postage ▶ stamp was issued in 1940 to celebrate the 400th anniversary of the Coronado expedition.

Spain's Influence Expands

Spain's American colonies helped make it the richest, most powerful nation in the world during much of the 16th century. Ships filled with treasures from the Americas continually sailed into Spanish harbors. This newfound wealth helped usher in a golden age of art and culture in Spain. (See Chapter 21.)

Throughout the 16th century, Spain also increased its military might. To protect its treasure-filled ships, Spain built a powerful navy. The Spanish also strengthened their other military forces, creating a skillful and determined army. For a century and a half, Spain's army seldom lost a battle. Meanwhile, Spain enlarged its American empire by settling in parts of what is now the United States.

Conquistadors Push North Dreams of new conquests prompted Spain to back a series of expeditions into the southwestern United States. The Spanish actually had settled in parts of the United States before they even dreamed of building an empire on the American mainland. In 1513, Spanish explorer Juan Ponce de León landed on the coast of modern-day Florida and claimed it for Spain.

By 1540, after building an empire that stretched from Mexico to Peru, the Spanish once again looked to the land that is now the United States. In 1540–1541, Francisco Vásquez de Coronado led an expedition throughout much of present-day Arizona, New Mexico, Texas, Oklahoma, and Kansas. He was searching for another wealthy empire to conquer. Coronado found little gold amidst the dry deserts of the Southwest. As a result, the Spanish monarchy assigned mostly priests to explore and colonize the future United States.

Catholic priests had accompanied conquistadors from the very beginning of American colonization. The conquistadors had come in search of wealth. The priests who accompanied them had come in search of converts. In the winter of 1609–1610, Pedro de Peralta, governor of Spain's northern holdings, called New Mexico, led settlers to a tributary on the upper Rio Grande. They built a capital called Santa Fe, or "Holy Faith." In the next two decades, a string of Christian missions arose among the Pueblo, the native inhabitants of the region. Scattered missions, forts, and small ranches dotted the lands of New Mexico. These became the headquarters for advancing the Catholic religion. **C**

MAIN IDEA

Contrasting
C How did Spain's colony in New Mexico differ from its colonies in New Spain?

Opposition to Spanish Rule

Spanish priests worked to spread Christianity in the Americas. They also pushed for better treatment of Native Americans. Priests spoke out against the cruel treatment of natives. In particular, they criticized the harsh pattern of labor that emerged under the *encomienda* system. "There is nothing more detestable or more cruel," Dominican monk Bartolomé de Las Casas wrote, "than the tyranny which the Spaniards use toward the Indians for the getting of pearl [riches]."

African Slavery and Native Resistance The Spanish government abolished the *encomienda* system in 1542. To meet the colonies' need for labor, Las Casas suggested Africans. "The labor of one . . . [African] . . . [is] more valuable than that of four Indians," he said. The priest later changed his view and denounced African slavery. However, others promoted it.

Opposition to the Spanish method of colonization came not only from Spanish priests, but also from the natives themselves. Resistance to Spain's attempt at domination began shortly after the Spanish arrived in the Caribbean. In November of 1493, Columbus encountered resistance in his attempt to conquer the present-day island of St. Croix. Before finally surrendering, the inhabitants defended themselves by firing poison arrows.

As late as the end of the 17th century, natives in New Mexico fought Spanish rule. Although they were not risking their lives in silver mines, the natives still felt the weight of Spanish force. In converting the natives, Spanish priests and soldiers burned their sacred objects and prohibited native rituals. The Spanish also forced natives to work for them and sometimes abused them physically.

MAIN IDEA

Analyzing Causes
D Why did the natives of New Mexico revolt against Spanish settlers?

In 1680, Popé, a Pueblo ruler, led a well-organized rebellion against the Spanish. The rebellion involved more than 8,000 warriors from villages all over New Mexico. The native fighters drove the Spanish back into New Spain. For the next 12 years, until the Spanish regained control of the area, the southwest region of the future United States once again belonged to its original inhabitants. **D**

By this time, however, the rulers of Spain had far greater concerns. The other nations of Europe had begun to establish their own colonies in the Americas.

SECTION 1 ASSESSMENT

TERMS & NAMES 1. For each term or name, write a sentence explaining its significance.
• Christopher Columbus • colony • Hernando Cortés • conquistador • Francisco Pizarro • Atahualpa • mestizo • *encomienda*

USING YOUR NOTES

2. Which of these events do you think had the greatest impact?

MAIN IDEAS

3. What process did Columbus and his followers begin?

4. Why were most of the Spanish explorers drawn to the Americas?

5. Which country was the richest and most powerful in the 16th century, and why?

CRITICAL THINKING & WRITING

6. **ANALYZING PRIMARY SOURCES** Reread the primary source on page 553. How might Columbus's view of the Taino have led the Spanish to think they could take advantage of and impose their will on the natives?

7. **COMPARING** What might have been some similarities in character between Cortés and Pizarro?

8. **CLARIFYING** Through what modern-day states did Coronado lead his expedition?

9. **WRITING ACTIVITY** EMPIRE BUILDING Write a **dialogue** in which a Native American and a conquistador debate the merits of Spain's colonization of the Americas.

CONNECT TO TODAY MAKING A DATABASE
Use library resources to compile a **database** of places and geographical features in the Americas named after Columbus. Display your list in the classroom.

The Legacy of Columbus

In the years and centuries since Christopher Columbus's historic journeys, people still debate the legacy of his voyages. Some argue they were the heroic first steps in the creation of great and democratic societies. Others claim they were the beginnings of an era of widespread cruelty, bloodshed, and epidemic disease.

A SECONDARY SOURCE

Samuel Eliot Morison

Morison, a strong supporter of Columbus, laments that the sea captain died without realizing the true greatness of his deeds.

——

One only wishes that the Admiral might have been afforded the sense of fulfillment that would have come from foreseeing all that flowed from his discoveries; that would have turned all the sorrows of his last years to joy. The whole history of the Americas stems from the Four Voyages of Columbus; and as the Greek city-states looked back to the deathless gods as their founders, so today a score of independent nations and dominions unite in homage to Christopher, the stout-hearted son of Genoa, who carried Christian civilization across the Ocean Sea.

B PRIMARY SOURCE

Bartolomé de Las Casas

Las Casas was an early Spanish missionary who watched fellow Spaniards unleash attack dogs on Native Americans.

——

Their other frightening weapon after the horses: twenty hunting greyhounds. They were unleashed and fell on the Indians at the cry of *Tómalo!* ["Get them!"]. Within an hour they had preyed on one hundred of them. As the Indians were used to going completely naked, it is easy to imagine what the fierce greyhounds did, urged to bite naked bodies and skin much more delicate than that of the wild boars they were used to. . . . This tactic, begun here and invented by the devil, spread throughout these Indies and will end when there is no more land nor people to subjugate and destroy in this part of the world.

C SECONDARY SOURCE

Justin Winsor

In 1892, historian Justin Winsor was one of the first American writers to criticize Columbus.

——

He [Winsor] portrayed Columbus as a daring mariner with great powers of persuasion and extraordinary dedication to his goals. Winsor also revealed Columbus as an inept administrator, so sure of his own rectitude that he openly disobeyed royal instructions and brought many of his troubles on himself. Among his other failings, Columbus unashamedly waged war against the native inhabitants of the Caribbean and enslaved hundreds of them, hoping to profit from a transatlantic slave trade.

D PRIMARY SOURCE

Anonymous

Contemporary with the Spanish conquest of the Americas, this illustration depicts a medicine man tending to an Aztec suffering from smallpox, which killed millions of Native Americans.

Document-Based QUESTIONS

1. Based on Source A, was the legacy of Columbus a positive or negative thing?

2. In what ways do Sources B and C agree about Columbus?

3. Which aspect of the legacy of Columbus does the illustration in Source D show?

4. If you had to construct a balance sheet on Columbus, would you come up with a positive or negative balance? On a poster board, make up a list of positive and negative elements, and display your chart in the classroom.

European Nations Settle North America

MAIN IDEA	WHY IT MATTERS NOW	TERMS & NAMES
EMPIRE BUILDING Several European nations fought for control of North America, and England emerged victorious.	The English settlers in North America left a legacy of law and government that guides the United States today.	• New France • Jamestown • Pilgrims • Puritans • New Netherland • French and Indian War • Metacom

SETTING THE STAGE Spain's successful colonization efforts in the Americas did not go unnoticed. Other European nations, such as England, France, and the Netherlands, soon became interested in obtaining their own valuable colonies. The Treaty of Tordesillas, signed in 1494, had divided the newly discovered lands between Spain and Portugal. However, other European countries ignored the treaty. They set out to build their own empires in the Americas. This resulted in a struggle for North America.

Competing Claims in North America

Magellan's voyage showed that ships could reach Asia by way of the Pacific Ocean. Spain claimed the route around the southern tip of South America. Other European countries hoped to find an easier and more direct route to the Pacific. If it existed, a northwest trade route through North America to Asia would become highly profitable. Not finding the route, the French, English, and Dutch instead established colonies in North America.

hmhsocialstudies.com
TAKING NOTES
Use the graphic organizer online to take notes on information about early settlements.

Explorers Establish New France The early French explorers sailed west with dreams of reaching the East Indies. One explorer was Giovanni da Verrazzano (VEHR•uh•ZAHN•noh), an Italian in the service of France. In 1524, he sailed to North America in search of a sea route to the Pacific. While he did not find the route, Verrazzano did discover what is today New York harbor. Ten years later, the Frenchman Jacques Cartier (kahr•TYAY) reached a gulf off the eastern coast of Canada that led to a broad river. Cartier named it the St. Lawrence. He followed it inward until he reached a large island dominated by a mountain. He named the island Mont Real (Mount Royal), which later became known as Montreal. In 1608, another French explorer, Samuel de Champlain, sailed up the St. Lawrence with about 32 colonists. They founded Quebec, which became the base of France's colonial empire in North America, known as **New France**.

Then the French penetrated the North American continent. In 1673, French Jesuit priest Jacques Marquette and trader Louis Joliet explored the Great Lakes and the upper Mississippi River. Nearly 10 years later, Sieur de La Salle explored the lower Mississippi. He claimed the entire river valley for France. He named it Louisiana in honor of the French king, Louis XIV. By the early 1700s, New France covered much of what is now the midwestern United States and eastern Canada.

The Atlantic World **561**

A Trading Empire France's North American empire was immense. But it was sparsely populated. By 1760, the European population of New France had grown to only about 65,000. A large number of French colonists had no desire to build towns or raise families. These settlers included Catholic priests who sought to convert Native Americans. They also included young, single men engaged in what had become New France's main economic activity, the fur trade. Unlike the English, the French were less interested in occupying territories than they were in making money off the land. **Ⓐ**

MAIN IDEA

Summarizing

Ⓐ Why were France's North American holdings so sparsely populated?

The English Arrive in North America

The explorations of the Spanish and French inspired the English. In 1606, a company of London investors received from King James a charter to found a colony in North America. In late 1606, the company's three ships, and more than 100 settlers, pushed out of an English harbor. About four months later, in 1607, they reached the coast of Virginia. The colonists claimed the land as theirs. They named the settlement <u>**Jamestown**</u> in honor of their king.

The Settlement at Jamestown The colony's start was disastrous. The settlers were more interested in finding gold than in planting crops. During the first few years, seven out of every ten people died of hunger, disease, or battles with the Native Americans.

Despite their nightmarish start, the colonists eventually gained a foothold in their new land. Jamestown became England's first permanent settlement in North America. The colony's outlook improved greatly after farmers there discovered tobacco. High demand in England for tobacco turned it into a profitable cash crop.

Puritans Create a "New England" In 1620, a group known as <u>**Pilgrims**</u> founded a second English colony, Plymouth, in Massachusetts. Persecuted for their religious beliefs in England, these colonists sought religious freedom. Ten years later, a group known as <u>**Puritans**</u> also sought religious freedom from England's Anglican Church. They established a larger colony at nearby Massachusetts Bay.

▼ Henry Hudson's ship arrives in the bay of New York on September 12, 1609.

The Puritans wanted to build a model community that would set an example for other Christians to follow. Although the colony experienced early difficulties, it gradually took hold. This was due in large part to the numerous families in the colony, unlike the mostly single, male population in Jamestown.

The Dutch Found New Netherland Following the English and French into North America were the Dutch. In 1609, Henry Hudson, an Englishman in the service of the Netherlands, sailed west. He was searching for a northwest sea route to Asia. Hudson did not find a route. He did, however, explore three waterways that were later named for him—the Hudson River, Hudson Bay, and Hudson Strait.

The Dutch claimed the region along these waterways. They established a fur trade with the Iroquois Indians. They built trading posts along the Hudson River at Fort Orange (now Albany) and on Manhattan Island. Dutch merchants formed the Dutch West India Company. In 1621, the Dutch government granted the company permission to colonize the region and expand the fur trade. The Dutch holdings in North America became known as **New Netherland**.

Although the Dutch company profited from its fur trade, it was slow to attract Dutch colonists. To encourage settlers, the colony opened its doors to a variety of peoples. Gradually more Dutch, as well as Germans, French, Scandinavians, and other Europeans, settled the area. **B**

Colonizing the Caribbean During the 1600s, the nations of Europe also colonized the Caribbean. The French seized control of present-day Haiti, Guadeloupe, and Martinique. The English settled Barbados and Jamaica. In 1634, the Dutch captured what are now the Netherlands Antilles and Aruba from Spain.

On these islands, the Europeans built huge cotton and sugar plantations. These products, although profitable, demanded a large and steady supply of labor. Enslaved Africans eventually would supply this labor.

MAIN IDEA

Contrasting

B How were the Dutch and French colonies different from the English colonies in North America?

The Struggle for North America

As they expanded their settlements in North America, the nations of France, England, and the Netherlands battled each other for colonial supremacy.

The English Oust the Dutch To the English, New Netherland separated their northern and southern colonies. In 1664, the English king, Charles II, granted his brother, the Duke of York, permission to drive out the Dutch. When the duke's fleet arrived at New Netherland, the Dutch surrendered without firing a shot. The Duke of York claimed the colony for England and renamed it New York.

With the Dutch gone, the English colonized the Atlantic coast of North America. By 1750, about 1.2 million English settlers lived in 13 colonies from Maine to Georgia.

England Battles France The English soon became hungry for more land for their colonial population. So they pushed farther west into the continent. By doing so, they collided with France's North American holdings. As their colonies expanded, France and England began to interfere with each other. It seemed that a major conflict was on the horizon.

In 1754 a dispute over land claims in the Ohio Valley led to a war between the British and French on the North

History in Depth

Pirates

The battle for colonial supremacy occurred not only on land, but also on the sea. Acting on behalf of their government, privately owned armed ships, known as privateers, attacked merchant ships of enemy nations and sank or robbed them.

Also patrolling the high seas were pirates. They attacked ships for their valuables and did not care what nation the vessels represented. One of the best-known pirates was Edward B. Teach, whose prominent beard earned him the nickname Blackbeard. According to one account, Blackbeard attempted to frighten his victims by sticking "lighted matches under his hat, which appeared on both sides of his face and eyes, naturally fierce and wild."

Europeans in North America

1754

UNCLAIMED

Hudson Bay

NEW-FOUNDLAND

Quebec

ACADIA

Boston

New York

ATLANTIC OCEAN

Great Salt L.

Santa Fe

St. Augustine
FLORIDA

New Orleans

NEW SPAIN

Gulf of Mexico

HAITI

CUBA

JAMAICA

Santo Domingo

Mexico City

Caribbean Sea

N

0   500 Miles
0   1,000 Kilometers

- Disputed
- English
- French
- Spanish

1763

UNCLAIMED

ST-PIERRE AND MIQUELON

Hudson Bay

Quebec

Boston

New York

ATLANTIC OCEAN

ORIGINAL 13 COLONIES

Great Salt L.

Charleston

NEW SPAIN

Gulf of Mexico

HAITI

CUBA

JAMAICA

Mexico City

Caribbean Sea

N

0   500 Miles
0   1,000 Kilometers

- English
- French
- Russian
- Spanish

GEOGRAPHY SKILLBUILDER: Interpreting Maps
1. **Region** *Which nation claimed the largest area of the present-day United States in 1754?*
2. **Place** *How did Britain's North American empire change by 1763?*

American continent. The conflict became known as the **French and Indian War**. The war became part of a larger conflict known as the Seven Years' War. Britain and France, along with their European allies, also battled for supremacy in Europe, the West Indies, and India.

In North America, the British colonists, with the help of the British Army, defeated the French in 1763. The French surrendered their North American holdings. As a result of the war, the British seized control of the eastern half of North America.

Native Americans Respond

As in Mexico and South America, the arrival of Europeans in the present-day United States had a great impact on Native Americans. European colonization brought mostly disaster for the lands' original inhabitants.

A Strained Relationship French and Dutch settlers developed a mostly cooperative relationship with the Native Americans. This was due mainly to the mutual benefits of the fur trade. Native Americans did most of the trapping and then traded the furs to the French for such items as guns, hatchets, mirrors, and beads. The Dutch also cooperated with Native Americans in an effort to establish a fur-trading enterprise.

The groups did not live together in complete harmony. Dutch settlers fought with various Native American groups over land claims and trading rights. For the most part, however, the French and Dutch colonists lived together peacefully with their North American hosts. **C**

MAIN IDEA

Analyzing Issues
C Why were the Dutch and French able to coexist in relative peace with the Native Americans?

564 Chapter 20

The same could not be said of the English. Early relations between English settlers and Native Americans were cooperative. However, they quickly worsened over the issues of land and religion. Unlike the French and Dutch, the English sought to populate their colonies in North America. This meant pushing the natives off their land. The English colonists seized more land for their population—and to grow tobacco.

Religious differences also heightened tensions. The English settlers considered Native Americans heathens, people without a faith. Over time, many Puritans viewed Native Americans as agents of the devil and as a threat to their godly society. Native Americans developed a similarly harsh view of the European invaders. **D**

MAIN IDEA

Identifying Problems

D Why did the issues of land and religion cause strife between Native Americans and settlers?

Settlers and Native Americans Battle The hostility between the English settlers and Native Americans led to warfare. As early as 1622, the Powhatan tribe attacked colonial villages around Jamestown and killed about 350 settlers. During the next few years, the colonists struck back and massacred hundreds of Powhatan.

One of the bloodiest conflicts between colonists and Native Americans was known as King Philip's War. It began in 1675 when the Native American ruler **Metacom** (also known as King Philip) led an attack on colonial villages throughout Massachusetts. In the months that followed, both sides massacred hundreds of victims. After a year of fierce fighting, the colonists were victorious. During the 17th century, many skirmishes erupted throughout North America.

Diseases Strike Native Americans More destructive than the Europeans' weapons were their diseases. Like the Spanish in Central and South America, the Europeans who settled North America brought with them several diseases. The diseases devastated the native population in North America.

In 1616, for example, an epidemic of smallpox ravaged Native Americans living along the New England coast. The population of one tribe, the Massachusett, dropped from 24,000 to 750 by 1631. From South Carolina to Missouri, nearly whole tribes fell to smallpox, measles, and other diseases.

One of the effects of this loss was a severe shortage of labor in the colonies. In order to meet their growing labor needs, European colonists soon turned to another group: Africans, whom they would enslave by the millions.

SECTION 2 ASSESSMENT

TERMS & NAMES 1. For each term or name, write a sentence explaining its significance.
• New France   • Jamestown   • Pilgrims   • Puritans   • New Netherland   • French and Indian War   • Metacom

USING YOUR NOTES

2. What did these settlements have in common?

Name of Settlement	General Location	Reasons Settled
New France		
New Netherland		
Massachusetts Bay		

MAIN IDEAS

3. What was a basic difference between French and English attitudes about the land they acquired in North America?

4. What was the main result of the French and Indian War?

5. What were some of the results for Native Americans of European colonization of North America?

CRITICAL THINKING & WRITING

6. **MAKING INFERENCES** What may have been one reason the English eventually beat the French in North America?

7. **DRAWING CONCLUSIONS** What need drove the English farther west into the North American continent?

8. **COMPARING** In what ways did the colonies at Jamestown and Massachusetts Bay differ?

9. **WRITING ACTIVITY** EMPIRE BUILDING What were some of the grievances of Native Americans toward English colonists? Make a bulleted **list** of Native American complaints to display in the classroom.

 MULTIMEDIA ACTIVITY MAKING A POSTER

Use the Internet to research French Cajun culture in Louisiana. Make a **poster** displaying your findings.

INTERNET KEYWORD
Cajun

The Atlantic Slave Trade

MAIN IDEA	WHY IT MATTERS NOW	TERMS & NAMES
CULTURAL INTERACTION To meet their growing labor needs, Europeans enslaved millions of Africans in the Americas.	Descendants of enslaved Africans represent a significant part of the Americas' population today.	• Atlantic slave trade • triangular trade • middle passage

SETTING THE STAGE Sugar plantations and tobacco farms required a large supply of workers to make them profitable for their owners. European owners had planned to use Native Americans as a source of cheap labor. But millions of Native Americans died from disease, warfare, and brutal treatment. Therefore, the Europeans in Brazil, the Caribbean, and the southern colonies of North America soon turned to Africa for workers. This demand for cheap labor resulted in the brutalities of the slave trade.

The Causes of African Slavery

TAKING NOTES

Use the graphic organizer online to take notes on the effects of the slave trade.

Beginning around 1500, European colonists in the Americas who needed cheap labor began using enslaved Africans on plantations and farms.

Slavery in Africa Slavery had existed in Africa for centuries. In most regions, it was a relatively minor institution. The spread of Islam into Africa during the seventh century, however, ushered in an increase in slavery and the slave trade. Muslim rulers in Africa justified enslavement with the Muslim belief that non-Muslim prisoners of war could be bought and sold as slaves. As a result, between 650 and 1600, Muslims transported about 17 million Africans to the Muslim lands of North Africa and Southwest Asia.

In most African and Muslim societies, slaves had some legal rights and an opportunity for social mobility. In the Muslim world, a few slaves even occupied positions of influence and power. Some served as generals in the army. In African societies, slaves could escape their bondage in numerous ways, including marrying into the family they served.

The Demand for Africans The first Europeans to explore Africa were the Portuguese during the 1400s. Initially, Portuguese traders were more interested in trading for gold than for captured Africans. That changed with the colonization of the Americas, as native peoples began dying by the millions.

Europeans saw advantages in using Africans in the Americas. First, many Africans had been exposed to European diseases and had built up some immunity. Second, many Africans had experience in farming and could be taught plantation work. Third, Africans were less likely to escape because they did not know their way around the new land. Fourth, their skin color made it easier to catch them if they escaped and tried to live among others.

MAIN IDEA

Analyzing Motives

A What advantages did Europeans see in enslaving Africans?

In time, the buying and selling of Africans for work in the Americas—known as the <u>Atlantic slave trade</u>—became a massive enterprise. Between 1500 and 1600, nearly 300,000 Africans were transported to the Americas. During the next century, that number climbed to almost 1.3 million. By the time the Atlantic slave trade ended around 1870, Europeans had imported about 9.5 million Africans to the Americas. **A**

Spain and Portugal Lead the Way The Spanish took an early lead in importing Africans to the Americas. Spain moved on from the Caribbean and began to colonize the American mainland. As a result, the Spanish imported and enslaved thousands more Africans. By 1650, nearly 300,000 Africans labored throughout Spanish America on plantations and in gold and silver mines.

By this time, however, the Portuguese had surpassed the Spanish in the importation of Africans to the Americas. During the 1600s, Brazil dominated the European sugar market. As the colony's sugar industry grew, so too did European colonists' demand for cheap labor. During the 17th century, more than 40 percent of all Africans brought to the Americas went to Brazil.

Slavery Spreads Throughout the Americas

As the other European nations established colonies in the Americas, their demand for cheap labor grew. Thus, they also began to import large numbers of Africans.

England Dominates the Slave Trade As England's presence in the Americas grew, it came to dominate the Atlantic slave trade. From 1690 until England abolished the slave trade in 1807, it was the leading carrier of enslaved Africans. By the time the slave trade ended, the English had transported nearly 1.7 million Africans to their colonies in the West Indies.

African slaves were also brought to what is now the United States. In all, nearly 400,000 Africans were sold to Britain's North American colonies. Once in North America, however, the slave population steadily grew. By 1830, roughly 2 million slaves toiled in the United States.

History *in* Depth

Slavery

Slavery probably began with the development of farming about 10,000 years ago. Farmers used prisoners of war to work for them.

Slavery has existed in societies around the world. People were enslaved in civilizations from Egypt to China to India. The picture at the right shows slaves working in a Roman coal mine.

Race was not always a factor in slavery. Often, slaves were captured prisoners of war, or people of a different nationality or religion.

However, the slavery that developed in the Americas was based largely on race. Europeans viewed black people as naturally inferior. Because of this, slavery in the Americas was hereditary.

African Cooperation and Resistance Many African rulers and merchants played a willing role in the Atlantic slave trade. Most European traders, rather than travel inland, waited in ports along the coasts of Africa. African merchants, with the help of local rulers, captured Africans to be enslaved. They then delivered them to the Europeans in exchange for gold, guns, and other goods. **B**

As the slave trade grew, some African rulers voiced their opposition to the practice. Nonetheless, the slave trade steadily grew. Lured by its profits, many African rulers continued to participate. African merchants developed new trade routes to avoid rulers who refused to cooperate.

MAIN IDEA

Analyzing Issues

B Why did many African rulers participate in the Atlantic slave trade?

A Forced Journey

After being captured, African men and women were shipped to the Americas as part of a profitable trade network. Along the way, millions of Africans died.

The Triangular Trade Africans transported to the Americas were part of a transatlantic trading network known as the **triangular trade**. Over one trade route, Europeans transported manufactured goods to the west coast of Africa. There, traders exchanged these goods for captured Africans. The Africans were then transported across the Atlantic and sold in the West Indies. Merchants bought sugar, coffee, and tobacco in the West Indies and sailed to Europe with these products.

On another triangular route, merchants carried rum and other goods from the New England colonies to Africa. There they exchanged their merchandise for Africans. The traders transported the Africans to the West Indies and sold them for sugar and molasses. They then sold these goods to rum producers in New England.

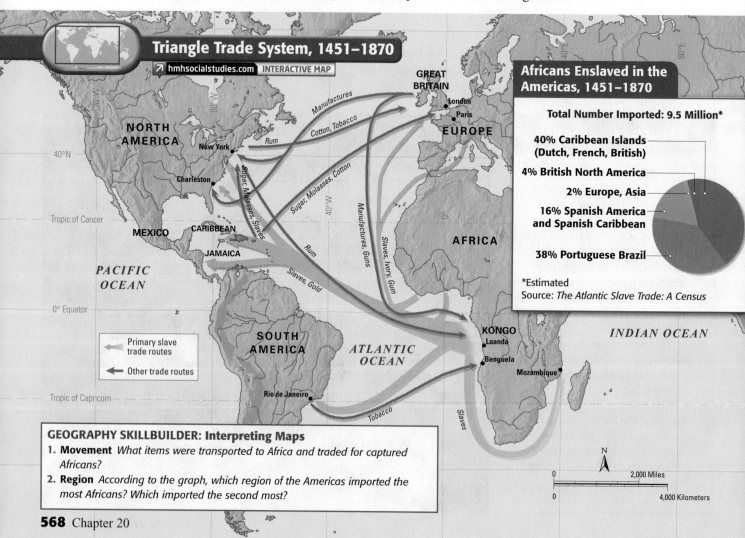

Triangle Trade System, 1451–1870

hmhsocialstudies.com INTERACTIVE MAP

Africans Enslaved in the Americas, 1451–1870

Total Number Imported: 9.5 Million*

40% Caribbean Islands (Dutch, French, British)

4% British North America

2% Europe, Asia

16% Spanish America and Spanish Caribbean

38% Portuguese Brazil

*Estimated
Source: *The Atlantic Slave Trade: A Census*

Primary slave trade routes

Other trade routes

GEOGRAPHY SKILLBUILDER: Interpreting Maps

1. **Movement** What items were transported to Africa and traded for captured Africans?
2. **Region** According to the graph, which region of the Americas imported the most Africans? Which imported the second most?

The Horrors of the Middle Passage

One African, Olaudah Equiano, recalled the inhumane conditions on his trip from West Africa to the West Indies at age 12 in 1762.

This diagram of a British slave ship shows how slave traders packed Africans onto slave ships in the hold below decks for the brutal middle passage.

PRIMARY SOURCE

I was soon put down under the decks, and there I received such a salutation [greeting] in my nostrils as I never experienced in my life; so that, with the loathsomeness of the stench, and crying together, I became so sick and low that I was not able to eat . . . but soon, to my grief, two of the white men offered me eatables; and on my refusing to eat, one of them held me fast by the hands, and laid me across . . . the windlass, while the other flogged me severely.

OLAUDAH EQUIANO, quoted in *Eyewitness: The Negro in American History*

DOCUMENT-BASED QUESTIONS

1. **Making Inferences** *Why might the white men have forced Equiano to eat?*
2. **Drawing Conclusions** *What does the diagram of the slave ship suggest about conditions on board?*

Various other transatlantic routes existed. The "triangular" trade encompassed a network of trade routes crisscrossing the northern and southern colonies, the West Indies, England, Europe, and Africa. The network carried a variety of traded goods.

The Middle Passage The voyage that brought captured Africans to the West Indies and later to North and South America was known as the **middle passage**. It was considered the middle leg of the transatlantic trade triangle. Sickening cruelty characterized this journey. In African ports, European traders packed Africans into the dark holds of large ships. On board, Africans endured whippings and beatings from merchants, as well as diseases that swept through the vessel. Numerous Africans died from disease or physical abuse aboard the slave ships. Many others committed suicide by drowning. Scholars estimate that roughly 20 percent of the Africans aboard each slave ship perished during the brutal trip.

Slavery in the Americas

Africans who survived their ocean voyage faced a difficult life in the Americas. Forced to work in a strange land, enslaved Africans coped in a variety of ways.

A Harsh Life Upon arriving in the Americas, captured Africans usually were auctioned off to the highest bidder. After being sold, slaves worked in mines or fields or as domestic servants. Slaves lived a grueling existence. Many lived on little food in small, dreary huts. They worked long days and suffered beatings. In much of the Americas, slavery was a lifelong condition, as well as a hereditary one.

Resistance and Rebellion To cope with the horrors of slavery, Africans developed a way of life based on their cultural heritage. They kept alive such things as their musical traditions as well as the stories of their ancestors.

Slaves also found ways to resist. They made themselves less productive by breaking tools, uprooting plants, and working slowly. Thousands also ran away.

Some slaves pushed their resistance to open revolt. As early as 1522, about 20 slaves on Hispaniola attacked and killed several Spanish colonists. Larger revolts occurred throughout Spanish settlements during the 16th century.

Occasional uprisings also occurred in Brazil, the West Indies, and North America. In 1739, a group of slaves in South Carolina led an uprising known as the Stono Rebellion. Uprisings continued into the 1800s.

Consequences of the Slave Trade

The Atlantic slave trade had a profound impact on both Africa and the Americas. In Africa, numerous cultures lost generations of their fittest members—their young and able—to European traders and plantation owners. In addition, countless African families were torn apart. Many of them were never reunited. The slave trade devastated African societies in another way: by introducing guns into the continent.

While they were unwilling participants in the growth of the colonies, African slaves contributed greatly to the economic and cultural development of the Americas. Their greatest contribution was their labor. Without their back-breaking work, colonies such as those on Haiti and Barbados may not have survived. In addition to their muscle, enslaved Africans brought their expertise, especially in agriculture. They also brought their culture. Their art, music, religion, and food continue to influence American societies.

The influx of so many Africans to the Americas also has left its mark on the very population itself. From the United States to Brazil, many of the nations of the Western Hemisphere today have substantial populations of African descent. Many Latin American countries have sizable mixed-race populations.

As the next section explains, Africans were not the only cargo transported across the Atlantic during the colonization of the Americas. The settlement of the Americas brought many different items from Europe, Asia, and Africa to North and South America. It also introduced items from the Americas to the rest of the world.

SECTION 3 ASSESSMENT

TERMS & NAMES 1. For each term or name, write a sentence explaining its significance.
• Atlantic slave trade   • triangular trade   • middle passage

USING YOUR NOTES	MAIN IDEAS	CRITICAL THINKING & WRITING
2. What seems to have been the most important consequence? Explain. Consequences of the slave trade I. in Africa 　A. 　B. II. in the Americas 　A. 　B.	3. What effect did the spread of Islam have on the slave trade? 4. How did enslaved Africans resist their bondage? 5. How did African slaves contribute to the development of the Americas?	6. **COMPARING AND CONTRASTING** How was slavery in the Americas different from slavery in Africa? 7. **SYNTHESIZING** What does the percentage of enslaved Africans imported to the Caribbean Islands and Brazil suggest about the racial makeup of these areas? 8. **MAKING INFERENCES** Why do you think the slave trade flourished for so long? 9. **WRITING ACTIVITY** CULTURAL INTERACTION Imagine you are an African ruler. Write a **letter** to a European leader in which you try to convince him or her to stop participating in the slave trade.

CONNECT TO TODAY MAKING A MAP

Research which of the original 13 colonies had the greatest numbers of slaves in the late 18th century. Then make a **map** of the colonies in which you show the numbers for each state.

The Columbian Exchange and Global Trade

MAIN IDEA	WHY IT MATTERS NOW	TERMS & NAMES
ECONOMICS The colonization of the Americas introduced new items into the Eastern and Western hemispheres.	This global exchange of goods permanently changed Europe, Asia, Africa, and the Americas.	• Columbian Exchange • capitalism • joint-stock company	• mercantilism • favorable balance of trade

SETTING THE STAGE The colonization of the Americas dramatically changed the world. It prompted both voluntary and forced migration of millions of people. It led to the establishment of new and powerful societies. Other effects of European settlement of the Americas were less noticeable but equally important. Colonization resulted in the exchange of new items that greatly influenced the lives of people throughout the world. The new wealth from the Americas resulted in new business and trade practices in Europe.

The Columbian Exchange

The global transfer of foods, plants, and animals during the colonization of the Americas is known as the **Columbian Exchange**. Ships from the Americas brought back a wide array of items that Europeans, Asians, and Africans had never before seen. They included such plants as tomatoes, squash, pineapples, tobacco, and cacao beans (for chocolate). And they included animals such as the turkey, which became a source of food in the Eastern Hemisphere.

Perhaps the most important items to travel from the Americas to the rest of the world were corn and potatoes. Both were inexpensive to grow and nutritious. Potatoes, especially, supplied many essential vitamins and minerals. Over time, both crops became an important and steady part of diets throughout the world. These foods helped people live longer. Thus they played a significant role in boosting the world's population. The planting of the first white potato in Ireland and the first sweet potato in China probably changed more lives than the deeds of 100 kings.

Traffic across the Atlantic did not flow in just one direction, however. Europeans introduced various livestock animals into the Americas. These included horses, cattle, sheep, and pigs. Foods from Africa (including some that originated in Asia) migrated west in European ships. They included bananas, black-eyed peas, and yams. Grains introduced to the Americas included wheat, rice, barley, and oats.

Some aspects of the Columbian Exchange had a tragic impact on many Native Americans. Disease was just as much a part of the Columbian Exchange as goods and food. The diseases Europeans brought with them, which included smallpox and measles, led to the deaths of millions of Native Americans.

hmhsocialstudies.com
TAKING NOTES

Use the graphic organizer online to take notes on the Columbian exchange.

The Columbian Exchange

Few events transformed the world like the Columbian Exchange. This global transfer of plants, animals, disease, and especially food brought together the Eastern and Western hemispheres and touched, in some way, nearly all the peoples of the world.

Frightening Foods

Several foods from the Americas that we now take for granted at first amazed and terrified Europeans. Early on, people thought the tomato was harmful to eat. One German official warned that the tomato "should not be taken internally." In 1619, officials in Burgundy, France, banned potatoes, explaining that "too frequent use of them caused the leprosy." In 1774, starving peasants in Prussia refused to eat the spud.

> *"The culinary life we owe Columbus is a progressive dinner in which the whole human race takes part but no one need leave home to sample all the courses."*
>
> *Raymond Sokolov*

The Columbian Exchange

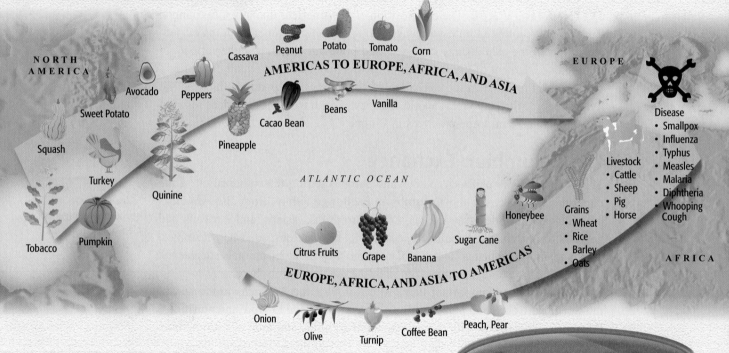

NORTH AMERICA

Avocado
Peppers
Sweet Potato
Squash
Turkey
Quinine
Tobacco
Pumpkin

Cassava
Peanut
Potato
Tomato
Corn

AMERICAS TO EUROPE, AFRICA, AND ASIA

Cacao Bean
Pineapple
Beans
Vanilla

ATLANTIC OCEAN

Citrus Fruits
Grape
Banana
Sugar Cane
Honeybee
Grains
• Wheat
• Rice
• Barley
• Oats

EUROPE, AFRICA, AND ASIA TO AMERICAS

Onion
Olive
Turnip
Coffee Bean
Peach, Pear

EUROPE

Disease
• Smallpox
• Influenza
• Typhus
• Measles
• Malaria
• Diphtheria
• Whooping Cough

Livestock
• Cattle
• Sheep
• Pig
• Horse

AFRICA

The Geography of Food

Think about your favorite foods. Chances are that at least one originated in a distant land. Throughout history, the introduction of new foods into a region has dramatically changed lives—for better and worse. Dependence on the potato, for example, led to a famine in Ireland. This prompted a massive migration of Irish people to other countries. In the Americas, the introduction of sugar led to riches for some and enslavement for many others.

Connect *to* Today

1. **Forming Opinions** Have students work in small groups to pose and answer questions about the beneficial and harmful aspects of the Columbian Exchange.

   See Skillbuilder Handbook, page R20.

2. **Comparing and Contrasting** Find out what major items are exchanged or traded between the United States and either Asia, Africa, or Europe. How do the items compare with those of the Columbian Exchange? Report your findings to the class.

A Spanish missionary in Mexico described the effects of smallpox on the Aztecs:

PRIMARY SOURCE
There was a great havoc. Very many died of it. They could not walk. . . . They could not move; they could not stir; they could not change position, nor lie on one side; nor face down, nor on their backs. And if they stirred, much did they cry out. Great was its destruction.

BERNARDINO DE SAHAGUN, quoted in *Seeds of Change*

MAIN IDEA

Making Inferences
A Why is the Columbian Exchange considered a significant event?

Other diseases Europeans brought with them included influenza, typhus, malaria, and diphtheria. **A**

Global Trade

The establishment of colonial empires in the Americas influenced the nations of Europe in still other ways. New wealth from the Americas was coupled with a dramatic growth in overseas trade. The two factors together prompted a wave of new business and trade practices in Europe during the 16th and 17th centuries. These practices, many of which served as the root of today's financial dealings, dramatically changed the economic atmosphere of Europe.

The Rise of Capitalism One aspect of the European economic revolution was the growth of **capitalism**. Capitalism is an economic system based on private ownership and the investment of resources, such as money, for profit. No longer were governments the sole owners of great wealth. Due to overseas colonization and trade, numerous merchants had obtained great wealth. These merchants continued to invest their money in trade and overseas exploration. Profits from these investments enabled merchants and traders to reinvest even more money in other enterprises. As a result, businesses across Europe grew and flourished.

The increase in economic activity in Europe led to an overall increase in many nations' money supply. This in turn brought on inflation, or the steady rise in the price of goods. Inflation occurs when people have more money to spend and thus demand more goods and services. Because the supply of goods is less than the demand for them, the goods become both scarce and more valuable. Prices then rise. At this time in Europe, the costs of many goods rose. Spain, for example, endured a crushing bout of inflation during the 1600s, as boatloads of gold and silver from the Americas greatly increased the nation's money supply.

Joint-Stock Companies Another business venture that developed during this period was known as the **joint-stock company**. The joint-stock company worked much like the modern-day corporation, with investors buying shares of stock in a company. It involved a number of people combining their wealth for a common purpose.

Three Worlds Meet, 1492–1700

1492 (Europeans)
Columbus embarks on voyage.

1511 (Africans)
Africans begin working as slaves in the Americas.

1521 (Americans)
The Aztec Empire in Mexico is conquered by Hernando Cortés.

1533 (Americans)
The Inca Empire in South America falls to Francisco Pizarro.

1630 (Europeans)
Puritans establish the Massachusetts Bay Colony in North America.

1650 (Africans)
The number of Africans toiling in Spanish America reaches 300,000.

1675 (Americans)
Native Americans battle colonists in King Philip's War.

The Atlantic World **573**

Mercantilism

As you have read, mercantilism was an economic theory practiced in Europe from the 16th to the 18th centuries. Economists of the period believed that a country's power came from its wealth. Thus, a country would do everything possible to acquire more gold, preferably at the expense of its rivals. A mercantilist country primarily sought gold in two ways: establishing and exploiting colonies, and establishing a favorable balance of trade with a rival country. In the example to the right, England is the home country, America is England's colony, and France is England's rival.

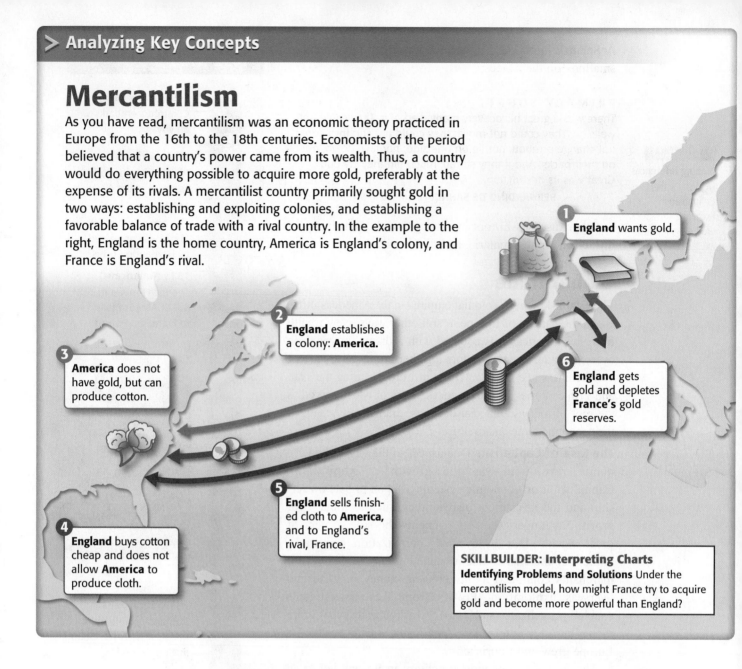

1 **England** wants gold.

2 **England** establishes a colony: **America.**

3 **America** does not have gold, but can produce cotton.

4 **England** buys cotton cheap and does not allow **America** to produce cloth.

5 **England** sells finished cloth to **America,** and to England's rival, France.

6 **England** gets gold and depletes **France's** gold reserves.

SKILLBUILDER: Interpreting Charts
Identifying Problems and Solutions Under the mercantilism model, how might France try to acquire gold and become more powerful than England?

In Europe during the 1500s and 1600s, that common purpose was American colonization. It took large amounts of money to establish overseas colonies. Moreover, while profits may have been great, so were risks. Many ships, for instance, never completed the long and dangerous ocean voyage. Because joint-stock companies involved numerous investors, the individual members paid only a fraction of the total colonization cost. If the colony failed, investors lost only their small share. If the colony thrived, the investors shared in the profits. It was a joint-stock company that was responsible for establishing Jamestown, England's first North American colony. **B**

The Growth of Mercantilism

During this time, the nations of Europe adopted a new economic policy known as **mercantilism**. The theory of mercantilism (shown above) held that a country's power depended mainly on its wealth. Wealth, after all, allowed nations to build strong navies and purchase vital goods. As a result, the goal of every nation became the attainment of as much wealth as possible.

MAIN IDEA

Making Inferences-
B Why would a joint-stock company be popular with investors in overseas colonies?

Balance of Trade According to the theory of mercantilism, a nation could increase its wealth and power in two ways. First, it could obtain as much gold and silver as possible. Second, it could establish a **favorable balance of trade**, in which it sold more goods than it bought. A nation's ultimate goal under mercantilism was to become self-sufficient, not dependent on other countries for goods. An English author of the time wrote about the new economic idea of mercantilism:

> **PRIMARY SOURCE**
> Although a Kingdom may be enriched by gifts received, or by purchases taken from some other Nations . . . these are things uncertain and of small consideration when they happen. The ordinary means therefore to increase our wealth and treasure is by Foreign Trade, wherein we must ever observe this rule: to sell more to strangers yearly than we consume of theirs in value.
>
> **THOMAS MUN,** quoted in *World Civilizations*

Mercantilism went hand in hand with colonization, for colonies played a vital role in this new economic practice. Aside from providing silver and gold, colonies provided raw materials that could not be found in the home country, such as wood or furs. In addition to playing the role of supplier, the colonies also provided a market. The home country could sell its goods to its colonies. **C**

MAIN IDEA

Summarizing
C) What role did colonies play in mercantilism?

Economic Revolution Changes European Society The economic changes that swept through much of Europe during the age of American colonization also led to changes in European society. The economic revolution spurred the growth of towns and the rise of a class of merchants who controlled great wealth.

The changes in European society, however, only went so far. While towns and cities grew in size, much of Europe's population continued to live in rural areas. And although merchants and traders enjoyed social mobility, the majority of Europeans remained poor. More than anything else, the economic revolution increased the wealth of European nations. In addition, mercantilism contributed to the creation of a national identity. Also, as Chapter 21 will describe, the new economic practices helped expand the power of European monarchs, who became powerful rulers.

SECTION 4 ASSESSMENT

TERMS & NAMES 1. For each term or name, write a sentence explaining its significance.
- Columbian Exchange
- capitalism
- joint-stock company
- mercantilism
- favorable balance of trade

USING YOUR NOTES	**MAIN IDEAS**	**CRITICAL THINKING & WRITING**
2. Which effect do you think had the greatest impact on history?	3. What were some of the food items that traveled from the Americas to the rest of the world?	6. **MAKING INFERENCES** Why were colonies considered so important to the nations of Europe?
	4. What food and livestock from the rest of the world traveled to the Americas?	7. **DRAWING CONCLUSIONS** Why might establishing overseas colonies have justified high profits for those who financed the colonies?
	5. What were some of the effects on European society of the economic revolution that took place in the 16th and 17th centuries?	8. **COMPARING** What were some of the positive and negative consequences of the Columbian Exchange?
		9. **WRITING ACTIVITY** [ECONOMICS] Do you think the economic changes in Europe during the era of American colonization qualify as a revolution? Why or why not? Support your opinions in a two-paragraph **essay**.

Using Your Notes table:

Food/ Livestock/ Disease	Place of Origin	Effect
Potato		
Horse		
Smallpox		

CONNECT TO TODAY MAKING A POSTER

Research one crop that developed in the Americas (such as corn or potatoes) and its impact on the world today. Show your findings in a **poster**.

TERMS & NAMES

For each term or name below, briefly explain its connection to the Atlantic world from 1492 to 1800.

1. conquistador
2. *encomienda*
3. Jamestown
4. French and Indian War
5. Atlantic slave trade
6. triangular trade
7. Columbian Exchange
8. mercantilism

MAIN IDEAS

Spain Builds an American Empire Section 1
(pages 553–560)

9. Why did Columbus set sail westward?
10. What were three goals of the Spanish in the Americas?
11. Why did Popé lead a rebellion against the Spanish?

European Nations Settle North America Section 2
(pages 561–565)

12. What did the Europeans mostly grow in their Caribbean colonies?
13. What was the result of the French and Indian War?

The Atlantic Slave Trade Section 3 (pages 566–570)

14. What factors led European colonists to use Africans to resupply their labor force?
15. What were the conditions on board a slave ship?
16. What were several ways in which enslaved Africans resisted their treatment in the Americas?

The Columbian Exchange and Global Trade Section 4
(pages 571–575)

17. Why was the introduction of corn and potatoes to Europe and Asia so significant?
18. What was the economic policy of mercantilism?

CRITICAL THINKING

1. USING YOUR NOTES

Use the chart to identify which nation sponsored each explorer and the regions he explored.

Explorer	Nation	Regions
Cabral		
Magellan		
Cartier		

2. DRAWING CONCLUSIONS

EMPIRE BUILDING What factors helped the Europeans conquer the Americas? Which was the most important? Why?

3. RECOGNIZING EFFECTS

ECONOMICS Explain the statement, "Columbus's voyage began a process that changed the world forever." Consider all the peoples and places American colonization affected economically.

4. COMPARING AND CONTRASTING

CULTURAL INTERACTION What might have been some of the differences in the Europeans' and Native Americans' views of colonization?

5. SYNTHESIZING

How did enslaved Africans help create the societies in the New World?

VISUAL SUMMARY

The Atlantic World

Global Interaction

Europeans

- Beginning around 1500, the Spanish and Portuguese colonize Central and South America and establish prosperous overseas empires.
- Throughout the 1600s and 1700s, the English, French, and Dutch battle for control of North America, with the English emerging victorious.

Native Americans

- Between 1521 and 1533, the once mighty Aztec and Incan empires fall to the invading Spanish.
- Throughout the Americas, the native population is devastated by European conquests and diseases.

Africans

- Beginning around 1500, millions of Africans are taken from their homeland and forced to labor as slaves in the Americas.
- Africans eventually become an important part of the Americas, as they populate the various regions and share aspects of their culture.

Use the quotation and your knowledge of world history to answer questions 1 and 2.

PRIMARY SOURCE

Where there is a vacant place, there is liberty for . . . [Christians] to come and inhabit, though they neither buy it nor ask their leaves. . . . Indeed, no nation is to drive out another without special commission from Heaven . . . unless the natives do unjustly wrong them, and will not recompense the wrongs done in a peaceable fort [way]. And then they may right themselves by lawful war and subdue the country unto themselves.

JOHN COTTON, from "God's Promise to His Plantation"

1. What do you think Native Americans might have said about Cotton's statement that America was a "vacant place"?

A. agreed that the continent was largely empty

B. discussed development plans with him

C. pointed out that they inhabited the land

D. offered to sell the land to him

2. How might the last part of Cotton's statement have helped the Puritans justify taking land from the Native Americans?

A. Puritans could claim natives had wronged them.

B. Natives could claim Puritans had wronged them.

C. Puritans believed war was wrong in all circumstances.

D. Native Americans were willing to negotiate their grievances.

Use the Aztec drawing below and your knowledge of world history to answer question 3.

3. How does the artist depict the clash of Aztec and Spanish cultures?

A. meeting to negotiate peace

B. meeting as warriors

C. engaging in a sports competition

D. meeting as friends

 hmhsocialstudies.com **TEST PRACTICE**

For additional test practice, go online for:

• Diagnostic tests

• Strategies

• Tutorials

Interact *with* History

On page 552 you examined the choices some Native Americans faced during the invasion by Spanish conquistadors. Now that you have read the chapter, rethink the choice you made. If you chose to side with the Spaniards, would you now change your mind? Why? If you decided to fight with the Aztecs, what are your feelings now? Discuss your thoughts and opinions with a small group.

FOCUS ON WRITING

An English colony would have looked strange and different to a Native American of the time. Write a **paragraph** describing an English colony of the 17th century. In your paragraph, provide details about the following:

• clothes

• food

• shelter

• weapons

MULTIMEDIA ACTIVITY

21ST CENTURY

Participating in a WebQuest

Introduction The Columbian Exchange marked the beginning of worldwide trade. Imagine that you are an exporter of a product and want to know how tariffs will affect your sales in various countries.

Task Collect and organize data about a particular product, including how much of the product various countries import and the tariff each country imposes.

Process and Resources With a team of four other students, use the Internet to research your product. Internet keyword: *customs tariffs various countries.* Identify at least five countries that import the product. Organize your findings in a spreadsheet.

Evaluation and Conclusion How did this project contribute to your understanding of global trade? How do you think tariffs will affect demand for your product in each country?

Ponce de Leon

The Spanish conquistador Juan Ponce de Leon was the first European to set foot on land that later became part of the United States. Ponce de Leon first sailed to the Americas with Christopher Columbus on his second voyage in 1493. Once in the Caribbean region, he helped conquer what is now Puerto Rico and was named ruler of the island. In Puerto Rico, Ponce de Leon heard about a nearby island that supposedly held the legendary Fountain of Youth. Its waters were said to make old people young again. In 1513, Ponce de Leon set out to find the island but instead landed in what is now Florida. He named Florida and claimed it for Spain.

Explore important events in the life of Ponce de Leon online. You can find a wealth of information, video clips, primary sources, activities, and more at ↗ hmhsocialstudies.com .

📹 Caribbean Island Encounters

Watch the video to learn about the first encounters between Spanish explorers and the people of the Caribbean.

📹 Claiming Florida for Spain

Watch the video to learn about Ponce de Leon's first landing on the coast of what is now Florida.

🌎 Ponce de Leon's 1513 Route

Study the map to learn about the region of the Americas that Ponce de Leon explored in 1513.

Four Governments

In Unit 4, you studied how cultures around the world organized and governed themselves. The next six pages focus on four of those governments—the Incan Empire, Italian city-states, Tokugawa Japan, and the Ottoman Empire. How they functioned and the physical symbols they used to communicate their power are important themes. The chart below identifies some key characteristics of the four different governments, and the map locates them in time and place. Take notes on the similarities and differences between the four governments.

Key Characteristics			
	Incan Empire	**Italian City-States**	**Tokugawa Japan**	**Ottoman Empire**
Title of Ruler	• Inca	• varied by city: some had title of nobility, others of an elected position	• Shogun; emperor was a figurehead only	• Sultan
Ruling Structure	• monarchical	• oligarchic	• militaristic	• bureaucratic
Basis of Authority	• ruler believed to be descendant of the Sun god	• inheritance or social status supported by financial influence	• absolute loyalty and devoted service of samurai to their daimyo	• military power
Distinctive Feature of Government	• Officials reported from the village level up to the king. • Members of an ethnic group were moved from their homes to other areas to increase agricultural output or put down rebellions. • Children of Inca, local officials, and some others were taken to Cuzco for training.	• Power was in the hands of the ruling family or of a few wealthy families of bankers and merchants. • Many cities had constitutions and elected assemblies with little power.	• Daimyo were the shogun's vassals and local administrators. • Shogun controlled daimyo's marriage alliances and the number of samurai each had. • To ensure cooperation, daimyo's families were held hostage at court while daimyos administered their home regions.	• Sultan owned everything of value (such as land and labor); his bureaucracy was in charge of managing and protecting it. • Members of the bureaucracy derived status from the sultan but were his slaves along with their families. • Heads of *millets* governed locally.

SKILLBUILDER: Interpreting Charts
Drawing Conclusions *How did the rulers of most of these governments keep themselves in power?*

Monarchy in the Incan Empire, 1438–1535

The Incan monarchy was different from European monarchies. In the Incan Empire, all people worked for the state, either as farmers, or artisans making cloth, for example. Men also served as road builders, as messengers, or as soldiers. The state provided clothing, food, and any necessities in short supply. Every year, the amount of land every family had was reviewed to make sure it could produce enough food to live on.

SOUTH AMERICA

Oligarchy in the Italian City-States, 1000–1870

Oligarchy is government by a small group of people. In Venice, citizens elected a great council, but real power was held by the senate, which made all decisions. Only members of 125 to 150 wealthy and cultured families were eligible for membership.

Militarism in Tokugawa Japan, 1603–1867

A militaristic government is run by the military. All those in power under the Tokugawa shoguns were samurai. As the samurais' work became more administrative than military, the Tokugawa rulers encouraged cultural pursuits such as poetry, calligraphy, and the tea ceremony to keep warlike tendencies in check.

EUROPE

ASIA

Sea of Japan

40°N

Mediterranean Sea

AFRICA

PACIFIC OCEAN

Bureaucracy in the Ottoman Empire, 1451–1922

A bureaucratic government is organized into departments and offices staffed by workers who perform limited tasks. Because of the size of the empire, the Ottoman bureaucracy required tens of thousands of civil servants. The empire also supported and encouraged the arts.

0°

INDIAN OCEAN

Comparing & Contrasting

1. In what ways did the Incan government resemble the Ottoman bureaucracy?

2. What similarities and differences were there in the way the sultans and shoguns controlled government officials?

3. What characteristic did the ruling class of the Italian city-states and Tokugawa Japan have in common?

40°S

Structures of Government

All of the governments have officials at different levels with varying degrees of power and responsibility. Compare the governmental structure of the Ottoman bureaucracy with that of Tokugawa Shogunate's militaristic government using the charts below.

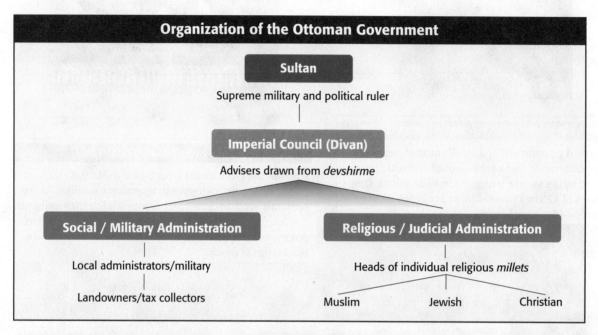

Organization of the Ottoman Government

Sultan
Supreme military and political ruler

Imperial Council (Divan)
Advisers drawn from *devshirme*

Social / Military Administration
Local administrators/military
Landowners/tax collectors

Religious / Judicial Administration
Heads of individual religious *millets*
Muslim   Jewish   Christian

Organization of the Tokugawa Shogunate

Emperor
Held highest rank in society but had no political power

Shogun
Actual ruler

Daimyo
Large landowners

Samurai Warriors
Loyal to daimyo and shogun

Peasants
Four-fifths of the population

Merchants
Low status gradually gained influence

Artisans
Craftspeople such as artists and blacksmiths

SKILLBUILDER: Interpreting Charts
1. **Clarifying** *To whom were the heads of the* millets *answerable?*
2. **Drawing Conclusions** *How might the samurai's loyalty to his daimyo conflict with his loyalty to the shogun?*

Artifacts of Power

The everyday objects used by members of government often serve a symbolic purpose. Note how the objects below communicated the rank and importance of the person who used them. Examine them and consider the effect they probably had on the people who saw them.

◄ Japanese Sword
Beautiful weapons and armor were symbols of status and power in Tokugawa Japan. Swords were the special weapons of the samurai, who were the only people allowed to carry arms. Daimyo had artisans make fine swords with expensively decorated hilts and scabbards for ceremonial occasions.

◄ Incan Headdress
All of the people in the Incan Empire were required to wear the clothing of their particular ethnic group. The patterns on clothes and headdresses immediately identified a person's place of birth and social rank.

Italian Medici Pitcher ▲
As well as being great patrons of the fine arts, wealthy Italians surrounded themselves with luxurious practical objects. Even ordinary items, like a pitcher, were elaborately made of expensive materials.

Comparing & Contrasting

1. How did the role of the sultan compare with the role of the Japanese emperor?

2. What message were expensive personal items meant to convey?

3. How does a household item like the pitcher differ from a sword or headdress as a symbol of power?

Architecture of Government

A ruler's castle or palace was a luxurious and safe home where he was surrounded by vassals who protected him. It was also a center of government where his administrators carried on their work under his supervision. Castles and palaces are a show of greatness. Large rooms that accommodate many guests demonstrate the ruler's authority over many people. Rich decorations display the ruler's wealth, refinement, and superior rank.

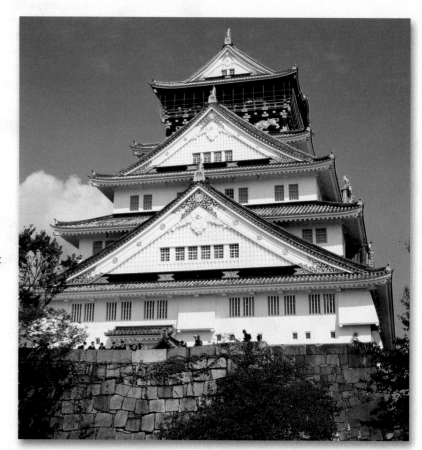

Japanese Palace ▶
Osaka Castle was originally built by Toyotami Hideyoshi and has been rebuilt twice since then due to fire. It is surrounded by gardens, and the interior was known for its wall paintings and painted screens. During the Tokugawa period, the city of Osaka was a center of trade for agricultural and manufactured goods. The city was governed directly by the shoguns who owned the castle.

◀ Ottoman Palace
Topkapi Palace in modern Istanbul, Turkey, was the home of the Ottoman sultans. The buildings were built around several courtyards. Within the outer walls were gardens, a school for future officials, the treasury, and an arsenal. Elaborate paintings, woodwork, and tile designs decorated the walls and ceilings of rooms used by the sultan and his high officials.

Descriptions of Government

↗ hmhsocialstudies.com **INTERACTIVE**
Go online to listen to selected audio excerpts.

The following passages were written by writers who were reflecting not only on the past, but also on places and events they had personally witnessed.

PRIMARY SOURCE

Machiavelli

In this excerpt from *The Discourses,* Italian writer Niccolò Machiavelli discusses six types of government—three good and three bad.

[T]he three bad ones result from the degradation of the other three. . . . Thus monarchy becomes tyranny; aristocracy degenerates into oligarchy; and the popular government lapses readily into licentiousness [lack of restraint].

   [S]agacious legislators . . . have chosen one that should partake of all of them, judging that to be the most stable and solid. In fact, when there is combined under the same constitution a prince, a nobility, and the power of the people, then these three powers will watch and keep each other reciprocally in check.

DOCUMENT-BASED QUESTION
Why does Machiavelli think a combined government is the best type of government?

PRIMARY SOURCE

Garcilaso de la Vega

This description of government administration comes from Garcilaso's history of the Inca.

[Local administrators] were obliged each lunar month to furnish their superiors . . . with a record of the births and deaths that had occurred in the territory administered by them. . . .

   [E]very two years . . . the wool from the royal herds was distributed in every village, in order that each person should be decently clothed during his entire life. It should be recalled that . . . the people . . . possessed only very few cattle, whereas the Inca's and the Sun's herds were . . . numerous. . . . Thus everyone was always provided with clothing, shoes, food, and all that is necessary in life.

DOCUMENT-BASED QUESTION
What and how did the Incan authorities provide for the common people's needs?

Comparing & Contrasting

1. How do Osaka Castle and Topkapi Palace project the importance of their owners? Explain.
2. Does Machiavelli favor a system of government that would provide directly for people's needs? Explain.

EXTENSION ACTIVITY

Use the library to get some additional information about the government structure of the Incan Empire and Renaissance Venice. Then draw an organizational chart for each of those governments like the charts on page 580.

Absolutism to Revolution
1500–1900

On July 14, 1789, an angry French mob attacked the Bastille, a state prison in Paris, because it was looking for arms and gunpowder. The capture of this prison is considered the beginning of the French Revolution.

Comparing & Contrasting

Political Revolutions
In Unit 5, you will learn that new ideas about human rights and government led to political revolutions in many countries during the late 1700s and the 1800s. At the end of the unit, you will have a chance to compare and contrast those revolutions. (See pages 706–711.)

585

Absolute Monarchs in Europe, 1500–1800

Essential Question

What were the causes and effects of absolute monarchies in Europe from 1500 until 1800?

? What You Will Learn

In this chapter you will learn about absolute monarchs in Europe.

SECTION 1 Spain's Empire and European Absolutism

Main Idea During a time of religious and economic instability, Philip II ruled Spain with a strong hand.

SECTION 2 The Reign of Louis XIV

Main Idea After a century of war and riots, France was ruled by Louis XIV, the most powerful monarch of his time.

SECTION 3 Central European Monarchs Clash

Main Idea After a period of turmoil, absolute monarchs ruled Austria and the Germanic state of Prussia.

SECTION 4 Absolute Rulers of Russia

Main Idea Peter the Great made many changes in Russia to try to make it more like western Europe.

SECTION 5 Parliament Limits the English Monarchy

Main Idea Absolute rulers in England were overthrown, and Parliament gained power.

Previewing Themes

POWER AND AUTHORITY As feudalism declined, stronger national kingdoms in Spain, France, Austria, Prussia, and Russia emerged under the control of absolute rulers.

Geography *Study the map. What large empire was surrounded by many of these national kingdoms?*

ECONOMICS Absolute rulers wanted to control their countries' economies so that they could free themselves from limitations imposed by the nobility. In France, Louis XIV's unrestrained spending left his country with huge debts.

Geography *What other evidence of unrestrained spending by an absolute ruler does the time line suggest?*

REVOLUTION In Great Britain, Parliament and the British people challenged the monarch's authority. The overthrow of the king led to important political changes.

Geography *Study the map and the time line. Which British Stuart lands were most affected by the event occurring in 1649?*

1588
◄ British defeat Philip II's Spanish Armada.

EUROPE

1500

1600

WORLD

1521
Cortés conquers Aztec Empire.

1533
Pizarro conquers Incan Empire. ►

1603
Tokugawa shoguns rule Japan.

Europe, 1650

Legend:
- Austrian Hapsburg lands
- British Stuart lands
- French Bourbon lands
- Prussian lands
- Russian lands
- Spanish Hapsburg lands
- Boundary of Holy Roman Empire

0   250   500 Miles
0   250   500 Kilometers
Conic Projection

60°N
45°N
15°W

North Sea
Baltic Sea
ATLANTIC OCEAN
Adriatic Sea
Mediterranean Sea

SCOTLAND
IRELAND
ENGLAND
London
UNITED NETHERLANDS
Amsterdam
Utrecht
SPANISH NETH.
Hamburg
DENMARK–NORWAY
SWEDEN
ESTONIA
INGRIA
LIVONIA
LITHUANIA
RUSSIA
Moscow
PRUSSIA
Danzig
BRANDENBURG
Magdeburg
Warsaw
POLAND
Kiev
HOLY ROMAN EMPIRE
Paris
Nantes
FRANCHE-COMTÉ
CHAROLAIS
FRANCE
Augsburg
SWISS CONFED.
Milan
Prague
AUSTRIA
Vienna
HUNGARY
ITALIAN STATES
PAPAL STATES
CORSICA
Rome
Naples
SARDINIA (SPAIN)
KINGDOM OF NAPLES
PORTUGAL
Lisbon
Madrid
SPAIN
Balearic Is.

HISTORY
Ivan the Terrible: Might and Madness
↗ hmhsocialstudies.com VIDEO

1643
Louis XIV begins to rule France.

1649
Puritans under Oliver Cromwell (at right) execute English king. ▶

1696
Peter the Great becomes sole czar of Russia.

1756
Prussian king Frederick the Great begins Seven Years' War against Austria.

1700

1800

1631
Shah Jahan orders construction of Taj Mahal. ▶

1776
American colonists declare their independence from England.

What are the benefits and drawbacks of having an absolute ruler?

You live under the most powerful monarch in 17th-century Europe, Louis XIV of France, shown below. As Louis's subject, you feel proud and well protected because the French army is the strongest in Europe. But Louis's desire to gain lands for France and battle enemies has resulted in costly wars. And he expects you and his other subjects to pay for them.

hmhsocialstudies.com INTERACTIVE

1 Louis XIV uses his clothing to demonstrate his power and status, as his portrait shows. The gold flower on his robe is the symbol of French kings.

2 Louis's love of finery is apparent not only in his clothing but also in the ornate setting for this painting. As absolute ruler, Louis imposes taxes to pay for the construction of a magnificent new palace and to finance wars.

3 The government of Louis XIV enforces laws and provides security. His sword, scepter, and crown symbolize the power he wields. Yet the French people have no say in what laws are passed or how they are enforced.

EXAMINING *the* ISSUES

- **What might people gain from having a ruler whose power is total, or absolute?**

- **What factors might weaken the power of an absolute monarch?**

As a class, discuss these questions. You may want to refer to earlier rulers, such as those of the Roman, Ottoman, and Carolingian empires. As you read about absolute monarchs in Europe, notice what strengthened and weakened their power.

Spain's Empire and European Absolutism

1

MAIN IDEA	WHY IT MATTERS NOW	TERMS & NAMES
ECONOMICS During a time of religious and economic instability, Philip II ruled Spain with a strong hand.	When faced with crises, many heads of government take on additional economic or political powers.	• Philip II • divine right • absolute monarch

SETTING THE STAGE As you learned in Chapter 18, from 1520 to 1566, Suleyman I exercised great power as sultan of the Ottoman Empire. A European monarch of the same period, Charles V, came close to matching Suleyman's power. As the Hapsburg king, Charles inherited Spain, Spain's American colonies, parts of Italy, and lands in Austria and the Netherlands. As the elected Holy Roman emperor, he ruled much of Germany. It was the first time since Charlemagne that a European ruler controlled so much territory.

A Powerful Spanish Empire

A devout Catholic, Charles not only fought Muslims but also opposed Lutherans. In 1555, he unwillingly agreed to the Peace of Augsburg, which allowed German princes to choose the religion for their territory. The following year, Charles V divided his immense empire and retired to a monastery. To his brother Ferdinand, he left Austria and the Holy Roman Empire. His son, <u>Philip II</u>, inherited Spain, the Spanish Netherlands, and the American colonies.

Philip II's Empire Philip was shy, serious, and—like his father—deeply religious. He was also very hard working. Yet Philip would not allow anyone to help him. Deeply suspicious, he trusted no one for long. As his own court historian wrote, "His smile and his dagger were very close."

Perhaps above all, Philip could be aggressive for the sake of his empire. In 1580, the king of Portugal died without an heir. Because Philip was the king's nephew, he seized the Portuguese kingdom. Counting Portuguese strongholds in Africa, India, and the East Indies, he now had an empire that circled the globe.

Philip's empire provided him with incredible wealth. By 1600, American mines had supplied Spain with an estimated 339,000 pounds of gold. Between 1550 and 1650, roughly 16,000 tons of silver bullion were unloaded from Spanish galleons, or ships. The king of Spain claimed between a fourth and a fifth of every shipload of treasure as his royal share. With this wealth, Spain was able to support a large standing army of about 50,000 soldiers.

Defender of Catholicism When Philip assumed the throne, Europe was experiencing religious wars caused by the Reformation. However, religious conflict was not new to Spain. The Reconquista, the campaign to drive Muslims from Spain, had been completed only 64 years before. In addition, Philip's great-grandparents

hmhsocialstudies.com
TAKING NOTES
Use the graphic organizer online to take notes on the conditions that allowed European monarchs to gain power.

Route of the Armada
Route of the English fleet
Some shipwreck sites
Spanish Hapsburg lands

SCOTLAND

IRELAND

ATLANTIC
OCEAN

ENGLAND

North
Sea

Plymouth

London

Dover

Calais

SPANISH
NETHERLANDS

English
Channel

0   200 Miles
0   400 Kilometers

Bay of
Biscay

FRANCE

La Coruña

42°N

Santander
Late September, 1588

PORTUGAL

Lisbon
Late May, 1588

SPAIN

In the summer of 1588, Philip II sent about 130 ships carrying 19,000 soldiers to the English Channel. English warships, however, outmaneuvered the Spanish vessels and bombarded the Armada with their heavier long-range cannons.

hmhsocialstudies.com

INTERACTIVE HISTORY
Follow the events that led to the wreck of the Spanish Armada.

Inset map

ENGLAND

52°N

0   50 Miles
0   100 Kilometers

London

Dover

Aug. 8

Calais

Gravelines

SP.
NETH.

Major battles

Plymouth

Portland Bill

Isle of Wight

Aug. 2

Aug. 3

Aug. 4

July 31

English Channel

FRANCE

**GEOGRAPHY SKILLBUILDER:
Interpreting Maps**

1. **Location** *Off what English town did the first clash between the Spanish Armada and the English fleet take place?*
2. **Movement** *Why do you think the Spanish captains chose to sail north around Scotland rather than take the more direct route home back through the English Channel?*

Isabella and Ferdinand had used the Inquisition to investigate suspected heretics, or nonbelievers in Christianity.

Philip believed it was his duty to defend Catholicism against the Muslims of the Ottoman Empire and the Protestants of Europe. In 1571, the pope called on all Catholic princes to take up arms against the mounting power of the Ottoman Empire. Philip responded like a true crusader. More than 200 Spanish and Venetian ships defeated a large Ottoman fleet in a fierce battle near Lepanto. In 1588, Philip launched the Spanish Armada in an attempt to punish Protestant England and its queen, Elizabeth I. Elizabeth had supported Protestant subjects who had rebelled against Philip. However, his fleet was defeated. (See map opposite.)

Although this setback seriously weakened Spain, its wealth gave it the appearance of strength for a while longer. Philip's gray granite palace, the Escorial, had massive walls and huge gates that demonstrated his power. The Escorial also reflected Philip's faith. Within its walls stood a monastery as well as a palace. **A**

MAIN IDEA

Making Inferences

A What did Philip want his palace to demonstrate about his monarchy?

Golden Age of Spanish Art and Literature

Spain's great wealth did more than support navies and build palaces. It also allowed monarchs and nobles to become patrons of artists. During the 16th and 17th centuries, Spain experienced a golden age in the arts. The works of two great painters show both the faith and the pride of Spain during this period.

El Greco and Velázquez Born in Crete, El Greco (GREHK•oh) spent much of his adult life in Spain. His real name was Domenikos Theotokopoulos, but Spaniards called him El Greco, meaning "the Greek." El Greco's art often puzzled the people of his time. He chose brilliant, sometimes clashing colors, distorted the human figure, and expressed emotion symbolically in his paintings. Although unusual, El Greco's techniques showed the deep Catholic faith of Spain. He painted saints and martyrs as huge, long-limbed figures that have a supernatural air.

The paintings of Diego Velázquez (vuh•LAHS•kehs), on the other hand, reflected the pride of the Spanish monarchy. Velázquez, who painted 50 years after El Greco, was the court painter to Philip IV of Spain. He is best known for his portraits of the royal family and scenes of court life. Like El Greco, he was noted for using rich colors.

Don Quixote The publication of *Don Quixote de la Mancha* in 1605 is often called the birth of the modern European novel. In this book, Miguel de Cervantes (suhr•VAN•teez) wrote about a poor Spanish nobleman who went a little crazy after reading too many books about heroic knights.

▼ In *Las Meninas (The Maids of Honor)*, Velázquez depicts King Philip IV's daughter and her attendants.

Hoping to "right every manner of wrong," Don Quixote rode forth in a rusty suit of armor, mounted on a feeble horse. At one point, he mistook some windmills for giants:

PRIMARY SOURCE
He rushed with [his horse's] utmost speed upon the first windmill he could come at, and, running his lance into the sail, the wind whirled about with such swiftness, that the rapidity of the motion presently broke the lance into shivers, and hurled away both knight and horse along with it, till down he fell, rolling a good way off in the field.

MIGUEL DE CERVANTES, *Don Quixote de la Mancha*

Some critics believe that Cervantes was mocking chivalry, the knightly code of the Middle Ages. Others maintain that the book is about an idealistic person who longs for the romantic past because he is frustrated with his materialistic world.

The Spanish Empire Weakens

Certainly, the age in which Cervantes wrote was a materialistic one. The gold and silver coming from the Americas made Spain temporarily wealthy. However, such treasure helped to cause long-term economic problems.

Inflation and Taxes One of these problems was severe inflation, which is a decline in the value of money, accompanied by a rise in the prices of goods and services. Inflation in Spain had two main causes. First, Spain's population had been growing. As more people demanded food and other goods, merchants were able to raise prices. Second, as silver bullion flooded the market, its value dropped. People needed more and more amounts of silver to buy things.

Spain's economic decline also had other causes. When Spain expelled the Jews and Moors (Muslims) around 1500, it lost many valuable artisans and business-people. In addition, Spain's nobles did not have to pay taxes. The tax burden fell on the lower classes. That burden prevented them from accumulating enough wealth to start their own businesses. As a result, Spain never developed a middle class.

Global Impact

Tulip Mania

Tulips came to Europe from Turkey around 1550. People went wild over the flowers and began to buy rare varieties. However, the supply of tulips could not meet the demand, and prices began to rise. Soon people were spending all their savings on bulbs and taking out loans so that they could buy more.

Tulip mania reached a peak between 1633 and 1637. Soon after, tulip prices sank rapidly. Many Dutch families lost property and were left with bulbs that were nearly worthless.

Making Spain's Enemies Rich Guilds that had emerged in the Middle Ages still dominated business in Spain. Such guilds used old-fashioned methods. This made Spanish cloth and manufactured goods more expensive than those made elsewhere. As a result, Spaniards bought much of what they needed from France, England, and the Netherlands. Spain's great wealth flowed into the pockets of foreigners, who were mostly Spain's enemies.

To finance their wars, Spanish kings borrowed money from German and Italian bankers. When shiploads of silver came in, the money was sent abroad to repay debts. The economy was so feeble that Philip had to declare the Spanish state bankrupt three times. **B**

The Dutch Revolt In the Spanish Netherlands, Philip had to maintain an army to keep his subjects under control. The Dutch had little in common with their Spanish rulers. While Spain was Catholic, the Netherlands had many Calvinist congregations. Also, Spain had a sluggish economy, while the Dutch had a prosperous middle class.

Philip raised taxes in the Netherlands and took steps to crush Protestantism. In response, in 1566, angry Protestant mobs swept through Catholic churches. Philip then sent an

MAIN IDEA

Identifying Problems
B Why didn't Spain's economy benefit from the gold and silver from the Americas?

army under the Spanish duke of Alva to punish the rebels. On a single day in 1568, the duke executed 1,500 Protestants and suspected rebels.

The Dutch continued to fight the Spanish for another 11 years. Finally, in 1579, the seven northern provinces of the Netherlands, which were largely Protestant, united and declared their independence from Spain. They became the United Provinces of the Netherlands. The ten southern provinces (present-day Belgium) were Catholic and remained under Spanish control.

The Independent Dutch Prosper

The United Provinces of the Netherlands was different from other European states of the time. For one thing, the people there practiced religious toleration. In addition, the United Provinces was not a kingdom but a republic. Each province had an elected governor, whose power depended on the support of merchants and landholders.

Dutch Art During the 1600s, the Netherlands became what Florence had been during the 1400s. It boasted not only the best banks but also many of the best artists in Europe. As in Florence, wealthy merchants sponsored many of these artists.

Rembrandt van Rijn (REHM•BRANT vahn RYN) was the greatest Dutch artist of the period. Rembrandt painted portraits of wealthy middle-class merchants. He also produced group portraits. In *The Night Watch* (shown below), he portrayed a group of city guards. Rembrandt used sharp contrasts of light and shadow to draw attention to his focus.

Another artist fascinated with the effects of light and dark was Jan Vermeer (YAHN vuhr•MEER). Like many other Dutch artists, he chose domestic, indoor settings for his portraits. He often painted women doing such familiar activities as pouring milk from a jug or reading a letter. The work of both Rembrandt and Vermeer reveals how important merchants, civic leaders, and the middle class in general were in 17th-century Netherlands.

◄ In *The Night Watch*, Rembrandt showed the individuality of each man by capturing distinctive facial expressions and postures.

Dutch Trading Empire The stability of the government allowed the Dutch people to concentrate on economic growth. The merchants of Amsterdam bought surplus grain in Poland and crammed it into their warehouses. When they heard about poor harvests in southern Europe, they shipped the grain south while prices were highest. The Dutch had the largest fleet of ships in the world—perhaps 4,800 ships in 1636. This fleet helped the Dutch East India Company (a trading company controlled by the Dutch government) to dominate the Asian spice trade and the Indian Ocean trade. Gradually, the Dutch replaced the Italians as the bankers of Europe.

Absolutism in Europe

Even though Philip II lost his Dutch possessions, he was a forceful ruler in many ways. He tried to control every aspect of his empire's affairs. During the next few centuries, many European monarchs would also claim the authority to rule without limits on their power.

The Theory of Absolutism These rulers wanted to be **absolute monarchs**, kings or queens who held all of the power within their states' boundaries. Their goal was to control every aspect of society. Absolute monarchs believed in **divine right**, the idea that God created the monarchy and that the monarch acted as God's representative on Earth. An absolute monarch answered only to God, not to his or her subjects. **C**

MAIN IDEA

Drawing Conclusions
C How was Philip II typical of an absolute monarch?

> ## Analyzing Key Concepts

Absolutism

Absolutism was the political belief that one ruler should hold all of the power within the boundaries of a country. Although practiced by several monarchs in Europe during the 16th through 18th centuries, absolutism has been used in many regions throughout history. In ancient times, Shi Huangdi in China, Darius in Persia, and the Roman caesars were all absolute rulers. (See Chapters 4, 5, and 6.)

SKILLBUILDER: Interpreting Charts
1. **Making Inferences** *Why do you think absolute rulers controlled social gatherings?*
   See Skillbuilder Handbook, page R10.

2. **Hypothesizing** *Today several nations of the world (such as Saudi Arabia) have absolute rulers. Judging from what you know of past causes of absolutism, why do you think absolute rulers still exist today?*

Causes

- Religious and territorial conflicts created fear and uncertainty.
- The growth of armies to deal with conflicts caused rulers to raise taxes to pay troops.
- Heavy taxes led to additional unrest and peasant revolts.

ABSOLUTISM

Effects

- Rulers regulated religious worship and social gatherings to control the spread of ideas.
- Rulers increased the size of their courts to appear more powerful.
- Rulers created bureaucracies to control their countries' economies.

Growing Power of Europe's Monarchs As Europe emerged from the Middle Ages, monarchs grew increasingly powerful. The decline of feudalism, the rise of cities, and the growth of national kingdoms all helped to centralize authority. In addition, the growing middle class usually backed monarchs, because they promised a peaceful, supportive climate for business. Monarchs used the wealth of colonies to pay for their ambitions. Church authority also broke down during the late Middle Ages and the Reformation. That opened the way for monarchs to assume even greater control. In 1576, Jean Bodin, an influential French writer, defined absolute rule:

PRIMARY SOURCE
The first characteristic of the sovereign prince is the power to make general and special laws, but—and this qualification is important—without the consent of superiors, equals, or inferiors. If the prince requires the consent of superiors, then he is a subject himself; if that of equals, he shares his authority with others; if that of his subjects, senate or people, he is not sovereign.

JEAN BODIN, *Six Books on the State*

Crises Lead to Absolutism The 17th century was a period of great upheaval in Europe. Religious and territorial conflicts between states led to almost continuous warfare. This caused governments to build huge armies and to levy even heavier taxes on an already suffering population. These pressures in turn brought about widespread unrest. Sometimes peasants revolted.

In response to these crises, monarchs tried to impose order by increasing their own power. As absolute rulers, they regulated everything from religious worship to social gatherings. They created new government bureaucracies to control their countries' economic life. Their goal was to free themselves from the limitations imposed by the nobility and by representative bodies such as Parliament. Only with such freedom could they rule absolutely, as did the most famous monarch of his time, Louis XIV of France. You'll learn more about him in the next section.

SECTION 1 ASSESSMENT

TERMS & NAMES 1. For each term or name, write a sentence explaining its significance.
• Philip II   • absolute monarch   • divine right

USING YOUR NOTES

2. Which condition is probably most necessary for a monarch to gain power? Why?

MAIN IDEAS

3. What is the significance of England's defeat of the Spanish Armada?

4. Why did the Dutch revolt against Spain?

5. Why did absolute monarchs believe that they were justified in exercising absolute power?

CRITICAL THINKING & WRITING

6. **DRAWING CONCLUSIONS** What does the art described in this section reveal about the cultures of Spain and the Netherlands?

7. **ANALYZING CAUSES** What role did religion play in the struggle between the Spanish and the Dutch?

8. **MAKING INFERENCES** How did the lack of a middle class contribute to the decline of Spain's economy?

9. **WRITING ACTIVITY** `ECONOMICS` Write a **comparison-contrast paragraph** on the economies of Spain and the Netherlands around 1600.

MULTIMEDIA ACTIVITY CREATING A GRAPH

Use the Internet to identify the religious affiliations of people in Spain and in the Netherlands today. Create a **graph** for each country showing the results of your research.

INTERNET KEYWORD
religion in Spain; religion in the Netherlands

The Reign of Louis XIV

MAIN IDEA	WHY IT MATTERS NOW	TERMS & NAMES
POWER AND AUTHORITY After a century of war and riots, France was ruled by Louis XIV, the most powerful monarch of his time.	Louis's abuse of power led to revolution that would inspire the call for democratic government throughout the world.	• Edict of Nantes • Cardinal Richelieu • skepticism • Louis XIV • intendant • Jean Baptiste Colbert • War of the Spanish Succession

SETTING THE STAGE In 1559, King Henry II of France died, leaving four young sons. Three of them ruled, one after the other, but all proved incompetent. The real power behind the throne during this period was their mother, Catherine de Médicis. Catherine tried to preserve royal authority, but growing conflicts between Catholics and Huguenots—French Protestants—rocked the country. Between 1562 and 1598, Huguenots and Catholics fought eight religious wars. Chaos spread through France.

Religious Wars and Power Struggles

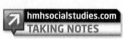
hmhsocialstudies.com
TAKING NOTES

Use the graphic organizer online to take notes on the major events of Louis XIV's reign.

In 1572, the St. Bartholomew's Day Massacre in Paris sparked a six-week, nationwide slaughter of Huguenots. The massacre occurred when many Huguenot nobles were in Paris. They were attending the marriage of Catherine's daughter to a Huguenot prince, Henry of Navarre. Most of these nobles died, but Henry survived.

Henry of Navarre Descended from the popular medieval king Louis IX, Henry was robust, athletic, and handsome. In 1589, when both Catherine and her last son died, Prince Henry inherited the throne. He became Henry IV, the first king of the Bourbon dynasty in France. As king, he showed himself to be decisive, fearless in battle, and a clever politician.

Many Catholics, including the people of Paris, opposed Henry. For the sake of his war-weary country, Henry chose to give up Protestantism and become a Catholic. Explaining his conversion, Henry reportedly declared, "Paris is well worth a mass."

In 1598, Henry took another step toward healing France's wounds. He declared that the Huguenots could live in peace in France and set up their own houses of worship in some cities. This declaration of religious toleration was called the **Edict of Nantes**.

Aided by an adviser who enacted wise financial policies, Henry devoted his reign to rebuilding France and its prosperity. He restored the French monarchy to a strong position. After a generation of war, most French people welcomed peace. Some people, however, hated Henry for his religious compromises. In 1610, a fanatic leaped into the royal carriage and stabbed Henry to death.

Louis XIII and Cardinal Richelieu After Henry IV's death, his son Louis XIII reigned. Louis was a weak king, but in 1624, he appointed a strong minister who made up for all of Louis's weaknesses.

<u>Cardinal Richelieu</u> (RIHSH•uh•LOO) became, in effect, the ruler of France. For several years, he had been a hard-working leader of the Catholic church in France. Although he tried sincerely to lead according to moral principles, he was also ambitious and enjoyed exercising authority. As Louis XIII's minister, he was able to pursue his ambitions in the political arena.

Richelieu took two steps to increase the power of the Bourbon monarchy. First, he moved against Huguenots. He believed that Protestantism often served as an excuse for political conspiracies against the Catholic king. Although Richelieu did not take away the Huguenots' right to worship, he forbade Protestant cities to have walls. He did not want them to be able to defy the king and then withdraw behind strong defenses.

Second, he sought to weaken the nobles' power. Richelieu ordered nobles to take down their fortified castles. He increased the power of government agents who came from the middle class. The king relied on these agents, so there was less need to use noble officials.

Richelieu also wanted to make France the strongest state in Europe. The greatest obstacle to this, he believed, was the Hapsburg rulers, whose lands surrounded France. The Hapsburgs ruled Spain, Austria, the Netherlands, and parts of the Holy Roman Empire. To limit Hapsburg power, Richelieu involved France in the Thirty Years' War. **A**

MAIN IDEA

Making Inferences

A How did Richelieu's actions toward Huguenots and the nobility strengthen the monarchy?

▲ Cardinal Richelieu probably had himself portrayed in a standing position in this-painting to underscore his role as ruler.

Writers Turn Toward Skepticism

As France regained political power, a new French intellectual movement developed. French thinkers had witnessed the religious wars with horror. What they saw turned them toward <u>skepticism</u>, the idea that nothing can ever be known for certain. These thinkers expressed an attitude of doubt toward churches that claimed to have the only correct set of doctrines. To doubt old ideas, skeptics thought, was the first step toward finding truth.

Montaigne and Descartes Michel de Montaigne lived during the worst years of the French religious wars. After the death of a dear friend, Montaigne thought deeply about life's meaning. To communicate his ideas, Montaigne developed a new form of literature, the essay. An essay is a brief work that expresses a person's thoughts and opinions.

In one essay, Montaigne pointed out that whenever a new belief arose, it replaced an old belief that people once accepted as truth. In the same way, he went on, the new belief would also probably be replaced by some different idea in the future. For these reasons, Montaigne believed that humans could never have absolute knowledge of what is true.

Another French writer of the time, René Descartes, was a brilliant thinker. In his *Meditations on First Philosophy,* Descartes examined the skeptical argument that one could never be certain of anything. Descartes used his observations and his reason to answer such arguments. In doing so, he created a philosophy that influenced modern thinkers and helped to develop the scientific method. Because of

Louis XIV
1638–1715

Although Louis XIV stood only 5 feet 5 inches tall, his erect and dignified posture made him appear much taller. (It also helped that he wore high-heeled shoes.)

Louis had very strong likes and dislikes. He hated cities and loved to travel through France's countryside. The people who traveled with him were at his mercy, however, for he allowed no stopping except for his own comfort.

It is small wonder that the vain Louis XIV liked to be called the Sun King. He believed that, as with the sun, all power radiated from him.

↗ **hmhsocialstudies.com**

RESEARCH WEB LINKS Go online for more on Louis XIV.

this, he became an important figure in the Enlightenment, which you will read about in Chapter 22.

Louis XIV Comes to Power

The efforts of Henry IV and Richelieu to strengthen the French monarchy paved the way for the most powerful ruler in French history—<u>Louis XIV</u>. In Louis's view, he and the state were one and the same. He reportedly boasted, *"L'état, c'est moi,"* meaning "I am the state." Although Louis XIV became the strongest king of his time, he was only a four-year-old boy when he began his reign.

Louis, the Boy King When Louis became king in 1643 after the death of his father, Louis XIII, the true ruler of France was Richelieu's successor, Cardinal Mazarin (MAZ•uh•RAN). Mazarin's greatest triumph came in 1648, with the ending of the Thirty Years' War.

Many people in France, particularly the nobles, hated Mazarin because he increased taxes and strengthened the central government. From 1648 to 1653, violent anti-Mazarin riots tore France apart. At times, the nobles who led the riots threatened the young king's life. Even after the violence was over, Louis never forgot his fear or his anger at the nobility. He determined to become so strong that they could never threaten him again.

In the end, the nobles' rebellion failed for three reasons. Its leaders distrusted one another even more than they distrusted Mazarin. In addition, the government used violent repression. Finally, peasants and townspeople grew weary of disorder and fighting. For many years afterward, the people of France accepted the oppressive laws of an absolute king. They were convinced that the alternative—rebellion—was even worse. **B**

Louis Weakens the Nobles' Authority When Cardinal Mazarin died in 1661, the 22-year-old Louis took control of the government himself. He weakened the power of the nobles by excluding them from his councils. In contrast, he increased the power of the government agents called <u>intendants</u>, who collected taxes and administered justice. To keep power under central control, he made sure that local officials communicated regularly with him.

Economic Growth Louis devoted himself to helping France attain economic, political, and cultural brilliance. No one assisted him more in achieving these goals than his minister of finance, <u>Jean Baptiste Colbert</u> (kawl•BEHR). Colbert believed in the theory of mercantilism. To prevent wealth from leaving the country, Colbert tried to make France self-sufficient. He wanted it to be able to manufacture everything it needed instead of relying on imports.

To expand manufacturing, Colbert gave government funds and tax benefits to French companies. To protect France's industries, he placed a high tariff on goods from other countries. Colbert also recognized the importance of colonies, which provided raw materials and a market for manufactured goods. The French government encouraged people to migrate to France's colony in Canada. There the fur trade added to French trade and wealth.

MAIN IDEA

Recognizing Effects

B What effects did the years of riots have on Louis XIV? on his subjects?

Vocabulary

mercantilism: the economic theory that nations should protect their home industries and export more than they import

After Colbert's death, Louis announced a policy that slowed France's economic progress. In 1685, he canceled the Edict of Nantes, which protected the religious freedom of Huguenots. In response, thousands of Huguenot artisans and business people fled the country. Louis's policy thus robbed France of many skilled workers.

The Sun King's Grand Style

In his personal finances, Louis spent a fortune to surround himself with luxury. For example, each meal was a feast. An observer claimed that the king once devoured four plates of soup, a whole pheasant, a partridge in garlic sauce, two slices of ham, a salad, a plate of pastries, fruit, and hard-boiled eggs in a single sitting! Nearly 500 cooks, waiters, and other servants worked to satisfy his tastes.

Louis Controls the Nobility Every morning, the chief valet woke Louis at 8:30. Outside the curtains of Louis's canopy bed stood at least 100 of the most privileged nobles at court. They were waiting to help the great king dress. Only four would be allowed the honor of handing Louis his slippers or holding his sleeves for him.

Meanwhile, outside the bedchamber, lesser nobles waited in the palace halls and hoped Louis would notice them. A kingly nod, a glance of approval, a kind word— these marks of royal attention determined whether a noble succeeded or failed. A duke recorded how Louis turned against nobles who did not come to court to flatter him:

▼ Though full of errors, Saint-Simon's memoirs provide valuable insight into Louis XIV's character and life at Versailles.

MAIN IDEA

Analyzing Primary Sources

C How did Louis's treatment of the nobles reflect his belief in his absolute authority?

PRIMARY SOURCE C
He looked to the right and to the left, not only upon rising but upon going to bed, at his meals, in passing through his apartments, or his gardens. . . . He marked well all absentees from the Court, found out the reason of their absence, and never lost an opportunity of acting toward them as the occasion might seem to justify. . . . When their names were in any way mentioned, "I do not know them," the King would reply haughtily.

DUKE OF SAINT-SIMON, *Memoirs of Louis XIV and the Regency*

Having the nobles at the palace increased royal authority in two ways. It made the nobility totally dependent on Louis. It also took them from their homes, thereby giving more power to the intendants. Louis required hundreds of nobles to live with him at the splendid palace he built at Versailles, about 11 miles southwest of Paris.

As you can see from the pictures on the following page, everything about the Versailles palace was immense. It faced a huge royal courtyard dominated by a statue of Louis XIV. The palace itself stretched for a distance of about 500 yards. Because of its great size, Versailles was like a small royal city. Its rich decoration and furnishings clearly showed Louis's wealth and power to everyone who came to the palace.

Patronage of the Arts Versailles was a center of the arts during Louis's reign. Louis made opera and ballet more popular. He even danced the title role in the ballet *The Sun King*. One of his favorite writers was Molière (mohl•YAIR), who wrote some of the funniest plays in French literature. Molière's comedies include *Tartuffe,* which mocks religious hypocrisy.

Not since Augustus of Rome had there been a European monarch who supported the arts as much as Louis. Under Louis, the chief purpose of art was no longer to glorify God, as it had been in the Middle Ages. Nor was its purpose to glorify human potential, as it had been in the Renaissance. Now the purpose of art was to glorify the king and promote values that supported Louis's absolute rule.

The Palace at Versailles

Louis XIV's palace at Versailles was proof of his absolute power. Only a ruler with total control over his country's economy could afford such a lavish palace. It cost an estimated $2.5 billion in 2003 dollars. Louis XIV was also able to force 36,000 laborers and 6,000 horses to work on the project.

Many people consider the Hall of Mirrors the most beautiful room in the palace. Along one wall are 17 tall mirrors. The opposite wall has 17 windows that open onto the gardens. The hall has gilded statues, crystal chandeliers, and a painted ceiling.

It took so much water to run all the fountains at once that it was done only for special events. On other days, when the king walked in the garden, servants would turn on fountains just before he reached them. The fountains were turned off after he walked away.

The gardens at Versailles remain beautiful today. Originally, Versailles was built with:
• 5,000 acres of gardens, lawns, and woods
• 1,400 fountains

SKILLBUILDER: Interpreting Visuals

1. **Analyzing Motives** *Why do you think Louis XIV believed he needed such a large and luxurious palace? Explain what practical and symbolic purposes Versailles might have served.*

2. **Developing Historical Perspective** *Consider the amount of money and effort that went into the construction of this extravagant palace. What does this reveal about the way 17th-century French society viewed its king?*

Louis Fights Disastrous Wars

Under Louis, France was the most powerful country in Europe. In 1660, France had about 20 million people. This was four times as many as England and ten times as many as the Dutch republic. The French army was far ahead of other states' armies in size, training, and weaponry.

Attempts to Expand France's Boundaries In 1667, just six years after Mazarin's death, Louis invaded the Spanish Netherlands in an effort to expand France's boundaries. Through this campaign, he gained 12 towns. Encouraged by his success, he personally led an army into the Dutch Netherlands in 1672. The Dutch saved their country by opening the dikes and flooding the countryside. This was the same tactic they had used in their revolt against Spain a century earlier. The war ended in 1678 with the Treaty of Nijmegen. France gained several towns and a region called Franche-Comté.

Louis decided to fight additional wars, but his luck had run out. By the end of the 1680s, a Europeanwide alliance had formed to stop France. By banding together, weaker countries could match France's strength. This defensive strategy was meant to achieve a balance of power, in which no single country or group of countries could dominate others.

In 1689, the Dutch prince William of Orange became the king of England. He joined the League of Augsburg, which consisted of the Austrian Hapsburg emperor, the kings of Sweden and Spain, and the leaders of several smaller European states. Together, these countries equaled France's strength.

MAIN IDEA

Recognizing Effects

D How did Louis's wars against weaker countries backfire?

France at this time had been weakened by a series of poor harvests. That, added to the constant warfare, brought great suffering to the French people. So, too, did new taxes, which Louis imposed to finance his wars. **D**

War of the Spanish Succession Tired of hardship, the French people longed for peace. What they got was another war. In 1700, the childless king of Spain, Charles II, died after promising his throne to Louis XIV's 16-year-old grandson, Philip of Anjou. The two greatest powers in Europe, enemies for so long, were now both ruled by the French Bourbons.

Other countries felt threatened by this increase in the Bourbon dynasty's power. In 1701, England, Austria, the Dutch Republic, Portugal, and several German and Italian states joined together to prevent the union of the French and Spanish thrones. The long struggle that followed is known as the **War of the Spanish Succession**.

The costly war dragged on until 1714. The Treaty of Utrecht was signed in that year. Under its terms, Louis's grandson was allowed to remain king of Spain so long as the thrones of France and Spain were not united.

The big winner in the war was Great Britain. From Spain, Britain took Gibraltar, a fortress that controlled the entrance to the Mediterranean. Spain also granted a British company an *asiento*, permission to send enslaved Africans to Spain's American colonies. This increased Britain's involvement in trading enslaved Africans.

▼ The painting below shows the Battle of Denain, one of the last battles fought during the War of the Spanish Succession.

Debt of the Royal Family, 1643–1715

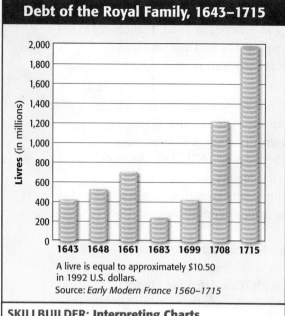

A livre is equal to approximately $10.50 in 1992 U.S. dollars.

Source: *Early Modern France 1560–1715*

SKILLBUILDER: Interpreting Charts

1. **Comparing** How many times greater was the royal debt in 1715 than in 1643?
2. **Synthesizing** What was the royal debt of 1715 equal to in 1992 dollars?

In addition, France gave Britain the North American territories of Nova Scotia and Newfoundland, and abandoned claims to the Hudson Bay region. The Austrian Hapsburgs took the Spanish Netherlands and other Spanish lands in Italy. Prussia and Savoy were recognized as kingdoms.

Louis's Death and Legacy Louis's last years were more sad than glorious. Realizing that his wars had ruined France, he regretted the suffering he had brought to his people. He died in bed in 1715. News of his death prompted rejoicing throughout France. The people had had enough of the Sun King.

Louis left a mixed legacy to his country. On the positive side, France was certainly a power to be reckoned with in Europe. France ranked above all other European nations in art, literature, and statesmanship during Louis's reign. In addition, France was considered the military leader of Europe. This military might allowed France to develop a strong empire of colonies, which provided resources and goods for trade.

On the negative side, constant warfare and the construction of the Palace of Versailles plunged France into staggering debt. Also, resentment over the tax burden imposed on the poor and Louis's abuse of power would plague his heirs—and eventually lead to revolution.

Absolute rule didn't die with Louis XIV. His enemies in Prussia and Austria had been experimenting with their own forms of absolute monarchy, as you will learn in Section 3.

SECTION 2 ASSESSMENT

TERMS & NAMES 1. For each term or name, write a sentence explaining its significance.
• Edict of Nantes • Cardinal Richelieu • skepticism • Louis XIV • intendant • Jean Baptiste Colbert • War of the Spanish Succession

USING YOUR NOTES

2. Which events on your time line strengthened the French monarchy? Which weakened it?

MAIN IDEAS

3. What impact did the French religious wars have on French thinkers?

4. How did Jean Baptiste Colbert intend to stimulate economic growth in France?

5. What was the result of the War of the Spanish Succession?

CRITICAL THINKING & WRITING

6. **SUPPORTING OPINIONS** Many historians think of Louis XIV as the perfect example of an absolute monarch. Do you agree? Explain why or why not.

7. **RECOGNIZING EFFECTS** How did the policies of Colbert and Louis XIV affect the French economy? Explain both positive and negative effects.

8. **SYNTHESIZING** To what extent did anti-Protestantism contribute to Louis's downfall?

9. **WRITING ACTIVITY** POWER AND AUTHORITY Write a **character sketch** of Louis XIV. Discuss his experiences and character traits.

CONNECT TO TODAY CREATING AN ORAL PRESENTATION
Research to find out what happened to Versailles after Louis's death and what its function is today. Then present your findings in an **oral presentation.**

Central European Monarchs Clash

MAIN IDEA	WHY IT MATTERS NOW	TERMS & NAMES
POWER AND AUTHORITY After a period of turmoil, absolute monarchs ruled Austria and the Germanic state of Prussia.	Prussia built a strong military tradition in Germany that contributed in part to world wars in the 20th century.	• Thirty Years' War • Maria Theresa • Frederick the Great • Seven Years' War

SETTING THE STAGE For a brief while, the German rulers appeared to have settled their religious differences through the Peace of Augsburg (1555). They had agreed that the faith of each prince would determine the religion of his subjects. Churches in Germany could be either Lutheran or Catholic, but not Calvinist. The peace was short-lived—soon to be replaced by a long war. After the Peace of Augsburg, the Catholic and Lutheran princes of Germany watched each other suspiciously.

The Thirty Years' War

Both the Lutheran and the Catholic princes tried to gain followers. In addition, both sides felt threatened by Calvinism, which was spreading in Germany and gaining many followers. As tension mounted, the Lutherans joined together in the Protestant Union in 1608. The following year, the Catholic princes formed the Catholic League. Now, it would take only a spark to set off a war.

Bohemian Protestants Revolt That spark came in 1618. The future Holy Roman emperor, Ferdinand II, was head of the Hapsburg family. As such, he ruled the Czech kingdom of Bohemia. The Protestants in Bohemia did not trust Ferdinand, who was a foreigner and a Catholic. When he closed some Protestant churches, the Protestants revolted. Ferdinand sent an army into Bohemia to crush the revolt. Several German Protestant princes took this chance to challenge their Catholic emperor.

Thus began the **Thirty Years' War**, a conflict over religion and territory and for power among European ruling families. The war can be divided into two main phases: the phase of Hapsburg triumphs and the phase of Hapsburg defeats.

Hapsburg Triumphs The Thirty Years' War lasted from 1618 to 1648. During the first 12 years, Hapsburg armies from Austria and Spain crushed the troops hired by the Protestant princes. They succeeded in putting down the Czech uprising. They also defeated the German Protestants who had supported the Czechs.

Ferdinand II paid his army of 125,000 men by allowing them to plunder, or rob, German villages. This huge army destroyed everything in its path.

Hapsburg Defeats The Hapsburg triumph would not last. In 1630, the Protestant Gustavus Adolphus of Sweden and his army shifted the tide of war.

> **hmhsocialstudies.com**
> **TAKING NOTES**
> Use the graphic organizer online to take notes on the reigns of Maria Theresa and Frederick the Great.

They drove the Hapsburg armies out of northern Germany. However, Gustavus Adolphus was killed in battle in 1632.

Cardinal Richelieu and Cardinal Mazarin of France dominated the remaining years of the war. Although Catholic, these two cardinals feared the Hapsburgs more than the Protestants. They did not want other European rulers to have as much power as the French king. Therefore, in 1635, Richelieu sent French troops to join the German and Swedish Protestants in their struggle against the Hapsburg armies.

Peace of Westphalia The war did great damage to Germany. Its population dropped from 20 million to about 16 million. Both trade and agriculture were disrupted, and Germany's economy was ruined. Germany had a long, difficult recovery from this devastation. That is a major reason it did not become a unified state until the 1800s.

The Peace of Westphalia (1648) ended the war. The treaty had these important consequences:

- weakened the Hapsburg states of Spain and Austria;
- strengthened France by awarding it German territory;
- made German princes independent of the Holy Roman emperor;
- ended religious wars in Europe;
- introduced a new method of peace negotiation whereby all participants meet to settle the problems of a war and decide the terms of peace. This method is still used today. **A**

Beginning of Modern States The treaty thus abandoned the idea of a Catholic empire that would rule most of Europe. It recognized Europe as a group of equal, independent states. This marked the beginning of the modern state system and was the most important result of the Thirty Years' War.

MAIN IDEA

Drawing Conclusions

A Judging from their actions, do you think the two French cardinals were motivated more by religion or politics? Why?

Europe After the Thirty Years' War, 1648

hmhsocialstudies.com INTERACTIVE MAP

— The Holy Roman Empire

Population Losses

- Up to 15%
- 15–33%
- 34–66%
- Over 66%
- — The Holy Roman Empire

GEOGRAPHY SKILLBUILDER: Interpreting Maps

1. **Place** Name at least five modern European countries that existed at the end of the Thirty Years' War.
2. **Region** Refer to the inset map. Which regions lost the most population in the Thirty Years' War?

604

States Form in Central Europe

Strong states formed more slowly in central Europe than in western Europe. The major powers of this region were the kingdom of Poland, the Holy Roman Empire, and the Ottoman Empire. None of them was very strong in the mid-1600s.

Economic Contrasts with the West One reason for this is that the economy of central Europe developed differently from that of western Europe. During the late Middle Ages, serfs in western Europe slowly won freedom and moved to towns. There, they joined middle-class townspeople, who gained economic power because of the commercial revolution and the development of capitalism.

By contrast, the landowning aristocracy in central Europe passed laws restricting the ability of serfs to gain freedom and move to cities. These nobles wanted to keep the serfs on the land, where they could produce large harvests. The nobles could then sell the surplus crops to western European cities at great profit.

Several Weak Empires The landowning nobles in central Europe not only held down the serfs but also blocked the development of strong kings. For example, the Polish nobility elected the Polish king and sharply limited his power. They allowed the king little income, no law courts, and no standing army. As a result, there was not a strong ruler who could form a unified state.

The two empires of central Europe were also weak. Although Suleyman the Magnificent had conquered Hungary and threatened Vienna in 1529, the Ottoman Empire could not take its European conquest any farther. From then on, the Ottoman Empire declined from its peak of power.

In addition, the Holy Roman Empire was seriously weakened by the Thirty Years' War. No longer able to command the obedience of the German states, the Holy Roman Empire had no real power. These old, weakened empires and kingdoms left a power vacuum in central Europe. In the late 1600s, two German-speaking families decided to try to fill this vacuum by becoming absolute rulers themselves.

Austria Grows Stronger One of these families was the Hapsburgs of Austria. The Austrian Hapsburgs took several steps to become absolute monarchs. First, during the Thirty Years' War, they reconquered Bohemia. The Hapsburgs wiped out Protestantism there and created a new Czech nobility that pledged loyalty to them. Second, after the war, the Hapsburg ruler centralized the government and created a standing army. Third, by 1699, the Hapsburgs had retaken Hungary from the Ottoman Empire.

In 1711, Charles VI became the Hapsburg ruler. Charles's empire was a difficult one to rule. Within its borders lived a diverse assortment of people—Czechs, Hungarians, Italians, Croatians, and Germans. Only the fact that one Hapsburg ruler wore the Austrian, Hungarian, and Bohemian crowns kept the empire together.

Maria Theresa Inherits the Austrian Throne How could the Hapsburgs make sure that they continued to rule all those lands? Charles VI spent his entire reign working out an answer to this problem. With endless arm-twisting, he persuaded other leaders of Europe to sign an agreement that declared they would recognize Charles's eldest daughter as the heir to all his Hapsburg territories. That heir was a young woman named <u>**Maria Theresa**</u>. In theory, this agreement guaranteed Maria Theresa a peaceful reign. Instead, she faced years of war. Her main enemy was Prussia, a state to the north of Austria. (See map opposite.)

▼ The imperial crest of the Hapsburgs shows a double-headed eagle with a crown.

History Makers

Maria Theresa
1717–1780

An able ruler, Maria Theresa also devoted herself to her children, whom she continued to advise even after they were grown. Perhaps her most famous child was Marie Antoinette, wife of Louis XVI of France.

As the Austrian empress, Maria Theresa decreased the power of the nobility. She also limited the amount of labor that nobles could force peasants to do. She argued: "The peasantry must be able to sustain itself."

Frederick the Great
1712–1786

Although they reigned during the same time, Frederick the Great and Maria Theresa were very different. Where Maria was religious, Frederick was practical and atheistic. Maria Theresa had a happy home life and a huge family, while Frederick died without a son to succeed him.

An aggressor in foreign affairs, Frederick once wrote that "the fundamental role of governments is the principle of extending their territories." Frederick earned the title "the Great" by achieving his goals for Prussia.

↗ hmhsocialstudies.com

INTERNET ACTIVITY Go online to create a family tree showing Maria Theresa's parents and children.

Prussia Challenges Austria

Like Austria, Prussia rose to power in the late 1600s. Like the Hapsburgs of Austria, Prussia's ruling family, the Hohenzollerns, also had ambitions. Those ambitions threatened to upset central Europe's delicate balance of power.

The Rise of Prussia The Hohenzollerns built up their state from a number of small holdings, beginning with the German states of Brandenburg and Prussia. In 1640, a 20-year-old Hohenzollern named Frederick William inherited the title of elector of Brandenburg. After seeing the destruction of the Thirty Years' War, Frederick William, later known as the Great Elector, decided that having a strong army was the only way to ensure safety.

To protect their lands, the Great Elector and his descendants moved toward absolute monarchy. They created a standing army, the best in Europe. They built it to a force of 80,000 men. To pay for the army, they introduced permanent taxation. Beginning with the Great Elector's son, they called themselves kings. They also weakened the representative assemblies of their territories.

Prussia's landowning nobility, the Junkers (YUNG•kuhrz), resisted the king's growing power. However, in the early 1700s, King Frederick William I bought their cooperation. He gave the Junkers the exclusive right to be officers in his army. As a result, Prussia became a rigidly controlled, highly militarized society. **B**

Frederick the Great Frederick William worried that his son, Frederick, was not military enough to rule. The prince loved music, philosophy, and poetry. In 1730, when he and a friend tried to run away, they were caught. To punish Frederick, the king ordered him to witness his friend's beheading. Despite such bitter memories, Frederick II, known as **Frederick the Great**, followed his father's military policies when he came to power. However, he also softened some of his father's laws. With regard to domestic affairs, he encouraged religious toleration and legal reform. According to his theory of government, Frederick believed that a ruler should be like a father to his people:

MAIN IDEA

Clarifying

B What steps did the Prussian monarchs take to become absolute monarchs?

PRIMARY SOURCE
A prince . . . is only the first servant of the state, who is obliged to act with probity [honesty] and prudence. . . . As the sovereign is properly the head of a family of citizens, the father of his people, he ought on all occasions to be the last refuge of the unfortunate.

FREDERICK II, *Essay on Forms of Government*

War of the Austrian Succession In 1740, Maria Theresa succeeded her father, just five months after Frederick II became king of Prussia. Frederick wanted the Austrian land of Silesia, which bordered Prussia. Silesia produced iron ore, textiles, and food products. Frederick underestimated Maria Theresa's strength. He assumed that because she was a woman, she would not be forceful enough to defend her lands. In 1740, he sent his army to occupy Silesia, beginning the War of the Austrian Succession. **C**

MAIN IDEA

Clarifying

C Why would iron ore, agricultural lands, and textiles be helpful acquisitions for Frederick the Great?

Even though Maria Theresa had recently given birth, she journeyed to Hungary. There she held her infant in her arms as she asked the Hungarian nobles for aid. Even though the nobles resented their Hapsburg rulers, they pledged to give Maria Theresa an army. Great Britain also joined Austria to fight its longtime enemy France, which was Prussia's ally. Although Maria Theresa did stop Prussia's aggression, she lost Silesia in the Treaty of Aix-la-Chapelle in 1748. With the acquisition of Silesia, Prussia became a major European power.

The Seven Years' War Maria Theresa decided that the French kings were no longer Austria's chief enemies. She made an alliance with them. The result was a diplomatic revolution. When Frederick heard of her actions, he signed a treaty with Britain—Austria's former ally. Now, Austria, France, Russia, and others were allied against Britain and Prussia. Not only had Austria and Prussia switched allies, but for the first time, Russia was playing a role in European affairs.

In 1756, Frederick attacked Saxony, an Austrian ally. Soon every great European power was involved in the war. Fought in Europe, India, and North America, the war lasted until 1763. It was called the **Seven Years' War**. The war did not change the territorial situation in Europe.

It was a different story on other continents. Both France and Britain had colonies in North America and the West Indies. Both were competing economically in India. The British emerged as the real victors in the Seven Years' War. France lost its colonies in North America, and Britain gained sole economic domination of India. This set the stage for further British expansion in India in the 1800s, as you will see in Chapter 27.

SECTION 3 ASSESSMENT

TERMS & NAMES 1. For each term or name, write a sentence explaining its significance.
• Thirty Years' War   • Maria Theresa   • Frederick the Great   • Seven Years' War

USING YOUR NOTES	MAIN IDEAS	CRITICAL THINKING & WRITING
2. In what ways were the rulers similar?	3. What were the major conflicts in the Thirty Years' War? 4. What steps did the Austrian Hapsburgs take toward becoming absolute monarchs? 5. What countries were allies during the Seven Years' War?	6. **RECOGNIZING EFFECTS** How did the Peace of Westphalia lay the foundations of modern Europe? 7. **ANALYZING MOTIVES** Why did Maria Theresa make an alliance with the French kings, Austria's chief enemies? 8. **DRAWING CONCLUSIONS** Based on Frederick's assumption about Maria Theresa at the outset of the War of the Austrian Succession, what conclusions can you draw about how men viewed women in 1700s Europe? 9. **WRITING ACTIVITY** POWER AND AUTHORITY Write an **outline** for a lecture on "How to Increase Royal Power and Become an Absolute Monarch."

The note table contains:

Maria Theresa	Frederick the Great

CONNECT TO TODAY   CREATING A POSTER

Today much of western Europe belongs to an organization called the European Union (EU). Find out which countries belong to the EU and how they are linked economically and politically. Present your findings—including maps, charts, and pictures—in a **poster**.

Absolute Rulers of Russia

MAIN IDEA	WHY IT MATTERS NOW	TERMS & NAMES
POWER AND AUTHORITY Peter the Great made many changes in Russia to try to make it more like western Europe.	Many Russians today debate whether to model themselves on the West or to focus on traditional Russian culture.	• Ivan the Terrible • Peter the Great • boyar • westernization

SETTING THE STAGE Ivan III of Moscow, who ruled Russia from 1462 to 1505, accomplished several things. First, he conquered much of the territory around Moscow. Second, he liberated Russia from the Mongols. Third, he began to centralize the Russian government. Ivan III was succeeded by his son, Vasily, who ruled for 28 years. Vasily continued his father's work of adding territory to the growing Russian state. He also increased the power of the central government. This trend continued under his son, Ivan IV, who would become an absolute ruler.

The First Czar

hmhsocialstudies.com
TAKING NOTES

Use the graphic organizer online to take notes on the important events of Peter the Great's reign.

Ivan IV, called **Ivan the Terrible**, came to the throne in 1533 when he was only three years old. His young life was disrupted by struggles for power among Russia's landowning nobles, known as **boyars**. The boyars fought to control young Ivan. When he was 16, Ivan seized power and had himself crowned czar. This title meant "caesar," and Ivan was the first Russian ruler to use it officially. He also married the beautiful Anastasia, related to an old boyar family, the Romanovs.

The years from 1547 to 1560 are often called Ivan's "good period." He won great victories, added lands to Russia, gave Russia a code of laws, and ruled justly.

Rule by Terror Ivan's "bad period" began in 1560 after Anastasia died. Accusing the boyars of poisoning his wife, Ivan turned against them. He organized his own police force, whose chief duty was to hunt down and murder people Ivan considered traitors. The members of this police force dressed in black and rode black horses.

Using these secret police, Ivan executed many boyars, their families, and the peasants who worked their lands. Thousands of people died. Ivan seized the boyars' estates and gave them to a new class of nobles, who had to remain loyal to him or lose their land.

Eventually, Ivan committed an act that was both a personal tragedy and a national disaster. In 1581, during a violent quarrel, he killed his oldest son and heir. When Ivan died three years later, only his weak second son was left to rule.

Rise of the Romanovs Ivan's son proved to be physically and mentally incapable of ruling. After he died without an heir, Russia experienced a period of

MAIN IDEA

Recognizing Effects

A What were the long-term effects of Ivan's murder of his oldest son?

turmoil known as the Time of Troubles. Boyars struggled for power, and heirs of czars died under mysterious conditions. Several impostors tried to claim the throne.

Finally, in 1613, representatives from many Russian cities met to choose the next czar. Their choice was Michael Romanov, grandnephew of Ivan the Terrible's wife, Anastasia. Thus began the Romanov dynasty, which ruled Russia for 300 years (1613–1917). **A**

Peter the Great Comes to Power

Over time, the Romanovs restored order to Russia. They strengthened government by passing a law code and putting down a revolt. This paved the way for the absolute rule of Czar Peter I. At first, Peter shared the throne with his half-brother. However, in 1696, Peter became sole ruler of Russia. He is known to history as <u>Peter the Great</u>, because he was one of Russia's greatest reformers. He also continued the trend of increasing the czar's power.

Russia Contrasts with Europe When Peter I came to power, Russia was still a land of boyars and serfs. Serfdom in Russia lasted into the mid-1800s, much longer than it did in western Europe. Russian landowners wanted serfs to stay on the land and produce large harvests. The landowners treated the serfs like property. When a Russian landowner sold a piece of land, he sold the serfs with it. Landowners could give away serfs as presents or to pay debts. It was also against the law for serfs to run away from their owners.

Most boyars knew little of western Europe. In the Middle Ages, Russia had looked to Constantinople, not to Rome, for leadership. Then Mongol rule had cut Russia off from the Renaissance and the Age of Exploration. Geographic barriers also isolated Russia. Its only seaport, Archangel in northern Russia, was choked with ice much of the year. The few travelers who reached Moscow were usually Dutch or German, and they had to stay in a separate part of the city.

Religious differences widened the gap between western Europe and Russia. The Russians had adopted the Eastern Orthodox branch of Christianity. Western Europeans were mostly Catholics or Protestants, and the Russians viewed them as heretics and avoided them. **B**

MAIN IDEA

Summarizing

B Why was Russia culturally different from western Europe?

Peter Visits the West In the 1680s, people in the German quarter of Moscow were accustomed to seeing the young Peter striding through their neighborhood on his long legs. (Peter was more than six and a half feet tall.) He was fascinated by the modern tools and machines in the foreigners' shops. Above all, he had a passion for ships and the sea. The young czar believed that Russia's future depended on having a warm-water port. Only then could Russia compete with the more modern states of western Europe.

Peter was 24 years old when he became the sole ruler of Russia. In 1697, just one year later, he embarked on the "Grand Embassy," a long visit to western Europe. One of Peter's goals was to learn about European customs and manufacturing techniques. Never before had a czar traveled among Western "heretics."

VIDEO
Peter the Great:
The Tyrant Reformer

↗ hmhsocialstudies.com

History Makers

Peter the Great
1672–1725

Peter the Great had the mind of a genius, the body of a giant, and the ferocious temper of a bear. He was so strong that he was known to take a heavy silver plate and roll it up as if it were a piece of paper. If someone annoyed him, he would knock the offender unconscious.

The painting above represents Peter as he looked when he traveled through western Europe. He dressed in the plain clothes of an ordinary worker to keep his identity a secret.

↗ hmhsocialstudies.com

RESEARCH WEB LINKS Go online for more on Peter the Great.

Peter Rules Absolutely

Inspired by his trip to the West, Peter resolved that Russia would compete with Europe on both military and commercial terms. Peter's goal of **westernization**, of using western Europe as a model for change, was not an end in itself. Peter saw it as a way to make Russia stronger.

Peter's Reforms Although Peter believed Russia needed to change, he knew that many of his people disagreed. As he said to one official, "For you know yourself that, though a thing be good and necessary, our people will not do it unless forced to." To force change upon his state, Peter increased his powers as an absolute ruler. **C**

Peter brought the Russian Orthodox Church under state control. He abolished the office of patriarch, head of the Church. He set up a group called the Holy Synod to run the Church under his direction.

Like Ivan the Terrible, Peter reduced the power of the great landowners. He recruited men from lower-ranking families. He then promoted them to positions of authority and rewarded them with grants of land.

To modernize his army, Peter hired European officers, who drilled his soldiers in European tactics with European weapons. Being a soldier became a lifetime job. By the time of Peter's death, the Russian army numbered 200,000 men. To pay for this huge army, Peter imposed heavy taxes.

Westernizing Russia As part of his attempts to westernize Russia, Peter undertook the following:

- introduced potatoes, which became a staple of the Russian diet
- started Russia's first newspaper and edited its first issue himself
- raised women's status by having them attend social gatherings
- ordered the nobles to give up their traditional clothes for Western fashions
- advanced education by opening a school of navigation and introducing schools for the arts and sciences

MAIN IDEA

Analyzing Bias

C Judging from this remark, what was Peter's view of his people?

The Expansion of Russia, 1500–1800

hmhsocialstudies.com INTERACTIVE MAP

1462	Acquisitions to 1682
Acquisitions to 1505	Acquisitions to 1725
Acquisitions to 1584	Acquisitions to 1796

ARCTIC OCEAN

Arctic Circle

FINLAND

SWEDEN

St. Petersburg

Novgorod

Baltic Sea

Moscow

Warsaw

Kiev

POLAND

Dniester R.

AUSTRIA

Azov

Constantinople

Black Sea

OTTOMAN EMPIRE

Caspian Sea

Mediterranean Sea

RUSSIA

Volga R.

Ural R.

Ob R.

Yenisei R.

Tomsk

Irkutsk

MONGOLIA

Lena R.

Yakutsk

Amur R.

Nerchinsk

MANCHURIA

Okhotsk

Sea of Okhotsk

PACIFIC OCEAN

N

0   1,000 Miles

0   2,000 Kilometers

GEOGRAPHY SKILLBUILDER: Interpreting Maps

1. **Location** *Locate the territories that Peter added to Russia during his reign, from 1682 to 1725. What bodies of water did Russia gain access to because of these acquisitions?*

2. **Region** *Who added a larger amount of territory to Russia—Ivan III, who ruled from 1462 to 1505, or Peter the Great?*

Peter believed that education was a key to Russia's progress. In former times, subjects were forbidden under pain of death to study the sciences in foreign lands. Now subjects were not only permitted to leave the country, many were forced to do it.

Establishing St. Petersburg To promote education and growth, Peter wanted a seaport that would make it easier to travel to the West. Therefore, Peter fought Sweden to gain a piece of the Baltic coast. After 21 long years of war, Russia finally won the "window on Europe" that Peter had so desperately wanted.

Actually, Peter had secured that window many years before Sweden officially surrendered it. In 1703, he began building a new city on Swedish lands occupied by Russian troops. Although the swampy site was unhealthful, it seemed ideal to Peter. Ships could sail down the Neva River into the Baltic Sea and on to western Europe. Peter called the city St. Petersburg, after his patron saint.

To build a city on a desolate swamp was no easy matter. Every summer, the army forced thousands of luckless serfs to leave home and work in St. Petersburg. An estimated 25,000 to 100,000 people died from the terrible working conditions and widespread diseases. When St. Petersburg was finished, Peter ordered many Russian nobles to leave the comforts of Moscow and settle in his new capital. In time, St. Petersburg became a busy port. **D**

For better or for worse, Peter the Great had tried to westernize and reform the culture and government of Russia. To an amazing extent he had succeeded. By the time of his death in 1725, Russia was a power to be reckoned with in Europe. Meanwhile, another great European power, England, had been developing a form of government that limited the power of absolute monarchs, as you will see in Section 5.

MAIN IDEA

Synthesizing

D Which of Peter's actions in building St. Petersburg show his power as an absolute monarch?

Global Patterns

East Meets West

In the East, Western influence would affect not only Russia. Other eastern nations would give way—not always willingly—to the West and Western culture. In 1854, Japan was forced to open its doors to the United States. By 1867, however, Japan had decided to embrace Western civilization. The Japanese modernized their military based on the German and British models. They also adopted the American system of public education. China and Korea, on the other hand, would resist foreign intervention well into the 1900s.

SECTION 4 ASSESSMENT

TERMS & NAMES 1. For each term or name, write a sentence explaining its significance.
• Ivan the Terrible   • boyar   • Peter the Great   • westernization

USING YOUR NOTES

2. Which event had the most impact on modern Russia? Why?

Peter the Great

MAIN IDEAS

3. How did Ivan the Terrible deal with his enemies during his "bad period"?

4. Why did Peter the Great believe that Russia's future depended on having a warm-water port?

5. What were some of the ways Peter tried to westernize Russia?

CRITICAL THINKING & WRITING

6. **SUPPORTING OPINIONS** Who do you think was more of an absolute monarch: Ivan the Terrible or Peter the Great?

7. **DRAWING CONCLUSIONS** Which class of Russian society probably didn't benefit from Peter's reforms? Why?

8. **HYPOTHESIZING** How might Peter's attempts at westernization have affected his people's opinion of Christians in western Europe?

9. **WRITING ACTIVITY** POWER AND AUTHORITY Write a one-paragraph **expository essay** explaining which of Peter the Great's actions reveal that he saw himself as the highest authority in Russia.

CONNECT TO TODAY STAGING A DEBATE

Peter the Great's reforms were a first step toward Russia's westernization. Today the country continues the process by experimenting with democratization. Research to find out how Russia has fared as a democracy. Then stage a **debate** to argue whether the experiment is working.

Surviving the Russian Winter

Much of Russia has severe winters. In Moscow, snow usually begins to fall in mid-October and lasts until mid-April. Siberia has been known to have temperatures as low as -90°F. Back in the 18th century, Russians did not have down parkas or high-tech insulation for their homes. But they had other ways to cope with the climate.

For example, in the 18th century, Russian peasants added potatoes and corn to their diet. During the winter, these nutritious foods were used in soups and stews. Such dishes were warming and provided plenty of calories to help fight off the cold.

↗ hmhsocialstudies.com

RESEARCH WEB LINKS Go online for more on Russian winters.

Silver Samovar ▶
In the mid-18th century, samovars were invented in Russia. These large, often elaborately decorated urns were used to boil water for tea. Fire was kept burning in a tube running up the middle of the urn—keeping the water piping hot.

◄ Crimean Dress
These people are wearing the traditional dress of tribes from the Crimean Peninsula, a region that Russia took over in the 1700s. Notice the heavy hats, the fur trim on some of the robes, and the leggings worn by those with shorter robes. All these features help to conserve body heat.

▼ Troika
To travel in winter, the wealthy often used sleighs called troikas. *Troika* means "group of three"; the name comes from the three horses that draw this kind of sleigh. The middle horse trotted while the two outside horses galloped.

Winter Festival ▶

Russians have never let their climate stop them from having fun outdoors. Here, they are shown enjoying a Shrovetide festival, which occurs near the end of winter. Vendors sold food such as blinis (pancakes with sour cream). Entertainments included ice skating, dancing bears, and magic shows.

The people in the foreground are wearing heavy fur coats. Otter fur was often used for winter clothing. This fur is extremely thick and has about one million hairs per square inch.

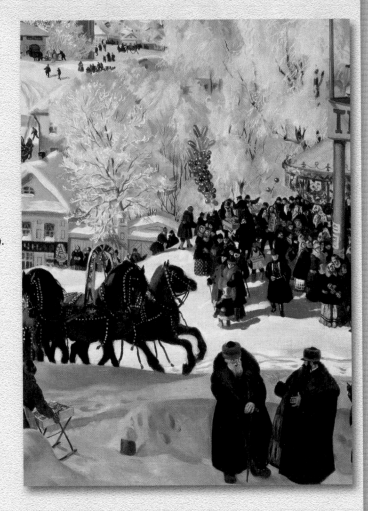

▼ Wooden House

Wooden houses, made of logs, were common in Russia during Peter the Great's time. To insulate the house from the wind, people stuffed moss between the logs. Russians used double panes of glass in their windows. For extra protection, many houses had shutters to cover the windows. The roofs were steep so snow would slide off.

> **DATA FILE**

FROSTY FACTS

- According to a 2001 estimate, Russian women spend about $500 million a year on fur coats and caps.

- The record low temperature in Asia of -90°F was reached twice, first in Verkhoyansk, Russia, in 1892 and then in Oimekon, Russia, in 1933.

- The record low temperature in Europe of -67°F was recorded in Ust'Shchugor, Russia.

- One reason for Russia's cold climate is that most of the country lies north of the 45° latitude line, closer to the North Pole than to the Equator.

Average High Temperature for January, Russian Cities

21°F	12°F	29°F
Moscow, Russia	Perm, Russia	Rostov, Russia

Source: *Worldclimate.com*

Average High Temperature for January, U.S. Cities

66°F	21°F	38°F
Los Angeles, California	Minneapolis, Minnesota	New York, New York

Source: *Worldclimate.com*

Connect *to* Today

1. **Making Inferences** In the 18th century, how did Russians use their natural resources to help them cope with the climate?

    See Skillbuilder Handbook, page R10.

2. **Comparing and Contrasting** How has coping with winter weather changed from 18th-century Russia to today's world? How has it stayed the same?

Parliament Limits the English Monarchy

MAIN IDEA	WHY IT MATTERS NOW	TERMS & NAMES
REVOLUTION Absolute rulers in England were overthrown, and Parliament gained power.	Many of the government reforms of this period contributed to the democratic tradition of the United States.	• Charles I • English Civil War • Oliver Cromwell • Restoration • *habeas corpus*	• Glorious Revolution • constitutional monarchy • cabinet

SETTING THE STAGE During her reign, Queen Elizabeth I of England had had frequent conflicts with Parliament. Many of the arguments were over money, because the treasury did not have enough funds to pay the queen's expenses. By the time Elizabeth died in 1603, she had left a huge debt for her successor to deal with. Parliament's financial power was one obstacle to English rulers' becoming absolute monarchs. The resulting struggle between Parliament and the monarchy would have serious consequences for England.

Monarchs Defy Parliament

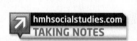
TAKING NOTES

Use the graphic organizer online to take notes on the causes of James I's, Charles I's, and James II's conflicts with Parliament.

Elizabeth had no child, and her nearest relative was her cousin, James Stuart. Already king of Scotland, James Stuart became King James I of England in 1603. Although England and Scotland were not united until 1707, they now shared a ruler.

James's Problems James inherited the unsettled issues of Elizabeth's reign. His worst struggles with Parliament were over money. In addition, James offended the Puritan members of Parliament. The Puritans hoped he would enact reforms to purify the English church of Catholic practices. Except for agreeing to a new translation of the Bible, however, he refused to make Puritan reforms.

Charles I Fights Parliament In 1625, James I died. <u>Charles I</u>, his son, took the throne. Charles always needed money, in part because he was at war with both Spain and France. Several times when Parliament refused to give him funds, he dissolved it.

By 1628, Charles was forced to call Parliament again. This time it refused to grant him any money until he signed a document that is known as the Petition of Right. In this petition, the king agreed to four points:
• He would not imprison subjects without due cause.
• He would not levy taxes without Parliament's consent.
• He would not house soldiers in private homes.
• He would not impose martial law in peacetime.

After agreeing to the petition, Charles ignored it. Even so, the petition was important. It set forth the idea that the law was higher than the king. This idea contradicted theories of absolute monarchy. In 1629, Charles dissolved Parliament and refused to call it back into session. To get money, he imposed all kinds of fees and fines on the English people. His popularity decreased year by year.

English Civil War

Charles offended Puritans by upholding the rituals of the Anglican Church. In addition, in 1637, Charles tried to force the Presbyterian Scots to accept a version of the Anglican prayer book. He wanted both his kingdoms to follow one religion. The Scots rebelled, assembled a huge army, and threatened to invade England. To meet this danger, Charles needed money—money he could get only by calling Parliament into session. This gave Parliament a chance to oppose him.

War Topples a King During the autumn of 1641, Parliament passed laws to limit royal power. Furious, Charles tried to arrest Parliament's leaders in January 1642, but they escaped. Equally furious, a mob of Londoners raged outside the palace. Charles fled London and raised an army in the north of England, where people were loyal to him.

From 1642 to 1649, supporters and opponents of King Charles fought the **English Civil War**. Those who remained loyal to Charles were called Royalists or Cavaliers. On the other side were Puritan supporters of Parliament. Because these men wore their hair short over their ears, Cavaliers called them Roundheads.

At first neither side could gain a lasting advantage. However, by 1644 the Puritans found a general who could win—**Oliver Cromwell**. In 1645, Cromwell's New Model Army began defeating the Cavaliers, and the tide turned toward the Puritans. In 1647, they held the king prisoner.

In 1649, Cromwell and the Puritans brought Charles to trial for treason against Parliament. They found him guilty and sentenced him to death. The execution of Charles was revolutionary. Kings had often been overthrown, killed in battle, or put to death in secret. Never before, however, had a reigning monarch faced a public trial and execution.

Cromwell's Rule Cromwell now held the reins of power. In 1649, he abolished the monarchy and the House of Lords. He established a commonwealth, a republican form of government. In 1653, Cromwell sent home the remaining members of Parliament. Cromwell's associate John Lambert drafted a constitution, the first written constitution of any modern European state. However, Cromwell eventually tore up the document and became a military dictator. **A**

Cromwell almost immediately had to put down a rebellion in Ireland. English colonization of Ireland had begun in the 1100s under Henry II. Henry VIII and his children had brought the country firmly under English rule in the 1500s. In 1649, Cromwell landed on Irish shores with an army and crushed the uprising. He seized the lands and homes of the Irish and gave them to English soldiers. Fighting, plague, and famine killed hundreds of thousands.

Puritan Morality In England, Cromwell and the Puritans sought to reform society. They made laws that promoted Puritan morality and abolished activities they found sinful, such as the theater, sporting events, and dancing. Although he was a strict

MAIN IDEA

Comparing

A What did Cromwell's rule have in common with an absolute monarchy?

▼ This engraving depicts the beheading of Charles I.

The English Civil War, 1642–1645

December 1642

SCOTLAND
North Sea
ENGLAND
Edgehill Oct. 1642
London

December 1643

SCOTLAND
IRELAND
North Sea
Adwalton Moor June 1643
ENGLAND
London

December 1644

SCOTLAND
IRELAND
North Sea
Marston Moor July 1644
ENGLAND
London

December 1645

SCOTLAND
IRELAND
ENGLAND
Naseby June 1645
London

58°N   0   250 Miles
0   500 Kilometers
50°N

- Area controlled by Puritans
- Area controlled by Royalists
- ✳ Battle

GEOGRAPHY SKILLBUILDER: Interpreting Maps
1. **Movement** *Explain which side gained and which side lost territory during each year from 1643 to 1645.*
2. **Place** *Which side maintained control of London? Why would this be important?*

Puritan, Cromwell favored religious toleration for all Christians except Catholics. He even allowed Jews to return; they had been expelled from England in 1290.

Restoration and Revolution

Oliver Cromwell ruled until his death in 1658. Shortly afterward, the government he had established collapsed, and a new Parliament was selected. The English people were sick of military rule. In 1659, Parliament voted to ask the older son of Charles I to rule England.

Charles II Reigns When Prince Charles entered London in 1660, crowds shouted joyfully and bells rang. On this note of celebration, the reign of Charles II began. Because he restored the monarchy, the period of his rule is called the **Restoration**.

During Charles II's reign, Parliament passed an important guarantee of freedom, ***habeas corpus***. *Habeas corpus* is Latin meaning "to have the body." This 1679 law gave every prisoner the right to obtain a writ or document ordering that the prisoner be brought before a judge to specify the charges against the prisoner. The judge would decide whether the prisoner should be tried or set free. Because of the Habeas Corpus Act, a monarch could not put someone in jail simply for opposing the ruler. Also, prisoners could not be held indefinitely without trials.

In addition, Parliament debated who should inherit Charles's throne. Because Charles had no legitimate child, his heir was his brother James, who was Catholic. A group called the Whigs opposed James, and a group called the Tories supported him. These two groups were the ancestors of England's first political parties.

James II and the Glorious Revolution In 1685, Charles II died, and James II became king. James soon offended his subjects by displaying his Catholicism. Violating English law, he appointed several Catholics to high office. When Parliament protested, James dissolved it. In 1688, James's second wife gave birth to a son. English Protestants became terrified at the prospect of a line of Catholic kings.

James had an older daughter, Mary, who was Protestant. She was also the wife of William of Orange, a prince of the Netherlands. Seven members of Parliament invited William and Mary to overthrow James for the sake of Protestantism. When William led his army to London in 1688, James fled to France. This bloodless overthrow of King James II is called the **Glorious Revolution**. **B**

MAIN IDEA

Contrasting
B How was the overthrow of James II different from the overthrow of Charles I?

616 Chapter 21

Limits on Monarch's Power

At their coronation, William and Mary vowed to recognize Parliament as their partner in governing. England had become not an absolute monarchy but a **constitutional monarchy**, where laws limited the ruler's power.

Bill of Rights To make clear the limits of royal power, Parliament drafted a Bill of Rights in 1689. This document listed many things that a ruler could not do:

- no suspending of Parliament's laws
- no levying of taxes without a specific grant from Parliament
- no interfering with freedom of speech in Parliament
- no penalty for a citizen who petitions the king about grievances

William and Mary consented to these and other limits on their royal power.

Cabinet System Develops After 1688, no British monarch could rule without the consent of Parliament. At the same time, Parliament could not rule without the consent of the monarch. If the two disagreed, government came to a standstill.

During the 1700s, this potential problem was remedied by the development of a group of government ministers, or officials, called the **cabinet**. These ministers acted in the ruler's name but in reality represented the major party of Parliament. Therefore, they became the link between the monarch and the majority party in Parliament.

Over time, the cabinet became the center of power and policymaking. Under the cabinet system, the leader of the majority party in Parliament heads the cabinet and is called the prime minister. This system of English government continues today.

Connect to Today

U.S. Democracy

Today, the United States still relies on many of the government reforms and institutions that the English developed during this period. These include the following:

- the right to obtain *habeas corpus*, a document that prevents authorities from holding a person in jail without being charged
- a Bill of Rights, guaranteeing such rights as freedom of speech and freedom of worship
- a strong legislature and strong executive, which act as checks on each other
- a cabinet, made up of heads of executive departments, such as the Department of State
- two dominant political parties

SECTION 5 ASSESSMENT

TERMS & NAMES 1. For each term or name, write a sentence explaining its significance.
• Charles I • English Civil War • Oliver Cromwell • Restoration • *habeas corpus* • Glorious Revolution • constitutional monarchy • cabinet

USING YOUR NOTES

2. What patterns do you see in the causes of these conflicts?

Monarch	Conflicts with Parliament
James I	
Charles I	
James II	

MAIN IDEAS

3. Why was the death of Charles I revolutionary?

4. What rights were guaranteed by the Habeas Corpus Act?

5. How does a constitutional monarchy differ from an absolute monarchy?

CRITICAL THINKING & WRITING

6. **EVALUATING DECISIONS** In your opinion, which decisions by Charles I made his conflict with Parliament worse? Explain.

7. **MAKING INFERENCES** Why do you think James II fled to France when William of Orange led his army to London?

8. **SYNTHESIZING** What conditions in England made the execution of one king and the overthrow of another possible?

9. **WRITING ACTIVITY** REVOLUTION Write a **persuasive essay** for an underground newspaper designed to incite the British people to overthrow Charles I.

CONNECT TO TODAY DRAWING A POLITICAL CARTOON

Yet another revolution threatens the monarchy today in Great Britain. Some people would like to see the monarchy ended altogether. Find out what you can about the issue and choose a side. Represent your position on the issue in an original **political cartoon.**

VISUAL SUMMARY

Absolute Monarchs in Europe

Long-Term Causes

- decline of feudalism
- rise of cities and support of middle class
- growth of national kingdoms
- loss of Church authority

Immediate Causes

- religious and territorial conflicts
- buildup of armies
- need for increased taxes
- revolts by peasants or nobles

European Monarchs Claim Divine Right to Rule Absolutely

Immediate Effects

- regulation of religion and society
- larger courts
- huge building projects
- new government bureaucracies appointed by the government
- loss of power by nobility and legislatures

Long-Term Effects

- revolution in France
- western European influence on Russia
- English political reforms that influence U.S. democracy

TERMS & NAMES

For each term or name below, briefly explain its connection to European history from 1500 to 1800.

1. absolute monarch
2. divine right
3. Louis XIV
4. War of the Spanish Succession
5. Thirty Years' War
6. Seven Years' War
7. Peter the Great
8. English Civil War
9. Glorious Revolution
10. constitutional monarchy

MAIN IDEAS

Spain's Empire and European Absolutism Section 1 (pages 589–595)

11. What three actions demonstrated that Philip II of Spain saw himself as a defender of Catholicism?
12. According to French writer Jean Bodin, should a prince share power with anyone else? Explain why or why not.

The Reign of Louis XIV Section 2 (pages 596–602)

13. What strategies did Louis XIV use to control the French nobility?
14. In what ways did Louis XIV cause suffering to the French people?

Central European Monarchs Clash Section 3 (pages 603–607)

15. What were six results of the Peace of Westphalia?
16. Why did Maria Theresa and Frederick the Great fight two wars against each other?

Absolute Rulers of Russia Section 4 (pages 608–613)

17. What were three differences between Russia and western Europe?
18. What was Peter the Great's primary goal for Russia?

Parliament Limits the English Monarchy Section 5 (pages 614–617)

19. List the causes, participants, and outcome of the English Civil War.
20. How did Parliament try to limit the power of the English monarchy?

CRITICAL THINKING

1. USING YOUR NOTES

POWER AND AUTHORITY In a chart, list actions that absolute monarchs took to increase their power. Then identify the monarchs who took these actions.

Actions of Absolute Rulers	Monarchs Who Took Them

2. DRAWING CONCLUSIONS

ECONOMICS What benefits might absolute monarchs hope to gain by increasing their countries' territory?

3. DEVELOPING HISTORICAL PERSPECTIVE

What conditions fostered the rise of absolute monarchs in Europe?

4. COMPARING AND CONTRASTING

Compare the reign of Louis XIV with that of Peter the Great. Which absolute ruler had a more lasting impact on his country? Explain why.

5. HYPOTHESIZING

Would Charles I have had a different fate if he had been king of another country in western or central Europe? Why or why not?

Use the excerpt from the English Bill of Rights passed in 1689 and your knowledge of world history to answer questions 1 and 2.

PRIMARY SOURCE

That the pretended power of suspending [canceling] of laws or the execution [carrying out] of laws by regal authority without consent of Parliament is illegal; . . .

That it is the right of the subjects to petition [make requests of] the king, and all commitments [imprisonments] and prosecutions for such petitioning are illegal;

That the raising or keeping a standing army within the kingdom in time of peace, unless it be with consent of Parliament, is against the law; . . .

That election of members of Parliament ought to be free [not restricted].

English Bill of Rights

1. According to the excerpt, which of the following is illegal?
   A. the enactment of laws without Parliament's permission
   B. the unrestricted election of members of Parliament
   C. the right of subjects to make requests of the king
   D. keeping a standing army in time of peace with Parliament's consent

2. The English Bill of Rights was passed as a means to
   A. limit Parliament's power.
   B. increase Parliament's power.
   C. overthrow the monarch.
   D. increase the monarch's power.

Use the map and your knowledge of world history to answer question 3.

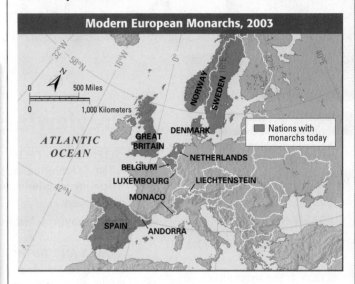

Modern European Monarchs, 2003

3. Of the countries that you studied in this chapter, which have monarchs today?
   A. Spain, Great Britain, the Netherlands
   B. Liechtenstein, Monaco
   C. Luxembourg, Andorra
   D. Great Britain, Norway, Sweden

hmhsocialstudies.com TEST PRACTICE

For additional test practice, go online for:
- Diagnostic tests
- Strategies
- Tutorials

Interact *with* History

On page 588, you thought about the advantages and disadvantages of absolute power. Now that you have read the chapter, what do you consider to be the main advantage and the main disadvantage of being an absolute ruler?

FOCUS ON WRITING

REVOLUTION Reread the information on Oliver Cromwell. Then write a **History Maker,** like the ones you've seen throughout this textbook, on Cromwell as a leader of a successful revolution. Be sure to
- include biographical information about Cromwell.
- discuss his effectiveness as a leader.
- use vivid language to hold your reader's attention.

MULTIMEDIA ACTIVITY

Creating a Television News Report

Use a video recorder to tape a television news report on the trial of Charles I. Role-play an announcer reporting a breaking news story. Relate the facts of the trial and interview key participants, including:
- a member of Parliament
- a Puritan
- a Royalist
- Charles I

CHAPTER 22

Enlightenment and Revolution, 1550–1789

Essential Question

What led Enlightenment scientists and thinkers to question old ideas?

 What You Will Learn

In this chapter you will learn how Enlightenment scientists and thinkers challenged old ideas in science, the arts, government, and religion.

SECTION 1 The Scientific Revolution

Main Idea In the mid-1500s, scientists began to question accepted beliefs and make new theories based on experimentation.

SECTION 2 The Enlightenment in Europe

Main Idea A revolution in intellectual activity changed Europeans' view of government and society.

SECTION 3 The Enlightenment Spreads

Main Idea Enlightenment ideas spread through the Western world and profoundly influenced the arts and government.

SECTION 4 The American Revolution

Main Idea Enlightenment ideas helped spur the American colonies to shed British rule and create a new nation.

Previewing Themes

SCIENCE AND TECHNOLOGY The Scientific Revolution began when astronomers questioned how the universe operates. By shattering long-held views, these astronomers opened a new world of discovery.
Geography *In what Russian city did Enlightenment ideas bloom?*

POWER AND AUTHORITY The thinkers of the Enlightenment challenged old ideas about power and authority. Such new ways of thinking led to, among other things, the American Revolution.
Geography *Where had Enlightenment ideas spread outside Europe?*

REVOLUTION Between the 16th and 18th centuries, a series of revolutions helped to usher in the modern era in Western history. Revolutions in both thought and action forever changed European and American society.
Geography *What city in Brandenburg-Prussia was an Enlightenment center?*

EUROPE AND NORTH AMERICA

1500

1543
Copernicus publishes heliocentric theory.

1609
◀ Galileo observes heavens through a telescope similar to this one.

1600

WORLD

1556
◀ Golden Age of Mughal Empire begins in India. (portrait of Mughal princess)

1603
Tokugawa Ieyasu becomes ruler of all Japan.

Centers of Enlightenment, c. 1740

British North American Colonies

Boston
Philadelphia

40°N
30°N
80°W

N

0   150   300 Miles
0 150 300 Kilometers
Conic Projection

HISTORY

Sir Isaac Newton: The Gravity of Genius

hmhsocialstudies.com   VIDEO

NORWAY

Edinburgh

North Sea

IRELAND

Dublin

Copenhagen

DENMARK

Baltic Sea

EAST PRUSSIA

GREAT BRITAIN

London

UNITED NETHERLANDS

Amsterdam

BRANDENBURG-PRUSSIA

Berlin

POLAND

AUSTRIAN NETH.

SMALL GERMAN STATES

SAXONY

Paris

FRANCE

SWITZERLAND

AUSTRIA

Vienna

HUNGARY

SAVOY

ITALIAN STATES

PAPAL STATES

OTTOMAN EMPIRE

◆ Enlightenment Centers

PORTUGAL

Lisbon

Madrid

SPAIN

Adriatic Sea

KINGDOM OF THE TWO SICILIES

N
W   E
S

SARDINIA (SAVOY)

0   250   500 Miles
0   250   500 Kilometers
Conic Projection

Mediterranean Sea

1687
Newton publishes treatise on law of gravity.

1776
◄ With Liberty Bell symbolizing their freedom, American colonies declare independence.

1789
Revolution erupts in France.

1700

1800

1644
Manchus invade China and establish Qing Dynasty. (Qing ruler Lohan) ►

1722
Chinese emperor Kangxi dies after a 61-year reign.

1776
Tukolor Kingdom arises in the former Songhai region of West Africa.

How would you react to a revolutionary idea?

You are a university student during the late 1600s, and it seems that the world as you know it has turned upside down. An English scientist named Isaac Newton has just theorized that the universe is not a dark mystery but a system whose parts work together in ways that can be expressed mathematically. This is just the latest in a series of arguments that have challenged old ways of thinking in fields from astronomy to medicine. Many of these ideas promise to open the way for improving society. And yet they are such radical ideas that many people refuse to accept them.

▲ This painting by English artist Joseph Wright depicts adults and children gazing at a miniature planetarium and its new ideas about the universe.

EXAMINING *the* ISSUES

- **Why might people have difficulty accepting new ideas or ways of thinking?**

- **What are the risks of embracing a different idea? What are some risks of always refusing to do so?**

Meet in small groups and discuss these questions. As you discuss these and other issues, recall other times in history when people expressed ideas that were different from accepted ones. As you read this chapter, watch for the effects of revolutionary ideas, beliefs, and discoveries.

The Scientific Revolution

MAIN IDEA	WHY IT MATTERS NOW	TERMS & NAMES
SCIENCE AND TECHNOLOGY In the mid-1500s, scientists began to question accepted beliefs and make new theories based on experimentation.	Such questioning led to the development of the scientific method still in use today.	• geocentric theory • Scientific Revolution	• heliocentric theory • Galileo Galilei • scientific method • Isaac Newton

SETTING THE STAGE As you recall, the period between 1300 and 1600 was a time of great change in Europe. The Renaissance, a rebirth of learning and the arts, inspired a spirit of curiosity in many fields. Scholars began to question ideas that had been accepted for hundreds of years. Meanwhile, the religious movement known as the Reformation prompted followers to challenge accepted ways of thinking about God and salvation. While the Reformation was taking place, another revolution in European thought had begun, one that would permanently change how people viewed the physical world.

The Roots of Modern Science

Before 1500, scholars generally decided what was true or false by referring to an ancient Greek or Roman author or to the Bible. Few European scholars challenged the scientific ideas of the ancient thinkers or the church by carefully observing nature for themselves.

The Medieval View During the Middle Ages, most scholars believed that the earth was an immovable object located at the center of the universe. According to that belief, the moon, the sun, and the planets all moved in perfectly circular paths around the earth. Common sense seemed to support this view. After all, the sun appeared to be moving around the earth as it rose in the morning and set in the evening.

This earth-centered view of the universe was called the **geocentric theory**. The idea came from Aristotle, the Greek philosopher of the fourth century B.C. The Greek astronomer Ptolemy (TOL•a•mee) expanded the theory in the second century A.D. In addition, Christianity taught that God had deliberately placed the earth at the center of the universe. Earth was thus a special place on which the great drama of life unfolded.

A New Way of Thinking Beginning in the mid-1500s, a few scholars published works that challenged the ideas of the ancient thinkers and the church. As these scholars replaced old assumptions with new theories, they launched a change in European thought that historians call the **Scientific Revolution**. The Scientific Revolution was a new way of thinking about the natural world. That way was based upon careful observation and a willingness to question accepted beliefs.

hmhsocialstudies.com
TAKING NOTES

Use the graphic organizer online to take notes on the events and circumstances that led to the Scientific Revolution.

A combination of discoveries and circumstances led to the Scientific Revolution and helped spread its impact. During the Renaissance, European explorers traveled to Africa, Asia, and the Americas. Such lands were inhabited by peoples and animals previously unknown in Europe. These discoveries opened Europeans to the possibility that there were new truths to be found. The invention of the printing press during this period helped spread challenging ideas—both old and new—more widely among Europe's thinkers.

The age of European exploration also fueled a great deal of scientific research, especially in astronomy and mathematics. Navigators needed better instruments and geographic measurements, for example, to determine their location in the open sea. As scientists began to look more closely at the world around them, they made observations that did not match the ancient beliefs. They found they had reached the limit of the classical world's knowledge. Yet, they still needed to know more.

A Revolutionary Model of the Universe

An early challenge to accepted scientific thinking came in the field of astronomy. It started when a small group of scholars began to question the geocentric theory.

The Heliocentric Theory Although backed by authority and common sense, the geocentric theory did not accurately explain the movements of the sun, moon, and planets. This problem troubled a Polish cleric and astronomer named Nicolaus Copernicus (koh•PUR•nuh•kuhs). In the early 1500s, Copernicus became interested in an old Greek idea that the sun stood at the center of the universe. After studying planetary movements for more than 25 years, Copernicus reasoned that indeed, the stars, the earth, and the other planets revolved around the sun.

Copernicus's **heliocentric**, or sun-centered, **theory** still did not completely explain why the planets orbited the way they did. He also knew that most scholars and clergy would reject his theory because it contradicted their religious views. Fearing ridicule or persecution, Copernicus did not publish his findings until 1543, the last year of his life. He received a copy of his book, *On the Revolutions of the Heavenly Bodies,* on his deathbed.

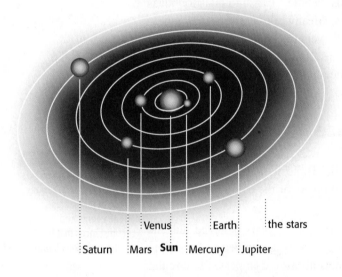

▲ This model shows how Copernicus saw the planets revolving around the sun.

Saturn Mars **Sun** Mercury Jupiter
Venus Earth the stars

While revolutionary, Copernicus's book caused little stir at first. Over the next century and a half, other scientists built on the foundations he had laid. A Danish astronomer, Tycho Brahe (TEE•koh brah), carefully recorded the movements of the planets for many years. Brahe produced mountains of accurate data based on his observations. However, it was left to his followers to make mathematical sense of them.

After Brahe's death in 1601, his assistant, a brilliant mathematician named Johannes Kepler, continued his work. After studying Brahe's data, Kepler concluded that certain mathematical laws govern planetary motion. One of these laws showed that the planets revolve around the sun in elliptical orbits instead of circles, as was previously thought. Kepler's laws showed that Copernicus's basic ideas were true. They demonstrated mathematically that the planets revolve around the sun. Ⓐ

MAIN IDEA

Recognizing Effects

Ⓐ How did Kepler's findings support the heliocentric theory?

Galileo's Discoveries An Italian scientist named <u>Galileo Galilei</u> built on the new theories about astronomy. As a young man, Galileo learned that a Dutch lens maker had built an instrument that could enlarge far-off objects. Galileo built his own telescope and used it to study the heavens in 1609.

Then, in 1610, he published a small book called *Starry Messenger,* which described his astonishing observations. Galileo announced that Jupiter had four moons and that the sun had dark spots. He also noted that the earth's moon had a rough, uneven surface. This shattered Aristotle's theory that the moon and stars were made of a pure, perfect substance. Galileo's observations, as well as his laws of motion, also clearly supported the theories of Copernicus.

Conflict with the Church Galileo's findings frightened both Catholic and Protestant leaders because they went against church teaching and authority. If people believed the church could be wrong about this, they could question other church teachings as well.

In 1616, the Catholic Church warned Galileo not to defend the ideas of Copernicus. Although Galileo remained publicly silent, he continued his studies. Then, in 1632, he published *Dialogue Concerning the Two Chief World Systems.* This book presented the ideas of both Copernicus and Ptolemy, but it clearly showed that Galileo supported the Copernican theory. The pope angrily summoned Galileo to Rome to stand trial before the Inquisition.

Galileo stood before the court in 1633. Under the threat of torture, he knelt before the cardinals and read aloud a signed confession. In it, he agreed that the ideas of Copernicus were false.

▲ Galileo stands before the papal court.

MAIN IDEA

Analyzing Primary Sources

B In what two ways does Galileo seek to appease the Church?

PRIMARY SOURCE B
With sincere heart and unpretended faith I abjure, curse, and detest the aforesaid errors and heresies [of Copernicus] and also every other error . . . contrary to the Holy Church, and I swear that in the future I will never again say or assert . . . anything that might cause a similar suspicion toward me.

GALILEO GALILEI, quoted in *The Discoverers*

Galileo was never again a free man. He lived under house arrest and died in 1642 at his villa near Florence. However, his books and ideas still spread all over Europe. (In 1992, the Catholic Church officially acknowledged that Galileo had been right.)

The Scientific Method

The revolution in scientific thinking that Copernicus, Kepler, and Galileo began eventually developed into a new approach to science called the <u>scientific method</u>. The scientific method is a logical procedure for gathering and testing ideas. It begins with a problem or question arising from an observation. Scientists next form a hypothesis, or unproved assumption. The hypothesis is then tested in an experiment or on the basis of data. In the final step, scientists analyze and interpret their data to reach a new conclusion. That conclusion either confirms or disproves the hypothesis.

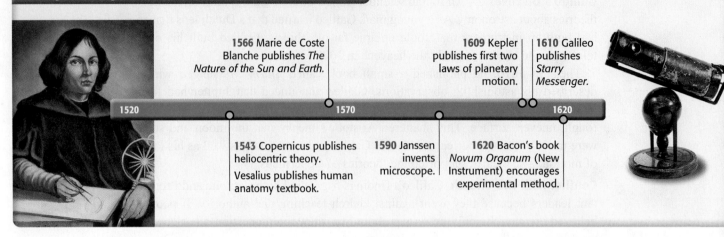

1566 Marie de Coste Blanche publishes *The Nature of the Sun and Earth.*

1609 Kepler publishes first two laws of planetary motion.

1610 Galileo publishes *Starry Messenger.*

1520   1570   1620

1543 Copernicus publishes heliocentric theory. Vesalius publishes human anatomy textbook.

1590 Janssen invents microscope.

1620 Bacon's book *Novum Organum* (New Instrument) encourages experimental method.

▲ Nicolaus Copernicus began the Scientific Revolution with his heliocentric theory.

Bacon and Descartes The scientific method did not develop overnight. The work of two important thinkers of the 1600s, Francis Bacon and René Descartes (day•KAHRT), helped to advance the new approach.

Francis Bacon, an English statesman and writer, had a passionate interest in science. He believed that by better understanding the world, scientists would generate practical knowledge that would improve people's lives. In his writings, Bacon attacked medieval scholars for relying too heavily on the conclusions of Aristotle and other ancient thinkers. Instead of reasoning from abstract theories, he urged scientists to experiment and then draw conclusions. This approach is called empiricism, or the experimental method.

In France, René Descartes also took a keen interest in science. He developed analytical geometry, which linked algebra and geometry. This provided an important new tool for scientific research.

Like Bacon, Descartes believed that scientists needed to reject old assumptions and teachings. As a mathematician, however, he approached gaining knowledge differently than Bacon. Rather than using experimentation, Descartes relied on mathematics and logic. He believed that everything should be doubted until proved by reason. The only thing he knew for certain was that he existed—because, as he wrote, "I think, therefore I am." From this starting point, he followed a train of strict reasoning to arrive at other basic truths. **C**

Modern scientific methods are based on the ideas of Bacon and Descartes. Scientists have shown that observation and experimentation, together with general laws that can be expressed mathematically, can lead people to a better understanding of the natural world.

MAIN IDEA

Contrasting
C How did Descartes's approach to science differ from Bacon's?

Newton Explains the Law of Gravity

By the mid-1600s, the accomplishments of Copernicus, Kepler, and Galileo had shattered the old views of astronomy and physics. Later, the great English scientist <u>Isaac Newton</u> helped to bring together their breakthroughs under a single theory of motion.

VIDEO
Sir Isaac Newton: The Gravity of Genius

↗ hmhsocialstudies.com

Changing Idea: Scientific Method	
Old Science	**New Science**
Scholars generally relied on ancient authorities, church teachings, common sense, and reasoning to explain the physical world.	In time, scholars began to use observation, experimentation, and scientific reasoning to gather knowledge and draw conclusions about the physical world.

1628 Harvey reveals how human heart functions.

1637 Descartes's book *Discourse on Method* sets forth his scientific method of reasoning from the basis of doubt.

1662 Boyle discovers mathematical relationship between the pressure and volume of gases, known as Boyle's law.

1674 Leeuwenhoek observes bacteria through microscope.

1714 Fahrenheit invents mercury thermometer.

1620   1670   1720

1633 Galileo faces Inquisition for support of Copernicus's theory.

1643 Torricelli invents barometer.

1666 France establishes Academy of Sciences.

1687 Newton publishes law of gravity.

1660 England establishes Royal Society to support scientific study.

Newton studied mathematics and physics at Cambridge University. By the time he was 26, Newton was certain that all physical objects were affected equally by the same forces. Newton's great discovery was that the same force ruled motion of the planets and all matter on earth and in space. The key idea that linked motion in the heavens with motion on the earth was the law of universal gravitation. According to this law, every object in the universe attracts every other object. The degree of attraction depends on the mass of the objects and the distance between them.

▲ Isaac Newton's law of gravity explained how the same physical laws governed motion both on earth and in the heavens.

In 1687, Newton published his ideas in a work called *The Mathematical Principles of Natural Philosophy*. It was one of the most important scientific books ever written. The universe he described was like a giant clock. Its parts all worked together perfectly in ways that could be expressed mathematically. Newton believed that God was the creator of this orderly universe, the clockmaker who had set everything in motion. **D**

MAIN IDEA

Clarifying

D Why was the law of gravitation important?

The Scientific Revolution Spreads

As astronomers explored the secrets of the universe, other scientists began to study the secrets of nature on earth. Careful observation and the use of the scientific method eventually became important in many different fields.

Scientific Instruments Scientists developed new tools and instruments to make the precise observations that the scientific method demanded. The first microscope was invented by a Dutch maker of eyeglasses, Zacharias Janssen (YAHN•suhn), in 1590. In the 1670s, a Dutch drapery merchant and amateur scientist named Anton van Leeuwenhoek (LAY•vuhn•HUK) used a microscope to observe bacteria swimming in tooth scrapings. He also examined red blood cells for the first time.

In 1643, one of Galileo's students, Evangelista Torricelli (TAWR•uh•CHEHL•ee), developed the first mercury barometer, a tool for measuring atmospheric pressure and predicting weather. In 1714, the German physicist Gabriel Fahrenheit (FAR•uhn•HYT) made the first thermometer to use mercury in glass. Fahrenheit's thermometer showed water freezing at 32°. A Swedish astronomer, Anders Celsius (SEHL•see•uhs), created another scale for the mercury thermometer in 1742. Celsius's scale showed freezing at 0°.

Medicine and the Human Body During the Middle Ages, European doctors had accepted as fact the writings of an ancient Greek physician named Galen. However, Galen had never dissected the body of a human being. Instead, he had studied the anatomy of pigs and other animals. Galen assumed that human anatomy was much the same. A Flemish physician named Andreas Vesalius proved Galen's assumptions wrong. Vesalius dissected human corpses and published his observations. His

Enlightenment and Revolution **627**

▲ The famous Dutch painter Rembrandt painted *Anatomy Lesson of Dr. Tulp* in 1632 from an actual anatomy lesson. The corpse was that of a criminal.

book, *On the Structure of the Human Body* (1543), was filled with detailed drawings of human organs, bones, and muscle.

In the late 1700s, British physician Edward Jenner introduced a vaccine to prevent smallpox. Inoculation using live smallpox germs had been practiced in Asia for centuries. While beneficial, this technique could also be dangerous. Jenner discovered that inoculation with germs from a cattle disease called cowpox gave permanent protection from smallpox for humans. Because cowpox was a much milder disease, the risks for this form of inoculation were much lower. Jenner used cowpox to produce the world's first vaccination.

Vocabulary
Inoculation is the act of injecting a germ into a person's body so as to create an immunity to the disease.

Discoveries in Chemistry Robert Boyle pioneered the use of the scientific method in chemistry. He is considered the founder of modern chemistry. In a book called *The Sceptical Chymist* (1661), Boyle challenged Aristotle's idea that the physical world consisted of four elements—earth, air, fire, and water. Instead, Boyle proposed that matter was made up of smaller primary particles that joined together in different ways. Boyle's most famous contribution to chemistry is Boyle's law. This law explains how the volume, temperature, and pressure of gas affect each other.

The notions of reason and order, which spurred so many breakthroughs in science, soon moved into other fields of life. Philosophers and scholars across Europe began to rethink long-held beliefs about the human condition, most notably the rights and liberties of ordinary citizens. These thinkers helped to usher in a movement that challenged the age-old relationship between a government and its people, and eventually changed forever the political landscape in numerous societies.

SECTION 1 ASSESSMENT

TERMS & NAMES 1. For each term or name, write a sentence explaining its significance.
• geocentric theory • Scientific Revolution • heliocentric theory • Galileo Galilei • scientific method • Isaac Newton

USING YOUR NOTES
2. Which event or circumstance do you consider to be the most significant? Why?

Causes of the Scientific Revolution

MAIN IDEAS
3. Before the 1500s, who and what were the final authorities with regard to most knowledge?
4. How did the heliocentric theory of the universe differ from the geocentric theory?
5. What are the main steps of the scientific method?

CRITICAL THINKING & WRITING
6. **DRAWING CONCLUSIONS** "If I have seen farther than others," said Newton, "it is because I have stood on the shoulders of giants." Could this be said of most scientific accomplishments? Explain.
7. **ANALYZING MOTIVES** Why might institutions of authority tend to reject new ideas?
8. **FORMING AND SUPPORTING OPINIONS** Do you agree with Galileo's actions during his Inquisition? Explain.
9. **WRITING ACTIVITY** SCIENCE AND TECHNOLOGY Create a television **script** for a discovery of the Scientific Revolution. Include key people, ideas, and accomplishments.

CONNECT TO TODAY CREATING A GRAPHIC
Research a modern-day invention or new way of thinking and then describe it and its impact on society to the class in a **poster** or **annotated diagram**.

The Enlightenment in Europe

MAIN IDEA	WHY IT MATTERS NOW	TERMS & NAMES
POWER AND AUTHORITY A revolution in intellectual activity changed Europeans' view of government and society.	The various freedoms enjoyed in many countries today are a result of Enlightenment thinking.	• Enlightenment • social contract • John Locke • philosophe • Voltaire • Montesquieu • Rousseau • Mary Wollstonecraft

SETTING THE STAGE In the wake of the Scientific Revolution, and the new ways of thinking it prompted, scholars and philosophers began to reevaluate old notions about other aspects of society. They sought new insight into the underlying beliefs regarding government, religion, economics, and education. Their efforts spurred the **Enlightenment**, a new intellectual movement that stressed reason and thought and the power of individuals to solve problems. Known also as the Age of Reason, the movement reached its height in the mid-1700s and brought great change to many aspects of Western civilization.

Two Views on Government

The Enlightenment started from some key ideas put forth by two English political thinkers of the 1600s, Thomas Hobbes and John Locke. Both men experienced the political turmoil of England early in that century. However, they came to very different conclusions about government and human nature.

Hobbes's Social Contract Thomas Hobbes expressed his views in a work called *Leviathan* (1651). The horrors of the English Civil War convinced him that all humans were naturally selfish and wicked. Without governments to keep order, Hobbes said, there would be "war . . . of every man against every man," and life would be "solitary, poor, nasty, brutish, and short."

Hobbes argued that to escape such a bleak life, people had to hand over their rights to a strong ruler. In exchange, they gained law and order. Hobbes called this agreement by which people created a government the **social contract**. Because people acted in their own self-interest, Hobbes said, the ruler needed total power to keep citizens under control. The best government was one that had the awesome power of a leviathan (sea monster). In Hobbes's view, such a government was an absolute monarchy, which could impose order and demand obedience.

hmhsocialstudies.com
TAKING NOTES
Use the graphic organizer online to take notes on the section's main ideas and details.

Changing Idea: The Right to Govern	
Old Idea	**New Idea**
A monarch's rule is justified by divine right.	A government's power comes from the consent of the governed.

Locke's Natural Rights The philosopher **John Locke** held a different, more positive, view of human nature. He believed that people could learn from experience and improve themselves. As reasonable beings, they had the natural ability to govern their own affairs and to look after the welfare of society. Locke criticized absolute monarchy and favored the idea of self-government.

According to Locke, all people are born free and equal, with three natural rights—life, liberty, and property. The purpose of government, said Locke, is to protect these rights. If a government fails to do so, citizens have a right to overthrow it. Locke's theory had a deep influence on modern political thinking. His belief that a government's power comes from the consent of the people is the foundation of modern democracy. The ideas of government by popular consent and the right to rebel against unjust rulers helped inspire struggles for liberty in Europe and the Americas. **A**

MAIN IDEA

Contrasting

A How does Locke's view of human nature differ from that of Hobbes?

The Philosophes Advocate Reason

History Makers

Voltaire
1694–1778

Voltaire befriended several European monarchs and nobles. Among them was the Prussian king Frederick II. The two men seemed like ideal companions. Both were witty and preferred to dress in shabby, rumpled clothes.

Their relationship eventually soured, however. Voltaire disliked editing Frederick's mediocre poetry, while Frederick suspected Voltaire of shady business dealings. Voltaire eventually described the Prussian king as "a nasty monkey, perfidious friend, [and] wretched poet." Frederick in turn called Voltaire a "miser, dirty rogue, [and] coward."

↗ hmhsocialstudies.com

RESEARCH WEB LINKS Go online for more on Voltaire.

The Enlightenment reached its height in France in the mid-1700s. Paris became the meeting place for people who wanted to discuss politics and ideas. The social critics of this period in France were known as **philosophes** (FIHL•uh•SAHFS), the French word for philosophers. The philosophes believed that people could apply reason to all aspects of life, just as Isaac Newton had applied reason to science. Five concepts formed the core of their beliefs:

1. **Reason** Enlightened thinkers believed truth could be discovered through reason or logical thinking.
2. **Nature** The philosophes believed that what was natural was also good and reasonable.
3. **Happiness** The philosophes rejected the medieval notion that people should find joy in the hereafter and urged people to seek well-being on earth.
4. **Progress** The philosophes stressed that society and humankind could improve.
5. **Liberty** The philosophes called for the liberties that the English people had won in their Glorious Revolution and Bill of Rights.

Voltaire Combats Intolerance Probably the most brilliant and influential of the philosophes was François Marie Arouet. Using the pen name **Voltaire**, he published more than 70 books of political essays, philosophy, and drama.

Voltaire often used satire against his opponents. He made frequent targets of the clergy, the aristocracy, and the government. His sharp tongue made him enemies at the French court, and twice he was sent to prison. After his second jail term, Voltaire was exiled to England for more than two years.

Although he made powerful enemies, Voltaire never stopped fighting for tolerance, reason, freedom of religious belief, and freedom of speech. He used his quill pen as if it were a deadly weapon in a thinker's war against humanity's worst enemies—intolerance, prejudice, and superstition. He summed up his staunch defense of liberty in one of his most famous quotes: "I do not agree with a word you say but will defend to the death your right to say it."

Vocabulary
Satire is the use of irony, sarcasm, or wit to attack folly, vice, or stupidity.

Montesquieu and the Separation of Powers Another influential French writer, the Baron de <u>Montesquieu</u> (MAHN•tuh•skYOO), devoted himself to the study of political liberty. Montesquieu believed that Britain was the best-governed and most politically balanced country of his own day. The British king and his ministers held executive power. They carried out the laws of the state. The members of Parliament held legislative power. They made the laws. The judges of the English courts held judicial power. They interpreted the laws to see how each applied to a specific case. Montesquieu called this division of power among different branches separation of powers.

Montesquieu oversimplified the British system. It did not actually separate powers this way. His idea, however, became a part of his most famous book, *On the Spirit of Laws* (1748). In his book, Montesquieu proposed that separation of powers would keep any individual or group from gaining total control of the government. "Power," he wrote, "should be a check to power." This idea later would be called checks and balances.

MAIN IDEA

Analyzing Issues
B What advantages did Montesquieu see in the separation of powers?

Montesquieu's book was admired by political leaders in the British colonies of North America. His ideas about separation of powers and checks and balances became the basis for the United States Constitution. **B**

Rousseau: Champion of Freedom A third great philosophe, Jean Jacques <u>Rousseau</u> (roo•SOH), was passionately committed to individual freedom. The son of a poor Swiss watchmaker, Rousseau won recognition as a writer of essays. A strange, brilliant, and controversial figure, Rousseau strongly disagreed with other

> Analyzing Primary Sources

Laws Protect Freedom

Both Montesquieu and Rousseau believed firmly that fair and just laws—not monarchs or unrestrained mobs—should govern society. Here, Rousseau argues that laws established by and for the people are the hallmark of a free society.

PRIMARY SOURCE

I . . . therefore give the name "Republic" to every state that is governed by laws, no matter what the form of its administration may be: for only in such a case does the public interest govern, and the *res republica* rank as a *reality*. . . . Laws are, properly speaking, only the conditions of civil association. The people, being subject to the laws, ought to be their author: the conditions of the society ought to be regulated . . . by those who come together to form it.

JEAN JACQUES ROUSSEAU, *The Social Contract*

Laws Ensure Security

While laws work to protect citizens from abusive rulers, Montesquieu argues that they also guard against anarchy and mob rule.

PRIMARY SOURCE

It is true that in democracies the people seem to act as they please; but political liberty does not consist in an unlimited freedom. . . . We must have continually present to our minds the difference between independence and liberty. Liberty is a right of doing whatever the laws permit, and if a citizen could do what they [the laws] forbid he would be no longer possessed of liberty, because all his fellow-citizens would have the same power.

BARON DE MONTESQUIEU, *The Spirit of Laws*

DOCUMENT-BASED QUESTIONS
1. **Analyzing Issues** *Why should citizens be the authors of society's laws, according to Rousseau?*
2. **Making Inferences** *Why does Montesquieu believe that disobeying laws leads to a loss of liberty?*

Enlightenment thinkers on many matters. Most philosophes believed that reason, science, and art would improve life for all people. Rousseau, however, argued that civilization corrupted people's natural goodness. "Man is born free, and everywhere he is in chains," he wrote.

Rousseau believed that the only good government was one that was freely formed by the people and guided by the "general will" of society—a direct democracy. Under such a government, people agree to give up some of their freedom in favor of the common good. In 1762, he explained his political philosophy in a book called *The Social Contract*.

Rousseau's view of the social contract differed greatly from that of Hobbes. For Hobbes, the social contract was an agreement between a society and its government. For Rousseau, it was an agreement among free individuals to create a society and a government.

Like Locke, Rousseau argued that legitimate government came from the consent of the governed. However, Rousseau believed in a much broader democracy than Locke had promoted. He argued that all people were equal and that titles of nobility should be abolished. Rousseau's ideas inspired many of the leaders of the French Revolution who overthrew the monarchy in 1789.

Beccaria Promotes Criminal Justice An Italian philosophe named Cesare Bonesana Beccaria (BAYK•uh•REE•ah) turned his thoughts to the justice system. He believed that laws existed to preserve social order, not to avenge crimes. Beccaria regularly criticized common abuses of justice. They included torturing of witnesses and suspects, irregular proceedings in trials, and punishments that were arbitrary or cruel. He argued that a person accused of a crime should receive a speedy trial, and that torture should never be used. Moreover, he said, the degree of punishment should be based on the seriousness of the crime. He also believed that capital punishment should be abolished.

Beccaria based his ideas about justice on the principle that governments should seek the greatest good for the greatest number of people. His ideas influenced criminal law reformers in Europe and North America.

Major Ideas of the Enlightenment

Idea	Thinker	Impact
Natural rights—life, liberty, property	Locke	Fundamental to U.S. Declaration of Independence
Separation of powers	Montesquieu	France, United States, and Latin American nations use separation of powers in new constitutions
Freedom of thought and expression	Voltaire	Guaranteed in U.S. Bill of Rights and French Declaration of the Rights of Man and Citizen; European monarchs reduce or eliminate censorship
Abolishment of torture	Beccaria	Guaranteed in U.S. Bill of Rights; torture outlawed or reduced in nations of Europe and the Americas
Religious freedom	Voltaire	Guaranteed in U.S. Bill of Rights and French Declaration of the Rights of Man and Citizen; European monarchs reduce persecution
Women's equality	Wollstonecraft	Women's rights groups form in Europe and North America

SKILLBUILDER: Interpreting Charts
1. **Analyzing Issues** *What important documents reflect the influence of Enlightenment ideas?*
2. **Forming Opinions** *Which are the two most important Enlightenment ideas? Support your answer with reasons.*

Women and the Enlightenment

The philosophes challenged many assumptions about government and society. But they often took a traditional view toward women. Rousseau, for example, developed many progressive ideas about education. However, he believed that a girl's education should mainly teach her how to be a helpful wife and mother. Other male social critics scolded women for reading novels because they thought it encouraged idleness and wickedness. Still, some male writers argued for more education for women and for women's equality in marriage.

Women writers also tried to improve the status of women. In 1694, the English writer Mary Astell published *A Serious Proposal to the Ladies*. Her book addressed the lack of educational opportunities for women. In later writings, she used Enlightenment arguments about government to criticize the unequal relationship between men and women in marriage. She wrote, "If absolute sovereignty be not necessary in a state, how comes it to be so in a family? . . . If all men are born free, how is it that all women are born slaves?"

During the 1700s, other women picked up these themes. Among the most persuasive was **Mary Wollstonecraft**, who published an essay called *A Vindication of the Rights of Woman* in 1792. In the essay, she disagreed with Rousseau that women's education should be secondary to men's. Rather, she argued that women, like men, need education to become virtuous and useful. Wollstonecraft also urged women to enter the male-dominated fields of medicine and politics. **C**

Women made important contributions to the Enlightenment in other ways. In Paris and other European cities, wealthy women helped spread Enlightenment ideas through social gatherings called salons, which you will read about later in this chapter.

One woman fortunate enough to receive an education in the sciences was Emilie du Châtelet (shah•tlay). Du Châtelet was an aristocrat trained as a mathematician and physicist. By translating Newton's work from Latin into French, she helped stimulate interest in science in France.

MAIN IDEA

Drawing Conclusions

C Why do you think the issue of education was important to both Astell and Wollstonecraft?

History Makers

Mary Wollstonecraft
1759–1797

A strong advocate of education for women, Wollstonecraft herself received little formal schooling. She and her two sisters taught themselves by studying books at home. With her sisters, she briefly ran a school. These experiences shaped much of her thoughts about education.

Wollstonecraft eventually took a job with a London publisher. There, she met many leading radicals of the day. One of them was her future husband, the writer William Godwin. Wollstonecraft died at age 38, after giving birth to their daughter, Mary. This child, whose married name was Mary Wollstonecraft Shelley, went on to write the classic novel *Frankenstein*.

hmhsocialstudies.com

RESEARCH WEB LINKS Go online for more on Mary Wollstonecraft.

Legacy of the Enlightenment

Over a span of a few decades, Enlightenment writers challenged long-held ideas about society. They examined such principles as the divine right of monarchs, the union of church and state, and the existence of unequal social classes. They held these beliefs up to the light of reason and found them in need of reform.

The philosophes mainly lived in the world of ideas. They formed and popularized new theories. Although they encouraged reform, they were not active revolutionaries. However, their theories eventually inspired the American and French revolutions and other revolutionary movements in the 1800s. Enlightenment thinking produced three other long-term effects that helped shape Western civilization.

Belief in Progress The first effect was a belief in progress. Pioneers such as Galileo and Newton had discovered the key for unlocking the mysteries of nature in the 1500s and 1600s. With the door thus opened, the growth of scientific knowledge seemed to quicken in the 1700s. Scientists made key new discoveries in chemistry, physics, biology, and mechanics. The successes of the Scientific Revolution gave people the confidence that human reason could solve social problems. Philosophes and reformers urged an end to the practice of slavery and argued for greater social equality, as well as a more democratic style of government.

A More Secular Outlook A second outcome was the rise of a more secular, or non-religious, outlook. During the Enlightenment, people began to question openly their religious beliefs and the teachings of the church. Before the Scientific Revolution, people accepted the mysteries of the universe as the workings of God. One by one, scientists discovered that these mysteries could be explained mathematically. Newton himself was a deeply religious man, and he sought to reveal God's majesty through his work. However, his findings often caused people to change the way they thought about God.

Meanwhile, Voltaire and other critics attacked some of the beliefs and practices of organized Christianity. They wanted to rid religious faith of superstition and fear and promote tolerance of all religions.

Importance of the Individual Faith in science and in progress produced a third outcome, the rise of individualism. As people began to turn away from the church and royalty for guidance, they looked to themselves instead.

The philosophes encouraged people to use their own ability to reason in order to judge what was right or wrong. They also emphasized the importance of the individual in society. Government, they argued, was formed by individuals to promote their welfare. The British thinker Adam Smith extended the emphasis on the individual to economic thinking. He believed that individuals acting in their own self-interest created economic progress. Smith's theory is discussed in detail in Chapter 25.

During the Enlightenment, reason took center stage. The greatest minds of Europe followed each other's work with interest and often met to discuss their ideas. Some of the kings and queens of Europe were also very interested. As you will learn in Section 3, they sought to apply some of the philosophes' ideas to create progress in their countries.

SECTION 2 ASSESSMENT

TERMS & NAMES 1. For each term or name, write a sentence explaining its significance.
• Enlightenment • social contract • John Locke • philosophe • Voltaire • Montesquieu • Rousseau • Mary Wollstonecraft

USING YOUR NOTES	MAIN IDEAS	CRITICAL THINKING & WRITING

2. Which impact of the Enlightenment do you consider most important? Why?
 	
Enlightenment in Europe
I. Two Views on Government
  A.
  B.
II. The Philosophes Advocate Reason
  A.
  B.
	3. What are the natural rights with which people are born, according to John Locke?
	
	4. Who were the philosophes and what did they advocate?
	
	5. What was the legacy of the Enlightenment?
		6. **SYNTHESIZING** Explain how the following statement reflects Enlightenment ideas: "Power should be a check to power."
		
		7. **ANALYZING ISSUES** Why might some women have been critical of the Enlightenment?
		
		8. **DRAWING CONCLUSIONS** Do you think the philosophes were optimistic about the future of humankind? Explain.
		
		9. **WRITING ACTIVITY** POWER AND AUTHORITY Compare the views of Hobbes, Locke, and Rousseau on government. Then write one **paragraph** about how their ideas reflect their understanding of human behavior.

CONNECT TO TODAY PRESENTING AN ORAL REPORT

Identify someone considered a modern-day social critic. Explore the person's beliefs and methods and present your findings to the class in a brief **oral report.**

↗ hmhsocialstudies.com INTERACTIVE

European Values During the Enlightenment

Writers and artists of the Enlightenment often used satire to comment on European values. Using wit and humor, they ridiculed various ideas and customs. Satire allowed artists to explore human faults in a way that is powerful but not preachy. In the two literary excerpts and the painting below, notice how the writer or artist makes his point.

A PRIMARY SOURCE

Voltaire

Voltaire wrote *Candide* (1759) to attack a philosophy called Optimism, which held that all is right with the world. The hero of the story, a young man named Candide, encounters the most awful disasters and human evils. In this passage, Candide meets a slave in South America, who explains why he is missing a leg and a hand.

———

"When we're working at the sugar mill and catch our finger in the grinding-wheel, they cut off our hand. When we try to run away, they cut off a leg. I have been in both of these situations. This is the price you pay for the sugar you eat in Europe. . . .

"The Dutch fetishes [i.e., missionaries] who converted me [to Christianity] tell me every Sunday that we are all the sons of Adam, Whites and Blacks alike. I'm no genealogist, but if these preachers are right, we are all cousins born of first cousins. Well, you will grant me that you can't treat a relative much worse than this."

B PRIMARY SOURCE

Jonathan Swift

The narrator of *Gulliver's Travels* (1726), an English doctor named Lemuel Gulliver, takes four disastrous voyages that leave him stranded in strange lands. In the following passage, Gulliver tries to win points with the king of Brobdingnag—a land of giants—by offering to show him how to make guns and cannons.

———

The king was struck with horror at the description I had given of those terrible engines. . . . He was amazed how so impotent and grovelling an insect as I (these were his expressions) could entertain such inhuman ideas, and in so familiar a manner as to appear wholly unmoved at all the scenes of blood and desolation, which I had painted as the common effects of those destructive machines; whereof, he said, some evil genius, enemy to mankind, must have been the first contriver [inventor].

C PRIMARY SOURCE

William Hogarth

The English artist William Hogarth often used satire in his paintings. In this painting, *Canvassing for Votes,* he comments on political corruption. While the candidate flirts with the ladies on the balcony, his supporters offer a man money for his vote.

Document-Based QUESTIONS

1. What is the main point that Voltaire is making in Source A? What technique does he use to reinforce his message?

2. What does the king's reaction in Source B say about Swift's view of Europe's military technology?

3. Why might Hogarth's painting in Source C be difficult for modern audiences to understand? Does this take away from his message?

The Enlightenment Spreads

MAIN IDEA	WHY IT MATTERS NOW	TERMS & NAMES
POWER AND AUTHORITY Enlightenment ideas spread through the Western world and profoundly influenced the arts and government.	An "enlightened" problem-solving approach to government and society prevails in modern civilization today.	• salon • baroque • neoclassical	• enlightened despot • Catherine the Great

SETTING THE STAGE The philosophes' views about society often got them in trouble. In France it was illegal to criticize either the Catholic Church or the government. Many philosophes landed in jail or were exiled. Voltaire, for example, experienced both punishments. Nevertheless, the Enlightenment spread throughout Europe with the help of books, magazines, and word of mouth. In time, Enlightenment ideas influenced everything from the artistic world to the royal courts across the continent.

A World of Ideas

hmhsocialstudies.com
TAKING NOTES
Use the graphic organizer online to take notes on the spread and influence of Enlightenment ideas on the monarchy and the arts.

In the 1700s, Paris was the cultural and intellectual capital of Europe. Young people from around Europe—and also from the Americas—came to study, philosophize, and enjoy the culture of the bustling city. The brightest minds of the age gathered there. From their circles radiated the ideas of the Enlightenment.

The buzz of Enlightenment ideas was most intense in the mansions of several wealthy women of Paris. There, in their large drawing rooms, these hostesses held regular social gatherings called **salons**. At these events, philosophers, writers, artists, scientists, and other great intellects met to discuss ideas.

Diderot's *Encyclopedia* The most influential of the salon hostesses in Voltaire's time was Marie-Thérèse Geoffrin (zhuh•frehn). She helped finance the project of a leading philosophe named Denis Diderot (DEE•duh•ROH). Diderot created a large set of books to which many leading scholars of Europe contributed articles and essays. He called it *Encyclopedia* and began publishing the first volumes in 1751.

The Enlightenment views expressed in the articles soon angered both the French government and the Catholic Church. Their censors banned the work. They said it undermined royal authority, encouraged a spirit of revolt, and fostered "moral corruption, irreligion, and unbelief." Nonetheless, Diderot continued publishing his *Encyclopedia*.

The salons and the *Encyclopedia* helped spread Enlightenment ideas to educated people all over Europe. Enlightenment ideas also eventually spread through newspapers, pamphlets, and even political songs. Enlightenment ideas about government and equality attracted the attention of a growing literate middle class, which could afford to buy many books and support the work of artists.

Cybercafés

These days, when people around the world gather to explore new ideas and discuss current events, many do so at Internet cafés. These are coffee shops or restaurants that also provide access to computers for a small fee.

Internet cafés originated in the United States, but today they are more popular overseas. In China, for instance, there are roughly 113,000 licensed Internet cafés; and tens of thousands of unlicensed cafés have been shut down.

Like the French in the 1700s, the Chinese recognize the power of ideas and have tried to limit their spread. Licensed Internet cafés are monitored by video, and must register customers and keep records of all websites viewed. As well, an estimated 30,000–40,000 Internet police are employed by the government to monitor and censor Internet traffic.

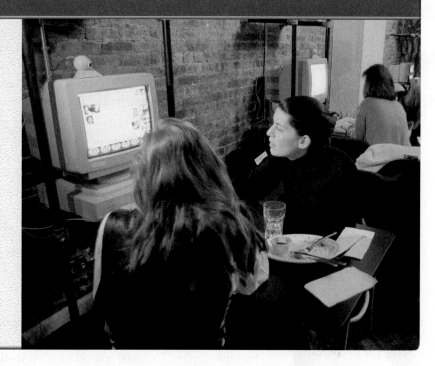

New Artistic Styles

The Enlightenment ideals of order and reason were reflected in the arts—music, literature, painting, and architecture.

Neoclassical Style Emerges European art of the 1600s and early 1700s had been dominated by the style called **baroque**, which was characterized by a grand, ornate design. Baroque styles could be seen in elaborate palaces such as Versailles (see page 600) and in numerous paintings.

Under the influence of the Enlightenment, styles began to change. Artists and architects worked in a simple and elegant style that borrowed ideas and themes from classical Greece and Rome. The artistic style of the late 1700s is therefore called **neoclassical** ("new classical").

Changes in Music and Literature Music styles also changed to reflect Enlightenment ideals. The music scene in Europe had been dominated by such composers as Johann Sebastian Bach of Germany and George Friedrich Handel of England. These artists wrote dramatic organ and choral music. During the Enlightenment, a new, lighter, and more elegant style of music known as *classical* emerged. Three composers in Vienna, Austria, rank among the greatest figures of the classical period in music. They were Franz Joseph Haydn, Wolfgang Amadeus Mozart, and Ludwig van Beethoven.

Writers in the 18th century also developed new styles and forms of literature. A number of European authors began writing novels, which are lengthy works of prose fiction. Their works had carefully crafted plots, used suspense, and explored characters' thoughts and feelings. These books were popular with a wide middle-class audience, who liked the entertaining stories written in everyday language. Writers, including many women, turned out a flood of popular novels in the 1700s.

Samuel Richardson's *Pamela* is often considered the first true English novel. It tells the story of a young servant girl who refuses the advances of her master. Another English masterpiece, *Tom Jones,* by Henry Fielding, tells the story of an orphan who travels all over England to win the hand of his lady.

Enlightenment and Monarchy

From the salons, artists' studios, and concert halls of Europe, the Enlightenment spirit also swept through Europe's royal courts. Many philosophes, including Voltaire, believed that the best form of government was a monarchy in which the ruler respected the people's rights. The philosophes tried to convince monarchs to rule justly. Some monarchs embraced the new ideas and made reforms that reflected the Enlightenment spirit. They became known as **enlightened despots**. Despot means "absolute ruler."

The enlightened despots supported the philosophes' ideas. But they also had no intention of giving up any power. The changes they made were motivated by two desires: they wanted to make their countries stronger and their own rule more effective. The foremost of Europe's enlightened despots were Frederick II of Prussia, Holy Roman Emperor Joseph II of Austria, and Catherine the Great of Russia. **A**

Frederick the Great Frederick II, the king of Prussia from 1740 to 1786, committed himself to reforming Prussia. He granted many religious freedoms, reduced censorship, and improved education. He also reformed the justice system and abolished the use of torture. However, Frederick's changes only went so far. For example, he believed that serfdom was wrong, but he did nothing to end it since he needed the support of wealthy landowners. As a result, he never tried to change the existing social order.

Perhaps Frederick's most important contribution was his attitude toward being king. He called himself "the first servant of the state." From the beginning of his reign, he made it clear that his goal was to serve and strengthen his country. This attitude was clearly one that appealed to the philosophes.

Joseph II The most radical royal reformer was Joseph II of Austria. The son and successor of Maria Theresa, Joseph II ruled Austria from 1780 to 1790. He introduced legal reforms and freedom of the press. He also supported freedom of worship, even for Protestants, Orthodox Christians, and Jews. In his most radical reform, Joseph abolished serfdom and ordered that peasants be paid for their labor with cash. Not surprisingly, the nobles firmly resisted this change. Like many of Joseph's reforms, it was undone after his death.

Catherine the Great The ruler most admired by the philosophes was Catherine II, known as **Catherine the Great**. She ruled Russia from 1762 to 1796. The well-educated empress read the works of philosophes, and she exchanged many letters with Voltaire. She ruled with absolute authority but also sought to reform Russia.

In 1767, Catherine formed a commission to review Russia's laws. She presented it with a brilliant proposal for reforms based on the ideas of Montesquieu and Beccaria. Among other changes, she recommended allowing religious toleration and abolishing torture and capital punishment. Her commission, however, accomplished none of these lofty goals.

Catherine eventually put in place limited reforms, but she did little to improve the life of the Russian peasants. Her views about enlightened ideas changed after a massive uprising of serfs in 1773. With great brutality, Catherine's army crushed the

▲ Joseph II

MAIN IDEA

Analyzing Motives
A Why did the enlightened despots undertake reforms?

Vocabulary
Serfdom was a system in which peasants were forced to live and work on a landowner's estate.

Changing Idea: Relationship Between Ruler and State	
Old Idea	**New Idea**
The state and its citizens exist to serve the monarch. As Louis XIV reportedly said, "I am the state."	The monarch exists to serve the state and support citizens' welfare. As Frederick the Great said, a ruler is only "the first servant of the state."

rebellion. Catherine had previously favored an end to serf-dom. However, the revolt convinced her that she needed the nobles' support to keep her throne. Therefore, she gave the nobles absolute power over the serfs. As a result, Russian serfs lost their last traces of freedom. **B**

MAIN IDEA

Synthesizing

B How accurately does the term enlightened despot describe Catherine the Great? Explain.

Catherine Expands Russia Peter the Great, who ruled Russia in the early 1700s, had fought for years to win a port on the Baltic Sea. Likewise, Catherine sought access to the Black Sea. In two wars with the Ottoman Turks, her armies finally won control of the northern shore of the Black Sea. Russia also gained the right to send ships through Ottoman-controlled straits leading from the Black Sea to the Mediterranean Sea.

Catherine also expanded her empire westward into Poland. In Poland, the king was relatively weak, and independent nobles held the most power. The three neighboring powers—Russia, Prussia, and Austria—each tried to assert their influence over the country. In 1772, these land-hungry neighbors each took a piece of Poland in what is called the First Partition of Poland. In further partitions in 1793 and 1795, they grabbed up the rest of Poland's territory. With these partitions, Poland disappeared as an independent country for more than a century.

By the end of her remarkable reign, Catherine had vastly enlarged the Russian empire. Meanwhile, as Russia was becoming an international power, another great power, Britain, faced a challenge from its North American colonies. Inspired by Enlightenment ideas, colonial leaders decided to do the unthinkable: break away from their ruling country and found an independent republic.

History Makers

Catherine the Great
1729–1796

The daughter of a minor German prince, Catherine was 15 when she was handed over to marry the Grand Duke Peter, heir to the Russian throne.

Peter was mentally unstable. Catherine viewed her husband's weakness as her chance for power. She made important friends among Russia's army officers and became known as the most intelligent and best-informed person at court. In 1762, only months after her husband became czar, Catherine had him arrested and confined. Soon afterward, Peter conveniently died, probably by murder.

SECTION 3 ASSESSMENT

TERMS & NAMES 1. For each term or name, write a sentence explaining its significance.
• salon   • baroque   • neoclassical   • enlightened despot   • Catherine the Great

USING YOUR NOTES

2. What are two generalizations you could make about the spread of Enlightenment ideas?

MAIN IDEAS

3. What were the defining aspects of neoclassical art?

4. What new form of literature emerged during the 18th century and what were its main characteristics?

5. Why were several rulers in 18th century Europe known as enlightened despots?

CRITICAL THINKING & WRITING

6. **DRAWING CONCLUSIONS** What advantages did salons have over earlier forms of communication in spreading ideas?

7. **ANALYZING ISSUES** In what way were the enlightened despots less than true reformers? Cite specific examples from the text.

8. **MAKING INFERENCES** How did the *Encyclopedia* project reflect the age of Enlightenment?

9. **WRITING ACTIVITY** POWER AND AUTHORITY Imagine you are a public relations consultant for an enlightened despot. Write a **press release** explaining why your client is "Most Enlightened Despot of the 1700s."

MULTIMEDIA ACTIVITY WRITING A CHARACTER SKETCH

Use the Internet to find out more about a composer or writer mentioned in this section. Then write a brief **character sketch** on that artist, focusing on interesting pieces of information about his or her life.

INTERNET KEYWORDS
biography European Enlightenment

Enlightenment and Revolution **639**

The American Revolution

MAIN IDEA	WHY IT MATTERS NOW	TERMS & NAMES

REVOLUTION Enlightenment ideas helped spur the American colonies to shed British rule and create a new nation.	The revolution created a republic, the United States of America, that became a model for many nations of the world.	• Declaration of Independence
		• Thomas Jefferson
		    • checks and balances
		    • federal system
		    • Bill of Rights

SETTING THE STAGE Philosophes such as Voltaire considered England's government the most progressive in Europe. The Glorious Revolution of 1688 had given England a constitutional monarchy. In essence, this meant that various laws limited the power of the English king. Despite the view of the philosophes, however, a growing number of England's colonists in North America accused England of tyrannical rule. Emboldened by Enlightenment ideas, they would attempt to overthrow what was then the mightiest power on earth and create their own nation.

Britain and Its American Colonies

hmhsocialstudies.com
TAKING NOTES

Use the graphic organizer online to take notes on the problems American colonists faced in shaping their republic and the solutions they found.

Throughout the 1600s and 1700s, British colonists had formed a large and thriving settlement along the eastern shore of North America. When George III became king of Great Britain in 1760, his North American colonies were growing by leaps and bounds. Their combined population soared from about 250,000 in 1700 to 2,150,000 in 1770, a nearly ninefold increase. Economically, the colonies thrived on trade with the nations of Europe.

Along with increasing population and prosperity, a new sense of identity was growing in the colonists' minds. By the mid-1700s, colonists had been living in America for nearly 150 years. Each of the 13 colonies had its own government, and people were used to a great degree of independence. Colonists saw themselves less as British and more as Virginians or Pennsylvanians. However, they were still British subjects and were expected to obey British law.

In 1651, the British Parliament passed a trade law called the Navigation Act. This and subsequent trade laws prevented colonists from selling their most valuable products to any country except Britain. In addition, colonists had to pay high taxes on imported French and Dutch goods. Nonetheless, Britain's policies benefited both the colonies and the motherland. Britain bought American raw materials for low prices and sold manufactured goods to the colonists. And despite various British trade restrictions, colonial merchants also thrived. Such a spirit of relative harmony, however, soon would change.

▼ This French snuffbox pictures (left to right) Voltaire, Rousseau, and colonial statesman Benjamin Franklin.

Americans Win Independence

In 1754, war erupted on the North American continent between the English and the French. As you recall, the French had also colonized parts of North America throughout the 1600s and 1700s. The conflict was known as the French and Indian War. (The name stems from the fact that the French enlisted numerous Native American tribes to fight on their side.) The fighting lasted until 1763, when Britain and her colonists emerged victorious—and seized nearly all French land in North America.

The victory, however, only led to growing tensions between Britain and its colonists. In order to fight the war, Great Britain had run up a huge debt. Because American colonists benefited from Britain's victory, Britain expected the colonists to help pay the costs of the war. In 1765, Parliament passed the Stamp Act. According to this law, colonists had to pay a tax to have an official stamp put on wills, deeds, newspapers, and other printed material. **A**

MAIN IDEA

Analyzing Causes
A How did the French and Indian War lead to the Stamp Act?

American colonists were outraged. They had never paid taxes directly to the British government before. Colonial lawyers argued that the stamp tax violated colonists' natural rights, and they accused the government of "taxation without representation." In Britain, citizens consented to taxes through their representatives in Parliament. The colonists, however, had no representation in Parliament. Thus, they argued they could not be taxed.

Growing Hostility Leads to War Over the next decade, hostilities between the two sides increased. Some colonial leaders favored independence from Britain. In 1773, to protest an import tax on tea, a group of colonists dumped a large load of British tea into Boston Harbor. George III, infuriated by the "Boston Tea Party," as it was called, ordered the British navy to close the port of Boston.

Such harsh tactics by the British made enemies of many moderate colonists. In September 1774, representatives from every colony except Georgia gathered in Philadelphia to form the First Continental Congress. This group protested the treatment of Boston. When the king paid little attention to their complaints, the colonies decided to form the Second Continental Congress to debate their next move.

On April 19, 1775, British soldiers and American militiamen exchanged gunfire on the village green in Lexington, Massachusetts. The fighting spread to nearby Concord. The Second Continental Congress voted to raise an army and organize for battle under the command of a Virginian named George Washington. The American Revolution had begun.

The Influence of the Enlightenment Colonial leaders used Enlightenment ideas to justify independence. The colonists had asked for the same political rights as people in Britain, they said, but the king had stubbornly refused. Therefore, the colonists were justified in rebelling against a tyrant who had broken the social contract.

In July 1776, the Second Continental Congress issued the **Declaration of Independence**. This document, written by political leader **Thomas Jefferson**,

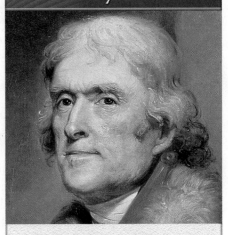

History Makers

Thomas Jefferson
1743–1826

The author of the Declaration of Independence, Thomas Jefferson of Virginia, was a true figure of the Enlightenment. As a writer and statesman, he supported free speech, religious freedom, and other civil liberties. At the same time, he was also a slave owner.

Jefferson was a man of many talents. He was an inventor as well as one of the great architects of early America. He designed the Virginia state capitol building in Richmond and many buildings for the University of Virginia. Of all his achievements, Jefferson wanted to be most remembered for three: author of the Declaration of Independence, author of the Statute of Virginia for Religious Freedom, and founder of the University of Virginia.

↗ hmhsocialstudies.com

INTERNET ACTIVITY Go online to create a time line of Jefferson's major achievements.

Changing Idea: Colonial Attachment to Britain	
Old Idea	**New Idea**
American colonists considered themselves to be subjects of the British king.	After a long train of perceived abuses by the king, the colonists asserted their right to declare independence.

was firmly based on the ideas of John Locke and the Enlightenment. The Declaration reflected these ideas in its eloquent argument for natural rights. "We hold these truths to be self-evident," states the beginning of the Declaration, "that all men are created equal, that they are endowed by their Creator with certain unalienable rights, that among these are life, liberty, and the pursuit of happiness."

Since Locke had asserted that people had the right to rebel against an unjust ruler, the Declaration of Independence included a long list of George III's abuses. The document ended by declaring the colonies' separation from Britain. The colonies, the Declaration said, "are absolved from all allegiance to the British crown."

Success for the Colonists The British were not about to let their colonies leave without a fight. Shortly after the publication of the Declaration of Independence, the two sides went to war. At first glance, the colonists seemed destined to go down in quick defeat. Washington's ragtag, poorly trained army faced the well-trained forces of the most powerful country in the world. In the end, however, the Americans won their war for independence.

hmhsocialstudies.com

INTERACTIVE HISTORY
Experience winter at Valley Forge with General Washington and his army.

Several reasons explain the colonists' success. First, the Americans' motivation for fighting was much stronger than that of the British, since their army was defending their homeland. Second, the overconfident British generals made several mistakes. Third, time itself was on the side of the Americans. The British could win battle after battle, as they did, and still lose the war. Fighting an overseas war, 3,000 miles from London, was terribly expensive. After a few years, tax-weary British citizens called for peace.

Finally, the Americans did not fight alone. Louis XVI of France had little sympathy for the ideals of the American Revolution. However, he was eager to weaken France's rival, Britain. French entry into the war in 1778 was decisive. In 1781, combined forces of about 9,500 Americans and 7,800 French trapped a British army commanded by Lord Cornwallis near Yorktown, Virginia. Unable to escape, Cornwallis eventually surrendered. The Americans had shocked the world and won their independence.

North America, 1783

ALASKA
Arctic Circle
UNCLAIMED
Hudson Bay
PACIFIC OCEAN
CANADA
Quebec
Boston
New York
UNITED STATES
ATLANTIC OCEAN
LOUISIANA TERRITORY
Charleston
FLORIDA
New Orleans
BAHAMAS
PUERTO RICO
Gulf of Mexico
NEW SPAIN
Tropic of Cancer
CUBA
Mexico City
JAMAICA
HISPANIOLA
HONDURAS
Caribbean Sea
SOUTH AMERICA
Rio Grande
Colorado R.
Missouri R.
Mississippi R.
Ohio
500 Miles
1,000 Kilometers

- British
- French
- Russian
- Spanish
- U.S. and Great Britain
- U.S. and Spain

GEOGRAPHY SKILLBUILDER: Interpreting Maps
1. **Region** What feature formed the western border of the United States?
2. **Human-Environment Interaction** What European countries had claims on the North American continent in 1783?

Democracy

Ancient Greece and Rome were strong influences on the framers of the U.S. system of government. Democracy as it is practiced today, however, is different from the Greek and Roman models.

The most famous democracy today is the United States. The type of government the United States uses is called a federal republic. "Federal" means power is divided between the national and state governments. In a republic, the people vote for their representatives. Two key components of democracy in the United States are the Constitution and voting.

Enlightenment Ideas and the U.S. Constitution

Many of the ideas contained in the Constitution are built on the ideas of Enlightenment thinkers.

Enlightenment Idea	U.S. Constitution
Locke A government's power comes from the consent of the people.	• Preamble begins "We the people of the United States" to establish legitimacy. • Creates representative government • Limits government powers
Montesquieu Separation of powers	• Federal system of government • Powers divided among three branches • System of checks and balances
Rousseau Direct democracy	• Public election of president and Congress
Voltaire Free speech, religious toleration	• Bill of Rights provides for freedom of speech and religion.
Beccaria Accused have rights, no torture	• Bill of Rights protects rights of accused and prohibits cruel and unusual punishment.

Who Votes?

Voting is an essential part of democracy. Universal suffrage means that all adult citizens can vote. Universal suffrage is part of democracy in the United States today, but that was not always the case. This chart shows how the United States gradually moved toward giving all citizens the right to vote.

Eligible Voters

1789	1870	1920	1924	1971
Only white, male property owners can vote.	The 15th Amendment stated African-American men could vote; however, many were still prevented.	The 19th Amendment was ratified, giving women the right to vote.	Citizenship and the vote were extended to include Native Americans.	The 26th Amendment is ratified, changing the legal voting age from 21 to 18. Today all citizens, 18 or older, can vote.

↗ hmhsocialstudies.com

RESEARCH WEB LINKS Go online for more on democracy.

> **DATA FILE**

U.S. Constitution
• There have been 27 amendments to the Constitution since its creation.
• The U.S. Constitution has been used by many other countries as a model for their constitutions.
• In 2002, over 120 established and emerging democracies met to discuss their common issues.

Voting
• In the 2000 U.S. presidential election, only 36.1 percent of people between 18 and 24 years old voted.
• Some countries, such as Australia, fine citizens for not voting. Australia's voter turnout has been over 90 percent since 1925.

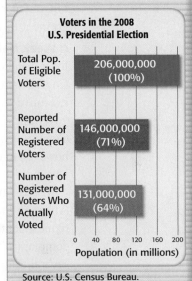

Voters in the 2008 U.S. Presidential Election

Total Pop. of Eligible Voters: 206,000,000 (100%)

Reported Number of Registered Voters: 146,000,000 (71%)

Number of Registered Voters Who Actually Voted: 131,000,000 (64%)

Population (in millions)

Source: U.S. Census Bureau.

Connect *to* Today

1. **Synthesizing** If so much of the U.S. Constitution can be found in European ideas, why were the framers of the U.S. Constitution so important?
   📄 See Skillbuilder Handbook, Page R21.

2. **Hypothesizing** Why is it important that every citizen has, and exercises, his or her right to vote?

The French Revolution

The American Revolution inspired the growing number of French people who sought reform in their own country. They saw the new government of the United States as the fulfillment of Enlightenment ideals, and longed for such a government in France.

The Declaration of Independence was widely circulated and admired in France. French officers like the Marquis de Lafayette (shown here), who fought for American independence, captivated his fellow citizens with accounts of the war. One Frenchman remarked about this time period, "We talked of nothing but America." Less than a decade after the American Revolution ended, an armed struggle to topple the government would begin in France.

Americans Create a Republic

Shortly after declaring their independence, the 13 individual states recognized the need for a national government. As victory became certain, all 13 states ratified a constitution in 1781. This plan of government was known as the Articles of Confederation. The Articles established the United States as a republic, a government in which citizens rule through elected representatives.

A Weak National Government To protect their authority, the 13 states created a loose confederation in which they held most of the power. Thus, the Articles of Confederation deliberately created a weak national government. There were no executive or judicial branches. Instead, the Articles established only one body of government, the Congress. Each state, regardless of size, had one vote in Congress. Congress could declare war, enter into treaties, and coin money. It had no power, however, to collect taxes or regulate trade. Passing new laws was difficult because laws needed the approval of 9 of the 13 states.

These limits on the national government soon produced many problems. Although the new national government needed money to operate, it could only request contributions from the states. Angry Revolutionary War veterans bitterly complained that Congress still owed them back pay for their services. Meanwhile, several states issued their own money. Some states even put tariffs on goods from neighboring states. **B**

A New Constitution Colonial leaders eventually recognized the need for a strong national government. In February 1787, Congress approved a Constitutional Convention to revise the Articles of Confederation. The Constitutional Convention held its first session on May 25, 1787. The 55 delegates were experienced statesmen who were familiar with the political theories of Locke, Montesquieu, and Rousseau.

Although the delegates shared basic ideas on government, they sometimes disagreed on how to put them into practice. For almost four months the delegates argued over important questions. Who should be represented in Congress? How many representatives should each state have? The delegates' deliberations produced not only compromises but also new approaches to governing. Using the political ideas of the Enlightenment, the delegates created a new system of government.

The Federal System Like Montesquieu, the delegates distrusted a powerful central government controlled by one person or group. They therefore established

MAIN IDEA

Making Inferences
B What was the main cause of the nation's problems under the Articles?

three separate branches—legislative, executive, and judicial. This setup provided a built-in system of **checks and balances**, with each branch checking the actions of the other two. For example, the president received the power to veto legislation passed by Congress. However, the Congress could override a presidential veto with the approval of two-thirds of its members.

Although the Constitution created a strong central government, it did not eliminate local governments. Instead, the Constitution set up a **federal system** in which power was divided between national and state governments.

The Bill of Rights The delegates signed the new Constitution on September 17, 1787. In order to become law, however, the Constitution required approval by conventions in at least 9 of the 13 states. These conventions were marked by sharp debate. Supporters of the Constitution were called Federalists. They argued in their famous work, the *Federalist Papers*, that the new government would provide a better balance between national and state powers. Their opponents, the Antifederalists, feared that the Constitution gave the central government too much power. They also wanted a bill of rights to protect the rights of individual citizens. **C**

In order to gain support, the Federalists promised to add a bill of rights to the Constitution. This promise cleared the way for approval. Congress formally added to the Constitution the ten amendments known as the **Bill of Rights**. These amendments protected such basic rights as freedom of speech, press, assembly, and religion. Many of these rights had been advocated by Voltaire, Rousseau, and Locke.

The Constitution and Bill of Rights marked a turning point in people's ideas about government. Both documents put Enlightenment ideas into practice. They expressed an optimistic view that reason and reform could prevail and that progress was inevitable. Such optimism swept across the Atlantic. However, the monarchies and the privileged classes didn't give up power and position easily. As Chapter 23 explains, the struggle to attain the principles of the Enlightenment led to violent revolution in France.

MAIN IDEA

Analyzing Issues

C What were the opposing views regarding ratification of the Constitution?

▼ Early copy of the U.S. Constitution

SECTION 4 ASSESSMENT

TERMS & NAMES 1. For each term or name, write a sentence explaining its significance.
• Declaration of Independence   • Thomas Jefferson   • checks and balances   • federal system   • Bill of Rights

USING YOUR NOTES	MAIN IDEAS	CRITICAL THINKING & WRITING
2. Which of the solutions that you recorded represented a compromise?	3. Why did the colonists criticize the Stamp Act as "taxation without representation"?	6. **MAKING INFERENCES** Why might it be important to have a Bill of Rights that guarantees basic rights of citizens?
	4. How did John Locke's notion of the social contract influence the American colonists?	7. **FORMING AND SUPPORTING OPINIONS** Do you think the American Revolution would have happened if there had not been an Age of Enlightenment?
	5. Why were the colonists able to achieve victory in the American Revolution?	8. **ANALYZING CAUSES** Why do you think the colonists at first created such a weak central government?
		9. **WRITING ACTIVITY** REVOLUTION Summarize in several **paragraphs** the ideas from the American Revolution concerning separation of powers, basic rights of freedom, and popular sovereignty.

Problem	Solution
1.	1.
2.	2.
3.	3.

CONNECT TO TODAY CELEBRATING AMERICA'S BIRTHDAY

Create a **birthday poster** to present to the United States this July 4th. The poster should include images or quotes that demonstrate the ideals upon which the nation was founded.

TERMS & NAMES

For each term or name below, briefly explain its connection to European history from 1550–1789.

1. heliocentric theory
2. Isaac Newton
3. social contract
4. philosophe
5. salon
6. enlightened despot
7. Declaration of Independence
8. federal system

MAIN IDEAS

The Scientific Revolution Section 1 (pages 623–628)

9. According to Ptolemy, what was the earth's position in the universe? How did Copernicus's view differ?

10. What are the four steps in the scientific method?

11. What four new instruments came into use during the Scientific Revolution? What was the purpose of each one?

The Enlightenment in Europe Section 2 (pages 629–635)

12. How did the ideas of Hobbes and Locke differ?

13. What did Montesquieu admire about the government of Britain?

14. How did the Enlightenment lead to a more secular outlook?

The Enlightenment Spreads Section 3 (pages 636–639)

15. What were three developments in the arts during the Enlightenment?

16. What sorts of reforms did the enlightened despots make?

The American Revolution Section 4 (pages 640–645)

17. Why did the Articles of Confederation result in a weak national government?

18. How did the writers of the U.S. Constitution put into practice the idea of separation of powers? A system of checks and balances?

CRITICAL THINKING

1. USING YOUR NOTES

List in a table important new ideas that arose during the Scientific Revolution and Enlightenment. In the right column, briefly explain why each idea was revolutionary.

New Idea	Why Revolutionary

2. RECOGNIZING EFFECTS

SCIENCE AND TECHNOLOGY What role did technology play in the Scientific Revolution?

3. ANALYZING ISSUES

POWER AND AUTHORITY How did the U.S. Constitution reflect the ideas of the Enlightenment? Refer to specific Enlightenment thinkers to support your answer.

4. CLARIFYING

How did the statement by Prussian ruler Frederick the Great that a ruler is only "the first servant of the state" highlight Enlightenment ideas about government?

VISUAL SUMMARY

Enlightenment and Revolution, 1550–1789

Scientific Revolution
- Heliocentric theory challenges geocentric theory.
- Mathematics and observation support heliocentric theory.
- Scientific method develops.
- Scientists make discoveries in many fields.

A new way of thinking about the world develops, based on observation and a willingness to question assumptions.

Enlightenment
- People try to apply the scientific approach to aspects of society.
- Political scientists propose new ideas about government.
- Philosophes advocate the use of reason to discover truths.
- Philosophes address social issues through reason.

Enlightenment writers challenge many accepted ideas about government and society.

Spread of Ideas
- Enlightenment ideas appeal to thinkers and artists across Europe.
- Salons help spread Enlightenment thinking.
- Ideas spread to literate middle class.
- Enlightened despots attempt reforms.

Enlightenment ideas sweep through European society and to colonial America.

American Revolution
- Enlightenment ideas influence colonists.
- Britain taxes colonists after French and Indian War.
- Colonists denounce taxation without representation.
- War begins in Lexington and Concord.

Colonists declare independence, defeat Britain, and establish republic.

Use the quotation and your knowledge of world history to answer questions 1 and 2.

PRIMARY SOURCE

We the People of the United States, in order to form a more perfect Union, establish Justice, insure domestic Tranquility, provide for the common defense, promote the general Welfare, and secure the Blessings of Liberty to ourselves and our Posterity, do ordain and establish this Constitution of the United States of America.
Preamble, *Constitution of the United States of America*

1. All of the following are stated objectives of the Constitution except
   A. justice.
   B. liberty.
   C. defense.
   D. prosperity.

2. With whom does the ultimate power in society lie, according to the Constitution?
   A. the church
   B. the military
   C. the citizens
   D. the monarchy

Use this engraving, entitled *The Sleep of Reason Produces Monsters,* and your knowledge of world history to answer question 3.

3. Which of the following statements best summarizes the main idea of this Enlightenment engraving?
   A. Nothing good comes from relaxation or laziness.
   B. A lack of reason fosters superstition and irrational fears.
   C. Dreams are not restricted by the boundaries of reason.
   D. Rulers that let down their guard risk rebellion and overthrow.

 hmhsocialstudies.com **TEST PRACTICE**

For additional test practice, go online for:
• Diagnostic tests
• Strategies
• Tutorials

Interact *with* History

On page 622, you examined how you would react to a different or revolutionary idea or way of doing things. Now that you have read the chapter, consider how such breakthroughs impacted society. Discuss in a small group what you feel were the most significant new ideas or procedures and explain why.

FOCUS ON WRITING

REVOLUTION Re-examine the material on the Scientific Revolution. Then write a three-paragraph **essay** summarizing the difference in scientific understanding before and after the various scientific breakthroughs. Focus on
• the ultimate authority on many matters before the Scientific Revolution.
• how and why that changed after the Revolution.

MULTIMEDIA ACTIVITY

21ST CENTURY

Writing an Internet-based Research Paper

Go to **hmhsocialstudies.com** to learn about conducting research on the Internet. Use the Internet to explore a recent breakthrough in science or medicine. Look for information that will help you explain why the discovery is significant and how the new knowledge changes what scientists had thought about the topic.

In a well-organized paper, compare the significance of the discovery you are writing about with major scientific or medical discoveries of the Scientific Revolution. Be sure to
• apply a search strategy when using directories and search engines to locate Web resources.
• judge the usefulness of each Web site.
• correctly cite your Web resources.
• revise and edit for correct use of language.

THE American REVOLUTION

The American Revolution led to the formation of the United States of America in 1776. Beginning in the 1760s, tensions grew between American colonists and their British rulers when Britain started passing a series of new laws and taxes for the colonies. With no representation in the British government, however, colonists had no say in these laws, which led to growing discontent. After fighting broke out in 1775, colonial leaders met to decide what to do. They approved the Declaration of Independence, announcing that the American colonies were free from British rule. In reality, however, freedom would not come until after years of fighting.

Explore some of the people and events of the American Revolution online. You can find a wealth of information, video clips, primary sources, activities, and more at **⬈ hmhsocialstudies.com**.

"I know not what course others may take; but as for me, give me liberty or give me death!"

— Patrick Henry

"Give Me Liberty or Give Me Death"

Read an excerpt from Patrick Henry's famous speech, which urged the colonists to fight against the British.

Seeds of Revolution

Watch the video to learn about colonial discontent in the years before the Revolutionary War.

Independence!

Watch the video to learn about the origins of the Declaration of Independence.

Victory!

Watch the video to learn how the American colonists won the Revolutionary War.

CHAPTER

23

The **French Revolution** and **Napoleon,** 1789–1815

Essential Question

What was the impact of the French Revolution, the rise and fall of Napoleon, and the Congress of Vienna?

 What You Will Learn

In this chapter you will learn about the French Revolution, Napoleon Bonaparte's empire, and the Congress of Vienna.

SECTION 1 The French Revolution Begins
Main Idea Economic and social inequalities in the Old Regime helped cause the French Revolution.

SECTION 2 Revolution Brings Reform and Terror
Main Idea The revolutionary government of France made reforms but also used terror and violence to retain power.

SECTION 3 Napoleon Forges an Empire
Main Idea Napoleon Bonaparte, a military genius, seized power in France and made himself emperor.

SECTION 4 Napoleon's Empire Collapses
Main Idea Napoleon's conquests aroused nationalistic feelings across Europe and contributed to his downfall.

SECTION 5 The Congress of Vienna
Main Idea After exiling Napoleon, European leaders at the Congress of Vienna tried to restore order and reestablish peace.

Previewing Themes

ECONOMICS The gap between rich and poor in France was vast. The inequalities of the economy of France were a major cause of the French Revolution.

Geography *Why do you think the royal palace at Versailles became a focal point for the anger of the poor people of Paris during the Revolution?*

REVOLUTION Driven by the example of the American Revolution and such Enlightenment ideas as liberty, equality, and democracy, the French ousted the government of Louis XVI and established a new political order.

Geography *Why do you think some historians cite the "wind from America" as a cause of the French Revolution?*

POWER AND AUTHORITY After seizing power in 1799, Napoleon conquered a huge empire that included much of Western Europe. His attempt to conquer Russia, however, led to his downfall.

Geography *What challenges and hazards of invading Russia might be inferred from the map?*

EUROPE

1789
Storming of the Bastille ignites the French Revolution.

1793
King Louis XVI is executed by guillotine; Reign of Terror begins. ▶

1796
Directory appoints Napoleon commander of French forces in Italy.

1789

WORLD

1789
George Washington is inaugurated as first U.S. president. ▶

1795
Great Britain seizes the Cape Colony in South Africa from the Dutch.

648

Napoleon's Empire, 1810

HISTORY
Napoleon Bonaparte:
The Glory of France

↗ hmhsocialstudies.com **VIDEO**

60°N

Legend:
- French Empire
- Countries allied with Napoleon
- Countries controlled by Napoleon
- Countries at war with Napoleon

KINGDOM OF DENMARK AND NORWAY

KINGDOM OF SWEDEN

North Sea

Baltic Sea

REP. OF DANZIG

UNITED KINGDOM OF GREAT BRITAIN AND IRELAND

15°W

N W E S

London

Brussels
• Amiens

PRUSSIA
Berlin
Elbe River

RUSSIAN EMPIRE

Warsaw
GRAND DUCHY OF WARSAW

ATLANTIC OCEAN

45°N

Paris
Versailles

CONFEDERATION OF THE RHINE

Prague

Loire River

Rhine River

Danube River

AUSTRIAN EMPIRE

FRENCH EMPIRE

HELVETIC REPUBLIC

Vienna

Milan • KINGDOM OF ITALY

Po River

Marseille

PORTUGAL

Madrid

Lisbon

SPAIN

Barcelona

CORSICA

KINGDOM OF SARDINIA

Adriatic Sea

ILLYRIAN PROVINCES

OTTOMAN EMPIRE

Black Sea

MONTENEGRO

Rome •

Naples
KINGDOM OF NAPLES

Mediterranean Sea

KINGDOM OF SICILY

0   250   500 Miles
0   250   500 Kilometers
Conic Projection

1799
Napoleon overthrows the Directory through a coup d'état.

1804
Napoleon crowns himself emperor, begins to create a vast European empire. ▶

1815
Napoleon is defeated at the Battle of Waterloo.

1800

1815

1800
Opium trade begins in China.

1804
Saint Domingue gains independence. (Toussaint L'Ouverture) ▶

1810
Padre Hidalgo calls for Mexican independence.

1814
War of 1812 between Great Britain and the United States ends.

How would you change an unjust government?

You are living in France in the late 1700s. Your parents are merchants who earn a good living. However, after taxes they have hardly any money left. You know that other people, especially the peasants in the countryside, are even worse off than you. At the same time, the nobility lives in luxury and pays practically no taxes.

Many people in France are desperate for change. But they are uncertain how to bring about that change. Some think that representatives of the people should demand fair taxes and just laws. Others support violent revolution. In Paris, that revolution seems to have begun. An angry mob has attacked and taken over the Bastille, a royal prison. You wonder what will happen next.

1. One of the mob leaders triumphantly displays the keys to the Bastille.

2. Although they were in search of gunpowder and firearms, the conquerors of the Bastille took whatever they could find.

3. One man drags the royal standard behind him.

▲ The conquerors of the Bastille parade outside City Hall in Paris.

EXAMINING *the* ISSUES

- **How would you define an unjust government?**

- **What, if anything, would lead you to take part in a violent revolution?**

Discuss these questions with your classmates. In your discussion, remember what you've learned about the causes of revolutionary conflicts such as the American Revolution and the English Civil War. As you read about the French Revolution in this chapter, see what changes take place and how these changes came about.

The French Revolution Begins

MAIN IDEA	WHY IT MATTERS NOW	TERMS & NAMES
ECONOMICS Economic and social inequalities in the Old Regime helped cause the French Revolution.	Throughout history, economic and social inequalities have at times led peoples to revolt against their governments.	• Old Regime • estate • Louis XVI • Marie Antoinette • Estates-General	• National Assembly • Tennis Court Oath • Great Fear

SETTING THE STAGE In the 1700s, France was considered the most advanced country of Europe. It had a large population and a prosperous foreign trade. It was the center of the Enlightenment, and France's culture was widely praised and imitated by the rest of the world. However, the appearance of success was deceiving. There was great unrest in France, caused by bad harvests, high prices, high taxes, and disturbing questions raised by the Enlightenment ideas of Locke, Rousseau, and Voltaire.

The Old Order

In the 1770s, the social and political system of France—the **Old Regime**—remained in place. Under this system, the people of France were divided into three large social classes, or **estates**.

The Privileged Estates Two of the estates had privileges, including access to high offices and exemptions from paying taxes, that were not granted to the members of the third. The Roman Catholic Church, whose clergy formed the First Estate, owned 10 percent of the land in France. It provided education and relief services to the poor and contributed about 2 percent of its income to the government. The Second Estate was made up of rich nobles. Although they accounted for just 2 percent of the population, the nobles owned 20 percent of the land and paid almost no taxes. The majority of the clergy and the nobility scorned Enlightenment ideas as radical notions that threatened their status and power as privileged persons.

The Third Estate About 97 percent of the people belonged to the Third Estate. The three groups that made up this estate differed greatly in their economic conditions. The first group—the bourgeoisie (BUR•zhwah•ZEE), or middle class—were bankers, factory owners, merchants, professionals, and skilled artisans. Often, they were well educated and believed strongly in the Enlightenment ideals of liberty and equality. Although some of the bourgeoisie were as rich as nobles, they paid high taxes and, like the rest of the Third Estate, lacked privileges. Many felt that their wealth entitled them to a greater degree of social status and political power.

The workers of France's cities formed the second, and poorest, group within the Third Estate. These urban workers included tradespeople, apprentices, laborers, and domestic servants. Paid low wages and frequently out of work, they often

hmhsocialstudies.com
TAKING NOTES
Use the graphic organizer online to take notes on the causes of the French Revolution.

The Three Estates

A FAUT ESPERER Q'EU JEU LA FINIRA BEN TOT.

Ⓐ First Estate
- made up of clergy of Roman Catholic Church
- scorned Enlightenment ideas

Ⓑ Second Estate
- made up of rich nobles
- held highest offices in government
- disagreed about Enlightenment ideas

Ⓒ Third Estate
- included bourgeoisie, urban lower class, and peasant farmers
- had no power to influence government
- embraced Enlightenment ideas
- resented the wealthy First and Second Estates.

Population of France, 1787

97% (Third Estate)

less than 1% (First Estate)

2% (Second Estate)

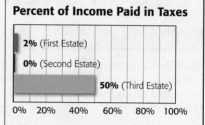

Percent of Income Paid in Taxes

2% (First Estate)

0% (Second Estate)

50% (Third Estate)

0% 20% 40% 60% 80% 100%

SKILLBUILDER: Interpreting Charts and Political Cartoons
1. **Drawing Conclusions** How do the chart and the graphs help explain the political cartoon?
2. **Making Inferences** Why might the First and Second Estates be opposed to change?

went hungry. If the cost of bread rose, mobs of these workers might attack grain carts and bread shops to steal what they needed.

Peasants formed the largest group within the Third Estate, more than 80 percent of France's 26 million people. Peasants paid about half their income in dues to nobles, tithes to the Church, and taxes to the king's agents. They even paid taxes on such basic staples as salt. Peasants and the urban poor resented the clergy and the nobles for their privileges and special treatment. The heavily taxed and discontented Third Estate was eager for change.

Vocabulary

tithe: a church tax, normally about one-tenth of a family's income

The Forces of Change

In addition to the growing resentment among the lower classes, other factors contributed to the revolutionary mood in France. New ideas about government, serious economic problems, and weak and indecisive leadership all helped to generate a desire for change.

Enlightenment Ideas New views about power and authority in government were spreading among the Third Estate. Members of the Third Estate were inspired by the success of the American Revolution. They began questioning long-standing notions about the structure of society. Quoting Rousseau and Voltaire, they began to demand equality, liberty, and democracy. The Comte D'Antraigues, a friend of Rousseau, best summed up their ideas on what government should be:

PRIMARY SOURCE
The Third Estate is the People and the People is the foundation of the State; it is in fact the State itself; the . . . People is everything. Everything should be subordinated to it. . . . It is in the People that all national power resides and for the People that all states exist.

COMTE D'ANTRAIGUES, quoted in *Citizens: A Chronicle of the French Revolution*

Economic Troubles By the 1780s, France's once prosperous economy was in decline. This caused alarm, particularly among the merchants, factory owners, and

652 Chapter 23

bankers of the Third Estate. On the surface, the economy appeared to be sound, because both production and trade were expanding rapidly. However, the heavy burden of taxes made it almost impossible to conduct business profitably within France. Further, the cost of living was rising sharply. In addition, bad weather in the 1780s caused widespread crop failures, resulting in a severe shortage of grain. The price of bread doubled in 1789, and many people faced starvation.

During the 1770s and 1780s, France's government sank deeply into debt. Part of the problem was the extravagant spending of **Louis XVI** and his queen, **Marie Antoinette**. Louis also inherited a considerable debt from previous kings. And he borrowed heavily in order to help the American revolutionaries in their war against Great Britain, France's chief rival. This nearly doubled the government's debt. In 1786, when bankers refused to lend the government any more money, Louis faced serious problems.

A Weak Leader Strong leadership might have solved these and other problems. Louis XVI, however, was indecisive and allowed matters to drift. He paid little attention to his government advisers, and had little patience for the details of governing. The queen only added to Louis's problems. She often interfered in the government, and frequently offered Louis poor advice. Further, since she was a member of the royal family of Austria, France's long-time enemy, Marie Antoinette had been unpopular from the moment she set foot in France. Her behavior only made the situation worse. As queen, she spent so much money on gowns, jewels, gambling, and gifts that she became known as "Madame Deficit."

Vocabulary
deficit: debt

Rather than cutting expenses, Louis put off dealing with the emergency until he practically had no money left. His solution was to impose taxes on the nobility. However, the Second Estate forced him to call a meeting of the **Estates-General**—an assembly of representatives from all three estates—to approve this new tax. The meeting, the first in 175 years, was held on May 5, 1789, at Versailles.

History Makers

Louis XVI
1754–1793

Louis XVI's tutors made little effort to prepare him for his role as king—and it showed. He was easily bored with affairs of state, and much preferred to spend his time in physical activities, particularly hunting. He also loved to work with his hands, and was skilled in several trades, including lock-making, metalworking, and bricklaying.

Despite these shortcomings, Louis was well intentioned and sincerely wanted to improve the lives of the common people. However, he lacked the ability to make decisions and the determination to see policies through. When he did take action, it often was based on poor advice from ill-informed members of his court. As one politician of the time noted, "His reign was a succession of feeble attempts at doing good, shows of weakness, and clear evidence of his inadequacy as a leader."

Marie Antoinette
1755–1793

Marie Antoinette was a pretty, lighthearted, charming woman. However, she was unpopular with the French because of her spending and her involvement in controversial court affairs. She referred to Louis as "the poor man" and sometimes set the clock forward an hour to be rid of his presence.

Marie Antoinette refused to wear the tight-fitting clothing styles of the day and introduced a loose cotton dress for women. The elderly, who viewed the dress as an undergarment, thought that her clothing was scandalous. The French silk industry was equally angry.

In constant need of entertainment, Marie Antoinette often spent hours playing cards. One year she lost the equivalent of $1.5 million by gambling in card games.

 hmhsocialstudies.com

RESEARCH WEB LINKS Go online for more on Louis XVI and Marie Antoinette.

Dawn of the Revolution

The clergy and the nobles had dominated the Estates-General throughout the Middle Ages and expected to do so in the 1789 meeting. Under the assembly's medieval rules, each estate's delegates met in a separate hall to vote, and each estate had one vote. The two privileged estates could always outvote the Third Estate.

The National Assembly The Third Estate delegates, mostly members of the bourgeoisie whose views had been shaped by the Enlightenment, were eager to make changes in the government. They insisted that all three estates meet together and that each delegate have a vote. This would give the advantage to the Third Estate, which had as many delegates as the other two estates combined. **A**

MAIN IDEA

Analyzing Motives

A Why did the Third Estate propose a change in the Estates-General's voting rules?

Siding with the nobles, the king ordered the Estates-General to follow the medieval rules. The delegates of the Third Estate, however, became more and more determined to wield power. A leading spokesperson for their viewpoint was a clergyman sympathetic to their cause, Emmanuel-Joseph Sieyès (syay•YEHS). In a dramatic speech, Sieyès suggested that the Third Estate delegates name themselves the **National Assembly** and pass laws and reforms in the name of the French people.

After a long night of excited debate, the delegates of the Third Estate agreed to Sieyès's idea by an overwhelming majority. On June 17, 1789, they voted to establish the National Assembly, in effect proclaiming the end of absolute monarchy and the beginning of representative government. This vote was the first deliberate act of revolution.

Three days later, the Third Estate delegates found themselves locked out of their meeting room. They broke down a door to an indoor tennis court, pledging to stay until they had drawn up a new constitution. This pledge became known as the **Tennis Court Oath**. Soon after, nobles and members of the clergy who favored reform joined the Third Estate delegates. In response to these events, Louis stationed his mercenary army of Swiss guards around Versailles.

Vocabulary

mercenary army: a group of soldiers who will work for any country or employer that will pay them

▼ The attack on the Bastille claimed the lives of about 100 people.

Storming the Bastille In Paris, rumors flew. Some people suggested that Louis was intent on using military force to dismiss the National Assembly. Others charged that the foreign troops were coming to Paris to massacre French citizens.

People began to gather weapons in order to defend the city against attack. On July 14, a mob searching for gunpowder and arms stormed the Bastille, a Paris prison. The mob overwhelmed the guard and seized control of the building. The angry attackers hacked the prison commander and several guards to death, and then paraded around the streets with the dead men's heads on pikes.

The fall of the Bastille became a great symbolic act of revolution to the French people. Ever since, July 14—Bastille Day—has been a French national holiday, similar to the Fourth of July in the United States.

A Great Fear Sweeps France

Before long, rebellion spread from Paris into the countryside. From one village to the next, wild rumors circulated that the nobles were hiring outlaws to terrorize the peasants. A wave of senseless panic called the **Great Fear** rolled through France. The peasants soon became outlaws themselves. Armed with pitchforks and other farm tools, they broke into nobles' manor houses and destroyed the old legal papers that bound them to pay feudal dues. In some cases, the peasants simply burned down the manor houses.

In October 1789, thousands of Parisian women rioted over the rising price of bread. Brandishing knives, axes, and other weapons, the women marched on Versailles. First, they demanded that the National Assembly take action to provide bread. Then they turned their anger on the king and queen. They broke into the palace, killing some of the guards. The women demanded that Louis and Marie Antoinette return to Paris. After some time, Louis agreed.

A few hours later the king, his family, and servants left Versailles, never again to see the magnificent palace. Their exit signaled the change of power and radical reforms about to overtake France. **B**

MAIN IDEA

Recognizing Effects

 How did the women's march mark a turning point in the relationship between the king and the people?

Social History

Bread

Bread was a staple of the diet of the common people of France. Most families consumed three or four 4-pound loaves a day. And the purchase of bread took about half of a worker's wages—when times were good. So, when the price of bread jumped dramatically, as it did in the fall of 1789, people faced a real threat of starvation.

On their march back from Versailles, the women of Paris happily sang that they were bringing "the baker, the baker's wife, and the baker's lad" with them. They expected the "baker"—Louis—to provide the cheap bread that they needed to live.

SECTION 1 ASSESSMENT

TERMS & NAMES 1. For each term or name, write a sentence explaining its significance.

• Old Regime • estates • Louis XVI • Marie Antoinette • Estates-General • National Assembly • Tennis Court Oath • Great Fear

USING YOUR NOTES

2. Select one of the causes you listed and explain how it contributed to the French Revolution.

Causes of Revolution

MAIN IDEAS

3. Why were members of the Third Estate dissatisfied with life under the Old Regime?

4. How did Louis XVI's weak leadership contribute to the growing crisis in France?

5. How did the purpose of the meeting of the Estates-General in 1789 change?

CRITICAL THINKING & WRITING

6. **FORMING AND SUPPORTING OPINIONS** Do you think that changes in the French government were inevitable? Explain.

7. **ANALYZING MOTIVES** Why do you think some members of the First and Second Estates joined the National Assembly and worked to reform the government?

8. **COMPARING AND CONTRASTING** How were the storming of the Bastille and the women's march on Versailles similar? How were they different?

9. **WRITING ACTIVITY** POWER AND AUTHORITY In the role of a member of the Third Estate, write a brief **speech** explaining why the French political system needs to change.

CONNECT TO TODAY CREATING A COLLAGE

Conduct research on how Bastille Day is celebrated in France today. Use your findings to create an **annotated collage** titled "Celebrating the Revolution."

The French Revolution and Napoleon **655**

Revolution Brings Reform and Terror

MAIN IDEA	WHY IT MATTERS NOW	TERMS & NAMES
REVOLUTION The revolutionary government of France made reforms but also used terror and violence to retain power.	Some governments that lack the support of a majority of their people still use fear to control their citizens.	• Legislative Assembly • guillotine • émigré • Maximilien Robespierre • sans-culotte • Reign of Terror • Jacobin

SETTING THE STAGE Peasants were not the only members of French society to feel the Great Fear. Nobles and officers of the Church were equally afraid. Throughout France, bands of angry peasants struck out against members of the upper classes, attacking and destroying many manor houses. In the summer of 1789, a few months before the women's march to Versailles, some nobles and members of clergy in the National Assembly responded to the uprisings in an emotional late-night meeting.

The Assembly Reforms France

TAKING NOTES

Use the graphic organizer online to take notes on the major events that followed the creation of the Constitution of 1791.

Throughout the night of August 4, 1789, noblemen made grand speeches, declaring their love of liberty and equality. Motivated more by fear than by idealism, they joined other members of the National Assembly in sweeping away the feudal privileges of the First and Second Estates, thus making commoners equal to the nobles and the clergy. By morning, the Old Regime was dead.

The Rights of Man Three weeks later, the National Assembly adopted a statement of revolutionary ideals, the Declaration of the Rights of Man and of the Citizen. Reflecting the influence of the Declaration of Independence, the document stated that "men are born and remain free and equal in rights." These rights included "liberty, property, security, and resistance to oppression." The document also guaranteed citizens equal justice, freedom of speech, and freedom of religion.

In keeping with these principles, revolutionary leaders adopted the expression "Liberty, Equality, Fraternity" as their slogan. Such sentiments, however, did not apply to everyone. When writer Olympe de Gouges (aw•LIMP duh GOOZH) published a declaration of the rights of women, her ideas were rejected. Later, in 1793, she was declared an enemy of the Revolution and executed.

A State-Controlled Church Many of the National Assembly's early reforms focused on the Church. The assembly took over Church lands and declared that Church officials and priests were to be elected and paid as state officials. Thus, the Catholic Church lost both its lands and its political independence. The reasons for the assembly's actions were largely economic. Proceeds from the sale of Church lands helped pay off France's huge debt.

The assembly's actions alarmed millions of French peasants, who were devout Catholics. The effort to make the Church a part of the state offended them, even

◄ One of the people who stopped Louis from escaping said that he recognized the king from his portrait on a French bank note.

though it was in accord with Enlightenment philosophy. They believed that the pope should rule over a church independent of the state. From this time on, many peasants opposed the assembly's reforms.

Louis Tries to Escape As the National Assembly restructured the relationship between church and state, Louis XVI pondered his fate as a monarch. Some of his advisers warned him that he and his family were in danger. Many supporters of the monarchy thought France unsafe and left the country. Then, in June 1791, the royal family tried to escape from France to the Austrian Netherlands. As they neared the border, however, they were apprehended and returned to Paris under guard. Louis's attempted escape increased the influence of his radical enemies in the government and sealed his fate.

Divisions Develop

For two years, the National Assembly argued over a new constitution for France. By 1791, the delegates had made significant changes in France's government and society.

A Limited Monarchy In September 1791, the National Assembly completed the new constitution, which Louis reluctantly approved. The constitution created a limited constitutional monarchy. It stripped the king of much of his authority. It also created a new legislative body—the **Legislative Assembly**. This body had the power to create laws and to approve or reject declarations of war. However, the king still held the executive power to enforce laws.

Factions Split France Despite the new government, old problems, such as food shortages and government debt, remained. The question of how to handle these problems caused the Legislative Assembly to split into three general groups, each of which sat in a different part of the meeting hall. Radicals, who sat on the left side of the hall, opposed the idea of a monarchy and wanted sweeping changes in the way the government was run. Moderates sat in the center of the hall and wanted some changes in government, but not as many as the radicals. Conservatives sat on the right side of the hall. They upheld the idea of a limited monarchy and wanted few changes in government. **A**

MAIN IDEA

Recognizing Effects

A How did differences of opinion on how to handle such issues as food shortages and debt affect the Legislative Assembly?

Connect to Today

Left, Right, and Center

The terms we use today to describe where people stand politically derive from the factions that developed in the Legislative Assembly in 1791.

- People who want to radically change government are called left wing or are said to be on the left.
- People with moderate views often are called centrist or are said to be in the center.
- People who want few or no changes in government often are called right wing or are said to be on the right.

The French Revolution and Napoleon **657**

In addition, factions outside the Legislative Assembly wanted to influence the direction of the government too. **Émigrés** (EHM•ih•GRAYZ), nobles and others who had fled France, hoped to undo the Revolution and restore the Old Regime. In contrast, some Parisian workers and small shopkeepers wanted the Revolution to bring even greater changes to France. They were called **sans-culottes** (SANZ-kyoo•LAHTS), or "those without knee breeches." Unlike the upper classes, who wore fancy knee-length pants, sans-culottes wore regular trousers. Although they did not have a role in the assembly, they soon discovered ways to exert their power on the streets of Paris.

War and Execution

Monarchs and nobles in many European countries watched the changes taking place in France with alarm. They feared that similar revolts might break out in their own countries. In fact, some radicals were keen to spread their revolutionary ideas across Europe. As a result, some countries took action. Austria and Prussia, for example, urged the French to restore Louis to his position as an absolute monarch. The Legislative Assembly responded by declaring war in April 1792.

France at War The war began badly for the French. By the summer of 1792, Prussian forces were advancing on Paris. The Prussian commander threatened to destroy Paris if the revolutionaries harmed any member of the royal family. This enraged the Parisians. On August 10, about 20,000 men and women invaded the Tuileries, the palace where the royal family was staying. The mob massacred the royal guards and imprisoned Louis, Marie Antoinette, and their children.

Shortly after, the French troops defending Paris were sent to reinforce the French army in the field. Rumors began to spread that supporters of the king held in Paris prisons planned to break out and seize control of the city. Angry and fearful citizens responded by taking the law into their own hands. For several days in early September, they raided the prisons and murdered over 1,000 prisoners. Many nobles, priests, and royalist sympathizers fell victim to the angry mobs in these September Massacres. **B**

Under pressure from radicals in the streets and among its members, the Legislative Assembly set aside the Constitution of 1791. It declared the king deposed, dissolved the assembly, and called for the election of a new legislature. This new governing body, the National Convention, took office on September 21. It quickly abolished the monarchy and declared France a republic. Adult male citizens were granted the right to vote and hold office. Despite the important part they had already played in the Revolution, women were not given the vote.

Jacobins Take Control Most of the people involved in the governmental changes in September 1792 were members of a radical political organization, the Jacobin (JAK•uh•bihn) Club. One of the most prominent **Jacobins**, as club members were called, was Jean-Paul Marat (mah•RAH). During the Revolution, he edited a newspaper called *L'Ami du Peuple* (Friend of the People). In his fiery editorials, Marat called for

MAIN IDEA

Analyzing Causes
B What did the September Massacres show about the mood of the people?

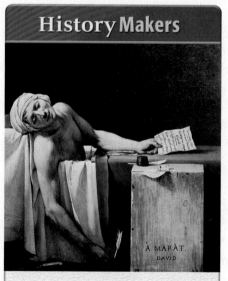

History Makers

Jean-Paul Marat
1743–1793

Marat was a thin, high-strung, sickly man whose revolutionary writings stirred up the violent mood in Paris. Because he suffered from a painful skin disease, he often found comfort by relaxing in a cold bath—even arranging things so that he could work in his bathtub!

During the summer of 1793, Charlotte Corday, a supporter of a rival faction whose members had been jailed, gained an audience with Marat by pretending to have information about traitors. Once inside Marat's private chambers, she fatally stabbed him as he bathed. For her crime, Corday went to the guillotine.

The Guillotine

If you think the guillotine was a cruel form of capital punishment, think again. Dr. Joseph Ignace Guillotin proposed a machine that satisfied many needs—it was efficient, humane, and democratic. A physician and member of the National Assembly, Guillotin claimed that those executed with the device "wouldn't even feel the slightest pain."

Prior to the guillotine's introduction in 1792, many French criminals had suffered through horrible punishments in public places. Although public punishments continued to attract large crowds, not all spectators were pleased with the new machine. Some witnesses felt that death by the guillotine occurred much too quickly to be enjoyed by an audience.

 hmhsocialstudies.com

RESEARCH WEB LINKS Go online for more on the guillotine.

Once the executioner cranked the blade to the top, a mechanism released it. The sharp weighted blade fell, severing the victim's head from his or her body.

Some doctors believed that a victim's head retained its hearing and eyesight for up to 15 minutes after the blade's deadly blow. All remains were eventually gathered and buried in simple graves.

Tricoteuses, or "woman knitters," were regular spectators at executions and knitted stockings for soldiers as they sat near the base of the scaffold.

Before each execution, bound victims traveled from the prison to the scaffold in horse-drawn carts during a one and one-half hour procession through city streets.

Beheading by Class

More than 2,100 people were executed during the last 132 days of the Reign of Terror. The pie graph below displays the breakdown of beheadings by class.

- ■ First Estate
- ■ Second Estate
- ■ Third Estate

Connect *to* Today

1. **Synthesizing** In what ways was the guillotine an efficient means of execution?

   See Skillbuilder Handbook, page R21.

2. **Comparing** France continued to use the guillotine until 1977. Four years later, France abolished capital punishment. Conduct research to identify countries where capital punishment is still used. Use your findings to create a map titled "Countries Using Capital Punishment."

the death of all those who continued to support the king. Georges Danton (zhawrzh-dahn•TAWN), a lawyer, was among the club's most talented and passionate speakers. He also was known for his devotion to the rights of Paris's poor people.

The National Convention had reduced Louis XVI's role from that of a king to that of a common citizen and prisoner. Now, guided by radical Jacobins, it tried Louis for treason. The Convention found him guilty, and, by a very close vote, sentenced him to death. On January 21, 1793, the former king walked with calm dignity up the steps of the scaffold to be beheaded by a machine called the **guillotine** (GIHL•uh•TEEN). (See the Science & Technology feature on page 659.)

The War Continues The National Convention also had to contend with the continuing war with Austria and Prussia. At about the time the Convention took office, the French army won a stunning victory against the Austrians and Prussians at the Battle of Valmy. Early in 1793, however, Great Britain, Holland, and Spain joined Prussia and Austria against France. Forced to contend with so many enemies, the French suffered a string of defeats. To reinforce the French army, Jacobin leaders in the Convention took an extreme step. At their urging, in February 1793 the Convention ordered a draft of 300,000 French citizens between the ages of 18 and 40. By 1794, the army had grown to 800,000 and included women.

The Terror Grips France

Foreign armies were not the only enemies of the French republic. The Jacobins had thousands of enemies within France itself. These included peasants who were horrified by the king's execution, priests who would not accept government control, and rival leaders who were stirring up rebellion in the provinces. How to contain and control these enemies became a central issue.

Robespierre Assumes Control In the early months of 1793, one Jacobin leader, **Maximilien Robespierre** (ROHBZ•peer), slowly gained power. Robespierre and his supporters set out to build a "republic of virtue" by wiping out every trace of France's past. Firm believers in reason, they changed the calendar, dividing the year into 12 months of 30 days and renaming each month. This calendar had no Sundays because the radicals considered religion old-fashioned and dangerous. They even closed all churches in Paris, and cities and towns all over France soon did the same.

In July 1793, Robespierre became leader of the Committee of Public Safety. For the next year, Robespierre governed France virtually as a dictator, and the period of his rule became known as the **Reign of Terror**. The Committee of Public Safety's chief task was to protect the Revolution from its enemies. Under Robespierre's leadership, the committee often had these "enemies" tried in the morning and guillotined in the afternoon. Robespierre justified his use of terror by suggesting that it enabled French citizens to remain true to the ideals of the Revolution. He also saw a connection between virtue and terror:

PRIMARY SOURCE C

The first maxim of our politics ought to be to lead the people by means of reason and the enemies of the people by terror. If the basis of popular government in time of peace is virtue, the basis of popular government in time of revolution is both virtue and terror: virtue without which terror is murderous, terror without which virtue is powerless. Terror is nothing else than swift, severe, indomitable justice; it flows, then, from virtue.

MAXIMILIEN ROBESPIERRE, "On the Morals and Political Principles of Domestic Policy" (1794)

MAIN IDEA

Analyzing Primary Sources

C How did Robespierre justify the use of terror?

The "enemies of the Revolution" who troubled Robespierre the most were fellow radicals who challenged his leadership. In 1793 and 1794, many of those who had led the Revolution received death sentences. Their only crime was that they were considered less radical than Robespierre. By early 1794, even Georges Danton found himself in danger. Danton's friends in the National Convention, afraid to defend him, joined in condemning him. On the scaffold, he told the executioner, "Don't forget to show my head to the people. It's well worth seeing."

The Terror claimed not only the famous, such as Danton and Marie Antoinette, the widowed queen. Thousands of unknown people also were sent to their deaths, often on the flimsiest of charges. For example, an 18-year-old youth was sentenced to die for cutting down a tree that had been planted as a symbol of liberty. Perhaps as many as 40,000 were executed during the Terror. About 85 percent were peasants or members of the urban poor or middle class—for whose benefit the Revolution had been launched.

End of the Terror

In July 1794, fearing for their own safety, some members of the National Convention turned on Robespierre. They demanded his arrest and execution. The Reign of Terror, the radical phase of the French Revolution, ended on July 28, 1794, when Robespierre went to the guillotine.

▲ At his trial, Georges Danton defended himself so skillfully that the authorities eventually denied him the right to speak.

French public opinion shifted dramatically after Robespierre's death. People of all classes had grown weary of the Terror. They were also tired of the skyrocketing prices for bread, salt, and other necessities of life. In 1795, moderate leaders in the National Convention drafted a new plan of government, the third since 1789. It placed power firmly in the hands of the upper middle class and called for a two-house legislature and an executive body of five men, known as the Directory. These five were moderates, not revolutionary idealists. Some of them were corrupt and made themselves rich at the country's expense. Even so, they gave their troubled country a period of order. They also found the right general to command France's armies—Napoleon Bonaparte.

SECTION 2 ASSESSMENT

TERMS & NAMES 1. For each term or name, write a sentence explaining its significance.
• Legislative Assembly   • émigré   • sans-culotte   • Jacobin   • guillotine   • Maximilien Robespierre   • Reign of Terror

USING YOUR NOTES
2. Do you think this chain of events could have been changed in any way? Explain.

Assembly Creates a Constitution

MAIN IDEAS
3. What major reforms did the National Assembly introduce?
4. What did the divisions in the Legislative Assembly say about the differences in French society?
5. How did the Reign of Terror come to an end?

CRITICAL THINKING & WRITING
6. **SYNTHESIZING** How did the slogan "Liberty, Equality, Fraternity" sum up the goals of the Revolution?
7. **COMPARING AND CONTRASTING** What similarities and differences do you see between the political factions in the Legislative Assembly and those in the U.S. government today?
8. **ANALYZING CAUSES** What factors led to Robespierre becoming a dictator?
9. **WRITING ACTIVITY** REVOLUTION Working in small teams, write short **biographies** of three revolutionary figures mentioned in this section.

MULTIMEDIA ACTIVITY PREPARING AN ORAL REPORT

Use the Internet to conduct research on governments that use terrorism against their own people. Prepare an **oral report** on the methods these countries use.

INTERNET KEYWORD
human rights

The French Revolution and Napoleon **661**

The French Revolution

Over time, people have expressed a wide variety of opinions about the causes and outcomes of the French Revolution. The following excerpts, dating from the 1790s to 1859, illustrate this diversity of opinion.

A SECONDARY SOURCE

Charles Dickens

In 1859, the English writer Dickens wrote *A Tale of Two Cities*, a novel about the French Revolution for which he did much research. In the following scene, Charles Darnay—an aristocrat who gave up his title because he hated the injustices done to the people—has returned to France and been put on trial.

———

His judges sat upon the bench in feathered hats; but the rough red cap and tricolored cockade was the headdress otherwise prevailing. Looking at the jury and the turbulent audience, he might have thought that the usual order of things was reversed, and that the felons were trying the honest men. The lowest, cruelest, and worst populace of a city, never without its quantity of low, cruel, and bad, were the directing spirits of the scene. . . .

Charles Evrémonde, called Darnay, was accused by the public prosecutor as an emigrant, whose life was forfeit to the Republic, under the decree which banished all emigrants on pain of Death. It was nothing that the decree bore date since his return to France. There he was, and there was the decree; he had been taken in France, and his head was demanded.

"Take off his head!" cried the audience. "An enemy to the Republic!"

▶ In this illustration from *A Tale of Two Cities*, Sidney Carton goes to the guillotine in Darnay's place.

B PRIMARY SOURCE

Edmund Burke

Burke, a British politician, was one of the earliest and most severe critics of the French Revolution. In 1790, he expressed this opinion.

———

[The French have rebelled] against a mild and lawful monarch, with more fury, outrage, and insult, than ever any people has been known to rise against the most illegal usurper, or the most [bloodthirsty] tyrant. . . .

They have found their punishment in their success. Laws overturned; tribunals subverted; . . . the people impoverished; a church pillaged, and . . . civil and military anarchy made the constitution of the kingdom. . . .

Were all these dreadful things necessary?

C PRIMARY SOURCE

Thomas Paine

In 1790, Paine—a strong supporter of the American Revolution—defended the French Revolution against Burke and other critics.

———

It is no longer the paltry cause of kings or of this or of that individual, that calls France and her armies into action. It is the great cause of all. It is the establishment of a new era, that shall blot despotism from the earth, and fix, on the lasting principles of peace and citizenship, the great Republic of Man.

The scene that now opens itself to France extends far beyond the boundaries of her own dominions. Every nation is becoming her ally, and every court has become her enemy. It is now the cause of all nations, against the cause of all courts.

Document-Based QUESTIONS

1. In your own words, summarize the attitude toward the French Revolution expressed in each of these excerpts.

2. Why might Edmund Burke (Source B) be so against the French Revolution?

3. In Source C, what is the distinction Thomas Paine is making between nations and courts?

Napoleon Forges an Empire

MAIN IDEA	WHY IT MATTERS NOW	TERMS & NAMES
POWER AND AUTHORITY Napoleon Bonaparte, a military genius, seized power in France and made himself emperor.	In times of political turmoil, military dictators often seize control of nations.	• Napoleon Bonaparte • coup d'état • plebiscite • lycée • concordat • Napoleonic Code • Battle of Trafalgar

SETTING THE STAGE Napoleon Bonaparte was quite a short man—just five feet three inches tall. However, he cast a long shadow over the history of modern times. He would come to be recognized as one of the world's greatest military geniuses, along with Alexander the Great of Macedonia, Hannibal of Carthage, and Julius Caesar of Rome. In only four years, from 1795 to 1799, Napoleon rose from a relatively obscure position as an officer in the French army to become master of France.

Napoleon Seizes Power

Napoleon Bonaparte was born in 1769 on the Mediterranean island of Corsica. When he was nine years old, his parents sent him to a military school. In 1785, at the age of 16, he finished school and became a lieutenant in the artillery. When the Revolution broke out, Napoleon joined the army of the new government.

Hero of the Hour In October 1795, fate handed the young officer a chance for glory. When royalist rebels marched on the National Convention, a government official told Napoleon to defend the delegates. Napoleon and his gunners greeted the thousands of royalists with a cannonade. Within minutes, the attackers fled in panic and confusion. Napoleon Bonaparte became the hero of the hour and was hailed throughout Paris as the savior of the French republic.

In 1796, the Directory appointed Napoleon to lead a French army against the forces of Austria and the Kingdom of Sardinia. Crossing the Alps, the young general swept into Italy and won a series of remarkable victories. Next, in an attempt to protect French trade interests and to disrupt British trade with India, Napoleon led an expedition to Egypt. But he was unable to repeat the successes he had achieved in Europe. His army was pinned down in Egypt, and the British admiral Horatio Nelson defeated his naval forces. However, Napoleon managed to keep stories about his setbacks out of the newspapers and thereby remained a great hero to the people of France.

Coup d'État By 1799, the Directory had lost control of the political situation and the confidence of the French people. When Napoleon returned from Egypt, his friends urged him to seize political power. Napoleon took action in early November 1799. His troops surrounded the national legislature and drove out most of its members. The remaining lawmakers voted to dissolve the Directory.

hmhsocialstudies.com
TAKING NOTES

Use the graphic organizer online to take notes on the events that led to Napoleon's crowning as emperor of France.

History Makers

Napoleon Bonaparte
1769–1821

Because of his small stature and thick Corsican accent, Napoleon was mocked by his fellow students at military school. Haughty and proud, Napoleon refused to grace his tormentors' behavior with any kind of response. He simply ignored them, preferring to lose himself in his studies. He showed a particular passion for three subjects—classical history, geography, and mathematics.

In 1784, Napoleon was recommended for a career in the army and he transferred to the Ecole Militaire (the French equivalent of West Point) in Paris. There, he proved to be a fairly poor soldier, except when it came to artillery. His artillery instructor quickly noticed Napoleon's abilities: "He is most proud, ambitious, aspiring to everything. This young man merits our attention."

HISTORY

VIDEO
Napoleon
Bonaparte: The
Glory of France

⤴ hmhsocialstudies.com

In its place, they established a group of three consuls, one of whom was Napoleon. Napoleon quickly took the title of first consul and assumed the powers of a dictator. A sudden seizure of power like Napoleon's is known as a *coup*—from the French phrase **coup d'état** (KOO day•TAH), or "blow to the state." Ⓐ

At the time of Napoleon's coup, France was still at war. In 1799, Britain, Austria, and Russia joined forces with one goal in mind, to drive Napoleon from power. Once again, Napoleon rode from Paris at the head of his troops. Eventually, as a result of war and diplomacy, all three nations signed peace agreements with France. By 1802, Europe was at peace for the first time in ten years. Napoleon was free to focus his energies on restoring order in France.

Napoleon Rules France

At first, Napoleon pretended to be the constitutionally chosen leader of a free republic. In 1800, a **plebiscite** (PLEHB•ih•SYT), or vote of the people, was held to approve a new constitution. Desperate for strong leadership, the people voted overwhelmingly in favor of the constitution. This gave all real power to Napoleon as first consul.

Restoring Order at Home Napoleon did not try to return the nation to the days of Louis XVI. Rather, he kept many of the changes that had come with the Revolution. In general, he supported laws that would both strengthen the central government and achieve some of the goals of the Revolution.

His first task was to get the economy on a solid footing. Napoleon set up an efficient method of tax collection and established a national banking system. In addition to ensuring the government a steady supply of tax money, these actions promoted sound financial management and better control of the economy. Napoleon also took steps to end corruption and inefficiency in government. He dismissed corrupt officials and, in order to provide the government with trained officials, set up **lycées**, or government-run public schools. These lycées were open to male students of all backgrounds. Graduates were appointed to public office on the basis of merit rather than family connections.

One area where Napoleon disregarded changes introduced by the Revolution was religion. Both the clergy and many peasants wanted to restore the position of the Church in France. Responding to their wishes, Napoleon signed a **concordat**, or agreement, with Pope Pius VII. This established a new relationship between church and state. The government recognized the influence of the Church, but rejected Church control in national affairs. The concordat gained Napoleon the support of the organized Church as well as the majority of the French people.

Napoleon thought that his greatest work was his comprehensive system of laws, known as the **Napoleonic Code**. This gave the country a uniform set of laws and eliminated many injustices. However, it actually limited liberty and promoted order and authority over individual rights. For example, freedom of speech and of the press, established during the Revolution, were restricted under the code. The code also restored slavery in the French colonies of the Caribbean.

MAIN IDEA

Analyzing Causes
Ⓐ How was Napoleon able to become a dictator?

Napoleon Crowned as Emperor In 1804, Napoleon decided to make himself emperor, and the French voters supported him. On December 2, 1804, dressed in a splendid robe of purple velvet, Napoleon walked down the long aisle of Notre Dame Cathedral in Paris. The pope waited for him with a glittering crown. As thousands watched, the new emperor took the crown from the pope and placed it on his own head. With this gesture, Napoleon signaled that he was more powerful than the Church, which had traditionally crowned the rulers of France. **B**

MAIN IDEA

Analyzing Motives

B Why do you think Napoleon crowned himself emperor?

Napoleon Creates an Empire

Napoleon was not content simply to be master of France. He wanted to control the rest of Europe and to reassert French power in the Americas. He envisioned his western empire including Louisiana, Florida, French Guiana, and the French West Indies. He knew that the key to this area was the sugar-producing colony of Saint Domingue (now called Haiti) on the island of Hispaniola.

Loss of American Territories In 1789, when the ideas of the Revolution reached the planters in Saint Domingue, they demanded that the National Assembly give them the same privileges as the people of France. Eventually, enslaved Africans in the colony demanded their rights too—in other words, their freedom. A civil war erupted, and enslaved Africans under the leadership of Toussaint L'Ouverture seized control of the colony. In 1801, Napoleon decided to take back the colony and restore its productive sugar industry. However, the French forces were devastated by disease. And the rebels proved to be fierce fighters.

After the failure of the expedition to Saint Domingue, Napoleon decided to cut his losses in the Americas. He offered to sell all of the Louisiana Territory to the United States, and in 1803 President Jefferson's administration agreed to purchase the land for $15 million. Napoleon saw a twofold benefit to the sale. First, he would gain money to finance operations in Europe. Second, he would punish the British. "The sale assures forever the power of the United States," he observed, "and I have given England a rival who, sooner or later, will humble her pride." **C**

MAIN IDEA

Recognizing Effects

C What effects did Napoleon intend the sale of Louisiana to have on France? on the United States? on Britain?

Conquering Europe Having abandoned his imperial ambitions in the New World, Napoleon turned his attention to Europe. He had already annexed the Austrian Netherlands and parts of Italy to France and set up a puppet government in Switzerland. Now he looked to expand his influence further. Fearful of his ambitions, the British persuaded Russia, Austria, and Sweden to join them against France.

Napoleon met this challenge with his usual boldness. In a series of brilliant battles, he crushed the opposition. (See the map on page 666.) The commanders of the enemy armies could never predict his next move and often took heavy losses. After the Battle of Austerlitz in 1805, Napoleon issued a proclamation expressing his pride in his troops:

PRIMARY SOURCE
Soldiers! I am pleased with you. On the day of Austerlitz, you justified everything that I was expecting of [you]. . . . In less than four hours, an army of 100,000 men, commanded by the emperors of Russia and Austria, was cut up and dispersed. . . . 120 pieces of artillery, 20 generals, and more than 30,000 men taken prisoner—such are the results of this day which will forever be famous. . . . And it will be enough for you to say, "I was at Austerlitz," to hear the reply: "There is a brave man!"

NAPOLEON, quoted in *Napoleon* by André Castelot

↗ hmhsocialstudies.com

INTERACTIVE MAP

Explore Napoleon's empire and meet the people he put into positions of power in Europe.

▼ This painting by Jacques Louis David shows Napoleon in a heroic pose.

hmhsocialstudies.com
INTERACTIVE MAP

■	French Empire
▨	Controlled by Napoleon
✶	French victory
✰	French defeat
🛡	British blockade

KINGDOM OF DENMARK AND NORWAY

KINGDOM OF SWEDEN

North Sea

Baltic Sea

REP. OF DANZIG

Neman R.

Moscow (1812)

Borodino (1812)

Friedland (1807)

RUSSIAN EMPIRE

PRUSSIA

UNITED KINGDOM OF GREAT BRITAIN AND IRELAND

London

Elbe R.

Berlin

GRAND DUCHY OF WARSAW

Brussels
Amiens

CONFEDERATION OF THE RHINE

Leipzig (1813)
Jena (1806)

Austerlitz (1805)

ATLANTIC OCEAN

Paris
Versailles

Seine R.

Loire R.

Rhine R.

Ulm (1805)

Wagram (1809)
Aspern (1809)

AUSTRIAN EMPIRE

Vienna

50°N

FRENCH EMPIRE

HELVETIC REPUBLIC

La Coruña (1809)

Milan

KINGDOM OF ITALY

ILLYRIAN PROVINCES

42°N

Ebro R.

Vitoria (1813)

Marseille

Po R.

Adriatic Sea

Danube R.

Black Sea

PORTUGAL

Talavera (1809)

Madrid (1808)

Tagus R.

CORSICA

Rome

MONTENEGRO

SPAIN

Valencia (1808)

SARDINIA

Naples

KINGDOM OF NAPLES

OTTOMAN EMPIRE

Trafalgar (1805)

Gibraltar

Mediterranean Sea

SICILY

N

0   500 Miles

0   1,000 Kilometers

Battle of Trafalgar, Oct. 21, 1805

🔸	British fleet
🔹	French and Spanish fleet
→	British thrust

Villeneuve

Nelson

Álava

Collingwood

By dividing Villeneuve's formation, Admiral Nelson captured nearly two-thirds of the enemy fleet.

Battle of Austerlitz, Dec. 2, 1805

▬	French forces
▬	Allied Russian, Prussian, and Austrian forces
→	French thrust
→	Allied thrust

Bernadotte
Lannes
Bagration

Austerlitz

Soult

Pratzen Plateau

Kollowrat

NAPOLEON (About 70,000 troops)

Goldbach Creek

Doctorov

CZAR ALEXANDER I (About 85,000 troops)

Davout

N

0   2 Miles

0   4 Kilometers

By drawing an Allied attack on his right flank, Napoleon was able to split the Allied line at its center.

GEOGRAPHY SKILLBUILDER: Interpreting Maps

1. **Region** What was the extent of the lands under Napoleon's control?
2. **Location** Where was the Battle of Trafalgar fought? What tactic did Nelson use in the battle, and why was it successful?

In time, Napoleon's battlefield successes forced the rulers of Austria, Prussia, and Russia to sign peace treaties. These successes also enabled him to build the largest European empire since that of the Romans. France's only major enemy left undefeated was the great naval power, Britain.

The Battle of Trafalgar In his drive for a European empire, Napoleon lost only one major battle, the <u>Battle of Trafalgar</u> (truh•FAL•guhr). This naval defeat, however, was more important than all of his victories on land. The battle took place in 1805 off the southwest coast of Spain. The British commander, Horatio Nelson, was as brilliant in warfare at sea as Napoleon was in warfare on land. In a bold maneuver, he split the larger French fleet, capturing many ships. (See the map inset on the opposite page.)

The destruction of the French fleet had two major results. First, it ensured the supremacy of the British navy for the next 100 years. Second, it forced Napoleon to give up his plans of invading Britain. He had to look for another way to control his powerful enemy across the English Channel. Eventually, Napoleon's extravagant efforts to crush Britain would lead to his own undoing.

The French Empire During the first decade of the 1800s, Napoleon's victories had given him mastery over most of Europe. By 1812, the only areas of Europe free from Napoleon's control were Britain, Portugal, Sweden, and the Ottoman Empire. In addition to the lands of the French Empire, Napoleon also controlled numerous supposedly independent countries. (See the map on the opposite page.) These included Spain, the Grand Duchy of Warsaw, and a number of German kingdoms in Central Europe. The rulers of these countries were Napoleon's puppets; some, in fact, were members of his family. Furthermore, the powerful countries of Russia, Prussia, and Austria were loosely attached to Napoleon's empire through alliances. Although not totally under Napoleon's control, they were easily manipulated by threats of military action. **D**

The French Empire was huge but unstable. Napoleon was able to maintain it at its greatest extent for only five years—from 1807 to 1812. Then it quickly fell to pieces. Its sudden collapse was caused in part by Napoleon's actions.

MAIN IDEA

Drawing Conclusions

D By 1805, how successful had Napoleon been in his efforts to build an empire?

SECTION ③ **ASSESSMENT**

TERMS & NAMES 1. For each term or name, write a sentence explaining its significance.
• Napoleon Bonaparte   • coup d'état   • plebiscite   • lycée   • concordat   • Napoleonic Code   • Battle of Trafalgar

USING YOUR NOTES	**MAIN IDEAS**	**CRITICAL THINKING & WRITING**
2. Which of these events do you think had the greatest impact on Napoleon's rise to power?	3. How did Napoleon become a hero in France? 4. What did Napoleon consider his greatest triumph in domestic policy? 5. How was Napoleon able to control the countries neighboring the French Empire?	6. **FORMING OPINIONS** In your opinion, was Napoleon the creator or the creation of his times? 7. **ANALYZING ISSUES** Napoleon had to deal with forces both inside and outside the French Empire. In your judgment, which area was more important to control? 8. **MAKING INFERENCES** If you had been a member of the bourgeoisie, would you have been satisfied with the results of Napoleon's actions? Explain. 9. **WRITING ACTIVITY** POWER AND AUTHORITY Look at the painting on page 665. Write a **paragraph** discussing why the painter portrayed Napoleon in this fashion.

CONNECT TO TODAY **CREATING A VENN DIAGRAM**

Identify and conduct research on a present-day world leader who has used dictatorial powers to rule his or her country. Use your findings to create a **Venn diagram** comparing this leader's use of power to Napoleon's use of power.

The French Revolution and Napoleon **667**

Napoleon's Empire Collapses

MAIN IDEA	WHY IT MATTERS NOW	TERMS & NAMES
POWER AND AUTHORITY Napoleon's conquests aroused nationalistic feelings across Europe and contributed to his downfall.	In the 1990s, nationalistic feelings contributed to the breakup of nations such as Yugoslavia.	• blockade • scorched-earth policy • Continental System • guerrilla • Waterloo • Peninsular War • Hundred Days

SETTING THE STAGE Napoleon worried about what would happen to his vast empire after his death. He feared it would fall apart unless he had an heir whose right to succeed him was undisputed. His wife, Josephine, had failed to bear him a child. He, therefore, divorced her and formed an alliance with the Austrian royal family by marrying Marie Louise, the grandniece of Marie Antoinette. In 1811, Marie Louise gave birth to a son, Napoleon II, whom Napoleon named king of Rome.

Napoleon's Costly Mistakes

hmhsocialstudies.com
TAKING NOTES

Use the graphic organizer online to take notes on Napoleon's three mistakes and the impact they had on the French Empire.

Napoleon's own personality proved to be the greatest danger to the future of his empire. His desire for power had raised him to great heights, and the same love of power led him to his doom. In his efforts to extend the French Empire and crush Great Britain, Napoleon made three disastrous mistakes.

The Continental System In November 1806, Napoleon set up a **blockade**—a forcible closing of ports—to prevent all trade and communication between Great Britain and other European nations. Napoleon called this policy the **Continental System** because it was supposed to make continental Europe more self-sufficient. Napoleon also intended it to destroy Great Britain's commercial and industrial economy.

Napoleon's blockade, however, was not nearly tight enough. Aided by the British, smugglers managed to bring cargo from Britain into Europe. At times, Napoleon's allies also disregarded the blockade. Even members of Napoleon's family defied the policy, including his brother, Louis, whom he had made king of Holland. While the blockade weakened British trade, it did not destroy it. In addition, Britain responded with its own blockade. And because the British had a stronger navy, they were better able than the French to make the blockade work.

To enforce the blockade, the British navy stopped neutral ships bound for the continent and forced them to sail to a British port to be searched and taxed. American ships were among those stopped by the British navy. Angered, the U.S.

▼ "Little Johnny Bull"—Great Britain—waves a sword at Napoleon as the emperor straddles the globe.

A STOPPAGE to a STRIDE over the GLOBE.

Congress declared war on Britain in 1812. Even though the War of 1812 lasted two years, it was only a minor inconvenience to Britain in its struggle with Napoleon.

The Peninsular War In 1808, Napoleon made a second costly mistake. In an effort to get Portugal to accept the Continental System, he sent an invasion force through Spain. The Spanish people protested this action. In response, Napoleon removed the Spanish king and put his own brother, Joseph, on the throne. This outraged the Spanish people and inflamed their nationalistic feelings. The Spanish, who were devoutly Catholic, also worried that Napoleon would attack the Church. They had seen how the French Revolution had weakened the Catholic Church in France, and they feared that the same thing would happen to the Church in Spain.

For six years, bands of Spanish peasant fighters, known as **guerrillas**, struck at French armies in Spain. The guerrillas were not an army that Napoleon could defeat in open battle. Rather, they worked in small groups that ambushed French troops and then fled into hiding. The British added to the French troubles by sending troops to aid the Spanish. Napoleon lost about 300,000 men during this **Peninsular War**—so called because Spain lies on the Iberian Peninsula. These losses weakened the French Empire.

In Spain and elsewhere, nationalism, or loyalty to one's own country, was becoming a powerful weapon against Napoleon. People who had at first welcomed the French as their liberators now felt abused by a foreign conqueror. Like the Spanish guerrillas, Germans and Italians and other conquered peoples turned against the French. **A**

The Invasion of Russia Napoleon's most disastrous mistake of all came in 1812. Even though Alexander I had become Napoleon's ally, the Russian czar refused to stop selling grain to Britain. In addition, the French and Russian rulers suspected each other of having competing designs on Poland. Because of this breakdown in their alliance, Napoleon decided to invade Russia.

In June 1812, Napoleon and his Grand Army of more than 420,000 soldiers marched into Russia. As Napoleon advanced, Alexander pulled back his troops, refusing to be lured into an unequal battle. On this retreat, the Russians practiced a **scorched-earth policy**. This involved burning grain fields and slaughtering livestock so as to leave nothing for the enemy to eat.

MAIN IDEA

Recognizing Effects

A How could the growing feelings of nationalism in European countries hurt Napoleon?

▼ Francisco Goya's painting *The Third of May, 1808* shows a French firing squad executing Spanish peasants suspected of being guerrillas.

669

Napoleon's Russian Campaign, 1812

130,000
Sept. 7, 1812 Napoleon's army fights the Battle of Borodino and suffers 30,000 casualties.

50,000
Napoleon sends troops to Polotsk to protect his left flank.

175,000
Reduced by desertion, disease, starvation, and capture, an army of 175,000 arrives in Smolensk. Another 30,000 die there.

422,000
June 1812 Napoleon and his troops march across the Neman River and into Russia.

Sept. 14, 1812 Napoleon enters Moscow to find it in ashes, torched by the czar. He waits, hoping to induce the czar to surrender.

Oct. 18, 1812 Frustrated and starving, having waited too long for the czar, the 100,000 survivors of the Grand Army begin their hellish retreat through the cruel Russia winter.

Dec. 6, 1812 Troops march for the Neman River. Only 10,000 make it out of Russia.
28,000

November 1812 The army returns to Smolensk and finds famine. The remaining 24,000 march on, abandoning their wounded.
37,000

The 30,000 in Polotsk join the 20,000 survivors. Thousands drown while crossing the Berezina River.
50,000

Western Dvina River · Polotsk · Glubokoye · Vitebsk · Smolensk · Vyazma · Borodino · Moscow · Maloyaroslavets · Moscow R. · Oku R.
Kovno · Vilna · Molodechno · Borisov · Minsk · Neman River · Dnieper River · Berezina River
PRUSSIA · GRAND DUCHY OF WARSAW · R U S S I A

Advancing troops
Retreating troops
= 10,000 soldiers
= 10,000 lost troops

0 100 Miles
0 200 Kilometers

GEOGRAPHY SKILLBUILDER: Interpreting Maps
1. **Movement** How long did it take the Grand Army to cover the distance between the Russian border and Moscow?
2. **Place** Why was it a mistake for Napoleon to stay in Moscow until mid-October?

On September 7, 1812, the two armies finally clashed in the Battle of Borodino. (See the map on this page.) After several hours of indecisive fighting, the Russians fell back, allowing Napoleon to move on Moscow. When Napoleon entered Moscow seven days later, the city was in flames. Rather than surrender Russia's "holy city" to the French, Alexander had destroyed it. Napoleon stayed in the ruined city until the middle of October, when he decided to turn back toward France.

As the snows—and the temperature—began to fall in early November, Russian raiders mercilessly attacked Napoleon's ragged, retreating army. Many soldiers were killed in these clashes or died of their wounds. Still more dropped in their tracks from exhaustion, hunger, and cold. Finally, in the middle of December, the last survivors straggled out of Russia. The retreat from Moscow had devastated the Grand Army—only 10,000 soldiers were left to fight.

Napoleon's Downfall

Napoleon's enemies were quick to take advantage of his weakness. Britain, Russia, Prussia, and Sweden joined forces against him. Austria also declared war on Napoleon, despite his marriage to Marie Louise. All of the main powers of Europe were now at war with France.

Napoleon Suffers Defeat In only a few months, Napoleon managed to raise another army. However, most of his troops were untrained and ill prepared for battle. He faced the allied armies of the European powers outside the German city of Leipzig (LYP•sihg) in October 1813. The allied forces easily defeated his inexperienced army and French resistance crumbled quickly. By January of 1814, the allied armies were pushing steadily toward Paris. Some two months later, King

Frederick William III of Prussia and Czar Alexander I of Russia led their troops in a triumphant parade through the French capital.

Napoleon wanted to fight on, but his generals refused. In April 1814, he accepted the terms of surrender and gave up his throne. The victors gave Napoleon a small pension and exiled, or banished, him to Elba, a tiny island off the Italian coast. The allies expected no further trouble from Napoleon, but they were wrong.

The Hundred Days Louis XVI's brother assumed the throne as Louis XVIII. (The executed king's son, Louis XVII, had died in prison in 1795.) However, the new king quickly became unpopular among his subjects, especially the peasants. They suspected him of wanting to undo the Revolution's land reforms.

The news of Louis's troubles was all the incentive Napoleon needed to try to regain power. He escaped from Elba and, on March 1, 1815, landed in France. Joyous crowds welcomed him on the march to Paris. And thousands of volunteers swelled the ranks of his army. Within days, Napoleon was again emperor of France. **B**

In response, the European allies quickly marshaled their armies. The British army, led by the Duke of Wellington, prepared for battle near the village of <u>Waterloo</u> in Belgium. On June 18, 1815, Napoleon attacked. The British army defended its ground all day. Late in the afternoon, the Prussian army arrived. Together, the British and the Prussian forces attacked the French. Two days later, Napoleon's exhausted troops gave way, and the British and Prussian forces chased them from the field.

This defeat ended Napoleon's last bid for power, called the <u>**Hundred Days**</u>. Taking no chances this time, the British shipped Napoleon to St. Helena, a remote island in the South Atlantic. There, he lived in lonely exile for six years, writing his memoirs. He died in 1821 of a stomach ailment, perhaps cancer.

Without doubt, Napoleon was a military genius and a brilliant administrator. Yet all his victories and other achievements must be measured against the millions of lives that were lost in his wars. The French writer Alexis de Tocqueville summed up Napoleon's character by saying, "He was as great as a man can be without virtue." Napoleon's defeat opened the door for the freed European countries to establish a new order.

MAIN IDEA

Analyzing Motives

B Why do you think the French people welcomed back Napoleon so eagerly?

▲ British soldiers who fought at the battle of Waterloo received this medal.

SECTION **4** **ASSESSMENT**

TERMS & NAMES 1. For each term or name, write a sentence explaining its significance.
• blockade • Continental System • guerrilla • Peninsular War • scorched-earth policy • Waterloo • Hundred Days

USING YOUR NOTES

2. Which of Napoleon's mistakes was the most serious? Why?

Napoleon's Mistakes	Effect on Empire

MAIN IDEAS

3. How did Great Britain combat Napoleon's naval blockade?

4. Why did Napoleon have trouble fighting the enemy forces in the Peninsular War?

5. Why was Napoleon's delay of the retreat from Moscow such a great blunder?

CRITICAL THINKING & WRITING

6. **ANALYZING MOTIVES** Why did people in other European countries resist Napoleon's efforts to build an empire?

7. **EVALUATING COURSES OF ACTION** Napoleon had no choice but to invade Russia. Do you agree with this statement? Why or why not?

8. **FORMING AND SUPPORTING OPINIONS** Do you think that Napoleon was a great leader? Explain.

9. **WRITING ACTIVITY** [POWER AND AUTHORITY] In the role of a volunteer in Napoleon's army during the Hundred Days, write a **letter** to a friend explaining why you are willing to fight for the emperor.

CONNECT TO TODAY **CREATING A MAP**

Conduct research on how nationalist feelings affect world affairs today. Create a **map** showing the areas of the world where nationalist movements are active. Annotate the map with explanations of the situation in each area.

The Congress of Vienna

MAIN IDEA	WHY IT MATTERS NOW	TERMS & NAMES
POWER AND AUTHORITY After exiling Napoleon, European leaders at the Congress of Vienna tried to restore order and reestablish peace.	International bodies such as the United Nations play an active role in trying to maintain world peace and stability today.	• Congress of Vienna • Klemens von Metternich • balance of power • legitimacy • Holy Alliance • Concert of Europe

SETTING THE STAGE European heads of government were looking to establish long-lasting peace and stability on the continent after the defeat of Napoleon. They had a goal of the new European order—one of collective security and stability for the entire continent. A series of meetings in Vienna, known as the **Congress of Vienna**, were called to set up policies to achieve this goal. Originally, the Congress of Vienna was scheduled to last for four weeks. Instead, it went on for eight months.

Metternich's Plan for Europe

hmhsocialstudies.com
TAKING NOTES
Use the graphic organizer online to take notes on how the three goals of Metternich's plan at the Congress of Vienna solved a political problem.

Most of the decisions made in Vienna during the winter of 1814–1815 were made in secret among representatives of the five "great powers"—Russia, Prussia, Austria, Great Britain, and France. By far the most influential of these representatives was the foreign minister of Austria, Prince **Klemens von Metternich** (MEHT•uhr•nihk).

Metternich distrusted the democratic ideals of the French Revolution. Like most other European aristocrats, he felt that Napoleon's behavior had been a natural outcome of experiments with democracy. Metternich wanted to keep things as they were and remarked, "The first and greatest concern for the immense majority of every nation is the stability of laws—never their change." Metternich had three goals at the Congress of Vienna. First, he wanted to prevent future French aggression by surrounding France with strong countries. Second, he wanted to restore a **balance of power**, so that no country would be a threat to others. Third, he wanted to restore Europe's royal families to the thrones they had held before Napoleon's conquests.

The Containment of France The Congress took the following steps to make the weak countries around France stronger:

- The former Austrian Netherlands and Dutch Republic were united to form the Kingdom of the Netherlands.
- A group of 39 German states were loosely joined as the newly created German Confederation, dominated by Austria.
- Switzerland was recognized as an independent nation.
- The Kingdom of Sardinia in Italy was strengthened by the addition of Genoa.

These changes enabled the countries of Europe to contain France and prevent it from overpowering weaker nations. (See the map on page 674.)

▲ Delegates at the Congress of Vienna study a map of Europe.

Balance of Power Although the leaders of Europe wanted to weaken France, they did not want to leave it powerless. If they severely punished France, they might encourage the French to take revenge. If they broke up France, then another country might become so strong that it would threaten them all. Thus, the victorious powers did not exact a great price from the defeated nation. As a result, France remained a major but diminished European power. Also, no country in Europe could easily overpower another.

Legitimacy The great powers affirmed the principle of <u>legitimacy</u>—agreeing that as many as possible of the rulers whom Napoleon had driven from their thrones be restored to power. The ruling families of France, Spain, and several states in Italy and Central Europe regained their thrones. The participants in the Congress of Vienna believed that the return of the former monarchs would stabilize political relations among the nations.

The Congress of Vienna was a political triumph in many ways. For the first time, the nations of an entire continent had cooperated to control political affairs. The settlements they agreed upon were fair enough that no country was left bearing a grudge. Therefore, the Congress did not sow the seeds of future wars. In that sense, it was more successful than many other peace meetings in history.

MAIN IDEA

Drawing Conclusions

A) In what ways was the Congress of Vienna a success?

By agreeing to come to one another's aid in case of threats to peace, the European nations had temporarily ensured that there would be a balance of power on the continent. The Congress of Vienna, then, created a time of peace in Europe. It was a lasting peace. None of the five great powers waged war on one another for nearly 40 years, when Britain and France fought Russia in the Crimean War. **A)**

Political Changes Beyond Vienna

The Congress of Vienna was a victory for conservatives. Kings and princes resumed power in country after country, in keeping with Metternich's goals. Nevertheless, there were important differences from one country to another. Britain and France now had constitutional monarchies. Generally speaking, however, the governments in Eastern and Central Europe were more conservative. The rulers of Russia, Prussia, and Austria were absolute monarchs.

Europe, 1810

hmhsocialstudies.com
INTERACTIVE MAP

UNITED KINGDOM OF GREAT BRITAIN AND IRELAND
KINGDOM OF DENMARK AND NORWAY
KINGDOM OF SWEDEN
North Sea
Baltic Sea
London
Brussels
Amiens
Paris
Versailles
ATLANTIC OCEAN
FRENCH EMPIRE
SWITZ.
Milan
ITALY
CONFEDERATION OF THE RHINE
Berlin
PRUSSIA
GRAND DUCHY OF WARSAW
RUSSIAN EMPIRE
AUSTRIAN EMPIRE
Vienna
ILLYRIAN PROVINCES
PORTUGAL
Madrid
SPAIN
CORSICA
SARDINIA
Rome
Naples
KINGDOM OF NAPLES
SICILY
Gibraltar
Mediterranean Sea
OTTOMAN EMPIRE

French Empire
Countries controlled by Napoleon
Countries allied with Napoleon
Countries at war with Napoleon
Neutral countries

0   400 Miles
0   800 Kilometers

Europe, 1817

hmhsocialstudies.com
INTERACTIVE MAP

KINGDOM OF NORWAY AND SWEDEN
UNITED KINGDOM OF GREAT BRITAIN AND IRELAND
North Sea
DENMARK
Baltic Sea
NETHERLANDS
London
Brussels
Amiens
Paris
Versailles
HANOVER
PRUSSIA
Berlin
SAXONY
RUSSIAN EMPIRE
ATLANTIC OCEAN
FRANCE
SWITZ.
Milan
BAVARIA
AUSTRIAN EMPIRE
Vienna
PARMA
LUCCA
TUSCANY
MODENA
PAPAL STATES
OTTOMAN EMPIRE
PORTUGAL
Madrid
SPAIN
KINGDOM OF SARDINIA
CORSICA
Rome
Naples
KINGDOM OF THE TWO SICILIES
Gibraltar
Mediterranean Sea

Small German states
Boundary of the German Confederation

0   400 Miles
0   800 Kilometers

GEOGRAPHY SKILLBUILDER: Interpreting Maps

1. **Region** *What parts of Napoleon's French Empire did France lose as a result of the Congress of Vienna?*
2. **Region** *In what sense did the territorial changes of 1815 reflect a restoration of order and balance?*

Conservative Europe The rulers of Europe were very nervous about the legacy of the French Revolution. They worried that the ideals of liberty, equality, and fraternity might encourage revolutions elsewhere. Late in 1815, Czar Alexander I, Emperor Francis I of Austria, and King Frederick William III of Prussia signed an agreement called the **Holy Alliance**. In it, they pledged to base their relations with other nations on Christian principles in order to combat the forces of revolution. Finally, a series of alliances devised by Metternich, called the **Concert of Europe**, ensured that nations would help one another if any revolutions broke out.

Across Europe, conservatives held firm control of the governments, but they could not contain the ideas that had emerged during the French Revolution. France after 1815 was deeply divided politically. Conservatives were happy with the monarchy of Louis XVIII and were determined to make it last. Liberals, however, wanted the king to share more power with the legislature. And many people in the lower classes remained committed to the ideals of liberty, equality, and fraternity. Similarly, in other countries there was an explosive mixture of ideas and factions that would contribute directly to revolutions in 1830 and 1848. **B**

Despite their efforts to undo the French Revolution, the leaders at the Congress of Vienna could not turn back the clock. The Revolution had given Europe its first experiment in democratic government. Although the experiment had failed, it had set new political ideas in motion. The major political upheavals of the early 1800s had their roots in the French Revolution.

Revolution in Latin America The actions of the Congress of Vienna had consequences far beyond events in Europe. When Napoleon deposed the king of Spain during the Peninsular War, liberal Creoles (colonists born in Spanish America)

MAIN IDEA

Making Inferences

B What seeds of democracy had been sown by the French Revolution?

seized control of many colonies in the Americas. When the Congress of Vienna restored the king to the Spanish throne, royalist *peninsulares* (colonists born in Spain) tried to regain control of these colonial governments. The Creoles, however, attempted to retain and expand their power. In response, the Spanish king took steps to tighten control over the American colonies.

This action angered the Mexicans, who rose in revolt and successfully threw off Spain's control. Other Spanish colonies in Latin America also claimed independence. At about the same time, Brazil declared independence from Portugal. (See Chapter 24.)

Long-Term Legacy The Congress of Vienna left a legacy that would influence world politics for the next 100 years. The continent-wide efforts to establish and maintain a balance of power diminished the size and the power of France. At the same time, the power of Britain and Prussia increased.

Nationalism began to spread in Italy, Germany, Greece, and to other areas that the Congress had put under foreign control. Eventually, the nationalistic feelings would explode into revolutions, and new nations would be formed. European colonies also responded to the power shift. Spanish colonies took advantage of the events in Europe to declare their independence and break away from Spain.

At the same time, ideas about the basis of power and authority had changed permanently as a result of the French Revolution. More and more, people saw democracy as the best way to ensure equality and justice for all. The French Revolution, then, changed the social attitudes and assumptions that had dominated Europe for centuries. A new era had begun. **C**

MAIN IDEA

Recognizing Effects
C How did the French Revolution affect not only Europe but also other areas of the world?

Connect to Today

Congress of Vienna and the United Nations

The Congress of Vienna and the Concert of Europe tried to keep the world safe from war. The modern equivalent of these agreements is the United Nations (UN), an international organization established in 1945 and continuing today, whose purpose is to promote world peace.

Like the Congress of Vienna, the United Nations was formed by major powers after a war—World War II. These powers agreed to cooperate to reduce tensions and bring greater harmony to international relations. Throughout its history, the United Nations has used diplomacy as its chief method of keeping the peace.

↗ **hmhsocialstudies.com**

INTERNET ACTIVITY Go online to create a graphic organizer to show the major agencies and functions of the United Nations.

SECTION 5 ASSESSMENT

TERMS & NAMES 1. For each term or name, write a sentence explaining its significance.
• Congress of Vienna • Klemens von Metternich • balance of power • legitimacy • Holy Alliance • Concert of Europe

USING YOUR NOTES	MAIN IDEAS	CRITICAL THINKING & WRITING
2. What was the overall effect of Metternich's plan on France? 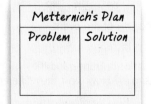 Metternich's Plan / Problem / Solution	**3.** What were the three points of Metternich's plan for Europe? **4.** Why was the Congress of Vienna considered a success? **5.** What was the long-term legacy of the Congress of Vienna?	**6. DRAWING CONCLUSIONS** From France's point of view, do you think the Congress of Vienna's decisions were fair? **7. ANALYZING ISSUES** Why did liberals and conservatives differ over who should have power? **8. MAKING INFERENCES** What do you think is meant by the statement that the French Revolution let the "genie out of the bottle"? **9. WRITING ACTIVITY** POWER AND AUTHORITY In the role of a newspaper editor in the early 1800s, write an **editorial**—pro or con—on the Congress of Vienna and its impact on politics in Europe.

CONNECT TO TODAY CREATING A SCRAPBOOK

Work in pairs to locate recent articles in newspapers and magazines on the peacekeeping efforts of the UN. Photocopy or clip the articles and use them to create a **scrapbook** titled "The UN as Peacekeeper."

VISUAL SUMMARY

The French Revolution and Napoleon

Long-Term Causes

- Social and economic injustices of the Old Regime
- Enlightenment ideas—liberty and equality
- Example furnished by the American Revolution

Immediate Causes

- Economic crisis—famine and government debt
- Weak leadership
- Discontent of the Third Estate

Revolution

- Fall of the Bastille
- National Assembly
- Declaration of the Rights of Man and of the Citizen and a new constitution

Immediate Effects

- End of the Old Regime
- Execution of monarch
- War with other European nations
- Reign of Terror
- Rise of Napoleon

Long-Term Effects

- Conservative reaction
- Decline in French power
- Spread of Enlightenment ideas
- Growth of nationalism
- Revolutions in Latin America

TERMS & NAMES

For each term or name below, briefly explain its connection to the French Revolution or the rise and fall of Napoleon.

1. estate
2. Great Fear
3. guillotine
4. Maximilien Robespierre
5. coup d'état
6. Napoleonic Code
7. Waterloo
8. Congress of Vienna

MAIN IDEAS

The French Revolution Begins Section 1 (pages 651–655)

9. Why were the members of the Third Estate dissatisfied with their way of life under the Old Regime?

10. Why was the fall of the Bastille important to the French people?

Revolution Brings Reform and Terror Section 2 (pages 656–662)

11. What political reforms resulted from the French Revolution?

12. What was the Reign of Terror, and how did it end?

Napoleon Forges an Empire Section 3 (pages 663–667)

13. What reforms did Napoleon introduce?

14. What steps did Napoleon take to create an empire in Europe?

Napoleon's Empire Collapses Section 4 (pages 668–671)

15. What factors led to Napoleon's defeat in Russia?

16. Why were the European allies able to defeat Napoleon in 1814 and again in 1815?

The Congress of Vienna Section 5 (pages 672–675)

17. What were Metternich's three goals at the Congress of Vienna?

18. How did the Congress of Vienna ensure peace in Europe?

CRITICAL THINKING

1. USING YOUR NOTES

Copy the chart of dates and events in Napoleon's career into your notebook. For each event, draw an arrow up or down to show whether Napoleon gained or lost power because of the event.

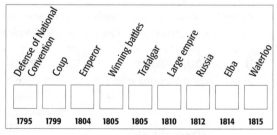

Defense of National Convention	Coup	Emperor	Winning battles	Trafalgar	Large empire	Russia	Elba	Waterloo
1795	1799	1804	1805	1805	1810	1812	1814	1815

2. COMPARING AND CONTRASTING

ECONOMICS How were the economic conditions in France and the American colonies before their revolutions similar? How were they different?

3. ANALYZING ISSUES

REVOLUTION There is a saying: "Revolutions devour their own children." What evidence from this chapter supports that statement?

4. RECOGNIZING EFFECTS

POWER AND AUTHORITY How did the Congress of Vienna affect power and authority in European countries after Napoleon's defeat? Consider who held power in the countries and the power of the countries themselves.

Use the excerpt—from the South American liberator Simón Bolívar, whose country considered giving refuge to Napoleon after Waterloo—and your knowledge of world history to answer questions 1 and 2.

PRIMARY SOURCE

If South America is struck by the thunderbolt of Bonaparte's arrival, misfortune will ever be ours if our country accords him a friendly reception. His thirst for conquest is insatiable [cannot be satisfied]; he has mowed down the flower of European youth . . . in order to carry out his ambitious projects. The same designs will bring him to the New World.

SIMÓN BOLÍVAR

1. In Bolívar's opinion, if his country gave Napoleon a friendly reception it would
   A. be beset by misfortune.
   B. become a great power in South America.
   C. become a part of the French Empire.
   D. be attacked by the United States.

2. Which of the following gives Bolívar's view of Napoleon?
   A. His desire for power cannot be satisfied.
   B. He is not ambitious.
   C. He cares for the lives of others.
   D. He does not want to come to the New World.

Use the map, which shows Great Britain and the French Empire in 1810, and your knowledge of world history to answer question 3.

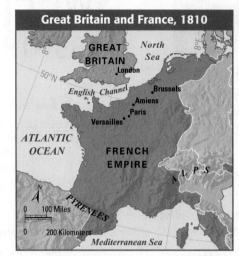

3. What geographical barrier helped to protect Britain from an invasion by Napoleon?
   A. Mediterranean Sea   C. Alps
   B. English Channel   D. Pyrenees

hmhsocialstudies.com **TEST PRACTICE**

For additional test practice, go online for:
- Diagnostic tests
- Strategies
- Tutorials

Interact *with* History

On page 650, you considered how to bring about change in the French government in the late 1700s. Now that you have read the chapter, reevaluate your thoughts on how to change an unjust government. Was violent revolution justified? effective? Would you have advised different actions? Discuss your opinions with a small group.

FOCUS ON WRITING

Imagine that you lived in Paris throughout the French Revolution. Write **journal entries** on several of the major events of the Revolution. Include the following events:
- the storming of the Bastille
- the women's march on Versailles
- the trial of Louis XVI
- the Reign of Terror
- the rise of Napoleon

MULTIMEDIA ACTIVITY

21st CENTURY

NetExplorations: The French Revolution

Go to *NetExplorations* at **hmhsocialstudies.com** to learn more about the French Revolution. Then plan a virtual field trip to sites in France related to the revolution. Be sure to include sites outside Paris. Begin your research by exploring the Web sites recommended at *NetExplorations*. Include the following in your field trip plan:
- a one-paragraph description of each site and the events that happened there
- specific buildings, statues, or other items to view at each site
- documents and other readings to help visitors prepare for each stop on the field trip
- topics to discuss at each site
- a list of Web sites used to create your virtual field trip

The French Revolution and Napoleon **677**

Nationalist Revolutions Sweep the West,
1789–1900

Essential Question

What great shifts in thinking altered politics and the arts between 1789 and 1900?

? What You Will Learn

In this chapter you will learn that nationalist revolutions, inspired by Enlightenment ideas, swept through Latin America and Europe.

SECTION 1 Latin American Peoples Win Independence

Main Idea Spurred by discontent and Enlightenment ideas, peoples in Latin America fought colonial rule.

SECTION 2 Europe Faces Revolutions

Main Idea Liberal and nationalist uprisings challenged the old conservative order of Europe.

SECTION 3 Nationalism Case Study: Italy and Germany

Main Idea Nationalism contributed to the formation of two new nations and a new political order in Europe.

SECTION 4 Revolutions in the Arts

Main Idea Artistic and intellectual movements both reflected and fueled changes in Europe during the 1800s.

Previewing Themes

REVOLUTION Inspired by Enlightenment ideas, the people of Latin America rebelled against European rule in the early 19th century. Rebels in Europe responded to nationalistic calls for independence.

Geography *Study the time line. What were the first two countries in Latin America and the Caribbean to work toward independence?*

POWER AND AUTHORITY Challenges by nationalist groups created unrest in Europe. Strong leaders united Italian lands and German-speaking lands.

Geography *Based on the map, in which area of Europe did the greatest number of revolts occur?*

CULTURAL INTERACTION Artists and intellectuals created new schools of thought. Romanticism and realism changed the way the world was viewed.

Geography *Which event shown on the time line involves a realistic way to view the world?*

LATIN AMERICA AND EUROPE

1804 Haiti wins freedom from France.

1810 Padre Hidalgo calls for Mexican independence. ▶

1837 Louis Daguerre perfects a method for photography.

1800

1825

WORLD

1804 Napoleon crowned Emperor. ▶

1815 Napoleon defeated and exiled.

Revolutions, 1848

Legend:
— Boundary of German Confederation
▪ Small German states
✴ Revolution in 1848–49

HISTORY

Miguel Hidalgo's Call to Arms

↗ hmhsocialstudies.com **VIDEO**

NORWAY

North Sea

UNITED KINGDOM

DENMARK

Hamburg

NETHERLANDS

London

PRUSSIA

Berlin

Warsaw

RUSSIAN EMPIRE

BELGIUM

Brussels

POLAND

Prague

Paris

LUX.

Stuttgart

ATLANTIC OCEAN

FRANCE

AUSTRIAN EMPIRE

Vienna

SWITZ.

Buda

Milan

ILLYRIAN PROVINCES

ITALY

PAPAL STATES

OTTOMAN EMPIRE

Adriatic Sea

PORTUGAL

Madrid

SPAIN

Rome

Naples

KINGDOM OF THE TWO SICILIES

GREECE

Mediterranean Sea

Scale:
0 — 200 — 400 Miles
0 — 200 — 400 Kilometers
Conic Projection

Timeline:

1848 Revolts shake Europe.

1861 Russia frees serfs.

1870 Italy unites.

1871 Wilhelm I crowned Kaiser of united Germany. ▶

1850

1875

1900

1863 ◀ Lincoln's Emancipation Proclamation frees enslaved persons in Confederate states.

1869 Suez Canal completed.

1884–1885 Berlin Conference divides Africa among European nations.

679

What symbolizes your country's values?

You are an artist in a nation that has just freed itself from foreign rule. The new government is asking you to design a symbol that will show what your country stands for. It's up to you to design the symbol that best suits the spirit and values of your people. Look at the symbols below. Will your symbol be peaceful or warlike, dignified or joyful? Or will it be a combination of these and other qualities?

Botswana
Industry and livestock are connected by water, the key to the country's prosperity. *Pula* in the Setswana language means "rain." But to a Setswana speaker, it is also a common greeting meaning luck, life, and prosperity.

Austria
The eagle was the symbol of the old Austrian Empire. The shield goes back to medieval times. The hammer and sickle symbolize agriculture and industry. The broken chains celebrate Austria's liberation from Germany at the end of World War II.

United States
The 13 original colonies are symbolized in the stars, stripes, leaves, and arrows. The Latin phrase *E pluribus unum* means "Out of many, one," expressing unity of the states. The American bald eagle holds an olive branch and arrows to symbolize a desire for peace but a readiness for war.

EXAMINING *the* ISSUES

- **What values and goals of your new country do you want to show?**

- **Will your symbols represent your country's past or future?**

As a class, discuss these questions. During the discussion, think of the role played by symbols in expressing a country's view of itself and the world. As you read about the rise of new nations in Latin America and Europe, think of how artists encourage national pride.

Latin American Peoples Win Independence

MAIN IDEA	WHY IT MATTERS NOW	TERMS & NAMES
REVOLUTION Spurred by discontent and Enlightenment ideas, peoples in Latin America fought colonial rule.	Sixteen of today's Latin American nations gained their independence at this time.	• *peninsulare* • José de San Martín • creole • Miguel Hidalgo • mulatto • José María Morelos • Simón Bolívar

SETTING THE STAGE The successful American Revolution, the French Revolution, and the Enlightenment changed ideas about who should control government. Ideas of liberty, equality, and democratic rule found their way across the seas to European colonies. In Latin America, most of the population resented the domination of European colonial powers. The time seemed right for the people who lived there to sweep away old colonial masters and gain control of the land.

Colonial Society Divided

In Latin American colonial society, class dictated people's place in society and jobs. At the top of Spanish-American society were the ***peninsulares*** (peh•neen•soo•LAH•rehs), people who had been born in Spain, which is on the Iberian peninsula. They formed a tiny percentage of the population. Only *peninsulares* could hold high office in Spanish colonial government. <u>Creoles</u>, Spaniards born in Latin America, were below the *peninsulares* in rank. Creoles could not hold high-level political office, but they could rise as officers in

hmhsocialstudies.com
TAKING NOTES
Use the graphic organizer online to take notes on Latin American independence movements.

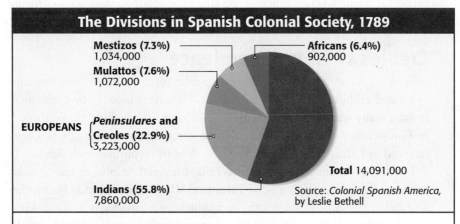

The Divisions in Spanish Colonial Society, 1789

Mestizos (7.3%) 1,034,000

Africans (6.4%) 902,000

Mulattos (7.6%) 1,072,000

EUROPEANS *Peninsulares* and Creoles (22.9%) 3,223,000

Indians (55.8%) 7,860,000

Total 14,091,000

Source: *Colonial Spanish America,* by Leslie Bethell

SKILLBUILDER: Interpreting Graphs
1. **Clarifying** *Which two groups made up the vast majority of the population in Spanish America?*
2. **Making Inferences** *Of the Europeans, which group—peninsulares or creoles—probably made up a larger percentage?*

Spanish colonial armies. Together these two groups controlled land, wealth, and power in the Spanish colonies.

Below the *peninsulares* and creoles came the mestizos, persons of mixed European and Indian ancestry. Next were the <u>**mulattos**</u>, persons of mixed European and African ancestry, and enslaved Africans. Indians were at the bottom of the social ladder.

Revolutions in the Americas

By the late 1700s, colonists in Latin America, already aware of Enlightenment ideas, were electrified by the news of the American and French Revolutions. The success of the American Revolution encouraged them to try to gain freedom from their European masters.

Revolution in Haiti The French colony called Saint Domingue was the first Latin American territory to free itself from European rule. The colony, now known as Haiti, occupied the western third of the island of Hispaniola in the Caribbean Sea.

Nearly 500,000 enslaved Africans worked on French plantations, and they outnumbered their masters dramatically. White masters used brutal methods to terrorize them and keep them powerless.

While the French Revolution was taking place, oppressed people in the French colony of Haiti rose up against their French masters. In August 1791, 100,000 enslaved Africans rose in revolt. A leader soon emerged, Toussaint L'Ouverture (too•SAN-loo•vair•TOOR). Formerly enslaved, Toussaint was unfamiliar with military and diplomatic matters. Even so, he rose to become a skilled general and diplomat. By 1801, Toussaint had taken control of the entire island and freed all the enslaved Africans.

In January 1802, 30,000 French troops landed in Saint Domingue to remove Toussaint from power. In May, Toussaint agreed to halt the revolution if the French would end slavery. Despite the agreement, the French soon accused him of planning another uprising. They seized him and sent him to a prison in the French Alps, where he died in April 1803.

Haiti's Independence Toussaint's lieutenant, Jean-Jacques Dessalines (zhahn•ZHAHK day•sah•LEEN), took up the fight for freedom. On January 1, 1804, General Dessalines declared the colony an independent country. It was the first black colony to free itself from European control. Dessalines called the country Haiti, which in the language of the Arawak natives meant "mountainous land."

Creoles Lead Independence

Even though they could not hold high public office, creoles were the least oppressed of those born in Latin America. They were also the best educated. In fact, many wealthy young creoles traveled to Europe for their education. In Europe, they read about and adopted Enlightenment ideas. When they returned to Latin America, they brought ideas of revolution with them.

Napoleon's conquest of Spain in 1808 triggered revolts in the Spanish colonies. Removing Spain's King Ferdinand VII, Napoleon made his brother Joseph king of Spain. Many creoles might have supported a Spanish king. However, they felt no loyalty to a king imposed by the French. Creoles, recalling Locke's idea of the consent of the governed, argued that when the real king was removed, power shifted to the people. In 1810, rebellion broke out in several parts of Latin America. The drive toward independence had begun. **Ⓐ**

▼ Toussaint L'Ouverture led enslaved Africans in a revolt against the French that ended slavery and resulted in the new nation of Haiti.

MAIN IDEA

Recognizing Effects

Ⓐ How did the French Revolution affect the colonists in the Americas?

Simón Bolívar
1783–1830

Called *Libertador* (Liberator), Bolívar was a brilliant general, a visionary, a writer, and a fighter. He is called the "George Washington of South America." Bolívar planned to unite the Spanish colonies of South America into a single country called Gran Colombia. The area of upper Peru was renamed Bolivia in his honor.

　　Discouraged by political disputes that tore the new Latin American nations apart, he is reported to have said, "America is ungovernable. Those who have served the revolution have ploughed the sea."

José de San Martín
1778–1850

Unlike the dashing Bolívar, San Martín was a modest man. Though born in Argentina, he spent much of his youth in Spain as a career military officer. He fought with Spanish forces against Napoleon. He returned to Latin America to be a part of its liberation from Spain. Fighting for 10 years, he became the liberator of Argentina, Chile, and Peru.

　　Discouraged by political infighting, San Martín sailed for Europe. He died, almost forgotten, on French soil in 1850.

　　The South American wars of independence rested on the achievements of two brilliant creole generals. One was **Simón Bolívar** (see•MAWN boh•LEE•vahr), a wealthy Venezuelan creole. The other great liberator was **José de San Martín** (hoh•SAY day san mahr•TEEN), an Argentinian.

Bolívar's Route to Victory Simón Bolívar's native Venezuela declared its independence from Spain in 1811. But the struggle for independence had only begun. Bolívar's volunteer army of revolutionaries suffered numerous defeats. Twice Bolívar had to go into exile. A turning point came in August 1819. Bolívar led over 2,000 soldiers on a daring march through the Andes into what is now Colombia. (See the 1830 map on page 685.) Coming from this direction, he took the Spanish army in Bogotá completely by surprise and won a decisive victory.

　　By 1821, Bolívar had won Venezuela's independence. He then marched south into Ecuador. In Ecuador, Bolívar finally met José de San Martín. Together they would decide the future of the Latin American revolutionary movement.

San Martín Leads Southern Liberation Forces San Martín's Argentina had declared its independence in 1816. However, Spanish forces in nearby Chile and Peru still posed a threat. In 1817, San Martín led an army on a grueling march across the Andes to Chile. He was joined there by forces led by Bernardo O'Higgins, son of a former viceroy of Peru. With O'Higgins's help, San Martín finally freed Chile.

　　In 1821, San Martín planned to drive the remaining Spanish forces out of Lima, Peru. But to do so, he needed a much larger force. San Martín and Bolívar discussed this problem when they met at Guayaquil, Ecuador, in 1822.

　　No one knows how the two men reached an agreement. But San Martín left his army for Bolívar to command. With unified revolutionary forces, Bolívar's army went on to defeat the Spanish at the Battle of Ayacucho (Peru) on December 9, 1824. In this last major battle of the war for independence, the Spanish colonies in Latin America won their freedom. The future countries of Venezuela, Colombia, Panama, and Ecuador were united into a country called Gran Colombia.

Struggling Toward Democracy

Revolutions are as much a matter of ideas as they are of weapons. Simón Bolívar, the hero of Latin American independence, was both a thinker and a fighter. By 1800, Enlightenment ideas spread widely across the Latin American colonies. Bolívar combined Enlightenment political ideas, ideas from Greece and Rome, and his own original thinking. The result was a system of democratic ideas that would help spark revolutions throughout Latin America.

▲ After winning South American independence, Simón Bolívar realized his dream of Gran Colombia, a sort of United States of South America.

Enlightenment Ideas Spread to Latin America, 1789–1810

hmhsocialstudies.com   INTERACTIVE MAP

NORTH AMERICA — Washington — Mexico City
ATLANTIC OCEAN
Thomas Jefferson, Benjamin Franklin
John Locke, Thomas Paine
Voltaire, Baron de Montesquieu
Jean-Jacques Rousseau
London — Paris — EUROPE — Madrid
AFRICA
PACIFIC OCEAN
Caracas — Bogotá — SOUTH AMERICA
Lima — La Paz — Ascunción — Santiago — Montevideo — Buenos Aires

❶ Bolívar's 1807 return from Europe by way of the United States allowed him to study the American system of government.

❷ In 1810, Bolívar went to London to seek support for the revolution in Latin America. At the same time, he studied British institutions of government.

Connect *to* Today

1. **Making Inferences** How are Enlightenment thought and the successes of the American and French Revolutions reflected in Bolívar's thinking?

   See Skillbuilder Handbook, page R10.

2. **Comparing** What recent events in today's world are similar to Simón Bolívar's movement for Latin American independence?

Mexico Ends Spanish Rule

In most Latin American countries, creoles led the revolutionary movements. But in Mexico, ethnic and racial groups mixed more freely. There, Indians and mestizos played the leading role.

A Cry for Freedom In 1810, Padre **Miguel Hidalgo** (mee•GEHL ee•THAHL•goh), a priest in the small village of Dolores, took the first step toward independence. Hidalgo was a poor but well-educated man. He firmly believed in Enlightenment ideals. On September 16, 1810, he rang the bells of his village church. When the peasants gathered in the church, he issued a call for rebellion against the Spanish. Today, that call is known as the *grito de Dolores* (the cry of Dolores).

The very next day, Hidalgo's Indian and mestizo followers began a march toward Mexico City. This unruly army soon numbered 80,000 men. The uprising of the lower classes alarmed the Spanish army and creoles, who feared the loss of their property, control of the land, and their lives. The army defeated Hidalgo in 1811. The rebels then rallied around another strong leader, Padre **José María Morelos** (moh•RAY•lohs). Morelos led the revolution for four years. However, in 1815, a creole officer, Agustín de Iturbide (ah•goos•TEEN day ee•toor•BEE•day), defeated him.

Mexico's Independence Events in Mexico took yet another turn in 1820 when a revolution in Spain put a liberal group in power there. Mexico's creoles feared the loss of their privileges in the Spanish-controlled colony. So they united in support of Mexico's independence from Spain. Ironically, Agustín de Iturbide—the man who had defeated the rebel Padre Morelos—proclaimed independence in 1821.

VIDEO
Miguel Hidalgo's
Call to Arms

↗ hmhsocialstudies.com

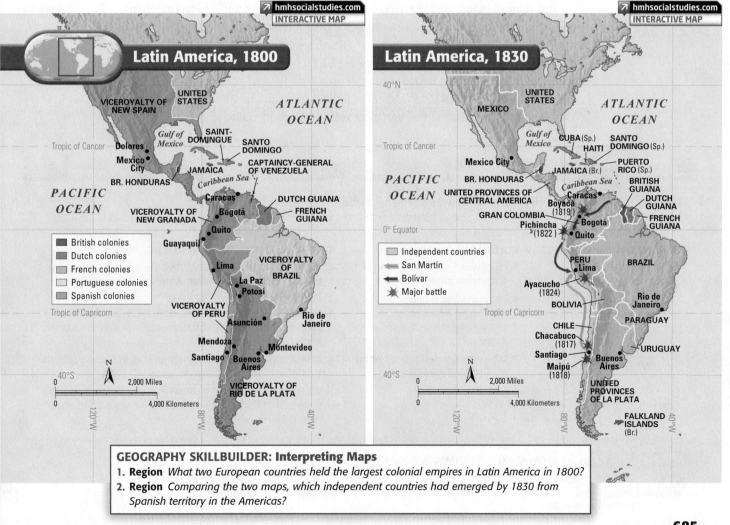

GEOGRAPHY SKILLBUILDER: Interpreting Maps
1. **Region** *What two European countries held the largest colonial empires in Latin America in 1800?*
2. **Region** *Comparing the two maps, which independent countries had emerged by 1830 from Spanish territory in the Americas?*

Before the Mexican revolution, Central America was part of the viceroyalty of New Spain. It had been governed by the Spanish from the seat of colonial government in Mexico. In 1821, several Central American states declared their independence from Spain—and from Mexico as well. However, Iturbide (who had declared himself emperor), refused to recognize the declarations of independence. Iturbide was finally overthrown in 1823. Central America then declared its absolute independence from Mexico. It took the name the United Provinces of Central America. The future countries of Nicaragua, Guatemala, Honduras, El Salvador, and Costa Rica would develop in this region.

Brazil's Royal Liberator

Brazil's quest for independence was unique in this period of Latin American history because it occurred without violent upheavals or widespread bloodshed. In fact, a member of the Portuguese royal family actually played a key role in freeing Brazil from Portugal.

In 1807, Napoleon's armies invaded both Spain and Portugal. Napoleon's aim was to close the ports of these countries to British shipping. As French troops approached Lisbon, the Portuguese capital, Prince John (later King John VI) and the royal family boarded ships to escape capture. They took their court and royal treasury to Portugal's largest colony, Brazil. Rio de Janiero became the capital of the Portuguese empire. For 14 years, the Portuguese ran their empire from Brazil. After Napoleon's defeat in 1815, King John and the Portuguese government returned to Portugal six years later. Dom Pedro, King John's son, stayed behind in Brazil.

King John planned to make Brazil a colony again. However, many Brazilians could not accept a return to colonial status. In 1822, creoles demanded Brazil's independence from Portugal. Eight thousand Brazilians signed a petition asking Dom Pedro to rule. He agreed. On September 7, 1822, he officially declared Brazil's independence. Brazil had won its independence in a bloodless revolution. **B**

Meanwhile, the ideas of the French Revolution and the aftermath of the Napoleonic Wars were causing upheaval in Europe, as you will learn in Section 2.

MAIN IDEA

Making Inferences

B In what way did the presence of the royal family in Brazil help Portugal's largest colony?

SECTION 1 ASSESSMENT

TERMS & NAMES 1. For each term or name, write a sentence explaining its significance.
• *peninsulare*   • creole   • mulatto   • Simón Bolívar   • José de San Martín   • Miguel Hidalgo   • José María Morelos

USING YOUR NOTES

2. Which independence movement was led by Toussaint L'Ouverture?

Who	Where
When	Why

MAIN IDEAS

3. How was Spanish colonial society structured?

4. How was the Haitian Revolution different from revolutions in the rest of Latin America?

5. Which groups led the quest for Mexican independence?

CRITICAL THINKING & WRITING

6. **COMPARING AND CONTRASTING** Compare and contrast the leadership of the South American revolutions to the leadership of Mexico's revolution.

7. **FORMING AND SUPPORTING OPINIONS** Would creole revolutionaries tend to be democratic or authoritarian leaders? Explain.

8. **ANALYZING CAUSES** How were events in Europe related to the revolutions in Latin America?

9. **WRITING ACTIVITY** REVOLUTION Write a **response** to this statement: "Through its policies, Spain gave up its right to rule in South America."

MULTIMEDIA ACTIVITY CREATING A MULTIMEDIA PRESENTATION

Use the Internet to find information on the Mexican Indian rebel group, the *Zapatistas*. Create a **multimedia presentation** describing the group and its goals.

INTERNET KEYWORD
Zapatistas

Europe Faces Revolutions

MAIN IDEA	WHY IT MATTERS NOW	TERMS & NAMES
REVOLUTION Liberal and nationalist uprisings challenged the old conservative order of Europe.	The system of nation-states established in Europe during this period continues today.	• conservative • nation-state • liberal • the Balkans • radical • Louis-Napoleon • nationalism • Alexander II

SETTING THE STAGE As revolutions shook the colonies in Latin America, Europe was also undergoing dramatic changes. Under the leadership of Prince Metternich of Austria, the Congress of Vienna had tried to restore the old monarchies and territorial divisions that had existed before the French Revolution. (See Chapter 23.) On an international level, this attempt to turn back history succeeded. For the next century, European countries seldom turned to war to solve their differences. Within countries, however, the effort failed. Revolutions erupted across Europe between 1815 and 1848.

Clash of Philosophies

In the first half of the 1800s, three schools of political thought struggled for supremacy in European societies. Each believed that its style of government would best serve the people. Each attracted a different set of followers. The list below identifies the philosophies, goals, and followers.

▼ Prince Clemens von Metternich shaped conservative control of Europe for almost 40 years.

- **Conservative**: usually wealthy property owners and nobility. They argued for protecting the traditional monarchies of Europe.
- **Liberal**: mostly middle-class business leaders and merchants. They wanted to give more power to elected parliaments, but only the educated and the landowners would vote.
- **Radical**: favored drastic change to extend democracy to all people. They believed that governments should practice the ideals of the French Revolution—liberty, equality, and brotherhood.

hmhsocialstudies.com
TAKING NOTES
Use the graphic organizer online to take notes on major revolutions in Europe.

Nationalism Develops

As conservatives, liberals, and radicals debated issues of government, a new movement called nationalism emerged. **Nationalism** is the belief that people's greatest loyalty should not be to a king or an empire but to a nation of people who share a common culture and history. The nationalist movement would blur the lines that separated the three political theories.

When a nation had its own independent government, it became a **nation-state**. A nation-state defends the nation's territory and way of life, and it represents the nation to the rest of the world. In Europe in 1815, only

Nationalism

Nationalism—the belief that people should be loyal to their nation—was not widespread until the 1800s. The rise of modern nationalism is tied to the spread of democratic ideas and the growth of an educated middle class. People wanted to decide how they were governed, instead of having monarchs impose government on them.

Bonds That Create a Nation-State

Culture
a shared way of life (food, dress, behavior, ideals)

History
a common past; common experiences

Religion
a religion shared by all or most of the people

NATION-STATE

Language
different dialects of one language; one dialect becomes "national language"

Nationality
belief in common ethnic ancestry that may or may not be true

Territory
a certain territory that belongs to the ethnic group; its "land"

Positive and Negative Results of Nationalism

Nationalism has not always been a positive influence. For example, extremely strong nationalistic feelings sometimes lead a group to turn against outsiders. The chart below lists some positive and negative results of nationalism. Note how some results, such as competition, can be both positive and negative.

Positive Results	Negative Results
• People within a nation overcoming their differences for the common good	• Forced assimilation of minority cultures into a nation's majority culture
• The overthrow of colonial rule	• Ethnic cleansing, such as in Bosnia and Herzegovina in the 1990s
• Democratic governments in nations throughout the world	• The rise of extreme nationalistic movements, such as Nazism
• Competition among nations spurring scientific and technological advances	• Competition between nations leading to warfare

hmhsocialstudies.com

RESEARCH WEB LINKS Go online for more on nationalism.

> **DATA FILE**

IMPACT OF NATIONALISM

• Between 1950 and 1980, 47 African countries overthrew colonial rulers and became independent nations.

• In the 1990s, the republics of Bosnia and Herzegovina, Croatia, Slovenia, and Macedonia broke away from Yugoslavia.

• In 2003, Yugoslavia changed its name to Serbia and Montenegro.

• Europe has 47 countries. (Some of those lie partially in Europe, partially in Asia.) About 50 languages are spoken in the region.

• In most of Latin America, Spanish or Portuguese is the official language. However, many native languages are still spoken. For example, Bolivia has three official languages: Spanish and the Indian languages of Aymara and Quechua.

Connect *to* Today

1. **Forming and Supporting Opinions**
   Do you think nationalism has had more of a positive or negative impact on the world? Support your opinion with evidence.

    See Skillbuilder Handbook, page R20.

2. **Comparing and Contrasting**
   Which of the bonds used to create nation-states are found in the United States?

France, England, and Spain could be called nation-states. But soon that would change as nationalist movements achieved success.

Most of the people who believed in nationalism were either liberals or radicals. In most cases, the liberal middle class—teachers, lawyers, and businesspeople— led the struggle for constitutional government and the formation of nation-states. In Germany, for example, liberals wanted to gather the many different German states into a single nation-state. Other liberals in large empires, such as the Hungarians in the Austrian Empire, wanted to split away and establish self-rule.

Nationalists Challenge Conservative Power

The first people to win self-rule during this period were the Greeks. For centuries, Greece had been part of the Ottoman Empire. The Ottomans controlled most of <u>the Balkans</u>. That region includes all or part of present-day Greece, Albania, Bulgaria, Romania, Turkey, and the former Yugoslavia. Greeks, however, had kept alive the memory of their ancient history and culture. Spurred on by the nationalist spirit, they demanded independence and rebelled against the Ottoman Turks in 1821.

Greeks Gain Independence The most powerful European governments opposed revolution. However, the cause of Greek independence was popular with people around the world. Russians, for example, felt a connection to Greek Orthodox Christians, who were ruled by the Muslim Ottomans. Educated Europeans and Americans loved and respected ancient Greek culture.

Eventually, as popular support for Greece grew, the powerful nations of Europe took the side of the Greeks. In 1827, a combined British, French, and Russian fleet destroyed the Ottoman fleet at the Battle of Navarino. In 1830, Britain, France, and Russia signed a treaty guaranteeing an independent kingdom of Greece. **Ⓐ**

MAIN IDEA

Analyzing Motives

Ⓐ Why would Europeans and Americans support the Greek revolutionary movement?

1830s Uprisings Crushed By the 1830s, the old order, carefully arranged at the Congress of Vienna, was breaking down. Revolutionary zeal swept across Europe. Liberals and nationalists throughout Europe were openly revolting against conservative governments.

Nationalist riots broke out against Dutch rule in the Belgian city of Brussels. In October 1830, the Belgians declared their independence from Dutch control. In Italy, nationalists worked to unite the many separate states on the Italian peninsula. Some were independent. Others were ruled by Austria, or by the pope. Eventually, Prince Metternich sent Austrian troops to restore order in Italy. The Poles living under the rule of Russia staged a revolt in Warsaw late in 1830. Russian armies took nearly an entire year to crush the Polish uprising. By the mid-1830s, the old order seemed to have reestablished itself. But the appearance of stability did not last long.

1848 Revolutions Fail to Unite In 1848, ethnic uprisings erupted throughout Europe. (See the map on page 679.) After an unruly mob in Vienna clashed with police, Metternich resigned and liberal uprisings broke out throughout the Austrian empire. In Budapest, nationalist leader Louis Kossuth called for a parliament and self-government

Social History

Nationalistic Music

As the force of nationalism began to rise in Europe, ethnic groups recognized their music as a unique element of their culture. Composers used folk melodies in their works. For example, Czech composer Antonín Dvořák (DVAWR•zhahk), pictured above, and the Norwegian composer Edvard Grieg incorporated popular melodies and legends into their works. These works became a source of pride and further encouraged the sense of nationalism. Richard Wagner created a cycle of four musical dramas called *Der Ring des Nibelungen*. His operas are considered the pinnacle of German nationalism.

▲ In *Combat Before the Hotel de Ville, July 28th, 1830*, Victor Schnetz portrays the riots in Paris that forced Charles X to flee to Great Britain.

for Hungary. Meanwhile in Prague, Czech liberals demanded Bohemian independence.

European politics continued to seesaw. Many liberal gains were lost to conservatives within a year. In one country after another, the revolutionaries failed to unite themselves or their nations. Conservatives regained their nerve and their power. By 1849, Europe had practically returned to the conservatism that had controlled governments before 1848. **B**

MAIN IDEA

Hypothesizing

B Why weren't the revolutions of 1830 and 1848 successful?

Radicals Change France

Radicals participated in many of the 1848 revolts. Only in France, however, was the radical demand for democratic government the main goal of revolution. In 1830, France's King Charles X tried to stage a return to absolute monarchy. The attempt sparked riots that forced Charles to flee to Great Britain. He was replaced by Louis-Philippe, who had long supported liberal reforms in France.

The Third Republic However, in 1848, after a reign of almost 18 years, Louis-Philippe fell from popular favor. Once again, a Paris mob overturned a monarchy and established a republic. The new republican government began to fall apart almost immediately. The radicals split into factions. One side wanted only political reform. The other side also wanted social and economic reform. The differences set off bloody battles in Parisian streets. The violence turned French citizens away from the radicals. As a result, a moderate constitution was drawn up later in 1848. It called for a parliament and a strong president to be elected by the people.

France Accepts a Strong Ruler In December 1848, <u>Louis-Napoleon</u>, the nephew of Napoleon Bonaparte, won the presidential election. Four years later, Louis-Napoleon Bonaparte took the title of Emperor Napoleon III. A majority of French voters accepted this action without complaint. The French were weary of instability. They welcomed a strong ruler who would bring peace to France. **C**

As France's emperor, Louis-Napoleon built railroads, encouraged industrialization, and promoted an ambitious program of public works. Gradually, because of Louis-Napoleon's policies, unemployment decreased in France, and the country experienced real prosperity.

MAIN IDEA

Summarizing

C How would you describe the political swings occurring in France between 1830 and 1852?

Reform in Russia

Unlike France, Russia in the 1800s had yet to leap into the modern industrialized world. Under Russia's feudal system, serfs were bound to the nobles whose land they worked. Nobles enjoyed almost unlimited power over them. By the 1820s, many Russians believed that serfdom must end. In their eyes, the system was morally wrong. It also prevented the empire from advancing economically. The czars, however, were reluctant to free the serfs. Freeing them would anger the landowners, whose support the czars needed to stay in power.

Defeat Brings Change Eventually, Russia's lack of development became obvious to Russians and to the whole world. In 1853, Czar Nicholas I threatened to take over part of the Ottoman Empire in the Crimean War. However, Russia's industries and transportation system failed to provide adequate supplies for the country's troops. As a result, in 1856, Russia lost the war against the combined forces of France, Great Britain, Sardinia, and the Ottoman Empire.

After the war, Nicholas's son, **Alexander II**, decided to move Russia toward modernization and social change. Alexander and his advisers believed that his reforms would allow Russia to compete with western Europe for world power.

Reform and Reaction The first and boldest of Alexander's reforms was a decree freeing the serfs in 1861. The abolition of serfdom, however, went only halfway. Peasant communities—rather than individual peasants—received about half the farmland in the country. Nobles kept the other half. The government paid the nobles for their land. Each peasant community, on the other hand, had 49 years to pay the government for the land it had received. So, while the serfs were legally free, the debt still tied them to the land.

Political and social reforms ground to a halt when terrorists assassinated Alexander II in 1881. His successor, Alexander III, tightened czarist control over the country. Alexander III and his ministers, however, encouraged industrial development to expand Russia's power. A major force behind Russia's drive toward industrial expansion was nationalism. Nationalism also stirred other ethnic groups. During the 1800s, such groups were uniting into nations and building industries to survive among other nation-states. **D**

MAIN IDEA

Analyzing Issues

D Why did czars push for industrialization?

History *in* Depth

Emancipation

In 1861, on the day before Abraham Lincoln became president of the United States, Czar Alexander II issued the Edict of Emancipation, freeing 20 million serfs. Less than two years later, President Lincoln issued the Emancipation Proclamation, freeing enslaved peoples living under the Confederacy.

The emancipation edicts did not entirely fulfill the hopes of Russian serfs or former slaves in the United States. Russian peasant communities, like the one pictured above, were still tied to the land. And Lincoln did not free enslaved people in the border states.

SECTION **2** ASSESSMENT

TERMS & NAMES 1. For each term or name, write a sentence explaining its significance.
• conservative   • liberal   • radical   • nationalism   • nation-state   • the Balkans   • Louis-Napoleon   • Alexander II

USING YOUR NOTES

2. Why did most of the revolts fail?

MAIN IDEAS

3. How were radicals different from liberals?

4. Why did France's Third Republic fail?

5. What was the driving force behind Russia's industrial expansion?

CRITICAL THINKING & WRITING

6. MAKING INFERENCES Why might liberals and radicals join together in a nationalist cause?

7. DRAWING CONCLUSIONS Why did some liberals disapprove of the way Louis-Napoleon ruled France after the uprisings of 1848?

8. EVALUATING DECISIONS What consequences did Alexander's reforms have on Russia?

9. WRITING ACTIVITY REVOLUTION Imagine you live in Europe in 1848. Write a **letter** to a friend, stating your political position—conservative, liberal, or radical. Express your feelings about the uprisings and the future of Europe.

CONNECT TO TODAY WRITING A TV NEWS SCRIPT

Early in the 21st century, hostility between Greeks and Turks on the island of Cyprus was reduced. Prepare a **TV news script** about the current status of governing the island.

3

Nationalism
CASE STUDY: Italy and Germany

MAIN IDEA	WHY IT MATTERS NOW	TERMS & NAMES
POWER AND AUTHORITY Nationalism contributed to the formation of two new nations and a new political order in Europe.	Nationalism is the basis of world politics today and has often caused conflicts and wars.	• Russification • Camillo di Cavour • Giuseppe Garibaldi • Junker • Otto von Bismarck • realpolitik • kaiser

SETTING THE STAGE Nationalism was the most powerful idea of the 1800s. Its influence stretched throughout Europe and the Americas. It shaped countries by creating new ones or breaking up old ones. In Europe, it also upset the balance of power set up at the Congress of Vienna in 1815, affecting the lives of millions. Empires in Europe were made up of many different groups of people. Nationalism fed the desire of most of those groups to be free of the rule of empires and govern themselves in their traditional lands.

Nationalism: A Force for Unity or Disunity

hmhsocialstudies.com
TAKING NOTES

Use the graphic organizer online to take notes on major events in the unification of Italy and Germany.

During the 1800s, nationalism fueled efforts to build nation-states. Nationalists were not loyal to kings, but to their people—to those who shared common bonds. Nationalists believed that people of a single "nationality," or ancestry, should unite under a single government. However, people who wanted to restore the old order from before the French Revolution saw nationalism as a force for disunity.

Gradually, authoritarian rulers began to see that nationalism could also unify masses of people. They soon began to use nationalist feelings for their own purposes. They built nation-states in areas where they remained firmly in control.

Types of Nationalist Movements		
Type	**Characteristics**	**Examples**
Unification	• Mergers of politically divided but culturally similar lands	• 19th century Germany • 19th century Italy
Separation	• Culturally distinct group resists being added to a state or tries to break away	• Greeks in the Ottoman Empire • French-speaking Canadians
State-building	• Culturally distinct groups form into a new state by accepting a single culture	• The United States • Turkey

SKILLBUILDER: Interpreting Charts
1. **Categorizing** *What types of nationalist movements can evolve in lands with culturally distinct groups?*
2. **Drawing Conclusions** *What must be present for state-building to take place?*

In the chart on page 692, you can see the characteristics and examples of three types of nationalist movements. In today's world, groups still use the spirit of nationalism to unify, separate, or build up nation-states.

Nationalism Shakes Aging Empires

Three aging empires—the Austrian Empire of the Hapsburgs, the Russian Empire of the Romanovs, and the Ottoman Empire of the Turks—contained a mixture of ethnic groups. Control of land and ethnic groups moved back and forth between these empires, depending on victories or defeats in war and on royal marriages. When nationalism emerged in the 19th century, ethnic unrest threatened and eventually toppled these empires.

The Breakup of the Austrian Empire The Austrian Empire brought together Slovenes, Hungarians, Germans, Czechs, Slovaks, Croats, Poles, Serbs, and Italians. In 1866, Prussia defeated Austria in the Austro-Prussian War. With its victory, Prussia gained control of the newly organized North German Confederation, a union of Prussia and 21 smaller German political units. Then, pressured by the Hungarians, Emperor Francis Joseph of Austria split his empire in half, declaring Austria and Hungary independent states, with himself as ruler of both. The empire was now called Austria-Hungary or the Austro-Hungarian Empire. Nationalist disputes continued to weaken the empire for more than 40 years. Finally, after World War I, Austria-Hungary broke into several separate nation-states.

The Russian Empire Crumbles Nationalism also helped break up the 370-year-old empire of the czars in Russia. In addition to the Russians themselves, the czar ruled over 22 million Ukrainians, 8 million Poles, and smaller numbers of Lithuanians, Latvians, Estonians, Finns, Jews, Romanians, Georgians, Armenians, Turks, and others. Each group had its own culture.

The ruling Romanov dynasty of Russia was determined to maintain iron control over this diversity. They instituted a policy of **Russification**, forcing Russian culture on all the ethnic groups in the empire. This policy actually strengthened ethnic nationalist feelings and helped to disunify Russia. The weakened czarist empire finally could not withstand the double shock of World War I and the communist revolution. The last Romanov czar gave up his power in 1917. **A**

The Ottoman Empire Weakens The ruling Turks of the Ottoman Empire controlled Greeks, Slavs, Arabs, Bulgarians, and Armenians. In 1856, under pressure from the British and French, the Ottomans granted equal citizenship to all the people under their rule. That measure angered conservative Turks, who wanted no change in the situation, and caused tensions in the empire. For example, in response to nationalism in

MAIN IDEA

Making Inferences

A Why might a policy like Russification produce results that are opposite those intended?

◄ Driven from their homes, Armenians beg for bread at a refugee center.

Armenia, the Ottomans massacred and deported Armenians from 1894 to 1896 and again in 1915. Like Austria-Hungary, the Ottoman Empire broke apart soon after World War I.

Cavour Unites Italy

While nationalism destroyed empires, it also built nations. Italy was one of the countries to form from the territory of crumbling empires. Between 1815 and 1848, fewer and fewer Italians were content to live under foreign rulers.

Cavour Leads Italian Unification Italian nationalists looked for leadership from the kingdom of Piedmont-Sardinia, the largest and most powerful of the Italian states. The kingdom had adopted a liberal constitution in 1848. So, to the liberal Italian middle classes, unification under Piedmont-Sardinia seemed a good plan.

In 1852, Sardinia's king, Victor Emmanuel II, named Count **Camillo di Cavour** (kuh•VOOR) as his prime minister. Cavour was a cunning statesman who worked tirelessly to expand Piedmont-Sardinia's power. Using skillful diplomacy and well-chosen alliances he set about gaining control of northern Italy for Sardinia.

Cavour realized that the greatest roadblock to annexing northern Italy was Austria. In 1858, the French emperor Napoleon III agreed to help drive Austria out of the northern Italian provinces. Cavour then provoked a war with the Austrians. A combined French-Sardinian army won two quick victories. Sardinia succeeded in taking all of northern Italy, except Venetia.

Garibaldi Brings Unity As Cavour was uniting northern Italy, he secretly started helping nationalist rebels in southern Italy. In May 1860, a small army of Italian nationalists led by a bold and visionary soldier, **Giuseppe Garibaldi** (GAR•uh• BAWL•dee), captured Sicily. In battle, Garibaldi always wore a bright red shirt, as did his followers. As a result, they became known as the Red Shirts.

From Sicily, Garibaldi and his forces crossed to the Italian mainland and marched north. Eventually, Garibaldi agreed to unite the southern areas he had conquered with the kingdom of Piedmont-Sardinia. Cavour arranged for King Victor Emmanuel II to meet Garibaldi in Naples. "The Red One" willingly agreed to step aside and let the Sardinian king rule. **B**

In 1866, the Austrian province of Venetia, which included the city of Venice, became part of Italy. In 1870,

The Unification of Italy, 1858–1870

hmhsocialstudies.com
INTERACTIVE MAP

FRANCE
SWITZERLAND
A L P S
AUSTRIAN EMPIRE
SAVOY
To France, 1860
Milan
Turin LOMBARDY
VENETIA
Venice
PIEDMONT PARMA
Po R.
MODENA
NICE
Genoa
LUCCA
Pisa
Florence
Arno R.
TUSCANY
PAPAL STATES
CORSICA (Fr.)
Rome
Tiber R.
Adriatic Sea
OTTOMAN EMPIRE
Mediterranean Sea
SARDINIA
Naples
KINGDOM
Tyrrhenian Sea
OF THE
TWO
Palermo SICILIES
SICILY
Drava R.
Sava R.
Danube R.
50° N
42° N
8° E
16° E

N

Kingdom of Sardinia, 1858
Added to Sardinia, 1859–1860
Added to Italy, 1866
Added to Italy, 1870
— Papal States

0   200 Miles
0   400 Kilometers

GEOGRAPHY SKILLBUILDER: Interpreting Maps
1. **Movement** *During what time period was the greatest share of territory unified in Italy?*
2. **Region** *Which territories did the Italians lose to France during their process of unification?*

MAIN IDEA

Hypothesizing

B What reasons might Garibaldi have had to step aside and let the Sardinian king rule?

"Right Leg in the Boot at Last"
In this 1860 British cartoon, the king of Sardinia is receiving control of lands taken by the nationalist Garibaldi. The act was one of the final steps in the unification of Italy.

SKILLBUILDER: Analyzing Political Cartoons
1. **Clarifying** *What symbol does the cartoonist use for the soon-to-be nation of Italy?*
2. **Making Inferences** *How is Garibaldi portrayed?*
3. **Analyzing Bias** *What does the title of the cartoon say about the cartoonist's view of Italian unification?*

 See Skillbuilder Handbook, page R29

Italian forces took over the last part of a territory known as the Papal States. With this victory, the city of Rome came under Italian control. Soon after, Rome became the capital of the united kingdom of Italy. The pope, however, would continue to govern a section of Rome known as Vatican City.

CASE STUDY: GERMANY

Bismarck Unites Germany

Like Italy, Germany also achieved national unity in the mid-1800s. Beginning in 1815, 39 German states formed a loose grouping called the German Confederation. The Austrian Empire dominated the confederation. However, Prussia was ready to unify all the German states.

Prussia Leads German Unification Prussia enjoyed several advantages that would eventually help it forge a strong German state. First of all, unlike the Austro-Hungarian Empire, Prussia had a mainly German population. As a result, nationalism actually unified Prussia. In contrast, ethnic groups in Austria-Hungary tore the empire apart. Moreover, Prussia's army was by far the most powerful in central Europe. In 1848, Berlin rioters forced a constitutional convention to write up a liberal constitution for the kingdom, paving the way for unification.

Bismarck Takes Control In 1861, Wilhelm I succeeded Frederick William to the throne. The liberal parliament refused him money for reforms that would double the strength of the army. Wilhelm saw the parliament's refusal as a major challenge to his authority. He was supported in his view by the <u>Junkers</u> (YUNG•kuhrz), strongly conservative members of Prussia's wealthy landowning class. In 1862, Wilhelm chose a conservative Junker named <u>Otto von Bismarck</u> as his prime minister. Bismarck was a master of what came to be known as <u>realpolitik</u>. This

Otto von Bismarck
1815–1898

To some Germans, Bismarck was the greatest and noblest of Germany's statesmen. They say he almost single-handedly unified the nation and raised it to greatness. To others, he was nothing but a devious politician who abused his powers and led Germany into dictatorship.

His speeches, letters, and memoirs show him to be both crafty and deeply religious. At one moment, he could declare, "It is the destiny of the weak to be devoured by the strong." At another moment he might claim, "We Germans shall never wage aggressive war, ambitious war, a war of conquest."

↗ hmhsocialstudies.com

INTERNET ACTIVITY Go online to create an interactive time line of Bismarck's actions to unite Germany.

German term means "the politics of reality." The term is used to describe tough power politics with no room for idealism. With realpolitik as his style, Bismarck would become one of the commanding figures of German history.

With the king's approval, Bismarck declared that he would rule without the consent of parliament and without a legal budget. Those actions were in direct violation of the constitution. In his first speech as prime minister, he defiantly told members of the Prussian parliament, "It is not by means of speeches and majority resolutions that the great issues of the day will be decided—that was the great mistake of 1848 and 1849—but by blood and iron." **C**

Prussia Expands In 1864, Bismarck took the first step toward molding an empire. Prussia and Austria formed an alliance and went to war against Denmark to win two border provinces, Schleswig and Holstein.

A quick victory increased national pride among Prussians. It also won new respect from other Germans and lent support for Prussia as head of a unified Germany. After the victory, Prussia governed Schleswig, while Austria controlled Holstein.

Seven Weeks' War Bismarck purposely stirred up border conflicts with Austria over Schleswig and Holstein. The tensions provoked Austria into declaring war on Prussia in 1866. This conflict was known as the Seven Weeks' War. The Prussians used their superior training and equipment to win a devastating victory. They humiliated Austria. The Austrians lost the region of Venetia, which was given to Italy. They had to accept Prussian annexation of more German territory.

With its victory in the Seven Weeks' War, Prussia took control of northern Germany. For the first time, the eastern and western parts of the Prussian kingdom were joined. In 1867, the remaining states of the north joined the North German Confederation, which Prussia dominated completely.

The Franco-Prussian War By 1867, a few southern German states remained independent of Prussian control. The majority of southern Germans were Catholics. Many in the region resisted domination by a Protestant Prussia. However, Bismarck felt he could win the support of southerners if they faced a threat from outside. He reasoned that a war with France would rally the south.

Bismarck was an expert at manufacturing "incidents" to gain his ends. For example, he created the impression that the French ambassador had insulted the Prussian king. The French reacted to Bismarck's deception by declaring war on Prussia on July 19, 1870.

The Prussian army immediately poured into northern France. In September 1870, the Prussian army surrounded the main French force at Sedan. Among the 83,000 French prisoners taken was Napoleon III himself. Parisians withstood a German siege until hunger forced them to surrender.

The Franco-Prussian War was the final stage in German unification. Now the nationalistic fever also seized people in southern Germany. They finally accepted Prussian leadership. On January 18, 1871, at the captured French palace of

MAIN IDEA

Hypothesizing
C Bismarck ignored both the parliament and the constitution. How do you think this action would affect Prussian government?

Versailles, King Wilhelm I of Prussia was crowned **kaiser** (KY•zuhr), or emperor. Germans called their empire the Second Reich. (The Holy Roman Empire was the first.) Bismarck had achieved Prussian dominance over Germany and Europe "by blood and iron."

A Shift in Power

The 1815 Congress of Vienna had established five Great Powers in Europe—Britain, France, Austria, Prussia, and Russia. In 1815, the Great Powers were nearly equal in strength. The wars of the mid-1800s greatly strengthened one of the Great Powers, as Prussia joined with other German states to form Germany.

By 1871, Britain and Germany were clearly the most powerful, both militarily and economically. Austria and Russia lagged far behind. France struggled along somewhere in the middle. The European balance of power had broken down. This shift also found expression in the art of the period. In fact, during that century, artists, composers, and writers pointed to paths that they believed European society should follow.

The Unification of Germany, 1865–1871

hmhsocialstudies.com
INTERACTIVE MAP

Legend:
- Prussia, 1865
- Annexed by Prussia, 1866
- Joined Prussia in North German Confederation, 1867
- South German States (joined Prussia to form German Empire, 1871)
- Conquered from France, 1871
- German Empire, 1871

0   200 Miles
0   400 Kilometers

GEOGRAPHY SKILLBUILDER: Interpreting Maps
1. **Location** What was unusual about the territory of Prussia as it existed in 1865?
2. **Movement** After 1865, what year saw the biggest expansion of Prussian territory?

SECTION 3 ASSESSMENT

TERMS & NAMES 1. For each term or name, write a sentence explaining its significance.
- Russification
- Camillo di Cavour
- Giuseppe Garibaldi
- Junker
- Otto von Bismarck
- realpolitik
- kaiser

USING YOUR NOTES
2. Identify an event that made the unification of Italy or Germany possible.

1800   1900

MAIN IDEAS
3. Which aging empires suffered from the forces of nationalism?
4. What role did Garibaldi play in the unification of Italy?
5. What advantages did Prussia have in leading the German states to unify?

CRITICAL THINKING & WRITING
6. **CLARIFYING** How can nationalism be both a unifying and a disunifying force?
7. **FORMING GENERALIZATIONS** Why did the Austrian, Russian, and Ottoman Empires face such great challenges to their control of land?
8. **EVALUATING COURSES OF ACTION** Many liberals wanted government by elected parliaments. How was Bismarck's approach to achieving his goals different?
9. **WRITING ACTIVITY** [POWER AND AUTHORITY] Write a one paragraph **biographical essay** on either Garibaldi or Cavour.

CONNECT TO TODAY CREATING A MAP AND DATABASE

Study the chart on page 692. Research the names of nations that have emerged in the last ten years. Categorize each nation's nationalist movement using the chart. Then create a **database** and **map** showing the location of the new nations and the category into which each new nation falls.

Revolutions in the Arts

MAIN IDEA	WHY IT MATTERS NOW	TERMS & NAMES
CULTURAL INTERACTION Artistic and intellectual movements both reflected and fueled changes in Europe during the 1800s.	Romanticism and realism are still found in novels, dramas, and films produced today.	• romanticism • impressionism • realism

SETTING THE STAGE During the first half of the 1800s, artists focused on ideas of freedom, the rights of individuals, and an idealistic view of history. After the great revolutions of 1848, political focus shifted to leaders who practiced realpolitik. Similarly, intellectuals and artists expressed a "realistic" view of the world. In this view, the rich pursued their selfish interests while ordinary people struggled and suffered. Newly invented photography became both a way to detail this struggle and a tool for scientific investigation.

The Romantic Movement

Use the graphic organizer online to take notes on movements in the arts.

At the end of the 18th century, the Enlightenment idea of reason gradually gave way to another major movement in art and ideas: <u>**romanticism**</u>. This movement reflected deep interest both in nature and in the thoughts and feelings of the individual. In many ways, romantic thinkers and writers reacted against the ideals of the Enlightenment. They turned from reason to emotion, from society to nature. Romantics rejected the rigidly ordered world of the middle class. Nationalism also fired the romantic imagination. For example, George Gordon, Lord Byron, one of the leading romantic poets of the time, fought for Greece's freedom.

The Ideas of Romanticism Emotion, sometimes wild emotion, was a key element of romanticism. However, romanticism went beyond feelings. Romantics expressed a wide range of ideas and attitudes. In general, romantic thinkers and artists:

- emphasized inner feelings, emotions, and imagination
- focused on the mysterious, the supernatural, and the exotic, grotesque, or horrifying
- loved the beauties of untamed nature
- idealized the past as a simpler and nobler time
- glorified heroes and heroic actions
- cherished folk traditions, music, and stories
- valued the common people and the individual
- promoted radical change and democracy

Romanticism in Literature Poetry, music, and painting were the most influential arts because they were able to capture the emotion of romanticism. To romantics, poetry was the highest

▼ Romantic poet Lord Byron fought with Greek nationalists. He did not live to see their victory.

form of expression. The British romantic poets William Wordsworth and Samuel Taylor Coleridge both honored nature as the source of truth and beauty. Later English romantic poets, such as Lord Byron, Percy Bysshe Shelley, and John Keats, wrote poems celebrating rebellious heroes, passionate love, and the mystery and beauty of nature. Like many romantics, many of these British poets lived stormy lives and died young. Byron, for example, died at the age of 36, while Shelley died at 29.

Germany produced one of the earliest and greatest romantic writers. In 1774, Johann Wolfgang von Goethe (YO•hahn-VUHLF•gahng-fuhn-GER•tuh) published *The Sorrows of Young Werther*. Goethe's novel told of a sensitive young man whose hopeless love for a virtuous married woman drives him to suicide. Also in Germany, the brothers Jakob and Wilhelm Grimm collected German fairy tales and created a dictionary and grammar of the German language. Both the tales and the dictionary celebrated the German spirit.

Victor Hugo led the French romantics. His works also reflect the romantic fascination with history and the individual. His novels *Les Misérables* and *The Hunchback of Notre Dame* show the struggles of individuals against a hostile society.

The Gothic Novel Gothic horror stories became hugely popular. These novels often took place in medieval Gothic castles. They were filled with fearful, violent, sometimes supernatural events. Mary Shelley, wife of the poet Percy Bysshe Shelley, wrote one of the earliest and most successful Gothic horror novels, *Frankenstein*. The novel told the story of a monster created from the body parts of dead human beings.

Composers Emphasize Emotion Emotion dominated the music produced by romantic composers. These composers moved away from the tightly controlled, formal compositions of the Enlightenment period. Instead, they celebrated heroism and national pride with a new power of expression.

As music became part of middle-class life, musicians and composers became popular heroes. Composer and pianist Franz Liszt (lihst), for example, achieved earnings and popularity comparable to those of today's rock stars.

One of the composers leading the way into the Romantic period was also its greatest: Ludwig van Beethoven (LOOD•vihg-vahn-BAY•toh•vuhn). His work evolved from the classical music of the Enlightenment into romantic compositions. His Ninth Symphony soars, celebrating freedom, dignity, and the triumph of the human spirit.

Later romantic composers also appealed to the hearts and souls of their listeners. Robert Schumann's compositions sparkle with merriment. Like many romantic composers, Felix Mendelssohn drew on literature, such as Shakespeare's A *Midsummer Night's Dream*, as the inspiration for his music. Polish composer and concert pianist Frederic Chopin (SHOH•pan) used Polish dance rhythms in his music. Guiseppe Verdi and Richard Wagner brought European opera to a dramatic and theatrical high point. **A**

MAIN IDEA

Summarizing

A What are some of the themes that are key to romantic literature and art?

History Makers

Ludwig van Beethoven
1770–1827

A genius of European music, Beethoven suffered the most tragic disability a composer can endure. At the age of 30, he began to go deaf. His deafness grew worse for 19 years. By 1819, it was total.

At first, Beethoven's handicap barely affected his career. By 1802, however, he knew that his hearing would only worsen. He suffered from bouts of depression. The depression would bring him to the brink of suicide. Nonetheless, he would rebound:

It seemed unthinkable for me to leave the world forever before I had produced all that I felt called upon to produce.

↗ hmhsocialstudies.com

RESEARCH WEB LINKS Go online for more on Ludwig van Beethoven.

The Shift to Realism in the Arts

By the middle of the 19th century, rapid industrialization deeply affected everyday life in Europe. The growing class of industrial workers lived grim lives in dirty, crowded cities. Industrialization began to make the dreams of the romantics seem pointless. In literature and the visual arts, **realism** tried to show life as it was, not as it should be. Realist painting reflected the increasing political importance of the working class in the 1850s. Along with paintings, novels proved especially suitable for describing workers' suffering.

Photographers Capture Reality As realist painters and writers detailed the lives of actual people, photographers could record an instant in time with scientific precision. The first practical photographs were called daguerreotypes (duh•GEHR•uh•TYPS). They were named after their French inventor, Louis Daguerre. The images in his daguerreotypes were startlingly real and won him worldwide fame.

British inventor William Talbot invented a light-sensitive paper that he used to produce photographic negatives. The advantage of his process was that many prints could be made from one negative. The Talbot process also allowed photos to be reproduced in books and newspapers. Mass distribution gained a wide audience for the realism of photography. With its scientific, mechanical, and mass-produced features, photography was the art of the new industrial age.

Writers Study Society Realism in literature flourished in France with writers such as Honoré de Balzac and Émile Zola. Balzac wrote a massive series of almost 100 novels entitled *The Human Comedy*. They describe in detail the brutal struggle for wealth and power among all levels of French society. Zola's novels exposed the

> Analyzing Photographs

Motion Studies

Eadweard Muybridge had a varied career as a photographer. He devoted part of his career to motion studies. These photographic studies froze the motion of an object at an instant in time. They allowed scientists to study motion and to better understand time. The equipment he built helped lead to the development of motion pictures.

This series of photographs taken in 1878, titled "The Horse in Motion," was designed to discover if all of a running horse's legs ever left the ground at the same time.

SKILLBUILDER: Interpreting Visual Sources

1. **Drawing Conclusions** *What do the series of photographs reveal about the question of whether all the legs of a horse ever left the ground at the same time?*
2. **Developing Historical Perspective** *What reaction do you think these pictures would have generated among the general public?*

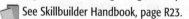 See Skillbuilder Handbook, page R23.

MAIN IDEA

Forming Opinions

B Which do you think would be more effective in spurring reforms—photographs or a realist novel? Explain.

miseries of French workers in small shops, factories, and coal mines. His revelations shocked readers and spurred reforms of labor laws and working conditions in France. The famous English realist novelist Charles Dickens created unforgettable characters and scenes of London's working poor. Many of the scenes were humorous, but others showed the despair of London's poor. In his book *Little Dorrit*, Dickens described the life of a working-class person as sheer monotony set in a gloomy neighborhood. **B**

Impressionists React Against Realism

Beginning in the 1860s, a group of painters in Paris reacted against the realist style. Instead of showing life "as it really was," they tried to show their impression of a subject or a moment in time. For this reason, their style of art came to be known as <u>impressionism</u>. Fascinated by light, impressionist artists used pure, shimmering colors to capture a moment seen at a glance.

Life in the Moment Unlike the realists, impressionists showed a more positive view of the new urban society in western Europe. Instead of abused workers, they showed shop clerks and dock workers enjoying themselves in dance halls and cafés. They painted performers in theaters and circuses. And they glorified the delights of the life of the rising middle class. Claude Monet (moh•NAY), Edgar Degas (duh•GAH), and Pierre-Auguste Renoir (ruhn•WHAR) were leaders in the movement that became very popular.

Composers also created impressions of mood and atmosphere. By using different combinations of instruments, tone patterns, and music structures, they were able to create mental pictures of such things as flashing lights, the feel of a warm summer day, or the sight of the sea. French composers Maurice Ravel and Claude Debussy are the most notable members of the impressionist music movement.

Changes in political, social, artistic, and intellectual movements during the 19th century signaled important changes in daily life. One of the most significant causes of change was industrialization, which you will learn about in Chapter 25.

SECTION 4 ASSESSMENT

TERMS & NAMES 1. For each term or name, write a sentence explaining its significance.
• romanticism   • realism   • impressionism

USING YOUR NOTES

2. What was the goal of realist writers?

I. The Romantic Movement

A.

B.

II. The Shift to Realism in the Arts

MAIN IDEAS

3. What was the key element of romanticism?

4. What characteristics did photography have that made it the art of the industrial age?

5. What was the goal of impressionist painters?

CRITICAL THINKING & WRITING

6. **COMPARING AND CONTRASTING** How are the movements of romanticism and realism alike and different?

7. **ANALYZING CAUSES** How might a realist novel bring about changes in society? Describe the ways by which this might happen.

8. **SUMMARIZING** How did nationalism influence the artistic movements you read about?

9. **WRITING ACTIVITY** CULTURAL INTERACTION Listen to a piece of music by Beethoven, and then listen to a piece of contemporary music that you like. Write a **comparison-and-contrast essay** on the two pieces of music.

CONNECT TO TODAY Creating an Arts Chart

Look at newspaper listings for films being shown today. Make a **chart** showing which of them might be categorized as romantic and which might be categorized as realistic. Present reasons why each film fell into the designated category.

Revolutions in Painting

European painting underwent revolutionary changes during the 1800s. In the early years, romanticism—which stressed emotion above all else—was the dominant style. As revolutions swept Europe in the 1840s, some artists rejected romanticism in favor of realism. They portrayed common people and everyday life in a realistic manner. Toward the end of the century, art underwent another revolution, influenced by scientific discoveries about vision. Impressionist painters experimented with light and color to capture their impressions of a passing moment.

⁊ **hmhsocialstudies.com**

RESEARCH WEB LINKS Go online for more on 19th-century painting.

▼ Romanticism

In their eagerness to explore emotion, romantic artists had certain favorite subjects: nature, love, religion, and nationalism. This painting, *The Lion Hunt* by Eugène Delacroix, shows that violence and exotic cultures were also popular themes. The swirling capes, snarling lions, and bold reds and yellows help convey the ferocity of the hunt.

▲ Realism

The Stone Breakers by Gustave Courbet shows that realist artists tried to portray everyday life just as it was, without making it pretty or trying to tell a moralistic story. Notice how the workers' clothes are torn and shabby. The boy rests the heavy basket of stones on his knee to ease his burden, while the man bends to his task. The colors are dull and gritty, just as the job itself is.

▼ Impressionism

The impressionists wanted to record the perceptions of the human eye rather than physical reality. To do this, they tried to portray the effect of light on landscapes and buildings. They combined short strokes of many colors to create a shimmering effect. They also used brighter, lighter colors than the artists before them had used. As the painting *Ducal Palace, Venice* by Claude Monet shows, the impressionists often painted water because of its reflective nature.

Connect *to* Today

1. **Developing Historical Perspective** If you were a political revolutionary of the 1800s, which of these artistic styles would you use for your propaganda posters? Why?

   See Skillbuilder Handbook, page R12.

2. **Drawing Conclusions** Impressionism remains extremely popular more than a century after it was first developed. What do you think accounts for its popularity today?

Chapter 24 Assessment

TERMS & NAMES

Briefly explain the importance of each of the following to the revolutions in Latin America or Europe.

1. conservative
2. liberal
3. nationalism
4. nation-state
5. realpolitik
6. romanticism
7. realism
8. impressionism

MAIN IDEAS

Latin American Peoples Win Independence
Section 1 (pages 681–686)

9. What caused the creoles in South America to rebel against Spain?
10. What role did Agustín de Iturbide play in the independence of Mexico?
11. Who was Dom Pedro, and what role did he play in Brazil's move to independence?

Europe Faces Revolutions Section 2 (pages 687–691)

12. How is a liberal different from a conservative?
13. How successful were the revolts of 1848? Explain.
14. Why did the French accept Louis-Napoleon as an emperor?

Case Study: Nationalism Section 3 (pages 692–697)

15. How did nationalism in the 1800s work as a force for both disunity and unity?
16. What approaches did Camillo di Cavour use to acquire more territory for Piedmont-Sardinia?
17. What strategy did Otto von Bismarck use to make Prussia the leader of a united Germany?

Revolutions in the Arts Section 4 (pages 698–703)

18. What are five elements of romanticism?
19. What are two ideas or attitudes of the romantic movement that reflect the ideals of nationalism?
20. What new conditions caused a change in the arts from romanticism to realism?

CRITICAL THINKING

1. USING YOUR NOTES
Using a chart, describe the nationalist movement in each of the countries listed and the results of each movement.

Country	Nationalism and Its Results
Mexico	
Greece	
Italy	
Germany	

2. EVALUATING DECISIONS
POWER AND AUTHORITY Why do you think Giuseppe Garibaldi stepped aside to let Victor Emmanuel II rule areas that Garibaldi had conquered in southern Italy?

3. ANALYZING MOTIVES
REVOLUTION How do you think nationalism might help revolutionaries overcome the disadvantages of old weapons and poor supplies to win a war for national independence? Explain.

4. MAKING INFERENCES
Do you believe the Latin American revolutions would have occurred without a push from European events? Explain.

5. SYNTHESIZING
CULTURAL INTERACTION How did artistic and intellectual movements reflect and fuel changes in Europe in the 1800s?

VISUAL SUMMARY

Nationalist Revolutions Sweep the West

NATIONALISM

Latin America
- Enlightenment ideas
- Haiti: slave-led
- South America: creole-led, especially Bolívar and San Martín
- Brazil: royalty-led

1830 & 1848 Revolutions
- Reactions against conservatives
- A few reforms
- Most failed

Unification Movements
- Garibaldi begins in Italy.
- Prime Minister Cavour completes the task.
- Prime Minister Bismarck leads the way in Germany.

The Arts
- Romantics inspired by emotion
- Dedication to common people or the group
- Realists see flaws and set new goals for nation.
- Impressionists capture the moment.

Use the quotation and your knowledge of world history to answer questions 1 and 2.

PRIMARY SOURCE

> When I say that we must strive continually to be ready for all emergencies, I advance the proposition that, on account of our geographical position, we must make greater efforts than other powers would be obliged to make in view of the same ends. We lie in the middle of Europe. We have at least three fronts on which we can be attacked. France has only an eastern boundary; Russia only its western, exposed to assault. . . . So we are spurred forward on both sides to endeavors which perhaps we would not make otherwise.
>
> **OTTO VON BISMARCK,** *speech to the German parliament on February 6, 1888*

1. According to Bismarck, what key factor makes Germany a potential target for invasion?

   A. dangerous neighbors

   B. three borders to protect

   C. location in the middle of Europe

   D. massive supplies of coal and iron

2. Based on his remarks above, what actions might Bismarck take?

   A. form alliances with other nations in Europe

   B. make peace with France

   C. make peace with England

   D. expand industry

Use this 20th-century mural titled *Grito de Dolores* painted by Juan O'Gorman and your knowledge of world history to answer question 3.

3. Look at the people portrayed in the mural. What does the artist suggest about the Mexican revolt against the Spanish?

   A. It was condemned by the Catholic Church.

   B. Only the poor fought against Spanish rule.

   C. People of all classes fought against Spanish rule.

   D. Only Indians fought Spanish rule.

 hmhsocialstudies.com | **TEST PRACTICE**

For additional test practice, go online for:

- Diagnostic tests
- Strategies
- Tutorials

Interact *with* History

On page 680, you were asked to create a symbol for your newly independent country. Show your symbol to the class. Explain the elements of your design and what they are intended to express. With your classmates' comments in mind, what might you change in your design?

FOCUS ON WRITING

Write a **speech** that might have been delivered somewhere in Europe at a rally for Greek independence. Urge the country's leaders to help the Greeks in their struggle for independence from the Ottoman Empire. Consider the following:

- the connections of Greece to Europeans
- the women's march on Versailles
- reasons to support Greek revolutionaries
- the cause of democracy

MULTIMEDIA ACTIVITY

21ST CENTURY

Creating a Web Page

Use the Internet, newspapers, magazines, and your own experience to make a list of movies that portray social and political conditions. Then create a Web page that classifies each portrayal as either romantic or realistic. Remember to focus on the meanings of the terms romantic and realistic as they apply to the two movements in art and literature. You may want to include on your Web page:

- descriptions of movie plots or character portrayals
- still shots from movies that support your conclusions
- romantic or realistic quotations from movies

Revolutions Across Time

Revolution—which is a sudden or significant change in the old ways of doing things—can occur in many areas, such as government, technology, or art. In Unit 5, you studied political revolutions in Europe and the Americas, in which people rebelled against unjust rulers to gain more rights. Each revolution led to major changes in governmental, social, and economic structures. In these six pages, you will gain a better understanding of those revolutions by examining their similarities and differences.

English Civil War and Glorious Revolution ▶

In 1642, civil war broke out between those who supported Parliament and those who supported the king. Parliament won and set up a commonwealth, led by Oliver Cromwell. In time, he became a dictator. After his death, the monarchy returned, but tensions built anew. In 1688, Parliament ousted King James II, shown at right, in the Glorious Revolution and invited William and Mary to rule.

1642   **1776**   **1789**

◀ American Revolution
After 1763, Americans began to resent British rule. Clashes such as the Boston Massacre, shown at left, took place. The colonies declared their independence **in 1776.** War ensued, and the United States won its freedom by defeating Britain.

▼ French Revolution
Beginning in 1789, the French people rose up to overthrow their king. The uprisings included the march by hungry women shown below. Differing goals soon split the revolutionaries. Several years of terror followed. Napoleon restored order and eventually made himself emperor of France.

1791

▲ **Latin American Revolutions**
From 1791 to 1824, revolutions took place in Haiti, Mexico, and the huge Spanish empire that spread across Central and South America. By the end of that period, nearly all of Latin America had gained its independence from European control. One of South America's great liberators was José de San Martín, shown in the painting above.

Model of a Revolution

From his study of the French Revolution, historian Crane Brinton developed a model of the stages that revolutions often go through. The model below is based on his work. Compare it with the revolutions you learned about in this unit.

 STAGE 1 **Fall of the Old Order**
Revolutions usually cannot occur until a ruler becomes weak. Often this weakness results in problems such as starvation and unfair taxes. Anger builds until the ruler is overthrown.

 STAGE 2 **Rule by Moderates**
The people relax because they think they have achieved their goal. A moderate group rules. But simply overthrowing the old order rarely solves the problems that led to the revolution.

 STAGE 3 **The Terror**
When people realize that the old problems still exist, they look for someone to blame. Radicals take control, push for more extreme changes, and execute "enemies of the revolution."

 STAGE 4 **Turn from Radical Rule**
In time, the violence sickens people, and the use of terror ends. The former radicals adopt a more gradual plan for effecting change.

STAGE 5 **Military Rule**
The terror often kills most of a country's leaders. Then the turn from radicalism makes people doubt revolutionary ideals. A military leader steps into the gap and becomes dictator.

STAGE 6 **Restoration**
When the dictatorship ends, through death or overthrow, a power vacuum results. The order that existed before the revolution is restored.

Comparing & Contrasting

1. Which of the revolutions on the time line, besides the French Revolution, is most like the model? Explain.

2. Which revolution is least like the model? Explain.

Causes of the Revolutions

Each of the revolutions you studied in this unit had political, economic, and social causes, as shown in the chart below. Some of the causes mentioned on the chart are the subjects of the primary sources located on the next page. Use the chart and the primary sources together to understand the causes of revolution more fully.

	England	North America	France	Latin America
Political	• King claimed divine right. • King dissolved Parliament. • Parliament sought guarantee of freedoms.	• Colonists accused British leaders of tyranny. • Colonists demanded the same rights as English citizens.	• Third Estate wanted greater representation. • Louis XVI was a weak ruler; his wife was unpopular. • American Revolution inspired political ideas.	• French Revolution inspired political ideas. • Royal officials committed injustices and repression. • Napoleon's conquest of Spain triggered revolts.
Economic	• King wanted money for wars. • King levied taxes and fines without Parliament's approval.	• Britain imposed mercantilism. • Britain expected colonies to pay for defense. • Colonists opposed taxation without representation.	• Wars and royal extravagance created debt. • Inflation and famine caused problems. • Peasants made little money but paid high taxes.	• Peninsulares and creoles controlled wealth. • Lower classes toiled as peasants with little income or as slaves.
Social	• Early Stuart kings refused to make Puritan reforms. • Parliament feared James II would restore Catholicism.	• Colonists began to identify as Americans. • Colonists were used to some independence. • Enlightenment ideas of equality and liberty spread.	• Third Estate resented the First and Second estates' privileges. • Enlightenment ideas of equality and liberty spread.	• Only peninsulares and creoles had power. • Mestizos, mulattos, Africans, and Indians had little status. • Educated creoles spread Enlightenment ideas.

SKILLBUILDER: Interpreting Charts

1. **Analyzing Causes** *What was the most frequent political cause of revolution? economic cause? social cause?*
2. **Contrasting** *How did the causes of the revolutions in Latin America differ from those of the other three revolutions?*

◄ In the 1780s, many French peasants could not afford bread to feed their families. At the same time, Marie Antoinette spent so much money on clothes that her enemies called her Madame Deficit. The harsh contrast between starvation and luxury sparked the anger that led to the Revolution.

Go online to listen to selected audio excerpts.

PRIMARY SOURCE

Political Cartoon, 1789

This French political cartoon portrayed the way the privileges of the First and Second estates affected the Third Estate.

DOCUMENT-BASED QUESTION

Do you think a member of the First, Second, or Third Estate created this cartoon? Interpret the cartoon and explain who was most likely to hold the viewpoint conveyed.

PRIMARY SOURCE

The English Bill of Rights, 1689

This excerpt from the English Bill of Rights attempted to justify the Glorious Revolution by describing the injustices King James II committed.

The late King James the Second, by the assistance of diverse evil counselors, judges and ministers employed by him, did endeavor to subvert and extirpate [destroy] the Protestant religion and the laws and liberties of this kingdom;

By assuming and exercising a power of dispensing with and suspending of laws and the execution of laws without consent of Parliament; . . .

By levying money for and to the use of the Crown by pretense of prerogative [privilege] for other time and in other manner than the same was granted by Parliament;

By raising and keeping a standing army within this kingdom in time of peace without consent of Parliament; . . .

By violating the freedom of election of members to serve in Parliament; . . .

And excessive bail hath been required of persons committed in criminal cases to elude the benefit of the laws made for the liberty of the subjects;

And excessive fines have been imposed;

And illegal and cruel punishments inflicted.

DOCUMENT-BASED QUESTION

According to this document, how did King James II take away power from Parliament? How did he violate the rights of citizens?

PRIMARY SOURCE

Political Cartoon, 1765

This political cartoon expressed an opinion about the Stamp Act. The act was a British law that required all legal and commercial documents in the American colonies to carry a stamp showing that a tax had been paid.

DOCUMENT-BASED QUESTION

What opinion does this cartoon express about the effect of the Stamp Act on the American economy?

Comparing & Contrasting

1. How are the opinions expressed by the three primary sources similar?

2. Reread the excerpt from the English Bill of Rights. Based on this document, what causes could you add to the chart on page 708?

Effects of Revolutions

The chart below shows political, economic, and social effects of the various revolutions. The primary sources on these two pages describe the political outcomes that three different revolutionaries expected to achieve. Use the chart and the primary sources together to understand the effects of revolution more fully.

	England	**North America**	**France**	**Latin America**
Political	• A constitutional monarchy was established. • The Bill of Rights increased Parliament's power and guaranteed certain rights. • The overthrow of a monarch helped inspire American revolutionaries.	• The United States gained independence. • The Constitution set up a republican government. • Revolutionary ideals continued to inspire groups seeking political equality. • The American Revolution inspired later revolutions.	• The Revolution led to a succession of governments: a republic, a dictatorship, a restored monarchy. • It created expectations for equality and freedom that sparked later uprisings in France. • It inspired later revolutions.	• Nearly all colonial rule in Latin America ended. • New countries were established. • Representative government was slow to develop. The military or the wealthy controlled much of the region until the late 1900s.
Economic	• Because it was answerable to taxpayers, Parliament encouraged trade.	• The removal of Britain's mercantilist policies allowed free enterprise to develop.	• The Revolution and ensuing wars with Europe devastated France's economy.	• Upper classes kept control of wealth. • Many places kept the plantation system.
Social	• England remained Protestant.	• The ideals of the Revolution continued to inspire groups seeking social equality.	• The French feudal system was abolished.	• Much of Latin America continued to have a strong class system.

SKILLBUILDER: Interpreting Charts
1. **Contrasting** *Which revolutions had positive economic effects, and which had negative? Explain.*
2. **Recognizing Effects** *What common political effect did the revolutions in North America and Latin America achieve?*

PRIMARY SOURCE

Thomas Paine

In this excerpt from the pamphlet *Common Sense,* Thomas Paine described the ideal government he wanted to see set up after the American Revolution.

But where, say some, is the king of America? I'll tell you, friend, he reigns above, and doth not make havoc of mankind like the Royal Brute of Great Britain. . . . Let a day be solemnly set apart for proclaiming the charter [constitution]; let it be brought forth placed on the divine law, the Word of God; let a crown be placed thereon, by which the world may know, that so far as we approve of monarchy, that in America THE LAW IS KING. For as in absolute governments the king is law, so in free countries the law *ought* to BE king, and there ought to be no other.

DOCUMENT-BASED QUESTION
What did Paine believe should be the highest power in a new American government?

PRIMARY SOURCE

Simón Bolívar

"The Jamaica Letter" is one of Simón Bolívar's most important political documents. In this excerpt, he discussed his political goals for South America after the revolution—and his fear that South Americans were not ready to achieve those goals.

The role of the inhabitants of the American hemisphere has for centuries been purely passive. Politically they were non-existent. . . . We have been harassed by a conduct which has not only deprived us of our rights but has kept us in a sort of permanent infancy with regard to public affairs. . . . Americans today, and perhaps to a greater extent than ever before, who live within the Spanish system occupy a position in society no better than that of serfs destined for labor. . . . Although I seek perfection for the government of my country, I cannot persuade myself that the New World can, at the moment, be organized as a great republic.

DOCUMENT-BASED QUESTION
Why did Bolívar believe that South Americans were not ready for a republican form of government?

PRIMARY SOURCE

Maximilien Robespierre

In a speech given on February 5, 1794, Robespierre described his goals for the French Revolution. In this excerpt, he explained his reasons for using terror.

It is necessary to annihilate both the internal and external enemies of the republic or perish with its fall. Now, in this situation your first political maxim should be that one guides the people by reason, and the enemies of the people by terror.

If the driving force of popular government in peacetime is virtue, that of popular government during a revolution is both virtue and terror: virtue, without which terror is destructive; terror, without which virtue is impotent. Terror is only justice that is prompt, severe, and inflexible; it is thus an emanation of virtue; it is less a distinct principle than a consequence of the general principle of democracy applied to the most pressing needs of the patrie [nation].

DOCUMENT-BASED QUESTION
Why did Robespierre believe the use of terror against his enemies was necessary?

Comparing & Contrasting

1. Judging from the information on the chart, which revolutions resulted in the establishment of representative government, and which resulted in a return to tyrannical rule?

2. How do the political goals of the revolutionary leaders quoted here differ?

3. Compare the types of government set up in the United States, France, and Latin America after their revolutions. Did Paine, Robespierre, and Bolívar achieve the political goals quoted? Explain.

EXTENSION ACTIVITY
Revolutionary activity continued after the period covered by this unit. Two major 20th-century revolutions were the Russian Revolution (see Chapter 30) and the Chinese revolution and civil war (see Chapter 30 and Chapter 33). Read about one of these revolutions either in this textbook or in an encyclopedia. Then create a chart comparing that revolution with either the American Revolution or the French Revolution.

ANCIENT WORLD HISTORY

PATTERNS OF INTERACTION

Skillbuilder Handbook — R1
Skills for reading, thinking, and researching

Online References — R39
Find the Economics and Primary Source Handbooks online

Glossary — R40
Important terms and definitions

Spanish Glossary — R51
Important terms and definitions translated into Spanish

Index — R61
Index of all topics in the textbook

Skillbuilder Handbook

Refer to the Skillbuilder Handbook when you need help in answering Main Idea questions or questions in Section Assessments and Chapter Assessments. In addition, the handbook will help you answer questions about maps, charts, and graphs.

SECTION 1: Reading Critically

1.1	Determining Main Ideas	R2
1.2	Following Chronological Order	R3
1.3	Clarifying; Summarizing	R4
1.4	Identifying Problems and Solutions	R5
1.5	Analyzing Causes and Recognizing Effects	R6
1.6	Comparing and Contrasting	R7
1.7	Distinguishing Fact from Opinion	R8

SECTION 2: Higher-Order Critical Thinking

2.1	Categorizing	R9
2.2	Making Inferences	R10
2.3	Drawing Conclusions	R11
2.4	Developing Historical Perspective	R12
2.5	Formulating Historical Questions	R13
2.6	Making Predictions	R14
2.7	Hypothesizing	R15
2.8	Analyzing Motives	R16
2.9	Analyzing Issues	R17
2.10	Analyzing Bias	R18
2.11	Evaluating Decisions and Courses of Action	R19
2.12	Forming and Supporting Opinions	R20
2.13	Synthesizing	R21

SECTION 3: Exploring Evidence: Print, Visual, Technology Sources

3.1	Analyzing Primary and Secondary Sources	R22
3.2	Visual, Audio, and Multimedia Sources	R23
3.3	Evaluating Internet Sources	R24
3.4	Interpreting Maps	R25
3.5	Interpreting Charts	R27
3.6	Interpreting Graphs	R28
3.7	Analyzing Political Cartoons	R29

SECTION 4: Creating Presentations

4.1	Writing for Social Studies	R30
4.2	Creating a Map	R31
4.3	Creating Charts and Graphs	R32
4.4	Creating and Using a Database	R33
4.5	Creating a Model	R34
4.6	Creating/Interpreting a Research Outline	R35
4.7	Creating Oral Presentations	R36
4.8	Creating Written Presentations	R37

1.1 Determining Main Ideas

The **MAIN IDEA** is a statement that sums up the most important point of a paragraph, a passage, an article, or a speech. Determining the main idea will increase your understanding as you read about historic events, people, and places. Main ideas are supported by details and examples.

Understanding the Skill

STRATEGY: IDENTIFY THE TOPIC. To find the main idea of a passage, first identify the topic. Then, as you read, define the central idea about the topic that the many details explain or support. The following passage contains information about the Renaissance. The diagram organizes the information to help you determine the main idea.

❶ **Identify the topic by first looking at the title or subtitle.** This title suggests a quick way to identify the topic by looking for the name of the Renaissance woman, Isabella d'Este.

❷ **Look at the beginning and ending sentences of each paragraph for possible clues to the main idea.**

❸ **Read the entire passage.** Look for details about the topic. What central idea do they explain or support?

> **❶** A Renaissance Woman
>
> Isabella d'Este was a woman who lived during the Renaissance. This historic period produced the ideal, or "universal," man—one who excelled in many fields. The concept of universal excellence applied almost exclusively to men. **❷** Yet a few women managed to succeed in exercising power.
>
> **❷** Isabella d'Este was one such woman. Born into the ruling family of the city-state of Ferrara, she married the ruler of Mantua, another city-state. Isabella brought many Renaissance artists to her court and acquired an art collection that was famous throughout Europe. She was also skilled in politics. When her husband was taken captive in war, Isabella defended Mantua and won his release. **❸**

STRATEGY: MAKE A DIAGRAM. State the topic and list the supporting details in a chart. Use the information you record to help you state the main idea.

Think how each detail supports the main idea.

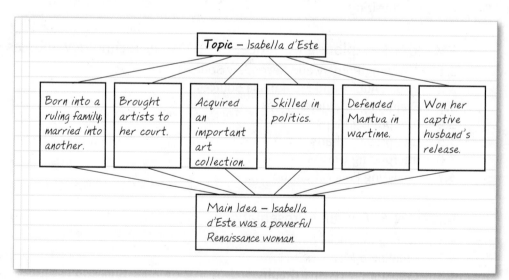

Topic – Isabella d'Este

| Born into a ruling family; married into another. | Brought artists to her court. | Acquired an important art collection. | Skilled in politics. | Defended Mantua in wartime. | Won her captive husband's release. |

Main Idea – Isabella d'Este was a powerful Renaissance woman.

Applying the Skill

MAKE YOUR OWN DIAGRAM. Turn to Chapter 19, page 530. Read "Technology Makes Exploration Possible." Make a diagram, like the one above, to identify the topic, the most important details, and the main idea of the passage.

1.2 Following Chronological Order

CHRONOLOGICAL ORDER is the order in which events happen in time. Historians need to figure out the order in which things happened to get an accurate sense of the relationships among events. As you read history, figure out the sequence, or time order, of events.

Understanding the Skill

STRATEGY: LOOK FOR TIME CLUES. The following paragraph is about the rulers of England after the death of Henry VIII. Notice how the time line that follows puts the events in chronological order.

1 **Look for clue words about time.** These are words like *first, initial, next, then, before, after, followed, finally,* and *by that time.*

2 **Use specific dates provided in the text.**

3 **Watch for references to previous historical events that are included in the background.**

Henry's Children Rule England

1 After the death of Henry VIII in **2** 1547, each of his three children eventually ruled. This created religious turmoil. Edward VI became king at age nine and ruled only six years. During his reign, the Protestants gained power. Edward's half-sister Mary **1** followed him to the throne. She was a Catholic who returned the English Church to the rule of the pope. Mary had many Protestants killed. England's **1** next ruler was Anne Boleyn's daughter, Elizabeth. After inheriting the throne in 1558, Elizabeth I returned her kingdom to Protestantism. In **2** 1559 Parliament followed Elizabeth's **3** request and set up a national church much like the one under Henry VIII.

STRATEGY: MAKE A TIME LINE.

If the events are complex, make a time line of them. Write the dates below the line and the events above the line.

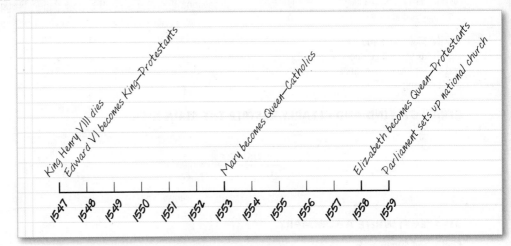

Applying the Skill

MAKE YOUR OWN TIME LINE. Skim Chapter 20, Section 1, "Spain Builds an American Empire," to find out about Spanish conquests in the Americas. List the important dates and events. Start with the arrival of Columbus in the Americas in 1492 and end with the rebellion led by Popé in 1680.

1.3 Clarifying; Summarizing

CLARIFYING means making clear and fully understanding what you read. One way to do this is by asking yourself questions about the material. In your answers, restate in your own words what you have read.

SUMMARIZING means condensing what you read into fewer words. You state only the main ideas and the most important details. In your own words, reduce the paragraph or section into a brief report of its general ideas.

Understanding the Skill

STRATEGY: UNDERSTAND AND CONDENSE THE TEXT. The passage below tells about trade in West Africa between 300 and 1600. Following the description is a summary that condenses and also clarifies the key information.

❶ Summarize: Look for topic sentences stating the main idea. These are often at the beginning of a section or paragraph. Restate each main idea briefly.

❷ Clarify: Look up words or concepts you don't know.

❸ Summarize: Include key facts and statistics. Watch for numbers, dates, quantities, percentages, and facts.

❹ Clarify: Make sure you understand. Ask yourself questions and answer them. For example, who's carrying what?

> West African Trade
>
> ❶ The wealth of the savanna empires was based on trade in two precious commodities, gold and salt. The gold came from a forest region south of the ❷ savanna between the Niger and Senegal rivers. Working in utmost secrecy, miners dug gold from shafts as much as 100 feet deep or sifted it from fast-moving streams. ❸ Until about 1350, at least two thirds of the world's supply of gold came from West Africa.
>
> Although rich in gold, the savanna and forest areas lacked salt, a material essential to human life. In contrast, the ❸ Sahara contained abundant deposits of salt. Arab traders, eager to obtain West African gold, carried salt across the Sahara by camel caravan. After a long journey, they reached the market towns of the savanna. ❹ Meanwhile, the other traders brought gold north from the forest region. The two sets of merchants met in trading centers such as Timbuktu. Royal officials made sure that all traders weighed goods fairly and did business according to law.

STRATEGY: FIND AND CLEARLY RESTATE THE MAIN IDEA.

> **MAIN IDEA**
> Gold and salt were traded in West Africa.

STRATEGY: WRITE A SUMMARY.

Clarify and Summarize: Write a summary to clarify your understanding of the main ideas.

> **Summary**
> Trade in West Africa was based on gold from the south and salt from the north. Gold was mined in the forest regions. Two thirds of all the world's gold supply came from West Africa. Salt came from the desert. Arab traders met with African traders at trade centers such as Timbuktu.

Applying the Skill

CLARIFY AND WRITE YOUR OWN SUMMARY. Turn to Chapter 17, page 484, and read "Printing Spreads Renaissance Ideas." Note the main ideas. Look up any words you don't recognize. Then write a summary of the section. Condense the section in your own words.

1.4 Identifying Problems and Solutions

IDENTIFYING PROBLEMS means finding and understanding the difficulties faced by a particular group of people at a certain time. Noticing how the people solved their problems is **IDENTIFYING SOLUTIONS.** Checking further to see how well those solutions worked is identifying outcomes.

Understanding the Skill

STRATEGY: LOOK FOR PROBLEMS AND SOLUTIONS. The passage below summarizes some economic problems facing Latin American nations during the early 20th century.

❶ Look for implied problems. Problems may be suggested indirectly. This sentence suggests that a serious problem in Latin America was the uneven division of wealth.

❷ Look for problems people face.

❸ Look for solutions people tried to deal with each problem.

❹ Check outcomes to the solutions. See how well the solutions worked. Sometimes the solution to one problem caused another problem.

> ### Land Reform In Latin America
>
> In Latin America, concentration of productive land in the hands of a ❶ few created extremes of wealth and poverty. Poor peasants had no choice but to work large estates owned by a few wealthy families. Landlords had no reason to invest in expensive farm machinery when labor was so cheap. ❷ Farming methods were inefficient and economic development was slow.
>
> As Latin American nations began to modernize in the 20th century, land ownership became a political issue. In response, a handful of countries began land reform programs. These programs ❸ divided large estates into smaller plots. Small plots of land were in turn distributed to farm families or granted to villages for communal farming. However, just turning over the land to the landless was not enough. ❹ Peasant farmers needed instruction, seeds, equipment, and credit. If the land and the people were to be productive, governments would have to provide assistance to the peasants.

STRATEGY: MAKE A CHART.

Summarize the problems and solutions in a chart. Identify the problem or problems and the steps taken to solve them. Look for the short- and long-term effects of the solutions.

Problems	Solutions	Outcomes
A few wealthy people owned most of the land.	Land reform programs divided large estates into smaller plots.	Peasants were given land, and communal farms were set up.
Inefficient farming resulted in slow economic development.		
Peasants lacked equipment, resources, skills.	Governments would have to assist with loans and instruction.	Not stated.

Applying the Skill

MAKE YOUR OWN CHART. Turn to Chapter 22, Section 4, "The American Revolution." Make a chart that lists the problems faced by the colonies before the American Revolution. List the solutions that were tried and whatever outcomes are mentioned.

1.5 Analyzing Causes and Recognizing Effects

CAUSES are the events, conditions, and other reasons that lead to an event. Causes happen before the event in time; they explain why it happened. **EFFECTS** are the results or consequences of the event. One effect often becomes the cause of other effects, resulting in a chain of events. Causes and effects can be both short-term and long-term. Examining **CAUSE-AND-EFFECT RELATIONSHIPS** helps historians see how events are related and why they took place.

Understanding the Skill

STRATEGY: KEEP TRACK OF CAUSES AND EFFECTS AS YOU READ. The passage below describes events leading to the rise of feudalism in Japan. The diagram that follows summarizes the chain of causes and effects.

1 **Causes: Look for clue words that show cause.** These include *because, due to, since,* and *therefore.*

2 **Look for multiple causes and multiple effects.** The weakness of the central government caused the three effects (a,b,c) shown here.

3 **Effects: Look for results or consequences.** Sometimes these are indicated by clue words such as *brought about, led to, as a result,* and *consequently.*

4 **Notice that an effect may be the cause of another event.** This begins a chain of causes and effects.

> **Feudalism Comes to Japan**
>
> For most of the Heian period, the rich Fujiwara family held the real power in Japan. Members of this family held many influential posts. By about the middle of the 11th century, the power of the central government and the Fujiwaras began to slip. This was **1** due in part to court families' greater interest in luxury and artistic pursuits than in governing.
>
> **2** Since the central government was weak, **(a)** large landowners living away from the capital set up private armies. **3** As a result, **(b)** the countryside became lawless and dangerous. Armed soldiers on horseback preyed on farmers and travelers, while pirates took control of the seas. **(c)** For safety, farmers and small landowners traded parts of their land to strong warlords in exchange for protection.
>
> **4** Because the lords had more land, the lords gained more power. This marked the beginning of a feudal system of localized rule like that of ancient China and medieval Europe.

STRATEGY: MAKE A CAUSE-AND-EFFECT DIAGRAM.

Summarize cause-and-effect relationships in a diagram. Starting with the first cause in a series, fill in the boxes until you reach the end result.

Cause ⟶	Effect/Cause ⟶	Effect/Cause ⟶	Effect
Ruling families had little interest in governing.	Weak central government was unable to control the land.	• Landowners set up private armies. • Countryside became dangerous. • Farmers traded land for safety under warlords.	Feudalism was established in Japan.

Applying the Skill

MAKE YOUR OWN CAUSE-AND-EFFECT DIAGRAM. Turn to Chapter 20, Section 3, "The Atlantic Slave Trade" (pages 566–570) and make notes about the causes and effects of the slave trade. Make a diagram, like the one shown above, to summarize the information you find.

1.6 Comparing and Contrasting

Historians compare and contrast events, personalities, ideas, behaviors, beliefs, and institutions in order to understand them thoroughly. **COMPARING** involves finding both similarities and differences between two or more things. **CONTRASTING** means examining only the differences between them.

Understanding the Skill

STRATEGY: LOOK FOR SIMILARITIES AND DIFFERENCES. The following passage describes life in the ancient Greek city-states of Sparta and Athens. The Venn diagram below shows some of the similarities and differences between the two city-states.

1 **Compare: Look for features that two subjects have in common.** Here you learn that both Athens and Sparta started out as farming communities.

2 **Compare: Look for clue words indicating that two things are alike.** Clue words include *all, both, like, as, likewise,* and *similarly.*

3 **Contrast: Look for clue words that show how two things differ.** Clue words include *unlike, by contrast, however, except, different,* and *on the other hand.*

4 **Contrast: Look for ways in which two things are different.** Here you learn that Athens and Sparta had different values.

Sparta and Athens

The Greek city-states developed separately but shared certain characteristics, **1** including language and religion. Economically, all began as farming economies, and all except Sparta eventually moved to trade. Politically, **2** all city-states, except for Sparta, evolved into early forms of democracies.

The leader in the movement to democracy was Athens. After a series of reforms, every Athenian citizen was considered equal before the law. However, as in the other Greek city-states, only about one fifth of the population were citizens. Slaves did much of the work, so Athenian citizens were free to create works of art, architecture, and literature, including drama.

3 By contrast, Sparta lived in constant fear of revolts by *helots,* people who were held in slave-like conditions to work the land. The city was set up as a military dictatorship, and Spartan men dedicated their lives to the military. **4** In Sparta, duty, strength, and discipline were valued over beauty, individuality, and creativity. As a result, Spartans created little art, architecture, or literature.

STRATEGY: MAKE A VENN DIAGRAM.

Compare and Contrast: Summarize similarities and differences in a Venn diagram. In the overlapping area, list characteristics shared by both subjects. Then, in one oval list the characteristics of one subject not shared by the other. In the other oval, list unshared characteristics of the second subject.

Athens Only

Economy: moved from farming to trade

Government: democracy

Values: beauty, individuality, creativity

Both

Language: Greek

Religion: same

Slavery: in both

Economy: began as farming communities

Sparta Only

Economy: remained farming community

Government: military dictatorship

Values: duty, strength, discipline

Applying the Skill

MAKE YOUR OWN VENN DIAGRAM. Turn to Chapter 20, pages 564–565, and read the section called "Native Americans Respond." Make a Venn diagram comparing and contrasting Dutch and English colonists' relations with Native Americans.

Skillbuilder Handbook

1.7 Distinguishing Fact from Opinion

FACTS are events, dates, statistics, or statements that can be proved to be true. Facts can be checked for accuracy. **OPINIONS** are judgments, beliefs, and feelings of the writer or speaker.

Understanding the Skill

STRATEGY: FIND CLUES IN THE TEXT. The following excerpt tells about the uprising of Jews in the Warsaw ghetto in 1943. The chart summarizes the facts and opinions.

1 **Facts: Look for specific names, dates, statistics, and statements that can be proved.** The first two paragraphs provide a factual account of the event.

2 **Opinion: Look for assertions, claims, hypotheses, and judgments.** Here Goebbels expresses his opinion of the uprising and of the Jews.

3 **Opinion: Look for judgment words that the writer uses to describe the people and events.** Judgment words are often adjectives that are used to arouse a reader's emotions.

The Warsaw Ghetto Uprising

With orders from Himmler to crush the Jews, **1** the Nazis attacked on April 19, 1943, at the start of the holiday of Passover. **1** Two thousand armed SS troops entered the ghetto, marching with tanks, rifles, machine guns, and trailers full of ammunition. The Jewish fighters were in position—in bunkers, in windows, on rooftops. **1** They had rifles and handguns, hand grenades and bombs that they had made. And they let fly. . . .

Unbelievably, the Jews won the battle that day. The Germans were forced to retreat. . . . **1** The Germans brought in more troops, and the fighting intensified. German pilots dropped bombs on the ghetto. . . .

2 On May 1, Goebbels [Nazi propaganda minister] wrote in his diary: "Of course this jest will probably not last long." He added a complaint. "But it shows what one can expect of the Jews if they have guns."

Goebbels' tone was mocking. But his forecast was inevitable—and correct. . . . Goebbels did not record in his diary, when the uprising was over, that the **3** starving Jews of the ghetto, with their **3** pathetic supply of arms, had held out against the German army for forty days, longer than Poland or France had held out.

Source: *A Nightmare in History,* by Miriam Chaikin. (New York: Clarion Books, 1987) pp. 77–78

STRATEGY: MAKE A CHART.

Divide facts and opinions in a chart. Summarize and separate the facts from the opinions expressed in a passage.

FACTS	OPINIONS
On April 19, 1943, 2,000 armed SS troops attacked the Warsaw ghetto. Jewish fighters held out for 40 days.	**Goebbels:** The uprising was a jest, but showed the danger of letting Jews get hold of guns. **Author:** It is difficult to believe that Warsaw Jews with their pathetic supply of arms were able to defeat the powerful Nazis.

Applying the Skill

MAKE YOUR OWN CHART. Turn to Chapter 20, "Different Perspectives" (page 560), and look at the primary and secondary sources. Make a chart in which you summarize the facts in your own words, and list the opinions and judgments stated. Look carefully at the language used in order to separate one from the other.

2.1 Categorizing

CATEGORIZING means organizing similar kinds of information into groups. Historians categorize information to help them identify and understand historical patterns.

Understanding the Skill

STRATEGY: DECIDE WHAT INFORMATION NEEDS TO BE CATEGORIZED. The following passage describes India's Taj Mahal, a memorial built by a Mughal ruler. As you read, look for facts and details that are closely related. Then choose appropriate categories.

1 Look at topic sentences for clues to defining categories.

2 Look at the type of information each paragraph contains. A paragraph often contains similar kinds of information.

Building the Taj Mahal

1 Some 20,000 workers labored for 22 years to build the famous tomb. It is made of white marble brought from 250 miles away. The minaret towers are about 130 feet high. The building itself is 186 feet square.

1 The design of the building is a blend of Hindu and Muslim styles. The pointed **2** arches are of Muslim design, and the perforated marble **2** windows and **2** doors are typical of a style found in Hindu temples.

The inside of the building is a glittering garden **2** thousands of carved marble flowers inlaid with tiny precious stones. One tiny flower, one inch square, had 60 different inlays.

STRATEGY: MAKE A CHART.

3 Add a title.

4 Sort information into the categories you have chosen.

5 Make one column for each category.

3 THE TAJ MAHAL

4 Labor	Dimensions	Design features
• 20,000 workers • 22 years to complete	• Minaret towers: 130 feet high • Building: 186 feet	• Made of white marble • Pointed arches (Muslim influence) • Perforated marble windows and doors (Hindu influence) • Interior: thousands of carved marble flowers inlaid with precious stones

Skillbuilder Handbook

Applying the Skill

MAKE YOUR OWN CHART. Turn to Chapter 22, page 637. Read "New Artistic Styles." Decide what categories you will use to organize the information. Then make a chart, like the one above, that organizes the information in the passage into the categories you have chosen.

2.2 Making Inferences

Inferences are ideas and meanings not stated in the material. **MAKING INFERENCES** means reading between the lines to extend the information provided. Your inferences are based on careful study of what is stated in the passage as well as your own common sense and previous knowledge.

Understanding the Skill

STRATEGY: DEVELOP INFERENCES FROM THE FACTS. This passage describes the Nok culture of West Africa. Following the passage is a diagram that organizes the facts and ideas that lead to inferences.

1 Read the stated facts and ideas.

2 Use your knowledge, logic, and common sense to draw conclusions. You could infer from these statements that the Nok were a settled people with advanced technology and a rich culture.

3 Consider what you already know that could apply. Your knowledge of history might lead you to infer the kinds of improvements in life brought about by better farming tools.

4 Recognize inferences that are already made. Phrases like "the evidence suggests" or "historians believe" indicate inferences and conclusions experts have made from historical records.

The Nok Culture

1 The earliest known culture of West Africa was that of the Nok people. They lived in what is now Nigeria between 900 B.C. and A.D. 200. Their name came from the village where the first artifacts from their culture were discovered by archaeologists. The **2** Nok were farmers. They were also **2** the first West African people known to smelt iron. The Nok began making iron around 500 B.C., using it to make tools for farming and weapons for hunting. **3** These iron implements lasted longer than wood or stone and vastly improved the lives of the Nok.

Nok artifacts have been found in an area stretching for 300 miles between the Niger and Benue rivers. **2** Many are sculptures made of terra cotta, a reddish-brown clay. Carved in great artistic detail, some depict the heads of animals such as elephants and others depict human heads. The features of some of the heads reveal a great deal about their history. One of the human heads, for example, shows an elaborate hairdo arranged in six buns, a style that is still worn by some people in Nigeria today. **4** This similarity suggests that the Nok may have been the ancestors of modern-day Africans.

STRATEGY: MAKE A CHART.

Summarize the facts and inferences you make in a chart.

Stated Facts and Ideas	Inferences
• iron farming tools • iron harder than wood • tools improved life	iron tools improved agriculture and contributed to cultural development
• Nok artifacts found in 300-mile radius	Nok culture spread across this area
• heads carved in great artistic detail	Nok were skilled potters and sculptors
• sculptures included elephant heads	elephants played a role in people's lives

Applying the Skill

MAKE YOUR OWN CHART. Read the Tamil poem from ancient India quoted in Chapter 7 on page 194. Using a chart like the one above, make inferences from the poem about its author, its subject, and the culture it comes from.

2.3 Drawing Conclusions

DRAWING CONCLUSIONS means analyzing what you have read and forming an opinion about its meaning. To draw conclusions, you look closely at the facts, combine them with inferences you make, and then use your own common sense and experience to decide what the facts mean.

Understanding the Skill

STRATEGY: COMBINE INFORMATION TO DRAW CONCLUSIONS. The passage below presents information about the reunification of East and West Germany in 1990. The diagram that follows shows how to organize the information to draw conclusions.

1 **Read carefully to understand all the facts.** Fact: Reunification brought social and political freedoms to East Germans.

2 **Read between the lines to make inferences.** Inference: After a market economy was introduced, many industries in eastern Germany failed, which put people out of work.

3 **Use the facts to make an inference.** Inference: Reunification put a strain on government resources.

4 **Ask questions of the material.** What are the long-term economic prospects for eastern Germany? Conclusion: Although it faced challenges, it seemed to have a greater chance for success than other former Communist countries.

> ### Germany is Reunified
>
> On October 3, 1990, Germany once again became a single nation. **1** After more than 40 years of Communist rule, most East Germans celebrated their new political freedoms. Families that had been separated for years could now visit whenever they chose.
>
> Economically, the newly united Germany faced serious problems. More than 40 years of Communist rule had left East Germany in ruins. Its transportation and telephone systems had not been modernized since World War II. State-run industries in East Germany had to be turned over to private control and operate under free-market rules. **2** However, many produced shoddy goods that could not compete in the global market.
>
> Rebuilding eastern Germany's bankrupt economy was going to be a difficult, costly process. **3** Some experts estimated the price tag for reunification could reach $200 billion. In the short-term, the government had to provide **2** unemployment benefits to some 1.4 million workers from the east who found themselves out of work.
>
> **4** In spite of these problems, Germans had reasons to be optimistic. Unlike other Eastern European countries, who had to transform their Communist economies by their own means, East Germany had the help of a strong West Germany. Many Germans may have shared the outlook expressed by one worker: "Maybe things won't be rosy at first, but the future will be better."

STRATEGY: MAKE A DIAGRAM.

Summarize the facts, inferences, and your conclusion in a diagram.

Facts ⟶	Inferences ⟶	Conclusion About Passage
East Germans gained freedoms.	East Germans welcomed the end of Communist rule.	Although eastern Germany was in bad shape at the time of reunification, it had the advantage of the strength of western Germany as it made the transition to democracy and capitalism.
Transportation and telephone systems were outmoded.	Rebuilding took time.	
State-run industries produced shoddy goods.	Industries couldn't compete in free-market economy.	
Unemployment skyrocketed.	Reunification put a great financial burden on Germany.	
Cost for reunification could be $200 billion.		

Applying the Skill

MAKE A DIAGRAM. Look at Chapter 6, pages 160–162, on the collapse of the Roman Republic. As you read, draw conclusions based on the facts. Use the diagram above as a model for organizing facts, inferences, and conclusions about the passage.

2.4 Developing Historical Perspective

DEVELOPING HISTORICAL PERSPECTIVE means understanding events and people in the context of their times. It means not judging the past by current values, but by taking into account the beliefs of the time.

Understanding the Skill

STRATEGY: LOOK FOR VALUES OF THE PAST. The following passage was written by Bartolomé de Las Casas, a Spanish missionary who defended the rights of Native Americans. It challenges an argument presented by a scholar named Sepúlveda, who held that the Spaniards had the right to enslave the Native Americans. Following the passage is a chart that summarizes the information from a historical perspective.

1 **Identify the historical figure, the occasion, and the date.**

2 **Look for clues to the attitudes, customs, and values of people living at the time.** As a Spanish missionary, Las Casas assumes that Europeans are more civilized than Native Americans and that Native Americans need to be converted to Catholicism.

3 **Explain how people's actions and words reflected the attitudes, values, and passions of the era.** Las Casas challenges prejudices about Native Americans that were widely held in Europe. His language emphasizes a favorable comparison between Native American and European societies.

> **1** In Defense of the Indians (1550)
> Bartolomé de Las Casas
>
> Now if we shall have shown that among our Indians of the western and southern shores **2** (granting that we call them barbarians and that they are barbarians) there are important kingdoms, large numbers of people who live settled lives in a society, great cities, kings, judges and laws, persons who engage in commerce, buying, selling, lending, and the other contracts of the law of nations, will it not stand proved that the Reverend Doctor Sepúlveda has spoken wrongly and viciously against peoples like these?. . . From the fact that the Indians are barbarians it does not necessarily follow that they are incapable of government and have to be ruled by others, **2** except to be taught about the Catholic faith and to be admitted to the holy sacraments. **3** They are not ignorant, inhuman, or bestial. Rather, long before they had heard the word Spaniard they had **3** properly organized states, wisely ordered by excellent laws, religion, and custom. They cultivated friendship and, bound together in common fellowship, lived in populous cities in which they wisely administered the affairs of both peace and war justly and equitably, truly governed by laws that at very many points surpass ours, and could have won **4** the admiration of the sages of Athens. . . .

4 **Notice words, phrases, and settings that reflect the period.** Las Casas speaks from a time when Europeans looked to classical Greece as a benchmark for civilization.

STRATEGY: WRITE A SUMMARY.

Use historical perspective to understand Las Casas's attitudes. In a chart, list key words, phrases, and details from the passage. In a short paragraph, summarize the basic values and attitudes of Las Casas.

Key Phrases	Las Casas's In Defense of the Indians
• barbarians • Catholic faith • not inhuman, ignorant, or bestial • properly organized states, wisely ordered • sages of Athens	Las Casas argues that Native Americans are not inhuman and do not deserve cruelty and slavery. Rather, they are fully capable of "coming up" to the level of Spanish civilization. Although he makes the statement that Native Americans are barbarians, his language and comparisons seem to suggest that he believes them to be highly civilized in many respects. At the same time, he believes in the importance of converting them to Catholicism.

Applying the Skill

WRITE YOUR OWN SUMMARY. Turn to Chapter 11, page 319, and read the excerpt from *Medieval Russia's Epics, Chronicles, and Tales*. Read the passage using historical perspective. Then summarize your ideas in a chart like the one above.

2.5 Formulating Historical Questions

FORMULATING HISTORICAL QUESTIONS is important as you examine primary sources—firsthand accounts, documents, letters, and other records of the past. As you analyze a source, ask questions about what it means and why it is significant. Then, when you are doing research, write questions that you want your research to answer. This step will help to guide your research and organize the information you collect.

Understanding the Skill

STRATEGY: QUESTION WHAT YOU READ. The Muslim scholar Ibn Battuta published an account of his journeys in Asia and Africa in the 1300s. The following passage is part of his description of China. After the passage is a web diagram that organizes historical questions about it.

❶ Ask about the historical record itself. Who produced it? When was it produced?

❷ Ask about the facts presented. Who were the main people? What did they do? What were they like?

❸ Ask about the person who created the record. What judgments or opinions does the author express?

❹ Ask about the significance of the record. How would you interpret the information presented? How does it fit in with the history of this time and place? What more do you need to know to answer these questions?

> **❶ Ibn Battuta in China, Around 1345**
>
> **❷** The Chinese themselves are infidels, who worship idols and burn their dead like the Hindus. . . . In every Chinese city there is a quarter for Muslims in which they live by themselves, and in which they have mosques both for the Friday services and for other religious purposes. The Muslims are honored and respected. **❸** The Chinese infidels eat the flesh of swine and dogs, and sell it in their markets. **❷** They are wealthy folk and well-to-do, but they make no display either in their food or their clothes. You will see one of their principal merchants, a man so rich that his wealth cannot be counted, wearing a coarse cotton tunic. But there is one thing that the Chinese take a pride in, that is gold and silver plate. Every one of them carries a stick, on which they lean in walking, and which they call "the third leg." **❹** Silk is very plentiful among them, because the silk-worm attaches itself to fruits and feeds on them without requiring much care. For that reason, it is so common as to be worn by even the very poorest there. Were it not for the merchants it would have no value at all, for a single piece of cotton cloth is sold in their country for the price of many pieces of silk.

STRATEGY: MAKE A WEB DIAGRAM.

Investigate a topic in more depth by asking questions. Ask a large question and then ask smaller questions that explore and develop from the larger question.

Applying the Skill

MAKE YOUR OWN WEB DIAGRAM. Turn to the quotation by Bernal Díaz in Chapter 16, page 455. Use a web diagram to write historical questions about the passage.

2.6 Making Predictions

MAKING PREDICTIONS means projecting the outcome of a situation that leaders or groups face or have faced in the past. Historians use their knowledge of past events and the decisions that led up to them to predict the outcome of current situations. Examining decisions and their alternatives will help you understand how events in the past shaped the future.

Understanding the Skill

STRATEGY: IDENTIFY DECISIONS. The following passage describes relations between Cuba and the United States following Fidel Castro's successful attempt to overthrow former Cuban dictator Fulgencio Batista. The chart lists decisions that affected U.S./Cuban relations, along with alternative decisions and predictions of their possible outcomes.

1 To help you identify decisions, look for words such as *decide, decision,* and *chose.*

2 Notice how one political decision often leads to another.

3 Notice both positive and negative decisions.

> **U.S./Cuban Relations under Castro**
>
> During the 1950s, Cuban dictator Fidel Castro **1** chose to nationalize the Cuban economy, which resulted in the takeover of U.S.-owned sugar mills and refineries. **2** U.S. President Eisenhower responded by ordering an embargo on all trade with Cuba. As relations between the two countries deteriorated, Cuba became more dependent on the USSR for economic and military aid. In 1960, the CIA trained anti-Castro Cuban exiles to invade Cuba. **3** Although they landed at Cuba's Bay of Pigs, the United States **1** decided not to provide them with air support. Castro's forces defeated the exiles, which humiliated the United States.

STRATEGY: MAKE A CHART.

4 Use a chart to record decisions.

5 Suggest alternative decisions.

6 Predict a possible outcome for each alternative decision.

4 Decisions	**5** Alternative Decisions	**6** Prediction of Outcome
Castro nationalized Cuban economy.	Castro did not nationalize Cuban economy.	There was no United States embargo of trade with Cuba.
The United States placed an embargo on trade with Cuba.	The United States continued to trade with Cuba.	Cuba continued to depend on the United States economically.
CIA trained Cuban exiles, who invaded Cuba.	The CIA did not train exiles to invade Cuba.	There was no invasion of Cuba.
The United States did not provide air support for the invasion.	The United States provided air support to the invaders.	The United States successfully invaded Cuba

APPLYING THE SKILL

MAKE A CHART like the one above. Turn to Chapter 21, page 615, and read the first four paragraphs of the section "English Civil War." Identify three decisions of England's King Charles I. Record them on your chart, along with an alternative decision for each. Then predict a possible outcome for each alternative decision.

2.7 Hypothesizing

HYPOTHESIZING means developing a possible explanation for historical events. A hypothesis is an educated guess about what happened in the past or a prediction about what might happen in the future. A hypothesis takes available information, links it to previous experience and knowledge, and comes up with a possible explanation, conclusion, or prediction.

Understanding the Skill

STRATEGY: FIND CLUES IN THE READING. In studying the Indus Valley civilization, historians do not yet know exactly what caused that culture to decline. They have, however, developed hypotheses about what happened to it. Read this passage and look at the steps that are shown for building a hypothesis. Following the passage is a chart that organizes the information.

1 **Identify the event, pattern, or trend you want to explain.**

2 **Determine the facts you have about the situation.** These facts support various hypotheses about what happened to the Indus Valley civilization.

3 **Develop a hypothesis that might explain the event.** Historians hypothesize that a combination of ecological change and sudden catastrophe caused the Indus Valley civilization to collapse.

4 **Determine what additional information you need to test the hypothesis.** You might refer to a book about India, for example, to learn more about the impact of the Aryan invasions.

> **1** Mysterious End to Indus Valley Culture
>
> **2** Around 1750 B.C., the quality of building in the Indus Valley cities declined. Gradually, the great cities fell into decay. What happened? Some historians think that the Indus River changed course, as it tended to do, so that its floods no longer fertilized the fields near the cities. Other scholars suggest that people wore out the valley's land. They overgrazed it, overfarmed it, and overcut its trees, brush, and grass.
>
> As the Indus Valley civilization neared its end, around 1500 B.C., a sudden catastrophe may have had a hand in the cities' downfall. **2** Archaeologists have found a half-dozen groups of skeletons in the ruins of Mohenjo-Daro, seemingly never buried. **3** Their presence suggests that the city, already weakened by its slow decline, may have been abandoned after a natural disaster or a devastating attack from human enemies. The Aryans, a nomadic people from north of the Hindu Kush mountains, swept into the Indus Valley at about this time. **4** Whether they caused the collapse of the Indus Valley civilization or followed in its wake is not known.

STRATEGY: MAKE A CHART.

Use a chart to summarize your hypothesis about events. Write down your hypothesis and the facts that support it. Then you can see what additional information you need to help prove or disprove it.

Hypothesis	Facts that support the hypothesis	Additional information needed
A combination of ecological change and sudden catastrophe caused the Indus Valley civilization to collapse	• Building quality declined • Indus River tended to change course • Unburied skeletons were found at Mohenjo-Daro • Aryan invasions occurred around same time	• What was Indus Valley culture like? • What were the geographical characteristics of the region? • How did overfarming tend to affect the environment? • What factors affected the decline of other ancient civilizations?

Applying the Skill

MAKE YOUR OWN CHART. Turn to Chapter 19, page 545, and read the Primary Source. Predict what impact the introduction of firearms might have had on Japan. Then read the surrounding text material. List facts that support your hypothesis and what additional information you might gather to help prove or disprove it.

Skillbuilder Handbook

2.8 Analyzing Motives

ANALYZING MOTIVES means examining the reasons why a person, group, or government takes a particular action. To understand those reasons, consider the needs, emotions, prior experiences, and goals of the person or group.

Understanding the Skill

STRATEGY: LOOK FOR REASONS WHY. On June 28, 1914, Serb terrorists assassinated Austria-Hungary's Archduke Franz Ferdinand and his wife when they visited Sarajevo, the capital of Bosnia. In the following passage, Borijove Jevtic, a Serb terrorist, explains why the assassination occurred. Before this passage, he explains that the terrorists had received a telegram stating that the Archduke would be visiting Sarajevo on June 28. The diagram that follows summarizes the motives of the terrorists for murdering the Archduke.

1 Look for motives based on basic needs and human emotions. Needs include food, shelter, safety, freedom. Emotions include fear, anger, pride, desire for revenge, and patriotism, for example.

2 Look for motives based on past events or inspiring individuals.

3 Notice both positive and negative motives.

> ### The Assassination of the Archduke
>
> How dared Franz Ferdinand, not only the representative of the oppressor but in his own person an **1** arrogant tyrant, enter Sarajevo on that day? Such an entry was a **1** studied insult.
>
> **2** 28 June is a date engraved deeply in the heart of every Serb, so that the day has a name of its own. It is called the vidovnan. It is the day on which the old Serbian kingdom was conquered by the Turks at the battle of Amselfelde in 1389. It is also the day on which in the second Balkan War the Serbian arms took glorious revenge on the Turk for his old victory and for the years of enslavement.
>
> **3** That was no day for Franz Ferdinand, the new oppressor, to venture to the very doors of Serbia for a display of the force of arms which kept us beneath his heel.
>
> Our decision was taken almost immediately. Death to the tyrant!

STRATEGY: MAKE A DIAGRAM.

Make a diagram that summarizes motives and actions. List the important action in the middle of the diagram. Then list motives in different categories around the action.

Applying the Skill

MAKE YOUR OWN DIAGRAM. Turn to Chapter 20, Section 2, ""European Nations Settle North America." Read the section and look for motives of European nations in acquiring lands in other parts of the world. Make a diagram, like the one above, showing the European nations' motives for taking the land.

2.9 Analyzing Issues

An issue is a matter of public concern or debate. Issues in history are usually economic, social, political, or moral. Historical issues are often more complicated than they first appear. **ANALYZING AN ISSUE** means taking a controversy apart to find and describe the different points of view about the issue.

Understanding the Skill

STRATEGY: LOOK FOR DIFFERENT SIDES OF THE ISSUE. The following passage describes working conditions in English factories in the early 1800s. The cluster diagram that follows the passage helps you to analyze the issue of child labor.

❶ Look for a central problem with its causes and effects.

❷ Look for facts and statistics. Factual information helps you understand the issue and evaluate the different sides or arguments.

❸ Look for different sides to the issue. You need to consider all sides of an issue before deciding your position.

Children at Work

❶ Child labor was one of the most serious problems of the early Industrial Revolution. Children as young as 6 years worked exhausting jobs in factories and mines. Because wages were very low, many families in cities could not survive unless all their members, including children, worked.

❷ In most factories, regular work hours were 6 in the morning to 6 in the evening, often with two "over-hours" until 8. It was common for 40 or more children to work together in one room—a room with little light or air. Those who lagged behind in their work were often beaten. Because safety was a low concern for many factory owners, accidents were common.

In 1831, Parliament set up a committee to investigate abuses of child labor. ❷ Medical experts reported that long hours of factory work caused young children to become crippled or stunted in their growth. They recommended that children younger than age 14 should work no more than 8 hours. ❸ Factory owners responded that they needed children to work longer hours in order to be profitable. As one owner testified, reduced working hours for children would "much reduce the value of my mill and machinery, and consequently of . . . my manufacture." As a result of the committee's findings, Parliament passed the Factory Act of 1833. The act made it illegal to hire children under 9 years old, and it limited the working hours of older children.

STRATEGY: MAKE A CLUSTER DIAGRAM.

If an issue is complex, make a cluster diagram. A cluster diagram can help you analyze an issue.

Issue: *Should Parliament restrict child labor?*

Facts: • *Children as young as 6 years worked.*
• *Working hours were typically 12 hours a day, often with 2 hours overtime.*
• *Working conditions were dangerous, unhealthy, and inhumane.*
• *Factory work caused deformities in young children.*

In favor of child labor:
Who: *factory owners, some parents*
Reasons: *Shorter hours would reduce profits. Children's income essential for families.*

Against child labor:
Who: *medical examiners*
Reasons: *Children working in factories suffered permanent deformities.*

Applying the Skill

MAKE YOUR OWN CLUSTER DIAGRAM. Chapter 14, Section 1, page 382–385, describes the Crusades. Make a cluster diagram to analyze the issue and the positions of the people involved.

Skillbuilder Handbook

2.10 Analyzing Bias

BIAS is a prejudiced point of view. Historical accounts that are biased tend to be one-sided and reflect the personal prejudices of the historian.

Understanding the Skill

STRATEGY: THINK ABOUT THE WRITER AS YOU READ. The European explorer Amerigo Vespucci reached the coast of Brazil in 1502, on his second voyage to the Americas. Below are his impressions of the people he met.

1 Identify the author and information about him or her. Does the author belong to a special-interest group, social class, political party, or movement that might promote a one-sided or slanted viewpoint on the subject?

2 Search for clues. Are there words, phrases, statements, or images that might convey a positive or negative slant? What might these clues reveal about the author's bias?

3 Examine the evidence. Is the information that the author presents consistent with other accounts? Is the behavior described consistent with human nature as you have observed it?

1 Amerigo Vespucci Reports on the People of Brazil

For twenty-seven days I ate and slept among them, and what I learned about them is as follows.

Having no laws and no religious faith, they live according to nature. **2** They understand nothing of the immortality of the soul. There is no possession of private property among them, for everything is in common. They have no boundaries of kingdom or province. They have no king, nor do they obey anyone. Each one is his own master. **3** There is no administration of justice, which is unnecessary to them, because in their code no one rules…

They are also **2** a warlike people and very cruel to their own kind… That which made me… astonished at their wars and cruelty was that I could not understand from them why they made war upon each other, considering that they held no private property or sovereignty of empire and kingdoms and **3** did not know any such thing as lust for possession, that is pillaging or a desire to rule, which appear to me to be the causes of wars and every disorderly act. When we requested them to state the cause, they did not know how to give any other cause than that this curse upon them began in ancient times and they sought to avenge the deaths of their forefathers.

STRATEGY: MAKE A CHART.

Make a chart of your analysis. For each of the heads listed on the left side of the chart, summarize information presented in the passage.

Vespucci's impressions of the native peoples of Brazil	
author, date	Amerigo Vespucci, 1502
occasion	exploration of coast of Brazil on second voyage to Americas
tone	judging, negative, superior
bias	Since the native people do not live in organized states and have no private property, they have no system of authority, laws, or moral principles. They have no apparent religious beliefs. They are warlike and cruel and seem to make war on one another for no reason. The author's comments about the soul seem to show a bias towards his own religious beliefs. He also reveals a prejudice that European customs and practices are superior to all others.

Applying the Skill

MAKE YOUR OWN CHART. Look at the quotation by the Qing emperor Kangxi in the Primary Source in Chapter 19, page 549. Summarize the underlying assumptions and biases using a chart like the one shown.

Skillbuilder Handbook

2.11 Evaluating Decisions and Courses of Action

EVALUATING DECISIONS means making judgments about the decisions that historical figures made. Historians evaluate decisions on the basis of their moral implications and their costs and benefits from different points of view.

EVALUATING VARIOUS COURSES OF ACTION means carefully judging the choices that historical figures had to make. By doing this, you can better understand why they made some of the decisions they did.

Understanding the Skill

STRATEGY: LOOK FOR CHOICES AND REASONS. The following passage describes the decisions U.S. President John Kennedy had to make when he learned of Soviet missile bases in Cuba. As you read it, think of the alternative responses he could have made at each turn of events. Following the passage is a chart that organizes information about the Cuban missile crisis.

1 Look at decisions made by individuals or by groups. Notice the decisions Kennedy made in response to Soviet actions.

2 Look at the outcome of the decisions.

3 Analyze a decision in terms of the choices that were possible. Both Kennedy and Khrushchev faced the same choice. Either could carry out the threat, or either could back down quietly and negotiate.

> ### The Cuban Missile Crisis
>
> During the summer of 1962, the flow of Soviet weapons into Cuba—including nuclear missiles—greatly increased. **1** President Kennedy responded cautiously at first, issuing a warning that the United States would not tolerate the presence of offensive nuclear weapons in Cuba. Then, on October 16, photographs taken by American U-2 planes showed the president that the Soviets were secretly building missile bases on Cuba. Some of the missiles, armed and ready to fire, could reach U.S. cities in minutes.
>
> **1** On the evening of October 22, the president made public the evidence of missiles and stated his ultimatum: any missile attack from Cuba would trigger an all-out attack on the Soviet Union. Soviet ships continued to head toward the island, while the U.S. navy prepared to stop them and U.S. invasion troops massed in Florida. To avoid confrontation, the Soviet ships suddenly halted. **2** Soviet Premier Nikita Khrushchev offered to remove the missiles from Cuba in exchange for a pledge not to invade the island. Kennedy agreed, and the crisis ended.
>
> **3** Some people criticized Kennedy for practicing brinkmanship, when private talks might have resolved the crisis without the threat of nuclear war. Others believed he had been too soft and had passed up a chance to invade Cuba and oust its Communist leader, Fidel Castro.

STRATEGY: MAKE A CHART.

Make a simple chart of your analysis. The problem was that Soviet nuclear missiles were being shipped to Cuba. The decision to be made was how the United States should respond.

Kennedy's Choices	Pros	Cons	My Evaluation
Publicly confront Khrushchev with navy and prepare for war.	Show Khrushchev and world the power and strong will of the U.S.; force him to back off.	Nuclear war could occur.	In your opinion, which was the better choice? Why?
Say nothing to U.S. public and negotiate quietly.	Avoid frightening U.S. citizens and avoid threat of nuclear war.	The U.S. would look weak publicly; Khrushchev could carry out plan.	

Applying the Skill

MAKE A CHART. Chapter 23, Section 2, pages 658–660, describes the decision made by French radicals to execute King Louis XVI. Make a chart, like the one shown, to summarize the pros and cons of their decision and evaluate their decision yourself.

Skillbuilder Handbook

2.12 Forming and Supporting Opinions

Historians do more than reconstruct facts about the past. They also **FORM OPINIONS** about the information they encounter. Historians form opinions as they interpret the past and judge the significance of historical events and people. They **SUPPORT THEIR OPINIONS** with logical thinking, facts, examples, quotes, and references to events.

Understanding the Skill

STRATEGY: FIND ARGUMENTS TO SUPPORT YOUR OPINION. In the following passage, journalist Paul Gray summarizes differing opinions about the significance and impact of Columbus's voyages. As you read, develop your own opinion about the issue.

1 **Decide what you think about a subject after reading all the information available to you.** After reading this passage, you might decide that Columbus's legacy was primarily one of genocide, cruelty, and slavery. On the other hand, you might believe that, despite the negatives, his voyages produced many long-term benefits.

2 **Consider the opinions and interpretations of historians and other experts.** Weigh their arguments as you form your own opinion.

3 **Support your opinion with facts, quotes, and examples, including references to similar events from other historical eras.**

How Should History View the Legacy of Columbus?

In one version of the story, Columbus and the Europeans who followed him **1** brought civilization to two immense, sparsely populated continents, in the process fundamentally enriching and altering the Old World from which they had themselves come.

Among other things, Columbus' journey was the first step in a long process that eventually produced the United States of America, **2** a daring experiment in democracy that in turn became a symbol and a haven of individual liberty for people throughout the world. But the revolution that began with his voyages was far greater than that. It altered science, geography, philosophy, agriculture, law, religion, ethics, government—the sum, in other words, of what passed at the time as Western culture.

Increasingly, however, there is a counterchorus, an opposing rendition of the same events that deems Columbus' first footfall in the New World to be fatal to the world he invaded, and even to the rest of the globe. The indigenous peoples and their cultures were doomed by European **3** arrogance, **3** brutality, and **3** infectious diseases. Columbus' gift was **3** slavery to those who greeted him; **1** his arrival set in motion the ruthless destruction, continuing at this very moment, of the natural world he entered. Genocide, ecocide, exploitation... are deemed to be a form of Eurocentric theft of history from [the Native Americans].

STRATEGY: MAKE A CHART.

Summarize your opinion and supporting information in a chart. Write an opinion and then list facts, examples, interpretations, or other information that support it.

Opinion: Voyages of Columbus brought more bad than good to the Americas	
Facts:	*Historical interpretations:*
• Europeans replaced existing cultures with their own.	• Europeans were arrogant and brutal.
• European diseases killed many Native Americans.	• Columbus's arrival set in motion ruthless destruction of environment.
• Columbus enslaved Native Americans.	• Through conquest and exploitation, Europeans "stole" Native Americans' history and culture.

Applying the Skill

MAKE YOUR OWN CHART. Look at the Different Perspectives on the Crusades in Chapter 14, page 386. Read the selections and form your own opinion about the Crusades. Summarize your supporting data in a chart like the one shown above.

2.13 Synthesizing

SYNTHESIZING is the skill historians use in developing interpretations of the past. Like detective work, synthesizing involves putting together clues, information, and ideas to form an overall picture of a historical event. A synthesis is often stated as a generalization, or broad summary statement.

Understanding the Skill

STRATEGY: BUILD AN INTERPRETATION AS YOU READ. The passage below describes the first settlement of the Americas. The highlighting indicates the different kinds of information that lead to a synthesis—an overall picture of Native American life.

1 **Read carefully to understand the facts.** Facts such as these enable you to base your interpretations on physical evidence.

2 **Look for explanations that link the facts together.** This statement is based on the evidence provided by baskets, bows and arrows, and nets, which are mentioned in the sentences that follow.

3 **Consider what you already know that could apply.** Your general knowledge will probably lead you to accept this statement as reasonable.

4 **Bring together the information you have about a subject.** This interpretation brings together different kinds of information to arrive at a new understanding of the subject.

The First Americans

1 From the discovery of chiseled arrowheads and charred bones at ancient sites, it appears that the earliest Americans lived as big game hunters. The woolly mammoth, their largest prey, provided them with food, clothing, and bones for constructing tools and shelters. **2** People gradually shifted to hunting small game and gathering available plants. They created baskets to collect nuts, wild rice, chokeberries, gooseberries, and currants. Later they invented bows and arrows to hunt small game such as jackrabbits and deer. They wove nets to fish the streams and lakes.

Between 10,000 and 15,000 years ago, a revolution took place in what is now central Mexico. People began to raise plants as food. Maize may have been the first domesticated plant, with pumpkins, peppers, beans, and potatoes following. Agriculture spread to other regions.

3 The rise of agriculture brought about tremendous changes to the Americas. Agriculture made it possible for people to remain in one place. It also enabled them to accumulate and store surplus food. As their surplus increased, people had the time to develop skills and more complex ideas about the world. **4** From this agricultural base rose larger, more stable societies and increasingly complex societies.

Skillbuilder Handbook

STRATEGY: MAKE A CLUSTER DIAGRAM.

Summarize your synthesis in a cluster diagram. Use a cluster diagram to organize the facts, opinions, examples, and interpretations that you have brought together to form a synthesis.

earliest Americans big game hunters

agriculture allowed people to settle, develop new skills and ideas

Synthesis: The shift from hunting and gathering to agriculture allowed for the development of more complex societies in the Americas.

shifted to hunting/gathering

agriculture began in Mexico

agriculture spread

Applying the Skill

MAKE YOUR OWN CLUSTER DIAGRAM. In Chapter 17 on pages 488–489, the beginnings of the Protestant Reformation are discussed. Read the passage and look for information to support a synthesis about its fundamental causes. Summarize your synthesis in a cluster diagram.

3.1 Analyzing Primary and Secondary Sources

PRIMARY SOURCES are written or created by people who lived during a historical event. The writers might have been participants or observers. Primary sources include letters, diaries, journals, speeches, newspaper articles, magazine articles, eyewitness accounts, and autobiographies.

SECONDARY SOURCES are derived from primary sources by people who were not present at the original event. They are written after the event. They often combine information from a number of different accounts. Secondary sources include history books, historical essays, and biographies.

Understanding the Skill

STRATEGY: EVALUATE THE INFORMATION IN EACH TYPE OF SOURCE. This passage describes political reforms made by Pericles, who led Athens from 461 to 429 B.C. It is mainly a secondary source, but it includes a primary source in the form of a speech.

1 **Secondary Source: Look for information collected from several sources.** Here the writer presents an overall picture of the reforms made by Pericles and the reasons for them.

2 **Secondary Source: Look for analysis and interpretation.** A secondary source provides details and perspective that are missing in a primary source. It also provides context for the primary source.

3 **Primary Source: Identify the author and evaluate his or her credentials.** How is the speaker connected to the event? Here, this speaker is Pericles himself.

4 **Primary Source: Analyze the source using historical perspective.** Read the source for factual information while also noting the speaker's opinions, biases, assumptions, and point of view.

Stronger Democracy in Athens

1 To strengthen democracy, Pericles increased the number of public officials who were paid salaries. Before, only wealthier citizens could afford to hold public office because most positions were unpaid. Now even the poorest could serve if elected or chosen by lot. **2** This reform made Athens one of the most democratic governments in history. However, political rights were still limited to those with citizenship status—a minority of Athens' total population.

The introduction of direct democracy was an important legacy of Periclean Athens. Few other city-states practiced this style of government. In Athens, male citizens who served in the assembly established all the important policies that affected the polis. In a famous "Funeral Oration" for soldiers killed in the Peloponnesian War, **3** Pericles expressed his great pride in Athenian democracy:

4 *Our constitution is called a democracy because power is in the hands not of a minority but of the whole people. When it is a question of settling private disputes, everyone is equal before the law; when it is a question of putting one person before another in positions of public responsibility, what counts is not membership of a particular class, but the actual ability which the man possesses. No one, as long as he has it in him to be of service to the state, is kept in political obscurity because of poverty.*

STRATEGY: MAKE A CHART.

Summarize information from primary and secondary sources on a chart.

Primary Source	Secondary Source
Author: Pericles	**Author:** world history textbook
Qualifications: main figure in the events described	**Qualifications:** had access to multiple accounts of event
Information: describes his view of Athenian democracy—power in the hands of "the whole people"	**Information:** puts events in historical perspective-Athens one of most democratic governments in history but limited rights to citizes

Applying the Skill

MAKE YOUR OWN CHART. Read the passage "Mehmed II Conquers Constantinople" in Chapter 18, pages 508–509, which includes a quote from the Greek historian Kritovoulos. Make a chart in which you summarize information from the primary and secondary sources.

3.2 Visual, Audio, and Multimedia Sources

In addition to written accounts, historians use many kinds of **VISUAL SOURCES.** These include paintings, photographs, political cartoons, and advertisements. Visual sources are rich with historical details and sometimes reflect the mood and trends of an era better than words can.

Spoken language has always been a primary means of passing on human history. **AUDIO SOURCES,** such as recorded speeches, interviews, press conferences, and radio programs, continue the oral tradition today.

Movies, CD-ROMs, television, and computer software are the newest kind of historical sources, called **MULTIMEDIA SOURCES.**

Understanding the Skill

STRATEGY: EXAMINE THE SOURCE CAREFULLY. Below are two portraits from the late 1700s, one of Marie Antoinette, the queen of France, and one of a woman who sells vegetables at the market. The chart that follows summarizes historical information gained from interpreting and comparing the two paintings.

1 **Identify the subject and source.**

2 **Identify important visual details.** Look at the faces, poses, clothing, hairstyles, and other elements.

3 **Make inferences from the visual details.** Marie Antoinette's rich clothing and her hand on the globe symbolize her wealth and power. The contrast between the common woman's ordinary clothing and her defiant pose suggests a different attitude about power.

Use comparisons, information from other sources, and your own knowledge to give support to your interpretation. Royalty usually had their portraits painted in heroic poses. Ordinary people were not usually the subjects of such portraits. David's choice of subject and pose suggests that he sees the common people as the true heroes of France.

A Woman of the Revolution [La maraîchère] (1795), Jacques Louis David **1**

Marie Antoinette, Jacques Gautier d'Agoty **1**

STRATEGY: MAKE A CHART.

Summarize your interpretation in a simple chart.

Subject	Visual Details	Inferences	Message
Common woman	Face is worn and clothing is plain, but her head is held high and she wears the red scarf of revolution	Has worked hard for little in life, but strong, proud, and defiant	Although the details are strikingly different, the two paintings convey similar characteristics about their subjects.
Marie Antoinette	Richly dressed and made up; strikes an imperial pose	Lives life of comfort and power; proud, strong, and defiant	

Applying the Skill

MAKE YOUR OWN CHART. Turn to the detail from a mural by Diego Rivera in Chapter 16, page 456. The painting shows the Aztec god Quetzalcoatl in many forms. Use a chart, like the one above, to analyze and interpret the painting.

Skillbuilder Handbook

3.3 Using the Internet

The **INTERNET** is a network of computers associated with universities, libraries, news organizations, government agencies, businesses, and private individuals worldwide. Each location on the Internet has a **HOME PAGE** with its own address, or **URL.**

With a computer connected to the Internet, you can reach the home pages of many organizations and services. You might view your library's home page to find the call number of a book or visit an online magazine to read an article. On some sites you can view documents, photographs, and even moving pictures with sound.

The international collection of home pages, known as the **WORLD WIDE WEB,** is a good source of up-to-the-minute information about current events as well as in-depth research on historical subjects. This textbook contains many suggestions for navigating the World Wide Web. Begin by entering **HMHSOCIALSTUDIES.COM** to access the home page for Holt McDougal World History.

Understanding the Skill

STRATEGY: EXPLORE THE ELEMENTS ON THE SCREEN. The computer screen below shows the "Issues & Press" page of the U.S. Department of State, the department of the executive branch responsible for international affairs.

1 **Go directly to a Web page.** If you know the address of a particular Web page, type the address in the box at the top of the screen and press ENTER (or RETURN). After a few seconds, the Web page will appear on your screen.

2 **Explore the links.** Click on any one of the images or topics to find out more about a specific subject. These links take you to another page at this Web site. Some pages include links to related information that can be found at other places on the Internet.

3 **Learn more about the page.** Scan the page to learn the types of information contained at this site. This site has information about current events, politics, and health and environmental issues.

4 **Explore the features of the page.** This page provides multimedia links and a chance to ask questions of State Department officials.

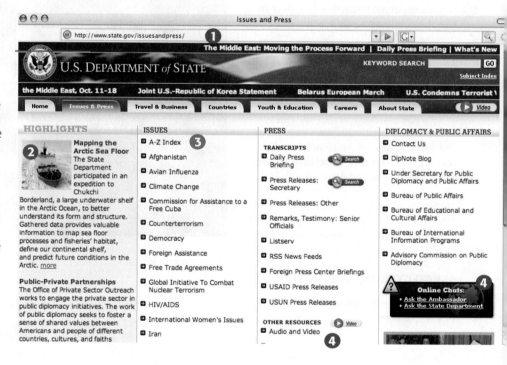

Applying the Skill

DO YOUR OWN

INTERNET RESEARCH. Explore the "World History" section of Houghton Mifflin Harcourt's Current Events website at **hmcurrentevents.com.** Find a story that interests you and follow the Related Links to learn more.

3.4 Interpreting Maps

MAPS are representations of features on the earth's surface. Historians use maps to locate historical events, to show how geography has influenced history, and to illustrate human interaction with the environment.

Different kinds of maps are used for specific purposes.

POLITICAL MAPS show political units, from countries, states, and provinces, to counties, districts, and towns. Each area is shaded a different color.

PHYSICAL MAPS show mountains, hills, plains, rivers, lakes, and oceans. They may use contour lines to indicate elevations on land and depths under water.

HISTORICAL MAPS illustrate such things as economic activity, political alliances, land claims, battles, population density, and changes over time.

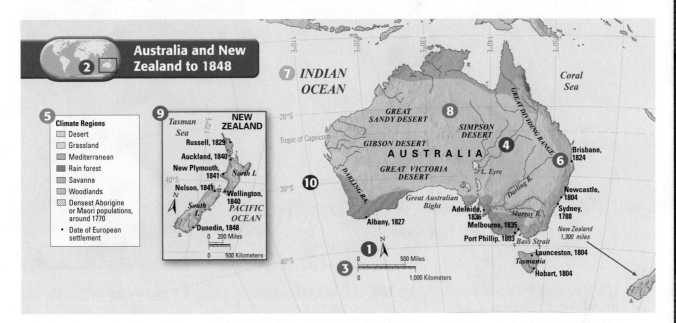

1 **Compass Rose** The compass rose is a feature indicating the map's orientation on the globe. It may show all four cardinal directions (N, S, E, W) or just indicate north.

2 **Locator** A locator map shows which part of the world the map subject area covers.

3 **Scale** The scale shows the ratio between a unit of length on the map and a unit of distance on the earth. The maps in this book usually show the scale in miles and kilometers.

4 **Lines** Lines indicate rivers and other waterways, political boundaries, roads, and routes of exploration or migration.

5 **Legend or Key** The legend or key explains the symbols, lines, and special colors that appear on the map.

6 **Symbols** Locations of cities and towns often appear as dots. A capital city is often shown as a star or as a dot with a circle around it. Picture symbols might be used to indicate an area's products, resources, and special features.

7 **Labels** Key places such as cities, bodies of water, and landforms are labeled. Key dates, such as those for the founding of cities, may also be labeled.

8 **Colors** Maps use colors and shading for various purposes. On physical maps, color may be used to indicate different physical regions or altitudes. On political maps, color can distinguish different political units. On specialty maps, color can show variable features such as population density, languages, or cultural areas.

9 **Inset** An inset is a small map that appears within a larger map. It often shows an area of the larger map in greater detail. Inset maps may also show a different area that is in some way related to the area shown on the larger map.

10 **Lines of Latitude and Longitude** Lines of latitude and longitude appear on maps to indicate the absolute location of the area shown.

• Lines of latitude show distance measured in degrees north or south of the equator.

• Lines of longitude show distance measured in degrees east or west of the prime meridian, which runs through Greenwich, England.

Skillbuilder Handbook

3.4 *(Continued)*

Understanding the Skill

STRATEGY: READ ALL THE ELEMENTS OF THE MAP. The historical maps below show European landholdings in North America in 1754 and after 1763. Together they show changes over time.

1 **Look at the map's title to learn the subject and purpose of the map.** What area does the map cover? What does the map tell you about the area? Here the maps show North America in 1754 and after 1763 with the purpose of comparing European claims at two different times.

2 **Look at the scale and compass.** The scale shows you how many miles or kilometers are represented. Here the scale is 500 actual miles to approximately 5/8 inch on the map. The compass shows you which direction on the map is north.

3 **Read the legend.** The legend tells you what the symbols and colors on the map mean.

4 **Find where the map area is located on the earth.** These maps show a large area from the Arctic Circle to below latitude 20°N and 40° to 140°W.

STRATEGY: MAKE A CHART. Study the maps and pose questions about how the geographic patterns and distributions changed. Use the answers to create a chart.

Relate the map to the five geography themes by making a chart. The five themes are described online and on the **Student One Stop DVD-ROM**. Ask questions about the themes and record your answers on the chart.

> **What Was the Location?** Large area from Arctic Circle to below 20° N, and 40° to 140° W
>
> **What Was the Place?** North American continent
>
> **What Was the Region?** Western Hemisphere
>
> **Was There Any Movement?** Between 1754 and 1763, land claimed by France was taken over by the other two colonial powers. Spain expanded its territories northward, while Britain expanded westward.
>
> **How Did Humans Interact with the Environment?** Europeans carved out political units in the continent, which already had inhabitants. They claimed vast areas, with waterways and large mountain ranges to cross.

Applying the Skill

MAKE YOUR OWN CHART. Turn to Chapter 12, page 334, and study the map titled "The Mongol Empire, 1294." Make a chart, like the one shown above, in which you summarize what the map tells you according to the five geography themes.

3.5 Interpreting Charts

CHARTS are visual presentations of materials. Historians use charts to organize, simplify, and summarize information in a way that makes it more meaningful or easier to remember. Several kinds of charts are commonly used.

SIMPLE CHARTS are used to summarize information or to make comparisons.

TABLES are used to organize statistics and other types of information into columns and rows for easy reference.

DIAGRAMS provide visual clues to the meaning of the information they contain. Venn diagrams are used for comparisons. Web diagrams are used to organize supporting information around a central topic. Illustrated diagrams or diagrams that combine different levels of information are sometimes called **INFOGRAPHICS.**

Understanding the Skill

STRATEGY: STUDY ALL THE ELEMENTS OF THE CHART. The infographic below conveys a great deal of information about the three estates, or classes, that existed in 18th-century France. The infographic visually combines a political cartoon, a bulleted chart, a pie graph, and a bar graph.

Read the title.

Identify the symbols and colors and what they represent. Here, three colors are used consistently in the infographic to represent the three estates.

Study each of the elements of the infographic. The political cartoon visually represents the power of the First and Second Estates over the Third Estate. The bulleted chart gives details about the estates. The two graphs give statistics.

Look for the main idea. Make connections among the types of information presented. What was the relationship among the three estates?

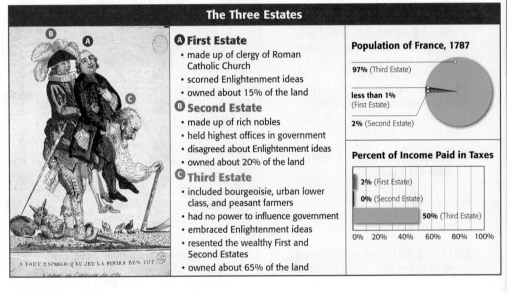

The Three Estates

Ⓐ First Estate
- made up of clergy of Roman Catholic Church
- scorned Enlightenment ideas
- owned about 15% of the land

Ⓑ Second Estate
- made up of rich nobles
- held highest offices in government
- disagreed about Enlightenment ideas
- owned about 20% of the land

Ⓒ Third Estate
- included bourgeoisie, urban lower class, and peasant farmers
- had no power to influence government
- embraced Enlightenment ideas
- resented the wealthy First and Second Estates
- owned about 65% of the land

A FAUT ESPERER Q'EU JEU LA FINIRA BEN TOT

Population of France, 1787

97% (Third Estate)

less than 1% (First Estate)

2% (Second Estate)

Percent of Income Paid in Taxes

2% (First Estate)

0% (Second Estate)

50% (Third Estate)

0% 20% 40% 60% 80% 100%

Look for geographic patterns and distributions. Pose questions about the way land is distributed among the three estates. Include your answers in your summary paragraph.

STRATEGY: WRITE A SUMMARY.

Write a paragraph to summarize what you learned from the chart.

> In 1787, French society was unevenly divided into three estates. Ninety-seven percent of the people belonged to the Third Estate. They had no political power, paid high taxes, and owned only 65 percent of the land. The First Estate, made up of the clergy, and the Second Estate, made up of rich nobles, held the power, the wealth, and more than their share of the land. Both opposed change and took advantage of the Third Estate.

Applying the Skill

WRITE YOUR OWN SUMMARY. Turn to Chapter 13, page 361, and look at the chart titled "Feudalism." Study the chart and write a paragraph in which you summarize what you learn from it.

3.6 Interpreting Graphs

GRAPHS show statistical information in a visual manner. Historians use graphs to show comparative amounts, ratios, economic trends, and changes over time.

LINE GRAPHS can show changes over time, or trends. Usually, the horizontal axis shows a unit of time, such as years, and the vertical axis shows quantities.

PIE GRAPHS are useful for showing relative proportions. The circle represents the whole, such as the entire population, and the slices represent the different groups that make up the whole.

BAR GRAPHS compare numbers or sets of numbers. The length of each bar indicates a quantity. With bar graphs, it is easy to see at a glance how different categories compare.

Understanding the Skill

STRATEGY: STUDY ALL THE ELEMENTS OF THE GRAPH. The line graphs below show average global temperatures and world population figures over a period of 25,000 years. Pose questions about geographic patterns and distributions shown on this graph; for example, when did worldwide temperature start to rise?

1 **Read the title to identify the main idea of the graph.** When two subjects are shown, look for a relationship between them. This set of graphs shows that the agricultural revolution had links to both global temperature and population.

2 **Read the vertical axis.** The temperature graph shows degrees Fahrenheit. The other shows population in millions, so that 125 indicates 125,000,000.

3 **Note any information that is highlighted in a box.**

4 **Read the horizontal axis.** Both graphs cover a period of time from 25,000 years ago to 0 (today).

5 **Look at the legend to understand what colors and certain marks stand for.**

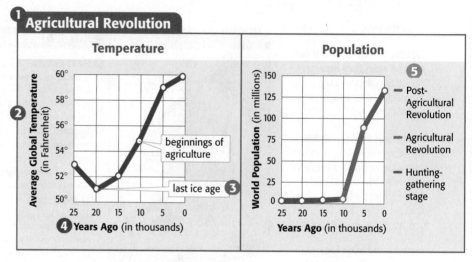

Summarize the information shown in each part of the graph. What trends or changes are shown in each line graph?

STRATEGY: WRITE A SUMMARY.

Use the answers to your questions about geographic patterns and distributions to write your summary paragraph.

Write a paragraph to summarize what you learned from the graphs.

> Some 20,000 years ago, after the last Ice Age, temperatures started to rise worldwide. This steady rise in average temperature from 51° to 55° made possible the beginnings of agriculture. As a result of the agricultural revolution, world population grew from about 2 million to about 130 million over a period of 10,000 years.

Applying the Skill

WRITE YOUR OWN SUMMARY. Turn to Chapter 20, page 556, and look at the graph "Native Populations of Central Mexico, 1500–1620." Study the graph and write a paragraph in which you summarize what you learn from it.

Skillbuilder Handbook

3.7 Analyzing Political Cartoons

POLITICAL CARTOONS are drawings that express the artist's point of view about a local, national, or international situation or event. They may criticize, show approval, or draw attention to a particular issue, and may be either serious or humorous. Political cartoonists often use symbols as well as other visual clues to communicate their message.

Understanding the Skill

STRATEGY: EXAMINE THE CARTOON CAREFULLY. The cartoon below was drawn during the period of détente—a lessening of Cold War tensions between the United States and the Soviet Union.

1 Look at the cartoon as a whole to determine the subject.

2 Look for symbols, which are especially effective in communicating ideas visually. In this cartoon, Szabo uses symbols that stand for two nations. The stars and stripes stand for the United States. The hammer and sickle stand for the Soviet Union.

3 Analyze the visual details, which help express the artist's point of view. The lit fuse suggests that the world is in immediate danger. The United States and the Soviet Union are cooperating to reduce the danger by cutting the fuse.

STRATEGY: MAKE A CHART.

Summarize your analysis in a chart. Look for details and analyze their significance. Then decide on the message of the cartoon.

Symbols and Visual Details	Significance	Message
• Stars and stripes	• United States	The United States and the
• Hammer and sickle	• Soviet Union	Soviet Union are trying to
• Lit fuse	• Danger	prevent their differences
• Both nations hold the scissors	• Cooperation	from destroying the world.

Applying the Skill

MAKE YOUR OWN CHART. Turn to the political cartoon in Chapter 23, page 652. Read the information provided in the chart and graphs to help you understand the basis for the cartoon. Note the clothing and apparent attitudes of the figures in the drawing, as well as how they relate to one another. Then make a chart like the one above.

4.1 Writing for Social Studies

WRITING FOR SOCIAL STUDIES requires you to describe an idea, a situation, or an event. Often, you will be asked to take a stand on a particular issue or to make a specific point. To successfully describe an event or make a point, your writing needs to be clear, concise, and accurate. When you write reports or term papers, you will also need to create a bibliography of your sources; and you need to evaluate how reliable those sources are.

Understanding the Skill

STRATEGY: ORGANIZE INFORMATION AND WRITE CLEARLY. The following passage describes the rise and fall of Napoleon Bonaparte. Notice how the strategies below helped the writer explain the historical importance of Napoleon's power.

① **Focus on your topic.** Be sure that you clearly state the main idea of your piece so that your readers know what you intend to say.

② **Collect and organize your facts.** Collect accurate information about your topic to support the main idea you are trying to make. Use your information to build a logical case to prove your point

To express your ideas clearly, use standard grammar, spelling, sentence structure, and punctuation when writing for social studies. Proofread your work to make sure it is well organized and grammatically correct.

> **①** The Rise and Fall of Napoleon, 1799–1814
>
> The power that Napoleon used to bring order to France after the Revolution ultimately proved to be his undoing. Under his command, the troops drove out members of the legislature in 1799 and helped Napoleon seize control of France. **②** As emperor of France, he stabilized the country's economy. He even created a code of laws. However, Napoleon wanted to control all of Europe. But he made mistakes that cost him his empire. He established a blockade in 1806 to prevent trade between Great Britain and other Europeans nations. But smugglers, aided by the British, managed to get cargo through. He angered Spain by replacing the country's king with his own brother. In 1812, Napoleon also invaded Russia by using many troops who were not French and who felt little loyalty to him. Eventually, all the main powers of Europe joined forces and defeated Napoleon in the spring of 1814.

STRATEGY: USE STANDARD FORMATS WHEN MAKING CITATIONS. Use standard formats when citing books, magazines, newspapers, electronic media, and other sources. The following examples will help you to interpret and create bibliographies.

③ Video

④ Newspaper

⑤ Magazine

⑥ Online database

⑦ Book

> **③** <u>Fire and Ice</u>. Prod. HistoryAlive Videocassette. BBC Video, 1998.
>
> **④** Gutierrez, Andrew R. "Memorial for Scott at Antarctic." <u>Los Angeles Times</u> 8 January 2001: 14A.
>
> **⑤** Hansen, Ron. "The Race for the South Pole." <u>Smithsonian Institute</u> 28 June 1999: 112.
>
> **⑥** "Scott's Run for the South Pole." <u>Facts on File</u>. Online. Internet. 28 February 2000.
>
> **⑦** Solomon, Susan. <u>The Coldest March: Scott's Fatal Antarctic Expedition</u>. New Haven, CT: Yale UP, 2001.

Applying the Skill

WRITE YOUR OWN RESPONSE. Turn to Chapter 23, Section 4, "Napoleon's Empire Collapses." Read the section and use the strategies above to write your answer to question 6 on page 671.

Find three or four different sources on the Internet or in the library relating to Napoleon's fall. Create a short bibliography and use standard formats for each type of source. Be sure to interpret, or evaluate, how reliable your sources are.

4.2 Creating a Map

CREATING A MAP can help you understand routes, regions, landforms, political boundaries, or other geographical information.

Understanding the Skill

STRATEGY: CREATE A MAP to clarify information and help you visualize what you read. Creating a map is similar to taking notes, except that you draw much of the information. After reading the passage below, a student sketched the map shown.

> **The French Explore North America**
>
> A number of Frenchmen were among the early explorers of North America. In 1534, Jacques Cartier sailed up a broad river that he named the St. Lawrence. When he came to a large island dominated by a mountain, he called the island Mont Real, which eventually became known as Montreal. In 1608, another French explorer, Samuel de Champlain, sailed further up the St. Lawrence and laid claim to a region he called Quebec. In 1673, Jacques Marquette and Louis Joliet explored the Great Lakes and the upper Mississippi River. Nearly 10 years later, Sieur de La Salle explored the lower Mississippi and claimed the entire river valley for France.

1 Create a title that shows the purpose of the map.

2 Consider the purpose of the map as you decide which features to include. Because the main purpose of this sketch map is to show the routes of early explorers, it includes a scale of distance.

3 Find one or more maps to use as a guide. For this sketch map, the student consulted a historical map and a physical map.

4 Create a legend to explain any colors or symbols used.

1 Early French Explorers in North America

KEY
• Cartier
• Champlain
• Marquette and Joliet
• La Salle

Applying the Skill

MAKE YOUR OWN SKETCH MAP. Turn to Chapter 20, page 556, and read the first three paragraphs of the section "Spanish Conquests in Peru." Create a sketch map showing the cities where Pizarro conquered the Inca. Use either a modern map of Peru or an historic map of the Incan Empire as a guide. (The conquered cities of the empire also belong to the modern nation of Peru.) Include a scale of miles to show the distance traveled by the Spanish to make their conquests. Add a legend to indicate which conquest involved a battle and which did not.

4.3 Creating Charts and Graphs

CHARTS and **GRAPHS** are visual representations of information. (See Skillbuilders 3.5, Interpreting Charts, and 3.6, Interpreting Graphs.) Three types of graphs are **BAR GRAPHS, LINE GRAPHS,** and **PIE GRAPHS.** Use a line graph to show changes over time, or trends. Use a pie graph to show relative proportions. Use a bar graph to display and compare information about quantities. Use a **CHART** to organize, simplify, and summarize information.

Understanding the Skill

STRATEGY: CREATE A BAR GRAPH. Choose the information that you wish to compare. After reading the following paragraph, a student created the bar graph below to compare population shifts in three European cities.

Population Shifts

The decline of the Roman Empire led to major population shifts. As Roman centers of trade and government collapsed, nobles retreated to the rural areas. Roman cities were left without strong leadership. The population of Rome dropped from 350,000 in A.D. 100 to 50,000 in A.D. 900. During the same period, other cities in the empire experienced similar declines. For example, the population of Trier, Germany, dropped from 100,000 to around 13,000. The population of Lyon, France, experienced an even greater decline, dropping from 100,000 to approximately 12,000.

STRATEGY: ORGANIZE THE DATA. Be consistent in how you present similar kinds of information.

1 Use a title that sums up the information.

2 Clearly label vertical and horizontal axes. Use the vertical axis to show increasing quantities. Label the horizontal axis with what is being compared.

3 Add a legend to indicate the meaning of any colors or symbols.

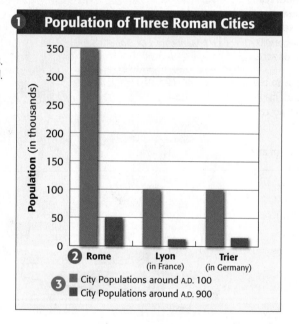

Applying the Skill

CREATE A BAR GRAPH. Turn to Chapter 23, page 670. Study the map "Napoleon's Russian Campaign, 1812." Use the information to create a bar graph showing the number of soldiers in Napoleon's army from June 1812 to December 6, 1812. Label the vertical axis Soldiers (in thousands) and show the grid in increments of 100, beginning with 0 and ending with 500. Provide a bar for each of the following dates: June 1812, September 7, 1812, November 1812, and December 6, 1812. Label each bar with the number of soldiers. Add a title. Be sure to read carefully the information in the boxes on the chart for each date you include in your graph.

4.4 Creating and Using a Database

A **DATABASE** is a collection of data, or information, that is organized so that you can find and retrieve information on a specific topic quickly and easily. Once a computerized database is set up, you can search it to find specific information without going through the entire database. The database will provide a list of all information in the database related to your topic. Learning how to use a database will help you learn how to create one.

Understanding the Skill

STRATEGY: CREATE THE DATABASE. First, identify the topic of the database. Both words in this title, "Five Empires," are important. These words were used to begin the research for this database.

1 Determine the order of presentation of information. For example, will you list items from largest to smallest? from oldest to newest? The five empires are listed in order of date, from earliest empire to latest.

2 Identify the entries included under each heading. Here, five empires from the text were chosen as topics for research.

3 Ask yourself what kind of data to include. For example, what geographic patterns and distributions will be shown? Your choice of data will provide the column headings. The key words *Dates, Greatest Territory,* and *Greatest Population* were chosen to focus the research.

Five Empires			
	1 Dates	**Greatest Territory*** **3**	**Greatest Population****
2 Persian	550 B.C.–330 B.C.	2.0	14.0
Roman	27 B.C.–A.D. 476	3.4	54.8
Byzantine	A.D. 395–A.D. 1453	1.4	30.0
Mongol	A.D. 1206–A.D. 1380	11.7	125.0
Aztec	A.D. 1325–A.D. 1521	0.2	6.0

4 * Estimated in millions of square miles
** Estimated in millions of people

4 Add labels or footnotes as necessary to clarify the nature of the data presented. Are the figures shown in thousands? hundreds of thousands? millions? Users of the database need to know what the figures represent.

STRATEGY: USE THE DATABASE. Use the database to help you find information quickly. For example, in this database you could search for "empires with populations of more than 10 million" and compile a list including the Persian, Roman, Byzantine, and Mongol empires.

Applying the Skill

CREATE A DATABASE for the wars of Napoleon that shows the dates and locations of important battles, the victor, and the significance of the outcome of each battle. Use information presented in Chapter 23 to find the data. Follow a chart format similar to the one above for your database.

Skillbuilder Handbook

4.5 Creating a Model

WHEN YOU CREATE A MODEL, you use information and ideas to show an event or a situation in a visual way. A model might be a poster or a diagram drawn to explain how something happened. Or, it might be a three-dimensional model, such as a diorama, that depicts an important scene or situation.

Understanding the Skill

STRATEGY: CREATE A MODEL. The poster below shows the hardships and dangers that children faced while working in the textile factories in the early 1800s. Use the strategies listed below to help you create your own model.

1 **Gather the information you need to understand the situation or event.** In this case, you need to be able to show the hardships and dangers of child labor.

2 **Visualize and sketch an idea for your model.** Once you have created a picture in your mind, make an actual sketch to plan how it might look.

3 **Think of symbols you may want to use.** Since the model should give information in a visual way, think about ways you can use color, pictures, or other visuals to tell the story.

Gather the supplies you will need and create the model. For example, you may need crayons and markers.

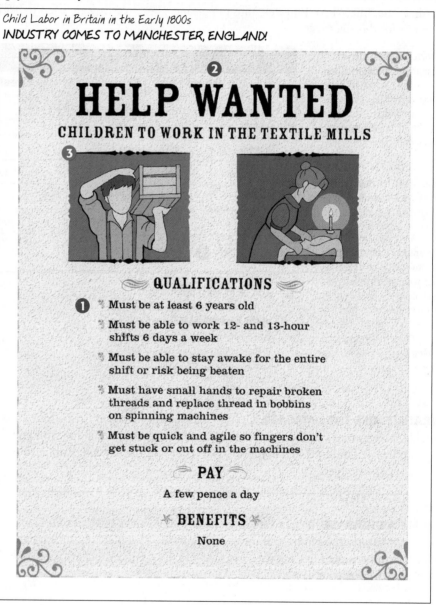

Child Labor in Britain in the Early 1800s

INDUSTRY COMES TO MANCHESTER, ENGLAND!

2

HELP WANTED
CHILDREN TO WORK IN THE TEXTILE MILLS

3

QUALIFICATIONS

1 ⚜ Must be at least 6 years old

⚜ Must be able to work 12- and 13-hour shifts 6 days a week

⚜ Must be able to stay awake for the entire shift or risk being beaten

⚜ Must have small hands to repair broken threads and replace thread in bobbins on spinning machines

⚜ Must be quick and agile so fingers don't get stuck or cut off in the machines

PAY

A few pence a day

✻ BENEFITS ✻

None

Applying the Skill

CREATE YOUR OWN MODEL. Read the Interact with History feature on page 378. Create a poster that appeals for recruits to join a Crusade. Show the rewards a crusader might expect to claim.

Skillbuilder Handbook

4.6 Creating/Interpreting a Research Outline

When you **CREATE A RESEARCH OUTLINE,** you arrange information you have gathered into an organized format. When you **INTERPRET A RESEARCH OUTLINE,** you use the outline's structure to guide you in writing a research report or paper that is clear and focused.

Understanding the Skill

STRATEGY: DECIDE HOW IDEAS ARE CONNECTED, THEN CREATE AN OUTLINE. As you research a topic, you are likely to gather names, dates, facts, and ideas. All of this information needs to be organized to show how the ideas connect to one another. To decide how the ideas connect, think about your purpose for writing the research report.

For example, suppose you are writing a report about Napoleon's retreat from Moscow. You might choose to create an outline using the sequence of events or using the causes and effects that led to the destruction of the Grand Army. Your outline would reflect your purpose.

❶ An outline begins with a statement of purpose.

❷ An outline is divided into two or more major sections, introduced by Roman numerals (I, II).

❸ Each major section is divided into two or more subsections introduced by capital letters (A, B).

❹ The subsections may be divided into sub-subsections introduced by Arabic numerals (1, 2).

Chronological outline

❶ Purpose: Describe the events that led to Napoleon's defeat in Russia.

❷ I. Napoleon's defeat in Russia
- A. June 1812
  1. march into Russia
  2. scorched-earth policy
- B. September 7, 1812
  1. Battle of Borodino
  2. narrow victory for the French
- C. September 14, 1812
  1. arrival in Moscow
  2. city in flames

❷ II. Napoleon's defeat in Russia
- A. mid-October 1812
  1. waiting for offer of peace
  2. too late to advance
  3. begins retreat from Moscow
- B. early November 1812
  1. retreat in snow storm
  2. attack by Russians

Cause-and-effect outline

Purpose: Describe the reasons for Napoleon's defeat in Russia.

I. Napoleon's mistakes
- **❸** A. troops not loyal to Napoleon
- B. waited too long to retreat
  - **❹** 1. starvation
  - 2. winter snows

II. Russian tactics
- A. scorched-earth policy
- B. no offer of peace from the czar
- C. attacks on the retreating army

STRATEGY: INTERPRET THE OUTLINE TO WRITE A RESEARCH REPORT.

Use the organization of the outline to choose signal words that match your purpose for writing.

Signal words to show time-order	*Signal words to show cause and effect*
dates: September 14, 1812	because
time frames: for five weeks	so
order: first, next, then, last	as a result

Applying the Skill

CREATE YOUR OWN OUTLINE. Read Chapter 22, Section 4, "The American Revolution." Create an outline that shows a sequence of events leading up to the Revolution or that shows the series of causes and effects that resulted in the Revolution. Choose appropriate signal words to write a rough draft from your outline.

Skillbuilder Handbook

4.7 Creating Oral Presentations

When you **CREATE AN ORAL PRESENTATION,** you prepare a speech or a talk to give before an audience. The object of an oral presentation is to provide information about a particular topic or to persuade an audience to think or act in a particular way.

Understanding the Skill

STRATEGY: CHOOSE A TOPIC. The following is an excerpt from a student's speech in support of recycling.

1 State your theme or point of view.

2 Include facts or arguments to support your theme.

3 Choose words and images that reflect the theme. The comparison to Disneyland is a visual image that helps to communicate the amount of waste in the Fresh Kills Landfill.

1 To help preserve the earth's dwindling natural resources, Americans need to get serious about recycling. At the moment, our track record is not very good. **2** Although people in the United States account for less than 5% of the world's population, they use 40% of the world's resources, and generate a huge amount of waste. The Fresh Kills Landfill, which serves New York City, is a prime example. It contains so much garbage that Fresh Kills Landfill is **3** four times the size of Disneyland. And that's just New York's garbage.

With so many people throwing so much away, is there any point in trying to change things? The answer is yes! Recycling one glass bottle saves enough energy to light a 100-watt light bulb for four hours. Twenty-five million trees could be saved every year by recycling just 10% of our newspapers. Making new aluminum products from recycled aluminum, rather than from bauxite, uses 95% less energy. By increasing the recycling of our bottles, jars, cans, and paper, we could dramatically reduce our demand for trees, fossil fuels, and other precious resources.

STRATEGY: USE THESE TIPS FOR SUCCESSFUL ORAL PRESENTATIONS.
- Maintain eye contact with your audience.
- Use gestures and body language to emphasize main points.
- Pace yourself. Speak slowly and distinctly.
- Vary your tone to help bring out the message you wish to make.

STRATEGY: PRACTICE THE PRESENTATION in front of a mirror or ask a friend or family member to listen to your presentation and give you feedback.

Applying the Skill

CREATE YOUR OWN ORAL PRESENTATION. Turn to Chapter 22. Choose a topic from the "New" section of one of the "Changing Idea" boxes on pages 626, 629, 638, or 642. Create an oral presentation in which you explain how the idea was new and why it was important. Use information from the chapter to support your chosen idea.

4.8 Creating Written Presentations

CREATING A WRITTEN PRESENTATION means writing an in-depth report on a topic in history. Your objective may be to inform or to support a particular point of view. To succeed, your writing must be clear and well organized. For additional information on creating a historical research paper, see Skillbuilder 4.1, Writing for Social Studies.

Understanding the Skill

STRATEGY: CREATE AN OUTLINE such as the one below. Use it as a guide to write your presentation.

1 State the main idea.

2 Organize the information by category.

3 Add supporting facts and details.

1 The Incan Empire

I. The Inca created a large and highly developed empire.

2 A. A Theocracy
  1. Members of only 11 families could rule
  2. Rulers believed to be descendants of the sun god
  3. Religion supported the state; worship of the sun god, Inti, amounted to worship of the king

B. Expansion
  1. Rulers conquered new territories to acquire wealth
  2. Pachacuti created the largest empire in the Americas
  3. Size by 1500: 2,500 miles along western coast, 16 million people

C. Unifying strategies
  3 1. Rulers practiced diplomacy
  2. Rulers imposed a single official language, Quechua
  3. Schools taught conquered peoples the Incan ways
  4. Extensive system of roads led to Cuzco, the capital

D. Early socialism
  1. Supported aged and disabled
  2. Rewarded citizens' labor with food and beer

E. Culturally advanced
  1. Elaborate calendar system
  2. Artisans created works in gold and silver
  3. Exception: no writing system, but oral tradition

Skillbuilder Handbook

4.8 *(Continued)*

STRATEGY: EDIT AND REVISE YOUR PRESENTATION.

Skillbuilder Handbook

1 **Use punctuation marks for their correct purposes.** A comma follows a prepositional phrase at the beginning of a sentence.

2 **Capitalize all proper nouns.** Three lines under a letter means to capitalize.

3 **Check spelling with both an electronic spell checker and a dictionary.**

4 **Use consistent verb tense.** Use past tense for events in the past.

5 **Check for common agreement errors.** Subjects and verbs must agree in person and number.

6 **Use correct sentence structure.** Every sentence must have a subject and a verb.

The Incan Empire

The Inca created the largest empire ever seen in the Americas. Despite its size **1** the Incan Empire was highly unified. Its government was diplomatic, bureaucratic, and socialist in nature, and its ruler was believed to be a god-king.

The Incan ruler was selected from one of 11 noble families, who were believed to have descended from **2** inti, the sun god. Religion therefore supported the state, for worship of the sun god amounted to worship of the king. Thus, the empire was a theocracy, which is a state believed to be ruled directly by divine guidance.

The empire's expansion was largely the result of an important tradition: dead rulers retained the wealth they **3** a͟c̬͟cumulated during their lives. To acquire wealth of their own, succeeding rulers often attempted to conquer new territories. One such ruler, Pachacuti, conquered all of Peru and many neighboring lands as well. By 1500, the Incan Empire extended 2,500 miles along the coast of western South America and included an estimated 16 million people.

Incan rulers used a number of strategies to achieve unification. They practiced diplomacy by allowing conquered peoples to retain their own customs as long as they were loyal to the state. The Inca imposed a single official language, Quechua, to be used throughout the empire. They founded schools to teach Incan ways. They **4** buil͟t 14,000 miles of roads and bridges, which connected cities in conquered areas with Cuzco, the Incan capital.

The government's concern for the welfare of its citizens suggests an early form of socialism. Citizens worked for the state and, in turn, were taken care of. At public feasts, food and beer **5** w̶a̶s̶ were distributed as a reward for labor. In addition, the aged and disabled often received state support.

Among the many cultural achievements of the Inca were the development of an elaborate calendar system and the creation of beautiful works in gold and silver. Surprisingly, **6** the Inca had no system of writing. They preserved their history and literature by means of an oral tradition.

Applying the Skill

CREATE A TWO-PAGE WRITTEN PRESENTATION on a topic of historical importance that interests you.

Online References

Economics Handbook

The Economics Handbook is a glossary of economic terms. Graphs and charts in the handbook provide a better understanding of these terms.

Primary Source Handbook

Rig Veda, *Creation Hymn*

Bible, *Psalm 23*

Confucius, *Analects*

Thucydides, *History of the Peloponnesian War*

Plato, *The Apology*

Tacitus, *Annals*

Qur'an

Sei Shōnagon, *The Pillow Book*

Magna Carta

Popol Vuh

Niccolò Machiavelli, *The Prince*

Sir Thomas More, *Utopia*

James Madison, *The Federalist,* "Number 51"

Mary Wollstonecraft, *A Vindication of the Rights of Woman*

Élisabeth Vigée-Lebrun, *Memoirs of Madame Vigée-Lebrun*

Sadler Committee, *Report on Child Labor*

Abraham Lincoln, *Second Inaugural Address*

Elizabeth Cady Stanton, *The Natural Rights of Civilized Women*

Woodrow Wilson, *The Fourteen Points*

Elie Wiesel, *Night*

Jeanne Wakatsuki Houston and James D. Houston, *Farewell to Manzanar*

Nelson Mandela, *Inaugural Address*

Martin Luther King, Jr., *I Have a Dream*

Cesar Chavez, *An Open Letter*

Online References

Glossary

The Glossary is an alphabetical listing of many of the key terms from the chapters, along with their meanings. The definitions listed in the Glossary are the ones that apply to the way the words are used in this textbook. The Glossary gives the part of speech of each word. The following abbreviations are used:

adj. adjective   *n.* noun   *v.* verb

Pronunciation Key

Some of the words in this book are followed by respellings that show how the words are pronounced. The following key will help you understand what sounds are represented by the letters used in the respellings.

Symbol	Examples	Symbol	Examples
a	apple [AP•uhl], catch [kach]	oh	road, [rohd], know [noh]
ah	barn [bahrn], pot [paht]	oo	school [skool], glue [gloo]
air	bear [bair], dare [dair]	ow	out [owt], cow [kow]
aw	bought [bawt], horse [hawrs]	oy	coin [koyn], boys [boyz]
ay	ape [ayp], mail [mayl]	p	pig [pihg], top [tahp]
b	bell [behl], table [TAY•buhl]	r	rose [rohz], star [stahr]
ch	chain [chayn], ditch [dihch]	s	soap [sohp], icy [EYE•see]
d	dog [dawg], rained [raynd]	sh	share [shair], nation [NAY•shuhn]
ee	even [EE•vuhn], meal [meel]	t	tired [tyrd], boat [boht]
eh	egg [ehg], ten [tehn]	th	thin [thihn], mother [MUH•thuhr]
eye	iron [EYE•uhrn]	u	pull [pul], look [luk]
f	fall [fawl], laugh [laf]	uh	bump [buhmp], awake [uh•WAYK],
g	gold [gohld], big [bihg]		happen [HAP•uhn], pencil [PEHN•suhl],
h	hot [haht], exhale [ehks•HAYL]		pilot [PY•luht]
hw	white [hwyt]	ur	earth [urth], bird [burd], worm [wurm]
ih	into [IHN•too], sick [sihk]	v	vase [vays], love [luhv]
j	jar [jahr], badge [baj]	w	web [wehb], twin [twihn]
k	cat [kat], luck [luhk]	y	As a consonant: yard [yahrd], mule [myool]
l	load [lohd], ball [bawl]		As a vowel: ice [ys], tried [tryd], sigh [sy]
m	make [mayk], gem [jehm]	z	zone [zohn], reason [REE•zuhn]
n	night [nyt], win [wihn]	zh	treasure [TREHZH•uhr], garage [guh•RAHZH]
ng	song [sawng], anger [ANG•guhr]		

Syllables that are stressed when the words are spoken appear in CAPITAL LETTERS in the respellings. For example, the respelling of *patterns* (PAT•uhrnz) shows that the first syllable of the word is stressed.

Syllables that appear in SMALL CAPITAL LETTERS are also stressed, but not as strongly as those that appear in capital letters. For example, the respelling of *interaction* (IHN•tuhr•AK•shuhn) shows that the third syllable receives the main stress and the first syllable receives a secondary stress.

A

Abbasids [uh•BAS•IHDZ] *n.* a dynasty that ruled much of the Muslim Empire from A.D. 750 to 1258. (p. 271)

absolute monarch [MAHN•uhrk] *n.* a king or queen who has unlimited power and seeks to control all aspects of society. (p. 594)

acropolis [uh•KRAHP•uh•lihs] *n.* a fortified hilltop in an ancient Greek city. (p. 127)

Aksum [AHK•SOOM] *n.* an African kingdom, in what is now Ethiopia and Eritrea, that reached the height of its power in the fourth century A.D. (p. 225)

al-Andalus [al•AN•duh•LUS] *n.* a Muslim-ruled region in what is now Spain, established in the eighth century A.D. (p. 271)

Allah [AL•uh] *n.* God (an Arabic word, used mainly in Islam). (p. 264)

Almohads [AL•moh•HADZ] *n.* a group of Islamic reformers who overthrew the Almoravid dynasty and established an empire in North Africa and southern Spain in the 12th century A.D. (p. 412)

Almoravids [AL•muh•RAHV•uhdz] *n.* an Islamic religious brotherhood that established an empire in North Africa and southern Spain in the 11th century A.D. (p. 412)

Anabaptist [AN•uh•BAP•tihst] *n.* in the Reformation, a member of a Protestant group that believed in baptizing only those persons who were old enough to decide to be Christian and believed in the separation of church and state. (p. 496)

Anasazi [AH•nuh•SAH•zee] *n.* an early Native American people who lived in the American Southwest. (p. 443)

Anatolia [AN•uh•TOH•lee•uh] *n.* the Southwest Asian peninsula now occupied by the Asian part of Turkey—also called Asia Minor. (p. 62)

Angkor Wat [ANG•kawr WAHT] *n.* a temple complex built in the Khmer Empire and dedicated to the Hindu god Vishnu. (p. 345)

Anglican [ANG•glih•kuhn] *adj.* relating to the Church of England. (p. 494)

animism [AN•uh•MIHZ•uhm] *n.* the belief that spirits are present in animals, plants, and other natural objects. (p. 216)

annul [uh•NUHL] *v.* to cancel or put an end to. (p. 492)

apostle [uh•PAHS•uhl] *n.* one of the followers of Jesus who preached and spread his teachings. (p. 168)

aqueduct [AK•wih•DUHKT] *n.* a pipeline or channel built to carry water to populated areas. (p. 181)

aristocracy [AR•ih•STAHK•ruh•see] *n.* a government in which power is in the hands of a hereditary ruling class or nobility. (p. 127)

artifact *n.* a human-made object, such as a tool, weapon, or piece of jewelry. (p. 5)

artisan [AHR•tih•zuhn] *n.* a skilled worker, such as a weaver or a potter, who makes goods by hand. (p. 20)

Aryans [air•ee•uhnz] *n.* an Indo-European people who, about 1500 B.C., began to migrate into the Indian subcontinent (p. 63)

assimilation [uh•SIHM•uh•LAY•shuhn] *n.* the adoption of a conqueror's culture by a conquered people. (p. 205)

Assyria [uh•SEER•ee•uh] *n.* a Southwest Asian kingdom that controlled a large empire from about 850 to 612 B.C. (p. 95)

Atlantic slave trade *n.* the buying, transporting, and selling of Africans for work in the Americas. (p. 567)

autocracy [aw•TAHK•ruh•see] *n.* a government in which the ruler has unlimited power and uses it in an arbitrary manner. (p. 109)

ayllu [EYE•loo] *n.* in Incan society, a small community or family group whose members worked together for the common good. (p. 460)

B

balance of power *n.* a political situation in which no one nation is powerful enough to pose a threat to others. (p. 672)

the Balkans [BAWL•kuhnz] *n.* the region of southeastern Europe now occupied by Greece, Albania, Bulgaria, Romania, the European part of Turkey, and the former republics of Yugoslavia. (p. 689)

Bantu-speaking peoples *n.* the speakers of a related group of languages who, beginning about 2,000 years ago, migrated from West Africa into most of the southern half of Africa. (p. 222)

baroque [buh•ROHK] *adj.* relating to a grand, ornate style that characterized European painting, music, and architecture in the 1600s and early 1700s. (p. 637)

barter *n.* a form of trade in which people exchange goods and services without the use of money. (p. 23)

Battle of Trafalgar [truh•FAL•guhr] *n.* an 1805 naval battle in which Napoleon's forces were defeated by a British fleet under the command of Horatio Nelson. (p. 667)

Benin [buh•NIHN] *n.* a kingdom that arose near the Niger River delta in the 1300s and became a major West African state in the 1400s. (p. 419)

Beringia [buh•RIHN•jee•uh] *n.* an ancient land bridge over which the earliest Americans are believed to have migrated from Asia into the Americas. (p. 235)

Bill of Rights *n.* the first ten amendments to the U.S. Constitution, which protect citizens' basic rights and freedoms. (p. 645)

bishop *n.* a high-ranking Christian official who supervises a number of local churches. (p. 171)

blockade [blah•KAYD] *n.* the use of troops or ships to prevent commercial traffic from entering or leaving a city or region. (p. 668)

boyar [boh•YAHR] *n.* a landowning noble of Russia. (p. 608)

Brahma [BRAH•muh] *n.* a Hindu god considered the creator of the world. (p. 194)

Brahmin [BRAH•mihn] *n.* in Aryan society, a member of the social class made up of priests. (p. 63)

Bronze Age *n.* a period in human history, beginning around 3000 B.C. in some areas, during which people began using bronze, rather than copper or stone, to fashion tools and weapons. (p. 21)

bubonic plague [boo•BAHN•ihk PLAYG] *n.* a deadly disease that spread across Asia and Europe in the mid-14th century, killing millions of people. (p. 399)

bureaucracy [byu•RAHK•ruh•see] *n.* a system of departments and agencies formed to carry out the work of government. (p. 105)

burgher [BUR•guhr] *n.* a medieval merchant-class town dweller. (p. 391)

Bushido [BUSH•ih•DOH] *n.* the strict code of behavior followed by samurai warriors in Japan. (p. 343)

C

cabinet *n.* a group of advisers or ministers chosen by the head of a country to help make government decisions. (p. 617)

caliph [KAY•lihf] *n.* a supreme political and religious leader in a Muslim government. (p. 269)

calligraphy [kuh•LIHG•ruh•fee] *n.* the art of beautiful handwriting. (p. 276)

Calvinism [KAL•vih•NIHZ•uhm] *n.* a body of religious teachings based on the ideas of the reformer John Calvin. (p. 495)

canon law *n.* the body of laws governing the religious practices of a Christian church. (p. 371)

capitalism *n.* an economic system based on private ownership and on the investment of money in business ventures in order to make a profit. (p. 573)

Carolingian [KAR•uh•LIHN•juhn] **Dynasty** *n.* a dynasty of Frankish rulers, lasting from A.D. 751 to 987. (p. 356)

caste [kast] *n.* one of the four classes of people in the social system of the Aryans who settled in India—priests, warriors, peasants or traders, and non-Aryan laborers or craftsmen. (p. 64)

Catholic Reformation [REHF•uhr•MAY•shuhn] *n.* a 16th-century movement in which the Roman Catholic Church sought to make changes in response to the Protestant Reformation. (p. 498)

centralized government *n.* a government in which power is concentrated in a central authority to which local governments are subject. (p. 200)

Chaldeans [kal•DEE•uhnz] *n.* a Southwest Asian people who helped to destroy the Assyrian Empire. (p. 97)

Chavín [chah•VEEN] *n.* the first major South American civilization, which flourished in the highlands of what is now Peru from about 900 to 200 B.C. (p. 246)

checks and balances *n.* measures designed to prevent any one branch of government from dominating the others. (p. 645)

chivalry [SHIHV•uhl•ree] *n.* a code of behavior for knights in medieval Europe, stressing ideals such as courage, loyalty, and devotion. (p. 365)

city-state *n.* a city and its surrounding lands functioning as an independent political unit. (p. 31)

civilization *n.* a form of culture characterized by cities, specialized workers, complex institutions, record keeping, and advanced technology. (p. 20)

civil service *n.* the administrative departments of a government—especially those in which employees are hired on the basis of their scores on examinations. (p. 203)

civil war *n.* a conflict between two political groups within the same country. (p. 161)

clan *n.* a group of people descended from a common ancestor. (p. 331)

classical art *n.* the art of ancient Greece and Rome, in which harmony, order, and proportion, were emphasized. (p. 136)

clergy [KLUR•jee] *n.* a body of officials who perform religious services—such as priests, ministers, or rabbis. (p. 370)

codex [KOH•DEHKS] *n.* a book with pages that can be turned, like the one you are reading now. (p. 448)

colony *n.* a land controlled by another nation. (p. 554)

Colossus of Rhodes [kuh•LAHS•uhs uhv ROHDZ] *n.* an enormous Hellenistic statue that formerly stood near the harbor of Rhodes. (p. 149)

Columbian Exchange *n.* the global transfer of plants, animals, and diseases that occurred during the European colonization of the Americas. (p. 571)

comedy *n.* a humorous form of drama that often includes slapstick and satire. (p. 136)

Commercial Revolution *n.* the expansion of trade and business that transformed European economies during the 16th and 17th centuries. (p. 389)

common law *n.* a unified body of law formed from rulings of England's royal judges that serves as the basis for law in many English-speaking countries today, including the United States. (p. 394)

Concert [KAHN•SURT] **of Europe** *n.* a series of alliances among European nations in the 19th century, devised by Prince Klemens von Metternich to prevent the outbreak of revolutions. (p. 674)

concordat [kuhn•KAWR•DAT] *n.* a formal agreement— especially one between the pope and a government, dealing with the control of Church affairs. (p. 664)

Congress of Vienna [vee•EHN•uh] *n.* a series of meetings in 1814–1815, during which the European leaders sought to establish long-lasting peace and security after the defeat of Napoleon. (p. 672)

conquistadors [kahng•KEE•stuh•DAWRZ] *n.* the Spanish soldiers, explorers, and fortune hunters who took part in the conquest of the Americas in the 16th century. (p. 554)

conservative *n.* in the first half of the 19th century, a European—mainly wealthy landowners and nobles—who wanted to preserve the traditional monarchies of Europe. (p. 687)

constitutional monarchy [MAHN•uhr•kee] *n.* a system of governing in which the ruler's power is limited by law. (p. 617)

consul [KAHN•suhl] *n.* in the Roman republic, one of the two powerful officials elected each year to command the army and direct the government. (p. 157)

Continental System *n.* Napoleon's policy of preventing trade between Great Britain and continental Europe, intended to destroy Great Britain's economy. (p. 668)

Council of Trent *n.* a meeting of Roman Catholic leaders, called by Pope Paul III to rule on doctrines criticized by the Protestant reformers. (p. 499)

coup d'état [KOO day•TAH] *n.* a sudden seizure of political power in a nation. (p. 664)

covenant [KUHV•uh•nuhnt] *n.* a mutual promise or agreement—such as the agreement between God and the Jewish people as recorded in the Hebrew Bible. (p. 78)

creole [KREE•OHL] *n.* in Spanish colonial society, a colonist who was born in Latin America to Spanish parents. (p. 681)

Crusade *n.* one of the expeditions in which medieval Christian warriors sought to recover control of the Holy Land from the Muslims. (p. 382)

cultural diffusion *n.* the spreading of ideas or products from one culture to another. (p. 31)

culture *n.* a people's unique way of life, as shown by its tools, customs, arts, and ideas. (p. 5)

cuneiform [KYOO•nee•uh•FAWRM] *n.* a system of writing with wedge-shaped symbols, invented by the Sumerians around 3000 B.C. (p. 20)

Cyrillic [suh•RIHL•ihk] **alphabet** *n.* an alphabet for the writing of Slavic languages, devised in the ninth century A.D. by Saints Cyril and Methodius. (p. 306)

czar [zahr] *n.* a Russian emperor (from the Roman title *Caesar*). (p. 311)

D

daimyo [DY•mee•OH] *n.* a Japanese feudal lord who commanded a private army of samurai. (p. 542)

Daoism [DOW•IHZ•uhm] *n.* a philosophy based on the ideas of the Chinese thinker Laozi, who taught that people should be guided by a universal force called the Dao (Way). (p. 106)

Declaration of Independence *n.* a statement of the reasons for the American colonies' break with Britain, approved by the Second Continental Congress in 1776. (p. 641)

delta *n.* a marshy region formed by deposits of silt at the mouth of a river. (p. 36)

democracy *n.* a government controlled by its citizens, either directly or through representatives. (p. 128)

devshirme [dehv•SHEER•meh] *n.* in the Ottoman Empire, the policy of taking boys from conquered Christian peoples to be trained as Muslim soldiers. (p. 510)

Diaspora [dy•AS•puhr•uh] *n.* the dispersal of the Jews from their homeland in Judea—especially during the period of more than 1,800 years that followed the

Romans' destruction of the Temple in Jerusalem in A.D. 70. (p. 170)

dictator *n.* in ancient Rome, a political leader given absolute power to make laws and command the army for a limited time. (p. 157)

direct democracy *n.* a government in which citizens rule directly rather than through representatives. (p. 135)

divine right *n.* the idea that monarchs are God's representatives on earth and are therefore answerable only to God. (p. 594)

domestication *n.* the taming of animals for human use. (p. 16)

Dorians [DAWR•ee•uhnz] *n.* a Greek-speaking people that, according to tradition, migrated into mainland Greece after the destruction of the Mycenaean civilization. (p. 125)

Dutch East India Company *n.* a company founded by the Dutch in the early 17th century to establish and direct trade throughout Asia. (p. 534)

dynastic [dy•NAS•tihk] **cycle** *n.* the historical pattern of the rise, decline, and replacement of dynasties. (p. 54)

dynasty [DY•nuh•stee] *n.* a series of rulers from a single family. (p. 31)

E

Edict of Nantes [EE•DIHKT uhv NAHNT] *n.* a 1598 declaration in which the French king Henry IV promised that Protestants could live in peace in France and could set up houses of worship in some French cities. (p. 596)

émigré [EHM•ih•GRAY] *n.* a person who leaves his native country for political reasons, like the nobles and others who fled France during the peasant uprisings of the French Revolution. (p. 658)

empire *n.* a political unit in which a number of peoples or countries are controlled by a single ruler. (p. 33)

encomienda [ehng•kaw•MYEHN•dah] *n.* a grant of land made by Spain to a settler in the Americas, including the right to use Native Americans as laborers on it. (p. 557)

English Civil War *n.* a conflict, lasting from 1642 to 1649, in which Puritan supporters of Parliament battled supporters of England's monarchy. (p. 615)

enlightened despot [DEHS•puht] *n.* one of the 18th-century European monarchs who was inspired by Enlightenment ideas to rule justly and respect the rights of subjects. (p. 638)

enlightenment [ehn•LYT•uhn•muhnt] *n.* in Buddhism, a state of perfect wisdom in which one understands basic truths about the universe. (p. 68)

Enlightenment *n.* an 18th-century European movement in which thinkers attempted to apply the principles of reason and the scientific method to all aspects of society. (p. 629)

epic *n.* a long narrative poem celebrating the deeds of legendary or traditional heroes. (p. 125)

estate [ih•STAYT] *n.* one of the three social classes in France before the French Revolution—the First Estate consisting of the clergy; the Second Estate, of the nobility; and the Third Estate, of the rest of the population. (p. 651)

Estates-General [ih•STAYTS•JEHN•uhr•uhl] *n.* an assembly of representatives from all three of the estates, or social classes, in France. (pp. 397, 653)

excommunication [EHKS•kuh•MYOO•nih•KAY•shuhn] *n.* the taking away of a person's right of membership in a Christian church. (p. 306)

F

Fatimid [FAT•uh•MIHD] *n.* a member of a Muslim dynasty that traced its ancestry to Muhammad's daughter Fatima and that built an empire in North Africa, Arabia, and Syria in the 10th–12th centuries. (p. 272)

favorable balance of trade *n.* an economic situation in which a country sells more goods abroad than it buys from abroad. (p. 575)

federal system *n.* a system of government in which power is divided between a central authority and a number of individual states. (p. 645)

Fertile Crescent [FUHR•tuhl KREHS•uhnt] *n.* an arc of rich farmland in Southwest Asia, between the Persian Gulf and the Mediterranean Sea. (p. 29)

feudalism [FYOOD•uhl•IHZ•uhm] *n.* a political system in which nobles are granted the use of lands that legally belong to their king, in exchange for their loyalty, military service, and protection of the people who live on the land. (p. 54)

fief [feef] *n.* an estate granted to a vassal by a lord under the feudal system in medieval Europe. (p. 360)

filial piety [FIHL•ee•uhl PY•ih•tee] *n.* respect shown by children for their parents and elders. (p. 104)

Franks *n.* a Germanic people who settled in the Roman province of Gaul (roughly the area now occupied by France) and established a great empire during the Middle Ages. (p. 354)

French and Indian War *n.* a conflict between Britain and France for control of territory in North America, lasting from 1754 to 1763. (p. 564)

G

gentry *n.* a class of powerful, well-to-do people who enjoy a high social status. (p. 327)

geocentric theory *n.* in the Middle Ages, the earth-centered view of the universe in which scholars believed that the earth was an immovable object located at the center of the universe. (p. 623)

Ghana [GAH•nuh] *n.* a West African kingdom that grew rich from taxing and controlling trade and that established an empire in the 9th–11th centuries A.D. (p. 413)

ghazi [GAH•zee] *n.* a warrior for Islam. (p. 507)

Glorious Revolution *n.* the bloodless overthrow of the English king James II and his replacement by William and Mary. (p. 616)

glyph [glihf] *n.* a symbolic picture—especially one used as part of a writing system for carving messages in stone. (p. 448)

Gothic [GAHTH•ihk] *adj.* relating to a style of church architecture that developed in medieval Europe, featuring ribbed vaults, stained glass windows, flying buttresses, pointed arches, and tall spires. (p. 380)

Great Fear *n.* a wave of senseless panic that spread through the French countryside after the storming of the Bastille in 1789. (p. 655)

Great Schism [SIHZ•uhm] *n.* a division in the medieval Roman Catholic Church, during which rival popes were established in Avignon and in Rome. (p. 399)

Greco-Roman culture *n.* an ancient culture that developed from a blending of Greek, Hellenistic, and Roman cultures. (p. 178)

griot [gree•OH] *n.* a West African storyteller. (p. 216)

guerrilla [guh•RIHL•uh] *n.* a member of a loosely organized fighting force that makes surprise attacks on enemy troops occupying his or her country. (p. 669)

guild [gihld] *n.* a medieval association of people working at the same occupation, which controlled its members' wages and prices. (p. 388)

guillotine [GIHL•uh•TEEN] *n.* a machine for beheading people, used as a means of execution during the French Revolution. (p. 660)

Gupta [GUP•tuh] **Empire** *n.* the second empire in India, founded by Chandra Gupta I in A.D. 320. (p. 191)

H

habeas corpus [HAY•bee•uhs KAWR•puhs] *n.* a document requiring that a prisoner be brought before a court or judge so that it can be decided whether his or her imprisonment is legal. (p. 616)

Hagia Sophia [HAY•ee•uh soh•FEE•uh] *n.* the Cathedral of Holy Wisdom in Constantinople, built by order of the Byzantine emperor Justinian. (p. 303)

haiku [HY•koo] *n.* a Japanese form of poetry, consisting of three unrhymed lines of five, seven, and five syllables. (p. 545)

hajj [haj] *n.* a pilgrimage to Mecca, performed as a duty by Muslims. (p. 267)

Han [hahn] **Dynasty** *n.* a Chinese dynasty that ruled from 202 B.C. to A.D. 9 and again from A.D. 23 to 220. (p. 200)

Harappan civilization *n.* another name for the Indus Valley civilization that arose along the Indus River, possibly as early as 7000 B.C.; characterized by sophisticated city planning. (p. 46)

Hausa [HOW•suh] *n.* a West African people who lived in several city-states in what is now northern Nigeria. (p. 417)

heliocentric [HEE•lee•oh•SEHN•trihk] **theory** *n.* the idea that the earth and the other planets revolve around the sun. (p. 624)

Hellenistic [HEHL•uh•NIHS•tihk] *adj.* relating to the civilization, language, art, science, and literature of the Greek world from the reign of Alexander the Great to the late second century B.C. (p. 146)

helot [HEHL•uht] *n.* in the society of ancient Sparta, a peasant bound to the land. (p. 129)

hieroglyphics [HY•uhr•uh•GLIHF•ihks] *n.* an ancient Egyptian writing system in which pictures were used to represent ideas and sounds. (p. 40)

Hijrah [HIHJ•ruh] *n.* Muhammad's migration from Mecca to Yathrib (Medina) in A.D. 622. (p. 265)

Hittites [HIHT•YTS] *n.* an Indo-European people who settled in Anatolia around 2000 B.C. (p. 62)

Holy Alliance *n.* a league of European nations formed by the leaders of Russia, Austria, and Prussia after the Congress of Vienna. (p. 674)

Holy Roman Empire *n.* an empire established in Europe in the 10th century A.D., originally consisting mainly of lands in what is now Germany and Italy. (p. 371)

hominid [HAHM•uh•nihd] *n.* a member of a biological group including human beings and related species that walk upright. (p. 7)

Homo sapiens [HOH•moh SAY•pee•uhnz] *n.* the biological species to which modern human beings belong. (p. 8)

House of Wisdom *n.* a center of learning established in Baghdad in the 800s. (p. 276)

humanism [HYOO•muh•NIHZ•uhm] *n.* a Renaissance intellectual movement in which thinkers studied classical texts and focused on human potential and achievements. (p. 472)

Hundred Days *n.* the brief period during 1815 when Napoleon made his last bid for power, deposing the French king and again becoming emperor of France. (p. 671)

Hundred Years' War *n.* a conflict in which England and France battled on French soil on and off from 1337 to 1453. (p. 401)

hunter-gatherer *n.* a member of a nomadic group whose food supply depends on hunting animals and collecting plant foods. (p. 14)

Hyksos [HIHK•sohs] *n.* a group of nomadic invaders from Southwest Asia who ruled Egypt from 1640 to 1570 B.C. (p. 89)

I

Ice Age *n.* a cold period in which huge ice sheets spread outward from the polar regions, the last one of which lasted from about 1,900,000 to 10,000 B.C. (p. 235)

I Ching [ee jihng] *n.* a Chinese book of oracles, consulted to answer ethical and practical problems. (p. 107)

icon [EYE•KAHN] *n.* a religious image used by eastern Christians. (p. 306)

impressionism [ihm•PREHSH•uh•NIHZ•uhm] *n.* a movement in 19th-century painting, in which artists reacted against realism by seeking to convey their impressions of subjects or moments in time. (p. 701)

Indo-Europeans [IHN•doh•YUR•uh•PEE•uhnz] *n.* a group of seminomadic peoples who, about 1700 B.C., began to migrate from what is now southern Russia to the Indian subcontinent, Europe, and Southwest Asia. (p. 61)

indulgence [ihn•DUHL•juhns] *n.* a pardon releasing a person from punishments due for a sin. (p. 489)

inflation *n.* a decline in the value of money, accompanied by a rise in the prices of goods and services. (p. 173)

Inquisition [IHN•kwih•ZIHSH•uhn] *n.* a Roman Catholic tribunal for investigating and prosecuting charges of heresy—especially the one active in Spain during the 1400s. (p. 384)

institution *n.* a long-lasting pattern of organization in a community. (p. 20)

intendant [ihn•TEHN•duhnt] *n.* a French government official appointed by the monarch to collect taxes and administer justice. (p. 598)

Iroquois [IHR•uh•KWOY] *n.* a group of Native American peoples who spoke related languages, lived in the eastern Great Lakes region of North America, and formed an alliance in the late 1500s. (p. 444)

Islam [ihs•LAHM] *n.* a monotheistic religion that developed in Arabia in the seventh century A.D. (p. 265)

Israel [IHZ•ree•uhl] *n.* a kingdom of the united Israelites, lasting from about 1020 to 922 B.C.; later, the northernmost of the two Israelite kingdoms; now, the Jewish nation that was established in the ancient homeland in 1948. (p. 81)

J

Jainism [JY•NIHZ•uhm] *n.* a religion founded in India in the sixth century B.C., whose members believe that everything in the universe has a soul and therefore should not be harmed. (p. 67)

janissary [JAN•ih•SEHR•ee] *n.* a member of an elite force of soldiers in the Ottoman Empire. (p. 510)

Jesuits [JEHZH•oo•ihts] *n.* members of the Society of Jesus, a Roman Catholic religious order founded by Ignatius of Loyola. (p. 499)

joint-stock company *n.* a business in which investors pool their wealth for a common purpose, then share the profits. (p. 573)

Judah [JOO•duh] *n.* an Israelite kingdom in Canaan, established around 922 B.C. (p. 81)

Justinian [juh•STIHN•ee•uhn] **Code** *n.* the body of Roman civil law collected and organized by order of the Byzantine emperor Justinian around A.D. 534. (p. 302)

K

kabuki [kuh•BOO•kee] *n.* a type of Japanese drama in which music, dance, and mime are used to present stories. (p. 545)

kaiser [KY•zuhr] *n.* a German emperor (from the Roman title *Caesar*). (p. 697)

karma [KAHR•muh] *n.* in Hinduism and Buddhism, the totality of the good and bad deeds performed by a person, which is believed to determine his or her fate after rebirth. (p. 67)

Khmer [kmair] **Empire** *n.* a Southeast Asian empire, centered in what is now Cambodia, that reached its peak of power around A.D. 1200. (p. 345)

knight *n.* in medieval Europe, an armored warrior who fought on horseback. (p. 360)

Koryu [KAWR•yoo] **Dynasty** *n.* a dynasty that ruled Korea from A.D. 935 to 1392. (p. 347)

Kush [kuhsh] *n.* an ancient Nubian kingdom whose rulers controlled Egypt between 2000 and 1000 B.C. (p. 92)

L

lay investiture [ihn•VEHS•tuh•chur] *n.* the appointment of religious officials by kings or nobles. (p. 372)

Legalism *n.* a Chinese political philosophy based on the idea that a highly efficient and powerful government is the key to social order. (p. 106)

legion *n.* a military unit of the ancient Roman army, made up of about 5,000 foot soldiers and a group of soldiers on horseback. (p. 157)

Legislative [LEHJ•ih•SLAY•tihv] **Assembly** *n.* a French congress with the power to create laws and approve declarations of war, established by the Constitution of 1791. (p. 657)

legitimacy [luh•JIHT•uh•muh•see] *n.* the hereditary right of a monarch to rule. (p. 673)

liberal *n.* in the first half of the 19th century, a European—mainly middle-class business leaders and merchants—who wanted to give more political power to elected parliaments. (p. 687)

lineage [LIHN•ee•ihj] *n.* the people—living, dead, and unborn—who are descended from a common ancestor. (p. 410)

loess [LOH•uhs] *n.* a fertile deposit of windblown soil. (p. 50)

lord *n.* in feudal Europe, a person who controlled land and could therefore grant estates to vassals. (p. 360)

Lutheran [LOO•thuhr•uhn] *n.* a member of a Protestant church founded on the teachings of Martin Luther. (p. 490)

lycée [lee•SAY] *n.* a government-run public school in France. (p. 664)

M

Macedonia [MAS•ih•DOH•nee•uh] *n.* an ancient kingdom north of Greece, whose ruler Philip II conquered Greece in 338 B.C. (p. 142)

Maghrib [MUHG•ruhb] *n.* a region of western North Africa, consisting of the Mediterranean coastlands of what is now Morocco, Tunisia, and Algeria. (p. 410)

Magna Carta [MAG•nuh KAHR•tuh] *n.* "Great Charter"—a document guaranteeing basic political rights in England, drawn up by nobles and approved by King John in A.D. 1215. (p. 394)

Mahabharata [muh•huh•BAH•ruh•tuh] *n.* a great Indian epic poem, reflecting the struggles of the Aryans as they moved south into India. (p. 64)

Mahayana [MAH•huh•YAH•nuh] *n.* a sect of Buddhism that offers salvation to all and allows popular worship. (p. 193)

maize [mayz] *n.* a cultivated cereal grain that bears its kernels on large ears—usually called corn in the United States. (p. 238)

Mali [MAH•lee] *n.* a West African empire that flourished from 1235 to the 1400s and grew rich from trade. (p. 415)

Manchus [MAN•chooz] *n.* a people, native to Manchuria, who ruled China during the Qing Dynasty (1644–1912). (p. 539)

Mandate of Heaven *n.* in Chinese history, the divine approval thought to be the basis of royal authority. (p. 54)

manor *n.* a lord's estate in feudal Europe. (p. 360)

matriarchal [MAY•tree•AHR•kuhl] *adj.* relating to a social system in which the mother is head of the family. (p. 192)

matrilineal [MAT•ruh•LIHN•ee•uhl] *adj.* relating to a social system in which family descent and inheritance rights are traced through the mother. (p. 410)

Mauryan [MAH•ur•yuhn] **Empire** *n.* the first empire in India, founded by Chandragupta Maurya in 321 B.C. (p. 189)

Medes [meedz] *n.* a Southwest Asian people who helped to destroy the Assyrian Empire. (p. 97)

mercantilism [MUR•kuhn•tee•LIHZ•uhm] *n.* an economic policy under which nations sought to increase their wealth and power by obtaining large amounts of gold and silver and by selling more goods than they bought. (p. 574)

mercenary [MUR•suh•NEHR•ee] *n.* a soldier who is paid to fight in a foreign army. (p. 173)

Meroë [MEHR–oh–EE] *n.* center of the Kush dynasty from about 250 B.C. to A.D. 150; known for its manufacture of iron weapons and tools. (p. 94)

Mesoamerica [MEHZ•oh•uh•MEHR•ih•kuh] *n.* an area extending from central Mexico to Honduras, where several of the ancient complex societies of the Americas developed. (p. 240)

mestizo [mehs•TEE•zoh] *n.* a person of mixed Spanish and Native American ancestry. (p. 557)

Middle Ages *n.* the era in European history that followed the fall of the Roman Empire, lasting from about 500 to 1500—also called the medieval period. (p. 353)

middle passage *n.* the voyage that brought captured Africans to the West Indies, and later to North and South America, to be sold as slaves—so called because it was considered the middle leg of the triangular trade. (p. 569)

migration *n.* the act of moving from one place to settle in another. (pp. 62, 220)

Ming Dynasty *n.* a Chinese dynasty that ruled from 1368 to 1644. (p. 536)

Minoans [mih•NOH•uhnz] *n.* a seafaring and trading people that lived on the island of Crete from about 2000 to 1400 B.C. (p. 72)

Mississippian [MIHS•ih•SIHP•ee•uhn] *adj.* relating to a Mound Builder culture that flourished in North America between A.D. 800 and 1500. (p. 443)

mita [MEE•tuh] *n.* in the Inca Empire, the requirement that all able-bodied subjects work for the state a certain number of days each year. (p. 461)

Moche [MOH•chay] *n.* a civilization that flourished on what is now the northern coast of Peru from about A.D. 100 to 700. (p. 247)

monarchy [MAHN•uhr•kee] *n.* a government in which power is in the hands of a single person. (p. 127)

monastery [MAHN•uh•STEHR•ee] *n.* a religious community of men (called monks) who have given up their possessions to devote themselves to a life of prayer and worship. (p. 354)

monopoly [muh•NAHP•uh•lee] *n.* a group's exclusive control over the production and distribution of certain goods. (p. 204)

monotheism [MAHN•uh•thee•IHZ•uhm] *n.* a belief in a single god. (p. 78)

monsoon [mahn•SOON] *n.* a wind that shifts in direction at certain times of each year. (p. 45)

mosque [mahsk] *n.* an Islamic place of worship. (p. 267)

movable type *n.* blocks of metal or wood, each bearing a single character, that can be arranged to make up a page for printing. (p. 325)

Mughal [MOO•guhl] *n.* one of the nomads who invaded the Indian subcontinent in the 16th century and established a powerful empire there. (p. 516)

mulattos [mu•LAT•ohz] *n.* persons of mixed European and African ancestry. (p. 682)

mummification [MUHM•uh•fih•KAY•shuhn] *n.* a process of embalming and drying corpses to prevent them from decaying. (p. 38)

Muslim [MUHZ•luhm] *n.* a follower of Islam. (p. 265)

Mutapa [moo•TAHP•uh] *adj.* relating to a southern African empire established by Mutota in the 15th century A.D. (p. 427)

Mycenaean [MY•suh•NEE•uhn] *n.* an Indo-European person who settled on the Greek mainland around 2000 B.C. (p. 124)

myth *n.* a traditional story about gods, ancestors, or heroes, told to explain the natural world or the customs and beliefs of a society. (p. 126)

N

Napoleonic [nuh•POH•lee•AHN•ihk] **Code** *n.* a comprehensive and uniform system of laws established for France by Napoleon. (p. 664)

National Assembly *n.* a French congress established by representatives of the Third Estate on June 17, 1789, to enact laws and reforms in the name of the French people. (p. 654)

nationalism *n.* the belief that people should be loyal mainly to their nation—that is, to the people with whom they share a culture and history—rather than to a king or empire. (p. 687)

nation-state *n.* an independent geopolitical unit of people having a common culture and identity. (p. 687)

Nazca [NAHS•kah] *n.* a civilization that flourished on what is now the southern coast of Peru from about 200 B.C. to A.D. 600. (p. 247)

neoclassical [NEE•oh•KLAS•ih•kuhl] *adj.* relating to a simple, elegant style (based on ideas and themes from ancient Greece and Rome) that characterized the arts in Europe during the late 1700s. (p. 637)

Neolithic [NEE•uh•LIHTH•ihk] **Age** *n.* a prehistoric period that began about 8000 B.C. and in some areas ended as early as 3000 B.C., during which people learned to polish stone tools, make pottery, grow crops, and raise animals—also called the New Stone Age. (p. 7)

Neolithic Revolution *n.* the major change in human life caused by the beginnings of farming—that is, by people's shift from food gathering to food producing. (p. 15)

New Kingdom *n.* the period of ancient Egyptian history that followed the overthrow of the Hyksos rulers, lasting from about 1570 to 1075 B.C. (p. 90)

nirvana [neer•VAH•nuh] *n.* in Buddhism, the release from pain and suffering achieved after enlightenment. (p. 69)

Nok [nahk] *n.* an African people who lived in what is now Nigeria between 500 B.C. and A.D. 200. (p. 217)

nomad *n.* a member of a group that has no permanent home, wandering from place to place in search of food and water. (p. 14)

O

obsidian [ahb•SIHD•ee•uhn] *n.* a hard, glassy volcanic rock used by early peoples to make sharp weapons. (p. 453)

Old Regime [ray•ZHEEM] *n.* the political and social system that existed in France before the French Revolution. (p. 651)

oligarchy [AHL•ih•GAHR•kee] *n.* a government in which power is in the hands of a few people—especially one in which rule is based upon wealth. (p. 127)

Olmec [AHL•mehk] *n.* the earliest-known Mesoamerican civilization, which flourished around 1200 B.C. and influenced later societies throughout the region. (p. 240)

oracle bone *n.* one of the animal bones or tortoise shells used by ancient Chinese priests to communicate with the gods. (p. 53)

P

Paleolithic [PAY•lee•uh•LIHTH•ihk] **Age** *n.* a prehistoric period that lasted from about 2,500,000 to 8000 B.C., during which people made use of crude stone tools and weapons—also called the Old Stone Age. (p. 7)

papyrus [puh•PY•ruhs] *n.* a tall reed that grows in the Nile delta, used by the ancient Egyptians to make a paperlike material for writing on. (p. 40)

parliament [PAHR•luh•muhnt] *n.* a body of representatives that makes laws for a nation. (p. 395)

pastoralist [PAS•tuhr•uh•lihst] *n.* a member of a nomadic group that herds domesticated animals. (p. 330)

patriarch [PAY•tree•AHRK] *n.* a principal bishop in the eastern branch of Christianity. (p. 306)

patriarchal [PAY•tree•AHR•kuhl] *adj.* relating to a social system in which the father is head of the family. (p. 192)

patrician [puh•TRIHSH•uhn] *n.* in ancient Rome, a member of the wealthy, privileged upper class. (p. 156)

patrilineal [PAT•ruh•LIHN•ee•uhl] *adj.* relating to a social system in which family descent and inheritance rights are traced through the father. (p. 410)

patron [PAY•truhn] *n.* a person who supports artists, especially financially. (p. 472)

Pax Mongolica [paks mahng•GAHL•ih-kuh] *n.* the "Mongol Peace"—the period from the mid-1200s to the mid-1300s when the Mongols imposed stability and law and order across much of Eurasia. (p. 333)

Pax Romana [PAHKS roh•MAH•nah] *n.* a period of peace and prosperity throughout the Roman Empire, lasting from 27 B.C. to A.D. 180. (p. 162)

Peace of Augsburg [AWGZ•BURG] *n.* a 1555 agreement declaring that the religion of each German state would be decided by its ruler. (p. 492)

Peloponnesian [PEHL•uh•puh•NEE•zhuhn] **War** *n.* a war, lasting from 431 to 404 B.C., in which Athens and its allies were defeated by Sparta and its allies. (p. 137)

peninsulares [peh•neen•soo•LAH•rehs] *n.* in Spanish colonial society, colonists who were born in Spain. (p. 681)

Peninsular [puh•NIHN•syuh•luhr] **War** *n.* a conflict, lasting from 1808 to 1813, in which Spanish rebels, with the aid of British forces, fought to drive Napoleon's French troops out of Spain. (p. 669)

Persian Wars *n.* a series of wars in the fifth century B.C., in which Greek city-states battled the Persian Empire. (p. 131)

perspective [puhr•SPEHK•tihv] *n.* an artistic technique that creates the appearance of three dimensions on a flat surface. (p. 474)

phalanx [FAY•LANGKS] *n.* a military formation of foot soldiers armed with spears and shields. (p. 131)

pharaoh [FAIR•oh] *n.* a king of ancient Egypt, considered a god as well as a political and military leader. (p. 37)

philosophe [FIHL•uh•SAHF] *n.* one of a group of social thinkers in France during the Enlightenment. (p. 630)

philosopher *n.* a thinker who uses logic and reason to investigate the nature of the universe, human society, and morality. (p. 138)

Phoenicians [fih•NIHSH•uhnz] *n.* a seafaring people of Southwest Asia, who around 1100 B.C. began to trade and established colonies throughout the Mediterranean region. (p. 73)

Pilgrims *n.* a group of people who, in 1620, founded the colony of Plymouth in Massachusetts to escape religious persecution in England. (p. 562)

plebeian [plih•BEE•uhn] *n.* in ancient Rome, one of the common farmers, artisans, and merchants who made up most of the population. (p. 156)

plebiscite [PLEHB•ih•SYT] *n.* a direct vote in which a country's people have the opportunity to approve or reject a proposal. (p. 664)

polis [POH•lihs] *n.* a Greek city-state—the fundamental political unit of ancient Greece after about 750 B.C. (p. 127)

polytheism [PAHL•ee•thee•IHZ•uhm] *n.* a belief in many gods. (p. 31)

pope *n.* the bishop of Rome, head of the Roman Catholic Church. (p. 171)

Popol Vuh [POH•pohl VOO] *n.* a book containing a version of the Mayan story of creation. (p. 448)

potlatch [PAHT•LACH] *n.* a ceremonial feast used to display rank and prosperity in some Northwest Coast tribes of Native Americans. (p. 441)

predestination [pree•DEHS•tuh•NAY•shuhn] *n.* the doctrine that God has decided all things beforehand, including which people will be eternally saved. (p. 495)

Presbyterian [PREHZ•bih•TEER•ee•uhn] *n.* a member of a Protestant church governed by presbyters (elders) and founded on the teachings of John Knox. (p. 496)

Protestant [PRAHT•ih•stuhnt] *n.* a member of a Christian church founded on the principles of the Reformation. (p. 490)

pueblo [PWEHB•loh] *n.* a village of large apartment-like buildings made of clay and stone, built by the Anasazi and later peoples of the American Southwest. (p. 443)

Punic Wars *n.* a series of three wars between Rome and Carthage (264–146 B.C.); resulted in the destruction of Carthage and Rome's dominance over the western Mediterranean. (p. 158)

Puritans *n.* a group of people who sought freedom from religious persecution in England by founding a colony at Massachusetts Bay in the early 1600s. (p. 562)

push-pull factors *n.* conditions that draw people to another location (pull factors) or cause people to leave their homelands and migrate to another region (push factors). (p. 220)

pyramid [PIHR•uh•mihd] *n.* a massive structure with a rectangular base and four triangular sides, like those that were built in Egypt as burial places for Old Kingdom pharaohs. (p. 37)

Qin [chihn] **Dynasty** *n.* a short-lived Chinese dynasty that replaced the Zhou Dynasty in the third century B.C. (p. 107)

Qing [chihng] **Dynasty** *n.* China's last dynasty, which ruled from 1644 to 1912. (p. 539)

Quetzalcoatl [keht•SAHL•koh•AHT•uhl] *n.* "the Feathered Serpent"—a god of the Toltecs and other Mesoamerican peoples. (p. 453)

quipu [KEE•poo] *n.* an arrangement of knotted strings on a cord, used by the Inca to record numerical information. (p. 461)

Qur'an [kuh•RAN] *n.* the holy book of Islam. (p. 267)

radical *n.* in the first half of the 19th century, a European who favored drastic change to extend democracy to all people. (p. 687)

realism *n.* a 19th-century artistic movement in which writers and painters sought to show life as it is rather than life as it should be. (p. 700)

realpolitik [ray•AHL•POH•lih•TEEK] *n.* "the politics of reality"—the practice of tough power politics without room for idealism. (p. 695)

Reconquista [reh•kawn•KEES•tah] *n.* the effort by Christian leaders to drive the Muslims out of Spain, lasting from the 1100s until 1492. (p. 384)

Reformation [REHF•uhr•MAY•shuhn] *n.* a 16th-century movement for religious reform, leading to the founding of Christian churches that rejected the pope's authority. (p. 489)

Reign [rayn] **of Terror** *n.* the period, from mid-1793 to mid-1794, when Maximilien Robespierre ruled France nearly as a dictator and thousands of political figures and ordinary citizens were executed. (p. 660)

reincarnation [REE•ihn•kahr•NAY•shuhn] *n.* in Hinduism and Buddhism, the process by which a soul is reborn continuously until it achieves perfect understanding. (p. 67)

religious toleration *n.* a recognition of people's right to hold differing religious beliefs. (p. 190)

Renaissance [REHN•ih•SAHNS] *n.* a period of European history, lasting from about 1300 to 1600, during which renewed interest in classical culture led to far-reaching changes in art, learning, and views of the world. (p. 471)

republic *n.* a form of government in which power is in the hands of representatives and leaders are elected by the citizens who have the right to vote. (p. 156)

Restoration [REHS•tuh•RAY•shuhn] *n.* the period of Charles II's rule over England, after the collapse of Oliver Cromwell's government. (p. 616)

romanticism [roh•MAN•tih•SIHZ•uhm] *n.* an early-19th-century movement in art and thought, which focused on emotion and nature rather than reason and society. (p. 698)

Royal Road *n.* a road in the Persian Empire, stretching over 1,600 miles from Susa in Persia to Sardis in Anatolia. (p. 101)

Russification [RUHS•uh•fih•KAY•shuhn] *n.* the process of forcing Russian culture on all ethnic groups in the Russian Empire. (p. 693)

sacrament [SAK•ruh•muhnt] *n.* one of the Christian ceremonies in which God's grace is transmitted to people. (p. 371)

Safavid [suh•FAH•VIHD] *n.* a member of a Shi'a Muslim dynasty that built an empire in Persia in the 16th–18th centuries. (p. 512)

Sahel [suh•HAYL] *n.* the African region along the southern border of the Sahara. (p. 213)

salon [suh•LAHN] *n.* a social gathering of intellectuals and artists, like those held in the homes of wealthy women in Paris and other European cities during the Enlightenment. (p. 636)

samurai [SAM•uh•RY] *n.* one of the professional warriors who served Japanese feudal lords. (p. 343)

sans-culottes [SANS•kyoo•LAHTS] *n.* in the French Revolution, a radical group made up of Parisian wage-earners and small shopkeepers who wanted a greater voice in government, lower prices, and an end to food shortages. (p. 658)

satrap [SAY•TRAP] *n.* a governor of a province in the Persian Empire. (p. 101)

savanna [suh•VAN•uh] *n.* a flat, grassy plain. (p. 215)

scholastics [skuh•LAS•tihks] *n.* scholars who gathered and taught at medieval European universities. (p. 392)

scientific method *n.* a logical procedure for gathering information about the natural world, in which experimentation and observation are used to test hypotheses. (p. 625)

Scientific Revolution *n.* a major change in European thought, starting in the mid-1500s, in which the study of the natural world began to be characterized by careful observation and the questioning of accepted beliefs. (p. 623)

scorched-earth policy *n.* the practice of burning crops and killing livestock during wartime so that the enemy cannot live off the land. (p. 669)

scribe *n.* one of the professional record keepers in early civilizations. (p. 20)

secular [SEHK•yuh•luhr] *adj.* concerned with worldly rather than spiritual matters. (pp. 355, 472)

Seljuks [SEHL•JOOKS] *n.* a Turkish group who migrated into the Abbasid Empire in the 10th century and established their own empire in the 11th century. (p. 315)

senate *n.* in ancient Rome, the supreme governing body, originally made up only of aristocrats. (p. 157)

serf *n.* a medieval peasant legally bound to live on a lord's estate. (p. 360)

Seven Years' War *n.* a conflict in Europe, North America, and India, lasting from 1756 to 1763, in which the forces of Britain and Prussia battled those of Austria, France, Russia, and other countries. (p. 607)

shah [shah] *n.* hereditary monarch of Iran. (p. 513)

shari'a [shah•REE•ah] *n.* a body of law governing the lives of Muslims. (p. 268)

Shi'a [SHEE•uh] *n.* the branch of Islam whose members acknowledge Ali and his descendants as the rightful successors of Muhammad. (p. 271)

Shinto [SHIHN•toh] *n.* the native religion of Japan. (p. 339)

Shiva [SHEE•vuh] *n.* a Hindu god considered the destroyer of the world. (p. 194)

shogun [SHOH•guhn] *n.* in feudal Japan, a supreme military commander who ruled in the name of the emperor. (p. 343)

Sikh [seek] *n.* a member of a nonviolent religious group whose beliefs blend elements of Buddhism, Hinduism, and Sufism. (p. 518)

Silk Roads *n.* a system of ancient caravan routes across Central Asia, along which traders carried silk and other trade goods. (p. 196)

simony [SY•muh•nee] *n.* the selling or buying of a position in a Christian church. (p. 379)

skepticism [SKEHP•tih•sIHZ•uhm] *n.* a philosophy based on the idea that nothing can be known for certain. (p. 597)

slash-and-burn farming *n.* a farming method in which people clear fields by cutting and burning trees and grasses, the ashes of which serve to fertilize the soil. (p. 15)

Slavs [slahvz] *n.* a people from the forests north of the Black Sea, ancestors of many peoples in Eastern Europe today. (p. 307)

social contract *n.* the agreement by which people define and limit their individual rights, thus creating an organized society or government. (p. 629)

Songhai [SAWNG•HY] *n.* a West African empire that conquered Mali and controlled trade from the 1400s to 1591. (p. 417)

specialization *n.* the development of skills in a particular kind of work, such as trading or record keeping. (p. 20)

stateless societies *n.* cultural groups in which authority is shared by lineages of equal power instead of being exercised by a central government. (p. 410)

steppes [stehps] *n.* dry, grass-covered plains. (p. 61)

stupa [STOO-puh] *n.* mounded stone structures built over Buddhist holy relics. (p. 193)

subcontinent *n.* a large landmass that forms a distinct part of a continent. (p. 44)

Sufi [SOO•fee] *n.* a Muslim who seeks to achieve direct contact with God through mystical means. (p. 271)

sultan *n.* "overlord," or "one with power"; title for Ottoman rulers during the rise of the Ottoman Empire. (p. 507)

Sunna [SUN•uh] *n.* an Islamic model for living, based on the life and teachings of Muhammad. (p. 268)

Sunni [SOON•ee] *n.* the branch of Islam whose members acknowledge the first four caliphs as the rightful successors of Muhammad. (p. 271)

Swahili [swah•HEE•lee] *n.* an Arabic-influenced Bantu language that is spoken widely in eastern and central Africa. (p. 422)

Taj Mahal [TAHZH muh•HAHL] *n.* a beautiful tomb in Agra, India, built by the Mughal emperor Shah Jahan for his wife Mumtaz Mahal. (p. 519)

Tamil [TAM•uhl] *n.* a language of southern India; also, the people who speak that language. (p. 191)

technology *n.* the ways in which people apply knowledge, tools, and inventions to meet their needs. (p. 8)

Tennis Court Oath *n.* a pledge made by the members of France's National Assembly in 1789, in which they vowed to continue meeting until they had drawn up a new constitution. (p. 654)

terraces *n.* a new form of agriculture in Aksum, in which stepped ridges constructed on mountain slopes help retain water and reduce erosion. (p. 228)

theocracy [thee•AHK•ruh•see] *n.* **1.** a government in which the ruler is viewed as a divine figure. (p. 37) **2.** a government controlled by religious leaders. (p. 496)

Theravada [THEHR•uh•VAH•duh] *n.* a sect of Buddhism focusing on the strict spiritual discipline originally advocated by the Buddha. (p. 193)

Thirty Years' War *n.* a European conflict over religion and territory and for power among ruling families, lasting from 1618 to 1648. (p. 603)

three-field system *n.* a system of farming developed in medieval Europe, in which farmland was divided into three fields of equal size and each of these was successively planted with a winter crop, planted with a spring crop, and left unplanted. (p. 387)

tithe [tyth] *n.* a family's payment of one-tenth of its income to a church. (p. 363)

Tokugawa Shogunate [TOH•koo•GAH•wah SHOH•guh•niht] *n.* a dynasty of shoguns that ruled a unified Japan from 1603 to 1867. (p. 544)

Torah [TAWR•uh] *n.* the first five books of the Hebrew Bible—the most sacred writings in the Jewish tradition. (p. 77)

totem [TOH•tuhm] *n.* an animal or other natural object that serves as a symbol of the unity of clans or other groups of people. (p. 445)

tournament *n.* a mock battle between groups of knights. (p. 367)

tragedy *n.* a serious form of drama dealing with the downfall of a heroic or noble character. (p. 136)

Treaty of Tordesillas [TAWR•day•SEEL•yahs] *n.* a 1494 agreement between Portugal and Spain, declaring that newly discovered lands to the west of an imaginary line in the Atlantic Ocean would belong to Spain and newly discovered lands to the east of the line would belong to Portugal. (p. 533)

triangular trade *n.* the transatlantic trading network along which slaves and other goods were carried between Africa, England, Europe, the West Indies, and the colonies in the Americas. (p. 568)

tribune [TRIHB•yoon] *n.* in ancient Rome, an official elected by the plebeians to protect their rights. (p. 156)

tribute *n.* a payment made by a weaker power to a stronger power to obtain an assurance of peace and security. (p. 82)

Triple Alliance *n.* an association of the city-states of Tenochtitlán, Texcoco, and Tlacopan, which led to the formation of the Aztec Empire. (p. 454)

triumvirate [try•UHM•vuhr•iht] *n.* in ancient Rome, a group of three leaders sharing control of the government. (p. 161)

Trojan War *n.* a war, fought around 1200 B.C., in which an army led by Mycenaean kings attacked the independent trading city of Troy in Anatolia. (p. 125)

troubadour [TROO•buh•DAWR] *n.* a medieval poet and musician who traveled from place to place, entertaining people with songs of courtly love. (p. 367)

tyrant [TY•ruhnt] *n.* in ancient Greece, a powerful individual who gained control of a city-state's government by appealing to the poor for support. (p. 127)

UV

Umayyads [oo•MY•adz] *n.* a dynasty that ruled the Muslim Empire from A.D. 661 to 750 and later established a kingdom in al-Andalus. (p. 271)

utopia [yoo•TOH•pee•uh] *n.* an imaginary land described by Thomas More in his book *Utopia*—hence, an ideal place. (p. 482)

vassal [VAS•uhl] *n.* in feudal Europe, a person who received a grant of land from a lord in exchange for a pledge of loyalty and services. (p. 360)

Vedas [VAY•duhz] *n.* four collections of sacred writings produced by the Aryans during an early stage of their settlement in India. (p. 63)

vernacular [vuhr•NAK•yuh•luhr] *n.* the everyday language of people in a region or country. (pp. 391, 475)

Vishnu [VIHSH•noo] *n.* a Hindu god considered the preserver of the world. (p. 194)

vizier [vih•ZEER] *n.* a prime minister in a Muslim kingdom or empire. (p. 315)

W

War of the Spanish Succession *n.* a conflict, lasting from 1701 to 1713, in which a number of European states fought to prevent the Bourbon family from controlling Spain as well as France. (p. 601)

westernization *n.* an adoption of the social, political, or economic institutions of Western—especially European or American—countries. (p. 610)

XYZ

yin and yang *n.* in Chinese thought, the two powers that govern the natural rhythms of life. (p. 107)

Yoruba [YAWR•uh•buh] *n.* a West African people who formed several kingdoms in what is now Benin and southern Nigeria. (p. 418)

Zapotec [ZAH•puh•TEHK] *n.* an early Mesoamerican civilization that was centered in the Oaxaca Valley of what is now Mexico. (p. 242)

ziggurat [ZIHG•uh•RAT] *n.* a tiered, pyramid-shaped structure that formed part of a Sumerian temple. (p. 23)

Spanish Glossary

A

Abbasids [abasidas] *s.* dinastía que gobernó gran parte del imperio musulmán entre 750 y 1258 d.C. (pág. 271)

absolute monarch [monarca absoluto] *s.* rey o reina que tiene poder ilimitado y que procura controlar todos los aspectos de la sociedad. (pág. 594)

acropolis [acrópolis] *s.* cima fortificada de las antiguas ciudades griegas. (pág. 127)

Aksum *s.* reino africano en lo que hoy es Etiopía y Eritrea, que alcanzó su mayor auge en el siglo 4. (pág. 225)

al-Andalus *s.* región gobernada por los musulmanes en lo que hoy es España, establecida en el siglo 8 d.C. (pág. 271)

Allah [Alah] *s.* Dios (palabra árabe usada en el islamismo). (pág. 264)

Almohads [almohades] *s.* grupo de reformadores islámicos que tumbaron la dinastía de los almorávides y que establecieron un imperio en el norte de África y en el sur de España en el siglo 12 d.C. (pág. 412)

Almoravids [almorávides] *s.* hermandad religiosa islámica que estableció un imperio en el norte de África y en el sur de España en el siglo 11 d.C. (pág. 412)

Anabaptist [anabaptista] *s.* en la Reforma, miembro de un grupo protestante que enseñaba que sólo los adultos podían ser bautizados, y que la Iglesia y el Estado debían estar separados. (pág. 496)

Anasazi [anasazi] *s.* grupo amerindio que se estableció en el Suroeste de Norteamérica. (pág. 443)

Anatolia *s.* península del suroeste de Asia actualmente ocupada por la parte asiática de Turquía; también llamada Asia Menor. (pág. 62)

Angkor Wat *s.* templo construido en el imperio Khmer y dedicado al dios hindú Visnú. (pág. 345)

Anglican [anglicano] *adj.* relacionado con la Iglesia de Inglaterra. (pág. 494)

animism [animismo] *s.* creencia de que en los animales, las plantas y otros objetos naturales habitan espíritus. (pág. 216)

annul [anular] *v.* cancelar o suspender. (pág. 492)

apostle [apóstol] *s.* uno de los seguidores de Jesús que predicaba y difundía sus enseñanzas. (pág. 168)

aqueduct [acueducto] *s.* tubería o canal para llevar agua a zonas pobladas. (pág. 181)

aristocracy [aristocracia] *s.* gobierno en que el poder está en manos de una clase dominante hereditaria o nobleza. (pág. 127)

artifact [artefacto] *s.* objeto hecho por el ser humano, como herramientas, armas o joyas. (pág. 5)

artisan [artesano] *s.* trabajador especializado, como hilandero o ceramista, que hace productos a mano. (pág. 20)

Aryans [arios] *s.* pueblo indoeuropeo que, hacia 1500 a.C., comenzó a emigrar al subcontinente de India. (pág. 63)

assimilation [asimilación] *s.* adopción de la cultura del conquistador por un pueblo conquistado. (pág. 205)

Assyria [Asiria] *s.* reino del suroeste de Asia que controló un gran imperio de aproximadamente 850 a 612 a.C. (pág. 95)

Atlantic slave trade [trata de esclavos del Atlántico] *s.* compra, transporte y venta de africanos para trabajar en las Américas. (pág. 567)

autocracy [autocracia] *s.* gobierno en el cual el gobernante tiene poder ilimitado y lo usa de forma arbitraria. (pág. 109)

ayllu *s.* en la sociedad inca, pequeña comunidad o clan cuyos miembros trabajaban conjuntamente para el bien común. (pág. 460)

B

balance of power [equilibrio de poder] *s.* situación política en que ninguna nación tiene suficiente poder para ser una amenaza para las demás. (pág. 672)

the Balkans [Balcanes] *s.* región del sureste de Europa ocupada actualmente por Grecia, Albania, Bulgaria, Rumania, la parte eureopea de Turquía y las antiguas repúblicas de Yugoslavia. (pág. 689)

Bantu-speaking peoples [pueblos de habla bantú] *s.* hablantes de un grupo de lenguas relacionadas, que hace aproximadamente 2,000 años emigraron de África occidental a casi toda la mitad sur del continente. (pág. 222)

baroque [barroco] *s.* estilo grandioso y ornamentado del arte, la música y la arquitectura a fines del siglo 17 y principios del 18. (pág. 637)

barter [trueque] *s.* forma de comercio en la cual se intercambian productos y servicios sin dinero. (pág. 23)

Battle of Trafalgar [Batalla de Trafalgar] *s.* batalla naval de 1805 en que las fuerzas de Napoleón fueron derrotadas por una flota inglesa al mando de Horacio Nelson. (pág. 667)

Benin *s.* reino que surgió en el siglo 14 cerca del delta del río Níger y llegó a ser un gran Estado de África occidental en el siglo 15. (pág. 419)

Beringia *s.* antiguo puente terrestre por el que se cree que los primeros habitantes de América migraron de Asia. (pág. 235)

Bill of Rights [Carta de Derechos] *s.* primeras diez enmiendas a la Constitución de E.U.A., que protegen los derechos y libertades básicos de los ciudadanos. (pág. 645)

bishop [obispo] *s.* autoridad eclesiástica cristiana que supervisa varias iglesias. (pág. 171)

blockade [bloqueo] *s.* desplazamiento de tropas o barcos para impedir para evitar la entrada o salida de todo tráfico comercial a una ciudad o región. (pág. 668)

boyar [boyardo] *s.* el noble terrateniente de Rusia. (pág. 608)

Brahma *s.* dios hindú considerado creador del mundo. (pág. 194)

Brahmin [brahamán] *s.* en la sociedad aria, miembro de la clase social formada por los sacerdotes. (pág. 63)

Bronze Age [Edad del Bronce] *s.* período de la historia humana, que comenzó aproximadamente en 3000 a.C. en algunas partes, en el cual se comenzó a usar el bronce, en vez del cobre o la piedra, para elaborar herramientas y armas. (pág. 21)

bubonic plague [peste bubónica] *s.* enfermedad mortal que se extendió por Asia y Europa a mediados del siglo 14 y que cobró millones de víctimas. (pág. 399)

bureaucracy [burocracia] *s.* sistema de departamentos y dependencias formado para realizar las labores del gobierno. (pág. 105)

burgher [burgués] *s.* habitante de un pueblo medieval. (pág. 391)

Spanish Glossary

Bushido *s.* estricto código de conducta de los guerreros samurai en Japón. (pág. 343)

cabinet [gabinete] *s.* grupo de asesores o ministros escogidos por el jefe de gobierno de un país para que participen en la toma de decisiones del gobierno. (pág. 617)

caliph [califa] *s.* líder político y religioso supremo de un gobierno musulmán. (pág. 269)

calligraphy [caligrafía] *s.* arte de escritura manuscrita. (pág. 276)

Calvinism [calvinismo] *s.* conjunto de enseñanzas religiosas basadas en las ideas del reformador Juan Calvino. (pág. 495)

canon law [derecho canónico] *s.* conjunto de leyes que gobierna una iglesia cristiana. (pág. 371)

capitalism [capitalismo] *s.* sistema económico basado en la propiedad privada y en la inversión de dinero en empresas comerciales con el objetivo de obtener ganancias. (pág. 573)

Carolingian Dynasty [dinastía carolingia] *s.* dinastía de los reyes francos que abarcó del 751 al 887 d.C. (pág. 356)

caste [casta] *s.* una de las cuatro clases del sistema social de los arios que se establecieron en India: sacerdotes, guerreros, campesinos o comerciantes, y trabajadores o artesanos no arios. (pág. 64)

Catholic Reformation [Contrarreforma] *s.* movimiento del siglo 16 en el que la Iglesia Católica intentó reformarse en respuesta a la Reforma protestante. (pág. 498)

centralized government [gobierno centralizado] *s.* gobierno en que el poder se concentra en una autoridad central a la cual se someten los gobiernos locales. (pág. 200)

Chaldeans [caldeos] *s.* pueblo del suroeste asiático que contribuyó a destruir el imperio asirio. (pág. 97)

Chavín *s.* primera de las grandes civilizaciones de Suramérica, que floreció en las montañas de lo que hoy es Perú, aproximadamente de 900 a 200 a.C. (pág. 246)

checks and balances [control y compensación de poderes] *s.* medidas para evitar que una rama del gobierno domine sobre las otras. (pág. 645)

chivalry [caballería] *s.* código de conducta de los caballeros de la Europa medieval que exaltaba ideales como el valor, la lealtad y la dedicación. (pág. 365)

city-state [ciudad Estado] *s.* ciudad y tierras de los alrededores que funcionaba como una unidad política independiente. (pág. 31)

civilization [civilización] *s.* forma de cultura que se caracteriza por tener ciudades, trabajadores especializados, instituciones complejas, un sistema de registro y tecnología avanzada. (pág. 20)

civil service [servicio público] *s.* departamentos administrativos del gobierno, especialmente los que requieren a los candidatos a empleo pasar ciertos exámenes. (pág. 203)

civil war [guerra civil] *s.* conflicto entre dos grupos políticos dentro de un mismo país. (pág. 161)

clan *s.* grupo de descendientes de un antepasado común. (pág. 331)

classical art [arte clásico] *s.* arte común de la antigua Grecia y Roma, que subraya la armonía, el orden y el equilibrio. (pág. 136)

clergy [clero] *s.* conjunto de eclesiásticos que celebran servicios religiosos, como sacerdotes, ministros o rabinos. (pág. 370)

codex [códice] *s.* libro de páginas que se pueden pasar, como éste. (pág. 448)

colony [colonia] *s.* tierra controlada por una nación distante. (pág. 554)

Colossus of Rhodes [Coloso de Rodas] *s.* enorme estatua helénica que se ubicaba cerca del puerto de Rodas. (pág. 149)

Columbian Exchange [trasferencia colombina] *s.* transferencia mundial de plantas, animales y enfermedades durante la colonización europea de América. (pág. 571)

comedy [comedia] *s.* forma humorística de drama con payasadas y sátira. (pág. 136)

Commercial Revolution [Revolución Comercial] *s.* expansión del comercio y los negocios que transformó las economías europeas en los siglos 16 y 17. (pág. 389)

common law [derecho consuetudinario] *s.* sistema de leyes desarrollado en Inglaterra, basado en costumbres y decisiones jurídicas anteriores. (pág. 394)

Concert of Europe [Concierto de Europa] *s.* serie de alianzas entre naciones europeas en el siglo 19, ideadas por el príncipe Klemens von Metternich para impedir revoluciones. (pág. 674)

concordat [concordato] *s.* acuerdo firmado entre Napoleón y el Papa para establecer una nueva relación entre la Iglesia y el Estado. (pág. 664)

Congress of Vienna [Congreso de Viena] *s.* serie de reuniones en 1814 y 1815 en las cuales los dirigentes europeos trataron de establecer una paz y seguridad duraderas tras la derrota de Napoleón. (pág. 672)

conquistadors [conquistadores] *s.* soldados, exploradores y aventureros españoles que participaron en la conquista de América en el siglo 16. (pág. 554)

conservative [conservadore] *s.* en la primera mitad del siglo 19, el europeo —principalmente los terratenientes y nobles acaudalados— que querían preservar las monarquías tradicionales. (pág. 687)

constitutional monarchy [monarquía constitucional] *s.* monarquía en que el poder del gobernante está limitado por la ley. (pág. 617)

consul [cónsul] *s.* en la república romana, uno de los dos poderosos funcionarios elegidos cada año para comandar el ejército y dirigir el gobierno. (pág. 157)

Continental System [Sistema Continental] *s.* política de Napoleón de impedir el comercio de Gran Bretaña con la Europa continental para destruir la economía británica. (pág. 668)

Council of Trent [Concilio de Trento] *s.* reunión de líderes de la Iglesia Católica Romana, convocada por el papa Pablo III, para fallar sobre varias doctrinas criticadas por los reformadores protestantes. (pág. 499)

coup d'etat [golpe de Estado] *s.* toma repentina del poder político de una nación. (pág. 664)

covenant [pacto] *s.* promesa o acuerdo mutuo, especialmente un acuerdo entre Dios y el pueblo hebreo, como los que registra la Biblia. (pág. 78)

creole [criollo] *s.* en la sociedad española colonial, el colono nacido en Latinoamérica de padres españoles. (pág. 681)

Crusade [cruzada] *s.* una de las expediciones de guerreros cristianos medievales para quitarle Jerusalén y la Tierra Santa a los musulmanes. (pág. 382)

cultural diffusion [difusión cultural] *s.* proceso de difusión de ideas o productos de una cultura a otra. (pág. 31)

culture [cultura] *s.* forma distintiva de la vida de un pueblo, representada en sus herramientas, costumbres, artes y pensamiento. (pág. 5)

cuneiform [cuneiforme] *s.* sistema de escritura que usa símbolos en forma de cuña inventado por los sumerios hacia 3000 a.C. (pág. 20)

Cyrillic alphabet [alfabeto cirílico] *s.* alfabeto inventado en el siglo 9 por los santos Cirilo y Metodio para la escritura de los idiomas eslavos. (pág. 306)

czar [zar] *s.* emperador ruso (de la palabra latina *Caesar*). (pág. 311)

D

daimyo *s.* señor feudal de Japón que comandaba un ejército privado de samurais. (pág. 542)

Daoism [taoísmo] *s.* filosofía basada en las ideas del pensador chino Laozi, quien enseñó a guiarse por una fuerza universal llamada Tao. (pág. 106)

Declaration of Independence [Declaración de Independencia] *s.* declaración de las razones de la ruptura de las colonias americanas con Gran Bretaña, aprobada por el Segundo Congreso Continental. (pág. 641)

delta *s.* zona pantanosa que se forma con los depósitos de légamo en la desembocadura de un río. (pág. 36)

democracy [democracia] *s.* gobierno controlado por sus ciudadanos, bien sea directa o indirectamente, por medio de sus representantes. (pág. 128)

devshirme *s.* en el imperio otomano, política de llevarse a los niños de los pueblos cristianos conquistados para entrenarlos como soldados musulmanes. (pág. 510)

Diaspora [diáspora] *s.* dispersión de los judíos fuera de Palestina, especialmente en los más de 1800 años que siguieron a la destrucción romana del Templo de Jerusalén en 70 d.C. (pág. 170)

dictator [dictador] *s.* en la antigua Roma, líder político con poder absoluto para decretar leyes y dirigir el ejército por un tiempo limitado. (pág. 157)

direct democracy [democracia directa] *s.* gobierno en el cual los ciudadanos gobiernan directamente, no a través de sus representantes. (pág. 135)

divine right [derecho divino] *s.* noción de que los monarcas son representantes de Dios en la Tierra y, por lo tanto, sólo le deben responder a él. (pág. 594)

domestication [domesticación] *s.* entrenamiento de animales para beneficio humano. (pág. 16)

Dorians [dorios] *s.* grupo de lengua griega que, según la tradición, emigró a Grecia después de la destrucción de la civilización micénica. (pág. 125)

Dutch East India Company [Compañía Holandesa de las Indias Orientales] *s.* empresa fundada por holandeses a principios del siglo 17 para establecer y dirigir comercio por todo Asia. (pág. 534)

dynastic cycle [ciclo dinástico] *s.* patrón histórico del surgimiento, caída y sustitución de dinastías. (pág. 54)

dynasty [dinastía] *s.* serie de gobernantes de una sola familia. (pág. 31)

E

Edict of Nantes [Edicto de Nantes] *s.* declaración en que el rey francés Enrique IV prometió que los protestantes podían vivir en paz en Francia y tener centros de veneración en algunas ciudades. (pág. 596)

émigré *s.* quien abandona su país de origen por razones políticas, como los nobles y otros que huyeron de Francia durante los levantamientos campesinos de la Revolución Francesa. (pág. 658)

empire [imperio] *s.* unidad política en que un solo gobernante controla varios pueblos o países. (pág. 33)

encomienda *s.* tierras otorgadas por España a un colonizador de América, con el derecho de hacer trabajar a los amerindios que vivían en ellas. (pág. 557)

English Civil War [Guerra Civil Inglesa] *s.* conflicto de 1642 a 1649 en que los seguidores puritanos del Parlamento lucharon contra los defensores de la monarquía de Inglaterra. (pág. 615)

enlightened despot [déspota ilustrado] *s.* uno de los monarcas europeos del siglo 18 inspirados por las ideas de la Ilustración a gobernar con justicia y respeto a los derechos de sus súbditos. (pág. 638)

enlightenment [iluminación] *s.* en budismo, estado de perfecta sabiduría en que se entienden las verdades básicas del universo. (pág. 68)

Enlightenment [Ilustración] *s.* movimiento del siglo 18 en Europa que trató de aplicar los principios de la razón y el método científico a todos los aspectos de la sociedad. (pág. 629)

epic [epopeya] *s.* poema narrativo extenso que celebran las hazañas de héroes tradicionales o legendarios. (pág. 125)

estate [estado] *s.* una de las tres clases sociales existentes en Francia antes de la Revolución Francesa; el primer estado era el de la clerecía; el segundo era el de la nobleza; y el tercero era del resto de la población. (pág. 651)

Estates-General [Estados Generales] *s.* asamblea de representantes de los tres estados, o clases sociales, de Francia. (págs. 397, 653)

excommunication [excomunión] *s.* expulsión de una iglesia cristiana. (pág. 306)

F

Fatimid [fatimitas] *s.* dinastía musulmana cuyos orígenes se remontan a Fátima, hija de Mahoma, y que construyó un imperio en África del Norte, Arabia y Siria en los siglos 9 a 12. (pág. 272)

favorable balance of trade [balanza comercial favorable] *s.* situación económica en la cual un país exporta más de lo que importa, es decir, que vende más productos de los que compra en el extranjero. (pág. 575)

federal system [sistema federal] *s.* sistema de gobierno en el que el poder se divide entre una autoridad central y varios estados. (pág. 645)

Fertile Crescent [Media Luna Fértil] *s.* arco de ricos terrenos de cultivo en el suroeste de Asia, entre el golfo Pérsico y el mar Mediterráneo. (pág. 29)

feudalism [feudalismo] *s.* sistema político en el cual a los nobles se les otorga el uso de tierras de propiedad del rey, a cambio de lealtad, servicio militar y protección de sus habitantes. (pág. 54)

fief [feudo] *s.* dominio concedido a un vasallo por un señor, conforme al sistema feudal de la Europa medieval. (pág. 360)

filial piety [amor filial] *s.* respeto de los hijos a los padres y a sus mayores. (pág. 104)

Franks [francos] *s.* pueblo germano que se asentó en la provincia romana de Galia (a grandes rasgos, donde está hoy Francia) y que formó un gran imperio durante la Edad Media. (pág. 354)

French and Indian War [Guerra contra Franceses e Indígenas] *s.* conflicto entre Gran Bretaña y Francia por control de territorio en Norteamérica, de 1754 a 1763. (pág. 564)

gentry [pequeña nobleza] *s.* clase de ricos y poderosos que gozan de alto nivel social. (pág. 327)

geocentric theory [teoría geocéntrica] *s.* teoría de la Edad Media en la que los eruditos creían que la Tierra era objeto fijo, localizado en el centro del universo. (pág. 623)

Ghana *s.* reino de África occidental que se enriqueció debido a recaudación de impuestos y al control del comercio, y que estableció un imperio en los siglos 9 a 11. (pág. 413)

ghazi *s.* guerrero del islam. (pág. 507)

Glorious Revolution [Revolución Gloriosa] *s.* derrocamiento incruento del rey Jacobo II de Inglaterra, quien fue reemplazado por Guillermo y María. (pág. 616)

glyph [glifo] *s.* dibujo simbólico, especialmente el usado como parte de un sistema de escritura para tallar mensajes en piedra. (pág. 448)

Gothic [gótico] *adj.* relacionado con un nuevo estilo de arquitectura religiosa surgido en la Europa medieval, caracterizado por bóvedas de nervadura, vitrales emplomados, contrafuertes volantes, arcos ojivales y altas agujas. (pág. 380)

Great Fear [Gran Miedo] *s.* ola de temor insensato que se extendió por las provincias francesas después de la toma de la Bastilla en 1789. (pág. 655)

Great Schism [Gran Cisma] *s.* división de la Iglesia Católica Romana medieval, durante la cual había dos Papas rivales, uno en Avignon y el otro en Roma. (pág. 399)

Greco-Roman culture [cultura greco-romana] *s.* antigua cultura producto de la mezcla de la cultura griega, helénica y romana. (pág. 178)

griot *s.* narrador de África occidental. (pág. 216)

guerrilla [guerrillero] *s.* miembro de una unidad de combate informal que ataca por sorpresa las tropas enemigas que ocupan su país. (pág. 669)

guild [gremio] *s.* asociación medieval de personas que laboraban en lo mismo; controlaba salarios y precios. (pág. 388)

guillotine [guillotina] *s.* máquina para decapitar con que se hicieron ejecuciones durante la Revolución Francesa. (pág. 660)

Gupta Empire [imperio gupta] *s.* el segundo imperio en India, fundado por Chandra Gupta I en el 320 d.C. (pág. 191)

habeas corpus *s.* documento que requiere que un detenido comparezca ante un tribunal o juez para que se determine si su detención es legal. (pág. 616)

Hagia Sophia [Santa Sofía] *s.* catedral de la Santa Sabiduría en Constantinopla, construida por orden del emperador bizantino Justiniano. (pág. 303)

haiku *s.* poema japonés que tiene tres versos no rimados de cinco, siete y cinco sílabas. (pág. 545)

hajj *s.* peregrinación a la Meca realizada como deber por los musulmanes. (pág. 267)

Han Dynasty [dinastía Han] *s.* dinastía china que gobernó del 202 a.C. al 9 d.C. y nuevamente del 23 al 220 d.C. (pág. 200)

Harappan civilization [civilización harappa] *s.* nombre alternativo de la civilización del valle del Indo que surgió a lo largo del río Indo, posiblemente hacia 7000 a.C; caracterizada por planificación urbana avanzada. (pág. 46)

Hausa [hausa] *s.* pueblo de África occidental que vivía en varias ciudades Estado en el actual norte de Nigeria. (pág. 417)

heliocentric theory [teoría heliocéntrica] *s.* idea de que la Tierra y los otros planetas giran en torno al Sol. (pág. 624)

Hellenistic [helénico] *adj.* relacionado con la civilización, el idioma, el arte, la ciencia y la literatura del mundo griego a partir del reino de Alejandro el Magno hasta el siglo 2 a.C. (pág. 146)

helot [ilota] *s.* en la antigua Esparta, campesino atado a la tierra. (pág. 129)

hieroglyphics [jeroglíficos] *s.* antiguo sistema de escritura egipcia en el cual se usan imágenes para representar ideas y sonidos. (pág. 40)

Hijrah *s.* migración de Mahoma de la Meca a Yathrib (Medina) en el 622 d.C. (pág. 265)

Hittites [hititas] *s.* pueblo indoeuropeo que se estableció en Anatolia hacia 2000 a.C. (pág. 62)

Holy Alliance [Alianza Sagrada] *s.* liga de naciones europeas formada por los dirigentes de Rusia, Austria y Prusia después del Congreso de Viena. (pág. 674)

Holy Roman Empire [Sacro Imperio Romano] *s.* imperio establecido en Europa en el siglo 10, que inicialmente se formó con tierras de lo que hoy es Alemania e Italia. (pág. 371)

hominid [homínido] *s.* miembro del grupo biológico que abarca a los seres humanos y especies relacionadas que caminan erguidas. (pág. 7)

Homo sapiens *s.* especie biológica de los seres humanos modernos. (pág. 8)

House of Wisdom [Casa de la Sabiduría] *s.* centro de enseñanza en Bagdad en el siglo 9. (pág. 276)

humanism [humanismo] *s.* movimiento intelectual del Renacimiento que estudió los textos clásicos y se enfocó en el potencial y los logros humanos. (pág. 472)

Hundred Days [Cien Días] *s.* corto período de 1815 en que Napoleón hizo su último intento de recuperar el poder, depuso al rey francés y de nuevo se proclamó emperador de Francia. (pág. 671)

Hundred Years' War [Guerra de los Cien Años] *s.* conflicto en el cual Inglaterra y Francia lucharon en territorio francés de 1337 a 1453, con interrupciones. (pág. 401)

hunter-gatherer [cazador-recolector] *s.* miembro de un grupo nómada que se alimenta de la caza de animales y la recolección de frutos. (pág. 14)

Hyksos [hicsos] *s.* grupo nómada de invasores del suroeste de Asia que gobernó Egipto de 1640 a 1570 a.C. (pág. 89)

Ice Age [Edad de Hielo] *s.* período de fríos en que enormes capas de hielo se desplazan de las regiones polares; la última fue de aproximadamente 1,900,000 a 10,000 a.C. (pág. 235)

I Ching *s.* libro chino de oráculos consultado para solucionar problemas éticos y prácticos. (pág. 107)

icon [icono] *s.* imagen religiosa usada por los cristianos de Oriente. (pág. 306)

impressionism [impresionismo] *s.* movimiento de la pintura del siglo 19 en reacción al realismo, que buscaba dar impresiones personales de sujetos o momentos. (pág. 701)

Indo-Europeans [indoeuropeos] *s.* grupo de pueblos seminómadas que, hacia 1700 a.C., comenzaron a emigrar de lo que es hoy el sur de Rusia al subcontinente hindú, Europa y el suroeste de Asia. (pág. 61)

indulgence [indulgencia] *s.* perdón que libera al pecador de la penitencia por un pecado. (pág. 489)

inflation [inflación] *s.* baja del valor de la moneda, acompañada de un alza de precios de bienes y servicios. (pág. 173)

Inquisition [Inquisición] *s.* tribunal de la Iglesia Católica para investigar y juzgar a los acusados de herejía, especialmente el establecido en España durante el siglo 15. (pág. 384)

institution [institución] *s.* patrón duradero de organización en una comunidad. (pág. 20)

intendant [intendente] *s.* funcionario del gobierno francés nombrado por el monarca para recaudar impuestos e impartir justicia. (pág. 598)

Iroquois [iroqueses] *s.* grupo de pueblos amerindios que hablaban lenguas relacionadas, vivían en la parte este de la región de los Grandes Lagos en Norteamérica y formaron una alianza a fines del siglo 16. (pág. 444)

Islam [islam] *s.* religión monoteísta que se desarrolló en Arabia en el siglo 7 d.C. (pág. 265)

Israel *s.* reino de los hebreos unidos en Palestina, de aproximadamente 1020 a 922 a.C.; después, el reino norte de los dos reinos hebreos; actualmente, la nación judía establecida en Palestina en 1948. (pág. 81)

Jainism [jainismo] *s.* religión fundada en India durante el siglo 6, cuyos miembros creen que todo en el universo tiene alma y por lo tanto no debe ser lastimado. (pág. 67)

janissary [janísero] *s.* miembro de una fuerza élite de soldados del imperio otomano. (pág. 510)

Jesuits [jesuitas] *s.* miembros de la Sociedad de Jesús, orden católica romana fundada por Ignacio de Loyola. (pág. 499)

joint-stock company [sociedad de capitales] *s.* negocio en el que los inversionistas reúnen capital para un propósito común y después comparten las ganancias. (pág. 573)

Judah [Judea] *s.* reino hebreo establecido en Palestina alrededor del 922 a.C. (pág. 81)

Justinian Code [Código Justiniano] *s.* cuerpo del derecho civil romano recopilado y organizado por órdenes del emperador bizantino Justiniano hacia el 534 d.C. (pág. 293)

kabuki *s.* forma de teatro japonés en que se representa una historia con música, danza y mímica. (pág. 545)

kaiser *s.* emperador alemán (del título romano Caesar). (pág. 697)

karma *s.* en hinduismo y budismo, la totalidad de actos buenos y malos que comete una persona, que determinan su destino al renacer. (pág. 67)

Khmer Empire [imperio Khmer] *s.* imperio del sureste asiático, centrado en la actual Camboya, que alcanzó su mayor auge hacia 1200 d.C. (pág. 345)

knight [caballero] *s.* en Europa medieval, guerrero con armadura y cabalgadura. (pág. 360)

Koryu dynasty [dinastía koryu] *s.* dinastía coreana del 935 a 1392 d.C. (pág. 347)

Kush *s.* antiguo reino nubio cuyos reyes gobernaron a Egipto del 751 a 671 a.C. (pág. 92)

lay investiture [investidura seglar] *s.* nombramiento de funcionarios de la Iglesia por reyes y nobles. (pág. 372)

Legalism [legalismo] *s.* filosofía política china basada en la idea de que un gobierno altamente eficiente y poderoso es la clave del orden social. (pág. 106)

legion [legión] *s.* unidad militar del ejército de la antigua Roma formada por aproximadamente 5,000 soldados de infantería y grupos de soldados de caballería. (pág. 157)

Legislative Assembly [Asamblea Legislativa] *s.* congreso creado por la Constitución francesa de 1791, con poder para emitir leyes y aprobar declaraciones de guerra. (pág. 657)

legitimacy [legitimidad] *s.* derecho hereditario de un monarca a gobernar. (pág. 673)

liberal [liberale] *s.* en la primera mitad del siglo 19, europeo —principalmente empresarios y comerciantes de clase media— que deseaba darle más poder político a los parlamentos elegidos. (pág. 687)

lineage [linaje] *s.* individuos —vivos, muertos y sin nacer— que descienden de un antepasado común. (pág. 410)

loess [loes] *s.* depósito fértil de tierra traída por el viento. (pág. 50)

lord [señor] *s.* en la Europa feudal, persona que controlaba tierras y por lo tanto podía dar feudos a vasallos. (pág. 360)

Lutheran [luterano] *s.* miembro de una iglesia protestante basada en las enseñanzas de Martín Lutero. (pág. 490)

lycée [liceo] *s.* escuela pública en Francia. (pág. 664)

Macedonia *s.* antiguo reino del norte de Grecia, cuyo rey Felipe II conquistó a Grecia en 338 a.C. (pág. 142)

Maghrib [Maghreb] *s.* región del norte de África que abarca la costa del Mediterráneo de lo que en la actualidad es Marruecos, Túnez y Argelia. (pág. 410)

Magna Carta [Carta Magna] *s.* "Gran Carta": documento de Inglaterra que garantiza derechos políticos elementales, elaborado por nobles ingleses y aprobado por el rey Juan en 1215 d.C. (pág. 394)

Mahabharata *s.* gran poema épico de India que relata las luchas arias durante su migración al sur de India. (pág. 64)

Mahayana *s.* secta del budismo que ofrece la salvación a todos y permite la veneración popular. (pág. 193)

maize [maíz] *s.* cereal cultivado cuyos granos se encuentran en grandes espigas, o mazorcas. (pág. 238)

Mali *s.* imperio de África occidental que floreció entre 1235 y el siglo 15, y se enriqueció con el comercio. (pág. 415)

Manchus [manchú] *s.* pueblo originario de Manchuria que gobernó en China durante la dinastía Qing (1644–1912). (pág. 539)

Mandate of Heaven [Mandato del Cielo] *s.* en China, creencia de que la autoridad real era producto de la aprobación divina. (pág. 54)

manor [señorío] *s.* dominios de un señor en la Europa feudal. (pág. 360)

matriarchal [matriarcal] *adj.* relacionado con un sistema social en el que la madre es jefa de la familia. (pág. 192)

matrilineal *adj.* relacionado con un sistema social en el que la descendencia familiar y los derechos de herencia se trasmiten a través de la madre. (pág. 410)

Mauryan Empire [imperio maurio] *s.* primer imperio de India, fundado por Chandragupta Mauria en 321 a.C. (pág. 189)

Medes [medos] *s.* pueblo del suroeste asiático que contribuyó a derrotar al imperio asirio. (pág. 97)

mercantilism [mercantilismo] *s.* política económica de aumentar la riqueza y poder de una nación obteniendo grandes cantidades de oro y plata, y vendiendo más bienes de los que se compran. (pág. 574)

mercenary [mercenario] *s.* soldado que recibe sueldo por pelear en un ejército extranjero. (pág. 173)

Meroë [Meroe] *s.* centro de la dinastía Kush de aproximadamente 250 a.C. a 150 d.C.; conocido por su manufactura de armas de hierro y herramientas. (pág. 94)

Mesoamerica [Mesoamérica] *s.* región que se extiende desde el centro de México hasta Honduras, donde se desarrollaron varias de las antiguas sociedades complejas de América. (pág. 240)

mestizo *s.* mezcla de español y amerindio. (pág. 557)

Middle Ages [Edad Media] *s.* era en la historia europea posterior a la caída del imperio romano, que abarca aproximadamente desde el 500 hasta 1500, también llamada época medieval. (pág. 353)

middle passage [travesía intermedia] *s.* viaje que trajo a africanos capturados al Caribe y, posteriormente, a América del Norte y del Sur, para venderlos como esclavos; recibió este nombre porque era considerada la porción media del triángulo comercial trasatlántico. (pág. 569)

migration [migración] *s.* acto de trasladarse de un lugar para establecerse en otro. (págs. 62, 220)

Ming Dynasty [dinastía Ming] *s.* dinastía que reinó en China desde 1368 hasta 1644. (pág. 536)

Minoans [minoicos] *s.* pueblo de navegantes y comerciantes que vivió en la isla de Creta de aproximadamente 2000 a 1400 a.C. (pág. 72)

Mississippian [misisipiense] *adj.* relacionado con una cultura constructora de túmulos que floreció en Norteamérica entre el 800 y 1500 d.C. (pág. 443)

mita *s.* en el imperio inca, obligación de todo súbdito de trabajar ciertos días al año para el Estado. (pág. 461)

Moche [moche] *s.* civilización que floreció en la actual costa norte de Perú de aproximadamente 100 a 700 d.C. (pág. 247)

monarchy [monarquía] *s.* gobierno en que el poder está en manos de una sola persona. (pág. 127)

monastery [monasterio] *s.* comunidad religiosa de hombres, llamados monjes, que ceden todas sus posesiones y se dedican a la oración y veneración. (pág. 354)

monopoly [monopolio] *s.* control exclusivo sobre la producción y distribución de ciertos bienes. (pág. 204)

monotheism [monoteísmo] *s.* creencia en un solo dios. (pág. 78)

monsoon [monzón] *s.* viento que cambia de dirección en ciertas épocas del año. (pág. 45)

mosque [mezquita] *s.* lugar de veneración islámica. (pág. 267)

movable type [tipo móvil] *s.* bloques de metal o de madera, cada uno con caracteres individuales, que pueden distribuirse para formar una página de impresión. (pág. 325)

Mughal [mogol] *s.* uno de los nómadas que invadieron el subcontinente de India en el siglo 16 y establecieron un poderoso imperio. (pág. 516)

mulattos [mulatos] *s.* personas de ascendencia europea y africana. (pág. 682)

mummification [momificación] *s.* proceso de embalsamamiento y secado de cadáveres para evitar su descomposición. (pág. 38)

Muslim [musulmán] *s.* devoto del islam. (pág. 265)

Mutapa [mutapa] *adj.* con un imperio de África del sur establecido por Mutota en el siglo 15 a.D. (pág. 427)

Mycenaean [micénicos] *s.* el grupo indoeuropeo que se estableció en Grecia hacia 2000 a.C. (pág. 124)

myth [mito] *s.* la narracion tradicional sobre dioses, antepasados o héroes, que explican el mundo natural o las costumbres y creencias de una sociedad. (pág. 126)

N

Napoleonic Code [código napoleónico] *s.* sistema extenso y uniforme de leyes establecido para Francia por Napoleón. (pág. 664)

National Assembly [Asamblea Nacional] *s.* congreso francés establecido el 17 de junio de 1789 por representantes del Tercer Estado para promulgar leyes y reformas en nombre del pueblo. (pág. 654)

nationalism [nacionalismo] *s.* creencia de que la principal lealtad del pueblo debe ser a su nación —es decir, a la gente con quien comparte historia y cultura— y no al rey o al imperio. (pág. 687)

nation-state [nación Estado] *s.* nación independiente de gente que tiene una cultura e identidad común. (pág. 687)

Nazca [nazca] *s.* civilización que floreció en la actual costa sur de Perú de 200 a.C. a 600 d.C. (pág. 247)

neoclassical [neoclásico] *adj.* relacionado con un estilo sencillo y elegante (inspirado en ideas y temas de la antigua Grecia y Roma) que caracterizó las artes en Europa a fines del siglo 18. (pág. 637)

Neolithic Age [Neolítico] *s.* período prehistórico que comenzó aproximadamente en 8000 a.C. y en algunas partes acabó desde 3000 a.C., durante el cual los grupos humanos aprendieron a pulir herramientas de piedra, hacer cerámica, cultivar alimentos y criar animales; también se llama Nueva Edad de Piedra. (pág. 7)

Neolithic Revolution [Revolución Neolítica] *s.* gran cambio en la vida humana causada por los comienzos de la agricultura; es decir, el cambio de recolectar a producir alimentos. (pág. 15)

New Kingdom [Reino Nuevo] *s.* período de la historia del antiguo Egipto tras la caída de los gobernantes hicsos, desde 1570 hasta 1075 a.C. (pág. 90)

nirvana *s.* en budismo, la liberación del dolor y el sufrimiento alcanzada después de la iluminación. (pág. 69)

Nok [nok] *s.* pueblo africano que vivió en lo que es hoy Nigeria entre 500 a.C. y 200 d.C. (pág. 217)

nomad [nómada] *s.* miembro de un grupo que no tiene hogar permanente y que va de un lugar a otro en busca de agua y alimento. (pág. 14)

obsidian [obsidiana] *s.* roca volcánica dura y vítrea con que los primeros seres humanos elaboraban herramientas de piedra. (pág. 453)

Old Regime [antiguo régimen] *s.* sistema político y social que existía en Francia antes de la Revolución Francesa. (pág. 651)

oligarchy [oligarquía] *s.* gobierno en que el poder está en manos de pocas personas, particularmente un gobierno que se basa en la riqueza. (pág. 127)

Olmec [olmeca] *s.* civilización mesoamericana más antigua que se conoce, que floreció hacia 1200 a.C. e influyó sobre las posteriores sociedades de la región. (pág. 240)

oracle bone [hueso de oráculo] *s.* hueso de animal o caparazón de tortuga que usaban los antiguos sacerdotes chinos para comunicarse con los dioses. (pág. 53)

Paleolithic Age [Paleolítico] *s.* período prehistórico que abarcó aproximadamente desde 2.5 millones hasta 8000 a.C., durante el cual los seres humanos hicieron rudimentarias herramientas y armas de piedra; también se llama Antigua Edad de Piedra. (pág. 7)

papyrus [papiro] *s.* carrizo alto que crece en el delta del Nilo, usado por los antiguos egipcios para hacer hojas de escribir similares al papel. (pág. 40)

parliament [parlamento] *s.* cuerpo de representantes que promulga las leyes de una nación. (pág. 395)

pastoralist [pastor] *s.* miembro de un grupo nómada que pastorea rebaños de animales domesticados. (pág. 330)

patriarch [patriarca] *s.* obispo principal de la rama oriental de la cristiandad. (pág. 306)

patriarchal [patriarcal] *adj.* relacionado con un sistema social en el que el padre es jefe de la familia. (pág. 192)

patrician [patricio] *s.* en la antigua Roma, miembro de la clase alta, privilegiada y rica. (pág. 156)

patrilineal [patrilineal] *adj.* relacionado con un sistema social en el que la descendencia y los derechos de herencia se trasmiten a través del padre. (pág. 410)

patron [mecenas] *s.* persona que apoya a los artistas, especialmente, en el aspecto financiero. (pág. 472)

Pax Mongolica [Paz Mongólica] *s.* período de mediados de 1200 a mediados de 1300 d.C., cuando los mongoles impusieron estabilidad y orden público en casi toda Eurasia. (pág. 333)

Pax Romana *s.* período de paz y prosperidad por todo el imperio romano, de 27 a.C. a 180 d.C. (pág. 162)

Peace of Augsburg [Paz de Augsburgo] *s.* acuerdo realizado en 1555 que declaró que la religión de cada Estado alemán sería decidida por su gobernante. (pág. 492)

Peloponnesian War [Guerra del Peloponeso] *s.* guerra de 431 a 404 a.C., en la cual Atenas y sus aliados resultaron derrotados por Esparta y sus aliados. (pág. 137)

peninsulares *s.* en la sociedad española colonial, colonos nacidos en España. (pág. 681)

Peninsular War [Guerra Peninsular] *s.* conflicto de 1808–1813 en que los rebeldes españoles lucharon con la ayuda de Gran Bretaña para expulsar de España las tropas de Napoleón. (pág. 669)

Persian Wars [Guerras Pérsicas] *s.* guerras del siglo 5 a.C. entre las ciudades Estado de Grecia y el imperio persa. (pág. 131)

perspective [perspectiva] *s.* técnica artística que crea la apariencia de tres dimensiones en una superficie plana. (pág. 474)

phalanx [falange] *s.* formación militar de soldados de infantería armados con lanzas y escudos. (pág. 131)

pharaoh [faraón] *s.* rey del antiguo Egipto, considerado dios, así como líder político y militar. (pág. 37)

philosophe *s.* miembro de un grupo de pensadores sociales de la Ilustración en Francia. (pág. 630)

philosophers [filósofos] *s.* pensadores que investigan la naturaleza del universo, la sociedad humana y la moral a través de la lógica y la razón. (pág. 138)

Phoenicians [fenicios] *s.* pueblo de navegantes del suroeste de Asia, que aproximadamente en 1100 a.C. comenzó a comerciar y a fundar colonias en la región mediterránea. (pág. 73)

Pilgrims [peregrinos] *s.* grupo que en 1620 fundó la colonia de Plymouth en Massachusetts para escapar de persecución religiosa en Inglaterra. (pág. 562)

plebeian [plebeyo] *s.* en la antigua Roma, uno de los agricultores, artesanos o comerciantes comunes que conformaban la mayoría de la población. (pág. 156)

plebiscite [plebiscito] *s.* voto directo mediante el cual la población de un país tiene la oportunidad de aceptar o rechazar una propuesta. (pág. 664)

polis *s.* ciudad Estado de Grecia; unidad política fundamental de la antigua Grecia a partir de 750 a.C. (pág. 127)

polytheism [politeísmo] *s.* creencia en muchos dioses. (pág. 31)

pope [Papa] *s.* obispo de Roma y dirigente de la Iglesia Católica Romana. (pág. 171)

Popol Vuh *s.* libro que narra una versión de la historia maya de la creación. (pág. 448)

potlatch *s.* fiesta ceremonial celebrada para mostrar rango y prosperidad en varias tribus del Noroeste de Norteamérica. (pág. 441)

predestination [predestinación] *s.* doctrina que postula que Dios ha decidido todo de antemano, incluso quiénes obtendrán la salvación eterna. (pág. 495)

Presbyterian [presbiteriano] *s.* miembro de una iglesia protestante gobernada por presbíteros conforme a las enseñanzas de John Knox. (pág. 496)

Protestant [protestante] *s.* miembro de una iglesia cristiana fundada de acuerdo a los principios de la Reforma. (pág. 490)

pueblos *s.* aldeas similares a complejos departamentales hechos de adobe, construidas por los anasazi y pueblos posteriores en el Suroeste de lo que hoy es Estados Unidos. (pág. 443)

Punic Wars [Guerras Púnicas] *s.* serie de tres guerras entre Roma y Cartago (264–146 a.C.); el resultado fue la destrucción de Cartago y la dominación romana de toda la región mediterránea occidental. (pág. 158)

Puritans [puritanos] *s.* grupo que, para liberarse de la persecución religiosa en Inglaterra, fundó una colonia en la bahía de Massachusetts a principios del siglo 17. (pág. 562)

push-pull factors [factores de empuje y de atracción] *s.* factores que hacen que la gente abandone sus hogares y emigre a otra región (factores de empuje); o factores que atraen a la gente a otros lugares (factores de atracción). (pág. 220)

pyramid [pirámide] *s.* enorme estructura de base rectangular y cuatro lados triangulares, como las que servían de tumba de los faraones del Reino Antiguo de Egipto. (pág. 37)

Q

Qin dynasty [dinastía Qin] *s.* dinastía china que reinó brevemente y sustituyó a la dinastía Zhou en el siglo 3 a.C. (pág. 107)

Qing dynasty [dinastía Qing] *s.* última dinastía china; reinó de 1644 a 1912. (pág. 539)

Quetzalcoatl [Quetzalcóatl] *s.* serpiente emplumada: dios de los toltecas y otros pueblos de Mesoamérica. (pág. 453)

quipu *s.* cuerda con nudos usadas para registrar información numérica por los incas. (pág. 461)

Qur'an [Corán] *s.* libro sagrado del islam. (pág. 267)

R

radical [radicale] *s.* en la primera mitad del siglo 19, el europeo a favor de cambios drásticos para extender la democracia a toda la población. (pág. 687)

realism [realismo] *s.* movimiento artístico del siglo 19 en que los escritores y pintores trataron de mostrar la vida como es, no como debiera ser. (pág. 700)

realpolitik *s.* "política de la realidad"; posición política dura que no da lugar al idealismo. (pág. 695)

Reconquista *s.* campaña de líderes cristianos para expulsar a los musulmanes de España, que empezó en el siglo 12 y terminó en 1492. (pág. 384)

Reformation [Reforma] *s.* movimiento del siglo 16 para realizar cambios religiosos que llevó a la fundación de iglesias cristianas que rechazaron la autoridad del Papa. (pág. 489)

Reign of Terror [Régimen del Terror] *s.* período entre 1793–1794 en que Maximilien Robespierre gobernó a Francia casi como dictador, durante el cual fueron ejecutados miles de personajes políticos y de ciudadanos comunes. (pág. 660)

reincarnation [reencarnación] *s.* en hinduismo y budismo, creencia de que el alma renace una y otra vez hasta alcanzar un conocimiento perfecto. (pág. 67)

religious toleration [tolerancia religiosa] *s.* reconocimiento del derecho de otros a tener creencias religiosas diferentes. (pág. 190)

Renaissance [Renacimiento] *s.* período de la historia europea de aproximadamente 1300 a 1600, durante el cual renació un interés en la cultura clásica que generó importantes cambios en el arte, la educación y la visión del mundo. (pág. 471)

republic [república] *s.* forma de gobierno en que el poder está en manos de representantes y líderes elegidos por los ciudadanos. (pág. 156)

Restoration [Restauración] *s.* en Inglaterra, período del reinado de Carlos II, después del colapso del gobierno de Oliver Cromwell. (pág. 616)

romanticism [romanticismo] *s.* movimiento de principios del siglo 19 en el arte y las ideas que recalca la emoción y la naturaleza, más que la razón y la sociedad. (pág. 698)

Royal Road [Camino Real] *s.* carretera de más de 1,600 millas que cruzaba el imperio persa, desde Susa en Persia hasta Sardes en Anatolia. (pág. 101)

Russification [rusificación] *s.* proceso que obliga a todos los grupos étnicos a adoptar la cultura rusa en el imperio ruso. (pág. 693)

S

sacrament [sacramento] *s.* una de las ceremonias cristianas en que se trasmite la gracia de Dios a los creyentes. (pág. 371)

Safavid [safávido] *s.* miembro de una dinastía musulmana shi'a que construyó un imperio en Persia del siglo 16 al 18. (pág. 512)

Sahel *s.* región africana a lo largo de la frontera sur del Sahara. (pág. 213)

salon [salón] *s.* reunión social de intelectuales y artistas, como las que celebraban en sus hogares señoras acaudaladas de París y otras ciudades europeas durante la Ilustración. (pág. 636)

samurai *s.* guerrero profesional que servía a los nobles en el Japón feudal. (pág. 343)

sans-culottes *s.* en la Revolución Francesa, grupo político radical de parisienses asalariados y pequeños comerciantes que anhelaban más voz en el gobierno, bajas de precios y fin a la escasez de alimentos. (pág. 658)

satrap [sátrapa] *s.* gobernador de una provincia en el imperio persa. (pág. 101)

savanna [sabana] *s.* planicie con pastizales. (pág. 215)

scholastics [escolásticos] *s.* académicos que se reunían y enseñaban en las universidades medievales de Europa. (pág. 392)

scientific method [método científico] *s.* procedimiento lógico para reunir información sobre el mundo natural, en que se usa experimentación y observación para poner a prueba hipótesis. (pág. 625)

Scientific Revolution [Revolución Científica] *s.* profundo cambio en el pensamiento europeo que comenzó a mediados del siglo 16, en que el estudio del mundo natural se caracterizó por cuidadosa observación y cuestionamiento de teorías aceptadas. (pág. 623)

scorched-earth policy [política de arrasamiento de campos] *s.* práctica de quemar campos de cultivo y de matar ganado durante la guerra para que el enemigo no pueda vivir de las tierras. (pág. 669)

scribe [escriba] *s.* profesional especializado en llevar registros en las civilizaciones tempranas. (pág. 20)

secular *adj.* relacionado con lo mundano más que con los asuntos espirituales. (págs. 355, 472)

Seljuks [seljucs] *s.* grupo turco que emigró al imperio abasida en el siglo 10 y estableció su propio imperio en el siglo 11. (pág. 315)

senate [senado] *s.* en la antigua Roma, organismo supremo de gobierno formado inicialmente sólo por aristócratas. (pág. 157)

serf [siervo] *s.* campesino medieval legalmente obligado a vivir en los dominios de un señor. (pág. 360)

Seven Years' War [Guerra de los Siete Años] *s.* conflicto en Europa, Norteamérica e India de 1756 a 1763, en que las fuerzas de Inglaterra y Prusia lucharon con las de Austria, Francia, Rusia y otros países. (pág. 607)

shah [sha] *s.* monarca hereditario de Irán. (pág. 513)

shari'a *s.* conjunto de leyes que rigen la vida de los musulmanes. (pág. 268)

Shi'a [shi'a] *s.* rama del islam que reconoce a los primeros cuatro califas como legítimos sucesores de Mahoma. (pág. 271)

Shinto [shintoísmo] *s.* religión oriunda de Japón. (pág. 339)

Shiva *s.* dios hindú considerado destructor del mundo. (pág. 194)

shogun [shogún] *s.* en el Japón feudal, jefe militar supremo que regía en nombre del emperador. (pág. 343)

Sikh [sikh] *s.* miembro de un grupo religioso no violento cuyas creencias combinaban elementos del budismo, el hinduismo y el sufismo. (pág. 518)

Silk Roads [Ruta de la Seda] *s.* sistema de antiguas rutas de las caravanas por Asia central, por las que se transportaban seda y otros productos comerciales. (pág. 196)

simony [simonía] *s.* venta o compra de una posición en una iglesia cristiana. (pág. 379)

skepticism [escepticismo] *s.* filosofía basada en la noción de que nada puede saberse con certeza. (pág. 597)

slash-and-burn farming [agricultura de tala y quema] *s.* método agrícola de desbrozar terrenos talando y quemando árboles y pastos, cuyas cenizas sirven como fertilizante. (pág. 15)

Slavs [eslavos] *s.* pueblo de los bosques al norte del mar Negro, origen de muchos pueblos de la Europa oriental de nuestros días. (pág. 307)

social contract [contrato social] *s.* acuerdo mediante el cual el pueblo define y limita sus derechos individuales, creando así una sociedad o gobierno organizados. (pág. 629)

Songhai *s.* imperio de África occidental que conquistó Malí y controló el comercio desde el siglo 15 hasta 1591. (pág. 417)

specialization [especialización] *s.* desarrollo de conocimientos para realizar determinado trabajo, como comerciar o llevar registros. (pág. 20)

stateless societies [sociedades sin Estado] *s.* grupos culturales en los que la autoridad es compartida por linajes de igual poder, en vez de ser ejercida por un gobierno central. (pág. 410)

steppes [estepas] *s.* llanuras secas de pastizales. (pág. 61)

stupa *s.* estructuras de piedra en forma de cúpula, construidas sobre reliquias budistas sagradas. (pág. 193)

subcontinent [subcontinente] *s.* gran masa que forma una parte claramente diferenciada de un continente. (pág. 44)

Sufi [sufí] *s.* musulmán que busca contacto directo con Dios por medio del misticismo. (pág. 271)

sultan [sultán] *s.* "jefe supremo" o "el que tiene poder"; título de los gobernantes otomanos durante el auge del imperio otomano. (pág. 507)

Sunna [sunna] *s.* modelo islámico de vida que se basa en las enseñanzas y vida de Mahoma. (pág. 268)

Sunni [sunni] *s.* rama del islam que reconoce a Alí y a sus descendientes como sucesores legítimos de Mahoma. (pág. 271)

Swahili [suahili] *s.* lengua bantú con influencias árabes que se usa en África oriental y central. (pág. 422)

Taj Mahal *s.* bella tumba en Agra, India, construida por el emperador mogol Shah Jahan para su esposa Mumtaz Mahal. (pág. 519)

Tamil [tamil o tamul] *s.* idioma del sur de India; grupo que habla dicho idioma. (pág. 191)

technology [tecnología] *s.* formas de aplicar conocimientos, herramientas e inventos para satisfacer necesidades. (pág. 8)

Tennis Court Oath [Juramento de la Cancha de Tenis] *s.* promesa hecha por los miembros de la Asamblea Nacional de Francia en 1789 de permanecer reunidos hasta que elaboraran una nueva constitución. (pág. 654)

terraces [cultivos en andenes/cultivos en terrazas] *s.* en Aksum, una técnica nueva para cultivar la tierra, utilizando campos horizontales a manera de peldaños, cortados en laderas o pendientes de montañas, para retener agua y reducir la erosión. (pág. 228)

theocracy [teocracia] *s.* **1.** gobierno en el cual se ve al gobernante como una figura divina (pág. 37). **2.** gobierno controlado por líderes religiosos. (pág. 496)

Theravada *s.* secta del budismo que se adhiere al énfasis original de Buda en la estricta disciplina espiritual. (pág. 193)

Thirty Years' War [Guerra de los Treinta Años] *s.* conflicto europeo de 1618 a 1648 por cuestiones religiosas, territoriales y de poder entre familias reinantes. (pág. 603)

three-field system [sistema de tres campos] *s.* sistema agrícola de la Europa medieval en que las tierras de cultivo se dividían en tres campos de igual tamaño y cada uno se sembraba sucesivamente con un cultivo de invierno, un cultivo de primavera y el tercero se dejaba sin cultivar. (pág. 387)

tithe [diezmo] *s.* pago de una familia a la Iglesia de la décima parte de sus ingresos. (pág. 363)

Tokugawa Shogunate [shogunato Tokugawa] *s.* dinastía de shogúns que gobernó un Japón unificado de 1603 a 1867. (pág. 544)

Torah *s.* cinco primeros libros de la Biblia hebrea, los más sagrados de la tradición judía. (pág. 77)

totem [tótem] *s.* la animale u otro objeto naturale que sirven de símbolo de unidad de clanes u otros grupos. (pág. 445)

tournament [torneo] *s.* justa deportiva entre grupos de caballeros. (pág. 367)

tragedy [tragedia] *s.* obra dramática seria profunda acerca de la caída de un personaje heroico o noble. (pág. 136)

Treaty of Tordesillas [Tratado de Tordesillas] *s.* acuerdo de 1494 entre Portugal y España que estableció que las tierras descubiertas al oeste de una línea imaginaria en el océano Atlántico pertenecerían a España y las tierras al este pertenecerían a Portugal. (pág. 533)

triangular trade [triángulo comercial] *s.* red comercial trasatlántica que transportaba esclavos y productos entre África, Inglaterra, Europa continental, el Caribe y las colonias de Norteamérica. (pág. 568)

tribune [tribuno] *s.* en la antigua Roma, funcionario elegido por los plebeyos para proteger sus derechos. (pág. 156)

tribute [tributo] *s.* pago de una potencia más débil a una potencia más fuerte para obtener una garantía de paz y seguridad. (pág. 82)

Triple Alliance [Triple Alianza] *s.* asociación de las ciudades Estado de Tenochtitlan, Texcoco y Tlacopan, que dio origen al imperio azteca. (pág. 454)

triumvirate [triunvirato] *s.* en la Roma antigua, grupo de tres líderes que compartían el control del gobierno. (pág. 161)

Trojan War [Guerra de Troya] *s.* guerra, aproximadamente en 1200 a.C., en que un ejército al mando de reyes micénicos atacó la ciudad comercial independiente de Troya, ubicada en Anatolia. (pág. 125)

troubadour [trovador] *s.* poeta y músico medieval que viajaba de un lugar a otro para divertir con sus cantos de amor cortesano. (pág. 367)

tyrant [tirano] *s.* en la antigua Grecia, individuo poderoso que ganaba el control del gobierno de una ciudad Estado apelando al apoyo de los pobres. (pág. 127)

Umayyads [omeyas] *s.* dinastía que gobernó el imperio musulmán del 661 al 750 d.C. y después estableció un reino en al-Andalus. (pág. 271)

utopia [Utopía] *s.* tierra imaginaria descrita por Tomás Moro en su libro del mismo nombre; lugar ideal. (pág. 482)

vassal [vasallo] *s.* en la Europa feudal, persona que recibía un dominio (tierras) de un señor a cambio de su promesa de lealtad y servicios. (pág. 360)

Vedas *s.* cuatro colecciones de escritos sagrados secretos, realizados durante la etapa temprana del asentamiento ario en India. (pág. 63)

vernacular *s.* lenguaje común y corriente de la gente de una región o país. (págs. 391, 475)

Vishnu [Visnú] *s.* dios hindú considerado responsable de conservar al mundo. (pág. 194)

vizier [visir] *s.* primer ministro de un reino o imperio musulmán. (pág. 315)

War of the Spanish Succession [Guerra de Sucesión Española] *s.* conflicto de 1701 a 1713 en que varios Estados europeos lucharon para impedir que la familia Borbón controlara a España, como a Francia. (pág. 601)

westernization [occidentalización] *s.* adopción de las instituciones sociales, políticas o económicas del Occidente, especialmente de Europa o Estados Unidos. (pág. 610)

yin and yang [yin y yang] *s.* en China, dos poderes que gobiernan los ritmos naturales de la vida; el yang representa las cualidades masculinas en el universo y el yin las femeninas. (pág. 107)

Yoruba [yoruba] *s.* pueblo del África occidental que formó varios reinos en lo que hoy es Benin y el sur de Nigeria. (pág. 418)

Zapotec [zapoteca] *s.* civilización mesoamericana centrada en el valle de Oaxaca de lo que hoy es México. (pág. 242)

ziggurat [zigurat] *s.* estructura de gradas en forma de pirámide, que formaba parte de un templo sumerio. (pág. 23)

Index

An *i* preceding an italic page reference indicates that there is an illustration, and usually text information as well, on that page. An *m* or a *c* preceding an italic page reference indicates a map or chart, as well as text information on that page.

A

Abbasid dynasty, 271–272, 273
Abbas the Great (Safavid Shah), 514–515
Aborigines, *i13*
absolute monarchs, 594–595, *c618. See also* monarchy.
absolute ruler, 161, 595
absolutism, 594–595, *c594*
Abraham, 77–78
Abu-Bakr (caliph), 269
acropolis, 127
Adena and Hopewell, 443
Adolphus, Gustavus, 603–604
Adulis, 226–227, 229
Aegean Sea, 72, *m72*
Aeschylus, 136
Aeneid **(Virgil),** 179
Africa, *m211. See also* East Africa; North Africa; South Africa; West Africa.
  age-set system, 410
  Christianity in, 227–228
  civilizations of, 210–229, *c230*
  comparative size of, 213, *m231*
  cultural developments of, 224
  desertification of, 217
  early art of, *i216, i217*
  early farming in, 16, 215
  economies of, 219, 413, 422
  empires of, 413–417, *m414,* 425–427, *c428*
  family organization, 216, 410
  geographic contrasts, 213–215, *m214*
  griots, 216
  human origins in, 7–11, *m10*
  hunter-gatherers, *i212,* 224, 409, *c411, m411*
  lineage, 410
  maps
    800–1500, *m407*
    East African Trade, *m423*
    West African Empires, 1000–1500, *m414*
    Western Africa, 2003, *m429*
  Muslim states, 410–412
  nomads, 215, 222
  political developments in, 216
  Portuguese in, 424, 427, 530, 532
  religions in, 216, 229, 410, 415
  role of slavery in, 566
  Sahara, 213, *i214,* 215
  Sahel, 213, *i214*
  societies of, 409–410, *m411, c428*
  stateless societies, 215, 410, *c410, c411, m411*
  trade in, 226, *i408,* 413–414
  vegetation regions, 213–215, *m214*
  weaving in, 422
afterlife. *See* burial rites.
Age of Faith, 379–386
Age of Reason, 629–635

Agricultural Revolution, 15, *c17*
agriculture. *See also* farming.
  in Africa, 16, 215, 222–223
  in the Americas, 16, 238–239
  in ancient China, 16, 50–51, 109
  beginnings, *c3,* 14–18, *m17*
  crops, 18, 571
  in Egypt, 35, 89
  as factor in social change, 18, *c239*
  of Han Dynasty, 204
  influence of Columbian Exchange on, 571, *i572*
  in Japan, 339
  Maya, 447
  revolution in, 15, *c17*
  in Roman Empire, 163, 173
  in Russia, 610
  slash-and-burn, 15, 222
Ahhotep (Egyptian queen), 89
Ainu people, 236
Akbar, 517–518, *i518*
Akkad, 33
Aksum, 225–229, *m226*
Alexander the Great, 139, 143–145, *i143*
  cultural influence of, 145, 146–149
  empire of, *c87, c121,* 143–145, *m144, c145*
Alexander II (Russian czar), 691
Alexander III (Russian czar), 691
Alexandria, 143, 146–148, *i262*
Alfred the Great, 393
algebra. *See* mathematics.
Allah, 264–268
Almohad dynasty, 412
Almoravid dynasty, 411–412
alphabet
  ancient and modern, *c74*
  Cyrillic, 306, *i306*
  Greek, 40, *c74*
  Phoenician, 74, *c74, i76, i116*
"America." *See* Americas, the; United States.
American Revolution, 640–645, *c706*
  causes of, 640–641
  effects of, 641–645
  Enlightenment, role of, 641–642, *c643*
  French influence on, 642, *c643*
Americas, the, *m233, c250. See also* Aztec civilization; Incan civilization; Maya civilization; North America.
  African influence on, 570
  agriculture's effect on, 238–239, *c239*
  ancient civilizations of, 20, *m233,* 240–251, *m241, m247, m251*
  astronomy in, 448
  colonization of, 554–558
  Columbian Exchange, 571–573, *i572*
  early Mesoamerican societies, 240–244

  early South American societies, 20
  empires in, 446–449, 459–453
  European exploration of, 553–558, *m555,* 561–563
  maps
    800 B.C. to A.D. 1535, *m439*
    Europeans in, *m564*
Amina (Zazzau queen), 418, *i418*
Amorites, 33
amphorae, *i75*
Anabaptists, 496
Analects **(Confucius),** 105, *i295*
Anasazi, 443
Anastasia, 608–609
Anatolia, *c58,* 62
Ancient World, *m59*
al-Andalus, 271–272
Andean civilizations
  Chavín period, *c59,* 246–247, *m247*
  headhunters, *i247*
  Moche culture, 247, 249
  Nazca culture, 247, *i248*
  religion, 246–249, *i248*
Andhra dynasty, 191
Angkor, 345
Angkor Wat, 70, 345, *i345*
Anglican Church, 494
Anglo-Saxons, 393–394
animals
  in agriculture, 21
  in ancient China, 52
  camels, *i433*
  domestication of, 16, 18, 46, 215
  in Egypt, 43
  horse, 364, 387
  importance to nomads of, 331
  in Indus Valley civilization, 48
  mammoth, *i234,* 235–236
  in Minoan civilization, 73, *i73*
  in prehistoric North America, 234–237, *i238*
  Punic War elephants, 158
  symbols of warriors, 454
animism, 216, 415
Annals **(Tacitus),** 181
annul, 492
anthropologists, 5–6, *i7,* 221
apostles, 168, *i169*
aqueducts, 47, 181, *i181*
Aquinas, Thomas, 392, *i392*
Arabian Peninsula, *m261,* 263
Arab scholars, 391
arch, 181
archaeological dig, 5, 16, 42, 167
archaeological evidence
  of Africa, *i426*
  of ancient China, 52
  of ancient Egypt, 42

of ancient Rome, 166–167, *i167*
of Aryan culture, 63
of Assyrian empire, 96
of Aztec civilization, *i457*
as clue to prehistory, 5
of Djenné-Djeno, 219, *i219*, *m219*
of Great Zimbabwe, *i426*
of Inca civilization, *i464–465*
of Indus civilization, *i27*, 46
at Jarmo, 16
of Maya society, 446, *i450*
of migration to the Americas, 235–237, *i237*
of Minoan culture, 72
at Monte Verde, 236, *i237*, *m237*
of Olmec culture, 240, *i244*
of Trojan War, 125
of Ur, 22–23
archaeologists, 5, 7–11, *m11*, 16, 18, 22
in the Americas, 236
in China, 52
archaeology, 5, 25
Archimedes, 148
architecture
Akbar period of, 518
Aksumite, *i228*
in Alexandria, 146–147, *i262*
in ancient Egypt, 37–38, *i39*, *i43*, 90–91, *i91*
of Angkor Wat, 345, *i345*
baroque, 637
Buddhist, *i198*
castle, *i366*, 367
cathedral, 380, *i381*
Chaldean, 98
church, 380, *i381*
Etruscan influence on Roman, 156
Gothic style, 380, *i381*
of government, *i582*
of Great Zimbabwe, *i426*
Greek, 135–136, 140, *i141*
Hindu, *i199*
Maya, 446–447, *i450–451*
Mesoamerican, 241, *i242*
Mughal Empire, 518–519, *i520*, *i522*
Muslim, *i266*, 276–278, *i276*, *i278*
neoclassical, 637
Parthenon, 135–136, *i141*
Persian, *i100*
pyramid, *i1*, 37–38, *i39*, *i92*, 444
Roman, 156, *i156*, 165, *i166–167*, 181, *i182*
Romanesque, 380
Sumerian, 22–23, 31, 32
Ziggurat, *i22*, 23, 31, 98
Argentina
independence of, 683
Aristarchus, 147
aristocracy, 127, *c128*
Aristophanes, 136
Aristotle, 139, *i139*, 151, 278–279, 623
arithmetic, 32
armor
Assyrian, 95
Mongol, *i332*
samurai, *i342*
art. *See also* drama; painting; propaganda; sculpture.
African, 15, *i216*, *i217*, *i420–421*
Akkadian, *i26*

Andean, 246–247, *i248*, 249
Assyrian, *i97*
Australian, *i13*, 15
Buddhist, *i198*
Buddhist influence on, 193
Catholic, 488, *i499*
cave painting, *i12–13*, 14
Chaldean, 98
Chavín, 246
Chinese, *i53*, *i209*, 326, *i326*
Christian, *i227*, *i286*, *i312–313*
civic duty to, 136
classical, 136, 178–179
Dutch, 593, *i593*
Egyptian, *i39*, *i42*, *i90*
Enlightenment values in, 637
Flemish, 481, *i481*
French, 701, *i703*
during French Revolution, *i665*
Greek (ancient), 136, *i140–141*
Hindu, *i199*
Hittite, *i58*, *i63*
impressionism in, 701
Islamic beliefs in, *i267*, *i277*
jewelry, 216
magical qualities of, *i12*
Meroë, *i94*
Minoan, 72, *i73*
mosaic, *i165*, 178
Muslim, 276, *i277*
nationalism and, 698
Nok, *i217*
Northern Renaissance, 481, *i481*
Nubian, *i87*, *i92–93*
Olmec, *i58*, 240–241, 243, *i244*
oracle bones, *i53*
Ottoman Empire, 511
Paleolithic, 11, *i12–13*
Persian, *i100*, *i102*
perspective, 474, *i474*
Phoenician, 74
photography, 700, *i700*
potter's wheel, 21
pottery, 72, *i140*
prehistoric, 11, *i12–13*, 14–15
realism in, 700
religious, *i312–313*
religious beliefs in, *i32*, *i39*
Renaissance, *i470*, 474–475, *i478–479*
revolution in, 698–703
Roman, *i165*, *i167*, 178–179
Romantic movement, 698
Russian, *i312–313*
Safavid Empire, 515, *i515*
Shang Dynasty, *i53*, *i117*
Spanish, 591, *i591*
Spartan, 131
stone age, 11, *i12–13*
Sumerian, *i3*, *i32*
West African, *i418–421*
Arthasastra **(Kautilya),** 189
artifacts, 5, 52, *i237*, *i581*
artisans, 20, 388
Aryans, 66
caste system, 63–64, *i64*
influence on Indian culture, 64–65, 193
invasions of India, *c58*, 63, *m65*
Vedas, 63
Ashurbanipal (Assyrian king), 96–97

Asia, *m321*
Askia Muhammad (Muslim ruler of Songhai), 417
Asoka, 190–191, 209
assimilation, 205
Assyria, 82, 95
Nineveh, 96–97
Assyrian empire, *c87*, 95–97, *m96*, *c121*
culture, 34, 96
military power, 82, 94, 95–97, *i97*
astrolabe, *i275*, *i433*, 530
astrology, 98
astronomy
Aristarchus, 147, *c147*
Chaldean, 98
Daoist effect on, 106
Egyptian, 40–41
of Hellenistic period, 147, *i147*
Indian, 195
Maya, 448
Muslim, 274, *i275*, 278
Ptolemy, 147, *c147*, 623
and Scientific Revolution, 624–625
Atahualpa, 556, *i557*
Athena, 126, 136
Athens, 133, 134–138, 142
plague in, 137
war with Sparta, 137–138, *m137*
Atlantic slave trade, 566–570. *See also* slavery; slaves.
Attila the Hun, 176
Augustine, St., 172
Augustus (Roman emperor), 162, *i162*. *See also* Octavian.
Aurangzeb, 520–521
Aurelius, Marcus, 173
australopithecines, *c2*, 7–8, *c8*, *m10*
Austria
Prussian control of, 607, 693
Austria-Hungary, 693
Austro-Hungarian Empire, 693
autocracy, 109
ayllu, 460
Aztec civilization, 452–458
art of, *i457*
Cortés' conquest of, *i552*, 556
cultural developments of, 454–456
fall of, 458, *c458*
political developments of, 454–455
religious beliefs of, 456, *i457*
society, 454–455
trade in, 454–455
Triple Alliance, 454

B

Babur, 516
Babylon, 62, 97–98
hanging gardens of, 98, *i98*
Babylonian captivity, 82, 100
Babylonian empire, 28
Assyrian defeat of, 95
Persian rule of, 82
rebirth of, 97–98
reign of Hammurabi, 33–34

Bacon, Francis, 626
Baghdad, 273–274, 276
balance of power, 672
  in 1800s, 672–673, 697
Balboa, Vasco Núñez de, 554
Balkans
  under Ottoman Empire, 508
Bantu-speaking peoples, 221–224
Ban Zhao, 204, 206
barbarian, 175
barometer, 627
baroque style, 637
barter, 23
Basil, St., 304, *i304*
bas-relief, 178
Bastille, storming of, 654–655,
  i654
Bathsheba, 81
battle
  Agincourt, 402–403
  Austerlitz, 665, *m666*
  Chaldiran, 514
  Crécy, 402–403
  Hastings, 394
  Peninsular, 669
  Poitiers, 402–403
  Tours, 356
  Trafalgar, *m666*, 667
Beccaria, Cesare Bonesana, 632
Bedouins, 263
Beethoven, Ludwig van, 637, 699, *i699*
Benedict (Italian monk), 355, *i355*
Benin, 419, *i420–421*
Berbers, 271, 411. *See also* Almohad
  dynasty; Almoravid dynasty.
Beringia, 235–237, *m237*
Bering Strait, 236
Bhutto, Benazir, *i519*
Bible, 85, 100, *i227. See also* Torah.
  as basis of truth, *i287, c491*
  destruction of Nineveh in, 97
  Gutenberg, 484
  Hebrew, 77, *c80*, 172
  King James, 614
  Philistines of, 77
  Protestant, *c491*
  Roman Catholic, *c491*
Bill of Rights
  English, 617, 619, 709
  United States, 645, *i645*
biological weapons. *See* weapons, of mass
  destruction.
bishop, 171
Bismarck, Otto von, 695–696, *i696*,
  705
Black Death. *See* bubonic plague.
blockade, 668
Boccaccio, Giovanni, 476
Bohemia, 603, 605
Boleyn, Anne, 493, *i493*
Bolívar, Simón, 677, 683, *i683, i684*
Bonaparte, Napoleon. *See* Napoleon I.
Book of the Dead, 38
books
  burning of, 107, 499
  history of making, 203, 484
  Maya, 448, *i448*
  in Middle Ages, *i354*, 355
"Boston Tea Party," 641

Bourbon dynasty, 596–597, 601
bourgeoisie, 651
boyars, 608–609
Boyle, Robert, 628
Brahma, 67, 194
Brahmin, 63, *i64*, 67
Braidwood, Robert, 16
Brazil
  independence of, 675, 686
  indians of, 566
  Portuguese in, 557, 567
Britain
  American colonies of, 562–565,
    640–641
  Anglo-Saxons, 393–394
  colonies of, 562–565, 640
  development of, *c397*
  East India Company, 535
  English Civil War, 615, *m616, c706*
  Hundred Years War, 401–403
  influence in East Asia, 535
  invasions, 393
  Magna Carta, 394–395, *i395*
  North American colonies of, 562–563,
    640
  Parliament, 395, 492–493, 614–617
  revolutions in, 615–616, *c706*
  role in slave trade, 567, 601
  territory of, 394, 601–602
bronze, *c3, i3*, 22
  first use of, 21, 32
  sculpture, *i420–421*
  in Shang dynasty, 52, *i117*
Bronze Age, 21
Bruegel, Pieter, 481, *i481*
Brutus, Marcus, 162
bubonic plague, 399–401
  in Byzantine Empire, 304
  death toll, *c400*, 401
  economic effect of, 401
  effects of, 401
Buddha, 68–69, *i69*, 193
Buddhism, 68–71, *c84, i284–285, c296*
  central ideas of, 68–69, *c84*
  enlightenment, 68
  historical origins of, 68
  in India, 70–71, 190–191
  in Japan, 71, 340, *i547*
  Mahayana, 193
  nirvana, 69, 193
  Siddhartha Gautama, 68, *i68*
  spread of, 70–71, 190, *m197*
  Theravada, 193
  in Vietnam, 346
  in the West, 71
  as world religion, 284–285
  Zen, *i547*
bull leapers of Knossos, *i73*
bureaucracy
  Abbasids, 271–272
  Chinese, 203
  Mauryan, 189
burghers, 391
Burke, Edmund, 662
burial rites
  Egyptian, 38–39, *i39*, 91
  Incan, *i464–465*
  Native American, 444
  Neanderthal, 9

Nubian, 92
  reliquary, *i313*
  Sumerian, 23, *i32*
Bushido, 343
Byzantine Empire, 301–306, 382
  in 1100, *m299*
  Byzantium, 175, 301
  education, 303
  emperors, 302–304
  fall of, 304
  Greek and Roman influence on, 176,
    301–303
  Justinian (emperor), 303–304
  Justinian Code of law, 302
  Muslim defeat of, 270, 304
  Turkish rule in, *i300*, 507

cabinet, 617
Caesar, Julius, 161–162, *i161*
Cahokia, 444
calendar
  Aztec, *i457*
  Egyptian, 40–41
  Incan, 461
  Indian, 195
  Maya, 448
  Muslim, *i275*
  Paleolithic, *i2*
  under Robespierre, 660
  Zapotec, 243
Caligula, *c164, i164*
caliph, 269, 271–272
calligraphy
  Islamic, 276, *i277*
Calvinism, 495–496
  in Germany, *m497*
  in Netherlands, 496, *m497*
Calvin, John, 495–496, *i496*
Cambyses, 100
camel, *i433*
Canaan, 77–78, *m78*, 79, 80, 81
Canada
  Quebec, 561
  trade and, 562
Canby, Thomas, 235–236, *i236*
cannons, 546, 556
canon law, 371
Canopic jars, *i39*
Canossa, 372
Canterbury Tales, The (Chaucer), 375,
  392
Canute (Danish king), 393
Capet, Hugh, 396
Capetian dynasty, 396
capitalism, 573
caravel, 530, *i531*
Caribbean
  colonization of, 563
Carolingian dynasty, 356–357
  fall of, 357
Carthage, *c59*, 74, 76, 158–159
Cartier, Jacques, 561
Cassius, Gaius, 162
caste system, 69. *See also* social classes.
  of India, 63–64, 67
Castiglione, Baldassare, 473, *i473*
cast iron, 55

castles, *i366*, 367
Catal Huyuk, 18
catapult, *i366*
cataract, 36
cathedrals, 380, *i381*
Catherine the Great (Russian empress),
    638–639, *i639*
Catholicism. *See also* Inquisition.
    in Spanish Empire, 589, 591
    in Spanish Netherlands, 592–593
Catholic League, 603
Catholic Reformation, 498–499
Caucasus Mountains, 61
caveman. *See* Neanderthal.
cave painting, *i12–13*, 14
Cavour, Camillo di, 694
censorship
    of Roman Catholic Church, 490
    Voltaire on, 630
Central America. *See also* Mesoamerican
    civilizations; Mexico.
    United Provinces of, 686
centralized government, 200, 397
Cervantes, Miguel de, 591–592
Ceylon. *See* Sri Lanka.
Chaldeans, 97–98, 99
Chaldiran, Battle of, 514
Champlain, Samuel de, 561
Champollion, Jean François, 40
Chandra Gupta (Indian king),
    191–192
Chandra Gupta II (Indian emperor),
    191–192
Chandragupta Maurya (Indian emperor),
    c121, 189–190
Chang Jiang. *See* Yangtze River.
chariot(s), 52, 61, 89
    charioteers, 63
    four-horse, 98
    in Hittite empire, 63, *i63*
    racing in Rome, 165
    two-wheeled, 90
Charlemagne (Holy Roman emperor),
    356–357, *i357*
    cultural revival, 357
    division of kingdom by Treaty of Verdun,
    357
    empire of, 356, *m356*
    Verdun, 357
Charles I (English king), 614–615
Charles II (English king), 616
Charles V (Holy Roman emperor), 490,
    492, 589
Charles VII (French king), 403
Charles X (French king), 690
Chartres Cathedral, 380, *i381*
Chaucer, Geoffrey, 375, 392
Chavín culture, *c59*, 246–247
checks and balances, 631, 645. *See also*
    political ideas.
chemistry, 628
Chichén Itzá, 446–447
children
    in African culture, 216
    in Confucian thought, 104
    in Crusades, 384
    in Han dynasty, 201
    slavery of, *i97*, 164
Children's Crusade, 384

China, *m51, m187. See also* names of
    dynasties.
    acupuncture, *i325*
    agriculture, 50, 204
    bureaucracy, 203
    coins, *i55*
    cultural developments, 52, 541
    dynastic cycle in, *c54*
    early cities, 52
    early farming, 16
    ethical systems, 105–107, *c106*
    foot-binding, 327
    Forbidden City, *i538*
    geography of, 50–51, *m51*
    Great Wall of, *i108*, 109, 323
    Han dynasty, 109, 200–207, *c208*,
    252–257
    inventions, 204, *i322*, 325, *i328–329*
    Mongol rule, 336–338
    peasants, 323
    political developments, 203, 323–324
    population, *c540*
    Qin dynasty, 107–109, *m108*, 200
    religious beliefs, 54, 71
    river dynasties of, 51–52, *i113*
    Sima Qian ("Grand Historian"), 202,
    205
    social changes, 327
    social values of ancient China, *c202*
    Wudi ("Martial Emperor"), 201–202
Chinese Heritage, The, 54
Chinese medicine, *i325*
chivalry
    age of, 365, 367–368
    decline of, 402–403
Christian humanists, 482
Christianity, 168–172, *i286–287, c296.*
See also church; Crusades; Roman Catholic
    Church.
    in Aksum, 227–228, *i227*
    under Constantine, 171–172
    and Enlightenment values, 634
    Hagia Sophia and, 303
    heresy, 172, 384
    in Japan, 546
    Jesus, 168–169, *i169*
    politics and spread of, 171, 354
    rise of, 168–172
    in Roman Empire, 169–171, 172
    schism, 399
    and science, 625
    sects, 490, 494–496
    spread of, 169–171, *m171*, 354, 530
    unifying force of, 170, 370–371
    Viking conversion to, 359
    widespread appeal of, 170
    as world religion, 286–287
Christians
    burial rites of, 169
    martyrs, 170
    missionaries, 354, 499, 546
    in Muslim culture, 268
    Roman persecution of, 170–171
church. *See also* Roman Catholic Church.
    division of, 304, *c305*
    Eastern Orthodox, 304–305, *c305*
    Great Schism, 399
    Hagia Sophia, 303
    lay investiture, 372

    Orthodox, 306
    reform, 379–380, 398
    Roman Catholic, 305–306, *c305*
    Russian Orthodox, *c305, i313*, 610
    tithes, 363, 379
citadel, 46
cities
    and absolute monarchy, 595
    of ancient China, 52
    definition of, 20
    early Mesoamerican, 242, *i242*
    in early Middle Ages, 353
    Forbidden, *i538*
    growth of, 19
    Muslim, 273–274
    planned, 46, 243, 455
    rise of, 20, *c24*
    Sumerian, *c3*, 20, 31
    Ur, *c3*, 19–22
citizens
    in ancient Greece, 127–128,
    134–135
    in ancient Rome, 156–157, *c157*, 158
    in Inca civilization, 461
    in limited democracy, 128
    rights and responsibilities, 135
    role in democracy, 128, 134, *c134*
    in United States, *c134*
city-state(s)
    African, 422–424
    Athens as, 133, 134–138, 142
    Carthage as, 76
    East African, 422–424
    Greek, *i87, c121, m121*, 127–133
    Hausa, 417–418
    Kilwa, 422, 424
    Maya, 446–447
    Northern Italian, *c578*
    Phoenician, 73
    Sparta as, 129, 131
    Sumerian, *c3*, 30–31
    Thebes as, 142
civic duty. *See* citizens.
civilization(s)
    American (1200 B.C. to A.D. 700),
    m233
    African, *c230*, 422–427
    agriculture's effect on, 18, 19
    ancient, 20–23, *c113*
    characteristics of, 20–21, *c21, c114*
    Confucian influence on, 105, 203
    of Indus Valley, *c27*, 44–49, *i112*
    prehistory to 2500 B.C., 5–23
    rise of, *i112–113*
    of river valleys (3500–500 B.C.),
    c26–27, c56
    in Ur, 22–23, 31
civil servants, 203
civil service, 203
    in Chinese empires, 203
    in Korea, 347
    in Tang dynasty, 324
civil war(s)
    English, 615, *m616*
    Incan, 463
    in Japan, 542
    Muslim, 270–271
    Roman, 161, 162
    Saint Domingue, 665, 682

clan, 331
Clare, 380
classical ages
    characteristics of, 252
    cultural achievements of, c254–255
    influence of, i252–253
    legacy of, 256–257, i256
    territory controlled by societies of, m253
    time line, c252–253
classical art, 136, 178–179
Cleisthenes, 128, 135
Cleopatra, 162
clergy, 370
climate
    influence on Greek life of, 124
    regions, world, m57
clock
    Chinese, 325, c328
    mechanical, c328
clothing, i581
Clovis culture, 236, i237, m237
Clovis (Germanic king), 354, 356
Cluny, 379
Code of Hammurabi. See Hammurabi's Code.
codex, 448, i448
coins
    Aksumite, 228
    first, 55, i55
    Persian, 101
    Roman, 163, 173, 196
Colbert, Jean Baptiste, 598–599
colonialism. See also colonies.
    British, 562–564
    and capitalism, 573
    effects of, 573–575
    of France, 561–562, 682
    impact on native Americans of, c556
    in Latin America, 554–558, 675
    of Netherlands, 563
    of Portugal, 427, 557
    resistance to, 559
    and slavery, 559, 566–570
    of Spain, 681–682
colonies, 554. See also colonialism.
    British, 562–563, 565, 640
    Dutch, 563–564
    French, 561–562, 564, 598, 682
    revolt in French, 682
Colonna, Vittoria, 477
Colosseum, 165, 181, i182
Colossus of Rhodes, 149
Columbian Exchange, 571–573, i572
    effect on food of, i572
Columbus, Christopher, 553–554, i554
    legacy of, 560
    native resistance to, 449
comedy, 136, i141
Commercial Revolution, 389–390, c390
common law, 394
compass
    magnetic, i322, 325, i328–329, i433
concordat, 664
Concordat of Worms, 372
Confucianism, i294–295, c296
    and agriculture, 204

and commerce, 204
    in China, 104–105, 203
    five relationships, 104
    and government, 105, 203
    in Korea, 346
    Legalists, 106–107, c106
    social order, 104
    values of, 104, c106
    as world ethical system, 294–295
    yin and yang, 107, i107, 109
Confucius, 104–105, i105, 115
    Analects, 105, i295
Congo, 409
Congress of Vienna, 672–675
conquistadors, 554–558
Conservatives, 657, 687, 690
Constantine (Roman emperor), 171–172, 174–175
    conversion of, 171
Constantinople, m302
    as capital, 175, 176, 301–304
    fall of, 304, 383, 385
    Hagia Sophia, 303
    Hippodrome, 303
    Nika Rebellion, 303
    Ottoman defeat of, 304, 508–509, i509
    Turkish threat to, 304, 315
constitution
    first, 615
    United States, c643, 644–645, 647
constitutional monarchy, 617, 657. See also monarchy.
consuls, 157
Continental System, 668
convents, 354
Copernicus, Nicolaus, 624–625
Coronado, Francisco Vásquez de, 558, i558
Cortés, Hernando, 554, 556
Council of Trent, 499
Counter Reformation. See Reformation, Catholic; Roman Catholic Church.
coup, 664
coup d'état, 664
covenant, 78
    Hebrew, 78–80
Creoles, 674–675, 681–682, c681
Crete, 72, m72
criminal justice, 632
Cro-Magnon, c3, i3, 9–10, c9
Cromwell, Oliver, 615–616
cross
    as Christian symbol, 171, i382
crossbow, 402
Crusades, 382–386, m383
    Children's, 383–384
    economic impact of, 385
    First Crusade, 382
    in the Middle Ages, 382–386, m383
    Muslim counterattacks, 316, 383
    political impact of, 385
    Second Crusade, 382
    in Seljuk Empire, 316, 383
    social impact of, i378, 385
    Spanish, 384
    Third Crusade, 383
Cry of Dolores. See Grito de Dolores.

cultural blending, 63, 512–513, c513. See also global culture.
    by Alexander the Great, 146
    in Mughal India, i522–523
    in Muslim Empire, 272, 273
    of Nubia and Egypt, 92–93, i92–93
    in Safavid Empire, 514–515
cultural diffusion, 31
culture(s), 5–6. See also Africa; Americas, the; China; Hellenistic Culture; India; Japan; Roman Empire.
    under Alexander the Great, 145, 146
    components of, c6
    means of expanding, 76
    and nationalism, 687, c688
cuneiform, 20, i21, 32, 40
cybercafés, i637
cyclops, i126
Cyrillic alphabet. See alphabet, Cyrillic.
Cyrus the Great (Persian king), 82, 99–100, 103
czar(s). See individual names of czars.

D

da Gama, Vasco, 532–533
daimyo, 542–546
Dai Viet, 346
Dante Alighieri, 392
Danton, Georges, 660–661, i661
Dao De Jing (Laozi), 105–106
Daoism, 105–106, c106
    Laozi, 105–106, 105
    in Song Dynasty, 326
Darius (Persian king), 100–101, 132
Darius III (Persian king), 143–144
David (Israeli king), 81
da Vinci, Leonardo, i286–287, 475, i475
death rituals. See burial rites.
Deborah (Hebrew judge), 80
Decameron (Boccaccio), 476
Deccan Plateau, 44
decimal system, 195
Declaration of Independence, 641–642
    Locke's influence on, 630, 642
Declaration of Rights of Man, 656
Delhi, 516
Delhi Sultanate, 516
Delian League, 133, 135
delta, 36
democracy, c180. See also democratic reforms; government, democratic and republican.
    in ancient Greece, 128, 134–135, c134
    Congress of Vienna and, 672
    and French Revolution, 652, 654, 656
    in United States, 617, c643
    Western, c180
democratic reforms
    in ancient Greece, 128, 135
    in ancient Rome, 156–157
    in England, 394–395, 617
    of French Revolution, 654, 656
    in Middle Ages, 394–397
Demosthenes, 142
de Pizan, Christine, 482, i482

Descartes, René, 626
desertification, 217
d'Este, Isabella, 473, *i473*
devshirme, 510
dharma, 70
Dias, Bartolomeu, 532
Diaspora, 170
dictators. *See also* individual names of dictators.
  in France, 664–667
  in Roman Republic, 157
Diderot, Denis, 636
Diocletian, 174–175
disease. *See also* bubonic plague.
  in Central Mexico, impact of, *c556*
  in Columbian Exchange, 571–573, *i573*
  inoculation against, 628
  in North America, 556, *c556*, 565, 571–573
  smallpox, 556, *i560*, 565, 571, 573, 628
Divine Comedy, The (Dante), 392
divine right, 594
Djenné-Djeno, 219, *i219*, *m219*
Dnieper River, 307, *m308*, 310
Dome of the Rock, *i266*
domestication, 16, 18, 46, 215
Domitian, *c164*
Don Quixote de la Mancha (Cervantes), 591–592
Dorians, 125
drama. *See also* art.
  Chinese, 541
  Greek, 136, *i141*
  Indian, 194, *i195*
  Japanese, 544, *i545*
Duke of Shao, 54
Dürer, Albrecht, 481
Dutch. *See also* Netherlands.
  colonies, 563–564
  East India Company, 534, 594
  in Southeast Asia, 534–535
dye, 74, *i75*
dynastic cycle, 54, *c54*
dynasties, 31, 90. *See also* empire(s).
  Abbasid, 271–272, 273
  Almohad, 412
  Almoravid, 411–412
  Bourbon, 596–597, 601
  Capetian, 396
  Carolingian, 356–357
  of China, *c338*
  Egyptian, 37, 90–91
  Fatimid, 272
  Han, 200–207, 252–257
  Korean, 346–347
  Ming, 536–539
  Muslim, 269–272
  Qin, *c87*, 107–109, *m108*, 200
  Qing, 539
  Romanov, 609
  Shang, 52
  Song, 324–327
  Tang, 323–327
  Umayyad, 271–272
  Xia, 51
  Zhou, *c27*, 54–55, 104, *c121*

Earth, planet, *c147*
  time line, *i9*
East Africa, 422–425. *See also* Africa.
  cultural blending in, 422
  human origins in, 7–8, *m10*, 11
  Islamic influences on, 424–425
  slavery in, 425
  trade in, 422, *m423*
East Asia, *m321*. *See also* empire(s).
Eastern Europe
  invasion by Vikings of, *m308*
Eastern Orthodox Church, 304–305, *c305*
economics
  capitalism, 573
  effects of migration on, 221
  in Han Dynasty, 204–205, *m204–205*
  inflation, 573, 592
  of manorialism, 360, 362–363
  in Middle Ages, 360, 362–363
economy. *See also* economics.
edict, 190
Edict of Milan, 171
Edict of Nantes, 596, 599
Edict of Worms, 490
education
  in Byzantium, 303
  under Charlemagne, 357
  in czarist Russia, 610–611
  in democracy, 128
  of girls, 129
  lycées, 664
  in Middle Ages, 391
  Spartan, 131
  Sumerian, 32
  in Tang Dynasty, 324, 327
Edward I (English king), 395, 405
Edward III (English king), 401
Edward VI (English king), 493
Efe, 409
Egypt, 35–41
  ancient, *c26*, 35–41, *c86*, 89–91, *i112*
  Cleopatra, 162
  cosmetics, *i43*
  culture of, 38
  divorce in, 40
  dynasties of, 37, 90–91
  geography of, 35, *m36*, *m91*
  Hebrew migration from, 89
  hieroglyphics, 40, *i40*
  invasion of ancient, 41, 89, 91
  inventions, 40–41
  kingdoms of, *c26*, 37, 90
  mummification, 38–39, *i39*
  Narmer, 37
  Nile River, importance of, 16, 35
  under Ottoman rule, 509
  pets, 43
  pharaohs of, 37, 39, 41, 90–91
  pyramids, *i1*, 37–38, *i39*
  religion of, 38–39
  social classes in, 40
Eightfold Path, 193
Eleanor of Aquitaine, 368, 394, *i394*
Elizabeth I (British queen), 483, 493–494, *i494*
Elizabethan Age
  Renaissance in England, 483, *i486–487*
El Salvador, 686

émigrés, 658
emperor(s). *See also* individual names of rulers.
  Byzantine, 301–304
  Chinese, 107, 109, 200–203, 539–541
  Holy Roman, 370–373, *m372*
  Japanese, 340
  Roman, *c164*
empire(s), 33
  Akkadian, 33
  of Alexander the Great, *c87*, *c121*, 143–145, *m144*, *c145*
  ancient, *m87*, 89–109
  Assyrian, *c87*, 95–97, *m96*, *c121*
  Aztec, 453–458, 556
  Babylonian, *c27*, 28
  builders of first, 32–33, *c110*
  Byzantine, 301–304
  characteristics of, 33, 90, *c110*
  Chinese, 104–109, 200–207, 323–329, 536–541
  comparison of, *c319*, *c525*
  East Asian, 330–343
  Egyptian, 37–38, 89–91
  First Age of Empires, 89–109
  French, 667
  of Ghana, 413–415, *m414*
  Greek, 142–149
  Gupta, 191–192, *c208*, 252–255
  Han, 200–207
  Hittite, 62–63
  Holy Roman, 371–373, 605
  Incan, 459–465
  Indian, 189–192, 516–521
  Khmer (Cambodia), 345
  Kush, *c87*, 92–94, *m93*
  Malian, 415–417, *m414*
  Mauryan, *c121*, 189–191, *m191*, *c208*
  Mongol, 309, *m309*, 332–334, *m334*, 335–338
  Mughal, 516–523
  Muslim, 269–272
  Mutapa, 427
  Napoleonic, *m649*, 665–671
  nationalism's effect on, 687, *c688*
  Nubian, *c87*, 92–94
  Ottoman, 507–511, 605
  Persian, *c87*, 99–103, *m101*, 143
  population of, *c319*
  Qin, *c87*, 107–109, *m108*, 200
  Roman, 160–165, 173–177, 252–257
  Russian, 693
  Safavid, 512–515, *m514*
  Seljuk, 314–316
  Songhai, *m414*, 417
  southern African, 425–427
  Spanish, 589–593
  trading, 413–416
  Turkish, 314–317
  West African, 413–417, *m414*
  Zhou, *c27*, 104, *c121*
empress. *See* individual names.
encomienda, 557, 559
Encyclopedia, 636
England. *See* Britain.
English Civil War. *See* civil war(s), Britain.
English language, 181
enlightened despot, 638
enlightenment, 68

Index

Enlightenment, 623–645
    and American Revolution, 641–642,
       c643
    architecture of, *i600*, 637
    centers of, *m621*, 630, 636
    and French Revolution, 652
    impact of, 633–634, 636–639
    literature of, 633, 636, 637
    music of, 637
    Paris during, 630, 636
    political ideas of, 629–632, *c632*
    and revolution, *c646*, *m684*
    values in, 639–635
    women's contributions to, 633, 636
environmental influences. *See also* flood-
    ing.
    in Africa, 213–216, 425
    on agricultural revolution, 15, *c17*
    in ancient China, 50–51, 207
    in ancient Egypt, 35–36, 89
    in ancient Greece, 123–124
    in ancient Sumer, 29
    in ancient trade, 76
    on Andean cultures, 246
    in Assyrian culture, 95
    and decline of Aksum, 229
    and decline of Mughal Empire, 521
    of disease, 556
    and end of Minoan culture, 73
    on fall of Roman Empire, 173
    in Han dynasty, *m204–205*, 207
    in India, 44–45, 195
    in Indus Valley, 45
    and isolationism, 339
    on Japan, 339
    in Kush, 92, 94
    in Mesopotamia, 29–30
    on migrations, 215, 220, *c221*, 223
    in native North America, 441, 443
    in North American colonies, 562–563
    in Olmec civilization, 240–241
    on Peloponnesian War, 137
    of the plague, 401
    on the Renaissance, 471
    on Southeast Asia, 344
    of the tsetse fly, 213, *i214*, 215
    on West African empires, 413, 415
    on Zapotec society, 242
Epic of Gilgamesh, 32, 83, 96
epics, 125–126, 179, *i179*, 367, *i367*
Epicurianism, 149
Epicurus, 149
epidemics. *See also* bubonic plague;
    influenza; smallpox.
Erasmus, Desiderius, 482
Eratosthenes, 147
Ericson, Leif, 359
Esfahan, 514
estates (French social classes), 397,
    651–652, *c652*
Estates-General, 397, 653–654
Este, Isabella d', 473, *i473*
ethical monotheism, 80
Ethiopia
    Christianity in, 228
    Haile Selassie, 225
    human origins in, *m10*
Ethiopian Orthodox Church, *i287*
Etruscans, 155–156

Euclid, 147–148
Euphrates River, 22, 29
Euripides, 136
Europe. *See also* European exploration;
    Western Europe.
    in the East, *m534*
    invasions in, *m359*
    and Japan, 545–547
    maps
        500, *m351*
        1500, *m469*
        1650, *m587*
        1805–1813, war in, *m666*
        1810/1817, *m674*
        1848, revolutions in, *m679*
        in the Middle Ages, *m351*, 353–373,
          m377
        post-Thirty Years' War, 604, *m604*
        religions in (1560), *m497*
European exploration, *m527*, *c548*. *See*
    also colonialism.
    of the Americas, *m555*
    causes of, 529–530
    cultural influence of, 558
    effects of, *c556*
    science and technology of, 530,
       i531
excavation, 5, 22, *i22*
excommunication, 306, 371
Exodus, 78
exploration, age of, 529–535, 553–558
extended family, 216
Eyck, Jan van, *i470*, 481
Ezana (Aksumite king), 226–228
Ezekiel, 82

family
    in African culture, 216, 410
    in Confucian thought, 104–105
    extended, 216
    in Germanic society, 354
    in Han dynasty, 206
    lineage system, 410
    matriarchal, 192
    matrilineal, 410
    in native America, 445
    patriarchal, 192
    patrilineal, 410
    and slave trade, 570
farming. *See also* agriculture; Neolithic
    Revolution.
    in the Americas, 16, 238–239, *c239*
    change brought by, 16
    crops, 18, 42
    early development of, 16, 18
    floating gardens, 239, 455
    of Indian empires, 190, 192
    in the Middle Ages, 362, 387
    role of slavery in, 164, 566
    terrace, 228
    three-field system of, 387
Fatimid caliphate, 272
federal system, 644–655
Ferrill, Arther, 177
Fertile Crescent, 29, 34, 88
    in 2500 B.C., *m30*
    Assyrian domination, 96

    Persian empire in, 100–101, *m101*
feudalism, 54. *See also* feudal society.
    Church authority, 363
    cultural effect of, 363
    decline of, 385
    economics, 362–363
    in Europe, *c361*, *i361*
    in Japan, 341, 343, *c361*, *i361*, 542
    manors, 360, 362, *i362*
    Russian, 690–691, *i691*
feudal society. *See also* feudalism.
    knights, 360, 364–365
    samurai, *i342*, 343, 542, *i542*
    women in, 368–369
fief, 360
filial piety, 104, 105
fire, mastery over, 7–8
firearms, 545
First Reich, 697
Five Pillars of Islam, 267, *i275*
flooding
    in the Americas, 240
    benefits of, 29
    in China, 50, 207
    control of, 51
    of Fertile Crescent, 29
    of Huang He, 50, *m51*
    of Indus River Valley, 44–45
    of Nile, 35–36
flood story, 83, *i83*
Florida, 558
Forbidden City, *i538*
forest dwellers, 409, *m411*
Forum, Roman, 156, *i156*
fossil hunters, 5
fossils, 5
Four Noble Truths, *c69*
France, *m677*. *See also* French Revolution.
    absolute monarchy in, 598–602
    in American Revolution, 642, 653
    art of prehistoric, *i13*
    Capetian dynasty, 396
    containment of, 672–673
    democracy in, 397, 654, 656, 690
    development of, *c397*
    as empire, *m649*, 664–667
    during Enlightenment, 630, 636
    Estates-General, 397, 653–654
        First, 397, 651, *c652*
        Second, 397, 651, *c652*
        Third, 651–652, *c652*
    in Hundred Years' War, 401–403
    in Indochina, *m797*
    instability of, 652–653
    Louis XIV of, *i588*, 598–602, *i598*
        debt incurred by, *c602*
    North American colonies of, 561–562,
        564, 641, 682
    reforms and revolution in, 651–661,
        690
    religions in, *m497*
    as republic, 690
    Third Republic, 690
    in Thirty Years' War, 604
    at war, 601, 658, 660
Francis I (French king), 480
Francis of Assisi, St., 380
***Frankenstein* (Shelley),** 699
Franks. *See* Germanic empire.

Index

Frederick I, "Barbarossa" (Holy Roman emperor), 373
Frederick William II, "Frederick the Great" (Prussian king), 606–607, *i606,* 638
French Revolution, *c706. See also* Napoleon I.
    Bastille, storming of, 654–655, *i654*
    causes of, 652–654
    democratic ideals of, 652–653
    effects of, 655–661
    Enlightenment ideas in, 652
    estates, 651–652, *c652,* 654
    Great Fear, 655
    guillotine, *i659,* 660
    influence of American Revolution on, *i644,* 652
    Legislative Assembly, 657–658
    National Assembly, 654, 656
    Old Regime, 651, 658
    opinions on, 662
    reforms of, 656–657
    Reign of Terror, 660–661
    Robespierre, Maximilien, 660–661, *i660, i711*
    social classes before, 651–652, *c652*
    Tennis Court Oath, 654
    war during, 658, 660
friars, 380
funeral rites. *See* burial rites.

Galilei, Galileo, 625, *i625*
Gandhi, Indira, *i519*
Ganges River, 44
Garibaldi, Giuseppe, 694, *i694*
gentry, 327
geocentric theory, 623–624
geographical isolation, 50
geography. *See also* environmental influences.
    of Africa, 213–215, *m214, m429*
    of Egypt, 35–36, *m36*
    influence on Greek life, 123–124
    influence on Indian culture, 197
geometry. *See* mathematics, geometry.
George III (English king), 539, 640
Germanic Empire. *See also* Prussia; reformation.
    Christianity in, 354–357
    Clovis, 354, 356
    Franks, 354–356
Germany. *See also* Prussia; reformation.
    Neanderthals in, 9, *m10*
    Renaissance in, 481–482
    Thirty Years' War in, 603–604
    unification of, 695–697, *m697*
Ghana
    empire of, 413–415, *m414*
    Islamic influences, 415
    Soninke people, 413
ghazi, 507
Gibbon, Edward, 177
"gift of the Nile," 35
glaciers, 236, *i237*
gladiators, 164, 165, *i165, i182*
Glorious Revolution, 616

glyphs. *See also* hieroglyphics.
    Maya, 448
Gobi Desert, 50, *m51*
gold trade, 227, 413
Gospels (New Testament), 169
Gothic, 380, *i381*
Gouges, Olympe de, 656
government, *c180. See also* democracy; political systems.
    of Africa, 216
    of ancient China, 54, 203
    architecture of, *i582*
    aristocracy, 127, *c128*
    of Assyrian empire, 96
    of Athens, 128, 133, 134–135
    under Augustus, 162, *i162*
    beginnings of organized, 30–31
    bureaucracy, 105, 203, *i579*
    centralized, 200, 397
    of China, 105, 200–203
    commonwealth, 615
    constitutional monarchy, 617
    democracy, 128, *c128,* 157, *c180*
    democratic, 128
    descriptions of, 583
    dictators in ancient Rome, 157
    of Egypt, *c26,* 37, 41, 89–91
    Incan, 460–461, *c578*
    of Indus Valley civilization, 48
    of Italian city-states, *c578*
    in the Middle Ages, 354
    military, 201–202
    monarchy, 127, *c128, i578,* 594–595
    natural rights in, 630, *c632*
    oligarchy, 127, *c128, i579*
    Ottoman, 510, *c578*
    papal, 379
    representative, 128
    republican, 157, *c157,* 644–645
    responsibility of, 630
    Roman influence of, 157
    social contract in, 629
    of Sparta, 131
    structures of, *c580*
    of Sumer, 32–34
    of Tokugawa Japan, *c578*
Goya, Francisco, *i669*
Gran Colombia, 683
gravitas, 163
Gravity, Law of, 626–627
Great Britain. *See* Britain.
Great Depression. *See* Depression, the.
Great Fear, 655
Great Plains, 443
Great Pyramid, 38, *i39. See also* pyramids.
Great Schism, 399
Great Wall of China, *i108,* 109, 323
Great Zimbabwe, 425–427, *i426*
Greco, El, 591
Greco-Roman civilization, 178–183. *See also* Greece; Roman Empire.
Greco-Roman culture, 178
Greece. *See also* Hellenistic culture.
    ancient, 122–126
    architecture, 135–136, 140, *i141*
    arts, *i122,* 136, *i140–141,* 178
    city-states, *c87, c121, m121,* 127–133
    classical age, 252–257
    democracy in, *i122,* 128, 134–135

    drama, 136, *i141*
    economy of ancient, 123, 125, 135
    environmental influences on, 123–124
    geography of, 121, 123–124
    independence of, 689
    legacy, 125, 134, *c150*
    Macedonia's conquest of, 142
    Minoan influence, 72, 123, 125
    Mycenaeans, 124, *m124*
    nationalism in, 689
    Parthenon, 135–136, *i141*
    Peloponnesian War, 137–138, *m137,* 142
    Pericles, 122, 134–135, *i135,* 136, *i252,* 257
    philosophy, 148, 149
    sculpture, *i122,* 136, *i140,* 149
    Sparta, 129, 131, 137–138
    sports in, 130
    values, 135
    war in, 131–133, 137–138
griots, 216
***Grito de Dolores* (Cry of Dolores),** 685, *i705*
guerrillas
    in Peninsular War, 669
guild, 388, *c388*
guillotine, *i659,* 660
Gulf War. *See* Persian Gulf War.
gunpowder, *i322,* 325, *i328–329*
Gupta Empire, 191–192, *c208,* 252–255
Gutenberg Bible, 484
Gutenberg, Johann, 484

habeas corpus, 616
Hadrian, *c164*
Hagia Sophia, 303
haiku, 544
Haile Selassie (Ethiopian emperor), 225
Hajj, 267
Hammurabi, 27, 33–34, *i34*
    reign of, 33
Hammurabi's Code, 28, *i33,* 33–34, 115, *c120*
    compared with Ten Commandments, 80
Han dynasty, 109, 200–207, *c208*
    as classical age, 252–257
    compared to Roman Empire, *c206*
Hannibal of Carthage, *i158*
    Punic Wars, 158–159, *m159*
    Rome's war with, 158–159, *m159*
    and war elephants, 158
Hapsburgs, 597, 605
    defeats, 603–604
    triumphs, 603
Harappan civilization. *See* Indus Valley.
Hatshepsut (Egyptian pharaoh), 90, *i90, c120*
Hausa, 417–418
Haydn, Joseph, 637
headhunters, *i247*
Hebrew Law, 169
Hebrews, 77–82. *See also* Jews; Judaism.
    Abraham, 77–79
    covenant, 78–80
    Exodus, 78–79, 89
    Israel, 81–82

kings, 81
monotheism, 78, 168
Moses, *i78*, 79
prophets, 80
Sumerian influence, 34
Ten Commandments, 79–80, *i79*, 168
Twelve Tribes, 80
heliocentric theory, 624–625
Hellenistic culture
in Alexandria, 146–147
arts, 149
Epicurianism, 149
library, 147
philosophy, 148–149, 179
science and technology in, 147–148
Stoicism, 148–149, 179
trade in, 146
helots, 129, 131
Henry II (English king), 394
Henry IV (French king of Bourbon dynasty), 596
Henry IV (German emperor), 372
Henry VIII (English king), 492–493, *c492–493*
Henry of Navarre, 596
Henry the Navigator, 530, *i530*, 532
Henry, Prince. *See* Henry the Navigator.
Herculaneum, 166
heresy, 172, 384
Herodotus, 35, *i38*, 74, 136
Hidalgo, Miguel, 685
hieroglyphics
Egyptian, 40, *i40*
Maya, 448
Hijrah, 265
Hildegard of Bingen, 380
Himalayas, 44, *m45*, 50, *m51*
Hinduism, 66–67, *c84, i288–289, c296*
central ideas of, 66–67, 193, *c289*
gods of, 67, 194, *c289*
moksha, 66–67
origins of, 66
rebirth of, 194
in Southeast Asia, *m197*
spread of, 197
Upanishads, 66–67
Vedas, 63, 66, *i289*
as world religion, 288–289
Hippodrome, 303
history
beginnings of written, 136
influence of migration on, 221–224
and nationalism, 687, *c688*
History, **Book IV (Herodotus),** 74
History of Herodotus, 38
HISTORY partnership, vi–vii, 111
MC1–111 MC2, 151 MC1–151 MC2,
185 MC1–185 MC2, 349 MC1–349
MC2, 405 MC1–405 MC2, 467
MC1–467 MC2, 577 MC1–577
MC2, 647 MC1–647 MC2
Hittites, *c58*, 62–63
Egyptians' battle with, 62, 90
Hobbes, Thomas, 629
Hohenzollerns, 606
Hohokam, 441
Holy Roman Empire, 371–373
in 1100, *m372*
Otto I, 371–372

weakening of, 373, 605
Homer, 125–126
hominids, *i2*, 7–11, *c8–9, m10, i11*
development of, *c2–3*, 7–9
Homo erectus, *c2*, 8, *c9, m10*, 51
Homo habilis, 8, *c8*
Homo sapiens, 8–10
Hongwu, 536
Hooper, Finley, 177
Hopewell. *See* Adena and Hopewell.
hoplites, 131
House of Commons, 395
House of Lords, 395
House of Wisdom, 276
Huang He river, 16, 50, *i51*
Huguenots, 496, 596–597, 599
Hulagu, 316–317
humanists
Christian, 482
Petrarch, Francesco, 475–476
humanities, 472
in Ottoman Empire, 694
Hundred Days, 671
Hundred Years' War, 401–403
effect of, 403
hunter-gatherers, 14, 16, 18, *c24*
of Africa, *i212*, 215, 224, 409, *c411, m411*
in the Americas, 236
modern, 215, 409
hunters, *i234*, 235–237, *m237*
Hus, Jan, 399
Hyksos, 89–90

Ibn al-Haytham, 278
Ibn Battuta, 416, 422, 424
Ibn Rushd, 278–279
Ibo. *See* Igbo.
Ice Age, 8–9, 236, *i237*
Ice Man, 4, *i15*
***I Ching* (Book of Changes),** 107
icons, 306, *i312*
democratic tradition of, 410
stateless society of, 410
Igbo, *m411*
Ignatius of Loyola, 498–499
Iliad, 125–126
immigration. *See* migration.
impressionism, 701
Inca civilization, *m439*, 459–465, *m461*
ayllu, 460–461
cultural developments of, 461–462
Cuzco, 462
economic developments of, 460
fall of, 463, *c463*
government of, 460–461, *c578*
Machu Picchu, 462, *i462*
mita, 461
mummies, *i464–465*
Pachacuti, 459–460, *i460*
Pizarro's conquest of, 556–557
quipu, i20, 461
religious beliefs of, 462
runner messengers, 461
trade in, 460
India
2500–1500 B.C., *m45*
321 B.C.–A.D. 9, *m187*

Alexander the Great's conquest of, 144, *m144*
ancient (2500–1500 B.C.), *m45*
Aryan invasion of, *c58*, 64, *m65*
Buddhism in, 70–71, 190–191, 193–194
caste system, 63–64
Delhi Sultanate, 516
empires, 189–192
geography of, *m187*
Hinduism, 66–67, 71, 194
Kalidasa, 194
lions as symbols of, *i190*
Mahabharata, 64–65
mathematics of, 195
Mughal Empire, 516–523
natural resources of, 195
Silk Roads, 71, 196
trade in, 195–197, *m196*
Indian culture
connection to Indus Valley, 49, 63
environmental influences on, 44–45, 61–62
Indians. *See* Native Americans; North America.
Indo-Europeans
language family, 61, *c61*
migrations of, 62, *m62*, 99, 124
indulgence, 489
Indus River Valley, 44–49, *m45*
centralized government in, 48
civilization, *c27*, 44–49
geography of, 44, *m45*
religious artifacts, 48, *i49*
seals, *i48, i116*
in France, 690
inflation, 173, 573, 592
Inquisition
of Galileo, 625, *i625*
in Papal states, 384
Spanish, 384, *i385*
institution, 20
intendants, 598
interdict, 371
invasions
of Britain, 393
Magyar, 359, *m359*
Muslim, 229, 269–270
Viking, *m308*, 358, *m359*
inventions. *See also* technology.
of ancient China, 204, *i322*, 325, *i328–329*
caravel, 530, *i531*
Egyptian, 40–41
gunpowder, *i322*, 325, *i328–329*
irrigation, 19, 22
magnetic compass, *i322*, 325, *i328–329, i433*
measurements of time, 325, *i328–329*
microscope, 627
movable type, 325, *i328–329*
photography, 700
printing, *i328–329*
printing press, 484, *i484*
saddle, 364
sail, 19, 32
steam engine, 148

wheel, 19, 32
wheelbarrow, 204
Iran. *See also* Persia.
Shi'a Muslim sect, 271
Iraq
ancient, 20, 23
Baghdad, 23
as birthplace of agriculture, 16
Iraqi National Museum, 23
Shanidar Cave, 9
Sunni Muslim sect, 271
Ireland
rebellion in, 615
iron
in ancient Africa, 217–218, *i218*
cast, 55
importance of, 55, *i218*
of Meroë, 94
weapons, 55, 63, 94
of Assyrian empire, 95
of ancient Greece, 131
ironworking, 63, 95, 217–218, *i218*
spread of, *m211*, 222–223
Iroquois League, 444, 445
irrigation
in ancient China, 51, 109
Incan, 460
invention of, 19, 22
Mongol destruction of, 333
of pueblos, 443
in Sumer, 21, 29–30, 31
in Ur, 21
Isabella (Spanish queen), 384
Isfahan, 315
Islam, 229, *i290–291, c296. See also* Muslim world; Muslims.
Allah, 264–268
in Byzantium, 304
central ideas of, 267–268
Dome of the Rock, *i266*
in East Africa, 424–425
and ethical monotheism, 80
Five Pillars of Islam, 267, *i275*
hajj, 267
historical origins of, 263–265
influence of, 270, 424–425
Mecca, 263–265, 267
Muhammad, 264–268, 269, 274
political influences of, 267, 271–272
Qur'an, 265, 267–268, 276
Ramadan, 267, *i275*
rise of, 263–268
role in slavery, 425, 566
shari'a, 268, 274
Shi'a Muslims, 271, *c271*, 272
spread of, 269–270, 410–411
Sufi sect, 271
Sunna, 268
Sunni Muslims, 271, *c271*
in West Africa, 417
as world religion, 290–291
Islamic law, 268, 411, *i424*, 510
Isma'il (Safavid ruler), 513–514, *i513*
isolationism
of Japan, 339, 547
Israel
Kingdom of, 81
kings, 81
promised land, 81

Istanbul, 510–511, *i511*
Italy. *See also* Rome.
Florence, 472
and Holy Roman Empire, 373
nationalism in, 689, 694–695
Renaissance in, 471–477
unification of, 694–695, *m694*
Iturbide, Agustín de, 685–686
Ivan I (Moscow prince), 310
Ivan III (Russian czar), 311, *i311*
Ivan IV "Ivan the Terrible" (czar), 608

J

Jacobin Club, 658, 660
Jahangir, 518–519
Jainism, 67–68
Mahavira, 67
James I (English king), 614
James II (English king), 616
Jamestown, 562
janissaries, 510
Japan
Buddhism in, 71, 340
Chinese influence on, 340
Christianity in, 546–547
"closed country policy," 547
contact with Europe, 545–547
daimyo, 542–546
defeats Mongols, 336
feudalism in, 341–343, *c361, i361,* 542
geography of, 339
Heian, 341
Heian period, 341
isolationism in, 547
natural resources of, 339
"rising sun," 339
samurai, *i342,* 343
Shinto, 339–340
social classes and values, 341, 343
"Warring States" period (Sengoku), 542
Jarmo, 16
Jefferson, Thomas, 641, *i641,* 665
Jenner, Edward, 628
Jerome, St., 177
Jerusalem, *c59*
Dome of the Rock, *i266*
Saladin's conquest of, 383
Western Wall (Wailing Wall), 170
Jesuits, 499, *i500*
Jesus of Nazareth, *i169. See also* Christianity.
apostles, 168
death, 169
disciples, 168
life and teachings, 168–169
Jews. *See also* Hebrews; Judaism.
with Arabs of Medina, 265
under Cromwell's rule, 616
Diaspora, 170
modern, *i292–293*
as moneylenders, 390
in Muslim culture, 268
persecution of, 384–385
purim, *i293*
rebellion, 170
under Roman rule, 168, 170

sects, 292
in Spain, 384–385, 592
Star of David, *i292*
Joan of Arc, 402–403, *i403*
Johanson, Donald, 7, *m10*
John (English king), 394–395
joint-stock companies, 573–574
Joseph II (Austrian king), 638
Judah, 81–82
Judaism, *c84, i292–293, c296. See also* Jews.
central ideas of, 79–80, *c84*
civil and religious laws of, 81, 169
and ethical monotheism, 80
origin of, 77–82
spread of, 82
Ten Commandments, 79–80, *i79*
Torah, 77, *i79, c80,* 83
as world religion, 292–293
yarmulke, *i293*
Junkers, 606, 695
jury, 394–395
Justinian (Byzantine emperor), 301–304
Justinian Code, 302

K

Kabuki, 544, *i545*
kaiser, 697. *See also* Wilhelm I; Wilhelm II.
Kalidasa, 194
Kamakura shogunate, 343
Kamose (Egyptian pharaoh), 89
Kangxi, 539, *i539,* 549
karma, 67
Kautilya, 189
Kenya
nomads, 215
Kepler, Johannes, 624
Khadija (wife of Muhammad), 264–265
Khan, Genghis, 309, 331–332, *i331*
"Khanate of the Golden Horde." *See* Mongols.
Khmer Empire (Cambodia), 345
Angkor Wat, 70, 345, *i345*
al-Khwarizimi, 278
Kiev
Byzantine influence, 307–308
Eastern Orthodox Church, 308
Mongol rule, 309–310, *m309,* 333
Olga (princess), 307–308
Russian, 308–311
Vladimir, 308
Yaroslav the Wise, 308–309
kingdom(s). *See also* dynasties.
Aksum, 225–229, *m226*
Aryan, 64
Benin, 419
of China, 51–55
of Egypt, *c26,* 37, 90
Germanic, 354–355
of Israel, 81
of the Jews, 81
of Judah, 81–82
of Kush, 92–94
matrilineal society, 410
Minoan, 72
patrilineal society, 410
Roman Catholic Church, 354–357
Seljuk, 315
of Southeast Asia, 344–347

Index

West African, 413, 415
Yoruban, 418–419
king(s). *See also* czar(s); emperor(s);
    monarchy.
    of Alexander the Great's empire,
      143–144
    of ancient Rome, 156
    Etruscan, 156
    Jewish, 81
    Mycenaean, 124
    Spartan, 131
    warrior-kings,124
King James Bible, 614
knights, 360, 367
    education, 365, 367
Knossos, 72
Knox, John, 496
Korea, *i347*
    Choson dynasty, 347
    dynasties, 346–347
    geography, 346
    Koryu dynasty, 346–347
    under Manchu rule, 540
Koryu dynasty, 346–347
Krishna, 65
Kublai Khan, 335–338, *i337*
Kush empire, 93–94
Kushites, 93–94
Kwakiutl, *i440*

Lady Hao, 52
language. *See also* writing.
    of Aksum, 228
    Arabic, 267–268, 276
    Bantu, 221–224
    Chinese, 53
    early spoken, 7–8, 10
    effects of migration on, 61, 221,
      223–224, *i223*
    English, 181
    French, 181
    Ge'ez, 228
    Greek, 40, 125, 146
    Hindi, 518
    Indo-European, 61, *c61*
    Latin, 181, 353
    Maya glyphs, 448
    and nationalism, *c688*
    Niger-Congo, 221
    Proto-Bantu, 221
    Romance, 181
    Sanskrit, 61, *c61*
    Slavic, 307
    Swahili, *i223*, 422, 427
    Tamil, 191
    Urdu, 518
    vernacular, 391–392, 475
    of woodlands tribes, 444
Laozi, 105–106, *i105*
Lascaux Cave, *i13*
Latin America
    colonial legacy of, 681–682
    maps
      in 1800 and 1830, *m685*
    revolutions in, 674–675, 681–686,
      c707
law(s), 28. *See also* constitution.
    canon, 371, 379

common, 394
    Draconian, 128
    Greek, 134–135, *c134*
    Hammurabi's Code, 33–34, 115
    Hebrew, 169
    Hittite, 63
    Islamic, 268, 411, *i424*, 510
    Justinian Code, 302
    Magna Carta's influence on, 395,
      i395
    Napoleonic Code, 664
    Petition of Right, 614
    Roman, 156–157, *c157*, 183
    of Suleyman, 510
    unwritten Germanic, 354
    written code of, 33–34, *i33*, 395
lay investiture, 372
Leakey, Louis, 7–8, 9
Leakey, Mary, 7–8, 9, *m10*
Leakey, Richard, 9, 25
legalism, 106–107, *c106*
Legion (Roman), 157
Legislative Assembly, 657–658
legitimacy, 673
Leo III (Byzantine emperor), 306
liberals, 687, 689–690
libraries
    of Alexandria, 147, *i262*
    of ancient world, 96
    monasteries and, 355
    Muslim, 276, 391
Libya
    invasion of Egypt, 91–92
Lighthouse of Alexandria, 146–147,
    i262
lineage, 410
literature. *See also* writers.
    of chivalry, 367–368
    of early China, 105, 205–206
    of the Enlightenment, 633, 637
    epic, 32, 64, 83, 125–126, 179, *i179*
    essay, 597
    French, 597–598, 599
    Greek influence on, 135, 178
    Hebrew, *c80,* 83
    in Heian-period Japan, 341, *i341*
    Hindu, 66–67, 518
    Indian, 64, 83, 194
    Japanese, 544
    Mesopotamia, 32, 83, 96
    Minoan influence on Greek, 125
    Muslim, 276
    novel, 637
    in Ottoman Empire, 511
    Persian, 315
    realism in, 700–701
    Renaissance, 475–477, 482–483
    Roman influence on, *i179*, *c180*
    Romanticism and, 698–699
    Spanish, 591–592
    Sumerian, 32
    vernacular in, 392, 475
Liu Bang, 200–201, *i200*
Livy, 155
Locke, John, 629, 630, 642
loess, 50
Lombard League, 373
London, *i486–487*
longbow, 402, *i402*

lord, 360
Louis IX (French king), 396
Louis XIII (French king), 597
Louis XIV (French king), *i588*, 598–602,
    i598
Louis XVI (French king), 642, 653, *i653*,
    657, 660
Louis XVIII (French king), 671
Louisiana
    Territory, 665
L'Ouverture, Toussaint, 665, 682, *i682*
Lower Egypt, 36–37. *See also* Egypt.
Lü, Empress, 201
"Lucy," 7, *m10*
Lutherans, 490
Luther, Martin, 489–490, *i489. See also*
    Reformation.
    95 Theses, 489
    excommunication, 490
lycées, 664

M

Macedonia, 142–145, *m142*
Machiavelli, Niccolò, 476, *i476*, 503,
    i583
Machu Picchu, 462, *i462*
Magadha, 64
Magellan, Ferdinand, 534, 554
Maghrib, 410–411
Magna Carta, 394–395, *i395*
Magyars, 359, *m359*
Mahabarata, 64–65
Mahavira, 67
Mahayana sect, 193
Maimonides (Moses Ben Maimon),
    279
maize, 238
major domo, 356
Mali empire, 414–417, *m414*
    Mansa Musa, 415–416, *m416*
    Sundiata, 415
Malik Shah, 315–316
mamelukes, 314
mammoth, 234–235, *i234*, *c238*
Manchuria, 539
Manchus, 539–540
Mandate of Heaven, 54, *c54*
Manicheanism, 103
manor, 360, 362, *i362*
manorial system
    Medieval, 360–363, *i362*
    effect of plague on, 401
Mansa Musa, 415–417, *m416*
maps
    ancient empires, *m87*
    prehistoric world, *m3*
    Spanish, *m416*
Marat, Jean-Paul, 658, *i658*
Marathon (Greek city), 132
marathon (race), 133
Marcus Aurelius, 173
Marguerite of Navarre, 498, *i498*
Maria Theresa (Austrian empress), 605,
    i606, 607
Marie Antoinette (French queen), 653,
    i653
Mark Antony, 162
Marrakech, 412

Martel, Charles, 356
martial emperor, 201–202
Masai, 215
masks
    Bantu, *i220, i224*
    of Benin, *i419*
    Maya, *i446*
mathematics
    algebra, 278
    in ancient Egypt, 41, *i148*
    in China, *i148,* 325
    decimal system, 195
    geometry, 32, 148, *i148*
    of Hellenistic period, 147–148, *i148*
    Indian, 195
    Maya, 448
    Muslim, *i148,* 278
    pi, 148, 195
    Pythagorean theorem, *i148*
    in Scientific Revolution, 624, 626–627
    in Sumer, 32
    zero, 195
matriarchal, 192
matrilineal society, 410
Mauryan Empire, *c121,* 189–191, *m191, c208*
Maya civilization, 446–450
    calendar, 448
    Classical Period, 446
    cultural developments of, 447–448, *c449*
    decline, 449, *c449*
    economic developments, 447
    hieroglyphs, 448
    political developments of, 446–447
    religious beliefs in, 447–448
    science and technology, 448
    Tikal, 446, *i450–451*
Mazarin, Cardinal, 598, 604
Mecca, 263–265, 267
Medes, 97, 99
Medici family, 472, *i472, i581*
medicine
    acupuncture, *i325*
    Daoist effect on, 106
    Egyptian, 41, 43
    of Enlightenment, 627–628
    heart function, 41
    Indian, 195
    Muslim, 274, 278
    in Scientific Revolution, 627–628
    Vesalius, Andreas, 627–628
Medieval period. *See* Middle Ages.
Medina, 265
Megasthenes, 189–190
Mehmed II, Mehmed the Conquerer (Ottoman emperor), 508–509
mercantilism, 574–575, *i574*
mercenary, 173
Meroë, 94
Mesoamerican civilizations, 240–244. *See also* Aztec, Maya, Olmec, and Zapotec civilizations.
    cultural developments in, 241–242
    economic developments in, 241
    legacy of, 243
    political developments of, 243
    trade in, 241
Mesopotamia, *c3,* 20, 29–34, *m96. See also* Sumer; Sumerians.

city-states in, *c26,* 31–33, *i112*
    kings of, 31–33
mestizo, 557, *c681,* 682
Metacom (King Philip), 565
Metternich, Klemens von, 672, 689
Mexico
    cultural blending in, 685
    early farming in, 16, 238–239
    independence of, 675, 685
    revolution in, 685–686
Michelangelo, 474, *i475*
microscope, 278, 627
Middle Ages, 353
    burghers, 391
    castles, *i366,* 367
    chivalry, 365, 367–368
    church authorities, 370–371, 379, 398
    cultural developments of, 364–368
    economic developments of, 388–390
    end of, 398–403
    European, *m351,* 353–373
    farming, 362
    feudalism, 360–363, *c361*
    guilds, 388, *c388*
    Hundred Years' War, 401–403
    monasteries, 354–355, 379, 380
    political developments of, 354, *c361,* 394–397
    population growth, 387, 390, *c405*
    Roman Catholic church in, 354–355, 370–373, 379–385, 398–399
    science and technology in, 623
    towns, 390–391
    trade in, 389–390, *c390*
    weaponry, 364, *i366,* 402, *i402*
middle class
    during Enlightenment, 636
    in French Revolution, 651–652, 654
    Dutch, 593
    and monarchy, 595
    rise of, 636
Middle Kingdom, 52
middle passage, 569, *i569*
migration(s), 62, 220
    from Asia to the Americas, 235–237, *m237*
    of Bantu speakers, 220–224, *m222*
    across Beringia, 235–237, *m237*
    cultural influence of, 221
    early human, 1,600,000–10,000 B.C., *m10*
    effect of colonization on, 562
    effects of large-scale, 221
    the Hijrah, 265
    historical influence of, 221
    of *Homo erectus,* 8, *m10*
    influence of, 221
    of Indo-Europeans, 62, *m62,* 99, 124
    of Jews to Palestine, 170
    of Mesoamerican people, 453–454
    push-pull factors in, 220, *c221*
    urbanization as factor in, 220
military power
    Assyrian, 94, 95–97, *i97*
    of Muslims, 270
    of Persian empire, 99
    of Roman legions, 157
    Spartan, 131, 132
Ming Dynasty, 536–539

Minoan culture, 72–73
Minos (Minoan king), 72
Minotaur, 72
missionaries
    Byzantine, 306
    Christian, 354, 546
    Jesuit, 499, *i500,* 537, 546
Mississippian culture, 443–444
mita, 461
Mithra, 103
Moche culture, 247, 249
moderates, 657
mohenjo-daro, *m46*
    plumbing of, *i47*
moksha, 66–67
Molière, 599
monarchs
    absolute, 594–595, *c618*
    European, 595
monarchy, 127, *c128. See also* kings.
    clothing and, *i588*
    constitutional, 617, 657
    divine origin of, 594
    end of Roman, 156
    and Enlightenment, 638–639
    limited, 617
    modern, 617
    after Napoleon I, 673
    in prehistory, *i578*
monasteries
    under Charlemagne, 357
    in Middle Ages, 354, 357, 379, 380
    monastic revival, 380
    as preservers of culture, 355
Monet, Claude, 701, *i703*
money, 163. *See also* coins.
    paper, 325, *c328*
    sakk, 272
Mongols
    and bubonic plague, 334, *m400*
    cavalry, *i332–333*
    in China, 333–334
    decline of, 337–338
    defeat by Japan of, 335–336, *i336*
    empire of Kublai Khan, 335–338
    Genghis Khan, 309, 331–332, *i331*
    Hulagu, 316–317
    "Khanate of the Golden Horde," 309, *m309,* 333
    in Korea, 347
    overthrow of Seljuk Empire, 316–317
    Pax Mongolica (Mongol Peace), 333
    in Russia, 309–311
monopoly, 204
monotheism, 78, 227. *See also* ethical monotheism; polytheism.
    in Aksum, 227–228
    Hindu move towards, 194
    of Muslims, Jews, and Christians, 268
    in teachings of Jesus, 168
monsoons
    of India, 45, *m45*
monsoon winds, 76
Montaigne, Michel de, 597
Monte Albán, *c59, c121,* 242–243, *i242*
Montesquieu, Baron de, 631, *i631*
Montezuma II (Aztec emperor), 456, 458, 556
More, Thomas, 482, *i482*

Morelos, Padre José Maria, 685
mosaics, *i165*, 178
Moscow, 310–311, 670. *See also* Russia.
mosque(s), 267, 273
    of Córdoba, *i278*
    of Damascus, 276
    of Suleyman, *i511*
    of Timbuktu, 416
mother goddess, 18
Mound Builders, 443–444, *i444*
Mount Vesuvius, 166–167, *c167*
movable type, 325, *i329*
movie industry
    Bollywood (India), *c195*, *i195*
Mozart, Wolfgang Amadeus, 637
Mughal Empire
    art of, *i522–523*
    cultural developments of, 518,
      i522–523
    decline of, 521
    economic developments of, 517, 519
    growth of, *m517*
    political developments of, 517
Muhammad, 264–268, 268, 274
    Hijrah, 265
    Medina, 265
mulattos, *c681*, 682
mummification
    Egyptian, 38–39
    Incan, *i464–465*
Muses, 147
music
    African, 570
    in age of chivalry, 368
    classical, 637
    impressionistic, 701
    nationalistic, *i689*
    neanderthal, 11
    neoclassical, 637
    Romanticism and, 699
    of Ur, 22
Muslims
    caliphs, 269, 271–272
    conflict among, 270–271
    conflict with Hindus, 516
    and Crusades, 316, 383, 385
    influence on sciences of, 274, 278
    invasions of, 229, 359, *m359*
    jihad, 269
    Ka'aba, 263–265, *i265*
    in Middle Ages, 263–279
    Mongol conversion to, 333
    in North Africa, 410–411
    population, *c281*
    prayer, *i268*
    and Reconquista, 384
    scholars, *i391*
    shari'a, 268, 274
    Spanish defeat of, 384
Muslim world, 263–279, *c280*, 507–523.
    See also Islam; Ottoman Empire.
    in 1200, *m261*
    al-Andalus, 271–272
    art and architecture, *i266*, 276–278,
      i277, *i278*
    civil war, 271–272
    Córdoba, 272, *i278*
    Damascus, 271, 276
    Dynasties, 271–272

empires of, 507–521
House of Wisdom, 276
imperialism in, 271–272
influence of, 273–279
mathematics in, 274, 278
population of, 272, *c273*, 274
religious tolerance in, 268, 270
science and technology in, 274, *i275*,
   276, 278
slavery in, 274, 425, 566
social classes, 274
urban centers, 273–274
Mutapa Empire, 427
Mycenaeans, 124–125, *m124*
myth(s)
    Greek, 122, 126
    of Minotaur, 72
    of Quetzalcoatl, 453
    Roman, 155

Napoleon I, Napoleon Bonaparte (French
    emperor), 663–671
    allies of, 667
    exile, 671
    nations controlled by, *m649*, 667
    nations at war with, 665, *m666*, 667,
     669
    restoring order, 664
    Russian campaign, 669–670, *m670*
    at Waterloo, 671
Napoleon III, Louis-Napoleon (French
    emperor), 690
Napoleonic Code, 664
Narmer, 37
National Assembly, 654, 656
National Convention, 658, 660
nationalism, 687, *c688,* 692
    and art, 698
    Balkan, 689
    in Europe, 687–691
    ideal of, 687–689
    impact of, *c688*
    against Napoleon I, 669
    postive and negative results of, *c688*
    and revolution, 682–686, 689–690
    rise of, 687, 689
nationalist movements, *c692*
nation-state, 687, *c688*
Native Americans. *See also* North
    America, native.
    burial rites of, 444
    colonialism and, 564–565
    slavery of, 557, 559
natural order, 105–106
natural resources. *See* environmental
    influences.
natural rights, 630
    Locke, John, 630, 642
nature. *See* environmental influences.
Nazca culture, 247, *i247*, *i248*
Nazca lines, *i248*
Neanderthals, 9–11, *c9*, *m10*
    musical expression of, 11
Nebuchadnezzar (Chaldean king), 82, 98
neoclassical style, 637
Neolithic Age, *c3*, 7, 15–16, *i17*
Neolithic Revolution, 15

Nero, *c164*
Netherlands, 534
    Asian trade with, 534–535
    French invasion of, 601
    Japanese trade with, 547
    republic of, 593
    trade in, 535, 594
    tulips of, *i592*
    United Provinces of, 592–593
Nevsky, Alexander, 310
New England, 562–563
New France, 561–562
New Kingdom of Egypt, *c86*, 90–91
New Netherland, 563
New Stone Age, 7, 15–16, *i17*
New Testament, 172
Newton, Isaac, 626–627, *i627*
Nicaragua, 686
Nicholas I (Russian czar), 691
Nike of Samothrace, *i140*, 149
Nile River, 35–37, 92. *See also* pyramids.
Nineveh, 96–97
nirvana, 69
Noah's Ark, *i83*
Nobunaga, Oda, 542–543
Nok, 217, *i217*, 222
nomads, 14. *See also* Mongols.
    of Africa, 215
    Aryan, 63
    of Asian steppe, 330–331
    Aztec, 453
    Bantu, 222–224
    Bedouins, 263
    conflict of empires with, 89
    Hyksos, 89
    influence on Indian culture of, 63–65
    in Iran, 99
    Magyar, 359, *m359*
    modern-day, 409
    Mongol, 175, 309, 331
    of North Africa, 409
    of North America, 235–236, 441,
     443
    pastoral, 330–331
    Seljuks, 314
    on Silk Roads, 196, *m204–205*
    transition of Jews from, 79
    warriors, 33, 331
    Xiongnu, 201–202
Normans, 393–394
North Africa
    Islam, 410–412
    Maghrib, 410–411
    Muslim reformers, 411–412
North America. *See also* North America,
    native.
    in 1783, *m642*
    colonization of, 554–558, 561–565
    maps, *m439*, *m442*, *m564*
North America, native. *See also* North
    America; Native Americans.
    colonization of, 554–558, 561–565
    cultural developments of, 444–445
    culture areas, *m442*
    early societies, 441–445
    Iroquois League, 444, 445
    Mound Builders, 443–444, *i444*
    Pacific Northwest, *i440*, 441
    political developments of, 441, 444

pueblo people of, 443
religion in, 444–445
trade in, 444
woodlands tribes of, 444–445
Northern Renaissance
art of, 480–481, *i481*
technology of, 484, *i484*
writers of, 482–483
Nubia, 90, 92–93
number systems, 41
base 60, 32
Nur Jahan, 518

O

oases, 263
obsidian, 18, 453, 456
Octavian, 162, *i162. See also* Augustus.
Oda Nobunaga, 542–543
Odyssey, 126
Oedipus the King, 136
Old Regime, 651
Old Stone Age, 7–15
Old Testament, 77, 172. *See also*
Bible.
Olduvai Gorge, 8, *m10*
oligarchy, 127, *c128, i579*
Olmec civilization, 240–241, *m241,* 243
as classical age, 252–255
decline of, 241
jaguar worship, 241, 243, *i244*
legacy, 243
sculpture, *i58,* 240–241, 243, *i244*
trade, 241
Olympic Games, 130
opposable thumb, 7
oracle bones, *i53*
Orthodox Church, 304–306, *c305*
Osiris, 38
Osman, 507
**Otto I, Otto the Great (Holy Roman
emperor),** 371–372
Ottoman Empire, 507–511
1451–1566, *m508*
in the Balkans, 508
cultural developments of, 511
decline of, 511, 605, 693–694
government of, 510
nationalism weakens, 693–694
social organization, 510
sultan, 507
Ovid, 179

P

Pachacuti (Inca ruler), 459–460, *i460*
Paine, Thomas, 662, *i710*
painters. *See* names of individual artists and
paintings.
painting. *See also* art.
African, *i216*
of Catal Huyuk, 18
cave, *i12–13, 14*
Chinese, *i107,* 326, *i326*
Dutch, 593, *i593*
Egyptian tomb, *i42*
of Enlightenment, 637
Flemish, 481, *i481*
French, 701

impressionism, 701, *i703*
Medieval, *i352, i357*
perspective in, 474, *i474*
realism in, *i703*
Renaissance, *i470,* 474–475, *i478–479,*
481, *i481*
of Richard the Lion-Hearted, *i384*
Roman, *i167,* 179
Romanticism and, *i702*
of Socrates, *i138*
of Song Dynasty, 326, *i326*
Spanish, 591, *i591*
Stone Age, *i12–13,* 14
of van Eyck, *i470,* 481
of Velázquez, 591, *i591*
Palembang, *i345,* 346
Paleolithic Age, *c2,* 7–15
paleontologists, 5
papacy, 355
papal authority, 372
dispute over, 398
Papal States, 695
Inquisition in, 384
paper, 203, *i203, i322*
papyrus, 40, 43, 147
parliament
and absolute monarchs, 595
and Bill of Rights, 617
British, 395, 614–617
democracy and, 395
and English monarchy, 395,
614–617
French, 690
Reformation, 492–493
under William and Mary, 617
Parthenon, 135–136, *i141*
Passover, 79
pastoralists, 330–331
patriarch (leading bishop of East), 306
patriarchal, 192
patricians, 156
patrilineal society, 410
patriotism
lack of and fall of Roman Empire, 173,
c174
patrons (of the arts), 472–473
Paul, the apostle, 170
Pax Mongolica, 333
Pax Romana, 162, 165, 170
Peace of Augsburg, 492
Peace of Westphalia, 604
peasant's revolt, 490
Peking man, 51
Peloponnesian War, 137–138, *m137,*
142
peninsula, 681
peninsulares, 675, 681–682, *c681*
Pepin the Short, 356
Pericles, 122, 134–135, *i135,* 137
Persia
carpets, 525
conquest of, 103
rise of, 99
Persian empire, *c87,* 99–103, *m101*
Alexander the Great's conquest of,
143–144
Muslim defeat of, 103
Royal Road, 101, *i102, m102*
Zoroaster, 103

Persian Gulf, *m30,* 48
Persian Gulf War, 23
Persian Wars, 131–133, *m132*
perspective (in art), 474, *i474*
Peru, 16, 246–249, *m247,* 683
Peter, the apostle, *i169,* 171
Peter I, "Peter the Great" (Russian czar),
609–611, *i609*
Petrarch, Francesco, 475–476
phalanx, 131–132, 142
pharaoh(s)
Alexander the Great as, 143
Egyptian, 37, 39, 89–91
Hatshepsut, 90, *i90, c120*
Ramses II, 90–91, *i91*
Pharos, 146, *i262*
Pheidippides, 132, 133
Philip II (French king), 396
Philip II (Macedonian king), 142–143
Philip II (Spanish king), 589, 591–592
Philip IV (French king), 398
Philistines, 77
philosopher-king, 138
philosophers, 138
Aristotle, 139, *i139,* 151, 278–279
Confucius, 104–105, *i105,* 115
Descartes, René, 626
Epicurus, 149
Plato, 138–139, *i139,* 278–279
Rousseau, Jean Jacques, 631–632,
i631
scholastics, 392
Socrates, 138, *i138, i139*
Zeno, 148
philosophes, 630–632, 638
philosophy
Chinese, 104–105
of Enlightenment, 630–632
Greek, 138–139, 148–149
Hellenistic, 148–149
Medieval, 392
Muslim, 278–279
Roman, 179
Phoenicia
alphabet, legacy of, 74, *c74, i76*
physics
of Hellenistic period, 148
in Scientific Revolution, 626–627
pi, 148, 195
Piankhi (Kushite king), 93–94
pictographs, *i53*
Piers Plowman (Langland), 363, *i363*
pilgrimages, 263, 267
pilgrims
religious, 263, 267, 562
Pilgrims, 562
pirates, *i563*
Pizarro, Francisco, 556–557, *i557*
plague. *See also* bubonic plague.
Black Death, 399
of Justinian, 304
in the Middle Ages, 399–401
in Peloponnesian War, 137
route of, *m400*
planned cities
of the Indus Valley, 46
Plato, 138–139, *i139,* 278–279
plebians, 156

plebiscite, 664
plow, 19, 32, 204
plumbing
    of ancient Rome, 47
    of Mohenjo-Daro, 46, *i47*
Plutarch, 148
polis. *See* city-state.
political ideas. *See also* political tolerance.
    of American Revolution, *c643*,
        644–645
    balance of power, 672–673
    checks and balances, 631, 645
    direct democracy, 135
    of English Civil War, 614–615
    during Enlightenment, 629–632
    of French Revolution, 652, 654
    greatest good, 632
    of Hammurabi's Code, 33–34, *i33*
    importance of the individual, 634
    in Kautilya's *Arthasastra*, 189
    of Machiavelli, *i583*
    monarchy, 127, *c128*, *i578*
    natural rights, 630
    progress, 630
    of Russian Revolution, *c872*
    scholarly influence on, 629–634
    secularism, 634
    separation of powers, 631, *c643*, 645
political systems, *c180*. *See also* democracy; government.
    absolute monarchy, 594–595
    aristocracy, 127, *c128*
    autocracy, 109
    direct democracy, 135
    federal system, 644–645
    feudalism, 54, 360
    of hunter-gatherers, 410, *c410*
    limited monarchy, 617
    military state, 201–202
    monarchy, 127, *c128*, *i578*
    in Muslim states, 271–272
    oligarchy, 127, *c128*, *i579*
    representative government, 128, 156
    republic, 156–157
    republican government, 157, *c157*
    in stateless societies, 410
    theocracy, 37, 496
    welfare state, 461
political tolerance. *See also* religious tolerance.
    in ancient Persia, 99, 101
politics
    Minoan influence on Greek, 125
    and spread of Christianity, 171
Polo, Marco, *i258–259*, 337, *i337*
polytheism, 31, 38, 78. *See also* monotheism.
Pompeii, 166–167, *c167*, *i167*, 179
Pontius Pilate, 169
pope(s), 171
    Benedict XVI, *i305*
    Boniface VIII, 398
    Byzantine, 306
    Clement V, 398
    Clement VII, 399
    controversy over, 398–399
    Council of Constance, 399
    and Galileo, 625, *i625*
    Gelasius I, 370
    Great Schism, 399

Gregory the Great, 355
Gregory VII, 372, 379
and Holy Roman Empire, 372–373
Leo III, 357, 371
Leo IX, 379
Leo X, 490
Martin V, 399
Paul III, 499
Paul IV, 499
Urban II, 382, 386
Popol Vuh, 448
popular culture
    movies, *c195*
population(s)
    of Aztec civilization, *c319*, 454
    of Byzantine Empire, *c319*
    of cities, *c273*
    during Agricultural Revolution, *c17*
    effect of farming on, *c17*, 387
    effect of trade on, 471
    in empires, *c319*
    in Europe, *c405*
    of Mongol Empire, *c319*
    of Monte Albán, 242
    Muslim, 272, 274, *c281*
    Persian, *c319*
    religious affiliations of world's,
        c282–283
    of Roman cities, 162
    of Roman Empire, *c319*
porcelain, 325, *i328*, *c329*, *i536*
Portugal
    Asian trade with, 532–533
    colonies of, 557, 686
    in European exploration, 530, 532, 554,
        557
    influence in Africa, 424, 427
    Japanese trade with, 545
    North American slaves, 567
    rivalry with Spain, 533
    slave trade of, 532, 566–567
    trade with India, 521, 533
potlatch, 441
poverty
    in ancient Rome, 164–165
    and Christianity, 170
predestination, 495
prehistoric civilizations
    economic changes in, 31
    social changes in, 32
prehistoric world
    tools in, *i4*, 7–11, 14, *i15*
    ways of investigating, 5, 22–23
Presbyterians, 496
priests
    lack of, in Islam, 267
    Roman, 164
    Sumerian, 23, 31–32
prime minister, 617
Prince, The (Machiavelli), 476, 503
printing
    in China, 484
    Gutenberg, 484, *i484*
    and Renaissance ideas, 484
printing press, 484, *i484*
Promised Land, 81
prophets, 80, *c80*
Protagoras, 138

Protestantism, *c491*
    Calvin's influence on, 495–496
    in Spanish Netherlands, 592–593
Protestants, 490, 596
Protestant Union, 603
Prussia
    alliances of, 607
    during the Enlightenment, 638
    rise of, 606, 696
Ptolemy, 147, *c147*
public works projects
    of Incan civilization, 461
    pyramids as, 38
pueblo, 443
pulley, 148
pump, 148
Punic Wars, 158–159, *m159*
Puritans
    in English Civil War, 615
    in "New England," 562–563
    victory over Metacom, 565
Purusha, *i64*
push-pull factors (in migration), 220,
    c221
pyramids
    Aztec, 455
    Egyptian, *i1*, 37–38, *i39*
    Maya, 446, *i450*
    in Mesoamerica, *i242*
    of North America, 444
    Nubian, *i92*
Pythagoras, *i148*
Pythagorean theorem, *i148*

Q

Qian-long, 539–540
Qin Dynasty, *c87*, 107–109, *m108*, 200
Qing Dynasty, 539
queens. *See* individual names.
Queen of Sheba, 225
Quetzalcoatl, *i452*, 453, 456, 458
quipu, i20, 461
quipucamayoc, 20
Qur'an, 265, 267–268, 276

R

Radicals, 657, 687
rain forest
    African, 213, *i214*
Ramses II (Egyptian pharaoh), 90–91,
    i91
Raphael, *i474*, 475
al-Razi, 278
realism, 700–701
realpolitik, 695–696
reconquista, 384, 557
record-keeping
    "checks" in, 272
    importance of paper to, 203
    Incan, *i20*, 461
    prehistoric, *i116*
    Sumerian, 20–21, 32
Red Shirts, 694
Reformation, the, 488–501
    and absolute monarchy, 493
    Catholic, 498–499
    causes of, 488–489, *c488*
    characteristics of, 489

effects of, 490–494, 500
indulgences, 489
Luther, Martin, 489–490
peasant's revolt, 490
values in, 489
women in, 494, 496, 498
Reformation Parliament, 492–493
Reign of Terror, 660–661
reincarnation, 67
religion. *See also* Buddhism; Christianity;
    Hinduism; Islam; Jainism; Judaism;
    Manicheanism; Zoroastrianism.
    and death, 9, 38–39, 67
    effect of printing press on, 485
    in Europe (1560), *m497*
    and nationalism, *c688*
    in native North America, 444–445
    Persian, 103
    reformers, 489–490
    Roman government and, 164, 170
    spread of Indian, 197, *c197*
    unifying force of, 371–372
    and women, 67, 72
    world, 282–296
religious affiliations, world's,
    c282–283
religious beliefs. *See also* religion;
    sacrifice.
    of ancient China, 52–53
    animism, 216, 415
    in art, *i312*
    Aztec, 456, *i457*
    effects of science on, 625
    empire worship, 164
    ethical monotheism, 80
    Incan, 462
    jaguar worship, 241, *i244*
    Maya, 447–448
    Minoan influence on Greek, 72, 125
    in native North America, 444–445
    of Persia, 103
    in prehistory, 9
    Roman, 168, 174
    sports in, 130
    Sumerian, 23, 31–32
religious persecution. *See also* Christianity;
    Inquisition.
    in Japan, 546
    in Spanish colonies, 559
religious rituals, 9. *See also* burial rites; sac-
    rifice.
    Sumerian, 23, 31–32
religious symbolism, *i287, c296*
    cross as, *i312*
religious tolerance, 68
    in Austria, 638
    of Cyrus the Great, 99–100
    in Edict of Nantes, 596
    and French Revolution, 656
    in Indian empires, 190
    in Islamic law, 268
    in Mughal Empire, 517
    under Muslim rule, 270, 274
    in Netherlands, 593
    in Ottoman Empire, 510
reliquary, *i313*
Rembrandt (van Rijn), 593, *i593, i628*
Remus, 155
Renaissance. *See also* Northern Renaissance.
    art, *i470,* 474, *i474, i478–479,* 481

British, 483
causes of, 471
characteristics of, 472–473, 475
Chinese, *i477*
da Vinci, Leonardo, 475, *i475, i478–479*
effects of, 485
European, 471–488
Flanders, 480–481
humanism, 472, 482
Italian, 471–477
literature, 475–477, 482–483
Michelangelo, 475, *i475, i478*
Muslim influence on, 279
Northern, 480–485
Petrarch, 475–476
Raphael, *i474,* 475, *i479*
themes of, 472
values of, 471–473, 480
women in, 473, *i473,* 477
"Renaissance men," 473, *i473*
"Renaissance women," 473, *i473*
republic
    French, 690
    Roman, 155–159, *c157*
    United States, *c157,* 644–645
***Republic, The* (Plato),** 138
res publica, 156
Restoration, 616
revolution(s)
    1848, *m679*
    agricultural, 15, *c17*
    American, 640–645, *c706*
    causes of, *c708*
    Commercial, 389–390, *c390*
    effects of, *c710*
    English, 615–616, *c706*
    and Enlightenment, 641–642, 652, *m684*
    failed, 689–690
    French, *i644,* 651–661, *c706*
    Glorious, 616, *c706*
    in Haiti, 682
    ideas and, 681, 684
    Latin American, 682–686, *c707*
    Mexican, 685–686
    model of, *c707*
    nationalist, 682–686
    role of Enlightenment in, 641–642, 652
    in Saint Domingue, 665, 682
    Scientific, 623–628, *c626–627*
    time line of, *c706–707*
Ricci, Matteo, 537, 539
Richardson, Samuel, 637
Richard the Lion-Hearted, *i378,* 383, *i384*
Richelieu, Cardinal, 597, *i597,* 604
Rig Veda, 63, *i289*
rights and responsibilities. *See also* Bill of
    Rights; constitution.
    in Declaration of the Rights of Man, 656
    in democracy, *c134*
    of *habeas corpus,* 616
    Locke's treatise on, 630
    under Magna Carta, 394–395, *i395*
    in Petition of Right, 614
    religious freedom, 630, *c632,* 638
Rio de Janeiro, 686
roads. *See also* Royal Road; Silk Roads.
    Incan, 461
    of Roman Empire, 163, 183
Robespierre, Maximilien, 660–661, *i660,*
    i711

Roman Catholic Church. *See also* church.
    in the Americas, 558–559
    authority of, 370–371, 399
    canon law, 371, 379
    division of, 398–399
    during French Revolution, 656–657
    effect of plague on, 401
    in Enlightenment, 636
    and fall of Roman Empire, 172
    and Galileo, 625
    and Holy Roman Empire, 371–372
    and Huguenots, 496, 597
    Inquisition in, 384, *i385*
    and Medieval women, 354–355
    in the Middle Ages, 354–355, 370–374,
        379–385
    problems in, 488–489
    Reformation in, 498–499
    reform of, 398, 489
    structure of, 370
    weakening of, 401
Roman Empire
    ancient, 160
    agriculture, 163, 164, 173
    aqueducts, 47, 181, *i181*
    army, 161, 173–174
    art and architecture, *i166–167,* 178–179,
        181, *i182,* 183
    Augustus, 162, *i162*
    beginnings, 160–161
    Caesar, Julius, 161–162, *i161*
    cities, 164, 165
    civil wars, 161, 162, 174
    as classical age, 252–257
    Colosseum, 165, 181, *i182*
    cultural influence of, 176, 178–181
    decline of, 168, 172, 173–177, *c174*
    economic developments of, 163
    education, 179
    emperors, 162, *c164*
    family life in, 162
    gladiators, 165, *i165, i182*
    government of, 161–162, *c164,* 174
    invasions into, 175–176, *m175,* 353
    Latin language in, 170, 181
    law in, 183
    legacy of, 178–183
    literature, 179, *c180,* 181
    mercenaries, 173
    Pax Romana, 162, 165, 170, 173
    political developments of, 162
    population of, 162, 164
    reforms, 161–162, 174
    religion in, 164, 168, 174
    slavery in, 160, 162, 164
    social classes, 164–165
    social life, 164–165
    triumvirate, 161–162
    values, 163, 178
Romanovs, 608–609, 693
Roman Republic, *c87,* 155–160
    army, 157–159
    collapse of, 160–161
    Etruscan influence on, 155–156
    government, 157
        compared with United States, *c157*
    Greek influence on, 155
    origins, 155–156
    Punic Wars, 158–159, *m159*
    Twelve Tables, 156

romanticism, 698–699
Rome. *See also* Roman Empire; Roman Republic.
Vatican City in, 695
Romulus, 155
Rosetta Stone, *i40*
Rousseau, Jean Jacques, 631–632, *i631*
Royal Road, 101, *i102*, *m102*
Rubicon River (Italy), 161
Russia. *See also* Russian empire.
boyars, 608–609
expansion of 1500–1800, *m610*, 639
Napoleon I invades, 669–670, *m670*
nationalism in, 691
Nevsky, Alexander, 310
Novgorod, 307
Peter the Great, 609–611, *i609*
reform in, 690–691
religious art of, *i312–313*
serfs in, 690–691, *i691*
Slavic and Greek traditions in, 307
winters of, *i612–613*
Russian Empire
under Catherine the Great, 638–639
fall of, 693
Russification, 693
Russification, 693

S

sacraments, 371
sacrifice
in Africa, 227
Aztec, 456
human, 73, 447–448, 456
Incan, 462, 464
Maya, 447–448
Minoan, 73
Sumerian, 23, 32
Safavid Empire, 512–515, *m514*
Sahara, 213, *i214*, 215
salt trade of, 413
Sahel, 213, *i214*
sail, *i117*
sailing
in ancient Greece, 123
Phoenician, *i117*
Saint Domingue, 665, 682
St. Petersburg, 611
Saladin, 383, *i384*, 386
Salamis, 132
salons, 636
salt, 413
trade, 413
samurai, *i342*, 343
Samyutta Nikaya, 69
San Martin, José de, 683, *i683*
San people, 215, 224, *c411*, *m411*
sans-culottes, 658
Sargon of Akkad, 33
Satrap, 101
Saul (Israelite king), 81
savannas, *i214*, 215
Schliemann, Heinrich, 125
Scholastica, 355, *i355*
scholastics, 392
science. *See also* Revolution, Scientific; technology; tools.
chemistry, 628

of Egypt, 41
in Indus Valley, 46
in Muslim world, 274, *i275, 278*
physics, 626–627
of Sumer, 32
scientific method, 625–626
Bacon, Francis, 626
Descartes, René, 626
old science and new science, *c626*
Scientific Revolution, 623–628, *c626–627*
advances in medicine, 627–628, *i628*
advances in chemistry, 628
tools and inventions, 627
Scipio, 159
scorched-earth policy, 669
Scorpion King, 37
scribes, 20–21
sculpture
Assyrian, 96, *i97*
Benin, *i419–421*
Buddhist, 193–194, *i194, i198*
Egyptian, *i90*
Greek, 136, *i140, 178*
Hellenistic, 149
Hittite, *i63*
Minoan, 72
Moche, 249
neoclassic, 637
Nok, *i217*
Nubian, *i92, i93*
Olmec, *i58*, 240–241, *i244*
Renaissance, 474, *i478–479*
Roman, 178
Second Reich, 697
secular, 355, 472, 634
Selim the Grim, 509, 514
Selim II, 511
Seljuk Empire
c.1100, *m299*
Crusaders in, 316, 383
Malik Shah, 315–316
Mongol overthrow of, 316–317
Senate
Roman, *i154*, 157, *c157*
United States, *c157*
Sennacherib (Assyrian king), 95–96
separation of powers. *See* political ideas.
serfs, 360, 362–363, 605, 690–691, *i691*
Seven Wonders of the World, 98, 149
sextant, *i531*
Shah Jahan, 519–520
Shah, Malik, 315–316
shahs, 514
Shakespeare, William, 483
Shang Di, 53
Shang dynasty, 52
artisans of, *i117*
social classes of, 52
Shanidar Cave, 9
shari'a, 268, 274
Shelley, Mary, 699
Shi'a Muslims, 271, *c271*, 272
Shi Huangdi, 107–109, *i107*, 200
Shinto, 339–340
shipbuilding, 74, *i75*
Shiva, 67, 194
shogun, 343
Siddhartha Gautama, 68. *See also* Buddha; Buddhism.

siege, *i366*, 367
Sikhs, 519, 521
silk
importance to China, 204–205, *m204–205*
Silk Roads
in Arabian trade, 263
Chinese commerce along, 205, *m204–205, i207*
in Indian trade, 196
in Muslim trade, 272
trade networks on, 71, *i88, m204–205*
silt, 29, 35, 36, 44
Sima Qian ("Grand Historian"), 202, 205
simony, 379
Sirius, 40
skepticism, 597
slash-and-burn farming, 15, 222
slavery, *i567*. *See also* slaves.
African, 418, 425, 566
in the Americas, 566–570
in Assyrian empire, 96
British role in, 567, 601
and colonialism, 566–570
in Egypt, 40, 89
Hebrews in, 78–79, 89
middle passage, 569, *i569*
under Napoleonic Code, 664
Portugal's role in, 566–567
slaves. *See also* slavery.
African, 425, 566
in the Americas, 566–570
in ancient Rome, 159, 160, 164
of Athens, 128
Aztec, 454
Carthaginian, 159
children as, 164
in civil service, 510
in Egypt, 40, 89
as gladiators, 164
native American, 557, 559
Nubian, *i93*
in Ottoman Empire, 510
resistance of, 569–570
revolt in Saint Domingue, 665, 682
ships bearing, 569, *i569*
in Sumer, 32
Turkish military, 314
in West Africa, 418
Slavic speakers, 306
Slavs, 306–307
language of, 306
and Vikings, 307, *m308*
smallpox, 556, *i560*, 565, 571, 573, 628
social classes. *See also* middle class.
Aztec, 454–455
and Buddhism, 70
clothing of, 93
during Commercial Revolution, 390, *c390*
of Egypt, 40
under feudalism, 360, *i361*
of Indus Valley, 48
in Japan, 341, 343
Maya, 447
in Middle Ages, 390–391
in Muslim society, 274
Platonic ideal of, 138
of Rome, 156, 164–165

of Shang dynasty, 52
of Sparta, 131
of Sumer, 32
in Tang and Song dynasties, 327
social contract, 629
in American Revolution, 641
Hobbes, Thomas, 629
Socrates, 138, *i138, i139*
solar system, *c147*
Solomon (Israelite king), 81, *i81,* 225
Solon, 128
Songhai, *m414,* 417
Askia Muhammad, 417
Sunni Ali, 417
Song dynasty
cultural advances in, 325–327
inventions of, 325, *i328–329*
population, 325
prosperity in, 325–326
renaissance of, 324–325
science and technology of, 325, *i328–329*
Sophists, 138
Sophocles, 136
South America
cultures, *m247, m461*
empires, 459–463
Southeast Asia
900–1200, *m345*
geography of, 344
influences on, 344–345
Khmer Empire (Cambodia), 345
kingdoms of, 344–347
Spain
in the Americas, 554–559
conquest patterns of, 557
Native resistance to, 559
Crusades in, 384–385
in Latin America, 675, 681–686
Napoleon's invasion of, 669
North American colonies of, 554,
556–558, 682–686
persecution of Jews in, 384
reconquista, 384, 557
rivalry with Portugal, 533
slave trade of, 567
Spanish Armada
defeat of, *m590,* 591
Spanish Empire, 589–593
Sparta
military state of, 129, 131
war with Athens, 137–138, *m137*
specialization, 20
Spice Islands, 533, *m534,* 535
sports
Maya ball game, 447, *i451*
Olmec, *i244*
Olympic games, 130, 133
Srivijaya, 345–346, *m345*
stateless society, 410
steam engine, 148
steppes, 61, 330
Stoicism, 148–149
Stone Age, Old and New. *See* Neolithic Age;
Paleolithic Age.
Straits of Hormuz, 533
Stuart lands, *m587*
stupas, 193, *i198*
stylus, 21
subcontinent, 44

Sufi, 271
sugar
in New World territories, 557, 563, 567
and slavery, 563, 567
Suleyman the Lawgiver, 510–511, *i510*
sultan, 507
Sumer, *c3,* 20–23, 48. *See also* Sumerians.
architecture of, 22–23, 31, 32
city-states of, *c26,* 30–31, *i112*
environmental challenges in, 29–30
geography of, 29, *m30*
poetry, 32
Sumerians, 20–23. *See also* Sumer.
culture of, 22–23, 31–32
influence on Mesopotamia of, 20, 29–30
religion of, 23, 31–32
social classes of, 32
Sundiata, 415
Sunna, 268
Sunni, 271, *c271*
Sunni Ali (Songhai ruler), 417
superstition, age of, *i371*
supreme court, *c180*
surnames, 388
Svetasvatara Upanishad, 67
Swahili, *i223,* 422, 427
Sweden, 358, *m610,* 611
symbols
alphabets, *c74, i116*
animal, 454
cuneiform, 20, *i21,* 32, 40, *i116*
glyphs, 448
hieroglyphs, 40, *i40,* 116
in language, *c74*
national, *i680*
pictographs, *i53*
in prehistoric art, 11, *i12–13*
in record keeping, 74, *i116*
religious, *i287, c296*
of warriors, 454
writing, 53
yin and yang, 107, *i107,* 109
Syracuse, 137

Tacitus, 181
Taj Mahal, 519, *i520*
Tamil, 191, 194
Tammarlane. *See also* Timur the Lame.
Tang dynasty, 323–327
expansion of China under, 323–324
influence on Japan, 340
inventions of, *i322,* 325, *i328–329*
population of, 325
renaissance in, 325–326
science and technology, 325,
i328–329
Tang Taizong, 323, *i324*
Tarquin the Proud, 156
technology, 8, 19, 21. *See also* inventions;
science; weapons.
of Africa, 217–218, *i218*
of Bronze Age, 21
of China, 52, 55, 203–204
of Egypt, 90
in European exploration, 530
of the harness, 203, 387
Hellenistic, 148

Hittite, 63
of *Homo erectus,* 8
horsepower, 387
of Indus Valley, 46, *i47*
of Islam, *i275,* 278
migration and, 221, 224
Muslim, *i275,* 278
of Northern Renaissance, 484
prehistoric, *i4,* 8, 14, *i15*
printing press, 484, *i484*
of Sumer, 19, 21, 32
of war, 89, 402
Tehuacan Valley, 238
telescope, 278
Ten Commandments, 79–80
as social code, 80
in teachings of Jesus, 168
Tennis Court Oath, 654
Tenochtitlán, 454–455, 458, *m467*
Teotihuacán, 452–453
theater
comedy and tragedy, 136, *i141*
French, 599
Greek, 136, *i141*
Kabuki, 544, *i545*
Molière, 599
Shakespeare, 483, *i483*
theocracy, 37, 48, 496
Theodora (Byzantine empress), 303, *i303,*
306
Theravada sect, 193
thermometer, 627
Thermopylae, 132
Theseus, 122
Third Republic, 690
Thousand and One Nights, The, 276, *i276*
three cardinal faults, *i285*
three-field system, 387
Thucydides, 122, 135, 136–138
Thutmose III (Egyptian pharaoh), 90, 91
Tiberius, 160
Tigris River, 29
Tikal, 446, *i450–451*
Timbuktu, 416
time
to Maya, 448
measuring, 325, *c328*
time lines
Africa
1500 B.C.–A.D. 500, *c210–211*
800–1500, *c406–407*
Africa, Southwest Asia, and China,
1570 B.C.–200 B.C., *c86–87*
Americas
10,000 B.C.–A.D. 700, *c232–233*
500–1500, *c438–439*
1500–1800, *c550–551*
Central Asia, 500–1500, *c298–299*
East and Southeast Asia, 600–1400, *c320-*
321
Eastern Hemisphere/Western Hemisphere,
2000 B.C.–250 B.C., *c58–59*
Europe
500–1100, *c350–351*
800–1500, *c376–377*
1300–1600, *c468–469*
1500–1800, *c586–587*
1789–1815, *c648–649*
Europe and Asia
1400–1800, *c526–527*

Index

Europe and North America, 1500–1800, *c620–621*
Greece, 2000 B.C.–300 B.C., *c120–121*
India and China, 400 B.C.–A.D. 500, *c186–187*
Latin America and Europe, 1800–1900, *c678–679*
Muslim World
    600–1250, *c260-261*
    1300–1700, *c504–505*
Rome, 500 B.C.–A.D. 500, *c152–153*
World
    4 million B.C.–2500 B.C., *c2–3*
    3500 B.C.–500 B.C., *c26–27*
Timur the Lame, 508
tithes, 363, 379
toilet, flush, 47
Tokugawa Ieyasu, 543–544, 546
Tokugawa Shogunate, 544, 546, *c578, i581*
Toltecs, 453
tools, 19, 21. *See also* technology.
    of exploration, *i531*
    prehistoric, *i4*, 5, 7–11, 14, *i17*
Torah, 77, 79, *i79*, *c80*, 83
Tories, 616
totems, 445
Toumai, 11
tournaments, 367
Toyotomi Hideyoshi, 543
trade. *See also* slavery; trade networks.
    African, 226–227, *i406*, 422
    Arabian, 263, *m264*
    Aztec, 454–455
    balance of, 575
    Buddhism and, 71, *m197*
    Chinese, 197, *m204–205*, 325–326
    colonial, 562–564
    Columbian Exchange, 571–573, *i572*
    and the Crusades, 385
    Dutch, 534–535, 594
    in the early Middle Ages, 353
    East African, 422, *m423*
    in Egypt, 37, 90, 92, 94
    French, 535, 562
    Ghana, 413–414
    global, 573–575
    gold, 227
    gold-salt, 413–414
    goods, *i434*
    Hellenistic, 146
    Incan, 460
    in India, 195–197, *m196*
    in Indus Valley, 48
    Japanese, 545
    under Kublai Khan, 336–337
    in Mesoamerica, 241
    in Middle Ages, 389–390
    Minoan, 72, 125
    Mongol effect on, 334, 336–337
    Muslim, 272, 424
    native North American, 444
    patterns of ancient, *m75*
    Phoenician, *c59*, 73–76, *i75*
    Portuguese, 424, 521, 533–534
    in Roman Empire, 162, 163, *m163*, 164, 197
    routes in Africa, Asia, Europe, *m430*

seafaring, 72–76, 163, 196–197
slave, 566–570
Triangular, 568–569, *m568*
in Ur, 23
Viking, 359
West African, 413–416
Zhou Dynasty, 55
trade networks
    components of, *c431*
    Indian Ocean, *c432*
    Mediterranean, *c432*
    modes of transport, *i433*
    Silk Roads, *c432*
    Trans-Arabia, *c432*
    Trans-Sahara, *c432*
    types of, *c431*
tragedy, 136, *i141*
Trajan, *c164*, *i164*
Treaty of Tordesillas, 533
Treaty of Verdun, 357
triangular trade, 568–569, *m568*
tribunes, 156
tribute, 82
Triple Alliance (Aztec), 454
    collapse of, 456, 458
triumvirate, 161–162
Trojan horse, *i125*
Trojan War, *c121*, 125
troubadours, 367–368
    love songs, 368
Troy, 125
tsetse fly, 213, *i214*, 215
Turkey, Republic of, *i317*
Turkish Empire, 314–317
Turks. *See also* Seljuk Empire.
    in Christian Byzantium, 304
    conflict with Greeks, 689, 693
    migrations, 314
    Seljuks, 314–316
Tutankhamen (Egyptian pharaoh), *i39*
Twelve Tables, 156, *c157*
tyrants, 127, 156, 514

Umayyad dynasty, 271
Umma, 265
United States. *See also* Native Americans; North America.
    Bill of Rights, 617, 645, *i645*
    colonies of, 640–642
    Constitution, *c643*, 644–645, 647
    democracy in, 617, *c643*
    government, *c643*, 644–645
    settlers in, 562–564
university, 391
untouchables, 64, *i64*
Upanishads, 66–67
Upper Egypt, 36–37. *See also* Egypt.
Ur, *c3*, 22–23
urban centers. *See also* cities.
    Muslim, 273–274
    Olmec design, 243
urbanization, 220
Urdu, 518
utopia, 482
Utopia **(More),** 482

Valley of the Kings, 91
Valley of Mexico, 452–453
values
    in ancient Greece, 129, *i130*, 134–136
    Chinese, 104–107
    during Enlightenment, 630–632, 635
    Medieval, 365
    of Persian Empire, 99, 103
    in Renaissance, 472–473, 480
    of samurai, *i342*, 343
    Spartan, 131
van Eyck, Jan, *i470*, 481
vassal, 360
Vedas, 63
Velázquez, Diego, 591, *i591*
Venezuela, 683
Vermeer, Jan, 593
vernacular, 391–392, 475
Verrazzano, Giovanni da, 561
Versailles
    Palace of, 47, 599, *i600*
Vesalius, Andreas, 627–628
Vespucci, Amerigo, 554
Vesuvius. *See* Mount Vesuvius.
Vikings
    Ericson, Leif, 359
    invasions, *m308*, 358, *m359*, 393
    longboats of, 358, *i358*
    Rurik (Viking chief), 307
    and Slavs, 307
villa (Roman), *i166–167*, 178
villages
    achievements of, 16, 18
    becoming cities, 19–20
    growth of, 16, *c24*
Virgil, 179
Vishnu, 67, 194
    fish incarnation of, 83
vizier, 315
Vladimir, 308
volcanoes, 166–167, *c167*
Voltaire, 630, *i630*
voting. *See also* suffrage.
    in ancient Rome, 156
    in United States, *c643*

Wang Mang, 206–207
war. *See also* civil war(s); empire(s); technology.
    American Revolutionary, 640–645
    in ancient China, 55, 201–202
    in ancient Sumer, 31, 32–33
    of the Austrian Succession, 607
    of Bantu-speaking peoples, 224
    elephants of, 158
    English Civil, 615, *m616*
    French and Indian, 564, 641
    Franco-Prussian, 696
    Hundred Years', 401–403
    in Incan civilization, 459–460, 463
    Peloponnesian, 137–138, *m137*, 142
    Peninsular, 669
    Persian, 131–133, *m132*
    Persian Gulf, 23

phalanx in, 131–132, 142
Punic, 158–159, *m159*
Roman civil, 161
of the Roses, 403
Seven Weeks', 696
Seven Years', 607
slave trade in, 566
of the Spanish Succession, 601
technology of, 63, 402, 542
Thirty Years', 603–604
war against terrorism
in Iraq, 23
warriors, feudal, 364–365, 367, 542
Waterloo, 671
weapons, 48. *See also* military power;
technology.
Assyrian, 95, *i97*
Bronze, 22, 90
caltrops, *i364*
catapult, *i366*
of Genghis Khan, 332, *i332*
iron, 55, 63, 94, 217
longbow, 402, *i402*
Mongol, *i332*
of samurai, *i342*
siege, *i366*, 366
Turkish, *i316*
welfare state, 461
West Africa. *See also* Africa.
in 2003, *m429*
empires of, 413–417, *m414*
societies in, 418–419
Western civilization, *c180*. *See also* Greece;
Roman Empire.
effect of Enlightenment on,
633–634
Greco-Roman influence on,
178–183
Greek influence on, 125, *c150*
Roman influence on, 181–183
and Russia, 610–611
values of, 183
Western Europe
a.d. 500, *m351*
in 14th century, *m377*
feudalism in, 360
formation of, 800–1500, 379–403
invasions of, 353, 358–359, *m359*
westernization, 610
wheel, 38
wheelbarrow, 204
Whigs, 616
Wilhelm I (kaiser), 695, 697
William the Conqueror (English king),
393–394
William of Orange (Dutch ruler), 616–617
Winged Victory, *i140*, 149
Wollstonecraft, Mary, 633, *i633*
women. *See also* queen(s); writers.
in agricultural revolution, 15
of ancient China, 52, 206, 327
in ancient Rome, 164
in ancient Sumer, 32
in Athens, 129, 131
in Buddhist society, 70
of China, 541
in czarist Russia, 610, 638–639
in Efe society, 409
in Egypt, 40, 89–90, *i90*
and the Enlightenment, 633

under feudalism, 363, 368–369
during French Revolution, 655, 656, 660
in Greek drama, 136
in Han Dynasty, 201, 206
in Hebrew society, 80
of India, 194, *i519*
Iroquois, 445
of Japan, *i341*, 544
in literature, 482
and manorialism, 363
in the Middle Ages, 354–355, 363,
368–369, *i368*
Minoan, 72
Mongol, *i333*
in Muslim countries, 274
of the Reformation, 494, 496, 498
religious orders of, 380
Renaissance, 473, *i473*, 477, 482
slavery of, *i97*, 164
in Sparta, 131
of Vietnam, 346, *i346*
warrior-women, *i342*, *i346*
Woolley, Leonard, 22
writers
Alighieri, Dante, 392
Aquinas, Thomas, 392, *i392*
Bacon, Francis, 626
Balzac, Honoré de, 700
Basho, Matsuo, 544, *i544*
Byron, Lord, 698, *i698*, 699
Cervantes, Miguel de, 591–592
Chaucer, Geoffrey, 375, 392
Colonna, Vittoria, 477
Dickens, Charles, 662, 701
Goethe, Johan Wolfgang von, 699
Homer, 125–126
Hugo, Victor, 699
Machiavelli, Niccolò, 476, *i476*, 503, *i583*
of Northern Renaissance, 482
Polo, Marco, 337, *i337*
of Renaissance, 475–477
Richardson, Samuel, 637
Shakespeare, William, 483
Shelley, Mary, 699
Shelley, Percy Bysshe, 699
Shikibu, Lady Murasaki, 342
Tocqueville, Alexis de, 671
Virgil, 179
Voltaire, 630, *i630*
Wollstonecraft, Mary, 633, *i633*
Wordsworth, William, 699
Zola, Émile, 700
writing. *See also* writers.
in ancient Greece, 125
Chinese, 53
cuneiform, 20, *i21*, 32, 40, *i116*
Etruscan influence on Roman, 156
hieroglyphics, 40, *i40*, *i116*
illuminated manuscripts, *i258–259*, *i312*
invention of, 20–21, *i21*
in Japan, 340
libraries, 96
of Alexandria, 147, *i262*
Maya, 448
Minoan, 72
Phoenician, 74, *c74*, *i76*, *i116*
pictographs, *i53*
record keeping, 20, 74, *i116*
in Roman Republic, 156
written records, 52, *i116*

writing systems
cuneiform, 20, *i21*, 32, 40, *i116*
hieroglyphics, 40, *i40*, *i116*
Wudi, 201–202
Wu Zhao (Chinese empress), 323,
i324
Wycliffe, John, 399

X

Xenophon, 129
Xerxes, 132–133
Xia Dynasty, 51
Xiongxu, 201–202, *m201*

Y

Yahweh, 78–79
Yamato clan (Japanese rulers), 340
Yangtze River, 50
Yaroslav the Wise, 308–309
Yellow River. *See* Huang He river.
Yemen, *i425*
yin and yang, 107, *i107*, 109
Yonglo, 536–537
Yoruba
Ife, 418–419
Oyo, 418
Yu, 51
Yuan Dynasty, 335–338
Yucatan Peninsula, 446, *m447*

Z

Zagros Mountains, 16, *m17*
early agriculture in, 16
Zapotec civilization, 242–243
Monte Albán, *c59*, *i59*, *c121*, 242–243,
i242
Oaxaca, 242
San José Mogote, 242
Zell, Katherina, 498
Zen Buddhism, *i547*
Zeno, 148, 179
zero, 195
Zeus, 126, 130
Zheng He, 537
Zhou Dynasty, *c27*, 54–55, 104, *c121*
feudalism in, 54
ziggurat, *i22*, 23, 31
of Babylon, 98
Zimbabwe, Great, 425–427, *i426*
Zola, Émile, 700
Zoroaster, 103
Zoroastrianism
Ahura Mazda, 103
Mithra cult, 103
in Muslim culture, 274
Parsi sect, 103
in Persian culture, 103
Zoskales (Aksumite king), 225

Index

Acknowledgments

 Unless otherwise indicated below, all video reference screens are © 2010 A&E Television Networks, LLC. All rights reserved.

Text Acknowledgments

Chapter 3, pages 77, 79, 83, 85: Excerpts from *Tanakh: A New Translation of the Holy Scriptures, According to the Traditional Hebrew Text.* Copyright © 1985 by The Jewish Publication Society. Reprinted by permission of the publisher.

Chapter 4, page 105: Excerpt from *The Analects of Confucius,* translated by Simon Leys. Copyright © 1997 by Pierre Ryckmans. Reprinted by permission of W. W. Norton & Company, Inc.

page 106: Excerpt from *Tao Te Ching* by Lao Tzu, A New English Version with Foreword and Notes by Stephen Mitchell. Translation copyright © 1988 by Stephen Mitchell. Reprinted by permission of HarperCollins Publishers, Pan Macmillan Ltd. and Michael Katz.

Chapter 5, page 126: Excerpt from the *Iliad* by Homer, translated by Ian Johnson, Malaspina University-College, Nanaimo, British Columbia.

Chapter 7, page 194: Excerpt from a Tamil poem from *The Wonder That Was India,* translated by A. L. Basham. Published by Sidgwick and Jackson. Reprinted by permission of Namita Catherine Basham.

Chapter 10, page 270: Excerpt from *Early Islam* by Desmond Stewart and The Editors of Time-Life Books. Copyright © 1967 by Time Inc. Reprinted by permission of Time Inc.

Chapter 11, page 315: Four lines from "Rumi Quatrain," from *Unseen Rain,* translated by John Moyne and Coleman Barks. Originally published by Threshold Books, 139 Main Street, Brattleboro, VT 05301. By permission of Threshold Books.

Chapter 12, page 326: "Moonlight Night," from *Tu Fu* by William Hung, Cambridge, Mass.: Harvard University Press. Copyright © 1952 by the President and Fellows of Harvard College.

Chapter 13, page 367: Seven lines from page 84 of *The Song of Roland* by Frederick Goldin, translator. Copyright © 1978 by W. W. Norton & Company, Inc. Reprinted by permission of W. W. Norton & Company, Inc.

page 375: Excerpt from "The Prologue," from *The Canterbury Tales* by Geoffrey Chaucer, translated by Nevill Coghill (Penguin Classics 1951). Copyright © 1951 by Nevill Coghill. Reprinted by permission of Penguin Books Ltd.

Chapter 19, page 544: Haiku poem, from *Matsuo Basho,* translated by Makoto Veda. By permission of Makoto Veda.

COMPARING & CONTRASTING FEATURES

Unit 1, Page 115: Excerpt from *The Analects of Confucius,* translated and annotated by Arthur Waley. Copyright © 1938 by George Allen & Unwin, copyright renewed 1966. Used with the permission of John Robinson, on behalf of the Arthur Waley Estate.
Excerpt from *Tanakh: A New Translation of the Holy Scriptures, According to the Traditional Hebrew Text.* Copyright © 1985 by The Jewish Publication Society. Reprinted by permission of the publisher.

Unit 5, Page 711: Excerpt from *The French Revolution,* edited by Paul H. Beik. Text copyright © 1971 by Paul H. Beik. Reprinted by permission of HarperCollins Publishers.

Art and Photography Credits

Maps supplied by Mapping Specialists

COVER

Machu Picchu © Jim Zuckerman/Corbis; sky © Digital Vision; Athena. Museo Archeologico Nazionale, Naples, Italy. Photo © Alinari/The Bridgeman Art Library; Olmec Warrior © Danny Lehman/Corbis; King Tut. Egypt Museum, Cairo. Photo by AKG London; Buddah. © Christie's Images/Corbis; Empress Theodora © Archivo Iconografico, S.A./Corbis;

FRONT MATTER

i-ii Machu Picchu © Jim Zuckerman/Corbis; sky © Digital Vision; **i** Athena. Museo Archeologico Nazionale, Naples, Italy. Photo © Alinari/The Bridgeman Art Library; Olmec Warrior © Danny Lehman/Corbis; King Tut. Egypt Museum, Cairo. Photo by AKG London; Buddah. © Christie's Images/Corbis; **ii** Empress Theodora © Archivo Iconografico, S.A./Corbis; **viii** *top left* Cave painting of Tassili n'Ajjer (2nd millenium B.C.). Musée de l'Homme, Paris. Henri Lhote Collection. Photo © Erich Lessing/Art Resource, New York; *top right* © Galen Rowell/Corbis; *center* Canopic sarcophagus containing the organs of Pharaoh Tutankhamun (18th dynasty), Egypt. Photo © Scala/Art Resource, New York; **ix** *top left* Cave painting of Tassili n'Ajjer (2nd millennium B.C.). Musée de l'Homme, Paris. Henri Lhote Collection. Photo © Erich Lessing/Art Resource, New York; *top right* © Galen Rowell/Corbis; *center* Noah's ark. Illumination from Add. MS 11639, f. 521r. By permission of the British Library; *bottom* © Joseph Mc Nally/Getty Images; **x** *top left* Asian and Nubian soldiers in the Egyptian army (2nd -1st millenium B.C.). Collection of Norbert Schimmel, New York. Photo © Erich Lessing/Art Resource, New York; *top left* © Michele Burgess/SuperStock; *center* © Mimmo Jodice/Corbis; *bottom* Pillar of Asoka © Borromeo/Art Resource, New York; **xi** *top left* Asian and Nubian soldiers in the Egyptian army (2nd -1st millennium B.C.). Collection of Norbert Schimmel, New York. Photo © Erich Lessing/Art Resource, New York; *top right* © Michele Burgess/SuperStock; *bottom, Ngady Amwaash.* Kuba Culture of Central Zaire. National Museum, Ghana. Photo © Werner Forman/Art Resource, New York; **xii** *left (top to bottom)* © Stone/Getty Images; © Buddy Mays; Greek cross (1000s), Byzantine. Museo della Civilta Romana, Rome. Photo © Gianni Dagli Orti/The Art Archive; *bottom left* Illustration by Peter Dennis; *top right* Steve Raymer/National Geographic Image Collection; **xiii** *top left* © Stone/Getty Images; *right (top to bottom)* Steve Raymer/National Geographic Image Collection; Golden Bull, (about 1390). Illumination on parchment. Bildarchiv der Osterreichische Nationalbibliothek, Vienna, Austria; *Portrait of Charlemagne,* Albrecht Durer. © Germanisches Nationalmuseum, Nuremberg, Germany. Photo © Lauros-Giraudon, Paris/SuperStock; *bottom* Benin, cast figure, bronze aquamanile. Photo © The British Museum; **xiv** *top left* © Explorer, Paris/SuperStock; *top right* © Tim Hursley/SuperStock; *center, Elizabeth I, 1533–1603 Queen of England,* Federico Zuccari. Pinacoteca Nacionale di Siena. Photo © Gianni Dagli Orti/The Art Archive; *bottom* Shah Tahmasp I receiving the Moghul Emperor Humayun (1660's). Period of Abbas II. Chihil Sutun, Isfahan, Iran. Photo © SEF/Art Resource, New York;

xv *top left* © Explorer, Paris/SuperStock; *top right* © Tim Hursley/SuperStock; *bottom* Globe by Martin Behaim (about 1492). Bibliothèque Nationale, Paris. Photo © Giraudon/Art Resource, New York; **xvi** *left (top to bottom)* Detail of *Marriage of Louis XIV, King of France and Marie Therese of Austria* (1600s), unknown artist. Musée de Tessé Le Mans. Photo © Gianni Dagli Orti/The Art Archive; *Louis XIV, King of France* (1701), Hyacinthe Rigaud. Louvre, Paris. Photo © Erich Lessing/Art Resource, New York; *right* Isaac Newton's reflecting telescope (1672). Royal Society. Photo by Eileen Tweedy/The Art Archive; *right Combat Before the Hotel de Ville, July 28th, 1830,* Victor Schnetz. Musée du Petit Palais, Paris. Photo by Bulloz. Photo © Réunion des Musées Nationaux/Art Resource, New York; *top right* © Todd A. Gipstein/Corbis; **xviii** *top, Alexander the Great,* Relief by Landolin Ohnmacht. Marble, 70 cm x 54 cm. Photo by AKG London; *bottom, Combat Before the Hotel de Ville, July 28th 1830,* Victor Schnetz. Musée du Petit Palais, Paris. Photo by Bulloz. Photo © Réunion des Musées Nationaux/Art Resource, New York; **xix** *top* © Chad Ehlers/Getty Images; *bottom* © Bettmann/Corbis;

UNIT ONE

0-1 spread © David Sutherland/Getty Images.

Chapter 1

2 *left* © John Reader/Photo Researchers; *right* Paleolithic engraving of a lunar calendar on a reindeer antler, (38,000 B.C.) Dordogne, France. Photo © Réunion des Musées Nationaux/Art Resource, New York; **3** *left* © John Reader/SPL/Photo Researchers; *center* National Museum of Iran, Tehran, Iran. Photo © The Bridgeman Art Library; *right* Head of a bull. Musical instrument. (2450 B.C.). Photo © Scala/Art Resource, New York; **4** Photo Archives, South Tyrol Museum of Archaeology; **5** *top left* Cave painting of Tassili n'Ajjer, (2nd millennium B.C.). Musée de l'Homme, Paris. Henri Lhote Collection. Photo © Erich Lessing/Art Resource, New York; *top right* © Galen Rowell/Corbis; **7** © Des Bartlett/Photo Researchers; **11** © AFP/Getty Images; **12** *top* Cave painting of Tassili n'Ajjer, (2nd millennium B.C.). Musée de l'Homme, Paris. Henri Lhote Collection. Photo © Erich Lessing/Art Resource, New York; *bottom* © Alberto Gandsas, Buenos Aires, Argentina, www.gandsas.com; **13** *top* © Sissie Brimberg/National Geographic Image Collection/Getty Images; *bottom* © Pam Gardner, Frank Lane Picture Agency/Corbis; **14** *top left* Cave painting of Tassili n'Ajjer, (2nd millennium B.C.). Musée de l'Homme, Paris. Henri Lhote Collection. Photo © Erich Lessing/Art Resource, New York; *top right* © Galen Rowell/Corbis;

15 *top* © Hanny Paul/Gamma-Liaison/Getty Images; *bottom* Getty Images/The Bridgeman Art Library/South Tyrol Museum of Archaeology, Bolzano, Italy; **16** University of Chicago News Office; **17** © Gianni Dagli Orti/Corbis; **18** © Sonia Halliday Photographs; **20** © Werner Forman/Art Resource, New York; **21** The British Museum, London. Photo © The Bridgeman Art Library; **22** *left* Courtesy of University of Pennsylvania Museum, Philadelphia (Neg.# S4-139540); *right* Ziggurat of Ur-Namu © The British Museum; **25** Bruce Coleman, Inc.

Chapter 2

26 *left* Head of Sargon the Great. (2300-2200 B.C.). Nineveh. Iraq Museum, Baghdad. Photo © Scala/Art Resource, New York; *right* Seated Scribe. Saqqara, Egypt, (5th dynasty). Painted limestone. Louvre, Paris. Photo © Erich Lessing/Art Resource, New York; **27** *left* Fragment of a vase depicting ibex, from Onengo-Daro. Indus Valley. Pakistan. National Museum of Karachi, Karachi, Pakistan. Photo © The Bridgeman Art Library; *right* Fandang (rectangular cooking vessel), Shang dynasty (1600-1100 B.C.). Bronze. From Ningxian, China. Photo © Giraudon/Art Resource, New York; **28** Illustration by Bill Cigliano; **29** *left* © Jose Fuste Raga/Corbis; *right* © Burstein Collection/Corbis; **31** Itur-Shamagen, King of Mari, in prayer. Sumerian. National Museum, Damascus, Syria. Photo © Giraudon/Art Resource, New York; **32** © The British Museum; **33** © Gianni Dagli Orti/Corbis; **34** Royal head, perhaps depicting Hammurabi (1792-1740 B.C.), from Susa. Diorite, 15 cm high. Louvre, Paris, France. Photo © Erich Lessing/Art Resource, New York; **35** *top left* © Jose Fuste Raga/Corbis; *top right* © Burstein Collection/Corbis; **36** Jacques Descloitres, MODIS Land Science Team/NASA; **38** Portrait bust of Herodotus, copy of Greek (fourth century B.C.). Museo Archeologico Nazional, Naples, Italy. Photo © The Bridgeman Art Library; **39** *top* © Bettmann/Corbis; *center left* © The British Museum; *center right* Canopic sarcophagus containing the organs of Pharaoh Tutankhamen. Egypt, (18th dynasty). Egyptian Museum, Cairo, Egypt. Photo © Scala/Art Resource, New York; *bottom* © David Sutherland/Getty Images; **40** The Granger Collection, New York; **42** *top center* © Gianni Dagli Orti/Corbis; *top right* © The British Museum; *center left* Victor R. Boswell, Jr./National Geographic Image Collection; *bottom* © Archivo Iconografico, S.A./Corbis; **42–43** © Corbis; **43** © The Image Works/Topham Picturepoint; **44** *left* © Jose Fuste Raga/Corbis; *right* © Burstein Collection/Corbis; **47** Illustration by Tom Jester; **48** *top* Seal depicting elephant and monograms, steatite (2500-200 B.C.). Indus Civilization, from Mohenjo Daro. National Museum, Karachi, Pakistan. Photo © Alfredo Dagli Orti/The Art Archive; *center* Seal depicting armor plated rhinoceros and monograms, steatite (2500-2000 B.C.). Indus Civilization, from Mohenjo Daro. National Museum Karachi, Pakistan. Photo © Alfredo Dagli Orti/The Art Archive; *bottom* Seal depicting zebu and monograms, steatite (2500-200 B.C.). Indus Civilization, from Mohenjo Daro. National Museum Karachi, Pakistan. Photo © Alfredo Dagli Orti/The Art Archive; **49** © Archivo Iconografico, S.A./Corbis; **50** *left* © Jose Fuste Raga/Corbis; *right* © Burstein Collection/Corbis; **51** © Julia Waterlow/ Eye Ubiquitous/Corbis; **53** © Royal Ontario Museum/Corbis; **55** © Lowell Georgia/Corbis.

Chapter 3

58 *left* Funerary stele of merchant holding weighing scales, (eighth century B.C.), Hittite culture. Musée du Louvre, Paris. Photo © Gianni Dagli Orti/The Art Archive; *right* Colossal Head No. 1, (1200-400 B.C.), Olmec culture. Archaeological garden of La Venta in Villahermosa, Mexico. Photo © Gianni Dagli Orti/The Art Archive; **59** *left* Bearded head pendant, (third century B.C.), Phoenician. National Museum of Carthage, Carthage, Tunisia. Photo © Erich Lessing/Art Resource, New York; *right* Jade mask of bat god (about 500 B.C.-800 A.D.), Zapotec culture. Museo Nacional de Antropologica, Mexico City. Photo © Michel Zabe/Art Resource, New York; **60** Illustration by Terence J. Gabbey; **61** *left* (Detail of) Hindu God Krishna surrounded by his milk carriers. Rajasthan, India. Private Collection, Paris. Photo © Gianni Dagli Orti/The Art Archive; *right* © Israelimages/Garo Nalbandian/Alamy Ltd; **63** Archer on a chariot (ninth century). Late Hittite. Museum of Oriental Antiquities, Istanbul, Turkey. Photo © Erich Lessing/Art Resource, New York; **64** Five-headed Brahma on his Vahana, the Cosmic Goose (1800s), Southern India. Photo © Victoria and Albert Museum, London/Art Resource, New York; **66** *left* (Detail of) Hindu God Krishna surrounded by his milk carriers, Indian. Private Collection, Paris. Photo © Gianni Dagli Orti/The Art Archive; *right* © Israelimages/Garo Nalbandian/Alamy Ltd; **67** Vishnu Visvarrupa, preserver of the universe, represented as the whole world, (early 1800s), Jaipur, India. Victoria and Albert Museum, London. Photo © Sally Chappell/The Art Archive; **68** © Ric Ergenbright/Corbis; **69** Reclining Buddha (1300s-1700s A.D.), Ayuthaya school. National Museum, Bangkok, Thailand. Photo © Scala/Art Resource, New York; **70** © Glen Allison/Stone/Getty Images; **72** *top left* (Detail of) Hindu God Krishna surrounded by his milk carriers. Rajasthan, India. Private Collection. Paris. Photo © Gianni Dagli Orti/The Art Archive; *top right* © Israelimages/Garo Nalbandian/Alamy Ltd; **73** Bull dancing (1700-1400 B.C.). Minoan fresco from Knossos, Crete. Heraklion (Crete) Museum. Photo © Gianni Dagli Orti/The Art Archive; **75** Illustration by Peter Dennis; **76** Detail of the inscription from the sarcophagus of Eshmunazar recounting how he and his mother Amashtarte built temples to the gods of Sidon, (3000-1200 B.C.),

Phoenician. Louvre, Paris. Photo © Lauros-Giraudon/The Bridgeman Art Library; **77** *left* (Detail of) Hindu God Krishna surrounded by his milk carriers. Rajasthan, India. Private Collection, Paris. Photo © Gianni Dagli Orti/The Art Archive; *right* © Israelimages/Garo Nalbandian/Alamy Ltd; **78** *Moses* The Santa Croce Altarpiece (1324-1325), Ugolino di Nerio. Tempera on wood, 54.4 cm x 31.4 cm. Bought, 1983 (NG6484). National Gallery, London. Photo © National Gallery, London/Art Resource, New York; **79** Keter Torah. © Zev Radovan, Jerusalem, Israel; **80** Mezuzah, (mid-late 1900s), Bezalel school. The Jewish Museum, New York, gift of Mrs. William Minder, 1987-57. Photo by John Parnell © The Jewish Museum of New York/Art Resource, New York; **81** *King Solomon* (1400s), Pedro Berruguete. Galleria Nazionale delle Marche, Urbino, Italy. Photo © Alinari/Art Resource, New York; **83** Noah's ark. Illumination from Add. MS 11639, f. 521r. By permission of the British Library; **85** Gold pendant (1600s B.C.), Hittite. From Yozgat, near Bogzkoy, Turkey. Musée Louvre, Paris. Photo © Erich Lessing/Art Resource, New York.

Chapter 4

86 *top* © Andrea Jemolo/Corbis; *bottom* Mask of Agamemnon, (1500s B.C.), Mycenaean. National Archaeological Museum, Athens. Photo © Gianni Dagli Orti/The Art Archive; **87** *top* Ceramic jar from Grave 566, Meroitic Period, Karanog, Nubia. Courtesy of University of Pennsylvania Museum, Philadelphia (Neg. #T4-55OC.2); *bottom* Alexander III, King of Macedonia, (338 B.C.), Roman, copied from Greek statue by Eufranor. Staatliche Glypothek, Munich. Photo © Alfredo Dagli Orti/The Art Archive; **88** Illustration by Peter Dennis; **89** *left* Detail of procession road to the Ishtar gate, (600s B.C.), Neo–Babylonian. Louvre, Paris. Photo © Erich Lessing/Art Resource, New York; *right* © Corbis; **90** *Hatshepsut*. Egyptian; from Deir el-Bahri, western Thebes, New Kingdom, Dynasty 18, reign of Hatshepsut, ca. 1473-1458 B.C. Indurated limestone, H. 76.75". (195 cm). The Metropolitan Museum of Art, Rogers Fund, 1929 (29.3.2). Photo © 1997 The Metropolitan Museum of Art; **91** Temple of Pharaoh Ramses II at Abu Simbel (1279-1213 B.C.). Photo © Alfredo Dagli Orti /The Art Archive; **92-93** *background* © Hugh Sitton/ImageState; **92** *left* © Paul Almasy/Corbis; *right* Photo by Derek A. Welsby © Derek A. Welsby; **93** Shawabits of King Taharka, (690-664 B.C.), Nubian, Napatan Period. Museum of Fine Arts, Boston. Harvard University Museum-Museum of Fine Arts Expedition. Photo © 2008 Museum of Fine Arts, Boston; **94** Gold ring shield from Queen Amanishakheto's pyramid. Staatliche Museen zu Berlin, Preussischer Kulturbesitz, Aegyptisches Museum, Berlin. Photo © Margarete Buesing/Art Resource, New York; **95** *left* Detail of procession road to the Ishtar gate (600s B.C.), Neo–Babylonian. Louvre, Paris. Photo © Erich Lessing/Art Resource, New York; *right* © Corbis; **97** Warriors scaling walls with ladders fighting hand-to-hand. Ashurnazirpal's assault on a city. Stone bas-relief from the palace of Ashurnazirpal II in Nimrud. The British Museum, London. Photo © Erich Lessing/Art Resource, New York; **98** © Bettmann/Corbis; **99** *left* Detail of procession road to the Ishtar gate (600s B.C.), Neo–Babylonian. Louvre, Paris. Photo © Erich Lessing/Art Resource, New York; *right* © Corbis; **100** © Corbis; **102** © The British Museum; **104** *left* Detail of procession road to the Ishtar gate (600s B.C.), Neo–Babylonian. Louvre, Paris. Photo © Erich Lessing/Art Resource, New York; *right* © Corbis; **105** *top* British Library HIP/The Image Works; *bottom* The Granger Collection, New York; **107** *top* © Photodisc/Getty Images; *bottom* Shi Huang-Di of the Qin Dynasty. By permission of the British Library; **108** *left* © Joseph McNally/Getty Images; *right* Illustration by Patrick Whelan; **111** Photo © Michael Holford/The British Museum, London; **111 MC1–111 MC2** © Ilya Terentyev/Getty Images; **112** *left* the gold mask, from the Treasure of Tutankhamen (c.1370-52 B.C.). Gold. Egyptian, 18th Dynasty. Egyptian National Museum, Cairo, Egypt, Bildarchiv Steffens. Photo © The Bridgeman Art Library; *center* © The British Museum; *right* Model of a cart pulled by two oxen, Harrappan. Mohenjo-Daro, Indus Valley, Pakistan. National Museum of Karachi, Karachi, Pakistan. Photo © The Bridgeman Art Library; *bottom* © The British Museum; **113** © John Slater/Corbis; **115** Miniature Torah Scroll, probably English (1765). Jewish Museum, London. Photo © The Bridgeman Art Library; **116** *top left* Man between tigers. Seal from Mohenjo-Daro. National Museum, New Delhi, India. Photo © Nimatallah/Art Resource, New York *center right* © Diego Lezama Orezzoli/Corbis; *bottom left* Hieroglyphs (Middle Kingdom). Thebes. Photo © Erich Lessing/Art Resource, New York; *bottom right* Detail of the inscription from the sarcophagus of Eshmunazar recounting how he and his mother Amashtarte built temples to the gods of Sidon (3000-1200 B.C.). Phoenician. Louvre, Paris. Photo © Lauros-Giraudon/The Bridgeman Art Library; **117** *left* © Asian Art & Archaeology, Inc./Corbis; *right* Model of a Phoenician ship of 900 B.C. Museo della Scienza e della Tecnica, Milan, Italy. Photo © Scala/Art Resource, New York.

UNIT TWO

118-119 *The Athenian Acropolis* (1846), Leo von Klenze. Neue Pinakothek, Munich. Photo © Joachim Blauel/Artothek.

Chapter 5

120 *top* Vase from Palaikastro, Minoan. Archaeological Museum, Heraklion, Crete. Photo © Nimatallah/Art Resource, New York; *bottom, Hatshepsut* (18th dynasty), from the temple of Hatshepsut. Deir el Bahari, West Thebes. Egyptian Museum, Cairo, Egypt. Photo © Scala/Art Resource, New York; **121** *left* Animal mask (about 1100–771 B.C.), Chinese, Western Zhou dynasty. Musée des Arts Asiatiques-Guimet, Paris. Photo by Richard Lambert © Werner Forman/Art Resource, New York; *right* Breastplate, Mixtec, Postclassic Monte Alban V, Yanhuitlan, Oaxaca. Museo Nacional de Antropologia, Mexico City. Photo © Réunion des Musées Nationaux/Art Resource, New York; **122** *left* American School of Classical Studies at Athens, Greece, Angora excavations; *center* Red-figure dish depicting Theseus slaying the Minotaur (400s B.C.). The British Museum, London. Photo © The Bridgeman Art Library; *right, Minerva with the Pectoral*, Pheidias. Louvre, Paris. Photo by Herve Lewandowski. Photo © Réunion des Musées Nationaux/Art Resource, New York; **123** *left* Young girl winning chariot race, Greek engraving from red-figure vase. Bibliothéque des Arts Décoratifs, Paris. Photo © Gianni Dagli Orti/The Art Archive; *right* © Corbis; **125** © Bettmann/Corbis; **126** Head of Polyphemos (about 150 B.C. or later), Hellenistic or Roman Period, Greece. Marble from Thasos, 15 1/8" (38.3 cm). Gift in Honor of Edward W. Forbes from his friends. Photo © Museum of Fine Arts, Boston; **127** *left* Young girl winning chariot race, Greek engraving from red-figure vase. Bibliothéque des Arts Décoratifs, Paris. Photo © Gianni Dagli Orti/The Art Archive; *right* © Corbis; **129** *top right* Funeral stele of Ktesileos and Theano (about 420). Greek, Attic, Classical. Marble, 93 cm H x 50 cm W. Found in Athens, 1921. National Archaeological Museum, Athens. Photo © Herve Champollion/akg-images, London; **130** *background* © Vanni Archive/Corbis; *top* Black-figured hydria (500s), Painter of Micali. Museo Gregoriano Etrusco, Vatican Museums, Rome. Photo © Scala/Art Resource, New York; **133** © AFP/Getty; **134** *left* Young girl winning chariot race, Greek engraving from red-figure vase. Bibliothéque des Arts Décoratifs, Paris. Photo © Gianni Dagli Orti/The Art Archive; *right* © Corbis; **135** Bust of Pericles (100s), Roman. Photo © British Museum, London/Bridgeman Art Library; **136** © Christie's Images/Corbis; **138** *The Death of Socrates* (1780), Francois-Louis Joseph Watteau. Musée des Beaux-Arts, Lille, France. Photo by P. Bernard © Réunion des Musées Nationaux/Art Resource, New York; **139** *left* © Museo Capitolino, Rome/SuperStock; *center* © Museo Capitolino, Rome/SuperStock; *top right* © SuperStock; **140** *left, Hydra with the Rape of Europa*. Museo Nazionale di Villa Giulia. Photo © Scala/Art Resource, New York; *left, inset* Fish plate. Red figure vase painting. (fourth century B.C.). Louvre, Paris. Photo © Réunion des Musées Nationaux/Art Resource, New York; *right* The Nike of Samothrace, goddess of Victory. Louvre, Paris.

Art and Photography Credits (Cont.)

Photo © Erich Lessing/Art Resource, New York; **141** *top* Parthenon © Werner Forman/Art Resource, New York; *center left* © R. Sheridan/Ancient Art and Architecture Collection Ltd.; *center right* © The Lowe Art Museum, The University of Miami/Superstock; *bottom* © Steve Vidler/Superstock; **142** *left* Young girl winning chariot race, Greek engraving from red-figure vase. Bibliothèque des Arts Décoratifs, Paris. Photo © Gianni Dagli Orti/The Art Archive; *right* © Corbis; **143** Detail of Alexander, from the Battle of Issus mosaic, House of the Faun, Pompeii (about 80 B.C.). Museo Archeologico Nazionale, Naples, Italy. Photo © Scala/Art Resource, New York; **146** *left* Young girl winning chariot race, Greek engraving from red-figure vase. Bibliothèque des Arts Décoratifs, Paris. Photo © Gianni Dagli Orti/The Art Archive; *right* © Corbis; **147** The Granger Collection, New York; **148** *top* MS D'Orville 301 f. 31v. Photo © Bodleian Library, Oxford, United Kingdom; *bottom left* The Granger Collection, New York; *bottom right* Smith Collection, Rare Book and Manuscript Library, Columbia University, New York; **150** © SuperStock; **151** *top right* Detail of warriors on Chigi vase, Greek. Museo Nazionale di Villa Giulia, Rome, Italy. Photo © Scala/Art Resource, New York; **151 MC1–151 MC2** © Goodshoot/Jupiterimages/Getty Images.

Chapter 6

152 Funerary figure (206 B.C.–220 A.D.), Han dynasty. Private Collection. Photo © Werner Forman/Art Resource, New York; **153** *top left* © Ancient Art & Architecture Collection Ltd.; *top right* Roman horseman (Soldier). Musée des Antiquities Nationales, Saint Germain-en-Laye, France. Photo © Erich Lessing/Art Resource, New York; *bottom* Small gold figure studded with turquoises in the form of a toucan (about 1400–1534 A.D.), Moche Culture. Private Collection. Photo © Werner Forman/Art Resource, New York; **154** *Cicero Denouncing Catalina Before the Senate* (1800s), Cesare Maccari. Wallpainting. Palazzo Madama, Rome. Photo © Scala/Art Resource, New York; **155** *left* © Vanni Archive/Corbis; *right* © Archivo Iconografico, S.A./Corbis; **156** Caesar's Forum and Temple of Venus Genetrix, Rome, Italy. Photo © Gianni Dagli Orti/The Art Archive; **158** *Hannibal* (about 1508–1513). Museo Capitolino, Rome. Photo © Gianni Dagli Orti/The Art Archive; **160** *left* © Vanni Archive/Corbis; *right* © Archivo Iconografico, S.A./Corbis; **161** *The Death of Julius Caesar* (1793), Vincenzo Camuccini. Galleria d'Arte Moderna, Rome. Photo © Alfredo Dagli Orti/The Art Archive; **162** Roman Emperor Augustus with laurel wreath (about 1000), German. Cameo from Lothair cross. Cathedral Treasury Aachen. Photo © Alfredo Dagli Orti/The Art Archive; **164** *left* © Charles & Josette Lenars/Corbis; *right* The Granger Collection, New York; **165** Gladiators fighting wild beasts (300s). Roman mosaic from Terranova, Italy. Galleria Borghese, Rome. Photo © Alfredo Dagli Orti/The Art Archive ; **166-167** Illustration by John James/Temple Rogers; **167** *top* © Mimmo Jodice/Corbis; *center, bottom* © Dorling Kindersley; **168** *left* © Vanni Archive/Corbis; *right* © Archivo Iconografico, S.A./Corbis; **169** *Christ's Charge to Saint Peter*, Raphael. Photo © Victoria and Albert Museum, London/Art Resource, New York; **172** *Saint Augustine of Hippo, Bishop and Doctor of the Church* (1400s), Swiss. Musée des Beaux Arts, Dijon, France. Photo © Gianni Dagli Orti/The Art Archive; **173** *left* © Vanni Archive/Corbis; *right* © Archivo Iconografico, S.A./Corbis; **176** © Stiftung Schleswig-Holsteinische Landesmuseen, Archaologisches Landesmuseum, Schloss Gottorf, Schleswig, Germany; **177** © Charles & Josette Lenars/Corbis; **178** *left* © Vanni Archive/Corbis; *right* © Archivo Iconografico, S.A./Corbis; **179** *left* © New Line Cinema/Courtesy of Photofest; *top right* El Cid in single combat with Martym Gomez at Callaforra (1344). From manuscript *Chronicle of Spain*. Science Academy, Lisbon, Portugal. Photo © Gianni Dagli Orti/The Art Archive; *bottom right* Illustration of the *Mahabharata* (1800s). Indian, Paithan school. Musée des Arts Asiatiques-Guimet, Paris. Photo by Richard Lambert. Photo © Réunion des Musées Nationaux/Art Resource, New York; **181** © Dennis Degnan/Corbis; **182** *top* © John Heseltine/Corbis; *bottom* Illustration by Phil Colprit/Wood Ronsaville Harlin, Inc.; **185** © Vittoriano Rastelli/Corbis; **185 MC1–185 MC2** © Images & Stories/Alamy.

Chapter 7

186 *Bronze Galloping Horse with One Hoof Resting on a Swallow* (second century A.D.). Chinese School. Late Han Dynasty, from the Tomb at Wuwei. Photo © Giraudon/The Bridgeman Art Library; **187** *left* Buff sandstone head of the Buddha (400s), Samath. National Museum of India, New Delhi, India. Photo © The Bridgeman Art Library; *center* Mask. Kuba people, West Africa. Wood with seashells and pearls. Rijksmuseum voor Volkenkunde Leiden (Leyden). Photo © Gianni Dagli Orti/The Art Archive; *right, Shiva Nataraja*, Indian, Tamilnadu, early 1200s, Chola period (ca. 890-1279). Bronze, height: 34.25 " (87.0 cm). The Nelson-Atkins Museum of Art, Kansas City, Missouri. Purchase: Nelson Trust, 34–7; **188** Illustration by Shannon Stirnweis; **189** *left* Brahma. Stone relief from Aihole (sixth to seventh century A.D.). Gupta Period, Prince of Wales Museum, Bombay, Maharashtra, India. Photo © Art Resource, New York; *right* © The Image Bank/Getty Images; **190** *top* Column of Asoka (200s B.C.). Photo © Borromeo/Art Resource, New York; *bottom* Pillar of Asoka. Photo © Borromeo/Art Resource, New York; **192** Terracotta tile with a musician (fifth century A.D.), Central India, Gupta period. © The British Museum, **193** *left* Brahma. Stone relief from Aihole (sixth to seventh century A.D.). Gupta Period, Prince of Wales Museum, Bombay, Maharashtra, India. Photo © Art Resource, New York; *right* © The Image Bank/Getty Images; **194** National Museum, New Delhi, India. Photo © Scala/Art Resource, New York; **195** © Monopole–Pathe/Photofest; **198** *top* Buddha (sixth century A.D.) Bronze. Gupta period. National Museum of India, New Delhi, India. Photo © The Bridgeman Art Library; *bottom* Stupe no. 3, Early Andhra dynasty. Sandhi, India. Photo © Scala/Art Resource, New York; **199** *top* © David Cumming/ Eye Ubiquitous/Corbis; *center left* Ganesa (fifth century A.D.). Gupta dynasty. From Itar. Museum and Picture Library. Photo © Borromeo/Art Resource, New York; *center right* © Arvind Garg/Corbis; **200** *top left* Brahma. Stone relief from Aihole (sixth to seventh century A.D.). Gupta Period, Prince of Wales Museum, Bombay, Maharashtra, India. Photo © Art Resource, New York; *top right* © The Image Bank/Getty Images; *bottom* By permission of the British Library; **203** © Bettmann/Corbis; **204–205** The Granger Collection, New York; **205** The Granger Collection, New York; **206** *left, Warrior* late Han dynasty, (206 BC–220 AD). Chinese. Terracotta. Musée Cernuschi, Paris. Photo © Gianni Dagli Orti/The Art Archive; *right* Bronze figurine of Roman legionnaire © The British Museum; **207** © Robert Harding Picture Library; **209** National Museum, Beijing, China. Photo © Erich Lessing/Art Resource, New York.

Chapter 8

210 *left* Massive stone head. Olmec. Anthropology Museum, Veracruz, Jalapa, Mexico. Photo © Werner Forman/Art Resource, New York; *right* Bust of Pericles (fifth century B.C.), Greek school. Vatican Museums and Galleries, Vatican City, Italy. Photo © Alinari/The Bridgeman Art Library; **211** *top left* Head (900 B.C.–200 A.D.), Nok. Nigeria. Entwistle Gallery, London. Photo © Werner Forman/Art Resource, New York; *bottom left* Bronze figurine of Roman legionnaire © The British Museum; *right* © Jane Taylor/Sonia Halliday Photographs; **212** *top* © David Turnley/Corbis; *bottom* © Paul Almasy/Corbis; **213** *left* Asian and Nubian soldiers in the Egyptian army. (second to first millennium B.C.) Collection of Norbert Schimmel, New York. Photo © Erich Lessing/Art Resource, New York; *right* © Michele Burgess/SuperStock; **214** *top left* © Martin Dohrn/Photo Researchers; *top right* © Photowood Inc./Corbis; *bottom left* © Michael Fogden/Bruce Coleman, Inc.; *bottom right* © Mary Ann McDonald/Corbis; **215** © Liba Taylor/Corbis; **216** Cave painting of Tassili n'Ajjer, (2nd millennium B.C.). Musée de l'Homme, Paris. Henri Lhote Collection. Photo © Erich Lessing/Art Resource, New York; **217** Nok Figure. Private Collection. Photo Joshua Nefsky, New York. Courtesy Entwistle, London; **218** Illustration by Terry Gabbey; **219** Charles Santore/National Geographic Image Collection; **220** Mask. Kuba culture, Zaire. Private Collection. Photo © Aldo Tutino/Art Resource, New

R84 ACKNOWLEDGMENTS

York; **223** *top left* © Joe Mc Donald/Corbis; *top right* © Photographers Library LTD/eStock Photography/PictureQuest/ JupiterImages; *bottom* © Staffan Widstrand/Corbis; **224** Ngady Amwaash. Kuba Culture of Central Zaire. National Museum, Ghana. Photo © Werner Forman/Art Resource, New York; **225** *top left* Asian and Nubian soldiers in the Egyptian army (second to first millennium B.C.). Collection of Norbert Schimmel, New York. Photo © Erich Lessing/Art Resource, New York; *top right* © Michele Burgess/SuperStock; **227** © George Gerster/Rapho/Eyedea; **228** Stela at Axum. Axum, Ethiopia. Photo © Werner Forman/Art Resource, New York; **230** *top* Charles Santore/National Geographic Image Collection; *center* © Photographers Library Ltd/eStock Photography/PictureQuest/JupiterImages ; *bottom* © George Gerster/Rapho/Eyedea.

Chapter 9

232 *left* The Giza Sphinx with the pyramid of Chephren (Old Kingdom, Fourth dynasty). Pyramid of Chefren, Giza, Egypt. Photo © Werner Forman/Art Resource, New York; *right* © National Museum of Anthropology, Mexico/Explorer, Paris/SuperStock; **233** *top* Gold monkey-head bead (100–600 A.D.), Mochia, La Mina, Jequetepeque Valley, north coast of Peru. Photo © Werner Forman/Art Resource, New York; *bottom* Bust of Emperor Hadrian (second century A.D.), Roman. Galleria degli Uffizi, Florence, Italy. Photo © Alinari/The Bridgeman Art Library; **234** © Chase Studio/Photo Researchers; **235** *left* © Philip Beaurline/SuperStock; *right* © Mark Newman/SuperStock; **236** © Steve McCurry/Magnum Photos; **237** *top right* Kenneth Garrett/National Geographic Image Collection; *center left* © Warren Morgan/Corbis; *center right* J. M. Adovasio, Mercyhurst Archaeological Institute; *bottom* Kenneth Garrett/National Geographic Image Collection; **238** Dale Walde/University of Calgary; **240** *left* © Philip Beaurline/SuperStock; *right* © Mark Newman/SuperStock; **242** © Robert Frerck/Odyssey/Chicago; **244** *top* Monolithic Olmec head found near La Venta. Mesoamerica, Pre-Columbian. La Venta, Mexico. Photo © SEF/Art Resource, New York; *center* Colossal Head. Olmec culture. Mesoamerica, Pre-Columbian. La Venta, Mexico. Photo © Scala/Art Resource, New York; *bottom* Dumbarton Oaks, Pre-Columbian Collection, Washington, D.C.; **245** *top* Altar no. 4 with Olmec lord in niche beneath jaguar pelt (about A.D. 500–1000), Pre-Columbian. Archaeological garden of La Venta in Villahermosa, Mexico. Photo © Gianni Dagli Orti/The Art Archive; *bottom* Standing figure holding a masked "baby" (800–500 B.C.), Olmec, Mexico. Jade, 8 5/8" x 3 3/16" x 1 5/8". On loan to the Brooklyn Museum of Art from the collection of Mr. Robin B. Martin (L47.6); **246** *left* © Philip Beaurline/SuperStock; *right* © Mark Newman/SuperStock; **247** *top* © Julio Donoso/Corbis Sygma; *center* © Jonathan Blair/Corbis; *bottom* © SuperStock; **248** *top* William Allard/ National Geographic Image Collection; *center* © Philip Baird/ www.anthroarcheart.org; *bottom* © Yann Arthus-Bertrand/ Corbis; **252** *top* Bust of Pericles (about 430 B.C.), Roman, copy of a Greek original. The British Museum, London. Photo © The Bridgeman Art Library; *bottom left* Dallas Museum of Art, gift of Ms. Eugene McDermott, The Roberta Coke Camp Fund, and The Art Museum League Fund; *bottom right* Emperor Liu Ban (1700s) China. British Library. Photo © The Art Archive; **253** *top* Augustus, Roman Emperor. Marble bust. Musei Capitolini, Rome. Photo © SEF/Art Resource, New York; *bottom* Courtesy Stephen Album Rare Coins, Santa Rosa, Calif.; **254** *top left* Pugilist resting (sixth–first century B.C.) Apollonios, or a Roman copy. Museo Nazionale Romano delle Terme, Rome. Photo © Erich Lessing/Art Resource, New York; *top center* © Archivo Iconografico, S.A./Corbis; *top right* Bronze figure of the seated Buddha (fifth century A.D.). Gupta Period, from Danesar Khera, Central India © The British Museum, London; *bottom, center* © John Heseltine/Corbis; *bottom right* Vishnu Temple (fifth century A.D.) Gupta Period. Photo © Borromeo/Art Resource, New York; **255** *top left* Flying horse. Easter Han dynasty. China. National Museum, Beijing, China. Photo © Erich Lessing/Art Resource, New York; *top right* Jade ceremonial axe in form of feline monster. Olmec culture. Veracruz, Mexico. Museum of Mankind, London. Photo © Eileen Tweedy/The Art Archive; *bottom left* Green glazed model of a tower in three detachable sections. Han Dynasty. Private Collection. Photo © The Bridgeman Art Library; *bottom right* © Bob Krist/Corbis; **256** *top left* © Paul Almasy/Corbis; *top right* © Lindsay Hebberd/Corbis; *bottom left* © Reuters NewMedia Inc./Corbis; *bottom right* © Vittoriano Rastelli/Corbis.

UNIT THREE

258–259 *Marco Polo Leaving Venice*, MS Bodl. 264, fol. 218r. Bodleian Library, University of Oxford.

Chapter 10

260 *top* © Bettmann/Corbis; *bottom* Detail of Scepter of King Charles V of France, surmounted by a statue of Charlemagne. Louvre, Paris. Photo © Erich Lessing/Art Resource, New York; **261** *top*, *Anatomy of the Eye* (592), Arabian manuscript. Of the *Hegira* (1214), Al-Mutadibih. Egyptian Museum, Cairo. Photo © Gianni Dagli Orti/The Art Archive; *bottom* © Stapleton Collection/Corbis; **262** Illustration by Yuan Lee; **263** *left* © Stone/Getty Images; *right* Steve Raymer/National Geographic Image Collection; **265** Abraham's elephants charging under the Ka'Bah (1368). From the Apostles Biography. Illuminated manuscript. Topkapi Museum, Istanbul, Turkey. Photo © Eileen Tweedy/The Art Archive; **266** *top left* © Ted Spiegel/Corbis; *top right* © Hanan Isachar/Corbis; *bottom* © Rostislav Glinsky/Shutterstock; **267** Qu'ran Ju/XXVII. Mamluk (1300s). Arabic School. Private Collection. Photo © Bonhams, London/The Bridgeman Art Library; **268** © Murat Ayranci/SuperStock; **269** *left* © Stone/Getty Images; *right* Steve Raymer/National Geographic Image Collection; **270** Battle of the tribes. Illumination from Add. Or 25900, f. 121v. By permission of the British Library; **272** © Sonia Halliday Photographs; **273** *left* © Stone/Getty Images; *right* Steve Raymer/National Geographic Image Collection; **274** *Persian Garden Party*. MS Elliott 189, f. 192. Photo © Bodleian Library, Oxford, United Kingdom; **275** *top* Photo © Gianni Dagli Orti/University Library, Istanbul, Turkey/ The Art Archive; *center, bottom* The Granger Collection, New York; **276** The Granger Collection, New York; **277** *left* © Arthur Thévenart/Corbis; *top right* © Peter Sanders; *center right, bottom right* © Arthur Thévenart/Corbis; **278** © Brian Lawrence/ImageState.

World Religions

284 © Adrienne McGrath; **284–285** *top* © Luca I. Tettoni/Corbis; *bottom* The Hutchison Library; **285** Oriental Museum, Durham University, England. The Bridgeman Art Library; **286** © Daniel Aguilar/Reuters; **286–287** *The Last Supper* (1498), Leonardo da Vinci. S. Maria delle Grazie, Milan, Italy. Photo © Scala/Art Resource, New York; **287** *top* © Jane Sweeney/Robert Harding; *center* The Granger Collection, New York; *bottom* © Photodisc/Getty Images; **288** © Gavin Hellier/Getty Images; **289** *top left* © Ric Ergenbright/Corbis; *right* Shiva as Mahesha or Brahma (900s). Indian, Tamil Nadu. Granite with gesso and red pigment. Worchester Art Museum, Massachusetts. Photo © Bridgeman Art Library; *bottom left* © Lindsay Hebberd/Corbis; **290** © AFP/Getty Images; **291** *top left* © Peter Sanders; *bottom left* James Stanfield/National Geographic Image Collection; *top right* From *Traditional Textiles of Central Asia* by Janet Harvey. Photo James Austin © 1996 Thames and Hudson Ltd., London. Reproduced by permission of the publishers; *bottom right* © World Religions Photo Library; **292** © Zbigniew Kosc/Circa Photo Library; **292-293** *top* © Rose Eichenbaum/Corbis; *bottom* © Zev Radovan; **293** *top* © Image Source/elektraVision/PictureQuest/JupiterImages; *bottom* The Granger Collection, New York; **294** © Xinhua/ Sovfoto; **295** *top* Confucius (1600s), from a Chinese scroll painting. Bibliothèque Nationale, Paris. Photo © Snark/Art Resource, New York; *bottom* Chinese painting showing filial piety (1100's). Photo © The Art Archive.

Art and Photography Credits (Cont.)

Chapter 11

298 © Ancient Art & Architecture Collection Ltd.; **299** *top left, Moorish Archer on Horseback.* Chinese, Ming Dynasty. Photo © Victoria and Albert Museum, London/Art Resource, New York; **299** *top right* Moorish forces surrounding Constantinople (1200s). folio 43V of *Canticles of Saint Mary,* manuscript by Alfonso X the Wise, King of Castile and Leon. Real Biblioteca de lo Escorial. Photo © Gianni Dagli Orti/The Art Archive; *bottom* Council of Clermont. Arrival of Pope Urban II in France. (1337) Miniature from the Toman de Godefroi de Bouillon. Bibliothéque Nationale, Paris. Photo © Giraudon/Art Resource, New York; **300** Timur's invasion of India. Victoria and Albert Museum, London. Photo © Eileen Tweedy/The Art Archive; **301** *top left* © Stone/Getty Images; *top right, The Archangel Michael* (2nd half 1300s). Russian Byzantine icon. Tretyakov Gallery, Moscow. Photo © Scala/Art Resource, New York; **bottom** Greek cross (1000s). Byzantine. Museo della Civilta Romana, Rome. Photo © Gianni Dagli Orti/The Art Archive; **302** © Sadik Demiroz/SuperStock; **303** *Theodora.* © R. Sheridan/Ancient Art & Architecture Collection Ltd.; **304** © Jonathan Blair/Corbis; **305** © Alessandro Bianchi/Reuters/Corbis; **306** Chalice (1000s). Byzantine. Basilica San Marco, Venice. Photo © Gianni Dagli Orti/The Art Archive; **307** *left* © Stone/Getty Images; *right, The Archangel Michael* (2nd half 1300s). Russian Byzantine icon. Tretyakov Gallery, Moscow. Photo © Scala/Art Resource, New York; **311** © Archivo Iconografico, S.A./Corbis; **312** *top* © Archivo Iconografico, S.A./Corbis; *center* © Massimo Listri/Corbis; *bottom* Scribe writing out the Gospel (late 1400s). Hermitage, St. Petersburg, Russia. Photo © The Bridgeman Art Library; **312–313** Church of the Assumption, Varzuga, Kola Peninsula, Russia. Photo © Vadim Gippenreiter/The Bridgeman Art Library; **313** © Elio Ciol/Corbis; **314** *left* © Stone/Getty Images; *right, The Archangel Michael* (2nd half 1300s). Russian Byzantine icon. Tretyakov Gallery, Moscow. Photo © Scala/Art Resource, New York; **315** © Jose Fuste Raga/Corbis; **316** *top* Or. MS 20,f. 124v. By permission of the Edinburgh University Library; **317** © The Image Bank/Getty Images.

Chapter 12

320 *left* Female polo player (700s). Tang Dynasty. Photo by Roger Asselberghe. Musée des Arts Asiatiques-Guimet, Paris. Photo © Erich Lessing/Réunion des Musées Nationaux/Art Resource, New York; *right* Quetzalcoatl, (post Classical period, ninth–13th century). Photo © Joseph Martin/The Art Archive; **321** *left* Pope Leo IX excommunicating Michael Keroularios (1400s). Greek manuscript. Biblioteca Nazionale, Palermo, Italy. Photo © Gianni Dagli Orti/The Art Archive; *right* Ariwara-no-Narihara, Japanese poet (1100s-1200s). Kamakura period. Silk painting. Photo © Gianni Dagli Orti/Paris/The Art Archive; **322** *left* © Dorling Kindersley; *center* © Keren Su/Corbis; *right* Photograph by Sharon Hoogstraten; **323** *left* © Kelly-Mooney Photography/Corbis; *right* © Ernest Manewal/SuperStock; **324** *top* Emperor Tang Taizong. National Palace Museum, Taipei. Photo © Wan-go Weng; *bottom* Empress Wu Zetian (1700s). Tang dynasty. Chinese. British Library. Photo © The Art Archive; **325** © William Whitehurst/Corbis; **326** *top* Tu Fu (1700s). Chinese. The British Museum, London. Photo © The Art Archive; *bottom* © Burstein Collection/Corbis; **328** *inset* Small plate. Northern Sung dynasty, China. Musée Guimet, Paris. Photo © Gianni Dagli Orti/The Art Archive; **328** *top* Porcelain flask (early 1400s), Ming dynasty. China. Photo © Victoria and Albert Museum, London/Art Resource, New York; *bottom* Ontario Science Center, Toronto, Canada; **329** Illustration by Peter Dennis; **330** *top* © Kelly-Mooney Photography/Corbis; *right* Temple of Angkor Wat, Cambodia. Photo © Ernest Manewal/SuperStock; **331** James L. Stanfield/National Geographic Image Collection; **332–333** Illustration by Patrick Whelan; **335** *left* © Kelly-Mooney Photography/Corbis; *right* Temple of Angkor Wat, Cambodia. © Ernest Manewal/SuperStock; **336** © The Granger Collection, New York; **337** *top* William H. Boyd/National Geographic Image Collection; *bottom* © Biblioteca Nazionale, Turin, Italy/Silvio Fiore/SuperStock; **339** *left* © Kelly-Mooney Photography/Corbis; *right* Temple of Angkor Wat, Cambodia. Photo © Ernest Manewal/SuperStock; **341** © Laurie Platt Winfrey, Inc.; **342** *top* Tomoe, a brave woman of the Genji and Heishi period (about 900 A.D.). Photo © The Art Archive; *bottom* Illustration by Peter Dennis; **344** *left* © Kelly-Mooney Photography/Corbis; *right* Temple of Angkor Wat, Cambodia.© Ernest Manewal/SuperStock; **345** *top* © Dave G. Houser/Corbis; *bottom* © Steve Vidler/SuperStock; **346** *The man god Dangun,* Korean School. Natural pigment on paper, 52 cm x 80 cm. Gahoe Museum, Jongnogu, South Korea. © The Bridgeman Art Library; **349 MC1–349 MC2** © Burstein Collection/Corbis.

Chapter 13

350 Feats of the noble prince Charles Martel. Musée Goya, Castres, France. Photo © Giraudon/Art Resource, New York; **351** *top left* Vendel warrior's helmet (seventh century). From the Vendel boat grave no. 1, Uppland, Sweden. Statens Historiska Museet, Stockholm, Sweden. Photo © Werner Forman/Art Resource, New York; *top right* Imperial orb (First half 1000s). Kunsthistorisches Museum, Vienna. Photo © Erich Lessing/Art Resource, New York; *bottom, The Genies Gathering Over the Sea.* Poem by Ma Lin on silk. (A.D. 960–1279), Chinese, Song dynasty. Calligraphy. Musée des Arts, Asiatiques–Guimet. Paris. Inv.: EG 2146. Photo by Michel Urtado. Photo © Réunion des Musées Nationaux/Art Resource, New York; **352** Month of June from the Grimani Breviary (1500s). Biblioteca Marciana, Venice. Photo © Scala/Art Resource, New York; **353** *left* © Chris Bland/Eye Ubiquitous/Corbis; *right* The army leaves after sack of town (1300s). Manuscript. Biblioteca Nazionale Marciana, Venice. Photo © Alfredo Dagli Orti/The Art Archive; **354** Golden Bull, (about 1390). Illumination on parchment. Bildarchiv der Osterreichische Nationalbibliothek, Vienna, Austria; **355** *left, Saint Benedict,* Hans Memling. Uffizi, Florence, Italy. Photo © Scala/Art Resource, New York; *right, St. Scholastica* © National Gallery Collection; By kind permission of the trustees of the National Gallery, London/Corbis; **357** *Portrait of Charlemagne,* Albrecht Durer. © Germanisches Nationalmuseum, Nuremberg, Germany. Photo © Lauros-Giraudon, Paris/SuperStock; **358** *top left* © Chris Bland/ Eye Ubiquitous/Corbis; *top right* The army leaves after sack of town (1300s) Manuscript. Biblioteca Nazionale Marciana, Venice. Photo © Alfredo Dagli Orti/The Art Archive; *bottom* © Dorling Kindersley; **361** Illustration by Terry Gabbey; **362** © North Wind Picture Archives; **363** Two men beating corn with flails (about 1320). From *The Luttrell Psalter.* The British Library, London. Photo © HIP/Art Resource, New York; **364** *top left* © Chris Bland/Eye Ubiquitous/Corbis; *top right* The army leaves after sack of town (1300s) Manuscript. Biblioteca Nazionale Marciana, Venice. Photo © Dagli Orti/The Art Archive; *bottom* Royal Armouries; **365** *St. George and the Dragon* (about 1460), Paolo Uccello. National Gallery, London. Photo © The Bridgeman Art Library; **366** Illustration by Wood Ronsaville Harlin, Inc.; **367** Courtesy of Photofest; **368** *left* © Archivo Iconografico, S.A./Corbis; *right, Peasant Woman With Scythe and Rake,* Alexei Venetsianov. Photo © The State Russian Museum/Corbis; **369** MS Bruxelles, B.R. 9961-62,fol.91v. Photo © Bibliothèque Royal Albert ler, Brussels, Belgium; **370** *top left* © Chris Bland/ Eye Ubiquitous/Corbis; *top right* The army leaves after sack of town (1300s) Manuscript. Biblioteca Nazionale Marciana, Venice. Photo © Alfredo Dagli Orti/The Art Archive; *bottom* Museo Tesoro di San Pietro, Vatican State. Photo © Scala/Art Resource, New York; **371** © Aaron Horowitz/Corbis; **372** Mapping Specialists; **373** *Frederick 1 Barbarossa and his Sons* (1100s). German School. Landes Bibliothek, Fulda, Germany. Photo © Alinari/The Bridgeman Art Library.

Chapter 14

376 *left* © Gianni Dagli Orti/Corbis; *right, William the Conqueror* (1289). Cloister of the Church of the Annunciation, Florence, Italy. Photo © Gianni Dagli Orti/The Art Archive; **377** *left* Portrait of Genghis Khan. National Palace Museum, Taipei, Taiwan. Photo © The Bridgeman Art Library; *right, Hours of Marguerite de Coetivy: The Final Moments* (1400s). Ms. 74/1088 f. 90. Musée Conde, Chantilly, France. Photo © Giraudon/Art Resource, New York; **378** *Richard Coeur de Lion on his* *way to Jerusalem*, James William Glass. Phillips, The International Fine Art Auctioneers, United Kingdom. Photo © The Bridgeman Art Library; **379** *left* © Corbis; *right* © Archivo Iconografico, S.A./Corbis; **381** *left* Harry Bliss/National Geographic Image Collection; *top right* © Daniel Thierry/Photononstop/Photolibrary; *center right, bottom right, Portrait of the Good Samaritan* (1200s). Stained glass. Chartres Cathedral, France. Photo © Giraudon/Art Resource, New York; **382** Mary Evans Picture Library; **384** *left* © Bettmann/Corbis; *right, Portrait of Saladin, Sultan of Egypt*. Museo di Andrea del Castagno, Uffizi, Florence. Photo © SEF/Art Resource, New York; **385** *Scene at Court* (1710–1720), Alessandro Magnasco. Kunthistorisches Museum, Vienna. Photo © Erich Lessing/Art Resource, New York; **386** By permission of the British Library; **387** *left* © Corbis; *right* © Archivo Iconografico, S.A./Corbis; **388** Illustration by Peter Dennis/Linda Rogers Associates; **389** *Fish Market*, Joachim Beuklelaer. Museo Nazionale de Capodimonte, Naples, Italy. Photo © Alinari/Art Resource, New York; **391** *Imaginary portrait of Avicenna* Ibn Sina. French School. Bibliothèque de la Faculte de Medecine, Paris. Photo © Archives Charmet/The Bridgeman Art Library; **392** St. Thomas Aquinas from the Demidoff Altarpiece, Carlo Crivelli. Photo © National Gallery Collection/By kind permission of the Trustees of the National Gallery, London/Corbis; **393** *left* © Corbis; *right* © Archivo Iconografico, S.A./Corbis; **394** Eleanor of Aquitaine (1800s), French School. Bibliothèque Nationale, Paris. Photo © The Bridgemann Art Library; **395** National Archives; **396** MS francais 6465, f. 212 v. Bibliothèque Nationale, Paris. Photo by AKG London; **398** *left* © Corbis; *right* © Archivo Iconografico, S.A./Corbis; **399** *The Triumph of Death* (late 1400s). Flemish. Musée du Berry, Bourges, France. Photo © Bridgeman-Giraudon/Art Resource, New York; **402** Illustration by Peter Dennis/Linda Rogers Associates; **403** © Christie's Images/Corbis; **405 MC1–405 MC2** © The Gallery Collection/Corbis.

Chapter 15

406 *top* © Paul Almasy/Corbis; *bottom* © Bettmann/Corbis; **407** *top* Mansu Musa, King of Mali. The Granger Collection, New York; *bottom* Death strangling a victim of the plague (1300s), Czechoslovakia. From the Stitny Codex. University Library, Prague, Czech Republic. Photo © Werner Forman/Art Resource, New York; **408** Illustration by Yuan Lee; **409** *left, right* © Michele Burgess/SuperStock; **412** © Richard Bickel/Corbis; **413** *left, right* © Michele Burgess/SuperStock; **416** Mansu Musa, King of Mali. The Granger Collection, New York; **418** © North Carolina Museum of Art/Corbis; **419** © Seattle Art Museum/Corbis; **420** *top* Benin, Queen Mother head. Photo © The British Museum; *bottom* Plaque which decorated the palace of Benin Obas © Werner Forman/Art Resource, New York; **421** *top* Illustration by Yuan Lee; *bottom left* Bronze figure of a horn blower (late 1500s–early 1600s A.D.), Edo. Benin Kingdom, Nigeria. Photo © The British Museum; *bottom right* Benin, cast figure, bronze aquamanile. Benin Kingdom, Nigeria. Photo © The British Museum; **422** *left, right* © Michele Burgess/SuperStock; **424, 425** The Granger Collection, New York; **426** *top left* © Colin Hoskins/Cordaiy Photo Library Ltd./Corbis; *top right* Anthony Bannister/Gallo Images/Getty Images; *bottom* © Robert Preston/Alamy Ltd; **433** *top* © Nik Wheeler/Corbis; *center right* Astrolabe (800s) Ahmad Ibu Khalaf. Bibliothèque Nationale de Cartes et Plans, Paris, France. Photo © The Bridgeman Art Library; *center left* Camel (700s A.D.) from tomb of Cungpu, Shaanxi province, China. Genius of China Exhibition. Photo © The Art Archive; *bottom* © Science & Society Picture Library, London; **434** *top left* Chinese moon flask decorated in famille rose colors with birds and flowers (1200s–1300s.) Yuan Dynasty. Percival David Foundation for Chinese Art/Harper Collins Publishers. Photo © The Art Archive; *top right* Spoon (1500-1600s) Edo peoples, Benin Kingdom, Nigeria. Bequest of Mrs. Robert Woods Bliss. National Museum of African Art, Smithsonian Institution, Washington, D.C. Photo © Aldo Tutino/Art Resource, New York; *bottom* Photograph by Sharon Hoogstraten.

UNIT FOUR

436–437 *La Salle's Louisiana Expedition* in 1684 (1844), J.A. Theodore Gudin. Photo © Réunion des Musées Nationaux/Art Resource, New York.

Chapter 16

438 *left* © Charles & Josette Lenars/Corbis; *right* Crown of the Holy Roman Empire (about 962). Kuntshistorisches Museum, Vienna, Austria. Photo © Erich Lessing/Art Resource, New York; **439** *top* Fertility goddess (pre-Columbian), Aztec. The British Museum, London. Photo © Werner Forman/Art Resource, New York; *bottom* © David Lees/Corbis; **440** Thunderbird Hamatsa headdress (early 1900s), Native American, Kwakwaka'wakw. Yellow cedar, cedar bark, cloth and paint, 10" x 14.5" x 24.5" (25.4 cm x 36.83 cm x 62.23 cm). Seattle Art Museum, Gift of John H. Hauberg. Photo © Paul Macapia; **441** *left* © Explorer, Paris/SuperStock; *right* © Tim Hursley/SuperStock; **443** © Corbis; **444** © Richard A. Cooke/Corbis; **446** *left* © Explorer, Paris/SuperStock; *right* © Tim Hursley/SuperStock; *bottom* Jade mask used in burial rituals (600s), Classic Maya. Excavated from the Temple of Inscriptions at Palenque. Museo Nacional de Antropologia, Mexico City. Photo © Werner Forman/Art Resource, New York; **448** (Detail of) Prisoners marching as a result of destruction of the land of Mu from Maya codex Troano or Tro-Cortesianus. Antochiw Collection, Mexico. Photo © Mireille Vautier/The Art Archive; **450** *left* The Granger Collection, New York; *right* Two-headed jaguar throne from Uxmal, Yucatan, Maya. Photo © Danielle Gustafson/Art Resource, New York; **450–451** © Alison Wright/Corbis; **451** *left* © Ludovic Maisant/Corbis; *right* Ball court at Chichen Itza, Maya, Yucatan, Mexico. Photo © Dagli Orti/The Art Archive; **452** *top left* © Explorer, Paris/SuperStock; *top right* © Tim Hursley/SuperStock; *bottom* Quetzalcoatl (900s), Toltec. Western Yucatan, Mexico. Photo © Dagli Orti/The Art Archive; **453** © Angelo Hornak/Corbis; **454** Eagle warrior (pre-Columbian), Aztec. Mueseo del Templo Mayor, Mexico City. Photo © Michel Zabe/Art Resource, New York; **456** Detail of *The Aztec World* (1929), Diego Rivera. Mural. National Palace Museum, Mexico City. © Banco de Mexico Trust. Photo © Schalkwijk/Art Resource, New York; **457** *top* (Detail of) Codex Vaticanus Mexico (before 1500), Aztec. Mexican National Library. Photo © Mireille Vautier/The Art Archive; *center* Aztec Calendar Stone, from Tenochtitlan (Mexico City), carved after 1502 under Montezuma II. Diameter, 11.5' (3.5 m). Museo Nacional de Antropologia, Mexico City. Photo © Michel Zabe/Art Resource, New York; *bottom* Solar calendar (reconstruction), Aztec, Mexica culture. National Anthropological Museum, Mexico. Photo © Dagli Orti/The Art Archive; **459** *left* © Explorer, Paris/SuperStock; *right* © Tim Hursley/SuperStock; **460** Pachacutic Inca IX, detail from Geneaology (1700s), Cuzco School. Museo Pedro de Osma, Lima, Peru. Photo © Mireille Vautier/The Art Archive; **462** Machu Picchu, Peru, seen from royal quarters and House of the Inca. Photo © Gianni Dagli Orti/The Art Archive; **464** *top* Parading a sacred Inca mummy on a litter (1565), Felipe Guanman Poma de Ayala. From *El Primer Nueva Coronica y buen Gobierno*, Perus codex facsimile. Royal Library, Copenhagen, Denmark. Photo © Nick Saunders Barbara Heller Photo Library, London/Art Resource, New York; *bottom* Stephen Alvarez/National Geographic Image Collection; **465** *top* © 2003 Ira Block; *center* Illustration by John Dawson/National Geographic Image Collection; *bottom* The Granger Collection; **466** *top* © Corbis; *2nd* Jade mask used in burial rituals (600s), Classic Maya. Excavated from the Temple of Inscriptions at Palenque. Museo Nacional de Antropologia, Mexico City. Photo © Werner Forman/Art Resource, New York; *3rd* Quetzalcoatl (900s), Toltec, Western Yucatan, Mexico. Photo © Dagli Orti/The Art Archive; *bottom* Machu Picchu, Peru, seen from royal quarters and House of the Inca. Photo © Gianni Dagli Orti/The Art Archive; **467** Map of Tenochtitlan and the Gulf of Mexico, from *Praeclara Ferdinadi Cortesii de Nova maris Oceani Hyspania Narratio* (1524), Hernando Cortes. Color lithograph. Photo © Newberry Library, Chicago/Bridgeman Art Library; **467 MC1–467 MC2** © imagebroker/Alamy.

Art and Photography Credits (Cont.)

Chapter 17

468 *top* Bust of Lorenzo de Medici (1400s or 1500s). Museo di Andrea del Castagno, Uffizi, Florence, Italy. Photo © Scala/Art Resource, New York; *bottom* Jar (1426–1435), Ming dynasty, Xuande mark and period. Chinese. Porcelain painted in underglaze blue; 19" high: Diameter 19". Gift of Robert E. Tod, 1937 (37.191.1), The Metropolitan Museum of Art, New York. Photo © 1986 The Metropolitan Museum of Art; **469** *left, Gutenberg Bible* (about 1455). Volume II, f. 45v–46. PML 818 ch1 ff1. The Pierpont Morgan Library, New York. Photo © The Pierpont Morgan Library/Art Resource, New York; *right* Detail of Nobles entertained in garden by musicians and dancers (about 1590), Mughal. Photo © British Library/The Art Archive; **470** *The Madonna of Chancellor Rolin* (about 1434), Jan van Eyck. Louvre, Paris. Photo © Scala/Art Resource, New York; **471** *left* © Photodisc/Getty Images; *right* © Ulf E. Wallin/The Image Bank/Getty Images; **472** (Detail of) *Lorenzo de Medici and the Arts in Florence* (about 1634) Giovanni da Sangiovanni. Palazzo Pitti, Florence, Italy. Photo © Alfredo Dagli Orti/The Art Archive; **473** *left, Portrait of Baldassare Castilione*, Raphael. Louvre, Paris. © Scala/ Art Resource, New York; *right* The Granger Collection, New York; **474** *Marriage of the Virgin* (1504), Raphael. Pinocoteca di Brera, Milan, Italy. Photo © Scala/Art Resource, New York; **475** *top* © Stephano Bianchetti/Corbis; *bottom* The Granger Collection, New York; **476** *Portrait of Niccolo Machiavelli*, Santi di Tito. Palazzo Vecchio, Florence, Italy. Photo © Erich Lessing/Art Resource, New York; **477** The Granger Collection, New York; **478** *left, Mona Lisa* (1503–1506), Leonardo da Vinci. Louvre, Paris. Photo by R. G. Ojeda. Photo © Réunion des Musées Nationaux/Art Resource, New York; **478–479** © SuperStock; **479** *top, The School of Athens* (1400s), Raphael. Stanza della Segnatura, Vatican Palace, Vatican State. Photo © Scala/Art Resource, New York; *bottom* © Bettmann/Corbis; **480** *left* © Photodisc/Getty Images; *right* © Ulf E. Wallin/The Image Bank/Getty Images; **481** *Peasant Wedding* (1568), Peter Bruegel the Elder. Kunsthistorisches Museum, Vienna, Austria. Photo © Saskia Ltd./Art Resource, New York; **482** *left* Christine de Pizan teaches her son (about 1430). Harley MS 4431, f. 26 ff. The British Library, London. Photo by AKG London/British Library; *right, Thomas More, Lord Chancellor* (late 1400s). Private Collection. Photo © The Stapleton Collection/The Bridgeman Art Library; **483** *left* © Castle Rock/Dakota Films/The Kobal Collection; *center* © Touchstone/The Kobal Collection; *top right* © Merick Morton/20th Century Fox/The Kobal Collection; *bottom right* © Herald Ace/Nippon Herald/Greenwich/The Kobal Collection; **484** Illustration by Peter Dennis/Linda Rogers Associates; **486** *top* KMSKA Antwerp-Image courtesy of Reproductiefonds; *center* By permission of the Folger Shakespeare Library, Washington, D.C.; *bottom* Pomander. Musée de la Parfumerie Fragonard, Paris. Photo © Gianni Dagli Orti/The Art Archive; **486–487** MS Sloane 2596, f. 52. British Library. Photo by AKG London/British Library; **487** *A Family Saying Grace Before the Meal* (1585), Anthuenis (Antoon) Claeissins or Claeissens. Oil on panel, 96.5 cm x 142 cm. Private Collection. Photo © Bridgeman Art Library; **488** *left* © Photodisc/Getty Images; *right* © Ulf E. Wallin/The Image Bank/Getty Images; **489** *Portrait of Martin Luther* (1529) Lucas Cranach the Elder. Museo Poldi Pezzoli, Milan, Italy. Photo © The Bridgeman Art Library; **492** *left, Portrait of Henry VIII, King of England* (1540), Hans Holbein the Younger. Galleria Nazionale d'Arte Antica, Rome. Photo © Scala/Art Resource, New York; *right, Anne Boleyn* (about 1530), unknown artist. Oil on wood panel. National Portrait Gallery, London. © National Portrait Gallery/SuperStock; **493** *top left* © Stapleton Collection/Corbis; **493** *bottom left, Mary I Tudor* (1554), Antonis Moro or Mor. Museo del Prado, Madrid. Photo © Gianni Dagli Orti/The Art Archive; *right, Elizabeth I, Queen of England*, Federico Zuccari. Pinacoteca Nacionale di Siena. Photo © Gianni Dagli Orti/The Art Archive; **494** *Elizabeth I* (about 1588), George Gower. Oil on wood panel. National Portrait Gallery, London. © National Portrait Gallery/SuperStock; **495** *left* © Photodisc/Getty Images; *right* © Ulf E. Wallin/The Image Bank/Getty Images; **496** *John Calvin as a young man*, Flemish School. Bibliothèque Publique et Universitaire, Geneva, Switzerland. Photo © Erich Lessing/Art Resource, New York; **498** *Marguerite d'Angouleme, Queen of Navarre* (1500s). Musée Condé, Chantilly, France. Photo © Réunion des Musées Nationaux/Art Resource, New York; **499** *Pope Paul III Farnese at the Council of Trent* (1560-1566), Taddeo and Federico Zuccari. Farnese Palace, Caprarola, Italy. Photo © Alfredo Dagli Orti/The Art Archive; **500** © Richard T. Nowitz/Corbis; **501** Martin Luther, German priest and Protestant reformer, caricature as seven-headed monster. Photo © The British Library/The Art Archive.; **502** *top* © SuperStock; *2nd,* Illustration by Peter Dennis/Linda Rogers Associates; *3rd, Portrait of Martin Luther* (1529) Lucas Cranach the Elder. Museo Poldi Pezzoli, Milan, Italy. Photo © The Bridgeman Art Library; *bottom* Detail of *Pope Paul III Farnese at the Council of Trent* (1560-1566), Taddeo and Federico Zuccari. Farnese Palace, Caprarola, Italy. Photo © Alfredo Dagli Orti/The Art Archive; © Bettmann/Corbis.

Chapter 18

504 *top* Topkapi Palace Museum, Istanbul, Turkey. Photo © Sonia Halliday and Laura Lushington; *bottom left* Pectoral ornament in the form of a double-headed serpent. Aztec. British Museum, London. Photo © Werner Forman/Art Resource, New York; *bottom right* By permission of the British Library; **505** © Burstein Collection/Corbis; **506** Shah Tahmasp I receiving the Moghul Emperor Humayun (1660s). Period of Abbas II. Chihil Sutun, Isfahan, Iran. Photo © SEF/Art Resource, New York; **507** *left* James L. Stanfield/National Geographic Image Collection; *right* © SuperStock; **509** Taking of Constantinople by the Turks, MS Fr. 9087 f.207. *Voyage d-Outremer de Bertrand de la Broquiere* Bibliothèque Nationale, Paris. Photo © Sonia Halliday Photographs; **510** *Sulieman the Magnificent*. Galleria degli Uffizi, Florence, Italy. Photo © Dagli Orti/The Art Archive; **511** © Sonia Halliday Photographs; **513** Shah Abbas I (1640s). Safavid mural. Chihil Sutun, Isfahan, Iran. Photo © SEF/Art Resource, New York; **514** Mapping Specialists; **515** Dome of south Iwan (1611–1638). Safavid dynasty. Majid-i Shah, Isfahan, Iran. Photo © SEF/Art Resource, New York; **516** *left* James L. Stanfield/National Geographic Image Collection; *right* © SuperStock; Portrait of Akbar and Prince Salim (1800s). India, Mughal. Gift of Sally Sample Aal, 1997. Inv. 97.19.16. The Newark Museum, Newark, New Jersey. Photo © The Newark Museum/Art Resource, New York; **519** *left* © Bettmann/Corbis; *center left, center right, right* AP/Wide World Photos; **520** © Brian A. Vikander/Corbis; **522** *top* Dagger handle in the form of a horse's head. Mughal. India. Victoria and Albert Museum, London. Photo © Victoria and Albert Museum, London/The Bridgeman Art Library; *bottom* © Abbie Enock/Travel Ink/Corbis; **523** *left* Akbar on the elephant Hawai pursuing the elephant rau Bagha (about 1590). Double page miniature from the Akbarnama. Mughal. Photo © Victoria and Albert Museum, London/Art Resource, New York; *right* Tent hanging (early 1700s). Mughal dynasty. Victoria and Albert Museum, London. Photo © Victoria and Albert Museum, London/Art Resource, New York.

Chapter 19

526 *left* Helmet (about 1500) Turkish. Photo © Victoria and Albert Museum, London/Art Resource, New York; *right* Detail of *St. Vincent Polyptych* (1400s), Nuno Goncalves. Museu Nacional de Arte Antiga, Lisbon, Portugal. Photo © Scala/Art Resource, New York; **527** *left* © The Flag Institute; *right, Washington Crossing the Delaware* (1851), Eastman Johnson. Copy after the Emmanuel Leutze painting in the Metropolitan Museum, New York. Private collection. Photo © Art Resource, New York; **528** India Orientalis (1606) Gerard Mercator and Jodocus Hondius from *Atlas sive cosmographicae Meditationes*; **529** *top left* © Culver Pictures, Inc./SuperStock; *top right* K'ossu (about 1600). Late Ming dynasty. China. Victoria and Albert Museum, London. Photo © Sally Chappell/The Art Archive; *bottom* Globe (about 1492), Martin Behaim. Bibliothèque Nationale, Paris. Photo © Giraudon/Art Resource, New York; **530** Detail of *St. Vincent Polyptych* (1400s), Nuno Goncalves. Museu Nacional de Arte Antiga, Lisbon, Portugal. Photo © Scala/Art Resource, New York; **531** *top* Demonstrating the usage of a sextant. Illustration from *Les Premieres oeuvres de Jacques Delvaux pillote en la marine*. 1583. Ms. fr. 150, fol. 21 r.

Bibliothèque National, Paris, France. Photo © Bridgeman-Giraudon/Art Resource; *center* © Bettmann/Corbis; *bottom left* Compass with sextant and dial (1617), Elias Allen. Photo © Victoria and Albert Museum, London/Art Resource, New York; *bottom right* © Dorling Kindersley; **533** © Stapleton Collection/Corbis; **535** © Morton Beebe/Corbis; **536** *top left* © Culver Pictures, Inc./Superstock; *top right* K'ossu (about 1600), Late Ming dynasty. China. Victoria and Albert Museum, London. Photo © Sally Chappell/The Art Archive; *bottom* Ming vase. Chinese School. Musée Guimet, Paris, France. Photo © The Bridgeman Art Library; **538** *top left* © Brian A. Vikander/Corbis; *bottom left* © John T. Young/Corbis; *bottom right* © Harvey Lloyd/Getty Images; 539 *Portrait of emperor Kangxi in casual dress reading books*, Qing Dynasty. Photo © Hu Weibiao/Panorama/The Image Works, Inc.; **540** Marriage ceremony (1800s), China. Victoria and Albert Museum, London. Photo © Eileen Tweedy/The Art Archive; **541** The Granger Collection, New York; **542** *top left* © Culver Pictures, Inc./SuperStock; *top right* K'ossu (about 1600), Late Ming dynasty. China. Victoria and Albert Museum, London. Photo © Sally Chappell /The Art Archive; *bottom* Japanese armor (1550, Muromachi period). Steel, silk and bronze, height 66". The Granger Collection, New York; **543** © B.S.P.I./Corbis; **544** © Asian Art & Archeology/Corbis; **545** *left* © Asian Art & Archaeology/Corbis; *right* © Michael S. Yamashita/Corbis; **546** © 1995 Christie's Images Limited; **547** *Monk Tokiyori*. Musée des Arts, Asiatiques-Guimet, Paris. Photo by Richard Lambert. Photo © Réunion des Musées Nationaux/Art Resource, New York; **548** Dutch Merchant ship plate (1756), Qing dynasty. China. Musée des Arts Asiatiques-Guimet, Paris. Photo by Richard Lambert. Photo © Réunion des Musées Nationaux/Art Resource, New York; **549** The Granger Collection, New York.

Chapter 20

550 *top* © Archivo Iconografico, S.A./Corbis; *bottom, Portrait of Tokugawa Ieyasu* (1600s), Japanese. Private Collection. Photo © The Bridgeman Art Library; **551** *top* The Granger Collection, New York; *bottom, The Taking of the Bastille, 14 July 1789* (1700s), French school. Musée de la Ville de Paris, Musée Carnavalet, Paris. Photo © The Bridgeman Art Library; **552** Battle for Tenochtitlan between Cortes and Spaniards and Aztecs. Antochiw Collection, Mexico. Photo © Mireille Vautier/The Art Archive; **553** *left* © Bettmann/Corbis; *right* (Detail of) Letter from Christopher Columbus to his son Diego (February 5, 1505). General Archive of the Indies, Seville, Spain. Photo © Gianni Dagli Orti/The Art Archive; **554** *Christopher Columbus* (1400s), Sebastiano del Piombo. Metropolitan Museum of Art, New York. Photo © The Bridgeman Art Library; **557** *left* The Granger Collection, New York; *right* South American Pictures; **558, 560** The Granger Collection, New York; **561** *left* © Bettmann/Corbis; *right* (Detail of) Letter from Christopher Columbus to his son Diego (February 5, 1505). General Archive of the Indies, Seville, Spain. Photo © Gianni Dagli Orti/The Art Archive; **562** The Granger Collection, New York; **563** North Carolina Collection, University of North Carolina, Chapel Hill; **566** *left* © Bettmann/Corbis; *right* (Detail of) Letter from Christopher Columbus to his son Diego (February 5, 1505). General Archive of the Indies, Seville, Spain. Photo © Gianni Dagli Orti/The Art Archive; **567** The Granger Collection, New York; **569** *left* The Granger Collection, New York; *right* The Newberry Library, Chicago; **571** *right* © Bettmann/Corbis; *left* (Detail of) Letter from Christopher Columbus to his son Diego (February 5, 1505). General Archive of the Indies, Seville, Spain. Photo © Gianni Dagli Orti/The Art Archive; **577** The Granger Collection, New York; **577 MC1–577 MC2** © Cummer Museum of Art & Gardens/SuperStock; **578** Portrait of the last Inca Chief, Atanualpa. Private Collection. Photo © The Bridgeman Art Library; **579** *top left, Cosimo de' Medici the Elder,* Agnolo Bronzino. Uffizi, Florence. Photo © Scala/Art Resource, New York; *top right* © Sakamoto Photo Research Laboratory/ Corbis; *bottom* © Bettmann/Corbis; **581** *top* © Araldo de Luca/Corbis; *bottom left* Nautilus Pitcher (about 1570). Francesco I de Medici Collection. Museo degli Argenti, Florence. Photo © Erich Lessing/Art Resource, New York; *bottom right* John Bigelow Taylor/American Museum of Natural History, NO. 4959(2); **582** *top* © Steve Vidler/SuperStock; *bottom* © Yann Arthur-Bertrand/Corbis; **583** © Archivo Iconografico, S.A./Corbis.

UNIT FIVE

584–585 *The Taking of the Bastille, July 14, 1789*, Anonymous French painter. Chateaux de Versailles et de Trianon, Versailles, France. Photo © Erich Lessing/Art Resource, New York.

Chapter 21

586 *top, Philip II, King of Spain and Portugal* (1500s), Alonso Sanchez Coello. Museo del Prado, Madrid, Spain. Photo © Erich Lessing/Art Resource, New York; *bottom, Francisco Pizarro* (1835), Amable-Paul Coutan. Chateau de Versailles et de Trianon, Versailles, France. Photo by Franck Raux. Photo © Réunion des Musées Nationaux/Art Resource, New York; **587** *top* The Granger Collection, New York; *bottom* © Pallava Bagla/Corbis; **588** *Louis XIV, King of France* (1701), Hyacinthe Rigaud. Louvre, Paris. Photo © Erich Lessing/Art Resource, New York; **589** *left* (detail of) *Marriage of Louis XIV, King of France and Marie Therese of Austria* (1600s), unknown artist. Musée de Tessé, Le Mans, France. Photo © Gianni Dagli Orti/The Art Archive; *right* © Todd A. Gipstein/Corbis; **590** The Granger Collection, New York; **591** *Las Meninas or The Family of Philip IV* (about 1656), Diego Rodriguez de Silva y Velasquez. Prado, Madrid, Spain. Photo © The Bridgeman Art Library; **592** *Tulipa gesaeriana no. 1908* (late 1500s-early 1600s), Jacopo Ligozzi. Gabinetto dei Disegni e delle Stampe. Ufizzi, Florence. Photo © Scala/Art Resource, New York; **593** The Granger Collection, New York; **596** *left* (detail of) *Marriage of Louis XIV, King of France and Marie Therese of Austria* (1600s), unknown artist. Musée de Tessé, Le Mans, France. Photo © Gianni Dagli Orti/The Art Archive; *right* © Todd A. Gipstein/Corbis; **597** *Cardinal Richelieu* (1636), Phillippe de Champaigne. Musée Condé, Chantilly, France. Photo © Erich Lessing/Art Resource, New York; **598** *Louis XIV, King of France* (1600s), follower of Pierre Mignard. Contemporary copy after a lost portrait by Mignard. Oil on canvas, 105 cm x 90 cm. Cat. 2299. Museo del Prado, Madrid. Photo © Erich Lessing/Art Resource, New York; **599** *Louis de Rouvroy, Duke of Saint-Simon* (1887), Viger du Vigneau. Chateaux de Versailles et de Trianon, Versailles, France. Photo © Réunion des Musées Nationaux/Art Resource, New York; **600** *top right* © Ben Mangor/SuperStock; *top center* © Adam Woolfitt/Corbis; *top left* © Archivo Iconografico, S.A./Corbis; *bottom* © Archivo Iconografico, S.A./Corbis; **601** *Battle of Denain, 24th July 1712* (1839), Jean Alaux. Chateau de Versailles, France. Photo © Giraudon/The Bridgeman Art Library; **603** *left* (detail of) *Marriage of Louis XIV, King of France and Marie Therese of Austria* (1600s), unknown artist. Musée de Tessé, Le Mans, France. Photo © Gianni Dagli Orti/The Art Archive; *right* © Todd A. Gipstein/Corbis; **605** Flag of the Imperial Hapsburg dynasty (about 1700). Heeresgeschichtliches Museum, Vienna, Austria. Photo © The Bridgeman Art Library; **606** *top* (detail of) *Empress Maria Theresa of Austria*. Museum der Stadt Wien. Photo © Alfredo Dagli Orti/The Art Archive; *bottom Frederick the Great* © Gianni Dagli Orti/Musée des Beaux Arts, Nantes, France/The Art Archive; **608** *left* (detail of) *Marriage of Louis XIV, King of France and Marie Therese of Austria* (1600s), unknown artist. Musée de Tessé, Le Mans, France. Photo © Gianni Dagli Orti/The Art Archive; *right* © Todd A. Gipstein/Corbis; **609** The Granger Collection, New York; **612** *top* © Dorling Kindersley; *center* Costumes of Crimean tribes (1888), A. Racinet. From Historical Costumes vol, V. Musée des Arts Décoratifs, Paris. Photo © Dagli Orti/The Art Archive; *bottom* © Historical Picture Archive/Corbis; **613** *top, Shrovetide* (1919), Boris Kustidiev. The I. Brodsky Museum, St. Petersburg, Russia. Photo Courtesy of the Smithsonian Institution Traveling Exhibition Service; *bottom* © Scheufler Collection/Corbis; **614** *left* (detail of) *Marriage of Louis XIV, King of France and Marie Therese of Austria* (1600s), unknown artist. Musée de Tessé, Le Mans, France. Photo © Gianni Dagli Orti/The Art Archive; *right* © Todd A.

Art and Photography Credits (Cont.)

Gipstein/Corbis; **615** The Granger Collection, New York.

Chapter 22

620 *left, Portrait of a Princess Holding a Wine Cup* (1600s-1700s), Mughal. India. The Newark Museum, Newark, New Jersey. Photo © The Newark Museum/Art Resource, New York; *right* Isaac Newton's reflecting telescope (1672) Royal Society. Photo © Eileen Tweedy/The Art Archive; **621** *left* Statuette of a Lohan, Ching dynasty. Musée des Arts Asiatiques-Guimet, Paris. Photo © Giraudon/Art Resource, New York; *right* © Leif Skoogfors/Corbis; **622** *A Philosopher Gives a Lecture on the Orrery* (1766), Joseph Wright of Derby. Canvas. Derby Museum and Art Gallery, Derby, Great Britain. Photo © Erich Lessing/Art Resource, New York; **623** *left* Copernican Solar System (1661). From *Harmonia Macronici*, Andreae Cellarius. Page 30. Photo © Victoria and Albert Museum, London/Art Resource, New York; *right* © Bettmann/Corbis; **625** *Galileo before the Holy Office of the Vatican.* John Nicolas Robert-Fleury. Oil on canvas. Louvre, Paris. Photo by Gerard Blot. Photo © Réunion des Musées Nationaux/Art Resource, New York; **626** *left* © Bettmann/Corbis; *right* Isaac Newton's reflecting telescope (1672). Royal Society. Photo © Eileen Tweed/The Art Archive; **627** © Bettmann/Corbis; **628** *The Anatomy Lesson of Dr. Tulp* (1632), Rembrandt van Rijn. Mauritshuis, The Hague, The Netherlands. Photo © Scala/Art Resource, New York; **629** *left* Copernican Solar System (1661). From *Harmonia Macronici*. Andreae Cellarius. Page 30. Victoria and Albert Museum, London. Photo © Art Resource, New York; *right* © Bettmann/Corbis; **630, 631** The Granger Collection, New York; **633** Mary Evans Picture Library; **635** The Granger Collection, New York; **636** *top left* Copernican Solar System (1661). From *Harmonia Macronici*. Andreae Cellarius. Page 30. Victoria and Albert Museum, London. Photo © Art Resource, New York; *right* © Bettmann/Corbis; **637** © Kevin Fleming/Corbis; **638** *Joseph II, Emperor of Austria and of the Holy Roman Empire, King of Hungary and Bohemia* (1700s), Austrian. Musée du Château de Versailles. Photo © Gianni Dagli Orti/The Art Archive; **639** © Anatoly Sapronenkov, Tomsk Regional Arts Museum/SuperStock; **640** *top left* Copernican Solar System (1661). From *Harmonia Macronici*. Andreae Cellarius. Page 30. Victoria and Albert Museum, London. Photo © Art Resource, New York; *top right* © Bettmann/Corbis; *bottom* Box with Medallion Top (1770-1800). French. 1" x 3 1/16". (2.5 x 7.8 cm). The Metropolitan Museum of Art, gift of William H. Huntington, 1883 (83.2.228). Photo © 1980 The Metropolitan Museum of Art; **641** Detail of *Thomas Jefferson* (1805), Rembrandt Peale. Oil on canvas, 71.1 cm x 59.7 cm. Photo © Collection of the New–York Historical Society/The Bridgeman Art Library; **644** © Corbis; **645** © Jon Feingersh/Stock Boston; **647** *El sueño de la razon produce monstuos* [The sleep of reason produces monsters] from *Los Caprichos* (1799) Francisco Jose de Goya y Lucientes. Etching and burnished aquatint, 21.5cm. x 15 cm. Bequest of William P. Babcock. Photo © Museum of Fine Arts, Boston; **647 MC1–647 MC2** © Ted Spiegel/Corbis.

Chapter 23

648 *left, George Washington,* George Healy. Musée du Château de Versailles. Photo © Gianni Dagli Orti/The Art Archive; *right* Reduced model of a guillotine. Musée de la Ville de Paris, Musée Carnavalet, Paris. Photo © Bridgeman-Giraudon/Art Resource, New York; **649** *top* Detail of *Napoleon Bonaparte, Emperor of France.* Musée du Château de Versailles. Photo © Gianni Dagli Orti/The Art Archive; *bottom* The Granger Collection, New York; **650** *The Conquerors of the Bastille Before the Hotel de Ville* (1839), Paul Delaroche. Musée du Petit Palais, Paris. Photo © Erich Lessing/Art Resource, New York; **651** *left* © SuperStock; *right* © Christie's Images/Corbis; **652** Detail of Caricature of the three estates: *A faut esperer que jeu la finira bientot* (1700s). Color engraving, Musée de la Ville de Paris, Musée Carnavalet, Paris. Photo by Bulloz. Photo © Réunion des Musées Nationaux/Art Resource, New York; **653** *left, Louis XVI, King of France.* Musée de Château de Versailles. Photo © Dagli Orti/The Art Archive; *right, Marie Antoinette, Queen of France* (replica of work painted in 1778) Musée du Château de Versailles. Photo © Gianni Dagli Orti/The Art Archive; **654** *The Storming of the Bastille, Paris, France, July 14, 1789.* Gouache. Musée Carnavalet, Paris. Photo © Gianni Dagli Orti°/The Art Archive; **656** *left* © SuperStock; *right* © Christie's Images/Corbis; **657** *Arrest of Louis XVI, King of France and his family attempting to flee the country at Varennes, France June 21-22, 1791.* Musée Carnavalet, Paris. Photo © Gianni Dagli Orti/The Art Archive; **658** *The Dead Marat* (1793), Jacques Louis David. Louvre, Paris. Photo © Erich Lessing/Art Resource, New York; **659** Illustration by Patrick Whelan; **660** *Portrait of Robespierre,* Louis L. Boilly. Musée des Beaux-Arts, Lille, France. Photo R. G. Ojeda. Photo © Réunion des Musées Nationaux/Art Resource, New York; **661** *Portrait of Danton* (1700s), Anonymous. Musée de la Ville de Paris, Musée Carnavalet, Paris. Photo by Bulloz. Photo © Réunion des Musées Nationaux/Art Resource, New York; **662** © Bettmann/Corbis; **663** *left* © SuperStock; *right* © Christie's Images/Corbis; **664** *Portrait of Bonaparte, premier consul* (1803), Francois Gerard. Oil on canvas. Musée Conde, Chantilly, France. Photo by Harry Breja. Photo © Réunion des Musées Nationaux./Art Resource, New York; **665** Detail of *Napoleon Crossing the Alps,* Jacques Louis David. Chateau de Malmaison et Bois–Preau, Rueil–Malmaison, France. Photo © Erich Lessing/Art Resource, New York; **668** *top left* © SuperStock; *top right* © Christie's Images/Corbis; *bottom, A Stoppage to a Stride over the Globe* (1803). English School. Color lithograph. Private collection. Photo © The Bridgeman Art Library; **669** © Archivo Iconografico, S.A./Corbis; **671** © Public Record Office/Topham-HIP/The Image Works; **672** *left* © SuperStock; *right* © Christie's Images/Corbis; **673** © Christel Gerstenberg/Corbis; **676** *left, Parisian sans culotte* (1700s), unknown artist. Musée de la Ville de Paris, Musée Carnavalet, Paris. Photo © Giraudon/Art Resource, New York; *right* Reduced model of a guillotine. Musée de la Ville de Paris, Musée Carnavalet, Paris. Photo © Bridgeman-Giraudon/Art Resource, New York.

Chapter 24

678 *left, Napoleon in his study at the Tuileries* (1812). Jacques Louis David. Collection of Prince and Princess Napoleon, Paris. Photo © Bridgeman-Giraudon/Art Resource, New York; *right, Miguel Hidalgo y Costilla* (1895). From Mexica publication *Patria e Independencia, folleto illustrado.* Antiochiw Collection, Mexico. Photo © Mireille Vautier/The Art Archive; **679** *left* © Francis G. Mayer/Corbis; *right* © Hulton-Deutsch Collection/Corbis; **680** Courtesy of the Flag Institute; **681** *left* © Michael S. Lewis/Corbis; *right* © Archivo Iconografico, S.A./Corbis; **682** *Portrait of Francois-Dominique Toussaint, known as Toussaint Louverture,* Anonymous. Musée du Quai Branly, Paris. Photo J. G. Berizzi. Photo © Réunion des Musées Nationaux/Art Resource, New York; **683** *left* © Christie's Images/Corbis; *right* The Granger Collection, New York; **684** © Bettmann/Corbis; **687** *top left* © Michael S. Lewis/Corbis; *top right* © Archivo Iconografico, S.A./Corbis; *bottom, Klemens Metternich, Austrian prince and statesman.* Museo Glauco, Lombardi, Parma, Italy. Photo © Gianni Dagli Orti/The Art Archive; **689** © Archivo Iconografico, S.A./Corbis; **690** *Combat Before the Hotel de Ville, July 28th, 1830,* Victor Schnetz. Musée du Petit Palais, Paris. Photo by Bulloz. Photo © Réunion des Musées Nationaux/Art Resource, New York; **691** © Corbis; **693** © Bettmann Corbis; **695** The Granger Collection, New York; **696** © Bettmann/Corbis; **698** *top left* © Michael S. Lewis/Corbis; *top right* © Archivo Iconografico, S.A./Corbis; *bottom* © Bettmann/Corbis; **699** *Portrait of Ludwig von Beethoven* (1819), Anonymous. Beethoven House, Bonn, Germany. Photo © Snark/Art Resource, New York; **700** © Hulton-Deutsch Collection/Corbis; **702** *Lion Hunt* (1860/1861) Eugene Delacroix. Potter Palmer Collection, 1922.404. Reproduction. The Art Institute of Chicago, Chicago, Illinois; **703** *top, The Stone Breakers* (1849), Gustave Courbet. Gemaldegalerie, Dresden, Germany. Photo © The Bridgeman Art Library; *bottom* © Francis G. Mayer/Corbis; **705** The Granger Collection, New York; **706** *top, Portrait of James II* (about 1685), Benedetto Gennari the Younger. Phillip Mould, Historical Portraits Ltd, London. Photo © The

Bridgeman Art Library; *left, The Bloody Massacre perpetrated in...Boston on March 5th, 1770* (1770), Paul Revere. Colored engraving. Private collection. Photo © Art Resource, New York; **706-707** The Granger Collection, New York; **707** The Granger Collection, New York; **708** *left, Marie-Antoinette Standing in her Court Robe with a Rose in her Hand* (1779) Louise Elizabeth Vigée-LeBrun. Châteaux de Versailles et de Trianon, Versailles, France. Photo © Réunion des Musées Nationaux/Art Resource, New York; *center* © Photodisc/Getty Images; **709** *top* Detail of Caricature of the three estates: *Il faut esperer que le jeu finira bientot* [Peasant carrying a nobleman and a cleric] (1789). Musée de la Ville de Paris, Musée Carnavalet, Paris. Photo © Giraudon/Art Resource, New York; *bottom* The Granger Collection, New York; **710** The Granger Collection, New York; **711** *top* The Granger Collection, New York; *bottom, Maximilien Robespierre.* Musée Carnavalet, Paris. Photo © Alfredo Dagli Orti/ The Art Archive.

END MATTER

R23 *left, La maraîchere* [Woman of the French Revolution]. Jacques Louis David. Musée de la Ville de Paris, Musée Carnavalet, Paris. Photo © Giraudon/Art Resource, New York; *right, Marie Antoinette,* Jacques Gautier d'Agoty. Château, Versailles, France. Photo © Giraudon/Art Resource, New York; **R24** U.S. State Department/Photo Courtesy U.S. Coast Guard; **R27** *Il faut esperer que jeu la finira bientôt.* Color engraving, 18th century. Musée de la Ville de Paris, Musée Carnavalet, Paris. Photo by Bulloz. Photo © Réunion des Musées Nationaux/Art Resource, New York; **R29** © Szabo/Rothco;

Holt McDougal has made every effort to locate the copyright holders of all copyrighted material in this book and to make full acknowledgment for its use. Omissions brought to our attention will be corrected in a subsequent edition.